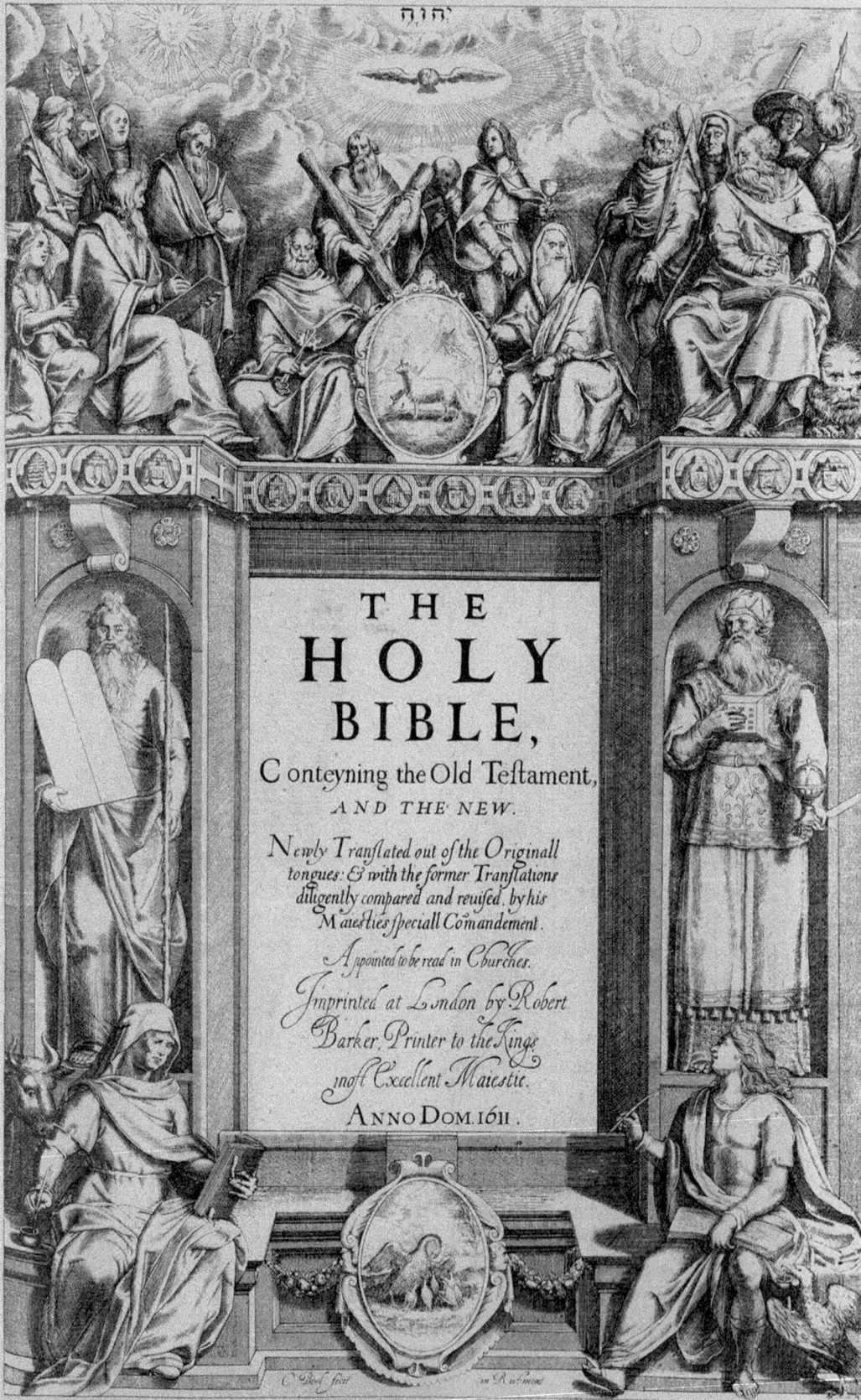

THE HOLY BIBLE,

C onteyning the Old Testament,

AND THE NEW.

Newly Tranſlated out of the Originall tongues: & with the former Tranſlations diligently compared and reuiſed, by his Maieſties ſpeciall Comandement.

Appointed to be read in Churches.

Jmprinted at London by Robert Barker, Printer to the Kings moſt Excellent Maieſtie.

ANNO DOM. 1611.

THE HOLY BIBLE CODE

God's Finished & Perfected Word as Revealed in the King James Version

Volume 7: Numbers 59-66 & Appendix

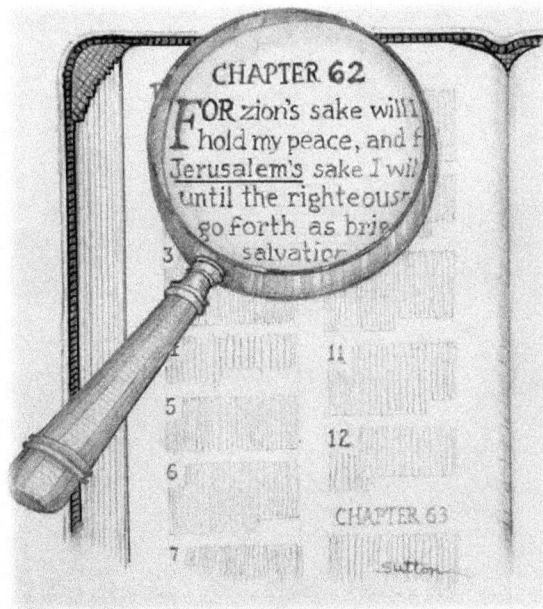

William K. Sutton, MTh, BTh

MEMBERS OF THE BODY PUBLISHING

Contents

Library of Congress Control Number: 2022922559

ISBN: 979-8-218-19344-7

First Printing, 2023

The author does not receive any proceeds of any sales, either ebook or print, and has made the entirety of this book freely available for viewing on his website, _theholybiblecode.com_.

Acknowledgements

Many thanks to Michael Hoggard for making freely available to the public his highly advanced Bible-search software program, *King James Pure Bible Search 2.0*.

Endless thanks and praise to the Holy Spirit, the Divine Revealer of Holy Truth, for His great enlightenment upon this Bible Numerics research project. Without His holy oversight and helpful underwriting, this published work could not have been accomplished.

This resource, *The Holy Bible Code*, only quotes from the 1769 edition of the King James Version Bible.

Authorship

As a young native of Eastern North Carolina, William K. Sutton's parents raised him in the ways of the Lord, themselves devoted members at their local Baptist church. He fully committed his heart and life to the Lord at the age of fifteen. Although he was afterwards baptized, he was not enrolled in any discipleship program; thus he fell woefully short in his walk with Christ. In due season the Good Shepherd found the twenty-five-year-old stray sheep and helped him rededicate his life to wholly serve the Lord Jesus Christ.

After reading the Bible daily for the next five years, the Lord called His reclaimed servant to preach the gospel. It was at that time he enrolled at *Trinity Baptist Bible College* to gain vital understanding of God's Holy Word. He graduated four years later with a Bachelor of Theology degree. He later obtained his Master of Theology degree from *Clarksville Theological Seminary* in Clayton, North Carolina, through correspondence courses.

As a missionary representative, Sutton departed with his wife and two young children in 2001 for the mission field of Australia, and they continue serving there today. Apart from his weekly pastoral and evangelistic work over the past two decades, he has extensively studied Jewish Religion, Bible Manners, and Near East Customs. This endeavor has aided him in writing gospel tracts, evangelistic booklets, and full-length books used in his ministry.

The Bible Numbers Chart

1: Unity	(Oneness)	1. Genesis	
2: Division	(Union, Witness)	2. Exodus	
3: Divine Perfection	(New Life)	3. Leviticus	
4: Earth	(World)	4. Numbers	
5: Grace	(God's Goodness)	5. Deuteronomy	
6: Man	(Weakness, Evils of Satan)	6. Joshua	
7: Spiritual Perfection	(Completion)	7. Judges	
8: New Beginnings		8. Ruth	
9: Spirit	(Fruit-Bearing)	9. 1 Samuel	
10: Ordinal Perfection	(Order)	10. 2 Samuel	
11: Judgment	(Disorder)	11. 1 Kings	
12: Governmental Perfection		12. 2 Kings	
13: Rebellion	(Anger)	13. 1 Chronicles	
14: Deliverance	(Salvation)	14. 2 Chronicles	
15: Rest	(Peace)	15. Ezra	
16: Love	(Obedience)	16. Nehemiah	
17: Victory	(Joy)	17. Esther	
18: Bondage	(Oppression)	18. Job	
19: Faith	(Trust)	19. Psalms	
20: Redemption	(Wisdom)	20. Proverbs	
21: Sin	(Lawlessness)	21. Ecclesiastes	
22: Understanding	(Light)	22. Song of Solomon	
23: Death		23. Isaiah	
24: Priesthood		24. Jeremiah	
25: Forgiveness		25. Lamentations	
26: Gospel	(Good News)	26. Ezekiel	
27: Preaching	(Holy Truth)	27. Daniel	
28: Eternal Life		28. Hosea	
29: Departure		29. Joel	
30: Dedication	(Blood)	30. Amos	
31: Family	(Children)	31. Obadiah	
32: Covenant	(Fellowship)	32. Jonah	
33: Promise		33. Micah	
34: Man's Religion		34. Nahum	
35: Hope	(Suffering)	35. Habakkuk	
36: Enemy	(Exaltation of Man)	36. Zephaniah	
37: Word of God		37. Haggai	
38: Unbelief		38. Zechariah	
39: Disease	(Adultery)	39. Malachi	

Legend of Canons

LAW: *Genesis-Deuteronomy*
OLD TESTAMENT NARRATIVE: *Joshua-Esther*
WISDOM BOOKS: *Job-Song of Solomon*
MAJOR PROPHETS: *Isaiah-Daniel*
MINOR PROPHETS: *Hosea-Malachi*

NEW TESTAMENT NARRATIVE: *Matthew-Acts*
SYNOPTIC GOSPELS: *Matthew-Luke*
PAULINE EPISTLES: *Romans-Hebrews*
GENERAL EPISTLES: *James-Jude*
APOCALYPTIC EPISTLE: *Revelation*

59—Oppressor

Oppressors and their acts of oppression are seen often throughout the Bible. Sometimes the Lord Himself oppresses men because of their sin. At certain appropriate times He permits others to oppress individuals as a form of chastisement for their sin and oversees the scope and severity of it. Throughout the Bible we consistently see that the Lord promises judgment upon those who oppress others, especially ones who oppress the Jews, widows, fatherless, and poor. Satan is also highly responsible for much of man's oppression; he too prompts other men to oppress people whether they are innocent or not. Kings are often found to be cruel oppressors.

You will recall that the Bible's number for Bondage and Oppression is 18. All forms of the word oppress point to the oppressor: *oppress* (23x), *oppressed* (38x), *oppresseth* (5x), *oppression* (24x), *oppressions* (3x), *oppressing* (3x), *oppressor* (14x), *oppressors* (8x) = 118, a multiple of 59.

The dictionary lists the following five definitions of the word OPPRESS:
> [1] to <u>burden</u> with <u>cruel</u> or unjust impositions or <u>restraints</u>, subject to a <u>burdensome</u> or harsh exercise of authority or <u>power</u>;
> [2] to lie <u>heavily</u> upon the mind, a person, etc.;
> [3] to weigh down, as sleep or <u>weariness</u> does;
> [4] to <u>put down, subdue</u>, or suppress; and
> [5] to press upon or <u>against</u>, crush.

The Old Testament combination *burden* (58 vs) and *burdensome* (1 v) = 59 verses.

The word *power* is mentioned in 59 verses of the Pauline Epistles.

All forms of the word heavy show the seal of the oppressor: *heavy* (39 vs), *heavily* (3 vs), *heavier* (3 vs), *heaviness* (14 vs) = 59 verses.

The word *against* is mentioned in 59 verses of Second Kings.

59th Verse of the Bible

"But of the fruit of the tree which is in the midst of the garden, <u>God</u> hath said, Ye shall not eat of it, neither shall ye touch it, lest ye <u>die</u>" (Gen. 3:3). Eve spoke of her potential oppression of death from God if she disobeyed. All forms of the word die show the seal of oppressor: *die* (321x), *died* (201x), *diest* (1x), *dieth* (30x), *dying* (6x) = 559.

> The title *God* is mentioned in 59 verses of Second Samuel.
> The title *God* is mentioned in 159 verses of Second Chronicles.

Satan Wears Down Eve's Mind

"And the <u>serpent</u> said unto the woman, Ye shall not surely die: For God doth know that in the day ye eat thereof, then your eyes shall be opened, and <u>ye shall be as gods</u>, <u>knowing good and evil</u>" (Gen. 3:4-5). Because the evil oppressor's first seed of doubt was latent and did not take root in Eve's mind, he had to plant a second one. This second seed of doubt which consisted of twice as many words was more potent. After these second words of doubt came to Eve she began

1

to look at the tree of knowledge in a different way. The Bible combination *that old serpent* (2x), *Devil* (2x), *Satan* (55x) = 59. The Bible combination *ye shall be as gods* (7x), *knowing* (51x), *good and evil* (1x) = 59.

God Oppresses the Serpent

"And the LORD God said unto the serpent, Because thou hast done this, thou art cursed above all cattle, and above every beast of the field; upon thy belly shalt thou go, and dust shalt thou eat all the days of thy life" (Gen. 3:14). The Bible combination *and the LORD God said unto the serpent* (1x), *serpent* (38x), *because thou hast done this* (3x), *thou art cursed* (1x), *above all cattle* (1x), *and above every beast of the field* (1x), *upon thy belly* (1x), *shalt thou go* (5x), *and dust shalt thou eat* (1x), *all the days of thy life* (7x) = 59.

God Oppresses the Woman

"Unto the woman he said, I will greatly multiply thy sorrow and thy conception; in sorrow thou shalt bring forth children; and thy desire shall be to thy husband, and he shall rule over thee" (Gen. 3:16). The word *woman* occurs 59 times in the Gospels. The Old Testament combination *I will greatly multiply thy* (1x), *sorrow* (54x), *and thy conception* (1x), *in sorrow thou shalt* (1x), *bring forth children* (2x) = 59.

God Oppresses the Man

"And unto Adam he said . . . cursed is the ground for thy sake; in sorrow shalt thou eat of it all the days of thy life; Thorns also and thistles shall it bring forth to thee; and thou shalt eat the herb of the field; In the sweat of thy face shalt thou eat bread, till thou return unto the ground; for out of it wast thou taken: for dust thou art, and unto dust shalt thou return. . . . Therefore the LORD God sent him forth from the garden of Eden, to till the ground from whence he was taken" (Gen. 3:17-19, 23).

The Bible combination *in sorrow shalt thou eat of it* (1x), *all the days of thy life* (7x), *thorns* (50x), *also and thistles shall it bring forth to thee* (1x) = 59.

Cain Oppresses His Brother with a Crushing Blow

"And Cain talked with Abel his brother: and it came to pass, when they were in the field, that Cain rose up AGAINST Abel his brother, and slew him" (Gen. 4:8). The brothers' religious discussion apparently grew worse with each passing day of Cain's unrepentant spirit. Coinciding with our fifth definition of the word oppress, Cain pressed upon Abel to crush the life out of him. The phrase *his brother* is mentioned in 59 chapters of the Old Testament. Again the word *against* is mentioned in 59 verses of Second Kings.

Lord Oppresses Fallen Mankind with Work

"And he called his name Noah, saying, This same shall comfort us concerning our work and toil of our hands, because of the ground which the LORD hath cursed" (Gen. 5:29). Lamech acknowledged mankind's oppression whereby men have to daily contend with weeds lest they overtake and choke the life out of the precious food-yielding crops. This form of work is laborious and discomforting. The title *LORD* occurs 559 times in First and Second Chronicles.

> The word *work* is mentioned in 59 verses of Exodus.
> The word *work* is mentioned in 59 verses of Major Prophets.
> The phrase *the work* occurs 159 times in the Bible.

The Mighty Oppressors of Old

"There were giants in the earth in those days; and also after that, when the sons of God came in unto the daughters of men, and they bare children to them, the same became mighty men which were <u>of old</u>, <u>men of</u> renown" (Gen. 6:4). Such mighty men exercised great rule over the people and maintained their rule through various oppressive measures. The phrase *of old* occurs 59 times in the Bible. The phrase *men of* is mentioned in 59 verses of the Major Prophets.

Mankind's Oppressive Spirit of Wickedness

"And GOD saw that <u>the wickedness</u> of <u>man</u> was great in the earth, and that every imagination of the thoughts of his heart was only <u>evil</u> continually. And it repented the LORD that he had made <u>man</u> on the earth, and it grieved him at his heart" (Gen. 6:5-6). Society had become so overrun with oppressive wickedness. Men were oppressors of mankind. Men's evil behavior was even oppressing the Lord by weighing down in His mind. The term *the wicked* occurs 259 times in the Bible. The word *evil* occurs 59 times in the NT Narrative.

The word *man* is mentioned in 59 verses of Second Samuel.
The word *man* occurs 559 times in the NT Narrative.

The Lord's Plan to Oppress Earth

"And the LORD said, I will destroy man whom I have created from the face of the <u>earth</u>; But Noah found grace in the eyes of the LORD. . . . And God said unto Noah, The end of all flesh is come before me; for the <u>earth</u> is filled with violence through them; and, behold, I will destroy them with the <u>earth</u>. . . . Make thee an ark of gopher wood; rooms shalt thou make in the ark, and shalt pitch it within and without with pitch. . . . And, behold, I, even I, do bring a flood of waters upon the <u>earth</u>, to destroy all flesh, wherein is the breath of life, from under heaven; and every thing that is in the earth shall <u>die</u>" (Gen. 6:7a-8, 13-14, 17).

The word *earth* is mentioned in 59 chapters of the OT Narrative. Again all forms of the word *die* occur a combined 559 times in the Bible. The Old Testament combination *die* (258 vs) and *diest* (1 v) = 259 verses.

Divine Oppressor Covers Earth with Troubled Waters

"And <u>the waters</u> prevailed exceedingly upon the earth; and all the high hills, that were under the whole heaven, were covered. . . . And all flesh died that moved upon the earth, both of fowl, and of cattle, and of beast, and of every creeping thing that creepeth upon the earth, and every man" (Gen. 7:19, 21). The phrase *the waters* occurs 59 times in the Law.

Oppressors Shed Innocent Blood

"Whoso sheddeth man's blood, by man shall his <u>blood</u> be shed: for in the image of God made he man" (Gen. 9:6). The murderous oppressor shall be judicially sentenced and swiftly put to death. The underlined word *blood* is the 5159th word of the Bible, and it refers to the oppressor's guilty blood.

Noah Becomes Furious Oppressor to His Wicked Son Ham

"And Noah awoke from his wine, and knew what his younger son had done unto him. And he said, Cursed be Canaan; a servant <u>of</u> servants shall he be unto his brethren" (Gen. 9:24-25). Here the word *of* is the 5599th word of the Bible, a number with 59 at its core, and congruently the 590th word of this chapter, a visual multiple of 59.

Citizens of Babel Provoke the Divine Oppressor

"Go to, let us go down, and there confound their language, that they may not understand one another's speech. So the LORD scattered them abroad from thence upon the face of all the earth: and they left off to build <u>the city</u>" (Gen. 11:7-8). The Lord's plan for the nations was for them to spread abroad not congregate in one place, as cities are breeding grounds for great oppression. The phrase *the city* occurs 459 times in the Old Testament.

Pharaoh Provokes the Divine Oppressor

"And the <u>LORD</u> <u>plagued</u> Pharaoh and his house with great plagues because of Sarai Abram's wife" (Gen. 12:17). Again the title *LORD* occurs 559 times in First and Second Chronicles. The phrase *the plague* is mentioned in 59 verses of the Old Testament.

The Oppressor King—Chedorlaomer

"And in the fourteenth year came Chedorlaomer, and the kings that were with him, and smote the Rephaims in Ashteroth Karnaim, and the Zuzims in Ham, and the Emims in Shaveh Kiriathaim, And the Horites in their mount Seir, unto El-paran, which is by the wilderness. And they returned, and came to En-mishpat, which is Kadesh, <u>and smote</u> <u>all the country of</u> the Amalekites, and also the Amorites, that dwelt in Hazezon-tamar" (Gen. 14:5-7). Most of these peoples which Chedorlaomer oppressed were giants. The OT Narrative combination *and smote* (56x), *all the country of* (3x) = 59.

Sarah Oppresses Her Maid Hagar

"But Abram said unto Sarai, Behold, thy <u>maid</u> is in thy hand; do to her as it pleaseth thee. <u>And when Sarai</u> <u>dealt</u> <u>HARDLY with her,</u> she fled from her face" (Gen. 16:6). Sarah oppressed Hagar by giving her glaring looks and harsh treatment to make her leave on her own. Sarah's oppressive scheme worked. All forms of the word *maid* are mentioned in 59 chapters of the Bible. The Bible combination *and when Sarai* (1x), *dealt* (57x), *hardly with her* (1x) = 59.

459th Verse of the Bible

"And there came two angels to Sodom at even; and Lot sat in the gate of Sodom: and Lot seeing them rose up to meet them; and he bowed himself with his face toward the ground" (Gen. 19:1). This 59th verse is the opening verse of a chapter which records the demise of five wicked cities at the hands of their divine Oppressor. These two angels were given an important mission to deliver Lot's family out of the oppressive city.

Lot's Sodomite Oppressors

"And they said, Stand back. And they said again, This one fellow came in to sojourn, and he will needs be a judge: now will we <u>deal</u> <u>worse with thee,</u> than with them. And they PRESSED sore upon the man, even Lot, and came near to break the door" (Gen. 19:9). The Old Testament combination *deal* (58x), *worse with thee* (1x) = 59.

Wicked Cities of the Plain Provoke the Divine Oppressor

"The sun was risen upon the earth <u>when Lot entered into Zoar. Then the LORD</u> <u>rained upon Sodom</u> <u>and upon Gomorrah</u> brimstone and fire <u>from the LORD</u> out of heaven; <u>And he overthrew those cities, and all the plain, and</u> <u>all the inhabitants of the cities, and that which grew upon the ground</u>" (Gen. 19:23-25). The Bible combination *when Lot entered into Zoar then the LORD* (1x), *rained upon* (3x), *Sodom* (48x), *and upon Gomorrah* (1x), *brimstone and fire* (1x), *from the LORD out of heaven* (1x), *and he overthrew those cities* (1x), *and all the plain and* (1x), *all the inhabitants of the cities* (1x), *and that which grew upon the ground* (1x) = 59.

Philistine King Provokes the Divine Oppressor

"And Abraham said of Sarah his wife, She is my sister: and Abimelech king of Gerar sent, and took Sarah. But God came to Abimelech in a dream by night, and said to him, Behold, thou art but a dead man, for the woman which thou hast taken; for she is a man's wife. . . . So Abraham prayed unto God: and God healed Abimelech, and his wife, and his maidservants; and they bare children. For the LORD had fast closed up all the wombs of the house of Abimelech, because of Sarah Abraham's wife" (Gen. 20:2-3, 17-18).

The Law combination *so Abraham* (2x), *prayed unto God* (1x), *and God healed* (1x), *Abimelech and his wife* (1x), *and his maidservants* (1x), *and they bare children* (2x), *for the LORD had* (4x), *fast* (1x), *closed* (3x), *up all the wombs* (1x), *of the house of* (17x), *Abimelech* (23x), *because of Sarah* (1x), *Abraham's wife* (1x) = 59.

Abraham—Deadly Oppressor to His Son

"And Abraham stretched forth his hand, and took the knife to slay his son" (Gen. 22:10). The two conjoined phrases *and Abraham stretched forth his hand, and took the knife to slay his son* consists of 59 characters! This oppressor verse presents the 59th occurrence of the name *Abraham*.

559th Verse of the Bible

"And the angel of the LORD called unto him out of heaven, and said, Abraham, Abraham: and he said, Here am I" (Gen. 22:11). At this very last moment Abraham was yet living out the role of his son's deadly oppressor.

King Threatens to Be the Oppressor of His People

"And Abimelech charged all his people, saying, He that toucheth this man or his wife shall surely be put to death" (Gen. 26:11). The phrase *his people* 159 times in the Bible.

Jacob's Oppressor Uncle

"And it came to pass in the evening, that he took Leah his daughter, and brought her to him; and he went in unto her. . . . And it came to pass, that in the morning, behold, it was Leah: and he said to Laban, What is this thou hast done unto me? did not I serve with thee for Rachel? wherefore then hast thou beguiled me?" (Gen. 29:23, 25) This act was only the first of many oppressive actions Laban would foist upon Jacob. The Bible combination *what is this thou hast* (2x), *done unto* (53x), *did not I serve with thee* (1x), *for Rachel* (3x) = 59.

Jacob's Oppressor Uncle Intensifies His Angry Countenance

"And he heard the words of Laban's sons, saying, Jacob hath taken away all that was our father's; and of that which was our father's hath he gotten all this glory. And Jacob beheld the countenance of Laban, and, behold, it was not toward him as before" (Gen. 31:1-2). The Bible combination *and Jacob beheld* (1x), *Laban's* (4x), *countenance* (53x), *it was not toward him as before* (1x) = 59.

Laban, the Son of Bethuel the Syrian

Because Jacob could no longer tolerate his uncle's spirit of oppression, he struck camp with all his family. Once Laban caught up to him, Jacob summarized the oppression he had been feeling over the past two decades. "Thus have I been twenty years in thy house; I served thee fourteen years for thy two daughters, and six years for thy cattle: and thou hast changed my wages ten times" (Gen. 31:41). The Bible titles *Laban* (51x), *Laban's* (4x), *son of Bethuel* (1x), [only in reference to Laban] *the Syrian* (3x) = 59.

Jacob's Oppressor Brother

"And the messengers returned to Jacob, saying, We came to thy brother Esau, and also he cometh to meet thee, and four hundred men with him. Then Jacob was greatly afraid and distressed: and he divided the people that was with him, and the flocks, and herds, and the camels, into two bands; And said, If Esau come to the one company, and smite it, then the other company which is left shall escape" (Gen. 32:6-8). The reason Jacob was so afraid of his brother was his brother's burning promise twenty years earlier to kill him. The Old Testament combination *Jacob was greatly* (1x), *afraid* (158x) = 159. The word *escape* occurs 59 times in Scripture.

Simeon & Levi Become Oppressors of Shechem's City

"And it came to pass on the third day, when they were sore, that two of the sons of Jacob, Simeon and Levi, Dinah's brethren, took each man his sword, and came upon the city boldly, and slew all the males" (Gen. 34:25). Again the phrase *the city* occurs 459 times in the Old Testament. The Bible combination *Simeon* (50x), *and Levi* (6x), *Dinah's brethren* (1x), *took each man his sword and came upon the city boldly* (1x), *and slew all the males* (1x) = 59.

Joseph's Oppressor Half-Brothers

"And when his brethren saw that their father loved him more than all his brethren, they hated him, and could not speak peaceably unto him. . . . And Joseph dreamed a dream, and he told it his brethren: and they hated him yet the more. . . . And they hated him yet the more. . . . Come now therefore, and let us slay him, and cast him into some pit. . . . And they took him, and cast him into a pit . . . and they drew and lifted up Joseph out of the pit, and sold Joseph to the Ishmeelites for twenty pieces of silver" (Gen. 37:4,5c, 8d, 20a, 24a, 28b).

The narrative details Joseph's oppression at his half-brothers' oppressor hands. The phrase *his brethren* is mentioned in 59 chapters of the Old Testament. The Old Testament combination *and they took him* (1x), *and cast him into* (6x), *the pit* (52x) = 59.

Jacob's Sons Oppress Him with Dreadful Untruthful News

The brothers knew Joseph's staged death would greatly oppress their father and weigh him down mentally. They proceeded with their plan anyway and showed their father the bloody tunic. "And he knew it, and said, It is my son's coat; an evil beast hath devoured him; Joseph is without doubt rent in pieces. And Jacob rent his clothes, and put sackcloth upon his loins, and mourned for his son many days. And all his sons and all his daughters rose up to comfort him; but he refused to be comforted; and he said, For I will go down into the grave unto my son mourning" (Gen. 37:33-35). The phrase *go down* is mentioned in 59 chapters of the Old Testament. The word *grave* occurs 59 times in the Old Testament.

Joseph's Master Becomes His Oppressor

"And Joseph's master took him, and put him into the prison, a place where the king's prisoners were BOUND: and he was there in the prison" (Gen. 39:20). The Bible combination *and Joseph's master* (1x), *took him* (8x), *and put him into* (2x), *the prison* (45x), *a place where the* (1x), *king's prisoners were bound* (1x), *and he was there in the prison* (1x) = 59.

Governor Joseph Oppresses His Half-Brothers

"And Joseph was the governor over the land, and he it was that sold to all the people of the land: and Joseph's brethren came, and bowed down themselves before him with their faces to the earth. And Joseph saw his brethren, and he knew them, but made himself strange unto them, and spake roughly unto them; and he said unto them, Whence come ye? And they said, From the land of Canaan to buy food. . . . Ye are spies; to see the nakedness of the land ye are come. . . . Hereby ye shall be proved: By the life of Pharaoh ye shall not go forth hence, except your youngest brother come hither. Send one of you, and let him fetch your brother, and ye shall be kept in prison, that your words may be proved, whether there be any truth in you: or else by the life of Pharaoh surely ye are spies. And he put them all together into ward three days" (Gen. 42:6-7, 9b, 15-17).

This was only the beginning of Joseph's oppression of his half-brothers, all in one grand attempt to bring them into full contrition and repentance over what they had done unto him. Joseph's motives were pure and true not malicious. The word *governor* occurs 59 times in the Bible.

Governor Joseph Further Oppresses His Half-Brothers

"And Joseph said unto them the third day, This do, and live; for I fear God: If ye be true men, let one of your brethren be BOUND in the house of your prison: go ye, carry corn for the famine of your houses: But bring your youngest brother unto me; so shall your words be verified, and ye shall not die. And they did so" (Gen. 42:18-20).

The Old Testament combination *if ye be true men* (1x), *let one of your brethren* (1x), *be bound in* (3x), *the house of your* (4x), *prison* (47x), *but bring your youngest brother unto me* (1x), *so shall your words be verified* (1x), *and ye shall not die* (1x) = 59.

Governor Joseph Feverishly Oppression of His Half-Brothers

"And he commanded the steward of his house, saying, Fill the men's sacks with food, as much as they can carry, and put every man's money in his sack's mouth. And put my cup, the silver cup, in the sack's mouth of the youngest, and his corn money. And he did according to the word that Joseph had spoken" (Gen. 44:1-2).

This opening passage which sets the stage for Joseph's last oppressive scheme is comprised of 59 words.

Oppressive Human Instruments in Satan's Cruel Hand

"Simeon and Levi are brethren; instruments of CRUELTY are in their habitations. . . . Cursed be their anger, for it was fierce; and their wrath, for it was CRUEL" (Gen. 49:5, 7a). On his deathbed Jacob spoke of this two sons' former behavior as oppressors of the city known as Shechem. All forms of the word instrument show the seal of oppressor: *instrument* (8x) and *instruments* (51x) = 59. The Bible combination *Simeon and Levi* (5x), *instruments* (51x), *of cruelty* (2x), *are in their habitations* (1x) = 59.

The Hebrews' Egyptian Oppressors

"Therefore they did set over them taskmasters to AFFLICT them with their BURDENS. And they built for Pharaoh treasure cities, Pithom and Raamses" (Exod. 1:11). Again the Old Testament combination *burden* (58 vs) and *burdensome* (1 v) = 59 verses.

Egypt Oppresses the Hebrews with Rigorous Service

"And they made their lives bitter with HARD BONDAGE, in morter, and in brick, and in all manner of <u>service</u> in the field: all their <u>service</u>, wherein they made them serve, was with rigour. And the king of Egypt spake to the Hebrew midwives. . . . And he said, When ye do the office of a midwife to the Hebrew women, and see them upon the stools; if it be a son, then ye shall . . . cast into the river" (Exod. 1:14-16, 22). The new king's goal was to oppress the Hebrews so badly that their health, strength, and numbers would quickly diminish. Pharaoh's scheme for their demise was dual: to place the adult males under a slow death by slavery and the newborn males under a quick death by drowning. The word *service* is mentioned in 59 verses of the Law.

Another Egyptian King Arises to Oppress the Hebrews

"And it came to pass in process of time, that the king of Egypt died: and the children of Israel sighed by reason of the BONDAGE, and they cried, and their cry came up unto God by reason of the BONDAGE. And God heard their groaning, and God remembered his covenant with Abraham, with Isaac, and with Jacob. And God looked upon the children of Israel, and God had respect unto them" (Exod. 2:23-25). All forms of the word bondage show the seal of the oppressor in the following way: *bond* (10 bks), *bonds* (11 bks), *bondage* (15 bks), *bondmaid* (2 bks), *bondmaids* (1 bk), *bondman* (3 bks), *bondmen* (10 bks), *bondservant* (1 bk), *bondservice* (1 bk), *bondwoman* (2 bks), *bondwomen* (3 bks) = 59 books.

Egyptian Oppressors Make Israel Cry

At the burning bush the Lord informed Moses that He was well aware of Israel's desperate and oppressive situation. "Now therefore, behold, the <u>cry</u> of the children of Israel is come unto me: and I have also seen the OPPRESSION wherewith the <u>Egyptians</u> OPPRESS them" (Exod. 3:9). The word *cry* is mentioned in 159 verses of the Old Testament. The Exodus combination *Egyptian/s* (58x), *oppress them* (1x) = 59.

59th Verse of Exodus

"And he said, Certainly I will be with thee; and this shall be a token unto thee, that I have sent thee: When thou <u>hast brought forth the people out of</u> <u>Egypt</u>, ye shall serve God upon this mountain" (Exod. 3:12). The Lord was overseeing a situation where Pharaoh was the oppressor and Moses was the deliverer. The phrase *brought forth* is mentioned in 59 verses of the Old Testament. The Bible combination *hast brought forth the people out of* (1x), *Egypt* (558x) = 559.

The Lord Looks upon Israel's Oppression

"And the people believed: and when they heard that the LORD had visited the children of Israel, and that he had looked upon their AFFLICTION, then they bowed their heads and worshipped" (Exod. 4:31). The word *affliction* is mentioned in 59 verses of the Old Testament.

Oppressor Pharaoh Increases Israel's Daily Workload

"And Pharaoh commanded the same day the TASKMASTERS of the people, and their officers, saying, Ye shall no more give the people straw to make brick, as heretofore: let them go and gather straw for themselves. And the tale of the bricks, which they did make heretofore, ye shall

LAY UPON them; ye shall not diminish ought thereof: for they be idle; therefore they cry, saying, Let us go and sacrifice to our God. Let there more <u>work</u> be LAID UPON the men, that they may labour therein" (Exod. 5:6-9a). This passage corresponds with our first definition of oppress: subject to a burdensome or harsh exercise of authority. We repeat the following seals.

The word *work* is mentioned in 59 verses of Exodus.
The word *work* is mentioned in 59 verses of Major Prophets.

Israel's Oppression Awaits Tangible Alleviation

"And Moses spake so unto the children of Israel: but they hearkened not unto Moses for anguish of spirit, and for CRUEL <u>BONDAGE</u>" (Exod. 6:9). The Israelites' minds were not encouraged by Moses' good-news message from the Lord. In accordance with our first, third, and fourth definitions of oppress, the Israelites' minds were heavily laid upon because of their cruel Egyptian oppressors, and their bodies were still physically weighed down with weariness. Again all forms of the word *bondage* are found collectively in 59 books of the Bible.

59th Chapter of the Bible

In this chapter the Lord continues to be the Oppressor over Israel's oppressor. Pharaoh is guilty of burdening Israel with cruel and unjust impositions and restraints. In response to the Egyptian oppressor's stubbornness the Divine Oppressor brings three more judgments upon Egypt.

The Fifth Judgment—"For if thou refuse to let them go, and wilt hold them still, Behold, the hand of the LORD is <u>upon</u> thy cattle which is in the field, <u>upon</u> the horses, <u>upon</u> the asses, <u>upon</u> the camels, <u>upon</u> the oxen, and <u>upon</u> the sheep: there shall be a very GRIEVIOUS murrain" (Exod. 9:2-3). This verse meets the conditions of our fifth definition of the word oppress: to press upon or against. The word *upon* is mentioned in 159 verses of Exodus!

The Sixth Judgment—Pharaoh's refusal caused God to bring about yet another oppressive judgment upon Egypt. "<u>And</u> the LORD said unto Moses and unto Aaron, Take to you handfuls of ashes of the furnace, and let Moses sprinkle it toward the heaven in the sight of Pharaoh. And it shall become small dust in all the land of Egypt, and shall be a boil breaking forth with blains upon man, and upon beast, throughout all the land of Egypt" (vv. 8-9). In this oppressor passage the leading word *And* is the 5959th word of Exodus.

"And they took ashes of the furnace, and stood before <u>Pharaoh</u>; and Moses sprinkled it up toward heaven; and it became a boil breaking forth with blains <u>upon</u> man, and <u>upon</u> beast" (v. 10). This verse presents the 59th occurrence of the oppressor name *Pharaoh* in Exodus, and it pertains to God's judgment upon Pharaoh's unabated oppression of Israel. Again the word *upon* is mentioned in 159 verses of Exodus!

For the first time in this oppressor-of-Israel story we see the Lord placing a specific judgment upon Pharaoh. "And the LORD hardened the heart of Pharaoh" (v. 12a). Pharaoh's heart now underwent oppression from the Lord, and it was soon to increase exponentially. "Thus saith the LORD God of the Hebrews, Let my people go, that they may serve me. For I will at this time send all my <u>plagues</u> upon thine heart, and upon thy servants, and upon thy people; that thou mayest know that there is none like me in all the earth" (vv. 13b-14). Again the phrase *the plague* is mentioned in 59 verses of the Old Testament.

The Seventh Judgment—"As yet exaltest thou thyself against my people, that thou wilt not let them go? Behold, to morrow about this time I will cause it to rain a very GRIEVOUS hail, such as hath not been in Egypt since the foundation thereof even until now. . . . And Moses stretched forth his rod toward heaven: and the LORD sent thunder and hail, and the fire ran along upon the ground; and the LORD rained hail upon the land of Egypt. So there was hail, and fire mingled with the hail, very grievous, such as there was none like it in all the land of Egypt since it became a nation" (vv. 17-18, 23-24). The Old Testament combination *rain* (58 chs), *a very grievous hail* (1 ch) = 59 chapters.

259th Verse of Exodus

"And the LORD said unto Moses, Stretch out thine hand over the land of Egypt for the locusts, that they may come up upon the land of Egypt, and eat every herb of the land, even all that the hail hath left. . . . And the locusts went up over all the land of Egypt, and rested in all the coasts of Egypt: very GRIEVOUS were they; before them there were no such locusts as they, neither after them shall be such" (Exod. 10:12, 14). This passage presents the Bible's 59th occurrence of the phrase *the land of Egypt*, and it pertains to the land's oppression at the hands of a divine Oppressor. The underlined words mark the 259th verse of Exodus.

Egypt's Divine Oppressor Devours the Land with Locusts

"For they covered the face of the whole earth, so that the land was darkened; and they did eat every herb of the land, and all the fruit of the trees which the hail had left: and there remained not any green thing in the trees, or in the herbs of the field, through all the land of Egypt" (Exod. 10:15). This oppressor-of-Egypt verse is comprised of 59 words.

Moses—Egypt's Hebrew Oppressor

"And the LORD said unto Moses, Stretch out thine hand toward heaven, that there may be darkness over the land of Egypt, even darkness which may be felt. And Moses stretched forth his hand toward heaven; and there was a thick darkness in all the land of Egypt three days" (Exod. 10:21-22). Moses was God's instrument to bring oppressive darkness upon the land. The underlined name *Moses* is the 7459th word of Exodus. The Old Testament combination *Moses* (158 chs), *of the sons of Amram* (1 ch) = 159 chapters.

Egypt's Divine Oppressor to Smite All Their Gods & Firstborn

"For I will pass through the land of Egypt this night, and will smite all the firstborn in the land of Egypt, both man and beast; and against all the gods of Egypt I will execute judgment: I am the LORD" (Exod. 12:12). The word *gods* is mentioned in 59 verses of the Law.

1859th Verse of the Bible

"It is a night to be much observed unto the LORD for bringing them out from the land of Egypt: this is that night of the LORD to be observed of all the children of Israel in their generations" (Exod. 12:42). This verse pertains to the original oppressive night which Israel was to annually memorialize, a night wherein the divine Oppressor killed all of Egypt's firstborn. The phrase *the night* is mentioned in 59 chapters of the Old Testament.

Hebrews' Egyptian Oppressor Chases Them Down

"But the Egyptians pursued after them, all the horses and chariots of Pharaoh, and his horsemen, and his army, and overtook them encamping by the sea, beside Pi-hahiroth, before Baal-zephon.

And when Pharaoh drew nigh, the children of Israel lifted up their eyes, and, behold, the Egyptians marched after them; and they were sore <u>afraid</u>: and <u>the children of Israel cried out</u> unto the LORD" (Exod. 14:9-10). The word *horsemen* occurs 59 times in the Bible. The Old Testament combination *afraid* (158x) and *the children of Israel cried out* (1x) = 159.

Pharaoh's Army Covered with a Flood by Their Divine Oppressor

"And Moses stretched forth his hand over the sea, and the sea returned to his strength when the morning appeared; and the Egyptians fled against it; and the LORD overthrew the Egyptians in the midst of the sea. And <u>the waters</u> returned, and <u>covered the chariots, and the</u> horsemen, and all the host of Pharaoh that came into the sea after them; there remained not so much as one of them" (Exod. 14:27-28). Again the phrase *the waters* occurs 59 times in the Law. The Bible combination *waters* (258 vs) and *covered the chariots and the horsemen* (1 v) = 259 verses.

459th Verse of Exodus

"Then came Amalek, and <u>fought</u> with Israel in Rephidim" (Exod. 17:8). This 59th verse introduces an oppressor nation that goes by the name of their evil forefather Amalek. The word *fought* occurs naturally 59 times in the Old Testament.

Amalekites Defeated by an Oppressor Named Joshua

"<u>And Joshua discomfited Amalek and his people with the edge of the sword</u>" (Exod. 17:13). The Amalekites attempted to oppress Israel, but Israel oppressed them with the edge of the sword under Joshua's leadership and Moses' upheld hands. Again the phrase *his people* 159 times in the Bible. The sentence *and Joshua discomfited Amalek and his people with the edge of the sword* consists of 59 letters!

Moses Oppressed by the People's Oppressive Problems

"Thou wilt surely wear away, both thou, and this <u>people</u> that is with thee: for this thing is too HEAVY for thee; thou art not able to perform it thyself alone" (Exod. 18:18). This verse meets the conditions of our second definition of the word oppress: to lie heavily upon the mind or a person. Here the word *people* is the 52,059th word of the Bible.

2059th Verse of the Bible

"Thou shalt not take the name of the LORD thy God in vain; for the LORD will not hold him guiltless that taketh his name in vain" (Exod. 20:7). If an Israelite entered into this oppressive form of speech, he would be judicially dealt with by the divine Oppressor.

Master Not to Be the Oppressor of His Servant

"And <u>if a man</u> <u>smite his servant, or his maid,</u> with a rod, and he die under his hand; he shall be surely punished" (Exod. 21:20). Because slaves and bondservants suffered so adversely under their masters, the Lord gave this law to prevent their oppression. The phrase *if a man* is mentioned in 59 verses of the Old Testament. The Bible combination *master* (157x), *smite his servant* (1x), *or his maid* (1x) = 159.

> The word *servant* occurs 59 times in the Wisdom Books.
> The word *servant* occurs 59 times in the Gospels.
> The word *servant* is mentioned in 59 verses of the NT Narrative.

Israel Not to Be the Oppressor of Strangers

"Thou shalt neither VEX a stranger, nor OPPRESS him: for ye were strangers in the land of Egypt" (Exod. 22:21). The Bible combination *thou shalt neither vex* (1x), *a stranger* (53x), *nor oppress him for* (1x), *ye were strangers in the land of Egypt* (4x) = 59.

God Will Kill the Widow's & Orphan's Oppressor

"Ye shall not afflict any widow, or fatherless child. If thou afflict them in any wise, and they cry at all unto me, I will surely hear their cry; And my wrath shall wax hot, and I will kill you with the sword" (Exod. 22:22-24a). The Old Testament combination *ye shall not afflict any* (1x), *widow/s* (58x) = 59. The Bible combination *I will kill you* (1x), *with the sword* (58x) = 59. Again the word *cry* is mentioned in 159 verses of the Old Testament.

The Lord Is Oppressor of His People

"And the LORD repented of the evil which he thought to do unto his people." (Exod. 32:14). Again the phrase *his people* 159 times in the Bible. The sentence *and the LORD repented of the evil which he thought to do unto his people.* consists of 59 characters!

Book of Leviticus' 859 Verses

The book of Leviticus contains oppressive content. Man's oppressive sin against both God and his neighbor are the subject of most of this book. Sin oppresses or weighs down the one who is sinned against; man's sin weighs down the Lord; sin even weighs down the sinner himself. Proper treatment of the widow, the fatherless, and the poor are discussed in this book. Throughout Leviticus various sins are listed with laws also given to prevent or rectify each sinful action and restore each sinned-against person. The tragic consequences of sin against God must be remedied in the strangest of ways—some animal from the flock must be oppressed unto death on the sinner's behalf. Thus the laws of sacrifice are described in detail. The oppressive book of Leviticus contains 859 verses.

The Priest as a Sacerdotal Oppressor

"And the priest shall bring it unto the altar, and wring off his head, and burn it on the altar; and the blood thereof shall be wrung out at the side of the altar" (Lev. 1:15). The title *the priest* is mentioned in 59 verses of Numbers.

Sacrificial Animals Killed by Oppressor Priesthood

"And if he bring a lamb for a sin offering, he shall bring it a female without blemish. And he shall lay his hand upon the head of the sin offering, and slay it for a sin offering in the place where they kill the burnt offering" (Lev. 4:32-33). Every day thousands of animals were oppressed to death at the hands of their ordained oppressors. The Lord established this bloody system so His wrath would be satisfied and guilty sinners could go out free and forgiven.

> The term *sin offering* occurs 118 times in the Bible, a multiple of 59.
> The word *kill* is mentioned in 118 verses of the Bible, a multiple of 59.

159th Verse of Leviticus

"For whosoever eateth the fat of the beast, of which men offer an offering made by fire unto the LORD, even the soul that eateth it shall be cut off from his people" (Lev. 7:25). Whoever broke this commandment would be oppressed unto death. The phrase *be cut off* is mentioned in 59 verses of the Bible.

Leviticus 13:59

"This is the law of <u>the plague</u> of leprosy in a garment of woollen or linen, either in the warp, or woof, or any thing of skins, to pronounce it clean, or to pronounce it unclean" (Lev. 13:59). Leprosy is perhaps the most oppressive ailment man can have. The person's flesh rots away before his eyes, and all hope is taken away. There is no cure apart from the Lord's intervention. Again the phrase *the plague* is mentioned in 59 verses of the Old Testament.

Thou Shalt Not Be the Oppressor of Thy Neighbor

"<u>Thou shalt not avenge, nor bear any</u> grudge <u>against the children of thy people,</u> but <u>thou shalt love thy neighbour as thyself</u>: I am the LORD" (Lev. 19:18). The Bible combination *thou shalt not avenge* (1x), *nor bear any* (1x), *grudge* (3x), *against thy neighbour* (4x), *thou shalt love* (14x), *thy neighbour* (25x), *own neighbour* (1x), *as thyself* (10x) = 59. The phrase *his neighbour* is mentioned in 59 verses of the Old Testament.

The Spiritually Oppressive Blasphemer

"And he that <u>blasphemeth</u> the name of the LORD, he shall surely be put to death, and all the congregation shall certainly stone him: as well the stranger, as he that is born in the land, when he <u>blasphemeth</u> the name of the LORD, shall be put to death" (Lev. 24:16). Blasphemy is a blatant form of spiritual oppression toward any listeners standing by. All forms of the word blasphemy show the seal of the oppressor: *blaspmeme* (10x), *blasphemed* (16x), *blasphemer* (1x), *blaspmemers* (2x), *blasphemest* (1x), *blasphemeth* (5x), *blasphemy* (14x), *blasphemies* (6x), *blaspheming* (1x), *blasphemous* (2x), and *blasphemously* (1x) = 59.

The Year of Jubilee & Release of Oppressed Servants

"And ye shall hallow the fiftieth year, and proclaim liberty throughout all the land unto all the inhabitants thereof: it shall be a jubile unto you; and ye shall <u>return</u> every man unto his possession, and ye shall <u>return</u> every man unto his family. And if thou sell ought unto thy neighbour, or buyest ought of thy neighbour's hand, ye shall not OPPRESS one another. . . . Ye shall not therefore OPPRESS one another; but thou shalt fear thy God: for I am the LORD your God" (Lev. 25:10, 14, 17).

Those who had suffered poverty and oppression over the previous decades had their land legally returned to them on the fiftieth year. Their financial oppression was suddenly turned into land possession. From Genesis to the Gospels the word *return* occurs 259 times.

The Bondservant's Oppressor Master

"And if thy brother that dwelleth by thee be waxen poor, and be sold unto thee; thou shalt not compel him <u>to</u> serve as a BONDSERVANT" (Lev. 25:39). Here the word *to* is the 21,859th word of Leviticus, and it pertains to being an oppressor of a poor fellow citizen.

No Oppressive Idols or Images

"Ye shall make you no <u>idols</u> nor graven <u>image,</u> neither rear you up a standing <u>image,</u> neither shall ye set up any <u>image</u> of stone in your land, to bow down unto it: for I am the LORD your God" (Lev. 26:1). Idols become the owner's spiritual oppressor.

The word *idols* is mentioned in 59 chapters of the Bible.

The word *image* is mentioned in 59 verses of the Old Testament.

Beasts Will Become Disobedient Israel's Oppressors
"I will also send wild <u>beasts</u> among you, which shall rob you of your children, and destroy your cattle, and make you few in number; and your high ways shall be desolate" (Lev. 26:22). The word *beasts* is mentioned in 59 verses of the Major and Minor Prophets.

Enemies Will Become Disobedient Israel's Oppressors
"Then shall the land enjoy her sabbaths, as long as it lieth desolate, and ye be in your enemies' land; even then shall the land rest, and enjoy her sabbaths" (Lev. 26:34). This oppressor verse is the 3559th verse of the Bible.

Nadab & Abihu Meet the Oppressor
"And Nadab and Abihu, the sons of Aaron, took either of them his censer, and put fire therein, and put incense thereon, and offered strange fire before the LORD, which he commanded them not. And there went out fire <u>from the LORD</u>, and devoured them, and they died before the LORD" (Num. 10:1-2).

The phrase *from the LORD* occurs 59 times in the Old Testament.

The phrase *from the LORD* is mentioned in 59 verses of the OT.

Israel's Enemy Oppressors
"And if ye go to war in your land against <u>the enemy</u> that <u>OPPRESSETH</u> you, then ye shall blow an alarm with the trumpets; and ye shall be remembered before the LORD your God, and ye shall be saved from your enemies" (Num. 10:9). The Lord promised to aid Israel against their oppressors when they sounded a holy alarm. The Bible combination *the enemy* (54x) and *oppresseth* (5x) = 59.

4059th Verse of the Bible
"And while the flesh was yet between their teeth, ere it was chewed, the wrath of the LORD was kindled against the people, and the LORD smote the people with a very great plague. <u>And he called the name of that place Kibroth-hattaavah: because there they buried the people that lusted</u>" (Num. 11:34). The underlined words mark the 4059th verse of the Bible, and they reveal the devastating results of murmuring Israel's plague which came from their divine Oppressor.

Israel Oppresses God with Murmurings
"How long shall I bear with this evil congregation, which murmur AGAINST me? I have heard <u>the murmurings of the children of Israel</u>, which they murmur <u>AGAINST me</u>" (Num. 14:27). Soon after Israel refused to enter Canaan their murmurings reached a new oppressive low weighing down the Lord's heart; this caused Him to issue a severe judgment upon them. No one older than twenty years of age would ever enter the Promised Land. The adult murmurers would all die in the wilderness. The phrases *the murmurings of the children of Israel* (2x) and *against me* (157x) = 159.

One Sabbath-Breaker Faced Mosaic Oppressors

"And the LORD said unto Moses, The man shall be surely put to death. . . . And all the congregation brought him without the camp, and <u>stoned him with stones</u>, and he died; as the LORD commanded Moses" (Num. 15:35a-36). The guilty man who dared break the national Sabbath law soon felt the oppressive wrath of the Sabbath-Maker's death penalty. The Bible words *stoning* (1 v) and *stones* (158 vs) = 159 verses.

Korah & His Band Faced the Divine Oppressor

"And there came out a fire <u>from the LORD,</u> and consumed the two hundred and fifty men that offered incense" (Num. 16:35). Again the phrase *from the LORD* occurs 59 times in the Old Testament.

Disgruntled Israelites Visited by the Divine Oppressor

"And Moses said unto Aaron, Take a censer, and put fire therein from off the altar, and put on incense, and go quickly unto the congregation, and make an atonement for them: for there is wrath gone out <u>from the LORD;</u> <u>the plague</u> is begun" (Num. 16:46). The next day many people blamed Moses and Aaron for the 250 men's deaths; therefore, the Lord oppressed those murmuring people in His anger. Again the phrase *from the LORD* occurs 59 times in the Old Testament. Again the phrase *the plague* is mentioned in 59 verses of the Old Testament.

Disgruntled Israelites Visited by the Divine Oppressor Yet Again

"And the people spake AGAINST God, and AGAINST Moses, Wherefore have ye brought us up out of Egypt to die in the wilderness? for there is no bread, neither is there any water; and our soul loatheth this light bread. And the LORD sent fiery serpents among the people, and they bit the people; and much people of Israel <u>died</u>" (Num. 21:5-6). The Lord oppressed the people according to our fourth definition of the word: to put down, subdue, or suppress. Their resistance quickly turned to repentance. Again all forms of the word *die* occur 559 times in the Bible.

Og & His People Face His Mosaic Oppressors

"And they turned and went up by the way of Bashan: and Og the king of Bashan went out AGAINST them . . . to the battle at Edrei. And the LORD said unto Moses, Fear him not: for I have delivered him into thy hand, and all <u>his people</u>, and his land; and thou shalt do to him as thou didst unto Sihon king of the Amorites, which dwelt at Heshbon. So they smote him, and his sons, and all <u>his people</u>, until there was none left him alive: and they possessed his land" (21:33-35). Again the phrase *his people* 159 times in the Bible.

Balaam—An Occultic Oppressor of Peoples

"Come now therefore, I pray thee, curse me this people; for they are too mighty for me: peradventure I shall prevail, that we may smite them, and that I may drive them out of the land: for I wot that he whom thou blessest is blessed, and he whom thou <u>cursest</u> is <u>cursed</u>" (Num. 22:6). The Old Testament combination *cursest* (1 ch) and *cursed* (58 chs) = 59 chapters.

Numbers 26:59

"And the name of <u>Amram's</u> wife was <u>Jochebed, the daughter of Levi</u>, whom her mother bare to Levi in Egypt: and she bare unto Amram <u>Aaron</u> and <u>Moses</u>, and <u>Miriam</u> their sister" (Num. 26:59). This family unit felt the weight of Egypt's oppressor king. When the evil Pharaoh ordered all the male babies to be cast into the river, Moses' whole family became oppressed as they frantically sought to keep him alive. The combined family titles *Amram* (4 bks), *Jochebed* (2 bks), *the daughter of Levi* (1 bk), *Aaron* (16 bks), *Moses* (31 bks), *Miriam* (5 bks) = 59 books.

4559th Verse of the Bible

"Why should the name of our father be done away from among his family, because he hath no son? Give unto us therefore a possession among the brethren of our father" (Num. 27:4). This verse recalls the words of the daughters of Zelophehad as they were oppressively weighed down with care.

Fleeing from an Oppressive Avenger

"Then ye shall appoint you cities to be cities of refuge for you; that the slayer may flee thither, which killeth any person at unawares. And they shall be unto you cities for refuge from the avenger; that the manslayer die not, until he stand before the congregation in judgment" (Num. 35:11-12). This law was to protect innocent manslayers from being wrongfully oppressed unto death. The Bible combination *then ye shall appoint you cities* (1x), *to be cities of* (1x), *refuge for you* (1x), *that the slayer* (2x), *may flee thither* (1x), *which killeth any person at unawares* (1x), *and they shall be unto you cities for* (1x), *refuge* (47x), *from the avenger* (2x), *that the manslayer die not* (1x), *until he stand before the congregation in judgment* (1x) = 59.

4859th Verse of the Bible

"And of these cities which ye shall give six cities shall ye have for refuge" (Num. 35:13). These cities were designated places of long-term refuge for an innocent man fleeing from an avenger-oppressor.

Wilderness Generation Faced Their Divine Oppressor

"And the space in which we came from Kadesh-barnea, until we were come over the brook Zered, was thirty and eight years; until all the generation of the men of war were wasted out from among the host, as the LORD sware unto them. For indeed the hand of the LORD was against them, to destroy them from among the host, until they were consumed" (Deut. 2:13-15). The Bible combination *until all the generation* (2x), *of the men of war were wasted out* (1x), *from among the host* (2x), *as the LORD sware unto them* (1x), *for indeed* (4x), *the hand of the LORD* (36x), *was against them* (2x), *to destroy them* (7x), *from among the host* (2x), *until they were consumed* (2x) = 59.

4959th Verse of the Bible

"That also was accounted a land of giants: giants dwelt therein in old time; and the Ammonites call them Zamzummims" (Deut. 2:20). These giants were oppressors of natural men in a frightening way. The Old Testament combination *also was* (22x), *accounted* (6x), *a land of* (17x), *giants* (13x), *giants dwelt therein in old time* (1x) = 59.

Oppressor Kingdom of Bashan Suffers Defeat

"So the LORD our God delivered into our hands Og also, the king of Bashan, and all his people: and we smote him until none was left to him remaining" (Deut. 3:3). The oppressor kingdom of Bashan experienced a crushing oppression at the hands of the Israelites. The joined phrases *so the LORD our God delivered into our hands Og also, the king of Bashan,* consist of 59 characters!

16

The name *Bashan* occurs 59 times in the Bible.

5059ᵗʰ Verse of the Bible

"I stood between the LORD and you at that time, to shew you the word of the LORD: for ye were afraid by reason of the fire, and went not up into the mount" (Deut. 5:5). In that day, the nation was experiencing fearful emotions while their Oppressor God was speaking to them from the mountaintop flames.

"Thou Shalt Not Kill"

In repeating the Ten Commandments to the new generation Moses said, "Thou shalt not <u>kill</u>" (Deut. 5:17). The Lord would not tolerate such murderous oppressors. Again the word *kill* is mentioned in 118 verses of the Bible, a multiple of 59.

159ᵗʰ Chapter of the Bible

"Then beware lest thou forget the LORD, which brought thee forth out of the land of Egypt, from the house of BONDAGE" (Deut. 6:12). New generation is encouraged to remember their Lord who mightily delivered them from their Egyptian oppressors.

Oppressor

"And the LORD will take away from thee all sickness, and will put none of the evil <u>diseases</u> of Egypt, which thou knowest, upon thee; but will lay them upon all them that hate thee" (Deut. 7:15). The Lord recalls how He oppressed Egypt with horrible diseases. Here the oppressive word *diseases* is the 6659ᵗʰ word of Deuteronomy.

Do Not Forsake the Levite

"Take heed to thyself that thou <u>forsake</u> not <u>the Levite</u> as long as thou livest upon the earth" (Deut. 12:19). Because Levites were not granted any allotment of land, the people were to aid them in various ways. If the Levite's hometown did not help him, the people would subsequently be his oppressors. The Bible combination *forsake* (58x) and *the Levite thy brother* (1x) = 59. The title *Levite(s)* is mentioned in 59 verses of Second Chronicles.

His Relief from Oppressor Neighbor in the Sabbatic Year

"At the end of every seven years thou shalt make a release. And this is the manner of the release: Every creditor that lendeth ought unto <u>his neighbour</u> shall release it; he shall not exact it of <u>his neighbour</u>, or of his brother; because it is called the LORD'S release" (Deut. 15:1-2). During this year of release indebted Hebrews were to have their oppressive financial obligations wiped clean. Such a law would prevent a creditor from being an oppressor. Again the phrase *his neighbour* is mentioned in 59 verses of the Old Testament.

The Bread of Affliction

"Thou shalt eat no leavened bread with it; seven days shalt thou eat unleavened bread therewith, even the bread of AFFLICTION; for thou camest forth out of the land of Egypt in haste: that thou mayest remember the day when thou camest forth out of the land of Egypt all the days of thy life" (Deut. 16:3). The annual Passover observance and subsequent eating of unleavened bread for a week was to be a parabolic memorial of Israel's deliverance from her Egyptian oppressors. Again the word *affliction* is mentioned in 59 verses of the Old Testament.

Let Not Your Hearts Be Oppressed with Fear

Before going into battle against vastly armed Canaanite nations, the high priest was to encourage the Israelites with the following words to alleviate their mental oppression. "And shall say unto them, Hear, O Israel, ye approach this day unto battle against your enemies: let not your hearts faint, <u>fear</u> not, and do not tremble, neither be ye terrified because of them; For the LORD your God is he that goeth with you, to fight for you against your enemies, to save you" (Deut. 20:3-4). A promise is given that the Lord would oppress Israel's enemies for them. The word *fear* occurs 59 times in the Law.

559th Verse of Deuteronomy

"And the elders of that city shall bring down the heifer unto a rough valley, which is neither eared nor sown, and shall strike off the heifer's neck there in the valley" (Deut. 21:4). In the matter of inquest for the slain victim, a ceremonial act was to be undertaken wherein a heifer was oppressed unto death on behalf of the innocent victim's family to legally satisfy their desire to avenge his blood.

Do Not Oppress a Poor, Needy Servant

"Thou shalt not OPPRESS an hired <u>servant</u> that is poor and needy, whether he be of thy brethren, or of thy strangers that are in thy land within thy gates" (Deut. 24:14). Again the word *servant* is mentioned in 59 verses of the NT Narrative.

Oppressor Not to Beat Criminal Overbearingly

"Forty stripes he may give him, and not exceed: lest, if he should exceed, and <u>beat</u> him above these with many stripes, then thy brother should seem vile unto thee" (Deut. 25:3). All forms of the word *beat* are mentioned in 59 chapters of the Bible.

659th Verse of Deuteronomy

"Thou shalt not muzzle the <u>ox</u> when he treadeth out the corn" (Deut. 25:4). This injunction protected a beast of burden from unnecessary oppression at his master's hands. The title *ox* occurs naturally 59 times in the Old Testament.

Formerly Afflicted by Egyptians Oppressors

"And <u>the Egyptians</u> <u>evil entreated us,</u> and AFFLICTED us, and laid upon us hard BONDAGE: And when we cried unto the LORD God of our fathers, the LORD heard our voice, and looked on our AFFLICTION, and our labour, and our OPPRESSION" (Deut. 26:6-7). The Exodus combination *Egyptian/s* (58x), *evil entreated this people* (1x) = 59.

Mosaic Laws Were Oppressive toward the Disobedient

"Cursed be he that confirmeth not all the words of <u>this law</u> to do them. And all the people shall say, Amen" (Deut. 27:26). The Lord promised oppression to the man or woman who dared break any one of His holy laws. The term *the law* is mentioned in 59 verses of the OT Narrative.

Deuteronomy 28:59

"Then the LORD will make thy <u>plagues</u> wonderful, and <u>the plagues</u> of thy seed, even great <u>plagues</u>, and of long continuance, and sore sicknesses, and of long continuance" (Deut. 28:59). The Lord Himself pledged to become Israel's Oppressor if they did not walk uprightly before

Him. Again the phrase *the plague* is mentioned in 59 verses of the Old Testament.

Disobedient Nation to Be Oppressed in Heart & Mind

"And among these nations shalt thou find no ease, neither shall the sole of thy foot have rest: but the LORD shall give thee there a trembling heart, and failing of eyes, and SORROW OF MIND" (Deut. 28:65). The Lord promised to become the Oppressor of anyone who habitually broke His holy laws and refused to repent. This verse meets the conditions of our second definition of the word oppress: to lie heavily upon the mind or a person. The joined phrases *give thee there a trembling heart, and failing of eyes, and sorrow of mind* consist of 59 letters!

5959th Verse of the Bible

"And the armed men went before the priests that blew with the trumpets, and the rereward came after the ark, the priests going on, and blowing with the trumpets" (Josh. 6:9). Jericho's Israelite oppressors circled the city in a unique military way—with the trumpets of God and the Ark of God.

5968th Verse of the Bible

"And ye, in any wise keep yourselves from the accursed thing, lest ye make yourselves accursed, when ye take of the accursed thing, and make the camp of Israel a curse, and trouble it" (Josh. 6:18). The person who violated this command would become an oppressor of the people; his fault would bring oppression from the Lord upon all the people. The Old Testament combination *curse* (58 chs), *and trouble it* (1 ch) = 59 chapters.

Achan Brings Oppression on the Camp

"But the children of Israel committed a trespass in the accursed thing: for Achan . . . took of the accursed thing: and the anger of the LORD was kindled against the children of Israel. . . . And the men of Ai smote of them about thirty and six men: for they chased them from before the gate even unto Shebarim, and smote them in the going down: wherefore the hearts of the people melted, and became as water" (Josh. 7:1, 5). These two oppression verses are the 5978th and 5982nd verses of the Bible, numbers from the 59-hundred range.

Israel Oppresses Achan unto Death

"And Joshua said, Why hast thou TROUBLED us? the LORD shall TROUBLE thee this day. And all Israel stoned him with stones, and burned them with fire, after they had stoned them with stones" (Josh. 7:25).

Joshua used the choice words troubled and trouble as a play on Achan's name which means troubler. Achan's disobedience brought about the nation's great oppression from the Lord. Joshua sought to alleviate it by oppressing Achan unto death. The Bible combination *troubled* (58 chs) and *troubler* (1 ch) = 59 chapters. All forms of the word *trouble* are collectively mentioned in 59 chapters of the Wisdom Books.

Joshua—Fiery Oppressor of the Canaanite Nations

"And the LORD said unto Joshua, Stretch out the spear that is in thy hand toward Ai; for I will give it into thine hand. And Joshua stretched out the spear that he had in his hand toward the city. . . . And Joshua burnt Ai, and made it an heap for ever, even a desolation unto this day" (Josh.

8:18, 28). Joshua's divine ordination sanctioned him to become the great oppressor of Canaan. The phrase *and Joshua* occurs 59 times in the book of Joshua. The Bible combination *stretched out the* (6x), *spear* (45x), *that he had in his hand* (1x), *toward the city* (3x), *and Joshua burnt Ai and made it* (1x), *an heap for ever* (2x), *even a desolation unto this day* (1x) = 59.

Oppressors Smite & Burn City of Jerusalem

"Now the children of Judah had <u>fought</u> against <u>Jerusalem</u>, and had taken it, and smitten it with the edge of the sword, and set the city on fire" (Judg. 1:8). Again the word *fought* occurs naturally 59 times in the Old Testament.

> The name *Jerusalem* is mentioned in 59 verses of Acts.
> The phrase *of Jerusalem* occurs 159 times in the Old Testament.
> The phrase *of Jerusalem* is mentioned in 59 chapters of Major/Minor Prophets.

59th Verse of Judges

"Therefore the LORD left those <u>nations</u>, without driving them out hastily; neither delivered he them into the hand of Joshua" (Judg. 2:23). The Lord allowed some heathen nations to remain in the land to become Israel's punitive oppressors. The phrase *the nations* is mentioned in 159 verses of the Old Testament.

6559th Verse of the Bible

"<u>And they forsook the LORD, and served Baal and Ashtaroth</u>. And the anger of the LORD was hot against Israel, and he delivered them into the hands of SPOILERS that spoiled them, and he sold them into the hands of their enemies round about, so that they could not any longer stand before their enemies. Whithersoever they went out, the hand of the LORD was AGAINST them for evil, as the LORD had said, and as the LORD had sworn unto them: and they were greatly DISTRESSED" (Judg. 2:13-15). The underlined words indicate the 6559th verse of the Bible, and they reveal the reason the Lord became Israel's Oppressor.

Israel's Oppressor Judges

"And when the LORD raised them up <u>judges</u>, then the LORD was with the <u>judge</u>, and <u>delivered them out of the hand of their enemies all the days of the judge</u>: for it repented the LORD because of their groanings by reason of them that OPPRESSED them and vexed them" (Judg. 2:18). The words *delivered them out of the hand of their enemies all the days of the judge* consist of 59 letters! The Old Testament title *judge* (112 vs) and *judges* (47 vs) = 159 verses.

Israel's Oppressor Judge—Othniel

"And when the children of Israel cried unto the LORD, the <u>LORD raised up a deliverer to the children of Israel, who delivered them</u>, even Othniel the son of Kenaz, Caleb's younger brother. And the Spirit of the LORD came upon him, and he judged Israel, and went out to war: and the LORD delivered Chushan-rishathaim king of Mesopotamia into his hand; and his hand prevailed against Chushan-rishathaim. And the land had rest forty years. And Othniel the son of Kenaz died" (Judg. 3:9-11). The word *LORD raised up a deliverer to the children of Israel, who delivered them* consists of 59 letters!

Israel's Oppressor Judge—Ehud

"But when the children of Israel cried unto the LORD, the LORD raised them up a deliverer, EHUD the son of Gera, a Benjamite, a man lefthanded: and by him the children of Israel sent a present unto Eglon the king of Moab. But EHUD made him a dagger which had two edges, of a cubit length; and he did gird it under his raiment upon his right thigh. And he brought the present unto Eglon king of Moab: and Eglon was a very fat man. And when he had made an end to offer the present, he sent away the people that bare the present. But he himself turned again from the quarries that were by Gilgal, and said, I have a secret errand unto thee, O king: who said, Keep silence. And all that stood by him went out from him. And EHUD came unto him; and he was sitting in a summer parlour, which he had for himself alone. And EHUD said, I have a message from God unto thee. And he arose out of his seat. And EHUD put forth his left hand, and took the dagger from his right thigh, and thrust it into his belly: And the haft also went in after the blade; and the fat closed upon the blade, so that he could not draw the dagger out of his belly; and the dirt came out. Then EHUD went forth through the porch, and shut the doors of the parlour upon him, and locked them. When he was gone out, his servants came; and when they saw that, behold, the doors of the parlour were locked, they said, Surely he covereth his feet in his summer chamber. And they tarried till they were ashamed: and, behold, he opened not the doors of the parlour; therefore they took a key, and opened them: and, behold, their lord was fallen down dead on the earth. And EHUD escaped while they tarried, and passed beyond the quarries, and escaped unto Seirath. And it came to pass, when he was come, that he blew a trumpet in the mountain of Ephraim, and the children of Israel went down with him from the mount, and he before them. And he said unto them, Follow after me: for the LORD hath delivered your enemies the Moabites into your hand. And they went down after him, and took the fords of Jordan toward Moab, and suffered not a man to pass over. And they slew of Moab at that time about ten thousand men, all lusty, and all men of valour; and there escaped not a man. So Moab was subdued that day under the hand of Israel. And the land had rest fourscore years. And after HIM was Shamgar the son of Anath" (Judg. 3:15-31a).

From the beginning of this passage where we find the first mention of the name *Ehud* unto the last reference to *him* is comprised of 459 words!

Israel's Oppressor Judge—Shamgar

"And after him was Shamgar the son of Anath, which slew of the Philistines six hundred men with an ox goad: and he also delivered Israel" (Judg. 3:31). Again the title *ox* occurs naturally 59 times in the Old Testament.

Israel's Oppressor Judge—Deborah

"And the LORD sold them into the hand of Jabin king of Canaan, that reigned in Hazor; the captain of whose host [was] Sisera, which dwelt in Harosheth of the Gentiles. And the children of Israel cried unto the LORD: for he had nine hundred chariots of iron; and twenty years he mightily oppressed the children of Israel. And DEBORAH, a prophetess, the wife of Lapidoth, she judged Israel at that time. And she dwelt under the palm tree of Deborah between Ramah and Beth-el in mount Ephraim: and the children of Israel came up to her for judgment" (Judg. 4:2-5). In this introductory passage there are 59 words preceding the name *Deborah*. In this introductory passage there are 59 naturally occurring words upon reaching the name of *Deborah*; the translators supplied the word in brackets.

Israel's Oppressor Judge—Barak

"And she sent and called Barak the son of Abinoam out of Kedesh-naphtali, and said unto him, Hath not the LORD God of Israel commanded, saying, Go and draw toward mount Tabor, and take with thee ten thousand men of the children of Naphtali and of the children of Zebulun? And I will draw unto thee to the river Kishon Sisera, the captain of Jabin's army, with his chariots and his multitude; and I will deliver him into thine hand" (Judg. 4:6-7). The opening words *and she sent and called Barak the son of Abinoam out of Kedesh-naphtali* consist of 59 characters!

Children of Israel Suffer under Canaanite Oppressor Jabin

"And the children of Israel again did evil in the sight of the LORD, when Ehud was dead. And the LORD sold them into the hand of Jabin king of Canaan, that reigned in Hazor; the captain of whose host was Sisera, which dwelt in Harosheth of the Gentiles. And the children of Israel cried unto the LORD: for he had nine hundred chariots of iron; and twenty years he mightily OPPRESSED the children of Israel" (Judg. 4:1-3). Here the underlined word *the* is the 178,159th word of the Bible, and it supports the keyword oppressed.

God Subdues Israel's Canaanite Oppressor

"And when he came into her tent, behold, Sisera lay dead, and the nail was in his temples. So God SUBDUED on that day Jabin the king of Canaan before the children of Israel" (Judg. 4:22d-23). Again the title *God* is mentioned in 59 verses of Second Samuel.

6659th Verse of the Bible

"And so it was, when Israel had sown, that the Midianites came up, and the Amalekites, and the children of the east, even they came up AGAINST them; And they encamped AGAINST them, and destroyed the increase of the earth, till thou come unto Gaza, and left no sustenance for Israel, neither sheep, nor ox, nor ass. . . . And Israel was greatly impoverished because of the Midianites; and the children of Israel cried unto the LORD" (Judg. 6:3-4, 6). The underlined words mark the 6659th verse of the Bible, and it describes how an enemy nation mightily oppressed the Hebrews for seven years.

Israel's Oppressor Judge—Gideon

"Thus was Midian SUBDUED before the children of Israel, so that they lifted up their heads no more. And the country was in quietness forty years in the days of Gideon" (Judg. 8:28). Here the word *before* is the 182,659th word of the Bible, and it supports the oppressor-related word subdued.

Abimelech Oppressed His 70 Brothers unto Death

"Then God sent an evil spirit between Abimelech and the men of Shechem; and the men of Shechem dealt treacherously with Abimelech: That the CRUELTY done to the threescore and ten sons of Jerubbaal might come, and their blood be laid upon Abimelech their brother, which slew them; and upon the men of Shechem, which aided him in the killing of his brethren" (Judg. 9:23-24). From Genesis to Judges the name *Abimelech('s)* is mentioned in 59 verses.

City of Shechem Beaten Down & Oppressed

"And Abimelech fought against the city all that day; and he took the city, and slew the people that was therein, and beat down the city, and sowed it with salt" (Judges 9:45). Again the word *fought* occurs naturally 59 times in the Old Testament. All forms of the word *beat* are mentioned in 59 chapters of the Bible.

The Children of Israel's Oppressor, Ammon

"And the anger of the LORD was hot against Israel, and he sold them into the hands of the Philistines, and into the hands of the children of Ammon. And that year they vexed and OPPRESSED the children of Israel: eighteen years" (Judg. 10:7-8a). The Judges combination *oppressed* (4 vs), *the children of Israel* (55 vs) = 59 verses.

Israel's Oppressor Judge—Jephthah

"So Jephthah passed over unto the children of Ammon to fight against them; and the LORD delivered them into his hands. And he smote them from Aroer, even till thou come to Minnith, even twenty cities, and unto the plain of the vineyards, with a very great slaughter. Thus the children of Ammon were SUBDUED before the children of Israel" (Judg. 11:32-33). In this verse there are 59 words surrounding the oppressor-related word *subdued*.

Israel's Oppressor Judge—Samson

"For, lo, thou shalt conceive, and bear a son; and no razor shall come on his head: for the child shall be a Nazarite unto God from the womb: and he shall begin to deliver Israel out of the hand of the Philistines" (Judg. 13:5). Here the word *out* is the 11,159th word of Judges, and it refers to being delivered out from under the control of an oppressor people.

Samson Oppresses 1000 Philistines in One Day

"And when he came unto Lehi, the Philistines shouted AGAINST him: and the Spirit of the LORD came mightily upon him. . . . And he found a new jawbone of an ass, and put forth his hand, and took it, and slew a thousand men therewith" (Judg. 15:14a, 15). The Bible combination *and he found a* (2x), *new jawbone of an ass* (1x), *and put forth his hand and took it* (1x), *and slew a* (3x), *thousand men* (52x) = 59.

Philistines' Failed Attempt to Oppress Samson

"Now there were men lying in wait, abiding with her in the chamber. And she said unto him, The Philistines be upon thee, Samson. And he brake the withs, as a thread of tow is broken when it toucheth the fire. So his strength was not known" (Judg. 16:9). This is the 6959th verse of the Bible.

Delilah Oppressed Samson with Her Persistent Prying

"And it came to pass, when she PRESSED him daily with her words, and urged him, so that his soul was VEXED unto death" (Judg. 16:16). The phrases *pressed him daily with her words, and urged him, so that his soul was vexed* consists of 59 letters!

Delilah Oppresses Samson While He Sleeps

"And she made him sleep upon her knees; and she called for a man, and she caused him to shave off the seven locks of his head; and she began to AFFLICT him, and his strength went from him" (Judg. 16:19). By remaining steadfast with her calculated plan, Delilah finally succeeded at oppressing the champion of Israel. According to our fourth definition, she subdued or suppressed him. Again the word *affliction* is mentioned in 59 verses of the Old Testament. This is the 459th verse of Judges.

Philistines Become Samson's Oppressor

"But the <u>Philistines</u> took him, and put out his eyes, and brought him down to Gaza, and BOUND him with fetters of brass; and he did grind in the prison house" (Judg. 16:21). Fitting our first definition of oppress, the Philistines burdened Samson with cruel impositions and restraints. The name *Philistines* occurs 118 times in First Samuel, a multiple of 59.

Samson Oppresses More Than 3000 Philistines

"And Samson took hold of the two middle pillars upon which the house stood, and on which it was borne up, of the one with his right hand, and of the other with his left. And Samson said, Let me die with the Philistines. And he bowed himself with all his might; and the house <u>fell</u> upon the lords, and upon all the people that were therein. So the dead which he slew at his death were more than they which he slew in his life" (Judg. 16:29-30). The word *fell* occurs 159 times in the Old Testament.

7059th Verse of the Bible

"And the Levite, the husband of the woman that was slain, answered and said, I came into Gibeah that belongeth to Benjamin, I and my concubine, to lodge" (Judg. 20:4). This poor Levite begins to explain how he had suffered mental oppression from the Benjamite oppressors who assaulted his handmaid.

Men of Israel Become Benjamin's Oppressors

"And the <u>men of Israel</u> <u>went out to battle AGAINST</u> <u>Benjamin</u>; and the men of Israel put themselves in array to fight AGAINST them at Gibeah" (Judg. 20:20). Because Benjamin's wickedness had reached such an incredible low, the other tribes were sent to oppress them or subdue them. The Old Testament combination *went out to battle against* (1x), *Benjamin* (158x) = 159.

The phrase *men of Israel* occurs 59 times in the Old Testament.
The phrase *of Israel* occurs 59 times in the Minor Prophets.

59th Verse of Ruth

"And she lay at <u>his feet</u> until the morning: and she rose up before one could know another. And he said, Let it not be known that a woman came into the floor" (Ruth 3:14). Showing the spirit of a true servant, Ruth placed herself in a subdued or subservient position at Boaz's feet. She was desperately seeking him to become her kinsman redeemer and thereby deliver her from an oppressive life of widowhood, childlessness, and poverty. Throughout the Bible, being under someone's foot symbolizes oppression. From Genesis to the Gospels the phrase *his feet* is mentioned in 59 verses.

Peninnah Becomes Hannah's Oppressor

"And she was in BITTERNESS OF SOUL, and prayed unto the LORD, and wept sore. And she vowed a vow, and said, O LORD of hosts, if thou wilt indeed look on the AFFLICTION of thine handmaid, and remember me, and not forget thine handmaid, but wilt give unto thine handmaid a man child, then I will give him unto the LORD all the days of his life, and there shall no razor come upon his head" (1 Sam. 1:10-11). Barren Hannah drew the Lord's attention to her daily oppressor. Peninnah had been afflicting Hannah with constant taunts and reproaches concerning her barrenness. Again the word *affliction* is mentioned in 59 verses of the Old Testament.

59th Verse of First Samuel

"Behold, the days come, that I will cut off thine arm, and the arm of thy father's house, that there shall not be an old man in thine house" (1 Sam. 2:31). God prophesied that He would oppress, that is, suppress the rule of Eli's priestly line.

The Lord, Eli's Oppressor

"And the man of thine, whom I shall not cut off from mine altar, shall be to consume thine eyes, and to GRIEVE thine heart: and all the increase of thine house shall die in the flower of their age. And this shall be a sign unto thee, that shall come upon thy two sons, on Hophni and Phinehas; in one day they shall die both of them" (1 Sam. 2:33-34). The word *heart* occurs 159 times in the Major Prophets. Again all forms of the word *die* occur 559 times in the Bible.

The Lord, Philistines' Oppressor

"And the Philistines took the ark of God, and brought it from Eben-ezer unto Ashdod. . . . But the hand of the LORD was HEAVY upon them of Ashdod, and he destroyed them, and smote them with emerods, even Ashdod and the coasts thereof. And when the men of Ashdod saw that it was so, they said, The ark of the God of Israel shall not abide with us: for his hand is sore upon us, and upon Dagon our god" (1 Sam. 5:1, 6-7). The Lord greatly oppressed the Philistines for their pride and presumption. The phrase *upon them* is mentioned in 159 verses of the Old Testament. The Bible combination *his hand is sore* (1x), *upon us* (58x) = 59.

"So the Philistines were SUBDUED, and they came no more into the coast of Israel: and the hand of the LORD was AGAINST the Philistines all the days of Samuel" (1 Sam. 7:13). Again the name *Philistines* occurs 118 times in the First Samuel, a multiple of 59.

Make Us a King Like the Other Nations

Israel's elders went to Samuel at Ramah "and said unto him, Behold, thou art old, and thy sons walk not in thy ways: now make us a king to judge us like all the nations" (1 Sam. 8:5). The Lord counseled Samuel, "Now therefore hearken unto their voice: howbeit yet protest solemnly unto them, and shew them the manner of the king that shall reign over them" (v. 9). God wanted to let the people know that their earthly king would typically be of the oppressive sort. The Bible phrases *a king* (47 vs) and *a * king* (12 vs) = 59 verses.

The Oppressive Manner of Israel's Earthly Kings

"Now therefore hearken unto their voice: howbeit yet protest solemnly unto them, and shew them the manner of the king that shall reign over them. . . . And Samuel told all the words of the LORD unto the people that asked of him a king. And he said, This will be the manner of the king that shall reign over you: He will take your sons, and appoint them for himself, for his chariots, and to be his horsemen; and some shall run before his chariots. . . . And he will take your daughters to be confectionaries, and to be cooks, and to be bakers. And he will take your fields, and your vineyards, and your oliveyards, even the best of them, and give them to his servants. And he will take the tenth of your seed, and of your vineyards, and give to his officers, and to his servants. And he will take your menservants, and your maidservants, and your goodliest young men, and your asses, and put them to his work. He will take the tenth of your sheep: and ye shall be his servants. And ye shall cry out in that day because of your king which ye shall have chosen you" (1 Sam. 8:9, 10-11, 13-18a).

Recalling that the number 18 stands for oppression, the phrase *manner of* occurs 118 times in the Bible, a multiple of 59. Again the word *cry* is mentioned in 159 verses of the Old Testament.

Israel's Former Deliverance from Their Egyptian Oppressors

"And Samuel called the people together unto the LORD to Mizpeh; And said unto the children of Israel, Thus saith the LORD God of Israel, I brought up Israel out of Egypt, and delivered you <u>out of the hand of</u> <u>the Egyptians</u>, and out of the hand of all kingdoms, and of them that OPPRESSED you: And ye have this day rejected your God" (1 Sam. 10:17-19a). The Exodus combination *out of the hand of* (6x), *the Egyptians* (53x) = 59.

Samuel Oppresses Israel with Thunder & Rain

"Is it not wheat harvest to day? I will call unto the LORD, and he shall send <u>thunder</u> and <u>rain</u>; that ye may perceive and see that your wickedness is great, which ye have done in the sight of the LORD, in asking you a king. So Samuel called unto the LORD; and the LORD sent <u>thunder</u> and <u>rain</u> <u>that day</u>: and all the people greatly feared the LORD and Samuel" (1 Sam. 12:17-18). The Lord showed His great displeasure when He oppressed the people by ruining their wheat crops. The Old Testament words *rain* (58 chs) and *rainy* (1 ch) = 59 chapters. The Major and Minor Prophets combination *that day* (58 chs) and *thunder* (1 ch) = 59 chapters.

Saul, the Oppressor King

"And <u>Saul</u> answered, God do so and more also: for thou shalt surely <u>die</u>, Jonathan" (1 Sam. 14:44). Soon after becoming king, Saul's nature greatly transformed from a healthy spirit to a heavy spirit of oppression which never parted from him. Here Saul desired to oppress the spirit of victory with the spirit of death, even the death of his own heroic son. The Second Samuel combination *Saul* (57x) and *of death* (2x) = 59. Again all forms of the word *die* occur 559 times in the Bible.

7659th Verse of the Bible

"And he took his staff in his hand, and chose him five smooth stones out of the brook, and put them in a shepherd's bag which he had, even in a scrip; and his sling was in his hand: and he drew near to the Philistine" (1 Sam. 17:40). A young man prepares to oppress a giant unto death.

Saul's First Attempt to Oppress David

"And it came to pass on the morrow, that the evil spirit from God came upon Saul, Saul, and he prophesied in the midst of the house: and David played with his hand, as at other times: <u>and there was a javelin</u> <u>in Saul's hand</u>. <u>And Saul cast the javelin</u>; <u>for he said, I will</u> <u>smite</u> <u>David even</u> <u>to the wall</u> <u>with it</u>. And David avoided out of his presence" (1 Sam. 18:10-11). The OT Narrative combination *and there was a javelin* (1x), *in Saul's hand* (1x), *and Saul cast the javelin* (1x), *for he said I will* (1x), *smite* (42x), *David even* (4x), *to the wall* (7x), *with it* (2x) = 59.

Saul's Third Attempt to Oppress David

"And Saul spake to Jonathan his son, and to all his servants, that they should <u>kill</u> David" (1 Sam. 19:1). Again the word *kill* is mentioned in 118 verses of the Bible, a multiple of 59.

Saul's Fifth Attempt to Oppress David

"Saul also sent messengers unto David's house, to watch him, and to slay him in the morning: and Michal David's wife told him, saying, If thou save not thy life to night, <u>to morrow thou shalt be</u> <u>slain</u>" (1 Sam. 19:11). The OT Narrative combination *to morrow thou shalt be* (1x), *slain* (58x) = 59.

Saul's Seventh Attempt to Oppress David

"For as long as the son of Jesse liveth upon the ground, thou shalt not be established, nor thy kingdom. Wherefore now send and fetch him unto me, for he shall surely die" (1 Sam. 20:31). The Bible combination *for as long as the son of Jesse liveth upon the ground* (1x), *thou shalt not be established nor thy kingdom* (1x), *wherefore now send* (1x), *and fetch him* (4x), *for he shall* (30x), *surely die* (22x) = 59.

Saul's Ninth Attempt to Oppress David

"And David saw that Saul was come out to seek his life: and David was in the wilderness of Ziph in a wood" (1 Sam. 23:15). The Bible combination *was come out to seek* (1 v), *his life* (58 vs) = 59 verses.

Saul's Eleventh Attempt to Oppress David

"And it came to pass, when Saul was returned from following the Philistines, that it was told him, saying, Behold, David is in the wilderness of En-gedi. Then Saul took three thousand chosen men out of all Israel, and went to seek David and his men upon the rocks of the wild goats" (1 Sam. 24:1-2). The OT Narrative combination *and it came to pass when Saul* (1x), *was returned from following the Philistines* (1x), *that it was told him saying* (1x), *behold David is* (2x), *in the wilderness of En-gedi* (1x), *then Saul took* (1x), *three thousand chosen men* (2x), *out of all Israel and went* (1x), *to seek* (30x), *David and his men* (17x), *upon the rocks* (1x), *of the wild goats* (1x) = 59.

David Plans to Flee beyond the Reach of His Oppressor

"And David said in his heart, I shall now perish one day by the hand of Saul: there is nothing better for me than that I should speedily escape into the land of the Philistines; and Saul shall despair of me, to seek me any more in any coast of Israel: so shall I escape out of his hand" (1 Sam. 27:1). Again the word *escape* occurs 59 times in Scripture. There are 59 words in this oppressor verse.

> The phrase *of David* occurs 59 times in First/Second Chronicles.
> The name *David('s)* is mentioned in 459 verses of First/Second Samuel.

59th Verse of Second Samuel

"And they took up Asahel, and buried him in the sepulchre of his father, which was in Beth-lehem. And Joab and his men went all night, and they came to Hebron at break of day" (2 Sam. 2:32). This verse speaks of Asahel's oppression unto death. He was killed by Abner in hand-to-hand combat. Thus Abner became Asahel's oppressor. The name *Abner('s)* occurs a combined 59 times in First and Second Samuel.

God Will Save His People Israel from Their Oppressors

"Now then do it: for the LORD hath spoken of David, saying, By the hand of my servant David I will save my people Israel out of the hand of the Philistines, and out of the hand of all their enemies" (2 Sam. 3:18). The phrase *people Israel* is mentioned in 59 verses of the Bible.

Joab—Abner's Oppressor

"And when Abner was returned to Hebron, Joab took him aside in the gate to speak with him quietly, and smote him there under the fifth rib, that he <u>died</u>, for the blood of Asahel his brother" (2 Sam. 3:27). Again the name *Abner('s)* occurs a combined 59 times in First and Second Samuel. Again all forms of the word *die* occur 559 times in the Bible.

Sons of Rimmon—Ishbosheth's Oppressors
"And the sons of Rimmon the Beerothite, <u>Rechab and Baanah, went, and came about</u> <u>the heat of</u> <u>the day</u> to the house of Ish-bosheth, <u>who lay on a bed at noon. And they came thither into the</u> <u>midst of the house,</u> as though <u>they would have</u> <u>fetched wheat; and they</u> <u>smote him</u> <u>under the fifth</u> <u>rib</u>: and Rechab and Baanah his brother escaped. . . . and took his head, and gat them away through the plain all night" (2 Sam. 4:5-6, 7d). The Old Testament combination *Rechab and Baanah went and came about* (1x), *the heat of the day* (3x), *to the house of Ish-bosheth* (1x), *who lay on a bed at noon* (1x), *and they came thither into the midst of the house* (1x), *as though* (11x), *they would have* (2x), *fetched wheat and they* (1x), *smote him* (35x), *under the fifth rib* (3x) = 59.

David Subdued the Philistines Time after Time
"<u>And after this it came to pass, that</u> <u>David smote</u> <u>the Philistines, and SUBDUED them:</u> <u>and</u> <u>David took Metheg-ammah out of the hand of the Philistines</u>" (2 Sam. 8:1). The First and Second Samuel and First and Second Kings combination and after this it came to pass that (1x), *David smote* (5x), *the Philistines* (151x), *and subdued them* (1x), *and David took Metheg-ammah out of the hand of the Philistines* (1x) = 159.

8259th Verse of the Bible
"And the Syrians fled before Israel; and David slew the men of seven hundred chariots of the Syrians, and forty thousand horsemen, and smote Shobach the captain of their host, who <u>died</u> there" (2 Sam. 10:18). On this day the Israelites became the Syrians' oppressors. Again all forms of the word *die* occur 559 times in the Bible.

Amnon, Tamar's Oppressor
Tamar was filled with fear and dread. "And she answered him, <u>Nay, my brother, do not force me;</u> <u>for no such thing ought to be done in Israel</u>: do not thou this folly" (2 Sam. 13:12). The oppressive words *nay, my brother, do not force me; for no such thing ought to be done in Israel* consist of 59 letters!

Absalom—Amnon's Oppressor
"Now Absalom had commanded his servants, saying, Mark ye now when Amnon's heart is merry with wine, and <u>when I say unto you, Smite</u> <u>Amnon;</u> <u>then kill him,</u> <u>fear not:</u> <u>have not I</u> <u>commanded you?</u> <u>be courageous,</u> <u>and be valiant. And the servants of Absalom</u> <u>did unto Amnon</u> <u>as Absalom had commanded,</u> <u>and every man gat</u> <u>him up upon</u> <u>his mule, and fled</u>" (2 Sam. 13:28-29a). The OT Narrative combination *when I say unto you smite* (1x), *Amnon* (25x), *then kill him* (1x), *fear not* (13x), *have not I* (3x), *commanded you* (8x), *be courageous* (1x), *and be valiant* (1x), *and the servants of Absalom* (1x), *did unto Amnon* (1x), *as Absalom had commanded* (1x), *and every man gat* (1x), *him up upon* (1x), *his mule and fled* (1x) = 59.

Joab—Absalom's Oppressor
"Then said Joab, I may not tarry thus with thee. <u>And he took three darts</u> <u>in his hand, and thrust</u>

them through the heart of Absalom, while he was yet alive in the midst of the oak. And ten young men that bare Joab's armour compassed about and smote Absalom, and slew him" (2 Sam. 18:14-15). The OT Narrative combination *and he took three darts* (1x), *in his hand* (27x), *and thrust them through* (1x), *the heart* (18x), *of Absalom* (7x), *while he was* (3x), *yet alive in the* (1x), *midst of the oak* (1x) = 59.

David Deeply Oppressed by Absalom's Death

"And the king was much moved, and went up to the chamber over the gate, and wept: and as he went, thus he said, O my son Absalom, my son, my son Absalom! would God I had died for thee, O Absalom, my son, my son!" (2 Sam. 18:33) David became oppressed or weighed down in his mind. This oppressed verse presents the Bible's 59th occurrence of the phrase *my son*, and it recalls a father's great oppression while mourned his dead son.

Joab—Amasa's Oppressor

"And Joab said to Amasa, Art thou in health, my brother? And Joab took Amasa by the beard with the right hand to kiss him. But Amasa took no heed to the sword that was in Joab's hand: so he smote him therewith in the fifth rib, and shed out his bowels to the ground, and struck him not again; and he died" (2 Sam. 20:9-10d). Amasa was David's nephew and had joined Absalom's revolt. As a result Joab rewarded him with a crushing judgment. The OT Narrative combination *Amasa* (16x), *took no heed* (2x), *to the sword* (2x), *that was in* (29x), *Joab's hand* (1x), *so he smote him* (1x), *therewith in* (1x), *the fifth rib* (4x), *and shed out* (1x), *his bowels to the ground* (1x), *and struck him not again* (1x) = 59.

The Angel of the Lord, Israel's Oppressor

"And David spake unto the LORD when he saw the angel that smote the people, and said, Lo, I have sinned, and I have done wickedly: but these sheep, what have they done? let thine hand, I pray thee, be against me, and against my father's house" (2 Sam. 24:17). In the wilderness the Lord warned Israel to beware of the Angel of the Lord because He would punitively oppress them following any sort of disobedience. The title *the angel of the LORD/Lord* occurs 59 times in the Bible. The Old Testament combination *angel of the LORD* (56x), *smote the people* (3x) = 59.

59th Verse of First Kings

"Do therefore according to thy wisdom, and let not his hoar head go down to the grave in peace" (1 Kings 2:6). David assigned Solomon the role of becoming Joab's deadly oppressor. Again the phrase *go down* is mentioned in 59 chapters of the Old Testament. Again the word *grave* occurs 59 times in the Old Testament.

Benaiah—Joab's Oppressor

Solomon was speaking to Benaiah about Joab: "And the LORD shall return his blood upon his own head, who fell upon two men more righteous and better than he, and slew them with the sword, my father David not knowing thereof, to wit, Abner the son of Ner, captain of the host of Israel, and Amasa the son of Jether, captain of the host of Judah" (1 Kings 2:32). There are 59 words in this oppressor verse.

Benaiah—Shimei's Oppressor

"The king said moreover to Shimei, Thou knowest all the wickedness which thine heart is privy to, that thou didst to David my father: therefore the LORD shall return thy wickedness <u>upon</u> thine own head . . . . So the king commanded <u>Benaiah</u> the son of Jehoiada; which went out, and <u>fell</u> <u>upon</u> him, that he died" (1 Kings 2:44, 46ab). Here the word *upon* is the 2959th word of First Kings and congruently the 1459th word of this chapter. The OT Narrative combination *Benaiah* (40x) and *fell upon* (19x) = 59.

Solomon—Jeroboam's Oppressor

"<u>Solomon sought</u> <u>therefore to</u> <u>kill</u> <u>Jeroboam. And Jeroboam arose, and fled into Egypt</u>, unto Shishak king of Egypt, and was in Egypt until the death of Solomon" (1 Kings 11:40). The First Kings combination *Solomon sought* (1x), *therefore to* (2x), *kill* (2x), *Jeroboam* (53x), *and Jeroboam arose and fled into Egypt* (1x) = 59.

The Man of God—Jeroboam's Oppressor

"And it came to pass, when king Jeroboam heard the saying of <u>the man of God</u>, which had cried against the altar in Beth-el, that he put forth his hand from the altar, saying, Lay hold on him. And his hand, which he put forth against him, dried up, so that he could not pull it in again to him. The altar also was rent, and the ashes poured out from the altar, according to the sign which <u>the man of God</u> had given by the word of the LORD" (1 Kings 13:4-5). The title *the man of God* occurs 59 times in the Bible.

Baasha—Asa's Oppressor

"And there was war between Asa and Baasha king of Israel all their days. And Baasha king of Israel went up <u>AGAINST</u> Judah, and built Ramah, that he might not suffer any to go out or come in to Asa king of Judah" (1 Kings 15:16-17). Again the word *against* is mentioned in 59 verses of Second Kings.

559th Verse of First Kings

"And Baasha the son of Ahijah, of the house of Issachar, conspired against him; and Baasha smote him at Gibbethon, which belonged to the Philistines; for Nadab and all Israel laid siege to Gibbethon" (1 Kings 15:27). Baasha became King Nadab's deadly oppressor.

Baasha—Jeroboam's Oppressor

"<u>And it came to pass, when he reigned, that he smote all the house of Jeroboam; he left not to Jeroboam any that breathed, until he had destroyed him</u>, according unto the saying of the LORD, which he spake by his servant Ahijah the Shilonite: Because of the sins of Jeroboam which he sinned, and which he made Israel sin, by his provocation wherewith he provoked the LORD God of Israel to anger" (1 Kings 15:29-30). The First Kings combination *and it came to pass when he reigned* (1x), *that he smote* (1x), *all the house* (7x), *of Jeroboam* (26x), *he left not* (1x), *to Jeroboam* (2x), *any* (20x), *that breathed until he had destroyed him* (1x) = 59.

Zimri—Elah's Oppressor

Baasha died, and then "began Elah the son of Baasha to reign over Israel in Tirzah, two years. And his servant Zimri, captain of half his chariots, conspired against him, as he was in Tirzah, drinking himself drunk in the house of Arza steward of his house in Tirzah. And <u>Zimri</u> went in and smote him, and killed him . . . and reigned in his stead" (1 Kings 16:8b-10). Here the underlined name *Zimri* is the 259,810th word of the Bible, a number from the 259,000 range.

Zimri—House of Baasha's Oppressor

"And it came to pass, when he began to reign, as soon as he sat on his throne, that he slew all the house of Baasha: he left him not one that pisseth against a wall, neither of his kinsfolks, nor of his friends. Thus did <u>Zimri</u> destroy all the house of Baasha, according to the word of the LORD . . . For all the sins of Baasha, and the sins of Elah his son, by which they sinned, and by which they made Israel to sin" (1 Kings 16:11-13d). Here the underlined name *Zimri* is the 259,879th word of the Bible, a number from the 259,000 range.

Omri—Zimri's Oppressor

"And the people that were encamped heard say, Zimri hath conspired, and hath also slain the king: wherefore all Israel made Omri, the captain of the host, king over Israel that day in the camp. And Omri went up from Gibbethon, and all Israel <u>with</u> him, and they besieged Tirzah. And it came to pass, when Zimri saw that the city was taken, that he went into the palace of the king's house, and burnt the king's house over him with fire, and died, For his sins which he sinned in doing evil in the sight of the LORD, in walking in the way of Jeroboam, and in his sin which he did, to make Israel to sin" (1 Kings 16:16-19).

The underlined word *with* is the 260,059th word of the Bible, and it refers to being with a newly appointed king who goes forth on this day as an oppressor of usurper king.

Elijah, the Northern Tribes' Oppressor Prophet

"And <u>Elijah</u> the Tishbite, who was of the inhabitants of Gilead, said unto Ahab, As the LORD God of Israel liveth, before whom I stand, there shall not be dew nor rain these years, but according to my word" (1 Kings 17:1). The First Kings combination *Elijah* (38 vs), *the prophet* (21 vs) = 59 verses.

"And it came to pass, when Ahab saw Elijah, that Ahab said unto him, Art thou he that <u>TROUBLETH</u> Israel?" (1 Kings 18:17) This verse corresponds with our second definition of oppress: to lie heavily upon the mind or a person. Again all forms of the word *trouble* are collectively mentioned in 59 chapters of the Wisdom Books. This oppressor verse is the 9359th verse of the Bible.

Elijah Oppresses the Prophets of Baal

"And Elijah said unto them, Take the prophets of Baal; let not one of them <u>escape</u>. And they took them: and Elijah brought them down to the brook Kishon, and slew them there" (1 Kings 18:40). Again the word *escape* occurs 59 times in Scripture.

Jezebel—Elijah's Oppressor

"And Ahab told Jezebel all that Elijah had done, and withal how he had slain all the prophets with the sword. Then Jezebel sent a messenger unto Elijah, saying, So let the gods do to me, and more also, if I make not thy life as the life of one of them by to morrow about this time. And when he saw that, he arose, <u>and went for</u> <u>his life</u>" (1 Kings 19:1-3b). The Bible combination *and went for* (1 v), *his life* (58 vs) = 59 verses.

Elijah Becomes Mentally Oppressed

"But he himself went a day's journey into the wilderness, and came and sat down under a juniper tree: and <u>he requested</u> <u>for himself that</u> <u>he might die</u>; and said, <u>It is enough</u>; <u>now, O LORD, take</u> <u>away</u> <u>my life</u>; <u>for I am not better than my fathers</u>" (1 Kings 19:4). The Old Testament combination *he requested* (4x), *for himself that* (1x), *he might die* (1x), *it is enough* (7x), *now O LORD take away* (1x), *my life* (44x), *for I am not better than my fathers* (1x) = 59.

9359th Verse of the Bible

"And Jezebel his wife said unto him, Dost thou now govern the kingdom of Israel? arise, and eat bread, and let thine heart be merry: I will give thee the vineyard of Naboth the Jezreelite" (1 Kings 21:7). Ahab's wife encouraged him to dismiss his sadness, his mental oppression.

Ahab—Micaiah's Oppressor

"And the king of Israel said, Take Micaiah, and carry him back unto Amon the governor of the city, and to Joash the king's son; And say, Thus saith the king, Put this fellow in the prison, and feed him with bread of AFFLICTION and with water of AFFLICTION, until I come in peace" (1 Kings 22:26-27). Over the coming days Micaiah's scant provision of food would make him mentally oppressed. Again the word *affliction* is mentioned in 59 verses of the Old Testament. The words *and feed him with bread of affliction and with water of affliction, until* consists of 59 letters!

Elisha—The Northern Tribes' Next Troubling Oppressor

"And he went up from thence unto Beth-el: and as he was going up by the way, there came forth little children out of the city, and mocked him, and said unto him, Go up, thou bald head; go up, thou bald head. And he turned back, and looked on them, and cursed them in the name of the LORD. And there came forth two she bears out of the wood, and tare forty and two children of them" (2 Kings 2:23-24). Because the northern tribes preferred worshiping Baal over Jehovah, they viewed Elijah's departure as a victory for them. Here young adolescents joyfully repeated what they heard their parents say, how they wished the Lord would also take up Elisha from their midst. The Old Testament combination *Elisha* (58x) and *the son of Shaphat of Abel-meholah* (1x) = 59.

Elisha—Gehazi's Unexpected Oppressor

"The leprosy therefore of Naaman shall cleave unto thee, and unto thy seed for ever. And he went out from his presence a leper as white as snow" (2 Kings 5:27). The word *thy* is the 959th word of this chapter.

The Lord Oppresses Northern Tribes with Famine

"Then spake Elisha unto the woman, whose son he had restored to life, saying, Arise, and go thou and thine household, and sojourn wheresoever thou canst sojourn: for the LORD hath called for a famine; and it shall also come upon the land seven years" (2 Kings 8:1). The phrase *the land* occurs 1259 times in the Bible!

Jehu—Jehoram's Oppressor

"And Jehu drew a bow with his full strength, and smote Jehoram between his arms, and the arrow went out at his heart, and he sunk down in his chariot" (2 Kings 9:24). The name *Jehu* occurs 59 times in Scripture.

Jehu—Jezebel's Oppressor

"Wherefore they came again, and told him. And he said, This is the word of the LORD, which he spake by his servant Elijah the Tishbite, saying, In the portion of Jezreel shall dogs eat the flesh of Jezebel" (2 Kings 9:36). This oppression verse is the 259th verse of Second Kings.

Jehu—Ahab's Oppressor
"So Jehu slew all that remained of the house of Ahab in Jezreel, and all his great men, and his kinsfolks, and his priests, until he left him none remaining" (2 Kings 10:11). By divine order Jehu brought a full and oppressive end to Ahab's dynasty. Again the name *Jehu* occurs 59 times in Scripture.

Jeroboam Spiritually Oppresses the Northern Tribes
"Howbeit from the sins of Jeroboam the son of Nebat, who made Israel to sin, Jehu departed not from after them, to wit, the golden calves that were in Beth-el, and that were in Dan" (2 Kings 10:29). The name *Bethel* is mentioned in 59 verses of the Bible.

Athaliah—The House of Judah's Evil Oppressor
"And when Athaliah the mother of Ahaziah saw that her son was dead, she arose and destroyed all the seed royal" (2 Kings 11:1). The OT Narrative combination *Athaliah* (17x), *that wicked woman* (1x), *the mother of Ahaziah* (2x), *saw that her son* (2x), *was dead* (32x), *she arose and destroyed all* (2x), *the seed royal* (3x) = 59.

Hazael—Jehoahaz's Oppressor
"And Jehoahaz besought the LORD, and the LORD hearkened unto him: for he saw the OPPRESSION of Israel, because the king of Syria OPPRESSED them. . . . Hazael king of Syria OPPRESSED Israel all the days of Jehoahaz" (2 Kings 13:4, 22). The phrase *all the days of* occurs 59 times in the Old Testament.

Shallum—Zachariah's Oppressor
"Zachariah the son of Jeroboam reign over Israel in Samaria six months. And he did that which was evil in the sight of the LORD, as his fathers had done: he departed not from the sins of Jeroboam the son of Nebat, who made Israel to sin. And Shallum the son of Jabesh conspired against him, and smote him before the people, and slew him, and reigned in his stead" (2 Kings 15:8b-10). The Old Testament combination *smote him* (35x), *and slew him* (24x) = 59.

Menahem—Shallum's Oppressor
"Shallum the son of Jabesh began to reign . . . and he reigned a full month in Samaria. For Menahem the son of Gadi went up from Tirzah, and came to Samaria, and smote Shallum the son of Jabesh in Samaria, and slew him, and reigned in his stead" (2 Kings 15:13-14). The OT Narrative combination *smote Shallum the son of Jabesh in Samaria* (1x), *and slew him and reigned* (3x), *reigned in his stead* (55x) = 59.

Pekah—Pekahiah's Oppressor
"Pekahiah the son of Menahem began to reign over Israel in Samaria, and reigned two years. And he did that which was evil in the sight of the LORD: he departed not from the sins of Jeroboam the son of Nebat, who made Israel to sin. But Pekah the son of Remaliah, a captain of his, conspired against him, and smote him in Samaria, in the palace of the king's house, with Argob and Arieh, and with him fifty men of the Gileadites: and he killed him, and reigned in his

room" (2 Kings 15:23b-25). The Second Kings combination *Pekahiah the son of Menahem began to reign* (1x), *but Pekah* (1x), *the son of Remaliah* (6x), *a captain of his* (1x), *conspired* (6x), *against him* (8x), *and smote him* (3x), *in Samaria* (23x), *in the palace of the king's house* (1x), *with Argob* (1x), *and Arieh* (1x), *and with him* (1x), *fifty men* (3x), *of the Gileadites* (1x), *and he killed him* (1x), *and reigned in his room* (1x) = 59.

Tiglath-Pileser—Israel's Oppressor

"In the days of Pekah king of Israel came Tiglath-pileser king of Assyria, and took Ijon, and Abel-beth-maachah, and Janoah, and Kedesh, and Hazor, and Gilead, and Galilee, all the land of Naphtali, and carried them CAPTIVE to Assyria" (2 Kings 15:29). In accordance with our first definition of oppress, the Assyrians burdened the Israelites with cruel impositions and restraints. The word *captive* occurs 59 times in the Bible.

Hoshea—Pekah's Oppressor

"And Hoshea the son of Elah made a conspiracy against Pekah the son of Remaliah, and smote him, and slew him, and reigned in his stead" (2 Kings 15:30abcd). The Old Testament combination *smote him* (35x), *and slew him* (24x) = 59.

The Angel of the Lord—Assyrian Army's Mighty Oppressor

"And it came to pass that night, that the angel of the LORD went out, and smote in the camp of the Assyrians an hundred fourscore and five thousand: and when they arose early in the morning, behold, they were all dead corpses" (2 Kings 19:35). Again the title *the angel of the LORD/Lord* occurs 59 times in the Bible.

Manasseh—Judah's Spiritual Oppressor

"And he made his son pass through the fire, and observed times, and used enchantments, and dealt with familiar spirits and wizards: he wrought much wickedness in the sight of the LORD, to provoke him to anger" (2 Kings 21:6). Again the word *wickedness* occurs 118 times in the Old Testament, a multiple of 59.

Oppressor Kings of Judah

"And he PUT DOWN the idolatrous priests, whom the kings of Judah had ordained to burn incense in the high places in the cities of Judah, and in the places round about Jerusalem; them also that burned incense unto Baal, to the sun, and to the moon, and to the planets, and to all the host of heaven" (2 Kings 23:5). The phrase *of Judah* 259 verses of the OT Narrative.

Judah Spiritually Oppressed by Idols

"Moreover the workers with familiar spirits, and the wizards, and the images, and the idols, and all the abominations that were spied in the land of Judah and in Jerusalem, did Josiah put away, that he might perform the words of the law which were written in the book that Hilkiah the priest found in the house of the LORD" (2 Kings 23:24). After Josiah heard the Law read aloud, he sought to put away both the idols and their oppressive spirits from the land. Josiah's obedience helped bring about a great revival. Again the phrase *the work* occurs 159 times in the Bible. Again the word *idols* is mentioned in 59 chapters of the Bible.

Babylonian Oppressor Carries Judah Away in Chains

"And the king of Babylon smote them, and slew them at Riblah in the land of Hamath. So Judah was carried away out of their land" (2 Kings 25:21). This was Judah's third and final deportation. Here the remaining Judean resisters suffered great oppression, being defeated and carried away into distant captivity. The title *the king of Babylon* is mentioned in 59 verses of the Major Prophets. The phrase *carried away* occurs 59 times in the Old Testament.

The Mighty & Valiant Men

"The sons of Reuben, and the Gadites, and half the tribe of Manasseh, of valiant men, men able to bear buckler and sword, and to shoot with bow, and skilful in war, were four and forty thousand seven hundred and threescore, that went out to the war" (1 Chron. 5:18). The mighty and valiant men were trained soldiers who knew how to oppress or crush an enemy. The OT Narrative combination *mighty men* (45x) and *valiant men* (14x) = 59.

Philistines Oppress Saul & His Sons in Battle

"Now the Philistines fought AGAINST Israel; and the men of Israel fled from before the Philistines, and fell down slain in mount Gilboa. And the Philistines followed hard after Saul, and after his sons; and the Philistines slew Jonathan, and Abinadab, and Malchi-shua, the sons of Saul. And the battle went sore AGAINST Saul, and the archers hit him, and he was wounded of the archers" (1 Chron. 10:1-3). Again the word *fought* occurs naturally 59 times in the Old Testament. Again the word *fell* occurs 159 times in the Old Testament. The underlined word *the* is the 7059th word of First Chronicles, and it refers to the king's three oppressed sons.

David—The Philistines' Oppressor

"Now after this it came to pass, that David smote the Philistines, and SUBDUED them, and took Gath and her towns out of the hand of the Philistines. And he smote Moab; and the Moabites became David's servants, and brought gifts" (1 Chron. 18:1-2). Again the name *David('s)* is mentioned in 459 verses of First and Second Samuel.

659th Verse of First Chronicles

"Wherefore Hanun took David's servants, and shaved them, and cut off their garments in the midst hard by their buttocks, and sent them away. Then there went certain, and told David how the men were served. And he sent to meet them: for the men were greatly ashamed. And the king said, Tarry at Jericho until your beards be grown, and then return" (1 Chron. 19:4). The underlined words indicate the 59th verse of the Bible. All forms of the word *shame* and *ashamed* are mentioned in 59 collective verses of the Wisdom Books.

Oppressor Giant Meets His Fatal End

"And it came to pass after this, that there arose war at Gezer with the Philistines; at which time Sibbechai the Hushathite slew Sippai, that was of the children of the giant: and they were SUBDUED" (1 Chron. 20:4). The First Chronicles combination *Sippai that was of* (1x), *the children of* (55x), *the giant* (3x) = 59.

359th Chapter of the Bible

"And Satan stood up AGAINST Israel, and provoked David to number Israel" (1 Chron. 21:1). Satan wanted to oppress Israel at this time, and so he began scheming.

Rehoboam's Oppressive Tax Plan

"For whereas my father put a HEAVY yoke upon you, I will put more to your yoke: my father chastised you with whips, but I will chatise you with scorpions" (2 Chron. 10:11). Rehoboam followed his young counselors bad advice and chose to oppress the northern tribes by weighing heavily upon them with greatly increased taxes. Thus they promptly withdrew from the united kingdom and made Jeroboam king over them. Again the word *yoke* occurs 59 times in the Bible.

Shishak—Rehoboam's & Jerusalem's Oppressor

"And it came to pass, when Rehoboam had established the kingdom, and had strengthened himself, he forsook the law of the LORD, and all Israel with him. And it came to pass, that in the fifth year of king Rehoboam Shishak king of Egypt came up against Jerusalem, because they had transgressed against the LORD, With twelve hundred chariots, and threescore thousand horsemen: and the people were without number that came with him out of Egypt; the Lubims, the Sukkiims, and the Ethiopians. And he took the fenced cities which pertained to Judah, and came to Jerusalem" (2 Chron. 12:1-4).

Again the word *horsemen* occurs 59 times in the Bible. Again the name *Jerusalem* is mentioned in 59 verses of Acts.

Asa, Good King Suddenly Turns into Oppressor

"Then Asa was wroth with the seer, and put him in a prison house; for he was in a rage with him because of this thing. And Asa OPPRESSED some of the people the same time" (2 Chron. 16:10). The name *Asa* occurs 59 times in the Bible.

11,559th Verse of the Bible

"Then he said, I did see all Israel scattered upon the mountains, as sheep that have no shepherd: and the LORD said, These have no master; let them return therefore every man to his house in peace" (2 Chron. 18:16). Micaiah prophesied the oppression Israel would suffer if they went into battle against the Syrians, a battle wherein their king, Ahab, would become oppressed unto death.

For Jehoshaphat, the Lord Oppressed Three Enemy Armies

"For the children of Ammon and Moab stood up AGAINST the inhabitants of mount Seir, utterly to slay and destroy them: and when they had made an end of the inhabitants of Seir, every one helped to destroy another. And when Judah came toward the watch tower in the wilderness, they looked unto the multitude, and, behold, they were dead bodies fallen to the earth, and none escaped" (2 Chron. 20:23-24). For godly Jehoshaphat's benefit the Lord brought confusion upon Judah's three confederated enemies wherein they oppressed each other unto death. Again the word *escape* occurs 59 times in Scripture.

The Lord Oppressed Jehoram with Three Enemy Armies

"Moreover the LORD stirred up AGAINST Jehoram the spirit of the Philistines, and of the Arabians, that were near the Ethiopians: And they came up into Judah, and brake into it, and carried away all the substance that was found in the king's house, and his sons also, and his wives; so that there was never a son left him, save Jehoahaz, the youngest of his sons" (2 Chron. 21:16-17). Jehoram was an ungodly and oppressive Judean king, and the Lord rewarded him accordingly with oppression to subdue him. Again the phrase *carried away* occurs 59 times in the Old Testament.

Wicked Oppressor Queen—Athaliah

"But when Athaliah the mother of Ahaziah saw that her son was dead, she arose and destroyed all the seed royal of the house of Judah" (2 Chron. 22:10). Athaliah's rule was insufferably wicked and spiritually oppressive. The singular title *ruler('s)* is mentioned in 59 chapters of the Bible.

Joash, Good King Suddenly Turns into Oppressor

"And they conspired against him, and stoned him with stones at the commandment of the king in the court of the house of the LORD. Thus Joash the king remembered not the kindness which Jehoiada his father had done to him, but slew his son. And when he died, he said, The LORD look upon it, and require it" (2 Chron. 24:21-22). There are 59 words in this oppressor passage.

Joash's Reign Cut Short by Avenger Oppressors

"And when they were departed from him, for they left him in great diseases, his own servants conspired against him for the blood of the sons of Jehoiada the priest, and slew him on his bed, and he died: and they buried him in the city of David, but they buried him not in the sepulchres of the kings" (2 Chron. 24:25). There are 59 words in this oppressor verse.

God Has the Power to Oppress

"But if thou wilt go, do it, be strong for the battle: God shall make thee fall before the enemy: for God hath <u>POWER</u> to help, and to cast DOWN" (2 Chron. 25:8). This verse pertains to our first definition of oppress: subject to a burdensome or harsh exercise of authority or power. Again the word *power* is mentioned in 59 verses of the Pauline Epistles. We repeat the following seals.

> The title *God* is mentioned in 59 verses of Second Samuel.
> The title *God* is mentioned in 159 verses of Second Chronicles.

559th of Second Chronicles

"And Uzziah the king was a leper unto the day of his death, and dwelt in a several house, being a leper; for he was <u>cut off</u> from the house of the LORD: and Jotham his son was over the king's house, judging the people of the land" (2 Chron. 26:21). The Lord oppressed this good king after his pride caused him to commit a great sin. Again the phrase *be cut off* is mentioned in 59 verses of the Bible.

Sennacherib Attempts to Oppress Judah

"After these things, and the establishment thereof, <u>Sennacherib</u> <u>king of Assyria</u> came, and entered into Judah, and encamped AGAINST the fenced cities, and thought to win them for himself" (2 Chron. 32:1). Sennacherib began his oppressive campaign to frighten Jerusalem into surrendering. The OT Narrative combination *Sennacherib* (9 vs), *king of Assyria* (50 vs) = 59 verses.

Jews' & Jerusalem's Mental Oppression

The Assyrian army tried to oppress Jerusalem with their taunts. "Then they cried with a loud voice in <u>the Jews</u>' speech unto the people <u>of Jerusalem</u> that were on the wall, to AFFRIGHT them, and to TROUBLE them; that they might take the city" (2 Chron. 32:18). The Assyrians exceeded all other nations in their cruelty to enemy captives. Again all forms of the word *trouble* are collectively mentioned in 59 chapters of the Wisdom Books. The title *the Jews* is mentioned in 59 verses of Acts. Again the phrase *of Jerusalem* is mentioned in 59 chapters of the Major and Minor Prophets.

The Oppressed Remnant

"Now in the second year of their coming unto the house of God at Jerusalem, in the second month, began Zerubbabel the son of Shealtiel, and Jeshua the son of Jozadak, and the <u>remnant</u> of their brethren the priests and the Levites, and all they that were come out of the CAPTIVITY unto Jerusalem; and appointed the Levites, from twenty years old and upward, to set forward the work of the house of the LORD" (Ezra 3:8). Here the word *remnant* is the 1659th word of Ezra. The title *remnant* is mentioned in 59 verses of the Major and Minor Prophets. Again the word *captive* occurs 59 times in the Bible.

Tattenai—Ezra's Oppressor

"The copy of the letter that Tatnai, <u>governor</u> on this side the river, and Shethar-boznai, and his companions the Apharsachites, which were on this side the river, sent unto Darius the king" (Ezra 5:6). At the time when the Jews returned from exile, Tattenai governed the northern part of Israel for Persia. He wrote a letter to Darius asking him to search the records to see if Cyrus had authorized this rebuilding project. Tattenai was acting as an oppressor, but Darius wrote back telling him to leave the Jews alone so they could rebuild without any further hindrances by him. Again the word *governor* occurs 59 times in the Bible.

Our God Has the Power to Oppress

"For I was ashamed to require of the king a band of soldiers and horsemen to help us against the enemy in the way: because we had spoken unto the king, saying, The hand of our God is upon all them for good that seek him; but his <u>POWER</u> and his wrath is AGAINST all them that forsake him" (Ezra 8:22). Again the word *power* is mentioned in 59 verses of the Pauline Epistles. This oppressor verse consists of 59 words.

Ezra Prays That the Divine Oppressor Will Show Mercy

"Should we again break thy commandments, and join in affinity with the people of these abominations? wouldest not thou be angry with us till thou hadst consumed us, so that there should be no <u>remnant</u> nor escaping?" (Ezra 9:14) Again the title *remnant* 59 verses of the Major and Minor Prophets.

Residue Scorch Marks of the Oppressor

"And they said unto me, The <u>remnant</u> that are left of the CAPTIVITY there in the province are in great AFFLICTION and reproach: the wall <u>of Jerusalem</u> also is broken down, and the gates thereof are burned with fire" (Neh. 1:3). Again the title *remnant* 59 verses of the Major and Minor Prophets. Again the word *captive* occurs 59 times in the Bible. Again the phrase *of Jerusalem* occurs 159 times in the Old Testament.

The Governor's Throne

"And next unto them repaired Melatiah the Gibeonite, and Jadon the Meronothite, the men of Gibeon, and of Mizpah, unto <u>the throne</u> of <u>the governor</u> on this side the river" (Neh. 3:7). The throne was the place from which an oppressor could maintain his power and control over his subjects. The phrase *the throne* is mentioned in 59 chapters of the Bible. Again the word *governor* occurs 59 times in the Bible.

Judean Remnant Over-Burdened & Oppressed with Rubbish Removal

"And Judah said, The strength of the bearers of BURDENS is decayed, and there is much rubbish; so that we are not able to build the wall" (Neh. 4:10). The abundant rubbish of broken and charred stones from Jerusalem's walls required more strength to remove than the remnant seemed able to put forth. They were greatly discouraged. Here the word rubbish is the 346,959th word of the Bible.

Rich Jews Became Oppressors to the Poor Jews

"And there was a great cry of the people and of their wives against their brethren the Jews. For there were that said, We, our sons, and our daughters, are many: therefore we take up corn for them, that we may eat, and live. Some also there were that said, We have mortgaged our lands, vineyards, and houses, that we might buy corn, because of the dearth. There were also that said, We have borrowed money for the king's tribute, and that upon our lands and vineyards. Yet now our flesh is as the flesh of our brethren, our children as their children: and, lo, we bring into BONDAGE our sons and our daughters to be servants, and some of our daughters are brought unto BONDAGE already: neither is it in our power to redeem them; for other men have our lands and vineyards" (Neh. 5:1-4).

Again the word *cry* is mentioned in 159 verses of the Old Testament. Again the word *servant* occurs 59 times in the Wisdom Books, occurs 59 times in the Gospels, and is mentioned in 59 verses of the NT Narrative.

Sanballat—Nehemiah's Oppressor

"Then sent Sanballat his servant unto me in like manner the fifth time with an open letter in his hand" (Neh. 6:5). Operating in Samaria, Sanballat held some seat of influence for Persia at the time of the remnant's return from Babylon. He was a very vindictive oppressor. After his legal efforts to stop the rebuilding project failed he resorted to assassinating Nehemiah. This attempt also failed miserably. The phrase *in his hand* is mentioned in 59 chapters of the Bible.

Haman—The Jews' Wicked Oppressor

"And he thought scorn to lay hands on Mordecai alone; for they had shewed him the people of Mordecai: wherefore Haman sought to destroy all the Jews that were throughout the whole kingdom of Ahasuerus, even the people of Mordecai" (Est. 3:6). The word *destroy* is the 159th word in this chapter.

59th Verse of Esther

"The copy of the writing for a commandment to be given in every province was published unto all people, that they should be ready AGAINST that day" (Est. 3:14). Here the Jews' kingdom-wide oppressors were carefully certified and notified by letters.

A Time to Resist the Oppressor

"For if thou altogether holdest thy peace at this time, then shall there enlargement and deliverance arise to the Jews from another place; but thou and thy father's house shall be destroyed: and who knoweth whether thou art come to the kingdom for such a time as this?" (Est. 4:14) The phrase *a time* occurs 59 times in the Bible.

Oppressors of the Jews

"Now in the twelfth month, that is, the month Adar, on the thirteenth day of the same, when the king's commandment and his decree drew near to be put in execution, in the day that the enemies of the Jews hoped to have POWER over them, though it was turned to the contrary, that the Jews had rule over them that hated them" (Est. 9:1). Again the word *power* is mentioned in 59 verses of the Pauline Epistles. Here the word *hoped* is the 359,759th word of the Bible, and it. The phrase *of the Jews* is mentioned in 59 verses of the New Testament!

Haman—Jews' Agagite Oppressor

"Because Haman the son of Hammedatha, the Agagite, the enemy of all the Jews, had devised AGAINST the Jews to destroy them, and had cast Pur, that is, the lot, to consume them, and to destroy them" (Est. 9:24). Mordecai's refusal to bow before Haman provoked Haman to oppress the Jews unto a crushing death. The Bible combination *Haman* (50x), *the son of Hammedatha the Agagite* (4x), *the enemy of all the Jews* (1x), *had devised against the* (1x), *Jews to destroy them* (1x), *and had cast Pur that is the lot* (1x), *to consume them and to destroy them* (1x) = 59.

Sabeans—Oppressors of Job's Servants

"And the Sabeans fell upon them, and took them away; yea, they have slain the servants with the edge of the sword; and I only am escaped alone to tell thee (Job 1:15). This verse presents the Bible's 59th chapter-mention of the phrase *the sword*.

Satan Given Permission to Become Job's Oppressor

"And Satan answered the LORD, and said, Skin for skin, yea, all that a man hath will he give for his life. But put forth thine hand now, and touch his bone and his flesh, and he will curse thee to thy face. And the LORD said unto Satan, Behold, he is in thine hand; but save his life" (Job 2:4-6). There are 59 words in this Satanic-oppressor passage.

Satan—Job's Oppressor

"So went Satan forth from the presence of the LORD, and smote Job with sore boils from the sole of his foot unto his crown" (Job 2:7). The Bible combination *so went* (3x), *Satan* (55x), *and smote Job with sore boils* (1x) = 59.

Job's Great Oppression

Job's name is synonymous with oppression. His oppression was so great that he wished for the grave. "There the prisoners rest together; they hear not the voice of the OPPRESSOR" (Job 3:18). This is the Bible's first mention of the keyword oppressor. The 59th letter in this verse falls inside the keyword oppressor! The name *Job* occurs 59 times in Scripture!

Oppressive Power of the Sword

"In famine he shall redeem thee from death: and in war from the POWER of the sword" (Job 5:20). Again the word *power* is mentioned in 59 verses of the Pauline Epistles. The Old Testament combination *in famine he shall redeem thee from death* (1x), *and in war* (1x), *from the power* (7x), *of the sword* (50x) = 59.

Job Oppressed by Wearisome Nights

"So am I made to possess months of vanity, and wearisome nights are appointed to me. When I lie down, I say, When shall I arise, and the night be gone? and I am full of tossings to and fro unto the dawning of the day" (Job 7:3-4). Job's bright world had suddenly turned into one endless and oppressive night. As a thief in the night, Satan had come and stolen from him everything good in his life. The Wisdom Books combination *wearisome* (1x), *night/s* (58x) = 59. The phrase *the night* is mentioned in 59 chapters of the Old Testament.

159th Verse of Job

"I have sinned; what shall I do unto thee, O thou preserver of men? why hast thou set me as a mark against thee, so that I am a BURDEN to myself?" (Job 7:20) Job speaks miserably out of his oppression.

Wicked Oppressor Dreads His Unknown End

"The wicked man travaileth with pain all his days, and the number of years is hidden to the OPPRESSOR" (Job 15:20). Again the term *the wicked* occurs 259 times in the Bible. The word *man* is mentioned in 59 verses of Second Samuel. The Bible combination *his days* (37x), *the number of years* (4x), *hidden* (17x), *to the oppressor* (1x) = 59.

Job Thinks God Is His Oppressor

"Then Job answered and said . . . But now he hath made me WEARY: thou hast made desolate all my company. And thou hast filled me with wrinkles, which is a witness against me: and my leanness rising up in me beareth witness to my face. He teareth me in his wrath, who hateth me: he gnasheth upon me with his teeth; mine enemy sharpeneth his eyes upon me. They have gaped upon me with their mouth; they have smitten me upon the cheek reproachfully; they have gathered themselves together against me. God hath delivered me to the ungodly, and turned me over into the hands of the wicked. I was at ease, but he hath broken me asunder: he hath also taken me by my neck, and shaken me to pieces, and set me up for his mark. His archers compass me round about, he cleaveth my reins asunder, and doth not spare; he poureth out my gall upon the ground. He breaketh me with breach upon breach, he runneth upon me like a giant" (Job 16:1a, 7-14).

Again the title *God* is mentioned in 59 verses of Second Samuel and 159 verses of Second Chronicles.

Wicked Man—Oppressor of the Poor

"Because he hath OPPRESSED and hath forsaken the poor; because he hath violently taken away an house which he builded not" (Job 20:19). The Job combination *because* (28x), *he hath* (28x), *oppressed* (2x), *and hath forsaken the poor* (1x) = 59.

459th Chapter of the Bible

"They drive away the ass of the fatherless, they take the widow's ox for a pledge. They turn the needy out of the way: the poor of the earth hide themselves together. . . . They cause the naked to lodge without clothing, that they have no covering in the cold. They are wet with the showers of the mountains, and embrace the rock for want of a shelter. They pluck the fatherless from the breast, and take a pledge of the poor. They cause him to go naked without clothing, and they take away the sheaf from the hungry; Which make oil within their walls, and tread their winepresses, and suffer thirst. Men groan from out of the city, and the soul of the wounded crieth out: yet God layeth not folly to them. . . . The murderer rising with the light killeth the poor and needy, and in the night is as a thief" (Job 24:3-4, 7-12, 14).

The pronoun *they* is mentioned in 859 verses of the Law and in 159 verses of Judges.

The Cry of the Oppressed Ones

"By reason of the multitude of OPPRESSIONS they make the OPPRESSED to cry: they cry out by reason of the arm of the mighty" (Job 35:9). Again the word *cry* is mentioned in 159 verses of the Old Testament. The Old Testament combination *arm* (58 vs), *of the oppressors* (1 v) = 59 verses.

Why Do the Nations Rage?

"Why do the heathen rage, and the people imagine a vain thing? The kings of the earth set themselves, and the rulers take counsel together, AGAINST the LORD, and AGAINST his anointed, saying, Let us break their bands asunder, and cast away their cords from us" (Ps. 2:1-3). The nations rage against Israel whenever Satan moves their leaders to do so. Again the phrase *the nations* is mentioned in 159 verses of the Old Testament. The Old Testament combination *rulers* (57x), *take counsel together against the LORD* (1x), *and against his anointed* (1x) = 59.

Oppressed Ones' Refuge from the Oppressor

"The LORD also will be a refuge for the OPPRESSED, a refuge in times of trouble" (Ps. 9:9). Here the keyword *oppressed* is the 159th word of this chapter.

Finding Safety from the Oppressor

"For the OPPRESSION of the poor, for the sighing of the needy, now will I arise, saith the LORD; I will set him in safety from him that puffeth at him" (Ps. 12:5). The phrase *him that* is mentioned in 59 verses of the Law.

14,159th Verse of the Bible

"For thou hast girded me with strength unto the battle: thou hast SUBDUED under me those that rose up against me. Thou hast also given me the necks of mine enemies; that I might destroy them that hate me" (Ps. 18:39-40). In the underlined 59th verse David thanks the Lord for helping him to oppress or subdue his enemies.

Roman Oppressors Have Nailed Lowly Messiah to a Tree

"Deliver my soul from the sword; my darling from the POWER of the dog" (Ps. 22:20). In keeping with our first definition of oppress, Messiah speaks of the Roman leaders' harsh exercise of authority and power over Him as He hangs with cruel and unjust restraints from their cruelly made cross. The phrase *my soul* is mentioned in 159 verses of the Old Testament.

The Enemy Oppresses with Their Reproachful Words

"As with a sword in my bones, mine enemies reproach me; while they say daily unto me, Where is thy God?" (Ps. 42:10) The Bible combination *mine enemies* (57x) and *mine enemies reproach me* (2x) = 59.

Oppressors Seek My Soul

"For strangers are risen up AGAINST me, and OPPRESSORS seek after my soul: they have not set God before them. Selah" (Ps. 54:3). Again the word *against* is mentioned in 59 verses of Second Kings. Again the phrase *my soul* is mentioned in 159 verses of the Old Testament.

Because of the Enemy Oppressor

"Give ear to my prayer, O God; and hide not thyself from my supplication. Attend unto me, and hear me: <u>I mourn in my complaint, and make a noise; Because of the voice of the enemy</u>, because of the OPPRESSION of the wicked: for they cast iniquity upon me, and in wrath they hate me" (Ps. 55:1-3). The phrases *I mourn in my complaint, and make a noise; because of the voice of the enemy* consist of 59 letters! The phrase *because of* occurs 59 times in the Major Prophets.

59th Psalm

The superscription to this Psalm shows it to be written about David's relentless oppressor: *To the chief Musician, Al-taschith, Michtam <u>of David</u>; when Saul sent, and they watched the house to kill him*. We repeat the following seal.

The phrase *of David* occurs 59 times in the Chronicles.

Nothing could be more oppressive than to see your own house surrounded by your enemies. David described his oppressors with terms like "mine enemies . . . <u>them that rise up AGAINST me</u> . . . workers of iniquity . . . bloody men . . . the mighty . . . the heathen . . . wicked transgressors" (Ps. 59:1-5). The Wisdom Books combination *them that rise up* (1x), *against me* (58x) = 59.

David made his complaint and prayer to God, saying, "For, lo, <u>they</u> lie in wait for <u>my soul</u>: the mighty are gathered AGAINST me. . . . <u>They</u> run and prepare themselves: awake to help me, and behold" (vv. 3a, 4). Oppressors tend to work more wilily at night. David spoke of this very brand of oppression he felt. "<u>They</u> return at evening: they make a noise like a dog, and go round about the city" (v. 6). Again the pronoun *they* is mentioned in 159 verses of Judges. Again the phrase *my soul* is mentioned in 159 verses of the Old Testament.

This 59th chapter celebrates God's timely mercy in view of David's many oppressors. "The God of my <u>mercy</u> shall . . . let me see my desire upon mine enemies. . . . I will sing aloud of thy <u>mercy</u> in the morning: for thou hast been my defence and refuge in the day of my trouble. . . . for God is my defence, and the God of my <u>mercy</u>" (vv. 10a, 16, 17). Webster's Dictionary gives two definitions of mercy that pertain to David's plea: compassion or forbearance shown especially to one subject to one's power and compassionate treatment shown of those in distress. The word *mercy* occurs 59 times in the New Testament.

The Cruel Man

"<u>Deliver me</u>, <u>O my God</u>, out of the hand of the wicked, out of the hand of the unrighteous and CRUEL <u>man</u>" (Ps. 71:4). The Old Testament combination *deliver me* (38x), *O my God* (21x) = 59. Again the word *man* occurs 559 times in the NT Narrative.

God Will Break in Pieces the Oppressor

"He shall judge the poor of the people, he shall save the children of <u>the</u> needy, and shall break in pieces the OPPRESSOR" (Ps. 72:4). The underlined word *the* is the 59th word of this Psalm, and it refers to the object of the Oppressor's attack.

559th Chapter of the Bible

"I should soon have SUBDUED their enemies, and turned my hand against their adversaries"

(Ps. 81:14). The oppressor-related word *subdued* actually occurs in this 59th chapter.

Spiritually Oppressive Idols

"And shed innocent blood, even the blood of their sons and of their daughters, whom they sacrificed unto the <u>idols</u> of Canaan: and the land was polluted with blood" (Ps. 106:38). Again the word *idols* is mentioned in 59 chapters of the Bible.

Don't Follow the Oppressor's Evil Ways

"Envy thou not the OPPRESSOR, and choose none of his ways" (Prov. 3:31). The definite article *the* is mentioned in 1559 verses of the Pauline Epistles.

Some Oppressors Only Seek Gain

"He that OPPRESSETH the poor to <u>increase</u> his riches, and he that giveth to the rich, shall surely come to want" (Prov. 22:16). Here the word *increases* is the 10,159th word of Proverbs, and it pertains to an oppressor's ill-gotten gain.

Mad Man Oppresses His Neghbor

"As a <u>mad</u> man who casteth firebrands, arrows, and death, So is the man that deceiveth his neighbour, and saith, Am not I in sport?" (Prov. 26:18-19) Here the word *mad* is the 434,959th word of the Bible.

A Wicked Ruler over the Poor

"<u>As a roaring</u> <u>lion</u>, and a ranging bear; so is a <u>wicked</u> <u>ruler</u> over the poor people" (Prov. 28:15). This ancient proverb speaks of the oppressor's easy prey. The Old Testament combination *as a roaring* (1 ch), *lion* (58 chs) = 59 chapters. Again the term *the wicked* occurs 259 times in the Bible. From Genesis to the Major Prophets the word *ruler* is mentioned in 59 verses.

The Unwise Prince Who Oppresses His People

"<u>The prince</u> that wanteth understanding is also a great OPPRESSOR" (Prov. 28:16a). The Hebrew word here for "prince" can be applied to any number of commanders such as a captain, leader, governor, noble, prince, or ruler.

> The title *princes* occurs 59 times in the Major Prophets.
> The title *princes* is mentioned in 159 chapters of the OT.
> The title *the princes* is mentioned in 59 verses of the OTN.

Works That Are Unsatisfactory & Oppressive

"I have seen all <u>the works</u> that are done under the sun; and, behold, all is <u>vanity</u> and VEXATION of spirit" (Eccles. 1:14). Again the phrase *the work* occurs 159 times in the Bible. The word *vanity* occurs 59 times in the Wisdom Books.

The Oppressor's Power to Oppress

"So I returned, and considered all the OPPRESSIONS that are done under the sun: and behold the tears of such as were OPPRESSED, and they had no comforter; and on the side of their OPPRESSORS there was <u>POWER</u>; but they had no comforter. Wherefore I praised <u>the dead</u> which are already dead more than the living which are yet alive" (Eccles. 4:1-2). Again the word *power* is mentioned in 59 verses of the Pauline Epistles. The phrase *the dead* is mentioned in 59 chapters of the New Testament.

Help the Oppressed Orphans & Widows

"Learn to do well; seek judgment, relieve the <u>OPPRESSED</u>, judge the fatherless, plead for <u>the widow</u>" (Isa. 1:17). The Bible combination *oppressed* (38x) and *the widow* (21x) = 59.

59th Verse of Isaiah

"When a man shall take hold of his brother of the house of his father, saying, Thou hast clothing, be thou our <u>ruler</u>, and let this ruin be under thy hand" (Isa. 3:6). In the preceding related verse we are told, "the people shall be OPPRESSED, every one by another." Hence the brother appointed to rule over his family's house shall become the family's oppressor. This comes as a form of God's punishment upon Israel for their disobedience. Again from Genesis to the Major Prophets the word *ruler* is mentioned in 59 verses.

Oppressors in the House of Israel & Judah

"For the vineyard of the LORD of hosts is the house of Israel, and the men of Judah his pleasant plant: and he looked for judgment, but behold OPPRESSION; for righteousness, but behold a <u>cry</u>" (Isa. 5:7). Again the word *cry* is mentioned in 159 verses of the Old Testament.

The Oppressor Lays Yokes & Burdens on Others

"For thou hast broken the <u>yoke</u> of his BURDEN, and the staff of his shoulder, the rod of his OPPRESSOR, as in the day of Midian" (Isa. 9:4). Again the word *yoke* occurs 59 times in the Bible.

Sennacherib's Oppressive Threat to Zion

"Therefore thus saith the Lord GOD of hosts, O my people that dwellest in <u>Zion</u>, be not afraid of <u>the Assyrian</u>: he shall smite thee with a <u>rod</u>, and shall lift up his staff AGAINST thee, after the manner of Egypt" (Isa. 10:24). This verse presents the Bible's 59th occurrence of the word *rod*, and it refers to an oppressive threat from an enemy nation's ruler. The OT Narrative combination *Sennacherib* (9 vs) and *king of Assyria* (50 vs) = 59 verses.

> The phrase *of Zion* occurs 59 times in the Bible.
> The phrase *of Zion* is mentioned in 59 verses of the Bible.

5959th Word of Isaiah

"And it shall come to pass in that day, that his <u>BURDEN</u> shall be taken away from off thy shoulder, and his yoke from off thy neck, and the yoke shall be destroyed because of the anointing" (Isa. 10:27). Here the oppressor-related *word burden* is the 5959th word of Isaiah.

The Lord Will Oppress Babylon

"<u>Behold, the day of the LORD cometh, CRUEL both with wrath and fierce anger</u>, to lay the land desolate: and he shall destroy the sinners thereof out of it" (Isa. 13:9). Phrases *behold, the day of the LORD cometh, cruel both with wrath and fierce anger* consist of 59 letters!

Lucifer, Oppressor of the Nations

"How art thou fallen from heaven, O Lucifer, son of the morning! how art thou cut down to the ground, which didst weaken the nations!" (Isa. 14:12) Lucifer is the great oppressor of the nations. He seeks to weaken them through his schemes of violence, war, and much more. The Bible combination *Lucifer* (1 v) and [all forms of the word] *weak* (58 vs) = 59 verses.

Moab Will Face an Oppressor

"For the waters of Dimon shall be full of blood: for I will bring more upon Dimon, lions upon him that escapeth of Moab, and upon the remnant of the land" (Isa. 15:9). Again the title *remnant* 59 verses of the Major and Minor Prophets.

18,059th Verse of the Bible

"And Elam bare the quiver with chariots of men and horsemen, and Kir uncovered the shield" (Isa. 22:6). Oppressors prepared for the war. Again the word *horsemen* occurs 59 times in the Bible.

Beasts Oppressed with Heavy Burdens

"Bel boweth down, Nebo stoopeth, their idols were upon the beasts, and upon the cattle: your carriages were HEAVY loaden; they are a BURDEN to the WEARY beast" (Isa. 46:1). Again the word *beasts* is mentioned in 59 verses of the Major and Minor Prophets.

959th Verse of Isaiah

"Behold, they shall be as stubble; the fire shall burn them; they shall not deliver themselves from the POWER of the flame: there shall not be a coal to warm at, nor fire to sit before it" (Isa. 47:14). When divine judgment comes Babylon will fall under the power and destruction of an oppressor army.

Messiah's Wicked Oppressors

"I gave my back to the smiters, and my cheeks to them that plucked off the hair: I hid not my face from shame and spitting" (Isa. 50:6). The Heaven-sent Messiah permitted this to happen that His atoning blood my flow freely.

> The word *them* occurs 59 times in Proverbs.
> The word *them* occurs 259 times in Isaiah.
> The word *them* occurs 259 times in the Minor Prophets.

Where Is the Oppressor?

"And forgettest the LORD thy maker, that hath stretched forth the heavens, and laid the foundations of the earth; and hast feared continually every day because of the fury of the OPPRESSOR, as if he were ready to destroy? and where is the fury of the OPPRESSOR?" (Isa. 51:13) The phrase *where is* is mentioned in 59 verses of the Bible.

Messiah's Oppressors & Oppression Foretold

"Surely he hath BORNE our griefs, and carried our sorrows: yet we did esteem him STRICKEN, SMITTEN of God, and AFFLICTED. But he was WOUNDED for our transgressions, he was BRUISED for our iniquities: the CHASTISEMENT of our peace was upon him; and with his stripes we are healed. . . . He was OPPRESSED, and he was

AFFLICTED, yet he opened not his mouth: he is brought as a <u>lamb</u> to the slaughter, and as a sheep before her shearers is dumb, so he openeth not his mouth" (Isa. 53:4-5, 7).

Just five verses prior to this oppressed verse is the 1059th verse of Isaiah. Again the word *affliction* is mentioned in 59 verses of the Old Testament. The title *lamb* occurs 59 times in the Law. The Law combination *he was* (47x) and [all available forms of the word] *oppress* (12x) = 59.

The Lord Responsible for Messiah's Oppression

"Yet it pleased the LORD to BRUISE him; he hath put him to GRIEF: when thou shalt make his soul an offering for sin, he shall see his seed, he shall prolong his days, and the pleasure of the LORD shall prosper in his hand" (Isa. 53:10). This painful oppression unto death was substitutionary on behalf of all the sinners in the world so they might have the legal right to go free. Again the title *LORD* occurs 559 times in First and Second Chronicles.

The Lord Will Let the Oppressed Go Free

"Is not this the fast that I have chosen? to <u>loose</u> the bands of wickedness, to undo the HEAVY BURDENS, and to let the OPPRESSED go <u>free</u>, and that ye break every <u>yoke</u>?" (Isa. 58:6) All forms of the word *loose* are mentioned in 59 verses of the Bible. The word *free* occurs 59 times in the Bible. Again the word *yoke* occurs 59 times in the Bible.

59th Chapter of Isaiah

It had not been long since the nation's Assyrian oppressors came to carry off the northern tribes into captivity. The spirit of oppression still filled the land at this time, but it was mainly a result of Israel's depravity and sin. "Behold, the LORD'S hand is not shortened, that it cannot save; neither his ear heavy, that it cannot hear: But your <u>iniquities</u> have separated between you and your God, and your sins have hid his face from you, that <u>he will not hear</u>" (Isa. 59:1-2). The Bible combination *iniquities* (56x) and *he will not hear* (3x) = 59.

The Lord revealed to the nation that it was now guilty of being oppressors to its own countrymen. "Their works are works of iniquity, and the act of violence is in their hands. <u>Their feet run to evil, and they</u> <u>make haste to</u> <u>shed</u> innocent blood: their thoughts are thoughts of iniquity; wasting and destruction are in their paths" (vv. 6-7). The Bible combination *their feet run to evil and they* (1x), *make haste to* (6x), *shed* (52x) = 59.

The people lamented their oppressive, sinful situation. "We grope for the wall like the blind, and we grope as if we had no eyes: we stumble at noonday as in the night; we are in desolate places as dead men. . . . For our transgressions are multiplied before thee, and our sins testify against us: for our transgressions are with us; and as for our iniquities, we know them; In transgressing and lying against the LORD, and departing away from our God, speaking OPPRESSION and revolt, conceiving and uttering from the heart words of falsehood" (vv. 10, 12-13). A related keyword of our study *oppression* actually occurs in this 59th chapter.

As the chapter begins to close, God promised the people that He would relieve them of evil oppressors if they only began to fear His holy name. "When <u>the enemy</u> shall come in like a flood, the Spirit of the LORD shall lift up a standard AGAINST him" (v. 19). The singular Bible terms *the enemy* (54x), *the * enemy* (3x), *the enemy's* (2x) = 59.

The Lord truly wants the Holy City to be liberated of all its many sinful oppressors. This comes by true repentance. Thus He said, "And the Redeemer shall come to Zion, and <u>unto them that</u>

turn from <u>transgression</u> <u>in Jacob</u>, saith the LORD" (v. 20). The Bible combination *unto them that turn from* (1x), *transgression* (51x), *in Jacob* (7x) = 59.

59th Verse of Jeremiah

After accusing Israel of polluting the land with her idolatry and wickedness, the Lord went on to reveal her oppressive punishment. "Therefore the showers have been withholden, and there hath been no latter rain" (Jer. 3:3).

19,059th Verse of the Bible

"For I have heard a voice as of a woman in travail, and the anguish as of her that bringeth forth her first child, the voice of the daughter <u>of Zion,</u> that bewaileth herself, that spreadeth her hands, saying, Woe is me now! for my soul is WEARIED because of murderers" (Jer. 4:31). Zion felt the wrath of God when their Babylonian oppressors came breaking in with devouring force. Again the phrase *of Zion* occurs 59 times in the Bible.

Jerusalem Filled with Spiritual Oppressors

"For thus hath the LORD of hosts said, Hew ye down trees, and cast a mount against <u>Jerusalem</u>: this is the city to be visited; she is wholly OPPRESSION in the midst of her" (Jer. 6:6). Again the name *Jerusalem* is mentioned in 59 verses of Acts.

"Oppress Not the Stranger"

"If ye <u>OPPRESS not</u> <u>the stranger</u>, the fatherless, and the widow, and shed not innocent blood in this place, neither walk after other gods to your hurt: Then will I cause you to dwell in this place, in the land that I gave to your fathers, for ever and ever" (Jer. 7:6-7). The Bible combination *oppress not* (2x), *the stranger* (57x) = 59.

Delivered out of the Hand of the Oppressor

"And I will deliver thee <u>out of the hand of</u> <u>the wicked</u>, and I will redeem thee out of the hand of the terrible" (Jer. 15:21). God promised to deliver Israel from their Chaldean oppressors. In seventy years' time He did just that. This verse presents the Bible's 59th occurrence of the phrase *out of the hand of*, and it refers to an oppressor. Again the phrase *the wicked* occurs 259 times in Scripture.

459th Verse of Jeremiah

"Therefore deliver up their children to the famine, and pour out their blood by the force of the sword; and let their wives be BEREAVED of their children, and be widows; and let their men be put to death; let their young men be slain by the sword in battle" (Jer. 18:21). Jeremiah calls for Jerusalem's disobedient leaders' severe oppression in retribution for their wrongful and oppressive treatment toward him.

Zedekiah, Jeremiah's Oppressor

"Thus saith the LORD; Execute ye judgment and righteousness, and deliver the spoiled out of the hand of the OPPRESSOR: and do no wrong, do no violence to the stranger, the fatherless, nor the widow, neither shed innocent blood in this place" (Jer. 22:3). This oppressor verse immediately precedes the 19,459th verse of the Bible.

Judah's Fierce Oppressor, Babylon

"He hath forsaken his covert, as the lion: <u>for their land is desolate because of the fierceness of the OPPRESSOR,</u> and because of his fierce anger" (Jer. 25:38). The phrase *for their land is desolate because of the fierceness of the oppressor,* consists of 59 characters!

Jacob's End-Time Oppressor

"Alas! for that day is great, so that none is like it: it is even the time of Jacob's trouble; but he shall be saved out of it. For it shall come to pass in that day, saith the LORD of hosts, that I will break his <u>yoke</u> from off thy neck, and will burst thy BONDS, and strangers shall no more serve themselves of him" (Jer. 30:7-8). Jacob's end-time oppressor will be the false messiah, otherwise known as the antichrist. Again the word *yoke* occurs 59 times in the Bible.

Judah's Divine Oppressor

"All thy lovers have forgotten thee; they seek thee not; <u>for I have</u> <u>wounded thee with</u> <u>the wound of</u> <u>an enemy,</u> <u>with the chastisement of</u> <u>a CRUEL one,</u> for the multitude of thine iniquity; because thy sins were increased" (Jer. 30:14). The Major Prophets combination *for I have* (25x), *wounded thee with* (1x), *the wound of an* (1x), *enemy* (30x), *with the chastisement of* (1x), *a cruel one* (1x) = 59.

Nebuchadnezzar, Zedekiah's Babylonian Oppressor

"And <u>the king of Babylon</u> slew the sons of Zedekiah before his eyes: he slew also all the princes of Judah in Riblah. Then he put out the eyes of Zedekiah; and <u>the king of Babylon</u> BOUND him in CHIANS, and carried him to Babylon, and put him in prison till the day of his death" (Jer. 52:10-11). Again the title *the king of Babylon* is mentioned in 59 verses of the Major Prophets.

Oppressing Sword to Come upon Babylon

"<u>Cut off</u> the sower from Babylon, and him that handleth the sickle in the time of harvest: for fear of the OPPRESSING sword they shall turn every one to <u>his people</u>, and they shall flee every one to his own land" (Jer. 50:16). Again the phrase *be cut off* is mentioned in 59 verses of the Bible. Again all forms of the word *oppress* occur 118 times, a multiple of 59. The phrase *his people* occurs 159 times in the Bible.

Israel & Judah Held Captive by Relentless Oppressors

"Thus saith the LORD of hosts; The children of Israel and the children of Judah were OPPRESSED together: and all that took them <u>CAPTIVES</u> held them fast; they refused to let them go" (Jer. 50:33). Again the word *captive* occurs 59 times in the Bible.

Babylon's Coming Persian Oppressors

"They shall hold the bow and the lance: they are CRUEL, and will not shew mercy: their voice shall roar like the sea, <u>and they shall ride upon horses,</u> <u>every one put in array,</u> <u>like a man to the battle,</u> AGAINST thee, O daughter of Babylon" (Jer. 50:42). Again the word *horsemen* occurs 59 times in the Bible. The Major Prophets combination *and they shall ride upon horses* (1x), *every one put in array* (1x), *like a man to the battle* (1x), *against thee* (55x), *O daughter of Babylon* (1x) = 59.

59th Verse of Lamentations

"He hath filled me with <u>bitterness</u>, he hath made me drunken with wormwood" (Lam. 3:15). Along with all Judea, the prophet had experienced the great oppression of Jerusalem. All forms of the word *bitter* are mentioned in 59 chapters of the Bible.

20,559th Verse of the Bible

"A third part of thee shall <u>die</u> with the pestilence, and with famine shall they be consumed in the midst of thee: and a third part <u>shall fall</u> by the sword round about thee; and I will <u>scatter</u> a third part into all the winds, and I will draw out a sword after them" (Ezek. 5:12). This verse refers to Jerusalem's coming third oppression. Again all forms of the word *die* occur 559 times in the Bible. The phase *shall fall* is mentioned in 59 chapters of the Old Testament. The word *scattered* occurs 59 times in the Old Testament.

Land of Israel to Be Oppressed by Beasts

"If I cause noisome <u>beasts</u> to pass through the land, and they spoil it, so that it be desolate, that no man may pass through because of the <u>beasts</u>" (Ezek. 14:15). Again the word *beasts* is mentioned in 59 verses of the Major and Minor Prophets.

Judah Despised God's Word as Much as an Oppressor

"For thus saith the Lord GOD; I will even deal with thee as thou hast done, which hast <u>despised</u> the oath in breaking the covenant" (Ezek. 16:59). Judah's despising God's Word was not dissimilar to their despising of enemy oppressors. The word *despised* is mentioned in 59 verses of the Bible.

A Son's Father Who Cruelly Oppressed Others

"<u>As for his father</u>, <u>because he CRUELLY OPPRESSED</u>, <u>spoiled his brother by violence</u>, <u>and did that which is not good among his people</u>, lo, even he shall die in his iniquity" (Ezek. 18:18). The Old Testament combination *as for his father* (1x), *because he cruelly oppressed* (1x), *spoiled* (54x), *his brother by violence* (1x), *and did that which is not good among his people* (1x) = 59.

Judah's Oppressors Within

"Behold, <u>the princes</u> of Israel, every one were in thee to their POWER to shed blood. . . . Her <u>princes</u> in the midst thereof are like wolves ravening the prey, to shed blood, and to destroy <u>souls</u>, to get dishonest gain. . . . The people of the land have used OPPRESSION, and <u>exercised</u> robbery, and have vexed the poor and needy: yea, they have OPPRESSED the stranger wrongfully" (Ezek. 22:16, 27, 29). Judah's civil rulers oppressed the people for their own selfish desires of monetary gain. Again the title *the princes* is mentioned in 59 verses of the OT Narrative. The word *souls* occurs 59 times in the Old Testament. Here the word *exercised* is the 259th word of this chapter.

The Lord, Tyre's Oppressor

"When I shall bring thee DOWN with them that descend into the pit, with the people of old time, and shall set thee in the low parts of the earth, in places desolate of old, with them that go DOWN to the pit, that thou be not inhabited; and I shall set glory in the land of the living" (Ezek. 26:20). There are 59 words in this oppression verse.

759th Verse of Ezekiel

"Thus will I execute judgments in Egypt: and they shall know that I am the LORD" (Ezek. 30:19). The Lord pledged to oppress Egypt in the day of her judgment. The phrases *in Egypt* (58x) and *in * Egypt* (1x) = 59.

859th Verse of Ezekiel

"Thus saith the Lord GOD; Behold, I am AGAINST the shepherds; and I will require my flock at their hand, and cause them to cease from feeding the flock; neither shall the shepherds feed themselves any more; for I will deliver my flock from their mouth, that they may not be meat for them" (Ezek. 34:10). Both the nation's civil and ecclesiastical leaders were oppressive toward them. All of them were bad shepherds over God's sheepfold. The Lord therefore pledged to remedy the dire situation.

> The terms *the flock* (57x), *the * flock* (2x) occur 59 times in the Bible.
> The term *flocks* is mentioned in 59 chapters of the Old Testament.

Israel's Princes Will No More Oppress the People

"In the land shall be his possession in Israel: and my princes shall no more OPPRESS my people; and the rest of the land shall they give to the house of Israel according to their tribes" (Ezek. 45:8). Again the title *princes* occurs 59 times in the Major Prophets.

An End-Times Oppressor King Shall Arise

"And the ten horns out of this kingdom are ten kings that shall arise: and another shall rise after them; and he shall be diverse from the first, and he shall SUBDUE three kings." (Dan. 7:24). The phrases *and he shall be diverse from the first, and he shall subdue three kings.* consist of 59 characters!

21,959th Verse of the Bible

"And he shall speak great words AGAINST the most High, and shall WEAR out the saints of the most High, and think to change times and laws: and they shall be given into his hand until a time and times and the dividing of time" (Dan. 7:25). This cruel end-times overlord will oppress all the nations but especially Israel. Again the phrase *a time* occurs 59 times in the Bible.

Israel's End-Time Oppressor Will Be Satanically Empowered

"And in the latter time of their kingdom, when the transgressors are come to the full, a king of fierce countenance, and understanding dark sentences, shall stand up. And his POWER shall be mighty, but not by his own POWER: and he shall destroy wonderfully, and shall prosper, and practise, and shall destroy the mighty and the holy people" (Dan. 8:23-24). The Old Testament combination *a king* (41x), *of fierce countenance* (2x), *and understanding dark sentences* (1x), *shall stand up* (8x), *and his power* (1x), *shall be mighty* (2x), *but not by his own power* (1x), *and he shall destroy wonderfully* (1x), *and shall prosper and practice* (1x), *and shall destroy the mighty and the holy people* (1x) = 59.

22,059th Verse of the Bible

"And with the arms of a flood shall they be overflown from before him, and shall be broken; yea, also the prince of the covenant" (Dan. 11:22). The end-times oppressor will have devastating power.

59th Verse of Hosea

"Hear ye this, O priests; and hearken, ye house of Israel; and give ye ear, O house of the king; for judgment is toward you, because ye have been a snare on Mizpah, and a net spread upon Tabor" (Hos. 5:1). The priesthood and the people were both accused of being spiritual oppressors by ensnaring Hebrews and causing them to practice idolatry.

Ephraim Loves to Financially Oppress Others

"He is a merchant, the balances of deceit are in his hand: he loveth to OPPRESS" (Hos. 12:7). The name *Ephraim* is mentioned in 159 verses of the Bible.

The Lord, Ephraim's Just Oppressor

"I will meet them as a bear that is bereaved of her whelps, and will rend the caul of their heart, and there will I devour them like a lion: the wild beast shall tear them" (Hos. 13:8). The Lord declared His oppressive intentions for Ephraim—the wayward northern tribes. The idolatrous northern tribes provoked the Divine Oppressor to action because their heart was rebellious and resistant toward Him. The phrase *their heart* occurs 59 times in the Bible. The words *devour* (58 chs) and *devourer* (1 ch) = 59 chapters of the Bible. The Bible combination *rend the caul* (1x), *a bear* (8x), *a lion* (43x), *wild beast* (5x), *tear them* (2x) = 59.

The Beasts, Herds, Flocks & Sheep All Suffer Oppression

"How do the beasts groan! the herds of cattle are perplexed, because they have no pasture; yea, the flocks of sheep are made desolate" (Joel 1:18). Again the word *beasts* is mentioned in 59 verses of the Major and Minor Prophets. All forms of the word *herd* are mentioned collectively in 59 verses of the Bible. The word *flocks* is mentioned in 59 chapters of the Old Testament. All available forms of the word *sheep* occur 59 times in the Law.

59th Verse of Joel

"Behold, I will raise them out of the place whither ye have sold them, and will return your recompence upon your own head" (Joel 3:7). The Lord was upset with the nations for selling His people into captivity as slaves. He promised to deliver the Israelites and punish the guilty oppressor nations. On Judgment Day the Lord will become the guilty nations' Oppressor. The Bible combination *ye have sold them* (1x), *I will return* (7x), *recompence* (20x), *upon your* (18x), *own head* (13x) = 59.

Israel's Capital City Leaders Oppress the Poor

"Hear this word, ye kine of Bashan, that are in the mountain of Samaria, which OPPRESS the poor, which CRUSH the needy, which say to their masters, Bring, and let us drink" (Amos 4:1). This verse corresponds with our fifth definition of oppress: to crush. The Major and Minor Prophets combination *ye kine of Bashan that are in* (1x), *the mountain of Samaria which* (2x), *oppress* (9x), *the poor* (34x), *which crush* (1x), *the needy* (9x), *which say to their masters* (1x), *bring and* (1x), *let us drink* (1x) = 59.

Assyria, Israel's Coming Oppressor

"For thus Amos saith, Jeroboam shall die by the sword, and Israel shall surely be led away CAPTIVE out of their own land" (Amos 7:11). Amos prophesied during the days of Jeroboam's evil reign over the northern tribes. The king did die, and some sixty years later Amos' prophesy fully came to pass when Assyria became Israel's oppressor. Again the word *captive* occurs 59 times in the Bible.

Israel's Oppression of Their Own People

"Woe to them that devise iniquity, and work evil upon their beds! when the morning is light, they practise it, because it is in the POWER of their hand. And they covet fields, and take them by violence; and houses, and take them away: so they OPPRESS a man and his house, even a man and his heritage" (Mic. 2:1-2). The Old Testament combination *they practise it because it is* (1x), *in the power of* (4x), *their hand* (46x), *and they covet fields* (1x), *and take them by violence* (1x), *and houses* (3x), *and take them away* (1x), *so they oppress a man and his house* (1x), *even a man and his heritage* (1x) = 59.

The Lord Will Become Ninevah's Oppressor

"God is jealous, and the LORD revengeth; the LORD revengeth, and is furious; the LORD will take vengeance on his adversaries, and he reserveth wrath for his enemies. The LORD is slow to anger, and great in POWER, and will not at all acquit the wicked: the LORD hath his way in the whirlwind and in the storm, and the clouds are the dust of his feet" (Nah. 1:2-3). Because the Assyrians oppressed Israel by carrying her away into captivity, the Lord would reward them by oppressing their capital city. Again the title *LORD* occurs 559 times in First and Second Chronicles.

The Lord Is an All-Powerful Oppressor

"God came from Teman, and the Holy One from mount Paran. . . . And his brightness was as the light; he had horns coming out of his hand: and there was the hiding of his POWER. Before him went the pestilence, and burning coals went forth at his feet" (Hab. 3:3a, 4-5). Again the word *power* is mentioned in 59 verses of the Pauline Epistles.

The Oppressing City of Jerusalem

"Woe to her that is filthy and polluted, to the OPPRESSING city! . . . Her princes within her are roaring lions; her judges are evening wolves; they gnaw not the bones till the morrow" (Zeph. 3:1, 3). Again the name *Jerusalem* is mentioned in 59 verses of Acts.

The Lord Will Be an End-Times Oppressor of Nations

"For thus saith the LORD of hosts; Yet once, it is a little while, and I will shake the heavens, and the earth, and the sea, and the dry land; And I will shake all nations" (Hag. 2:6-7a). Again the title *LORD* occurs 559 times in First and Second Chronicles.

Do Not Oppress These Disadvantaged People

"And the word of the LORD came unto Zechariah, saying, Thus speaketh the LORD of hosts, saying, Execute true judgment, and shew mercy and compassions every man to his brother: And OPPRESS not the widow, nor the fatherless, the stranger, nor the poor; and let none of you imagine evil against his brother in your heart. But they refused to hearken" (Zech. 7:8-11a). The

Bible combination *and oppress not the* (1x), *widow* (50x), *nor the fatherless* (1x), *the stranger nor the poor* (1x), *and let none of you* (2x), *imagine evil against his brother* (1x), *in your heart* (3x) = 59.

No More Oppressors to Pass through Israel

"And I will encamp about mine house because of the army, because of him that passeth by, and because of him that returneth: and no OPPRESSOR shall pass through them any more: for now have I seen with mine eyes" (Zech. 9:8). The Bible combination *and I will encamp about mine house* (1x), *because of the army* (1x), *because of him that passeth by* (1x), *and because of him that returneth* (1x), *and no oppressor* (1x), *shall pass* (53x), *through them any more* (1x) = 59.

Oppressors Will Be Judged

"And I will come near to you to judgment; and I will be a swift witness against the adulterers, and against false swearers, and against those that OPPRESS the hireling in his wages, the widow, and the fatherless, and that turn aside the stranger from his right, and fear not me, saith the LORD of hosts" (Mal. 3:5). In this oppressive verse there are 59 words surrounding the keyword *oppress*.

The New Testament

"The book of the generation of Jesus Christ, the son of David, the son of Abraham" (Matt. 1:1). During Christ's public ministry He became the oppressor of devils as He subdued them and made them leave their human captives. Throughout this same period the religious leaders became His oppressors as they repeatedly attempted to deny His entry into His rightful place as King over Israel. At last they oppressed Him unto death—the crushing cruelty of a Roman crucifixion.

The title *the Lord Jesus* occurs 59 times in the New Testament.
The name *Jesus* is mentioned in 59 chapters of the Synoptic Gospels.

59th Verse of Matthew

"I indeed baptize you with water unto repentance: but he that cometh after me is mightier than I, whose shoes I am not worthy to bear: he shall baptize you with the Holy Ghost, and with fire" (Matt. 3:11). John spoke of the Messiah's dual nature; He is both the Deliverer of the righteous and the Oppressor of the unrighteous. John had two audiences before him, the repentant people and the unrepentant religious leaders. Because the repentant had already met Messiah's preconditions of confession and baptism, the aim of John's warning was directed only toward the unrighteous religious emissaries from Jerusalem. The Baptizer warned them, saying that the Messiah "will burn up the chaff with unquenchable fire" (v. 12d). Whether these leaders would meet the Deliverer or the Oppressor on Judgment Day depended on whether or not they would repent. The Bible phrases *the fire* (156x) and *the * fire* (3x) = 159.

Bethlehem Children Crushed by an Edomite Oppressor

"Then Herod, when he saw that he was mocked of the wise men, was exceeding wroth, and sent forth, and slew all the children that were in Bethlehem, and in all the coasts thereof, from two years old and under, according to the time which he had diligently enquired of the wise men. Then was fulfilled that which was spoken by Jeremy the prophet, saying, <u>In Rama was there a voice heard</u>, <u>lamentation, and</u> <u>weeping</u>, <u>and great mourning</u>, <u>Rachel weeping for her children</u>, <u>and would not be comforted</u>, <u>because they are not</u>" (Matt. 2:16-19).

The Bible combination *in Rama* (1x), *was there a voice heard* (1x), *lamentation and* (8x), *weeping* (44x), *and great mourning* (1x), *Rachel weeping for her children* (1x), *and would not be comforted* (1x), *because they are not* (2x) = 59.

The Devil, Jesus' Foremost Oppressor

"Then was Jesus led up of the Spirit into the wilderness to be tempted of <u>the devil</u>. And when he had fasted forty days and forty nights, he was afterward an hungred. And when the tempter came to him" (Matt. 4:1-3a). The oppressive title "devil" belongs to the fallen angel Lucifer. The Devil has subjects under him who also work to oppress humanity; these carry his name's sake and are known as devils. Jesus' public ministry both began and ended underneath the devil's dark oppression.

The lowercase title *devil* occurs 59 times in the Bible.
The title *the devil(s)* is mentioned in 59 verses of the Bible.

People Oppressed with Darkness & Death

"<u>The people which</u> <u>sat in</u> <u>darkness</u> saw great light; and <u>to them which</u> <u>sat in the</u> <u>region</u> <u>and shadow of</u> <u>death</u> <u>light is</u> <u>sprung up</u>" (Matt. 4:16). With His divine light Christ came to this Gentile area because it was full of spiritually oppressed people. The devil had blinded their Gentile minds from the knowledge of salvation. For this reason Christ sought to bring them radiant and eternal hope. The New Testament combination *the people which* (3x), *sat in* (5x), *darkness* (51x) = 59. The Gospels combination *to them which* (4x), *sat in the* (2x), *region* (7x), *and shadow of* (1x), *death* (44x), *light is sprung up* (1x) = 59. This relief-from-oppression passage consists of 59 words.

Mankind's Devilish Oppressors

"When the even was come, they brought unto him many that <u>were POSSESSED with</u> <u>devils</u>: and he cast out the spirits with his word, and healed all that were sick" (Matt. 8:16). The Bible combination *were possessed with* (4x), *devils* (55x) = 59.

259th Verse of the New Testament

"He said unto them, Give place: for the maid is not <u>dead</u>, but sleepeth. And they laughed him to scorn" (Matt. 9:24). The girl was oppressed unto death, but Christ would raise her up again as if she were only sleeping. He alone had this power of life. Again the phrase *the dead* is mentioned in 59 chapters of the New Testament.

Man Tongue-Tied by Devilish Oppressor

"As they went out, behold, they brought to him a <u>dumb man</u> POSSESSED with a <u>devil</u>" (Matt. 9:32). The Bible combination *dumb man* (2 vs) and *devil* (57 vs) = 59 verses. The 59th letter in this oppressor verse falls in the oppressive word *devil*.

Apostles Given Oppressor Power to Subdue Demons

"And when he had called unto him his twelve disciples, he gave them POWER against unclean spirits, to cast them out, and to heal all manner of sickness and all manner of disease" (Matt. 10:1). Again the word *power* is mentioned in 59 verses of the Pauline Epistles.

Governors Will Be Oppressors of Gospel Workers

"But beware of men: for they will deliver you up to the councils, and they will SCOURGE you in their synagogues; And ye shall be brought before governors and kings for my sake, for a testimony against them and the Gentiles" (Matt. 10:17-18). Again the word *governor* occurs 59 times in the Bible.

Jesus Gives the Oppressed Rest from their Oppressor

"Come unto me, all ye that labour and are HEAVY LADEN, and I will give you rest" (Matt. 11:28). Jesus promised to give spiritual rest to those who had been spiritually oppressed by the nation's oppressive, legalistic, religious leaders. The term "heavy laden" corresponds with our third definition of oppress: to weigh down. Again all forms of the word *heavy* show the seal of oppression with their Bible total of 59 verse-mentions.

359th Verse of the New Testament

"Then the Pharisees went out, and held a council AGAINST him, how they might destroy him" (Matt. 12:14). Jesus' oppressors were politically motivated. They wanted to keep their power, control, and influence over the people. The title *the Pharisees* is mentioned in 59 verses of the New Testament.

Israel's Oppressive Religious Leaders

Jesus scolded Israel's many religious oppressors: "O generation of vipers, how can ye, being evil, speak good things? for out of the abundance of the heart the mouth speaketh" (Matt. 12:34). Again the word *evil* occurs 59 times in the NT Narrative. The term *my heart* is mentioned in 59 chapters of the Old Testament.

Herod, The Baptizer's Oppressor

"For Herod had LAID HOLD on John, and BOUND him, and put him in prison for Herodias' sake, his brother Philip's wife" (Matt. 14:3). According to our fourth definition of the word "oppress," Herod's intention was to put down, subdue, or suppress John's voice of dissent. The New Testament combination *Herod* (40x), *laid hold* (6x), *bound him* (7x), *put him in prison* (2x), *for Herodias' sake* (2x), *his brother Philip's wife* (2x) = 59.

Jesus—Oppressor of the Oppressor

"And when they were come to the multitude, there came to him a certain man, kneeling down to him, and saying, Lord, have mercy on my son: for he is lunatick, and sore vexed: for ofttimes he falleth into the fire, and oft into the water. . . . And Jesus rebuked the devil; and he departed out of him: and the child was cured from that very hour" (Matt. 17:14-15, 18). Again the name *Jesus* is mentioned in 59 chapters of the Synoptic Gospels. Again the title *the devil(s)* is mentioned in 59 combined verses of the Bible.

Woe unto Oppressors of Christ's Little Ones

"But whoso shall offend one of these little ones which believe in me, it were better for him that a millstone were hanged about his neck, and that he were drowned in the depth of the sea" (Matt. 18:6). Jesus warns wicked oppressors who would think of coming against little children; a curse awaits them if they do. The Bible combination *but whoso* (9x), *shall offend one of these* (2x), *little ones* (40x), *which believe in me* (1x), *it were better for him* (2x), *that a millstone were hanged about his neck* (3x), *and that he were drowned* (1x), *in the depth of the sea* (1x) = 59.

The Scribes, Jesus' Chief Oppressors

"Behold, we go up; and the Son of man shall be betrayed unto the chief priests and unto the scribes, and they shall condemn him to death, And shall deliver him to the Gentiles to mock, and to SCOURGE, and to crucify him: and the third day he shall rise again" (Matt. 20:18-19). The title *scribes* occurs 59 times in the Gospels.

Scribes & Pharisees, Religious Oppressors

"Then spake Jesus to the multitude, and to his disciples, Saying, The scribes and the Pharisees sit in Moses' seat: All therefore whatsoever they bid you observe, that observe and do; but do not ye after their works: for they say, and do not. For they bind HEAVY BURDENS and grievous to be borne, and lay them on men's shoulders; but they themselves will not move them with one of their fingers" (Matt. 23:1-4). Jesus' indictment revealed how oppressive the religious leadership had become over the nation. Again the title *the Pharisees* is mentioned in 59 verses of the New Testament. Again the title *scribes* occurs 59 times in the Gospels. The NT Narrative combination *for they* (58x), *bind heavy burdens* (1x) = 59 chapters.

Woe unto the Oppressors come Judgment Day

"But woe unto you, scribes and Pharisees, hypocrites! for ye shut up the kingdom of heaven against men: for ye neither go in yourselves, neither suffer ye them that are entering to go in" (Matt. 23:13). Corresponding with our first definition of oppress, Jesus speaks of the religious leaders' harsh exercise of authority or power. The phrase *woe unto* occurs 59 times in the Bible. Again the title *scribes* occurs 59 times in the Gospels. Again the title *the Pharisees* is mentioned in 59 verses of the New Testament.

The Church's Future Hateful Oppressors

Jesus described oppressors' evil nature during the Church Age. "Then shall they deliver you up to be AFFLICTED, and shall kill you: and ye shall be hated of all nations for my name's sake" (Matt. 24:9). Again the word *affliction* is mentioned in 59 verses of the Old Testament. Again the word *kill* is mentioned in 118 verses of the Bible, a multiple of 59.

Christ's Oppressors Will Soon Shed His Blood

"And as they were eating, Jesus took bread, and blessed it, and brake it, and gave it to the disciples, and said, Take, eat; this is my body. And he took the cup, and gave thanks, and gave it to them, saying, Drink ye all of it; For this is my blood of the new testament, which is shed for many for the remission of sins" (Matt. 26:26-28). Right on cue, the word *blood* is mentioned in 159 chapters from Genesis to the Gospels.

Jesus Meets the Oppressor in Garden of Gethsemane

"And he took with him Peter and the two sons of Zebedee, and began to be sorrowful and very HEAVY" (Matt. 26:37). This verse corresponds with our third definition of oppress: to weigh down, as sleep or weariness does. Again all forms of the word *heavy* are mentioned together in 59 verses of the Bible.

Matthew 26:59

"Now the chief priests, and elders, and all the council, sought false witness AGAINST Jesus, to put him to death" (Matt. 26:59). At this point in time Christ's oppressors were the Jerusalem council or Sanhedrin, and they would not be satisfied with anything less oppressive than the death penalty. Even when Pilate later scourged Jesus and tried to release Him back into their custody, the council members still clamored for the death penalty. From Genesis to the NT Narrative the phrase *to death* is mentioned in 59 chapters.

Pilate's Judgment Seat

"When he was set down on the judgment seat, his wife sent unto him, saying, Have thou nothing to do with that just man: for I have suffered many things this day in a dream because of him" (Matt. 27:19). According to our second definition Pilate was mentally oppressed that day. The matter of Jesus' innocence continued to weigh heavily upon his mind. His wife's declaration further oppressed him. Right on cue from Genesis to the Synoptic Gospels the word *judgment* is mentioned in 159 chapters.

24,159th Verse of the Bible

"And when they had platted a crown of thorns, they put it upon his head, and a reed in his right hand: and they bowed the knee before him, and mocked him, saying, Hail, King of the Jews!" (Matt. 27:29) Jesus' Roman oppressors took cruel delight in His suffering.

Roman Oppressors Nail Jesus' Feet to a Cross

"He saved others; himself he cannot save. If he be the King of Israel, let him now come down from the cross, and we will believe him" (Matt. 27:42). The lowly Savior would not come down from the Cross because He had been nailed to it by His Roman oppressors. In the sense of our first definition of the word oppress, Jesus' body was oppressed with cruel and unjust restraints— nails into His hands and feet. Again from Genesis to the Gospels the phrase *his feet* is mentioned in 59 verses.

Matthew 27:59

"And when Joseph had taken the body, he wrapped it in a clean linen cloth" (Matt. 27:59). At this time Jesus' body had been oppressed unto death. The New Testament combination *Joseph had taken* (1 v), *the body* (58 vs) = 59 verses.

1159th Verse of the New Testament

"And he ordained twelve . . . that he might send them forth to preach, And to have POWER to heal sicknesses, and to cast out devils" (Mark 3:14-15). The underlined 59th verse pertains to ordained men having power over supernatural, satanic oppressors. Again the word *power* is mentioned in 59 verses of the Pauline Epistles.

Master of the Sea Oppresses the Wind

"And they <u>feared</u> exceedingly, and said one to another, What manner of man is this, that even <u>the wind</u> and the sea obey him?" (Mark 4:41) The Incarnate Creator oppressed or subdued the prevailing and oppressive winds. This verse presents the Bible's 59th occurrence of the word *feared*. The term *the wind(s)* is mentioned in 59 combined verses from Genesis to the Gospels.

Maniac of Gadara Tormented by Supernatural Oppressors

"And they came over unto the other side of the sea, into the country of the Gadarenes. And when he was come out of the ship, immediately there met him out of the tombs a man with an unclean spirit, Who had his dwelling among the tombs; and no man could BIND him, no, not with CHAINS: Because that he had been often BOUND with FETTERS and CHAINS, and the CHAINS had been plucked asunder by him, and the FETTERS broken in pieces: neither could any man tame him. And always, night and day, he was in the mountains, and in the tombs, <u>crying</u>, and cutting himself with stones" (Mark 5:1-5).

Again the word *cry* is mentioned in 159 verses of the Old Testament.

159th Verse of Mark

"What have I to do with thee, Jesus, thou Son of the most high God? I adjure thee by God, that thou TORMENT me not. For he said unto him, Come out of the man, thou unclean spirit. And he asked him, What is thy name? And he answered, saying, My name is Legion: for we are many. <u>And he besought him much that he would not send them away out of the country</u>" (Mark 5:7b-10). The underlined 159th verse makes reference to supernatural oppressors.

Syrophenician Girl Vexed with Devilish Oppressor

"And from thence he arose, and went into the borders of Tyre and Sidon, and entered into an house, and would have no man know it: but he could not be hid. For a certain woman, whose young daughter had an unclean spirit, heard of him, and came and fell at his feet: The woman was a Greek, a Syrophenician by nation; and she besought him that he would cast forth the <u>devil</u> out of her daughter" (Mark 7:24-26). Again the lowercase title *devil* occurs 59 times in the Bible.

The Son of Man's Deadly Oppressors

"For he taught his disciples, and said unto them, The Son of man is delivered into the hands of men, and they shall <u>kill</u> him; and after that he is killed, he shall rise the third day" (Mark 9:31). Jesus spoke many times of His coming death at the hands of oppressors. Again the word *kill* is mentioned in 118 verses of the Bible, a multiple of 59.

459th Verse of Mark

"<u>And he began to speak unto them by parables. A certain man planted a vineyard, and set an hedge about it, and digged a place for the winefat, and built a tower, and let it out to husbandmen, and went into a far country.</u> And at the season he sent to the husbandmen a servant, that he might receive from the husbandmen of the fruit of the vineyard. And they caught him, and <u>BEAT</u> him, and sent him away empty. And again he sent unto them another servant; and at him they cast stones, and WOUNDED him in the head, and sent him away shamefully handled. And again he sent another; and him they killed, and many others; <u>BEATING</u> some, and killing some. Having yet therefore one son, his wellbeloved, he sent him also last unto them, saying, They will reverence my son. But those husbandmen said among themselves, This is the heir; come, let us kill him, and the inheritance shall be ours. And they took him, and killed him, and cast him out of the vineyard" (Mark 12:1-8).

This underlined 59th introduces the parable on Jerusalem's religious oppressors. Again all forms of the word *beat* are mentioned in 59 chapters of the Bible.

The End-Times Antichrist Oppressor

"But when ye shall see the abomination of desolation, spoken of by Daniel the prophet, standing where it ought not . . . then let them that be in Judæa flee to the mountains. . . . For in those days shall be AFFLICTION, such as was not from the beginning of the creation which God created unto this time, neither shall be" (Mark 13:14, 19). Again the word *affliction* is mentioned in 59 verses of the Old Testament.

The Good Shepherd's Wrath-Filled Oppressor

"And Jesus saith unto them, <u>All ye shall be</u> <u>offended</u> <u>because of</u> <u>me this night</u>: <u>for it is written</u>, <u>I will smite</u> <u>the shepherd</u>, <u>and the sheep</u> <u>shall be scattered</u>" (Mark 14:27). The Gospels combination *all ye shall be* (2x), *offended* (14x), *because of* (21x), *me this night* (2x), *for it is written* (6x), *I will smite* (2x), *the shepherd* (4x), *and the sheep* (5x), *shall be scattered* (3x) = 59.

Jesus' Soul Weighed down by the Dark Oppressor

"And they came to a place which was named Gethsemane: and he saith to his disciples, Sit ye here, while I shall pray. And he taketh with him Peter and James and John, and began to be sore amazed, and to be very <u>HEAVY</u>; And saith unto them, <u>My soul</u> is exceeding sorrowful unto death: tarry ye here, and watch" (Mark 14:32-34). Again all forms of the word *heavy* are mentioned together in 59 verses of the Bible. Again the phrase *my soul* is mentioned in 159 verses of the Old Testament.

1659th Verse of the New Testament

"And Jesus answered and said unto them, Are ye come out, as AGAINST a thief, with swords and with staves to take me? <u>I was daily with you in the temple teaching, and ye took me not: but the scriptures must be fulfilled</u>. And they all forsook him, and fled" (Mark 14:48-50). The words of the underlined 59th verse were directed at Jesus' religious oppressors who had come to restrain Him and suppress Him.

Mark 14:59

"But neither so did their witness agree together" (Mark 14:59). These religious oppressors were inserting fabricated witnesses into Christ's religious trial.

Pontius Pilate, Judaea's Roman Oppressor

"And so <u>Pilate</u>, willing to content the people, released Barabbas unto them, and delivered Jesus, when he had SCOURGED him, to be crucified" (Mark 15:15). Pilate had killed many Jews during his rule, but he was determined to let Jesus go free. He unfortunately succumbed to the oppressive circumstances that day, and in the end he became Jesus' legal and judicial oppressor as he consented to His death. The NT Narrative combination *Pontius* (3x), *Pilate* (55x), *governor of Judaea* (1x) = 59.

Israel's Spiritual Oppression to Be Reversed

"And he shall go before him in the spirit and power of Elias, to turn the <u>hearts</u> of the fathers to the children, and the disobedient to the wisdom of the just; to make ready a people prepared for the Lord" (Luke 1:17). This verse presents the Bible's 59th chapter-mention of the word *hearts*, and it pertains to a reversal of Israel's spiritual oppression. From Genesis to the Synoptic Gospels the word *hearts* is mentioned in 59 chapters.

Saved from Our Oppressors

"That we should be <u>saved</u> <u>from our enemies, and from the hand of all that hate us</u>. . . . That he would grant unto us, that we being delivered out of the hand of our enemies might serve him without fear" (Luke 1:71, 74). This part of Zacharias' prayer proclaimed the Davidic Savior who had come to save the nation from its occupying Roman oppressors. The New Testament combination *saved* (57x), *from our enemies* (1x), *and from the hand of all that hate us* (1x) = 59.

Messiah & Israelite Followers to Fall by the Oppressor

"And Simeon blessed them, and said unto Mary his mother, Behold, this child is set for the fall and rising again of many in Israel; and for a sign which shall be spoken AGAINST; Yea, a <u>sword</u> shall <u>pierce through</u> thy own <u>soul</u> also, that the thoughts of many hearts may be revealed" (Luke 2:34-35). The aged priest prophesied the oppressor coming against the Messiah directly, an event which would indirectly affect His followers and His mother. Her Son's agonizing death would greatly oppress her mind. The singular word *soul('s)* occurs 459 times in the Bible. The Bible combination *with the sword* (58x) and *pierce through* (1x) = 59.

Messiah Comes to Relieve Captives from Their Oppressors

"The Spirit of the Lord is upon me, because he hath anointed me to preach the gospel to the poor; he hath sent me to heal the brokenhearted, to preach deliverance to the <u>CAPTIVES</u>, and recovering of sight to the blind, to set at liberty <u>them that are BRUISED</u>" (Luke 4:18). Again the word *captive* occurs 59 times in the Bible. The Luke combination *them* (258 vs), *that are bruised* (1 v) = 259 verses.

Omnipotent Son Versus Oppressor Spirit

"And in the synagogue there was a man, which had a spirit of an unclean devil, and cried out with a loud voice, Saying, Let us alone; what have we to do with thee, thou Jesus of Nazareth? art thou come to destroy us? I know thee who thou art; the Holy One of God. And Jesus rebuked him, saying, Hold thy peace, and come out of him. . . . And they were all amazed, and spake among themselves, saying, What a word is this! for with authority and <u>POWER</u> he commandeth the <u>unclean</u> <u>spirits</u>, and they come out" (Luke 4:33-35a, 36).

Again the word *power* is mentioned in 59 verses of the Pauline Epistles. The New Testament combination *possessed with* (8 chs), *unclean* (23 chs), *spirits* (28 chs) = 59 chapters.

259th Verse of Luke

"And it came to pass also on another sabbath, that he entered into the synagogue and taught: and there was a man whose right hand was withered" (Luke 6:6). This poor man had likely been afflicted by that same diabolical oppressor who had smitten so many in Israel around that era.

Man of the Tombs Beset with Many Devilish Oppressors

"And Jesus asked him, saying, What is thy name? And he said, Legion: because <u>many</u> <u>devils</u> were entered into him" (Luke 8:30). Again the title *the devil(s)* is mentioned in 59 verses of the Bible.

The word *many* is mentioned in 59 chapters of the Major Prophets.

The word *many* is mentioned in 259 verses of the Old Testament.

2159th Verse of the New Testament

"Then he called his twelve disciples together, and gave them <u>POWER</u> and authority over all devils, and to cure diseases. <u>And he sent them to preach the kingdom of God, and to heal the sick</u>" (Luke 9:1-2). The underlined words mark the 59th verse. Again the word *power* is mentioned in 59 verses of the Pauline Epistles.

Luke 9:59

"And he said unto another, Follow me. But he said, Lord, suffer me first to go and <u>bury</u> my father" (Luke 9:59). His father was not dead but only quite aged. According to the Near East custom this firstborn son merely expressed his birthright obligation to stay at home until his father's passing. Before this would-be disciple would follow the Prince of Life he had to await his father's oppressor to come whose name was Death. Again the word *grave* occurs 59 times in the Old Testament.

2259th Verse of the New Testament

"But Martha was cumbered about much serving, and came to him, and said, Lord, dost thou not care that my sister hath left me to serve alone? bid her therefore that she help me" (Luke 10:40). This verse concerns a believer's unnecessary mental oppression while serving alone without help.

Beelzebub, the Chief of Oppressors

"And he was casting out a devil, and it was dumb. And it came to pass, when <u>the devil</u> was gone out, the dumb spake; and the people wondered. But some of them said, He casteth out devils through Beelzebub the chief of <u>the devils</u>" (Luke 11:14-15). Beelzebub literally means lord of the flies and refers to a Philistine deity worshiped at Ekron. The name, however, has come to mean the prince of evil spirits. Matthew and Mark employed the name "the prince of the devils." Again the title *the devil(s)* is mentioned in 59 verses of the Bible.

Rich Lawyers Oppress Debtors with Internments to Debtors' Prison

"And he said, Woe unto you also, ye lawyers! for <u>ye</u> lade men with BURDENS grievous to be borne, and ye yourselves touch not the BURDENS with one of your fingers" (Luke 11:46). Here the underlined word *ye* is the 51,959th word of the New Testament, and it refers to civil oppressors.

559th Verse of Luke

"Woe unto you! for ye build the sepulchres of the prophets, and your fathers killed them" (Luke 11:47). Jesus denounces lawyers whose forefathers were oppressors of holy prophets.

Luke 12:59

"I tell thee, thou shalt not depart thence, till thou hast paid the very last mite" (Luke 12:59). Jesus spoke of the debtors' prison where the debtor would become subject to harsh restraints and cruel oppressors.

Woman Physically & Physiologically Bound by the Oppressor

"And, behold, there was a <u>woman</u> which had a <u>spirit</u> <u>of infirmity</u> eighteen years, and was bowed together, and could in no wise lift up herself. And when Jesus saw her, he called her to him, and said unto her, Woman, thou art loosed from thine infirmity. . . . And ought not this woman, being a daughter of Abraham, whom <u>Satan hath BOUND</u>, lo, these eighteen years, be loosed from this BOND on the sabbath day?" (Luke 13:11-12, 16) Again the word *woman* occurs 59 times in the Gospels. The New Testament Narrative combination [lowercase only] *spirit* (57x), *of infirmity* (1x), *Satan hath bound* (1x) = 59.

Parable of the Judicial Oppressor

"And he spake a parable unto them to this end, that men ought always to pray, and not to faint; Saying, <u>There was in a city a judge, which feared not God, neither regarded man:</u> And there was a widow in that city; and she came unto him, saying, Avenge me of mine adversary. And he would not for a while: but afterward he said within himself, Though I fear not God, nor regard man; Yet because this widow troubleth me, I will avenge her, lest by her continual coming she WEARY me. And the Lord said, Hear what the unjust judge saith" (Luke 18:1-6).

This judge wearied people with his oppressive judgments. In this parable the adamant widow was oppressing the judge with her loud, persistent voice. The joined phrases *there was in a city a judge, which feared not God, neither regarded man:* consists of 59 characters!

Parable of the Noble Oppressor

"And another came, saying, Lord, behold, here is thy pound, which I have kept laid up in a napkin: <u>For I feared thee, because thou art an AUSTERE MAN: thou takest up that thou layedst not down, and reapest that thou didst not sow</u>. And he saith unto him, Out of thine own mouth will I judge thee, thou wicked servant. Thou knewest that I was an AUSTERE MAN, taking up that I laid not down, and reaping that I did not sow: Wherefore then gavest not thou my money into the bank, that at my coming I might have required mine own with usury? And he said unto them that stood by, Take from him the pound, and give it to him that hath ten pounds" (Luke 19:20-24).

Webster's Dictionary defines the word austere as stern, grave, or morally strict. This noble land owner was just and fair but also capable of becoming an oppressor toward those who dared challenge his authoritative rule. The underlined words indicate the 859th verse of Luke.

Son of Man Returns to Oppress the Wicked

"And there shall be signs in the sun, and in the moon, and in the stars; and upon the earth distress of nations, with perplexity; the sea and the waves roaring; <u>Men's hearts</u> failing them for fear, and for looking after those things which are coming on the earth: for the powers of heaven shall be shaken. And then shall they see the Son of man coming in a cloud with <u>POWER</u> and great glory" (Luke 21:25-27). When the Lord Jesus returns to Earth He will take on the role of an Oppressor of wicked men. Again the phrase *their heart* occurs 59 times in the Bible. Again the word *power* is mentioned in 59 verses of the Pauline Epistles.

Luke 22:59

"And about the space of one hour after another confidently affirmed, saying, Of a truth this fellow also was with him: for he is a Galilæan" (Luke 22:59). Here yet another accuser seeks to get Peter arrested. This accuser, like the two beforehand, greatly oppressed Peter's heart and mind.

This Man Was Beset with Vocal Oppressors

"And they cried out all at once, saying, Away with this man, and release unto us Barabbas" (Luke 23:18). At this moment Jesus' oppressors were great in number. The phrase *this man* occurs 59 times in the NT Narrative.

Calvary's Noonday Oppression of Darkness

"And it was about the sixth hour, and there was a darkness over all the earth until the ninth hour. And the sun was darkened. . . . And all the people that came together to that sight, beholding the things which were done, smote their breasts" (Luke 23:44-45a, 48). God brought darkness at noonday to oppress the people for their complicity in killing His heaven-sent Son. The following seal employs all available forms of the word dark. The Major and Minor Prophets combination *dark* (15x), *darken* (1x), *darkened* (7x), *darkness* (35x), *noonday as in the night* (1x) = 59. The word *hour* occurs in 59 verses of the Gospels.

Jesus' Body Quenched of Life by Deadly Oppressors

"And they found the stone rolled away from the sepulchre. And they entered in, and found not the body of the Lord Jesus" (Luke 24:3). Again the title *the Lord Jesus* occurs 59 times in the New Testament.

The Jews, Christ's Constant Oppressors

"The man departed, and told the Jews that it was Jesus, which had made him whole. And therefore did the Jews PERSECUTE Jesus, and sought to SLAY him, because he had done these things on the sabbath day" (John 5:15-16). John uses the term "the Jews" when referring to the nation's religious leadership. Again the title *the Jews* is mentioned in 59 verses of Acts.

Christ's Many Oppressors in the World

"The world cannot hate you; but me it hateth, because I testify of it, that the works thereof are evil" (John 7:7). John identified a satanic system in this world which hates Jesus outright and seeks to oppress His worldwide followers. The word *world* is mentioned in 59 verses of John's Gospel. Again the phrase *the work* occurs 159 times in the Bible. Again the word *evil* occurs 59 times in the NT Narrative.

The Adulteress' Judgmental Religious Oppressors

"And the scribes and Pharisees brought unto him a woman taken in adultery; and when they had set her in the midst, They say unto him, Master, this woman was taken in adultery, in the very act. Now Moses in the law commanded us, that such should be stoned: but what sayest thou?" (John 8:3-5) Again the word *woman* occurs 59 times in the Gospels.

John 8:59

"Then took they up stones to cast at him: but Jesus hid himself, and went out of the temple, going through the midst of them, and so passed by" (John 8:59). Having rejected Christ's saying the Pharisees once again became His fierce oppressors. The Bible combination *stones* (158 vs), *to cast at him* (1 v) = 159 verses.

People's Fear of the Religious Oppressors

"These words spake his parents, because they feared the Jews: for the Jews had agreed already, that if any man did confess that he was Christ, he should be put out of the synagogue" (John 9:22). Here the word *feared* is the 8659th word of John's Gospel, and it pertains to fear of oppressors. Again the title *the Jews* is mentioned in 59 verses of Acts.

Satanic Oppressor's Three Evil Objectives
"All that ever came before me are thieves and robbers: but the sheep did not hear them. . . . The thief cometh not, but for to steal, and to <u>kill</u>, and to destroy" (John 10:8, 10a). Again the word *kill* is mentioned in 118 verses of the Bible, a multiple of 59.

Christ's Oppressors Seek to Stone Him
"I and my Father are one. Then <u>the Jews took up</u> <u>stones</u> again to stone him" (John 10:30-31). The Bible combination *the Jews took up* (1 v), *stones* (158 vs) = 159 verses.

Lazarus Oppressively Bound with Restraining Graveclothes
"<u>And he that was dead came forth, BOUND hand and foot with graveclothes:</u> and his face was BOUND about with a napkin. Jesus saith unto them, Loose him, and let him go" (John 11:44). Lazarus had recently been oppressed unto death. The word *bound* is mentioned in 59 chapters from Genesis to the Gospels. The phrases *and he that was dead came forth, bound hand and foot with graveclothes:* consists of 59 characters!

Christ's Political Oppressors Become Dead Serious
"Then from that day forth they took counsel together for to put him <u>to death</u>" (John 11:53). Again from Genesis to the NT Narrative the phrase *to death* is mentioned in 59 chapters.

Jesus to Be Oppressed for the World's Sins
"<u>Now is</u> <u>the judgment of</u> <u>this world</u>: now shall the prince of this world be cast out" (John 12:31). Keeping the second half of this verse in context with the verse which follows it, Jesus, the Prince of Peace, is to be cast out of the kingdom by way of a crucified death. Though He is physically cast out of this world, His bloody death will become the means whereby He can legally redeem the world. The New Testament combination *now is* (15x), *the judgment of* (6x), *this world* (38x) = 59.

The Oppressor Works Mostly in the Night
"And when he had dipped the sop, he gave it to Judas Iscariot, the son of Simon. And after the sop Satan entered into him. . . . He then having received the sop went immediately out: and it was <u>night</u>" (John 13:26b-27a, 30). Again the phrase *the night* is mentioned in 59 chapters of the Old Testament.

26,759th Verse of the Bible
"Behold, the <u>hour</u> cometh, yea, is now come, that ye shall be <u>scattered</u>, every man to his own, and shall leave me alone: and yet I am not alone, because the Father is with me" (John 16:32). This 59th verse speaks of the fast-approaching hour of satanic darkness and oppression. Again the word *hour* is mentioned in 59 verses of the Gospels. Again the word *scattered* occurs 59 times in the Old Testament.

Christ's Prayer of Protection from the Oppressor—for Believers

"I pray not that thou shouldest take them out of the <u>world</u>, but that thou shouldest keep <u>them from the evil</u>" (John 17:15). Again the word *world* is mentioned in 59 verses of John. The John combination *them* (158 vs), *from the evil* (1 v) = 259 verses. Again the word *evil* occurs 59 times in the NT Narrative.

Caiaphas, the Oppressor High Priest

"Then <u>the band and the captain and</u> <u>officers</u> <u>of the Jews</u> took Jesus, and BOUND him, And led him away to Annas first; for he was father in law to Caiaphas, which was the high priest that same year. Now Caiaphas was he, which gave counsel to the Jews, that it was expedient that one man should die for the people. . . . Now Annas had sent him BOUND unto Caiaphas the high priest" (John 18:12-14, 24). Again the word *bound* is mentioned in 59 chapters from Genesis to the Gospels. The Bible combination *the band and the captain and* (1x), *officers* (58x) = 59. Again the phrase *of the Jews* is mentioned in 59 verses of the New Testament.

Pilate, the Oppressor Governor

"Then saith Pilate unto him, Speakest thou not unto me? knowest thou not that I have <u>POWER</u> to crucify thee, and have power to release thee?" (John 19:10) The governor boasted in his sovereign power to oppress whom he would, but Jesus corrected his miscalculation. Again the word *power* is mentioned in 59 verses of the Pauline Epistles.

Jesus Oppressed & Thirsty

"After this, Jesus knowing that all things were now accomplished, that the scripture might be fulfilled, saith, I <u>thirst</u>" (John 19:28). Jesus' thirst stood as a great sign of His subjugation to His evil oppressors. All forms of the word thirst reveal the numeric seal of the oppressor: *thirst* (31x), *thirsted* (2x), *thirsteth* (4x), *thirsty* (17x), *athirst* (5x) = 59.

The Church's First Oppression

Peter and John had drawn a great preaching audience after healing the lame man at the golden gate.

> "And as they spake unto the people, the priests, and the captain of the temple, and the Sadducees, <u>came upon them</u>, Being grieved that they taught the people, and preached through Jesus the resurrection from the dead. And they <u>laid hands on them, and put them in hold</u> unto the next day: for it was now eventide. . . . But that it spread no further among the people, let us straitly <u>threaten them</u>, that they speak henceforth to no man in this name. And they called them, <u>and commanded them</u> <u>not to speak</u> <u>at all nor teach</u> <u>in the name of Jesus</u>" (Acts 4:1-3, 17-18).

The Bible combination *came upon them* (5x), *laid hands on them* (1x), *and put them in hold* (1x), *threaten them* (1x), *and commanded them* (39x), *not to speak* (5x), *at all nor teach* (1x), *in the name of Jesus* (6x) = 59.

The Church's Second Oppression

The church was gaining great interest among the surrounding cities of Jerusalem. They had been bringing their sick folk to the apostles and seeing them all get healed.

> "<u>Then the high priest rose up, and all they that were with him, which is the sect</u> <u>of the Sadducees, and were filled with</u> <u>indignation, And</u> <u>laid their hands</u> <u>on the apostles, and put</u>

them in the common prison" (Acts 5:17-18).

Caiaphas was of the Sadducee party, and they sought to oppress the Jewish church. The Bible combination *then the high priest rose up, and all they that were with him which is the sect* (1x), *of the Sadducees* (5x), *and were filled with* (2x), *indignation* (41x), *laid their hands* (8x), *on the apostles* (1x), *and put them in the common prison* (1x) = 59.

Moses Helped a Fellow Hebrew Who Had Been
Attacked by an Egyptian Oppressor

"And seeing one of them suffer wrong, he <u>defended him, and avenged him that was OPPRESSED, and smote the Egyptian</u>" (Acts 7:24). The words *defended him, and avenged him that was oppressed, and smote the Egyptian* consist of 59 letters!

Acts 7:59
The Church's Third Oppression

"And they <u>stoned</u> <u>Stephen, calling upon God, and saying, Lord Jesus, receive my spirit</u>" (Acts 7:59). Stephen's dreadful oppressors began a third wave of oppression by stoning this church deacon to death. The Bible combination *stoned* (22x), *Stephen* (7x), *unto death* (28x), *calling upon God and saying* (1x), *Lord Jesus receive my spirit* (1x) = 59.

The Church's Fourth Oppression

"And Saul was consenting unto his death. And at that time there was a great <u>PERSECUTION</u> AGAINST the church which was at Jerusalem; and they were all <u>scattered</u> abroad throughout the regions of Judæa and Samaria, except the apostles. . . . As for Saul, he made havock of the church, entering into every house, and haling men and women committed them to prison. . . . And Saul, yet breathing out THREATENINGS and slaughter AGAINST the disciples of the Lord, went unto the high priest, And desired of him letters to Damascus to the synagogues, that if he found any of this way, whether they were men or women, he might bring them BOUND unto <u>Jerusalem</u>" (Acts 8:1, 3; 9:1-2).

This man instigated the Church's fourth wave of oppression. He desperately wanted to suppress the gospel's advancement. All forms of the word persecute show the seal of the oppressor: *persecute* (24x), *persecuted* (19x), *persecutest* (6x), *persecution* (10x) = 59. Again the word *scattered* occurs 59 times in the Old Testament. Again the name *Jerusalem* is mentioned in 59 verses of Acts.

Jesus Christ Had Divine Oppressor Powers

"How God anointed Jesus of Nazareth with the Holy Ghost and with <u>POWER</u>: who went about doing good, and healing all that were OPPRESSED of the devil; for God was with him" (Acts 10:38). Again the word *power* is mentioned in 59 verses of the Pauline Epistles.

The Church's Fifth Oppression

"Now about that time Herod the king stretched forth his hands to VEX certain of the church. And he <u>killed</u> James the brother of John with the sword. And because he saw it pleased the Jews, he proceeded further to take Peter also. Then were the days of unleavened bread. And when he had apprehended him, he put him in prison, and delivered him to four quaternions of soldiers to keep him; intending after Easter to bring him forth to the people" (Acts 12:1-4).

Again the word *kill* is mentioned in 118 verses of the Bible, a multiple of 59.

The Jews, Paul's Oppressors

"But when the Jews saw the multitudes, they were filled with envy, and spake AGAINST those things which were spoken by Paul, contradicting and blaspheming" (Acts 13:45). The Jews became Paul's vocal oppressors, particularly so when they blasphemed the worthy name of Jesus Christ and said He was not God Incarnate. Again all forms of the word *blasphemy* have the numeric seal of the oppressor, occurring 59 times. Again the title *the Jews* is mentioned in 59 verses of Acts.

The Gentiles, Paul's Oppressors

Paul was initially met with great gospel success among the Gentiles of Iconium. "But the unbelieving Jews stirred up the Gentiles, and made their minds evil affected AGAINST the brethren" (Acts 14:2). The title *the Gentiles* occurs 118 times in the Bible, a multiple of 59.

4359th Verse of the New Testament

"And when her masters saw that the hope of their gains was gone, they caught Paul and Silas, and drew them into the marketplace unto the rulers, And brought them to the magistrates, saying, These men, being Jews, do exceedingly trouble our city" (Acts 16:19-20). The underlined 59th verse reveals the chief apostle's Roman oppressors in Philippi.

Paul & Silas Suffered under Philippian Oppressors

"And when her masters saw that the hope of their gains was gone, they caught Paul and Silas, and drew them into the marketplace unto the rulers, And brought them to the magistrates, saying, These men, being Jews, do exceedingly trouble our city, And teach customs, which are not lawful for us to receive, neither to observe, being Romans. And the multitude rose up together against them: and the magistrates rent off their clothes, and commanded to BEAT them. And when they had laid many STRIPES upon them, they cast them into prison, charging the jailor to keep them safely: Who, having received such a charge, thrust them into the inner prison, and made their feet fast in the STOCKS" (Acts 16:19-24). The name *Paul('s)* is mentioned in 159 verses of the New Testament.

4559th Verse of the New Testament

"But Paul said, I am a man which am a Jew of Tarsus, a city in Cilicia, a citizen of no mean city: and, I beseech thee, suffer me to speak unto the people" (Acts 21:39). Paul desired to preach the gospel to his multitudinous oppressors who had just tried to stone him.

Paul's Roman Oppressors Prepare to Scourge Him

"The chief captain commanded him to be brought into the castle, and bade that he should be examined by SCOURGING; that he might know wherefore they cried so AGAINST him. And as they BOUND him with THONGS, Paul said unto the centurion that stood by, Is it lawful for you to SCOURGE a man that is a Roman, and uncondemned?" (Acts 22:24-25) The phrase *a man* is mentioned in 59 chapters of the NT Narrative, and this is its 59th chapter-mention.

4659th Verse of the New Testament

"And when he was come, the Jews which came down from Jerusalem stood round about, and laid many and grievous complaints AGAINST Paul, which they could not prove" (Acts 25:7). Paul's Jewish enemies from Jerusalem came to Ceasarea to oppress his gospel ministry with their accusatory words.

Satan's Oppressor Power Weakened by Gospel Preaching of Christ

"To open their eyes, and to turn them from darkness to light, and from the <u>POWER</u> of Satan unto God, that they may receive forgiveness of sins, and inheritance among them which are sanctified by faith that is in me" (Acts 26:18). Again the word *power* is mentioned in 59 verses of the Pauline Epistles.

4759th Verse of the New Testament

"And when the barbarians saw the venomous beast hang on his hand, they said among themselves, No doubt this man is a murderer, whom, though he hath escaped the sea, yet vengeance suffereth not to live" (Acts 28:4). The islanders thought Paul was being judged by the gods, that is, unseen oppressors.

59th Verse of Romans

"And shall not uncircumcision which is by nature, if it fulfil the law, judge thee, who by the letter and circumcision <u>dost transgress</u> <u>the law</u>" (Rom. 2:27). Paul spoke to the Jews who knew the law yet were condemned by it. The Law was their oppressor because the Law was only meant to show men where they were guilty and was not designed to save. The New Testament phrases *dost transgress* (1 ch), *the law* (58 chs) = 59 chapters.

1059th Chapter of the Bible

The theme of this chapter is obedience to civil authorities. The believer is to demonstrate his obedience to God through his obedience toward good government. By contrast God will oppress the lawless and rebellious ones through good governance which He has established on Earth. By design, good governance will show itself to be the oppressor of evil ones.

> "Whosoever therefore resisteth the POWER, resisteth the ordinance of God: and they that resist shall receive to themselves damnation. For rulers are not a TERROR to good works, but to the evil. Wilt thou then not be <u>afraid</u> <u>of the POWER</u>? do that which is good, and thou shalt have praise of the same: For he is the minister of God to thee for good. But if thou do that which is evil, be afraid; for he beareth not <u>the sword</u> in vain: for he is the minister of God, a REVENGER to execute WRATH upon him that doeth evil. Wherefore ye must needs be subject, not only for WRATH, but also for conscience sake" (Rom. 13:2-5).

The Old Testament combination *afraid* (158x) and *the power of the sword* (1x) = 159. Again the word *power* is mentioned in 59 verses of the Pauline Epistles.

God to Subdue All People under His Son's Universal Kingdom Rule

"And when all things shall be SUBDUED unto him, then shall <u>the Son</u> also himself be subject unto him that put <u>all things</u> <u>under him</u>, that God may be all in all" (1 Cor. 15:28). This verse corresponds with our fourth definition of oppress: to put down, subdue, or suppress. The Old Testament combination *all things* (49x), *under him* (10x) = 59.

The title *T/the Son* is mentioned in 159 verses of the New Testament!

Final Victory over the Grave Oppressor

"So when this corruptible shall have put on incorruption, and this mortal shall have put on immortality, then shall be brought to pass the saying that is written, <u>Death</u> is swallowed up in victory. O <u>death,</u> where is thy sting? O <u>grave,</u> where is thy victory? The sting of <u>death</u> is sin; and the strength of sin is the law" (1 Cor. 15:54-56). Again the word *grave* occurs 59 times in the Old Testament. Again the phrase *the dead* is mentioned in 59 chapters of the New Testament.

The Gospel Mission Team's Asian Oppressors

"For we would not, brethren, have you ignorant of our trouble which came to us in Asia, that <u>we were</u> PRESSED <u>out of measure, above strength,</u> insomuch that we despaired even of life" (2 Cor. 1:8). The naturally occurring Bible combination *we were* (43x), *pressed* (15x), *out of measure above strength* (1x) = 59. Again the name *Paul('s)* is mentioned in 159 verses of the New Testament.

Paul's Jewish Oppressors Gave Him Many Stripes

"<u>Of the Jews</u> five times received I forty stripes save one" (2 Cor. 11:24). The chief apostle recalls his intermittent suffering while being under the control of his wrath-filled Jewish oppressors. Again the phrase *of the Jews* is mentioned in 59 verses of the New Testament. Again the title *the Jews* is mentioned in 59 verses of Acts.

Christ Saved Us from the Mosaic Oppressor's Curse

"Christ hath redeemed us from the <u>curse</u> <u>of the law,</u> being made a curse for us: for it is written, Cursed is <u>every one that</u> <u>hangeth on a tree</u>" (Gal. 3:13). Jesus Christ subjected Himself to the oppressor so we could escape safely with our lives. The Old Testament combination *curse* (58 chs) and *sentence of the law* (1 ch) = 59 chapters. Again the term *the law* is mentioned in 59 verses of the OT Narrative. The Law combination *cursed* (35x), *every one that* (23x), *hang thee on a tree* (1x) = 59.

This World' Invincible & Invisible Oppressor

"Wherein in time past ye walked according to the course of this world, according to the prince of the POWER of the air, the spirit that now worketh in the children of disobedience" (Eph. 2:2). Here the oppressor-related word *power* is the 136,759th word of the New Testament. Again the word *power* is mentioned in 59 verses of the Pauline Epistles.

59th Verse of Ephesians

"For this cause I bow my knees unto the Father of our Lord Jesus Christ" (Eph. 3:14). This verse's connecting word "For" directs us to look back at what the suffering apostle mentioned in the previous verse: "I desire that ye faint not at my tribulations for you" (v. 13). The book of Ephesians is known as one of Paul's prison epistles. Both the apostle and his gospel message were oppressed while in unjust bonds and imprisonments.

59th Verse of Philippians

"Receive him therefore in the Lord with all gladness; and hold such in reputation" (Phil. 2:29). The Christians at Philippi were to greatly honor the gospel laborer Epaphroditus when they saw him because he had suffered an ailment which may have been caused by the dark oppressor.

The Satanic Oppressor's Power of Darkness

"Who hath delivered us <u>from the</u> POWER <u>of darkness,</u> and hath translated us into the kingdom of his dear Son" (Col. 1:13). Again the word *power* is mentioned in 59 verses of the Pauline

Epistles. The Bible combination *from the* (1157x), *power of darkness* (2x) = 1159.

59th Verse of Colossians

"In the which ye also walked some time, when ye <u>lived</u> <u>in them</u>" (Col. 3:7). The previous two verses frame this verse as they mention certain sins that oppress God's mind and bring about His oppressor wrath. These same sins also oppress the sinner. The Bible combination *lived* (58x) and *no pleasure in them* (1x) = 59.

59th Verse of First Thessalonians

"For the Lord himself shall descend from heaven with a shout, with the voice of the archangel, and with the trump of God: and <u>the dead</u> in Christ shall rise first" (1 Thess. 4:16). On this notable day the underworld oppressor will have to let go of his captives' oppressed bodies. Again the phrase *the dead* is mentioned in 59 chapters of the New Testament.

Beware—The Divine Oppressor Is Coming

"Seeing it is a righteous thing with God to recompense tribulation to them that TROUBLE you; And to you who are TROUBLED rest with us, when the Lord Jesus shall be revealed from heaven with his mighty angels, <u>In flaming fire</u> <u>taking</u> <u>vengeance</u> <u>on them</u> <u>that know not God, and</u> <u>that obey not</u> <u>the gospel of our Lord Jesus Christ</u>: <u>Who shall be punished</u> <u>with everlasting destruction</u> <u>from the presence of the Lord,</u> <u>and from the glory of his POWER</u>" (2 Thess. 1:6-9).

The New Testament combination *in flaming fire* (1x), *taking* (14x), *vengeance* (7x), *on them* (28x), *that know not God and* (1x), *that obey not* (2x), *the gospel of our Lord Jesus Christ* (1x), *who shall be punished* (1x), *with everlasting destruction* (1x), *from the presence of the Lord* (2x), *and from the glory of his power* (1x) = 59.

Don't Be Weary in Well Doing

"But ye, brethren, be <u>not</u> WEARY in well doing" (2 Thess. 3:13). Here the word *not* is the 259th word in this chapter, and it supports the oppressor-related word weary.

The Law Was Designed to Oppress Men's Sin

"Knowing this, that <u>the law</u> is not made for a righteous man, but for the lawless and disobedient, for the ungodly and for sinners, for unholy and profane, for murderers of fathers and murderers of mothers, for manslayers, For whoremongers, for them that defile themselves with mankind, for menstealers, for liars, for perjured persons, and if there be any other thing that is contrary to sound doctrine" (1 Tim. 1:9-10). In accordance with our fourth definition of oppress, the Law was designed in a fearful way to 'suppress' men's sin. Again the term *the law* is mentioned in 59 verses of the OT Narrative.

The Gospel & Gospel Worker Suffer Trouble from the Oppressor

"Wherein I suffer <u>TROUBLE</u>, as an evil doer, even unto BONDS; but the word of God is not BOUND. Therefore I endure all things for the elect's sakes, that they may also obtain the salvation which is in Christ Jesus with eternal glory" (2 Tim. 2:9-10). Again all forms of the word *trouble* are mentioned in 59 collective chapters of the Wisdom Books.

The False Teacher's Oppressive Words

"For there are many unruly and vain talkers and deceivers, specially they of the circumcision: Whose mouths must be stopped, who subvert whole houses, teaching things which they ought not, for filthy lucre's sake. One of themselves, even a prophet of their own, said, The Cretians are alway liars, evil beasts, slow bellies" (Titus 1:10-12). The underlined verse is the 6759th verse of the New Testament.

The Satanic Oppressor's Former Power of Death

"Forasmuch then as the children are partakers of flesh and blood, he also himself likewise took part of the same; that through death he might destroy him that had the POWER of death, that is, the devil" (Heb. 2:14). Again the word *power* is mentioned in 59 verses of the Pauline Epistles. Again the title *the devil(s)* is mentioned in 59 verses of the Bible.

59th Verse of Hebrews

"For if Jesus had given them rest, then would he not afterward have spoken of another day" (Heb. 4:8). Here Paul refers to the wilderness pilgrims who refused to enter into their place of blessing. Instead of going into the green land of milk and honey, they had to remain in the oppressive and barren wilderness. During that time the Arabian wilderness was their strange oppressor. The Bible combination *afterward* (58 chs) and *spoken of another day* (1 ch) = 59 chapters.

Judges & Prophets Oppressed Enemy Kingdoms

"And what shall I more say? for the time would fail me to tell of Gedeon, and of Barak, and of Samson, and of Jephthae; of David also, and Samuel, and of the prophets: Who through faith SUBDUED kingdoms" (Heb. 11:32-33a). The New Testament combination *through faith subdued* (1x), *the prophets* (56x), *subdued* (2x) = 59.

Old Testament Saints Faced Cruel Oppressors

"And others had trial of CRUEL mockings and SCOURGINGS, yea, moreover of BONDS and imprisonment" (Heb. 11:36). The New Testament combination *and others* (54x), *had trial of* (1x), *cruel mockings* (1x), *and scourgings* (1x), *yea moreover* (1x), *of bonds and imprisonment* (1x) = 59.

The 59th Book of the Bible

JAMES is the 59th BOOK of the Bible because of who its recipients are—Jewish believers who dwelled in the oppressive, idol-worshiping lands among the Gentiles. The theme of James' writing could easily be entitled Overcoming the Oppressor. Because the evil one's oppressive assaults abound in so many aspects of the believer's life, faith, love, obedience, and prayer must be exercised to overcome the oppressor. Each assault upon the believer presents a test.

Oppressive Lands—This letter is addressed to the "twelve tribes which are scattered abroad" (James 1:1). There can be little doubt that these chosen ones were experiencing the continual heat of their oppressors the Gentiles. Wherever Jews are found outside the land of Israel they are in the minority; thus they are easily oppressed by their Gentile overlords. Again the word *scattered* occurs 59 times in the Old Testament.

Oppressive Trials—"My brethren, count it all joy when ye fall into divers temptations;

Knowing this, that the <u>trying of</u> <u>your faith</u> worketh <u>patience</u>" (1:2-3). The Bible combination *trying of* (1x), *your faith* (24x), *patience* (34x) = 59. If a persecuted one thinks his faith is insufficient for an oppressive trial, "let him ask in faith, nothing <u>wavering</u>. For he that <u>wavereth</u> is like a <u>wave</u> of the sea driven with <u>the wind</u> and tossed" (1:6). The combined Bible words *wavereth* (1x), *wave* (32x), *waves* (26x) = 59. This verse presents the Bible's 59th occurrence of the oppressive phrase *the wind*.

Oppressive Temptations—Believers will be oppressed and tempted to give into their own lusts, but "blessed is the man that <u>endureth</u> temptation: for when he is TRIED, he shall receive the crown of life, which the Lord hath promised to them that love him. . . . But every man is tempted, when he is drawn away of his own lust, and enticed. Then when lust hath conceived, it bringeth forth sin: and sin, when it is finished, bringeth forth death" (1:12, 14-15). The word *endureth* occurs 59 times in the Bible. James gave the remedy against such temptations from the oppressor. "Wherefore lay apart all filthiness and superfluity of naughtiness, and <u>receive with meekness the engrafted word, which is able to save your</u> souls" (v. 21). The Bible combination *receive with meekness* (1 v), *the engrafted word which is* (1 v), *able* (155 vs), *to save your* (2 vs) = 159 verses.

Oppressive Disobedience—If the evil oppressor cannot stop you from hearing the Word he will try to prevent you from obeying the Word. "But be ye doers of the word, and not hearers only, deceiving your own selves" (1:22). Acts of omission are equally as bad as acts of commission. James offers the struggling believer a remedy: "But whoso looketh into the perfect law of liberty, and continueth therein, he being not a forgetful hearer, but a doer of the work, this man shall be blessed in his deed" (1:25). If the believer is not being blessed, he is still being oppressed. Obedience to God's Word makes the critical difference.

Oppressive Religions—James knew these scattered Jewish believers were living in lands which practiced strange and oppressive religions. He did not want these scattered believers to be victims of their own pride by looking down upon the Gentiles among whom they lived. Thus he warned, "If any man among you seem to be religious, and bridleth not his tongue, but deceiveth his own heart, this man's religion is vain" (1:26). Because the New Covenant faith is intended for all men, James challenges Jewish believers to show the love of God by reliving the oppressions of the oppressed: "Pure religion and undefiled before God and the Father is this, To visit the <u>fatherless</u> and <u>widows</u> in their AFFLICTION" (v. 27). The combined Bible words *fatherless* (43x) and *needs* (16x) = 59. The Bible's singular words *widow* (50x), *widow's* (5x), *widowhood* (4x) = 59. Again the word *affliction* is mentioned in 59 verses of the Old Testament.

Oppressive Treatment of the Poor—The apostle James challenged his Jewish brethren not to be oppressors of those poor strangers who sometimes came to visit their assembly services. "My brethren, have not the faith of our Lord Jesus Christ, the Lord of glory, with respect of persons" (2:1). It is wrong to show partiality toward any attendees, whether they are rich or are poor. If men do show respect of persons, James said, "Are ye not then partial in yourselves, and are become judges of evil thoughts? Hearken, my beloved brethren, Hath not God chosen the poor of this world rich in faith, and heirs of the kingdom which he hath promised to them that love him? But ye have <u>despised</u> the poor. Do not rich men OPPRESS you, and draw you before the judgment seats? Do not they blaspheme that worthy name by the which ye are called? (2:4-7). James taught the twelve tribes not to oppress others in a reciprocal fashion by giving them the golden rule: "Thou shalt love thy neighbour as thyself" (2:8b). Again the word *despised* is mentioned in 59 verses of the Bible. Again all forms of the word *blaspheme* show the seal of the oppressor, occurring 59 times. The keyword *oppress* actually occurs in this 59th book of the Bible.

The apostle also challenged his Jewish brethren not to be oppressors of the poor by disrespectfully sending them away from their synagogue service with their needs unmet. "If a brother or sister be <u>naked,</u> and <u>destitute of daily food,</u> And one of you say unto them, Depart in peace, be ye warmed and filled; notwithstanding <u>ye give them not those things which are needful to the body</u>; what doth it profit? Even so faith, if it hath not works, is dead, being alone" (2:15-17). In verse 25 the apostle gave the reverse illustration of Rahab, a Gentile who met the needs of two destitute Jewish spies who had come into her place of rest. The Bible combination *naked* (47x), *destitute* (8x), *of daily food* (1x), *ye give them not those things which are needful* (1x), *to the body* (2x) = 59.

Oppressive Tongues—Because the tongue is powerful, perverse, and polluted it can be extremely oppressive. The 59th verse of James has this oppressive thing to say: "And the <u>tongue</u> is a <u>fire</u>, a <u>world</u> of iniquity: so is the tongue among our members, that it defileth the whole body, and setteth on fire the course of nature; and it is set on fire of hell" (3:6). James was talking about how the untamed tongue can oppress an entire city as nature knows no bounds. James gave the remedy to this oppressive problem: "And the fruit of righteousness is sown in peace of them that make peace" (3:18). Again the word *world* is mentioned in 59 verses of John's Gospel. The Law combination *his tongue* (2 ch) and *fire* (57 chs) = 59 chapters.

Oppressive Behaviour—James warned of those who engage in acts of bitterness, envy, and strife, then he says this: "This wisdom descendeth not from above, but is earthly, sensual, devilish" (3:15). This oppressor verse is composed of 59 letters!

Oppressive Worldliness—James knew that the scattered believers had not yet to mature in their faith. However, this did not excuse them from ungodly living. "From whence come wars and fightings <u>among you</u>? come they not hence, even of your lusts that war in your members? Ye lust, and have not: ye <u>kill</u>, and desire to have, and cannot obtain: ye fight and war, yet ye have not, because ye ask not" (4:1-2). This is very strong language to use of believers, but James was trying to vividly describe how believers can sometimes oppress others along the way to getting what they want in life. The phrase *among you* is mentioned in 59 chapters of the Old Testament and occurs 59 times in the New Testament. Again the word *kill* is mentioned in 118 verses of the Bible, a multiple of 59. The devil is the great oppressor who inspires fighting and killing, yet the apostle gave the remedy: "<u>Submit yourselves therefore to God.</u> <u>Resist</u> the devil, <u>and he will flee from you</u>" (4:7). The lowercase name *devil* occurs 59 times in Scripture. The combination *submit yourselves therefore to God* (1x), *resist* (10x), *the devil* (46x), *resist the devil* (1x), *and he flee from you* (1x) = 59.

Oppressive Attitudes—James used more strong language regarding the proud ones. He wanted them to oppress their sin nature. "Cleanse your hands, ye sinners; and purify your hearts, ye double minded. Be AFFLICTED, and <u>mourn</u>, and weep: let your laughter be turned to MOURNING, and your joy to <u>HEAVINESS</u>" (4:8-9). The Bible words *mourn* (45x) and *heaviness* (14x) = 59. Hoping to ward off other possible oppressive behavior within the early church, James gave yet another command. "Speak not <u>evil</u> one of another, brethren. He that speaketh <u>evil</u> of <u>his brother</u>, and judgeth his brother, speaketh <u>evil</u> of the law, and judgeth the law: but if thou judge the law, thou art not a doer of the law, but a judge. There is one lawgiver, who is able to save and to destroy: who art thou that judgest another" (4:11-12). Again the word *affliction* is mentioned in 59 verses of the Old Testament. Again the phrase *his brother* is mentioned in 59 chapters of the Old Testament. Again the word *evil* occurs 59 times in the NT Narrative.

Oppressive Extravagance—"Go to now, ye <u>rich</u> men, weep and howl for your miseries that shall come upon you. Your riches are corrupted, and your garments are motheaten. Your gold and silver is cankered; and the rust of them shall be a witness AGAINST you, and shall eat your flesh as it were fire. Ye have heaped treasure together for the last days. Behold, the hire of the labourers who have reaped down your fields, which is of you kept back by fraud, crieth: and the cries of them which have reaped are entered into the ears of the Lord of sabaoth. Ye have lived in pleasure on the earth, and been wanton; ye have nourished your hearts, as in a day of slaughter. Ye have condemned and killed the just; and he doth not resist you" (5:1-6). These are oppressive words indeed, but the apostle was serious about relieving the poor from their rich oppressors. From Genesis to the NT Narrative the word *rich* occurs 59 times.

Oppressive Sickness & Sin—James presented the problem and the remedy: "Is any among you AFFLICTED? let him pray. Is any merry? let him sing psalms. Is any sick among you? let him call for the elders of the church; and let them pray over him, anointing him with oil in the name of the Lord: And the prayer of faith shall save the sick, and the Lord shall raise him up; and if he have committed sins, they shall be forgiven him" (5:13-15). Again the word *affliction* is mentioned in 59 verses of the Old Testament.

59th Verse of First Peter

"Not rendering <u>evil</u> for <u>evil</u>, or railing for railing: but contrariwise blessing; knowing that ye are thereunto called, that ye should inherit a blessing" (1 Pet. 3:9). Peter warned the Jewish strangers scattered abroad about their potentially oppressive behavior. Again the word *evil* occurs 59 times in the NT Narrative.

59th Verse of Second Peter

"As also in all his epistles, speaking in them of these things; in which are some things hard to be understood, which they that are unlearned and unstable wrest, as they do also the other scriptures, unto their own destruction" (2 Pet. 3:16). Peter mentions Paul's warnings which the many oppressive false teachers did not heed.

Overcoming the Oppressive Wicked One's Strength

"I have written unto you, fathers, because ye have known him that is from the beginning. I have written unto you, young men, because ye are <u>strong</u>, and the word of God abideth in you, and ye have overcome <u>the wicked</u> one" (1 John 2:14). This verse presents the Bible's 259th occurrence of the title *the wicked*, and it refers to the great oppressor of mankind—Satan. Again the phrase *the wicked* occurs 259 times in Scripture. The word *strong* occurs 59 times in the OT Narrative.

59th Verse of First John

"For if our heart condemn us, God is greater than our heart, and knoweth all things" (1 John 3:20). Tragically many Christians live defeated lives as they condemn themselves for their lack of victory over sin's dreadful pull. With self-defeated attitudes, such believers wrongly oppress themselves.

Oppressive Men of Old

"For there are certain men crept in unawares, who were before <u>of old</u> ordained to this condemnation, ungodly men, turning the grace of our God into lasciviousness, and denying the only Lord God, and our Lord Jesus Christ" (Jude 4). Jude was speaking of present-day apostates who oppressed local churches with their damnable doctrines. Even though their final judgment is certain, believers today should yet beware of them and contend for the true faith. Again the phrase *of old* occurs 59 times in Scripture.

59th Verse of Revelation

"Because thou hast kept the word of my patience, I also will keep thee from the <u>hour</u> of temptation, which shall come upon all the <u>world,</u> to try them that dwell upon the earth" (Rev. 3:10). The Lord speaks of a specific time when Earth will experience the wrath of that Tribulation oppressor known as the antichrist. Again the word *hour* is mentioned in 59 verses of the Gospels. Again the word *world* is mentioned in 59 verses of John's Gospel.

The Oppressor Lion-King from Judah's Royal Tribe

"And one of the elders saith unto me, Weep not: behold, the <u>Lion of the tribe of Juda</u>, the Root of David, hath prevailed to open the book, and to loose the seven seals thereof" (Rev. 5:5). When Jesus Christ was born on earth He came out from Judah's ruling tribe. At this critical end-time in history He will oppress the unbelieving, wicked world with untold oppression. The Bible combination *a lion* (43x), *the tribe of Juda/h* (16x) = 59. The Old Testament combination *lion* (58 chs), *out of the tribe of Judah* (1 ch) = 59 chapters.

The White Horse Rider

"And I saw, and behold a white <u>horse</u>: and <u>he that sat on him</u> had a bow; and a crown was given unto him: and he went forth conquering, and to conquer" (Rev. 6:2). This horseman is the first mentioned in a series of four horse riders who go out to oppress the whole world. Collectively they are known as the Four Horsemen of the Apocalypse. Again the word *horsemen* occurs 59 times in the Bible.

The Red Horse Rider

"And there went out another horse that was red: and <u>POWER</u> was given to him that sat thereon to take peace from the earth, and that they should kill one another: and there was given unto him a great sword" (Rev. 6:4). Again the word *power* is mentioned in 59 verses of the Pauline Epistles.

The Black Horse Rider

"And I beheld, and lo a <u>black</u> <u>horse</u>; and he that sat on him had a pair of balances in his hand. And I heard a voice in the midst of the four beasts say, A measure of wheat for a penny, and three measures of barley for a penny" (Rev. 6:5). This oppressor will starve the multitudes. The Bible combination *black* (18 vs), *horse* (41 vs) = 59 verses.

The Pale Horse Rider

"And I looked, and behold a pale horse: and his name that sat on him was Death, and Hell followed with him. And <u>POWER</u> was given unto them over the fourth part of the earth, to kill with sword, and with hunger, and with death, and with the <u>beasts</u> of the earth" (Rev. 6:8). Again the word *power* is mentioned in 59 verses of the Pauline Epistles. Again the word *beasts* is mentioned in 59 verses of the Major and Minor Prophets.

Winged Oppressors Inflict Pain on Men for Five Months

"And there came out of the smoke locusts upon the earth: and unto them was given <u>POWER</u>, as the scorpions of the earth have <u>POWER</u>. . . . And they had tails like unto scorpions, and there were stings in their tails: and their <u>POWER</u> was to hurt men five months" (Rev. 9:3, 10). Again the word *power* is mentioned in 59 verses of the Pauline Epistles.

Two Hundred Million Oppressors Rise up from the Euphrates

"And the number of the army of the <u>horsemen</u> were two hundred thousand thousand: and I heard the number of them. And thus I saw the horses in the vision, and them that sat on them, having breastplates of fire, and of jacinth, and brimstone: and the heads of the horses were as the heads of lions; and out of their mouths issued fire and smoke and brimstone. By these three was the third part of men killed, by the fire, and by the smoke, and by the brimstone, which issued out of their mouths. For their <u>POWER</u> is in their mouth, and in their tails: for their tails were like unto serpents, and had heads, and with them they do hurt" (Rev. 9:16-19).

Again the word *horsemen* occurs 59 times in the Bible. Again the word *power* is mentioned in 59 verses of the Pauline Epistles.

Two Powerful Oppressor Witnesses in the End-Times

"And I will give <u>POWER</u> unto my two witnesses, and they shall prophesy a thousand two hundred and threescore days, clothed in sackcloth. . . . And if any man will hurt them, fire proceedeth out of their mouth, and devoureth their enemies: and if any man will hurt them, he must in this manner be killed. These have <u>POWER</u> to shut heaven, that it rain not in the days of their prophecy: and have <u>POWER</u> over waters to turn them to blood, and to smite the earth with all <u>plagues</u>, as often as they will" (Rev. 11:3, 5-6). Again the word *power* is mentioned in 59 verses of the Pauline Epistles. Again the phrase *the plague* is mentioned in 59 verses of the Old Testament.

The Great Dragon's Oppressor Power

"And <u>the great dragon</u> <u>was cast out</u>, <u>that old serpent</u>, called <u>the Devil</u>, <u>and Satan</u>, which deceiveth the whole world: he <u>was cast out into the earth</u>, and his angels were cast out with him" (Rev. 12:9). This point in time marks the beginning of God's great oppression of Satan. Soon after this event he will be cast into the oppressive bottomless pit for a thousand years. The Bible combination *the great dragon* (2x), *was cast out into the earth* (1x), *that old serpent* (2x), *the d/ Devil* (46x), *and Satan* (8x) = 59.

The All-Powerful Oppressor—Lord Jesus Christ

"And I heard a loud voice saying in heaven, Now is come salvation, and strength, and the kingdom of our God, and the <u>POWER</u> of his <u>Christ</u>: for the accuser of our brethren is cast down, which accused them before our God day and night" (Rev. 12:10). Again the word *power* is mentioned in 59 verses of the Pauline Epistles. Again the title *the Lord Jesus* occurs 59 times in the New Testament.

The Antichrist's Oppressor Power

"And they worshipped the dragon which gave <u>POWER</u> unto the beast: and they worshipped the beast, saying, Who is like unto the beast? who is able to make war with him? And there was given unto him a mouth speaking great things and blasphemies; and <u>POWER</u> was given unto him to continue forty and two months" (Rev. 13:4-5). This oppressor beast is the antichrist. Again the word *power* is mentioned in 59 verses of the Pauline Epistles.

The False Prophet's Oppressor Power

"And I beheld another beast coming up out of the earth; and he had two horns like a lamb, and he spake as a dragon. And he exerciseth all the <u>POWER</u> of the first beast before him . . . And he doeth great wonders, so that he maketh fire come down from heaven on the earth in the sight of men. . . . And he had <u>POWER</u> to give life unto the image of the beast, that the image of the beast should both speak, and cause that as many as would not worship the image of the beast should be killed" (Rev. 13:11-13, 15). Again the word *power* is mentioned in 59 verses of the Pauline Epistles.

Hour of the Divine Oppressor's Worldwide Judgment

"And I saw another angel fly in the midst of heaven . . . Saying with a loud voice, Fear God, and give glory to him; for the <u>hour</u> of his judgment is come: and worship him that made heaven, and earth, and the sea, and the fountains of waters" (Rev. 14:6a, 7). Again the word *hour* occurs in 59 verses of the Gospels.

Seven Oppressor Angels Pour out God's Wrath

"And one of the four beasts gave unto the <u>seven angels</u> seven golden vials full of the wrath of God, who liveth for ever and ever. And the temple was filled with smoke from the glory of God, and from his power; and no man was able to enter into the temple, till the seven <u>plagues</u> of the seven angels were fulfilled. . . . And I heard a great voice out of the temple saying to the <u>seven angels</u>, Go your ways, and <u>pour out the</u> <u>vials of the</u> <u>wrath</u> of God upon the earth" (Rev. 15:7-8; 16:1). Again the phrase *the plague* is mentioned in 59 verses of the Old Testament. The New Testament combination *seven angels* (9x), *go your ways and* (1x), *pour out the* (1x), *vials of the* (1x), *wrath* (47x) = 59.

Wounded Beast Regains His Oppressive Power

"The beast that thou sawest was, and is not; and shall ascend out of the bottomless pit, and go into perdition: and they that dwell on the earth shall wonder, whose names were not written in the book of life from the foundation of the world, when they behold the beast that was, and is not, and yet is" (Rev. 17:8). This oppressor verse consists of 59 words.

Almighty Oppressor King Who Is Lord of All

"And I saw heaven opened, and behold a white horse; and he that sat upon him was called Faithful and True, and in righteousness he doth judge and make war. His eyes were as a flame of fire, and on his head were many crowns; and he had a name written, that no man knew, but he himself. And he was clothed with a vesture dipped in blood: and his name is called The Word of God. And the armies which were in heaven followed him upon white horses, clothed in fine linen, white and clean. And out of his mouth goeth a sharp sword, that with it he should smite the nations: and he shall rule them with a rod of iron: and he treadeth the winepress of the fierceness and wrath of <u>Almighty</u> God. And he hath on his vesture and on his thigh a name written, <u>KING OF KINGS, AND LORD OF LORDS</u>" (Rev. 19:11-16).

Again the title *LORD* occurs 559 times in First and Second Chronicles. The Bible combination *Almighty* (57x), *King of Kings and Lord of Lords* (2x) = 59.

Thousand-Year Oppression of Satan

"And he laid hold on the <u>dragon,</u> <u>that old serpent</u>, which is the <u>Devil</u>, and <u>Satan</u>, and BOUND him a thousand years" (Rev. 20:2). John saw an angel descend from heaven with a great chain in his hand with which he oppresses Satan for the next one thousand years. The Bible combination *dragon* (19x), *serpent* (38x), [uppercase] *Devil* (2x) = 59. Again the combination *that old serpent* (2x), [uppercase] *Devil* (2x), *Satan* (55x) = 59.

Everlasting Oppression of Satan, Beast & False Prophet

John writes with certainty: "and fire came down from God out of heaven, and devoured them. <u>And the devil</u> <u>that deceived them</u> <u>was cast into the</u> <u>lake of fire and brimstone,</u> <u>where the beast and the false prophet are,</u> <u>and shall be tormented day and night</u> <u>for ever and ever</u>" (Rev. 20: 9c-10). The Bible combination *and the devil* (4x), *that deceived them* (1x), *was cast into the* (4x), *lake of fire and brimstone* (1x), *where the beast and* (1x), *the false prophet are* (1x), *and shall be tormented day and night* (1x), *for ever and ever* (46x) = 59.

The Day God Oppresses the Wicked Dead

"And the sea gave up <u>the dead</u> which were in it; and death and hell delivered up <u>the dead</u> which were in them: and they were judged every man according to their works" (Rev. 20:13). Again the phrase *the dead* is mentioned in 59 chapters of the New Testament.

60—Earthly King

God established human government on this fallen chaotic planet to bring about measurable peace and order. As city-states developed so did the idea of a king. Over the millennia, rule by a king's decree has been widely accepted by the nations as a form of good governance. Satan thwarts God's peace plan by attempting to install particularly evil kings upon the nations' thrones. Yet it is only when godly kings sit upon their thrones that nations can rejoice. It is God's timely goal to install His Son upon Earth's singular throne, with its capital being in Jerusalem. He will reign there for 1000 years and with His divine scepter maintain peace and prosperity all over the earth.

> The word *earth* is mentioned in 60 chapters of the Law.
> The word *earth* occurs 60 times in the Minor Prophets.
> The phrase *in the earth* is mentioned in 60 verses of the Old Testament.
> The phrase *all the earth* occurs 60 times in the Old Testament.
> The Jeremiah combination *king of* (157x), *the whole earth* (3x) = 160.
>
> ~~~~~
>
> The word *king* occurs 60 times in First Chronicles.
> The word *king* occurs 60 times in Isaiah.
> The term *king over* is mentioned in 60 verses of the Bible.
> The word *the* occurs 1060 times in Daniel.
> The term *the king* occurs 60 times in Joshua.
> The term *the king* is mentioned in 60 chapters of the Major Prophets.
> The term *the kings* is mentioned in 60 chapters of the OT Narrative.
> The phrase *of the king* occurs 60 times in the Kings and Chronicles.
> The phrases *to the king* (56 chs), *to the kings* (4 chs) = 160 chapters of the Bible.
> The phrases *a king* (48x), *a * king* (12x) = 60 times in the Bible.
> The phrases *a king* (48x), *a kingdom* (12x) = 60 times in the Bible.
> The word *kingdom* is mentioned in 60 chapters of the OT Narrative.
> The phrase *the kingdom of* is mentioned in 60 chapters of the New Testament.

The word KING means a male sovereign or monarch; a <u>man</u> who holds by life tenure, and usually by hereditary right, the <u>chief</u> <u>authority</u> over a <u>country</u> and <u>people</u>.

> The word *man* occurs 60 times in First Kings.
> The word *man* is 360 verses of Wisdom Books.
> The word *man* is found in 60 books of the Bible.
> The word *country* is mentioned in 160 verses from Genesis to Synoptic Gospels.
> The phrase *of the people* is mentioned in 60 chapters of the OT Narrative.

The word KINGLY is an adjective and means [1] stately or splendid as resembling, suggesting, or befitting a king, regal; [2] pertaining or proper to a king; [3] having the rank of king; and [4] consisting of kings or others of <u>royal</u> rank. This descriptive word *kingly* occurs only one time in the Bible, and there it reveals a numeric seal of 60; we will reveal this in Daniel.

The number SIXTY occurs twice in Leviticus, and the combined words in these two verses present a total yield of 60 words.

Nimrod's Kingdom

"And Cush begat Nimrod: he began to be a mighty one in the earth. He was a mighty hunter before the LORD . . . And the beginning of his KINGDOM was Babel, and Erech, and Accad, and Calneh, in the land of Shinar" (Gen. 10:8-10). The Old Testament combination *the beginning of* (29 vs), *his kingdom* (31 vs) = 60 verses. Again the word *kingdom* is mentioned in 60 chapters of the OT Narrative. The phrase *the land of* occurs 260 times in the Law.

Abram, Head of a Great Nation

"And I will make of thee a great nation, and I will bless thee, and make thy name great; and thou shalt be a blessing" (Gen. 12:2). This verse corresponds with our first definition of kingly: stately or splendid as resembling, suggesting, or befitting a king. The phrase *a great* occurs 160 times in the Old Testament.

Tidal, King of Nations

"And it came to pass in the days of Amraphel KING of Shinar, Arioch KING of Ellasar, Chedorlaomer KING of Elam, and Tidal KING of nations" (Gen. 14:1). This verse presents the Bible's first mention of the word "king." The fourth king mentioned in this verse gave himself a grand title—king of nations. The Joshua combination *the king of* (52x), *nations* (8x) = 60. The word *nations* is mentioned in 160 verses of the Major and Minor Prophets.

Kings Joined Together in the War Effort

"That these made war with Bera KING of Sodom, and with Birsha KING of Gomorrah, Shinab KING of Admah, and Shemeber KING of Zeboiim, and the KING of Bela, which is Zoar. All these were joined together in the vale of Siddim, which is the salt sea" (Gen. 14:2-3). The Wisdom Books combination *joined* (6x), *together* (54x) = 60.

Melchizedek, King of Salem

"And Melchizedek KING of Salem brought forth bread and wine: and he was the priest of the most high God" (Gen. 14:18). The Numbers combination *the priest* (59 vs), *of the most h/High* (1 v) = 60 verses.

Sarah, a Mother of Kings

"And God said unto Abraham, As for Sarai thy wife, thou shalt not call her name Sarai, but Sarah shall her name be. And I will bless her, and give thee a son also of her: yea, I will bless her, and she shall be a mother of nations; KINGS of people shall be of her" (Gen. 17:16). Sarah was the chief matriarch of the Israelite nation. This nation soon became divided into two nations, each bringing forth a succession of earthly kings over the course of one thousand years. The Bible combination *Sarai/'s* (17x), *Sarah/'s* (39x), *I will bless her* (2x), *and she shall be a mother of nations* (1x), *kings of people shall be of her* (1x) = 60. The Old Testament combination *and she shall be a* (1x), *mother* (159x) = 160.

Ishmael to Beget Twelve Kingly Sons

"And as for Ishmael, I have heard thee: Behold, I have blessed him, and will make him fruitful, and will multiply him exceedingly; twelve PRINCES shall he beget, and I will make him a great nation" (Gen. 17:20). The Lord consoled Abraham by pledging that his firstborn son would also enjoy a royal destiny. As kings beget princely sons so would Ishmael. The word "princes" fits our fourth definition of the word kingly: consisting of kings or others of royal rank. The title *the prince('s)* occurs 60 times in the Bible. Again the phrase *a great* occurs 160 times in the Old Testament.

Abimelech—King of Gerar

"And Abraham said of Sarah his wife, She is my sister: and <u>Abimelech</u> KING of Gerar sent, and took Sarah" (Gen. 20:2). Gerar was a city among the Philistines. This is the first mention of the name Abimelech in the Bible. This popular name means 'my father is king.' It was common practice for a king to name his son with such a name. The kingly name *Abimelech* is mentioned in 60 verses of the Bible!

Genesis 24:60

"And they blessed Rebekah, and said unto her, Thou art our sister, be thou the mother of thousands of millions, and let thy <u>seed</u> possess the gate of those which hate them" (Gen. 24:60). The family spoke of Rebekah as though she would become the queen of a great people. In reality this bride was preparing to marry a princely man whose very wealthy father was the chieftain of a large tribe, held divine rights to a vast land, and was the progenitor of a royal nation. Such a man could easily be considered a king by the very definition of the word. The fact remains: Rebekah was a matriarch of the Hebrew people, and her husband Isaac was a patriarch of the Hebrew people. In effect, at the height of their adult lives they played the role of a queen and a king. The word *seed* occurs 60 times in the Major and Minor Prophets.

Israel, a Prince with God

"And he said, Thy name shall be called no more Jacob, but <u>Israel</u>: <u>for as a</u> <u>PRINCE</u> hast thou POWER <u>with God</u> and with men, and hast prevailed" (Gen. 32:28). The Lord assigned a regal name to Abraham's grandson, making the Hebrews a kingly people. The meaning of the name Israel is 'he shall rule with God.' The Bible combination *for as a* (3x), *a prince* (15x), *he shall rule* (3x), *with God* (39x) = 60.

> The name *Israel* [all available forms] occurs 160 times in Joshua.
> The name *Israel* is mentioned in 260 verses of First/Second Chronicles.
> The name *Israel* is mentioned in 60 verses of the Psalms.
> The name *Israel* is mentioned in 160 chapters of Major/Minor Prophets.

Hamor, Prince of the Hivites

"And Dinah the daughter of Leah, which she bare unto Jacob, went out to see the daughters of the land. And when Shechem the son of Hamor the Hivite, PRINCE of the COUNTRY, saw her, he took her, and lay with her, and defiled her" (Gen. 34:1-2). Hamor was the princible man of that country. Josephus calls him a king. Perhaps Hamor bore the title prince because his aged father, the king, was still alive at that time. Again the kingly title *the prince('s)* occurs 60 times in the Bible.

1060th Verse of the Bible

"These are <u>the sons of</u> Esau, who is Edom, and these are their DUKES" (Gen. 36:19). Webster's dictionary gives us two kingly meanings of the title duke: a sovereign male <u>ruler</u> and a nobleman of the highest hereditary rank. This 60th verse fits our fourth definition of the word kingly:

consisting of kings or others of royal rank. The phrase *the sons of* occurs 560 times in the Bible. The word *ruler* is mentioned naturally in 60 verses of the Old Testament.

The Early Kings Who Reigned in Edom

"And these are the KINGS that <u>REIGNED in the land of</u> Edom, before there <u>REIGNED</u> any <u>KING over</u> the children of Israel" (Gen. 36:31). The word *reigned* is mentioned in 60 chapters of the OT Narrative. The Genesis combination *in the land of* (49 vs), *Edom* (11 vs) = 60 verses. Again the phrase *king over* is mentioned in 60 verses of the Bible.

Names of the Early Kings Who Reigned in Edom

"And <u>Bela the son of Beor REIGNED in Edom: and the name of his city was Dinhabah</u>. And Bela died, and Jobab the son of Zerah of Bozrah REIGNED <u>in his stead</u>. And Jobab died, and Husham of the land of Temani REIGNED <u>in his stead</u>. And Husham died, and Hadad the son of Bedad, who smote Midian in the field of Moab, REIGNED <u>in his stead</u>: and the name of his city was Avith. And Hadad died, and Samlah of Masrekah REIGNED <u>in his stead</u>. And Samlah died, and Saul of Rehoboth by the river REIGNED <u>in his stead</u>. And Saul died, and Baal-hanan the son of Achbor REIGNED <u>in his stead</u>. And Baal-hanan the son of Achbor died, and Hadar REIGNED <u>in his stead</u>: and the name of his city was Pau" (Gen. 36:32-39c).

This Edomite or Idumean monarchy eventually ceased and returned to regional governance by dukes. The joined phrases *Bela the son of Beor reigned in Edom: and the name of his city was Dinhabah* consist of 60 characters!

> The phrase *in his stead* occurs 60 times in the OT Narrative.
> The phrase *in his stead* is mentioned in 60 verses of the OT Narrative.

Joseph's Future Reign & Kingdom Dominion

"And his brethren said to him, Shalt thou <u>indeed REIGN</u> over us? or shalt thou indeed have DOMINION over us? And they hated him yet the more for his dreams, and for <u>his words</u>" (Gen. 37:8). The Law combination *and Joseph* (59x) and *indeed reign* (1x) = 60. The kingly phrase *his word(s)* is mentioned in 60 verses from Genesis to the NT Narrative.

Joseph, Governor of Egypt

"Thou shalt be over my house, and according unto thy word shall all my people be RULED: only in the throne will I be greater than thou. And Pharaoh said unto <u>Joseph</u>, See, I have set thee over all the land of Egypt. And Pharaoh took off his ring from his hand, and put it upon Joseph's hand, and arrayed him in vestures of fine linen, and put a gold chain about his neck; And he made him to ride in the second <u>chariot</u> which he had; and they cried before him, Bow the knee: and he made him RULER over all <u>the land of</u> Egypt . . . GOVERNOR <u>over all the land of Egypt</u>" (Gen. 41:40-43; 45:26c).

According to our first definition Joseph's new position was indeed kingly: stately or splendid as resembling, suggesting, or befitting a king, regal. The word *chariot* occurs naturally 60 times in the Old Testament. Again the word *ruler* is mentioned naturally in 60 verses of the Old Testament. Again the phrase *the land of* occurs 260 times in the Law. The Law combination *and Joseph* (59x) and *ruler over all the land of Egypt* (1x) = 60.

> The title *governor('s)* occurs 60 times in the Bible.
> The word *govern** occurs 60 times in the Old Testament.
> The word *govern** is mentioned in 60chapters of the Bible.

Joseph Ruled Like a Powerful King

"And Joseph was thirty years old when he stood before Pharaoh KING of Egypt. And Joseph went out from the presence of Pharaoh, and went throughout all the land of Egypt" (Gen. 41:46). The phrase *the land of Egypt* occurs 60 times in Exodus.

1260th Verse of the Bible

"And Joseph saw his brethren, and he knew them, but made himself strange unto them, and spake roughly unto them; and he said unto them, Whence come ye? And they said, From the land of Canaan to buy food" (Gen. 42:7). The leading word of this kingly 1260th verse of the Bible *And* is the 31,060th word of the Bible.

1360th Verse of the Bible

"Then Joseph could not refrain himself before all them that stood by him; and he cried, Cause every man to go out from me. And there stood no man with him, while Joseph made himself known unto his brethren" (Gen. 45:1). The regal ruler was about to reveal his true identity. The sentence Then *Joseph could not refrain himself before all them that stood by him;* consists of 60 characters! The Old Testament combination *his brethren* (59 chs) and *his father's brethren* (1 ch) = 60 chapters.

The King's Scepter Belongs to Judah

"Judah, thou art he whom thy brethren shall praise: thy hand shall be in the neck of thine enemies; thy father's children shall bow down before thee. Judah is a lion's whelp: from the prey, my son, thou art gone up: he stooped down, he couched as a lion, and as an old lion; who shall rouse him up? The SCEPTRE shall not depart from Judah, nor a lawgiver from between his feet, until Shiloh come; and unto him shall the gathering of the people be. Binding his foal unto the vine, and his ass's colt unto the choice vine; he washed his garments in wine, and his clothes in the blood of grapes: His eyes shall be red with wine, and his teeth white with milk" (Gen. 49:8-12).

The patriarchal father prophesied that the Israelite nation would in the future be ruled from within Judah's tribe. Jacob also prophesied that Judah's succession of kings would not end until they had brought forth their Messianic King. In this kingdom-rule passage there are 60 words preceding the kingly word *scepter*. Right on cue from Genesis to the NT Narrative the word *gather* occurs 160 times.

> The title *King of Judah* occurs 60 times in First and Second Kings.
> The title *Judah* is mentioned in 60 verses of the Minor Prophets.
> The phrase *and Judah* occurs 60 times in the Bible.

Asher's Kingly Tribe

"Out of Asher his bread shall be fat, and he shall yield ROYAL dainties" (Gen. 49:20). Like earthly kings, the Asherites would never want for bread. They would enjoy a delightful provision. The Old Testament combination *out of Asher* (2x), *his bread shall* (1x), *be fat* (5x), *yield* (23x), *royal* (26x), *dainties* (3x) = 60.

A New King Who Knew Nothing of Joseph

"Now there arose up a new KING over Egypt, which knew not Joseph" (Exod. 1:8). Again the phrase *king over* is mentioned in 60 verses of the Bible.

The King of Egypt Refuses to Let Israel Go

"And the LORD said unto Moses, Pharaoh's heart is hardened, he <u>refuseth</u> to let the people go" (Exod. 7:14). Earthly kings are prone to having hardened hearts. All available forms of the word *refuse* are mentioned in 60 verses of the Old Testament.

60ᵗʰ Chapter of the Bible

Exodus chapter ten is the 60ᵗʰ chapter of the Bible because of its a great stand off between the earthly King of Egypt and the heavenly King of Israel. "<u>And the LORD said</u> unto Moses, Go in unto Pharaoh: for I have hardened his heart, and the heart of his servants, that I might shew these my signs before him: And that thou mayest tell in the ears of thy son, and of thy son's son, what things I have wrought in Egypt, and my signs which I have done among them; that ye may know how that <u>I am</u> the <u>LORD</u>" (Exod. 10:1-2). The phrase *and the LORD/Lord/lord said* occurs naturally 160 times in the Bible. The kingly phrase *I am* is mentioned in 60 verses of Psalms. The title *LORD* occurs 60 times in Amos.

An interesting feature of this 60ᵗʰ chapter of the Bible is the kingless army which came out of nowhere against Egypt. It was an absolutely innumerable and ruthless army whose sweeping destruction robbed the nation of its entire supply of fresh food. This was God's eighth judgment upon Egypt, implemented with Moses' kingly scepter. "And Moses stretched forth his rod over the land of Egypt, and the LORD brought an east wind upon the land all that day, and all that night; and when it was morning, the east wind brought the <u>locusts</u>. And the <u>locusts</u> went up over all the land of Egypt, and rested in all the coasts of Egypt: very grievous were they; before them there were no such <u>locusts</u> as they, neither after them shall be such" (vv. 13-14). We are expressly told in Proverbs, "The locusts have no KING, yet go they forth all of them by bands." Even though locusts have no king they still carry out their battle assignments with a tenacious mindset. "For they covered the face of the whole EARTH, so that the land was darkened; and they did eat every herb of the land, and all the fruit of the trees which the hail had left: and there remained not any green thing in the trees, or in the herbs of the field, through all the land of Egypt" (Exod. 10:15). This verse consists of 59 words—just one word short of having 60—in keeping with the locusts' lack of a king.

The long stand off between the two kings ended with the heavenly King's horrifying sign of darkness, the ninth Judgment upon Egypt. "And the LORD said unto Moses, Stretch out thine hand toward <u>heaven,</u> that there may be darkness over <u>the land of Egypt,</u> even darkness which may be felt. And Moses stretched forth <u>his hand</u> toward heaven; and there was a thick <u>darkness</u> in all the land of Egypt three days: They saw not one another, neither rose any from his place for three days: but all the <u>children of Israel</u> had light in their dwellings" (vv. 21-23). The King of Heaven made sure His covenant children had light in their homes. The word *heaven* occurs 60 times in the Wisdom Books. Again the phrase *the land of Egypt* occurs 60 times in Exodus. The phrase *his hand* is mentioned in 60 verses of the Law.

> The title *children of Israel* occurs 600 times in Bible, multiple of 60.
> The title *the children of Israel* occurs 60 times in Judges.
> The phrase *children of the* occurs 60 times in the Bible.

King of Egypt Pursues in His Chariots

"For Pharaoh will say of the children of Israel, They are entangled in the land, the wilderness hath shut them in. . . . And it was told the KING of Egypt that the people fled: and the heart of Pharaoh and of his servants was turned against the people, and they said, Why have we done this, that we have let Israel go from serving us? And he made ready his <u>chariot</u>, and took his people with him: And he took SIX HUNDRED chosen <u>chariots</u>, and all the <u>chariots</u> of Egypt, and <u>captains</u> over every one of them" (Exod. 14:3, 5-7).

600 is a visual multiple of 60. Again the word *chariot* occurs naturally 60 times in the Old Testament. The word *captains* is mentioned in 60 chapters of the Old Testament.

Theocratic King's Excellent Hand

"<u>Thy right hand</u>, <u>O LORD</u>, is become glorious in power: <u>thy right hand</u>, <u>O LORD</u>, hath dashed in pieces the enemy. And in the greatness of thine <u>excellency</u> thou hast overthrown them that rose up against thee" (Exod. 15:6-7a). Since antiquity the right hand has represented a person's righteous hand. Here the Song of Moses celebrated the king of Egypt's defeat by the mighty right hand of the King of Heaven. The Lord is spoken of in 'regal' terms in this verse, according to our first definition of the word kingly. The phrase *O LORD/Lord* is mentioned in 60 verses of the Major Prophets. Again the title *LORD* occurs 60 times in Amos. All forms of the word excellent show the seal of earthly king: *excellent* (34x) and *excellency* (26x) = 60.

> The phrase *the right hand* occurs 60 times in the Bible.
> The phrase *his hand* is mentioned in 60 verses of the Law.

Theocratic King's Peculiar Treasure

"Now therefore, if ye will obey my voice indeed, and keep my covenant, then ye shall be a peculiar <u>treasure</u> unto me above all people: for <u>all the EARTH</u> is <u>mine</u>" (Exod. 19:5). The Lord's plan was for the Hebrews to be a faithful and obedient people and thereby exist as kingly treasure to His heart. From Genesis to the NT Narrative the word *treasures* occurs 60 times. Again the phrase *all the earth* occurs 60 times in the Old Testament. The word *mine* is mentioned in 60 chapters of the OT Narrative.

Israel, A Priestly Kingdom

"And ye shall be unto me a KINGDOM of <u>priests</u>, and an holy nation. These are the words which thou shalt speak unto the children of Israel" (Exod. 19:6).

> The title *the priests* occurs 60 times in Second Chronicles.
> The phrase *the high priest* occurs 60 times in the Bible.
> All forms of word *priest** in 60 chapters of New Testament.

Theocratic King's Trumpet Voice

"And Moses brought forth the people out of the camp to meet with God; and they stood at the nether part of the mount. And mount Sinai was altogether on a smoke, because the LORD descended upon it in fire: and the smoke thereof ascended as the smoke of a furnace, and the whole mount quaked greatly. And when <u>the voice</u> of the <u>trumpet</u> sounded long, and waxed louder and louder. . . . the <u>LORD</u> came down upon mount Sinai, on the top of the mount" (Exod. 19:17-20a).

This great trumpet blasting was to motivate the people to prepare to receive the King of Heaven's earthly laws. Trumpets are typically made to announce a king's eminence. The Major Prophets phrases *the voice* (59x) and *the * voice* (1x) = 60. The word *trumpet* is mentioned in 60 verses of the Bible. Again the title *LORD* occurs 60 times in Amos.

The Ruler of the People

"Thou shalt not revile the gods, nor curse the <u>RULER</u> of thy people" (Exod. 22:28). Again the word *ruler* is mentioned naturally in 60 verses of the Old Testament.

Theocratic King's Words of Judgment

"And Moses came and told the people all <u>the words of the</u> LORD, and all the judgments: and all the people answered with one voice, and said, All the <u>words</u> which the LORD hath said will we do" (Exod. 24:3).

The phrase *my words* occurs 60 times in the Bible.

The phrase *my words* is mentioned in 60 verses of the Bible.

The phrase *the words of the* is mentioned in 60 verses of the OT.

The phrase *the word/s of the LORD/Lord* is in 260 verses of the OT.

The phrase *the word of the LORD/Lord* occurs 60 times in Ezekiel.

The phrase *the word of the LORD/Lord* is in 60 verses of Ezekiel.

The word *words* is mentioned naturally in 60 verses of NT Narrative.

Theocratic King's Ten Commandments

"And the LORD said unto Moses, Come up to me into the mount, and be there: and I will give thee tables of stone, and a <u>law</u>, and commandments which I have written; that thou mayest teach them" (Exod. 24:12). With His own fiery finger the Theocratic King wrote ten obligations that His people must follow. The Bible combination *law* (459 vs) and *there is one lawgiver* (1 v) = 460 verses. The Bible combination *law* (459 vs) and *the LORD is our lawgiver* (1 v) = 460 verses. The Bible combination *law* (459 vs) and *the LORD is king* (1 v) = 460 verses.

Theocratic King's Earthly Throne

"And thou shalt make a <u>mercy seat</u> of pure gold: two cubits and a half shall be the length thereof, and a cubit and a half the breadth thereof. And thou shalt make two cherubims of gold, of beaten work shalt thou make them, in the two ends of the <u>mercy seat</u>. And make one cherub on the one end, and the other cherub on the other end: even of the <u>mercy seat</u> shall ye make the cherubims on the two ends thereof. And the cherubims shall stretch forth their wings on high, covering the <u>mercy seat</u> with their wings, and their faces shall look one to another; toward the <u>mercy seat</u> shall the faces of the cherubims be. And thou shalt put the <u>mercy seat</u> above upon the ark; and in the ark thou shalt put the testimony that I shall give thee. And there I will meet with thee, and I will commune with thee" (Exod. 25:17-22a).

This divine King's earthly throne was flanked symbolically with two heavenly guards or cherubs. More importantly it was covered with a mercy seat which is highly symbolic of the great mercy King Jehovah wished to extend to His wayward people. The conjoined word "mercyseat" only occurs one time in Scripture.

The Bible combination *mercyseat* (1x), *of gold* (159x) = 160.

The Bible combination *seat* (58x), *seated* (1x), *mercyseat* (1x) = 60.

The Bible combination *seat* (58x), *mercyseat* (1x), *mercy seatward* (1x) = 60.

The New Testament combination *mercy* (59x) and *mercyseat* (1x) = 60.

Theocratic King's Earthly Tabernacle

"According to all that I shew thee, after the pattern of <u>the tabernacle</u>, and the pattern of all the instruments thereof, even so shall ye make it" (Exod. 25:9). Although this Tabernacle was for the

Lord's habitation it was known as the tabernacle of the congregation because the people were supposed to encamp and assemble around it. The phrase *the tabernacle of the* is mentioned in 60 verses of Numbers.

Theocratic King's 60-Foot-Long Interior Tent

"Moreover thou shalt make the tabernacle with <u>ten curtains</u> of fine twined linen, and blue, and purple, and scarlet: with cherubims of cunning work shalt thou make them. The length of one curtain shall be eight and twenty cubits, and the breadth of one curtain <u>four cubits</u>: and every one of the curtains shall have one measure. The five curtains shall be coupled together one to another; and other five curtains shall be <u>coupled one to another</u>. . . . And thou shalt make fifty taches of gold, and couple the curtains together with the taches: and it shall be one tabernacle" (Exod. 26:1-3, 6).

What is described here is not to be confused with the hangings for the outer courtyard. When connected together these regal linen curtains formed the beautiful inner tent and served to cover the interior ceiling, sides, and back wall. Altogether it was sixty feet long and forty-two feet wide: (10) curtains x four cubits each (6 feet) = 60 feet long!

Theocratic King's Most Holy Place

Moses was further instructed, "And thou shalt put the mercy seat upon the ark of the testimony in the most <u>holy place</u>" (Exod. 26:34). The Most Holy Place was cubical in shape: 15' wide x 15' deep x 15' high. When we consider the perimeter of its interior walls we find the seal of earthly king: (4) walls x fifteen feet each (15ft) = 60 feet in perimeter. The phrase *holy place* occurs 60 times in the Bible.

Theocratic King's Intercessory Priest

"Make Aaron's garments to consecrate him, that he may minister unto me in the priest's office. And these are the garments which they shall make; a breastplate, and an ephod, and a robe, and a broidered coat, a mitre, and a girdle. . . . And thou shalt make a plate of pure gold, and grave upon it, like the engravings of a signet, HOLINESS TO THE LORD. And thou shalt put it on a blue lace, that it may be upon the mitre; upon the forefront of the mitre it shall be. And it shall be upon Aaron's forehead" (Exod. 28:3b-4a, 36-38a).

The plate of gold served as a holy crown. The Lord's intercessory high priest was arrayed in kingly clothing because he was His intermediary holy king. He was to portray the King of Heaven's holy nature to the people. The uppercase word *Holy* is mentioned in 60 chapters of the New Testament.

"And thou shalt take <u>the</u> garments, and put upon Aaron the coat, and the robe of the ephod, and the ephod, and the breastplate, and gird him with the curious girdle of the ephod: And thou shalt put the mitre upon his head, and put the holy <u>CROWN</u> upon the mitre. Then shalt thou take the anointing oil, and pour it upon his head, and anoint him" (29:5-7). Here the underlined word *the* is the 60,360th word of the Bible. Here the word *crown* is the 60,403rd word of the Bible, a number from the 60,000 range. All forms of the word *crown* are mentioned in 60 verses of the Old Testament.

Theocratic King's Golden Furniture

"And thou shalt make an altar to burn incense upon: of shittim wood shalt thou make it. . . . And thou shalt overlay it with <u>pure gold</u>, the top thereof, and the sides thereof round about, and the horns thereof; and thou shalt <u>make unto it a CROWN of gold</u> round about" (Exod. 30:1, 3). The top surfaces of the Ark, table, and altar each had crowns around them, making them regal in nature. Remember the word kingly means 'stately, splendid, or regal.'

The words *pure* (59 chs) and *purely* (1 ch) = 60 chapters of the Bible.
The words *gold* (59x) and *golden* (1x) = 60 times in First/Second Kings.
The words *make unto it a crown* (1x), *of gold* (159x) = 160 times in the Bible.

Service unto the Theocratic King

"And they spake unto Moses, saying, The people bring much more than enough for the <u>service</u> of <u>the work</u>, which the LORD commanded to make" (Exod. 36:5). The people began serving the Lord in the very early stages by making their donations toward His kingdom work, that is, the building His earthly house of worship. The words *service* (59 vs) and *servant's* (1 v) = 60 verses of the Law. The Bible phrases *the work* (159x) and *the king's work* (1x) = 160.

Burnt Offerings & Sacrifices unto the Holy King

"Speak unto the children of Israel, and say unto them, If any man of you bring an <u>offering</u> unto the LORD, ye shall bring your offering of the cattle, even of the herd, and of the flock. If his offering be a <u>burnt sacrifice</u> of the herd, let him offer a male without blemish: he shall offer it of his own voluntary will at the door of the tabernacle of the congregation before the LORD . . . an <u>offering</u> made by fire, of a sweet savour <u>unto the LORD</u>" (Lev. 1:2-3, 9c). The Wisdom Books combination *unto the LORD/Lord* (56x), *burnt offerings* (3x), *burnt sacrifices* (1x) = 60. The word *sacrifices* is mentioned in 60 chapters of the Bible.

The phrase *an offering* is in 60 verses of the Old Testament.
The word *offerings* occurs 60 times in the Old Testament.

2760th Verse of the Bible

"And if the burnt sacrifice <u>for his offering</u> to the LORD be of <u>fowls</u>, then he shall bring his offering of turtledoves, or of young pigeons" (Lev. 1:14). The sinning kingdom subject is to bring a sweet-savor offering to satiate the Theocratic King's wrath. The Bible combination *for his offering* (5x) and *fowls* (55x) = 60.

Holy King Gives His Kingdom Subjects Feast Days

"And the LORD spake unto Moses, saying, Speak unto the children of Israel, and say unto them, Concerning <u>the feasts</u> of the LORD, which ye shall proclaim to be holy convocations, even these are <u>my feasts</u>" (Lev. 23:1-2). As earthly kings often desire to do with their loving subjects, they establish national feast days to celebrate together. The Bible combination *the feast* (59 vs) and *my feasts* (1 v) = 60 verses. The Bible phrase *of the Lord* (159x) and *of the * Lord* (1x) = 160. Again the title LORD occurs 60 times in Amos.

Holy King Gives His Kingdom Subjects Weekly Rest Day

"Six days shall work be done: but the seventh day is the <u>sabbath</u> of rest, an holy convocation; ye shall do no work therein: it is the <u>sabbath</u> of the LORD in all your dwellings" (Lev. 23:3). Because the Theocratic King delights to commune with His earthly people, He granted them a no-work day so they might rest in Him and worship Him.

The word *sabbath* is mentioned in 60 verses of the OT.

The word *sabbath* occurs 60 times in the New Testament.

Holy King Proclaims a Year of Release

"Then shalt thou cause the <u>trumpet</u> of the jubile to sound on the tenth day of the seventh month, in the day of atonement shall ye make the <u>trumpet</u> sound throughout all your land. And ye shall hallow the fiftieth year, and proclaim liberty throughout all the land unto all the inhabitants thereof: it shall be a jubile unto you; and ye shall return every man unto his possession, and ye shall return every man unto his family" (Lev. 25:9-10). The Lord is a compassionate and considerate King. Here He is seen as the Champion of the Poor in that He proclaimed a national release of all who were indentured servants to others. The sounding of a trumpet is generally associated with a king's eminent presence and is also hopeful of some proclamation he is soon to make. Again the word *trumpet* is mentioned in 60 verses of the Bible.

Holy King's Land & Tenant Blessing

"Then I will command my <u>blessing</u> upon you in the sixth year, and it shall bring forth fruit for three years. And ye shall sow the eighth year, and eat yet of old fruit until the ninth year; until her fruits come in ye shall eat of the old store. <u>The land</u> <u>shall not be sold for ever</u>: for <u>the land</u> <u>is mine</u>; for <u>ye are strangers and sojourners</u> <u>with me</u>" (Lev. 25:21-23). The land belongs to the Theocratic King. He would bless the holy land for the holy people's sake as long as they remained holy before Him. The word *blessing(s)* is mentioned in 60 verses of the Old Testament. The Bible combination *the land* (1259x), *shall not be sold for ever* (1x) = 1260. The Law combination *the land* (158x), *is mine* (2x) = 160. The Minor Prophets combination *the land* (57 vs), *is mine* (3 vs) = 60 verses. The word *mine* is mentioned in 60 chapters of the OT Narrative. The Old Testament combination *ye are strangers and sojourners* (1x), *with me* (159x) = 160.

Holy King's Warning & Law of the Land

"And if ye shall despise my statutes, or if your soul abhor <u>my judgments</u>, so that ye will not do all <u>my commandments</u>, but that ye break <u>my</u> covenant: I also will do this unto you; I will even appoint over you terror, consumption, and the burning ague, that shall consume the eyes, and cause sorrow of heart: and ye shall sow your seed in vain, for your enemies shall eat it. And I will set <u>my face</u> against you, and ye shall be slain before your enemies" (Lev. 26:15-17a). This is the first of five progressive stages of chastisement which would come from the Theocratic King if His kingdom subjects did not do well in the land of their inheritance. The Bible phrases *my judgments* (29 vs) and *my commandments* (31 vs) = 60 verses. The phrase *my face* is mentioned in 60 verses of the Bible.

The word *my* occurs 60 times in Second Chronicles.
The word *my* is found in 60 books of the Bible.

Holy King Claims All the Levites for Himself

"And the LORD spake unto Moses, saying, And I, behold, I have taken the <u>Levites</u> from among the children of Israel instead of all the firstborn that openeth the matrix among the children of Israel: therefore the <u>Levites</u> shall be <u>mine</u>; Because all the firstborn are <u>mine</u>; for on the day that I smote all the firstborn in the land of Egypt I hallowed unto me <u>all the firstborn in Israel</u>, both man and beast: <u>mine shall they be</u>: <u>I am the LORD</u>" (Num. 3:11-13). Earthly kings are known for laying claim to certain things, even people. Their governing power permits them to conscript large numbers of men into their full-time service. Here the Theocratic King assigned the Levites to be His personal ministers. Again the word *mine* is mentioned in 60 chapters of the OT Narrative. The Old Testament combination *all the firstborn in Israel* (1x), *mine shall they be* (1x), *I am the LORD* (158x) = 160.

The title *the Levites* is mentioned in 60 verses of the Law.
The title *the Levites* occurs 160 times in the OT Narrative.

Numbers 7:60

"On the ninth day Abidan the son of Gideoni, PRINCE of the children of Benjamin, offered" (Num. 7:60). Upon completion of the Theocratic King's earthly tabernacle Moses conducted a ceremony for the dedication of His holy altar. For twelve successive days each of the twelves princes over the tribes of Israel brought their offerings to the King. These twelve princes lived regal lives as they served as noble heads over their royal families. Again the title *the prince('s)* occurs 60 times in the Bible. Again the phrase *an offering* is mentioned in 60 verses of the Old Testament. The kingly word *prince* actually occurs in this 60th verse.

Holy King's Brazen Altar Dedicated

"And all the oxen for the sacrifice of the peace offerings were twenty and four bullocks, the rams SIXTY, the he goats SIXTY, the lambs of the first year SIXTY. This was the dedication of the altar, after that it was anointed" (Num. 7:88). Here we see the obvious numerical token between the Holy King and the His holy altar—60. The phrase *the altar* occurs precisely 260 times in the Old Testament.

Holy King's Manifest Glory Cloud

"And on the day that the tabernacle was reared up the cloud covered the tabernacle, namely, the tent of the testimony: and at even there was upon the tabernacle as it were the appearance of fire, until the morning. So it was alway: the cloud covered it by day, and the appearance of fire by night" (Num. 9:15-16). The Holy King of Heaven and Earth manifested His glory to the nation by way of a divine cloud, one that shrouded His holy presence. The word *cloud* is mentioned in 60 chapters of the Bible.

Holy King's Rising & Resting

"And it came to pass, when the ark set forward, that Moses said, Rise up, LORD, and let thine enemies be scattered; and let them that hate thee flee before thee. And when it rested, he said, Return, O LORD, unto the many thousands of Israel" (Num. 10:35-36). The Ark served as the Holy King's earthly throne. He would rise from it to go into battle and then victoriously return to it and resume His holy rest. From Genesis to the Gospels the phrase *rise up* is mentioned in 60 chapters. The word *rest* (as in cessation from labor) occurs 60 times from Genesis to the end of the OT Narrative! Again the phrase *O LORD/Lord* is mentioned in 60 verses of the Major Prophets.

Holy King's Chief Servant Moses

"My servant Moses is not so, who is faithful in all mine house" (Num. 12:7). The Holy King needed many earthly servants, but He particularly needed one earthly servant whom He could count on for things of the highest priority. Moses was that man, even that servant. The title *servant* occurs 60 times in the NT Narrative.

Holy King's Children to Be Royally Dressed

"Speak unto the children of Israel, <u>and bid them that they make them</u> <u>fringes</u> <u>in the borders</u> <u>of their garments</u> throughout their generations, <u>and that they put upon the</u> <u>fringe</u> <u>of the</u> <u>borders</u> <u>a ribband</u> <u>of blue</u>: And it shall be unto you for a fringe, that ye may look upon it, and remember all <u>the commandments of the LORD</u>, and do them; and that ye seek not after your own heart and your own eyes, after which ye use to go a whoring" (Num. 15:38-39).

The Holy King wanted His covenant people to be holy; therefore, He ordained suitable kingly clothing for them as a reminder to be holy. The royal color blue was symbolically selected, and princely fringes were prescribed. This verse fits our first definition of the word kingly: stately or splendid as resembling, suggesting, or befitting a king; regal. The Law combination *garment* (26x), *and bid them that they make them* (1x), *fringes* (2x), *in the borders of their garments* (1x), *and that they put upon the* (1x), *fringe* (2x), *of the border* (1x), *a ribband* (1x), *of blue* (25x) = 60. The phrase *the commandment(s) of the LORD/Lord* occurs 60 times in the Bible.

King of Edom

"And Moses sent messengers from Kadesh <u>unto the</u> KING of Edom, Thus saith thy brother Israel, Thou knowest all the travail that hath befallen us" (Num. 20:14).

The phrase *unto the* is mentioned in 60 verses of Second Samuel.
The phrase *unto the* occurs 60 times in Jeremiah.

The King's Highway

The Messengers' letter from Moses read: "Let us pass, I pray thee, through thy country: we will not pass through the fields, or through the vineyards, neither will we drink of the water of the wells: we will go by <u>the KING'S</u> high way, we will not turn to the right hand nor to the left, until we have passed thy borders" (Num. 20:17). The Old Testament combination *the king's* (256 vs), *high way* (4 vs) = 260 verses.

King Fought with King

"For Heshbon was the city of Sihon the KING of the Amorites, who had <u>fought</u> against the former KING of Moab, and taken all his land out of his hand, even unto Arnon" (Num. 21:26). The word *fought* occurs 60 times in the Old Testament.

King of Bashan

"And they turned and went up by the way of Bashan: <u>and Og</u> <u>the KING of</u> Bashan went out against them, he, and all his people, to the battle at Edrei" (Num. 21:33). The Old Testament combination *and Og* (7x), *the king of* (453x) = 460.

King of the Moab

"And Moab said unto the elders of Midian, Now shall this company lick up all that are round about us, as the ox licketh up the grass of the field. And <u>Balak</u> <u>the son of Zippor</u> <u>was KING</u> <u>of</u> <u>the Moabites</u> at that time" (Num. 22:4). The Old Testament combination *Balak* (42x), *the son of Zippor was* (1x), *was king* (10x), *of the Moabites* (7x) = 60.

The Messianic King's Coming Rule

"I shall see him, but not now: I shall behold him, but not nigh: there shall come a Star out of Jacob, and a SCEPTRE shall rise out of Israel, and shall smite the corners of Moab. And Edom shall be a possession, Seir also shall be a possession for his enemies; and Israel shall do valiantly. Out of Jacob shall come he that shall have DOMINION, and shall destroy him that remaineth of the city" (Num. 24:17-19). This verse is prophetic of King Messiah who was to come to Earth in an incarnate form. At His second earthly coming this Incarnate King will be victorious in battle. The star represents the Messianic King's glory, and the scepter represents His rule. Again from Genesis to the Gospels the phrase *rise up* is mentioned in 60 chapters. The underlined words indicate the 860th verse of Numbers, and they speak of the Messianic King's lasting possession—His annexed land.

Making a Vow to the Holy King

"If a man vow a vow unto the LORD, or swear an oath to bind his soul with a bond; he shall not break his word, he shall do according to all that proceedeth out of his mouth" (Num. 30:2). Vows made to the Holy King become holy vows; they are anything but ordinary. The phrase *if a man* occurs 60 times in the Old Testament. The Bible combination *vow* (41x), *a vow* (18x), *or swear an oath* (1x) = 60. The phrase *shall do* occurs 60 times in the Old Testament.

Kings of Midian

"And they slew the kings of Midian, beside the rest of them that were slain; namely, Evi, and Rekem, and Zur, and Hur, and Reba, five kings of Midian: Balaam also the son of Beor they slew with the sword" (Num. 31:8). Again the term *the kings* is mentioned in 60 chapters of the OT Narrative.

King of the Amorites

"And Moses gave unto them, even to the children of Gad, and to the children of Reuben, and unto half the tribe of Manasseh the son of Joseph, the KINGDOM of Sihon KING of the Amorites, and the kingdom of Og king of Bashan, the land, with the cities thereof in the coasts, even the cities of the country round about" (Num. 32:33). In this verse there are 60 words surrounding the Amorite king's name *Sihon*.

60th Verse of Deuteronomy

"And the space in which we came from Kadesh-barnea, until we were come over the brook Zered, was thirty and eight years; until all the generation of the men of war were wasted out from among the host, as the LORD sware unto them" (Deut. 2:14). A king is the supreme lord over his army. Here the Theocratic King of Israel dispensed of His army because their allegiance to Him had become faithless. Again the title *LORD* occurs 60 times in Amos.

4960th Verse of the Bible

"A people great, and many, and tall, as the Anakims; but the LORD destroyed them before them; and they succeeded them, and dwelt in their stead" (Deut. 2:21). As it was the king's duty to go out to the battle with his people in the lead position, the Lord did so here and in all-victorious power and glory. Again the title *LORD* occurs 60 times in Amos.

Og's Kingdom of 60 Cities

"And we took all his cities at that time, there was not a city which we took not from them, THREESCORE cities, all the region of Argob, the KINGDOM of Og in Bashan" (Deut. 3:4). The Jeremiah combination *threescore* (1x), *cities* (59x) = 60. The Bible combination *all the region of Argob* (2x), *the kingdom of* (36x), *Og* (22x) = 60.

160th Chapter of the Bible

This chapter is about the Holy King and His kingly people. He promised them victory in the Canaan conquest. "When the LORD thy God shall bring thee into the land whither thou goest to possess it, and hath cast out many nations before thee, the Hittites, and the Girgashites, and the Amorites, and the Canaanites, and the Perizzites, and the Hivites, and the Jebusites, seven nations greater and mightier than thou" (Deut. 7:1).

The kingdom was theirs if they could keep it! All they had to do was be a separated and holy people before Him. This could be achieved by keeping the Holy King's holy commandments.

> "For thou art an holy people unto the LORD thy God: the LORD thy God hath chosen thee to be a special people unto himself, above all people that are upon the face of the EARTH. . . . Know therefore that the LORD thy God, he is God, the faithful God, which keepeth covenant and mercy with them that love him and keep his commandments to a thousand generations; And repayeth them that hate him to their face, to destroy them: he will not be slack to him that hateth him, he will repay him to his face. Thou shalt therefore keep the commandments, and the statutes, and the judgments, which I command thee this day, to do them" (vv. 6, 9-11).

The Bible combination *know therefore that the LORD thy God* (1x), *he is God* (6x), *the faithful God* (1x), *which keepeth covenant and mercy with them* (1x), *that love him and keep* (1x), *his commandments* (45x), *to a thousand generations* (3x), *and repayeth them that hate him* (1x), *to their face* (1x) = 60.

Follow Every Word That Proceeds out of the King's Mouth

"And he humbled thee, and suffered thee to hunger, and fed thee with manna, which thou knewest not, neither did thy fathers know; that he might make thee know that man doth not live by bread only, but by every word that proceedeth out of the mouth of the LORD doth man live" (Deut. 8:3). The Luke combination *by* (59x) and *every word of God* (1x) = 60. The OT Narrative combination *words* (59x) and *out of the king's mouth* (1x) = 60.

> The word *but* is mentioned in 160 chapters of the Law.
> The word *by* is mentioned in 60 verses of Hebrews.
> The word *every* is mentioned in 1060 verses of the Bible.
> The word *word* occurs 60 times in the Psalms.
> The word *that* occurs 600 times in Psalms, a visual multiple of 60.
> The word *come* is mentioned in 1260 verses of the Old Testament.
> The phrase *out of the* is mentioned in 360 chapters of Old Testament.
> The word *mouth* occurs 160 times in the Wisdom Books.
> The phrase *the mouth of* is mentioned in 60 chapters of the Bible.
> The phrase *of the LORD* is mentioned in 1460 verses of the Bible.

Only God May Choose Israel's Earthly Kings

"When thou art come unto the land which the LORD thy God giveth thee, and shalt possess it, and shalt dwell therein, and shalt say, I will set <u>a KING</u> over me, like as all the nations that are about me; Thou shalt in any wise set him KING over thee, <u>whom the LORD thy God shall choose</u>: one from among thy brethren shalt thou set KING over thee: thou mayest not set a stranger over thee, which is not thy brother" (Deut. 17:14-15). The Lord made it clear that the people were not to choose the king. Rather they were to allow Him to do this for them. Again the Bible phrases *a king* (48x) and *a * king* (12x) = 60. The Bible combination *whom the LORD thy God shall* (1x), *choose* (59x) = 60.

The Throne of His Kingdom

"And it shall be, when he sitteth upon the <u>throne of</u> his KINGDOM, that he shall write him a copy of this law in a book out of that which is before the priests the Levites" (Deut. 17:18). The phrase *throne(s) of* occurs 60 times in the Bible.

560ᵗʰ Verse of Deuteronomy

"And the priests the sons of <u>Levi</u> shall <u>come near</u>; for them the LORD thy God hath chosen to minister <u>unto him</u>, and to bless in the name of the LORD; and by their word shall every controversy and every stroke be tried" (Deut. 21:5). Only the Holy King's chosen religious tribe was to approach near Him to worship Him. Again the title *the Levites* is mentioned in 60 verses of the Law. The Bible combination *near* (158 chs), *come unto the king* (1 ch), *come in unto the king* (1 ch) = 160 chapters.

Holy King's Peculiar People

"And the LORD hath avouched thee this day to be <u>his peculiar people</u>, as he hath promised thee, and that thou shouldest keep all his commandments" (Deut. 26:18). The Bible combination *his people* (159x), *his peculiar people* (1x) = 160.

All of the Holy King's Men

"Ye stand this day all of you before the LORD your God; your captains of your tribes, your elders, and your officers, with <u>all the men of Israel</u>" (Deut. 29:10).

> The phrase *all the men* is mentioned in 60 verses of the Old Testament.
> The phrase *the men of Israel* is mentioned in 60 verses of the Bible.
> The phrase *the men of* is mentioned in 60 chapters of the OT Narrative.
> The phrase *men of the* is mentioned naturally in 60 verses of the Bible.

Holy King Leads His People

"So the LORD alone did <u>lead</u> him, and there was no strange god with him" (Deut. 32:12). Moses' song celebrated the victorious way in which the nation's Holy King led them through the wilderness. The word *lead* occurs 60 times in the Bible.

Holy King's Glittering Sword

"If I whet my glittering <u>sword</u>, and mine hand take hold on judgment; I will render vengeance to mine enemies, and will reward them that hate me" (Deut. 32:41). Moses' song spoke of the Holy King's needful earthly vengeance and justice. The phrase *the sword* is mentioned in 260 verses of the Bible.

Jehovah Was King in Jeshurun

"And he was KING in Jeshurun, when the heads of the people and the tribes of Israel were gathered together" (Deut. 33:5). The Hebrew names Yeshurun and Yishrael share a common root —'yashar' meaning upright. The Old Testament combination *and he was* (55x), *king in Israel* (4x), *in Jeshurun* (1x) = 60.

The phrase *the tribes of* occurs 60 times in the Old Testament.
The phrase *the tribes of* is mentioned in 60 verses of the Old Testament.

King of Jericho

"And it was told the KING of Jericho, saying, Behold, there came men in hither to night of the children of Israel to search out the country" (Josh. 2:2). The word *told* is mentioned in 60 verses of the New Testament. The Bible combination *and it was told the king of Jericho* (1 v) and *Jericho* (59 vs) = 60 verses.

60ᵗʰ Verse of Joshua

"And it came to pass, when all the people were clean passed over Jordan, that the LORD spake unto Joshua, saying" (Josh. 4:1). The Theocratic King of Israel spoke to the top general of His earthly army host. Again the title *LORD* occurs 60 times in Amos. The OT Narrative combination *that the LORD spake* (2x), *spake unto* (51x), *Joshua saying* (7x) = 60.

5960ᵗʰ Verse of the Bible

"And Joshua had commanded the people, saying, Ye shall not shout, nor make any noise with your voice, neither shall any word proceed out of your mouth, until the day I bid you shout; then shall ye shout" (Josh. 6:10). Joshua served the nation much like a king would, only he wore no crown. He led the troops out into battle as any king would do. On that coming appointed day the Israelites were to lift up a great unified shout of victory to their abiding Theocratic King, even the Lord. The Bible combination *ye shall not shout* (1x), *nor make any noise* (1x), *with your voice* (1x), *neither shall any word* (1x), *proceed out of your mouth* (2x), *until the day I* (1x), *bid you shout* (1x), *then shall ye* (16x), *shout* (36x) = 60.

Theocratic King Conquers with His General's Spear

"And the LORD said unto Joshua, Stretch out the spear that is in thy hand toward Ai; for I will give it into thine hand. And Joshua stretched out the spear that he had in his hand toward the city. . . . And so it was, that all that fell that day, both of men and women, were twelve thousand, even all the men of Ai. For Joshua drew not his hand back, wherewith he stretched out the spear, until he had utterly destroyed all the inhabitants of Ai" (Josh. 8:18, 25-26).

General Joshua followed the express military instructions from his Theocratic King. The word *spear(s)* occurs 60 times in the Old Testament.

Five Kings of Canaan

"And they did so, and brought forth those five KINGS unto him out of the cave, the KING of Jerusalem, the KING of Hebron, the KING of Jarmuth, the KING of Lachish, and the KING of Eglon" (Josh. 10:23). The nations occupying Canaan were generally comprised of city-states. The Lord gave Joshua and the Israelites victory over all these earthly kings. Again the term *the kings* is mentioned in 60 chapters of the OT Narrative. The phrase *of Canaan* occurs 60 times in the Law.

The King of Eglon

"The KING of Jericho, <u>one</u>; the king of Ai, which is beside Beth-el, <u>one</u>; The KING of Jerusalem, <u>one</u>; the KING of Hebron, <u>one</u>; The KING of Jarmuth, <u>one</u>; the KING of Lachish, <u>one</u>; **The KING of Eglon**, <u>one</u>; the KING of Gezer, <u>one</u>; The KING of Debir, <u>one</u>; the KING of Geder, <u>one</u>; The KING of Hormah, <u>one</u>; the KING of Arad, <u>one</u>; The KING of Libnah, <u>one</u>; the KING of Adullam, <u>one</u>; The KING of Makkedah, <u>one</u>; the KING of Beth-el, <u>one</u>; The KING of Tappuah, <u>one</u>; the KING of Hepher, <u>one</u>; The KING of Aphek, <u>one</u>; the KING of Lasharon, <u>one</u>; The KING of Madon, <u>one</u>; the KING of Hazor, <u>one</u>; The KING of Shimron-meron, <u>one</u>; the KING of Achshaph, <u>one</u>; The KING of Taanach, <u>one</u>; the KING of Megiddo, <u>one</u>; The KING of Kedesh, <u>one</u>; The KING of Jokneam of Carmel, <u>one</u>; The KING of Dor in the coast of Dor, <u>one</u>; the KING of the nations of Gilgal, <u>one</u>; The KING of Tirzah, <u>one</u>: all the KINGS thirty and one" (Josh. 12:9-24).

The bolded phrase of this kingly passage presents the Bible's 60th occurrence of the phrase *the king of*, and we find its complimentary seal: The Joshua combination *the king of* (52x), *Eglon* (8x) = 60. Because there can only be one king at a time over a people, the word *one* occurs 1360 times in the Old Testament.

60 Cities Belonging to King Og's Expansive Kingdom

"<u>And</u> their coast was from Mahanaim, all Bashan, all the KINGDOM of Og king of Bashan, and all the towns of Jair, which are in Bashan, THREESCORE cities" (Josh. 13:30). The lead word of this 60-city-kingdom verse *And* is the 167,060th word of the Bible.

Theocratic King Fulfilled All His Good Promises

"<u>There failed not ought of any</u> good thing which the LORD <u>had spoken</u> <u>unto the house of Israel;</u> <u>all came to pass</u>" (Josh. 21:45). Israel's Theocratic King is recorded as having fulfilled all His royal promises to give His people victory in the conquest of Canaan. The Bible combination *there failed not ought of any* (1x), *good thing which the LORD* (2x), *had spoken* (40x), *unto the house of Israel* (16x), *all came to pass* (1x) = 60.

Judges—An Early Type of the Israelite Kings

"Nevertheless <u>the LORD raised up</u> <u>judges,</u> <u>which delivered them</u> <u>out of the hand of those</u> <u>that spoiled them</u>. . . . And the Spirit of the LORD came upon him, and he <u>judged</u> Israel, and went out to war: and the LORD delivered Chushan-rishathaim KING of Mesopotamia into his hand" (Judg. 2:16, 3:10a). Before God allowed Israel to have a succession of kings He first gave them a succession of judges. These judges served as civil and military leaders and were chosen and anointed by the Lord himself just as Israel's future kings were to be. In the same manner as a king would rule, only one judge ruled at a time. Counting backward from the end of the Old Testament, in the above passage the word *judged* occurs for its 60th time. The Bible combination *the LORD raised up* (2x), *judges* (52x), *which delivered* (2x), *delivered them out of the hand of* (4x) = 60. The Bible combination *the LORD raised up* (2x), *judges* (52x), *which delivered them* (1x), *out of the hand of those* (2x), *those that spoiled them* (3x) = 60.

King of Canaan

"And the LORD sold them into the hand of Jabin KING <u>of Canaan</u>, that REIGNED in Hazor; the captain of whose host was Sisera, which dwelt in Harosheth of the Gentiles" (Judg. 4:2). Hazor was the chief city where most of the northern-dwelling Canaanites lived. Again the phrase *of Canaan* occurs 60 times in the Law.

The Confederated Kings of Canaan Land

Deborah's song tells of Canaan's many kings who confederated with Jabin in their attempt to defeat the Israelites. "The KINGS came and fought, then fought the KINGS of Canaan in Taanach by the waters of Megiddo; they took no gain of money" (Judg. 5:19). Again the term *the kings* is mentioned in 60 chapters of the OT Narrative. Again the word *fought* occurs 60 times in the Old Testament.

The Sword of the Lord & of Gideon

"When I blow with a trumpet, I and all that are with me, then blow ye the trumpets also on every side of all the camp, and say, The sword of the LORD, and of Gideon" (Judg. 7:18). Gideon instructed his small army to blow their trumpets in honor of their Theocratic King. Again the word *trumpet* is mentioned in 60 verses of the Bible. Again the phrase *the sword* is mentioned in 260 verses of the Bible.

Kings of Midian

"Then said he unto Zebah and Zalmunna, What manner of men were they whom ye slew at Tabor? And they answered, As thou art, so were they; each one resembled the children of a KING" (Judg. 8:18). These two Midianites kings flattered their captor king in hopes of assuaging his anger and reducing the severity of their judgment. The phrase *of men* occurs 160 times in the Bible.

There Was No Visible Earthly King in Israel

"In those days there was no KING in Israel: every man did that which was right in his own eyes" (Judg. 21:25). In those days Israel had no mortal king. The people had no more judges to serve as kings after Samson's demise. This verse confirms that the judges of Israel were viewed as kings over the nation. The word *no* is found in 60 books of the Bible. The positive OT Narrative combination *a king to judge* (2x) and *in Israel* (58x) = 60.

> The Job combination *no* (54x), *king* (5x), *in God's stead* (1x) = 60.
> The Psalms combination *no* (57x), *king in* (2x), *the land of Canaan* (1x) = 60.

60ᵗʰ Verse of Ruth

"Also he said, Bring the vail that thou hast upon thee, and hold it. And when she held it, he measured six measures of barley, and laid it on her: and she went into the city" (Ruth 3:15). Boaz was a wealthy, powerful, noble, dignified, and stately Judean man—much like a king. Kings were responsible for feeding their people, and in any well-ordered kingdom a king's resources are always distributed in a measured fashion. Here the stately man Boaz carefully measured out a healthy provision of grain for one of his most devoted subjects.

We Want an Earthly King Like All the Nations!

"Then all the elders of Israel gathered themselves together, and came to Samuel unto Ramah, And said unto him, Behold, thou art old, and thy sons walk not in thy ways: now make us a KING to judge us like all the nations" (1 Sam. 8:4-5). The people came to the prophet so he might play the part of a king-maker.

> The word *make* is mentioned in 60 verses of the Gospels.
> The word *made* occurs 460 times in the OT Narrative.

99

Theocratic King's Rule Rejected

"And the LORD said unto Samuel, Hearken unto the voice of the people in all that they say unto thee: for they have not rejected thee, but they have rejected me, that I should not <u>REIGN over them</u>" (1 Sam. 8:7). The people's demand for a visible king was an unforeseen mistake. Their Theocratic King had never failed them not even once. The first seal below is repeated.

The word *reigned* is mentioned in 60 chapters of the OTN.
The phrase *over them* is mentioned in 60 verses of the Bible.

Saul, Israel's First Mortal Earthly King

"And he had a son, whose name was <u>Saul</u>, a choice young man, and a goodly: and there was not among the children of Israel a goodlier person than he: from his shoulders and upward he was higher than any of the people. . . . Then Samuel took a vial of oil, and poured it upon his head" (1 Sam. 9:2; 10:1a). Because the Hebrews did not want to follow God with eyes of faith, He gave them a king whom they would have naturally chosen with their own eyes, a man who was tall, strong, and handsome—a champion.

The name *Saul* occurs 360 times in the OT Narrative.
The name *Saul('s)* is mentioned in 60 chapters of the OT Narrative.

The Man Whom the Lord Chose to Be King

"And Samuel said to all the people, See ye him <u>whom</u> the LORD hath chosen, that there is none like him among all the people? And all the people shouted, and said, God save the KING" (1 Sam. 10:24). The word *whom* is found in 60 books of the Bible.

260th Verse of First Samuel

Samuel reminded the people of their faithlessness when he said, "And when ye saw that Nahash the KING of the children of Ammon came against you, ye said unto me, Nay; but a KING shall REIGN over us: when <u>the LORD your God</u> was <u>your</u> KING" (1 Sam. 12:12). Three different *kings* are actually mentioned in this 260th verse. The title *the LORD your God* is mentioned in 60 chapters of the Old Testament.

The word *your* is mentioned in 60 chapters of the Pauline Epistles.
The word *your* occurs 60 times in the General Epistles.

Saul, a Willful & Disobedient King

"Then came <u>the word of the LORD</u> unto Samuel, saying, It repenteth me that I have set up Saul to be KING: for he is turned back from following me, and hath not performed my commandments. And it grieved Samuel; and he cried unto the LORD all night" (1 Sam. 15:10-11). Saul turned out to be a willful and disobedient king. Moreover, he made an astonishing series of poor judgments, strange decisions, and sinful acts. Again the title *the word of the LORD* occurs 60 times in Ezekiel.

David, God's Choice for King

"Then Samuel took the horn of oil, and anointed him in the midst of his brethren: and the Spirit of the LORD came upon <u>David</u> from that day forward. So Samuel rose up, and went to Ramah" (1 Sam. 16:13). Whereas Saul came from a proud family of wealth and influence, David came from an ordinary working family.

The name *David('s)* occurs 360 times in Kings and Chronicles.
The name *David('s)* occurs naturally 1060 times in the Bible!

"And the King Said"

"<u>And the king said,</u> <u>Enquire thou</u> <u>whose son the stripling is</u>" (1 Sam. 17:56). The Bible combination *and the king said* (58x), *enquire thou* (1x), *whose son the stripling is* (1x) = 60.

The King's Enemies

"And Saul said, Thus shall ye say to David, The KING desireth not any dowry, but an hundred foreskins of the Philistines, to be avenged of the KING'S <u>enemies</u>. But Saul thought to make David fall by the hand of the Philistines" (1 Sam. 18:25). Every earthly king has enemies. Israelite kings, however, had more than most. The Philistines were greatly against Saul for the duration of his rule. Here Saul was not all that concerned with his enemy's army but was rather concerned with David. Saul had unnecessarily made David his enemy because he thought David wanted to take his throne. The word *enemies* is mentioned in 260 verses of the Bible.

7760th Verse of the Bible

"And he said, Let me go, I pray thee; for our family hath a sacrifice in the city; and my brother, he hath commanded me to be there: and now, if I have found favour in thine eyes, let me get away, I pray thee, and see my brethren. Therefore he cometh not unto the KING'S table" (1 Sam. 20:29). In this 60th verse a king's son spoke with the king. The keyword *king's* actually occurs in this 60th verse.

Jonathan Was Next in Line to Be King

"Then Saul's anger was kindled against <u>Jonathan</u>, and he said unto him, Thou son of the perverse rebellious woman, do not I know that thou hast chosen the son of Jesse to thine own confusion, and unto the confusion of thy mother's nakedness? For as long as the son of Jesse liveth upon the ground, thou shalt not be established, nor thy KINGDOM" (1 Sam. 20:30-31b). The name *Jonathan* is mentioned in 60 verses of First Samuel.

260th Chapter of the Bible

"And it came to pass, when Saul was returned from following the Philistines, that it was told him, saying, Behold, David is in the wilderness of En-gedi. Then Saul took three thousand chosen men out of all Israel, and went to seek David and his men upon the rocks of the wild goats" (1 Sam. 24:1-2).

7860th Verse of the Bible

"And now, behold, I know well that thou shalt surely be KING, and that the KINGDOM of Israel shall be established in thine hand" (1 Sam. 24:20). Saul understood and acknowledged David's destiny and divine appointment. The keyword *king* and related keyword *kingdom* actually occur in this 60th verse.

The Lord Had Appointed David to Be King

Abigail proclaimed, "And it shall come to pass, when the LORD shall have done to my lord according to all the good that he <u>hath spoken concerning thee</u>, <u>and shall have</u> <u>appointed</u> thee <u>RULER over Israel</u>" (1 Sam. 25:30). The OT Narrative combination *hath spoken concerning thee* (1x), *and shall have* (1x), *appointed* (56x), *ruler over Israel* (2x) = 60.

7960th Verse of the Bible
"And the LORD hath done to him, as he spake by me: for the LORD hath rent the KINGDOM out of thine hand, and given it to thy neighbour, even to David" (1 Sam. 28:17). The related keyword *kingdom* actually occurs in this 60th verse. The OT Narrative combination *the kingdom* (56x), *out of thine hand* (4x) = 60.

Earthly Kings Die as Mere Mortals
"So Saul <u>died</u>, and his three sons, and his armourbearer, and all his men, that same day together" (1 Sam. 31:6). The word *died* is mentioned in 60 chapters of the OT Narrative.

David Was King in Hebron
"And it came to pass after this, that David enquired of the LORD, saying, Shall I go up into any of the cities of Judah? And the LORD said unto him, Go up. And David said, Whither shall I go up? And he said, Unto <u>Hebron</u>. . . . And the time that David was KING in <u>Hebron</u> over the house of Judah was seven years and SIX months" (2 Sam. 2:1, 11). The word *Hebron* is mentioned in 60 verses of the OT Narrative.

8060th Verse of the Bible
"Ish-bosheth Saul's son was forty years old when he began to REIGN over <u>Israel</u>, and <u>REIGNED</u> two years. But the house of Judah followed David" (2 Sam. 2:10). This 60th verse pertains to the beginning of a king's earthly reign. Again the word *reigned* is mentioned in 60 chapters of the OT Narrative. Again the name *Israel* is mentioned in 60 verses of the Psalms.

60th Verse of Second Samuel
"Now there was long war between the <u>house of Saul</u> and the <u>house of David</u>: but David <u>waxed stronger</u> and stronger, and the <u>house of Saul</u> waxed <u>weaker</u> and weaker" (2 Sam. 3:1). Two kingly lines are compared in this 60th verse. Even though the balance of warring tribes was eleven to one at this time, Judah's tribe yet thrived. The Bible combination *house of David* (25x), *waxed strong* (2x), *stronger than* (15x), *King Saul* (2x), *house of Saul* (13x), *weaker* (3x) = 60.

Abner's Kingdom Allegiance Shifted to David
Abner told Ish-bosheth, "So do God to Abner, and more also, except, as the LORD hath sworn <u>to David</u>, even so I do to him; To translate the KINGDOM from the house of Saul, and to set up the throne of David over Israel and over Judah, from Dan even to Beer-sheba" (2 Sam. 3:9). Abner was now prepared to withdraw his political support from one earthly king and give it to another. He did this knowing which kingly line the Lord had already chosen in advance. The phrase *to David* occurs 60 times in the Old Testament! Again the related keyword *kingdom* is mentioned in 60 chapters of the OT Narrative.

Abner's Kingdom Allegiance Offered to David
"So Abner came to David to Hebron, and twenty men with him. And David made Abner and the men that were with him a feast. And Abner said unto David, <u>I will arise and go</u>, <u>and will gather</u>

all Israel unto <u>my lord the KING</u>, <u>that they may make</u> <u>a league with thee</u>, and <u>that thou mayest</u> <u>REIGN over all that thine heart desireth</u>" (2 Sam. 3:20-21). Abner desired to use his political influence to solidify a united kingdom rule under David. The Bible combination *I will arise and go* (2x), *and will gather all Israel unto* (1x), *my lord the king* (51x), *that they may make* (3x), *a league with thee* (2x), *that thou mayest reign over all that thine heart desireth* (1x) = 60.

United Kingdom Rule Comes to David

"Then came all the tribes of Israel to David unto Hebron, and spake, saying, Behold, we are thy bone and thy flesh. Also in time past, when Saul was KING over us, thou wast he that leddest out and broughtest in Israel: and the LORD said to thee, Thou shalt feed my people Israel, and thou shalt be a captain over Israel. So all the elders of Israel came <u>to the KING</u> to Hebron; and KING David made a league with them in Hebron before the LORD: and they anointed David KING over Israel" (2 Sam. 5:1-3).

The phrase *to the king* occurs 60 combined times in the kingly two-volume writings of Samuel, Kings, and Chronicles.

8160th Verse of the Bible

"<u>And David</u> arose, and went with all the people that were with him from Baale of Judah, to bring up from thence the ark of God, whose name is called by the name of the LORD of hosts that dwelleth between the cherubims" (2 Sam. 6:2). The Israelite kings always felt comforted having the Ark near their place of residence. The phrase *and David* is mentioned in 60 chapters of the Bible.

The King—Chosen One of the Lord

"And David said unto Michal, It was before the LORD, which <u>chose</u> me before thy father, and before all his house, to appoint me RULER over the people of the LORD, over Israel: therefore will I play before the LORD" (2 Sam. 6:21). All forms of the word *chose* occur 60 times in the OT Narrative: *chose* (13x), *chosen* (47x) = 60.

160th Verse of Second Samuel

"That the KING said unto Nathan the prophet, See now, I dwell in <u>an house of</u> <u>cedar</u>, but the ark of God dwelleth within curtains" (2 Sam. 7:2). The keyword *king* actually occurs in this 60th verse. The Bible combination *an house of* (12 vs), *cedar* (48 vs) = 60 verses.

David's House & Kingdom Established Forever

"And <u>thine house</u> and <u>thy KINGDOM</u> shall be established for ever before thee: thy throne shall be established for ever. According to all these words, and according to all this vision, so did Nathan speak unto David" (2 Sam. 7:16-17). This proclamation from the Lord revealed the continuance of David's family line and earthly kingdom rule. The Old Testament combination *thine house* (46x) and *thy kingdom* (14x) = 60.

King of Ammon

"And it came to pass after this, that the KING of the children of Ammon died, and Hanun his son REIGNED <u>in his stead</u>" (2 Sam. 10:1). This is the Bible's first mention of the expression "in his stead." Again the phrase *in his stead* occurs 60 times in the OT Narrative.

8260th Verse of the Bible

"And when all the KINGS that were servants to Hadarezer saw that they were smitten before Israel, they made peace with Israel, and served them. So the Syrians feared to help the children of Ammon any more" (2 Sam. 10:19). The keyword *kings* actually occurs in this 60th verse. Again the term *the kings* is mentioned in 60 chapters of the OT Narrative.

The Kings' Ancient Battle Tradition

"And it came to pass, after the year was expired, at the time when KINGS go forth to battle, that David sent Joab, and his servants with him, and all Israel; and they destroyed the children of Ammon, and besieged Rabbah. But David tarried still at Jerusalem" (2 Sam. 11:1). It was the custom of kings to go into the battle with their troops. Here King David departed from this ancient tradition. The word *battle* is mentioned naturally in 160 verses of the Bible.

A Crown for the King's Head

"And he took their KING'S CROWN from off his head, the weight whereof was a talent of gold with the precious stones: and it was set on David's head. And he brought forth the spoil of the city in great abundance" (2 Sam. 12:30). A king's crown represents his power and glory. Again all forms of the word *crown* are mentioned in 60 verses of the Old Testament. The Old Testament combination *weight* (54x), *whereof was a* (1x), *talent of gold* (4x), *with the precious stones* (1x) = 60. The word *head* occurs 60 times in the Major Prophets. The OT Narrative combination *and it was* (53x), *set on* (5x), *David's head* (2x) = 60.

8360th Verse of the Bible

"And come to the KING and speak on this manner unto him. So Joab put the words in her mouth" (2 Sam. 14:3). The keyword *king* actually occurs in this 60th verse. The word *speak* is mentioned in 60 verses of the Pauline Epistles.

Absalom Becomes a Usurper King

"But Absalom sent spies throughout all the tribes of Israel, saying, As soon as ye hear the sound of the trumpet, then ye shall say, Absalom reigneth in Hebron" (2 Sam. 15:10). Again the word *trumpet* is mentioned in 60 verses of the Bible.

The King's Faithful Servants

David spoke to Ittai. "And Ittai answered the KING, and said, As the LORD liveth, and as my lord the KING liveth, surely in what place my lord the KING shall be, whether in death or life, even there also will thy servant be" (2 Sam. 15:21). The plural phrase *thy servants* is mentioned in 60 chapters of the Bible.

Kings Should Rule Justly & Fearfully before God

"He that RULETH over men must be just, RULING in the fear of God. And he shall be as the light of the morning, when the sun riseth, even a morning without clouds; as the tender grass springing out of the EARTH by clear shining after rain" (2 Sam. 23:3b-4). David's last words were rehearsed from what the Lord had earlier told him about a king's authority. The Old Testament combination *he that ruleth over men must be* (1x), *just* (59x) = 60.

Kingdom Subjects Made to Suffer for the King's Sin

"So the LORD sent a pestilence upon Israel from the morning even to the time appointed: and there died of the people from Dan even to Beer-sheba seventy thousand men. . . . And David spake unto the LORD when he saw the angel that smote the people, and said, Lo, I <u>have sinned</u>, and I have done wickedly: but these sheep, what have they done? let thine hand, I pray thee, be against me, and against my father's house" (2 Sam. 24:15, 17). The phrase *have sinned* is mentioned in 60 verses of the Old Testament.

Another Son Becomes a Usurper King

"Now king David was old and stricken in years; and they covered him with clothes, but he gat no heat. . . . Then Adonijah the son of Haggith exalted himself, saying, I will be KING: and he prepared him chariots and horsemen, and fifty men to run before him. . . . And he conferred with Joab the son of Zeruiah, and with Abiathar the priest: and they following Adonijah helped him" (1 Kings 1:1, 5, 7). After Absalom's death Adonijah became the eldest son of David. Thus he considered this position an entitlement. Again the word *chariot* occurs naturally 60 times in the Old Testament.

Bowing before the King with One's Face to the Ground

"And they <u>told</u> the king, saying, Behold Nathan the prophet. <u>And when he was come in before the king,</u> he <u>bowed himself</u> <u>before the king</u> with his face to the ground" (1 Kings 1:23). Again the word *told* is mentioned in 60 verses of the New Testament. The Bible combination *and when he was come in before the king* (1x), *he bowed him*self (5x), *before the king* (50x), *with his face to the ground* (4x) = 60.

Solomon Shall Be King

"Then ye shall come up after him, that he may come and sit upon my throne; for he <u>shall be</u> KING in my stead: and I have appointed him <u>to be</u> <u>RULER</u> over Israel and over Judah" (1 Kings 1:35). Again the word *ruler* is mentioned naturally in 60 verses of the Old Testament.

> The word *be* is mentioned in 160 verses of Proverbs.
> The word *be* is mentioned in 60 chapters of the Minor Prophets.
> The phrase *shall be* occurs 2460 times in the Bible.
> The phrase *to be* is seen naturally in 60 verses of Synoptic Gospels.

Solomon Now Sits as King upon the Throne

"And also <u>Solomon sitteth on</u> <u>the throne</u> of the KINGDOM" (1 Kings 1:46). Here the kingly name *Solomon* is the 244,060th word of the Bible. The name *Solomon* occurs naturally 260 times in the OT Narrative. The Bible combination *Solomon sitteth on* (1 ch), *the throne* (59 chs) = 60 chapters.

60th Verse of First Kings

"But shew kindness unto the sons of Barzillai the Gileadite, and let them be of those that eat at thy table: for so they came to me when I fled because of Absalom thy brother" (1 Kings 2:7). Absalom led a revolt against his father through subtlety. So strong was Absalom's following that David felt the need to speedily flee Jerusalem. The usurper king did not remain king for very long—less than a month.

King Solomon Issues a Death Penalty

"And the KING sent and called for Shimei, and said unto him, Did I not make thee to swear by the LORD, and protested unto thee, saying, Know for a certain, on the day thou goest out, and walkest abroad any whither, that thou shalt surely die? and thou saidst unto me, The word that I have heard is good" (1 Kings 2:42). These words were the beginning of Shimei's death sentence at the mouth of an earthly king. This kingly verse consists of 60 words.

King Solomon Needs Godly Wisdom

"In Gibeon the LORD appeared to Solomon in a dream by night: and God said, Ask what I shall give thee. . . . Give therefore thy servant an <u>understanding</u> heart to judge thy people, that I may discern between good and bad: for who is able to judge this thy so great a people? . . . Behold, I have done according to thy words: lo, I have given thee a wise and an <u>understanding</u> heart" (1 Kings 3:5, 9, 12a). To rule effectively, youthful King Solomon knew the two things he needed most were wisdom and understanding. The word *understanding* occurs 160 times in the Bible.

King Solomon's Expansive Kingdom Reign

"<u>And Solomon REIGNED</u> <u>over all</u> KINGDOMS from the river unto the land of the Philistines, and unto the border of Egypt: they brought presents, and served Solomon all the days of his life" (1 Kings 4:21). Here the kingly word *reigned* is the 360th word of this chapter. The Old Testament combination *and Solomon reigned* (2x), *over all* (58x) = 60.

King Solomon's Daily Provision of 60 Measures of Meal

"<u>And Solomon's provision for one day was thirty measures of fine flour, and</u> THREESCORE measures of meal, Ten fat oxen, and twenty oxen out of the pastures, and an hundred sheep, beside harts, and roebucks, and fallowdeer, and fatted fowl" (1 Kings 4:22-23). In this verse there are 60 letters preceding *threescore*—the word meaning 60.

King Solomon's Dominion over all the Region

"<u>For he had DOMINION</u> <u>over all</u> <u>the region on this side the river</u>, from Tiphsah even to Azzah, over all the KINGS on this side the river: and he had peace on all sides round about him" (1 Kings 4:24). The Old Testament combination *for he had dominon* (1x), *over all* (58x), *the region on this side the river* (1x) = 60.

All the Days of the King's Life

"And Judah and Israel dwelt safely, every man under his vine and under his fig tree, from Dan even to Beer-sheba, <u>all the days of</u> Solomon" (1 Kings 4:25). The phrase *all the days of* occurs 60 times in the Bible. Again the name *Solomon* occurs naturally 260 times in the OT Narrative.

160th Verse of First Kings

"And he spake three thousand proverbs: and his songs were a thousand and five. <u>And he spake of trees, from the cedar tree that is in Lebanon even unto the hyssop that springeth out of the wall: he spake also of beasts, and of fowl, and of creeping things, and of fishes.</u> And there came of all people to hear the wisdom of Solomon, from all KINGS of the EARTH, which had heard of his wisdom" (1 Kings 4:32-34). The underlined words indicate the 160th verse of First Kings, and the verse pertains to an earthly king's proverbial wisdom.

Earthly Temple of 60 Cubits Length for the King of Heaven & Earth

"And the house which king Solomon built for the LORD, the length thereof was THREESCORE cubits, and the breadth thereof twenty cubits, and the height thereof thirty cubits" (1 Kings 6:2). The phrase *the length* occurs 60 times in the Bible.

The Heavenly King's Earthly Oracle

"And the oracle in the forepart was twenty cubits in length, and twenty cubits in breadth, and twenty cubits in the height thereof: and he overlaid it with pure gold" (1 Kings 6:20). The Lord's Most Holy Place was of architectural perfection and cube shaped. This threefold measurement of 20 draw for us a mental picture of 60.

First Kings 8:60

In Solomon's blessing after the prayer he said, "That all the people of the EARTH may know that the LORD is God, and that there is none else" (1 Kings 8:60). The following numeric seals show that the Lord God is Earth's Greatest King. Again the phrase *all the earth* occurs 60 times in the Old Testament.

King Solomon's Great Throne of Ivory

"Moreover the KING made a great throne of ivory, and overlaid it with the best gold. The throne had six steps, and the top of the throne was round behind: and there were stays on either side on the place of the seat, and two lions stood beside the stays. And twelve lions stood there on the one side and on the other upon the six steps: there was not the like made in any KINGDOM" (1 Kings 10:18-20). Here the underlined word *the* is the 11,060th word of First Kings, and it serves as the definite article for the keyword king. The Old Testament combination *throne of* (47x), *ivory* (12x), *and overlaid it with the best gold* (1x) = 60.

All of King Solomon's Chariots & Horsemen

"And Solomon gathered together chariots and horsemen: and he had a thousand and four hundred chariots, and twelve thousand horsemen, whom he bestowed in the cities for chariots, and with the KING at Jerusalem" (1 Kings 10:26). Again the word *chariot* occurs naturally 60 times in the Old Testament. The Bible combination *horsemen* (59x) and *horsehoofs* (1x) = 60. The Old Testament combination *and with the king* (3x), *at Jerusalem* (57x) = 60.

King Solomon Received Foreign Merchandise

"And Solomon had horses brought out of Egypt, and linen yarn: the king's merchants received the linen yarn at a price" (1 Kings 10:28). The word *received* occurs 160 times in the Bible.

A Davidic King Forever in Jerusalem

The prophet Ahijah foretold that the united kingdom would become divided again under the reign of Solomon's son: "And unto his son will I give one tribe, that David my servant may have a light alway before me in Jerusalem, the city which I have chosen me to put my name there" (1 Kings 11:36).

The name *Jerusalem* occurs 60 times in Acts of the Apostles.
The phrase *in Jerusalem* is mentioned in 160 verses of the Bible.

King Rehoboam

"And the time that Solomon REIGNED in Jerusalem over all Israel was forty years. And Solomon slept with his fathers, and was buried in the city of David his father: his son REIGNED in his stead" (1 Kings 11:42-43). Again the phrase *in his stead* occurs 60 times in the OT Narrative.

9160th Verse of the Bible

"But he forsook the counsel of the old men, which they had given him, and consulted with the young men that were grown up with him, and which stood before him" (1 Kings 12:8). Here a king forsakes the good advice of aged counselors.

United Kingdom Becomes Divided into Two Kingdoms

"So when all Israel saw that the king hearkened not unto them, the people answered the KING, saying, What portion have we in David? neither have we inheritance in the son of Jesse: to your tents, O Israel: now see to thine own house, David. So Israel departed unto their tents. . . . So Israel rebelled against the house of David unto this day. And it came to pass, when all Israel heard that Jeroboam was come again, that they sent and called him unto the congregation, and made him KING over all Israel: there was none that followed the house of David, but the tribe of Judah only" (1 Kings 12:16, 19-20).

Solomon's death brought an end to an era. Only under the nation's first three kings was the kingdom united. The First Kings combination *Jeroboam* (53x), *called him unto the congregation and* (1x), *made him king* (1x), *over all Israel* (5x) = 60.

Note: For the remainder of First and Second Kings we will mainly make mention only of the northern kings as do these two books so treat them.

King Jeroboam

"And it came to pass, when KING Jeroboam heard the saying of the man of God, which had cried against the altar in Beth-el, that he put forth his hand from the altar, saying, Lay hold on him. And his hand, which he put forth against him, dried up, so that he could not pull it in again to him" (1 Kings 13:4). This smitten-king verse consists of 60 words.

*** The Kings of Israel ***

"And the rest of the acts of Jeroboam, how he warred, and how he reigned, behold, they are written in the book of the chronicles of the KINGS of Israel" (1 Kings 14:19). Here the word *book* is the 15,460th word of First Kings, and it pertains to a book which records all the details of the kings of Israel.

King Nadab

"And the days which Jeroboam reigned were two and twenty years: and he slept with his fathers, and Nadab his son reigned in his stead" (1 Kings 14:20). Here the underlined word *and* is the 660th word of this chapter; it supports the name of the new king Nadab.

9260th Verse of the Bible

"And forty and one years REIGNED he in Jerusalem. And his mother's name was Maachah, the daughter of Abishalom" (1 Kings 15:10). This verse speaks of the beginning of a godly Judean king's reign—Asa's. Again the phrase *in Jerusalem* is mentioned in 160 verses of the Bible.

560th Verse of First Kings

"Even in the third year of Asa KING of Judah did Baasha slay him, and REIGNED in his stead" (1 Kings 15:28). Baasha killed Nadab in order to seize control of the kingdom. The keyword *king* actually occurs in this 60th verse. Again the phrase *in his stead* occurs 60 times in the OT Narrative.

King Baasha

A grim prophecy was proclaimed before the evil king: "Behold, I will take away the posterity of Baasha, and the posterity of his house; and will make thy house like the house of Jeroboam the son of Nebat. Him that dieth of Baasha in the city shall the dogs eat; and him that dieth of his in the fields shall the fowls of the air eat" (1 Kings 16:3-4). The First and Second Kings combination *behold I will* (8x), *take away* (9x), *the posterity of* (2x), *Baasha* (23x), *and the posterity of* (1x), *his house* (15x), *and will make thy/thine house like the house of Jeroboam the son of Nebat* (2x) = 60.

King Elah

"So Baasha slept with his fathers, and was buried in Tirzah: and Elah his son REIGNED in his stead" (1 Kings 16:6). Again the phrase *in his stead* occurs 60 times in the OT Narrative.

King Zimri

"Baasha . . . REIGN over Israel in Tirzah, two years. And his servant Zimri, captain of half his chariots, conspired against him, as he was in Tirzah, drinking himself drunk in the house of Arza steward . . . And Zimri went in and smote him, and killed him . . . and REIGNED in his stead" (1 Kings 16:8b-10). Again the word *chariot* occurs naturally 60 times in the Old Testament. Again the word *reigned* is mentioned in 60 chapters of the OT Narrative.

King Omri

"And the people that were encamped heard say, Zimri hath conspired, and hath also slain the king: wherefore all Israel made Omri, the captain of the host, KING over Israel that day in the camp. And Omri went up from Gibbethon, and all Israel with him, and they besieged Tirzah. And it came to pass, when Zimri saw that the city was taken, that he went into the palace of the king's house, and burnt the king's house over him with fire, and died" (1 Kings 16:16-18). The underlined word *him* is the 260,060th word of the Bible, and it refers to a newly crowned king.

The Evil-Hearted Northern Kings

"But Omri wrought evil in the eyes of the LORD, and did worse than all that were before him" (1 Kings 16:25). Omri was just one of the twenty-one evil-hearted kings who reigned over the northern kingdom. The word *evil* is found in 60 books of the Bible.

King Ahab

"So Omri slept with his fathers, and was buried in Samaria: and Ahab his son REIGNED in his stead. And . . . Ahab the son of Omri reigned over Israel in Samaria twenty and two years. And Ahab the son of Omri did evil in the sight of the LORD above all that were before him" (1 Kings 16:28-30). The First Kings combination *Ahab* (49x), *reigned in his stead* (11x) = 60.

Earthly Kings versus Godly Prophets

"And it came to pass at the time of the offering of the evening sacrifice, that <u>Elijah</u> the prophet came near, and said, LORD God of Abraham, Isaac, and of Israel, let it be known this day that thou art God in Israel, and that I am thy servant, and that I have done all these things at thy word" (1 Kings 18:36). The prophets of God were not to fear the king's wrath but rather fear God and deliver His messages undiluted to the king's ear. It was the Lord's design that the kings expressly heed the prophet's warnings and counsels. The name *Elijah* is mentioned in 60 verses of the Kings. There are 60 words in this king-challenger verse.

9460th Verse of the Bible

"So she wrote letters in Ahab's name, and sealed them with his seal, and sent the letters unto the elders and to the nobles that were in his city, dwelling with Naboth" (1 Kings 21:8). This 60th verse mentions a king's authoritative name and seal.

The Book of the Chronicles of the Kings of Israel

"Now the rest of the acts of Ahab, and all that he did, and the ivory house which he made, and all the cities that he built, <u>are they not written in the book of the chronicles of the KINGS of Israel?</u>" (1 Kings 22:39) Again the title *the kings* is mentioned in 60 chapters of the OT Narrative. The kingly question *are they not written in the book of the chronicles of the kings of Israel?* consists of 60 characters!

King Ahaziah

"So Ahab slept with his fathers; and Ahaziah his son REIGNED <u>in his stead</u>. . . . Ahaziah the son of Ahab began to REIGN over Israel in Samaria . . . and REIGNED two years over Israel. And he did evil in the sight of the LORD, and walked in the way of his father, and in the way of his mother" (1 Kings 22:40, 51-52c). Again the phrase *in his stead* occurs 60 times in the OT Narrative.

King Jehoram

"And Ahaziah fell down through a lattice in his upper chamber that was in Samaria, and was sick . . . <u>So he died according to the word of the LORD</u> which Elijah had spoken. And <u>Jehoram REIGNED in his stead</u> . . . <u>because he had no son</u>" (2 Kings 1:2a, 17). Ahaziah and Jehoram were brothers. One reigned after the other. The First and Second Kings combination *so he died* (1x), *according to the word of the LORD* (13x), *which Elijah had spoken and* (1x), *Jehoram* (10x), reigned *in his stead* (33x), *because he had* (1x), *no son* (1x) = 60.

Ben-Hadad II, King of Syria

"And it came to pass after this, that <u>Ben-hadad KING of Syria gathered all his host, and went up,</u> and besieged Samaria" (2 Kings 6:4). There were three kings of Syria who bore this name; this was Ben-hadad II. The OT Narrative *Ben-hadad* (24 vs), *king of Syria* (35 vs), *gathered all his host and went up* (1 v) = 60 verses.

The King Asked a Question

"<u>And when the king asked</u> the woman, she told him. So the king appointed unto her a certain officer, saying, Restore all that was hers, and all the fruits of the field since the day that she left the land, even until now" (2 Kings 8:6). The Old Testament combination *and when the king* (6x), *asked* (54x) = 60.

Hazael, King of Syria

"And Elisha answered, <u>The LORD hath shewed me that</u> thou shalt be KING over <u>Syria</u>. . . . And it came to pass on the morrow, that he took a thick cloth, and dipped it in water, and spread it on his face, so that he died: and Hazael REIGNED in his stead" (2 Kings 8:13, 15). The OT Narrative combination *the LORD hath shewed me that* (1x), *thou shalt be king over* (2x), *Syria* (57x) = 60.

King Jehu

"And Jehu drew a bow with his full strength, and smote Jehoram between his arms, and the arrow went out at his heart, and he sunk down in his chariot. Then said Jehu to Bidkar his captain, Take up, and cast him in the portion of the field of Naboth the Jezreelite . . . And the time that <u>Jehu REIGNED over Israel in Samaria</u> was twenty and eight years" (2 Kings 9:24-25b, 36). The OT Narrative combination *Jehu* (58x), *reigned over Israel in Samaria* (2x) = 60.

When the King Was Come

"<u>And when Jehu</u> <u>was come</u> to Jezreel, Jezebel heard of it; and she painted her face, and tired her head, and looked out at a window" (2 Kings 9:30). The Old Testament combination *and when Jehu* (1x), *was come* (59x) = 60.

King Jehoahaz

"And <u>Jehu slept with his fathers: and</u> they buried him in Samaria. And <u>Jehoahaz</u> <u>his son REIGNED in his stead</u>" (2 Kings 10:35). The Second Kings combination *Jehu slept with his fathers and* (1x), *Jehoahaz* (16x), *his son* (21x), *reigned in his stead* (22x) = 60.

King Jehoash

"And Jehoahaz slept with his fathers; and they buried him in Samaria: and Joash his son REIGNED <u>in his stead</u> . . . began Jehoash the son of Jehoahaz to REIGN over Israel in Samaria, and REIGNED sixteen years" (2 Kings 13:9-10b). Again the phrase *in his stead* occurs 60 times in the OT Narrative.

360th Verse of Second Kings

"But <u>Hazael KING of Syria oppressed Israel all the days of Jehoahaz</u>" (2 Kings 13:22). The keyword *king* actually occurs in this 60th verse. The OT Narrative combination *Hazael* (22x), *king of Syria* (36x), *oppressed Israel* (1x), *all the days of Jehoahaz* (1x) = 60.

Ben-Hadad III, King of Syria

"So Hazael KING of Syria died; and Ben-hadad his son <u>REIGNED</u> in his stead" (2 Kings 13:24). Again the word *reigned* is mentioned in 60 chapters of the OT Narrative.

Jeroboam II

"And Jehoash slept with his fathers, and was buried in Samaria with the KINGS of Israel; and Jeroboam his son REIGNED in his stead. . . . in Samaria, <u>and REIGNED</u> <u>forty and one</u> <u>years</u>. And he did that which was evil in the sight of the LORD" (2 Kings 14:16, 23c-24a). The Second Kings combination *and reigned* (14x), *forty and one* (1x), *years* (45x) = 60.

King Zachariah

"And Jeroboam slept with his fathers, even with the KINGS of Israel; and Zachariah his son REIGNED in his stead. . . . over Israel in Samaria six months. And he did that which was evil in the sight of the LORD, as his fathers had done" (2 Kings 14:29; 15:8c-9b). The Second Kings combination *Jeroboam slept with his fathers even* (1x) *with the kings of Israel* (3x), *Zachariah* (4x), *his son* (21x), *reigned in his stead* (22x), *over Israel in Samaria* (7x), *six months* (1x), *and he did that which was evil in the sight of the LORD as his fathers had done* (1x) = 60.

King Shallum

"And Shallum the son of Jabesh conspired against him, and smote him before the people, and slew him, and REIGNED in his stead. . . . and he REIGNED a full month in Samaria" (2 Kings 15:10, 13c). The OT Narrative combination *and Shallum the son of Jabesh* (1x), *conspired against him and smote him* (2x), *before the people and slew him and* (1x), *reigned in his stead* (55x), *and he reigned a full month* (1x) = 60.

King Menahem

"For Menahem the son of Gadi went up from Tirzah, and came to Samaria, and smote Shallum the son of Jabesh in Samaria, and slew him, and REIGNED in his stead. . . . and REIGNED ten years in Samaria. And he did that which was evil in the sight of the LORD" (2 kings 15:14, 17c-18a). Again the word *reigned* is mentioned in 60 chapters of the OT Narrative.

King Pekahiah

"And Menahem slept with his fathers; and Pekahiah his son REIGNED in his stead. . . . began to REIGN over Israel in Samaria, and REIGNED two years. And he did that which was evil in the sight of the LORD" (2 Kings 15:22, 23c-24a). The phrases *Menahem slept with his fathers; and Pekahiah his son reigned in his stead* consist of 60 letters!

King Pekah

"But Pekah the son of Remaliah, a captain of his, conspired against him, and smote him in Samaria, in the palace of the king's house, with Argob and Arieh, and with him fifty men of the Gileadites: and he killed him, and REIGNED in his room. . . . and REIGNED twenty years. And he did that which was evil in the sight of the LORD" (2 Kings 15:25, 27c-28a). Here the underlined word *and* is the 281,060th word of the Bible; it supports the kingly word reigned.

King Hoshea

"And Hoshea the son of Elah made a conspiracy against Pekah the son of Remaliah, and smote him, and slew him, and REIGNED in his stead" (2 Kings 15:30). Again the phrase *in his stead* occurs 60 times in the OT Narrative.

9960th Verse of the Bible

"And he did that which was right in the sight of the LORD: he did according to all that his father Uzziah had done" (2 Kings 15:34). This verse speaks of the godly Judean king Jotham.

10,060th Verse of the Bible

"Who are they among all the gods of the countries, that have delivered their country out of mine hand, that the LORD should deliver Jerusalem out of mine hand?" (2 Kings 18:35) This 60th verse recalls the king of Assyria's frightening message to the king of Judah.

An Earthly King's Earthly Treasure

"At that time Berodach-baladan, the son of Baladan, KING of Babylon, sent letters and a present unto Hezekiah: for he had heard that Hezekiah had been sick. And Hezekiah hearkened unto them, and shewed them all the house of his precious things, the silver, and the gold, and the spices, and the precious ointment, and all the house of his armour, and all that was found in his <u>treasures</u>: there was nothing in his house, nor in all his DOMINION, that Hezekiah shewed them not" (2 Kings 20:12-13).

Chapter twenty records two events: the first is King Hezekiah's earthly prayer to God and his miraculous recovery from sickness; the second event is King Hezekiah giving a grand tour of all his splendid treasures to representatives of Babylon's king. Again the word *treasures* occurs 60 times from Genesis to the NT Narrative. This chapter consists of 660 words.

The Early Kings of Edom

"Now <u>these are the KINGS that</u> <u>REIGNED</u> <u>in the land of</u> <u>Edom</u> before any king reigned over the children of Israel; Bela the son of Beor: and the name of his city was Dinhabah. And when Bela was dead, Jobab the son of Zerah of Bozrah reigned in his stead. And when Jobab was dead, Husham of the land of the Temanites reigned in his stead. And when Husham was dead, Hadad the son of Bedad, which smote Midian in the field of Moab, reigned in his stead: and the name of his city was Avith. And when Hadad was dead, Samlah of Masrekah reigned in his stead. And when Samlah was dead, Shaul of Rehoboth by the river reigned in his stead. And when Shaul was dead, Baal-hanan the son of Achbor reigned in his stead. And when Baal-hanan was dead, Hadad reigned in his stead" (1 Chron. 1:43-50a).

The Bible combination *these are the* (156x), *kings that reigned* (2x), *reigned in the land of Edom* (2x) = 160. Again the Genesis combination *in the land of* (49 vs), *Edom* (11 vs) = 60 verses.

Judah's Tribe Gave Rise to the Chief Ruler over Israel

"For <u>Judah</u> prevailed above his brethren, and of him came <u>the CHIEF RULER</u>; but the birthright was Joseph's" (1 Chron. 5:2). This verse corresponds with our third definition of kingly: having the rank of king. The phrase *the chief of* occurs 60 times in the Old Testament. Again the word *ruler* is mentioned naturally in 60 verses of the Old Testament. We repeat the following two seals.

> The title *Judah* is mentioned in 60 verses of the Minor Prophets.
> The title *King of Judah* occurs 60 times in First and Second Kings.

10,660th Verse of the Bible

"And Azel had six sons, whose names are these, Azrikam, Bocheru, and Ishmael, and Sheariah, and Obadiah, and Hanan: these were the sons of Azel" (1 Chron. 9:44). This 60th verse speaks of royal descendants from King Saul.

King David's Coronation over All Israel

"Then all Israel gathered themselves to David unto Hebron, saying, Behold, we are thy bone and thy flesh. And moreover in time past, even when Saul was KING, <u>thou [wast] he that leddest out and broughtest in Israel: and the LORD thy God said unto thee, Thou shalt feed my people Israel, and thou shalt be ruler over my people Israel. Therefore came all the elders of Israel to the king to Hebron; and David made a covenant with them in Hebron before the LORD; and they anointed</u>

David KING over Israel, according to the word of the LORD by Samuel" (1 Chron. 11:1-3). In this passage there are 60 naturally occurring words resting between the two bookend-like words *king*; the bracketed word was supplied by the translators. Again the word *ruler* is mentioned naturally in 60 verses of the Old Testament.

King David's Castle

"And David said, Whosoever smiteth the Jebusites first shall be chief and captain. So Joab the son of Zeruiah went first up, and was chief. And David dwelt in the castle; therefore they called it the city of David" (1 Chron. 11:6-7). The First Chronicles combination *and David* (54x), *dwelt in the* (3x), *castle* (2x), *therefore they called it the city of David* (1x) = 60. The First and Second Chronicles combination *they called it the city* (1x), *of David* (59x) = 60.

King David's Mighty Men

"These also are the chief of the mighty men whom David had, who strengthened themselves with him in his KINGDOM, and with all Israel, to make him KING, according to the word of the LORD concerning Israel" (1 Chron. 11:10). The OT Narrative combination *these also are the chief of the* (1x), *mighty men* (45x), *whom David had* (4x), *who strengthened themselves with him* (1x), *in his kingdom* (2x), *and with all Israel* (1x), *to make him king* (5x), *according to the word of the LORD concerning Israel* (1x) = 60.

10,760th Verse of the Bible

"All these men of war, that could keep rank, came with a perfect heart to Hebron, to make David KING over all Israel: and all the rest also of Israel were of one heart to make David KING. And there they were with David three days, eating and drinking: for their brethren had prepared for them" (1 Chron. 12:38-39). The underlined 60th verse pertains to a celebration which followed a king's coronation.

King David's Wives

"And David took more wives at Jerusalem: and David begat more sons and daughters" (1 Chron. 14:3). The First and Second Chronicles combination *the king's* (42x), *wife* (18x) = 60. The First and Second Chronicles combination *took* (59 vs), *more wives* (1 v) = 60 verses.

King David's Choir

"And he appointed certain of the Levites to minister before the ark of the LORD, and to record, and to thank and praise the LORD God of Israel: Asaph the chief, and next to him Zechariah, Jeiel, and Shemiramoth, and Jehiel, and Mattithiah, and Eliab, and Benaiah, and Obed-edom: and Jeiel with psalteries and with harps; but Asaph made a sound with cymbals" (1 Chron. 16:4-5). The OT Narrative combination *appointed* (56x), *certain of the* (4x) = 60. The Psalms combination *praise* (158x), *the LORD God of Israel* (2x) = 160.

King David's Kingdom Established by Divine Covenant

"And it shall come to pass, when thy days be expired that thou must go to be with thy fathers, that I will raise up thy seed after thee, which shall be of thy sons; and I will establish his KINGDOM. He shall build me an house, and I will stablish his throne for ever. I will be his father, and he shall be my son: and I will not take my mercy away from him, as I took it from him that was before thee: But I will settle him in mine house and in my KINGDOM for ever: and his throne shall be established for evermore" (1 Chron. 17:11-14).

The Bible combination *I will establish* (10x), *his kingdom* (40x), *and I will stablish* (2x), *his throne for ever* (1x), *I will be his father and he shall be my son* (2x), *and I will not take my mercy away from him* (1x), *as I took it from him that was before thee* (1x), *but I will settle him in mine house* (1x), *and in my kingdom for ever* (1x), *and his throne shall be established for evermore* (1x) = 60.

King David's Dominion

"And David smote Hadarezer king of Zobah unto Hamath, <u>as he went to</u> <u>stablish his</u> <u>DOMINION</u> <u>by the river Euphrates</u>. . . . So David REIGNED over all Israel, and executed judgment and justice among all his people" (1 Chron. 18:3, 14). The Old Testament combination *as he went to* (3x), *stablish his* (2x), *dominion* (51x), *by the river Euphrates* (4x) = 60.

The King's Word

"And David said to Joab and to the rulers of the people, Go, number Israel from Beer-sheba even to Dan; and bring the number of them to me, that I may know it. And Joab answered, The LORD make his people an hundred times so many more as they be: but, my lord the king, are they not all my lord's servants? why then doth my lord require this thing? why will he be a cause of trespass to Israel? Nevertheless the king's <u>word</u> prevailed against Joab. Wherefore Joab departed, and went throughout all Israel, and came to Jerusalem" (1 Chron. 21:2-4) Again the word *word* occurs 60 times in the Psalms.

King David's Army Officers

and Jehiel the son of :and a scribe ,a wise man ,s uncle was a counsellor'Also Jonathan David" and Hushai the :s counsellor'And Ahithophel was the king :s sons'Hachmoni was with the king :s companion'Archite was the king <u>And after Ahithophel was Jehoiada</u> the son of Benaiah, <u>and</u> <u>Abiathar: and the general of</u> the <u>KING'S</u> <u>army</u> <u>was Joab</u>" (1 Chron. 27:32-34). The First and Second Chronicles combination *and after Ahithophel was Jehoiada* (1x), *the son of Benaiah* (2x), *and Abiathar* (2x), *and the general of* (1x), *the king's* (42x), *army* (11x), *was Joab* (1x) = 60.

The Throne of the Kingdom Belongs to the Lord

"And of all my sons, for the LORD hath given me many sons, he hath chosen Solomon my son to sit upon the throne of the KINGDOM of the <u>LORD</u> over Israel" (1 Chron. 28:5). Here the kingly title *Lord* is the 309,560th word of the Bible.

The Holy King's Chief Pleasure

David blessed the Lord before all the congregation of Israel. Of great importance he said, "I know also, my God, that thou triest the heart, and hast <u>pleasure</u> in uprightness" (1 Chron. 29:17). Here it is made evident that the righteous King of Heaven and Earth finds His greatest delight when His children walk in righteousness before Him. The word *pleasure* is mentioned in 60 verses of the Bible.

King David's Reign Reaches an Honorable End

"Thus David the son of Jesse <u>REIGNED</u> over all Israel. And the time that he REIGNED over Israel was forty years; seven years REIGNED he in Hebron, and thirty and three years REIGNED he in Jerusalem. And he died in a good old age, full of days, riches, and honour" (1

Chron. 29:26-28a). The underlined kingly word *reign* is the 311,060th word of the Bible.

God Magnified Solomon's Kingdom Exceedingly

"And Solomon the son of David was strengthened in his KINGDOM, and the LORD his God was with him, and magnified him exceedingly" (2 Chron. 1:1). Again the name *Solomon* occurs naturally 260 times in the OT Narrative. The Bible combination *magnified* (21x) and *exceedingly* (39x) = 60.

A 60-Cubits-Long Temple for the High King of Glory

"Now these are the things wherein Solomon was instructed for the building of the house of God. The length by cubits after the first measure was THREESCORE cubits, and the breadth twenty cubits" (2 Chron. 3:3). Here the word *cubits* is the 1260th word of this chapter.

60th Verse of Second Chronicles

"He made also ten tables, and placed them in the temple, five on the right side, and five on the left. And he made an hundred basons of gold" (2 Chron. 4:8). Solomon built the Temple for the High King of Glory, and if any king was worthy of gold it was Him. The Bible combination *an hundred basons* (1x), *of gold* (159x) = 160.

God's Everlasting Commitment to David's Kingly Dynasty

"Then will I stablish the throne of thy KINGDOM, according as I have covenanted with David thy father, saying, There shall not fail thee a man to be RULER in Israel" (2 Chron. 7:18). The OT Narrative combination *there shall not fail thee a man to* (1x), *be ruler in* (1x), *in Israel* (58x) = 60. Again the word *ruler* is mentioned naturally in 60 verses of the Old Testament.

11,360th Verse of the Bible

"Then Solomon offered burnt offerings unto the LORD on the altar of the LORD, which he had built before the porch, Even after a certain rate every day, offering according to the commandment of Moses, on the sabbaths, and on the new moons, and on the solemn feasts, three times in the year, even in the feast of unleavened bread, and in the feast of weeks, and in the feast of tabernacles" (2 Chron. 8:12-13). The underlined words indicate the 11,360th verse of the Bible, and they describe the king's recommendation concerning the sacrifices.

The King's Commandment & Order

"And he appointed, according to the order of David his father, the courses of the priests to their service, and the Levites to their charges, to praise and minister before the priests, as the duty of every day required: the porters also by their courses at every gate: for so had David the man of God commanded. And they departed not from the commandment of the KING unto the priests and Levites concerning any matter, or concerning the treasures" (2 Chron. 8:14-15). The word *order* occurs naturally 60 times in the Bible.

The King at Jerusalem

"And Solomon had four thousand stalls for horses and chariots, and twelve thousand horsemen; whom he bestowed in the chariot cities, and with the KING at Jerusalem" (2 Chron. 9:25). The phrase *at Jerusalem* occurs 60 times from Genesis to the Synoptic Gospels.

King Rehoboam

"And Solomon slept with his fathers, and he was buried in the city of David his father: and Rehoboam his son REIGNED in his stead" (2 Chron. 9:31). The OT Narrative combination *and Solomon slept with his fathers* (2x), *and he was buried in the city of David his father* (1x), *and Rehoboam his son* (2x), *reigned in his stead* (55x) = 60.

King Rehoboam's 60 Concubines & 60 Daughters

"And Rehoboam loved Maachah the daughter of Absalom above all his wives and his concubines: for he took eighteen wives, and THREESCORE concubines; and begat twenty and eight sons, and THREESCORE daughters" (2 Chron. 11:21). The word *daughters* occurs 60 times in the Major Prophets.

King Shishak's 60,000 Horsemen

"And it came to pass, that in the fifth year of king Rehoboam Shishak king of Egypt came up against Jerusalem, because they had transgressed against the LORD, With twelve hundred chariots, and THREESCORE thousand horsemen: and the people were without number that came with him out of Egypt; the Lubims, the Sukkiims, and the Ethiopians" (2 Chron. 12:2-3). The Bible combination *and threescore thousand* (1x), *horsemen* (59x) = 60.

King Abijah

"And Rehoboam slept with his fathers, and was buried in the city of David: and Abijah his son REIGNED in his stead. . . . Now in the eighteenth year of KING Jeroboam began Abijah to REIGN over Judah. He reigned three years in Jerusalem" (2 Chron. 12:16; 13:1-2a). In the underlined 260th verse of Second Chronicles the keyword *king* occurs.

11,460th Verse of the Bible

"Yet Jeroboam the son of Nebat, the servant of Solomon the son of David, is risen up, and hath rebelled against his lord" (2 Chron. 13:6). This 60th verse of the Bible records the rebellion of a king's servant.

King Asa

"So Abijah slept with his fathers, and they buried him in the city of David: and Asa his son REIGNED in his stead. In his days the land was quiet ten years. And Asa did that which was good and right in the eyes of the LORD his God" (2 Chron. 14:1-2). The name *Asa('s)* occurs 60 times in the Bible.

*** The Kings of Judah ***

"And, behold, the acts of Asa, first and last, lo, they are written in the book of the kings of Judah and Israel" (2 Chron. 16:11). As the book of Second Kings gives greater attention to the kings of Israel, Second Chronicles gives greater attention to the kings of Judah. Again the title *King of Judah* occurs 60 times in First and Second Kings.

King Jehoshaphat

"And Jehoshaphat his son reigned in his stead . . . And the LORD was with Jehoshaphat, because he walked in the first ways of his father David, and sought not unto Baalim; But sought to the LORD God of his father, and walked in his commandments . . . Therefore the LORD stablished the

KINGDOM in his hand; and all Judah brought to Jehoshaphat presents; and he had riches and honour in abundance" (2 Chron. 17:1a, 3-5). Again the phrase *in his stead* occurs 60 times in the OT Narrative.

11,560th Verse of the Bible

"And the KING of Israel said to Jehoshaphat, Did I not tell thee that he would not prophesy good unto me, but evil?" (2 Chron. 18:17). This 60th verse actually contains the keyword *king*.

King Jehoram

"Now Jehoshaphat slept with his fathers, and was buried with his fathers in the city of David. And Jehoram his <u>son</u> REIGNED in his stead. . . . Now when Jehoram was risen up to the kingdom of his father, he strengthened himself, and slew all his brethren with the sword, and divers also of the princes of Israel. Jehoram was thirty and two years old when he began to REIGN, and he REIGNED eight years in Jerusalem" (2 Chron. 21:1, 4-5). Here the word *son* is the 12,960th word of Second Chronicles, and it pertains to a king's son.

King Ahaziah

"And after all this the LORD smote him in his bowels with an incurable disease. And it came to pass, that in process of time, after the end of two years, his bowels fell out by reason of his sickness: so he died of sore diseases. And his people made no burning for him, like the burning of his fathers. . . . And the inhabitants of Jerusalem made Ahaziah his youngest son KING in his stead: for the band of men that came with the Arabians to the camp had slain all the eldest. So Ahaziah the son of Jehoram <u>KING of Judah</u> REIGNED" (2 Chron. 21:18-19; 22:1).

Again the title *King of Judah* occurs 60 times in First and Second Kings.

They Made Him King & Shouted "God Save the King"

It was little Joash's crowning day. "Then they brought out the KING'S son, and put upon him the CROWN, and gave him the testimony, and <u>made him</u> KING. And Jehoiada and his sons anointed him, and said, God <u>save</u> the KING" (2 Chron. 23:11). The unison blessing from the people was a prayer to God that praised His ability alone to preserve the king's life. The phrase *made him* occurs 60 times in the Bible. The word *save* occurs 60 times in the OT Narrative.

King Joash

"Joash was seven years old when he began to REIGN, and he REIGNED forty years in Jerusalem. His mother's name also was Zibiah of Beer-sheba. And <u>Joash did that which was right in the sight of the LORD all the days of Jehoiada the priest</u>" (2 Chron. 24:1-2). The OT Narrative combination *Joash* (47x), *did that which was right in the sight of the LORD* (12x), *all the days of Jehoiada the priest* (1x) = 60.

King Amaziah

"<u>And Amaziah his son REIGNED in his stead. Amaziah was twenty and five years old when he began to REIGN, and he REIGNED twenty and nine years</u> in Jerusalem. And his mother's name was Jehoaddan of Jerusalem. And he did that which was right in the sight of the LORD, but not with a perfect heart. The OT Narrative combination *and Amaziah his son* (2x), *reigned in his stead* (55x), *Amaziah was* (2x), *twenty and five years old when he began to reign and he reigned twenty and nine years* (1x) = 60.

King Uzziah

"Then all the people of Judah took Uzziah, who was sixteen years old, and made him king in the room of his father Amaziah. . . . Sixteen years old was Uzziah when he began to REIGN, and he REIGNED fifty and two years <u>in Jerusalem</u>. His mother's name also was Jecoliah of Jerusalem. And he did that which was right in the sight of the LORD" (2 Chron. 26:1, 3-4a). Again the phrase *in Jerusalem* is mentioned in 160 verses of the Bible.

King Jotham

"So Uzziah slept with his fathers . . . and Jotham his son <u>REIGNED in his stead</u> . . . Jotham was twenty and five years old when he began to REIGN, and he REIGNED <u>sixteen years in Jerusalem</u>. His mother's name also was Jerushah, the daughter of Zadok" (2 Chron. 26:23—27:1). The OT Narrative combination *reigned in his stead* (55x), *sixteen years in Jerusalem* (5x) = 60.

King Ahaz

"And Jotham slept with his fathers, and they buried him in the city of David: and Ahaz his son <u>REIGNED in his stead</u>. Ahaz was twenty years old when he began to REIGN, and he REIGNED <u>sixteen years in Jerusalem</u>: but he did not that which was right in the sight of the LORD, like David his father" (2 Chron. 27:9—28:1). Here the underlined word *in* is the 17660th word of Second Chronicles, and it is a grammatical part of a kingly expression. The OT Narrative combination *reigned in his stead* (55x), *sixteen years in Jerusalem* (5x) = 60.

King Hezekiah

"<u>And</u> Ahaz slept with his fathers . . . and Hezekiah his son <u>REIGNED in his</u> stead. Hezekiah began to REIGN when he was five and twenty years old, and he REIGNED nine and twenty years in Jerusalem. . . . And he did that which was right in the sight of the LORD, according to all that David his father had done. He in the first year of his REIGN, in the first month, opened the doors of the house of the LORD, and repaired them" (2 Chron. 28:27—28:1-3). Hezekiah is counted as the godliest Davidic king to rule over Judah. This verse presents the Bible's 60th occurrence of the phrase *reigned in his*, and the leading word of this verse *and* is the 860th word of Second Chronicles chapter twenty-eight.

King Manasseh

"<u>Manasseh</u> was twelve years old when he began to REIGN, and he REIGNED fifty and five years in Jerusalem: But did that which was evil in the sight of the LORD, like unto the abominations of the heathen, whom the LORD had cast out before the children of Israel. For he built again the high places which Hezekiah his father had broken down, and he reared up altars for Baalim, and made groves, and worshipped all the host of heaven, and served them" (2 Chron. 33:1-3). Just over half of Judah's kings were bad kings. Manasseh was the worst of them all. The name *Manasseh* is mentioned in 60 chapters of the Bible.

King Amon

"So Manasseh slept with his fathers, and they buried him in his own house: <u>and Amon his son REIGNED in his</u> stead. Amon was two and twenty years old when he began to REIGN, and REIGNED two years in Jerusalem. But he did that which was evil in the sight of the LORD, as did Manasseh his father: for Amon sacrificed unto all the carved images which Manasseh his

119

father had made, and served them" (2 Chron. 33:20-22). The Bible combination *and Amon his son reigned in his* (2 chs), *stead* (58 chs) = 60 chapters.

King Josiah

"Josiah was eight years old when he began to REIGN, and he REIGNED in Jerusalem one and thirty years. And he did that which was right in the sight of the LORD, and walked in the ways of David his father, and declined neither to the right hand, nor to the left. For in the eighth year of his REIGN, <u>while he was yet young, he began to seek after the God of David his father:</u> and in the twelfth year he began to purge Judah and Jerusalem from the high places, and the groves, and the carved images, and the molten images" (2 Chron. 34:1-3). The joined phrases *while he was yet young, he began to seek after the God of David his father:* consist of 60 characters!

The Scribe Told the King

"Then Shaphan the scribe <u>told</u> the KING, saying, Hilkiah the priest hath given me a book. And Shaphan read it KING" (2 Chron. 34:18). Again the word *told* is mentioned in 60 verses of the New Testament.

King Jehoahaz

"Then the people of the land took Jehoahaz the son of Josiah, and made him king in his father's stead in Jerusalem. Jehoahaz was twenty and three years old when he <u>began</u> to REIGN and he REIGNED three months in Jerusalem. . . . And the king of Egypt made Eliakim his brother king over Judah and Jerusalem, and turned his name to Jehoiakim. And Necho took Jehoahaz . . . and carried him to Egypt" (2 Chron. 36:1-2, 4). Here the word *began* is the 25,360th word of Second Chronicles, and it refers to the time when a king began to reign.

King Jehoiakim

"Jehoiakim was twenty and five years old when he began to REIGN, and he <u>REIGNED</u> eleven years in Jerusalem: and he did that which was evil in the sight of the LORD his God. Against him came up Nebuchadnezzar king of Babylon, and bound him in fetters, to carry him to Babylon" (2 Chron. 36:5-6). Again the word *reigned* is mentioned in 60 chapters of the OT Narrative.

King Jehoiachin

"Jehoiachin his son REIGNED in <u>his stead</u>. Jehoiachin was eight years old when he began to REIGN, and he REIGNED three months and ten days in Jerusalem: and he did that which was evil in the sight of the LORD. And when the year was expired, king Nebuchadnezzar sent, and brought him to Babylon, with the goodly vessels of the house of the LORD, and made Zedekiah his brother king over Judah and Jerusalem" (2 Chron. 36:8e-10). Not seen heretofore, the phrase *his stead* occurs 60 times in the OT Narrative.

King Zedekiah

"Zedekiah was one and twenty years old when he began to REIGN, and REIGNED eleven years <u>in Jerusalem.</u> And he did that which was evil in the sight of the LORD his God, and humbled not himself before Jeremiah the prophet speaking from the mouth of the LORD. And he also rebelled against king Nebuchadnezzar, who had made him swear by God . . . Therefore he brought upon them the KING of the Chaldees . . . And they burnt the house of God, and brake down the wall of Jerusalem . . . And them that had escaped from the sword carried he away to Babylon" (2 Chron.

36:11-13b, 17a, 19a, 20a). Again the phrase *in Jerusalem* is mentioned in 160 verses of the Bible.

The King's Saying
"Now in the first year of Cyrus KING of Persia, that the word of the LORD by the mouth of Jeremiah might be fulfilled, the LORD stirred up the spirit of Cyrus KING of Persia, that he made a proclamation throughout all his KINGDOM, and put it also in writing, saying, Thus saith Cyrus KING of Persia, The LORD God of heaven hath given me all the KINGDOMS of the EARTH; and he hath charged me to build him an house at Jerusalem, which is in Judah" (Ezra 1:1-2). Here an earthly king admitted he had been dictated to by the heavenly King. The word *saying* occurs naturally 60 times in First and Second Chronicles.

A Remnant of the Children of the Kingdom Returns—42,360
"The whole congregation together was forty and two thousand three hundred and THREESCORE" (Ezra 2:64). Their servants and maids accompanied them on the journey.

Kings of Persia—Cyrus & Darius
"And hired counsellors against them, to frustrate their purpose, all the days of Cyrus king of Persia, even until the REIGN of Darius king of Persia" (Ezra 4:5). The Bible combination *king/s of Persia* (16 vs), *Cyrus* (19 vs), *Darius* (25 vs) = 60 verses.

The King's Servants
"This is the copy of the letter that they sent unto him, even unto Artaxerxes the KING; Thy servants the men on this side the river, and at such a time" (Ezra 4:11). Earthly kings have servants of every sort. Again the phrase *thy servants* is mentioned in 60 chapters of the Bible.

The King's Decree
In the first year of Cyrus the KING the same Cyrus the KING made a decree concerning the house of God at Jerusalem, Let the house be builded, the place where they offered sacrifices, and let the foundations thereof be strongly laid; the height thereof THREESCORE cubits, and the breadth thereof THREESCORE cubits" (Ezra 6:3). This earthly king permitted the King of Israel's Temple to be, if necessary, a maximum of 60 cubits tall and 60 cubits wide!

The King's Realm
"Whatsoever is commanded by the God of heaven, let it be diligently done for the house of the God of heaven: for why should there be wrath against the REALM of the KING and his sons?" (Ezra 7:23) Here the underlined word *the* is the 660th word of this chapter, and it serves as the definite article for the keyword king.

Repairing the Royal City of King David
"But the gate of the fountain repaired Shallun the son of Col-hozeh, the ruler of part of Mizpah; he built it, and covered it, and set up the doors thereof, the locks thereof, and the bars thereof, and the wall of the pool of Siloah by the KING'S garden, and unto the stairs that go down from the city of David" (Neh. 3:15). The phrase *the city of* occurs 60 times in the OT Narrative. In this verse there are 60 words preceding the kingly name *David*.

Nehemiah 7:60

"All the Nethinims, and the children of Solomon's servants, were three hundred ninety and two" (Neh. 7:60). The Nethinims were Temple servants brought back from Babylon. By their kingly registry these servants held a more noble degree than ordinary servants did in the land.

The Queen

"To bring Vashti the QUEEN before the KING with the CROWN ROYAL, to shew the people and the princes her beauty: for she was fair to look on" (Est. 1:11). The Bible combination *for she was* (6x), *fair* (53x), *to look on* (1x) = 60.

The King's Harem

"Now when every maid's turn was come to go in to KING Ahasuerus, after that she had been twelve months, according to the manner of the women, for so were the days of their purifications accomplished, to wit, six months with oil of myrrh, and six months with sweet odours, and with other things for the purifying of the women" (Est. 2:12). This kingly verse consists of 60 words.

The King's Scribes

"Then were the KING'S scribes called on the thirteenth day of the first month, and there was written according to all that Haman had commanded unto the king's lieutenants, and to the governors that were over every province, and to the RULERS of every people of every province according to the writing thereof, and to every people after their language; in the name of king Ahasuerus was it written, and sealed with the KING'S ring" (Est. 3:12). The Gospels combination *scribes* (59x) and *the writing* (1x) = 60. This kingly verse is the 12,760th verse of the Bible.

60th Verse of Esther

"The posts went out, being hastened by the KING'S commandment, and the decree was given in Shushan the palace. And the KING and Haman sat down to drink; but the city Shushan was perplexed" (Est. 3:15). The keyword *king* actually occurs in this 60th verse.

Making Supplications to the King

"Also he gave him the copy of the writing of the decree that was given at Shushan to destroy them, to shew it unto Esther, and to declare it unto her, and to charge her that she should go in unto the KING, to make supplication unto him, and to make request before him for her people" (Est. 4:8). The word *supplication(s)* occurs 60 combined times in the Bible.

King Offers Queen Half of His Kingdom

"And the KING said again unto Esther on the second day at the banquet of wine, What is thy petition, QUEEN Esther? and it shall be granted thee: and what is thy request? and it shall be performed, even to the half of the KINGDOM" (Est. 7:2). The OT Narrative combination *what is thy petition queen Esther* (1x), *what is thy request and it shall be performed* (1x), *even to the half of* (2x), *the kingdom* (56x) = 60.

Mordecai's Kingly & Royal Appearance

"And Mordecai went out from the presence of the KING in ROYAL apparel, and with a great CROWN of gold, and with a garment of fine linen and purple: and the city of Shushan rejoiced and was glad" (Est. 8:15). This verse corresponds with our first definition of kingly: stately or splendid as resembling, suggesting, or befitting a king, regal. The name *Mordecai('s)* occurs 60 times in the Bible! The Bible combination *royal* (29x), *apparel* (28x), *and with a great crown of gold and with a garment* (1x), *of fine linen and purple* (2x) = 60.

The King Grants Esther Multiple Requests

"And the KING said unto Esther the queen, The Jews have slain and destroyed five hundred men in Shushan the palace, and the ten sons of Haman; what have they done in the rest of the KING'S provinces? now what is thy petition? and it shall be granted thee: or what is thy request further? and it shall be done" (Est. 9:12). There are 60 words in this king's-favor verse.

The King's Authority

"Then Esther the QUEEN, the daughter of Abihail, and Mordecai the Jew, wrote with all AUTHORITY, to confirm this second letter of Purim" (Est. 9:29). Here the king-related word *authority* is the 60,610th word of the Bible, a number from the 60,000 range.

The King's Right-Hand Man

After all the dust settled Mordecai became great in the kingdom of Persia. "For Mordecai the Jew was next unto KING Ahasuerus, and great among the Jews, and accepted of the multitude of his brethren, seeking the wealth of his people, and speaking peace to all his seed" (Est. 10:3). Mordecai was promoted from a humble position to a stately position next to the king. His rule at the king's right hand was splendid and regal. Again the name *Mordecai('s)* occurs 60 times in the Bible.

The King's Rest

"For now should I have lain still and been quiet, I should have slept: then had I been at rest, With KINGS and counsellors of the earth, which built desolate places for themselves; Or with princes that had gold, who filled their houses with silver" (Job 3:13-15). The Old Testament combination *have been* (59 vs), *at rest in mine house* (1 v) = 60 verses. Here the 362,060th word of the Bible rests next to the keyword king—*with*.

A King Ready for Battle

"Trouble and anguish shall make him afraid; they shall prevail against him, as a KING ready to the battle" (Job 15:24). Here the keyword *king* is the 60th word of this chapter.

Kings of the Earth Fight Together against God

"The KINGS of the earth set themselves, and the RULERS take counsel together, against the LORD, and against his anointed, saying" (Ps. 2:2). The Wisdom Books combination *the kings of the earth* (5x), *set themselves and the rulers take counsel* (1x), *together* (54x) = 60.

God's King Set upon His Holy Hill of Zion

"Yet have I set my KING upon my holy hill of Zion" (Ps. 2:6). This declaration refers to Messiah's post-resurrection days wherein He ascended to heaven and was placed at the Father's right hand to share His heavenly throne. The word *set* is mentioned in 60 chapters of the Wisdom Books. The word *upon* is found in 60 books of the Bible. The name *Zion* (59 chs) and *Zion's* (1 ch) = 60 chapters of the Major/Minor Prophets. The Bible combination *I set my king* (1x), *upon my* (5x), *holy hill* (54x) = 60.

Prophecy of the Messianic King's Pierced Hands & Feet

"<u>For dogs have compassed me: the assembly of the wicked have inclosed me:</u> they pierced my <u>hands</u> and my feet" (Ps. 22:16) The phrases *for dogs have compassed me: the assembly of the wicked have inclosed me:* consists of 60 characters! The phrase *his hands* occurs naturally 60 times in the Old Testament.

Earth's Globally Governing King

"For the KINGDOM is the LORD'S: and he is the <u>GOVERNOR</u> among the nations" (Ps. 22:28). The Lord's governorship over the nations will be clearly demonstrated at the end of days. Again the kingly title *governor('s)* occurs 60 times in the Bible.

The King of Glory

"Lift up your heads, O ye gates; and be ye lift up, ye everlasting doors; and the KING of glory shall come in. <u>Who is</u> this KING of glory? The LORD strong and mighty, the LORD mighty in battle. Lift up your heads, O ye gates; even lift them up, ye everlasting doors; and the KING of glory shall come in. <u>Who is</u> this KING of glory? The LORD *of hosts,* <u>he is</u> the KING of glory. Selah" (Ps. 24:7-10). The phrase *of hosts* is mentioned in 60 verses of Isaiah.

The NT combination *who is* (59x), *the King of kings* (1x) = 60.
The Bible combination *he is* (359x), *Christ the King* (1x) = 360!

The King's Scepter

"Thy throne, O God, is <u>for ever and ever: the sceptre of thy KINGDOM</u> is a right sceptre" (Ps. 45:6). The Bible combination *for ever and ever* (46x), *the scepter* (8x), *of thy kingdom* (6x) = 60.

City of the Great King

"Beautiful for <u>situation,</u> the joy of <u>the whole EARTH,</u> is mount Zion, on the sides of the north, <u>the city of the great KING</u>" (Ps. 48:2). Zion is a euphemistic name for Jerusalem. God delighted to dwell there among His people in joyful Spirit. Again the phrase *the city of* occurs 60 times in the OT Narrative. The Bible combination *situation* (2x) and *habitation* (58x) = 60. The Bible combination *habitation* (58x) and *city of the great King* (2x) = 60. Again the Jeremiah combination *king of* (157x) and *the whole earth* (3x) = 160. The New Testament combination *name of* (59x) and *the great King* (1x) = 60.

Psalm 60

David wrote about a difficult time he faced in war. It was a time when he had to greatly rely on his Theocratic King in heaven of whom he said, "Thou hast given a banner to them that fear thee, that it may be displayed because of the truth. Selah. That thy beloved may be delivered; save with thy <u>right hand,</u> and hear me" (Ps. 60:4-5). Kings, generals, and captains had their military banners in time of war. Each flag had its own insignia and was displayed atop a staff or pole so their troops could better follow them. As kings usually went out in the midst of the battle, David spoke thus of the Theocratic King's unseen presence leading the people's way into battle. Again the phrase *the right hand* occurs 60 times in the Bible.

"God hath spoken in his holiness; I will rejoice, I will divide Shechem, and mete out the valley of Succoth. Gilead is <u>mine</u>, and Manasseh is <u>mine</u>; Ephraim also is the strength of <u>mine</u> head; Judah is my lawgiver; Moab is my washpot; over Edom will I cast out my shoe: Philistia, triumph thou because of me" (vv. 6-8). God spoke as a King who had recently conquered territories and now sought to divide up the newly conquered lands and do with them as He pleased. Again the word *mine* is mentioned in 60 chapters of the OT Narrative.

David ends this Psalm by placing all hope in his valiant Theocratic King. "Give us help from trouble: for vain is the help of man. Through God we <u>shall do</u> valiantly: for he <u>it is</u> that shall tread down our <u>enemies</u>" (vv. 11-12). Again the phrase *shall do* occurs 60 times in the Old Testament. The phrase *it is* can be found in 60 books of the Bible. Again the word *enemies* is mentioned in 260 verses of the Bible.

Psalm 78:60

"So that he forsook <u>the tabernacle of Shiloh, the</u> <u>tent</u> which he placed among men" (Ps. 78:60). The Theocratic King of Israel is described as having departed the place of His earthly habitation. Again the phrase *the tabernacle of the* is mentioned in 60 verses of Numbers. The law combination *Shiloh* (1x) and *tent* (59x) = 60.

Psalm 119:60 & 119:160

"I made haste, and delayed not to keep <u>thy</u> <u>commandments</u>. . . . <u>Thy</u> word is true from the beginning: and every one of <u>thy</u> righteous <u>judgments</u> endureth for ever" (Ps. 119:60, 160). David delighted in keeping the Theocratic King's commandments. Again the Bible phrases *my commandments* (31 vs) and *my judgments* (29 vs) = 60 verses. The word *thy* is mentioned in 60 verses of Second Chronicles.

600th Chapter of the Bible

"I was glad when they said unto me, Let us go into the house of the LORD. Our feet shall stand within thy <u>gates</u>, O Jerusalem. Jerusalem is builded as a city that is compact together: Whither the tribes go up, the tribes of the LORD, unto the testimony of Israel, to give thanks unto the name of the LORD. For there are set <u>thrones of</u> judgment, the <u>thrones of</u> the house of David. <u>Pray for the peace</u> of Jerusalem: they shall prosper that love thee. Peace be within thy walls, and prosperity within thy palaces. For my brethren and companions' sakes, I will now say, Peace be within thee. Because of the house of the LORD our God I will seek thy good" (Ps. 122).

This Psalm pays homage to the holy House belonging to Israel's great Theocratic King. To pray for the peace of Jerusalem is to pray for King Messiah to take up His residence there, ruling and reigning in prosperity. The word *gate* occurs 260 times in the Old Testament. Again the phrase *throne(s) of* occurs 60 times in the Bible. The Old Testament combination *pray for the peace* (1x), *of Jerusalem* (159x) = 160.

Theocratic King's Everlasting Kingdom & Dominion

"Thy KINGDOM is an <u>everlasting</u> <u>KINGDOM</u>, and thy DOMINION endureth throughout all generations" (Ps. 145:13). The Matthew's Gospel combination *everlasting* (4x), *kingdom* (56x) = 60.

Praise the Great King on High!

"<u>Praise ye the LORD</u>. <u>Praise God</u> <u>in his sanctuary</u>: <u>praise him</u> <u>in the firmament of his POWER</u>"

(Ps. 150:1). The Old Testament combination *praise ye the LORD* (25x), *praise God* (1x), *in his sanctuary* (2x), *praise him* (22x), *in the firmament* (5x), *of his power* (5x) = 60!

"Praise him for his mighty acts: praise him according to his excellent greatness" (v. 2). The Old Testament combination *praise him for his/the* (2x), *mighty acts* (4x), *praise him* (22x), *according to his excellent* (1x), *greatness* (31x) = 60!

"Praise him with the sound of the trumpet: praise him with the psaltery and harp" (v. 3). The Old Testament combination *praise him* (22x), *with the sound* (5x), *of the trumpet* (19x), *praise him with* (4x), *the psaltery* (5x), *and harp* (5x) = 60!

"Praise him with the timbrel and dance: praise him with stringed instruments and organs" (v. 4). The Old Testament combination *praise him* (22x), *with timbrels* (4x), *with the timbrel and* (2x), *dance* (8x), *praise him* (22x), *with stringed instruments* (1x), *and organs* (1x) = 60!

2460th Verse of Psalms

"Praise him upon the loud cymbals: praise him upon the high sounding cymbals" (Ps. 150:5). The pomp and ceremony of any king's honor was typically accompanied by blaring brass instruments such as trumpets and cymbals. Again the word *trumpet* is mentioned in 60 verses of the Bible. The word *loud* occurs 60 times in the Bible and is mentioned in 60 verses thereof. The Psalms combination *praise* (158x) and *cymbals* (2x) = 160!

Earthly Kings Put on the Throne by Divine Oversight

"By me KINGS REIGN, and princes decree justice. By me princes rule, and nobles, even all the judges of the earth" (Prov. 8:15-16). The Old Testament combination *princes* (159 chs), *decree justice* (1 ch) = 160 chapters.

The King's Favor

"The KING'S favour is toward a wise servant: but his wrath is against him that causeth shame" (Prov. 13:45). Here the 560th word of this chapter is *toward*.

The King's Delight

"Righteous lips are the delight of KINGS; and they love him that speaketh right" (16:13). The Old Testament combination *delight* (49 vs), *of kings* (11 vs) = 60 verses.

The King's Grandchildren

"Children's children are the CROWN of old men; and the glory of children are their fathers" (Prov. 17:6). Again all forms of the word *crown* are mentioned in 60 verses of the Old Testament. The New Testament combination *children's* (3x), *children* (157x) = 160.

The King's Wrath

"The KING'S wrath is as the roaring of a lion; but his favour is as dew upon the grass" (Prov. 19:12). The word *wrath* is mentioned in 60 verses of the Wisdom Books.

The King's Heart

"The KING'S heart is in the hand of the LORD, as the rivers of water: he turneth it whithersoever he will" (Prov. 21:1). The word *heart* is mentioned in 360 chapters of the Old Testament.

The King's Righteousness

"When the <u>righteous</u> are in AUTHORITY, the people rejoice: but when the wicked beareth rule, the people mourn" (Prov. 29:2). The word *righteous* occurs 60 times in the Psalms.

The King's Judgment

"The KING by <u>judgment</u> establisheth the land: but he that receiveth gifts overthroweth it" (Prov. 29:4). The word *judgment* is mentioned in 60 chapters of the Major and Minor Prophets.

660th Chapter of the Bible

"The words of the <u>Preacher</u>, the son of David, KING <u>in Jerusalem</u>. . . . I the Preacher was <u>KING over</u> Israel in Jerusalem" (Eccles. 1:1, 12). This 660th chapter of the Bible was written by a king. The word *preached* occurs 60 times in the New Testament. Again the phrase *in Jerusalem* is mentioned in 160 verses of the Bible. Again the phrase *king over* is mentioned in 60 verses of the Bible.

The King's Commandment

"I counsel thee to keep the KING'S <u>commandment</u>, and that in regard of the oath of God" (Eccle. 8:2). The word *commandment* is mentioned naturally in 60 verses of the OT Narrative.

The King's Word & Power

"Where the <u>word</u> of a KING is, there is <u>power</u>: and who may say unto him, What doest thou?" (Eccle. 8:4) Again the word *word* occurs 60 times in the Psalms. The word *power* is mentioned in 260 verses of the Bible.

King Solomon's 60 Chamber Guards & 60 Queens

"Behold his bed, which is <u>Solomon's</u>; THREESCORE valiant men are about it, of the valiant of Israel. . . . There are THREESCORE queens, and fourscore <u>concubines</u>, and virgins without number" (Song 3:7; 6:8). Solomon wrote this love song in the early part of his reign. Thus the full number of his wives and concubines is fewer here than it would eventually become. The Bible combination *concubines* (17x) and *of Solomon* (43x) = 60.

Behold King Solomon & His Wedding-Day Chariot

"KING Solomon made himself a <u>chariot</u> of the wood of Lebanon. He made the pillars thereof of silver, the bottom thereof of gold, the covering of it of purple, the midst thereof being paved with love, for the daughters of Jerusalem. Go forth, O ye <u>daughters</u> of Zion, and <u>behold</u> KING Solomon with the CROWN wherewith his mother CROWNED him in the day of his espousals, and in the day of the gladness of his heart" (Song 3:9-11). Again the word *chariot* occurs naturally 60 times in the Old Testament. The word *behold* occurs 60 times in Matthew. Again the word *daughters* occurs 60 times in the Major Prophets.

60th Verse of Isaiah

"In that day shall he swear, saying, I will not be an healer; for in my house is neither bread nor clothing: make me not a <u>RULER</u> OF THE PEOPLE" (Isa. 3:7). In that day of calamity no person will want to inherit society's problems. Again the word *ruler* is mentioned naturally in 60 verses of the Old Testament.

King Whose Title Is the Lord of Hosts

"Then said I, Woe is me! for I am undone; because I am a man of unclean lips, and I dwell in the midst of a people of unclean lips: for mine eyes have seen the KING, the LORD <u>of hosts</u>" (Isa. 6:5). Again the phrase *of hosts* is mentioned in 60 verses of Isaiah.

King Immanuel, the Virgin-Born Son of God

"Therefore the Lord himself shall give you a sign; Behold, a virgin shall <u>conceive</u>, and bear <u>a son</u>, and shall call his name Immanuel" (Isa. 7:14). The virgin's miraculous conception was for the purpose of bringing unto Israel their divinely promised King. The word *conceive(ed)* occurs a combined 60 times in the Bible. This kingly verse presents the Bible's 60th occurrence of the phrase *a son*, and it refers to the Kingly Son.

160th Verse of Isaiah

"Now therefore, behold, the Lord bringeth up upon them the waters of the river, strong and many, even <u>the KING of Assyria</u>, <u>and all his glory</u>: and he shall come up over all his channels, and go over all his banks" (Isa. 8:7). The Bible combination *the king of Assyria* (59 vs), *and all his glory* (1 v) = 60 verses.

Messianic Prince of Peace

"For unto us a child is born, unto us a son is given: and the <u>government</u> shall be upon his shoulder: and his name shall be called Wonderful, Counsellor, The mighty God, The everlasting Father, The PRINCE of <u>Peace</u>" (Isa. 9:6). These titles exemplify the heavenly glory of earth's Incarnate King. Again the title *governor('s)* occurs a combined 60 times in the Bible. The words *peace* (59 bks) and *peacemakers* (1 bk) = 60 books.

The Messianic King's Perfect Government

"Of the <u>increase</u> <u>of his government</u> and peace there shall be no end, upon the throne of David, and upon his KINGDOM, to order it, and to establish it with judgment and with justice from henceforth even for ever. The zeal of the LORD of hosts will perform this" (Isa. 9:7). The Incarnate King will install peace on the earth such as has never been seen before in the history of human government. The Old Testament combination *increase* (59 chs), *of his government* (1 ch) = 60 chapters.

King of Babylon

"That thou shalt take up this proverb against the KING of <u>Babylon</u>, and say, How hath the oppressor ceased! the golden city ceased!" (Isa. 14:4) The name *Babylon* occurs 60 times in the OT Narrative.

The Name of Israel's Divine King

"O LORD our God, other lords beside thee have had DOMINION over us: but by thee only will we make mention of thy <u>name</u>" (Isa. 26:13). The Isaiah combination *name* (57x), *of the king* (3x) = 50.

Israel's Gloriously Crowned King

"In that day shall the LORD of hosts be for a <u>CROWN</u> of glory, and for a DIADEM of beauty, unto the residue of his people" (Isa. 28:5). Again all forms of the word *crown* are mentioned in

60 verses of the Old Testament.

Behold the Messianic King Who Reigns in Righteousness!

"Behold, a KING shall REIGN in righteousness, and princes shall rule in judgment" (Isa. 32:1). Again the word *behold* occurs 60 times in Matthew. The Bible combination *shall reign* (22x), *in righteousness* (25x), *and princes* (12x), *shall rule in judgment* (1x) = 60.

The King of Heaven & Earth

"O LORD of hosts, God of Israel, that dwellest between the cherubims, thou art the God, even thou alone, of all the KINGDOMS of the EARTH: thou hast made heaven and EARTH" (Isa. 37:16).

The word *heaven* occurs 60 times in the Wisdom Books.

The word *earth* occurs 60 times in the Minor Prophets.

Prepare the Highway for Our Heaven-Sent King

"The voice of him that crieth in the wilderness, Prepare ye the way of the LORD, make straight in the desert a highway for our God. Every valley shall be exalted, and every mountain and hill shall be made low: and the crooked shall be made straight, and the rough places plain: And the glory of the LORD shall be revealed, and all flesh shall see it together: for the mouth of the LORD hath spoken it" (Isa. 40:3-5). Here the word valley implies a pothole in the road, and the mountain and hill implies a big or small bump in the road. Again the Old Testament combination *the king's* (256 vs), *high way* (4 vs) = 260 verses. The phrase *for our* occurs 60 times in the Bible.

1060th Verse of Isaiah

"He is despised and rejected of men; a man of sorrows, and acquainted with grief: and we hid as it were our faces from him; he was despised, and we esteemed him not" (Isa. 53:3). This prophecy foretold that Israel's Messianic King would be despised by His own people. The word *despised* occurs 60 times in Scripture.

Messianic King Offered up for His People's Sin

"Yet it pleased the LORD to bruise him; he hath put him to grief: when thou shalt make his soul an offering for sin, he shall see his seed, he shall prolong his days, and the pleasure of the LORD shall prosper in his hand" (Isa. 53:10). The Lord offered up Israel's Messianic King as a ransom for the people's sin, so they might thereafter go out justified and free. The phrase *an offering* is mentioned in 60 verses of the Old Testament.

60th Chapter of Isaiah

This 60th chapter describes the golden millennial age when the Messianic King will have returned to Earth to set up His worldwide kingdom in the land of Israel among His covenant Hebrew people.

As it is universally customary to rise from one's seated position in a king's presence, so the prophet told Israel, "Arise, shine; for thy light is come, and the glory of the LORD is risen upon thee . . . and his glory shall be seen upon thee" (Isa. 60:1-2). Right on cue the uppercase word *Arise* occurs 60 times from Genesis to Matthew. The Bible combination *the glory* (59 chs) and *is risen upon thee* (1 ch) = 60 chapters.

"And the Gentiles shall come to thy light, and KINGS to the brightness of thy rising" (v. 3). During the coming golden age, earthly kings will desperately long to make their way to Israel to behold the glory of the Incarnate King. When these earthly Gentile kings come before the Great Messianic King they will bow low before Him in humble adoration. The keyword *kings* is found three additional places in this 60th chapter.

Not only will nobility come to pay homage to Israel and her reigning Messianic King but also less desirable ones will come. "The sons also of them that afflicted thee shall come bending unto thee; and all they that despised thee shall bow themselves down at the soles of thy feet; and they shall call thee, The city of the LORD, The Zion of the Holy One of Israel" (v. 14). Again the phrase *the city of* occurs 60 times in the OT Narrative.

The Messianic King will bring abounding peace and safety to Israel. "Violence shall no more be heard in thy land, wasting nor destruction within thy borders; but thou shalt call thy walls Salvation, and thy gates Praise" (v. 18). Again the word *gate* occurs 260 times in the Old Testament.

The Lord Is an Everlasting King

Jeremiah testified to Israel, "But the LORD is the true God, he is the living God, and an everlasting KING: at his wrath the EARTH shall tremble, and the nations shall not be able to abide his indignation" (Jer. 10:10). The joined phrases *but the LORD is the true God, he is the living God, and an everlasting king* consist of 60 characters!

The King of Righteousness

"Behold, the days come, saith the LORD, that I will raise unto David a righteous Branch, and a KING shall REIGN and prosper, and shall execute judgment and justice in the earth. In his days Judah shall be saved, and Israel shall dwell safely: and this is his name whereby he shall be called, THE LORD OUR RIGHTEOUSNESS" (Jer. 23:5-6). Again the Bible combination *a king* (48x) and *a kingdom* (12x) = 60. Again the word *righteous* occurs 60 times in the Psalms.

Surrender to the King of Babylon

"Hearken not unto them; serve the KING of Babylon, and live: wherefore should this city be laid waste?" (Jer. 27:17) This verse presents the 60th occurrence of the word *king* in Jeremiah, and it is a command from Jeremiah to King Zedekiah summarizing the theme of Jeremiah's whole ministry. He was to convince the king of Judah not to listen to his false prophets but rather Jeremiah—the true prophetic voice of God—and surrender to Babylon's army when it arrived. Again the name *Babylon* occurs 60 times in the OT Narrative.

All the Kingdoms of King Nebuchadnezzar's Dominion

"The word which came unto Jeremiah from the LORD, when Nebuchadnezzar KING of Babylon, and all his army, and all the kingdoms of the EARTH of his DOMINION, and all the people, fought against Jerusalem, and against all the cities thereof, saying" (Jer. 34:1). Again the name *Babylon* occurs 60 times in the OT Narrative. The Major Prophets combination *the king of Babylon* (59 vs) and *all the kingdoms of the earth of his dominion* (1v) = 60 verses.

All the Kingdoms of the Earth

"Therefore thus saith the LORD; Ye have not hearkened unto me, in proclaiming liberty, every one to his brother, and every man to his neighbour: behold, I proclaim a liberty for you, saith the LORD, to the sword, to the pestilence, and to the famine; and I will make you to be removed into <u>all</u> the KINGDOMS of <u>the earth</u>" (Jer. 34:17). Again the phrase *all the earth* occurs 60 times in the Old Testament. This kingdom verse is comprised of 60 words.

Zedekiah, the Last King of Judah

"Then he put out the eyes of <u>Zedekiah</u>; and the KING of Babylon bound him in chains, and carried him to Babylon, and put him in prison till the day of his death" (Jer. 52:11). The name *Zedekiah* is mentioned in 60 verses of the Bible. This is the 60th verse-mention of his name.

Last King of Judah Comes Forth out of Prison

"And it came to pass in the seven and thirtieth year of the captivity of Jehoiachin <u>KING of Judah</u>, in the twelfth month, in the five and twentieth day of the month, that Evil-merodach KING of Babylon in the first year of his reign lifted up the head of Jehoiachin <u>KING of Judah</u>, and brought him forth out of prison" (Jer. 52:31). Again the title *King of Judah* occurs 60 times in First and Second Kings. There are 60 words in this captor-king verse.

Jerusalem's King Has Been Taken Captive

"Her gates are sunk into the ground; he hath destroyed and broken her bars: <u>her</u> KING and her princes are among the Gentiles: the law is no more; her prophets also find no vision from the LORD" (Lam. 2:9).

The word *her* is mentioned in 160 verses of the NTN.
The word *her* is mentioned in 360 chapters of the Bible.

The Son of God's Kingly Throne

"And above the firmament that was over their heads was the likeness of a throne, as the appearance of a sapphire stone: and upon the likeness of the THRONE was the likeness as the appearance of a MAN above upon it. And I saw as the colour of amber, as the appearance of fire round about within it, from the appearance of his loins even upward, and from the appearance of his loins even downward, I saw as it were the appearance of fire, and it had brightness round about. As the appearance of the bow that is in the cloud in the day of rain, so was the appearance of the brightness round about. This was the appearance of the likeness of the glory of the LORD. And when I saw it, I fell upon my face, and I heard a voice of one that spake" (Ezek. 1: 26-28).

Again the word *man* is found in 60 books of the Bible.

Israel's Faithful Shepherd King

"As the holy flock, as the flock of Jerusalem in her solemn feasts; so shall the waste cities be filled with flocks of men: and they <u>shall know that I am</u> the LORD" (Ezek. 36:38). A king's scepter symbolizes the shepherd's rod with which he protects his flock from predators. The phrase *shall know that I am* occurs 60 times in the Bible.

One Kingdom & One King over Israel

The Lord promised that in the latter days the Israelites will be a united people. "And I will make them <u>one</u> nation in the land upon the mountains of Israel; and <u>one</u> KING shall be KING to them all: and they shall be no more two nations, neither shall they be divided into two KINGDOMS any more at all" (Ezek. 37:22).

The word *one* occurs 60 times in the Chronicles.
The word *one* is mentioned in 60 verses of Jeremiah.
The word *one* occurs 1360 times in the Old Testament.
The word *one* occurs 60 times in John's Gospel.

Temple Court Posts of 60 Cubits

"He made also posts of THREESCORE cubits, even unto the post of the court round about the gate" (Ezek. 40:14). Here the key number *threescore* is the 560,420th word of the Bible, a number from the 560,000 range.

All Kingdoms Will Crumble at King Messiah's Coming

Nebuchadnezzar lost memory of his dream until Daniel retold it to him: "Then was the iron, the clay, the brass, the silver, and the gold, broken to pieces together, and became like the chaff of the summer threshingfloors; and the wind carried them away, that no place was found for them: and the stone that smote the image became a great <u>mountain</u>, and filled the whole EARTH" (Dan. 2:35). The Bible sometimes uses a mountain as a metaphor for a kingdom. The phrase *the mountain* is mentioned in 60 verses of the Bible.

60th Verse of Daniel

"And after thee shall arise <u>another</u> <u>KINGDOM</u> inferior to thee, and <u>another</u> third <u>KINGDOM</u> of brass, which shall bear all the EARTH" (Dan. 2:39). Here Daniel referred to the kingdom of Persia being followed by the kingdom of Greece. The word *another* occurs 60 times in the Major Prophets. Again the word *kingdom* is mentioned in 60 chapters of the OT Narrative.

Nebuchadnezzar's Kingly Image—60 Cubits High

"<u>Nebuchadnezzar</u> the KING made <u>an image of gold, whose</u> <u>height</u> was THREESCORE cubits, and the breadth thereof six cubits: he set it up in the plain of Dura, in the province of Babylon" (Dan. 3:1). The name *Nebuchadnezzar* occurs 60 times in the Bible. The Old Testament combination *an image of gold whose* (1x), *height* (59x) = 60.

The Most High King's Everlasting Dominion

"And at the end of the days I Nebuchadnezzar lifted up mine eyes unto heaven, and mine understanding returned unto me, and I blessed the most High, and I praised and honoured him that liveth for ever, whose DOMINION is an <u>everlasting</u> <u>DOMINION</u>, and his KINGDOM is from generation to generation" (Dan. 4:34). The Major and Minor Prophets combination *everlasting* (36x), *dominion* (24x) = 60.

King Belshazzar's Great Feast for a Thousand Lords

"Belshazzar the <u>KING</u> made a great feast to a thousand of his lords, and drank wine before the thousand. Belshazzar, whiles he tasted the wine, commanded to bring the golden and silver vessels which his father Nebuchadnezzar had taken out of the temple which [was] in Jerusalem; that the KING, and his princes, his wives, and his concubines, might drink therein" (Dan. 5:1-2). Here the underlined keyword *king* is the 572,760th word of the Bible. There are 60 naturally occurring words in this king's-feast passage; the bracketed word was supplied by the translators.

Belshazzar's Kingly Throne

"But when his heart was lifted up, and his mind hardened in pride, he was deposed from his KINGLY throne, and they took his glory from him" (Dan. 5:20). This verse presents the Bible's only occurrence of the adjective *kingly*, and it is the 573,460th word of the Bible!

Belshazzar Promoted Daniel to Kingly Status

"Then commanded Belshazzar, and they clothed Daniel with scarlet, and put a chain of gold about his neck, and made a proclamation concerning him, that he should be the third RULER in the KINGDOM" (Dan. 5:29). This verse corresponds with our first definition of kingly: stately or splendid as resembling, suggesting, or befitting a king, regal. The Bible combination *they clothed Daniel with* (1x), *scarlet* (52x), *and put a chain of gold* (1x), *about his neck* (6x) = 60. Again the word *ruler* is mentioned naturally in 60 verses of the Old Testament.

Darius Promoted Daniel to Kingly Status

"Then this Daniel was preferred above the presidents and princes, because an excellent spirit was in him; and the KING thought to set him over the whole REALM" (Dan. 6:3). Again the word *set* is mentioned in 60 chapters of the Wisdom Books.

Saints to Reign with Messiah in His Forever Kingdom

"And the KINGDOM and DOMINION, and the greatness of the KINGDOM under the whole heaven, shall be given to the people of the saints of the most High, whose KINGDOM is an everlasting KINGDOM, and all DOMINIONS shall serve and obey him" (Dan. 7:27). Again the word *heaven* occurs 60 times in the Wisdom Books. The title *saints* occurs 60 times in the New Testament.

King over the Chaldeans

"In the first year of Darius the son of Ahasuerus, of the seed of the Medes, which was made KING over the REALM of the Chaldeans" (Dan. 9:1). Again the phrase *king over* is mentioned in 60 verses of the Bible.

Fortress of the King

"But out of a branch of her roots shall one stand up in his estate, which shall come with an army, and shall enter into the fortress of the KING of the north, and shall deal against them, and shall prevail" (Dan. 11:7). Here the definite article *the* is the 260th word of this chapter, and it serves as the definite article for the keyword king.

Israel's Northern Kingdom to Cease

"And the LORD said unto him, Call his name Jezreel; for yet a little while, and I will avenge the blood of Jezreel upon the house of Jehu, and will cause to cease the KINGDOM of the house of Israel" (Hos. 1:4). The word *cease* is mentioned in 60 chapters of the Old Testament.

God Gives Disobedient Nations Bad King as a Form of Judgment

"I gave thee a KING in mine anger, and took him away in my wrath" (Hos. 13:11). Here the keyword *king* is the 260th word of this chapter.

The Theocratic King's Coming Judgment

As it is customary to sound a trumpet to recognize that a king is about to enter his people's presence, so the Theocratic King of Israel warns Israel to prepare against His coming judgment day. "Blow ye the <u>trumpet</u> in Zion, and sound an alarm in my holy mountain: let all the inhabitants of the land tremble: for the day of the LORD cometh, for it is nigh at hand" (Joel 2:1). Again the word *trumpet* is mentioned in 60 verses of the Bible.

The LORD Is King in Zion

"And he said, The <u>LORD</u> will roar from Zion, and utter his voice from Jerusalem; and the habitations of the shepherds shall mourn, and the top of Carmel shall wither" (Amos 1:2). Again the kingly title *LORD* occurs 60 times in Amos.

The King's Chapel & Court

"But prophesy not again any more at Beth-el: for it is the KING'S chapel, and it is the KING'S <u>court</u>" (Amos 7:13). The word *court* occurs 60 times in the Major and Minor Prophets.

When the Kingdom of Israel Becomes Overruled by the Lord

"And saviours shall come up on mount Zion to judge the mount of Esau; and the KINGDOM shall be the LORD'S" (Obad. 1:21). Again the kingly title *LORD* occurs 60 times in Amos.

King of Assyria Gives Nineveh a Dire Decree

"And he caused it to be <u>proclaimed</u> and published through Nineveh by the decree of the <u>KING</u> and his NOBLES, saying, Let neither man nor beast, herd nor flock, taste any thing: let them <u>not feed, nor drink water</u>: But let man and beast be covered with sackcloth, and cry mightily unto God: yea, let them turn every one from his evil way, and from the violence that is in their hands. Who can tell if God will turn and repent, and turn away from his fierce anger, that we perish not?" (Jonah 3:7-9) The OT Narrative combination *king of Assyria* (56x), *proclaimed a fast* (3x), *Nineveh* (1x) = 60.

The Messianic King Will Be Born in a City near Jerusalem

"And thou, O tower of the flock, the strong hold of the daughter of Zion, unto thee shall it come, even the first DOMINION; <u>the KINGDOM shall come to the daughter of Jerusalem</u>" (Mic. 4:8). As it turned out, that city was Bethlehem. The Old Testament combination *the kingdom shall come to the daughter* (1x), *of Jerusalem* (159x) = 160.

Heaven's King to Become the Earth's Incarnate King

"But thou, Beth-lehem Ephratah, though thou be little among the thousands of Judah, yet out of thee <u>shall he</u> come forth unto me that is to be <u>RULER</u> in Israel; whose goings forth <u>have been from of old</u>, from everlasting" (Mic. 5:2). This Messianic verse presents the Bible's 60th verse-mention of the word *ruler*, and it speaks of the eternal King of Heaven. Again the word *ruler* is mentioned naturally in 60 verses of the Old Testament. The phrase *shall he* occurs 60 times in the Major and Minor Prophets. The Bible combination *have been from* (1 v), *of old* (59x) = 60.

The King's Scoffers

"And they shall scoff at <u>the</u> KINGS, and the princes shall be a scorn unto them: they shall deride every strong hold; for they shall heap dust, and take it" (Hab. 1:10). Here the word *the* is the

598,060th word of the Bible, and it serves as the definite article for the keyword king.

The King's Children
"And it shall come to pass in the day of the LORD'S sacrifice, that I will punish the princes, and the KING'S children, and all such as are clothed with strange apparel" (Zeph. 1:8). The New Testament combination *the king's* (3x), *children* (157x) = 160.

Kingdoms Overthrown
"And I will overthrow the throne of KINGDOMS, and I will destroy the strength of the KINGDOMS of the heathen; and I will overthrow the chariots, and those that ride in them; and the horses and their riders shall come down, every one by the sword of his brother" (Hag. 2:22). Again the phrase *throne(s) of* occurs 60 times in the Bible.

Zerubbabel & the King's Authoritative Signet Ring
"In that day, saith the LORD of hosts, will I take thee, O Zerubbabel, my servant, the son of Shealtiel, saith the LORD, and will make thee as a signet: for I have chosen thee, saith the LORD of hosts" (Hag. 2:23). This verse presents the Bible's 60th verse-mention of the phrase *my servant*, and it refers to the Lord's a special servant who was charged with overseeing the nation's governmental affairs. Although Zerubbabel was only a governor, he was to rule like a king—with full authority, power, and confidence.

Prophecy of the Priestly King
"Behold the man whose name is The BRANCH; and he shall grow up out of his place, and he shall build the temple of the LORD: Even he shall build the temple of the LORD; and he shall bear the glory, and shall sit and RULE upon his throne; and he shall be a priest upon his throne: and the counsel of peace shall be between them both" (Zech. 6:12b-13). This prophecy speaks of Messiah coming to Earth and building His Temple to sit in it acting as both Priest and King. The title *the high priest* occurs 60 times in Scripture. Verse twelve is the 22,960th verse of the Bible.

King Messiah Will Ride into Jerusalem upon a Donkey
"Rejoice greatly, O daughter of Zion; shout, O daughter of Jerusalem: behold, thy KING cometh unto thee: he is just, and having salvation; lowly, and riding upon an ass, and upon a colt the foal of an ass" (Zech. 9:9). The word *having* is mentioned in 60 verses of the NT Narrative. Here the word *riding* is the 605,760th word of the Bible, and it refers a king's riding.

The Lord to Be King over All the Earth
"And the LORD shall be KING over all the earth: in that day shall there be one LORD, and his name one" (Zech. 14:9). Again the word *one* occurs 60 times in John's Gospel. Again the Jeremiah combination *king of* (157x) and *the whole earth* (3x) = 160.

The Great King
"But cursed be the deceiver, which hath in his flock a male, and voweth, and sacrificeth unto the Lord a corrupt thing: for I am a GREAT KING, saith the LORD of hosts, and my name is dreadful among the heathen" (Mal. 1:14).

The word *great* occurs 260 times in the OT Narrative.

The word *great* occurs 60 times in the Chronicles.
The phrase *a great* occurs 160 times in the OT.

The New Testament

"The book of the generation of Jesus <u>Christ</u>, <u>the son of</u> David, the son of Abraham" (Matt. 1:1). Matthew wrote his Gospel record to prove that Jesus of Nazareth was the long-awaited Messianic King, even the Christ. Both the titles Messiah and Christ mean anointed one. For this reason in this section we will refer to Christ as the Messianic King. The Messianic King must be a royal descendant of King David; through Mary's family line Jesus certainly was.

The title *Christ* occurs 60 times in the Gospels.
The title *King of Judah* occurs 60 times in First and Second Kings.
The phrase *the Son of* is mentioned in 60 chapters of the Bible.
The title *s/Son* is mentioned in 260 verses of the NT Narrative.

The Messianic King Is Now Incarnate

The wise men came to Herod "Saying, <u>Where is</u> <u>he that is</u> <u>born KING</u> of the Jews? for we have seen his star in the east, and are come <u>to</u> worship <u>him</u>" (Matt. 2:2). During the Hebrews' time of captivity in Babylon they became referred to as Jews, meaning Judeans. The phrase *where is* occurs 60 times from Genesis to the Gospels. The phrase *he that is* occurs 60 times from Genesis to Matthew. The NT Narrative combination *where is he that is* (1x), *born king* (1x), *of the Jews* (58x) = 60. The NT Narrative combination *unto him* (459x) and *Christ the King of Israel* (1x) = 460.

He Shall Rule the People of Israel

"And thou Bethlehem, in the land of Juda, art not the least among the PRINCES of Juda: for out of thee shall come a <u>Governor</u>, that shall <u>RULE</u> my <u>people Israel</u>" (Matt. 2:6). Matthew cites Jesus' birth as a fulfillment of Micah's kingly prophecy. Again the title *governor('s)* occurs a combined 60 times in the Bible. Again the word *ruler* is mentioned naturally in 60 verses of the Old Testament. The phrase *people Israel* occurs 60 times in the Old Testament.

Wise Men Worshiped the Messianic King

"And when they were come into the house, they saw the young child with Mary his mother, and <u>fell down</u>, and <u>worshipped</u> him: and when they had opened their <u>treasures</u>, they presented unto him gifts; gold, and frankincense, and myrrh" (Matt. 2:11). The phrase *fall/fell down* occurs 60 combined times in the Bible. The word *worshipped* is mentioned in 60 chapters of the Bible. Again from Genesis to the NT Narrative the word *treasures* occurs 60 times.

King Herod

"Then Herod, when he saw that he was mocked of the wise men, was <u>exceeding wroth, and sent forth, and slew all the children</u> that were in Bethlehem, and in all the coasts thereof, from two years old and under, according to the time which he had diligently enquired of the wise men" (Matt. 2:16). Bearing the Hebrew name Herodos, this man was Jewish and born in Edom. He was a Roman citizen; under his governorship of Judea he successfully pressed Caesar for the title King of Jews. Other successors of Herod the Great were not afforded this same privileged title. The Bible combination *exceeding* (59x), *wroth and sent forth and slew slew all the children* (1x) = 60.

Ethnarch Archelaus

"But when he heard that Archelaus <u>did</u> REIGN in Judaea in the room of his father Herod, he was afraid to go thither: notwithstanding, being warned of God in a dream, he turned aside into the parts of Galilee" (Matt. 2:22). Archelaus was governor of Judea, Samaria, and Idumea. He was the son Herod the Great. Ethnarch means ruler of a tribe or nation—the Greek word for tribe or nation being 'ethnos.' Here the word *did* is the 560th word of this chapter, and it.

Satan Tempts Messiah with Becoming King of the World

"Again, the devil taketh him up into an exceeding high mountain, and <u>sheweth him all the KINGDOMS of the world</u>, and the glory of them; And saith unto him, <u>All these things will I give thee</u>, if thou wilt fall down and worship me" (Matt. 4:8-9). Here the word *of* is the 1660th word of the New Testament, and it supports the keyword kingdoms. The New Testament combination *sheweth him all the* (1 v), *kingdoms* (4 vs), *of the world* (54 vs), *all these things will I give thee* (1 v) = 60 verses.

The Messianic King's Kingdom Teachings & Expectations

"And seeing the multitudes, he went up into a <u>mountain</u>: and when he was set, his disciples came unto him: And he opened his mouth, and <u>taught</u> them, saying, Blessed are the poor in spirit: for theirs is the KINGDOM of heaven" (Matt. 5:1-3). The Messianic King began to explain what He looks for in the lives of His kingdom subjects. Again we see the word "mountain" in symbolic relation to a kingdom. Again the phrase *the mountain* is mentioned in 60 verses of the Bible. Right on cue the word *taught* is mentioned in 60 chapters from Genesis to the NT Narrative.

The Messianic King Will Fulfil the Law to Perfection

"Think not that I am come to destroy <u>the law</u>, or the prophets: I am not come to destroy, but <u>to fulfil</u>" (Matt. 5:17). The OT Narrative combination *to fulfill the statutes and judgments* (1 v), the law (58 vs) = 60 verses.

The Name of the Great King

"But I say unto you, Swear not at all; neither by heaven; for it is God's throne: Nor by the earth; for it is his footstool: neither by Jerusalem; for it is the city <u>of the great King</u>" (Matt. 5:34-35). Again the New Testament combination *name of* (59x) and *the great King* (1x) = 60.

The Messianic King's Heavenly Father

"Not every one that saith unto me, Lord, Lord, shall enter into the KINGDOM of heaven; but he that doeth the will of <u>my Father</u> which is in heaven" (Matt. 7:21). The Earthly King tells all kingdom seekers some vital information on entrance into His Father's kingdom. All Bible references to the capitalized word *Father* which are preceded by the word *my* look like this: *my Father* (52x) and *my Father's* (8x) = 60.

The Messianic King's Great Authority

"And it came to pass, when Jesus had ended these sayings, the people were astonished at his doctrine: For he taught them as one <u>having</u> AUTHORITY, and not as the scribes" (Matt. 7:28-29). Again the word *having* is mentioned in 60 verses of the NT Narrative.

The Messianic King's Twelve Commissioners

"Now the names of <u>the twelve apostles</u> are these; The first, Simon, who is called Peter, and Andrew his brother; James the son of Zebedee, and John his brother; Philip, and Bartholomew; Thomas, and Matthew the publican; James the son of Alphaeus, and Lebbaeus, whose surname was Thaddaeus; Simon the Canaanite, and Judas Iscariot, who also betrayed him" (Matt. 10:2). The plural New Testament title *apostles* (55x) and *the twelve/other apostles* (5x) = 60.

The Messianic King's Divine Sword

"Think not that I am come to send peace on EARTH: I came not to send peace, but a <u>sword</u>. For I am come to set a man at variance against his father, and the daughter against her mother, and the daughter in law against her mother in law" (Matt. 10:34). In the Orient a Samurai soldier's sword was the symbol of his full allegiance to the emperor, the king. Again the phrase *the sword* is mentioned in 260 verses of the Bible.

23,460ᵗʰ Verse of the Bible

"And whosoever shall give to drink unto one of these little ones a cup of cold water only in the name of a disciple, verily I say unto you, he shall in no wise lose his <u>reward</u>" (Matt. 10:42). King Messiah gives a promise concerning rewards. Right on cue the word *reward* is mentioned in 60 verses from Genesis to the NT Narrative.

They That Live in Kings' Houses

"<u>But what went ye out for to see? A man clothed in soft raiment? behold, they that wear soft clothing are in KINGS'</u> houses" (Matt. 11:8). The New Testament combination *but what went ye out for to* (4x), *see a man* (3x), *clothed in* (10x), *soft* (3x), *raiment* (21x), *behold they that* (1x), *wear* (2x), *soft clothing* (1x), *are in kings'* (2x), *houses* (13x) = 60.

The Messianic King's Engrafted Family

"And he stretched forth <u>his hand</u> toward his disciples, and said, Behold my mother and my brethren! For whosoever <u>shall do</u> the will of my Father which is in heaven, the same is my brother, and sister, and mother" (Matt. 12:49-50). Again the phrase *his hand* is mentioned in 60 verses of the Law. The phrase *shall do* occurs 60 times in the Old Testament.

Bringing Forth 60-Fold Fruit in Faithful Service to the King

"But other <u>fell into good ground, and brought forth fruit</u>, some an hundredfold, some SIXTYFOLD, some thirtyfold" (Matt. 13:8). The New Testament combination *fell into good ground and brought forth* (1 v), *fruit* (58 vs), *sixtyfold* (1 v) = 60 verses.

460th Verse of the New Testament

"Whereupon <u>he promised with an</u> <u>oath</u> to give her whatsoever she would ask" (Matt. 14:7). Herod Antipas, son of Herod the Great, was a very wealthy king. He made an irrevocable promise to his daughter-in-law. The Bible combination *he promised with an* (1x), *oath* (59x) = 60.

The Messianic King's Power to Draw Multitudes

"And he commanded <u>the multitude</u> to sit down on the grass, and took the five loaves, and the two fishes, and looking up to heaven, he blessed, and brake, and gave the loaves to his disciples, and the disciples to <u>the multitude</u>" (Matt. 14:19). This Messianic King loves His earthly subjects and greatly desires to meet their most basic needs. The phrase *the multitude* is mentioned in 60 chapters of the Old Testament.

The Messianic King's Merciful Nature

"And, behold, a woman of Canaan came out of the same coasts, and cried unto him, saying, Have <u>mercy</u> on me, O Lord, thou Son of David; my daughter is grievously vexed with a devil. . . . Then Jesus <u>answered and said unto</u> her, O woman, great is thy faith: <u>be it unto thee</u> even as thou wilt. And her daughter was made whole from that very hour" (Matt. 15:22, 28). The New Testament combination *mercy* (59x) and *be it unto thee* (1x) = 60. The phrase *answered and said unto* occurs 60 times in the New Testament.

The Messianic King's Divine Credentials

"And Simon Peter answered and said, Thou art the <u>Christ</u>, <u>the Son of</u> the living God" (Matt. 16:16). Again the title *Christ* occurs 60 times in the Gospels. The phrase *the Son of* is mentioned in 60 chapters of the Bible.

The Messianic King's Divine Unveiling

"And after six days Jesus taketh Peter, James, and John his brother, and bringeth them up into an high <u>mountain</u> apart, And was transfigured before them: and his face did shine as the sun, and his raiment was white as the light" (Matt. 17:1-2). Again the phrase *the mountain* is mentioned in 60 verses of the Bible.

The Messianic King's Divine Charge

"And as they came down from the mountain, Jesus charged them, saying, <u>Tell the vision to no man, until the Son of man be risen again from the dead</u>" (Matt. 17:9). The command *tell the vision to no man, until the Son of man be risen again from the dead* consists of 60 characters!

The Messianic King's Spiritual Children

"At the same time came the disciples unto Jesus, saying, Who is the greatest in the KINGDOM of heaven? And Jesus called a little child unto him, and set him in the midst of them, And said, Verily I say unto you, Except ye be converted, and become as little <u>children</u>, ye shall not enter into the KINGDOM of heaven" (Matt. 18:1-3). The phrase *the children* occurs naturally 60 times in the New Testament.

The Messianic King's Earthly Judgment Thrones

"Behold, we have forsaken all, and followed thee; what shall we have therefore? And Jesus said unto them, Verily I say unto you, That ye which have followed me, in the regeneration when the Son of man shall sit in the throne of his glory, ye also shall sit upon twelve thrones, judging the twelve tribes of Israel" (Matt. 19:27b-28). From Genesis to the NT Narrative the phrase *the throne* occurs 60 times. Again the phrase *throne(s) of* occurs 60 times in the Bible. The Bible combination *ye also shall sit* (1x), *upon twelve thrones* (1x), *judging* (6x), *tribes of Israel* (52x) = 60.

The Messianic King's Galilean Followers

"All this was done, that it might be fulfilled which was spoken by the prophet, saying, Tell ye the daughter of Sion, Behold, thy KING cometh unto thee, meek, and sitting upon an ass, and a colt the foal of an ass. And the disciples went, and did as Jesus commanded them, And brought the ass, and the colt, and put on them their clothes, and they set him thereon. And a very great multitude spread their garments in the way; others cut down branches from the trees, and strawed them in the way. And the multitudes that went before, and that followed, cried, saying, Hosanna to the Son of David: Blessed is he that cometh in the name of the Lord; Hosanna in the highest" (Matt. 21:4-9).

This kingly passage presents the Bible's 60th verse-mention of the word *followed*. The Gospels combination *tell ye the daughter* (1x), *of Sion behold thy* (1x), *king* (55x), *cometh unto thee* (1x), *meek and sitting upon an ass* (1x), *and a colt the foal of an ass* (1x) = 60.

The Messianic King's Due Praise

"And when the chief priests and scribes saw the wonderful things that he did, and the children crying in the temple, and saying, Hosanna to the Son of David; they were sore displeased, And said unto him, Hearest thou what these say? And Jesus saith unto them, Yea; have ye never read, Out of the mouth of babes and sucklings thou hast perfected praise?" (Matt. 21:15-16) Again the word *worshipped* is mentioned in 60 chapters of the Bible. The Psalms combination *babes* (2x) and *praise* (158x) = 160.

The King Who Made a Marriage Banquet for His Son

"The KINGDOM of heaven is like unto a certain KING, which made a marriage for his son" (Matt. 22:2). The Bible combination *the kingdom of heaven* (32x), *is like unto a certain king* (1x), *which made a* (1x), *marriage* (19x), *marriage supper* (1x), *for his son* (6x) = 60.

The King's Salvation Message Goes out to the Nations

"And this gospel of the KINGDOM shall be preached in all the world for a witness unto all nations; and then shall the end come" (Matt. 24:14). Again the word *preached* occurs 60 times in the New Testament. Again the word *nations* is mentioned in 160 verses of the Major and Minor Prophets.

Sign of the Messianic King's Second Coming

"And then shall appear the sign of the Son of man in heaven: and then shall all the tribes of the EARTH mourn, and they shall see the Son of man coming in the clouds of heaven with POWER and great glory. And he shall send his angels with a great sound of a trumpet, and they shall gather together his elect from the four winds, from one end of heaven to the other" (Matt. 24:30-31). From Genesis to the Synoptic Gospels the word *sign* is mentioned in 60 verses. The phrase *shall see* is mentioned in 60 verses of the Old Testament. Again the word *cloud* is mentioned in 60 chapters of the Bible. Again the word *trumpet* is mentioned in 60 verses of the Bible.

Hour of the Messianic King's Second Coming

"Watch therefore, for ye know neither the day nor <u>the hour wherein the Son of man</u> <u>cometh</u>" (Matt. 25:13). The term son of man carries earthly implications because man came from the soil of the earth. This term is used often regarding Ezekiel, yet Jesus used it concerning Himself because He was born of an earthly woman. The Old Testament combination *the hour wherein the Son of man* (1x), *cometh* (159x) = 160.

Angels Accompany the Messianic King's Second Coming

"When the Son of <u>man</u> shall come in his glory, and all <u>the</u> holy <u>angels</u> <u>with him</u>, then shall he sit <u>upon the throne</u> of his glory" (Matt. 25:31). The NT Narrative combination *a man* (59 ch), *upon the throne* (1 ch) = 60 chapters. The title *the angel('s/s)* occurs 160 times in the Bible. The phrase *with him* occurs 60 times in the Synoptic Gospels.

The Returning King Shall Say unto Them

"And the KING shall answer and <u>say unto</u> them, Verily I say unto you, Inasmuch as ye have done it unto one of the least of these my brethren, ye have done it unto me" (Matt. 25:40). When the Heavenly King returns to Earth to be its earthly king He will judge the nations based on how they treated His Jewish kinsmen. The phrase *say unto* occurs 160 times in the Synoptic Gospels.

The Messianic King's Ceremonial Anointing

"<u>Now when Jesus was</u> <u>in Bethany,</u> <u>in the house of Simon the leper,</u> <u>There came unto him</u> <u>a</u> <u>woman having an</u> <u>alabaster</u> <u>box</u> of very <u>precious</u> <u>ointment,</u> <u>and poured it</u> <u>on his head,</u> <u>as he sat at</u> <u>meat</u>" (Matt. 26:6-7). Tragically this holy anointing was not for the Messianic King's inaugural ascension to the throne but instead for His ascension to Calvary and subsequent burial. The New Testament combination *now when Jesus was* (3x), *in Bethany* (2x), *in the house of Simon the leper* (2x), *there came unto him* (2x), *a woman having an* (3x), *alabaster* (3x), *box* (4x), *of very* (1x), *precious* (17x), *ointment* (12x), *and poured it* (2x), *on his head* (6x), *as he sat at meat* (3x) = 60.

The Messianic King's Guardian Angels await Instruction

"Then said Jesus unto him, Put up again thy sword into his place: for all they that take the sword shall perish with the sword. Thinkest thou that I cannot now pray to my Father, and he shall presently give me more than twelve legions of angels? But how then shall the scriptures be fulfilled, that thus it must be?" (Mark 26:52-54) In this Messianic King passage there are 60 words.

Matthew 26:60

"But found none: yea, though many false witnesses came, yet found they none. At the last came two false witnesses" (Matt. 26:60). The wicked religious leaders put the Messianic King on trial seeking to get a conviction of guilt at any cost.

Roman Governor Gave Jesus His Due Title—King of the Jews

"And set up over his head his accusation written, THIS IS JESUS THE KING OF THE JEWS" (Matt. 27:37). This verse presents the New Testament's 60th occurrence of the title *king*.

The phrase *the Jews* is mentioned in 60 verses of John.
The phrase *the Jews* occurs 60 times in Acts.

Sun Testifies That Jesus of Nazareth Is King of All Earth's Kings

"Now from the sixth hour there was darkness over all the land unto the ninth hour" (Matt. 27:45). This verse presents the Bible's 60th occurrence of the phrase *over all*, and it coincides with the darkened sun testifying that Jesus of Nazareth was the King over all the kings of the earth. Again the Jeremiah combination *king of* (157x) and *the whole earth* (3x) = 160. The word *sun* occurs 160 times in the Bible!

The Messianic King's Last Dying Breath

"Jesus, when he had cried again with a loud voice, yielded up the ghost" (Matt. 27:50). The NT Narrative combination *Jesus when he had* (3x), *cried* (56x), *again with a loud voice yielded up the ghost* (1x) = 60.

Matthew 27:60

"And laid it in his own new tomb, which he had hewn out in the rock: and he rolled a great stone to the door of the sepulchre, and departed" (Matt. 27:60). Here we see a burial fit for any earthly king. This King received a burial presided over by two religious heads of state, had His body wrapped in new cloth, and was laid in a brand-new tomb. Another Gospel tells us they administered about one hundred pounds of myrrh and aloes to His body, something befitting of a king. The combination *sepulchre* (54x) and *burial* (6x) = 60.

1060th Verse of the New Testament

"And as they went to tell his disciples, behold, Jesus met them, saying, All hail. And they came and held him by the feet, and worshipped him" (Matt. 28:9). The Risen King demands worship from His followers as He now possesses a glorified body. Again the word *worshipped* is mentioned in 60 chapters of the Bible.

The Risen King Issues a Great Commission
(Part 1)

"All POWER is given unto me in heaven and in EARTH. Go ye therefore, and teach all nations, baptizing them in the name of the Father, and of the Son, and of the Holy Ghost: Teaching them to observe all things whatsoever I have commanded you: and, lo, I am with you alway, even unto the end of the world. Amen" (Matt. 28:18b-19). In a red-letter Bible, the last word "Amen" appears in black letters; this is because Matthew added it as part of his narration. Again the word *power* is mentioned in 260 verses of the Bible. The Risen King's declarative words of gospel commission consist of precisely 60 words!

The Kingdom of God & Its Servant King Come to Galilee

"Jesus came into Galilee, preaching the gospel of the KINGDOM of God, And saying, The time is fulfilled, and the KINGDOM of God is at hand: repent ye, and believe the gospel" (Mark

1:14b-15). Mark wrote his Gospel record to reveal Jesus of Nazareth as the perfect Servant. Jesus came from heaven to earth to serve others. Thus the Servant King is a fitting title for Him; for this reason we will refer to Jesus as such in this Gospel section. The kingdom of God could begin on Earth in its spiritual form because its heaven-sent Servant King was standing in the people's midst ready to forgive sins and change their hearts through His special brand of love. The name *Galilee* is mentioned in 60 verses of the Gospels. The phrase *the kingdom of God* is mentioned in 60 verses of the NT Narrative.

60th Verse of Mark

"And it came to pass, that, as Jesus <u>sat</u> <u>at meat in his house</u>, many publicans and sinners sat also together with Jesus and his disciples: for there were many, and they followed him" (Mark 2:15). At His ministry headquarters, the lowly Servant King hosted with all gladness the so-called 'undesirable' people of the Israelite kingdom. The New Testament combination *sat* (59 chs), *at meat in his house* (1 ch) = 60 chapters.

960th Chapter of the Bible

"For he had healed many; insomuch that they pressed upon him for to touch him, as many as had plagues" (Mark 3:10). It is customary in any land that no one touch the king's person, especially commoners. Here in this 60th chapter we see the opposite action taking place. The common people crowded tightly just to touch the Servant King. Christ served the people as a kind and caring King, even as a Physician possessing special healing powers in His body which the people were excitedly aware of. He served the people well by making Himself so available to the needy.

"And he goeth up into a <u>mountain</u>, and calleth unto him whom he would: and they came unto him. And he ordained twelve, that they should be with him, and that he might send them forth to preach, And to have POWER to heal sicknesses, and to cast out devils" (vv. 13-15). With a mountain being biblically representative of a kingdom, Jesus ascended one on this occasion to perform an important governmental ceremony. The Servant King needed to ordain twelve underling servants to help Him with His special kingdom work. Again the phrase *the mountain* is mentioned in 60 verses of the Bible.

The Servant King Spoke Mysteriously with Parables

"And with many such <u>parables</u> <u>spake he</u> the word unto them, as they were able to hear it. But without a <u>parable</u> <u>spake he</u> not unto them: and when they were alone, he expounded all things to his disciples" (Mark 4:33-34). A parable is a fictitious story which carries a firm moral or religious principle. The Servant King served His disciples by giving the interested ones further teaching and explanation during later private sessions.

> The OT combination *he spake* (59x), *parables* (1x) = 60.
> The Bible combination *spake he* (11x), *parable* (49x) = 60.

The Servant King Adopts Spiritual Daughters on Simple Merit of Faith

"And he said unto her, <u>Daughter</u>, thy <u>faith</u> hath made thee whole; go in peace, and be whole of thy plague" (Mark 5:34). The Servant King yet again served His people in the role of a caring Physician. Again the word *daughters* occurs 60 times in the Major Prophets. The word *faith* occurs 160 times in the Pauline Epistles.

The Servant King Leads a Blind Man by the Hand

"And he cometh to Bethsaida; and they bring a blind man unto him . . . And he took the blind man by the <u>hand</u>, and led him out of the town; and when he had spit on his eyes, and put <u>his hands</u> upon him, he asked him if he saw ought" (Mark 8:22-23). When the Servant King reached the edge of town, having led him like a good servant, He began performing His servant-like physician work on the needy man. Here the word *hand* is the 30,460th word of the New Testament, and it is reflective of a kind King's hand. Again the phrase *his hand* is mentioned in 60 verses of the Law.

Seeing the Kingdom of God

"And he said unto them, Verily I say unto you, That there be some of them that stand here, which shall not taste of death, till they have seen the KINGDOM <u>of</u> God come with power" (Mark 9:1). Here the underlined word *of* is the 641,160th word of the Bible, and it supports the keyword kingdom.

The Servant King Teaches a Lesson on Servanthood

"And he came to Capernaum: and being in the house he asked them, What was it that ye disputed among yourselves by the way? But they held their peace: for by the way they had disputed among themselves, who should be the greatest. And he sat down, and called the twelve, and saith unto them, If any man desire to be first, <u>the same shall be</u> <u>last of all, and servant of all</u>" (Mark 9:33-35). This servant saying was Jesus' own daily habit. He practiced what He preached. The New Testament combination *the same shall be* (6x), *last* (53x), *of all and servant of all* (1x) = 60. Again the title *servant* occurs 60 times in the NT Narrative.

The King Promises Reward to All Servants Who Engage in Active Duty

"For whosoever shall give you a cup of water to drink in my name, because ye belong to Christ, verily I say unto you, he shall not lose his <u>reward</u>" (Mark 9:41). The King of Israel promises to reward His covenant ones for performing even the simplest acts of servitude. From Genesis to the NT Narrative the word *reward* is mentioned in 60 verses.

Criteria for Entering the Kingdom of God—A Pure Heart

"And if thine eye offend thee, pluck it out: it is better for thee to enter into the KINGDOM <u>of</u> God with one eye, than having two eyes to be cast into hell fire" (Mark 9:47). Jesus' hard-hitting kingdom teachings fall under the dispensation of the Law not the dispensation of grace. Here the word *of* is the 8260th word of Mark, and it supports the keyword kingdom.

1460th Verse of the New Testament

"Suffer the little children to come unto me, and forbid them not: for of such is the KINGDOM of God. Verily I say unto you, Whosoever shall not receive the KINGDOM of God as a little child, he shall not enter therein. <u>And he took them up in his arms, put his hands upon them, and blessed them</u>" (Mark 10:14b-16). With a smile on His face the Servant King gathered up several children in His arms in a show of genuine love.

The King's Right-Hand & Left-Hand Men

The brothers James and John came to King Jesus. "And he said unto them, What would ye that I should do for you? They said unto him, Grant unto us that we may sit, one on <u>thy right hand, and</u>

the other on thy left hand, in thy glory" (Mark 10:36-37). Again the phrase *the right hand* occurs 60 times in the Bible. The New Testament combination *and the other on thy left* (1x), *hand* (158x), *in thy glory* (1x) = 160.

The Servant King's Summarized Manifesto

"For even the Son of man came not to be ministered unto, but to minister, and to give his life a ransom for many" (Mark 10:45). All forms of the word minister show the seal of king in the following way: *minister* (68 chs), *ministers* (21 chs), *ministered* (34 chs), *ministereth* (2 chs), *ministering* (9 chs), *ministry* (19 chs), *ministration* (4 chs), *administration* (1 ch), *administrations* (1 ch), *administered* (1 ch) = 160 chapters.

The King Sends Two Runners on an Important Task

"And saith unto them, Go your way into the village over against you: and as soon as ye be entered into it, ye shall find a colt tied, whereon never man sat; loose him, and bring him. And if any man say unto you, Why do ye this? say ye that the Lord hath need of him; and straightway he will send him hither" (Mark 11:2-3). The King spoke precisely 60 words as He explained the two men's assignment.

The Servant King Rides a Humble Donkey Not a High Horse

"And they brought the colt to Jesus, and cast their garments on him; and he sat upon him. And many spread their garments in the way: and others cut down branches off the trees, and strawed them in the way. And they that went before, and they that followed, cried, saying, Hosanna; Blessed is he that cometh in the name of the Lord" (Mark 11:7-9). Here the name *Jesus* is the kingly 643,660th word of the Bible.

This King's Words Are Eternal

"Heaven and earth shall pass away: but my words shall not pass away" (Mark 13:31). Again the word *my* is found in 60 books of the Bible. Again the phrase *my words* occurs 60 times in the Bible.

560th Verse of Mark

"The Son of man indeed goeth, as it is written of him: but woe to that man by whom the Son of man is betrayed! good were it for that man if he had never been born" (Mark 14:21). This 60th verse pertains to the King's betrayal by a trusted friend.

The Servant King's Parting Passover Blessing

"And as they did eat, Jesus took bread, and blessed, and brake it, and gave to them, and said, Take, eat: this is my body. And he took the cup, and when he had given thanks, he gave it to them: and they all drank of it. And he said unto them, This is my blood of the new testament, which is shed for many" (Mark 14:22-24). Again the word *blessing(s)* is mentioned in 60 verses of the Old Testament. The word *blessed* occurs 60 times in the OT Narrative.

1660th Verse of the New Testament

"And they all forsook him, and fled" (Mark 14:50). This 60th verse recalls how the King's closest confidantes left Him in His hour of need.

Mark 14:60

"And the high priest <u>stood</u> up in the midst, and asked Jesus, saying, Answerest thou nothing? what is it which these witness against thee?" (Mark 14:60) It was the most infamous trial in history, and Israel's Supreme Court judge was astonished at the silent, servant-like nature of the Great Davidic King. As it is universally customary to rise from one's seated position in the presence of a sovereign head or king, so here the high priest unwittingly stood up before the Sovereign King of Heaven and Earth. The word *stood* occurs 60 times in the Major and Minor Prophets.

The Servant King Will One Day Return as Sovereign King

"And Jesus said, I am: and ye shall see the Son of man sitting on <u>the right hand</u> of POWER, and coming in the <u>clouds</u> of heaven" (Mark 14:62). Again the phrase *the right hand* occurs 60 times in the Bible. Again the word *cloud* is mentioned in 60 chapters of the Bible.

The Suffering King's Crown of Braided Thorns

"And the soldiers led him away into the hall, called Prætorium; and they call together the whole band. And they clothed him with purple, and platted <u>a CROWN of</u> <u>thorns</u>, and put it about his head, And began to salute him, Hail, KING of the Jews!" (Mark 15:16-17) Again all forms of the word *crown* are mentioned in 60 verses of the Old Testament. The Bible combination *platted a crown of* (3x), *thorn/s* (57x) = 60.

The Crucified King of the Jews

"And it was the third hour, and they crucified him. And the superscription of his accusation was written over, <u>THE</u> KING OF THE <u>JEWS</u>" (Mark 15:25-26). Here the underlined word *THE* is the 14,260th word of Mark, and it serves as the definite article for the keyword king. Here the title *Jews* is the 460th word of Mark, and it refers to the Jews' King.

"Christ the King"

"Let <u>Christ the KING</u> of Israel descend now from the cross, that we may see and believe. And they that were crucified with him reviled him" (Mark 15:32). Descending from the Cross would have been much easier for Christ than remaining nailed to it. Jesus' voluntary and substitutionary death on the Cross was what gained Him such enduring fame among believers over the subsequent ages. This verse marks the Bible's only occurrence of the title, "Christ the King." You will recall that the name Christ means 'anointed one.' The Kings of Israel and Judah were always anointed for installation into their civil office. Thus Christ is synonymous with the word King. Again the title *Christ* occurs 60 times in the Gospels.

24,860th Verse of the Bible

"And when the sixth hour was come, there was darkness over the whole land until the ninth hour" (Mark 15:33). The supernatural, celestial darkness testified to the nation their great error in rejecting their rightful heaven-sent King.

The Risen King Issues a Great Commission
(Part 2)

"And he said unto them, Go ye into all the world, and preach <u>the gospel</u> <u>to every creature</u>. He that believeth and is baptized shall be saved; but he that believeth not shall be damned. And these signs shall follow them that believe; In my name shall they cast out devils; they shall speak with new tongues; They shall take up serpents; and if they drink any deadly thing, it shall not hurt them; they shall lay hands on the sick, and they shall recover" (Mark 16:15-18).

These words of commission were spoken in the late afternoon of the King's resurrection day. The Risen King wanted His disciples to go to all nations and all peoples with the good news of His blood-bought salvation. The Pauline and General Epistles combination *the gospel* (59 vs), *to every creature* (1 v) = 60 verses. The Bible combination *to every* (59x), *creature of God* (1x) = 60.

The Davidic King

"Hail, thou that art highly favoured, the Lord is with thee: blessed art thou among women . . . . Fear not, Mary: for thou hast found favour with God. And, behold, thou shalt conceive in thy womb, and bring forth a son, and shalt call his name JESUS. He shall be great, and shall be called the Son of the Highest: and the Lord God shall give unto him the THRONE of his father <u>David</u>: And he shall REIGN over the house of Jacob for ever; and of his KINGDOM there shall be no end. . . . The Holy Ghost shall come upon thee, and the power of the Highest shall overshadow thee: therefore also that holy thing which shall be born of thee shall be called the Son of God. And, behold, thy cousin Elisabeth, she hath also conceived a son in her old age: and this is the sixth month with her, who was called barren. For with God nothing shall be impossible" (Luke 1:28b, 30b-33, 35b-37).

You will recall that Matthew presents Jesus as the Messianic King and Mark presents Him as the Servant King. Luke presents Jesus as the Davidic King—the perfect Man to rule over the people. Gabriel's announcement of Earth's Highest King consists of 160 words! We repeat the following seals.

The name *David('s)* occurs 360 times in the Kings/Chronicles.
The name *David('s)* occurs naturally 1060 times in the Bible!

The Davidic King's Priestly Prophet

"And his mother answered and said, Not so; but he shall <u>be called</u> John" (Luke 1:60). John was ordained from birth to become the Davidic King's forerunner or herald, and it was important that he be named according to the angel's directive. John's Hebrew name was Yohanan, meaning Jehovah is Gracious. John's ministry was to be kingly in accordance with our first definition of the word: stately or splendid, befitting a king, regal. The Bible combination *be called* (59x) and *be * called* (1x) = 60.

Zacharias' Royal Announcement of the Davidic King

"Blessed be the Lord God of Israel; for he hath <u>visited and redeemed</u> <u>his people</u>, And hath raised up an horn of salvation for us in the house of his servant David; As he spake by the mouth of his holy prophets, which have been since the world began: That we should be saved from our enemies, and from the hand of all that hate us; To perform the mercy promised to our fathers, and to remember his holy covenant; The oath which he sware to our father Abraham, That he would grant unto us, that we being delivered out of the hand of our enemies might serve him without fear, In holiness and righteousness before him, all the days of our life" (Luke 1:69-75).

Zacharias prophesies with an attitude of thanksgiving regarding the coming Davidic King. Following these words he will prophesy of John. The Bible phrases *visited and redeemed* (1x), *his people* (159x) = 160.

Davidic King Brought forth in the Royal City of David

"And Joseph also went up from Galilee, out of the city of Nazareth, into Judæa, unto the city of David, which is called Bethlehem; because he was of the house and lineage of David: To be taxed with Mary his espoused wife, being great with child. And so it was, that, while they were there, the days were accomplished that she should be delivered. And she brought forth her firstborn son, and wrapped him in swaddling clothes, and laid him in a manger; because there was no room for them in the inn" (Luke 2:7).

Again the phrase *the city of* occurs 60 times in the OT Narrative. The phrase *brought forth* occurs 60 times in the Old Testament.

Regal Announcement Given to the Shepherds

"Fear not: for, behold, I bring you good tidings of great joy, which shall be to all people. For unto you is born this day in the city of David a Saviour, which is Christ the Lord. And this shall be a sign unto you; Ye shall find the babe wrapped in swaddling clothes, lying in a manger. And suddenly there was with the angel a multitude of the heavenly host praising God, and saying, Glory to God in the highest, and on EARTH peace, good will toward men" (Luke 2:10b-14).

The Bible combination *fear not for behold* (1x), *I bring you good tidings of great joy* (1x), *which shall be to all people* (1x), *for unto you is born this day in* (1x), *the city of David* (46x), *a s/ Saviour* (6x), *which is Christ* (3x), *the only Lord* (1x) = 60.

Davidic King Filled with Wisdom & Grace

"And when they had performed all things according to the law of the Lord, they returned into Galilee, to their own city Nazareth. And the child grew, and waxed strong in spirit, filled with wisdom: and the grace of God was upon him" (Luke 2:39-40). The Bible combination *filled* (159x), *with wisdom and the grace* (1x) = 160.

Davidic King Is the Son of God

Luke gives us a genealogy of Jesus of Nazareth. Whereas Matthew's genealogy ties Christ's lineage back to Abraham, Luke goes all the way back to that former perfect holy man Adam. "And Jesus himself began to be about thirty years of age, being as was supposed the son of Joseph, which was the son of Heli . . . Which was the son of Enos, which was the son of Seth, which was the son of Adam, which was the son of God" (Luke 3:23, 38). Adam's Father was not earthly but heavenly. The same was true of Jesus. Again the phrase *the Son of* is mentioned in 60 chapters of the Bible. The phrase *of God* is mentioned in 60 verses of the Wisdom Books.

This Davidic King Knows the Word of God!

"And the devil said unto him, If thou be the Son of God, command this stone that it be made bread. And Jesus answered him, saying, It is written, That man shall not live by bread alone, but by every word of God" (Luke 4:3-4). The Mosaic Law mandated that every Israelite king write his own copy of the Law and to continually read it and live by it. Here the Davidic King shows His perfect working knowledge of the Law. The Bible combination *the king should* (2x), *live by* (12x), *the word of God* (46x) = 60.

"Thou Art Christ the Son of God"

"And devils also came out of many, crying out, and saying, Thou art Christ the Son of God. And he rebuking them suffered them not to speak: for they knew that he was Christ" (Luke 4:41). You will recall that the name Christ is synonymous with the word King, meaning 'anointed one.' Again the name *Christ* occurs 60 times in the Gospels.

260th Verse of Luke

"And the scribes and Pharisees watched him, whether he would heal on the sabbath day; that they might find an accusation against him" (Luke 6:7). This verse emphasizes the merciful nature of the Davidic King because He longed to heal visibly sick people sitting in the Synagogue. Such illustrative healings gave His sermon words irrefutable credibility.

2060th Verse of the New Testament

"When Jesus heard these things, he marvelled at him, and turned him about, and said unto the people that followed him, I say unto you, I have not found so great faith, no, not in Israel" (Luke 7:9). Every king has expectations of his people. Here the King of the Jews compliments a Gentile man for his great confidence in the King.

2160th Verse of the New Testament

"Then he called his twelve disciples together, and gave them POWER and AUTHORITY over all devils, and to cure diseases. And he sent them to preach <u>the</u> KINGDOM of God, and to heal the sick. <u>And he said unto them, Take nothing for your journey, neither staves, nor scrip, neither bread, neither money; neither have two coats apiece</u>" (Luke 9:1-2). The King conferred His healing power upon His twelve high commissioners. The underlined words mark the 2160th verse of the New Testament. Here the underlined word *the* is the 9560th word of Luke, and it serves as the definite article for the keyword kingdom.

The Kingdom of God & Its Transcendent King

"But I tell you of a truth, there be some standing here, which shall not taste of death, till they see <u>the KINGDOM of God</u>. And it came to pass about an eight days after these sayings, he took Peter and John and James, and went up into a mountain to pray. And as he prayed, the fashion of his countenance was altered, and his raiment was white and glistering" (Luke 9:27-29). Jesus' unveiling of His divinity demonstrated He was no mere earthly king but rather immortal and eternal. Again the phrase *the kingdom of* is mentioned in 60 chapters of the New Testament. Again the term *the kingdom of God* is mentioned in 60 verses of the NT Narrative.

Davidic King Prophesies Being Quickly Raised from the Dead

"The Son of man must suffer many things, and be rejected of the elders and chief priests and scribes, and be slain, and be <u>raised</u> the third day" (Luke 9:22). The word *raised* is mentioned in 60 chapters of the Bible.

25,360th Verse of the Bible

"And Jesus said unto him, <u>Foxes have holes, and birds of the air have nests; but the Son of man hath not where to lay his head</u>" (Luke 9:58). This King was lowly much like David was during the early years of his anointing as king—living in fields and forests. The NT Narrative combination *foxes have holes* (2x), *and [the] birds of the air have nests* (2x), *but the Son of man hath not* (2x), *where to* (4x), *lay* (36x), *his head* (14x) = 60.

Luke 9:60

A man expressed his willingness to follow the Davidic King but held one reservation. "Jesus said unto him, Let the dead bury their dead: but go thou and preach the KINGDOM of God" (Luke 9:60). Because the Davidic King was now in the nation's midst, there could be no delay in getting the vital news of His emerging kingdom to everyone. The related keyword *kingdom* actually occurs in this 60th verse.

The King Sends Seventy Messengers before Him

"After these things the Lord appointed other seventy also, and sent them two and two before his face into every city and place, whither he himself would come" (Luke 10:1). The word *seventy* is mentioned in 60 verses of the Bible. The Bible combination *after these things the Lord* (1x), *appointed other seventy also and* (1x), *sent them* (41x), *two and two* (6x), *before his face* (8x), *into every city* (1x), *and place whither* (1x), *he himself would come* (1x) = 60.

Christ—A Greater King than Solomon

"The QUEEN of the south shall rise up in the judgment with the men of this generation, and condemn them: for she came from the utmost parts of the earth to hear the wisdom of Solomon; and, behold, a greater than Solomon is here" (Luke 11:31). Right on cue from Genesis to the NT Narrative the word *greater* is mentioned in 60 verses.

2360th Verse of the New Testament

"But and if that servant say in his heart, My lord delayeth his coming; and shall begin to beat the menservants and maidens, and to eat and drink, and to be drunken" (Luke 12:45). This verse employs the kingly title "my lord" as was so often used in the Old Testament when a man spoke directly to his king.

Coming from Earth's Four Corners to the Kingdom Capital

"And they shall come from the east, and from the west, and from the north, and from the south, and shall sit down in the KINGDOM of God" (Luke 13:29). The Old Testament combination *from the east* (22x), *from the west* (12x), *from the north* (16x), *from the south* (10x) = 60.

Blessed Is the King Who Comes in the Name of the Lord

"O Jerusalem, Jerusalem, which killest the prophets, and stonest them that are sent unto thee; how often would I have gathered thy children together, as a hen doth gather her brood under her wings, and ye would not! Behold, your house is left unto you desolate: and verily I say unto you, Ye shall not see me, until the time come when ye shall say, Blessed is he that cometh in the name of the Lord" (Luke 13:34-35). The Luke combination *ye shall not* (5x), *see* (38x), *me* (109x), *until the time come* (1x), *when ye shall say* (1x), *blessed is he that* (2x), *cometh in* (2x), *the name of the Lord* (2x) = 160.

A King Considers His War Options

"Or what KING, going to make war against another KING, sitteth not down first, and consulteth whether he be able with ten thousand to meet him that cometh against him with twenty thousand? Or else, while the other is yet a great way off, he sendeth an ambassage, and desireth conditions of peace" (Luke 14:31-32). In Jesus' parable of a king preparing for war the king contemplates with his war council whether to send ten thousand soldiers or one small team of peacekeeping ambassadors. The word *able* occurs 160 times in the Bible. The Bible combination *ten thousand* (48x) and *footmen* (12x) = 60.

Invisible Nature of the Kingdom of God

"And when he was demanded of the Pharisees, when the <u>KINGDOM of God</u> should come, he answered them and said, The <u>KINGDOM of God</u> cometh not with observation: Neither shall they say, Lo here! or, lo there! for, behold, the kingdom of God is within you" (Luke 17:20-21). The kingdom of God has spiritual aspects which the kingdom of heaven does not. The Kingdom of God can only be entered into via the new birth, that is, a spiritual birth. At such a time the Spirit of God also enters into your soul. Both of these entrances are invisible yet nonetheless real and experiential. Again the term *the kingdom of God* is mentioned in 60 verses of the NT Narrative.

2560th Verse of the New Testament

"But Jesus called them unto him, and said, Suffer little children to come unto me, and forbid them not: for of such is the <u>KINGDOM of God</u>" (Luke 18:16). The related keyword *kingdom* actually occurs in this 60th verse.

The Merciful Davidic King from Nazareth Passes By

"And it came to pass, that as he was come nigh unto Jericho, a certain blind man sat by the way side begging. . . . And they told him, that <u>Jesus of Nazareth</u> <u>passeth by</u>. <u>And he cried, saying, Jesus, thou</u> <u>Son of David</u>, <u>have mercy on me</u>" (Luke 18:35, 37-38). The Bible combination *Jesus of Nazareth* (17x), *passeth by* (10x), *and he cried saying Jesus thou* (1x), *Son of David* (26x), *have mercy on me* (6x) = 60.

This Davidic King Will Not Reign over Us

"But his citizens <u>hated</u> him, and sent a message after him, saying, <u>We will not have</u> <u>this man</u> to REIGN over us" (Luke 19:14). Jesus' parable portrayed the Judean people's coming rejection of His kingship. However, the Galilean Jews loved Him. The opposite was true for David; his Judean people loved him and the northern tribes so often despised him. The NT Narrative combination *we will not have* (1x), *this man* (59x) = 60.

> The word *hated* is in 60 chapters of the Old Testament.
> The word *hated* occurs 60 times in the Bible.

Blessed Is the Lord's Incoming King!

"And they brought him to Jesus: and they cast their garments upon the colt, and they set Jesus thereon. And as he went, they spread their clothes in the way. And when he was come nigh, even now at the descent of the mount of Olives, the whole multitude of the disciples began to rejoice and praise God with a loud voice for all the mighty works that they had seen; Saying, <u>Blessed</u> be the KING that <u>cometh</u> <u>in the name of the Lord</u>: peace in heaven, and glory in the highest" (Luke 19:35-38). Again the word *blessed* occurs 60 times in the OT Narrative. The Old Testament combination *cometh* (159x), *in the name of the Lord God* (1x) = 160.

Man Journeys to a Far Country to Obtain Legal Rights to a Kingdom

"He said therefore, A certain noble<u>man</u> went into a <u>far country</u> <u>to receive for himself a</u>

KINGDOM, and to <u>return</u>" (Luke 20:12). Again the word *man* occurs 60 times in First Kings. Again the word *country* is mentioned in 160 verses from Genesis to the Synoptic Gospels. The Gospels combination *to receive for himself a kingdom* (1x), *return* (259x) = 260.

David's Two Sovereign Kings

"And he said unto them, How say they that Christ is David's son? And David himself saith in the book of Psalms, The LORD said unto my Lord, Sit thou on my <u>right hand</u>, Till I make thine enemies thy footstool. David therefore calleth him Lord, how is he then his son?" (Luke 20:41-43) Jesus' exposition of Psalm 110 reveals that David served not one but two co-ruling Heavenly Kings—Father and Son. Again the phrase *the right hand* occurs 60 times in the Bible.

The Kings of the Gentiles

"And he said unto them, <u>The KINGS</u> of the Gentiles exercise LORDSHIP <u>over them</u>; and they that exercise AUTHORITY upon them are called benefactors" (Luke 22:25). Again the term *the kings* is mentioned in 60 chapters of the OT Narrative. This verse presents the Bible's 160th verse-mention of the term *the kings*. Again the phrase *over them* is mentioned in 60 verses of the Bible.

Luke 22:60

"And Peter said, Man, I know not what thou sayest. And immediately, while he yet spake, the cock crew" (Luke 22:60). The man who wanted to sit on the King's right hand now denied for the third time even knowing Him.

The Lowly Davidic King Rejected & Put to Death

"And there were also two other, malefactors, led with him to be <u>put to death</u>" (Luke 23:32). David's life was once sought after by the cruel, mad leader of Israel. The lowly King suffered humiliation and shame as He was rejected by His people and put to a cruel death. Rather than giving Him the crown they instead gave Him the Cross. The phrase *put to death* occurs 60 times in the Old Testament.

Jesus Was a Most Merciful & Forgiving King

"Then said Jesus, Father, <u>forgive</u> them; for they know not what they do. And they parted his raiment, and cast lots" (Luke 23:34). The meek and lowly King had always taught forgiveness, and here at His lowest point in life He found room in His kingly heart to forgive His enemies. The Bible combination *forgive* (56x) and *forgiving* (4x) = 60.

2860th Verse of the New Testament

"And, behold, two of them went that same day to a village called Emmaus, which was from Jerusalem about THREESCORE furlongs" (Luke 24:13). At this moment in time, little did these two believers realize that the risen King of the Jews was walking just behind them. Emmaus was a city lying 60 furlongs from the City of the Great King. This 60th verse actually contains the key number *threescore*.

The Risen King Issues a Great Commission
(Part 3)

"Thus it is written, and thus it behoved Christ to suffer, and to rise from the dead the third day:

And that repentance and remission of sins should be preached in his name among all nations, beginning <u>at Jerusalem</u>. And ye are witnesses of these things" (Luke 24:46-48). These royal words of commission were proclaimed on the late afternoon of the King's resurrection day. Again from Genesis to the Synoptic Gospels the phrase *at Jerusalem* occurs 60 times; this is its 60th occurrence, and it relates to the Earthly King's Great Commission.

Andrew Heralds the King's Arrival

"He first findeth his own brother Simon, and saith unto him, We have found the MESSIAS, which is, being interpreted, the <u>Christ</u>" (John 1:41). You will recall that both the titles Messiah and Christ mean anointed one. Again the title *Christ* occurs 60 times in the Gospels.

Nathanael's Great Confession

"Nathanael answered and saith unto him, Rabbi, <u>thou art</u> the Son of God; <u>thou art</u> the <u>KING of Israel</u>" (John 1:49). John wrote his Gospel record to prove that Jesus of Nazareth was the eternal Incarnate God, thus the truly Divine King. The phrase *thou art* is mentioned in 60 verses of the Major and Minor Prophets. Again the title *king of Israel* is mentioned in 120 verses of the OT Narrative, a multiple of 60.

The Divine King's Heavenly Host

The Divine King responded to Nathanael's confession of faith, saying, "Verily, verily, I say unto you, Hereafter ye shall see <u>heaven</u> open, and the angels of God ascending and descending upon the Son of man" (John 1:51). Again the word *heaven* occurs 60 times in the Wisdom Books.

The Divine King's Miracle Powers

"<u>And there were set there six waterpots of stone, after the manner of the purifying of the Jews, containing two or three firkins apiece. Jesus saith unto them, Fill the waterpots with water. And they filled them up to the brim. And he saith unto them,</u> *Draw out now*, <u>and bear unto the governor of the feast. And they bare it. When the ruler of the feast had tasted the water that was made wine</u>" (John 2:6-9a). The King of the Jews could turn water into wine because He was in reality the Divine Creator. The Gospels combination *and there were set there* (1x), *six waterpots* (1x), *of stone* (1x), *after the manner of* (1x), *the purifying of the Jews* (1x), *containing* (1x), *two or three firkins apiece* (1x), *Jesus saith unto them fill* (1x), *the waterpots* (1x), *with water* (8x), *and they filled them up* (1x), *to the brim* (1x), *and he saith unto them* (11x), *draw out now* (1x), *and bear unto* (1x), *the governor of the feast* (2x), *and they bare it* (1x), *when the ruler of the feast* (1x), *had tasted* (2x), *the water that was made* (1x), *wine* (21x) = 60.

One Must Be Spiritually Reborn into the Kingdom of God

"Jesus answered and said unto him, Verily, verily, I say unto thee, Except a man be born again, he cannot see the KINGDOM of <u>God</u>" (John 3:3). Here the title *God* is the 676,660th word of the Bible, and it refers to the Divine King of Heaven.

Christ Is King above All Earthly Kings

"He that cometh from above is above all: he that is of the EARTH is EARTHLY, and speaketh of the EARTH: he that cometh from <u>heaven</u> is above all" (John 3:31). Here the keyword *earthly* is the 66,960th word of the New Testament. Again the word *heaven* occurs 60 times in the Wisdom Books.

153

Woman of Samaria Meets the Divine King

"The woman saith unto him, I know that MESSIAS cometh, which is called Christ: when he is come, he will tell us all things. Jesus saith unto her, I that speak unto thee am he" (John 4:25). The Synoptic Gospels combination *I know that Messias* (1x), *cometh* (59x) = 60.

The Divine King's Authority to Judge All Men

"And hath given him AUTHORITY to execute judgment also, because he is the Son of man" (John 5:27). Here the word *him* is the 68,760th word of the New Testament. Again the word *judgment* is mentioned in 60 chapters of the Major and Minor Prophets.

Heavenly Father Bears Witness of His Divine, Kingly Son

"But I have greater witness than that of John: for the works which the Father hath given me to finish, the same works that I do, bear witness of me, that the Father hath sent me" (John 5:36). Right on cue from Genesis to the NT Narrative the word *greater* is mentioned in 60 verses. Right on cue from Genesis to the NT Narrative the phrase *of me* occurs 60 times.

Satisfied Crowd Wanted to Make Jesus King

"When Jesus therefore perceived that they would come and take him by force, to make him a KING, he departed again into a mountain himself alone" (John 6:15). The time was not yet ordained for Jesus to present Himself to the nation as its rightful King. The Bible combination *that they would come and* (1x), *take him by force* (2x), *to make him* (9x), *a king* (48x) = 60.

John 6:60

"Many therefore of his disciples, when they had heard this, said, This is an hard saying; who can hear it?" (John 6:60) Although the masses had tasted and eaten of the Divine King's earthly bread they refused to consume His heavenly bread. Again the word *saying* occurs naturally 60 times in First and Second Chronicles.

The Divine, Earthly King's Festive Fountain

"In the last day, that great day of the feast, Jesus stood and cried, saying, If any man thirst, let him come unto me, and drink" (John 7:37). This verse presents the Bible's 60th occurrence of the phrase *the feast*, and it pertains to a Divine King's invitation to freely come and drink. Again the word *drink* occurs 300 times in the Old Testament, a multiple of 60.

3260th Verse of the New Testament

"And he said unto them, Ye are from beneath; I am from above: ye are of this world; I am not of this world" (John 8:23). The Divine King emphasized His heavenly nature. This verse is also congruently 360th verse of John.

The Divine King Receives Earthly Worship

After performing a miracle on the man born blind, the Divine Earthly King approached the seeing man and asked him if he believed on the Son of God. "And he said, Lord, I believe. And he worshipped him" (John 9:38). The Divine King received worship from man. Jesus rightfully received worship from others and never refused it. The case-sensitive title *the Son* occurs 160 times in the New Testament. Again the word *worshipped* is mentioned in 60 chapters of the Bible.

Joyful Shouts of Hosanna to the King of Israel

Jesus' Galilean followers were many in number, and they "Took branches of palm trees, and went forth to meet him, and cried, Hosanna: Blessed is the KING of Israel that cometh in the name of the Lord. And Jesus, when he had found a young ass, sat thereon; as it is written, Fear not, daughter of Sion: behold, thy KING cometh, sitting on an ass's colt" (John 12:13-15). Here the Divine King was properly revered and adored. Again the title *the king* occurs 60 times in Joshua. Again the Old Testament combination *cometh* (159x), *in the name of the Lord God* (1x) = 160. This kingly chapter consists of 1060 words.

The Divine King's New Commandment

"A new commandment I give unto you, That ye love one another; as I have loved you, that ye also love one another. By this shall all men know that ye are my disciples, if ye have love one to another" (John 13:34-35). The Bible combination *a new commandment* (3 vs) and *given unto* (57 vs) = 60 verses. Again the word *commandment* is mentioned naturally in 60 verses of the OT Narrative.

Make Your Humble Petition in the Divine King's Name

"And whatsoever ye shall ask in my name, that will I do, that the Father may be glorified in the Son. If ye shall ask any thing in my name, I will do it" (John 14:13-14). This Divine King loves to grant His devotees' hearts' desires. All they need do is to delight in His name. The New Testament combination *the name* (59x) and *Christ the King* (1x) = 60.

The Divine King's Kingdom Exists in another World

"Jesus answered, My KINGDOM is not of this world: if my KINGDOM were of this world, then would my servants fight, that I should not be delivered to the Jews: but now is my KINGDOM not from hence. Pilate therefore said unto him, Art thou a KING then? Jesus answered, Thou sayest that I am a KING. To this end was I born, and for this cause came I into the world, that I should bear witness unto the truth. Every one that is of the truth heareth my voice" (John 18:36-37). Again the Bible combination *a king* (48x) and *a kingdom* (12x) = 60. The word *cause* is mentioned in 60 verses of the Wisdom Books.

Behold the Jews' Great Passover King

"And it was the preparation of the passover, and about the sixth hour: and he saith unto the Jews, Behold your KING!" (John 19:14)

> The phrase *the passover* is mentioned in 60 verses of the Bible.
> The phrase *the Jews* is mentioned in 60 verses of John.
> The word *behold* occurs 60 times in Matthew!
> The word *your* occurs 60 times in the General Epistles.
> The word *king* occurs 60 times in Isaiah.

"Shall I Crucify Your King?"

"But they cried out, Away with him, away with him, crucify him. Pilate saith unto them, Shall I crucify your KING? The chief priests answered, We have no KING but Cæsar" (John 19:15). The New Testament combination *Pilate* (56x), *saith unto the Jews* (1x), *shall I crucify* (1x), *your King* (2x) = 60. The word *your* is mentioned in 60 chapters of Pauline Epistles and occurs 60 times in the General Epistles.

Jesus of Nazareth, The King of The Jews

"And Pilate wrote a title, and put it on the cross. And the writing was, JESUS OF <u>NAZARETH</u> THE KING OF THE JEWS. This title then read many of the Jews: for the place where Jesus was crucified was nigh to the city: and it was written in Hebrew, and Greek, and Latin" (John 19:19-20). Here the word *Nazareth* is the 11,860th word of the New Testament, and it is used in conjunction with the keyword king.

The Reincarnate King

"Then the same day at evening, being the first day of the week, when the doors were shut where the disciples were assembled for fear of the Jews, came Jesus and stood <u>in the midst</u>, and saith unto them, Peace be unto you. And when he had so said, he shewed unto them <u>his hands</u> and his side" (John 20:19-20). The King of the Jews was back from the dead and in record time. Now there could be no question of His divine nature. The phrase *in the midst* is mentioned in 60 chapters of the Major Prophets. Again the phrase *his hands* occurs naturally 60 times in the Old Testament.

The Risen King Issues a Great Commission
(Part 4)

"<u>Then said Jesus to them again, Peace be unto you</u>: <u>as my Father hath sent me</u>, <u>even so</u> <u>send I you</u>. And when he had said this, he breathed on them, and saith unto them, Receive ye the Holy Ghost: Whose soever sins ye remit, they are remitted unto them; and whose soever sins ye retain, they are retained" (John 20:21-23). The Risen King commissioned His apostolic commissioners and sent them to the nations as His royal ambassadors. The Bible combination *then said Jesus to them again peace be unto you* (1x), *as my Father hath sent me* (1x), *even so* (57x), *send I you* (1x) = 60.

Divine King Received up into Heaven with Grand Processional

"And when he had spoken these things, while they beheld, he was taken <u>up</u>; and a <u>cloud</u> received him out of their sight. And while they looked stedfastly toward heaven as he went <u>up</u>, behold, two men stood by them in white apparel. Which also said, Ye men of Galilee, why stand ye gazing <u>up</u> into heaven? this same Jesus, which is taken <u>up</u> from you into heaven, shall so come in like manner as ye have seen him go into heaven" (Acts 1:9-11). Again the word *cloud* is mentioned in 60 chapters of the Bible. Again the word *received* occurs 160 times in the Bible. The word *up* is found in 60 books of the Bible.

60th Verse of Acts

"For David is not <u>ascended into the heavens</u>: but he saith himself, <u>The LORD</u> said unto my Lord, Sit thou on my right hand" (Acts 2:34). Again the phrase *the right hand* occurs 60 times in the Bible. The New Testament combination *the Lord Jesus* (59x) and *ascended into the heavens* (1x) = 60.

Kings of the Earth Stood against the King of the Jews

"The KINGS of the EARTH stood up, and the RULERS were gathered together against the Lord, and against his <u>Christ</u>" (Acts 4:26). Here the word *kings* is the 697,060th word of the Bible. Again the title *Christ* occurs 60 times in the Gospels.

Acts 7:60

"And he kneeled down, and cried with a loud voice, <u>Lord</u>, lay not this sin to their charge. And when he had said this, he fell asleep" (Acts 7:60). According to the Oriental custom, this devotee knelt before Christ the King and asked Him to grant government pardons for his own executioners' hateful deed. Again the title *LORD* occurs 60 times in Amos.

Saul Meets Christ the King on the King's Highway

"And as he journeyed, he came near Damascus: and suddenly there shined round about him a light from heaven: And he fell to the earth, and heard a voice saying unto him, Saul, Saul, why persecutest thou me? And he said, Who art thou, Lord? And the Lord said, I am Jesus whom thou persecutest: it is hard for thee to kick against the pricks. And he trembling and astonished said, Lord, what wilt thou have me to do? And the Lord said unto him, Arise, and go into the city, and it shall be <u>told</u> thee what thou must do" (Acts 9:3-7).

The Damascus Road was part of an ancient highway running between Egypt and Syria, a trade route known as the King's High Way. On this life-changing occasion Saul received a commission from the King but was not given any immediate specifics. Again the word *told* is mentioned in 60 verses of the New Testament.

King Herod, Agrippa I

"Now about that time Herod the KING stretched forth <u>his hands</u> to vex certain of the church" (Acts 12:1). Agrippa I was the grandson of Herod the Great and the last ruler in Judea to hold a title of royalty—King of the Jews. Again the phrase *his hands* occurs naturally 60 times in the Old Testament.

27,360th verse of the Bible

"And the people gave a shout, saying, It is the voice of a god, and not of a man" (Acts 12:22). The people from Tyre and Sidon gave a shout of praise which elevated a Judean King to a status which he did not deserve. Herod Agrippa I gladly received it to his own downfall.

David Their King

"And when he had removed him, he raised up unto them David to be their KING; to whom also he gave testimony, and said, I have found David the son of Jesse, a <u>man</u> after mine own heart, which shall fulfil all my will" (Acts 13:22). At Antioch Pisidia Paul preached about King Jesus' earthly Davidic forebear. Again the word *man* is found in 60 books of the Bible.

Thessalonian Jews Resist Giving Allegiance to another King

"Whom Jason hath received: and these all do contrary to the decrees of Cæsar, saying that there is <u>another</u> KING, one Jesus" (Acts 17:7). Again the word *another* occurs 60 times in the Major Prophets.

King Herod, Agrippa II

"Then Agrippa said unto Paul, Thou art permitted to speak for thyself. Then Paul stretched forth the hand, and answered for himself: I think myself happy, KING Agrippa, because I shall answer for myself this day before thee touching all the things whereof I am accused of the Jews. . . . Which knew me from the beginning, if they would testify, that after the most straitest sect of our religion I lived a Pharisee. And now I stand and am judged for the hope of the promise made of God unto our fathers: Unto which promise our twelve tribes, instantly serving God day and night, hope to come. For which hope's sake, KING Agrippa, I am accused of the Jews" (Acts 26:1-2, 5-7). Claudius gave Agrippa II the title king over certain parts of Israel which Phillip once ruled. In verse seven the underlined name *Agrippa* is the 160th word of this chapter, the name of the king.

1060th Chapter of the Bible

The theme of this chapter concerns Christ the King being the judge of every Christian. At the heart of this kingly chapter it says, "We shall all stand before the judgment seat of Christ. For it is written, As I live, saith the Lord, every knee shall bow to me, and every tongue shall confess to God. So then every one of us shall give account of himself to God. Let us not therefore judge one another any more: but judge this rather, that no man put a stumblingblock or an occasion to fall in his brother's way" (Rom. 14:10b-13). The New Testament combination *as I live* (1x), *saith the Lord* (13x), *every knee shall bow* (1x), *to me* (45x) = 60.

"For the KINGDOM of God is not meat and drink; but righteousness, and peace, and joy in the Holy Ghost. For he that in these things serveth Christ is acceptable to God, and approved of men" (vv. 17-18). The related keyword *kingdom* actually occurs in this 1060th chapter of the Bible. Again the title *Christ* occurs 60 times in the Gospels.

The King's Gentile Devotees

"And again, Esaias saith, There shall be a root of Jesse, and he that shall rise to REIGN over the Gentiles; in him shall the Gentiles trust" (Rom. 15:12). Paul referred to Isaiah's repeated prophesies where he talked of the future Messianic King of Israel finding fame among the nations. The Pauline Epistles combination *root of Jesse* (1x), *in him shall* (1x), *the Gentiles* (37x), *trust* (21x) = 60.

The King's Christian Ministers

"Let a man so account of us, as of the ministers of Christ, and stewards of the mysteries of God" (1 Cor. 4:1). Paul's use of the term ministers of Christ and stewards of God falls in line with our fourth definition of kingly: consisting of kings or others of royal rank. Again all forms of the word *minister* are mentioned in 160 chapters of the Bible. Again the title *Christ* occurs 60 times in the Gospels.

The King's Enemies

"Then cometh the end, when he shall have delivered up the KINGDOM to God, even the Father; when he shall have put down all RULE and all AUTHORITY and power. For he must REIGN, till he hath put all enemies under his feet" (1 Cor. 15:24-25). Again the word *enemies* is mentioned in 260 verses of the Bible.

The King's Faithful Men

"Watch ye, stand fast in the faith, quit you like men, be strong" (1 Cor. 16:13). Again the word *faith* occurs 160 times in the Pauline Epistles.

60th Verse of Second Corinthians

"Therefore seeing we have this <u>ministry</u>, as we have received mercy, we faint not" (2 Cor. 4:1). When kings ascend to their throne they quickly pick key people to become their ministers. Christ the King has duly appointed all believers to become ministers over His kingdom affairs. Here the ministry which Paul refers to is a ministry of reconciliation whereby people's souls are reconciled to God through ministers of the gospel preaching about the King's Cross. Again all forms of the word *minister* are mentioned in 160 chapters of the Bible.

Aretas, King of Damascus

"In <u>Damascus</u> the governor under Aretas the KING kept the city of the Damascenes with a garrison, desirous to apprehend me" (2 Cor. 11:32). This kingly verse falls in the 160th chapter of the New Testament. The name *Damascus* occurs 60 times in the Bible.

These Shall Not Inherit the Kingdom of God

"Envyings, murders, drunkenness, <u>revellings</u>, <u>and such like</u>: of the which I tell you before, as I have also told you in time past, that <u>they which</u> <u>do such things</u> <u>shall not inherit the KINGDOM of God</u>" (Gal. 5:21). The New Testament combination *revellings* (2x), *and such like* (1x), *they which* (53x), *do such things* (2x), *shall not inherit the kingdom of God* (2x) = 60.

60th Verse of Ephesians

Paul spoke of bowing his knees to the Father of our Lord Jesus Christ: "Of whom <u>the whole</u> family in heaven and <u>EARTH</u> is named" (Eph. 3:15). Christians are named with the name of Christ the King. Again the Jeremiah combination *king of* (157x) and *the whole earth* (3x) = 160.

Christ the King Distributes Gifts

"Wherefore he saith, When he ascended up on high, he led captivity captive, and <u>gave gifts unto men</u>" (Eph. 4:8). Paul quotes from Psalm 68 and tells of the Ascended King distributing gifts to the Old Testament saints who ascended with Him so they could share in His great victory celebration. The Bible combination *gave unto them* (7x), *gifts* (53x) = 60. The Bible combination *gift* (59x) and *worthy portion* (1x) = 60.

"The Kingdom of Christ"

"For this ye know, that no whoremonger, nor unclean person, nor covetous man, who is an idolater, hath any inheritance in <u>the KINGDOM of Christ</u> and of <u>God</u>" (Eph. 5:5). Again the phrase *the kingdom of* is mentioned in 60 chapters of the New Testament. Again the term *the kingdom of God* is mentioned in 60 verses of the NT Narrative. Again the title *Christ* occurs 60 times in the Gospels.

Every Knee Shall Bow before King Jesus

"Wherefore God also hath highly exalted him, and given him a name which is above every name: That at <u>the name of Jesus every knee should bow</u>, of things in heaven, and things <u>in EARTH</u>, and things under <u>the EARTH</u>; And that every tongue should confess that Jesus Christ is Lord, to the glory of God the Father" (Phil. 2:9-11). The New Testament combination *the name of* (59x), *Jesus every knee should bow* (1x) = 60. Again the phrase *in the earth* is mentioned in 60 verses of the Old Testament.

The King's Saints

"Giving thanks unto the Father, which hath made us meet to be partakers of the inheritance of the saints in light: Who hath delivered us from the power of darkness, and hath translated us into the KINGDOM of his dear Son: In whom we have redemption through his blood, even the forgiveness of sins" (Col. 1:12-14). Again the title *saints* occurs 60 times in the New Testament.

Thrones & Dominions

"For by him were all things created, that are in heaven, and that are in earth, visible and invisible, whether they be THRONES, or DOMINIONS, or principalities, or powers: all things were created by him, and for him" (Col. 1:16). Here the word *or* is the 752,060th word of the Bible, and it rests between the two king-related words thrones and dominions.

The Returning King & the Sabbath

"Let no man therefore judge you in meat, or in drink, or in respect of an holyday, or of the new moon, or of the sabbath days: Which are a shadow of things to come; but the body is of Christ" (Col. 2:16-17). Paul speaks to the Gentiles, urging them not to be drawn into the Old Testament form of worship wherein the seventh day was esteemed above all others. The Sabbath Day has been temporarily postponed along with the literal kingdom until Christ returns. In contrast, Paul explains that the Sabbath days (whether they be weekly, monthly, or annual) point toward the millennium. The Sabbath is thus linked to the Heavenly King reigning on Earth. Again the word *sabbath* occurs 60 times in the New Testament.

Walk Worthy of Christ's Kingdom Glory

"That ye would walk worthy of God, who hath called you unto his KINGDOM and glory" (1 Thess. 1:12). The Pauline Epistles combiantion *walk worthy of God who hath* (1x), *called* (55x), *you unto* (3x), *his kingdom and glory* (1x) = 60.

Trumpet to Announce Christ the King's Coming

"For the Lord himself shall descend from heaven with a shout, with the voice of the archangel, and with the trump of God: and the dead in Christ shall rise first" (1 Thess. 4:16). Again the word *trumpet* is mentioned in 60 verses of the Bible.

Be Found Worthy of the Kingdom

"Which is a manifest token of the righteous judgment of God, that ye may be counted worthy of the KINGDOM of God, for which ye also suffer" (2 Thess. 1:5). The New Testament combination *worthy* (54x), *of the kingdom of God* (6x) = 60.

The Eternal, Immortal, Invisible King

"Now unto the KING eternal, immortal, invisible, the only wise God, be honour and glory for ever and ever. Amen" (1 Tim. 1:17). The Bible combination *now unto the* (4x), *King eternal* (1x), *immortal* (1x), *invisible* (5x), *the only wise God* (2x), *be honour and glory* (1x), *for ever and ever* (46x) = 60.

Pray for All Kings So that Peace May Prevail

"I exhort therefore, that, first of all, supplications, prayers, intercessions, and giving of thanks, be made for all men; For KINGS, and for all that are in AUTHORITY; that we may lead a quiet and peaceable life in all godliness and honesty" (1 Tim. 2:1-2). The New Testament combination *supplications* (3x), *prayers* (22x), *intercessions* (1x), *and giving of thanks* (1x), *be made for all men for* (1x), *kings* (31x), *and for all that are in authority* (1x) = 60.

6660th Verse of the New Testament

"That thou keep this commandment without spot, unrebukeable, until the appearing of our Lord Jesus Christ: Which in his times he shall shew, who is the <u>blessed</u> and only POTENTATE, the KING OF KINGS, and Lord of lords; <u>Who only hath immortality, dwelling in the light which no man can approach unto; whom no man hath seen, nor can see: to whom be honour and power everlasting. Amen</u>" (1 Tim. 6:14-16). Again the word *blessed* occurs 60 times in the OT Narrative. The underlined words mark the 6660th verse of the New Testament, and that verse refers to the King of Kings.

Gospel of the Incarnate King's Resurrection from the Dead

"Remember that <u>Jesus Christ</u> of <u>the seed</u> of David was <u>raised</u> from the dead according to my gospel" (2 Tim. 2:8). Christ the King's seed was royal in both its earthly and heavenly aspects. The phrase *the seed(s)* is mentioned in 60 verses of the Bible. Again the word *raised* is mentioned in 60 chapters of the Bible.

The King of Salem

"For this Melchisedec, KING of Salem, priest of the most high God, who met Abraham . . . and blessed him; To whom also Abraham gave a tenth part of all; first being by interpretation KING of <u>righteousness</u>, and after that also KING of Salem, which is, KING of peace" (Heb. 7:1-2). Again the word *righteous* occurs 60 times in the Psalms.

Christ, the Priestly King of Heaven

"For those priests were made without an oath; but this with an oath by him that said unto him, The Lord sware and will not repent, <u>Thou art</u> a priest for ever after the order of MELCHISEDEC" (Heb. 7:21). The title Melchisedec means my king is righteous. This verse presents the New Testament's 60th verse-mention of the phrase *thou art*, and it refers to the heavenly King Melchisedec.

Jesus, High Priest & King

"But into the second went <u>the high priest</u> alone once every year, not without blood, which he offered for himself, and for the errors of the people" (Heb. 9:7). Jesus was not an earthly priest after the order of Aaron but after the order of Melchesidec. This allowed Him to be both Israel's royal Priest and Israel's royal King. Again the title *the high priest* occurs 60 times in Scripture.

The Twelve Tribes Still Have an Earthly King

"James, a servant of God and of the Lord Jesus Christ, to the twelve <u>tribes</u> which are scattered abroad, greeting" (James 1:1). Christ reigns supreme over the twelve tribes of Israel, but He will not return until they welcome Him to return to their midst. Jesus is also King over all the tribes of the earth. Again the phrase *the tribes of* occurs 60 times in the Old Testament.

The Crown of Life

"Blessed is the man that endureth temptation: for when he is tried, he shall receive the <u>CROWN</u> of life, which the Lord hath promised to them that love him" (James 1:12). This verse presents the Bible's 60th occurrence of the word *crown*. Again all forms of the word *crown* are mentioned in 60 verses of the Old Testament.

Heirs of the Kingdom

"Hearken, my beloved brethren, Hath not God chosen the poor of this world rich in faith, and heirs of <u>the</u> KINGDOM which he hath promised to them that love him?" (James 2:5) Here the underlined *the* is the 660th word of James, and it serves as the definite article of the keyword kingdom.

60th Book of the Bible

FIRST PETER is the 60th BOOK of the Bible as it focuses upon the believer's readiness to suffer on Christ the King's behalf. Because a holy war taking place Peter wrote to scattered and fearful believers that he might encourage them and embolden their faith. The believer is to endure, not shun, persecution for the greater good of Christ and the overspreading of His kingdom. The theme of this book is Victory over Suffering.

Faith & Hope in Christ the King (1:3-25)—Not only did Christ suffer and die for us, but He also rose again from the dead so we might obtain greater hope and faith in the face of looming threats of persecution and death. Peter celebrated this idea: "Blessed be the God and Father of our Lord Jesus Christ, which according to his abundant mercy hath begotten us again unto a lively <u>hope</u> by the resurrection of Jesus Christ from the dead. To an inheritance incorruptible, and undefiled, and that fadeth not away, reserved in <u>heaven</u> for you, Who are kept by the power of God through <u>faith</u> unto salvation ready to be revealed in the last time" (1:3-5). The word *hope* occurs 60 times in the New Testament. Again the word *heaven* occurs 60 times in the Wisdom Books. Again the word *faith* occurs 160 times in the Pauline Epistles.

Peter wanted the suffering saints to look beyond their immediate dark horizons and display greater faith in and allegiance toward Christ their King. "Wherein ye greatly rejoice, though now for a season, if need be, ye are in heaviness through manifold temptations: That <u>the trial</u> of your <u>faith</u>, being <u>much more precious than</u> <u>of gold</u> that perisheth, though it be tried with fire, might be found unto praise and honour and glory at the appearing of Jesus Christ" (1:6-7). These are two of the key verses in this Epistle. Again the word *faith* occurs 160 times in the Pauline Epistles. The Old Testament combination *the trial* (1x) and *precious* (59x) = 60. The Bible combination *much more precious than* (1x), *of gold* (159x) = 160.

A few verses later Peter repeats this Coming-King theme. This time he includes some key instructions: "Wherefore gird up the loins of your mind, be sober, and hope to the end for the <u>grace</u> <u>that is to be brought unto you</u> at the revelation of Jesus <u>Christ</u>" (1:13). The Bible combination *grace* (159 vs), *that is to be brought unto you* (1 v) = 160 verses. Again the name *Christ* occurs 60 times in the Gospels.

Holiness unto Christ the King (2:1-3:9)—Peter encouraged the scattered pilgrims to holiness by emphasizing that they were not only part of Christ's earthly kingdom but also part of His earthly Melchisedec priesthood. "Ye also, as lively stones, are built up a spiritual house, an <u>holy</u> <u>priesthood,</u> <u>to offer</u> <u>up spiritual sacrifices,</u> <u>acceptable to God</u> by Jesus Christ" (2:5). This is the 7260th verse of the New Testament, and it refers to Christ's kingly order of priests. The uppercase word *Holy* is mentioned in 60 chapters of the New Testament. The Bible combination *priesthood* (16x), *to offer* (41x), *up spiritual sacrifices* (1x), *acceptable to God* (2x) = 60.

Peter shows the suffering saints one way they can honor their New Covenant King, and this by not having a rebellious attitude toward their present earthly king. Kingdom saints are to enter into suffering not sedition. "Submit yourselves to every ordinance of man for the Lord's sake: whether it be to the KING, as supreme. . . . Honour all men. Love the brotherhood. Fear God. Honour the KING" (2:13, 17). The keyword *king* actually occurs in this 60th book of the Bible. Again the phrase *the king* is mentioned in 60 chapters of the Major Prophets. All available forms of the word *honour* are mentioned in 60 collective verses of the New Testament.

Victory for Christ the King (3:10-4:19)—The 60th verse of First Peter says, "For he that will love life, and see good days, let him refrain his tongue from evil, and his lips that they speak no guile" (3:10). The victorious life which pleases Christ is the guile-free life. No one kept his tongue from evil and his lips from speaking guile better than Christ during the time of His suffering. He even prayed for His enemies and spoke kindly of them. In this 60th verse Peter impresses suffering soldiers to imitate their Great King's former godly behavior even as He did during the time of His great suffering.

Christ the King has done much for us by His suffering. Shall we not likewise do so for Him? "Forasmuch then as Christ hath suffered for us in the flesh, arm yourselves likewise with the same mind: for he that hath suffered in the flesh hath ceased from sin" (4:1). Peter used a military term here—arm yourselves. This victorious weapon of royal warfare is not physical but spiritual. From Genesis to the NT Narrative the phrase *for us* occurs 60 times.

Peter emphasizes "that God in all things may be glorified through Jesus Christ, to whom be praise and DOMINION for ever and ever. Amen" (4:11b). Here the title *Christ* is the 260th word of this chapter, and Christ is King.

The other key verses of this kingly Epistle are these: "Beloved, think it not strange concerning the fiery trial which is to try you, as though some strange thing happened unto you: But rejoice, inasmuch as ye are partakers of Christ's sufferings; that, when his glory shall be revealed, ye may be glad also with exceeding joy" (4:12-13). As in the other key verses of this Epistle, these also speak of Christ the King's glorious return and the believer's associated rejoicing. The word *joy* is mentioned in 60 verses of the New Testament. The underlined words indicate the 30,460th verse of the Bible.

Service toward Christ the King (5:1-7)—"The ELDERS which are among you I exhort, who am also an ELDER. . . . Feed the flock of God which is among you. . . . Neither as being lords over God's heritage, but being ensamples to the flock. And when the CHIEF Shepherd shall appear, ye shall receive a CROWN of glory that fadeth not away" (5:1a, 2a, 3-4). The mature, faithful leaders are to serve the King's spiritual children by feeding them the pure bread of God without fear or favor. Again the word *elders* occurs 60 times in the New Testament. Again the phrase *the chief of* occurs 60 times in the Old Testament. Here the word *crown* is the 2260th word in First Peter.

"Likewise, ye younger, submit yourselves unto the ELDER. Yea, all of you be subject one to another, and be clothed with humility: for God resisteth the proud, and giveth grace to the humble. Humble yourselves therefore under the mighty hand of God, that he may exalt you in due time: Casting all your care upon him; for he careth for you" (5:5-7). Our Majestic King stands ready to aid His servants as they stand ready to serve Him. The Bible combination *grace* (159 vs), *to the humble* (1 v) = 160 verses.

Conflict because of Christ the King (5:8-11)—Persecution of Christians was fierce under Nero's reign. Many believers thought he was the infamous antichrist. Accordingly Peter counseled the saints, saying, "Be sober, be vigilant; because your adversary the devil, as a roaring lion, walketh about, seeking whom he may devour: Whom resist stedfast in the <u>faith</u>" (5:8-9a). Again the word *faith* occurs 160 times in the Pauline Epistles. The King of Saints will help His devotees hold fast amidst the continuous conflict waged by the Roman Empire's evil king. "But the God of all grace, who hath called us unto his eternal glory by Christ Jesus, after that ye have suffered a while, make you perfect, stablish, strengthen, settle you. To him be glory and DOMINION for ever and ever. Amen" (5:10-11).

60th Verse of Second Peter

"Ye therefore, beloved, seeing ye know these things before, beware lest ye also, being led away with the error of the wicked, fall from your own stedfastness" (2 Pet. 3:17). Peter mentions steadfastness—an attribute that can easily apply to being steadfast in the King's service. The Wisdom Books combination *service* (59x) and *of the great king* (1x) = 60.

1160th Chapter of the Bible

"That which was from the beginning, which <u>we have heard</u>, which <u>we have seen</u> <u>with our eyes</u>, which <u>we have looked upon</u>, and <u>our hands have handled, of the Word of life</u>" (1 John 1:1). The aged apostle expressed such joy when he thought about how he and the other apostles dwelt so closely and interactively with the King of Kings. They were even privileged to touch the Incarnate King! The Bible combination *we have heard* (26x), *we have seen* (15x), *with our eyes* (1x), *we have looked upon* (1x), *our hands* (16x), *have handled of the word of life* (1x) = 60.

The Only Wise & Glorious Savior-King

"Now unto him that is able to keep you from falling, and to present you faultless before the presence of his glory with exceeding joy, To the only <u>wise</u> <u>God our Saviour</u>, be glory and majesty, DOMINION and POWER, both now and ever. Amen" (Jude 24-25). The New Testament combination *wise* (54 vs), *God our Saviour* (6 vs) = 60 verses.

Prince of the Kings of the Earth

John addressed his letter as being from his hand "and from Jesus Christ, who is the faithful witness, and the first begotten of the dead, and the <u>PRINCE</u> of <u>the KINGS</u> OF THE EARTH. Unto him that loved us, and washed us from our sins in his own blood" (Rev. 1:5). The word *prince('s)* is mentioned in 60 chapters of the Bible. Again the phrase *the kings* is mentioned in 60 chapters of the OT Narrative. This verse presents the Bible's 160th occurrence of the phrase *kings of*, and it speaks of Christ as the Prince among all earthly kings.

60th Verse of Revelation

The Ascended King brings encouragement to His devoted subjects: "Behold, I come quickly: hold that fast which thou hast, that no man take thy CROWN" (Rev. 3:11). Not only is the King coming, but He is also coming quickly. Again all forms of the word *crown* are mentioned in 60 verses of the Old Testament.

The King Stands at the Door

"Behold, I stand at <u>the door</u>, and knock: if any man hear my voice, and open <u>the door</u>, I will come in to him, and will sup <u>with him</u>, and he with me" (Rev. 3:20). The King of Saints stands ready to visit each and every one of His devotees. All they have to do is extend a proper invitation for Him to come and dine. The phrase *the door* occurs 160 times in the Bible; this verse presents its 160th occurrence.

Granted a Place to Sit with Christ the King

"To him that overcometh will I grant to <u>sit</u> with me in my THRONE, even as I also overcame, and am <u>set down</u> with my Father in his THRONE" (Rev. 3:21). The wonder and amazement of this promise leaves the believer breathless. The phrase *sat/set/sit down* is mentioned in 60 verses from Genesis to the NT Narrative.

The Lion King

"And one of the elders saith unto me, Weep not: behold, the <u>Lion</u> of the tribe <u>of Juda</u>, the Root of David, hath prevailed to open the book, and to loose the seven seals thereof" (Rev. 5:5). Judah is the kingly tribe. From this tribe a king is chosen to rule over all Israel's other tribes. The OT Narrative combination *lion roared* (1 v) and *of Judah* (259 vs) = 260 verses.

King of the Bottomless Pit

"And they had a KING <u>over them,</u> which is the angel of the bottomless pit, whose name in the Hebrew tongue is Abaddon, but in the Greek tongue hath his name Apollyon" (Rev. 9:11). Again the phrase *over them* is mentioned in 60 verses of the Bible.

Christ the King Grants His Two End-time Witnesses
Heavenly Power for 1260 Days

"And I will give power unto my two <u>witnesses,</u> and they shall prophesy a thousand two hundred and THREESCORE days, clothed in sackcloth" (Rev. 11:3). All available forms of the word *witness* are mentioned in 60 verses of the New Testament Narrative.

Earthly Kings Will Surrender Their Earthly Reigns Forever

"And the seventh angel sounded; and there were great voices in heaven, saying, The KINGDOMS of this world are become the KINGDOMS of our Lord, and of HIS CHRIST; and he shall REIGN for ever and ever" (Rev. 11:15). You will recall that the word Christ is synonymous with the word king. This verse presents the Bible's 160th verse-mention of the word *reign*, and it speaks of all earthly reigns being handed over to the forever-reigning King called Christ.

The King of Saints

"And they sing the song of Moses the servant of God, and the song of the Lamb, saying, Great and marvellous are thy works, Lord God Almighty; just and true are thy ways, thou KING of <u>saints</u>" (Rev. 15:3). Besides being King of Israel, King of Jacob, King of Glory, King of Nations, King of Kings, and King of Righteousness, Jesus is also the King of Saints. Again the word *saints* occurs 60 times in the New Testament.

Kings of the East

"And the sixth angel poured out his vial upon the great river Euphrates; and the water thereof was dried up, that the way of the KINGS of <u>the east</u> might be prepared" (Rev. 16:12) The phrase *the east* is mentioned in 60 verses of the Major Prophets.

The Millennial King's Iron Scepter

"And out of his mouth goeth a sharp sword, that with it he should smite the nations: and he shall RULE them with a rod of <u>iron</u>: and he treadeth the winepress of the fierceness and wrath of Almighty God" (Rev. 19:15). Throughout the Orient, kings' scepters were made of iron and overlaid with silver or gold. The word *iron* is mentioned in 60 chapters of the Old Testament.

Earth's Coming King of Kings & Lord of Lords

John saw the King coming in His glory with all of His armies behind Him. "And he hath on his vesture and on his thigh a name written, <u>KING</u> OF <u>KINGS</u>, AND LORD OF LORDS" (Rev. 19:16). Again the title *the king* occurs 60 times in Joshua.

Christ, King over the Earth for 1000 Years

"Blessed and holy is he that hath part in the first resurrection: on such the second death hath no POWER, but they shall be priests of God and of <u>Christ</u>, and shall REIGN with him a thousand years" (Rev. 20:6). This privileged group fits our fourth definition of the word "kingly": consisting of kings or others of royal rank. Again the name *Christ* occurs 60 times in the Gospels.

The City of the Great King

"And I John saw <u>the</u> holy <u>city</u>, new Jerusalem, coming down from God out of heaven, prepared as a bride adorned for her husband" (Rev. 21:2). Again the Bible combination *habitation* (58x) and *city of the great King* (2x) = 60. Again the phrase *the city of* occurs 60 times in the OT Narrative.

Their God Is Their King

"And I heard a great voice out of heaven saying, Behold, the tabernacle of God is with men, and he will dwell with them, and they shall be his people, and God himself shall be with them, and be <u>their God</u>" (Rev. 21:3). The phrase *their God* is mentioned in 60 chapters of the Bible!

King David's Offspring

"I Jesus have sent mine angel to testify unto you these things in the churches. I am the root and the offspring of David, and the bright and morning star" (Rev. 22:16). This kingly verse rests in the 260th chapter of the New Testament.

61—God

(King of the Jews)

In every way the eternal God is a mystery. Yet He chooses to reveal to mankind what He wants us to know. He gives us knowledge about Himself little by little. The more receptive we are to Him the more knowledge He gives us. In the Bible we learn about God as He gives us progressive revelation. From Genesis chapter one to Revelation chapter one, our understanding of Him unfolds in a splendid way. Behold now with wonder the following 61 numeric seals which employ any reference to the title God, Lord, and Spirit.

The title *God* is mentioned in 661 verses of the Law.
The title *God* occurs 427 times in the Psalms, a multiple of 61.
The title *God* is mentioned in 161 chapters of the Wisdom Books.
The title *God* occurs 427 times in the Major/Minor Prophets, a multiple of 61.
The title *God* is mentioned in 161 chapters of the Major/Minor Prophets.
The title *God* is mentioned in 61 verses of Second Corinthians.
The title *God/GOD/god* is mentioned in 661 verses of the Major/Minor Prophets.
The title *the God* occurs 61 times in the OT Narrative.
The title *the God of Israel* is mentioned in 61 chapters of the Old Testament.
The phrase *God is* occurs 61 times in the New Testament.
The phrase *God of* is mentioned in 61 verses of Isaiah.
The phrase *God hath* is mentioned naturally in 61 and ½ verses of the Law.
The phrase *God/GOD hath* occurs 122 times in the Old Testament, a multiple of 61.
The phrase *And God/GOD* occurs 61 times in the Law.
The phrase *O God/GOD* is mentioned in 61 chapters of the Bible.
The phrase *his God/god* occurs 61 times in the Old Testament.
The phrase *to God* is mentioned in 61 chapters of the Bible.
The phrase *the kingdom of God* occurs 61 times in the NT Narrative.

~~~~~

The title *LORD* occurs 161 times in Genesis.
The title *LORD* occurs 6461 times in the Old Testament.
The title *LORD/Lord/lord* occurs 2161 times in the OT Narrative.
The title *LORD/Lord/lord* is found in 61 books of the Bible.
The title *LORD/Lord our God* is mentioned in 61 chapters of the Bible.
The title *LORD('S)* occurs 561 times in First and Second Chronicles.
The title *the LORD* is mentioned in 1561 verses of the OT Narrative.
The title *the LORD* occurs 6090 times in the Old Testament, nearly 6100 times.
The title *the LORD/Lord* is found in 61 books of the Bible.
The title *the Lord/Lord's/lord* occurs 61 times in Luke.
The title *the Lord* occurs 366 times in the Old Testament, a multiple of 61.
The phrase *my Lord/lord* occurs 183 times in the Bible, a multiple of 61.
The phrase *I am the LORD/Lord* is mentioned in 161 verses of the Bible.
The phrase *the LORD/Lord of* is mentioned in 61 chapters of the Major Prophets.
The title *the word of the LORD* is mentioned in 61 verses of the Kings/Chronicles.
The title *the word of the LORD/Lord* is mentioned in 161 chapters of the Bible.

The phrase *the words of the* occurs 61 times in the Old Testament.

The phrase *the LORD/Lord is* is mentioned in 61 verses of the Wisdom Books.

The phrase *the LORD spake unto Moses* is mentioned in 61 chapters of the Law.

The phrase *LORD of* is mentioned in 61 chapters of the Major Prophets.

The phrase *before the LORD* occurs 61 times in the book of Leviticus.

The phrase *before the LORD* occurs 161 times in the Law.

The phrase *unto the LORD* is mentioned in 61 verses of Numbers.

The phrase *unto the LORD* is mentioned in 461 verses of the Old Testament.

The phrase *of the LORD/Lord* is mentioned in 1610 verses of the Bible.

The phrase *of the Lord* occurs 61 times in the Pauline and General Epistles.

The phrase *from the LORD/Lord* is mentioned in 61 chapters of the Bible.

The phrase *thus saith the LORD/Lord* is mentioned in 161 chapters of the Bible.

The phrase *saith the Lord* is mentioned in 61 chapters of the Old Testament.

The phrase *saith the Lord GOD/LORD God* is mentioned in 61 chapters of Major Prophets.

The phrase *saith the* is mentioned in 161 chapters of the Major/Minor Prophets.

The title *LORD/ Lord our God* is mentioned in 61 chapters of the Bible.

The title *the Lord GOD* is mentioned in 61 chapters of the Major Prophets.

The title *the LORD/Lord of hosts* occurs 122 times in the Major Prophets, multiple of 61.

The phrase *for the LORD/Lord* is mentioned naturally in 161 chapters of the Old Testament.

The phrase *the LORD/Lord that* occurs 122 times in the Old Testament, a multiple of 61.

The phrase *and the LORD/Lord* is mentioned in 261 chapters of the Old Testament.

The phrase *and the LORD/Lord/lord said* occurs naturally 161 times in the Bible.

~~~~~

The title *the Spirit* is mentioned in 61 collective of chapters of the New Testament.

The title *spirit* is mentioned in 61 verses of the Wisdom Books.

The title *S/spirit* occurs 261 times in the New Testament.

The title *S/spirit* is mentioned naturally in 61 verses of the Gospels.

The title *Spirit* occurs 161 times from Genesis to Jude.

The Golden Ratio or Divine Proportion
1.618034

There is a number so perfect and flawless that it forms a foundation for many different studies such as mathematics, physics, music, art, architecture, and more. This number is so prolific, profound, and purpose-filled throughout the natural world that it gives mankind clear evidence of creation's intelligent design. God uses this ratio number to reveal Himself to man; it is 1.618034. It forms what is most commonly referred to as the GOLDEN RATIO. Plato and others called it the GOLDEN MEAN; around 300 BC Euclid described it as 'division according to the outer and middle proportion.' In the 1200s Fibonacci codified it and called it the GOLDEN SEQUENCE; in the 1400s Luca Pacioli called it the DIVINE PROPORTION; in 1835 mathematician Martin Ohm called it the GOLDEN SECTION. It is God's special number. Some people call it the God Number! Indeed it is. Scientists and mathematicians typically do not associate this number to God, but that error is cleared up upon seeing its prolific use in the King James Version Bible. The scientific world calls this number the most astonishing number in the world. Indeed it is. We stand amazed to find the root of this number, 61 or 161, in so many of the above-mentioned numeric seals pertaining to God's titles.

The word *golden* is mentioned in 61 verses of the King James Bible!

The golden ratio or divine proportion is a special arrangement considered to be esthetically pleasing. Any structure which has a ratio close to this perfect number is also considered to have perfect proportions.

The golden ratio is a mathematical term used to describe the relationship of two figures where the numbers appear to have some form of complimentary ratio. This golden ratio is associated with a patterned arrangement of things in nature having what is known as the golden spiral; things like an ocean wave, a hurricane, a galaxy, a snail's shell, a seashell, a flower's petals, a plant's leaves, a sunflower's seeds, a pinecone's rows, a tree's branches, and even a human's arms hand and fingers. Some creatures even live according to the golden ratio like honey bees whose colonies are known to maintain a ratio of males to females at a ratio of 1:1.618. The golden ratio is also seen at the quantum level. The double-helix spirals of our DNA and the composition of a single DNA molecule both seem to have been made in accordance with the divine proportion of the golden ratio.

In the appendix we allow someone else more qualified to reveal the specific details of this unique number. Beside the appendix much secular information exists on the subject of the golden ratio. Various books both in the past and recently have written about it. The numeric-seal, even golden seal, evidence in the King James Bible is overwhelming and proves that man is not responsible for its content but rather only an infinitely wise God.

The Holy Bible
[King James Version]
AD 1611

Not long after its initial printing, the royally authorized English version of THE HOLY BIBLE came to be called more familiarly as *The King James Bible*. This English rendering was completed by the scholarly translation committee in the divinely proportioned year 1610. It was then sent to a certified publisher and made available to the public in the following year 1611. Both these dates reveal the base number of the golden ration or divine proportion! The word *holy* occurs 611 times in Scripture, a number crowned with a 61. From the Bible's first and earliest canonical publishing by Moses in approximately 1450 BC until its epic English publishing in 1611 spans a divinely proportioned time of 3061 years!

About one and one-half centuries later in the year 1769 [a multiple of 61], this translation was updated with consistent and contemporary English spelling. This would be the last time God's fingerprints ever touched the Holy Bible! This updated rendering of the Holy Bible was 'also' to be surely included in God's final biblical work; this we know because the word *also* occurs 1769 times in the Bible. Accordingly the equation 1769 ÷ 61 = 29 with 29 being the Bible's number for Departure! Upon His completion of the 1769 edition of The Holy Bible the Divine Author permanently departed from His creative work of the Bible. Thus it stands divinely authorized, complete, and perfect! The equation 1769 - 161 = 1608 with 1608 being the year God was overseeing the KJV translators' ongoing, in-depth Bible work.

Modern English editions of the Bible beginning with the RSV in 1881 and all three hundred plus editions that have followed after it are not the works of God but of misguided men. Rather these have all altered God's perfect Bible by removing or changing His divinely proportioned words. Consider the following numeric seal which testifies to God's authorship of the KJV Holy Bible.

Its Old Testament canon consists of <u>61</u>0,281 divinely proportioned words, a number crowned with a crystal-clear 61.

In the Beginning God Made Heaven & Earth

"In the <u>beginning</u> GOD created <u>the heaven</u> and the <u>earth</u>" (Gen. 1:1). The phrase *the heaven* is mentioned in 61 chapters of the Bible. The Wisdom Books combination *the LORD made* (1x) and *heaven* (60x) = 61. The word *earth* occurs 61 times in Jeremiah.

> The word *begin** is mentioned in 61 chapters of the Old Testament.
> The word *began* occurs 61 times in the Gospels.
> The word *began* is mentioned in 61 verses of the Gospels.

God Is Divine Light

"And GOD said, Let there be <u>light</u>: and there was <u>light</u>" (Gen. 1:3). This light was not that of the planetary bodies but that emanating from His countenance. The phrase *the light* occurs 61 times in the Old Testament.

61st Word of the Bible

"And GOD saw the light, that it was good: and <u>GOD</u>" (Gen. 1:4). As seen underlined here, the 61st word of the Bible is *God*.

God Made the Evening & Morning

"And GOD <u>called the</u> light <u>Day</u>, and the darkness <u>he called</u> <u>Night</u>. And the <u>evening</u> and the <u>morning</u> were the first day" (Gen. 1:5). The phrase *called the* is mentioned in 61 verses of the Old Testament. The phrase *he called* is mentioned in 61 verses from Genesis to the Gospels. The word *evening(s)* occurs 61 times in the Bible. The word *night* is mentioned in 61 verses of the New Testament. The word *morning* is mentioned in 161 chapters of the Bible.

> The phrase *the day* is mentioned in 261 chapters of the Bible.
> The word *day* is found in 61 books of the Bible.

And God Said

"And GOD <u>said</u>, Let there be a firmament in the midst of the waters, and let it divide the waters from the waters" (Gen. 1:6).

> The word *said* is mentioned in 61 verses of Job.
> The word *said* occurs 1061 times in the New Testament.
> The phrase *said I* is mentioned in 61 verses of the OTN.

And God Made

"And GOD <u>made</u> the firmament, and divided the <u>waters</u> which were under the firmament from the waters which were above the firmament: and it was so" (Gen. 1:7). The singular word *water* is mentioned in 61 verses of the Major and Minor Prophets.

> The word *made* is mentioned in 611 chapters of the Bible.
> The word *made* is mentioned in 461 chapters of the Old Testament.
> The phrase *he made* occurs 161 times from Genesis to the NT Narrative.

And God Saw

"And GOD said, Let the waters under the heaven be gathered together unto one place, and let the dry land appear: and it was so. And GOD called the dry land Earth; and the gathering together of the waters called he Seas: and GOD saw that it was good" (Gen. 1:9-10). The word *saw* is mentioned in 61 verses of the Major and Minor Prophets. The word *it* is mentioned in 61 chapters of Isaiah. The phrase *is/was good* is mentioned in 61 chapters of the Old Testament.

God Created Fruit Trees

"And GOD said, Let the earth bring forth grass, the herb yielding seed, and the fruit tree yielding fruit after his kind, whose seed is in itself, upon the earth: and it was so. And the earth brought forth grass, and herb yielding seed after his kind, and the tree yielding fruit, whose seed was in itself, after his kind: and GOD saw that it was good" (Gen. 1:11-12). In this passage there are 61 words from one occurrence of *God* to its next occurrence. The singular word *seed('s)* occurs 61 times in the Major and Minor Prophets. The word *fruit* occurs naturally 61 times in the Major and Minor Prophets.

And God

"And GOD made two great lights; the greater light to rule the day, and the lesser light to rule the night: he made the stars also" (Gen. 1:16). Again the phrase *And God/GOD* occurs 61 times in the Law. In the Kings James Version—God is responsible for the placement of every "and" that we see. The following golden numeric seals are case-sensitive.

The word *and* is mentioned in 16150 verses of the Old Testament.
The word *and* occurs 761 times in Daniel.
The word *and* is mentioned in 61 verses of Joel.
The word *and* occurs 361 times in First and Second Corinthians.
The word *And* is mentioned in 1161 verses of Genesis.
The word *And* occurs 1361 times in the Major and Minor Prophets.
The phrase *And he* is mentioned in 361 chapters of the OT.
The phrase *And the* is mentioned in 61 chapters of the Gospels.

God Let All Creation Happen at His Command

"And God blessed them, saying, Be fruitful, and multiply, and fill the waters in the seas, and let fowl multiply in the earth" (Gen. 1:22). The lowercase word *let* occurs 261 times in the OT Narrative.

61st Verse of the Bible

"For GOD doth know that in the day ye eat thereof, then your eyes shall be opened, and ye shall be as gods, knowing good and evil" (Gen. 3:5). The keyword *God* actually occurs in this 61st verse. Both the singular title God and the plural title gods share the same Hebrew word elohim. The word *then* occurs 661 times in the OT Narrative. The word *opened* is mentioned in 61 verses of the New Testament. The phrase *they shall be* is mentioned in 61 chapters of the Major and Minor Prophets.

Man Made in Divine Proportion to God

"This is the book of the generations of Adam. In the day that GOD created man, in the likeness of GOD made he him" (Gen. 5:1). The first man upon the earth was given a measure of God's divine proportion. Originally there was neither sin nor sin nature in Adam. In the New Testament's genealogy of man, Adam is referred to as "the son of God." The reason for this was simply that he came from God and not man. The phrase *the day that* is mentioned in 61 chapters of the Bible. This verse presents to us the Bible's 61st occurrence of the name *God*. The word *like* is mentioned in 61 chapters of the New Testament. The Bible combination *Adam* (30x), *was made in the* (2x), *likeness of* (26x), *image of God* (3x) = 61.

The title *man('s)* occurs 61 times in First Kings.
The phrase *a man* occurs 61 times in the Synoptic Gospels.

Finding Grace in the Eyes of God

"But Noah found grace in the eyes of the LORD" (Gen. 6:8). The Hebrew word for grace means favor. Favor is not always earned; sometimes it is simply given because of the giver's love, pity, or compassion for another. The word *found* occurs 61 times in the Major and Minor Prophets. The word *grace* is mentioned in 122 chapters of the New Testament, a multiple of 61. The phrase *eyes of* is mentioned in 61 chapters of the Old Testament. Again the phrase *of the LORD/Lord* is mentioned in 1610 verses of the Bible. Again the title *LORD* occurs 161 times in Genesis.

God Prepares to Destroy all the Earth

"And, behold, I, even I, do bring a flood of waters upon the earth, to destroy all flesh, wherein is the breath of life, from under heaven; and every thing that is in the earth shall die" (Gen. 6:17). The phrase *to destroy* is mentioned in 61 chapters of the Old Testament.

All That God Commanded Moses

"Thus did Noah; according to all that GOD commanded him, so did he" (Gen. 6:22). The phrase *all that* occurs 561 times in the Bible.

God Spares a Righteous Man's Family

"And the LORD said unto Noah, Come thou and all thy house into the ark; for thee have I seen righteous before me in this generation" (Gen. 7:1). The Genesis combination *for thee* (3x), *have I* (15x), *seen* (11x), *righteous* (10x), *before me* (7x), *in this* (10x), *generation* (3x) = 61.

God Remembers His Covenants

"And I will remember my covenant, which is between me and you and every living creature of all flesh; and the waters shall no more become a flood to destroy all flesh" (Gen. 9:15). All available tenses of the word *remember* occur 61 times in the Wisdom Books.

God Shall Dwell in the Hebrew's Camp

"GOD shall enlarge Japheth, and he shall dwell in the tents of Shem; and Canaan shall be his servant" (Gen. 9:27). The Hebrews descended from Shem's line. The word *shall* is mentioned in 6061 verses of the Bible! The phrase *dwell in* occurs 161 times in the Old Testament.

The phrase *he shall* is mentioned in 61 verses of Isaiah.
The phrase *and he shall* is mentioned naturally in 161 chapters of the Bible.

Let's Go down to Babel

"And the LORD said, Behold, the people is one, and they have all one language; and this they begin to do: and now nothing will be restrained from them, which they have imagined to do. Go to, let us go down, and there confound their language, that they may not understand one another's speech" (Gen. 11:6-7). God referred to Himself in a plural form of existence. As the whole of Scripture reveals, God exists as three inseparable Persons: Father, Son, and Spirit.

The term *let us* is mentioned in 61 verses of the New Testament.

The word *let* occurs 61 times in First Samuel.

The word *let* is mentioned in 61 verses of First and Second Kings.

The word *let* is mentioned in 61 chapters of the Pauline/General Epistles.

The word *us* occurs 61 times in Deuteronomy.

The word *us* occurs 961 times in the Old Testament.

The Lord Came down to Babel

"And the LORD came down to see the city and the tower, which the children of men builded" (Gen. 11:5). Again the title *LORD* occurs 161 times in Genesis. The word *came* is mentioned in 161 verses of Genesis. The word *down* occurs 61 times in Judges.

The Lord Had Said unto Abram

"Now the LORD had said unto Abram, Get thee out of thy country, and from thy kindred, and from thy father's house, unto a land that I will shew thee" (Gen. 12:1). The Bible phrase *had said* (59x) and *had thus said* (2x) = 61.

The phrase *said unto* is mentioned in 161 chapters of the OT Narrative.

The phrase *said unto* is mentioned in 61 chapters of Synoptic Gospels.

Abram Called on the Name of the Lord

"And Abram went up out of Egypt . . . Unto the place of the altar, which he had made there at the first: and there Abram called on the name of the LORD" (Gen. 13:1a, 4). The word *called* is mentioned in 61 verses of the Pauline and General Epistles.

Melchizedek—Prototype King of the Jews

"And Melchizedek king of Salem brought forth bread and wine: and he was the priest of the most high GOD. And he blessed him, and said, Blessed be Abram of the most high GOD, possessor of heaven and earth: And blessed be the most high GOD, which hath delivered thine enemies into thy hand. And he gave him tithes of all" (Gen. 14:18-20). Salem was the early name for Jerusalem. Jerusalem means flowing with peace. When Abraham, the first Jew, paid covenant tithes to the king of Salem, Melchizedek thus became the King of the Jews to the Jewish people. This passage consists of 61 words!

The Words of the Lord

"After these things the word of the LORD came unto Abram in a vision, saying, Fear not, Abram: I am thy shield, and thy exceeding great reward" (Gen. 15:1). God holds many titles in the Bible. As a Person, He often refers to Himself as the Word of the Lord. Again the title *the word of the LORD/Lord* is mentioned in 161 chapters of the Bible. The phrase *came unto* occurs 61 times in the Major Prophets. The encouraging phrase *fear not* occurs 61 times from Genesis to the NT Narrative.

> The word *word* occurs naturally 61 times in the Pauline Epistles.
> The word *words* is mentioned naturally in 61 verses of the NT Narrative.
> The word *word(s)* is mentioned in 61 verses of Acts.
> The phrase *the words of the* occurs 61 times in the Old Testament.
> The phrase *words of the* is mentioned in 61 verses of Old Testament.

God's Divine Messenger

In the Old Testament we are presented with a heavenly Person Who shares unique divine proportions with God. He is called *the Angel of the LORD*. In reality He is the second Person of the Godhead—the Son of God. The Hebrew root word for "angel" is malakh, meaning to dispatch as a deputy. This Hebrew root word is translated in various ways: angel, ambassador, messenger, and king. At times the Lord himself made appearances to men on Earth, and at other times He dispatched His Son as Heaven's Chief Messenger to come below and accomplish some needful earthly task. Throughout the Old Testament we will look at clues which lead us to firmly believe that the Angel of the Lord is none other than God's eternally existent and divine Son.

God's Divine Messenger
(Part 1)

"And <u>the angel of the LORD</u> found her by a fountain of water in the wilderness, by the fountain in the way to Shur. And he said, Hagar, Sarai's maid, whence camest thou? and whither wilt thou go? And she said, I flee from the face of my mistress Sarai. And <u>the angel of the LORD</u> said unto her, Return to thy mistress, and submit thyself under her hands. And <u>the angel of the LORD</u> said unto her, I will multiply thy seed exceedingly, that it shall not be numbered for multitude. . . . And she called the name of the LORD that spake unto her, <u>Thou GOD seest</u> me: for she said, Have I also here looked after him that <u>seeth</u> me?" (Gen. 16:7-10, 13)

This passage presents the first occurrence of the title "the Angel of the Lord." The biblical principle of first mention is vital to our understanding of any subject. Here the maid calls the Angel of the Lord by two clear titles of deity—God and LORD, the latter title signifying the sacred name Jehovah. The narrative does not correct Hagar's supposed 'misuse' use of these titles of deity because she was absolutely correct in her speech. Such interchangeable usage will be shown time and again as we study the Angel of the Lord. The Old Testament titles *the angel of God* (5x) and *angel of the LORD* (56x) = 61. The word *thou* occurs 61 times in Revelation. The word *Thou* [uppercase only] is mentioned in 61 verses of the Gospels. The word *seest/seeth* is mentioned in 61 verses of the Old Testament.

The Almighty God Appeared to Abram

"And when Abram was ninety years old and nine, the <u>LORD</u> <u>appeared</u> to Abram, and said unto him, I am the Almighty GOD; walk before me, and be thou perfect" (Gen. 17:1). Here the title *LORD* is the 9261st word of the Bible. All forms of the word *appear* are mentioned in 161 verses of the Bible.

God Changes Abram's Name to Abraham

"Neither shall thy name any more be called <u>Abram</u>, but thy name shall be <u>Abraham</u>; for a father of many nations have I made thee" (Gen. 17:5). God added the letter 'h,' the breath sound, from

His own holy name. Abraham became known as the Friend of God.

The name *Abram('s)* occurs 61 times in the Bible.
The name *Abraham* occurs naturally 161 times in the Old Testament.

God Promises to Give

"And GOD said unto Abraham, As for Sarai thy wife, thou shalt not call her name Sarai, but Sarah shall her name be. And I will bless her, and give thee a son also of her" (Gen 17:15-16a). The phrase *and give* occurs 61 times in the Old Testament.

The phrase *And I will* occurs 161 times in Major/Minor Prophets.
The phrase *And I will* is seen in 161 verses of Major/Minor Prophets.
The phrase *A/and I will* occurs 61 times in Isaiah.

The Lord Made It Rain Fire & Brimstone

"And the LORD went his way, as soon as he had left communing with Abraham: and Abraham returned unto his place. . . . Then the LORD rained upon Sodom and upon Gomorrah brimstone and fire from the LORD out of heaven" (Gen. 18:33; 19:24). The OT combination *the LORD went* (11x), *his way* (44x), *as soon as he had left* (1x), *communing with Abraham* (1x), *and Abraham returned unto his place* (1x), *then the LORD rained* (1x), *upon Sodom and upon Gomorrah* (1x), *brimstone and fire from the LORD out of heaven* (1x) = 61.

God's Divine Messenger
(Part 2)

Hagar and little Ishmael had been exiled from the camp. When her water ran out she placed her boy under a shrub to shield him from the sun. He lay their crying. "And GOD heard the voice of the lad; and the angel of GOD called to Hagar out of heaven, and said unto her, What aileth thee, Hagar? fear not; for GOD hath heard the voice of the lad where he is" (Gen. 21:17). On this occasion God hears but the Angel of God speaks. This is amazing! Indeed the Angel of God shares a divine proportion to God. They are a single entity within the Elohim. The word *heard* is mentioned in 61 chapters of the Gospels. Again the Old Testament titles *the angel of God* (5x) and *angel of the LORD* (56x) = 61.

God's Divine Messenger
(Part 3)

"And it came to pass after these things, that GOD did tempt Abraham, and said unto him . . . Take now thy son, thine only son Isaac, whom thou lovest, and get thee into the land of Moriah; and offer him there for a burnt offering . . . And the angel of the LORD called unto him out of heaven, and said, Abraham, Abraham: and he said, Here am I. And he said, Lay not thine hand upon the lad, neither do thou any thing unto him: for now I know that thou fearest GOD, seeing thou hast not withheld thy son, thine only son from me" (Gen. 22:1-2c, 11-12).

At the beginning of this story the Lord himself tells Abraham to go sacrifice his son; but later at the climatic point of sacrifice the Angel of the Lord speaks to Abraham in the same divine capacity by His use of the word "me." Here in this passage we again see the interchangeable voice of God and His Chief Messenger. The phrase *the angel* is mentioned in 122 verses of the Bible, a multiple of 61.

The God of Heaven & Earth

"And <u>swear</u> by the LORD, the GOD <u>of heaven</u>, and the GOD <u>of the earth</u>, that thou shalt not take a wife unto my son of the daughters of the Canaanites, among whom I dwell" (Gen. 24:3). All forms of the word swear/sware show the golden seal of God: *sware* (56 chs), *swarest* (5 chs), *sworn* (43 chs), *swear* (45 chs), *swearers* (1 ch), *sweareth* (7 chs), *swearing* (4 chs) = 161 chapters.

> The phrase *of heaven* is mentioned in 61 chapters of the Bible.
> The phrase *of the earth* is mentioned in 61 verses of the Wisdom Books.

The Lord Appeared unto Isaac

"And there was a famine in the land, beside the first famine that was in the days of Abraham. And Isaac went unto Abimelech king of the Philistines unto Gerar. And the LORD <u>appeared</u> unto him, and said, Go not down into Egypt; dwell in the land which I shall tell thee of: Sojourn in this land, and I will be with thee, and will bless thee" (Gen. 26:1-3a). Again all forms of the word *appear* are mentioned in 161 verses of the Bible.

The Lord Hath Blessed

"And his father Isaac said unto him, Come near now, and kiss me, my son. And he came near, and kissed him: and he smelled the smell of his raiment, and blessed him, and said, See, the smell of my son is as the smell of a field which the LORD hath <u>blessed</u>" (Gen. 27:26-27). All available forms of the word *bless* occur 61 times in the NT Narrative.

The Stairway to Heaven

"And he <u>dreamed, and behold a ladder set up</u> on the earth, <u>and the top of it reached to heaven:</u> <u>and behold the angels of GOD ascending and descending on it</u>. <u>And, behold, the LORD stood</u> <u>above it, and said, I am the LORD GOD</u> of Abraham thy father, <u>and the GOD of Isaac</u>" (Gen. 28:12-13a). The Major and Minor Prophets combination *stood* (60x), *above it* (1x) = 61. The Old Testament combination *dreamed* (20x), *and behold a ladder set up* (1x), *on the earth* (15x), *and the top of it* (1x), *reached to heaven and behold* (1x), *the angels of God* (2x), *ascending* (2x), *and descending* (1x), *on it* (10x), *and behold the* L*ORD* (3x), *stood above it* (1x), *and said I am the* L*ORD God* (1x), *of Abraham thy father* (2x), *and the God of Isaac* (1x) = 61.

The House of God at Bethel

"And Jacob awaked out of his sleep, and he said, Surely the LORD is in this place; and I knew it not. And he was afraid, and said, How dreadful is this place! this is none other but <u>the house of</u> GOD, and this is the gate of heaven" (Gen. 28:16-17).

> The phrase *the house of* is seen naturally in 161 verses of the Chronicles.
> The phrase *the house of* occurs 61 times in Jeremiah and Lamentations.
> The phrase *the house* occurs naturally 61 times in the NT Narrative.

God's Divine Messenger
(Part 4)

"And the angel of GOD <u>spake</u> unto me in a dream, <u>saying</u>, Jacob . . . I am the GOD of Beth-el, where thou anointedst the pillar, and where thou vowedst a vow <u>unto me</u>: now arise, get thee out from this land, and return unto the land of thy kindred" (Gen. 31:11a, 13). Here we see again the alternate title to the Angel of the Lord—the Angel of God. This Heavenly Messenger expressed His divine proportion to God by declaring to be the very God. If He was not God it would be a great blasphemy for Him to say so. As stated earlier, we know this Person to be the Son of God. The phrase *unto me* is mentioned in 61 chapters of the Law.

> The word *spake* is mentioned in 61 verses of the Synoptic Gospels.
> The word *saying* is mentioned in 61 verses of Second Kings
> The word *saying* is mentioned in 61 verses of the Chronicles.

The Hebrews' Divine Watcher

Laban's parting covenant words to Jacob were these: "The LORD <u>watch</u> between me and thee, when we are absent one from another" (Gen. 31:49). Laban, a Hebrew of nominal faith, acknowledged that the Hebrews' God watched over His people from one day to the next and from one generation to the next. The word *watch* occurs 61 times in the Bible.

Having Seen God Face to Face

".and there wrestled a man with him until the breaking of the day ;And Jacob was left alone" . . . And Jacob called the name of the place Peniel: for I have <u>seen</u> <u>GOD face to face</u>, and my life is preserved" (Gen. 32:24, 30). Jacob marveled that he had looked God in the face and not died. According to the whole passage, the heavenly Person whom Jacob had wrestled with was both Man and God. Two verses forward is the related 961st verse of the Bible. The Bible combination *seen* (259 vs), *God face to face* (1 v), *the LORD face to face* (1 v) = 261 verses. The NT Narrative combination *seen* (59 vs) and *the Lord God* (2 vs) = 61 verses.

> The phrase *my face* occurs 61 times in the OT.
> The phrase *thy face* occurs 61 times in the Bible.

The Altar of God

"And GOD said unto Jacob, Arise, go up to Beth-el, and dwell there: and make there an <u>altar</u> unto GOD. . . . And GOD <u>went up</u> from him in the place <u>where</u> he <u>talked</u> with him" (Gen. 35:1a, 13). The word *altar* is mentioned in 161 verses of the Law. The phrase *went up* is mentioned in 161 verses from Genesis to the Gospels. The word *where* occurs 61 times in the Major Prophets. All forms of the word *talk* occur 61 times in the Old Testament.

Again God Appeared unto Jacob

"And GOD <u>appeared</u> unto Jacob <u>again</u>, when he came out of Padan-aram, and blessed him" (Gen. 35:9). Again all forms of the word *appear* are mentioned in 161 verses of the Bible. The word *again* occurs 161 times in the NT Narrative.

The Lord Was with Joseph

"And the LORD <u>was with</u> Joseph, and he was a prosperous man; and he was in the house of his master the Egyptian. . . . But the LORD <u>was with</u> Joseph, and shewed him mercy, and gave him favour in the sight of the keeper of the prison" (Gen. 39:2, 21). The phrase *was with* occurs 61 times from Genesis to the Gospels.

Interpretations Belong to God

"And they said unto him, We have dreamed a dream, and there is no interpreter of it. And Joseph said unto them, Do not interpretations belong <u>to</u> GOD? tell me them, I pray you" (Gen. 41:8).

> The word *to* is mentioned in 361 verses of Exodus.
> The word *to* is mentioned in 361 verses of Second Kings.
> The word *to* occurs 61 times in Galatians.

A Dream from God

"And Joseph said unto Pharaoh, The <u>dream</u> of Pharaoh is one: GOD hath <u>shewed</u> Pharaoh what he is about <u>to do</u>" (Gen. 41:25). Joseph let the king know his dream actually came from God. The word *dream* is mentioned in 61 verses of the Bible. All available forms of the word *shew* occur 61 times in the Wisdom Books. The phrase *to do* occurs naturally 61 times in the OT Narrative.

Established by God

"And for that the dream was doubled unto Pharaoh twice; it is because the thing is established <u>by</u> GOD, shortly bring it to pass" (Gen. 41:32).

> The word *by* occurs 61 times in Deuteronomy.
> The word *by* occurs 61 times in Second Kings.
> The word *by* is mentioned in 61 verses of Second Chronicles.
> The word *by* occurs 61 times in Second Corinthians.

Joseph Had the Spirit of God

"And Pharaoh said unto his servants, Can we find such a one as this is, a man in whom <u>the Spirit</u> of GOD is?" (Gen. 41:38) Again the title *the Spirit* is mentioned in 61 collective chapters of the New Testament.

God Did Send Me

"And Joseph said unto his brethren, Come near to me, I pray you. And they came near. And he said, I am Joseph your brother, whom ye sold into Egypt. Now therefore be not grieved, nor angry with yourselves, that ye sold me hither: for GOD <u>did</u> <u>send</u> me before you to preserve life" (Gen. 45:4-5). The word *send* is mentioned in 161 verses of the Old Testament.

> The word *did* occurs 461 times in the OT Narrative.
> The word *did* is mentioned naturally in 61 verses of Second Chronicles.
> The phrase *he did* occurs 61 times in First and Second Kings.

God Speaks in Visions of the Night

"<u>And</u> GOD spake unto Israel in the <u>visions</u> of the night, and said, Jacob, Jacob. And he said, Here am I" (Gen. 46:2). Again Genesis contains 1161 verse mentions of the uppercase word *And*. Again the phrase *And God/GOD* occurs 61 times in the Law. The word *vision(s)* is mentioned in 61 verses of the Major and Minor Prophets.

God's Divine Messenger
(Part 5)

Jacob proclaimed to Joseph, "<u>The Angel which redeemed me from all evil</u>, bless the lads; and let my name be named on them, and the name of my fathers Abraham and Isaac; and let them grow into a multitude in the midst of the earth" (Gen. 48:16). God's Divine Messenger is revealed here as fulfilling the role of a Redeemer, a title which rightly belongs to God. Hence the Angel of the Lord is once again shown to hold a divine proportion with God. The combined Bible titles *the angel of the LORD/Lord* (59x), *the Angel which redeemed me from all evil* (1x), *the angel of his presence* (1x) = 61. The word *redeemed* is mentioned in 61 verses of the Bible.

Future Jews to Gather around the Divine King of the Jews

"Judah, thou art he whom thy brethren shall praise. . . . The sceptre shall not depart from Judah, nor a lawgiver from between his feet, until Shiloh come; and unto him shall the gathering of the people be" (Gen. 49:8a, 10). Jacob prophesied about Judah's Everlasting Jewish King. Alas, when the Incarnate King of the Jews walked about the Galilean hills during the days of His public ministry, multitudes of Jews followed after Him and gathered around Him. The underlined name *Judah* is the 161st word in this prophetic Jacobean chapter.

> The word *him* occurs naturally 61 times in Joshua.
> The word *him* is mentioned in 61 verses of Daniel.
> The word *him* occurs 6661 times in the Bible!
> The phrase *to him* is mentioned in 61 verses of the Gospels.
> The New Testament: *unto him* (459x), *gathering* (2x) = 461.

The Servants of God

"So shall ye say unto Joseph, Forgive, I pray thee now, the trespass of thy brethren, and their sin; for they did unto thee evil: and now, we pray thee, forgive the trespass of the servants of the GOD of thy father. And Joseph wept when they spake unto him" (Gen. 50:17). Counting backward from Revelation this verse presents the Bible's 61st occurrence of the phrase *the servants of,* and it is clearly identified with God.

The Children of Israel

"And Joseph took an oath of the children of Israel, saying, GOD will surely visit you" (Gen. 50:25a). The children of Israel are vitally linked to *El*—a Hebrew name for God.

> The phrase *children of Israel* occurs 61 times in Leviticus.
> The phrase *children of Israel* occurs 61 times in Judges.
> The phrase *of the children of Israel* is mentioned in 161 verses of the Bible.
> The phrase *and the children of Israel* is in 61 chapters of the Old Testament.
> The phrase *of Israel* is mentioned naturally in 161 verses of the Old Testament.

God Remembered & Heard & Looked

"And it came to pass in process of time, that the king of Egypt died: and the children of Israel sighed by reason of the bondage, and they cried, and their cry came up unto GOD by reason of the bondage. And GOD heard their groaning, and GOD remembered his covenant with Abraham, with Isaac, and with Jacob. And GOD looked upon the children of Israel, and GOD had respect unto them" (Exod. 2:23-25). Again the word *heard* is mentioned in 61 chapters of the Gospels. Again all available tenses of the word *remember* occurs 61 times in the Wisdom Books. All tenses of the word *look* are mentioned naturally in 61 chapters of the New Testament.

God's Divine Messenger
(Part 6)

"And the angel of the LORD <u>appeared unto him in a flame of fire out of the midst of a bush: and he looked, and, behold, the bush burned with fire, and the bush was not consumed. And Moses said, I will now turn aside, and see this great sight, why the bush is not burnt. And when the LORD saw that he turned aside to see</u>, GOD called unto him out of the midst of the bush, and said, Moses, Moses" (Exod. 3:2-4). Here again the Angel of the Lord is seen to share a divine proportion with God. The Bible is clearly trying to teach us that the Angel of the Lord is not only divine but one-and-the-same with God. Again all forms of the word *appear* show the golden seal of God, being mentioned in 161 verses of the Bible. The word *burnt* occurs 361 times in the Old Testament. In this passage there are 61 underlined words of divine proportion which link the Angel of the Lord to God.

God's Holy Ground

"And he said, Draw not nigh hither: put off thy shoes from off thy feet, for the place whereon thou standest is <u>holy</u> ground" (Exod. 3:5). Again the word *holy* occurs 611 times in Scripture, a number crowned with a 61. Here the word *holy* is the 1261st word of Exodus.

61st Verse of Exodus

"And God said unto Moses, <u>I AM THAT I AM</u>: and he said, Thus shalt thou say unto the children of Israel, I AM hath sent me unto you" (Exod. 3:14). This 61st verse gives us an understanding of God's nature and is found nowhere else in Scripture. God ever was, ever is, and ever shall be. He exists beyond the confines of time. Behold the following divine coincidence. Strong's Concordance Hebrew word #1961 *haya* ['to exist'] is the root from which the name *Yehovah*—the Existing One—is derived. The phrase *to be* occurs 61 times in the Major Prophets. The phrase *to be* is mentioned in 61 verses of Synoptic Gospels.

> The word *I* is mentioned in 961 verses of the OT Narrative.
> The word *am* occurs 611 times in the Old Testament.
> The word *am* occurs naturally 61 times in the Synoptic Gospels.
> The word *that* occurs 61 times in First Peter.
> The term *that I* is mentioned naturally in 61 chapters of the Law.
> The word *am* [lowercase only] occurs 161 times in the NT Narrative.

Israel Is God's Firstborn Nation

"And thou shalt say unto Pharaoh, <u>Thus</u> saith the LORD, <u>Israel</u> is my son, even my firstborn" (Exod. 4:22). Here the word *thus* is the 661st word in this chapter, and it relates to God. The title *Israel** is mentioned 1161 verses of the OT Narrative.

> The name *Israel* occurs 261 times in First/Second Samuel.
> The name *Israel* occurs 161 times in Second Kings.

The Covenant Name of God

"And I appeared unto Abraham, unto Isaac, and unto Jacob, by <u>the name</u> of GOD Almighty, but by my name JEHOVAH was I not known to them" (Exod. 6:3). At this important time God revealed His covenant name to Moses. This is the first visual occurrence of the name Jehovah in the King James Bible; it is only presented this way four times in Scripture.

The phrase *the name* occurs 261 times from Genesis to the Gospels.

The phrase *the name* is mentioned in 161 chapters from Genesis to the Gospels.

The phrase *the name of* is mentioned naturally in 261 verses of the Bible.

1661st Verse of the Bible

"And I have also heard the groaning of the children of Israel, whom the Egyptians keep in bondage; and I have remembered my covenant" (Exod. 6:5). God is speaking in this 61st verse.

The phrase *I have* is mentioned in 61 verses of the Pauline Epistles.

The phrase *I have* is found in 61 books of the Bible.

Israel's Redeemer-God

"I will redeem you with a stretched out arm" (Exod. 6:6). From Exodus to the end of the Bible all forms of the word *redeem* occur 161 times. Again the word *redeemed* is mentioned in 61 verses of the Bible.

And I Will Be

"And I will take you to me for a people, and I will be to you a GOD: and ye shall know that your GOD, which bringeth you out from under the burdens of the Egyptians" (Exod. 6:7).

The word *will* is mentioned in 261 verses of Ezekiel.

The word *will* is mentioned in 61 chapters of the Pauline Epistles.

The phrase *and I will* occurs 61 times in Isaiah.

The phrase *I will be* occurs 61 times in the Old Testament.

The word *be* occurs naturally 61 times in the Apocalyptic Epistle.

God Spake unto Moses

"And the LORD spake unto Moses, Say unto Aaron, Take thy rod, and stretch out thine hand upon the waters of Egypt, upon their streams, upon their rivers, and upon their ponds, and upon all their pools of water, that they may become blood; and that there may be blood throughout all the land of Egypt, both in vessels of wood, and in vessels of stone" (Exod. 7:19). Again the phrase *the LORD spake unto Moses* is mentioned in 61 chapters of the Bible. Again the word *spake* is mentioned in 61 verses of the Synoptic Gospels. The name *Moses(')* is mentioned in 261 verses of Exodus. In this verse there are 61 words surrounding the phrase *the LORD spake unto Moses.*

Meeting God in the Wilderness

"We will go three days' journey into the wilderness, and sacrifice to the LORD our GOD, as he shall command us" (Exod. 8:27). Again the title *LORD/Lord our God* is mentioned in 61 chapters of the Bible.

The phrase *the wilderness* is mentioned in 61 verses of OT Narrative.

The phrase *the wilderness* is mentioned in 161 chapters of the Bible.

Ye May Know That I Am God

"And that thou mayest tell in the ears of thy son, and of thy son's son, what things I have wrought in Egypt, and my signs which I have done among them; that ye may know how that I am the LORD" (Exod. 10:2). God wanted future generations of Jews to know with certainty that He is their heavenly King. The phrase *may know* occurs 61 times in the Bible. Again the phrase *I am the LORD/Lord* is mentioned in 161 verses of the Bible.

61st Chapter of the Bible

The pharaohs were worshipped as the embodiments of the gods. Exodus chapter eleven is the 61st chapter of the Bible because of a great turn of events which will first prove the Lord is King over the Jews not Pharaoh and then will further prove the Lord to be God over all Egypt's gods. The Lord God was about to bring His tenth judgment upon Egypt. From Exodus to Deuteronomy the word *judgment(s)* is mentioned in 61 verses.

> "And the LORD said unto Moses, Yet will I bring one <u>plague</u> more upon <u>Pharaoh</u>, and upon Egypt; afterwards he will let you go hence. . . . <u>Thus saith the LORD</u>, About midnight will I go out into the midst of Egypt: And all the firstborn in the land of Egypt shall die, from the firstborn of <u>Pharaoh</u> that sitteth upon his throne, even unto the firstborn of the maidservant that is behind the mill; and all the firstborn of beasts. And there shall be a great cry throughout all the land of Egypt, such as there was none like it, nor shall be like it any more" (Exod. 11:1a, 4-6).

Here God's judgment upon all the firstborn sons is foretold. The word *plague(s)* occurs 61 times in Leviticus. Again the phrase *thus saith the LORD/Lord* is mentioned in 161 chapters of the Bible. The title *Pharaoh* is mentioned in 161 verses of the Law.

King of the Jews' Freedom Feast

"And they shall eat the flesh in that night, roast with <u>fire</u>, and <u>unleavened</u> <u>bread</u>; and with <u>bitter</u> herbs they shall eat it" (Exod. 12:8). On the eve of the nation's liberation from slavery the Lord called for a national feast, one that would become a memorial to be observed throughout future generations. This feast marks a great victory, yet it is framed with very somber features. This Passover Feast was made as a living parable to prophetically portray the nation's future Messianic King of the Jews dying for the nation to bring about its release from bondage to sin. Because leaven is a corruptive agent it pictures sin; as leaven was not to be found in the Jews' Passover bread, neither was there found any sin within the divine life of the Messianic Lamb of God. The fire speaks of the Messianic King of the Jews' suffering on the Cross, and the bitter herbs typify His bitter bondage.

> The word *fire* is mentioned in 427 verses of the OT, a multiple of 61.
> The word *unleavened* occurs 61 times in the Bible.
> The word *bread* occurs 361 times in the Bible.
> All forms of the word *bitter* are mentioned in 61 chapters of the Bible.

King of the Jews' Future Saving Blood

"And the <u>blood</u> shall be to you for a token upon the houses where ye are: and when I see the <u>blood</u>, I will pass over you, and the <u>plague</u> shall not be upon you to destroy you, when I smite the land of Egypt" (Exod. 12:13). Every family had to slay a lamb for its house's safety. If a man lived alone he still had to slay a lamb and apply its blood to the front door. Moreover, one lamb also had to be sacrificed on the whole nation's behalf. It was this latter lamb in particular that typified the future Messianic King's meritorious death for the nation. Again the word *plague(s)* occurs 61 times in Leviticus. The word *blood* occurs 61 times in the Old Testament Narrative.

God's Divine Messenger
(Part 7)

"And the angel of GOD, which went before the camp of Israel, removed and went behind them; and the <u>pillar of the cloud</u> went from before their face, and stood behind them. . . . And it came to pass, that in the morning watch the LORD looked unto the host of the Egyptians through <u>the pillar of fire</u> and of the cloud, and troubled the host of the Egyptians" (Exod. 14:19, 24). Just as both God and the Angel of God were in the burning bush, so they were both together in the cloudy pillar. Deductive reasoning here reveals that the One is divinely proportionate to the Other.

The Bible combination: *pillar* (47x), *of the cloud* (14x) = 61 times.
The OT combination: *the pillar* (10 vs), *of fire* (51 vs) = 61 verses.

Do Right by God

"And said, If thou wilt diligently hearken to the voice of the LORD thy GOD, and wilt <u>do</u> that which is right in his sight, and wilt give ear to his commandments, and keep all his statutes, I will put none of these diseases upon thee, which I have brought upon the Egyptians: for I am the LORD that healeth thee" (Exod. 15:26). There are 61 words in this God verse.

The word *do* is mentioned in 261 verses of the OTN.
The word *do* occurs 61 times in Luke.
The word *do* is mentioned in 1261 verses of the Bible.
The word *do* is found in 61 books of the Bible.

All That God Had Done to the Egyptians

"And Moses told his father in law <u>all that</u> the LORD <u>had done</u> unto Pharaoh and to the Egyptians for Israel's sake, and all the travail that had come upon them by the way, and how the LORD delivered them" (Exod. 18:8). God had successfully brought judgment upon the land of Egypt, the Egyptians, and their underworld gods. The phrase *all that* occurs 561 times in the Bible. The phrase *had done* occurs 61 times in the Old Testament!

The Priesthood of God

"And ye shall be <u>unto me</u> a kingdom of <u>priests,</u> and an holy nation. These are the words which thou shalt speak unto the children of Israel" (Exod. 19:6). God wanted not just the Levites but the whole nation to be spiritual and to walk holy before Him. Again the phrase *unto me* is mentioned in 61 chapters of the Law. The Old Testament combination *the priests* (260x) and *the LORD'S priests* (1x) = 261.

The Voice of God

"<u>And when the voice of the trumpet sounded long, and waxed louder and louder,</u> Moses spake, and GOD answered him by a voice" (Exod. 19:19). God was about to issue His holy laws to be observed throughout His kingdom. Just before doing so He announced His eminent presence with the sound of a great trumpet. The phrase *the voice of* occurs 161 times in the Old Testament. The word *trumpet* occurs 61 times in the Bible. The word *sound* is mentioned in 61 verses of the Old Testament. The word *loud(er)* is mentioned in 61 verses of the Bible. The phrase *and when the voice of the trumpet sounded long and waxed louder and louder* consists of 61 letters!

Moses Went up to See the God of the Mountain

"And the LORD came down upon mount Sinai, on the top of the mount: and the LORD called Moses up to the top of the mount; and Moses went up" (Exod. 19:20). Again the word *down* occurs 61 times in Judges. The title *the mountain* occurs 61 times from Genesis to the Gospels.

The word *went* occurs 61 times in the Acts of the Apostles.

The phrase *went up* is in 161 verses from Genesis to the Gospels.

The word *up* is mentioned in 61 verses of the Pauline Epistles.

God's Holy Commandments

"Thou shalt not bow down thyself to them, nor serve them: for I the LORD thy GOD am a jealous GOD, visiting the iniquity of the fathers upon the children unto the third and fourth generation of them that hate me; And shewing mercy unto thousands of them that love me, and keep my commandments" (Exod. 20:6). This chapter consists of 561 words. The word *commandment* is mentioned in 61 verses of the OT Narrative.

The word *keep* occurs 61 times in the OT Narrative.

The phrase *keep the* is mentioned in 61 chapters of the Bible.

The phrase *to keep* is mentioned in 61 chapters of the Bible.

2061st Verse of the Bible

"Remember the sabbath day, to keep it holy. Six days shalt thou labour, and do all thy work: But the seventh day is the sabbath of the LORD thy GOD" (Exod. 20:8-10a). The underlined words indicate the short 2061st verse of the Bible, and they are words spoken by God.

God's Divine Messenger
(Part 8)

"Behold, I send an Angel before thee, to keep thee in the way, and to bring thee into the place which I have prepared. Beware of him, and obey his voice, provoke him not; for he will not pardon your transgressions: for my name is in him. But if thou shalt indeed obey his voice, and do all that I speak; then I will be an enemy unto thine enemies, and an adversary unto thine adversaries. For mine Angel shall go before thee" (Exod. 23:20-23a). Since God's name is synonymous with His Person, the Angel of the Lord is equated with God. Here the Angel's voice is also equated with God's speech. Since this Angel had the ability to forgive Israel's sin, He must undoubtedly share a divine proportion with God. The Bible combination *I send* (22x), *an a/ Angel* (34x), *mine A/angel* (3x), *before thee to keep thee in the way* (1x), *and to bring thee into the place which I have prepared* (1x) = 61. The phrase *will not* is mentioned in 61 verses of the OT Narrative. The phrase *my name('s)* occurs 122 combined times in the Bible, a multiple of 61. The phrase *is in* is mentioned in 61 verses of the OT Narrative.

God's Sapphire Throne

"And they saw the GOD of Israel: and there was under his feet as it were a paved work of a sapphire stone, and as it were the body of heaven in his clearness" (Exod. 24:10). Although the word throne is not mentioned in this striking passage, later in Ezekiel 1:26 and 10:1 God's sapphire throne is described, and the King of the Jews is seen sitting upon it "as the appearance of a man" who we understand to be God's Son. Again the title *the God of Israel* is mentioned in 61 chapters of the Old Testament. From Genesis to the Gospels the phrase *his feet* occurs 61 times. Again the phrase *of heaven* is mentioned in 61 chapters of the Bible. From Genesis to the OT Narrative the word *throne* is mentioned in 61 verses.

They Saw God

"And . . . the nobles of the children of Israel . . . they <u>saw</u> GOD, and did eat and drink" (Exod. 24:11). The word *saw* is mentioned in 61 verses of the Major and Minor Prophets.

God's Ark

"And they shall make an <u>ark</u> of shittim wood: two cubits and a <u>half</u> shall be the length thereof, and a cubit and a <u>half</u> the breadth thereof, and a cubit and a <u>half</u> the height thereof" (Exod. 25:10). The Ark was to be God's earthly transportable throne. The word *half* is mentioned in 61 chapters of the Bible.

> The title *the ark* occurs 61 times in First and Second Samuel.
> The title *ark* occurs 61 times in the Kings and Chronicles.
> The title *ark* is mentioned in 61 chapters of the Bible.

God's Mercy Seat

"And thou <u>shalt make</u> <u>a mercy seat</u> <u>of</u> <u>pure</u> <u>gold</u>: two cubits and a half shall be the length thereof, and a cubit and a half the breadth thereof" (Exod. 25:17). The word *mercy* is mentioned in 261 verses of the Bible. The Exodus combination *shalt make* (60x), *a mercy seat* (1x) = 61. The word *of* occurs precisely 6100 times in the New Testament, a hundredfold multiple of 61. The word *pure* occurs 61 times beyond the Law. The word *gold* is mentioned in 361 verses of the Bible.

God's Heave Offering

"And thou shalt take the breast of the ram of Aaron's consecration, and wave <u>it</u> for a wave offering <u>before the LORD</u>: and it shall be thy part. And thou shalt sanctify the breast of the wave offering, and the shoulder of the heave offering, which is waved, and which is heaved up, of the ram of the consecration, even of that which is for Aaron, and of that which is for his sons: And it shall be Aaron's and his sons' by a statute for ever from the children of Israel" (Exod. 29:26-28a). Here the underlined word *it* is the 61,000st word of the Bible, and it belongs to God. Again the phrase *before the LORD* occurs 161 times in the Law.

God's Anointed High Priest

"And <u>the holy garments of</u> <u>Aaron</u> shall be his sons' after him, to be anointed therein, and to be consecrated in them" (Exod. 29:29). The high priest was to visually represent God to the people, that is, in a divine proportion. He was to be holy and atone for the sins of the people just as God would also do for them. The Law combination *the holy garments of* (1 v), *Aaron* (260 vs) = 261 verses.

God's Holy Place

"And that son that is priest in his stead shall put them on seven days, when he cometh into the tabernacle of the congregation to minister in the <u>holy place</u>" (Exod. 29:30). Here the word *place* is the 61,161st word of the Bible, and it refers to God's very own place. The titles *holy place* (60x) and *holy dwelling place* (1x) occur a combined 61 times in the Bible.

God's Continual Burnt Offering

"And the other lamb thou shalt offer at even, and shalt do thereto according to the meat offering of the morning, and according to the drink offering thereof, for a sweet savour, an offering made by fire unto the LORD. This shall be a continual burnt offering throughout your generations at the door of the tabernacle of the congregation before the LORD" (Exod. 29:41-42). Again the phrase *before the LORD* occurs 61 times in Leviticus.

God's Earthly Children

"And I will dwell among the children of Israel, and will be their GOD" (Exod. 29:45). Again the phrase *children of Israel* occurs 61 times in Leviticus. The word *their* is mentioned in 561 verses of the Law.

I Am the Lord

"And they shall know that I am the LORD their GOD, that brought them forth out of the land of Egypt, that I may dwell among them: I am the LORD their GOD" (Exod. 29:46). The Bible combination *shall know that I am* (60x), *the LORD their God that brought them forth out of the land of Egypt* (1x) = 61. Again the phrase *I am the LORD/Lord* is mentioned in 161 verses of the Bible.

God's Incense Altar

"And thou shalt make an altar to burn incense upon: of shittim wood shalt thou make it. . . . And thou shalt overlay it with pure gold, the top thereof, and the sides thereof round about, and the horns thereof; and thou shalt make unto it a crown of gold round about" (Exod. 30:1, 3). Again the word *altar* is mentioned in 161 verses of the Law. Here the underlined word *and* is the 61,661st word of the Bible.

God's Testimony

"And thou shalt put it before the vail that is by the ark of the testimony, before the mercy seat that is over the testimony, where I will meet with thee" (Exod. 30:6). Here the word *over* is the 61,761st word of the Bible.

God's Annual Atonement

"And Aaron shall make an atonement upon the horns of it once in a year with the blood of the sin offering of atonements: once in the year shall he make atonement upon it throughout your generations: it is most holy unto the LORD" (Exod. 30:10). Here the word *shall* is the 61,861st word of the Bible. The phrase *an atonement for* occurs 61 times in the Bible.

God's Ransomed Ones

"When thou takest the sum of the children of Israel after their number, then shall they give every man a ransom for his soul unto the LORD, when thou numberest them; that there be no plague among them, when thou numberest them. This they shall give, every one that passeth among them that are numbered, half a shekel after the shekel of the sanctuary: a shekel is twenty gerahs: an half shekel shall be the offering of the LORD" (Exod. 30:12-13). Here the underlined word *the* is the 61,961st word of the Bible, and it serves as the definite article for the divine title Lord.

God Personally Wrote the Ten Commandments

"And he gave unto Moses, when he had made an end of communing with him upon mount Sinai, <u>two tables of</u> <u>testimony</u>, <u>tables of</u> stone, <u>written</u> <u>with the finger of GOD</u>" (Exod. 31:18). The Law combination *two tables of* (13x), *testimony* (32x), *written* (14x), *with the finger of God* (2x) = 61.

Moses Goes up Again to See God

"And it came to pass on the morrow, that Moses said unto the people, Ye have sinned a great sin: and now I will <u>go up</u> unto the LORD; peradventure I shall make an atonement for your sin" (Exod. 32:30). The phrase *go up* is mentioned in 61 verses of the OT Narrative.

God Passed by Moses

"And the LORD <u>passed</u> by before him, and proclaimed, The LORD, The LORD GOD, <u>merciful and gracious</u>, <u>longsuffering</u>, <u>and abundant in goodness and truth</u>" (Exod. 34:6). The word *passed* occurs 161 times in the Bible. The Bible combination *merciful* (40x), *and gracious* (3x), *longsuffering* (17x), *and abundant in goodness and truth* (1x) = 61.

God's Holiness

"And they made the plate of the holy crown of pure gold, and wrote upon it a writing, like to the engravings of a signet, <u>HOLINESS</u> TO THE LORD" (Exod. 39:30). The Law combination *holiness* (3 vs) and *holy* (158 vs) = 161 verses.

God's Glory Cloud

"Then a <u>cloud</u> <u>covered the tent of the congregation</u>, and the glory of the LORD filled the tabernacle" (Exod. 40:34). The Bible combination *cloud* (60 chs), *covered the tent of the congregation* (1 ch) = 61 chapters.

God's Burnt Offering

"If his offering be a burnt sacrifice of the herd, let him offer a male without blemish: he shall offer it of his own voluntary will at the door of the tabernacle of the congregation before the LORD. And he shall put his hand upon the head of <u>the burnt offering</u>; and it shall be accepted for him to make atonement for him" (Lev. 1:3-4).

> The term *burnt offering* is mentioned in 61 chapters of the Bible.
> The term *the burnt offering* is mentioned in 61 verses of the Bible.

God's Meal Offering

"And when any will offer a meat offering unto the LORD, his offering <u>shall be of fine</u> <u>flour</u>; and he shall pour oil upon it, and put frankincense thereon: And he shall bring it to Aaron's sons the priests: and he shall take thereout his handful of the flour thereof, and of the oil thereof, with all the frankincense thereof; and the priest shall burn the memorial of it upon the altar, to be an offering made by fire, of a sweet savour unto the LORD" (Lev. 2:1-2). The Bible often uses the word meat when referring to any form of food; here it refers to wheat meal. The Bible combination *shall be of fine* (3x), *flour* (58x) = 61.

God's Peace Offering

"And he <u>shall offer</u> of <u>the sacrifice of the</u> <u>peace offering</u> <u>an offering</u> <u>made by fire</u> <u>unto the LORD</u>"

(Lev. 3:9). To satisfy God's divine wrath against the nation's sin, the people were to offer Him a peace offering. The Law combination *the sacrifice of the* (8 vs), *peace offering/s* (53 vs) = 61 verses. From Genesis to the NT Narrative the phrase *an offering* is mentioned in 61 verses. The phrase *made by fire* occurs 61 times in the Law. Again the phrase *unto the LORD/Lord* is mentioned in 61 verses of Numbers.

The phrase *shall offer* is mentioned in 61 verses of the Law.
All available forms of the word *offer* occur 61 times in NT.

God's Sin Offering

"Even the whole bullock shall he carry forth without the camp unto a clean place, where the ashes are poured out, and burn him on the wood with fire: where the ashes are poured out shall he be burnt" (Lev. 4:12).

The word *wood* occurs 61 times in the Law.
The phrase *the fire* occurs naturally 61 times in Major/Minor Prophets.
The word *burnt* occurs 361 times in the Old Testament.

God's Trespass Offering

"And he shall bring a ram without blemish out of the flock, with thy estimation, for a trespass offering, unto the priest: and the priest shall make an atonement for him concerning his ignorance wherein he erred and wist it not, and it shall be forgiven him. It is a trespass offering: he hath certainly trespassed against the LORD" (Lev. 5:18-19). Here the underlined word *trespass* is the 3361st word of Leviticus. Again the phrase *an atonement for* occurs 61 times in the Bible. All available forms of the word *forgive* occurs 61 times in the New Testament.

2961st Verse of the Bible

"And Moses said unto Aaron, Go unto the altar, and offer thy sin offering, and thy burnt offering, and make an atonement for thyself, and for the people: and offer the offering of the people, and make an atonement for them; as the LORD commanded" (Lev. 9:7). This 61st verse speaks of something that God had commanded. The word *commanded* occurs naturally 61 times in the New Testament.

God's Love Shown to Your Neighbor

"Thou shalt not avenge, nor bear any grudge against the children of thy people, but thou shalt love thy neighbour as thyself: I am the LORD" (Lev. 19:18b). To love God is to love your neighbor. The word *neighbour* is mentioned in 61 chapters of the Old Testament.

God's Appointed Feasts

"Speak unto the children of Israel, and say unto them, Concerning the feasts of the LORD, which ye shall proclaim to be holy convocations, even these are my feasts" (Lev. 23:2). The Law combination *feast/s* (41x), *convocation/s* (19x), *appointment/s* (1x) = 61.

God's Freewill Offering

"Beside the sabbaths of the LORD, and beside your gifts, and beside all your vows, and beside all your freewill offerings, which ye give unto the LORD" (Lev. 23:38). The Bible combination *free* (58 vs) and *your freewill* (3 vs) = 61 verses.

God's Bread of Presence

"And thou shalt take fine flour, and bake twelve cakes thereof: two tenth deals shall be in one cake. And thou shalt set them in two rows, six on a row, upon the pure table before the LORD. And thou shalt put pure frankincense upon each row, that it may be on the bread for a memorial, even an offering made by fire unto the <u>LORD. Every sabbath he shall set it in order before the LORD continually, being taken from the children of Israel by an everlasting covenant. And it shall be Aaron's and his sons'; and they shall eat it in the holy place: for it is most holy unto him of the offerings of the LORD made by fire by a perpetual statute</u>" (Lev. 24:5-9).

From the keyword *LORD* unto the end of the instructive passage comprises 61 words.

God's Commandments Not to Be Broken

"And if ye shall despise my statutes, or if your soul abhor my judgments, so that ye will not do all my commandments, but that ye <u>break</u> my covenant: I also will do this unto you; I will even appoint over you terror, consumption, and the burning ague, that shall consume the eyes, and cause sorrow of heart: and ye shall sow your seed in vain, for your enemies shall eat it. And I will set my face against you" (Lev. 26:15-17a).

The word *break* occurs 61 times in the Major Prophets.
The word *broken* occurs 161 times in the Old Testament.

God's Tithe

"And all the tithe <u>of the land</u>, whether of the <u>seed</u> <u>of the land</u>, or of the <u>fruit</u> of the tree, is the LORD'S: it is holy unto the LORD" (Lev. 27:30). The tithe or tenth belongs to God. It is never man's to keep. Again the singular word *seed('s)* occurs 61 times in the Major and Minor Prophets. Again the word *fruit* occurs naturally 61 times in the Major/Minor Prophets.

The phrase *of the land* is seen in 61 chapters of the Law.
The word *land* occurs 61 times in the Wisdom Books.

61st Verse of Numbers

"Then the tribe of Zebulun: and <u>Eliab</u> the son of Helon shall be captain of the children of Zebulun" (Num. 2:7). Eliab's name is comprised of two words; *Eli* meaning 'my God,' and *ab* meaning 'father.' The literal translation of his name is rendered 'my God is father,' but it may be understood as 'God of my father.'

God's Tabernacle

"And on the eighth day he shall bring two turtles, or two young pigeons, to the priest, to the door <u>of the tabernacle of the congregation</u>" (Num. 6:10).

The phrase *of the tabernacle of the congregation* occurs 61 times in the Bible.
The phrase *of the tabernacle of the congregation* is seen in 61 verses of the Bible.

God's Shining Face

"The LORD make <u>his face</u> <u>shine</u> upon thee, and be <u>gracious</u> <u>unto thee</u>" (Num. 6:25). No face among men or angels shines so brightly and beautifully as does God's heavenly face. Again the phrase *thy face* occurs 61 times in the Bible. All forms of the word *shine* occur 61 times in the Bible. The NT Narrative combination *gracious* (1 v), *unto thee* (60 vs) = 61 verses.

Numbers 7:61

His" offering one ,the weight whereof was an hundred and thirty shekels ,was one silver charger both of them full of fine flour ;after the shekel of the sanctuary ,silver bowl of seventy shekels offering mingled with oil for a meat" (Num. 7:61). The prince of the tribe of Benjamin brought his offering as gifts to God for the Tabernacle's dedication ceremony. Again all available forms of the word *offer* occur 61 times in New Testament.

God's Enemies

"And it came to pass, when the ark set forward, that Moses said, Rise up, LORD, and let thine enemies be scattered; and let them that hate thee flee before thee" (Num. 10:35). The phrase *thine enemies* is mentioned in 61 verses of the Bible.

God's Mouth

"And he said, Hear now my words: If there be a prophet among you, I the LORD will make myself known unto him in a vision, and will speak unto him in a dream. My servant Moses is . . . faithful in all mine house. With him will I speak mouth to mouth, even apparently, and not in dark speeches; and the similitude of the LORD shall he behold" (Num. 12:6-8c). Again the word *word(s)* is mentioned in 61 verses of Acts. The underlined verse marks the 461st verse of Numbers and pertains to God's words spoken through His prophet.

The phrase *mouth of* is mentioned in 61 chapters of the Bible.
The word *mouth(s)* is mentioned in 161 verses of Wisdom Books.

God's Forgiving Power

"And now, I beseech thee, let the power of my Lord be great, according as thou hast spoken, saying" (Num. 14:17). Because the nation had just greatly sinned by refusing to enter Canaan, God pronounced its complete annihilation. For this cause Moses began to speak to God by appealing to His great mercy and forgiveness. The phrase *the power* is mentioned in 61 verses of the Bible. Again the phrase *my Lord/lord* occurs 183 times in Scripture, a multiple of 61.

God's Divine Messenger
(Part 9)

"And GOD came unto Balaam at night, and said unto him, If the men come to call thee, rise up, and go with them; but yet the word which I shall say unto thee, that shalt thou do. . . . And the angel of the LORD said unto Balaam, Go with the men: but only the word that I shall speak unto thee, that thou shalt speak. So Balaam went with the princes of Balak" (Num. 22:20, 35). God personally delivered a message to Balaam. The next day God's divine Messenger delivered the very same message using a strikingly similar fourteen-word sentence. By this mirror action and mirror words the Angel of the Lord reveals His divine proportion to God.

God's Presence

"He hath not beheld iniquity in Jacob, neither hath he seen perverseness in Israel: the LORD his GOD is with him, and the shout of a king is among them" (Num. 23:21). The phrase *with him* occurs 61 times in First and Second Samuel. From Genesis to Job [Job being the man in whom God found no perverseness] the phrase *among them* occurs 61 times. The title *king* is mentioned in 61 verses of the Law.

God's 61 Tributary Donkeys

"And <u>THREESCORE AND ONE THOUSAND</u> asses . . . of which the LORD'S tribute was <u>THREESCORE AND ONE</u>" (Num. 31:34, 39b). The total number of donkeys which the Israelite soldiers spoiled from the Midianites was 61,000. They took half for themselves and gave the other half to the people. As tribute God received one donkey out of every five hundred (61) from the soldiers, and one out of every fifty (610) from the people. This valuable tribute of donkeys demonstrated the nation's willing subjugation to God.

The God of Your Fathers

"<u>The LORD GOD of your fathers make you a thousand times so many more as ye are</u>, and bless you, as he hath promised you!" (Deut. 1:11) The phrase *of your* occurs 61 times in the New Testament. The phrase *a thousand* is mentioned in 61 chapters of the Old Testament. The phrase *the LORD God of your fathers make you a thousand times so many more as ye are* consists of 61 letters!

61st Verse of Deuteronomy

"For indeed the hand of the LORD was against them, <u>to destroy</u> them from among the host, until they were consumed" (Deut. 2:15). Because the wilderness generation rebelled against God they became judged by God's hand of justice so future generations would learn to obey Him. Again the phrase *to destroy* is mentioned in 61 chapters of the Old Testament.

God Will Fight for the New Generation

Moses reminded the young nation what He told Joshua about the gigantic inhabitants of Canaan: "Ye shall not fear them: for the LORD your GOD <u>he shall</u> <u>fight</u> for you" (Deut. 3:22). Again the phrase *he shall* is mentioned in 61 verses of Isaiah.

The word *fight* is mentioned in 61 chapters of the OT.
The word *fought* is mentioned in 61 verses of the Bible.

God's Promised Land

"Now therefore hearken, O Israel, unto the statutes and unto the judgments, which I teach you, for to do them, that ye may live, and go in and possess the <u>land</u> <u>which the LORD GOD of your</u> <u>fathers</u> <u>giveth you</u>" (Deut. 4:1). Again the word *land* occurs 61 times in the Wisdom Books. The Bible combination *the land* (1259x), *which the LORD God of your fathers giveth you/hath given you* (2x) = 1261.

God's Voice

Moses encouraged the new generation, "Did ever people hear <u>the voice of</u> GOD speaking out of the midst of the fire, as thou hast heard, and live?" (Deut. 4:33) Again the phrase *the voice of* occurs 161 times in the Old Testament.

5061st Verse of the Bible

"Thou shalt have none other <u>gods</u> before me" (Deut. 5:7). In this 61st verse God commands that Israel worship no other gods. Again the title *God/GOD/god* is mentioned in 661 verses of the Major/Minor Prophets.

God Talks with Man

"And ye said, Behold, the LORD our God hath shewed us his glory and his greatness, and we have heard his voice out of the midst of the fire: we have seen this day that GOD doth <u>talk</u> with man, and he liveth" (Deut. 5:24). Again all forms of the word *talk* occur 61 times in the Old Testament.

The Triune God

"Hear, O Israel: The LORD our GOD is <u>one</u> LORD" (Deut. 6:4). The Hebrew name for God is plural—Elohim. Here the Hebrew word for "one" is 'echad' which properly means united. This fact reveals to us that God is a composite Being comprised of more than one personality. God is in fact three Persons in one—united altogether as one. The word *we* is mentioned in 61 chapters of the Law. The phrase *if we* occurs 61 times in the Bible. The Old Testament combination *three* (360 vs), *dwell in one* (1 v) = 361 verses. The Old Testament combination *three* (360 vs), *be one LORD* (1 v) = 361 verses.

> The word *one* occurs 61 times in First Corinthians.
> The word *two* occurs 61 times in the Major Prophets.
> The word *three* [lowercase only] occurs 61 times in Major/Minor Prophets.

Lest God's Wrath Be Kindled against Thee

"For the LORD thy GOD is a jealous GOD among you lest the anger of the LORD thy GOD be kindled <u>against thee</u>, and destroy thee from off the face of the earth" (Deut. 6:15). The phrase *against thee* occurs 61 times in the Major and Minor Prophets.

161st Chapter of the Bible

"And thou shalt remember all the way which the LORD thy GOD led thee these forty years in the wilderness, to humble thee, and to prove thee, to know what was in thine heart, whether thou wouldest keep his commandments, or no. And <u>he</u> humbled thee, and suffered thee to hunger, and fed thee with manna, which thou knewest not, neither did thy fathers know; that <u>he</u> might make thee know that man doth not live by bread only, but by every word that proceedeth out of the mouth of the LORD doth man live" (Deut. 8:2-3). The word *he* is mentioned in 961 verses of the Wisdom Books.

5161st Verse of the Bible

"Understand therefore this day, that the LORD thy GOD is <u>he</u> which goeth over before thee; as a consuming fire <u>he</u> shall destroy them, and <u>he</u> shall bring them down before thy face: so shalt thou drive them out, and destroy them quickly, as the LORD hath said unto thee" (Deut. 9:3). The key titles *God* and *Lord* actually occur in this 61st verse. Again the word *he* is mentioned in 961 verses of the Wisdom Books.

A Restful Place for God's Name

"Then there shall be <u>a place which the LORD your GOD shall</u> <u>choose</u> <u>to cause his name to dwell there</u>; thither shall ye bring all that I command you; your burnt offerings, and your sacrifices, your tithes, and the heave offering of your hand, and all your choice vows which ye vow unto the LORD" (Deut. 11:12). The Bible combination *a place which the LORD your God shall* (1x), *choose* (59x), *to cause his name to dwell there* (1x) = 61.

5261st Verse of the Bible

"When the LORD thy GOD shall enlarge thy border, as he hath promised thee, and thou shalt say, I will eat flesh, because thy soul longeth to eat flesh; thou mayest eat flesh, whatsoever thy soul lusteth after" (Deut. 12:20). This 61st verse actually contains the key titles *God* and *LORD*.

God's Nighttime Passover

"Observe the <u>month</u> of Abib, and keep the passover unto the LORD thy GOD: for in the month of Abib the LORD thy GOD brought thee forth out of <u>Egypt</u> <u>by night</u>" (Deut. 16:1). The word *month* is mentioned in 61 verses of the Law. Again the word *night* is mentioned in 61 verses of the New Testament. The phrase *by night* occurs 61 times in Scripture.

> The name *Egypt* occurs 61 times in Jeremiah.
> The name *Egypt* is mentioned in 61 chapters of Major/Minor Prophets.

The Lord Thy God

"And thou shalt keep the feast of weeks unto <u>the LORD thy GOD</u> with a tribute of a freewill offering of thine hand, which thou shalt give <u>unto the LORD thy GOD</u>, according as <u>the LORD thy GOD</u> hath blessed thee" (Deut. 16:10). Again the phrase *unto the LORD* is mentioned in 61 verses of Numbers. The all-inclusive Bible combination *the LORD thy God* (296x), *the LORD thy GOD* (1x), *the Lord thy God* (7x), *the Lord and thy God* (1x) = 305, a multiple of 61. Again the term *thy God* is mentioned naturally in 305 verses of the Old Testament, a multiple of 61.

God's Gift to the Levites

"And, behold, I have given the children of <u>Levi</u> all the tenth in Israel for an <u>inheritance</u>, for their service which they serve, even the service of the tabernacle of the congregation" (Deut. 18:21). The name *Levi* is mentioned in 61 verses of the Old Testament.

> The word *inheritance* is mentioned in 61 verses of the Law.
> The word *inherit* is mentioned in 61 verses of the Bible.

Coming Prophet Who Will Be the King of the Jews

"I will raise them up a Prophet from among their brethren, like unto thee, and will put my words in his mouth; and he shall speak unto them all that I shall command him. <u>And it shall come to pass, that</u> <u>whosoever</u> <u>will not</u> <u>hearken</u> <u>unto my words</u> <u>which he shall</u> <u>speak in</u> <u>my name</u>, <u>I will require it</u> <u>of him</u>" (Deut. 18:18-19). The Deuteronomy combination *and it shall come to pass that* (1x), *whosoever* (1x), *will not* (19x), *hearken* (20x), *unto my words* (1x), *which he shall* (6x), *speak in* (3x), *my name* (2x), *I will require it* (1x), *of him* (7x) = 61.

God's Heavenly Habitation

"Look down <u>from</u> thy holy habitation, <u>from heaven,</u> and bless thy people Israel, and the land <u>which thou hast</u> given us, as thou swarest unto our fathers, a land that floweth with milk and honey" (Deut. 26:15). The word *from* is mentioned in 161 verses of Isaiah. The phrase *from heaven* is mentioned in 61 verses of the New Testament. The phrase *which thou hast* is mentioned in 61 chapters from Genesis to the NT Narrative.

Deuteronomy 28:61
God Has Written Every Word in the Book of the Law

"Also every sickness, and every plague, which <u>is</u> not <u>written in the book of</u> <u>this law</u>, them will the LORD bring upon thee, until thou be destroyed" (Deut. 28:61). God promised these punishments if the Israelites remained disobedient and defiant during their chastisement.

The phrase *it is written* is mentioned in 61 chapters of the Bible.
The phrase *written in the book* occurs 61 times in the OT Narrative.
The phrase *written in the book* is mentioned in 61 verses of the OTN.
The phrase *the book* is mentioned in 61 chapters of the Old Testament.
The phrase *the book of* occurs 61 times in the Kings and Chronicles.
The phrase *book of* is mentioned in 61 chapters of the Old Testament.
The word *book(s)* occurs 161 times from Genesis to the NT Narrative.
The phrase *the law* occurs 61 times in the OT Narrative.

Our God

"Because I will publish the name of the LORD: ascribe ye greatness unto <u>our</u> GOD" (Deut. 32:3). All available forms of the word *our* occur 161 times in the Wisdom Books.

A God of Truth

"He is the Rock, his work is perfect: for all his ways are judgment: a <u>GOD</u> of <u>truth</u> and without iniquity, just and right is he" (Deut. 32:4). Again the phrase *God of* is mentioned in 61 verses of Isaiah. The phrase *the truth* is mentioned in 61 verses of the New Testament.

A God Who Gathers Together

"And he was KING in Jeshurun, when the heads of the people and the tribes of Israel were <u>gathered together</u>" (Deut. 33:5). This poetic verse refers to God being the King of the Jews. The phrase *gathered together* is mentioned in 61 verses of the Old Testament.

A God among Whom There Is None Like

"<u>There is none</u> <u>like</u> unto the GOD of Jeshurun, who rideth upon the heaven in thy help, and in his excellency on the sky" (Deut. 33:26). Jeshurun is a symbolic name for Israel meaning upright. The phrase *there is none* is mentioned in 61 verses of the Old Testament. God's Son is however just like Him! Again the word *like* is mentioned in 61 chapters of the New Testament.

5861st Verse of the Bible

"<u>Have</u> not I commanded thee? Be strong and of a good courage; be not afraid, neither be thou dismayed: for the LORD thy <u>GOD is with thee</u> <u>whithersoever thou goest</u>" (Josh. 1:9). These are the very last words of encouragement which God spoke to Joshua concerning his task at hand. The word *have* is mentioned in 161 chapters of the Wisdom Books.

The phrase *God is* occurs 61 times in the New Testament.
The phrase *is with* occurs 61 times from Genesis to the NT Narrative.
The OT: *with thee* (160 chs), *whithersoever thou goest* (1 ch) = 161 chapters.

God's Mighty Hand

"For the LORD your God dried up the waters of Jordan from before you, until ye were passed over, as the LORD your God did to the Red sea, which he dried up from before us, until we were gone over: That all the people of the earth might know the hand of the LORD, that it is mighty: that ye might fear the LORD your God for ever" (Josh. 4:23-24). The phrase *the hand of the* occurs 161 times in the Old Testament.

The Army Captain over God's Host

"And the captain of the LORD'S host said unto Joshua, Loose thy shoe from off thy foot; for the place whereon thou standest is holy. And Joshua did so" (Josh. 5:15). At the burning bush God spoke these nearly identical words to Moses. Here the Angel of the Lord by a different title gave Joshua an order which indicated preparation to worship Him. Right on cue from Genesis to the NT Narrative the title *the captain* occurs 61 times.

5961st Verse of the Bible

"So the ark of the LORD compassed the city, going about it once: and they came into the camp, and lodged in the camp" (Josh. 6:11). The Ark of God is the subject of this 61st verse. Again the title *the ark* occurs 61 times in First and Second Samuel. Again the title *ark* is mentioned in 61 chapters of the Bible.

God's Country

"So the LORD was with Joshua; and his fame was noised throughout all the country" (Josh. 6:27). At this time Canaan Land had become God's country, and His goal was for His covenant people to possess it. The word *country* occurs naturally 61 times in the OT Narrative.

161,061st Word of the Bible—"God"

"And Joshua said, Alas, O Lord GOD, wherefore hast thou at all brought this people over Jordan, to deliver us into the hand of the Amorites, to destroy us? would to GOD we had been content, and dwelt on the other side Jordan!" (Josh. 7-7) Here the underlined keyword *God* is the 161,061st word of the Bible!

161,161th Word of the Bible

"Israel hath sinned, and they have also transgressed my covenant which I commanded them: for they have even taken of the accursed thing, and have also stolen, and dissembled also, and they have put it even among their own stuff" (Josh. 7:11). Here the word *thing* is the 161,161st word of the Bible, and it refers to things which belonged exclusively to God.

> The word *thing* occurs 61 times in Major Prophets.
> The word *things* occurs 1161 times in the Bible.

The 161,803rd Word of the Bible

"And thou shalt do to Ai and her king as thou didst unto Jericho and her king: only the spoil thereof, and the cattle thereof, shall ye take for a prey unto yourselves: lay thee an ambush for the city behind it" (Josh. 8:2). The sentence *and thou shalt do to Ai and her king as thou didst unto Jericho and her king:* consists of 61 characters! We now recall the decimal number for the golden ration, the divine proportion—1.618034. The word *shall* is the 161,803rd word of the Bible, and God is speaking it to Joshua. The phrase *shall ye* occurs naturally 161 times in the Bible!

God's Golden Leader Joshua

"And the LORD said unto <u>Joshua</u>, Stretch out the <u>spear</u> that is in thy hand toward Ai; for I will give it into thine hand. And <u>Joshua</u> stretched out the <u>spear</u> that he had in his hand toward the city" (Josh. 8:18). Joshua was God's golden leader over the nation! His name displays the basis of the golden ratio number. The name *Joshua* is mentioned in 161 verses of the OT Narrative. All forms of the word *spear* occur naturally 61 times in the Old Testament.

6061st Verse of the Bible

"Now therefore ye are cursed, and there shall none of you be freed from being bondmen, and hewers of wood and drawers of water for the house of my GOD" (Josh. 9:23). The key name *God* actually occurs in this 61st verse.

The God of Israel Fought for Israel

"And all these kings and their land did Joshua take at one time, because <u>the LORD GOD of Israel fought</u> for <u>Israel</u>" (Josh. 10:42). Again the word *fought* is mentioned in 61 verses of the Bible. Again the title *the God of Israel* is mentioned in 61 chapters of the Old Testament. Again the name *Israel* occurs 161 times in Second Kings.

6161st Verse of the Bible

"All the inhabitants of the hill country from Lebanon unto Misrephoth-maim, and all the Sidonians, them will I drive out from before the children of Israel: only divide thou it by lot unto the Israelites for an inheritance, as I have commanded thee" (Josh. 13:6). God is speaking in this 61st verse.

God's Divine Messenger
(Part 10)

"And an angel of the LORD <u>came up</u> from Gilgal to Bochim, and said, I made you to go up out of Egypt, and have brought you unto the land which I sware unto your fathers; and I said, I will never break my covenant with you. . . . but ye have not obeyed my voice: why have ye done this? Wherefore I also said, I will not drive them out from before you; but they shall be as thorns in your sides, and their gods shall be a snare unto you" (Judg. 2:1, 2c-3).

In the latter part of this passage the Angel of the Lord speaks in the past tense. What He speaks mirrors the Lord's former words spoken to Israel in Numbers 33:55. What He speaks also mirrors the Lord's words spoken to Israel in Judges 2:20-21. Again we are shown that the Angel of the Lord shares a divine proportion to the Lord. Again the word *came* is mentioned in 161 verses of Genesis. Again the word *up* is mentioned in 61 verses of the Pauline Epistles.

6661st Verse of the Bible

"And Israel was greatly impoverished because of the Midianites; <u>and the children of Israel</u> cried <u>unto the LORD</u>" (Judg. 6:6). In this 61st verse the Israelites cried out to God for help. Again the phrase *and the children of Israel* is mentioned in 61 chapters of the Old Testament. Again the phrase *unto the LORD* is mentioned in 61 verses of Numbers.

God's Divine Messenger
(Part 11)

"Gideon threshed wheat by the winepress, to hide it from the Midianites. . . . And the angel of the LORD appeared unto him, and said unto him, The LORD is <u>with thee</u>, thou mighty man of valour. . . . And the LORD looked upon him, and said, Go in this thy might, and thou shalt <u>save</u> Israel from the hand of the Midianites: have not I sent thee?" (Judg. 6:11d-12, 14) Yet again the Angel of the Lord and the Lord are indeed shown to be One Lord. The phrase *with thee* is mentioned in 183 chapters of the Bible, a multiple of 61. All forms of the word *save* [with an 'e'] are mentioned in 61 verses of the Wisdom Books.

God Determines Who Possesses What

"Wilt not thou possess that which Chemosh thy god giveth thee to <u>possess</u>? So whomsoever the LORD our GOD shall drive out from before us, them will we <u>possess</u>" (Judg. 11:24). The word *possess* is mentioned in 61 chapters of the Old Testament.

God's Divine Messenger
(Part 12)

"And Manoah said unto the angel of the LORD, <u>What is thy name</u>, that when thy sayings <u>come to pass</u> we may do thee honour? And the angel of the LORD said unto him, Why askest thou thus after my name, seeing it is <u>secret</u>?" (Judg. 13:17-18) In Revelation 19:12c we discover the continued secrecy of this divine Person's name; that narrative tells us that the returning Christ "had a name written that no man knew but he himself." The New Testament combination *what is thy name* (2 vs) and *name* (159 vs) = 161 verses. The phrase *thy name* occurs 122 times in the Bible, a multiple of 61. The phrase *come to pass* occurs 161 times in the Bible. The Old Testament combination *secret/s* (60x), *hiding of his power* (1x) = 61.

God's Divine Messenger
(Part 13)

"But the angel of the LORD did no more appear to Manoah and to his wife. Then Manoah knew that he was an angel of the LORD. And Manoah said unto his wife, We shall surely die, because we have seen GOD" (Judg. 13:21-22). Manoah knew the Angel of the Lord was actually the Lord, even the very God. Rightly so, the narrative does not inform us otherwise because she indeed was correct in her declaration. Scripture is building a case for us that we might know for sure this Heavenly Messenger's divine nature.

The Lord Had Visited His People

"Then she arose with her daughters in law, that she might return from the country of Moab: for she had heard in the country of Moab how that the LORD <u>had visited</u> <u>his people</u> in giving them bread" (Ruth 1:6). All forms of the word *visit* are mentioned in 61 collective chapters of the Old Testament. The Bible combination *had visited* (2x), *his people* (159x) = 161.

The God of Knowledge

"Talk no more so exceeding proudly; let not arrogancy come out of your mouth: for the LORD is a GOD of <u>knowledge</u>, and by him actions are weighed" (1 Sam. 2:3).

The phrase *I know* occurs naturally 61 times in the New Testament.

The word *know* is mentioned in 61 verses of John's Gospel.

All forms of the word *know* occur 261 times in the Wisdom Books.

The word *knoweth* is mentioned in 61 verses of the Old Testament.

The word *knew* is mentioned in 61 verses of the NT Narrative.

God's Ark Taken Away

"And she said, The glory is departed from Israel: for <u>the ark</u> of GOD is <u>taken</u>" (1 Sam. 4:22). Phinehas' wife lamented over the emblem of God's mercy—the Ark of God—being taken away from the nation. Again the title *the ark* occurs 61 times in First and Second Samuel. The word *taken* occurs 61 times in the Law and 61 times in the Major and Minor Prophets.

God's Ark Returns

"And the men of Kirjath-jearim came, and fetched up the ark of the LORD, and brought it <u>into the house of</u> <u>Abinadab in the hill</u>, and sanctified Eleazar his son to keep the ark of the LORD" (1 Sam. 7:1). The Old Testament combination *into the house of* (60x), *Abinadab in the hill* (1x) = 61.

7361st Verse of the Bible

"And the children of Israel said to Samuel, Cease not to cry unto the LORD our GOD for us, that he will save us out of the hand of the Philistines" (1 Sam. 7:8). Again the phrase *unto the LORD* is mentioned in 461 verses of the Old Testament. The key titles *Lord* and *God* actually occur in this 61st verse.

God's Theocratic Rule Rejected

"But the thing displeased Samuel, when they said, Give us a king to judge us. And Samuel prayed unto the LORD. And the LORD said unto Samuel, Hearken unto the voice of the people in all that they say unto thee: for they have not rejected thee, but they have rejected me, that I should not <u>reign over</u> them" (1 Sam. 8:6-7). All tenses of the phrase "reign over" show the seal of God in the following way: *reign over* (38 vs), *reigned over* (18 vs), *reignest over* (1 v), *reigneth over* (3 vs), *reigning over* (1 v) = 61 verses.

The Man of God

Saul's servant told him, "Behold now, there is in this city <u>a man of GOD</u>, and he is an honourable man" (1 Sam. 9:6a). The term man of God generally describes a person who had open communication with God and thus had obtained divine knowledge and foreknowledge from Him. As needed, God spoke to that man and also through him. God's Spirit also rested upon that man of God throughout the duration of his ministry. Within the OT Narrative the titles *the man of God* (52 vs) and *a man of God* (9 vs) = 61 verses. The title *the man of* is mentioned in 61 verses of the Bible.

God Controls What Comes to Pass

The narrative continues to say of the man of God, "<u>all that he</u> saith <u>cometh</u> surely <u>to pass</u>: now let us go thither; peradventure he can shew us our way that we should go" (1 Sam. 9:6b). The phrase *all that he* occurs 61 times in the Old Testament.

The phrase *come to pass* occurs 161 times in the Bible.

The phrase *it came to pass* is mentioned in 261 chapters of the Bible.

The phrase *and it came to pass that* occurs 61 times in the Bible.

The phrase *and it came to pass that* is mentioned in 61 verses of the Bible.

The Word of God

"And as they were going down to the end of the city, Samuel said to Saul, Bid the servant pass on before us . . . but stand thou still a while, that I may shew thee the word of God" (1 Sam. 9:27). The God Number 61 divided by the Golden Ratio 1.618034 = 37.7000731. The Bible number representing the Word of God is 37. The number 1037 is a perfect multiple of 61. Herein lays the divine proportion of God to the Word of God.

The Transforming Spirit of God

"And the Spirit of the LORD will come upon thee, and thou shalt prophesy with them, and shalt be turned into another man. And let it be, when these signs are come unto thee, that thou do as occasion serve thee; for GOD is with thee" (1 Sam. 10:6-7). Again the title *the Spirit* is mentioned in 61 chapters of the New Testament.

261st Verse of First Samuel

Samuel reminded the people that God had chosen their king for them according to their carnal desires. "Now therefore behold the king whom ye have chosen, and whom ye have desired! and, behold, the LORD hath set a king over you" (1 Sam. 12:13). Israel was no longer interested in their Heavenly King's rule over them. They wanted an earthly king. Again the title *LORD* occurs 6461 times in the Old Testament. The word *over* occurs 61 times in Deuteronomy.

The Abiding God

"Behold, I have seen a son of Jesse the Beth-lehemite, that is cunning in playing, and a mighty valiant man, and a man of war, and prudent in matters, and a comely person, and the LORD is with him" (1 Sam. 16:18). Again the phrase *with him* occurs 61 times in First and Second Samuel.

The Living God

"And David spake to the men that stood by him, saying, What shall be done to the man that killeth this Philistine, and taketh away the reproach from Israel? for who is this uncircumcised Philistine, that he should defy the armies of the living GOD?" (1 Sam. 17:26) The word *living* occurs 61 times in the Wisdom Books.

7861st Verse of the Bible

"Swear now therefore unto me by the LORD, that thou wilt not cut off my seed after me, and that thou wilt not destroy my name out of my father's house" (1 Sam. 24:21). Swearing by the name of God is the subject of this 61st verse. Again all forms of the word *swear/sware* show the golden seal of God being mentioned in 161 chapters of the Bible.

7961st Verse of the Bible

"Because thou obeyedst not the voice of the LORD, nor executedst his fierce wrath upon Amalek, therefore hath the LORD done this thing unto thee this day" (1 Sam. 28:18). Not obeying the voice of God is the subject of this verse. Again the phrase *the voice of* occurs 161 times in the Old Testament.

David—Prototype King of the Jews

"And it came to pass after this, that David enquired of the LORD, saying, Shall I go up into any of the cities of Judah? And the LORD said unto him, Go up. And David said, Whither shall I go up? And he said, Unto Hebron. . . . And the men of Judah came, and there they anointed <u>David KING over the house of</u> <u>Judah</u>" (2 Sam. 2:1, 4a). Saul was the prototype King of Israel, but David was the prototype King of the Jews, that is, the Judeans. Many other Judean kings would descend from his royal line. The New Testament titles *David* (58x), *David's* (1x), *son of Jesse* (2x) = 61. The phrase *the tribe of* occurs 161 times in the Old Testament.

> The phrase *king over* occurs 61 times in the Old Testament.
> The phrase *the house of* occurs 61 times in Jeremiah/Lamentations.
> The name *Judah* occurs 161 times in Second Chronicles.

61st Verse of Second Samuel

And the time that David was" <u>KING</u> in Hebron over the house of Judah was seven years and six months" (2 Sam. 2:11). The key word *king* actually occurs in this 61st verse.

8061st Verse of the Bible

"And un<u>to David</u> were sons born in Hebron: and his firstborn was Amnon, of Ahinoam the Jezreelitess" (2 Sam. 3:2). The prototype King of the Jews is named in this 61st verse.

> The phrase *to David* occurs 61 times in the Bible.
> The phrase *to David* is mentioned in 61 verses of the Bible.

A Judean King over All Israel

Abner told Ishbosheth that his new goal was "to translate <u>the kingdom</u> from the house of Saul, and to set up <u>the throne</u> of David over Israel and over Judah, from Dan even to Beer-sheba" (2 Sam. 3:10). From the time of Saul's death the Lord sought to establish His plan that all future kings come only from the tribe of Judah. Abner's change of heart revealed the work of Lord through him. The phrase *the kingdom* occurs 122 times in the New Testament, a multiple of 61. The phrase *the throne* (60x) and *the * throne* (1x) = 61 times from Genesis to the Gospels.

King of the Jews Chooses Jerusalem

"And the KING and his men went to <u>Jerusalem</u> unto the Jebusites, the inhabitants of the land . . . David took the strong hold of Zion . . . So David dwelt in the fort, and called it the city of David" (2 Sam. 5:6a, 7a, 9a). This prototype King of the Jews chose Jerusalem to be the capital of his kingdom. This city was situated inside Judah's tribal allotment.

> The name *Jerusalem* is mentioned in 61 verses of the Minor Prophets.

God Speaks 61 Words of Instruction to David

"And the Philistines came up yet again, and spread themselves in the valley of Rephaim. And when David enquired of the LORD, he said, <u>Thou shalt not go up; but fetch a compass behind them, and come upon them over against the mulberry trees. And let it be, when thou hearest the sound of a going in the tops of the mulberry trees, that then thou shalt bestir thyself: for then</u>

shall the LORD go out before thee, to smite the host of the Philistines. And David did so, as the LORD had commanded him; and smote the Philistines from Geba until thou come to Gazer" (2 Sam. 5:22-25).

8161st Verse of the Bible

"And they set the ark *of* GOD upon a new cart, and brought it out of the house of Abinadab that was in Gibeah: and Uzzah and Ahio, the sons of Abinadab, drave the new cart" (2 Sam. 6:3). The underlined word *of* is the 61st word in this chapter, and it rests next to the key title God. The key name *God* actually occurs in this 61st verse.

161st Verse of Second Samuel

"And Nathan said to the KING, Go, do all that is in thine heart; for the LORD is with thee" (2 Sam. 7:3). The keyword *king* actually occurs in this 61st verse, and it is a king of the Jews.

God Reigns over Israel as Lord of Hosts

As David communed with the Lord in the Tabernacle he said, "The LORD of hosts is the GOD over Israel" (2 Sam. 7:26b). The title *the LORD of hosts* occurs 122 times in the Major Prophets, a multiple of 61. The phrase *over Israel* is mentioned in 61 verses of the Bible.

God's Tent

"Go and tell my servant David, Thus saith the LORD, Shalt thou build me an house for me to dwell in? Whereas I have not dwelt in any house since the time that I brought up the children of Israel out of Egypt, even to this day, but have walked in a tent and in a tabernacle" (2 Sam. 7:5-6). The Law combination *tent* (59x) and *my tabernacle* (2x) = 61.

8361st Verse of the Bible

"And when the woman of Tekoah spake to the KING, she fell on her face to the ground, and did obeisance, and said, Help, O KING" (2 Sam. 14:4). The keyword *king* actually occurs in this 61st verse.

The Lord Answered

"Then there was a famine in the days of David three years, year after year; and David enquired of the LORD. And the LORD answered, It is for Saul, and for his bloody house, because he slew the Gibeonites" (2 Sam. 21:1). The underlined word *the* is the 17,161st word of Second Samuel, and it supports the key title *Lord*.

The God of Salvation

"The LORD liveth; and blessed be my rock; and exalted be the GOD of the rock of my salvation" (2 Sam. 22:47). The word *salvation* [lowercase only] occurs 61 times in the Psalms and is mentioned in 61 verses thereof.

Solomon—First Successor King of the Jews

"And Zadok the priest took an horn of oil out of the tabernacle, and anointed Solomon. And they blew the trumpet; and all the people said, God save KING Solomon. And all the people came up after him, and the people piped with pipes, and rejoiced with great joy, so that the earth rent with the sound of them" (1 Kings 1:39-40). The name *Solomon* occurs 261 times in the OT Narrative.

8761st Verse of the Bible

"And Jonathan answered and said to Adonijah, Verily our lord <u>KING</u> David hath made Solomon <u>KING</u>" (1 Kings 1:43). The keyword *king* occurs twice in this 61st verse, and both kings are kings over the Jews.

161st Verse of First Kings

"And there came of all people to hear the wisdom of Solomon, from all kings of the earth, which had heard of his wisdom" (1 Kings 4:34). This verse refers to the exceeding wisdom of one very special King of the Jews.

Concerning What Belongs to God

"<u>Concerning</u> this house which thou art in building, if thou wilt walk in my statutes, and execute my judgments, and keep all my commandments to walk in them; then will I perform my word with thee, which I spake unto David thy father" (1 Kings 6:12). The word *concerning* is mentioned in 61 verses of the OT Narrative.

The House of the Lord

"And it came to pass, when the priests were come out of the holy place, that the cloud filled <u>the house of</u> the LORD" (1 Kings 8:10). We repeat the following two seals.

The phrase *the house of* is mentioned naturally in 161 verses of the Chronicles.
The phrase *the house* occurs naturally 61 times in the NT Narrative.

First Kings 8:61

"Let your heart therefore be perfect with the LORD our <u>GOD</u>, to walk in <u>his</u> statutes, and to keep <u>his</u> <u>commandments</u>, as at this day" (1 Kings 8:61). Solomon's blessing included this challenge to adhere closely to God's holy laws. The key name *God* actually occurs in this 61st verse. The word *his* occurs 610 times in the Psalms, a visual multiple of 61. Again the word *commandment* is mentioned in 61 verses of the OT Narrative.

9061st Verse of the Bible

"And they shall answer, Because they <u>forsook</u> the LORD their GOD, who brought forth their fathers out of the land of Egypt, and have taken hold upon other gods, and have worshipped them, and served them: therefore hath the LORD brought upon them all this evil" (1 Kings 9:9). The key titles *LORD* and *God* actually occur in this 61st verse. The word *forsaken* is mentioned in 61 chapters of the Bible.

King of the Jews' Great Ivory Throne

"Moreover the <u>KING</u> made a great throne of ivory, and overlaid it with the best gold" (1 Kings 10:18). Here the keyword *king* is the 11,061st word of First Kings, and it refers to a beloved king of the Jews, even Solomon.

461st Verse of First Kings

"If this people go up to do sacrifice <u>in the house of the</u> LORD at Jerusalem, then shall the heart of this people turn again unto their lord, even unto Rehoboam <u>KING</u> of Judah, and they shall kill me, and go again to Rehoboam <u>king</u> of Judah" (1 Kings 12:27). The phrase *in the house of the* is mentioned in 61 verses of the Bible. This is the 461st verse of First Kings, and it mentions a king of the Jews.

9261st Verse of the Bible

"And <u>Asa</u> <u>did that which was right in the eyes of the LORD</u>, as did David his father" (1 Kings 15:11). Asa was a godly king who reigned over the Jews. The Bible combination *Asa* (59x), *did that which was right in the eyes of the LORD* (2x) = 61.

561st Verse of First Kings

"And it came to pass, when he reigned, that he smote all the house of Jeroboam; he left not to Jeroboam any that breathed, until he had destroyed him, according unto the <u>saying</u> of the LORD, which <u>he spake</u> by his servant Ahijah the Shilonite" (1 Kings 15:29). In this 61st verse, the saying of God is shown to have been fulfilled. Again the word *saying* is mentioned in 61 verses of Second Kings and in 61 verses of First and Second Chronicles. The Old Testament phrase *he spake* (59x) and *he yet spake* (2x) = 61. This 61st verse actually contains the key title *Lord*.

The God of Elijah

"And it came to pass at the time of the offering of the evening sacrifice, that <u>Elijah</u> the prophet came near, and said, LORD GOD of Abraham, Isaac, and of Israel, let it be known this day that thou art GOD in Israel, and that I am thy servant, and that I have done all these things at thy word. <u>Hear me, O LORD, hear me, that this people may know that thou art the LORD GOD, and that thou hast turned their heart back again</u>" (1 Kings 18:36-37). Again the phrase *may know* occurs 61 times in the Bible. The underlined words indicate the 661st verse of First Kings. The name *Elijah* is mentioned in 61 verses of the Kings and Chronicles.

The Fire of God

"Then <u>the fire</u> of the LORD fell, and consumed the burnt sacrifice, and the wood, and the stones, and the dust, and licked up the water that was in the trench" (1 Kings 18:38). Again the phrase *the fire* occurs naturally 61 times in the Major and Minor Prophets.

A Little Cloud like a Man's Hand

"And it came to pass at the seventh time, that he said, Behold, <u>there ariseth a little</u> <u>cloud</u> out of the sea, like a <u>man's</u> hand. And he said, Go up, say unto Ahab, Prepare thy chariot, and get thee down, that the rain stop thee not" (1 Kings 18:44). The Bible combination *there ariseth a little* (1 ch), *cloud* (60 chs) = 61 chapters. The word *man('s)* occurs 61 times in First Kings.

God of the Hills & the Valleys

"And there came a man of God, and spake unto the king of Israel, and said, Thus saith the LORD, Because the Syrians have said, The LORD is GOD of the hills, but he is not GOD of <u>the</u> <u>valleys</u>, therefore will I deliver all this great multitude into thine hand, and ye shall know that <u>I</u> <u>am the LORD</u>" (1 Kings 20:28). The phrase *in the valley(s)* is mentioned in 61 verses of the Bible. Again the phrase *I am the LORD/Lord* is mentioned in 161 verses of the Bible.

Jehoshaphat—King of the Jews

"And the king of Israel and <u>Jehoshaphat</u> the <u>king of Judah</u> sat each on his throne, having put on their robes, in a void place in the entrance of the gate of Samaria; and all the prophets prophesied before them" (1 Kings 22:10). Here *Jehoshaphat* is the 261 word of the chapter.

The title *king of Judah('s)* occurs 61 times in the Major and Minor Prophets.
The phrase *of Judah* is mentioned in 61 chapters of the Kings and Chronicles.

Where Is the God of Elijah?

"And he took the mantle of Elijah that fell from him, and smote the waters, and said, Where is the LORD GOD of <u>Elijah</u>? And when he also had smitten the waters, they parted hither and thither: and Elisha went over" Again the name *Elijah* is mentioned in 61 verses of the Kings and Chronicles.

61st Verse of Second Kings

"And this is but a light thing in the sight of the LORD: he will deliver the Moabites also into your hand" (2 Kings 3:18). Elisha promised the king of Israel and the king of the Jews that God would perform a supernatural victory on their behalf. This 61st verse actually contains the key title *Lord*.

The Heavenly Host & Chariots of God

The Assyrians had come with a great army to arrest Elisha. "And when the servant of the man of GOD was risen early, and gone forth, behold, an <u>host</u> compassed the city both with horses and chariots. And his servant said unto him, Alas, my master! How shall we do? And he answered, Fear not: for they that be with us are more than they that be with them. And Elisha prayed, and said, LORD, I pray thee, open his eyes, that he may see. And the LORD opened the eyes of the young man; and he saw: and, behold, the mountain was full of horses and <u>chariots</u> of fire <u>round about</u> Elisha" (2 Kings 6:15-17). The word *host* occurs 122 times in the OT Narrative, a multiple of 61. The word *chariot* occurs 61 times in the Old Testament. The phrase *round about* is mentioned in 61 verses of Ezekiel.

God Delights

Amaziah, king of the Jews, "He was twenty and five years old when he began to reign, and reigned twenty and nine years in Jerusalem. And his mother's name was <u>Jehoaddan</u> of Jerusalem" (2 Kings 14:2). The mother's name *Jehoaddan* means 'Jehovah delights' and is the 12,161st word of Second Kings.

Their God

"For so it was, that the children of Israel had sinned against the LORD <u>their GOD</u> . . . And the children of Israel did secretly those things that were not right against the LORD <u>their GOD</u> . . . Notwithstanding they would not hear, but hardened their necks, like to the neck of their fathers, that did not believe in the LORD <u>their GOD</u>. . . . And they left all the commandments of the LORD <u>their GOD</u>, and made them molten images, even two calves, and made a grove, and worshipped all the host of heaven, and served Baal" (2 Kings 17:7a, 9a, 14, 16). Only the first seal below is repeated.

The word *their* occurs 461 times in the Wisdom Books.
The word *I* mentioned in 561 verses of the Law.
The word *I* mentioned in 761 verses of the Major/Minor Prophets.
The word *I* mentioned in 61 chapters of the Synoptic Gospels.

The word *I* mentioned in 161 verses of Pauline/General/Apocalyptic Epistles.

10,061ˢᵗ Verse of the Bible

"But the people held their peace, and answered him not a word: for the <u>KING'S</u> commandment was, saying, Answer him not" (2 Kings 18:36). In this 61ˢᵗ verse the current king of the Jews Hezekiah is mentioned. In this 61ˢᵗ verse the key word *king's* actually occurs. The word *king's* is mentioned in 261 verses of the Bible. Again the word *commandment* is mentioned in 61 verses of the OT Narrative.

God Has Heard Thy Prayer

"Turn again, and tell Hezekiah the captain of my people, Thus saith the LORD, the GOD of David thy father, I have <u>heard</u> thy prayer, I have seen thy tears: behold, I will heal thee: on the third day thou shalt go up unto the house of the LORD" (2 Kings 20:5). Again the word *heard* is mentioned in 61 chapters of the Gospels.

Zedekiah—Last King of the Jews for 600 Years

"And they slew the sons of <u>Zedekiah</u> before his eyes, and put out the eyes of <u>Zedekiah</u>, and bound him with fetters of brass, and carried him to Babylon" (2 Kings 25:7). The name *Zedekiah* occurs 61 times in the Bible.

Judah Prevails as Chief Ruler

"For <u>Judah</u> prevailed above his brethren, and of him came <u>the chief</u> <u>ruler</u>; but the birthright was Joseph's" (1 Chron. 5:2). Here again we see that Judah's Jewish line was meant to be the kingly line. Again the name *Judah* occurs 161 times in Second Chronicles.

> The word *chief* occurs 61 times in the Gospels.
> The word *ruler* appears in 61 verses of the Old Testament.

First Chronicles 6:61

"And unto the sons of Kohath, which were left of the family of that tribe, were cities given out of the half tribe, namely, out of the half tribe of Manasseh, by lot, ten cities" (1 Chron. 6:61). The Kohaths were one of the three priestly families unto God.

David Anointed as King over Israel & the Jews

"Therefore came all the elders of Israel to the king to Hebron; and David made a covenant with them in Hebron before the LORD; and they anointed David KING <u>over Israel</u>, according to the word of the LORD by Samuel" (1 Chron. 11:3). The phrase *king over* occurs 61 times in the Old Testament.

King David's Army & the Host of God

"And they helped David against the <u>band</u> of the rovers: for they were <u>all mighty men of valour</u>, and were <u>captains</u> in the <u>host</u>. For at that time day by day there came <u>to David</u> to help him, until <u>it was a great host</u>, <u>like the</u> <u>host</u> of GOD" (1 Chron. 12:21-22). David never lost a single battle because he was helped by the army of God. The Hebrew word for "host" is also translated as band, camp, company, or tents. Thus the word host refers to a large number of army men. The phrase *like the* occurs 61 times in the Major and Minor Prophets. The Bible combination *camp*

(60 chs) and *the host of God* (1 ch) = 61 chapters. Again the word *host* occurs 122 times in the OT Narrative, a multiple of 61. The OT Narrative combination *the host of* (46x), *the camp of* (13x), *the company of* (2x) = 61. The Old Testament combination *the tent/s* (59x), *all mighty men of valour* (1x), *it was a great host* (1x) = 61. Again the phrase *to David* occurs 61 times in the Bible.

> All forms of the word *band* are mentioned in 61 verses of the Bible.
> The phrase *all the men* occurs 61 times in the Bible.
> The word *company* occurs naturally 61 times in the Old Testament.
> The phrase *the captains* occurs 61 times in the Bible.
> The phrase *captains of* occurs 61 times in the Old Testament.

God Owns the Land of Canaan

"Unto thee will I give <u>the land of Canaan,</u> the lot of your inheritance" (1 Chron. 16:18). This verse is part of David's psalm of thanksgiving to the Lord. It presents the Bible's 61st verse-mention of the phrase *the land of Canaan*, and it speaks of God as its rightful Owner. The phrase *the land of Canaan* is mentioned in 61 verses from Genesis to the OT Narrative.

Give unto the Lord the Glory He Deserves

"<u>Give unto the LORD,</u> ye kindreds of the people, <u>give unto the LORD</u> glory and strength. <u>Give unto the LORD</u> the glory due unto his name: bring an offering, and come before him: worship the LORD in the beauty of holiness" (1 Chron. 16:28-29). This verse is also part of David's psalm of thanksgiving to the Lord. Right on cue the phrase *give unto* occurs 61 times from Genesis to the NT Narrative. Again the phrase *unto the LORD* is mentioned in 61 verses of Numbers and in 461 verses of the Old Testament.

Blessed Be the Lord God

"<u>Blessed</u> be the LORD GOD of Israel for ever and ever. And all the people said, Amen, and praised the LORD" (1 Chron. 16:36). This verse is also part of David's psalm of thanksgiving to the Lord. Again all available forms of the word *bless* occur 61 times in the NT Narrative.

God Has Chosen Jerusalem

"And David lifted up his eyes, and saw the angel of the LORD stand between the earth and the heaven, having a drawn sword in his hand stretched out over <u>Jerusalem</u>. . . . Then the angel of the LORD commanded Gad to say to David, that David should go up, and set up an altar unto the LORD in the threshingfloor of Ornan the Jebusite. . . . And David built there an altar unto the LORD, and offered burnt offerings and peace offerings, and called upon the LORD; and he answered him from heaven by fire upon the altar of <u>burnt offering</u>. . . . Then David said, <u>This is the</u> house of the LORD GOD, and <u>this is the altar of the burnt offering for Israel</u>" (1 Chron. 21:16a, 18, 26; 22:1).

Again the name *Jerusalem* is mentioned in 61 verses of the Minor Prophets. Verse twenty-six is the 10,961st verse of the Bible. The phrase *this is the* occurs 61 times in the Law. Again the term *burnt offering* is mentioned in 61 chapters of the Bible. Again the phrase *the burnt offering* is mentioned in 61 verses of the Bible. Again the word *altar* is mentioned in 161 verses of the Law. The Bible combination *the altar of* (60x), *the burnt offering for Israel* (1x) = 61.

God's Divine Messenger
(Part 14)

"<u>Then</u> the angel of the LORD commanded Gad to say to David, that David should go up, and set up an altar unto the LORD in the threshingfloor of Ornan the Jebusite. And David went up at the saying of Gad, which he spake in the name of the LORD" (1 Chron. 21:18-19). The Angel of the Lord spoke to Gad in His own name, but then in the very next verse the narrative attributes His saying as coming from the Lord himself. As we have seen time and again, these two Persons are one and the same. The leading word of this divine proportion passage *Then* is the 14,261st word of First Chronicles.

10,961st Verse of the Bible

"And David built there an altar unto the LORD, and offered burnt offerings and peace offerings, and <u>called</u> upon the LORD; and he answered him from heaven by fire upon the altar of burnt offering" (1 Chron. 21:26). The key title *LORD* actually occurs in this 61st verse. Again the word *called* is mentioned in 61 verses of the Pauline and General Epistles.

11,161st Verse of the Bible

"Also pure gold for the fleshhooks, and the bowls, and the cups: <u>and for the</u> <u>golden basons</u> <u>he gave</u> <u>gold</u> <u>by weight</u> <u>for every bason</u>; <u>and likewise</u> <u>silver</u> <u>by weight</u> <u>for every bason</u> <u>of silver</u>" (1 Chron. 28:17). David communicated to Solomon every detail of the pattern for God's Temple and holy furnishings. Again the word *golden* is mentioned in 61 verses of the Bible!

> The OTN: *and for the* (60x), *golden basons* (1x) = 61.
> The OTN: *gold* (58 chs), *by weight* (3 chs) = 61 chapters.
> The OTN: *silver* (58 chs), *by weight* (3 chs) = 61 chapters.
> The OTN: *he gave gold by weight* (1x), *for every bason* (2x), *of silver* (58x) = 61.
> The OTN: *and likewise silver by weight* (1x), *for every bason* (2x), *of silver* (58x) = 61.

The Kingdom of God

"Thine, O LORD, is the greatness, and the power, and the glory, and the victory, and the majesty: for all that is in the heaven and in the earth is thine; <u>thine</u> is <u>the KINGDOM</u>, O LORD, and thou art exalted as head above all" (1 Chron. 29:11). The word *thine* is mentioned in 61 verses of the NT Narrative. Again the phrase *the kingdom of God* occurs 61 times in the NT Narrative.

God's Pleasure toward Man's Righteousness

"I know also, my GOD, that thou triest the heart, and hast <u>pleasure</u> in uprightness. As for me, in the uprightness of mine heart I have willingly offered all these things: and now have I seen with joy thy people, which are present here, to offer willingly unto thee" (1 Chron. 29:17).

> The word *pleasure* occurs 61 times in the Bible.
> The word *pleased* is mentioned in 61 verses of the Bible.

God Appeared to Solomon

"In that night did GOD <u>appear</u> unto <u>Solomon</u>, and said unto him, Ask what I shall give thee" (2 Chron. 1:7). Again all forms of the word *appear* are mentioned in 161 verses of the Bible. Here the word *appear* is the 311,361st word of the Bible, and it refers to God. Again the name *Solomon* occurs 261 times in the OT Narrative.

Burden Bearers for God's House Construction

"And Solomon determined to build an house for the name of the LORD, and an house for his KINGDOM. And Solomon told out threescore and ten thousand men to bear <u>burdens</u>" (2 Chron. 2:1-2a). Sometimes we bear our burdens for God, and at other times God bears our burdens. The word *burden* occurs naturally 61 times in the Old Testament.

The Temple of God

"And he reared up the pillars before the <u>temple</u>, one on the right hand, and the other on the left; and called the name of that on the right hand Jachin, and the name of that on the left Boaz" (2 Chron. 3:17).

The word *temple* is mentioned in 161 verses from Genesis to NTN.

The word *temple* is mentioned in 61 verses of the Gospels.

61st Verse of Second Chronicles

"Furthermore he made the <u>court</u> of the priests, and the great <u>court</u>, and doors for the <u>court</u>, and overlaid the <u>doors of</u> them with <u>brass</u>" (2 Chron. 4:9). This 61st verse pertains to God's House. The word *court* occurs 61 times from Genesis to the OT Narrative. The singular phrase *door of* occurs 61 times in the Law. The Bible combination *burnished* (1 ch) and *brass* (60 chs) = 61 chapters.

Treasures of the House of God

"Thus all the work that Solomon made for the house of the LORD was finished: and Solomon brought in all the things that David his father had dedicated; and the silver, and the gold, and all the instruments, put he among the treasures <u>of the house</u> of GOD" (2 Chron. 5:1). The phrase *of the house* is mentioned in 61 verses of the Major Prophets.

Invitation for God to Be Seated upon the Ark

As Solomon closed out his dedication sermon he said, "Now therefore arise, O LORD GOD, into thy resting place, thou, and <u>the ark</u> of thy strength: let thy priests, O LORD GOD, be clothed with salvation, and let thy saints <u>rejoice</u> in goodness" (2 Chron. 6:41). Again the phrase *the ark* occurs 61 times in First and Second Samuel. From Genesis to the NT Narrative the word *rejoice* occurs 161 times. All available forms of the word *rejoice* occur 61 times in the Psalms.

11,361st Verse of the Bible

"And he appointed, according to the <u>order</u> of David his father, the courses of the priests to their service, and the Levites to their charges, to praise and <u>minister</u> before the priests, as the duty of every day required: the porters also by their courses at every gate: for so had David the man of God commanded" (2 Chron. 8:14). This verse describes the orchestration of various services to be performed at God's House. The word *order* occurs 61 times in Scripture. All forms of the word *minister* are mentioned collectively in 161 verses of the Bible.

361st Verse of Second Chronicles

"And Micaiah said, As the LORD <u>liveth</u>, even what my GOD saith, that will I speak" (2 Chron. 18:13). The key titles *LORD* and *God* actually occur in this 61st verse. Again the word *living* occurs 61 times in the Wisdom Books.

11,561ˢᵗ Verse of the Bible

"Again he said, Therefore hear <u>the word of the LORD</u>; I saw the LORD sitting upon his throne, and all the host of heaven standing on his right hand and on his left" (2 Chron. 18:18). Again the title *the word of the LORD* is mentioned in 61 verses of the Kings and Chronicles. The key title *LORD* actually occurs in this 61ˢᵗ verse.

God Is Able

"And Amaziah said to the man of GOD, But what shall we do for the hundred talents which I have given to the army of Israel? And the man of GOD answered, The LORD is <u>able to</u> give thee much more than this" (2 Chron. 25:9).

> The phrase *able to* is mentioned in 61 chapters of the Old Testament.
> The word *able* occurs 61 times in the New Testament.

Zedekiah—Last King of the Jews for a Long While

"Zedekiah was one and twenty years old when he began to reign, and reigned eleven years in Jerusalem. <u>And he did that which was evil in the sight of the LORD his GOD, and humbled not himself before Jeremiah the prophet speaking from the mouth of the LORD. And he also rebelled against king Nebuchadnezzar, who had made him swear by God: but he stiffened his neck, and hardened his heart from turning unto the LORD GOD of Israel</u>" (2 Chron. 36:11-13). Again the name *Zedekiah* occurs 61 times in the Bible. Verses twelve through thirteen consist of 61 words.

61,000 Drams of Gold for God's House Reconstruction

"They gave after their ability unto the treasure of the work THREESCORE AND ONE THOUSAND drams of <u>gold, and</u> five thousand pound of silver, and one hundred priests' garments" (Ezra 2:9). This gold was used to beautify God's rebuilt Temple.

> The word *gold* is mentioned in 361 verses of the Bible.
> The phrase *gold and* occurs 161 times in the Bible.

Ezra 2:61

"And of the children of <u>the priests</u>: the children of Habaiah, the children of Koz, the children of Barzillai; which took a wife of the daughters of Barzillai the Gileadite, and was called after their name" (Ezra 2:61). This 61ˢᵗ verse begins to list certain priests of God who lost their pedigrees. Again the Old Testament combination *the priests* (260x) and *the LORD'S priests* (1x) = 261.

The Prophets of God

"Then rose up Zerubbabel the son of Shealtiel, and Jeshua the son of Jozadak, and began to build the house of GOD which is at Jerusalem: and with them were <u>the prophets of GOD</u> helping them" (Ezra 5:2). This verse presents to us the Bible's only occurrence of the term *prophet/s of God*.

> The title *prophets* occurs 61 times in the NT Narrative.
> The title *prophet* is mentioned in 61 verses of the Major Prophets.

The God of Jerusalem

"The vessels also that are given thee for the service of the house of thy GOD, those deliver thou before the GOD of <u>Jerusalem</u>" (Ezra 7:19). Again the name *Jerusalem* is mentioned in 61 verses of the Minor Prophets.

God's Jewish Remnant

"And they said unto me, <u>The remnant</u> that are left of the captivity there in the province are in great affliction and reproach: the wall of Jerusalem also is broken down, and the gates thereof are burned with fire" (Neh. 1:3). From the beginning of the OT Narrative to the end of the Old Testament the term *the remnant* occurs 61 times.

Jews—The People of God

"But it came to pass, that when Sanballat heard that we builded the wall, he was wroth, and took great indignation, and mocked <u>the Jews</u>" (Neh. 4:1). The name Jews is regularly employed by Scripture from the time of Judah's Babylonian captivity onward.

> The title *Jews* occurs 61 times in the post-exilic books Ezra/Nehemiah/Esther.
> The title *the Jews* is mentioned in 61 verses of the Old Testament.
> The title *Jews* is mentioned in 61 verses of John's Gospel.

Taking Refuge in God's Temple

"Afterward I came unto the house of Shemaiah the son of Delaiah the son of Mehetabeel, who was shut up; and he said, Let us meet together in the house of GOD, within the <u>temple</u>, and let us shut the doors of the temple: for they will come to slay thee; yea, in the night will they come to slay thee" (Neh. 6:10). Again the word *temple* is mentioned in 61 verses of the Gospels. This temple-of-God verse consists of 61 words.

Nehemiah 7:61

"And these were they which went up also from Tel-melah, Tel-haresha, Cherub, Addon, and Immer: but they could not shew their father's house, nor their <u>seed</u>, whether they were of Israel" (Neh. 7:61). These descendants of Solomon's servants could not prove their genealogy was Jewish, the people of God. Again the singular word *seed('s)* occurs 61 times in the Major and Minor Prophets.

God Alone Made All Things

"Thou, even thou, art LORD alone; thou hast made heaven, the heaven of heavens, with all their host, the earth, and all <u>things</u> that are therein, the seas, and all that is therein, and thou preservest them all; and the host of heaven worshippeth thee" (Neh. 9:6). Again the word *things* occurs 1161 times in the Bible.

Mordecai—Became Like the King of the Persian Jews

"And let this apparel and horse be delivered to the hand of one of the KING'S most noble princes, that they may array the man withal whom the KING delighteth to honour, and bring him on horseback through the street of the city, and proclaim before him, Thus shall it be done to the man whom the KING delighteth to honour" (Est. 6:9). As it turned out, things could not have been better for the Jews at this time if Mordecai had been declared to be their de facto king.

There are 61 words in this King-of-the-Jews verse.

Mordecai Paraded around Like a King of the Jews

"Then took Haman the apparel and the horse, and arrayed <u>Mordecai</u>, and brought him on horseback through the street of the city, and <u>proclaimed</u> before him, Thus shall it be done unto the man whom the KING delighteth to honour. . . . for he had told them that <u>he was a Jew</u>" (Est. 6:11, 3:4d). Here the word *proclaimed* is the 361st word in this chapter, and it refers to a Jewish man being paraded on horseback like a king of the Jews. The Old Testament combination *Mordecai/'s* (60x), *he was a Jew* (1x) = 61.

Mordecai—Apparent King of the Persian Jews

"And Mordecai went out from the presence of the KING in royal apparel of blue and white, and with a great crown of gold, and with a garment of fine linen and purple: and the city of Shushan rejoiced and was glad <u>The JEWS</u> had light, and gladness, and joy, and honour. . . . <u>Then Esther the queen, the daughter of Abihail, and Mordecai the Jew, wrote with all authority, to confirm this second letter of Purim.</u> And he sent the letters unto all <u>the JEWS</u> . . . For Mordecai the JEW was next unto KING Ahasuerus, and great among <u>the JEWS</u>, and accepted of the multitude of his brethren, seeking the wealth of his people, and speaking peace to all his seed" (Est. 8:15-16; 9:29-30a, 10:3).

Wonderful imagery of a King of the Jews is pictured in these selected passages. Mordecai appeared to the Jewish remnant as if he was their beloved king. No other specific individual in the Bible is ever given the surname the Jew. Again the title *the Jews* is mentioned in 61 verses of the Old Testament. The underlined verse is the 161st verse of Esther.

The Sons of God

"Now there was a day when the <u>sons of</u> GOD <u>came to</u> present themselves <u>before the LORD</u>, and Satan came also among them" (Job 1:6). The phrase *came to* occurs 61 times in First and Second Chronicles. Again the phrase *before the LORD* occurs 61 times in Leviticus.

> The phrase *sons of* is mentioned in 61 verses of Numbers.
> The phrase *sons of* occurs naturally 261 times in the Chronicles.

The Hand of God

"What? shall we receive good at <u>the hand of</u> GOD, and shall we not receive evil? In all this did not Job sin with his lips" (Job 2:10b).

> The word *hand* is mentioned in 61 verses of Judges.
> The phrase *the hand of the* occurs 161 times in the Old Testament.
> The phrase *of the hand of* is mentioned in 61 verses of the Old Testament.
> The phrase *the hands of* is mentioned in 61 verses from Genesis to NTN.
> The word *hands* occurs 461 times in the Bible.

The Secret of God

"<u>Hast thou heard the</u> <u>secret</u> <u>of GOD</u>? and dost thou restrain wisdom to thyself?" (Job 15:8) The Old Testament combination *hast thou heard the* (1x), *secret/s* (60x) = 61.

Where Is God—The Song Giver

"But none saith, <u>Where</u> is GOD my maker, who giveth <u>songs</u> in the night" (Job 35:10). Again the word *where* occurs 61 times in the Major Prophets. The word *song(s)* is mentioned in 61 verses of the Bible.

The Unsearchable Number of God's Years

"Behold, GOD is great, and we know him not, neither can the <u>number of</u> <u>his years be searched out</u>" (Job 36:26). The Bible combination *number of* (60 chs), *his years be searched out* (1 ch) = 61 chapters.

God Saith

"For <u>he saith</u> to the snow, Be thou on the earth; likewise to the small rain, and to the great rain of his strength" (Job. 37:6).

The phrase *he saith* occurs 61 times in the Gospels.
The word *saith* is mentioned in 361 chapters of the Bible.

The Stars of God

"Where wast thou when . . . the morning <u>stars</u> <u>sang</u> together, <u>and all the</u> sons of GOD shouted for joy?" (Job 38:4a, 7) The Bible combination *stars* (50 vs), *sang* (11 vs) = 61 verses. The phrase *and all the* occurs 561 times in the Bible.

The Majesty of God

"Then answered the LORD unto Job out of the whirlwind, and said . . . Hast thou an arm like GOD? or canst thou thunder with a voice like him? Deck thyself now with majesty and excellency; and array thyself with glory and beauty" (Job 40:6, 9-10). Job chapter forty has 361 words in it, and God does most of the speaking.

The Ways of God

"He is the chief of <u>the ways of</u> GOD: he that made him can make his sword to approach unto him" (Job 40:19).

The word *way* is mentioned in 61 chapters of the NTN.
The phrase *the way of* occurs 161 times in the Bible.
The word *ways* occurs 61 times in the Major Prophets.

1061st Verse of Job

"Therefore take unto you now seven bullocks and seven rams, and go to my servant Job, and offer up for yourselves a burnt offering; and my servant Job shall pray for you: for him will I accept: lest I deal with you after your folly, in that ye have not spoken of me the thing which is right, like my servant Job" (Job 42:8). In this 61st verse God demands a sacrifice from three hypocrites lest He suddenly deal with them in displeasure.

Nations Rage against God

"Why do the heathen rage, and the people imagine a vain thing? The kings of the earth set themselves, and the rulers take counsel together, <u>against</u> the LORD, and <u>against</u> his anointed, saying, Let us break their bands asunder, and cast away their cords from us" (Ps. 2:1-3).

The word *against* is mentioned in 61 verses of First Samuel.

The word *against* is mentioned in 61 chapters of the NT Narrative.

Divine King of the Jews' Resurrection Day Foretold

A two-way conversation between God and His newly Reincarnate Son transpires in this resurrection-day passage. [God's proclamation]: "Yet have I <u>set my KING</u> <u>upon my holy hill of Zion</u>. [risen King of the Jews' response] <u>I will</u> declare the decree: the LORD hath said unto me, <u>Thou art my Son</u>; this day have I begotten thee. [God's bequeath] "Ask of me, and <u>I shall</u> give thee the heathen for <u>thine inheritance</u>, and the uttermost parts of the earth for thy <u>possession</u>" (Ps. 2:6-8).

The phrase *his father* is mentioned in 61 chapters of the OT Narrative. The Bible phrases *thy holy hill* (2x), *of Zion* (59x) = 61. The Bible name *Zion* (152x) and *Sion* (9x) = 161. Again the phrase *unto me* is mentioned in 61 chapters of the Law. The phrase *I will* occurs 183 times in Psalms, a multiple of 61. The phrase *thou art* occurs 61 times in the OT Narrative. The phrase *my son* is mentioned in 122 verses of the Bible, a multiple of 61. The phrase *I shall* is mentioned in 161 verses of the Bible. Again the word *thine* is mentioned in 61 verses of the NT Narrative. Again the word *inheritance* is mentioned in 61 verses of the Law. Again the word *possess* is mentioned in 61 chapters of the Old Testament. The Bible combination *set my king* (1x), *upon my holy hill of Zion* (1x), *I will declare* (10x), *the decree* (16x), *this day have I begotten thee* (3x), *ask of me* (5x), *I will give thee* (22x), *uttermost parts of the earth* (2x), *for thy possession* (1x) = 61.

The Throne of God

"<u>The LORD is in</u> <u>his holy temple</u>, <u>the LORD'S throne is in heaven</u>: his eyes behold, his eyelids try, the children of men" (Ps. 11:4). Again the phrase *the LORD/Lord is* is mentioned in 61 verses of the Wisdom Books. Again from Genesis to the Gospels the combination *the throne* (60x) and *the LORD'S throne* (1x) = 61. The phrase *is in* is mentioned in 61 verses of the OT Narrative.

> The Wisdom Books combination *is in* (60x), *his holy temple* (1x) = 61.
> The Wisdom Books combination *the LORD'S throne is in* (1x), *heaven* (60x) = 61.

Asking God, "Why?"

"My GOD, my GOD, <u>why</u> hast thou <u>forsaken</u> me? <u>why</u> art thou so far from helping me, and from the words of my roaring?" (Ps. 22:1) These sad words of prophesy were uttered by the lowly Incarnate King of the Jews as He cried out from His cruel Roman-style cross. Again the word *forsaken* is mentioned in 61 chapters of the Bible. The word *why* is mentioned in 261 verses of the Bible.

Crucified King of the Jews' Lamentation

From the Cross the lowly King of the Jews lamented His dire situation: "they pierced my <u>hands</u> and my <u>feet</u>. I may tell all my <u>bones</u>: they look and stare upon <u>me</u>. They part my <u>garments</u> among them, and cast lots <u>upon my vesture</u>" (Ps. 22:16-18). Proof that the Person mentioned in this prophetic Psalm is the Incarnate Son of God, even the King of the Jews, is revealed by the following numeric seals. The phrase *his hands* occurs 61 times in the Old Testament. Again from Genesis to the Gospels the phrase *his feet* occurs 61 times. The word *bones* is mentioned in 61 chapters of the Old Testament. The word *me* is mentioned in 161 verses of the Pauline Epistles. The word *garments* is mentioned in 61 chapters of the Bible. The Bible combination *upon my* (53 vs), *vesture* (8 vs) = 61 verses.

The Worship of God

"All the ends of the world shall remember and turn unto the LORD: and all the kindreds of the nations shall <u>worship</u> before thee" (Ps. 22:7). The word *worship* is mentioned naturally in 61 verses of the Old Testament.

The King of Glory

"Lift up your heads, O ye gates; and be ye lift up, ye everlasting doors; <u>and the KING of</u> glory shall come in. Who is this KING of glory? The LORD strong and mighty, the LORD mighty in battle. Lift up your heads, O ye gates; even lift them up, ye everlasting doors; <u>and the KING of</u> glory shall come in. Who is this KING of glory? The LORD of hosts, he is the KING of glory. Selah" (Ps. 24:7-10). The phrase *and the king of* is mentioned naturally in 61 verses of the Bible.

God's Divine Messenger
(Part 15)

"This poor man cried, and the LORD heard him, and saved him out of all his troubles. The angel of the LORD encampeth <u>round about</u> them that fear him, and delivereth them" (Ps. 34:6-7). In verse six the Lord saved the people and in verse seven the Angel of the Lord delivers them. By this we are again shown the heavenly Messenger's divine proportion to God. Again the phrase *round about* is mentioned in 61 verses of Ezekiel.

The Fear of God

"Come, ye children, <u>hearken unto</u> me: I will teach you the <u>fear of</u> the LORD" (Ps. 34:11). These wise words were prophetically uttered by the Son of God so the Jews would learn a lesson in reverencing God. The phrase *hearken unto* is mentioned in 61 chapters of the Bible. Again the phrase *unto me* is mentioned in 61 chapters of the Law. Again the word *me* is mentioned in 161 verses of the Pauline Epistles. The phrase *fear of* is mentioned in 61 chapters of the Bible.

The Orderliness of God

"The steps of a good man are <u>ordered</u> <u>by the</u> LORD: and he delighteth in his way" (Ps. 37:23). Again the word *order* occurs 61 times in Scripture. The phrase *by the* is mentioned in 61 chapters of the Pauline Epistles and in 861 verses of the Bible.

The Whole Bible Is about God's Son

"Then said <u>I, Lo, I</u> <u>come</u>: in the volume of <u>the book</u> <u>it is written</u> <u>of me</u>" (Ps. 40:7). The Son of God uttered these inspiring words so the Jews would begin searching the Scriptures and find Him there. The Psalms combination *I lo I* (1x), *come* (60x) = 61. The third and fourth seal below are repeated.

> The word *come* occurs naturally 61 times in Numbers.
> The word *read* occurs 61 times from Genesis to the NT Narrative.
> The phrase *the book* is mentioned in 61 chapters of Old Testament.
> The phrase *it is written* is mentioned in 61 chapters of the Bible.
> The phrase *of me* is mentioned in 61 chapters of the Bible.

The Incarnate Son of God Preached to Jews

"<u>I have</u> <u>preached</u> righteousness in the great congregation: lo, I have not refrained my lips, O

LORD, thou knowest" (Ps. 40:9). This verse is prophetic. The Son of God, the Incarnate King of the Jews, preached to His Jewish kinsmen for more than three full years on how to be right with God. Many times He preached in the great open courts of the Temple where the Jews congregated daily. Again the phrase *I have* is found in 61 books of the Bible. The word *preached* occurs 61 times in the Bible.

The City of God

"There is a river, the streams whereof shall make glad <u>the city of GOD</u>, <u>the holy place</u> of the tabernacles of <u>the most High</u>" (Ps. 46:4). The Bible reveals that there are actually two Jerusalems, one earthly and one heavenly. Each is considered to be the City of God. The OT Narrative combination *the city of* (60x) and *the most High* (1x) = 61. Again the Bible terms *holy place* (60x) and *holy dwelling place* (1x) = 61.

> The term *the holy* is mentioned in 61 verses of the Law.
> The term *the holy* is mentioned in 61 verses of the Major Prophets.
> The word *city* is mentioned in 61 verses of the Synoptic Gospels.

God Has Gone up with a Shout

"GOD is <u>gone up</u> <u>with a</u> <u>shout</u>, the LORD with the <u>sound</u> of a <u>trumpet</u>" (Ps. 47:5). The word *gone* occurs 61 times in the Major Prophets. The Wisdom Books combination *gone up* (1x), *with a* (52x), *shout* (8x) = 61. Again the phrase *go up* is mentioned in 61 verses of the OT Narrative. Again the word *up* is mentioned in 61 verses of the Pauline Epistles. Again the word *sound* is mentioned in 61 verses of the Old Testament. The OT Narrative combination *trumpet/s* (58x) and *trumpeters* (3x) = 61. Again the word *trumpet* occurs 61 times in the Bible.

Heavenly King of the Jews Shares Equality with God

"Sing praises <u>to GOD</u>, sing praises: <u>sing praises</u> un<u>to</u> <u>our KING</u>, sing praises" (Ps. 47:6). The King of Heaven shares a divine proportion to the God of Heaven. Again the phrase *to God* is mentioned in 61 chapters of the Bible. The Psalms combination *sing* (56 vs), *praises to* (4 vs), *our King* (1 v) = 61.

Deliver Me, O God

"<u>Deliver me</u> from bloodguiltiness, O GOD, thou GOD of my salvation: and my tongue shall sing aloud of thy righteousness" (Ps. 51:14). All tenses of the phrase *deliver me* are mentioned in 61 verses of the Bible.

None Can Understand God

"GOD looked down <u>from heaven</u> upon the children of men, to see if there were any that did <u>understand</u>, <u>that did</u> <u>seek</u> GOD" (Ps. 53:2). No one can understand God unless He reveals Himself to that person. Again the phrase *from heaven* is mentioned in 61 verses of the New Testament. The word *understand* is mentioned in 61 verses of the Old Testament. The New Testament combination *that did* (4x), *seek* (57x) = 61.

Through God

"<u>Through</u> GOD we shall do valiantly: for he it is that shall tread down our enemies" (Ps. 60:12). Alternatively this verse stands as an immediate introduction to Psalm 61.

The word *through* occurs 61 times in the OT Narrative.

The word *through* occurs 61 times in the NT Narrative.

Psalm 61

Beneath the literal rendering of a passage may lie some prophetic implication. Such is the case in this Psalm. Listen to the pitiful words of the King of the Jews as He cried to His heavenly Father from the Cross: "Hear my cry, <u>O GOD</u>; attend unto my prayer. From the end of the earth will I cry unto thee, when my heart is overwhelmed" (Ps. 61:1-2a). Many medical experts agree that the Incarnate King of the Jews died of a broken heart. Again the expression *O God* is mentioned in 61 chapters of the Bible.

From His garden tomb the resting King of the Jews gave confident thanks to His Father. "For thou, O GOD . . . Thou wilt prolong the <u>KING'S</u> life: and his years as many generations. He shall abide before GOD for ever" (vv. 6-7a). Again the word *king's* occurs 61 times in Second Kings. The word *life* occurs naturally 61 times in the Law. The key title *God* actually occurs in this 61st Psalm. Examining this entire 61st psalm, after the middle mention of the title *God* there are 61 words flowing to the end of the Psalm!

My God

"O GOD, thou art <u>my</u> GOD; early will I seek thee: my soul thirsteth for thee, my flesh longeth for thee in a dry and thirsty land, where no water is" (Ps. 63:1). The word *my* is mentioned in 161 chapters of the Wisdom Books.

Resurrected Son of God's Ascension to Heaven

"The <u>chariots</u> of GOD are twenty thousand, even thousands of angels: the LORD is among them, as in Sinai, in the holy place. <u>Thou hast</u> ascended on high, <u>thou hast</u> led captivity captive: <u>thou hast</u> received <u>gifts</u> for men" (Ps. 68:17-18a). The word *gift(s)* occurs 61 times in the New Testament. Again the word *chariot* occurs 61 times in the Old Testament. Again the word *Thou* [uppercase only] is mentioned in 61 verses of the Gospels. The phrase *thou hast* is mentioned in 161 verses of the Major Prophets.

The word *hast* occurs 261 times in the Major Prophets.

The word *hast* is mentioned in 61 verses of First/Second Samuel.

The word *hast* is mentioned in 61 verses of First/Second Kings.

Asking God, "How Long?"

"O GOD, <u>how long</u> shall the adversary reproach? shall the enemy blaspheme thy name for ever?" (Ps. 74:10) Whenever the believer faces adversity his or her favorite question to ask God is "How long?" The phrase *how long* occurs 61 times in the Bible.

Can God?—Yes He Can!

"Yea, they spake against GOD; they said, <u>Can</u> GOD furnish a <u>table</u> in <u>the wilderness</u>?" (Ps. 78:19) The word *can* is mentioned in 61 verses of the Wisdom Books. The word *table* occurs 61 times in the Old Testament. Again the phrase *the wilderness* is mentioned in 161 chapters of the Bible.

Psalm 78:61

"And delivered his strength into captivity, and his glory into the <u>enemy's</u> hand" (Ps. 78:61). God allowed His Ark to be taken away from Israel's possession. Again the phrase *thine enemies* is mentioned in 61 verses of the Bible.

The Children of God

"GOD standeth in the congregation of the mighty. . . . I have said, <u>Ye are gods</u>; and <u>all of you</u> are <u>children of</u> the <u>most High</u>. But ye shall die like men, and fall like one of the princes" (Ps. 82:1a, 6-7). The Hebrew word for gods—*elohim*—means rulers. Verse one speaks of the ruling angels in heaven who were created as children in God's image, and the latter two verses speak of the rulers on Earth who were chiefs over the children of Israel. Indeed God considered the children of Israel to be His peculiar children. The New Testament combination *ye are gods* (1x), *all of you* (1x), *children of* (55x), *the most high* (4x) = 61.

> The word *children* occurs 61 times in Genesis.
> The word *children* occurs 61 times in Leviticus.
> The word *children* is mentioned in 61 verses of the Kings.
> The word *children* is mentioned in 61 verses of Synoptic Gospels.
> The title *the children* occurs naturally 61 times in the New Testament.
> The phrase *of the children* is mentioned in 61 chapters of the Law.
> The phrase *of the children of* is mentioned in 61 chapters of the Law.
> The phrase *and the children of* is mentioned in 61 chapters of the OT.

561st Chapter of the Bible

"That men <u>may know</u> that thou, whose name alone is JEHOVAH, art the most high over all the earth" (Ps. 83:18). This verse is one of the four times the translators actually showed the Lord's covenant name. The covenant name of *God* is seen in this 61st verse. Again the phrase *may know* occurs 61 times in the Bible.

A God Ready to Forgive

"For thou, LORD, art good, and ready to <u>forgive</u>; and plenteous in mercy unto all them that call upon thee" (Ps. 86:5). All available forms of the word *forgive* occur 61 times in the New Testament.

The Eternal Nature of God

"<u>But thou art</u> <u>the same, and thy years shall have no end</u>" (Ps. 102:27). The New Testament combination *but thou art the* (1x), *the same* (159x), *and thy years shall not fail* (1x) = 161.

The 1610th Verse of Psalms

"The children of thy servants shall continue, and their <u>seed shall be established before thee</u>" (Ps. 102:28). This 61st verse speaks of the longevity of God's spiritually reborn children. Again the word *seed('s)* occurs 61 times in the Major and Minor Prophets. The Law combination *thy seed shall be* (2x), *be established* (2x), *before thee* (57x) = 61.

Rejected King of the Jews Becomes Co-King of Heaven

"<u>The LORD</u> said unto my Lord, <u>Sit thou at my right hand, until</u> <u>I make thine enemies thy</u>

217

footstool. . . . The LORD hath sworn, and will not repent, <u>Thou art</u> a <u>priest</u> <u>for ever</u> after the <u>order</u> of Melchizedek" (Ps. 110:1, 4). David heard a future conversation taking place in heaven at the moment of the risen Son of God's full ascension into heaven. David's two Lords share a divine proportion to one another as Father and Son. The Bible combination *sit thou at my right hand until* (1x), *I make* (55x), *thine enemies thy footstool* (5x) = 61. The Bible phrases *the right hand* (60x) and *the LORD'S right hand* (1x) = 61.

The phrase *right hand* is mentioned in 161 verses of the Bible.
Again the phrase *thine enemies* is mentioned in 61 verses of the Bible.
Again the phrase *thou art* occurs 61 times in the OT Narrative.
The title *priest* is mentioned in 61 verses of Numbers.
The phrase *for ever* is mentioned in 61 verses of Major/Minor Prophets.
Again the word *order* occurs 61 times in the Bible.

God Hath Done

"But our GOD is in the heavens: <u>he hath done</u> whatsoever he hath pleased" (Ps. 115:3).

The phrase *he hath* is mentioned in 461 verses of the Bible.
The phrase *hath done* occurs 61 times in the Old Testament.

The Jews' Rejected Kingly Head & Chief Cornerstone

"<u>The stone</u> which the builders <u>refused</u> is become the <u>head stone</u> of the <u>corner</u>" (Ps. 118:22). Messiah came to Earth to be the Jews' earthly King, but they refused to have Him reign over them. Thus He ascended back to heaven to reign as King from there until such a time as He should return to Earth. The Bible combination *the stone* (32x) and *rejected* (29x) = 61. All forms of the word *refuse* occur 61 times in the Old Testament. All forms of the word *refuse* are mentioned collectively in 61 chapters of the Bible. The Major Prophets combination *head* (60x) and *corner stone* (1x) = 61.

Psalm 119:161

"Princes have persecuted <u>me</u> without a cause: but my heart standeth in <u>awe</u> of <u>thy word</u>" (Ps. 119:161). The lowly Incarnate King of the Jews was hated without a cause by His princely kinsmen the Pharisees and Sadducees. Messiah's love of God's Word was His daily staying power. Again the word *me* is mentioned in 161 verses of the Pauline Epistles. The Bible combination *awe* (3x) and *thy word* (58x) = 61.

16,100th Verse of the Bible

"Unto thee lift I up mine eyes, O <u>thou that</u> dwellest in the heavens" (Ps. 123:1). Hope in the God above is the subject of this 161st verse. The phrase *thou that* is mentioned in 61 verses of the Bible.

16,111st Verse of the Bible

"Our help is in <u>the name of the LORD,</u> who made heaven and earth" (Ps. 124:8). In this 161st verse we find the Bible's 61st occurrence of the phrase *the name of the LORD*.

16,161st Verse of the Bible

"Let thy priests be clothed with righteousness; and let <u>thy saints</u> <u>shout</u> <u>for joy</u>" (Ps. 132:9).

Rejoicing in God's uprightness is the subject of this 161st verse. The Bible combination *thy saints* (6x), *shout* (36x), *for joy* (19x) = 61.

16,180th Verse of the Bible

"For the LORD hath chosen Jacob unto himself, and Israel for his peculiar treasure" (Ps. 135:4). Understanding God's choice among nations is the subject of this 161st verse. Again the phrase *for the LORD/Lord* is mentioned naturally in 161 chapters of the Old Testament.

2461 Psalm Verses with Which to Praise God

The Psalms are songs which were written to accompany the plucking of a stringed instrument. Their entire collection was ultimately organized into a Temple hymnbook so God could be daily praised by a choral gathering. Here we cite the last verse of all the Psalms, the 2461st verse of Psalm: "Let every thing that hath breath praise the LORD. Praise ye the LORD" (Ps. 150:6). This 61st verse actually contains the key title *Lord*. The phrase *that hath* occurs 161 times in the Bible.

61st Verse of Proverbs

"In all thy ways acknowledge him, and he shall direct thy paths" (Prov. 3:6). A challenge is given to the believer to ask God for guidance through each day's forward journey. The phrase *in all* is mentioned in 61 chapters of the New Testament. Again the word *ways* occurs 61 times in the Major Prophets. Again the word *him* occurs 6661 times altogether in the Bible! Again the phrase *and he shall* is mentioned naturally in 161 chapters of the Bible.

Proverbs 16:10

"A divine sentence is in the lips of the king: his mouth transgresseth not in judgment" (Prov. 16:10). At this golden-seal location [161] we are shown a divine proportion between what the king spoke and what God had given him to decisively say regarding a pending matter of judgment. King Solomon's specially acquired wisdom actually allowed this saying to be particularly true of him, yet only ideally true for all other Israelite kings. The indefinite article *a* occurs 261 times in Deuteronomy, 361 times in Psalms, and 261 times in Acts. The First and Second Corinthians combination *a* (160x) and *sentence* (1x) = 161. Again the phrase *is in* is mentioned in 61 verses of the OT Narrative. The phrase *of the king* occurs 122 times in the Old Testament, a multiple of 61. The Major Prophets combination *sentence* (1 v), *lips* (15 vs), *of the king* (45 vs) = 61 verses.

God Knows All Men's Hearts

"Every way of a man is right in his own eyes: but the LORD pondereth the hearts" (Prov. 21:2).

> The word *heart* is mentioned in 161 verses of the Major/Minor Prophets.
> The word *hearts* occurs 61 times in the New Testament.
> The word *hearts* is mentioned in 61 verses of the New Testament.

What Is the Name of God's Son?

"Who hath ascended up into heaven, or descended? who hath gathered the wind in his fists? who hath bound the waters in a garment? who hath established all the ends of the earth? what is his name, and what is his son's name, if thou canst tell?" (Prov. 30:4) Agur's prophecy put forth a most-intriguing riddle. If God's covenant name Yehovah was made known to mankind, so in time would His Son's name be revealed. We now know His name to be Yeshua. The phrase *his son* is mentioned naturally in 161 verses of the Old Testament! Again the word *son* is mentioned in 61 verses of the Wisdom Books. The lowercase-only phrase *what is* is mentioned in 61 chapters of the Bible. The Bible combination *What is* (54x), *his son's name* (2x), *who can tell* (5x) = 61. Behold with wonder the following uppercase seals.

The Bible combination *God's* (24 chs), *Son* (137 chs) = 161 chapters!
The title *Son* is mentioned naturally in 161 verses of the NT Narrative.

Making Vows to God
"When thou vowest a <u>vow</u> unto GOD, defer not to pay it; for he hath no pleasure in fools: pay that which thou hast vowed. Better is it that thou shouldest not <u>vow</u>, than that thou shouldest <u>vow</u> and not pay" (Eccles. 5:4-5). The word *vow(s)* is mentioned in 61 verses of the Old Testament.

17,461st Verse of the Bible
"I counsel thee to keep the KING'S <u>commandment</u>, and that in regard of the oath of GOD" (Eccles. 8:2). Again the word *commandment* is mentioned in 61 verses of the OT Narrative. This 61st verse actually contains the key titles *God* and *king's*.

God's Oath to Man
"I counsel thee to keep the KING'S commandment, and that in regard of the <u>oath</u> of GOD" (Eccles. 8:2). The word *oath('s)* occurs 61 times in the Bible.

161st Verse of Ecclesiastes
"For <u>all this</u> I considered in my heart even to declare <u>all this</u>, that the righteous, and the wise, and their works, are in the hand of GOD: no man knoweth either love or hatred by all that is before them" (Eccles. 9:1). The wise ones of this earth are those who believe in the One True God and put their trust in Him. All of this—every word of the King James Version—has been written by the hand of God! The phrase *all this* is mentioned in 61 chapters of the Old Testament.

The Whole Matter of Fearing God
"Let us hear the conclusion of the <u>whole matter</u>: Fear <u>GOD, and keep his commandments</u>: for this is the whole duty of man" (Eccles. 12:13). The word *whole* occurs 61 times in the Gospels. The word *matter* is mentioned in 61 verses of the Old Testament. The following seal employs only the capitalized word Fear. The Bible combination *Fear* (59x), *God and keep his commandments* (2x) = 61. Again the word *commandment* is mentioned in 61 verses of the OT Narrative.

The Daughters of Jerusalem
The contemplative bride describes the King of the Jews' wedding-day chariot. "He made the pillars thereof of silver, the bottom thereof of gold, the covering of it of purple, the midst thereof being paved with love, for <u>the daughters of</u> Jerusalem" (SOS 3:10). The title *the daughter(s) of* is mentioned in 61 verses of the OTN.

61st Verse of Song of Solomon
"Awake, O north wind; and come, thou south; blow upon my garden, that the spices thereof may

flow out. Let my <u>beloved</u> come into his <u>garden</u>, and eat <u>his pleasant fruits</u>" (Song 4:16). The bride desires for the king to come to her, and she speaks metaphorically knowing that every king had his own private garden. She waits for Solomon, the beloved king of the Jews. The word *beloved* is mentioned in 61 verses of the New Testament. The Bible combination *garden* (47 vs), *gardens* (12 vs), *gardener* (1 v), *his pleasant fruits* (1 v) = 61 verses.

God's Spiritual Challenge to Sin-Sick Israel

"Come now, and let us reason together, <u>saith the LORD</u>: though your sins be as scarlet, they shall be as white as snow; though they be red like crimson, they shall be as wool" (Isa. 1:18). Again the phrase *saith the Lord* is mentioned in 61 chapters of the Old Testament.

God's Incarnate Son to Be Born of a Virgin

"Therefore the LORD himself shall give you a sign; <u>Behold, a</u> <u>virgin</u> <u>shall conceive, and bear</u> <u>a</u> <u>son, and shall call</u> <u>his name</u> <u>Immanuel</u>" (Isa. 7:14). This miracle Son will be born in divine proportion to His heavenly Father. The Major Prophets combination *behold a* (17x), *virgin* (13x), *shall conceive and bear* (1x), *a son* (7x), *and shall call* (1x), *his name* (20x), *Immanuel* (2x) = 61.

God's Son Is Given to Israel

"For <u>unto us</u> a child is born, <u>unto us</u> <u>a son</u> is given: and the government shall be upon his shoulder: and his name shall be called Wonderful, Counsellor, The mighty GOD, The everlasting Father, The Prince of Peace" (Isa. 9:6). The phrase *unto us* is mentioned in 61 chapters of the Old Testament. This verse presents the Bible's 61st naturally occurring phrase *a son*, and it refers to God's Son.

Divine King of the Jews Shall Exercise Global Governance

"Of the increase of his <u>government</u> and peace there shall be no end, upon the throne of David, and upon his KINGDOM, to <u>order</u> it, and to establish it with judgment and with justice from henceforth even for ever. The zeal of the LORD of hosts will perform this" (Isa. 9:7). All forms of the word govern show the seal of God and King of the Jews: *govern* (3 chs), *governor* (37 chs), *governnor's* (1 ch), *governors* (16 chs), *government* (3 chs), *governments* (1 ch) = 61 chapters. Again the word *order* occurs 61 times in Scripture.

Divine King of the Jews Shall Have Sevenfold Spirit of God

"And there shall come forth a rod out of the stem of Jesse, and a Branch shall grow out of his roots: And the <u>spirit</u> of the LORD shall rest upon him, the <u>spirit</u> of wisdom and understanding, the <u>spirit</u> of counsel and might, the <u>spirit</u> of knowledge and of the fear of the LORD" (Isa. 11:1-2). Again the lowercase title *spirit* is mentioned in 61 verses of the Wisdom Books.

Divine King of the Jews Shall Slay the Wicked with a Word

Isaiah speaks of the wondrous millennial reign of the divine King of the Jews. "But with righteousness <u>shall he</u> judge the poor, and reprove with equity for the meek of the earth: and he shall smite the earth with the rod of his mouth, and with the breath of his lips shall he slay the wicked" (Isa. 11:4). The phrase *shall he* occurs 161 times in the Old Testament.

This Is Our God

"And it shall be said in that day, Lo, <u>this</u> is our GOD; we have waited for him, and he will save us: <u>this is the</u> LORD; we have waited for him, we will be glad and rejoice in his salvation" (Isa. 25:9). Here the word *this* is the 261st word in the chapter, and it refers to title God. Again the phrase *this is the* occurs 61 times in the Law.

18,261st Verse of the Bible

"Behold, a KING shall reign in righteousness, and princes shall rule in judgment" (Isa. 32:1). This 61st verse foretells the nature of the divine King of the Jews' millennial reign. The key title *king* actually occurs in this 61st verse.

God Is Our King

"For the LORD <u>is our</u> judge, the LORD <u>is our</u> lawgiver, the LORD <u>is our</u> KING; he will save us" (Isa. 33:22). Right on cue the word *is* is mentioned in 61 verses of Judges. Again all available forms of the word *our* occur 161 times in the Wisdom Books.

If You Say to God

"But if thou <u>say to</u> me, We trust in the <u>LORD our GOD</u>" (Isa. 36:7a). The phrase *say to* is mentioned in 61 chapters of the Bible. Again the title *LORD/Lord our God* is mentioned in 61 chapters of the Bible.

Word of God Stands Forever

"The grass withereth, the flower fadeth: but the word of our GOD shall stand <u>for ever</u>" (Isa. 40:8). Again the phrase *for ever* is mentioned in 61 verses of the Major and Minor Prophets.

Behold Your God!

"O Zion, that bringest good tidings, get thee up into the high mountain; O Jerusalem, that bringest good tidings, lift up thy voice with strength; lift it up, be not afraid; say unto the cities of Judah, <u>Behold</u> your GOD!" (Isa. 40:9)

> The word *Behold* occurs 61 times in Isaiah.
> The word *b/Behold* occurs 61 times in Minor Prophets.

Youthfulness Given & Sustained by God

"Even the <u>youths</u> shall faint and be weary, and the young men shall utterly fall: But they that wait upon the LORD shall renew their strength; they shall mount up with wings as eagles; they shall run, and not be weary; and they shall walk, and not faint" (Isa. 40:30-31). The word *youth* is mentioned in 61 chapters of the Old Testament.

861st Verse of Isaiah

"Ye are my witnesses, saith the LORD, and my servant whom I have chosen: that ye may know and believe me, and understand that I am he: before me there was no GOD formed, neither shall there be after me" (Isa. 43:10). This 61st verse makes a great declaration concerning the existence of God.

God Will Do a New Thing

"Behold, I will do a new thing; now it shall spring forth; shall ye not know it? I will even make a way in the wilderness, and rivers in the desert" (Isa. 43:19). Here the word *do* is the 24,161st word of Isaiah. Again the word *do* is mentioned in 1261 verses of the Bible.

There Is No God beside Me

"I am the LORD, and there is none else, there is no God beside me: I girded thee, though thou hast not known me: That they may know from the rising of the sun, and from the west, that there is none beside me. I am the LORD, and there is none else. I form the light, and create darkness: I make peace, and create evil: I the LORD do all these things" (Isa. 45:5-7). Isaiah wrote this while the Israelites were in Assyrian captivity. The Assyrians believed that there were two gods, one good and the other evil. Isaiah corrected that errant view with this declaration. Again the phrase *there is none* is mentioned in 61 verses of the Old Testament. Again the word *me* is mentioned in 161 verses of the Pauline Epistles.

God Sends the Son of God to Israel

God said, "Hearken unto me, O Jacob and Israel, my called; I am he; I am the first, I also am the last. . . . Come ye near unto me, hear ye this; I have not spoken in secret from the beginning; from the time that it was, there am I: and now the Lord GOD, and his Spirit, hath sent me" (Isa. 48:12, 16). As God speaks of Himself, He suddenly becomes the Sent One, a reference to His Incarnate Son. The divine proportion between God and His Son are wonderfully revealed here. Again the phrase *hearken unto* is mentioned in 61 chapters of the Bible. Again the word *me* is mentioned in 161 verses of the Pauline Epistles. The phrase *the first* occurs 61 times in Numbers.

Messianic King of the Jews Scourged & Mocked

"I gave my back to the smiters, and my cheeks to them that plucked off the hair: I hid not my face from shame and spitting" (Isa. 50:6). The sentance *I gave my back to the smiters, and my cheeks to them that plucked off the hair* consists of 61 letters!

God Put His Own Son to Grief

"Yet it pleased the LORD to bruise him; he hath put him to grief" (Isa. 53:10a).

Here the word *him* is the 47,6061st word of the Bible, and it refers to God's sent Son.

Crucified King of the Jews Astonishes the World

"Behold, my servant shall deal prudently, he shall be exalted and extolled, and be very high. As many were astonied at thee; his visage was so marred more than any man, and his form more than the sons of men" (Isa. 52:14-15). All forms of the word *astonish* occur 61 times from Genesis to the Gospels.

Crucified King of the Jews Suffered for Israel's Sin

"Surely he hath borne our griefs, and carried our sorrows: yet we did esteem him stricken, smitten of GOD, and afflicted" (Isa. 53:4). The word *carried* is mentioned in 61 verses of the OT Narrative. The word *smitten* occurs 61 times in the Old Testament. This King-of-the-Jews, smitten-of-God verse is the 1061st verse of Isaiah.

The word *affliction* occurs 61 times in the Old Testament.

The word *affliction* is mentioned in 61 chapters of the Bible.

The word *affliction(s)* is mentioned in 61 verses of Old Testament.

Crucified King of the Jews Bore Israel's Sin

"But he was wounded for our transgressions, he was bruised for our iniquities: the chastisement of our peace was <u>upon him</u>; and with his stripes we are healed. All we like sheep have gone astray; we have turned every one to his own way; and the LORD hath laid on <u>him</u> the iniquity of us all. . . . He was <u>taken</u> from prison and from judgment: and who shall declare his generation? he was <u>cut off</u> out of the land of the living: for the transgression of my people was he stricken" (Isa. 53:5-6, 8).

The weight of the world's sin was placed upon the lowly Messianic King of the Jews' shoulders for the benefit of the world's salvation. He was also laden with the literal and physical weight of the Cross and soon fell under its crushing load. The phrase *upon him* is mentioned in 161 verses from Genesis to the Gospels. The underlined word *him* is the 161st word in this chapter. Again the word *taken* occurs 61 times in the Law and 61 times in the Major and Minor Prophets. The phrase *be cut off* occurs 61 times in the Bible.

Messianic King of the Jews' Suffering Pleased God

"Yet it <u>pleased</u> the LORD to bruise him; he hath put him to grief: when thou shalt make his soul an offering for sin. . . . He <u>shall see</u> of the travail of his soul, and shall be <u>satisfied</u>: by his knowledge shall my righteous servant justify many; for he shall bear their iniquities" (Isa. 53:10a, 11).

This verse reveals who was ultimately responsible for Messiah's sacrificial death. Again the word *pleased* is mentioned in 61 verses of the Bible. All forms of the word satisfy show the King of the Jews seal: *satisfaction* (2x), *satisfied* (43x), *satisfiest* (1x), *satisfieth* (3x), *satisfy* (10x), *satisfying* (2x) = 61.

61st Chapter of Isaiah

This chapter presents the two comings of the heavenly King of the Jews; first His incarnate coming and then His reincarnate return.

The Message of God—"<u>The Spirit</u> of the LORD GOD is upon me; because the LORD hath anointed me to <u>preach</u> good tidings unto the meek; he hath <u>sent</u> me to bind up the brokenhearted, to proclaim liberty to the captives, and the opening of the prison to them that are bound; To proclaim the acceptable year of the LORD, and the day of vengeance of our GOD" (Isa. 61:1-2a). These prophetic words comprised the Messianic King of the Jews' very first sermon which took place in Nazareth; but it should be duly noted that at that time Messiah stopped reading upon reaching the words "the day of vengeance of our God" because this pointed to His reincarnate return when He would install global peace and righteousness on the earth. Again the title *the Spirit* is mentioned in 61 chapters of the New Testament. Again the word *preached* occurs 61 times in Scripture. The NT Narrative combination *sent* (160 vs), *his only begotten Son* (1 v) = 161 verses.

The Beauty of God—The majority of this 61st chapter anticipates Israel's long-awaited restoration and blessing which culminates at the ascended King of the Jews' return in power and glory. His millennial work will be "to appoint unto them that mourn in Zion, to give unto them <u>beauty</u> for ashes, the oil of joy for mourning, the <u>garment</u> of praise for the spirit of heaviness; that they might be called trees of righteousness, the planting of the LORD, that he might be glorified" (v. 3). All forms of the word *beauty* are mentioned in 61 chapters of the Bible. Again the word *garments* is mentioned in 61 chapters of the Bible.

The Ministers of God—"But ye shall be named the Priests of the LORD: men shall call you the <u>Ministers</u> of our GOD: ye shall eat the riches of the Gentiles, and in their glory shall ye boast yourselves" (v. 6). Again all forms of the word *minister* are mentioned collectively in 161 verses of the Bible.

<h2 style="text-align:center">God's Divine Messenger
(Part 16)</h2>

"In all their affliction he was afflicted, and the angel <u>of his</u> <u>presence</u> saved them: in his love and in his pity he redeemed them; and he bare them, and carried them all the days of old" (Isa. 63:9). Here the Angel of the Lord is shown to possess a divine proportion with God's very presence. The phrase *of his* occurs 61 times in Leviticus and is mentioned in 61 verses of Isaiah. The phrase *the presence of* is mentioned in 61 verses of the Bible.

<h2 style="text-align:center">Messianic King of the Jews' Divine Title</h2>

"Behold, the days come, saith the <u>LORD</u>, that I will raise unto David a righteous Branch, and a KING shall reign and prosper, and shall execute judgment and justice in the <u>earth</u>. In his days Judah shall be saved, and Israel shall dwell safely: and this is his name whereby he shall be called, THE LORD OUR RIGHTEOUSNESS" (Jer. 23:5-6). This King of the Jews will bear the title LORD because He is the Incarnate Lord. The underlined title *LORD* is the 499,161st word of the Bible.

> The Bible combination *earthly* (5x), *king* (2256x) = 2261 times.
> The Bible combination *earthly* (5 vs), *king* (1756 vs) = 1761 verses.

<h2 style="text-align:center">God's Drawing Love for the Jews</h2>

"The LORD hath appeared of old unto me, saying, Yea, I have loved thee with an everlasting love: therefore with lovingkindness have I <u>drawn</u> thee" (Jer. 31:3). The word *draw* occurs 61 times in the Old Testament and is mentioned in 61 verses thereof; it is also mentioned in 61 chapters of the Bible. The word *drew* is mentioned in 61 chapters of the Bible.

<h2 style="text-align:center">God Serves as a Father to Israel</h2>

"They shall come with weeping, and with supplications will I lead them: I will cause them to walk by the rivers of waters in a straight way, wherein they shall not stumble: for I am <u>a father</u> to Israel, and Ephraim is my firstborn" (Jer. 31:9).

> The phrase *the father* is mentioned in 61 verses of the Old Testament.
> The case-sensitive phrase *the Father* is mentioned in 61 verses of the NT Narrative.

<h2 style="text-align:center">King of the Jews Mediates the Jews' New Covenant</h2>

"Behold, the days come, saith the LORD, that I will make a <u>new</u> covenant with the house of Israel, and with the house of Judah" (Jer. 31:31). Right on cue the word *new* occurs 61 times in the New Testament.

God Is a Faithful Witness

"Then they said to Jeremiah, The LORD be a true and <u>faithful</u> <u>witness</u> between us, if we do not even according to all things for the which the LORD thy GOD shall send thee to us" (Jer. 42:5). The word *faithful* is the 161st word of this chapter, and it refers to God. The NT Narrative combination *faithful* (12x), *witness* (49x) = 61.

Lamentations 3:61

"Thou hast <u>heard</u> their reproach, O LORD, and all their imaginations against me" (Lam. 3:61). Again the word *heard* is mentioned in 61 chapters of the Gospels. The key title *LORD* actually occurs in this 61st verse.

The Son of God's Fiery Appearance

"And above the firmament that was over their heads was the likeness of a throne, as the appearance of a sapphire stone: and <u>upon the likeness of the throne was the likeness as the appearance of a man</u> above upon it. And I saw as the colour of amber, as the appearance of fire <u>round about</u> within it, from the appearance of his <u>loins</u> even upward, and from the appearance of his <u>loins</u> even downward, I saw as it were the appearance of fire, and it had brightness round about" (Ezek. 1:26-27).

The words *upon the likeness of the throne was the likeness as the appearance of a man* consists of 61 letters! Again the phrase *a man* occurs 61 times in the Synoptic Gospels. Again the phrase *round about* is mentioned in 61 verses of Ezekiel. The word *loins* is mentioned in 61 verses of the Bible.

The Unbelieving Nation Shall Know God

"And ye <u>shall know</u> that <u>I am the LORD</u>, when I have wrought with you for my name's sake, not according to your wicked ways, nor according to your corrupt doings, O ye house of Israel, saith the LORD GOD" (Ezek. 20:44). The phrase *shall know* occurs 61 times in Ezekiel and is mentioned in 61 verses thereof. Again the phrase *I am the LORD/Lord* is mentioned in 161 verses of the Bible.

God's Holy Mountain & Stones of Fire

"Thou art the anointed cherub that covereth; and I have set thee so: thou wast upon the holy mountain of GOD; thou hast walked up and down in the midst of the <u>stones</u> of fire" (Ezek. 28:14). The word *stones* occurs 161 times in the Old Testament.

God's New Spirit within You

"A <u>new</u> heart also will I give you, and a <u>new</u> <u>spirit</u> will I put within you: and I will take away the stony heart out of your flesh, and I will give you an heart of flesh" (Ezek. 36:26). A prophecy is given here concerning the New Covenant gift of God's permanently abiding Spirit. Again the word *new* occurs 61 times in the New Testament. Again the lowercase title *spirit* is mentioned in 61 verses of the Wisdom Books. Again the title *the Spirit* is mentioned in 61 chapters of the New Testament.

Millennial King of the Jews' Exclusive Gate

"Then he brought me back <u>the way of</u> <u>the gate</u> of the outward sanctuary which looketh toward the east; and it was shut. . . . This gate shall be shut, it shall not be opened, and no man shall enter in by it; because the LORD, the GOD of Israel, hath entered in by it, therefore it shall be shut. It is for the prince" (Ezek. 44:1, 2b-3a). Again the phrase *the way of* occurs 161 times in the Bible. From Genesis to the NT Narrative the phrase *the gate* occurs 161 times.

God's Son—Fourth Man in the Fire

"He answered and said, Lo, I see four men loose, walking in the midst of the fire, and they have no hurt; and the form of the fourth is like the Son of GOD" (Dan. 3:25). Again the phrase *the fire* occurs naturally 61 times in the Major and Minor Prophets. The phrase *the fourth* is mentioned in 61 chapters of the Bible.

God's Handwriting on the Wall

"In the same hour came forth fingers of a man's hand, and wrote over against the candlestick upon the plaister of the wall of the king's palace: and the king saw the part of the hand that wrote" (Dan. 5:5). Again the word *man('s)* occurs 61 times in First Kings. Again the phrase *a man* occurs 61 times in the Synoptic Gospels. The phrase *part of* is mentioned in 61 chapters of the Bible. Again the phrase *of the hand of* is mentioned in 61 verses of the Old Testament.

Daniel's God

"Then said these men, We shall not find any occasion against this Daniel, except we find it against him concerning the law of his GOD" (Dan. 6:5). Again the word *concerning* is mentioned in 61 verses of the OT Narrative. The phrase *concerning the* occurs 61 times in the Old Testament. Again the phrase *his God/god* occurs 61 times in the Old Testament.

The Ancient of Days

"I beheld till the thrones were cast down, and the Ancient of days did sit, whose garment was white as snow, and the hair of his head like the pure wool: his throne was like the fiery flame, and his wheels as burning fire. . . . I saw in the night visions, and, behold, one like the Son of man came with the clouds of heaven, and came to the Ancient of days, and they brought him near before him" (Dan. 7:9, 13). Daniel had a vision of the Son of God standing before the eternal throne of God receiving His commission and anointing to rule the earth from the holy city of Jerusalem. The term *the throne(s)* is mentioned in 61 chapters of the Bible. The word *days* occurs 61 times in Genesis. Again the word *pure* occurs 61 times outside the Law. The capitalized title *Son of man* occurs 61 times in Ezekiel; this title refers to the incarnate Son of God in the New Testament and is always capitalized there. Again the phrase *came to* occurs 61 times in First and Second Chronicles.

29,161st Verse of the Bible

"And the kingdom and dominion, and the greatness of the kingdom under the whole heaven, shall be given to the people of the saints of the most High, whose kingdom is an everlasting kingdom, and all dominions shall serve and obey him" (Dan. 7:27). This prophecy refers to the heaven-sent Messiah, the Eternal King of Kings. Again the phrase *the kingdom of God* occurs 61 times in the NT Narrative.

Being Wise toward God

"Many shall be purified, and made white, and tried; but the wicked shall do wickedly: and none of the wicked shall understand; but the wise shall understand" (Dan. 12:10). The wise ones of this earth are those who believe in the God of Israel and put their trust in Him. The phrase *the wise* occurs 61 times in the Old Testament.

Rejected King of the Jews Returns to Heaven
"I will go and return to my place, till they acknowledge their offence, and seek my face: in their affliction they will seek me early" (Hos. 5:15). This verse prophesies Israel's offensive rejection of her Messianic King of the Jews and His subsequent departure and return to heaven. The phrase *will go* is mentioned in 61 chapters of the Bible. Again the phrase *my face* occurs 61 times in the Old Testament.

22,361st verse of the Bible
"So shall ye know that I am the LORD your GOD dwelling in Zion, my holy mountain: then shall Jerusalem be holy, and there shall no strangers pass through her any more" (Joel 3:17). The key titles *LORD* and *God* actually occur in this 61st verse.

God's Devouring Fire
"But I will send a fire into the house of Hazael, which shall devour the palaces of Ben-hadad" (Amos 1:4). The word *devour* is mentioned in 61 verses of the Old Testament.

God's Eternal Kingly Reign over the Jews
"And I will make her that halted a remnant, and her that was cast far off a strong nation: and the LORD shall reign over them in mount Zion from henceforth, even for ever" (Mic. 4:7). During the Golden Age the divine King of the Jews will reign over His Jewish people. Again all tenses of the phrase *reign over* are mentioned in 61 verses of the Bible.

Messianic King of the Jews Is from Eternity Past
"But thou, Beth-lehem Ephratah, though thou be little among the thousands of Judah, yet out of thee shall he come forth unto me that is to be ruler in Israel; whose goings forth have been from of old, from everlasting" (Mic. 5:2). Again the word *ruler* is mentioned in 61 verses of the Old Testament. The Minor Prophets combination *ruler in Israel whose* (1x), *goings* (1x), *forth* (53x), *have been* (6x), *from old* (1x) = 61. The Minor Prophets combination *goings* (1x), *forth* (53x), *have been* (6x), *from everlasting* (2x) = 61.

Wait for God
"Therefore I will look unto the LORD; I will wait for the GOD of my salvation: my GOD will hear me" (Mic. 7:7). The word *wait* is mentioned in 61 chapters of the Old Testament.

God Walks on the Clouds
The prophet declared, "the LORD hath his way in the whirlwind and in the storm, and the clouds are the dust of his feet" (Nah. 3:1b). The phrase *the dust* is mentioned in 61 chapters of the Bible. Again from Genesis to the Gospels the phrase *his feet* occurs 61 times.

God & His Holy One
"GOD came from Teman, and the Holy One from mount Paran. Selah. His glory covered the heavens, and the earth was full of his praise. And his brightness was as the light; he had horns coming out of his hand: and there was the hiding of his power. Before him went the pestilence,

and burning coals went forth at his feet" (Hab. 3:3-5). The Bible combination *H/holy O/one* (51 vs) and *Paran* (10 vs) = 61 verses. Again the phrase *the light* occurs 61 times in the Old Testament. This passage on God's glory consists of 61 words.

The Great & Terrible Day of the Lord
"The great day of the LORD is near, it is near, and hasteth greatly, even the voice of the day of the LORD: the mighty man shall cry there bitterly. That day is a day of wrath, a day of trouble and distress, a day of wasteness and desolation, a day of darkness and gloominess, a day of clouds and thick darkness, A day of the trumpet and alarm against the fenced cities, and against the high towers" (Zeph. 1:14-16). Again the word *trumpet* occurs 61 times in the Bible.

22,961st verse of the Bible
"Even he shall build the temple of the LORD; and he shall bear the glory, and shall sit and rule upon his throne; and he shall be a priest upon his throne: and the counsel of peace shall be between them both" (Zech. 6:13). The key title *LORD* actually occurs in this 61st verse.

God's Pierced Hands
"And I will pour upon the house of David, and upon the inhabitants of Jerusalem, the spirit of grace and of supplications: and they shall look upon me whom they have pierced, and they shall mourn for him, as one mourneth for his only son, and shall be in bitterness for him, as one that is in bitterness for his firstborn" (Zech. 12:10). When the heavenly King of the Jews returns to Israel, the people will recognize Him as Yeshua because He will have the nail prints or covenant scars in His hands. The Person who has been speaking throughout the entirety of this chapter is God, thus this returning King shares a divine proportion to God. He is the Son of God, the formerly crucified King of the Jews. Again the word *me* is mentioned in 161 verses of the Pauline Epistles.

The One Man Who Is God's Equal
"Awake, O sword, against my shepherd, and against the man that is my fellow, saith the LORD of hosts: smite the shepherd, and the sheep shall be scattered: and I will turn mine hand upon the little ones" (Zech. 13:7). The word fellow implies an equal. The Shepherd referred to in this verse is the lowly incarnate Son of God. The phrase *the man that* is mentioned in 61 verses of the Bible.

God Will Be King over the Jews
"And the LORD shall be KING over all the earth: in that day shall there be one LORD, and his name one" (Zech. 14:9). Again the phrase *king over* occurs 61 times in the Old Testament, and this verse presents its 61st occurrence.

Up to Jerusalem to Worship the Heaven-Sent King of the Jews
"And it shall come to pass, that every one that is left of all the nations which came against Jerusalem shall even go up from year to year to worship the KING, the LORD of hosts, and to keep the feast of tabernacles. And it shall be, that whoso will not come up of all the families of the earth unto Jerusalem to worship the KING, the LORD of hosts, even upon them shall be no rain. And if the family of Egypt go not up, and come not, that have no rain; there shall be the plague, wherewith the LORD will smite the heathen that come not up to keep the feast of tabernacles. This shall be the punishment of Egypt, and the punishment of

all nations that come not <u>up</u> to keep the feast of tabernacles" (Zech. 14:16-19).

Regardless of where a person is on the earth, the Bible always exalts Jerusalem by saying that a person must go up to reach it. Jerusalem is the city of the Great King, even the heavenly King of the Jews. Again the word *up* is mentioned in 61 verses of the Pauline Epistles. The word *upward* occurs 61 times in Scripture. Again the phrase *go up* is mentioned in 61 verses of the OT Narrative. The phrase *come up* is mentioned in 61 chapters of the Old Testament. The word *nations* is mentioned in 61 verses of the Law. Again the word *worship* is mentioned naturally in 61 verses of the Old Testament.

God's Holy Table
"Ye offer polluted bread upon mine altar; and ye say, Wherein have we polluted thee? In that ye say, The <u>table</u> of the LORD is contemptible" (Mal. 1:7). Again the word *table* occurs 61 times in the Old Testament.

God's Divine Messenger
(Part 17)
"Behold, I will send my messenger, and he shall prepare the way before me: and the LORD, whom ye seek, <u>shall</u> suddenly <u>come</u> to his temple, even the messenger of the covenant, whom ye delight in: behold, he <u>shall come</u>, saith the LORD of hosts" (Mal. 3:1). This New Covenant Messenger of the Lord is in reality the Incarnate Lord, the Son of God. The phrase *shall come* occurs naturally 161 times in the Major Prophets.

Son of God Will Return
"Even from the days of your fathers ye are gone away from mine ordinances, and have not kept them. Return unto me, and I <u>will return</u> unto you, saith the LORD of hosts. But ye said, Wherein shall we return?" (Mal. 3:7). The phrase *will/shall return* occurs 61 times in the Old Testament.

God's Holy Storehouse
"Bring ye all the tithes into the storehouse, that there may be meat <u>in mine</u> house, and prove me now herewith, saith the LORD of hosts, if I will not open you the windows of heaven, and pour you out a blessing, that there shall not be room enough to receive it" (Mal. 3:10). The phrase *in mine* is mentioned in 61 chapters of the Old Testament.

Is It Vain to Serve God?
"Ye have said, It is vain to serve GOD: and what profit <u>is it</u> that we have kept his ordinance, and that we have walked mournfully <u>before the LORD</u> of hosts?" (Mal. 3:14). The phrase *is it* is mentioned in 61 chapters of the Old Testament; this verse presents its 61st chapter-mention, and it pertains to God. Again the phrase *before the LORD* occurs 61 times in Leviticus.

God's Numeric Seal upon the Old Testament Canon
"And he shall turn the heart of the fathers to <u>the</u> children, and the heart of the children to their fathers, lest I come and smite the earth with a curse" (Mal. 4:6). Here the underlined word *the* is the 610,261st word of the Old Testament. The Old Testament canon closes with this verse, and it contains altogether 610,281 words, a number from the 61-hundred range.

The New Testament

"The book of the generation of Jesus Christ, the son of David, the son of Abraham" (Matt. 1:1). Jesus Christ was proven to be the King of the Jews by His genealogy and the Scriptures. Matthew wrote his book specifically to prove that Jesus was the Messianic King foretold. Further, Jesus was proven to be the Son of God by His mighty miracles and His royal resurrection from the dead.

The phrase *the book* is mentioned in 61 chapters of the Old Testament.
The phrase *of Jesus* occurs 61 times from Acts to the Apocalypse.
The title *Christ* is mentioned naturally in 161 chapters of the New Testament.

Son of God
The title *Son of* is mentioned in 61 chapters of the NT Narrative.
The title *Son* occurs 61 times in Ezekiel.
The title *Son* is mentioned in 61 verses of Ezekiel.
The title *Son* is mentioned naturally in 161 verses of the NT Narrative.
The word *son* occurs 161 combined times in Ezra and Nehemiah.
The word *son* is mentioned in 61 verses of the Wisdom Books.
The title *s/Son* occurs 261 times in the Synoptic Gospels.
The phrase *thy s/Son* is mentioned in 61 verses of the Bible.
The phrase *his son* is mentioned naturally in 161 verses of the Old Testament.

King of the Jews
The title *king* is mentioned in 61 verses of the Law.
The title *King* occurs 61 times from Genesis to the Gospels.
The title *King* is mentioned in 61 verses from Genesis to the NT Narrative.
The word *king('s)* is mentioned in 61 verses of First Chronicles.
The word *king's* is mentioned in 261 verses of the Bible.
The phrase *king over* occurs 61 times in the Old Testament.
The phrase *the kingdom of God* occurs 61 times in the NT Narrative.
The phrase *kingdom of* is mentioned in 61 chapters of the New Testament.
* The word *of* occurs precisely 6100 times in the New Testament!
The title *king of Judah('s)* occurs 61 times in the Major and Minor Prophets.
The titles *king of Judah* (60x), *king of the city* (1x) = 61 in First and Second Kings.
The phrase *of Judah* is mentioned in 61 chapters of the Kings and Chronicles.
The name *Judah* occurs 161 times in Second Chronicles.
The phrase *the tribe of* occurs 161 times in the Old Testament.
The phrase *the Jews* is mentioned in 61 verses of the Old Testament.
The name *Jews* occurs 61 combined times in Ezra, Nehemiah, and Esther.
The name *Jews* is mentioned in 61 verses of John's Gospel.

23,161st Verse of the Bible
"And Jacob begat Joseph the husband of Mary, of whom was born Jesus, who is called Christ" (Matt. 1:16). In this 61st verse we are told of the documented birth of the King of the Jews! The

231

phrase *is called* occurs 61 times in the Bible. Again the title *Christ* is mentioned naturally in 161 chapters of the New Testament.

King of the Jews' Jewish Genealogy

"So all the generations from Abraham to David are fourteen generations; and from David until the carrying away into Babylon are fourteen generations; and from the carrying away into Babylon unto Christ are fourteen generations" (Matt. 1:17). Matthew verified Jesus' Jewish genealogy all the way back to the first Jew Abraham. Again the phrase *to David* occurs 61 times in the Bible. The name *Babylon* occurs 161 times in Jeremiah. Again the title *Christ* is mentioned naturally in 161 chapters of the New Testament. Matthew's complete genealogy of Christ in verses one through seventeen consists of precisely 261 words!

Son of God's Earthly Conception & Birth

"Now the birth of Jesus Christ was on this wise: When as his mother Mary was espoused to Joseph, before they came together, she was found with child of the Holy Ghost. . . . And knew her not till she had brought forth her firstborn son: and he called his name JESUS" (Matt. 1:18, 25). In the Greek New Testament text this full passage on the Son of God's divine conception and birth [vv. 18-25] consists of precisely 161 Greek words.

God Is with Us!

"Behold, a virgin shall be with child, and shall bring forth a son, and they shall call his name Emmanuel, which being interpreted is, GOD with us" (Matt. 1:23). Matthew emphasized Jesus' divine proportion to God by using this prophetic word from Isaiah. The New Testament combination *Behold* (60 chs), *a virgin shall be with child* (1 ch) = 61 chapters. We repeat the following seals.

> The phrase *God is* occurs 61 times in the New Testament.
> The phrase *is with* occurs 61 times from Genesis to NT Narrative.
> The word *us* occurs 61 times in Deuteronomy.

King of the Jews' Far-Reaching Fame

"Where is he that is born KING OF THE JEWS? for we have seen his star in the east, and are come to worship him" (Matt. 2:2). The New Testament combination *worship* (44x), *the king of the Jews/Israel* (17x) = 61.

King of the Jews Born in the Land of the Jews

"And thou Bethlehem, in the land of JUDA, art not the least among the princes of JUDA: for out of thee shall come a Governor, that shall rule my people Israel" (Matt. 2:6). The phrase *in the land* is mentioned in 61 verses of Genesis. Again the phrase *of Judah* is mentioned in 61 chapters of the Kings and Chronicles. Again all forms of the word *govern* are mentioned in 61 chapters of the Bible.

Infant King of the Jews Worshiped by Foreigners

"And when they were come into the house, they saw the young child with Mary his mother, and fell down, and worshipped him: and when they had opened their treasures, they presented unto him gifts; gold, and frankincense, and myrrh" (Matt. 2:11). Each man had a gift with which to worship the young Jewish King. Again the word *gift(s)* occurs 61 times in the New Testament. Again the word *gold* is mentioned in 361 verses of the Bible.

Infant King of the Jews Ushered to Safety

"And when they were departed, behold, the angel of the Lord appeareth to Joseph in a dream, saying, Arise, and take the young child and his mother, and flee into Egypt, and be thou there until I bring thee word: for Herod will seek the young child to destroy him" (Matt. 2:13). The 611, 061st word of the Bible occurs within this King-of-the-Jews verse.

Youthful King of the Jews Taken Back to Israel

"Arise, and take the young child and his mother, and go into the land of Israel: for they are dead which sought the young child's life" (Matt. 2:20). The word *take* occurs 161 times in the New Testament. The sentence *arise and take the young child and his mother and go into the land of Israel* consists of 61 letters!

King of the Jews' Ceremonial Baptism

"Then cometh Jesus from Galilee to Jordan unto John, to be baptized of him. But John forbad him, saying, I have need to be baptized of thee, and comest thou to me?" (Matt. 3:14)   The sentence *then cometh Jesus from Galilee to Jordan unto John, to be baptized of him.* consists of 61 characters! The word *baptized* occurs 61 times in the Bible.

God's Beloved Son

"And lo a voice from heaven, saying, This is my beloved Son, in whom I am well pleased" (Matt. 3:17). The phrase *a * voice* occurs 61 times in the Bible. Again the word *beloved* is mentioned in 61 verses of the New Testament. Again the title *Son* is mentioned naturally in 161 verses of the NT Narrative. The phrase *whom I* is mentioned in 61 verses of the Old Testament. Again the word *pleased* is mentioned in 61 verses of the Bible.

God's Son Can Turn Stones to Bread

"And when the tempter came to him, he said, If thou be the Son of GOD, command that these stones be made bread" (Matt. 4:3). The phrase *if thou* occurs 61 times in the Law. Again the word *stones* occurs 161 times in the Old Testament. Again the word *made* is mentioned in 461 chapters of the Old Testament.

Every Word out of the Mouth of God

"But he answered and said, It is written, Man shall not live by bread alone, but by every word that proceedeth out of the mouth of GOD" (Matt. 4:4). Again the word *word* occurs naturally 61 times in the Pauline Epistles. The phrase *out of* occurs naturally 61 times in First Samuel and is mentioned in 61 verses of Minor Prophets. The phrase *mouth of* is mentioned in 61 chapters of the Bible.

King of the Jews' Galilean Headquarters

The religious leaders at Nazareth had outright rejected Jesus' lordship and kingship over them. Their refusal caused the King of the Jews to move His ministry headquarters from the tribe of Zebulon just across the border into the neighboring tribe of Naphtali.

"Now . . . Jesus . . . leaving Nazareth . . . came and dwelt in Capernaum, which is upon the sea coast, in the borders of Zabulon and Nephthalim: That it might be fulfilled which was spoken by Esaias the prophet, saying, The land of Zabulon, and the land of Nephthalim, by the way of the sea, beyond Jordan, Galilee of the Gentiles; The people which sat in darkness saw great light; and to them which sat in the region and shadow of death light is sprung up" (Matt. 4:12-16).

Again the phrase *the way of* occurs 161 times in the Bible. The name *Galilee* occurs 61 times in the Gospels. Again the phrase *the light* occurs 61 times in the Old Testament.

King of the Jews Began His Ministry

"From that time Jesus began to preach, and to say, Repent: for the kingdom of heaven is at hand" (Matt. 4:17). Again the word *began* occurs 61 times in the Gospels. Again the phrase *kingdom of* is mentioned in 61 chapters of the New Testament. The words *Jesus began to preach and to say repent for the kingdom of heaven is at hand* consists of 61 letters!

Son of God Went About Teaching, Preaching & Healing

"And Jesus went about all Galilee, teaching in their synagogues, and preaching the gospel of the kingdom, and healing all manner of sickness and all manner of disease among the people" (Matt. 4:23). The word *about* occurs 161 times in the New Testament. Again the name *Galilee* occurs 61 times in the Gospels. The phrases *healing all manner of sickness and all manner of disease among the people* consists of 61 letters!

God Wrote Every Jot & Tittle of the KJV Holy Bible

"Think not that I am come to destroy the law, or the prophets: I am not come to destroy, but to fulfil. For verily I say unto you, Till heaven and earth pass, one jot or one tittle shall in no wise pass from the law, till all be fulfilled" (Matt. 5:17-18). A jot refers to the yod—the smallest letter in the Hebrew alphabet—and the tittle is the tiny ornamental mark made at the apex of many Hebrew letters.

> The phrase *the law* occurs 61 times in the OT Narrative.
> The phrase *it is written* is mentioned in 61 chapters of the Bible.
> The phrase *written in the book* occurs 61 times in the OT Narrative.
> The word *write* is mentioned naturally in 61 chapters of the Bible.
> The word *wrote* occurs naturally 61 times in the Bible.

God, Give Us Our Daily Bread

"Our Father which art in heaven, Hallowed be thy name. Thy kingdom come. Thy will be done in earth, as it is in heaven. Give us this day our daily bread" (Matt. 6:9b-11). Here the word *bread* is the 613,661st word of the Bible, and God is the Giver of it.

This King of the Jews Worshipped as God

"And, behold, there came a leper and worshipped him, saying, Lord, if thou wilt, thou canst make me clean" (Matt. 8:2). Again the word *worship* is mentioned naturally in 61 verses of the Old Testament. Again the word *him* occurs 6661 times altogether in the Bible!

Son of God's Omnipotence

"When the even was come, they brought unto him many that were possessed with devils: and he cast out the spirits with his word, and healed all that were sick" (Matt. 8:16). The narrative speaks of the King of the Jews' mighty power over the forces of darkness. The phrase *cast out* is mentioned in 61 chapters of the Bible.

Son of God Sleeps through a Storm

"And, behold, there arose a great tempest in the sea, insomuch that the ship was covered with the waves: but he was asleep" (Matt. 8:24). The word *sleep* occurs 61 times in the Old Testament.

Son of God Is Able

"And when he was come into the house, the blind men came to him: and Jesus saith unto them, Believe ye that I am able to do this? They said unto him, Yea, Lord" (Matt. 9:28). Again the phrase *to him* is mentioned in 61 verses of the Gospels. We repeat the following seals.

The phrase *able to* is mentioned in 61 chapters of the OT.
The word *able* occurs 61 times in the New Testament.

23,461st Verse of the Bible

"And it came to pass, when Jesus had made an end of commanding his twelve disciples, he departed thence to teach and to preach in their cities" (Matt. 11:1). This 61st verse speaks about the King of the Jews' twelve high-ranking government appointees. Again the phrase *and it came to pass that* occurs 61 times in the Bible.

Son of God Invites All to Come to Him

"Come unto me, all ye that labour and are heavy laden, and I will give you rest" (Matt. 11:28). Again the word *come* occurs naturally 61 times in Numbers. The phrase *to me* occurs 61 times in the OT Narrative. Again the phrase *and I will* occurs 61 times in Isaiah.

King of the Jews' Awaiting Destroyers

"Then the Pharisees went out, and held a council against him, how they might destroy him" (Matt. 12:14). The word *destroy* occurs 261 times in the Bible.

361st Verse of the New Testament

"And charged them that they should not make him known" (Matt. 12:16). After healing a multitude of sick people, the King of the Jews issued a decree that they keep His location concealed for the present time. Again the word *commandment* is mentioned in 61 verses of the OT Narrative.

God's Own Soul

"Behold my servant, whom I have chosen; my beloved, in whom my soul is well pleased: I will put my spirit upon him, and he shall shew judgment to the Gentiles" (Matt. 12:18). This verse presents the Bible's 161st occurrence of the phrase *my soul*, and it refers to God's very own soul.

Multitudes Gathered unto the King of the Jews

"And great multitudes were gathered together, so that he went into a ship, and sat; and the whole multitude stood on the shore" (Matt. 13:2). Jacob's deathbed prophecy foretold that the people would gather unto Shiloh, the Preeminent King of Judah. This verse reveals that prophecy's fulfillment. The New Testament combination *many were gathered together* (2x), *unto him* (459x) = 461. Again the phrase *gathered together* is mentioned in 61 verses of the Old Testament.

King of the Jews' Kingdom Mysteries

"And the disciples came, and said unto him, Why <u>speakest</u> thou unto them in parables? He <u>answered and said</u> unto them, Because it is given unto you to know the mysteries of the <u>kingdom of</u> heaven, but to them it is not given" (Matt. 13:10-11). The King of the Jews' kingdom unfolded daily with Christ's careful explanations and revelations about it. The word *speak* occurs 161 times in the New Testament. The phrase *answered and said* is mentioned in 61 chapters of the Old Testament. Again the phrase *kingdom of* is mentioned in 61 chapters of the New Testament.

Son of God Walks upon the Sea like God Does

"But the ship was now in the midst of the sea, tossed with waves: for the wind was contrary. And in the fourth watch of the night Jesus went unto them, <u>walking</u> <u>on the sea</u>. And when the disciples saw him <u>walking</u> <u>on the sea</u>" (Matt. 14:24-26a). Jesus' miracle walk revealed He had passed the test of divinity set forth in Job chapter nine where it declares that "God . . . alone . . . treadeth upon the waves of the sea." The phrase *the sea* occurs 61 times in the NT Narrative. Again the word *water* is mentioned in 61 verses of the Major and Minor Prophets.

The Major/Minor Prophets combination *walk* (60x), *on the sea* (1x) = 61.
The Major/Minor Prophets combination *walk* (60x), *upon the water* (1x) = 61.

23,661st Verse of the Bible

"And she said, Truth, <u>Lord</u>: yet the dogs eat of the crumbs which fall from their masters' table" (Matt. 15:27). This 61st verse records the words of a desperate woman seeking help from the incarnate Son of God. She called Him by a very respectful title. Again the title *the Lord/lord* occurs 61 times in Luke.

Lowly Son of God Leaves His Adversaries

"A wicked and adulterous generation seeketh after a sign; and there shall no sign be given unto it, but the sign of the prophet Jonas. And he <u>left</u> them, and departed" (Matt. 16:4). The word *left* is mentioned in 61 verses of the NT Narrative.

That He Was the Anointed King of the Jews

"Then charged he his disciples that they should tell no man <u>that he was</u> Jesus the Christ" (Matt. 16:20). The phrase *that he was* occurs 61 times in the Bible!

Lowly King of the Jews' Transfiguration to Undiminished Deity

"And was transfigured before them: and <u>his face</u> did shine as the sun, and his raiment was white as the light" (Matt. 17:2). Jesus was not just a lowly, earthly King among the Jews. His sudden transformation gave the disciples a grand, once-in-a-lifetime opportunity to behold His heavenly nature and Godlikeness. Again the phrase *my face* occurs 61 times in the Old Testament.

561st Verse of the New Testament

"While he yet spake, behold, a bright cloud overshadowed them: and behold a voice out of the cloud, which said, This is my beloved Son, in whom I am well <u>pleased</u>; hear ye him" (Matt.

17:5). In this 61st verse God audibly testified to Jesus' unique Sonship with Him. Again the word *pleased* is mentioned in 61 verses of the Bible.

Disciples' Mountaintop Vision of the Heavenly Son of God

"And as they came down from the mountain, Jesus charged them, saying, Tell the vision to no man, until the Son of man be risen again from the dead" (Matt. 17:9). In the Bible a mountain represents a kingdom. On this occasion the Son of God had taken His disciples up an exceeding high mountain to demonstrate the exceeding highness of His heavenly kingdom. Again the title *the mountain* occurs 61 times from Genesis to the Gospels. Again the word *vision(s)* is mentioned in 61 verses of the Major and Minor Prophets. The word *vision* is mentioned in 61 verses from Genesis to the Gospels.

For Heaven's Sake

"For there are some eunuchs, which were so born from their mother's womb: and there are some eunuchs, which were made eunuchs of men: and there be eunuchs, which have made themselves eunuchs for the kingdom of heaven's sake. He that is able to receive it, let him receive it" (Matt. 19:12). The New Testament combination *heaven's* (1x), *sake* (60x) = 61.

With God All Things Are Possible

"But Jesus beheld them, and said unto them, With men this is impossible; but with GOD all things are possible" (Matt. 19:26). Again the word *things* occurs 1161 times in the Bible.

> The word *with* is mentioned in 61 chapters of the Chronicles.
> The word *with* occurs 61 times in Isaiah.
> The word *with* is mentioned in 161 verses of Luke.

King of the Jews' Triumphal Entry

"All this was done, that it might be fulfilled which was spoken by the prophet, saying, Tell ye the daughter of Sion, Behold, thy KING cometh unto thee, meek, and sitting upon an ass, and a colt the foal of an ass. . . . And when he was come into Jerusalem, all the city was moved, saying, Who is this?" (Matt. 21:4-5, 10) Again the phrase *all this* is mentioned in 61 chapters of the Old Testament. Again the title *the daughter(s) of* is mentioned in 61 verses of the OTN. The Bible combination *sitting* (43 vs) and *an ass* (18 vs) = 61 verses. Again the name *Jerusalem* is mentioned in 61 verses of the Minor Prophets.

> The phrase *when he was* occurs 61 times in the New Testament
> The phrase *when he was* is mentioned in 61 chapters of the Bible.
> The phrase *was come* occurs 61 times in the New Testament.

Whose Son Is Christ?

"Saying, What think ye of Christ? whose son is he? They say unto him, The Son of David" (Matt. 22:42). This verse presents the Bible's 161st chapter-mention of the word *whose*, and it refers to God's Son. Again the title *Christ* is mentioned naturally in 161 chapters of the New Testament.

God's Son Sits at God's Right Hand

Jesus quotes from Psalm 110, saying, "The LORD said unto my Lord, Sit thou on my right hand, till I make <u>thine enemies</u> thy footstool?" (Matt. 22.44) From Genesis to Matthew the phrases *my hand* (50 vs) and *my right hand* (11 vs) = 61 verses. Again the phrase *thine enemies* is mentioned in 61 verses of the Bible.

God's Throne—He Sits Thereon

"And he that shall swear by heaven, sweareth by the throne of God, and by him that sitteth <u>thereon</u>" (Matt. 23:22). The word *thereon* is mentioned in 61 verses of the Bible.

King of the Jews' Second Coming

"And then shall appear the sign of the Son of man in heaven: and <u>then shall all the tribes of the earth mourn, and they shall see the Son of man</u> <u>coming in the</u> <u>clouds</u> <u>of heaven with</u> <u>power and great glory</u>" (Matt. 24:30). When the Son of Man comes again He will appear unmistakably as the Son of God. The Bible combination *then shall all the tribes of the earth mourn* (1x), *and they shall see the Son of man* (1x), *coming in the* (6x), *clouds* (49x), *of heaven with* (2x), *power and great glory* (2x) = 61.

King of the Jews' Coming Glory

"When the Son of man <u>shall come in</u> <u>his glory</u>, and all the holy angels with him, then shall he sit upon the throne of his glory" (Matt. 25:31). The Bible combination *shall come in* (17 vs), *his glory* (44 vs) = 61 verses.

Judas Conspired against the King of the Jews

"Then one of the twelve, called Judas Iscariot, went unto the chief priests, And said unto them, What will ye give me, and I will deliver him unto you? And they covenanted with him for thirty pieces of silver. And from that time he sought opportunity to betray him" (Matt. 26:14-16). The OT Narrative combination *conspired* (17x) and *against him* (44x) = 61.

King of the Jews' Victory Cup

"And he took the cup, and gave thanks, and gave it to them, saying, <u>Drink</u> ye all of it" (Matt. 26:27). The disciples were given opportunity to drink from the King of the Jews' Passover cup. It was representative both of suffering and of victory to follow.

> The word *drink* occurs 61 times in the OT Narrative.
> The word *drink* is mentioned in 61 verses of the NT.
> The phrase *to drink* occurs 61 times in the Bible.

King of the Jews' Anguished Soul

"Then saith he unto them, <u>My soul</u> is exceeding sorrowful, even unto death: tarry ye here, and watch with me" (Matt. 26:38). This verse presents the Bible's 161st verse-mention of the expression *my soul*, and it refers to the King of the Jews own soul.

King of the Jews' Legions of Angels

"Thinkest thou that I cannot now pray to my Father, and he shall presently <u>give me</u> more than twelve legions of angels?" (Matt. 26:53) The Son of God was the Captain of the angelic armies until He forfeited that control, leaving heaven for Earth to become a lowly Man. The phrase *give me* is mentioned in 61 verses of the Bible.

Matthew 26:61

"This fellow said, I am able <u>to destroy</u> the <u>temple</u> of God, and to <u>build it</u> in <u>three days</u>" (Matt. 26:61). This false witness did not accurately recall what Jesus had said. Jesus had raised a hypothetical scenario whereby others might destroy the temple. He in turn would miraculously rebuild it. Again the phrase *to destroy* is mentioned in 61 chapters of the Old Testament. Again the word *temple* is mentioned in 61 verses of the Gospels. The combination *build it* (7x) and *three days* (54x) = 61.

King of the Jews' Chief Adversaries

"But <u>the chief priests</u> and elders persuaded the multitude that they should ask Barabbas, and destroy Jesus" (Matt. 27:20). The chief priests were among the King of the Jews' chief adversaries. Instead they should have been His chief advocates. The phrase *the chief priests* occurs 61 times in the New Testament.

24,161st Verse of the Bible

"And when they had platted a crown of thorns, they put it upon his head, and a reed in his right hand: and they bowed the knee before him, and mocked him, saying, Hail, KING OF THE JEWS! And they spit upon him, and took the reed, and smote him on the head. <u>And after that they had mocked him, they took the robe off from him, and put his own raiment on him, and led him away to crucify him</u>" (Matt. 27:29-21). The underlines words mark the 24,161st verse of the Bible, and they are associated with the King of the Jews.

King of the Jews' Daytime Nightmare

"Now from the sixth hour there was darkness over all the land unto the ninth hour" (Matt. 27:45). The Jewish nation and all the earth came under a curse while the Incarnate Son of God hung upon the Tree. The noonday sky became black as midnight. Just before the sun returned to its former strength the King of the Jews gave up His spirit. Again the word *night* is mentioned in 61 verses of the New Testament.

Declaration of Truth about the King of the Jews

"Jesus, when he had cried again with a loud voice, yielded up the ghost. . . . Now when the centurion, and they that were with him, watching Jesus, saw the earthquake, and those things that were done, they feared greatly, saying, Truly this was the <u>Son of</u> GOD" (Matt. 27:50, 54). The death of God's Incarnate Son is revealed in the following numeric seal. The God Number 161 is a multiple of 23, the Bible's number for death. Again the title *Son of* is mentioned in 61 chapters of the NT Narrative. Again the Bible combination *God's* (24 chs), *Son* (137 chs) = 161 chapters!

King of the Jews' Body Was Taken to Burial

"And when Joseph had <u>taken</u> the body, he wrapped it in a clean linen cloth" (Matt. 27:59). Again the word *taken* occurs 61 times in the Law and 61 times in the Major and Minor Prophets.

Matthew 27:61

"And there was Mary Magdalene, and the other Mary, sitting <u>over against</u> the <u>sepulchre</u>" (Matt. 27:61). Two lady disciples sat just outside the King of the Jews' closed tomb. The great Passover feast began in a couple of hours, but they were too heartbroken to be concerned with that. From Genesis to the Gospels the phrase *over against* is mentioned in 61 chapters. From Genesis to the

Gospels the word *sepulchre(s)* is mentioned in 61 verses.

Place Where the Son of God's Dead Body Lay

"He is not here: for he is risen, as he said. Come, see the place where the Lord lay" (Matt. 28:6). This verse presents the Bible's 161st occurrence of the phrase *the place,* and it refers to the place where the Son of God's body once lay lifeless. The Old Testament combination *the place* (160x), *he was laid down* (1x) = 161. This verse *he is not here for he is risen as he said come see the place where the Lord lay* consists of 61 letters!

1061st Verse of the New Testament

"Then said Jesus unto them, Be not afraid: go tell my brethren that they go into Galilee, and there shall they see me" (Matt. 28:10). In this 61st verse the newly risen Son of God gives instructions for His disciples to meet Him soon. Again the name *Galilee* occurs 61 times in the Gospels.

King of the Jews' Great Commission
(Part 1)

"All power is given unto me in heaven and in earth. Go ye therefore, and teach all nations, baptizing them in the name of the Father, and of the Son, and of the Holy Ghost: Teaching them to observe all things whatsoever I have commanded you: and, lo, I am with you alway, even unto the end of the world. Amen" (Matt. 28:18b-20). The Son of God's Great Commission along with the narrator's confirming word Amen consists of 61 words. Again the phrase *the power* is mentioned in 61 verses of the Bible. Again the phrase *unto me* is mentioned in 61 chapters of the Law. Again the phrase *the heaven* is mentioned in 61 chapters of the Bible. The phrase *in the earth* occurs 61 times in the Old Testament. Again the word *earth* occurs 61 times in Jeremiah. Again from Genesis to the Gospels the phrase *the name* occurs 261 times and is mentioned in 161 chapters.

The Gospel of God's Incarnate Servant-Son

"The beginning of the gospel of Jesus Christ, the Son of GOD" (Mark 1:1). Whereas Matthew's Gospel portrays Jesus as the Perfect King, Mark's Gospel portrays Him as the Perfect Servant. Jesus served both God and man with all grace and glory. This opening verse of Mark's Gospel presents the Bible's 61st occurrence of the word *beginning*, and it pertains to the Son of God's public ministry beginning. The phrase *the gospel* occurs 61 times in the Pauline Epistles. Again from Acts to the Apocalypse the phrase *of Jesus* occurs 61 times.

The Gospel of the Kingdom of God

Jesus went to Galilee preaching "And saying, The time is fulfilled, and the KINGDOM of GOD is at hand: repent ye, and believe the gospel" (Mark 1:15). Again the phrase *kingdom of* is mentioned in 61 chapters of the New Testament. Again the phrase *the kingdom of God* occurs 61 times in the NT Narrative.

But God

"Why doth this man thus speak blasphemies? who can forgive sins but God only?" (Mark 2:7). This Man was authorized to forgive sins because He was the God-Man. The NT Narrative combination *this man* (59x), *can forgive sins* (2x) = 61. The New Testament combination *but God* (25x), *but the Lord* (3x), *but Christ* (5x), *but Jesus* (28x) = 61.

61st Verse of Mark

"And when the scribes and Pharisees saw him <u>eat</u> with publicans and sinners, they said unto his disciples, How is it that he <u>eateth</u> and drinketh <u>with publicans and sinners</u>?" (Mark 2:16) The lowly Son of God came with a specific mission objective—to turn sinners' hearts toward Him. If He loved them enough to die for them, He could easily eat with them. The word *eaten* is mentioned in 61 chapters of the Old Testament. The Bible combination *eateth* (56x), *with publicans* (4x), *with sinners* (1x) = 61.

Servant-Son of God Needs Underling Servants

"And he goeth up into a mountain, and calleth unto him whom he would: and they <u>came unto</u> him. And he ordained twelve, that they should be with him, and that he might <u>send</u> them forth to preach, And to have power to heal sicknesses, and to cast out devils" (Mark 3:13-15). Again the phrase *came unto* occurs 61 times in the Major Prophets. Again the word *send* is mentioned in 161 verses of the Old Testament.

Do the Will of God

"For whosoever shall <u>do</u> the <u>will</u> of GOD, the same is my brother, and my sister, and mother" (Mark 3:35). Again the word *do* is mentioned in 1261 verses of the Bible and occurs 61 times in the Gospel of Luke. Again the word *will* is mentioned in 261 verses of Ezekiel.

Reverential Fear of God's Son

"And they <u>feared</u> exceedingly, and said one to another, What manner of <u>man</u> is this, that even the wind and <u>the sea</u> obey him?" (Mark 4:41) Again the phrase *the sea* occurs 61 times in the NT Narrative. Again the phrase *a man* occurs 61 times in the Synoptic Gospels.

> The word *fear* is mentioned in 61 verses of the Psalms.
> The word *fear* is mentioned in 61 chapters of the Major/Minor Prophets.
> The phrase *fear of* is mentioned in 61 chapters of the Bible.

Needy Man Runs to the Son of God

"But when he saw Jesus afar off, he <u>ran</u> and worshipped him" (Mark 5:6). The word *ran* occurs 61 times in the Bible and is mentioned in 61 verses thereof.

Servant-Son of God Has Done Great Things

"Howbeit Jesus suffered him not, but saith unto him, Go home to thy friends, and tell them how great things the Lord <u>hath done</u> for thee, and hath had compassion on thee" (Mark 5:19). Again the phrase *hath done* occurs 61 times in the Old Testament.

"It Is I"

"But when they saw him walking upon the sea, they supposed it had been a spirit, and cried out: For they all saw him, and were troubled. And immediately he talked with them, and saith unto them, Be of good cheer: <u>it is I</u>; be not afraid" (Mark 6:49-50). The Incarnate Son of God borrows a three-word phrase from Isaiah 52:6 where God used it to bring glory to Himself. In doing so, Jesus proclaimed His deity. Again the word *I* is mentioned in 961 verses of the OT Narrative.

> The phrase *it is* is mentioned in 61 chapters of the Gospels.
> The phrase *it is* is mentioned in 261 verses of the New Testament.

Bearing Shame for the Crucified King of the Jews

"Whosoever will come after me, let him deny himself, and take up his cross, and <u>follow</u> me" (Mark 8:34b). The lowly Son of God referred to the general day-to-day public shame His followers must be willing to endure on His behalf. The New Testament combination *whosoever will* (11x), *come after me* (4x), *let him deny himself* (3x), *take up* (14x), *his cross* (10x), *follow me* (19x) = 61. All forms of the word *follow* occur 261 times in the Bible.

The Son of God's Glory with His Father

"Whosoever therefore shall be ashamed of me and of my words in this adulterous and sinful generation; of him also shall the Son of man be ashamed, when he cometh in the glory of <u>his Father</u> with the holy angels" (Mark 8:38). Again the phrase *his father* is mentioned in 61 chapters of the OT Narrative.

Desiring to Sit Next to the King of the Jews

"They said unto him, Grant unto us that we may sit, one on thy <u>right hand</u>, and the other on thy left <u>hand</u>, in thy glory" (Mark 10:37). Again the phrase *right hand* is mentioned in 161 verses of the Bible. Here the word *hand* is the 9161st word of Mark's Gospel.

Have Faith in God

"And Jesus answering saith unto them, <u>Have faith in GOD</u>" (Mark 11:22).

> The word *Have* occurs 61 times in the Bible.
> The word *faith* is mentioned in 61 chapters of the Pauline Epistles.
> The word *in* occurs 161 times in Romans.
> The title *God* is mentioned in 61 verses of Second Corinthians.

The Way of God

"Master, we know that thou art true, and carest for no man: for thou regardest not the person of men, but teachest <u>the way of</u> GOD in truth" (Mark 12:14b). Again the phrase *the way of* occurs 161 times in the Bible.

Son of God Going on a Far Journey

"For the Son of man is as <u>a man taking a far journey</u>, who left his house, and gave authority to his servants, and to every man his work, and commanded the porter to watch" (Mark 13:34). Again the phrase *a man* occurs 61 times in the Synoptic Gospels. The Bible combination *taking a far* (1x), *journey* (60x) = 61.

Precious Anointing Oil for the King of the Jews

"And being in Bethany in the house of Simon the leper, as he sat at meat, there came a woman <u>having</u> an alabaster box of ointment of spikenard very <u>precious</u>; and she brake the box, and poured it on his head" (Mark. 14:3). The word *having* occurs 61 times in the NT Narrative. This verse presents the Bible's 61st occurrence of precious, and it pertains to expensive ointment lavished upon the King of the Jews. This is 1613rd verse of the New Testament.

They Went with the King of the Jews

"And when they had sung an hymn, <u>they went</u> out into the mount of Olives" (Mark 14:26). The phrase *they went* is mentioned in 61 verses of the OT Narrative. Again the word *went* occurs 61 times in Acts.

Mark 14:61

"But he held his peace, and answered nothing. Again the high priest asked him, and said unto him, Art thou the Christ, the Son of the <u>Blessed</u>?" (Mark 14:61) In this 61st verse Israel's high priest asked Jesus if He was indeed God's Son. Again all available forms of the word *bless* occur 61 times in the NT Narrative.

Servant-Son of God to Be Exalted to God's Right Hand

"And Jesus said, I am: and ye shall see the Son of man sitting on <u>the right hand</u> of power, and coming in the clouds of heaven" (Mark 14:62). Again the phrase *right hand* is mentioned in 161 verses of the Bible. The phrases *the right hand* (60x) and *the LORD'S right hand* (1x) = 61.

Pilate Willing to Release the King of the Jews

"But Pilate answered them, saying, Will ye that I release unto you the KING <u>OF</u> THE JEWS?" (Mark 15:9) Here the word *of* is the 161st word in this chapter, and it pertains to the King of the Jews.

Servant-King of the Jews' Strange Coronation

"And they clothed him with purple, and platted a <u>crown</u> of <u>thorns,</u> and put it about his head, And began to salute him, Hail, KING OF THE JEWS! And they smote him on the head with a reed, and did spit upon him, and bowing their knees worshipped him" (Mark 15:17-19).

Tragically Jesus was given a sinner's crown not a Savior's crown. Nevertheless, this was the King of the Jews' coronation day. It was His strange exaltation on the way to His eternal throne of glory. From this day forward He would reign in the hearts of faithful men and women, His kingdom subjects. The Father had spoken of this time as Christ's exaltation. On this day we see Him robed in splendor, a crown upon His head, and a scepter in His hand. Then He was hailed King of the Jews and worshiped as such. He was soon given a king's retinue, being crucified between two other men. All of this was done by irreverent men, yet it was all in God's divine plan to exalt Him for all ages. From Genesis to the Gospels the combination *crown* (55x) and *thorn* (6x) = 61.

Servant-King of the Jews' Superscription

"And the superscription of his accusation was written over, THE <u>KING</u> OF THE JEWS" (Mark 15:26). Again the phrase *king over* occurs 61 times in the Old Testament. Again the title *king of Judah('s)* occurs 61 times in the Major and Minor Prophets. Here the key title *King* is the 14,261st word in Mark's Gospel.

Servant-King Challenged to Come Down

"Save thyself, and <u>come down</u> from the cross. . . . Let Christ the KING of Israel descend now from the cross, that we may see and believe" (Mark 15:30, 32a). This is the Bible's 61st occurrence of the phrase *come down*, and it is a command directed at the miracle-working King of the Jews.

Servant-King of the Jews Given Offer to Drink Vinegar

"And one ran and filled a spunge full of vinegar, and put it on a reed, and <u>gave him</u> to <u>drink</u>, saying, Let alone; let us see whether Elias will come to take him down" (Mark 15:36). The combined past-tense phrases *gave him* (59x) and *gavest him* (2x) = 61. Again the word *drink* is mentioned in 61 verses of the New Testament.

Divine King of the Jews Rises up from His Grave

"Now when Jesus was <u>risen</u> <u>early the first day of the week</u>, he appeared first to Mary Magdalene" (Mark 16:9). From Genesis to the Gospels the combination *rise up* (60 chs) and *early the first day of the week* (1 ch) = 61 chapters.

The King of the Jews' Great Commission
(Part 2)

"<u>Go</u> ye into all the world, and preach <u>the gospel</u> to every creature. He that believeth and is <u>baptized</u> shall be saved; but he that believeth not shall be damned" (Mark 16:15-16). This is the first half of the King's Great Commission presented by Mark. The uppercase word *Go* is mentioned in 61 chapters of the OT Narrative. Again the phrase *the gospel* occurs 61 times in the Pauline Epistles. Again the word *baptized* occurs 61 times in the Bible.

King of the Jews' Reserved Throne

"He shall be great, and shall <u>be called</u> <u>the Son of the Highest</u>: and the LORD GOD shall give unto him the throne of his father David" (Luke 1:32). Luke wrote his gospel account with emphasis on Jesus as being the Perfect Man. He was perfect because He was God's incarnate Son. Again the title *Son of* is mentioned in 61 chapters of the NT Narrative. The Bible combination *son of Mary* (1x), *be called* (59x), *the Son of the Highest* (1x) = 61.

That Holy Thing

"And the angel answered and said unto her, The Holy Ghost shall come upon thee, and the power of the Highest shall <u>overshadow</u> thee: therefore also that holy <u>thing</u> which shall be born of thee shall be called the Son of GOD" (Luke 1:35). The word *shadow* is mentioned in 61 chapters of the Bible. Back in Joshua, in one location we saw how the word *thing* was positioned as the 161,161st word of the Bible.

King of the Jews' Earthly Nativity

"<u>For unto you is born this day</u> in the city of David a Saviour, which is Christ the LORD. And this shall be a sign unto you; Ye shall find the babe wrapped in swaddling clothes, lying in a manger" (Luke 2:11-12). The Bible combination *for unto you* (2x), *is born this day* (1x), *in the city of David* (46x), *a s/Saviour* (6x), *which is Christ the Lord* (1x), *and this shall be a sign unto you* (1x), *ye shall find the babe* (1x), *wrapped in swaddling clothes* (1x), *lying in a manger* (2x) = 61.

Youthful King Filled with God's Spirit

"And the child grew, and waxed strong in <u>spirit</u>, <u>filled with</u> wisdom: and the grace of GOD was <u>upon him</u>" (Luke 2:40). The phrase *filled with* is mentioned in 61 chapters of the Bible. Again the title *s/Spirit* occurs 261 times in the New Testament. Again from Genesis to the Gospels the phrase *upon him* is mentioned in 161 verses.

Youthful King of the Jews Tarries in Jerusalem

"And when they had fulfilled the days, as they returned, the child Jesus tarried behind <u>in</u> <u>Jerusalem</u>; and Joseph and his mother knew not of it" (Luke 2:43). The Bible phrases *in Jerusalem* (160 vs) and *in * Jerusalem* (1 v) = 161.

The Importance of God's Word

"And Jesus answered him, saying, <u>It is written, That man shall not live by bread alone, but by every word of GOD</u>" (Luke 4:4). The phrase *shall not* is mentioned in 61 verses of Jeremiah. There are 61 letters here in Jesus' kingly declaration.

1961st Verse of the New Testament

"And when it was day, he <u>departed</u> and went into a desert place: and the people sought him, and came unto him, and stayed him, that he should not depart from them" (Luke 4:42). Shortly after the King of the Jews departed the people went after Him to convince Him to return. Here the word *departed* is the 4661st word of Luke.

Jesus Is God of the Sabbath

"<u>And he said unto them,</u> That the Son of man is LORD also of the sabbath" (Luke 6:5).

The phrase *And he said* is mentioned in 161 verses of the OT Narrative.
The phrase *And he said* is mentioned in 61 chapters of the New Testament.
The phrase *and he said unto them* occurs 61 times in the NT Narrative.
The phrase *and he said unto them* is mentioned in 61 verses of the NTN.
The phrase *he said* is mentioned in 161 verses of the Synoptic Gospels.

God Has Visited His People

"And there came a fear on all: and they glorified GOD, saying, That a great prophet is risen up among us; and, That GOD hath <u>visited</u> his people" (Luke 7:16). After God's Son raised a young man up from his burial stretcher, the people began to shout God's praises. Again all forms of the word *visit* are mentioned in 61 collective chapters of the Old Testament.

Luke 9:61

"And another also said, LORD, I will follow <u>thee</u>; but let me first go bid them farewell, which are at home at my house" (Luke 9:61). Many Jews greatly desired to follow the King of the Jews, but certain things hindered them.

The word *thee* is mentioned in 661 verses of the Law.
The word *thee* occurs 61 times in Proverbs.
The word *thee* occurs 61 times in John.

Son of God Is Lord of the Harvest

"Therefore said he unto them, The <u>harvest</u> truly is great, but the labourers are few: pray ye therefore the <u>LORD of</u> the <u>harvest</u>, that he would <u>send</u> forth labourers into his <u>harvest</u>" (Luke 10:2). Again the phrase *LORD of* is mentioned in 61 chapters of the Major Prophets. The word *harvest* occurs 61 times in Scripture. Again the word *send* is mentioned in 161 verses of the Old Testament.

King of the Jews Selects Seventy Men as Goodwill Ambassadors

"And the <u>seventy</u> returned again with joy, saying, Lord, even the devils are subject unto us through thy name" (Luke 10:17). The word *seventy* occurs 61 times in Scripture; this verse presents its 61st occurrence, and it refers to the number of appointees representing the King of the Jews.

Our Father in Heaven

"And he said unto them, When ye pray, say, Our Father which <u>art</u> in heaven, Hallowed be thy name. Thy kingdom come. Thy will be done, as in heaven, so in earth" (Luke 11:2). Here the word *art* is the 661,161st word of the Bible, and pertains to God.

Coming from the Four Corners to Partake in God's Kingdom

"And they shall come from the east, and from the west, and from the north, and from the south, and shall sit down in the KINGDOM of GOD" (Luke 13:29). Here the title *God* is the 54,261th word of the New Testament.

Son of God Rebukes the Pharisees

"<u>And the Lord said</u> unto him, Now do ye Pharisees make clean the outside of the cup and the platter; but your inward part is full of ravening and wickedness" (Luke 11:39). Again the phrase *and the LORD/Lord/lord said* occurs naturally 161 times in the Bible.

2561st Verse of the New Testament

"Verily I say unto you, Whosoever shall not receive the KINGDOM of GOD as a little child shall in no wise enter therein" (Luke 18:17). The key words *kingdom* and *God* actually occur in this 61st verse.

King of the Jews Shall Not Reign over Us

Christ's parable is full of import: "But his citizens hated him, <u>and sent</u> a message after him, saying, We will not have this man to <u>reign over</u> us" (Luke 19:14). The phrase *and sent* is mentioned in 61 verses of the Bible. All tenses of the phrase *reign over* occur 61 times from Genesis to the NT Narrative. Again the phrase *king over* occurs 61 times in the Old Testament.

The Things Which Belong to God

"And he said unto them, Render therefore unto Cæsar the things which be Cæsar's, and unto GOD the <u>things</u> which be GOD'S" (Luke 20:25). Again the word *things* occurs 1161 times in the Bible.

The Son of God's Temple-Destruction Prophecy

The Son of God gave forth a chilling prophecy to His disciples concerning the Temple's destruction. "As for these things which ye behold, the days <u>will come</u>, in the which there shall not be left one stone upon another, that shall not be thrown down" (Luke 21:6). Again the phrase *come to pass* occurs 161 times in Scripture.

The Son of God's Words

"Heaven and earth shall pass away: but my <u>words</u> shall not pass away" (Luke 21:33). Again the word *words* is mentioned naturally in 61 verses of the NT Narrative.

King of the Jews' Communion Table

Jesus said, "That ye may eat and drink at my <u>table</u> in my KINGDOM" (Luke 22:30a). Again the word *table* occurs 61 times in the Old Testament.

Luke 22:61

"And the LORD turned, and looked upon <u>Peter</u>. And Peter remembered <u>the word of the LORD</u>, how he had said unto him, Before the cock crow, thou shalt deny me thrice" (Luke 22:61). The term Word of the Lord is synonymous with the Word of God. The name *Peter* is mentioned in 61 verses of the Synoptic Gospels. Again the phrase *the word of the LORD/Lord* is mentioned in 161 chapters of the Bible.

Women Lament the King of the Jews' Plight

"And there followed him a great company of people, and of women, which also bewailed and <u>lamented</u> him" (Luke 23:27). The lowly King of the Jews had already been severely beaten with whips. Even more unbearable to these lady disciples was the thought of His fast-approaching and painful execution. All forms of the word lament have the numeric seal of the King of the Jews: *lament* (21x), *lamentable* (1x), *lamented* (11x), *lamentation* (25x), *lamentations* (3x) = 61.

God's Son Put to Death for All Mankind

"And there were also two other, malefactors, led <u>with him</u> to be <u>put to death</u>" (Luke 23:32). When the lowly Son of God challenged the Pharisees to name one Mosaic Law He had broken they could not do it. Their silent affirmation gave Jesus the legal right to die in the place of all Jews who had broken the Law. Again the phrase *with him* occurs 61 times in First and Second Samuel. The phrase *put to death* is mentioned in 61 verses of the Bible.

This Is the King of the Jews

"And a superscription also was written over him in letters of Greek, and Latin, and Hebrew, THIS IS <u>THE</u> KING OF THE JEWS" (Luke 23:38). Here the underlined word *the* is the 673,661st word of the Bible, and it supports the title *King of the Jews*.

Son of God's Spirit of Forgiveness Even unto Death

"Then said Jesus, Father, <u>forgive</u> them; for they know not what they do. And they parted his raiment, and cast lots" (Luke 23:34). Again all available forms of the word *forgive* in the New Testament = 61.

Darkened Sun Testifies to the Son of God's Tragedy

"And it was about the sixth hour, and there was a darkness over <u>all the earth</u> until the ninth hour" (Luke 23:44). This verse presents the Bible's 61st occurrence of the phrase *all the earth*, and it refers to a worldwide darkness which testified to Jesus' deity. The phrase *all the earth* occurs 61 times from Genesis to the Gospels.

Rent Veil Testifies to the Son of God's Divinity

"And the sun was darkened, and the veil of the temple was <u>rent</u> in the midst" (Luke 23:45). This verse presents the Bible's 61st occurrence of the word *rent*, and it testifies to the ending of the Aaronic Priesthood and the beginning of a new one where the Son of God presides as Great High Priest after the order of Melchisedec. From Genesis to the Gospels the word *rent* is mentioned in

61 verses.

Risen Son of God Testifies to His Suffering & Glorification

On the King of the Jews' glorious resurrection day He found two disheartened disciples and said to them, "Ought not Christ to have suffered these things, and to enter into his glory?" (Luke 24:26) The Bible phrases *his glory* (45x) and *glory of God* (16x) = 61.

King of the Jews Reincarnated Himself

"And as they thus spake, Jesus himself stood in the midst of them, and saith unto them, Peace be unto you" (Luke 24:36). The word *himself* occurs 61 times in the Synoptic Gospels; this verse presents is 61st occurrence.

Law & Prophets Were Written Concerning the Son of God

"These are the words which I spake unto you, while I was yet with you, that all things must be fulfilled, which were written in the law of Moses, and in the prophets, and in the psalms, concerning me" (Luke 24:44). Again the word *concerning* is mentioned in 61 verses of the OT Narrative. Again the word *me* is mentioned in 161 verses of the Pauline Epistles.

King of the Jews' Great Commission
(Part 3)

"Thus it is written, and thus it behoved Christ to suffer, and to rise from the dead the third day: And that repentance and remission of sins should be preached in his name among all nations, beginning at Jerusalem. And ye are witnesses of these things" (Luke 24:46-48). The King of the Jews told His ambassadors that their preaching must include the doctrine of repentance. If the Son of God is to forgive sin, man must first repent of sin. Again the title *Christ* is mentioned naturally in 161 chapters of the New Testament.

Jesus' Divine Proportion to God

"In the beginning was the Word, and the Word was with GOD, and the Word was GOD. The same was in the beginning with GOD. All things were made by him; and without him was not any thing made that was made" (John 1:1-3). John wrote his Gospel record on the premise that Jesus is the very God, God incarnate. Accordingly John does not give Christ's genealogy but rather cites His dateless past. Some of the following seals have already been shown.

> The phrase *in the* is mentioned naturally in 61 verses of Daniel.
> The phrase *the beginning(s)* is mentioned in 61 chapters from Genesis to NTN.
> The word *was* is mentioned in 261 verses of Genesis.
> The title *the word of the LORD* is mentioned in 61 verses of Kings/Chronicles.
> The phrase *and the* is mentioned in 61 chapters of the Minor Prophets.
> The word *word* occurs naturally 61 times in the Pauline Epistles.
> The phrase *was with* occurs 61 times from Genesis to the Gospels.
> The title *God* is mentioned in 661 verses of the Law.
> The phrase *and the* is mentioned in 61 chapters of the Minor Prophets.
> The word *was* is found in 61 books of the Bible.
> The title *God* is mentioned in 61 verses of Second Corinthians.
> The phrase *the same* is mentioned in 61 verses of the Gospels.

The phrase *was in the* is mentioned in 61 chapters of the Bible.

The word *begin* [including present & infinite forms] is seen in 61 chapters of OT.

The word *with* [lowercase only] occurs 5961 times in the Bible!

The title *God* is mentioned in 161 chapters of the Wisdom Books.

The NTN combination *all things* (57 vs), *all the things* (4 vs) = 61 verses.

The word *were* is mentioned in 61 chapters of the Synoptic Gospels.

The phrase *he made* occurs 161 times from Genesis to the NT Narrative.

The word *by* occurs 61 times in the book of Deuteronomy.

The word *him* occurs 6661 times altogether in the Bible.

The word *and* is mentioned in 61 verses of Joel.

The word *without* (262 chs) – *without him* (1 ch) = 261 chapters of Bible.

The word *him* is mentioned in 61 verses of Daniel.

The word *was* is mentioned in 261 verses of Genesis.

The word *not* occurs 61 times in the Apocalyptic Epistle.

The word *any* is mentioned in 261 verses of the New Testament.

The word *thing* occurs 61 times in the Major Prophets.

The word *made* is mentioned in 461 chapters of the Old Testament.

The title *that was* occurs 61 times in the Kings and Chronicles.

The word *made* is mentioned in 611 chapters of the Bible.

The Son of God & the Spirit of God

"And John bare record, saying, I saw <u>the Spirit</u> descending <u>from heaven</u> <u>like</u> a dove, and it abode <u>upon him</u>" (John 1:32). All four Gospel writers recorded this divine event. Here the Spirit of God revealed His divine proportion to the Son of God. Again the title *the Spirit* is mentioned in 61 chapters of the New Testament. Again the phrase *from heaven* is mentioned in 61 verses of the New Testament. Again the word *like* is mentioned in 61 chapters of the New Testament. Again from Genesis to the Gospels the phrase *upon him* is mentioned in 161 verses.

We Have Found God's Anointed One

"He first findeth his own brother Simon, and saith unto him, We have <u>found</u> the Messias, which is, being interpreted, the Christ" (John 1:41). Again the word *found* occurs 61 times in the Major and Minor Prophets.

Son of God Did Go Forth

"The day following Jesus would <u>go forth</u> into Galilee, and findeth Philip, and saith unto him, Follow me" (John 1:43). The phrase *go forth* is mentioned in 61 chapters of the Bible.

Son of God Went down from Jerusalem

"This beginning of miracles did Jesus in Cana of Galilee, and manifested forth his glory; and his disciples believed on him. After this <u>he went down</u> to Capernaum" (John 2:11-12a).

> The phrase *he went* occurs 61 times in the Gospels.
> The phrase *went down* occurs 61 times in the Old Testament.

Son of God Purged His Father's House

"And said unto them that sold doves, Take these things hence; make not my <u>Father's house</u> an house of merchandise" (John 2:16). This statement confirmed yet again that Jesus was in fact God's heaven-sent Son.

The word *father's* occurs 61 times in the Law.
The term *father's house* occurs 61 times in the Old Testament.

Son of God Told Men Heavenly Things

"If I have <u>told</u> you earthly <u>things</u>, and ye believe not, how shall ye believe, if I tell you of heavenly <u>things</u>?" (John 3:12) The word *told* occurs 61 times in the New Testament. Again the word *things* occurs 1161 times in the Bible.

Son of God Became Son of Man

"And no man hath ascended up to heaven, but he that came down <u>from heaven,</u> even the <u>Son of man</u> which is in heaven" (John 3:13). In this statement Jesus reveals that He has divine origins. As it transpired, the Son of God became the Son of Man to die for all mankind. Again the phrase *from heaven* is mentioned in 61 verses of the New Testament. Again the capitalized title *Son of man* occurs 61 times in Ezekiel.

The Seal that God Is True

"He that hath received his <u>testimony</u> hath set to his seal <u>that GOD</u> is <u>true</u>" (John 3:33). All forms of the word *test** are mentioned in 61 chapters of the New Testament. The phrase *that God* occurs naturally 61 times in the Bible. The word *true* is mentioned in 61 chapters of the Bible.

The Anointed King of the Jews

"Come, see a man, which told me all things that ever I did: is not this the Christ?" (John 4:28 or 29) This verse *come, see a man, which told me all things that ever I did: is not this the Christ* consists of 61 letters!

Son of God Made Water into Wine

"So Jesus came again into Cana of Galilee, where he <u>made the</u> water wine. And there was a certain nobleman, whose son was sick at Capernaum" (John 4:46). As we have recently stated, Jesus was able to turn water into wine because He was the Creator God. The phrase *made the* is mentioned in 61 chapters of the Bible.

2061ˢᵗ Verse of the New Testament

"<u>The nobleman saith unto him, Sir, come down ere my child die</u>. Jesus saith unto him, Go thy way; thy son liveth" (John 4:49-50). The Son of God is pictured here as the Great Physician, that is to say, Jehovah Rapha—the God Who Heals. The underlined 2061ˢᵗ verse of the New Testament is also congruently the 161ˢᵗ verse of John.

Son of God Performs the Works of God

"But I have greater witness than that of John: for <u>the works</u> which the Father hath given me to finish, <u>the same</u> <u>works</u> that I do, bear witness of me, that the Father hath sent me" (John 5:36). Again the phrase *the same* is mentioned in 61 verses of the Gospels. The phrase *the works* occurs 61 times in the Bible.

God the Father

"Do not think that I will accuse you to the <u>Father</u>: there is one that accuseth you, even Moses, in whom ye trust" (John 5:45). Here the word *Father* is the 961st word in this chapter.

The Divine Bread of Life

"For the bread of GOD is he which cometh down from heaven, and giveth life unto the world. . . . <u>I am that bread of life</u>" (John 6:33, 48). Bread generally symbolizes fellowship. Hence the Son of God invites people of faith to share in His divine life by having communion with Him. The underlined five-word verse is the 3161st verse of the New Testament and concurrently the 261st verse of John; it refers to God. Again the word *bread* occurs 361 times in the Bible. Again the word *life* occurs naturally 61 times in the Law.

Son of God Makes Blood-Oath Pact with Man

"I am the living <u>bread</u> which <u>came down</u> from heaven: if any man eat of this bread, he shall live for ever: and the bread that I will give is my flesh, which I will give for the life of the world. . . . Verily, verily, I say unto you, Except ye eat <u>the flesh</u> of the <u>Son of man</u>, <u>and drink</u> his <u>blood</u>, ye have no life in you. Whoso eateth my flesh, and drinketh my <u>blood</u>, hath eternal life; <u>and I will</u> raise him up at the last day. For my flesh is meat indeed, and my blood is drink indeed" (John 6:51, 53-55).

Jesus speaks in metaphorical terms regarding two men making a sacred blood-covenant pact. When two such covenant partners consumed bread and wine together it symbolized that each person was partaking in the other's life. Again the word *bread* occurs 361 times in the Bible. From Genesis to the NT Narrative the phrase *came down* occurs 61 times. The phrase *the flesh* is mentioned in 61 verses of the Old Testament. Again the capitalized title *Son of man* occurs 61 times in Ezekiel. The phrase *and drink* occurs 61 times in the Bible. Again the word *drink* is mentioned in 61 verses of the New Testament. The word *blood* occurs 61 times in the OT Narrative. Again the phrase *and I will* occurs 61 times in Isaiah.

John 6:61

"When Jesus <u>knew</u> in <u>himself</u> that his disciples murmured at it, he said unto them, Doth this offend you" (John 6:61). The people were discomforted by the illustration Jesus gave about His metaphorical claim to be the supernatural Bread having come down from the God of heaven. Again the word *knew* is mentioned in 61 verses of the NT Narrative. The word *himself* occurs 61 times in the Synoptic Gospels.

God's One & Only Divine Prophet

"Many of the people therefore, when they heard this saying, said, Of a truth this is <u>the Prophet</u>" (John 7:40). Moses had predicted that God would raise up a future prophet like him, having great authority and miracle-working powers. When the people heard Jesus' claim that He could create living waters to flow from their soul's inner sanctum, many perceived Him to be this very Prophet Moses had said God would dispatch. The phrase *the prophet* occurs 61 times in the Major Prophets.

Son of God Sets Men Free

"If the <u>Son</u> therefore shall make you <u>free</u>, ye shall be <u>free</u> indeed" (John 8:36). Again the title *Son* is mentioned naturally in 161 verses of the NT Narrative. The word *free(d)* occurs 61 times in the Bible.

Son of God Heals Man Born Blind

"Since the world began was it not heard that any man <u>opened</u> the eyes of one that was born blind. If this man were not of GOD, he could do nothing" (John 9:32-33). Jesus' deity was greatly proven by the abundance of miracles He did like this one. Again the word *opened* is mentioned in 61 verses of the New Testament.

Son of God Is the Door of Heaven

"I am <u>the door</u>: by me if any man enter in, he shall be saved, and shall go in and out, and find pasture" (John 10:9). If Jesus claimed to be the door of heaven, He was claiming to be God because God alone determines who enters heaven. Again the phrase *of heaven* is mentioned in 61 chapters of the Bible. Again the phrase *door of* occurs 61 times in the Law.

How Long?

"Then came the Jews round about him, and said unto him, <u>How long</u> dost thou make us to doubt? <u>If thou</u> be the Christ, tell us plainly" (John 10:24). Because the name Christ means anointed one, the religious leaders wanted to know if Jesus was the anointed Messiah whom god had promised to send. Again the phrase *how long* occurs 61 times in the Bible. Again the phrase *if thou* occurs 61 times in the Law.

Son of God Wept

"Jesus <u>wept</u>" (John 11:35). This is the shortest verse in the Bible, and it refers to the lowly Son of God. All forms of the word weep show the golden seal of God: *weep* (45 vs), *weepest* (3 vs), *weepeth* (4 vs), *weeping* (41 vs), *wept* (68 vs) = 161.

Lazarus Hears Son of God's Voice Calling

"And when he thus had spoken, he cried with a loud <u>voice</u>, Lazarus, come forth. And he that was dead came forth" (John 11:43-44a). When the Son of God's voice reached Lazarus' ears he suddenly began to live again. This exceeding miracle proved Jesus was the Son of the Living God. Again the phrase *the voice of* occurs 161 times in the Old Testament.

Burial Rite Fit for a Godly Jewish King

It was just one week before the King of the Jews' sacrificial death, and at that time the Spirit of God moved a believer to pour an entire bottle of special ointment over His head and body. Judas was enraged. "Why was not this ointment sold for <u>three hundred</u> pence, and given to the poor?" (John 12:5) Jesus answered Judas by telling him that the woman had done this in view of His burial. Godly Judean kings were given worthy burials. The Incarnate King of the Jews was given an exemplary one. The word *three hundred* is mentioned in 61 verses of the Bible.

The Jewish King of Jerusalem

"On the next day much people that were come to the feast, when they heard that Jesus was coming to <u>Jerusalem</u>, Took branches of palm trees, and went forth to meet him, and cried, Hosanna: Blessed is the <u>King</u> of Israel that cometh in the name of the Lord. And Jesus, when he had found a young ass, sat thereon; as it is written, Fear not, daughter of Sion: behold, thy King cometh, sitting on an ass's colt" (John 12:12-15). The Joshua combination *the king of* (52x),

Jerusalem (9x) = 61.

Drawn to the Crucified Son of God

"And I, if I be lifted up from the earth, will <u>draw</u> all men <u>unto me</u>" (John 12:32). Indeed wherever the story of the Crucified Son of God has been told, men of all countries, creeds, and colors have repentantly drawn to Him. Again the phrase *unto me* is mentioned in 61 chapters of the Law of Moses. We repeat the following seals.

> The word *draw* occurs 61 times in the Old Testament.
> The word *draw* is mentioned in 61 verses of the Old Testament.
> The word *draw* is also mentioned in 61 chapters of the Bible.
> The word *drew* is mentioned in 61 chapters of the Bible.

Son of God to Come Again

"And if I go and prepare a place for you, I will come <u>again</u>, and receive you unto myself; that where I am, there ye may be also" (John 14:3). Again the word *again* occurs 161 times in the NT Narrative.

Jesus Is the Truth of God

During His conversation with Thomas, "Jesus saith unto him, I am the way, <u>the truth</u>, and the life: no man cometh unto the Father, but by me" (John 14:6). Again the phrase *the truth* is mentioned in 61 verses of the New Testament.

Jesus Is the Visible God

In the Upper Room Jesus told Philip in most definitive terms that He was God in the flesh: "he <u>that hath</u> <u>seen</u> me hath seen <u>the Father</u>?" (John 14:9) Jesus spoke in specific golden-ratio terms. He is divinely proportional to God. Again the phrase *that hath* occurs 161 times in the Bible. Again the Bible combination *seen* (259 vs), *God face to face* (1 v), *the LORD face to face* (1 v) = 261 verses. Again the NT Narrative combination *seen* (59 vs) and *the Lord God* (2 vs) = 61 verses. Again the case-sensitive phrase *the Father* is mentioned in 61 verses of the NT Narrative.

Jesus Issues New Commandments of God

"If ye love me, keep <u>my</u> commandments" (John 14:15). Jesus never couched His speech. He said exactly what He meant to say. His use of the word commandments was to advocate His Godhood status. The word *my* occurs 3748 times in the Old Testament; $3748 \div 61 = 61.44$. Again the word *my* is mentioned in 161 chapters of the Wisdom Books.

Jesus Will Give Men the Spirit of God

"I will pray the Father, and he shall give you <u>another</u> Comforter, that he may abide <u>with you</u> for ever" (John 14:16). The Greek text uses two separate words which are both translated in English as another. The word 'heteros' means another of a different kind, and 'allos' means another of the same kind. Here the Comforter Jesus promised to send was another of the same kind—another of the same divine proportion. He would send the Spirit of God. The word *another* is mentioned in 261 chapters of the Bible. The phrase *with you* is mentioned in 122 chapters of the Bible, a multiple of 61.

Son of God's Holy Engrafting

"At that day ye <u>shall know</u> that I am in my Father, and ye in me, and I in you" (John 14:20). Again the phrase *shall know* occurs 61 times in Ezekiel.

The Vine, the Branches & the Vine Keeper

"I am the true <u>vine</u>, and my Father is the <u>husbandman</u>. Every branch in me that beareth not fruit he taketh away: and every branch that beareth fruit, he purgeth it, that it may bring forth more fruit. . . . Abide in me, and I in you. As the branch cannot bear <u>fruit of</u> itself, except it abide in the vine; no more can ye, <u>except ye abide in me</u>" (John 15:1-2, 4). Jesus speaks first of His divinely proportional relationship with God. The Son is like a planted vineyard, and the Father is like its patient farmer. Jesus speaks further of the branches' proportional relationship to the vine. The children of God may only nourish and flourish as they closely relate with Christ. From Genesis to the NT Narrative the phrase *the fruit of* is mentioned in 61 verses. From Genesis to the Gospels the combination *vine* (55 vs), *husbandman* (5 vs), *except ye abide in me* (1 v) = 61 verses.

26,761ˢᵗ Verse of the Bible

"These words spake Jesus, and lifted up his eyes to heaven, and said, Father, the hour is come; glorify <u>thy Son</u>, that <u>thy Son</u> also may glorify thee" (John 17:1). This 61ˢᵗ verse reflects the Son of God's divine proportion with God the Father. Again the phrase *thy s/Son* is mentioned in 61 verses of the Bible.

To Know God & His Son

Jesus prayed to his Father, "And this is life eternal, that they might <u>know</u> thee the only true GOD, and Jesus Christ, whom thou hast sent" (John 17:3). Again the word *know* is mentioned in 61 verses of John's Gospel.

God Is the Divine Keeper of Souls

"And now I am no more in the world, but these are in the world, and I come to thee. Holy Father, <u>keep</u> through thine own name those whom thou hast given me, that they may be one, as we are" (John 17:11). Jesus speaks of the divine proportion between Himself and His born-again followers.

> The word *keep* occurs 61 times in the OT Narrative.
> The phrase *to keep* is mentioned in 61 chapters of the Bible.
> The phrase *keep thee* is mentioned in 61 chapters of the Bible.
> The word *kept* is mentioned in 161 verses from Genesis to the NTN.

761ˢᵗ Verse of John

"Jesus answered him, I <u>spake</u> openly to the world; I ever taught in the synagogue, and in the temple, whither the Jews always resort; and in secret have I said nothing" (John 18:20). The Son of God is speaking in this 61ˢᵗ verse. Again the word *spake* is mentioned in 61 verses of the Synoptic Gospels.

Born King of the Jews

"Pilate therefore said unto him, Art thou a KING then? Jesus answered, Thou sayest that <u>I am</u> a

KING. To this end was I born, and for this cause came I into the world, that I should bear witness unto the truth. Every one that is of the truth heareth my voice" (John 18:37). This verse presents the 61st occurrence of the phrase *I am* in John's Gospel, and it pertains to the King of the Jews. The Bible combination *to this end* (4x), *was I born* (1x), *born* (154x), *and for this cause came* (1x), *I into the world* (1x) = 161. Again the phrase *the truth* is mentioned in 61 verses of the New Testament.

King of the Jews Becomes National Passover Lamb

"But ye have a custom, that I should release unto you one at the passover: will ye therefore that I release unto you the KING OF THE JEWS?" (John 18:39) The title *the passover* occurs 61 times from Genesis to the NT Narrative.

Faultless King of the Jews

After investigating claims of the lowly Nazarene, Pilate testified three times to Jesus' perfection: "I find no fault in him" (John 19:6d). Pilate could find no fault in Jesus because in Him was no sin. He was the faultless King of the Jews and the perfect Son of God. Again the word *him* is mentioned in 61 verses of Daniel.

Behold the King of the Jews' Accusation

"The Jews answered him, We have a law, and by our law he ought to die, because he made himself the Son of GOD" (John 19:7). The word *die* is mentioned in 261 verses from Genesis to the Synoptic Gospels. Again the word *himself* occurs 61 times in the Synoptic Gospels. This is the New Testament's 161st occurrence of the phrase *of God*.

Behold the King of the Jews' Affliction

Pilate had just scourged Jesus hoping to pacify the Judean leaders' anger. He brought Him out on display. "And it was the preparation of the passover, and about the sixth hour: and he saith unto the Jews, Behold your KING!" (John 19:14) Again the word *behold* occurs 61 times in the Minor Prophets. The Matthew combination *behold* (60x), *thy king* (1x) = 61.

Pilate Wrote King of the Jews' Execution Inscription

"And Pilate wrote a title, and put it on the cross. And the writing was, JESUS OF NAZARETH THE KING OF THE JEWS" (John 19:19). The word *wrote* occurs naturally 61 times in the Bible. Here the underlined word *the* is the 81,861st word of the New Testament, and it supports the title *King of the Jews*!

Behold the King of the Jews' Inscription

"Then said the chief priests of the Jews to Pilate, Write not, The KING OF THE JEWS; but that he said, I am KING OF THE JEWS" (John 19:21). Again from Genesis to the Gospels the capitalized title *King* occurs 61 times; this verse presents its 61st occurrence.

Behold the King of the Jews' Kingly Burial

"And after this Joseph of Arimathaea . . . and took the body of Jesus. And there came also Nicodemus . . . and brought a mixture of myrrh and aloes, about an hundred pound weight. Then took they the body of Jesus, and wound it in linen clothes with the spices, as the manner of the Jews is to bury. Now in the place where he was crucified there was a garden; and in the garden a new sepulchre, wherein was never man yet laid. There laid they Jesus"

(John 19:38-42a).

Every Jewish king of Jerusalem had a garden; it symbolized his royal existence and was a private, sacred space where he alone could rest leisurely. Again the Bible combination *garden* (47 vs), *gardens* (12 vs), *gardener* (1 v), *his pleasant fruits* (1 v) = 61 verses.

Behold the King of the Jews' Resurrection

"And the napkin, that was about his head, not lying with the linen clothes, but wrapped together in a <u>place</u> by itself. . . . For as yet they knew not the scripture, that he must rise again from the dead" (John 20:7, 9). This verse presents the New Testament's 61st occurrence of the word *place*, and the word occurs 61 times in the Gospels.

Behold the King of the Jews' Nearing Ascension

"Jesus saith unto her, Touch me not; for I am not yet ascended to <u>my Father</u>: but go to my brethren, and say unto them, I ascend unto my Father, and your Father; and to my GOD, and your GOD" (John 20:17). The risen Son of God speaks of the proportional relationship that both He and His born-again followers have to the Divine Father in heaven. It is a golden ratio based upon both Christ's humanity and His deity. The underlined phrase *my Father* presents the Bible's 161st occurrence thereof.

King of the Jews' Great Commission
(Part 4)

"Then said Jesus to them again, Peace be unto you: <u>as my Father hath sent</u> me, even so <u>send</u> I you. . . . Whose soever sins ye remit, they are remitted unto them; and whose soever sins ye retain, they are retained" (John 20:21, 23). The Bible combination *as my Father* (4x), *hath sent* (57x) = 61. Again the word *send* is mentioned in 161 verses of the Old Testament.

Son of God Will Restore the Kingdom

"When they therefore were come together, they asked of him, saying, LORD, wilt thou at this time <u>restore</u> again <u>the KINGDOM</u> to Israel?" (Acts 1:6) All forms of the word *restore* occur 61 times in the Old Testament. Again the phrase *the kingdom of God* occurs 61 times in the NT Narrative.

Son of God Received up into Heaven

"And when he had spoken these things, while they beheld, he was taken <u>up</u>; and a cloud <u>received</u> him out of their sight" (Acts 1:9). Again the word *up* is mentioned in 61 verses of the Pauline Epistles. The word *received(dst)* occurs 161 times in the Bible.

Son of God Loved the Olivet Mountain

"Then returned they unto Jerusalem from the mount called <u>Olivet</u>, which is from Jerusalem a sabbath day's journey" (Acts 1:12). The Incarnate Son of God loved this mountain. It rises above Jerusalem some three hundred feet to overlook the city. Jesus resorted there, prayed there, preached there, surrendered to the Cross there, and ultimately ascended back to God from there. He is predicted to return and land at this same location. Olive trees on this very mountain have lived for more than 2000 years and so has the gospel story of God's Son. All forms of the word "olive" show the seal of God: *olive* (38x), *olives* (15x), *olivet* (2x), *oliveyard* (1x), *oliveyards*

(5x) = 61.

God's Spirit Permanently Abides with Men

"And when the day of Pentecost was fully come, they were all with one accord in one place. . . . And they were all filled with the Holy Ghost, and began to speak with other <u>tongues,</u> as <u>the Spirit</u> gave them utterance" (Acts 2:1, 4). God's devoted followers began to enjoy the special privilege of God's permanently indwelling Spirit. The word *tongue* occurs 61 times in the Wisdom Books. Again the title *the Spirit* is mentioned in 61 chapters of the New Testament.

God Adds Saved Souls to the Church of God

"Praising GOD, and having favour with all the people. And the LORD added to <u>the church</u> daily such as should be saved" (Acts 2:47). From Matthew to the General Epistles the title *the church* occurs 61 times.

Don't Be Found Fighting Against God

"But <u>if it be</u> of GOD, ye cannot overthrow it; lest haply ye be found even to <u>fight</u> against GOD" (Acts 5:39). The Proverbs combination *if it* (1 v) and *be* (160 vs) = 161 verses. Again the word *fight* is mentioned in 61 chapters of the Old Testament.

27,361st Verse of the Bible

"And immediately the angel of the LORD smote him, because he gave not GOD the glory: and he was eaten of worms, and gave up the ghost" (Acts 12:23). This 61st verse actually contains the key titles *Lord* and *God*.

61st Verse of Romans

"But he is a <u>Jew,</u> which is one inwardly; and circumcision is that of the <u>heart,</u> in the spirit, and not in the letter; whose praise is not of men, but <u>of GOD</u>" (Rom. 2:29). Again the phrase *the Jews* is mentioned in 61 verses of the Old Testament. The phrase *heart of* is mentioned in 61 chapters of the Bible. The Bible combination *the heart* (11 bks) and *of God* (50 bks) = 61 books. The keyword *God* actually occurs in this 61st verse.

God's True Nature

"GOD forbid: yea, let GOD be <u>true,</u> but every man a liar; as it is written" (Rom. 3:4a). Again the word *true* is mentioned in 61 chapters of the Bible.

God's Salvation Gift

"For the wages of sin is death; but the <u>gift</u> of GOD is eternal life through Jesus Christ our Lord" (Rom. 6:23). Again the word *gift(s)* occurs 61 times in the New Testament.

God's Grand Purpose

"And we know that all things work together for good to them that love GOD, to them who are the <u>called</u> <u>according to his</u> <u>purpose</u>" (Rom. 8:28). The first seal is repeated.

The word *called* is mentioned in 61 verses of the Pauline/General Epistles.
The phrase *according to* occurs 61 times in First and Second Chronicles.
The phrase *to his* occurs 361 times in the Bible.

All forms of the word *purpose* are mentioned in 61 verses of the Bible.

God's Favoritism

"What shall we then say to these things? If GOD be for <u>us</u>, who can be against <u>us</u>?" (Rom. 8:31) Again the word *us* occurs 61 times in Deuteronomy. Again the word *us* occurs 961 times in the Old Testament.

5061st Verse of the New Testament

"So then faith cometh by hearing, and hearing by the word of GOD" (Rom. 10:17). The keyword *God* actually occurs in this 61st verse.

God's Distribution of Faith

Paul challenged men to act "according as GOD hath dealt to every man the measure of <u>faith</u>" (Rom. 12:3e). Again the word *faith* is mentioned in 61 chapters of the Pauline Epistles.

God's Governmental Powers

"Let every soul be subject unto the higher powers. For there is no power but of <u>GOD</u>: the powers that be are ordained of <u>GOD</u>. Whosoever therefore resisteth the power, resisteth the ordinance of <u>GOD</u>: and they that resist shall receive to themselves damnation" (Rom. 13:1-2). Romans chapter thirteen consists of 361 words.

Every Tongue Shall Confess That Jesus Is God

"But . . . we shall all stand before the judgment seat of Christ. For it is written, As I live, saith the Lord, <u>every</u> <u>knee</u> <u>shall bow to</u> <u>me</u>, <u>and every tongue shall confess to GOD</u>" (Rom. 14:10-11). Again the phrase *to me* occurs 61 times in the OT Narrative. Again the word *tongue* occurs 61 times in the Wisdom Books. The Romans combination *every* (18x), *knee* (2x), *shall bow to* (1x), *me* (28x), *and every tongue shall confess* (1x), *to God* (11x) = 61.

1061st Chapter of the Bible

The theme of the first part of this chapter is the Christian Law of Love. It is to be daily lived out between the Jewish and Gentile children of God. "Now the GOD of patience and consolation grant you to be likeminded one toward another according to <u>Christ</u> Jesus: That ye may with one mind and one mouth glorify GOD, even the Father of our LORD Jesus <u>Christ</u>. Wherefore receive ye one another, as <u>Christ</u> also received us to the glory of GOD. . . . And that the Gentiles might glorify <u>GOD</u> for his mercy" (Rom. 15:5-7, 9a). The keyword *God* occurs many times in this 1061st chapter of the Bible. The underlined title *God* indicates the 3361st occurrence of the case-sensitive title of deity. Again the title *Christ* is mentioned naturally in 161 chapters of the New Testament.

The theme of the second part of this chapter is the Gospel of God. Paul emphasized that his gospel calling was specifically to the Gentiles. "I have written the more boldly unto you in some sort, as putting you in mind, because of the grace that is given to me of GOD, That I should be the minister of Jesus Christ to the Gentiles, ministering <u>the gospel</u> of GOD, that the offering up of the Gentiles might be acceptable, being sanctified by the Holy Ghost. I have therefore whereof I may glory through Jesus Christ in those things which pertain to GOD" (vv. 15-17). Again the term *the gospel* occurs 61 times in the Pauline Epistles.

The Wisdom of God
"But we speak the wisdom of GOD in a mystery, even the hidden wisdom, which God ordained before the world unto our glory" (1 Cor. 2:7). The Old Testament combination *the wisdom of God* (1x) and *wise man/men* (60x) = 61.

The Deep Things of God
"But God hath revealed them unto us by his Spirit: for the Spirit searcheth all things, yea, the deep things of GOD" (1 Cor. 2:10). Again the word *things* occurs 1161 times in the Bible.

The Spirit of God
"For what man knoweth the things of a man, save the spirit of man which is in him? even so the things of GOD knoweth no man, but the Spirit of GOD" (1 Cor. 2:11). This is the 5261st verse of the New Testament, and it regards God. Again the title *the Spirit* is mentioned in 61 chapters of the New Testament.

61st Verse of First Corinthians
"If any man's work abide which he hath built thereupon, he shall receive a reward" (1 Cor. 3:14). God will reward all His faithful servants for their steadfast work. From Genesis to the Gospels the word *reward* occurs 61 times.

The Ministers of God
"Let a man so account of us, as of the ministers of Christ, and stewards of the mysteries of GOD" (1 Cor. 4:1). Again all forms of the word *minister* are mentioned collectively in 161 verses of the Bible.

One God & One Lord Jesus Christ
"But to us there is but one GOD, the Father, of whom are all things, and we in him; and one LORD Jesus Christ, by whom are all things, and we by him" (1 Cor. 8:6). Again the word *one* occurs 61 times in First Corinthians. The Bible combination *Father* (260x), *of whom are all things* (1x) = 261.

The Church of God
"Give none offence, neither to the Jews, nor to the Gentiles, nor to the church of GOD" (1 Cor. 10:32). Again from Matthew to the General Epistles the title *the church* occurs 61 times.

Son of God's Broken Communion Bread
"And when he had given thanks, he brake it, and said, Take, eat: this is my body, which is broken for you: this do in remembrance of me" (1 Cor. 11:24). We repeat the following seals.

The word *break* occurs 61 times in the Major Prophets.
The word *broken* occurs 161 times in the Old Testament.

The Grace of God
"But by the grace of GOD I am what I am: and his grace which was bestowed upon me was not in vain; but I laboured more abundantly than they all: yet not I, but the grace of GOD which was with me" (1 Cor. 15:10). The Gospels combination *the grace* (4 vs), *of God* (157 vs) = 161 verses.

The Knowledge of God

"Awake to righteousness, and sin not; for some have not the <u>knowledge</u> of GOD: I speak this to your shame" (1 Cor. 15:34). Again the phrase *shall know* occurs 61 times in Ezekiel.

The Will of God

"Paul, an apostle of Jesus Christ by the <u>will</u> of GOD, and Timothy our brother, unto the church of God which is at Corinth, with all the saints which are in all Achaia" (2 Cor. 1:1). Again the word *will* is mentioned in 261 verses of Ezekiel.

The Promises of God

"For all the <u>promises</u> of GOD in him are <u>yea</u>, and in him Amen, unto the glory of GOD by us" (2 Cor. 1:20). The Psalms combination *promise* (2x) and *yea* (59x) = 61.

The Image of God

"In whom the god of this world hath blinded the minds of them which believe not, lest the light of the glorious gospel of Christ, <u>who is the</u> <u>image</u> <u>of GOD</u>, should shine unto them" (2 Cor. 4:4). Again the title *Christ* is mentioned naturally in 161 chapters of the New Testament. The Old Testament combination *who is the son* (1 v), *image* (59 vs), *face of God* (1 v) = 61.

The Face of God

"For GOD, who commanded the light to shine out of darkness, hath shined in our hearts, to give the light of the knowledge of the glory of GOD in the <u>face of Jesus</u> Christ" (2 Cor. 4:6). The light of God was manifest by the incarnate Son of God. Again the phrase *thy face* occurs 61 times in the Bible. From Acts to the Apocalypse the phrase *of Jesus* occurs 61 times.

The Building of God

"For we know that if our earthly house of this tabernacle were dissolved, <u>we have a</u> <u>building of GOD, an house</u> <u>not made with hands, eternal</u> <u>in the heavens</u>" (2 Cor. 5:1). The Bible combination *we have a* (7x), *building* (37x), *of God an house* (1x), *not made with hands eternal* (1x), *in the heavens* (15x) = 61.

The Temple of God

"And what agreement hath the temple of GOD with idols? for ye are the <u>temple</u> of the <u>living</u> GOD; as GOD hath said, I will <u>dwell in</u> them, and walk in them; <u>and I will</u> be <u>their</u> GOD, and they shall be my people" (2 Cor. 6:16). The apostle instructively reminded the carnal Corinthians that God's Spirit indwelled them like a temple. Again the word *temple* is mentioned in 61 verses of the Gospels. Again the word *living* occurs 61 times in the Wisdom Books. Again the phrase *dwell in* occurs 161 times in the Old Testament. The phrase *and I will* occurs 61 times in Isaiah. Again the word *their* is mentioned in 161 verses of Pauline/General/Apocalyptic Epistles.

The Warfare of God

"For the weapons of our warfare are not carnal, but mighty <u>through GOD</u> to the pulling down of strong holds" (2 Cor. 10:4). Again the word *through* occurs 61 times in the OT Narrative.

161st Chapter of the New Testament

This chapter begins with a story of a man who was called up to heaven unto the presence of the

Son of God.

> "It is not expedient for me doubtless to glory. I will come to visions and revelations of the Lord. I knew a man in <u>Christ</u> above fourteen years ago, whether in the body, I cannot tell; or whether out of the body, I cannot tell: GOD knoweth; such an one caught up to the third heaven. And I knew such a man, whether in the body, or out of the body, I cannot tell: GOD knoweth; How that he was caught up into paradise, and heard unspeakable words, which it is not lawful for a man to utter" (2 Cor. 12:1-4).

Again the title *Christ* is mentioned naturally in 161 chapters of the New Testament. Again the title *God* is mentioned in 61 verses of Second Corinthians.

The Triune Existence of God

"The grace of the LORD Jesus Christ, and the love of GOD, and the communion of the Holy Ghost, be with you all. Amen" (2 Cor. 13-14). This verse presents Second Corinthian's 61st verse-mention of the title *God*, and it speaks of the triune Godhead.

The Seed of God

"Now to Abraham and his <u>seed</u> were the promises made. He saith not, And to seeds, as of many; but as of one, And to thy <u>seed</u>, <u>which is</u> Christ" (Gal. 3:16). Paul reminded the Gentile believers of Galatia that God's promises are entrusted to people who exercise faith in Christ. They are the offspring of God. Again the singular word *seed('s)* occurs 61 times in the Major and Minor Prophets. This seed-of-God verse is the 61st verse of Galatians. The phrase *which is* occurs 261 times in the New Testament.

The Household of God

"Now therefore ye are no more strangers and foreigners, but fellowcitizens with the saints, and of the <u>household</u> of GOD" (Eph. 2:19). Gentile believers are encouraged to know that they are now as much a part of the family of God as Israel is. The Bible uses the word household to imply one's family, even extended family. The word *household* occurs 61 times in Bible.

The Fullness of God

"And to know the love of Christ, which passeth knowledge, that ye might be <u>filled with all the fulness</u> of GOD" (Eph. 3:19).

> The phrase *filled with* is mentioned in 61 chapters of the Bible.
> The phrase *with all* is mentioned in 161 verses of the Bible.
> The NT combination *filled* (59x) and *all the fullness of* (2x) = 61.
> The phrase *full of* is mentioned naturally in 161 verses of the Bible.

6161st Verse of the New Testament

"Be ye therefore followers of GOD, as dear children" (Eph. 5:1). The key title God actually occurs in this 6161st verse.

The Armor of God

"<u>Put on the whole armour of GOD</u>, that ye may be able to stand against the wiles of the devil. . . . Wherefore <u>take</u> unto you <u>the whole</u> armour of God, that ye may be able to withstand in the evil day, and having done all, to stand" (Eph. 6:11, 13). The First and Second Kings combination *take the whole* (1x), *put on armour* (1x), *of God* (59x) = 61.

The Equal of God

"Let this mind be in you, which was also in <u>Christ Jesus</u>: <u>Who, being in the form of GOD,</u> <u>thought it not robbery to</u> <u>be equal with GOD</u>: But made himself of no reputation, and took upon him the form of a servant, and was made in the likeness of men" (Phil. 2:5-7). The Bible combination *Christ Jesus* (58x), *who being in the form of God* (1x), *thought it not robbery to* (1x), *be equal with God* (1x) = 61.

The Name of God

"<u>Wherefore</u> GOD also hath highly exalted him, <u>and given him</u> a <u>name</u> <u>which is above every</u> <u>name</u>" (Phil. 2:19). The word *wherefore* is mentioned in 61 verses of the Major and Minor Prophets. Again the phrase *of Jesus* occurs 61 times from Acts to the Apocalypse. The New Testament combination *and given him* (1x), *the name* (59x), *which is above every name* (1x) = 61.

61st Verse of Philippians

"Finally, my brethren, <u>rejoice</u> in the Lord. To write the same things to you, to me indeed is not grievous, but for you it is safe" (Phil. 3:1). The persecuted Philippians would find their strength by rejoicing in God. Again from Genesis to the NT Narrative the word *rejoice* occurs 161 times.

The Hope of God

"To whom GOD would make known what is the riches of the glory of this mystery among the Gentiles; which is Christ <u>in you, the hope of glory</u>" (Col. 1:27). The Bible phrases *in you* (60x) and *in among you* (1x) = 61. The Bible phrases *in you* (60x), *the hope of glory* (1x) = 61.

The Gospel of God

"But even after that we had suffered before, and were shamefully entreated, as ye know, at Philippi, we were bold in our GOD to speak unto you <u>the gospel</u> of GOD with much contention" (1 Thess. 2:2). Again the phrase *the gospel* occurs 61 times in the Pauline Epistles.

End-Time Man Who Will Imitate God

"Who opposeth and exalteth himself above all that <u>is called</u> GOD, or that is worshipped; so that he as GOD sitteth in the temple of GOD, shewing himself that he is GOD" (2 Thess. 2:4). Again the phrase *is called* occurs 61 times in the Bible.

The Trump of God

"In a moment, in the twinkling of an eye, at the last <u>TRUMP</u>: for the trumpet shall sound, and the dead shall be raised incorruptible, and we shall be changed. . . . For the Lord himself shall descend from heaven with a shout with the voice of the archangel, and with the <u>TRUMP</u> of GOD and the dead in Christ shall rise first" (1 Cor. 15:52; Thess. 4:16). These two verses comprise the Bible's only mentions of the word *trump*, and they total 61 words! Again the word *trumpet* occurs 61 times in Scripture.

The Only Wise God

"Now unto the King eternal, immortal, invisible, <u>the</u> only <u>wise</u> GOD, be honour and glory for ever and ever. Amen" (1 Tim. 1:17). Here the word *wise* is the 361st word in this chapter, and it is an adjective of God. Again the phrase *the wise* occurs 61 times in the Old Testament.

The Manifestation of God

"And without controversy great is the mystery of godliness: GOD was manifest in the flesh, justified in the Spirit, seen of angels, preached unto the Gentiles, believed on in the world, received up into glory" (1 Tim. 3:16). Again the phrase *the flesh* is mentioned in 61 verses of the Old Testament.

61st Verse of First Timothy

"For therefore we both labour and suffer reproach, because we trust in the living GOD, who is the Saviour of all men, specially of those that believe" (1 Tim. 4:10). The keyword *God* actually occurs in this 61st verse. The Old Testament combination *those that* (160x), *believe in the LORD their God* (1x) = 161.

The Universal & Omnipotent Jewish King

"Which in his times he shall shew, who is the blessed and only Potentate, the KING of kings, and LORD of lords" (1 Tim. 6:15). The Pauline/General Epistles combination *Jesus Christ* (160 vs) and *King of kings* (1 v) = 161 verses.

The Living God

"Charge them that are rich in this world, that they be not highminded, nor trust in uncertain riches, but in the living GOD, who giveth us richly all things to enjoy" (1 Tim. 6:17). Again the word *living* occurs 61 times in the Wisdom Books.

The Man of God

"That the man of GOD may be perfect, throughly furnished unto all good works" (2 Tim. 3:17). The keyword *God* actually occurs in this 61st verse of Second Timothy. Again the title *the man of* is mentioned in 61 verses of the Bible.

The Commandment of God

"But hath in due times manifested his word through preaching, which is committed unto me according to the commandment of GOD our Saviour" (Titus 1:3). In the very next verse Paul called Jesus by the same title "our Saviour," giving Him equal status with God. The phrase *the commandment of* is mentioned in 61 verses of the Bible.

The Express Image of God

"GOD . . . Hath in these last days spoken unto us by his Son, whom he hath appointed heir of all things, by whom also he made the worlds; Who being the brightness of his glory, and the express image of his person" (Heb. 1:1a, 2-3). The Bible combination *who being the* (1x), *brightness of his glory* (1x), *and the express* (1x), *image of his* (2x), *person* (56x) = 61.

Son of God's Holy Brethren

Those who have made covenant with the Son of God are counted as His brothers being born again into His family. "For both he that sanctifieth and they who are sanctified are all of one: for which cause he is not ashamed to call them brethren" (Heb. 2:11).

The phrase *his brethren* occurs 61 times in the Law.

The phrase *and his brethren* occurs 61 times in the OT.

The Rest of God

"For he that is entered into his rest, he also hath ceased from his own works, as <u>GOD</u> <u>did</u> from his" (Heb. 4:10). Again the word *did* is mentioned naturally in 61 verses of Second Chronicles.

The High Priest of God

"Seeing then that we have a <u>great high priest</u>, that is passed into the heavens, Jesus the Son of GOD, let us hold fast our profession" (Heb. 4:14). The New Testament combination *mercy* (59x), *mercyseat* (1x), *great high priest* (1x) = 61.

The Better Covenant of God

"But now hath he obtained a more excellent ministry, by how much also he is the mediator of a better <u>covenant</u>, which was established upon better promises" (Heb. 8:6). The better covenant of God is the one which was mediated by the Son of God.

The word *covenant* occurs 61 times in the Major Prophets.

The term *of the covenant* is mentioned in 61 verses of Old Testament.

King of the Jews' Last Will & Testament

"For where a testament is, there must <u>also of</u> necessity be the death of the testator" (Heb. 9:16). The phrase *also of* is mentioned in 61 chapters of the Bible; this verse presents it 61st chapter-mention, and it speaks of the death of the King of the Jews.

The Presence of God

"For Christ is not entered into the holy places made with hands, which are the figures of the true; but into heaven itself, now to appear in <u>the presence of</u> GOD for us" (Heb. 9:24). Again the phrase *the presence of* is mentioned in 61 verses of the Bible.

God Is

"But without faith it is impossible to please him: for he that cometh to <u>GOD</u> must believe that he <u>is</u>, and that he is a rewarder of them that diligently seek him" (Heb. 11:6). Again the phrase *God is* occurs 61 times in the New Testament.

The Celestial City of God

"But ye are come unto mount <u>Sion</u>, and unto <u>the city</u> of the living GOD, the heavenly Jerusalem, and to an innumerable company of angels" (Heb. 12:22). This is the 61st occurrence of the phrase *the city* in the New Testament, and it refers to the celestial city of God. Again the names *Zion* (152x) and *Sion* (9x) = 161.

Ask Something of God

"If any of you lack wisdom, let him <u>ask</u> of GOD, that giveth to all men liberally, and upbraideth not; and it shall be given him" (James 1:5). The word *ask* occurs naturally 61 times in the New Testament.

You Should Show Evidence of God in Your Life

"But ye are a chosen generation, a royal priesthood, an holy nation, a peculiar people; that ye <u>should</u> shew forth the praises of him who hath called you out of darkness into his marvellous light" (1 Pet. 2:9). Here *should* is the 161,610 word of the New Testament.

The People of God

"Which in time past were not a people, <u>but</u> are <u>now</u> <u>the people of</u> GOD: which had not obtained mercy, <u>but now</u> have obtained mercy" (1 Pet. 2:10). The phrase *but now* occurs naturally 61 times in the Bible. This verse presents the New Testament's 161st verse-mention of the title *the people*, and it refers to the people of God.

> The phrase *people of* occurs 161 times in the Bible.
> The phrase *the people of the* is mentioned in 61 chapters of the Bible.
> The phrase *the people* is mentioned naturally 61 times in Second Chronicles.

Going Astray from God

"For ye were as sheep going astray; but are now returned unto the Shepherd and Bishop <u>of your</u> souls" (1 Pet. 2:25). Again the phrase *of your* occurs 61 times in the New Testament.

Son of God Was Put to Death

"For Christ also hath once suffered for sins, the just for the unjust, that he might bring us to GOD, being <u>put to death</u> in the flesh, but quickened by the Spirit" (1 Pet. 3:18). Again the phrase *put to death* is mentioned in 61 verses of the Bible.

30,461st Verse of the Bible

"If ye be reproached for the name of Christ, happy are ye; for the spirit of glory and of GOD resteth upon you: on their part he is evil spoken of, but on your part he is glorified" (1 Pet. 4:14). The keyword *God* is actually mentioned in this 61st verse of First Peter.

61st Book of the Bible

SECOND PETER is the 61st BOOK of the Bible because of its climactic theme in the final chapter—the Son of God's glorious return and fiery judgment of the wicked. This return of the Lord is known as "The Day of God" (2 Pet. 3:12). In this letter Peter wrote to the same audience as his previous letter: Jewish believers scattered abroad. He wrote on the overall theme of the knowledge of God by which believers would be able to overcome the sway of false teachers and rampant apostasy within the Church. This 61st book of the Bible consists of 61 verses! We now use W. Graham Scroggie's outline for Second Peter.

Knowledge of God & the Christian's Growth—Chapter One

Peter began by drawing attention to the foundation of the Christian's spiritual growth—his faith in God. "Simon Peter, a servant and an apostle of <u>Jesus Christ</u>, to them that have obtained like precious faith with us through the righteousness of GOD and our Saviour <u>Jesus Christ</u>" (2 Pet. 1:1). Jesus is seen here in His typical divine, proportional relationship to God. In this opening verse of the 61st book of the Bible we are presented with the Bible's 161st verse-mention of the name *Jesus Christ*, and it appears next to the name of God.

Peter introduced the subject of the knowledge of God and needful godliness: "Grace and peace be multiplied unto you through the knowledge of GOD, and of Jesus our LORD, According as his <u>DIVINE</u> power hath given unto us all things that pertain unto life and GODLINESS, through the knowledge of him that hath called us to glory and virtue . . . that by these ye might be partakers of the <u>DIVINE</u> nature" (1:3, 4b). Here in this 61st book of the Bible we find two of the rare mentions of the God-related word *divine* which are scattered throughout the Bible. These two complete verses each containing the word *divine* are comprised together of 61 naturally occurring words.

The believer's path to growth in godly virtues and Christian character is now presented. Peter lists them: "add to your <u>faith</u> virtue; and to virtue knowledge; And to knowledge temperance; and to temperance patience; and to patience GODLINESS; And to GODLINESS brotherly kindness; and to brotherly kindness charity. For if these things be in you, and abound, they make you that ye shall neither be barren nor unfruitful in the knowledge of our LORD Jesus Christ" (1:5b-8). Again the word *faith* is mentioned in 61 chapters of the Pauline Epistles.

The aged apostle recalls his personal knowledge of the reality of the Son of the God's first advent. He testifies: "For we have not followed cunningly devised fables, when we made known unto you <u>the power</u> and coming of our LORD Jesus Christ, but were eyewitnesses of his majesty" (1:16). Again the phrase *the power* is mentioned in 61 verses of the Bible.

Peter urges his readers to lean upon the Word of God for their Christian strength and stability. "We have also a more sure <u>word of</u> prophecy; whereunto ye do well that ye take heed, as unto a light that shineth in a dark place, until the day dawn, and the day star arise in your hearts. . . . For the prophecy came not in old time by the will of man: but holy <u>men of GOD</u> spake as they were moved by the Holy Ghost" (1:19, 21). Again the title *the word of the LORD/Lord* is mentioned in 161 chapters of the Bible. The phrase *men of* is mentioned in 61 verses of the Kings and Chronicles.

Knowledge of God & the Christian's Peril—Chapter Two
Peter now turns to expose heresy propagated by apostate false teachers. He wanted to encourage scattered believers to resist such rampant, erroneous teachings and continue trusting in the God of their salvation. "The LORD <u>knoweth</u> how to deliver the GODLY out of temptations, and to reserve the unjust unto the day of judgment to be punished" (2:9). The word *knoweth* is mentioned in 61 verses of the Old Testament.

Knowledge of God & the Christian's Hope—Chapter Three
False professors were propagating a heresy that the Son of God was delaying His Second Coming. Peter thus countered that harmful confusion with some reassuring truth. The promise of the Son of God's return is a matter of fact. "But, beloved, be not ignorant of this one thing, that one day is with the LORD as <u>a thousand</u> years, and <u>a thousand</u> years as one day" (3:8). Again the phrase *a thousand* is mentioned in 61 chapters of the Old Testament.

The Son of God's return that Peter describes is not the early one where the saints are caught up in the air but rather the latter-day judgment of unbelievers. "But <u>the day of</u> the LORD will come as a thief in the night; in the which the heavens shall pass away with a great noise, and the elements shall melt with fervent heat, the earth also and the works that are therein shall be burned up. . . . Looking for and hasting unto the coming of the day of GOD, wherein the heavens being on fire shall be dissolved, and the elements shall melt with fervent heat?" (3:10, 12) This passage in the

266

61st book of the Bible presents the Bible's 161st occurrence of the phrase *the day of*, and it refers to the day of God. Again the phrase *the day* is mentioned in 261 chapters of the Bible. Again the word *day* is found in 61 books of the Bible.

The Salutation

In the closing verse of his letter, Peter reiterates the theme of the Christian's growth in godly virtues and knowledge of God: "But grow in grace, and in the knowledge of our LORD and Saviour Jesus Christ. <u>To him</u> be glory both now and for ever. Amen" (3:18). Again the phrase *to him* is mentioned in 61 verses of the Gospels.

The Sons of God

"Beloved, now <u>are</u> we <u>the sons of</u> GOD, and it doth not yet appear what we shall be: but we know that, when he shall appear, we shall be like him; for we shall see him as he is" (1 John 3:2). The phrase *are the* is mentioned in 61 verses of the New Testament. The Bible combination *the sons of* (560x) and *the precious sons of* (1x) = 561. We repeat the following seals.

> The phrase *sons of* is mentioned in 61 verses of Numbers.
> The phrase *sons of* occurs naturally 261 times in the Chronicles.

Jesus Is the Very God

"Hereby perceive we the love of GOD, because he laid down his <u>life</u> for us: and we ought to lay down our lives for the brethren" (1 John 3:16). This verse presents the New Testament's 161st occurrence of the word *life*, thus making it a golden-ratio location wherein we discover yet again that Jesus is divinely proportional to the very God.

The Love of God

"No man hath seen GOD at any time. <u>If we love</u> one another, <u>GOD dwelleth in us</u>, and his love is perfected in us" (1 John 4:12). The phrase *if we* occurs 61 times in the Bible. The Bible combination *we love* (6x), *one another* (54x), *God dwelleth in us* (1x) = 61. All forms of the word *love* occur 261 times in the New Testament.

Proof That We Are the Children of God

"<u>By this we know that we love the children of GOD, when we love GOD, and keep his commandments</u>" (1 John 5:2). The Bible combination *by this we know* (1x), *know that we love* (1x), *the children of God* (9x), *when we* (49x), *love God and keep his commandments* (1x) = 61.

7561st Verse of the New Testament

"I am Alpha and Omega, the beginning and the ending, saith the LORD, <u>which is</u>, and which was, and which is to come, the Almighty" (Rev. 1:8). Again the phrase *which is* occurs 261 times in the New Testament.

Son of God's Trumpeting Voice

"I was in the Spirit on the Lord's day, and heard behind me a great voice, as of a <u>trumpet</u>, Saying, I am Alpha and Omega, the first and the last: and, What thou seest, write in a book, and send it unto the seven churches which are in Asia; unto Ephesus, and unto Smyrna, and unto Pergamos, and unto Thyatira, and unto Sardis, and unto Philadelphia, and unto Laodicea" (Rev. 1:10-11). This trumpet-like voice which John heard belonged to the Son of God. Again the word *trumpet* occurs 61 times in Scripture!

Son of God's Golden Garments

"And in the midst of the seven candlesticks one like unto the <u>Son of man</u>, clothed with a <u>garment</u> down to the foot, and girt about the paps with a <u>golden</u> girdle" (Rev. 1:13). Again the capitalized title *Son of man* occurs 61 times in Ezekiel. Again the word *garments* is mentioned in 61 chapters of the Bible. Again the word *golden* is mentioned in 61 verses of the Bible.

Son of God's Everlasting Nature

"And he laid his right hand upon me, saying unto me, <u>Fear not</u>; I am <u>the first</u> and the last" (Rev. 1:17b). Jesus verified His eternal nature as God the Son. Again the phrase *fear not* occurs 61 times from Genesis to the NT Narrative. The phrase *the first* occurs 61 times in Numbers.

Son of God's Glorious Feet

"And <u>his feet</u> like <u>unto</u> <u>fine</u> <u>brass</u>, as if they burned in a furnace; and his voice as the sound of many waters" (Rev. 1:15). Again from Genesis to the Gospels the phrase *his feet* occurs 61 times. The word *fine* occurs 61 times in the Law. The Bible combination *unto fine* (1 ch), *brass* (60 chs) = 61 chapters.

Son of God—He Ever Was, Ever Is & Ever Shall Be

Jesus declared, "I am <u>he</u> that liveth, and <u>was</u> dead; and, behold, I am alive for evermore, Amen; and have the keys of hell and of death" (Rev. 1:18).

> The phrase *he is* occurs 61 times in the OT Narrative.
> The phrase *for he is* occurs 61 times in the Bible.
> The word *is* is mentioned in 61 verses of Judges.
> The word *is* is mentioned in 61 verses of Second Corinthians.
> The phrase *he was* occurs 461 times in the Bible.
> The phrase *he shall* is mentioned in 61 verses of Isaiah.
> The word *shall* is mentioned in 61 verses of Revelation.
> The phrase *shall be* is found in 61 books of the Bible.

Son of God's Worldwide Rule

"And he shall <u>rule</u> them with a rod of iron; as the vessels of a potter shall they be broken to shivers: even as I received of my Father" (Rev. 2:27). This verse presents the Bible's 61st verse-mention of the word *rule*, and it pertains to the Son of God's worldwide sovereign rule. He will establish godly rulers over His worldwide realm. Again the word *ruler* is mentioned in 61 verses of the Old Testament.

61st Verse of Revelation

"Him that overcometh will I make a pillar in the temple of my GOD, and he shall go no more out: <u>and I will</u> write upon him the name of my GOD, and the name of the city of my GOD, which is new Jerusalem, which cometh down out of heaven from my GOD: <u>and I will</u> write upon him my new name" (Rev. 3:12). Again the phrase *and I will* occurs 61 times in Isaiah. The key title *God* occurs several times in this 61st verse.

Son of God's Healing Balm

"I counsel thee to buy of me gold tried in the fire, that thou mayest be rich; and white raiment, that thou mayest be clothed, and that the shame of thy nakedness do not appear; and anoint thine eyes with eyesalve, that thou mayest see" (Rev. 3:18). Again the phrase *of me* is mentioned in 61 chapters of the Bible.

The Door of God's Upward City

"After this I looked, and, behold, a door was opened in heaven" (Rev. 4:1a). The Bible terms *the door* (160x) and *the north door* (1x) = 161.

Untold Thousands of Angels around God

"And I beheld, and I heard the voice of many angels round about the throne and the beasts and the elders: and the number of them was ten thousand times ten thousand, and thousands of thousands" (Rev. 5:11). This verse presents the Bible's 61st occurrence of the word thousands, and it relates to thousands of angels surrounding God. Again the phrase *round about* is mentioned in 61 verses of Ezekiel. Again *a thousand* is mentioned in 61 chapters of the Old Testament.

The Measure of God's Temple

"And there was given me a reed like unto a rod: and the angel stood, saying, Rise, and measure the temple of GOD, and the altar, and them that worship therein" (Rev. 11:1). The word *measure* is mentioned naturally in 61 verses of the Bible. Again the word *temple* is mentioned in 61 verses of the Gospels.

God of the Earth

"These are the two olive trees, and the two candlesticks standing before the GOD of the earth" (Rev. 11:4). Again the phrase *of the earth* is mentioned in 61 verses of the Wisdom Books. Again the word *earth* occurs 61 times in Jeremiah.

The Kingdoms of Our God

"And the seventh angel sounded; and there were great voices in heaven, saying, The kingdoms of this world are become the kingdoms of our Lord, and of his Christ; and he shall reign for ever and ever" (Rev. 11-15).

The phrase *the kingdom(s) of* is mentioned in 161 verses of the Bible.
The phrase *the kingdom(s) of* is mentioned in 61 chapters of the New Testament.

God's Judgment Day Approaches

"And I heard the angel of the waters say, Thou art righteous, O LORD, which art, and wast, and shalt be, because thou hast judged thus" (Rev. 16:5). The word *judged* is mentioned in 61 verses of the Bible.

Give God Glory

"And men were scorched with great heat, and blasphemed the name of GOD, which hath power over these plagues: and they repented not to give him glory" (Rev. 16:9). All forms of the phrase *give him* are mentioned in 61 chapters of the Old Testament.

Son of God's Holy War

"And I saw heaven opened, and behold a white horse; and he that sat upon him was called <u>Faithful</u> and <u>True</u>, and in <u>righteousness</u> he doth judge and make war" (Rev. 19:11). The aged apostle saw the Son of God coming to Earth to judge it for its rebellion against Him, His covenant, and His Jewish people. Again the lowercase word *faithful* is mentioned in 61 chapters of the Bible. Again the word *true* is mentioned in 61 chapters of the Bible. Again the word *righteousness(es)* occurs 305 times in the Bible, a multiple of 61.

Son of God's Many Crowns

"His eyes were as a flame of fire, and on his head were many <u>crowns</u>; and he had a name written, that no man knew, but he himself" (Rev. 19:12). The word *crown(s)* occurs 61 times in the Old Testament.

Son of God's 1000-Year Reign

"Blessed and holy is he that hath part in the first resurrection: on such the second death hath no power, but they shall be priests of GOD and of Christ, and shall <u>reign</u> <u>with him</u> <u>a thousand</u> years" (Rev. 20:6). This verse presents the Bible's 161st verse-mention of the word *reign*. Again the phrase *with him* occurs 61 times in First and Second Samuel. Again the phrase *a thousand* is mentioned in 61 chapters of the Old Testament.

Son of God Rules All Three Heavens

"And I saw a great white throne, and him that sat on it, from whose face the earth and <u>the heaven</u> fled away; and there was found no place for them" (Rev. 20:11). At the end of His thousand-year reign the Son of God will judge fallen men and fallen angels who all occupy the earth and the lower heavens. Again the phrase *the heaven* is mentioned in 61 chapters of the Bible; this is its 61st chapter mention, and it has to do with the earthly heavens fleeing from God's Son.

The City of God

"And I John saw <u>the holy</u> <u>city</u>, <u>new</u> <u>Jerusalem</u>, coming down from GOD out of heaven, prepared as a bride adorned for her husband. We repeat the following seals.

> The term *the holy* is mentioned in 61 verses of the Law.
> The word *city* is mentioned in 61 verses of the Synoptic Gospels.
> The word *new* occurs 61 times in the New Testament.
> The name *Jerusalem* is mentioned in 61 verses of the Minor Prophets.

Tabernacle of God Is with Men

"And I heard a great voice out of heaven saying, Behold, <u>the tabernacle of</u> [GOD] <u>is</u> with men, and he will <u>dwell</u> with them, and they <u>shall be</u> his people, and GOD himself <u>shall be</u> with them, and be their GOD" (Rev. 21:3). Again the phrase *of the tabernacle of the congregation* occurs 61 times in the Bible. Again the phrase *God is* occurs 61 times in the New Testament; this is its 61st occurrence. This same case-sensitive title *[God]* is the Bible's 4061st occurrence thereof. Again the word *dwell* occurs 305 times in the Old Testament, a multiple of 61. Again the phrase *shall be* is found in 61 books.

God Is Going to Make All Things New

"And he that sat upon the throne said, Behold, I make all things <u>new</u>" (Rev. 21:5a). Again the word *new* occurs 61 times in the New Testament.

God's City Is Foursquare

"And the city lieth foursquare, and <u>the length</u> <u>is as large as the breadth</u>: and he <u>measured</u> the city with the reed, twelve thousand furlongs. The length and the breadth and the <u>height</u> of it are equal" (Rev. 21:16). Again the word *measure* is mentioned naturally in 61 verses of the Bible. The Bible combination *the length* (60x), *is as large as the breadth* (1x) = 61. Again the phrase *is as* is mentioned in 61 verses of the Bible. The word *height* occurs 61 times outside the book of Revelation. The word *height(s)* is mentioned in 61 verses of the Bible.

God's City Is Garnished with Transparent Gold

"And the building of the wall of it was of jasper: and the city was pure <u>gold</u>, like unto clear glass. . . . and the street of the city was pure <u>gold</u>, as it were transparent glass" (Rev. 21:18, 21b). Again the word *gold* is mentioned in 361 verses of the Bible.

God's City Has Gemstone Walls

"And the foundations of the wall of the city were garnished with all manner of precious <u>stones</u>. The first foundation was jasper; the second, sapphire; the third, a chalcedony; the fourth, an emerald" (Rev. 21:19). God so constructed the rich minerals of the earth that they might create gemstones over long spaces of time. Again the word *stones* occurs 161 times in the Old Testament.

God Controls the Time

"And he saith unto me, Seal not the sayings of the prophecy of this book: for <u>the time</u> is at hand" (Rev. 22:10). An angel had just prophesied to John about the King of the Jews' glorious Second Coming; yet the exact time of His return to Earth is undisclosed. It remains open-ended and therefore imminent. The King of Heaven can come at any given moment.

> The word *time* is found in 61 books of the Bible.
> The word *time* is mentioned in 61 chapters of the NTN.

The phrase *the time* is mentioned in 161 verses of the Bible.

62—Jerusalem

JERUSALEM is a name derived from two Hebrew root words: *yara* properly meaning to <u>flow</u> as water and *salam* meaning <u>peace</u> or to <u>be safe</u>. These two words combined form a beautiful picture of Jerusalem—'Flowing with Peace.' Gently flowing waters are themselves highly symbolic of peace. By God's grand design Jerusalem will one day return to being the spiritual capital of the world and flow with peaceful springs, streams, and rivers. This will happen during the Messiah's thousand-year reign in Jerusalem. We will look very close at Jerusalem's water-flowing prophesies in the Major and Minor Prophets.

> The Bible: *shall flow* (7x), *in peace* (54x), *be in safety* (1x) = 62.
> The word *peace* is mentioned in 62 verses of the Major Prophets.
> The word *peace* occurs 62 times in the Pauline/General Epistles.

~~~~~

> The phrase *of Jerusalem* appears in 162 verses from Genesis to Synoptic Gospels.
> The phrase *in Jerusalem* occurs 162 times after the Jebusites were driven out of it.

~~~~~

> All Jerusalem-related forms of the phrase "the city of" show the seal of Jerusalem: *the city of David* (46x), *the city of God* (2x), *the city of our God* (2x), *the city of my God* (1x), *the city of the living God* (1x), *the city of the great King* (2x), *the city of Jerusalem* (1x), *the city of the LORD* (2x), *the city of my joy* (1x), *the city of praise* (1x), *the city of righteousness* (1x), *the city of our solemnities* (1x), *the city of truth* (1x) = 62.

ZION is a name derived from a Hebrew word meaning conspicuousness. The Strong's Concordance gives the following description of the Hebrew word 'tsee-yone;' a monumental or guiding <u>pillar</u>:—sign, title, or way-mark. It is the same as 'tsee-yoon' giving the sense of conspicuousness. The word *pillar(s)* occurs 62 times in the Law.

The stronghold of Zion was quite conspicuous geographically. This fortress, originally occupied by the Jebusites, was situated on a hill at the intersection of two valleys, the Tyropoean and the Kidron. After David conquered the city and made it the place of his residence it became known as "The City of David." Zion also became known for the hill upon which it was situated. Later on in Israel's history, Zion became a companion name to Jerusalem; it also signified the land of Judah and the people of God. Originally it began with only political significance, being the seat of the king, but it grew in fame to take on great spiritual significance after Solomon built a Temple for God on the hill adjacent to Zion—Mount Moriah.

> The name *Zion* (152x), *Zion's* (1x), *Sion* (9x) = 162 times in the Bible.

The Gihon River

"<u>And a river went out of Eden to water the garden; and from thence it was parted</u>, and became into four heads. . . . And the name of the second river is Gihon: the same is it that compasseth the whole land of Ethiopia" (Gen. 2:10, 13). Some three thousand years later, in David's time, this name Gihon would entitle a peaceful low-pressure spring flowing along the slope just outside Jerusalem's eastern wall. The word Gihon means stream; its primitive root means 'to gush forth.'

273

The words *and a river went out of Eden to water the garden; and from thence it was parted* consist of 62 letters!

Jared's Years—162 & 962

"And Jared lived an hundred SIXTY and TWO years, and he begat Enoch. And Jared lived after he begat Enoch eight hundred years, and begat sons and daughters: And <u>all the days</u> of Jared <u>were</u> nine hundred SIXTY and TWO years: and he died" (Gen. 5:18-20). Jared stemmed from Seth's godly line from whence the Hebrews would later rise. The name Jared means to descend. The Bible always elevates Jerusalem above all other cities and places of the world regardless of their actual elevations. This is because God views Jerusalem as the physical and spiritual capital of the world. Time after time across the biblical narrative we see people going up to Jerusalem or descending from it. The dictionary defines the word "descend" as to come down. Still, any waters that flowed forth from Jerusalem must have flowed down for it was surrounded by valleys on three sides. The phrase *came down* occurs 62 times in the Bible. These two verses cite the only references of the number 62 in the whole Bible, and the verse between them presents the phrase *all the days* which mentioned in 62 verses of the Bible! Here the word *were* is the 3062nd word of the Bible, and it refers to a man's age which was 962.

King of Salem Brought Forth Symbols of Peace

"And Melchizedek <u>king of</u> SALEM <u>brought forth</u> bread and wine: and he was the priest of the most high God" (Gen. 14:18). The biblical narrative gives us our first glimpse of Jerusalem. Salem is either an early form of the name Jerusalem or it may have been a synonym with Jerusalem at the time. Salem means peaceful. The city was situated atop a mountain, being surrounded on three sides by valley terrain. Melchizedek offered Abraham a ceremonial meal highly representative of peace between two people. His title King of Salem means 'king of peace.' With such a king the city of Salem would have flowed with peace under his righteous reign. It is certain that the peaceful city flowed with gentle waters for there has always been a low-pressure spring located just outside the city called the Gihon Spring. The title *the king of* is mentioned in 62 chapters of the OT Narrative. Again the word *peace* is mentioned in 62 verses of the Major Prophets. The phrase *brought forth* is mentioned in 62 chapters of the Bible.

Mount Moriah

"And it came to pass after these things, that God did tempt Abraham, and said unto him, <u>Abraham</u>: and he said, Behold, here I am. And he said, Take now thy son, thine only son Isaac, whom thou lovest, and get thee into the land of MORIAH; and offer him there for a burnt offering upon one of <u>the mountains</u> which I will tell thee of" (Gen. 22:1-2). The mountain which God showed Abraham came to be called Mount Moriah. It was situated just north of Mount Zion and was slightly higher in elevation. Many centuries later Mount Moriah would become the location for the construction of Jerusalem's prized Temple. The phrase *the mountain* occurs 62 times in Scripture. The name *Abraham* occurs 162 times in the Old Testament.

Shiloh

"<u>The sceptre shall not depart from Judah</u>, nor a <u>lawgiver</u> <u>from between his feet</u>, until <u>Shiloh</u> come; and <u>unto him shall the</u> <u>gathering of the people be</u>" (Gen. 49:10). Jacob gave forth this promising prophecy in regards to Judah's anointed Messiah. This heaven-sent King would reign over Judah forever in Jerusalem, and there would be peace for evermore under His powerful rule.

Such a reign of peace corresponds with the meaning of the name Shiloh—tranquil. The Bible combination *the sceptre shall not depart from Judah* (1x), *from between his feet* (1x), *the king of Judah* (23x), *the lawgiver* (2x), *Shiloh* (33x), *unto him shall the* (1x), *gathering of the people be* (1x) = 62.

A Land Flowing with Milk & Honey

"And I am come down to deliver them out of the hand of the Egyptians, and to bring them up out of that land unto a good land and a large, unto a land FLOWING with milk and honey; unto the place of the Canaanites, and the Hittites, and the Amorites, and the Perizzites, and the Hivites, and the Jebusites" (Exod. 3:8). The heart and center of this good land will be a peaceful city called Jerusalem.

> The Bible combination *unto a land* (6x), *flowing with* (8x), *milk* (48x) = 62.
> The Bible combination *a land flowing with* (6x), *honey* (56x) = 62.

62ⁿᵈ Verse of Exodus

"And God said moreover unto Moses, Thus shalt thou say unto the children of Israel, The LORD God of your fathers, the God of Abraham, the God of Isaac, and the God of Jacob, hath sent me unto you: this is my name for ever, and this is my memorial unto all generations" (Exod. 3:15). Some time later God told Moses He would eventually place His great memorial name in one particular city within the Promised Land. That city will be Jerusalem.

> The word *name* is mentioned in 62 chapters of the Kings/Chronicles.
> The word *name* is mentioned in 362 chapters of the Old Testament.

62ⁿᵈ Chapter of the Bible

This 62ⁿᵈ chapter of the Bible covers the institution of the Passover, a feast which would later be permanently celebrated in the mandated city of Jerusalem.

"In the tenth day of this month they shall take to them every man a lamb, according to the house of their fathers, a lamb for an house: And if the household be too little for the lamb, let him and his neighbour next unto his house take it according to the number of the souls; every man according to his eating shall make your count for the lamb. Your lamb shall be without blemish, a male of the first year: ye shall take it out from the sheep, or from the goats" (Exod. 12:3b-5). As there were tens of thousands of Hebrew families, so there would have been tens of thousands of lambs offered to the Lord. The word *thousands* occurs 62 times in the Bible. The Bible combination *a lamb for a house* (1x) and *household* (61x) = 62.

"And thus shall ye eat it; with your loins girded, your shoes on your feet, and your staff in your hand; and ye shall eat it in haste: it is the LORD'S passover" (v. 11). On this first Passover observance Israel was still in servitude, and so the people were commanded to eat the supper standing not reclining.

The phrase *the passover* occurs 62 times in Scripture!

"And they shall take of the blood, and strike it on the two side posts and on the upper door post of the houses. . . . And the blood shall be to you for a token upon the houses where ye are: and when I see the blood, I will pass over you, and the plague shall not be upon you to destroy you, when I smite the land of Egypt" (vv. 7, 13). Over the millennia and even up until this present day, impressions of red handprints can be found stamped by the entrance of houses in the old city of Jerusalem. This was done with hope for the Lord's divine protection. The Bible combination *the door* (160x), *on the two side posts and* (1x), *on the upper door post* (1x) = 162.

"And this day shall be unto you for a memorial; and ye shall <u>keep</u> it a feast to the LORD throughout your generations; ye shall <u>keep</u> it a feast by an ordinance for ever" (v. 14). In the future, an Israelite could not keep this feast unless he was physically present in Jerusalem. The word *keep* occurs 62 times in the New Testament.

Passover came with a very frightful injunction: "<u>Seven days shall ye eat</u> <u>unleavened</u> bread; even the first day ye shall put away leaven out of your houses: for whosoever eateth leavened bread from the first day until the seventh day, that soul shall be cut off from Israel" (v. 15). The Bible combination *seven days shall ye eat* (1x), *unleavened* (61x) = 62.

God instructed Moses, saying, "It is a <u>night</u> to be much observed unto the LORD for bringing them out from the land of Egypt: this is that <u>night</u> of the LORD to be observed of all the children of Israel in their generations. And the LORD said unto Moses and Aaron, This is the ordinance of the passover" (v. 42-43a). The word *night* occurs 62 times in the New Testament.

62nd Verse of Leviticus
"Even the whole bullock shall he carry forth without the camp unto a clean place, where the ashes are poured out, and burn him on the wood with fire: where the ashes are poured out shall he be burnt" (Lev. 4:12). This rare temple ceremony would eventually be performed at Jerusalem.

Peace in the Land & Its Capital City
The Lord mentioned some of the conditions of His national blessing if Israel chose to truly walk in His ways. "And I will give PEACE in the land, and ye shall lie down, and none shall make you afraid: and I will rid evil beasts out of the land, neither shall the sword go through your land" (Lev. 26:6). At the very heart of this land lies Israel's future religious, economic, and political capital Jerusalem. Again the Jerusalem-related word *peace* is mentioned in 62 verses of the Major Prophets.

62nd Verse of Numbers
"And his <u>host</u>, and those that were numbered thereof, were fifty and seven thousand and four hundred" (Num. 2:8). In time Zebulun's host would assemble at Jerusalem to worship the Lord as would the hosts of all the tribes of Israel. The word *host* is mentioned in 62 chapters of the OT Narrative.

Numbers 7:62
"One golden spoon of ten shekels, full of incense" (Num. 7:62). In generations to come incense would burn sweetly within a permanent Temple in Jerusalem.

Numbers 26:62
"And those that were numbered of them were twenty and three thousand, all males from a month old and upward: for they were not numbered among the children of Israel, because there was no inheritance given them among the children of Israel" (Num. 26:62). All the males would one day

be required to appear before the Lord in Jerusalem three times a year for the festivals.

Mount Sion

"From Aroer, which is by the bank of the river Arnon, even unto mount SION, which is Hermon" (Deut. 4:48). The name Sion only occurs twice in the Old Testament; it occurs seven times in the New Testament. The name Sion means peak; its associated root means 'elevation:—excellency.' Hereafter in the biblical narrative, this striking name becomes synonymous with both earthly and heavenly Jerusalem. Here the word *which* is the 132,962nd word of the Bible, and it supports the Jerusalem-related name Sion.

The Place of God's Name to Rest
(Part 1)

"But unto the place which the LORD your God shall choose out of all your tribes to put his name there, even unto his habitation shall ye seek, and thither thou shalt come. . . . and when he giveth you rest from all your enemies round about, so that ye dwell in safety; Then there shall be a place which the LORD your God shall choose to cause his name to dwell there" (Deut. 12:5, 10b-11b). During the four-and-a-half-centuries era of the judges, the Lord would move His Tabernacle from one place to the next. The resting place for God's name moved from Gilgal to Shiloh to Gibeon and finally to Jerusalem. Jerusalem was the last city to be conquered because of its defensive terrain and fortified position. The Bible combination *but unto the place which the LORD your God shall* (1x), *choose* (59x), *out of all your tribes to put his name there* (1x), *even unto his habitation shall ye seek* (1x) = 62. The Law combination *a place* (7x), *to put his name there* (2x), *his name* (53x) = 62.

The Place of God's Name to Rest
(Part 2)

"If the place which the LORD thy God hath chosen to put his name there be too far from thee, then thou shalt kill of thy herd and of thy flock, which the LORD hath given thee, as I have commanded thee, and thou shalt eat in thy gates whatsoever thy soul lusteth after" (Deut. 12:21). This Jerusalem-related verse is the 5262nd verse of the Bible. The Old Testament combination *the place* (160x), *which the LORD thy God hath chosen* (2x) = 162. The Gospels combination *place* (61x) and *he hath chosen* (1x) = 62. Again the word *name* is mentioned in 362 chapters of the Old Testament.

All Males to Appear in Jerusalem

"Three times in a year shall all thy males appear before the LORD thy God in the place which he shall choose; in the feast of unleavened bread, and in the feast of weeks, and in the feast of tabernacles: and they shall not appear before the LORD empty" (Deut. 16:16). The Old Testament combination *three times in a year* (2x), *shall all thy males appear* (1x), *before the LORD thy God* (17x), *in the place* (40x), *which he shall choose to place his name there* (1x), *and they shall not appear before the LORD empty* (1x) = 62.

Deuteronomy 28:62

"And ye shall be left few in number, whereas ye were as the stars of heaven for multitude; because thou wouldest not obey the voice of the LORD thy God" (Deut. 28:62). Over time this prophecy tragically came true. When the Babylonians and Romans swept the land of Judea, the

Jews naturally gathered inside Jerusalem's defensive walls for refuge and safety. After both sieges were over Jerusalem's Jewish population was quickly decimated, leaving only a few poor souls to live therein. The word *few* is mentioned in 62 verses of the Bible.

The Place of God's Name to Rest
(Part 3)

"When all Israel is <u>come to</u> appear before the LORD thy God in the <u>place</u> which he shall <u>choose</u>, thou shalt read this law before all Israel in their hearing" (Deut. 33:11). The word *place* is mentioned in 162 verses of the Law; this is its 162nd verse-mention, and it refers ultimately to Jerusalem. All forms of the word *choose* are mentioned collectively in 62 verses of the Old Testament.

> The phrase *come to* is mentioned in 62 chapters of the OT Narrative.
> The phrase *come to* is mentioned in 62 chapters of the Major Prophets.

The Bible's First Mention of Jerusalem

"Now it came to pass, when Adoni-zedek king of JERUSALEM had heard how Joshua had <u>taken</u> Ai, and had utterly destroyed it" (Josh. 10:1a). This early king of Jerusalem had a very godly name. The name Adoni-zedek means *my lord is righteous*. It bears relation to an earlier king who once reigned there—Melchizedek. In the back of his mind Adonizedek feared Jerusalem being taken and destroyed. As it turned out, Jerusalem was the last fortified city Israel was able to take. The Law combination *the city was* (1x) and *taken* (61x) = 62.

The King of Jerusalem

"<u>The king of</u> JERUSALEM, <u>one</u>" (Josh. 12:10a). At this time Jerusalem was ruled by a succession of Gentile kings. As God's divine plan would have it, His only begotten Son would one day become Jerusalem's permanent King. Again from Genesis to the Synoptic Gospels the phrase *of Jerusalem* is mentioned in 162 verses. The word *one* occurs 62 times in the Minor Prophets and is mentioned in 162 verses of the Pauline Epistles.

> The word *king* occurs 62 times in the NT Narrative.
> The word *king* is mentioned in 362 verses of the Major Prophets.
> The phrase *the king of* is mentioned in 62 chapters of the OT Narrative.
> The phrase *And the king* is mentioned in 162 verses of the Old Testament.

The Jebusite Inhabitants of Jerusalem

"As for <u>the Jebusites</u> <u>the inhabitants of JERUSALEM</u>, the children of Judah could not drive them out: but the Jebusites dwell with the children of Judah at JERUSALEM unto this day" (Josh. 15:63). It seems that Judah could not accomplish taking this greatly fortified city until they had acquired their champion warrior king David. As for this city of God's own choosing, He was saving the best for last. The Bible combination *the Jebusites* (23x), *the inhabitants of Jerusalem* (39x) = 62.

> The phrase *the inhabitants of* is mentioned naturally in 62 verses of the OT.
> The phrase *the inhabitants of* occurs 62 times in the Major/Minor Prophets.

Jerusalem Smitten by the Sword & Set on Fire

"Now the children of Judah had fought against JERUSALEM, and had taken it, and had <u>smitten</u> it with the edge of <u>the sword</u>, and <u>set</u> the city <u>on fire</u>" (Judg. 1:8). Although Jerusalem had been conquered, the people had not because they stayed themselves up in the citadel, the city's large stronghold. It was not until David's time that Judah was able to breach the fortress. The word *smitten* is mentioned in 62 verses of Scripture. The phrase *the sword* occurs naturally 62 times in Ezekiel. The phrase *by fire* is mentioned in 62 verses of the Law. The Old Testament combination *smitten* (61x) and *set on fire* (1x) = 62. This chapter contains 962 words.

David Terrorizes the Jebusites with Goliath's Head

"And David took the head of the Philistine, and brought it to JERUSALEM; but he put his armour in his tent" (1 Sam. 17:54). At this time Judah was dwelling in Jerusalem, but Judah had yet to drive out the Jebusites from the stronghold of Zion. Some conjecture that David displayed the head of the infamous giant to terrorize the Jebusites. The name *Jerusalem* occurs only here in all of First Samuel.

David's Reign in Jerusalem

"<u>David was thirty years old when he began to reign, and he reigned forty years</u>. In Hebron he <u>reigned</u> over Judah seven years and six months: and in JERUSALEM he <u>reigned</u> thirty and three years over all Israel and Judah" (2 Sam. 5:4-5). The sentence *David was thirty years old when he began to reign, and he reigned forty years* consists of 62 letters! The word *reign* is mentioned in 162 verses of the Bible.

David Conquers Jerusalem's Jebusite-Held Fortress of Zion

"And the king and his men went to JERUSALEM unto the Jebusites, the inhabitants of the land: which spake unto David, saying, Except thou take away the blind and the lame, thou shalt not come in hither: thinking, David cannot come in hither. Nevertheless David took <u>the strong hold of ZION</u>: the same is the city of David. And David said on that day, Whosoever getteth up to the gutter, and smiteth the Jebusites . . . he shall be chief and captain" (2 Sam. 5:6-8d). This verse presents the Bible's first mention of the name Zion. Here the underlined word *of* is the 225,562nd word of the Bible, and it supports the related keyword Zion.

> The Bible name *Zion/'s* (153x) and *Sion/'s* (9x) = 162.
> The Bible combination *the strong hold of* (3x), *of Zion* (59x) = 62.

Jerusalem's Peacefully Flowing Waters
(Part 1)

Apart from underground cisterns which held rain water, Jerusalem possessed only one source of living waters. This was an underground stream that surfaced just outside the city's south-eastern wall and ran along the Ophel Hill. It was called the Gihon Spring and was so named after the stream which once flowed from Eden's paradise. This spring maintained very low head pressure and thus produced only a small yet sufficient supply of water to the city. The "gutter" David mentioned in the above verse was a culvert made to give the city's inhabitants private access to the spring away from the enemy's watchful eyes. David thus recognized that this steep gutter or vertical shaft was an entrance into the city that the people were not very worried about.

The City of David

"So David <u>dwelt in</u> the fort, and called it <u>the city of David</u>. And David built round <u>about</u> from

Millo and inward. And David went on, and grew great, and the LORD God of hosts was with him" (2 Sam. 5:9-10). The word *about* is mentioned in 62 verses of the Wisdom Books.

The word *city* occurs 362 times in the OT Narrative.
The phrase *in the city* is mentioned in 62 chapters of the Bible.
The name *David('s)* is mentioned in 162 verses of First Chronicles.

Sons & Daughters Born to David in Jerusalem

"And David took him more concubines and wives out of JERUSALEM, after he was come from Hebron: and there were yet <u>sons</u> and <u>daughters</u> born to David. And these be the names of those that were born unto him in JERUSALEM; Shammua, and Shobab, and Nathan, and <u>Solomon</u>, Ibhar also, and Elishua, and Nepheg, and Japhia, And Elishama, and Eliada, and Eliphalet" (2 Sam. 5:13-16). The word *sons* is mentioned in 62 chapters of the Kings and Chronicles. The phrase *daughters of* occurs 62 times in the Bible.

The Ark Finally Comes into Jerusalem

"And they brought it out of the house of Abinadab which was at Gibeah, accompanying the ark of God: and Ahio went before the ark. . . . And it was told king David, saying, The LORD hath blessed the house of Obed-edom, and all that pertaineth unto him, because of the ark of God. <u>So David went</u> <u>and brought up</u> <u>the ark of God</u> <u>from the house of Obed-edom</u> <u>into the city of David</u> <u>with gladness</u>" (2 Sam. 6:4, 12). Verse number four is the 8162nd verse of the Bible, and it relates to bringing an important vessel into Jerusalem. David had prepared a tent to house the Ark while allowing the Tabernacle to stay in Gibeon with its remaining holy furniture. The OT Narrative combination *so David went* (4x), *and brought up* (4x), *the ark of God* (37x), *from the house of Obed-edom* (1x), *into the city of David* (4x), *city of God* (2x), *with gladness* (10x) = 62. The First and Second Samuel combination *the ark* (61x) and *came into the city of David* (1x) = 62. The Kings and Chronicles combination *ark* (61x) and *into the city of David* (1x) = 62.

"And they brought in the ark of the LORD, and set it in his place, in the midst of the tabernacle that David had pitched for it: and David offered burnt offerings and PEACE offerings before the LORD. And as soon as David had made an end of offering burnt offerings and PEACE offerings, he blessed the people in the name of the LORD of hosts" (vv. 17-18). After these peace offerings were accepted of the Lord the city began flowing with the peace of God. Again the word *peace* occurs 62 times in the Pauline/General Epistles.

Shields of Gold Brought into Jerusalem

"And David took <u>the shields</u> of gold <u>that were on the servants of Hadadezer,</u> <u>and brought them to</u> JERUSALEM" (2 Sam. 8:7). The OT Narrative combination *the shields* (5x), *of gold* (53x), *that were on the servants of Hadadezer* (2x), *and brought them to Jerusalem* (2x) = 62.

Dwelt in Jerusalem

"So Mephibosheth <u>dwelt in</u> JERUSALEM: for he did eat continually at the king's table; and was lame on both his feet" (2 Sam. 9:13).

The phrase *dwelt in* occurs 62 times in the OT Narrative.
The phrase *dwell in* is mentioned in 162 verses of the Bible.

Came to Jerusalem

"And when the children of Ammon saw that the Syrians were fled, then fled they also before Abishai, and entered into the city. So Joab returned from the children of Ammon, and came to JERUSALEM" (2 Sam. 10:14). The phrase *and came to* occurs naturally 62 times in the Bible.

362nd Verse of Second Samuel

"So Absalom dwelt two full years in JERUSALEM, and saw not the king's face" (2 Sam. 14:28). The keyword *Jerusalem* actually occurs in this 62nd verse.

The Ark of God Came Again to Jerusalem

"Zadok therefore and Abiathar carried the ark of God again to JERUSALEM: and they tarried there" (2 Sam. 15:29). The phrase *again to* is mentioned naturally in 62 chapters of the Bible.

Return to Jerusalem

"And when they had sought and could not find them, they returned to JERUSALEM" (2 Sam. 17:20d). The joined phrases *and when they had sought and could not find them, they returned to Jerusalem* consists of 62 letters! The word *return* is mentioned in 162 chapters of the Bible.

Out of Jerusalem

"And said unto the king, Let not my lord impute iniquity unto me, neither do thou remember that which thy servant did perversely the day that my lord the king went out of JERUSALEM, that the king should take it to his heart" (2 Sam. 19:19).

> The phrase *out of* occurs 62 times in Second Samuel.
> The phrase *out of* occurs naturally 162 times in the NTN.
> The phrase *out of* is mentioned in 662 chapters of the Bible.

8562nd Verse of the Bible

"And there went out after him Joab's men, and the Cherethites, and the Pelethites, and all the mighty men: and they went out of JERUSALEM, to pursue after Sheba the son of Bichri" (2 Sam. 20:7). The keyword *Jerusalem* actually occurs in this 62nd verse.

Jerusalem's Sacred Altar

"And when the angel stretched out his hand upon JERUSALEM to destroy it, the LORD repented him of the evil, and said to the angel that destroyed the people, It is enough: stay now thine hand. And the angel of the LORD was by the threshingplace of Araunah the Jebusite. . . . And Gad came that day to David, and said unto him, Go up, rear an altar unto the LORD in the threshingfloor of Araunah the Jebusite. . . . And David built there an altar unto the LORD, and offered burnt offerings and PEACE offerings" (2 Sam. 24:16, 18, 25a).

The Old Testament phrases *rear an altar* (1 v), *unto the LORD* (461 vs) = 462 verses. The phrase *made by fire* is mentioned in 62 verses of the Bible. Here the Jerusalem-related word *peace* is the 242,762nd word of the Bible.

Jerusalem's Peacefully Flowing Waters
(Part 2)

"The king also said unto them, Take with you the servants of your lord, and cause Solomon my son to ride upon mine own mule, and bring him down to Gihon" (1 Kings 1:33). The Gihon

Spring was located just outside the wall of Jerusalem on its southeastern side. Spring water was considered holy water for it was pristine, pure, and came from a mystery source. Israelite kings were not only anointed with oil for their inauguration into the office of king, but they were also baptized with water. This was the reason for Solomon's needful journey to the Gihon Spring.

Jerusalem's Perimeter Walls

"And Solomon . . . made an end of building his own house, and the house of the LORD, and the wall of JERUSALEM round about" (1 Kings 3:1). Again the word *about* is mentioned in 62 verses of the Wisdom Books.

> The word *walls* is mentioned in 62 verses of the Old Testament.
> The phrase *wall(s) of* occurs 62 times in the Bible.

Solomon Made Peace Offerings in Jerusalem

"And Solomon awoke; and, behold, it was a dream. And he came to JERUSALEM, and stood before the ark of the covenant of the LORD, and offered up burnt offerings, and offered PEACE offerings, and made a feast to all his servants" (1 Kings 3:15). After these peace offerings were presented the peace of the Lord began flowing through Jerusalem. The phrases *and he came to Jerusalem, and stood before the ark of the covenant of the LORD* consists of 62 letters!

Peace Flowed Round about Jerusalem on All Sides

"For he had dominion over all the region on this side the river, from Tiphsah even to Azzah, over all the kings on this side the river: and he had PEACE on all sides round about him. And Judah and Israel dwelt SAFELY, every man under his vine and under his fig tree, from Dan even to Beer-sheba, all the days of Solomon" (1 Kings 4:25). You will recall that Jerusalem's root word *salam* means 'peace' or 'to be safe.' So here, we see the citizens of Jerusalem dwelling in safety. The Bible combination *dwelt* (226x), *safely* (21x), *every man under* (2x), *his vine* (3x), *and under his* (6x), *his fig tree* (4x) = 262.

Jerusalem's Wise Man

"And God gave Solomon wisdom and understanding exceeding much, and largeness of heart, even as the sand that is on the sea shore. And Solomon's wisdom excelled the wisdom of all the children of the east country, and all the wisdom of Egypt. For he was wiser than all men; than Ethan the Ezrahite, and Heman, and Chalcol, and Darda, the sons of Mahol: and his fame was in all nations round about" (1 Kings 4:31). The OT Narrative combination *Solomon* (261x) and *wiser than all men* (1x) = 262.

Jerusalem's Holy Temple

"And it came to pass in the . . . fourth year of Solomon's reign over Israel . . . that he began to build the house of the LORD. . . . And for the house he made windows of narrow lights. And against the wall of the house he built chambers round about, against the walls of the house round about, both of the temple and of the oracle: and he made chambers round about" (1 Kings 6:1, 4-5). The title *the house of the LORD* is mentioned in 162 verses of the OT Narrative. The word *temple* occurs 62 times in the Gospels.

Jerusalem's Holy Ark

"Then Solomon assembled the elders of Israel, and all the heads of the tribes, the chief of the fathers of the children of Israel, unto king Solomon in JERUSALEM, that they might bring up the ark of the covenant of the LORD out of the city of David, which is ZION. . . . And the priests brought in the ark of the covenant of the LORD unto his place, into the oracle of the house, to the most holy place, even under the wings of the cherubims" (1 Kings 8:1, 6). The Kings and Chronicles combination *the ark* (60x), *the holy ark* (1x), *into the oracle of the house* (1x) = 62.

People of Israel to Gather in Jerusalem at God's House

"Since the day that I brought forth my people Israel out of Egypt, I chose no city out of all the tribes of Israel to build an house, that my name might be therein; but I chose David to be over my people Israel. And it was in the heart of David my father to build an house for the name of the LORD God of Israel" (1 Kings 8:16-17). The title *the God of Israel* is mentioned in 62 chapters of the Bible. The phrase *people Israel* occurs 62 times in the Bible.

Jerusalem's Prayerful Place

"That thine eyes may be open toward this house night and day, even toward the place of which thou hast said, My name shall be there: that thou mayest hearken unto the prayer which thy servant shall make toward this place . . . and of thy people Israel, when they shall pray toward this place: and hear thou in heaven thy dwelling place: and when thou hearest, forgive" (1 Kings 8:29-30). Again the word *place* is mentioned in 162 verses of the Law.

First Kings 8:62

"And the king, and all Israel with him, offered sacrifice before the LORD" (1 Kings 8:62). It was the dedication day for God's finished House at Jerusalem.

> The word *offering* occurs 62 times in the Major Prophets.
> The word *sacrifices* is mentioned in 62 verses of the Old Testament.
> The term *before the LORD* occurs 262 times in the Old Testament.

Peace Offerings of Oxen & Sheep in Jerusalem

"And Solomon offered a sacrifice of PEACE offerings, which he offered unto the LORD, two and twenty thousand oxen, and an hundred and twenty thousand sheep. So the king and all the children of Israel dedicated the house of the LORD" (1 Kings 8:63). Again the word *peace* is mentioned in 62 verses of the Major Prophets. The word *offerings* occurs 62 times in the Kings and Chronicles. The Law combination *oxen* (31x) and *sheep* (31x) = 62.

Jerusalem's Silvery Appearance

"And the king made silver to be in JERUSALEM as stones, and cedars made he to be as the sycomore trees that are in the vale, for abundance" (1 Kings 10:27). The Major Prophets combination *to be* (61x) and *as silver* (1x) = 62. The OT Narrative combination *of silver* (58x), *to be in Jerusalem* (1x), *as stones* (3x) = 62.

Jerusalem's Unsanctioned High Places

"For it came to pass, when Solomon was old, that his wives turned away his heart after other gods. . . . Then did Solomon build an high place for Chemosh, the abomination of Moab, in the hill that is before JERUSALEM, and for Molech, the abomination of the children of Ammon" (1 Kings 11:7). From this time forward every king in Jerusalem had something to do with idol worship—either promoting it or eradicating it. The term *high place(s)* is mentioned in 62 verses of the OT Narrative.

Jerusalem, Capital of the Tribes of Israel

"But he shall have one tribe for my servant David's sake, and for JERUSALEM'S sake, the city which I have chosen out of all the tribes of Israel" (1 Kings 11:32). God chose Jerusalem to be Israel's capital.

> The title *the tribes of* occurs 62 times in the Bible.
> The title *Israel* occurs 62 times in the Psalms.

House of the Lord in Jerusalem

"If this people go up to do sacrifice in the house of the LORD at JERUSALEM" (1 Kings 12:27a).

> The word *house* occurs 162 times in First and Second Samuel.
> The title *the house* occurs 62 times in the NT Narrative.
> The title *the house of the LORD* is mentioned in 162 verses of OT Narrative.
> The phrase *of the house of the LORD* is mentioned in 62 verses of the Bible.

Against Jerusalem

"And it came to pass in the fifth year of king Rehoboam, that Shishak king of Egypt came up against JERUSALEM" (1 Kings 14:25). The First Samuel combination *against* (61 vs), *Jerusalem* (1 v) = 62 verses. The word *against* is mentioned in 62 verses of Deuteronomy.

Jerusalem's Establishment

"Nevertheless for David's sake did the LORD his God give him a lamp in JERUSALEM, to set up his son after him, and to establish JERUSALEM" (1 Kings 15:4). The word *established* is mentioned in 62 chapters of the Bible.

Jerusalem's Treasures

"And Jehoash king of Judah took all the hallowed things that Jehoshaphat, and Jehoram, and Ahaziah, his fathers, kings of Judah, had dedicated, and his own hallowed things, and all the gold that was found in the treasures of the house of the LORD, and in the king's house, and sent it to Hazael king of Syria: and he went away from JERUSALEM" (2 Kings 12:18). In this verse there are 62 words preceding the name *Jerusalem*. The word *treasures* occurs 62 times in Scripture.

In Jerusalem

"Sixteen years old was he when he began to reign, and he reigned two and fifty years in JERUSALEM. And his mother's name was Jecholiah of Jerusalem" (2 Kings 15:2).

> The word *in* is mentioned in 1762 verses of the Law.
> The word *in* occurs 562 times in the book of Isaiah.
> The word *in* occurs 1062 times in the Gospels.
> The word *in* is seen in 62 verses of First/Second Peter.

Jerusalem's Wars

"Then Rezin king of Syria and Pekah son of Remaliah king of Israel came up to JERUSALEM to <u>war</u>: and they besieged Ahaz, but could not overcome him" (2 Kings 16:5). Wikipedia writes that "throughout its long history Jerusalem has been destroyed at least twice, besieged 23 times, captured and recaptured 44 times, and attacked 52 times."

> The word *war* is mentioned in 62 chapters of the OT Narrative.
> The word *war(s)* occurs 62 times in the Kings and Chronicles.

Sennacherib King of Assyria Came against Jerusalem

"And the king of Assyria sent Tartan and Rabsaris and Rab-shakeh from Lachish to king Hezekiah with a great host <u>against</u> JERUSALEM" (2 Kings 18:17). Again the word *against* is mentioned in 62 verses of Deuteronomy.

Worship at Jerusalem

"Hezekiah . . . hath said to Judah and JERUSALEM, Ye shall <u>worship</u> before this altar in JERUSALEM" (2 Kings 18:22b). The word *worship* is mentioned in 62 verses of the Old Testament.

The Virgin Daughter of Zion

A prophecy is given concerning Sennacherib. "This is the word that the LORD hath spoken concerning him; <u>The virgin</u> the <u>daughter of ZION</u> hath despised thee, and laughed thee to scorn; the daughter of JERUSALEM hath shaken her head at thee" (2 Kings 19:21). This verse reveals the syncretized nature between Zion and Jerusalem. As a virgin, Zion's fortified walls had never been breached but Jerusalem's walls had. Again the phrase *daughters of* occurs 62 times in the Bible. The Bible combination *Zion/'s* (153x), *the virgin* (9x) = 162.

10,162th Verse of the Bible

"Thus saith the LORD, Behold, I will bring evil upon this place, and upon the inhabitants thereof, even all the words of the book which the king of Judah hath read" (2 Kings 22:16). Huldah gave a doom-and-gloom prophecy regarding Jerusalem's future.

A Remnant Will Go Forth from Jerusalem

"And the <u>remnant</u> that is escaped of the house of Judah shall yet again take root downward, and bear fruit upward. For <u>out of</u> JERUSALEM shall go forth a <u>remnant,</u> and they that escape out of mount <u>ZION</u>: the zeal of the LORD of hosts shall do this" (2 Kings 19:30-31). Sennacherib's first attack had done considerable harm to the Judean province (18:13). Those Jews who escaped from the defenced cities which Sennacherib overthrew would have sought new refuge in Jerusalem's greater walls. Again the phrase *out of* occurs 62 times in Second Samuel. Here the keyword *Zion* is the 962nd word of this chapter.

> The phrase *remnant of* occurs 62 times in the Old Testament.
> The phrase *remnant of* appears in 62 verses of the Old Testament.

Of Jerusalem

"And the king sent, and they gathered unto him all the elders of Judah and <u>of</u> JERUSALEM" (2 Kings 23:1). The word *of* is mentioned in 62 verses of John's Epistles.

Kings of Judah Rule from Jerusalem

"And he put down the idolatrous priests, whom <u>the kings of</u> Judah had ordained to burn incense in the high places in the cities of Judah, and in the places round about Jerusalem; them also that burned incense unto Baal, to the sun, and to the moon, and to the planets, and to all the host of heaven" (2 Kings 23:5).

The title *kings* occurs 162 times in the Old Testament Narrative.

The phrase *of the king of* is mentioned in 62 verses of the Old Testament.

From Jerusalem

"And he carried away Jehoiachin to Babylon, and the king's mother, and the king's wives, and his officers, and the mighty of the land, those carried he into captivity <u>from</u> JERUSALEM to Babylon" (2 Kings 24:15).

The word *from* is mentioned in 62 verses of Proverbs.

The word *from* occurs 462 times in the NT Narrative.

Nebuchadnezzar King of Babylon Came against Jerusalem

"At that time the servants of Nebuchadnezzar king of Babylon came up <u>against</u> JERUSALEM, and the city was besieged" (2 Kings 24:10). Again the word *against* is mentioned in 62 verses of Deuteronomy.

Defiant Jerusalem Burnt with Fire

"And in . . . the nineteenth year of king Nebuchadnezzar king of Babylon, came Nebuzar-adan, captain of the guard, a servant of the king of Babylon, unto JERUSALEM: And he <u>burnt</u> the house of the LORD, and the king's house, and all the houses of JERUSALEM" (2 Kings 25:8-9c). Again the phrase *by fire* is mentioned in 62 verses of the Law.

And Jerusalem

"And Jehozadak went into captivity, when the LORD carried away Judah <u>and</u> JERUSALEM by the hand of Nebuchadnezzar" (1 Chron. 6:15).

The word *and* is mentioned in 762 verses of Deuteronomy.

The word *and* is occurs 162 times in Micah.

Jerusalem—Place of Israel's Atonement

"But Aaron and his sons offered upon the altar of the burnt offering, and on the altar of incense, and were appointed for all the work of the place most holy, and to make <u>an atonement</u> for Israel, according to all that Moses the servant of God had commanded" (1 Chron. 6:49). Atonement was accomplished in a twofold way: through the high priest's burnt offering and through the high priest's intercessory prayer. The term *an atonement* occurs 62 times in the Law.

Went to Jerusalem

"And David and all Israel <u>went</u> to JERUSALEM, which is Jebus; where the Jebusites were, the inhabitants of the land. And the inhabitants of Jebus said to David, Thou shalt not come hither. Nevertheless David took the castle of ZION, which is the city of David" (1 Chron. 11:4).

The word *went* occurs 162 times in the Kings/Chronicles.

The word *went* occurs 1062 times in the Old Testament.

Jerusalem's Rebuilding Effort

"And David dwelt in the castle; therefore they called it the city of David. And he built the city round about, even from Millo round about: and Joab repaired the rest of the city" (1 Chron. 11:7-8). Millo was a natural rampart that supported the Jebusite fortress. David covered this sloping terrain with additional earth and stones to further fortify the stronghold of Zion. The rest of the city also underwent necessary repairs because of the significant destruction it had suffered in the process of conquering it. The word *build* occurs 162 times in the Bible! Again the word *about* is mentioned in 62 verses of the Wisdom Books.

Jerusalem's Levitical Orchestra & Choir of Praise

After David brought the Ark into Jerusalem he organized a holy choir to minister to the Lord. Asaph was appointed as conductor of Jerusalem's orchestra and choir.

> "And he appointed certain of the Levites to minister before the ark of the LORD, and to record, and to thank and praise the LORD God of Israel: Asaph the chief, and next to him Zechariah, Jeiel, and Shemiramoth, and Jehiel, and Mattithiah, and Eliab, and Benaiah, and Obed-edom: and Jeiel with psalteries and with harps; but Asaph made a sound with cymbals; Benaiah also and Jahaziel the priests with trumpets continually before the ark of the covenant of God" (1 Chron. 16:4-6).

The OT Narrative combination *Asaph* (17 chs), *the chief* (43 chs), *to thank and praise the LORD* (2 chs) = 62. The word *praise* occurs 162 times in the Wisdom Books.

Jerusalem's Coming Peace under Solomon's Reign

The Lord had promised David, saying, "Behold, a son shall be born to thee, who shall be a man of rest; and I will give him rest from all his enemies round about: for his name shall be Solomon, and I will give PEACE and quietness unto Israel in his days" (1 Chron. 22:9). The name Solomon means peace. The name *Solomon('s)* is mentioned in 262 verses of the Old Testament.

Jerusalem's Priests & Levites

"And he gathered together all the princes of Israel, with the priests and the Levites" (1 Chron. 23:2). The priests made their homes among all the various tribes of Israel, but they retained an obligation to go up to Jerusalem twice a year to fulfill their course of duty.

> The title *priests* occurs 62 times in the NT Narrative.
> The title *priests* is mentioned in 62 verses of the NT Narrative.
> The title *the priests and* appears in 62 verses of the OT Narrative.
> The title *the chief priests* occurs 62 times in the Bible.
> The phrase *and the Levites* occurs 62 times in the Bible.

At Jerusalem

"And Solomon gathered chariots and horsemen: and he had a thousand and four hundred chariots, and twelve thousand horsemen, which he placed in the chariot cities, and with the king at JERUSALEM" (2 Chron. 1:14). The word *at* is mentioned in 162 chapters of the New Testament.

Temple Building on Mount Moriah

"Then Solomon began to build the house of the LORD at JERUSALEM in mount Moriah, where the LORD appeared unto David his father, in the place that David had prepared in the threshingfloor of Ornan the Jebusite" (2 Chron. 3:1). In this special Jerusalem verse we find the Bible's 312,362nd word, and it refers to the *mount* upon which Jerusalem's Temple was built.

"The City of David Which Is Zion"

"Then Solomon assembled the elders of Israel, and all the heads of the tribes, the chief of the fathers of the children of Israel, unto JERUSALEM, to bring up the ark of the covenant of the LORD out of the city of David, which is ZION" (2 Chron. 5:2). The phrase *which is* occurs 62 times in the Major Prophets.

Choosing Jerusalem

"But I have chosen JERUSALEM, that my name might be there; and have chosen David to be over my people Israel" (2 Chron. 6:6). Again the phrase *people Israel* occurs 62 times in the Bible. All tenses of the word *choose* are mentioned in 62 verses of the Old Testament.

Praying toward Jerusalem's Temple

"That thine eyes may be open upon this house day and night, upon the place whereof thou hast said that thou wouldest put thy name there; to hearken unto the prayer which thy servant prayeth toward this place. Hearken therefore unto the supplications of thy servant, and of thy people Israel, which they shall make toward this place: hear thou from thy dwelling place, even from heaven; and when thou hearest, forgive" (2 Chron. 6:20-21). The Kings and Chronicles combination *pray* (56x), *toward this place* (6x) = 62.

The Chosen City

"If thy people go out to war against their enemies by the way that thou shalt send them, and they pray unto thee toward this city which thou hast chosen, and the house which I have built for thy name; Then hear thou from the heavens their prayer and their supplication, and maintain their cause" (2 Chron. 6:34-35). The OT Narrative combination *chosen* (45 vs) and *this city* (17 vs) = 62 verses.

God's Eyes Forever There on Jerusalem

Not long after dedicating the Temple, the Lord appeared unto Solomon and said, "For now have I chosen and sanctified this house, that my name may be there for ever: and mine eyes and mine heart shall be there perpetually" (2 Chron. 7:16). The word *sanctified* occurs 62 times in Scripture. The word *eyes* is mentioned in 62 chapters of the Law. From Genesis to the Synoptic Gospels the phase *eyes of* is mentioned in 62 chapters.

The word *there* occurs naturally 62 times in Luke.
The word *there* occurs naturally 62 times in John.

Silver in Jerusalem as Stones

"And the king made silver in JERUSALEM as stones, and cedar trees made he as the sycamore trees that are in the low plains in abundance" (2 Chron. 9:27). The Old Testament combination *made silver in Jerusalem as* (1x), *stones* (161x) = 162.

Jerusalem's Peace Maintained under Jehoshaphat's Godly Reign

"And Jehoshaphat the king of Judah returned to his house in PEACE to JERUSALEM" (2 Chron. 19:1). Again the word *peace* occurs 62 times in the Pauline and General Epistles.

Princes Gathered Together to Jerusalem

"Then came Shemaiah the prophet to Rehoboam, and to the <u>princes</u> of Judah, that were <u>gathered together</u> to JERUSALEM Shishak" (2 Chron. 12:5a). The title *princes* is mentioned in 162 chapters of the Bible. The phrase *gathered together* occurs 62 times in the Old Testament.

Jerusalem's True Prophets

"And they left the house of the LORD God of their fathers, and served groves and idols: and wrath came upon Judah and JERUSALEM for this their trespass. Yet he sent <u>prophets</u> to them, to bring them again unto the LORD; and they testified against them: but they would not give ear" (2 Chron. 24:18-19). The word *prophets* is mentioned in 62 verses of the OT Narrative.

Jerusalem Flows with Peace under Jehoshaphat's Godly Reign

"And also the burnt <u>offerings</u> were in abundance, with the fat of the PEACE <u>offerings</u>, and the drink offerings for every burnt offering. So the service of the house of the LORD was set in order. And Hezekiah rejoiced, and all the people, that God had prepared the people: for the thing was done suddenly" (2 Chron. 29:35-36). Again the word *offerings* occurs 62 times in the Kings and Chronicles.

Hezekiah's Great Passover Feast in Jerusalem

"And Hezekiah sent to all Israel and Judah, and wrote letters also to Ephraim and Manasseh, that they should come to the house of the LORD at JERUSALEM, to keep <u>the passover</u> unto the LORD God of Israel" (2 Chron. 30:1). Again the phrase *the Passover* occurs 62 times in Scripture.

Jerusalem's Storehouses

"And Hezekiah had exceeding much riches and honour: and he made himself treasuries for silver, and for gold, and for precious stones, and for spices, and for shields, and for all manner of pleasant jewels; Storehouses also for the increase of <u>corn</u>, and wine, and oil" (2 Chron. 32:27-28a). In the Bible the word "corn" often applies to any type of grain. The word *corn* is mentioned in 62 chapters of the Old Testament.

Jerusalem's Peacefully Flowing Waters
(Part 3)

"This same Hezekiah also stopped the upper watercourse of Gihon, and brought it straight down to the <u>west</u> side of the city of David. And Hezekiah prospered in all his works" (2 Chron. 32:30). Through considerable effort Jerusalem's spring had been redirected into two rivulets which led to an upper pool and a lower pool. Here a record is given of the king's completed work of sending the upper watercourse to a safer pool location called Siloam meaning sent. Hezekiah's carved tunnel was successfully completed under very heavy labor and cost. The new pool now lay safely inside a newly fortified wall which was constructed against Assyria's threatening invasion. Here the word *west* is the 333,462nd word of the Bible, and it refers to west side of Jerusalem.

Jerusalem's Temple Vessels Plundered

"And when the year was expired, king Nebuchadnezzar sent, and brought him to Babylon, with the goodly vessels of the house of the LORD, and made Zedekiah his brother king over Judah and JERUSALEM" (2 Chron. 36:10). This verse presents the Bible's 262nd verse-mention of the name *Jerusalem*, and it records the plundering of its Temple vessels. Again the word *treasures* occurs 62 times in Scripture.

Jerusalem's Walls Fell

"And they burnt the house of God, and brake down the wall of JERUSALEM, and burnt all the palaces thereof with fire, and destroyed all the goodly vessels thereof" (2 Chron. 36:19). Again the word *fell* occurs 62 times in the NT Narrative and is mentioned in 62 verses thereof.

Cyrus Supported Jerusalem's Temple-Rebuilding by Decree

"Now in the first year of Cyrus king of Persia, that the word of the LORD by the mouth of Jeremiah might be fulfilled, the LORD stirred up the spirit of Cyrus king of Persia, that he made a proclamation throughout all his kingdom, and put it also in writing, saying, Thus saith Cyrus king of Persia, The LORD God of heaven hath given me all the kingdoms of the earth; and he hath charged me to build him an house at JERUSALEM, which is in Judah. . . . And whosoever remaineth in any place where he sojourneth, let the men of his place help him with silver, and with gold, and with goods, and with beasts, beside the freewill offering for the house of God that is in JERUSALEM" (Ezra 1:1-2, 4).

This was the first of four decrees by four successive kings concerning Jerusalem's full restoration. The first three decrees pertained only to Jerusalem's Temple. The OT Narrative combination *the house of God that* (1 v), *is in* (61 v) = 62 verses.

Go Up to Jerusalem

"Who is there among you of all his people? his God be with him, and let him go up to JERUSALEM, which is in Judah, and build the house of the LORD God of Israel, he is the God, which is in JERUSALEM" (Ezra 1:3). This was part of Cyrus' decree. The OT Narrative combination *go up* (61 vs), *to Jerusalem which is in Judah* (1 v) = 62 verses.

> The word *go* is mentioned in 62 verses of Numbers.
> The word *go* occurs 162 times in the Kings and Chronicles.
> The word *up* is mentioned in 162 chapters of the New Testament.

Unto Jerusalem

"All the vessels of gold and of silver were five thousand and four hundred. All these did Sheshbazzar bring up with them of the captivity that were brought up from Babylon unto JERUSALEM" (Ezra 1:11).

> The word *unto* is mentioned in 162 verses of Second Kings.
> The word *unto* occurs 62 times in Proverbs.

Jerusalem's Genealogical Priesthood Records

"These sought their register among those that were reckoned by genealogy, but they were not found: therefore were they, as polluted, put from the priesthood" (Ezra 2:62). This verse pertains to some of the priests who had returned to Jerusalem. They needed to prove their decent from Aaron's family line but tragically could not. The Old Testament combination *the priests* (260x) and *that were reckoned by genealogy* (2x) = 262.

Darius Supported Jerusalem's Temple-Completion by Decree
"Also I have made a decree, that whosoever shall alter this word, let timber be pulled down from his house, and being set up, let him be hanged thereon; and let his house be made a dunghill for this. And the God that hath caused his name to dwell there destroy all kings and people, that shall put to their hand to alter and to destroy this house of God <u>which is</u> <u>at</u> JERUSALEM. I Darius have made a decree; let it be done with speed" (Ezra 6:11-12).

During his second year of reign, Darius' attention was brought to the matter of the unfinished House of God in Jerusalem. He answered Governor Tatnai's letter with this strong rebuke. Again the phrase *which is* occurs 62 times in the Major Prophets. Again the word *at* is mentioned in 162 chapters of the New Testament.

Jerusalem's Passover Restored
"And the children of the captivity kept <u>the passover</u> upon the fourteenth day of the first month" (Ezra 6:19). Here the word Passover is the 341,162nd word of the Bible. Again the phrase *the passover* occurs 62 times in Scripture.

Artaxerxes Supported Jerusalem's Temple-Beautification by Decree
"Now this is the copy of the letter that the king Artaxerxes gave unto Ezra the priest, the scribe, even a scribe of the words of the commandments of the LORD, and of his statutes to Israel. Artaxerxes, king of kings, unto Ezra the priest, a scribe of the law of the God of heaven, perfect <u>PEACE</u>, and at such a time. I make a decree, that all they of the people of Israel, and of his priests and Levites, in my realm, which are minded of their own freewill to go <u>up</u> to JERUSALEM, go with thee" (Ezra 7:11-13).

This passage presents the OT Narrative's 62nd chapter-mention of the word *peace*, and it refers to Jerusalem's peace. Again the word *peace* is mentioned in 62 verses of the Major Prophets. Again the word *up* is mentioned in 162 chapters of the New Testament.

Ezra's Thanksgiving
For the Beautification of God's House in Jerusalem
"Blessed be the LORD God of our fathers, which hath put such a thing as this in the king's heart, to beautify <u>the house of the LORD</u> which is in JERUSALEM" (Ezra 7:27). Again the title *the house of the LORD* is mentioned in 162 verses of OT Narrative.

Jerusalem's Children of the Captivity
"And they made proclamation throughout Judah and JERUSALEM unto all the children of the <u>captivity</u>, that they should gather themselves together unto Jerusalem" (Ezra 10:7). The word *captivity* occurs naturally 62 times in the Major Prophets.

Jerusalem's Impoverished Remnant
"And they said unto me, The <u>remnant</u> that are left of the <u>captivity</u> there in the province are in great affliction and reproach: the wall of JERUSALEM also is broken down, and the gates thereof are burned with fire" (Neh. 1:3). The king granted Nehemiah leave to return to Jerusalem with a small company of men and building supplies to reconstruct the gates and walls. Two remnant waves had already returned. The Major and Minor Prophets combination *remnant* (60x), *returned to Jerusalem* (1x), *returned unto Zion* (1x) = 62. The Major and Minor Prophets

combination *remnant* (60x), *residue of his people* (1x), *returned unto Zion* (1x) = 62. Again the phrase *remnant of* occurs 62 times in the Old Testament. Again the word *captivity* occurs naturally 62 times in the Major Prophets.

Artaxerxes Supported Jerusalem's Wall Rebuilding by Decree
"Moreover I said unto the king, If it please the king, let letters be given me to the governors beyond the river, that they may convey me over till I come into Judah; And a letter unto Asaph the keeper of the king's forest, that he may give me timber to make beams for <u>the gates</u> of the palace which appertained to the house, and for the wall of the city, and for the house that I shall enter into. And the king granted me, according to the good hand of my God upon me" (Neh. 2:7-8).

The phrase *the gates* is mentioned in 62 verses of the OT.
The phrase *the gate* occurs 162 times in the Bible.
The phrase *the gate of* occurs 62 times in the Old Testament.
The phrase *the gate of* is mentioned in 62 verses of the Bible.

Rulers of Jerusalem
"And next unto them repaired Rephaiah the son of Hur, the <u>ruler</u> of the half part of JERUSALEM. . . . And next unto him repaired Shallum the son of Halohesh, the <u>ruler</u> of the half part of JERUSALEM, he and his daughters" (Neh. 3:9, 12).

The word *ruler* occurs 62 times in the Old Testament.
The word *ruler(s)* occurs 62 times in the OT Narrative.

Jerusalem's Unrelenting Conspirators
"But it came to pass, that when Sanballat, and Tobiah, and the Arabians, and the Ammonites, and the Ashdodites, heard that the walls of Jerusalem were made up, and that the breaches began to be stopped, then they were very wroth, And conspired all of them together to come and to fight <u>against</u> JERUSALEM, and to hinder it" (Neh. 4:7-8). Again the word *against* is mentioned in 62 verses of Deuteronomy.

The Holy City
"And the rulers of the people dwelt at Jerusalem: the rest of the people also cast lots, to bring one of ten to dwell in JERUSALEM <u>THE HOLY CITY</u>, and nine parts to dwell in other cities. . . . All the Levites in <u>THE HOLY CITY</u> were two hundred fourscore and four" (Neh. 11:1, 18). This passage presents the Bible's first mention of the title the Holy City. The Major and Minor Prophets combination *the city* (60 chs) and *the holy city* (2 ch) = 62 chapters.

Jerusalem's Stationed Singers
"And the sons of the singers gathered themselves together, both out of the plain country <u>round about</u> JERUSALEM, and from the villages of Netophathi" (Neh. 12:28). This verse presents the OT Narrative's 62nd verse-mention of the phrase *round about*, and it pertains to Jerusalem.

Mordecai of Jerusalem
"Now in Shushan the palace there was a certain Jew, whose name was <u>Mordecai</u>, the son of Jair, the son of Shimei, the son of Kish, a Benjamite; <u>Who had been</u> <u>carried away from JERUSALEM</u> <u>with the captivity</u> which had been carried away with Jeconiah king of Judah" (Est. 2:5-6a). The

Bible combination *Mordecai* (58x), *who had been* (1x), *carried away from Jerusalem* (2x), *with the captivity* (1x) = 62. Again the word *captivity* occurs naturally 62 times in the Major Prophets.

"Walk about Zion"

"Walk about ZION, and go round about her: tell the towers thereof. Mark ye well her bulwarks, consider her palaces; that ye may tell it to the generation following. For this God is our God for ever and ever: he will be our guide even unto death" (Ps. 48:12-14). Again the word *about* is mentioned in 62 verses of the Wisdom Books. The Major and Minor Prophets combination *walk* (60x), *round about and behold/see* (2x) = 62. The OT Narrative combination *go round* (1x), *about* (159x), *the holy city* (2x) = 162. The Law combination *her* (61 chs), *bulwarks* (1 ch) = 62 chapters. The Old Testament combination *tower/s* (61x) and *about Zion* (1x) = 62. The Old Testament combination *consider* (56 vs), *her palaces* (6 vs) = 62 verses.

God Takes Pleasure in Building the Walls of Zion

"Do good in thy good pleasure unto ZION: build thou the walls of JERUSALEM" (Ps. 51:18). The Bible combination *in thy good* (1x), *pleasure* (61x) = 62. Again the word *build* occurs 162 times in the Bible. Again the word *walls* is mentioned in 62 verses of the Old Testament. Again the phrase *wall(s) of* occurs 62 times in the Bible.

Jerusalem's Peacefully Flowing Waters
(Part 4)

"There is a river, the streams whereof shall make glad the CITY OF GOD, the holy place of the tabernacles of the most High" (Ps. 46:4). As was explained in the introduction the name Jerusalem means flowing with peace. Here the Psalmist describes his desire to see Jerusalem's continual peace, sanctity, gentleness, and tranquility. He mentions streams because various channels were cut and pipes were laid to shed water into different parts of the city. The phrase *there is a* is mentioned in 62 verses of the Bible. The title *the tabernacle of* is mentioned naturally in 162 verses of the Old Testament.

Psalm 62

In this Psalm David presents the theme of salvation in a recurring way. He wrote, "Truly my soul waiteth upon God: from him cometh my salvation. . . . My soul, wait thou only upon God; for my expectation is from him. He only is my rock and my salvation: he is my defence; I shall not be moved. In God is my salvation and my glory: the rock of my strength, and my refuge, is in God" (Ps. 62:1, 5-6). David likened the safety he found in God to the safety he found in Jerusalem's greatly fortified enclosure. This warrior-king had many enemies, and he always felt protected behind Jerusalem's towering walls but more so with God's Ark of strength presiding close by in a Tabernacle. The Bible phrases *my expectation* (1x), *my rock* (12x), *my salvation* (33x), *my defence* (8x), *my refuge* (8x) = 62.

14,862nd Verse of the Bible

"Praise waiteth for thee, O God, in SION: and unto thee shall the vow be performed" (Ps. 65:1). The Zion-related name *Sion* only occurs twice in the Old Testament, yet it occurs here in a 62nd verse of Scripture.

1062nd Verse of Psalms

"Give the king thy judgments, O God, and thy righteousness unto the king's son. He shall judge thy people with righteousness, and thy poor with judgment. The mountains shall bring PEACE to the people, and the little hills, by righteousness. . . . He shall come down like rain upon the mown grass: as showers that water the earth. In his days shall the righteous flourish; and abundance of PEACE so long as the moon endureth. He shall have dominion also from sea to sea, and from the river unto the ends of the earth" (Ps. 72:1-3, 6-8). This psalm was written for Solomon who ruled from Jerusalem; it is also highly prophetic of the Messiah.

Salem

"In SALEM also is his tabernacle, and his dwelling place in ZION" (Ps. 76:2). The psalmist used the ancient name Salem to poetically denote Jerusalem. Here the name Salem has its second and last usage in the Old Testament. Again the word *in* occurs 1062 times in the Gospels.

Round about Jerusalem's Ruinous Heaps

"O God, the heathen are come into thine inheritance; thy holy temple have they defiled; they have laid JERUSALEM on heaps. . . . Their blood have they shed like water round about JERUSALEM; and there was none to bury them" (Ps. 79:1, 3). This psalm was written by Asaph who lived in the days of Jerusalem's destruction and captivity. All forms of the word heap show the seal of Jerusalem: *heap* (38x), *heaped* (2x), *heapeth* (2x), *heaps* (20x) = 62. Again the word *about* is mentioned in 62 verses of the Wisdom Books.

Jerusalem's Distinguished Citizens

"And of ZION it shall be said, This and that man was born in her: and the highest himself shall establish her. The LORD shall count, when he writeth up the people, that this man was born there. Selah" (Ps. 87:5-6). This passage has eschatological implications. Israel will dwell safely for one thousand years under her Messiah's reign. Strangers will also be born there and have their names written in Jerusalem's registry. The phrase *sons of* occurs naturally 262 times in First and Second Chronicles. In the Bible the word *born* has 62 chapter mentions prior to this passage. Again the word *established* is mentioned in 62 chapters of the Bible. Again the word *there* occurs naturally 62 times in Luke and naturally 62 times in John.

Jerusalem's Favorable Time

"Thou shalt arise, and have mercy upon ZION: for the time to favour her, yea, the set time, is come" (Ps. 102:13). Alas, the reunification of Jerusalem under Israel's favorable military control took place in AD 1967 following the Six-Day War. This historical event marked the end of an old era and the beginning of a new one. The last time the Jews controlled Jerusalem militarily was some twenty-six hundred years earlier. The Major and Minor Prophets combination *the time* (59x), *the LORD shall arise* (1x), *have mercy upon her* (2x) = 62. The New Testament combination *mercy* (59x), *mount Sion* (2x), *the city of Jerusalem* (1x) = 62. The NT Narrative combination *a set* (1 ch), *time* (61 chs) = 62 chapters. The Bible combination *set time* (7x), *for her* (55x) = 62. The Bible combination *the time* (161 vs), *to favour her* (1 v) = 162 verses. The word *favour* is mentioned in 62 chapters of the Bible!

The word *time* is mentioned in 562 verses of the Bible.

The word *time* is mentioned in 62 verses of the Pauline/General Epistles.

The phrase *the time of* occurs 62 times in the Old Testament.

Jerusalem's Ancient Stones

"For thy servants take pleasure in her stones, and favour the dust thereof" (Ps. 102:14). This is a prophecy which also looks toward the era of Israel's twentieth-century return from worldwide captivity. One consequence which accompanies Jerusalem's liberation from Gentile control is her undertaking of modern archaeology in and around Jerusalem. The dust mentioned here refers to the sifting process which fine soil undergoes during archaeological digs. Israel has built several museums and filled them with her findings from the environs of Jerusalem. The Old Testament combination *take pleasure in her* (1x), *stones* (161x) = 162. The Bible combination *pleasure* (61x), *in her stones* (1x) = 62. The term *the dust* occurs naturally 62 times in the Old Testament.

Jerusalem's Praiseworthy God

"To the name of the LORD in ZION, and his praise in JERUSALEM" (Ps. 102:21). The phrase *the name of* is mentioned in 262 verses of the Bible. Again the word *praise* occurs 162 times in the Wisdom Books.

Jerusalem's Division of East & West

"As far as the east is from the west, so far hath he removed our transgressions from us" (Ps. 103:12). Israel is a land bridge between three continents. It also serves as a boundary between east and west. At the heart of Israel lies its capital Jerusalem. There our sins were removed in a single day through the Messianic Savior's substitutional death. This verse presents the Bible's 62nd verse-mention of the phrase *the east*, and it refers indirectly to a city of the east—Jerusalem. The phrase *the west* occurs 62 times in Scripture.

The Jerusalem Temple's Chief Cornerstone

"The stone which the builders refused is become the head stone of the corner" (Ps. 118:22). This verse consists of 62 letters!

The Tribes Go through Jerusalem's Gates

"I was glad when they said unto me, Let us go into the house of the LORD. Our feet shall stand within thy gates, O JERUSALEM. JERUSALEM is builded as a city that is compact together: Whither the tribes go up, the tribes of the LORD, unto the testimony of Israel, to give thanks unto the name of the LORD" (Ps. 122:1-4). The title *the house of the LORD* is mentioned in 162 verses of the OT Narrative. Again the phrase *the gates* is mentioned in 62 verses of the Old Testament. Again the phrase *the tribes of* occurs 62 times in the Bible. Again the word *go* is mentioned in 62 verses of Numbers. Again the word *up* is mentioned in 162 chapters of the New Testament.

Jerusalem's Fleeting Peace

"Pray for the PEACE of JERUSALEM: they shall prosper that love thee. PEACE be within thy walls, and prosperity within thy palaces. For my brethren and companions' sakes, I will now say, PEACE be within thee" (Ps. 122:6-8). The Wisdom Books combination *pray for the peace of Jerusalem* (1x), *they shall* (54x), *prosper* (6x), *that love thee* (1x) = 62. The word *thee* is mentioned in 262 verses of the Psalms. The word *love* is mentioned in 162 chapters of the Bible.

Jerusalem's Surrounding Mountains

"As <u>the mountains</u> are round <u>about</u> JERUSALEM, so the LORD is round about his people from henceforth even for ever" (Ps. 125:2). Jerusalem is surrounded by mountains. Some are even higher in elevation than Jerusalem. Again the phrase *the mountain* occurs 62 times in the Bible. Again the word *about* is mentioned in 62 verses of the Wisdom Books.

Jerusalem's Goodness

"The LORD shall bless thee <u>out of ZION</u>: and thou <u>shalt see</u> <u>the good of JERUSALEM</u> <u>all the days</u> of thy <u>life</u>" (Ps. 128:5). The Bible combination *out of Zion/Sion* (12x) and *goodness* (50x) = 62. The word *good* occurs naturally 62 times in the Psalms. The Old Testament combination *shall see* (61x), *the good of Jerusalem* (1x) = 62. Again the phrase *all the days* is mentioned in 62 verses of the Bible. The word *life* occurs 62 times in the Law.

It Pleased the Lord to Establish Jerusalem

"Whatsoever the LORD <u>pleased</u>, that did he in heaven, and in earth, in the seas, and all deep places" (Ps. 135:6). The word *pleased* occurs 62 times in Scripture.

Jerusalem's Blessedness

"<u>Blessed be</u> the LORD <u>out of</u> ZION, which dwelleth at JERUSALEM. Praise ye the LORD" (Ps. 135:21). Again the phrase *out of* occurs naturally 162 times in the NT Narrative.

The phrase *blessed be* is mentioned in 62 verses of the Bible.
The word *blessed* is mentioned in 62 verses of the Wisdom Books.
The word *blessing* is mentioned naturally in 62 verses of the Bible.

"If I Forget Thee, O Jerusalem"

"If I forget <u>thee</u>, O JERUSALEM, let my right hand forget her cunning. If I do not remember <u>thee</u>, let my tongue cleave to the roof of my mouth; if I prefer not JERUSALEM above my chief <u>joy</u>" (Ps. 137:5-6). Again the word *thee* is mentioned in 262 verses of the Psalms. The phrase *my heart* is mentioned in 62 chapters of the Bible. The word *joy* occurs naturally 62 times in the New Testament.

Jerusalem's Joyful Israelite Children

"Let Israel rejoice in him that made him: let <u>the children</u> of ZION be <u>joyful</u> in their King" (Ps. 149:2). Again the word *joy* occurs naturally 62 times in the New Testament.

The word *children* is mentioned in 62 verses of Deuteronomy.
The phrase *the children* occurs 62 times in the New Testament.
The phrase *the children of* is mentioned in 62 verses of Nehemiah.
The phrase *the children of Israel* is naturally in 62 verses of Joshua.

~~~~~

The name *Israel* is mentioned in 162 verses of Second Chronicles.
The name *Israel* occurs 62 times in the Psalms.
The name *Israel* occurs 62 times in Ezra and Nehemiah.

Son of God's Name to Be Revealed in Jerusalem

"Who hath ascended up into heaven, or descended? who hath gathered the wind in his fists? who hath bound the waters in a garment? who hath established all the ends of the earth? what is his name, and what is his son's name, if thou canst tell?" (Prov. 30:4) Many centuries later the name of God's Son was revealed in Jerusalem. This took place forty days after His birth when He was taken from Bethlehem to Jerusalem for His mother's Mosaic purification ceremony. A priest held Him up in his arms and blessed Him after having been promised by the Spirit of God that he would not die until he had seen the Lord's Anointed One. This name was revealed in a much more public and profound way during His adult ministry.

The phrase *his son* is mentioned in 62 verses of First/Second Chronicles.
The phrase *his son* is mentioned in 162 verses of the Old Testament.

The Preacher-King of Jerusalem

"I the Preacher was king over Israel in JERUSALEM" (Eccles. 1:12). Solomon had much godly knowledge and wisdom to impart to the people of Jerusalem. The Bible combination *I the preacher* (1x) and *preached* (61x) = 62. The phrase *king over* occurs 62 times in the Bible. The phrase *over Israel* occurs 62 times in the OT Narrative.

The Daughters of Jerusalem

"He made the pillars thereof of silver, the bottom thereof of gold, the covering of it of purple, the midst thereof being paved with love, for the daughters of JERUSALEM" (Song 3:10). Again the word *love* is mentioned in 162 chapters of the Bible. The Bible: *the daughters* (58x), *the daughter/s of the king* (1x), *the king's daughters* (3x) = 62.

The OT Narrative: *the daughter of* (52 vs), *the daughters of* (10 v) = 62 verses.
The OT Narrative: *the daughter* (52 vs), *the daughters* (10 v) = 62 verses.

The Daughters of Zion

"Go forth, O ye daughters of ZION, and behold king Solomon with the crown wherewith his mother crowned him in the day of his espousals, and in the day of the gladness of his heart" (Song 3:11). Here the keyword *Zion* is the 444,162nd word of the Bible.

The phrase *daughters of* occurs 62 times in the Old Testament.

62nd Verse of Solomon's Song

"I am come into my garden, my sister, my spouse: I have gathered my myrrh with my spice; I have eaten my honeycomb with my honey; I have drunk my wine with my milk: eat, O friends; drink, yea, drink abundantly, O beloved" (Song 5:1). This verse concerns the king's grand wedding celebration in Jerusalem.

Love for the King of Jerusalem

"I charge you, O daughters of JERUSALEM, if ye find my beloved, that ye tell him, that I am sick of love" (Song 5:8). This verse presents the Wisdom Books' 62nd occurrence of the word *love*, and it pertains to one betrothed girl's love for the King of Jerusalem.

Rest & Sleep for the King of Jerusalem

"I charge you, O daughters of JERUSALEM, that ye stir not up, nor awake my love, until he please" (Song 8:4). This verse presents the Wisdom Books' 62nd verse-mention of the word *love*, and it pertains to love for the King of Jerusalem. The Old Testament combination *sleep* (61x) and *until he please* (1x) = 62.

Millennial City of Jerusalem Established

"The word that Isaiah the son of Amoz saw concerning Judah and JERUSALEM. And it shall come to pass in the last days, that <u>the mountain</u> of the LORD'S house shall be <u>established</u> in the top of the mountains, and shall be exalted above the hills; and all nations shall flow unto it" (Isa. 2:1-2). Again the phrase *the mountain* occurs 62 times in the Bible. Again the word *established* is mentioned in 62 chapters of the Bible.

Jerusalem's Final Sanctification

"When the Lord shall have washed away the filth of the daughters of ZION, and shall have purged the blood of JERUSALEM from the midst thereof by the spirit of judgment, and by the spirit of burning" (Isa. 4:4). Again the word *sanctified* occurs 62 times in Scripture.

Parable of God's Beloved Vineyard in Jerusalem

"Now will I sing to my wellbeloved a song of my <u>beloved</u> touching his vineyard. My wellbeloved hath a vineyard in a very fruitful hill. . . . And now, O inhabitants of Jerusalem, and men of Judah, judge, I pray you, betwixt me and my vineyard" (Isa. 5:1, 3). The word *beloved* is mentioned naturally in 62 chapters of the Bible.

Messiah Will Cause Jerusalem to Flow with Peace

"For unto us . . . a son is given: and the government shall be upon his shoulder: and his name shall be called . . . The Prince of PEACE. Of the increase of his government and PEACE there shall be no end . . . upon his kingdom, to order it, and to <u>establish it with judgment and with justice from henceforth even for ever</u>" (Isa. 9:6-7d). The words *establish it with judgment and with justice from henceforth even for ever* consist of 62 letters!

Jerusalem's Chief Administrator

"And the key of the house of David will I lay upon his shoulder; so he shall <u>open,</u> and none shall shut; and he shall shut, and none shall open" (Isa. 22:22). As was the custom, a chief steward over another's house would proudly walk about town displaying his master's household keys attached to a large ribbon and worn about his neck. This display was a symbol of his trustworthiness and high station. This verse presents the Bible's 62nd occurrence of the word *open*, and it refers to Jerusalem's faithful chief administrator Eliakim who replaced Shebna as Hezekiah's new prime minister. Revelation 3:7 repeats the latter portion of this verse, and the ascended King of the Jews is the One holding this prized key.

Jerusalem's Defensed Walls

"<u>In that day</u> shall this song be sung in the land of Judah; We have a strong <u>city</u>; salvation will God appoint for <u>walls</u> and bulwarks" (Isa. 26:1). This verse refers to the golden city of Jerusalem in the days when her Great Messianic King shall be reigning in her midst. The phrase *in that day* is mentioned in 62 chapters of the Old Testament. Again the word *city* occurs 362 times in the OT Narrative. Again the word *walls* is mentioned in 62 verses of the Old Testament.

Jerusalem's Sure Foundation

"Therefore thus saith the Lord GOD, Behold, <u>I lay in Zion</u> for a <u>foundation</u> a <u>stone</u>, a <u>tried stone</u>, a <u>precious corner stone</u>, a sure foundation: he that believeth shall not make haste" (Isa. 28:16). This verse presents the Bible's 62nd occurrence of the name *Zion*, and it speaks of Jerusalem's lowly yet exalted Messiah standing in her midst. The Bible's 162nd verse-mention of the word *stone* presents the accomplishment of this prophecy: "This is the <u>stone</u> which was set at nought of you builders, which is become the head of the corner" (Acts 4:11). The Bible combination *I lay in Zion* (1x), *foundation* (54x), *corner stone* (4x), *tried stone* (1x), *precious stone* (2x) = 62.

Jerusalem's Peacefully Flowing Waters
(Part 5)

"Look upon ZION, the city of our solemnities: <u>thine eyes shall see JERUSALEM a quiet habitation</u>. . . . But there the glorious LORD will be unto us a place of broad rivers and streams; wherein shall go no galley with oars, neither shall gallant ship pass thereby" (Isa. 33:20-21). Rivers and streams make for very peaceful habitations. This is the first of several prophecies concerning Jerusalem's glorious millennial future whereby she becomes the very source of mighty flowing waters during Messiah's peaceful reign. The Bible combination *thine eyes shall see Jerusalem* (1x), *a quiet* (3x), *habitation* (58x) = 62.

Mount Zion

"For <u>out of</u> JERUSALEM shall go forth a remnant, and they that escape out <u>of mount ZION</u>: the zeal of the LORD of hosts shall do this" (Isa. 37:32). Zion and Ophel were the first mountaintops upon which Jerusalem spanned. Over time it extended to include Moriah. Mount Zion became a favorite name for Jerusalem, outranking Mount Moriah eighteen to one in the biblical narrative. Again the phrase *out of* is mentioned in 662 chapters of the Bible. The Bible combination *of Zion* (59x) and *of mount Zion* (3x) = 62.

Messiah Will Bring Peaceful News to Jerusalem

"The first shall say to ZION, Behold, behold them: and I will give to JERUSALEM one that bringeth good tidings" (Isa. 41:27). The word *tidings* is the 762nd word in this chapter and congruently the 22,962nd word in Isaiah.

962nd Verse of Isaiah

"For they call themselves of <u>THE HOLY CITY</u>, and stay themselves upon the God of Israel; The LORD of hosts is his name" (Isa. 48:2). This 62nd verse speaks of the holy city of Jerusalem. Again the Major and Minor Prophets titles *the city* (60 chs) and *the holy city* (2 chs) = 62 chapters. The Bible phrases *be holy* (41x) and *be * holy* (21x) = 62.

Peace Flowing Like a River

"O that thou hadst hearkened to my commandments! then had thy PEACE been <u>as a</u> river, and thy righteousness as the waves of the sea" (Isa. 48:18). This prophetic word pertained to Israel and its ordained capital Jerusalem. The phrase *as a* occurs 62 times in Isaiah.

Jerusalem's Spiritual Uncleanness

"Awake, awake; put on thy strength, O ZION; put on thy beautiful garments, O JERUSALEM, THE HOLY CITY: for henceforth there shall no more come into thee the uncircumcised and the unclean" (Isa. 52:1). This end-time prophecy envisions the performance of Messiah's priestly service over the sinful people of Jerusalem. The word *unclean* occurs 162 times in the Old Testament.

Jerusalem's Spotless Lamb

"He was oppressed, and <u>he was afflicted, yet he opened not his mouth</u>: he is brought as a <u>lamb</u> to the slaughter, and as a sheep before her shearers is dumb, so he openeth not his mouth" (Isa. 53:7). This verse presents the Bible's 62nd verse-mention of the word *lamb*, and history reveals that it pertains to Jerusalem's Incarnate Messiah Who was offered up as a Sacrifice just outside her city walls. The Bible combination *he was* (461x), *afflicted yet he opened not his mouth* (1x) = 462.

Jerusalem's Redemptive Future

"Break forth into joy, sing together, ye waste places of JERUSALEM: <u>for the LORD</u> hath <u>comforted</u> his people, he hath <u>redeemed</u> JERUSALEM" (Isa. 52:9). Instead of destruction, Jerusalem could now enjoy redemption through the salvific work of her heaven-sent Messiah. The phrase *for the LORD/Lord* is mentioned in 162 chapters of the Old Testament. The word *comfort* is mentioned in 62 verses of the Bible. The word *redeemed* occurs 62 times in the Bible.

Messiah Arrested, Tried, Convicted, Executed & Buried in Jerusalem

"He was taken from prison and from judgment: and who shall declare his generation? for he was cut off out of the land of the living: for the transgression of my people was he stricken. And he made his grave with the wicked, and with the rich in his death; because he had done no violence, neither was any deceit in his mouth" (Isa. 53:8-9). The entirety of this Suffering Servant passage runs from 52:13 through 53:12 and consists of 462 words.

Jerusalem's Gates Continually Opened during Golden Age

"Therefore <u>thy gates</u> shall be open <u>continually</u>; they shall not be shut day nor night; that men may bring unto thee the forces of the Gentiles, and that their kings may be brought" (Isa. 60:11). Again the phrase *the gates* is mentioned in 62 verses of the Old Testament. The word *always* occurs 62 times in Scripture.

62nd Chapter of Isaiah

This chapter has Israel's final restoration in view, and its chief city—its spiritual capital Jerusalem—is the focus of attention. This 62nd chapter of Isaiah consists of 362 words!

"For <u>ZION'S sake</u> will I not hold my <u>PEACE</u>, and for JERUSALEM'S <u>sake</u> I will not rest, until the righteousness thereof go forth as brightness, and the salvation thereof as a lamp that burneth" (Isa. 62:1). The Lord expressed His unfailing commitment to see His people reach their ideal spiritual state and national restoration. Only in this way will the nations come to the city's perfect light. Again the Bible combination *Zion/'s* (153x) and *Sion/'s* (9x) = 162. This 62nd-chapter passage presents the Bible's 62nd chapter-mention of the word *sake*, and we see its relation to Jerusalem and Zion. Again the word *peace* is mentioned in 62 verses of the Major Prophets. The keyword *Jerusalem* actually occurs in this 62nd chapter.

The Lord encourages saints to pray until the city's momentous day culminates. He therefore declares, "I have set watchmen upon thy <u>walls</u>, O JERUSALEM, which shall never hold their

PEACE day nor night: ye that make mention of the LORD, keep not silence, <u>And give him no rest, till he establish, and till he make JERUSALEM a praise in the earth</u>" (vv. 6-7). Again the word *walls* is mentioned in 62 verses of the Old Testament. The underlined verse number seven is the 18,862nd verse of the Bible, and it employs the name *Jerusalem*. The word *make* occurs 62 times in the Gospels.

"Go through, go <u>through the gates</u>; prepare ye the way of the people; cast up, cast up the highway; gather out the stones; lift up a standard for the people" (v. 10).

>The phrase *through the* occurs 62 times in the New Testament.
>The NT Narrative: *through* (61x), *the gates of* (1x) = 62.
>The OT Narrative: *through* (61x), *the gates of Jerusalem be opened* (1x) = 62.

"Behold, the LORD hath proclaimed unto the end of the world, Say ye to <u>the daughter of</u> ZION, Behold, thy salvation cometh; behold, his reward is with him, and his work before him. And they shall call them, <u>The holy people</u>, The <u>redeemed</u> of the LORD: and thou shalt be called, Sought out, <u>A city</u> <u>not forsaken</u>" (vv. 11-12). The Bible likens earthly Zion as the daughter or offspring city from the heavenly Zion. Again the title *the daughter(s) of* is mentioned in 62 verses of the OT Narrative. Again the word *redeemed* occurs 62 times in the Bible! The Bible combination *the holy people* (3x), *a city* (54x), *not forsaken* (5x) = 62.

Zion's Travail

"Who hath heard such a thing? who hath seen such things? Shall the earth be made to bring forth in one day? or shall a nation be born at once? for as soon as ZION travailed, she <u>brought forth</u> her children. Shall I bring to the birth, and not cause to bring forth? saith the LORD: shall I cause to bring forth, and shut the womb? saith thy God" (Isa. 66:8-9). Again the phrase *brought forth* is mentioned in 62 chapters of the Bible.

Jerusalem's Peacefully Flowing Waters
(Part 6)

"Rejoice ye with JERUSALEM, and be glad with her, all ye that love her: rejoice for joy with her, all ye that mourn for her . . . . For thus saith the LORD, Behold, <u>I will extend PEACE to her like a river</u>, and the glory of the Gentiles like a FLOWING stream: then shall ye suck, ye shall be borne upon her sides, and be dandled upon her knees. As one whom his mother comforteth, so will I comfort you; and ye shall be comforted in JERUSALEM" (Isa. 66:10, 12-13). A descriptive promise is given that Jerusalem will one day flow with peace. The Bible combination *I will extend peace* (1x), *to her* (58x), *like a river* (3x) = 62.

Flee Jerusalem

"O ye children of Benjamin, gather yourselves to flee <u>out of</u> the midst of JERUSALEM, and blow the trumpet in Tekoa, and set up a sign of fire in Beth-haccerem: for evil appeareth out of the north, and great destruction" (Jer. 6:1). This is the 62nd occurrence of the name *Jerusalem* in the Major Prophets, and it is a command from God for Benjamin's tribe to forsake the city. Judah refuses to flee. Again the phrase *out of* is mentioned in 662 chapters of the Bible.

Jerusalem Crying

"<u>Behold the voice</u> <u>of the cry of</u> <u>the daughter of</u> <u>my people</u> because of them that dwell in a far country: Is not the LORD in ZION? is not her king in her? Why have they provoked me to anger with their graven images, and with strange vanities?" (Jer. 8:19) The Jeremiah combination *behold the voice* (1x), *of the cry of* (2x), *the daughter of* (14x), *my people* (45x) = 62.

Jerusalem Smitten

Jeremiah lamented, "Hast thou utterly rejected Judah? hath thy soul lothed ZION? why hast thou smitten us, and there is no healing for us? we looked for peace, and there is no good; and for the time of healing, and behold trouble!" (Jer. 14:19) Again the word *smitten* is mentioned in 62 verses of Scripture.

Jerusalem Entered

The first captivity had already transpired. There were two more to come if the leftover remnant did not do as divinely instructed. On a redemptive note, Jeremiah told the inhabitants of Jerusalem that if they would turn and hallow the Sabbath, "Then shall there enter into the gates of this city kings and princes sitting upon the throne of David, riding in chariots and on horses, they, and their princes, the men of Judah, and the inhabitants of JERUSALEM: and this city shall remain for ever" (Jer. 17:25). The word *enter* is mentioned in 62 chapters of the Old Testament.

Jerusalem Defiled

The Lord instructed Jeremiah to get a clay bottle and take it before the aged priests and elders of Jerusalem. There Jeremiah broke it as a token of God's next irreversible wave of wrath to come upon Jerusalem. Among the many things Jeremiah was instructed to say was this: "And the houses of JERUSALEM, and the houses of the kings of Judah, shall be defiled as the place of Tophet, because of all the houses upon whose roofs they have burned incense unto all the host of heaven, and have poured out drink offerings unto other gods" (Jer. 19:13). The drink offering was a daily act of devotion to God carried out at the great altar in Jerusalem. The word *defiled* is mentioned in 62 verses of the Old Testament.

Jerusalem Preserved

"Behold, the days come, saith the LORD, that I will raise unto David a righteous Branch, and a King shall reign and prosper, and shall execute judgment and justice in the earth" (Jer. 23:5). This verse refers to Messiah's millennial reign. The related Bible phrases *a king* (48x), *a king's* (2x), *a kingdom* (12x) = 62. Again the word *reign* is mentioned in 162 verses of the Bible.

Jerusalem Saved

"In his days Judah shall be saved, and Israel shall dwell SAFELY: and this is his name whereby he shall be called, THE LORD OUR RIGHTEOUSNESS" (Jer. 23:6). You will recall that Jerusalem's root word *salam* means 'peace' or 'to be safe.' So here, we see a promise that Jerusalem will one day dwell in perfect safety under Messiah's reign. The Old Testament combination *Judah shall be* (6x), *saved* (47x), *dwell safely* (9x) = 62.

Jerusalem Watered

"Therefore they shall come and sing in the height of ZION, and shall FLOW together to the goodness of the LORD, for wheat, and for wine, and for oil, and for the young of the flock and of the herd: and their soul shall be as a watered garden; and they shall not sorrow any more at all" (Jer. 31:12). Again the word *height* occurs 62 times in the Bible. The Old Testament combination *they shall come and sing* (1x), *and their soul shall be as a* (1x), *watered* (10x), *garden* (47x), *and they shall not sorrow* (1x), *any more at all* (2x) = 62.

Jerusalem Desolated

"For through the anger of the LORD it came to pass in JERUSALEM and Judah, till he had cast them out from his presence, that Zedekiah rebelled against the king of Babylon" (Jer. 52:3). This verse presents the Major Prophets' 62nd chapter-mention of the name *Jerusalem*. The Old Testament combination *for through the anger of the LORD* (2x), *it came to pass in* (52x), *Jersualem and Judah* (5x), *till he had cast them out from his presence* (1x), *that Zedekiah rebelled against the king of Babylon* (2x) = 62.

Jerusalem Lamenting

The weeping prophet began the first of his five lamentations: "How doth the city sit solitary, that was full of people! how is she become as a widow! she that was great among the nations, and princess among the provinces, how is she become tributary!" (Lam. 1:1) The combination of all forms of the word *lament* (61x) and *solitarily* (1x) = 62.

Jerusalem Mourning

"The ways of ZION do mourn, because none come to the solemn feasts: all her gates are desolate: her priests sigh, her virgins are afflicted, and she is in bitterness" (Lam. 1:4). The Old Testament combination *the ways of Zion do* (1x), *mourn* (39x), *because none come to* (1x), *the solemn feasts* (5x), *all her gates* (1x), *are desolate* (8x), *her priests sigh* (1x), *her virgins are afflicted and she is* (1x), *in bitterness* (5x) = 62.

Zion's Walls & Gates Destroyed

"The LORD hath purposed to destroy the wall of the daughter of ZION: he hath stretched out a line, he hath not withdrawn his hand from destroying: therefore he made the rampart and the wall to lament; they languished together. Her gates are sunk into the ground" (Lam. 2:8-9a). Here the word *the* is the 1062nd word of Lamentations, and it serves as the definite article for Zion's title.

Jerusalem No Longer the Perfection of Beauty

"All that pass by clap their hands at thee; they hiss and wag their head at the daughter of JERUSALEM, saying, Is this the city that men call The perfection of beauty, The joy of the whole earth?" (Lam. 2:15) This verse presents the Major Prophets' 162nd occurrence of the name *Jerusalem*, and it concerns her lamentation. The city had been burned with fire along with her beloved Temple. The Bible combination *perfection* (11x), *beauty* (49x), *the joy of the whole earth* (2x) = 62.

Jerusalem Remnant Now Faint-Hearted

In his fifth and final lamentation over Jerusalem Jeremiah said, The crown is fallen from our head: woe unto us, that we have sinned! For this our heart is faint; for these things our eyes are dim. Because of the mountain of ZION, which is desolate, the foxes walk upon it" (Lam. 5:16-18). All forms of the word faint show the numeric seal of Jerusalem: *faint* (41x), *fainted* (12x), *faintest* (1x), *fainteth* (4x), *faint-hearted* (3x), *faintness* (1x) = 62.

Jerusalem Set in the Midst of the Nations

"Thus saith the Lord GOD; This is JERUSALEM: I have set it in the midst of the nations and countries that are round about her" (Ezek. 5:5). The uppercase word *This* is mentioned in 62 verses of the Major and Minor Prophets and occurs 62 times in the NT Narrative. The NT Narrative combination *set* (57x) and *in the midst of the* (5x) = 62. Again the word *about* is mentioned in 62 verses of the Wisdom Books. The phrase *in the midst of* occurs 62 times in Ezekiel.

The Lord's Third Fury to Come upon Jerusalem

"And it came to pass, while they were slaying them, and I was left, that I fell upon my face, and cried, and said, Ah Lord GOD! wilt thou destroy all the residue of Israel in thy pouring out of thy fury upon JERUSALEM?" (Ezek. 9:8) There was one more Babylonian attack left to come upon Jerusalem. Ezekiel was given a vision of it. The word *upon* occurs 262 times in the New Testament.

Jerusalem a Burden Not a Blessing to the Lord

"Say thou unto them, Thus saith the Lord GOD; This burden concerneth the prince in JERUSALEM, and all the house of Israel that are among them" (Ezek. 12:10). The phrase *thus saith the LORD God/Lord GOD* occurs 162 times in the Old Testament and is mentioned in 162 verses thereof. The word *burden* occurs 62 times in the Old Testament.

A Prophecy Concerning Jerusalem

"To wit, the prophets of Israel which prophesy concerning JERUSALEM, and which see visions of peace for her, and there is no peace, saith the Lord GOD" (Ezek. 13:16). The phrase *concerning the* is mentioned in 62 chapters of the Bible.

Four Judgments Coming upon Jerusalem

"For thus saith the Lord GOD; How much more when I send my four sore judgments upon JERUSALEM, the sword, and the famine, and the noisome beast, and the pestilence, to cut off from it man and beast?" (Ezek. 14:21) The word *four* is mentioned in 62 verses of the Law. Again the word *upon* occurs 262 times in the New Testament.

> The word *judgment(s)* is seen in 62 verses of the Law.
> The word *judgment(s)* occurs 62 times in the Psalms.

Jerusalem Must Know Her Abominations

"Son of man, cause JERUSALEM to know her abominations" (Ezek. 16:2). The word *cause* occurs 62 times in the Wisdom Books. The word *abomination(s)* is mentioned in 62 verses of the Major Prophets.

His Holy Lordship of Jerusalem

"And I will establish my covenant with thee; and thou shalt know that I am the LORD" (Ezek. 16:62). The phrase *thou shalt* is mentioned in 62 verses of the Wisdom Books. The word *know* occurs 62 times in Judges and 262 times in the New Testament. The title *I am the LORD* occurs 62 times in Ezekiel.

The Holy Flock of Jerusalem

"As the holy <u>flock</u>, as the <u>flock</u> of JERUSALEM in her solemn feasts; so shall the waste cities be filled with <u>flocks</u> of men: and they shall know that I am the LORD" (Ezek. 36:38).

> The word *flock* is mentioned in 62 chapters from Genesis to NT Narrative.
> The word *flock(s)* is mentioned naturally in 162 verses of the Old Testament.

Jerusalem's Eastern Gate in the Millennium

During the millennium Jerusalem will be renewed and exist in dimensions far greater than ever before seen. The returned Messiah will have His very own gate, the outer Eastern Gate. However, the eastern gate of the inner court will be shared by all. Both these gates will only be open on the Sabbath and on the new moon. The word *moon(s)* occurs 62 times in the Bible.

"Then said the LORD unto me; This gate shall be shut, it shall not be opened, and no man shall <u>enter</u> in by it; because the LORD, <u>the God of Israel</u>, hath entered in by it, therefore it shall be shut" (Ezek. 44:2). Again the word *enter* is mentioned in 62 chapters of the Old Testament. Again the title *the God of Israel* is mentioned in 62 chapters of the Bible.

"Now when <u>the prince</u> shall prepare a voluntary burnt offering or PEACE <u>offerings</u> voluntarily unto the LORD, one shall then <u>open him the gate</u> that looketh toward the <u>east</u>, and he shall prepare his burnt offering and his PEACE <u>offerings</u>, as he did on the sabbath day: then he shall <u>go forth</u>; and after his going forth <u>one shall shut the gate</u>" (46:12). The prince may refer to either David or the Messiah; Scripture does not make this clear. The Bible combination *Messiah the Prince* (1x), *the prince* (58x), *the prince's* (2x), *open him the gate* (1x) = 62. The Bible titles *the prince* (58x) and *the * prince* (4x) = 62. Again the word *offerings* occurs 62 times in the Kings and Chronicles. The word *east* is mentioned in 62 verses of the Major Prophets. The combined phrases *go forth* (61 chs) and *one shall shut the gate* (1 ch) = 62 chapters. There are 62 words in this Jerusalem-Temple verse.

Jerusalem's Peacefully Flowing Waters
(Part 7)

"Afterward [566,562] he brought me again unto the door of the house; and, behold, <u>waters</u> <u>issued out from under the threshold</u> of the house eastward: for the forefront of the house stood toward the <u>east</u>, and the <u>waters</u> came down from under from the right side of the house, at the south side of the altar. Then brought he me out of the way of the gate northward, and led me about the way without unto the utter gate by the way that looketh eastward; and, behold, there ran out <u>waters</u> on the right side. And when the man that had the [566,662] line in his hand went forth eastward, he measured a thousand cubits, and he brought me through the <u>waters</u>; the <u>waters</u> were to the ankles. Again he measured a thousand, and brought me through the <u>waters</u>; the <u>waters</u> were to the knees. Again he measured a thousand, and brought me through; the <u>waters</u> were to the loins. Afterward he measured a thousand; and it was a river that I could not pass over: for the <u>waters</u> were risen, <u>waters</u> to swim in, a river that could not be passed over. And he said unto me, Son of man, hast thou [566,762] seen this? Then he brought me, and caused me to return to the brink of the river. Now when I had returned, behold, at the bank of the river were very many trees on the one side and on the other. Then said he unto me, These <u>waters</u> issue out toward the <u>east</u> country, and go down into the desert, and go into the sea: which being brought forth into the sea, the <u>waters</u> shall be healed. And it shall come to pass, that every thing that liveth, which moveth, whithersoever the rivers shall come, shall live: and there shall [566,862] be a very great multitude of fish, because these <u>waters</u> shall come thither: for they shall be healed; and every thing shall live whither the river cometh. And it shall come to pass, that the fishers shall stand upon it from En-gedi even unto En-eglaim; they shall be a place to spread forth nets; their fish shall be according to their kinds, as the fish of the great sea, exceeding many. But the miry places thereof and the marishes thereof shall not be healed; they shall be given to salt. And by the river upon the bank thereof, on this [566,962] side and on that side, shall grow all trees for meat, whose leaf shall not fade, neither shall the fruit thereof be consumed: it shall bring forth new fruit according to his months, because their <u>waters</u> they <u>issued out of the sanctuary</u>: and the fruit thereof shall be for meat, and the leaf thereof for medicine" (Ezek. 47:1-12).

In the ancient world temples were built very near a source of moving water and sometimes overtop an active spring. Ezekiel's prophecy gives us both more words and more information than all the other combined Bible prophecies regarding Jerusalem's flowing waters. Here it informs us that the source of this great flow of water was a strong spring bubbling forth from the main doorway of Messiah's east-facing Temple. Not only does this panoramic Jerusalem prophecy commence at a precise location of the Bible's 566,562nd word, but it also traverses four other locations yielding numbers suffixed with 62s. Behold the following exhaustive Bible combination of the word "spring" coupled with two important phrases from this prophecy: *spring* (22 vs), *springeth* (4 vs), *springing* (5 vs), *springs* (12 vs), *wellspring* (2 vs), *sprang* (7 vs), *sprung* (8 vs), *issued out of the sanctuary* (1 v), *issued out from under the threshold* (1 v) = 62 verses. Again the word *east* is mentioned in 62 verses of the Major Prophets.

> The word *water* occurs 62 times in the Major and Minor Prophets.
> The word *water* is mentioned in 62 verses of the New Testament.

Jerusalem's New Name in the Millennium
"It was round about eighteen thousand measures: and <u>the name of</u> the city from that day shall be, The LORD is <u>there</u>" (Ezek. 48:35). Messiah is the Lord's manifest Son, hence the second power of the Godhead. Again the phrase *the name of* is mentioned in 262 verses of the Bible. Again the word *there* occurs naturally 62 times in Luke and naturally 62 times in John.

King Darius Conquered Babylon at Age 62
"In that night was Belshazzar the king of the Chaldeans slain. And Darius the Median took the kingdom, being about THREESCORE AND TWO years old" (Dan. 5:30-31). As we saw earlier in Ezra, Darius looked favorably upon Jerusalem. Darius was 62 years old when he began to reign.

Daniel Prayed toward Jerusalem
"Now when Daniel knew that the writing was signed, he went into his house; and his windows being open in his <u>chamber</u> <u>toward JERUSALEM</u>, he kneeled upon his knees three times a day, and prayed, and gave thanks before his God, as he did aforetime" (Dan. 6:10). The Major/Minor Prophets combination *chamber/s* (59x), *toward Jerusalem* (3x) = 62. The New Testament combination *toward* (57x), *the holy city* (5x) = 62.

Daniel Prayed for Jerusalem's Past Sins
"O Lord, according to all thy righteousness, I beseech thee, let thine anger and thy fury be turned away from thy city JERUSALEM, thy holy mountain: because for our <u>sins</u>, and for the <u>iniquities</u> of our fathers, JERUSALEM and thy people are become a reproach to all that are about us" (Dan. 9:16). Confession of sin is always in order, even for a nation's sin.

> The word *sin* is mentioned in 62 verses of the Old Testament.
> The word *iniquity* occurs 262 times in the Old Testament.

The word *iniquity* is mentioned in 262 verses of the Bible.

62-Week Countdown to Messiah's Coronation

"Know therefore and understand, that from the going forth of the commandment to restore and to build JERUSALEM unto the Messiah the Prince shall be seven weeks, and THREESCORE AND TWO weeks: the street shall be built again, and the wall, even in troublous times" (Dan. 9:25). Messiah was indeed given a crown but not one that He deserved. Here we see an alignment of Jerusalem with the number 62. Again the Bible titles *the prince* (58x) and *the * prince* (4x) = 62. The word *street(s)* is mentioned in 62 chapters of the Old Testament. The word *again* occurs 62 times in the Major Prophets. The word *even* is mentioned in 162 chapters of the OT Narrative. Again the word *in* occurs 1062 times in the Gospels.

62-Week Countdown to Messiah's Crucifixion

"And after THREESCORE AND TWO weeks shall Messiah be cut off, but not for himself" (Dan. 9:26a). The word *threescore* is mentioned in 62 chapters of the Bible. The word *two* is mentioned in 262 chapters of the Old Testament. The word *be* occurs 862 times in the NT Narrative. The Bible combination *threescore and* (58x), *two weeks* (3x), *shall Messiah be cut off* (1x) = 62.

A Call for Spiritual Deliverance in Jerusalem

"And it shall come to pass, that whosoever shall call on the name of the LORD shall be delivered: for in mount ZION and in JERUSALEM shall be deliverance, as the LORD hath said, and in the remnant whom the LORD shall call" (Joel 2:32). Again the word *in* occurs 1062 times in the Gospels.

The Nations Will Divide Jerusalem

"I will also gather all nations, and will bring them down into the valley of Jehoshaphat, and will plead with them there for my people and for my heritage Israel, whom they have scattered among the nations, and parted my land" (Joel 3:2). This division of land will also include the capital Jerusalem. The word *part* occurs 62 times in the New Testament. The 62nd word in the Bible is *divided*.

As history bears out, Jerusalem became a divided city after Israel's final worldwide dispersion took place in AD 70. After putting down the final Jewish revolt in AD 135, the Romans banned Jews from living in or even entering Jerusalem. Later during medieval times, the city of Jerusalem was divided into four distinct quarters: Jewish, Muslim, Christian, and Armenian. This was done so Jerusalem's religiously diverse residences could attempt to live peaceably among each other.

After the Jewish people began to return to Israel from their worldwide dispersion in the beginning of the twentieth century AD a new problem arose. The Jewish people were not welcomed as they began to make their residences in and around the Old City. By 1947 the problem became of international interest at which time a political body known as the United Nations declared that not only Jerusalem but also the whole land should be divided into separate states—one for Israel and one for Palestine. The new lines of demarcation cut right through the city of Jerusalem, dividing it at the precise point between its old and new developments. From that time forward two names arose: East Jerusalem and West Jerusalem.

Jerusalem's Peacefully Flowing Waters
(Part 8)

"So shall ye know that I am the LORD your God dwelling in ZION, my holy mountain: then shall JERUSALEM be holy, and there shall no strangers pass through her any more. And it shall come to pass in that day, that the mountains shall drop down new wine, and the hills shall FLOW with milk, and all the rivers of Judah shall FLOW with waters, and a fountain shall come forth of the house of the LORD, and shall water the valley of Shittim" (Joel 3:17-18). Here a third prophet predicted Jerusalem's Messianic future of having a great source of flowing waters. You will recall that the first half of Jerusalem's name "yara" means to flow as water. Again the phrase *in that day* is mentioned in 62 chapters of the Old Testament. Again the title *the house of the LORD* is mentioned in 162 verses of the OT Narrative. Again the word *water* occurs 62 times in the Major and Minor Prophets. Again the word *water* is mentioned in 62 verses of the New Testament. Verse eighteen is the 22,362nd verse of the Bible.

The Lord Will Roar from Zion

"And he said, The LORD will roar from ZION, and utter his voice from JERUSALEM; and the habitations of the shepherds shall mourn, and the top of Carmel shall wither" (Amos 1:2).
The Old Testament combination *the LORD will/also shall roar* (2x), *from Zion and utter* (1x), *his voice* (38x), *from Jerusalem* (21x) = 62.

Raising David's Fallen Tabernacle in Jerusalem

"In that day will I raise up the tabernacle of David that is fallen, and close up the breaches thereof; and I will raise up his ruins, and I will build it as in the days of old" (Amos 9:11). This verse refers to David's dwelling place in Jerusalem being brought back to its former standing. For the past twenty-five years since its discovery, the ruins of David's palace have been undergoing a careful restoration process by various teams of archaeologists. This reconstruction effort includes Millo, the terraced-stone structure which supports it. Messiah will wonderfully restore it in the days of His millennial reign. The word *fallen* occurs 62 times in the Old Testament. Again the phrase *in that day* is mentioned in 62 chapters of the Old Testament. The Bible combination *will I raise up the tabernacle of David* (1x), *and I will raise up his ruins* (1x), *and I will build it as in the days* (1x), *of old* (59x) = 62.

Holiness Shall Be upon Mount Zion

"But upon mount ZION shall be deliverance, and there shall be holiness; and the house of Jacob shall possess their possessions. . . . And saviours shall come up on mount ZION to judge the mount of Esau; and the kingdom shall be the LORD'S" (Obad. 1:17, 21). Again the word *upon* occurs 262 times in the New Testament.

Jerusalem's Captive Host Shall Return

"And the captivity of this host of the children of Israel shall possess that of the Canaanites, Even unto Zarephath; and the captivity of JERUSALEM, which is in Sepharad, shall possess the cities of the south" (Obad. 20). Again the word *captivity* occurs naturally 62 times in the Major Prophets. Again the word *host* is mentioned in 62 chapters of the OT Narrative.

The Gates of Jerusalem to Suffer Evil

"For the inhabitant of Maroth waited carefully for good: but evil came down from the LORD unto the gate of JERUSALEM" (Mic. 1:12). Again the phrase *the gate of* occurs 62 times in the Old Testament; this is 62ⁿᵈ occurrence, and it refers so clearly to Jerusalem. Again the phrase *came down* occurs 62 times in the Bible.

Zion Shall Be Plowed

"Therefore shall ZION for your sake be <u>plowed</u> as a <u>field</u>, and JERUSALEM shall become heaps, and the mountain of the house as the high places of the forest" (Mic. 3:12). The Major and Minor Prophets combination *plowed* (3x) and *field* (59x) = 62. The word *field* is mentioned in 162 chapters of the Bible.

The Mountain of the House of the Lord

"But in the last days it shall come to pass, that <u>the mountain</u> of <u>the house of the LORD</u> shall be <u>established</u> in the <u>top</u> of the mountains, and <u>it shall be</u> <u>exalted</u> above the hills; and people shall FLOW unto it" (Mic. 4:1). During the forthcoming Messianic Age Jerusalem will finally live up to the meaning of its name, Flowing with Peace! This will give the people of the earth a great desire to flow to it. Again the phrase *the mountain* occurs 62 times in the Bible. Again the title *the house of the LORD* is mentioned in 162 verses of the OT Narrative. Again the word *established* is mentioned in 62 chapters of the Bible. The word *top* is mentioned in 62 chapters of the Bible. The phrase *it shall be* is mentioned in 62 chapters of the Law. The word *exalted* is mentioned in 62 verses of the Bible.

The Flock's Favorite Fold
The Stronghold of the Daughter of Zion

"And thou, O tower of the <u>flock</u>, <u>the strong hold of</u> the daughter <u>of ZION</u>, unto thee shall it come, even the first <u>dominion</u>; <u>the kingdom</u> shall come to the daughter of JERUSALEM" (Mic. 4:8). As Jerusalem's worldwide fame and dominion excelled under Solomon, so shall it excel all the more under King Messiah's millennial reign. Again the word *flock(s)* is mentioned naturally in 162 verses of the Old Testament. The word *dominion* occurs 62 times in the Bible. Again the Bible combination *the strong hold of* (3x) and *of Zion* (59x) = 62. From Genesis to the Gospels the phrase *the kingdom of* is mentioned in 62 chapters.

Jerusalem's Mountaintop Messiah

"Behold upon the mountains the feet of him that bringeth good tidings, that publisheth <u>PEACE</u>! O Judah, keep thy solemn feasts, perform thy vows: for the wicked shall no more pass through thee; he is utterly cut off" (Nah. 1:15). Again the word *peace* occurs 62 times in the Pauline/ General Epistles.

The Lord Will Save Jerusalem

"<u>In that day</u> it shall be said to JERUSALEM, Fear thou not: and to ZION, Let not thine hands be slack. The LORD thy God in the midst of thee is mighty; he will <u>save</u>, he will rejoice over thee with joy; he will rest in his love, he will joy over thee with singing" (Zeph. 3:16-17). Here salvation comes to Jerusalem in the form of God's incarnate presence. Again the phrase *in that day* is mentioned in 62 chapters of the Old Testament. The word *save* is mentioned in 62 verses of the New Testament.

The Remnant of Jerusalem

"And the LORD stirred up the spirit of Zerubbabel the son of Shealtiel, governor of Judah, and the spirit of Joshua the son of Josedech, the high priest, and the spirit of all the <u>remnant of</u> the people; and they came and did work in the house of the LORD of hosts, their God" (Hag. 1:14). Again the phrase *remnant of* occurs 62 times in the Old Testament.

Jerusalem's House of Peace

"The glory of this latter house shall be greater than of the former, saith the LORD of hosts: and in this <u>place</u> will I give PEACE, saith the LORD of hosts" (Hag. 2:9). Again the word *place* is mentioned in 162 verses of the Law.

The Measuring of Jerusalem

"Then said I, Whither goest thou? And he said unto me, To <u>measure</u> JERUSALEM, to see what is the breadth thereof, and what is the length thereof" (Zech. 2:2). Surveyors were needed to work in advance of the Temple's reconstruction. Moreover, the angel spoke of the city's prolific expansion during the golden age of Messiah's rule and reign. The word *measure* is mentioned in 62 verses of the Bible.

Messiah's Inheritance of Jerusalem

"And the LORD shall <u>inherit</u> Judah his portion in the holy land, and shall <u>choose</u> JERUSALEM again" (Zech. 2:12). At Messiah's Second Coming every Jew in Judea will readily receive Him and give Him the crown He so royally deserves. The word *inherit* occurs 62 times in Scripture. The combined words *choose* (59x) and *chooseth* (3x) = 62.

The Temple of Jerusalem

"And speak unto him, saying, Thus speaketh the LORD of hosts, saying, Behold the man whose name is The BRANCH; and he shall grow up out of his place, and he shall <u>build</u> <u>the temple</u> of the LORD" (Zech. 6:12). The majestic millennial Temple will be constructed in Jerusalem with Messiah's architectural oversight. Again the word *build* occurs 162 times in the Bible. The phrase *the temple* occurs 62 times in the Gospels.

The Lord Will Dwell in the Midst of Jerusalem

"Thus saith the LORD; I am returned unto ZION, and will <u>dwell in the midst of</u> JERUSALEM: and Jerusalem shall be called a <u>city of truth</u>; and the mountain of the LORD of hosts the holy mountain" (Zech. 8:3). The Lord will return one day and make Jerusalem His hometown, even His capital. Again the phrase *dwell in* is mentioned in 162 verses of the Bible. Again the phrase *in the midst of* occurs 62 times in Ezekiel. The Minor Prophets combination *Jerusalem* (61 vs) and *city of truth* (1 v) = 62 verses.

Many Nations Will Come to Jerusalem

"Yea, many people and strong nations shall <u>come to</u> seek the LORD of hosts in JERUSALEM, and to pray before the LORD" (Zech. 8:22). Again the phrase *come to* is mentioned in 62 chapters of the OT Narrative and in 62 chapters of the Major Prophets.

From Jerusalem's Messianic King Peace Will Flow to the Nations

"Rejoice greatly, O daughter of ZION; shout, O daughter of JERUSALEM: behold, thy <u>King</u>

cometh unto thee: he is just, and having salvation; lowly, and riding upon an ass, and upon a colt the foal of an ass. And I will cut off the chariot from Ephraim, and the horse from Jerusalem, and the battle bow shall be cut off: and he shall speak PEACE unto the heathen: and his dominion shall be from sea even to sea, and from the river even to the ends of the earth" (Zech. 9:9-10). Again the word *king* occurs 62 times in the NT Narrative.

Rain Will Bring Grassy Fields to Jerusalem
"Ask ye of the LORD <u>rain</u> in the time of the latter <u>rain</u>; so the LORD shall make bright clouds, and give them showers of <u>rain</u>, to every one <u>grass</u> in the field" (Zech. 10:1). As the worldwide remnant of Jews began to return to the land of Israel in the early 20th century, the rainfall began to increase incrementally and in sync with their increasing numbers. As the rains increased so the deserts were turned green, even in parched Jerusalem. All available forms of the word *rain* are mentioned in 62 chapters of the Old Testament. The word *grass* occurs 62 times in Scripture.

All Nations Will Gather Together against Jerusalem
"And <u>in that day</u> will I make JERUSALEM a burdensome stone for all people: all that <u>burden</u> themselves with it shall be cut in pieces, though all the people of the earth be <u>gathered together</u> against it" (Zech. 12:3). Again the phrase *in that day* is mentioned in 62 chapters of the Old Testament. Again the word *burden* occurs 62 times in the Old Testament. Again the phrase *gathered together* occurs 62 times in the Old Testament.

The Pierced Messiah Will Return to Jerusalem
"And I will pour upon the house of David, and upon the inhabitants of JERUSALEM, the spirit of grace and of supplications: and they shall look upon me whom they have pierced, and they shall mourn for him, as one mourneth for his only son, and shall be in bitterness for him, as one that is in bitterness for his firstborn" (Zech. 12:10). When the Great Messianic King returns to Jerusalem He will still have the covenant wounds in His hands and His feet. By these signs Jerusalem will know He is the same King who came the first time. The phrase *his feet* is mentioned in 62 chapters of the Bible.

In that day shall there be a great mourning in Jerusalem, as the mourning of Hadadrimmon in the valley of Megiddon. And the land shall mourn, every family apart; the family of the house of David apart, and their wives apart; the family of the house of Nathan apart, and their wives apart; The family of the house of Levi apart, and their wives apart; the family of Shimei apart, and their wives apart; All the <u>families</u> that remain, every family apart, and their wives apart" (12:11-13). The word *families* occurs 62 times in the OT Narrative.

Messiah Will Stand before Jerusalem
"And his feet shall stand in that day upon the mount of Olives, which is <u>before</u> JERUSALEM on the east, and the mount of Olives shall cleave in the midst thereof toward the east and toward the west, and there shall be a very great valley; and half of the mountain shall remove toward the north, and half of it toward the south" (Zech. 14:4). This prophecy foretells the Messianic King's powerful return to Jerusalem. It will cause a great earthquake, and so great will be the effect that a geographical change will take place to mark His arrival. The word *before* is found in 62 books of the Bible. In this Jerusalem verse there are 62 words surrounding the name *Jerusalem*.

Jerusalem's Peacefully Flowing Waters
(Part 9)

"And it shall be in that day, that living waters shall go out from JERUSALEM; half of them toward the former sea, and half of them toward the hinder sea: in summer and in winter shall it be" (Zech. 14:8). From the time of Solomon water was piped in to thirsty Jerusalem from two sources, Bethlehem and Hebron. During Messiah's glorious reign, Jerusalem itself will be the source of a vast amount of fresh water. Agricultural fields will not want for water as they presently do. The phrases *and it shall be in that day, that living waters shall go out from Jerusalem;* consist of 62 characters!

The Heavenly King of Jerusalem

"And it shall be, that whoso will not come up of all the <u>families</u> of the earth unto JERUSALEM to <u>worship</u> the <u>King</u>, the LORD of hosts, even upon them shall be no rain" (Zech. 14:17). Again the word *families* occurs 62 times in the OT Narrative. Again the word *worship* is mentioned in 62 verses of the Old Testament. Again the word *king* occurs 62 times in the NT Narrative.

Jerusalem Has Committed an Abomination

"Judah hath dealt treacherously, and an <u>abomination</u> is committed in Israel and in JERUSALEM; for Judah hath profaned the holiness of the LORD which he loved, and hath married the daughter of a strange god" (Mal. 2:11). Again the word *abomination(s)* is mentioned in 62 verses of the Major Prophets.

The New Testament

"The book of the generation of <u>Jesus Christ</u>, the son of David, the son of Abraham" (Matt. 1:1). A considerable amount of Jesus' ministerial work took place Him in Jerusalem. But because the religious leaders constantly sought to take Jesus' life, He never spent one night within it city walls. At nighttime He chose rather to take refuge in a garden adjacent to the city's Eastern Gate. He deserved to be coronated in Jerusalem, but instead they wrongly convicted Him as a criminal and then demanded His sacrificial death. His trial took place inside the city and His execution took place just outside the city.

> The title *Christ* is mentioned naturally in 162 chapters of the New Testament.
> The title *Jesus Christ('s)* is mentioned in 162 verses of the Pauline Epistles.
> The title *Lord* is mentioned in 620 verses of the New Testament.
> The title *Lord* occurs 62 times in the Pauline Epistles.
> The title *our Lord* is mentioned in 62 verses of the Pauline Epistles.

The Star of Jerusalem

"Now when Jesus was born in Bethlehem of Judaea in the days of Herod the king, behold, there came wise men from the <u>east</u> to JERUSALEM, Saying, Where is he that is born <u>King of</u> the Jews? for we have seen his star in the <u>east,</u> and are come to <u>worship</u> him" (Matt. 2:1-2). Because the star originally led the magi to Jerusalem, it could justifiably be called the Jerusalem Star. Again the word *east* is mentioned in 62 verses of the Major Prophets. Again the phrase *the king of* is mentioned in 62 chapters of the OT Narrative. Again the word *worship* is mentioned in 62 verses of the Old Testament.

All Jerusalem Was Troubled

"When Herod the king had heard these things, he was troubled, and <u>all</u> JERUSALEM with him" (Matt. 2:3). Herod had already killed some of his own family members to secure his reign. He was greatly paranoid and evil. This news may have caused parents of Davidic lineage to fear Herod's wrath, thinking he might go on a killing spree looking for any of their small baby boys. The word *all* occurs 162 times in First Samuel.

People Follow Jesus from Jerusalem

"And there followed him great multitudes of people from Galilee, and from Decapolis, and <u>from</u> JERUSALEM, and from Judaea, and from beyond Jordan" (Matt. 4:25). Again the word *from* occurs 462 times in the NT Narrative.

A City of Light Set upon the Hill

"Ye are <u>the light</u> of the world. A city that is set on an hill cannot be hid" (Matt. 5:14). This verse presents the Bible's 62nd occurrence of the phrase *the light*, and it shares an association with the city of Jerusalem which is set upon a holy hill.

> The word *light* is mentioned naturally in 62 verses of the Wisdom Books.
> The word *light* occurs 62 times in the NT Narrative.
> The word *light* is mentioned in 162 chapters of the Bible.

Jerusalem, City of the Great King

Jesus reminded the people how holy Jerusalem really is and that they should not swear by heaven because it is God's throne "nor by the earth; for it is <u>his footstool</u>: neither by JERUSALEM; for <u>it is</u> <u>the</u> <u>city of the great King</u>" (Matt. 5:35). The NT Narrative combination *worship at his footstool* (2 chs), *Jerusalem* (59 chs), *city of the great King* (1 ch) = 62 chapters. The Gospels combination *it is* (61 chs), *the city of the great King* (1 ch) = 62 chapters. Again the word *city* occurs 362 times in the OT Narrative.

The Kingdom of God & Its Jerusalem Capital

"<u>But seek ye first</u> <u>the kingdom of God,</u> and his righteousness; and all these things shall be added unto you" (Matt. 6:33). Moving beyond the spiritual aspects of this verse we look to one physical aspect related to it. Every kingdom has a capital city. Further, both the kingdom of God in heaven and the one on Earth have capitals named Jerusalem. Again from Genesis to the Gospels the phrase *the kingdom of* is mentioned in 62 chapters. From Genesis to the NT Narrative the combination *but seek ye first* (1x), *the kingdom of God* (61x) = 62. From Genesis to the NT Narrative the combination *the kingdom of God* (61x) and *the kingdom of my father* (1x) = 62.

The Gospel Harvest Begins in Jerusalem

"Then saith he unto his disciples, The harvest truly is plenteous, but the labourers are few; Pray ye therefore the <u>Lord of the harvest</u>, that he will send forth labourers into his harvest" (Matt. 9:37-38). The command for the gospel to specifically go forth from Jerusalem will come a little later in Jesus' instructions. The first harvest of barley and wheat took place ceremonially in Jerusalem every spring and summer; after these two annual one-day events were performed people could begin bringing in their own barley and wheat harvests. From Genesis to the Gospels the combination *harvestman* (2x) and *harvest* (60x) = 62.

The Scribes of Jerusalem

"Then came to Jesus <u>scribes</u> and Pharisees, which were <u>of</u> JERUSALEM, saying" (Matt. 15:1). Scribes of the Law naturally lived in Jerusalem because it was the religious capital. Again the word *of* is mentioned in 62 verses of John's Epistles.

> The title *scribes* occurs 62 times in the NT Narrative.
> The title *scribes* is mentioned in 62 verses of NT Narrative.

Christ Foretells His Death in Jerusalem

"From that time forth began Jesus to <u>shew</u> unto his disciples, how that he must go <u>unto</u> JERUSALEM, and suffer many things of the elders and chief priests and scribes, and be killed, and be raised again the third day" (Matt. 16:21). Matthew's Gospel segments Jesus' ministry into two distinct halves: first in Galilee and then in Jerusalem. The word *shew* occurs 162 times in the Old Testament. Again the word *unto* occurs 62 times in Proverbs. The phrase *to death* is mentioned in 62 chapters of the Bible.

The Up-to-Jerusalem Prophecy
(Part 1)

"And Jesus going up to JERUSALEM took the twelve disciples apart <u>in the way</u>, and said unto them, Behold, we go to JERUSALEM; and the Son of man shall be betrayed unto <u>the chief priests</u> and unto the scribes, and they shall condemn him <u>to death</u>, And shall deliver him to the Gentiles to mock, and to scourge, and to crucify him: and the third day he shall rise again" (Matt. 20:17-19). This passage presents the Bible's 62nd chapter-mention of the phrase *in the way*, and it refers to the way to Jerusalem. Again the title *the chief priests* occurs 62 times in the Bible. Again the phrase *to death* is mentioned in 62 chapters of the Bible.

Christ the King Enters Zion on a Donkey

"All this was done, that it might be <u>fulfilled</u> which was spoken by the prophet, saying, Tell ye the daughter of SION, Behold, thy <u>King</u> cometh unto thee, meek, and sitting upon an ass, and a colt the foal of an ass. And the disciples went, and did as Jesus commanded them, And brought the ass, and the colt, and put on them their clothes, and they set him thereon. . . . <u>And when he was come into JERUSALEM, all the city was moved, saying, Who is this?</u>" (Matt. 21:4-6, 10)

The name Zion does not occur in the New Testament, but its equivalent name Sion does. The word *fulfilled* is mentioned in 62 chapters of the Bible. Again the title *king* occurs 62 times in the NT Narrative. The Old Testament combination *was come* (59x), *into Jerusalem* (3x) = 62. The sentence *and when he was come into Jersualem, all the city was moved, saying, who is this* consists of 62 letters!

Christ Longed to Gather up Jerusalem

"O JERUSALEM, JERUSALEM, thou that killest the prophets, and stonest them which are sent unto thee, how often would I have gathered <u>thy children</u> together, even as a hen gathereth her chickens under her wings, and <u>ye</u> would not!" (Matt. 23:37) Again the phrase *the children* occurs 62 times in the New Testament. From Genesis to the Gospels the word *ye* is mentioned in 562 chapters.

One Night in Jerusalem

"Then saith Jesus unto them, All ye shall be offended because of me this <u>night</u>: for it is written, I will smite the shepherd, and the sheep of the flock shall be scattered abroad" (Matt. 26:31). The pinnacle of Christ's redemptive ministry commenced at night fall at His last Passover meal in Jerusalem. On this one night alone Christ would spend it inside the city's walls, even in a dungeon. Again the word *night* occurs 62 times in the New Testament.

Matthew 26:62

"And <u>the high priest</u> arose, and said unto him, Answerest thou nothing? what is it which these witness against thee?" (Matt. 26:62) The Scriptures had predicted that Messiah would undergo a mock trial. It happened in Jerusalem. Such a trial was destined to be led by a high priest. The title *the high priest('s)* is mentioned in 62 verses of the Bible.

Resurrected Saints Went into the Holy City

"And the graves were opened; and many bodies of the saints which slept arose, And came out of the graves after his resurrection, and <u>went into</u> THE HOLY CITY, and appeared unto many" (Matt. 27:52). From Genesis to the Gospels the phrase *went into* is mentioned in 62 chapters.

1062nd Verse of the New Testament

"Now when they were going, behold, some of the watch came <u>into THE CITY</u>, and shewed unto <u>the chief priests</u> all the things that were done" (Matt. 28:11). This 62nd verse makes reference to Jerusalem. Again the title *the chief priests* occurs 62 times in the Bible. Again the phrase *in the city* is mentioned in 62 chapters of the Bible.

"And They of Jerusalem"

"John did baptize in the wilderness, and preach the baptism of repentance for the remission of sins. And there went out unto him all the land of Judæa, <u>and they</u> of JERUSALEM, and were all baptized of him in the river of Jordan, confessing their sins" (Mark 1:4-5). The phrase *and they* is mentioned in 62 verses of Matthew. Again from Genesis to the Synoptic Gospels the phrase *of Jerusalem* is mentioned in 162 verses.

"And from Jerusalem"

Jesus was touring Galilee. "And from JERUSALEM, <u>and from Idumaea, and from beyond Jordan; and they about Tyre and Sidon, a great multitude, when they had heard what great things he did, came unto him. . . . And the scribes which came down from JERUSALEM</u>" (Mark 3:8-22a). Here in the referenced verses of Mark's Gospel there are 262 words following the name *Jerusalem* until arriving at the next mention of the name *Jerusalem*!

The Pharisees of Jerusalem

"Then came together unto him the Pharisees, and certain of the scribes, which came from JERUSALEM" (Mark 7:1). The Pharisees were both a religious and a political party. They demanded strict adherence to the Law. Their zeal reached back to the days of the Hassidic movement to counter backslidden Jews in Israel who were living according with the Hellenistic worldview instead of the Mosaic view. The NT Narrative titles *the Pharisees* (61x) and *the chief Pharisees* (1x) = 62.

The Up-to-Jerusalem Prophecy
(Part 2)

"And they were in the way going up to JERUSALEM; and Jesus went before them: and they were amazed; and as they followed, they were afraid. And he took again the twelve, and began to tell them what things should happen unto him" (Mark 10:32). On this day Jesus' stride was marked by faster and more determined steps than the disciples had ever witnessed before. The Master needed to explain to His students that this trip to Jerusalem was not going to turn out like any of the former trips. The Bible combination *were in* (161x), *the way going up* (1x) = 162. The Ecclesiastes combination *to* (157x), *Jerusalem* (5x) = 62. The word *tell* is mentioned in 62 verses of the Gospels. The phrase *unto him* is mentioned in 62 chapters of the Synoptic Gospels.

The Up-to-Jerusalem Prophecy
(Part 3)

"Behold, we go up to JERUSALEM; and the Son of man shall be delivered unto the chief priests, and unto the scribes; and they shall condemn him to death, and shall deliver him to the Gentiles: And they shall mock him, and shall scourge him, and shall spit upon him, and shall kill him: and the third day he shall rise again" (Mark 10:33-34). All tenses of the phrase "go up to" look like this: *go up to* (38x), *goeth up to* (7x), *going up to* (10x), *gone up to* (6x), *go/eth/ing/ gone * up to* (1x) = 62. Again the word *up* is mentioned in 162 chapters of the New Testament. There are 62 words in Jesus' up-to-Jerusalem prophecy!

"They Came Nigh to Jerusalem"

"And when they came nigh to JERUSALEM, unto Bethphage and Bethany, at the mount of Olives, he sendeth forth two of his disciples" (Mark 11:1). The phrase *they came* occurs 162 times in the Bible. This verse presents the Bible's 62nd verse-mention of the word *nigh*, and it refers to being nigh to Jerusalem!

They Went into & out of Jerusalem

It was the day of Christ's triumphal entry. "And Jesus entered into JERUSALEM, and into the temple: and when he had looked round about upon all things, and now the eventide was come, he went out unto Bethany with the twelve" (Mark 11:11). As we have recently stated, as far as Scripture reveals Jesus never spent a night inside Jerusalem's walls except on the eve of His crucifixion. This behavior stands as a token of His rejection by Jerusalem's religious leaders. The word *into* is mentioned in 62 verses of Exodus.

> The word *out* is mentioned in 162 verses of First/Second Samuel.
> The word *out* occurs naturally 62 times in the Pauline/General Epistles.

"They Come to Jerusalem"

"And they <u>come to</u> JERUSALEM: and Jesus went into the temple, and began to cast out them that sold and bought in the temple, and overthrew the tables of the moneychangers, and the seats of them that sold doves" (Mark 11:15). Again the phrase *come to* is mentioned in 62 chapters of the OT Narrative.

"They Come Again to Jerusalem"

"And they come <u>again</u> to JERUSALEM: and as he was walking in the temple, there come to him the chief priests, and the scribes, and the elders" (Mark 11:27).

The word *again* is mentioned in 62 chapters of the Major Prophets.
The word *again* occurs 62 times in the Pauline/General Epistles.

Jerusalem Temple's Second Destruction Foretold

"And Jesus answering said unto him, Seest thou these great buildings? there shall not be left one <u>stone</u> <u>upon another</u>, that shall not be thrown down" (Mark 13:2). Again the word *fell* occurs 62 times in the NT Narrative. The Old Testament combination *stones* (161x) and *fell one upon another* (1x) = 162.

Jesus' Glorious Return to Jerusalem Foretold

"And Jesus said, I am: and ye shall see the Son of man sitting on the right hand of power, and <u>in the clouds</u> of <u>heaven</u>" (Mark 14:62). Using well-known Old Testament terminology of God's deity and glory, the lowly Christ foretells His dynamic return to Jerusalem as the Cloud Rider. The Wisdom Books combination *in the clouds* (2x) and *heaven* (60x) = 62.

Women Disciples Also Came up with Jesus to Jerusalem

"And Jesus cried with a loud voice, and gave up the ghost. . . . There were also women looking on afar off: among whom was Mary Magdalene, and Mary the mother of James the less and of Joses, and Salome; Who also, when he was in Galilee, followed him, and ministered unto him; and many other women which <u>came up</u> with him unto JERUSALEM" (Mark 15:37, 40-41). The phrase *came up* is mentioned in 62 chapters of the Bible.

Infant Redeemer in Jerusalem

"And when the days of her purification according to the law of Moses were accomplished, they <u>brought him</u> to JERUSALEM, to present him to the Lord" (Luke 2:22). All firstborn males were considered the sole property of the Lord unless they were bought back from the Lord with five shekels after the Sanctuary measure. This is what Jesus' parents were doing on this day. The phrase *brought him* is mentioned in 62 verses of the Old Testament.

Israel's Redemption Announced in Jerusalem

Anna was an aged prophetess, and she understood the Messianic times in which she was living. "And she coming in that instant gave thanks likewise unto the Lord, and spake of him to all them that looked for <u>redemption</u> in JERUSALEM" (Luke 2:38). As Jerusalem was at the center of Israelite worship, so would the city be at the center of the nation's Messianic redemption. The word *redeemed* occurs 62 times in Scripture.

Christ's Transportation to Jerusalem

"Now his parents <u>went</u> to JERUSALEM every year at the feast of the passover. And when he was twelve years old, they <u>went up</u> to JERUSALEM after the custom of the feast. And when they had <u>fulfilled</u> the days, as they returned, <u>the child</u> Jesus tarried behind in JERUSALEM" (Luke 2:41-43a). Again the word *went* occurs 1062 times in the Old Testament. In the kingly books of Samuel, Kings, and Chronicles the phrase *went up* occurs 62 times. Again the phrase *the passover* occurs 62 times in Scripture. Again the word *fulfilled* is mentioned in 62 chapters of the Bible. The phrase *the child* occurs 62 times in the Old Testament.

Christ's Transmigration to Jerusalem

"And he <u>brought him</u> to JERUSALEM, and set him on a pinnacle of the temple, and said unto him, If thou be the Son of God, cast thyself down from hence" (Luke 4:9). Granted permission from God, Satan transported Christ from the Judean wilderness to the Judean capital. Again the phrase *brought him* is mentioned in 62 verses of the Old Testament.

Christ's Transfixion at Jerusalem

"And as he prayed, the fashion of his countenance was altered, and his raiment was white and glistering. And, behold, there talked with him two men, which were Moses and Elias: Who appeared in glory, and spake of his decease which he should accomplish <u>at</u> JERUSALEM" (Luke 9:29-31). These three disciples beheld Christ's transfiguration on Mount Hermon, yet they would in time behold His painful transfixion on Mount Calvary. Webster's Dictionary gives us a definition of transfix: to hold motionless by or as if by piercing. Again the word *at* is mentioned in 162 chapters of the New Testament.

Christ's Transfixion on Jerusalem

"And it came to pass, when the time was come that he should be received up, he stedfastly set his face to go to JERUSALEM, And sent messengers before his face: and they went, and entered into a village of the Samaritans, to make ready for him. And they did not receive him, because his face was as though he would go to JERUSALEM" (Luke 9:51-53). In this up-to-Jerusalem passage there are 62 words surrounding the twice-occurring word *Jerusalem*.

Luke 9:62

"And Jesus said unto him, No man, having put his hand to the plough, and looking back, is fit for <u>the kingdom of God</u>" (Luke 9:62). The capital of God's earthly kingdom is Jerusalem. The New Testament combination *the kingdom of God* (61x) and *the kingdom of our father* (1x) = 62.

Former Men Who Dwelt in Jerusalem

"Or those eighteen, upon whom the tower in Siloam fell, and slew them, think ye that they were sinners above <u>all men</u> that <u>dwelt in</u> JERUSALEM?" (Luke 13:4) The phrase *all men* occurs 62 times in the New Testament. Again the phrase *dwelt in* occurs 62 times in the OT Narrative.

Christ's Translocation to Jerusalem

"And he went through the cities and villages, teaching, and <u>journeying</u> toward JERUSALEM" (Luke 13:22). Jesus' sacrificial goal was to reach Jerusalem, but He did not proceed in haste until the final part of His journey from Jericho to Jerusalem. Meanwhile he travelled with the distinct purpose of preaching and teaching kingdom principles. All forms of the word *journey* are mentioned naturally in 62 collective chapters of the Bible.

Jerusalem to Kill their Supreme Prophet

Jesus gave a bold reply to His Pharisaic adversaries: "Nevertheless I must walk <u>to day</u>, and <u>to morrow</u>, and the day following: for it cannot be that a <u>prophet</u> perish <u>out of</u> JERUSALEM" (Luke 13:33). The title *prophet* is mentioned in 62 verses of the NT Narrative. Again the phrase *out of* is mentioned in 662 chapters of the Bible. The word *to day* is mentioned in 62 chapters of the Bible. The words *to/the morrow* are mentioned in 62 combined chapters of the Old Testament.

Jerusalem Killed Many of Her Past Prophets

"O JERUSALEM <u>JERUSALEM</u>, <u>which killest the</u> <u>prophets</u>, and stonest them that are <u>sent</u> <u>unto</u> <u>thee</u>; how often would I have gathered thy children together, as a hen doth gather her brood under her wings, and ye would not!" (Luke 13:34) Again the title *prophets* is mentioned in 62 verses of the OT Narrative. The phrase *unto thee* is mentioned in 62 verses of the Psalms. The NT Narrative combination *which killest the* (1x), *prophets* (61x) = 62. The Gospel of John combination *the prophets* (4x), *sent* (57x), *unto Jerusalem* (1x) = 62.

The Up-to-Jerusalem Prophecy
(Part 4)

"Then he took unto him the twelve, and said unto them, Behold, <u>we go up</u> to JERUSALEM, and all things that are written by the prophets concerning the Son of man shall be accomplished" (Luke 18:31). Again the word *go* is mentioned in 62 verses of Numbers and occurs 162 times in the Kings and Chronicles. Again the word *up* is mentioned in 162 chapters of the New Testament.

> The word *we* occurs 262 times naturally in the Law.
> The word *we* occurs 562 times in the Pauline/General Epistles.

Ascending to Jerusalem

"And when he had thus spoken, he went before, <u>ascending</u> up <u>to</u> JERUSALEM" (Luke 19:28). The New Testament combination *ascending* (3 chs) and *to* (259 chs) = 262 chapters.

Jerusalem Trodden down Until Times of the Gentiles Fulfilled

"And when ye shall see JERUSALEM compassed with armies, then know that the desolation thereof is nigh. . . . And they shall fall by the edge of <u>the sword</u>, and shall be led away <u>captive</u> into all nations: and JERUSALEM <u>shall be</u> trodden down of the Gentiles, until the <u>times</u> of the Gentiles be <u>fulfilled</u>" (Luke 21:20, 24). The times of the Gentiles refers to the nations' unfavorable political and military control over Israel's capital city Jerusalem. Since 606 BC various nations and empires have controlled Jerusalem. Of late, between the years 1948 and 1967 the Jordanians controlled Jerusalem at which time they took nearby Jewish gravestones and made pavers out of them for roads and latrines. The phrase *shall be* occurs 62 times in the Pauline Epistles. Again the phrase *the sword* occurs naturally 62 times in Ezekiel. Again the word *captivity* occurs naturally 62 times in the Major Prophets. Again the word *time* is mentioned in 562 verses of the Bible. Again the word *fulfilled* is mentioned in 62 chapters of the Bible.

Luke 22:62

"And <u>Peter</u> went out, and wept bitterly" (Luke 22:62). The backdrop setting of this 62nd verse of Scripture is Jerusalem. Peter was destined to be the pastor of the Jerusalem Church; therefore, he needed to repent of this sin of denial and be reconciled to the Lord of the Jerusalem Church. Peter's name carries the seal of Jerusalem: *Peter* (158x) and *Peter's* (4x) = 162.

Daughters of Jerusalem Told to Weep for the Children of Jerusalem

The lady disciples were wailing and lamenting because of Jesus' horrible plight. "But Jesus turning unto them said, <u>Daughters of</u> JERUSALEM, <u>weep</u> not for me, but <u>weep</u> for yourselves, and for your <u>children</u>" (Luke 23:28). This is the only usage of the term "daughters of Jerusalem" outside Solomon's Song. Again the phrase *daughters of* occurs 62 times in the Bible. With the exception of wept, all tenses of the word *weep* are mentioned in 62 verses of the Old Testament. Again the phrase *the children* occurs 62 times in the New Testament. Again the phrase *the children of* is mentioned in 62 verses of Nehemiah.

Christ's Transmutation in Jerusalem

"And, behold, two of them went that same day to a village called Emmaus, which was from JERUSALEM about threescore furlongs. . . . And it came to pass, that, while they communed together and reasoned, Jesus himself drew near, and went with them. But their eyes were holden that they should not know him. And he said unto them, What manner of communications are these that ye have one to another, as ye walk, and are sad? And the one of them, whose name was Cleopas, answering said unto him, Art thou only a stranger in Jerusalem, and hast not known the things which are come to pass there in these days? . . . Concerning Jesus of Nazareth, which was a prophet mighty in deed and word before God and all the people: And how the chief priests and our rulers delivered him to be condemned to death, and have crucified him. But we trusted that it had been he which should have redeemed Israel: and beside all this, to day is the third day since these things were done. Yea, and certain women also of our company made us astonished, which were early at the sepulchre; <u>And when they found not</u> his body, <u>they came, saying, that they had also</u> <u>seen a</u> <u>vision of angels, which said that he was alive</u>" (Luke 24:13, 15-18, 19b-23).

The Bible combination *and when they found not* (1x), *the Lord's body* (1x), *they came saying* (1x), *that they had also* (1x), *seen a* (8x), *visitation* (15x), *of angels* (9x), *which said* (16x), *said that he* (6x), *was alive* (4x) = 62.

Disciples' Sudden Transformation
Takes Them Back to Jerusalem with an Epic Message

"And their eyes were opened, and they knew him; and he vanished out of their sight. And they said one to another, Did not our heart burn within us, while he talked with us by the way, and while he opened to us the scriptures? And they rose up the same hour, and returned to JERUSALEM" (Luke 24:31-33a). The Bible combination *that he was* (61x) and *alive from the dead* (1x) = 62.

Beginning at Jerusalem

The risen King established a standard for the apostles to employ in their worldwide evangelism program; "that repentance and remission of sins should be <u>preached</u> in his name among all nations, <u>beginning</u> <u>at</u> JERUSALEM" (Luke 24:47). Again the word *at* is mentioned in 162 chapters of the New Testament.

The phrase *he began* occurs 62 times in the Bible.

320

The word *beginning* is mentioned in 62 chapters from Genesis to the Gospels.
The NT combination *began to* (58x), *preach the gospel to* (3x) = 62.

Disciples to Tarry in the City of Jerusalem

The risen King continued to give specific instructions regarding the apostles' and disciples' evangelism standards. "<u>I send the promise of my Father upon you: but tarry ye in THE CITY OF JERUSALEM</u>, until ye be endued with power from on high" (Luke 24:49). This verse presents the Bible's only occurrence of the title *the city of Jerusalem*. Again the phrase *in the city* is mentioned in 62 verses of the Bible. Again from Genesis to the Synoptic Gospels the phrase *of Jerusalem* is mentioned in 162 verses; this is its 162nd verse-mention. The words *I send the promise of my Father upon you: but tarry ye in the city of Jerusalem* consists of 62 letters!

Christ's Translation from Jerusalem to Bethany to Heaven

"And he led them out as far as to Bethany, and he lifted up his hands, and blessed them. And it came to pass, while he blessed them, he was parted from them, and carried up into heaven" (Luke 24:50-51). This verse presents the Bible's 62nd occurrence of the phrase *up into*, and it refers to the heavenly Jerusalem.

Disciples Return to Jerusalem

"And they worshipped him, and <u>returned</u> to JERUSALEM with great joy" (Luke 24:52). After Jesus' ascension had transpired the believers did what Jesus had told them to—return to Jerusalem. Again the word *return* is mentioned in 162 chapters of the Bible.

Priests from Jerusalem

"And this is the record of John, when the Jews sent <u>priests</u> and Levites from JERUSALEM to ask him, Who art thou?" (John 1:19) Again the title *priests* occurs 62 times in the NT Narrative.

The Father's House in Jerusalem

"And said unto them that sold doves, Take these things hence; make not my <u>Father's house</u> an house of merchandise" (John 2:16). The phrase *father's house* is mentioned in 62 verses of the Bible.

Jerusalem, the True Place of Worship

"Our fathers worshipped in this mountain; and ye say, that in JERUSALEM is <u>the place</u> where men ought to <u>worship</u>" (John 4:20). Upon Mount Gerizim the Samaritans once built their own Temple for Jehovah, but it had been destroyed about two centuries earlier according to Josephus. Jesus told this Samaritan woman that she was clearly in error. Jerusalem was unmistakably the true place of Israelite worship. This verse presents the Bible's 162nd verse-mention of the phrase *the place*, and it refers to Jerusalem. Again the word *place* is mentioned in 162 verses of the Law. Again the word *worship* is mentioned in 62 verses of the Old Testament.

Counting from One "Jerusalem" to the Next

"Woman, believe me, the hour cometh, when ye shall neither in this mountain, nor yet at JERUSALEM, <u>worship the Father. . . . Then when he was come into Galilee, the Galilæans received him, having seen all the things that he did at JERUSALEM</u> at the feast" (John 4:21, 4:45). After this fifth mention of the name *Jerusalem* there are 462 words until arriving at John's sixth mention of the name *Jerusalem*!

The Jews' Affinity with Jerusalem

"After this there was a feast of <u>the Jews</u>; and Jesus went up to JERUSALEM" (John 5:1). The term Jews is an abbreviation for Judeans. This shortened name was given to them during their Babylonian captivity. The Jews had an inherent fondness and attraction for Jerusalem because it was a beautiful part of their spiritual heritage from the Lord.

The title *the Jews* (61x), *the * Jews* (1x) = 62 times in the OT.
The name *Jews* is mentioned in 162 verses of the New Testament.

"Some of Them of Jerusalem"

"Then said some <u>of them</u> of JERUSALEM, Is not this he, whom they seek to kill?" (John 7:25) The city that should have welcomed the King of the Jews sought instead to kill Him. The phrase *of them* occurs 662 times in the Bible.

Jerusalem's Winter Festival

"And <u>it was at JERUSALEM</u> <u>the feast</u> <u>of the dedication</u>, <u>and it was winter</u>" (John 10:22). This eight-day feast was established in 165 BC after the Maccabean warriors recaptured the Temple compound from the Greco-Syrians. The Bible combination *it was at Jerusalem* (1 v), *the feast* (59 vs), *of the dedication* (1 v), *and it was winter* (1 v) = 62 verses.

Counting from "Jerusalem" to the End of the Chapter

"And the Jews' passover was nigh at hand: and many went out of the country up to JERUSALEM before the passover, to purify themselves. Then sought they for Jesus, and spake among themselves, as they stood in the temple, What think ye, that he will not come to the feast? Now both the chief priests and the Pharisees had given a commandment, that, if any man knew where he were, he should shew it, that they might take him" (John 11:55-57).

In this selected passage, from the word *Jerusalem* to the end of the chapter are 62 words.

They Heard Jesus Was Coming to Jerusalem

"On the next day much people that were come to the feast, when they heard that Jesus was coming to JERUSALEM, Took branches of palm trees, and went forth to meet him, and cried, Hosanna: <u>Blessed is</u> <u>the King</u> of Israel that cometh in the name of the Lord" (John 12:12-13). This passage presents the last mention of the name Jerusalem in John's Gospel. This passage presents the Bible's 1362nd occurrence of the title *the k/King*, and it pertains to the King of the Jews coming to Jerusalem. Again the phrase *blessed be* is mentioned in 62 verses of the Bible. Again the word *blessed* is mentioned in 62 verses of the Wisdom Books.

Pastor Peter Must Feed the Jerusalem Flock

"So when they had dined, Jesus saith to Simon <u>Peter</u>, Simon, son of Jonas, lovest thou me more than these? He saith unto him, Yea, Lord; thou knowest that I love thee. He saith unto him, Feed my <u>lambs</u>" (John 21:15). This was a reconciliation meal known as the Sulha, the Arabic word for table. Jesus had set a table of food over which the two were to eat and talk until peace between them was achieved. Jesus had invited all the disciples to come and dine because they all needed reconciling not just Peter. The narrator gives emphasis to Jesus' conversation with Peter because Peter was set to become the pastor of the Church at Jerusalem. Again the Bible names *Peter*

(158x) and *Peter's* (4x) = 162. Again the word *flock(s)* is mentioned naturally in 162 verses of the Old Testament.

Wait for My Holy Promise in Jerusalem

"And, being assembled together with them, commanded them that they should not depart from JERUSALEM, but <u>wait</u> for the <u>promise</u> of the Father, which, saith he, ye have heard of me. For John truly baptized with water; but ye shall be <u>baptized</u> <u>with the Holy Ghost</u> not many days hence" (Acts 1:4-5). The Old Testament combination *wait* (61 chs) and *his holy promise* (1 ch) = 62 chapters. The Bible combination *baptized* (61x) and *with the Spirit of the living God* (1x) = 62.

Be Witnesses for Me in Jerusalem

"But ye shall receive power, after that the Holy Ghost is come upon you: and <u>ye shall be</u> <u>witnesses</u> unto me both in Jerusalem, and in all Judæa, and in Samaria, and unto the uttermost part of the earth" (Acts 1:8). The phrase *ye shall be* occurs naturally 62 times in the Old Testament. The word *witness* occurs naturally 62 times in the Old Testament.

A Spirit-Filled House in Jerusalem

"And suddenly there came a sound from heaven as of a rushing mighty wind, and it filled all <u>the</u> <u>house</u> where they were sitting" (Acts 2:2). The house where the disciples were sitting was not the Upper Room but rather the House of God. This high feast day was a one-day festival, and at this important hour these orthodox believers would have been at the Temple precinct for the nation's special gathering. When the narrative speaks of a house it simply refers to one of the many covered porticos around the Temple compound. Again the phrase *the house* occurs 62 times in the NT Narrative.

The Spirit Poured out in Jerusalem

Peter spoke of the fulfillment of Joel's prophecy: "And it shall come to pass in the last days, saith God, <u>I will pour out of my Spirit upon all flesh</u>: and your sons and your daughters shall prophesy, and your <u>young men</u> shall see visions, and your old men shall dream dreams" (Acts 2:17). What Joel's prophecy did not say but is clear from history is that when God's Spirit was finally poured out, it was poured upon the city of Jerusalem; however, only those having faith in Christ received the Holy Spirit. The term *young men* is mentioned in 62 chapters of the Bible. The Bible combination *I will pour out of my* (1 v), *Spirit* (158 vs), *upon all flesh* (3 vs) = 162 verses.

"All Them That Dwell in Jerusalem"

The Sanhedrin was in a quandary, "Saying, What shall we do to these men? for that indeed a notable miracle hath been done by them is manifest to all them that <u>dwell in</u> JERUSALEM; and we cannot deny it" (Acts 4:16). We repeat the following two seals.

> The phrase *dwell in* is mentioned in 162 verses of the Bible.
> The phrase *dwelt in* occurs 62 times in the OT Narrative.

Paul Wants to Attend a Coming Feast in Jerusalem

"But bade them farewell, saying, I must by all means keep this feast that cometh in JERUSALEM: but I will <u>return</u> again unto you, if God will. And he sailed from Ephesus" (Acts

18:21). This verse presents the Bible's 262nd occurrence of the word *return*, and it mentions returning from Jerusalem.

Collection for the Poor Saints at Jerusalem
(Part 1)

"And herein do I exercise myself, to have always a conscience void of offence toward God, and toward men. Now after many years I came to bring alms to my nation, and offerings" (Acts 24:17-18). In Paul's appearance before Felix he spoke of his Jerusalem project and its completion. He had started a collection for the poor from among the Macedonian and Achaian churches. Paul's first missionary journey was a round trip from and back to Antioch Syria, but his second and third journeys brought him back to Jerusalem with his collection of alms for the poor saints of Jerusalem. Then he could fully return back to Antioch, his sending church. The word *poor* is mentioned in 162 verses of the Old Testament. The phrases *saints in* (2 chs), *in Jerusalem* (160 chs) = 162 chapters of the Bible.

Go Down from Jerusalem

"Let them therefore, said he, which among you are able, go down with me, and accuse this man, if there be any wickedness in him" (Acts 25:5). This verse presents the Bible's 62nd chapter-mention of the phrase *go down*, and it pertains to going down from Jerusalem.

Sion's Great Stumblingstone

"Wherefore? Because they sought it not by faith, but as it were by the works of the law. For they stumbled at that stumblingstone; As it is written, Behold, I lay in SION a stumblingstone and rock of offence: and whosoever believeth on him shall not be ashamed" (Rom. 9:32-33). The phrases *as it is written, behold, I lay in Sion a stumblingstone and rock of offence* consist of 62 characters!

Sion's Great Deliverer

"And so all Israel shall be saved: as it is written, There shall come out of SION the Deliverer, and shall turn away ungodliness from Jacob" (Rom. 11:26). The Bible combination *come out of* (43x), *Sion* (9x), *d/Deliverer* (10x) = 62.

From Jerusalem & Round About Jerusalem

Paul declared his finished work, saying that "through mighty signs and wonders, by the power of the Spirit of God; so that from JERUSALEM, and round about unto Illyricum, I have fully preached the gospel of Christ" (Rom. 15:19). Again the word *about* is mentioned in 62 verses of the Wisdom Books. The New Testament combination *through mighty signs and wonders* (1x), *by the power of the Spirit of God* (1x), *from Jerusalem* (15x), *round about* (36x), *unto Illyricum* (1x), *I have fully* (1x), *preached the gospel* (7x) = 62.

Collection for the Poor Saints at Jerusalem
(Part 2)

"But now I go unto JERUSALEM to minister unto the saints. For it hath pleased them of Macedonia and Achaia to make a certain contribution for the poor saints which are at JERUSALEM" (Rom. 15:25-26). The phrase *I go* occurs naturally 62 times in the Bible. Again the word *unto* occurs 62 times in Proverbs. Again the word *pleased* occurs 62 times in Scripture.

Again the word *poor* is mentioned in 162 verses of the Old Testament. Again the word *at* is mentioned in 162 chapters of the New Testament. The Psalms combination *poor* (37x), *saints* (20x), *in/of Jerusalem* (5x) = 62.

Collection for the Poor Saints at Jerusalem
(Part 3)

"That I may be delivered from them that do not believe in Judaea; and that my service which I have for JERUSALEM may be accepted of the saints" (Rom. 15:31). Paul had performed a great service for the poor of Jerusalem through the collection he gathered up for them. The Bible combination *service* (55 chs), *for the poor* (6 chs), *saints at Jerusalem* (1 ch) = 62 chapters.

The 1062nd Chapter of the Bible

Romans chapter sixteen is a very unique chapter in the Bible. It lists various Gentile saints, most of whom were servants within their local churches. Some of these saints were generous hosts who each allowed his house to become a meeting place for a local church. Although it is not stated as such in this chapter, these various Gentile churches owed their ultimate thanks to the mother church in Jerusalem from whence the gospel first went out into the world. "Greet Priscilla and Aquila my helpers in Christ Jesus. . . . Likewise greet the church that is in their house . . . Christ. Salute them which are of Aristobulus' household. . . . Greet them that be of the household of Narcissus, which are in the Lord" (Rom. 16:3, 5a, 10b, 11b). Each of these house churches were now considered the House of the Lord, and the title Lord is used many times in this chapter. The Bible combination *household* (61x) and *which are in the Lord* (1x) = 62. We repeat the following seals.

> The title *the house* occurs 62 times in the NT Narrative.
> The title *the house of the LORD* is mentioned in 162 verses of the OTN.
> The phrase *of the house of the LORD* is mentioned in 62 verses of the Bible.

Paul wrote to all Gentile believers in his summary: "The churches of Christ salute you. . . . the whole church saluteth you" (vv. 16b, 23b). The word *church* occurs 62 combined times in Acts and in Paul's writings which are the Pauline Epistles.

Collection for the Poor Saints at Jerusalem
(Part 4)

"Now concerning the collection for the saints, as I have given order to the churches of Galatia, even so do ye. Upon the first day of the week let every one of you lay by him in store, as God hath prospered him, that there be no gatherings when I come. And when I come, whomsoever ye shall approve by your letters, them will I send to bring your liberality unto JERUSALEM" (1 Cor. 16:3). The Corinthians had heard about Paul's collection for the poor saints at Jerusalem, and they enquired of him how they could properly participate in it. He gave them an answer here at the end of his letter. The phrase *send/t to* occurs 62 times in the Old Testament. The New Testament combination *concerning* (60x), *the collection* (1x), *for the poor saints* (1x) = 62.

Collection for the Poor Saints at Jerusalem
(Part 5)

"Insomuch that we desired Titus, that as he had begun, so he would also finish in you the same grace also. . . . For as touching the ministering to the saints, it is superfluous for me to write to you: For I know the forwardness of your mind. . . . Yet have I sent the brethren, lest our boasting of you should be in vain in this behalf; that, as I said, ye may be ready: Lest haply if they of Macedonia come with me, and find you unprepared, we that we say not, ye should be ashamed in this same confident boasting. . . . Every man according as he purposeth in his heart, so let him give; not grudgingly, or of necessity: for God loveth a cheerful giver" (2 Cor. 8:6; 9:1-2a, 3-4, 7).

Something had caused the Corinthians to become sidetracked with their personal collection for the poor saints at Jerusalem. Paul's words of encouragement and sending of Titus and others all worked together to bring their intended giving to fruition by the time of his eventual visit to Corinth. The Bible combination *for as touching the* (1x), *ministering* (9x), *the saints* (52x) = 62.

Collection for the Poor Saints at Jerusalem
(Part 6)

"Therefore I thought it necessary to exhort the brethren, that they would go before unto you, and make up beforehand your bounty, whereof ye had notice before, that the same might be ready, as a matter of bounty, and not as of covetousness" (2 Cor. 9:5). This is the 28,962nd verse of the Bible, and it pertains to a freewill gift for poor saints living in Jerusalem.

Collection for the Poor Saints at Jerusalem
(Part 7)

"But this I say, He which soweth sparingly shall reap also sparingly; and he which soweth bountifully shall reap also bountifully" (2 Cor. 9:6). This is the 162nd verse of Second Corinthians, and it pertains to giving alms for the poor saints living in Jerusalem. The Bible combination *and he which* (3x), *soweth* (15x), *bountifully* (6x), *reap* (32x), *bountifully* (6x) = 62.

Back to Jerusalem

"Then fourteen years after I went up again to JERUSALEM with Barnabas, and took Titus with me also" (Gal. 2:1). The word *again* occurs 62 times in the Pauline and General Epistles. Here the word *to* is the 462nd word of Galatians, and it supports the keyword Jerusalem.

Collection for the Poor Saints at Jerusalem
(Part 8)

"And when James, Cephas, and John, who seemed to be pillars, perceived the grace that was given unto me, they gave to me and Barnabas the right hands of fellowship; that we should go unto the heathen, and they unto the circumcision. Only they would that we should remember the poor; the same which I also was forward to do" (Gal. 2:9-10). Paul's organized collection for the poor saints at Jerusalem was a great fulfilling of the chief elders of the Jerusalem Church's request. Again the word *poor* is mentioned in 162 verses of the Old Testament.

Heavenly Jerusalem, the Mother Church of Earthly Jerusalem

"For this Agar is mount Sinai in Arabia, and answereth to JERUSALEM which now is, and is in bondage with her children. But JERUSALEM which is above is free, which is the mother of us all" (Gal. 4:26). The Bible combination *but Jerusalem* (2x), *the mother of us all* (1x), *free* (59x) = 62. As cities are traditionally given the personal pronoun she, the earthly Jerusalem has her mother city in heaven from which she draws her divine likeness. The name Jerusalem is not seen again until reaching the book of Hebrews. Here the word *to* is the 745,562nd word of the Bible, and it supports the keyword Jerusalem. The phrase *his mother* occurs 62 times in the Old Testament.

Christ's Triumphal Show in Jerusalem

"Blotting out the handwriting of ordinances that was against us, which was contrary to us, and took it out of the way, nailing it to his cross; And having spoiled principalities and powers, he made a <u>shew</u> of them openly, triumphing over them in it" (Col. 2:14-15). Christ's final triumph came when He arose from the dead just outside the city walls of Jerusalem to live forevermore! Thereafter He showed Himself alive in and around Jerusalem over the next forty days. Again the word *shew* occurs 162 times in the Old Testament.

Epicenter of the Rapture—Jerusalem's Open Air?

"Now we beseech you, brethren, by the coming of <u>our Lord</u> Jesus Christ, and by our gathering together unto him" (2 Thess. 2:1). If Jesus was introduced as an infant to Jerusalem, as a male made annual pilgrimage to Jerusalem, died in and arose from the dead at Jerusalem, ascended to heaven from a nearby suburb of Jerusalem, and was prophesied in the Old Testament to return in His second advent at Jerusalem, the Lord might in all likelihood hover in the air over Jerusalem at the moment of the catching away of the saints! But of course the elevation of His hovering might be thousands or even tens of thousands of feet in the air over Jerusalem, perhaps 6,200 ft. or even 62,000 ft. Again the title *our Lord* is mentioned in 62 verses of the Pauline Epistles.

The King of Salem

"To whom also Abraham gave a tenth part of all; first being by interpretation King of righteousness, and after that also <u>King of</u> SALEM, which is, <u>King of</u> PEACE; Without father, without mother, without descent, having neither beginning of days, nor end of life; but made like unto the Son of God; abideth a priest continually" (Heb. 7:2-3). The writer here compared the currently reigning Christ to the ancient reigning King of Jerusalem. Again the phrase *the king of* is mentioned in 62 chapters of the OT Narrative.

The Heavenly Jerusalem Church

"But ye <u>are come unto</u> <u>mount SION,</u> <u>and unto the city of the</u> <u>living God,</u> <u>the heavenly JERUSALEM,</u> and to an innumerable <u>company</u> of angels, To <u>the general assembly</u> and <u>church of the firstborn,</u> which are written in heaven, and to God the Judge of all, and to the spirits of just men made perfect" (Heb. 12:22-23). The heavenly Jerusalem is comprised of a heavenly company of saints and angels. This verse presents the Bible's 62nd occurrence of the term *firstborn*, and it is associated with the city of Jerusalem. The word *company* occurs 62 times in the Old Testament! The Bible combination *are come unto* (8x), *mount Sion* (3x), *and unto the city* (1x), *city of the* (17x), *living God* (30x), *the heavenly Jerusalem* (1x), *the general assembly* (1x), *church of the firstborn* (1x) = 62. The word *firstborn* is mentioned in 62 chapters of the Bible.

Zion's Chief Cornerstone

"Wherefore also it is contained in the scripture, Behold, I lay in SION a chief corner stone, elect, precious: and he that believeth on him shall not be confounded" (1 Pet. 2:6). This Zion verse immediately precedes the 7262nd verse of the New Testament.

New Heavens & New Earth = New Jerusalem

"Looking for and hasting unto the coming of the day of God, wherein the heavens being on fire shall be dissolved, and the elements shall melt with fervent heat? Nevertheless we, according to his promise, look for <u>new</u> heavens and a <u>new</u> earth, <u>wherein dwelleth righteousness</u>" (2 Pet. 3:12-13). The New Testament combination *new* (61x) and *wherein dwelleth righteousness* (1x) = 62.

62nd Book of the Bible

FIRST JOHN is the 62nd BOOK of the Bible because it speaks on a mystery level of Jerusalem. Be aware that John always wrote on the mystery level, whether in his Gospel Record, his three Epistles, or his Apocalyptic Letter. The mystery level is the fourth level in Hebraic interpretation; it is called Sod meaning deep. As you know, mysteries lie within the deep, the hidden, and the unknown. John's mysteries are all made accessible through seeking.

The aged apostle gave this book as an instructive, practical letter written by the heavenly Father and handed down to His heavenly family dwelling on Earth. Indeed it is a love letter from Jerusalem above written to Jerusalem below. The divine principle of the Father's heavenly will is this: As in Heaven, So on Earth. In C. I. Scofield's First John introductory notes he wrote, "John's Gospel leads across the threshold of the Father's house; his first Epistle makes us at home there." We know that the Father's earthly House was built in Jerusalem. In his Apocalyptic Letter John tells us that the city of God in heaven is called New Jerusalem, a place no doubt wherein stands God's eternal House. The controlling theme of First John is fellowship with the Father, experienced through walking in obedience toward His Son Jesus Christ and walking in love toward the brethren. In mystery form, John would see God's dear children walking in Jerusalem's pure light, love, and life!

Walking in Jerusalem's LIGHT—Chapters 1 & 2

"But if we <u>walk</u> in <u>the light</u>, as he is in <u>the light</u>, we have fellowship one with another, and <u>the blood</u> of Jesus Christ <u>his Son</u> cleanseth us from all sin" (1 John 1:7). To confirm the manner of light of which John now speaks, consider the following thought. In his mystical Apocalyptic Letter, John said that the saved nations shall all walk in New Jerusalem's holy and eternal light. The lowercase word *walk* occurs 62 times in the New Testament. Prior to this first mention of *the light*, in John's Epistle the phrase is mentioned in 62 previous chapters of the Bible. If anyone knows anything about the blood of Jesus Christ it was John because he was standing at the Cross when Christ's side was pierced and let to bleed. The blood of God's Son was shed in Jerusalem. The phrase *the blood* occurs 62 times in Leviticus! Again the phrase *his son* is mentioned in 62 verses of First and Second Chronicles.

"My <u>little children</u>, these things write I unto you, that ye sin not. And if any man sin, we have an advocate with the Father, Jesus Christ the righteous" (2:1). The heavenly Father seeks to maintain Jerusalem-wide fellowship with His citizen children as they maintain heartfelt confession before Him. The Bible phrases *little children* (20x), *little child* (40x), *little lad* (1x), *little sister* (1x) = 62. Again the phrase *the children* occurs 62 times in the New Testament.

"Brethren, I <u>write</u> no new commandment <u>unto you</u>, but an old commandment which ye had from the beginning. The old commandment is the word which ye have heard from the beginning. Again, a new commandment I write unto you, which thing is true in him and in you: because the darkness is past, and the true light now shineth" (2:7-8). The old commandment was the apostles' doctrine which was first delivered in Jerusalem some sixty years earlier. John's repeated use of the word "write" reminds us that he was writing this Letter to heaven-bound citizens of the New Jerusalem. The word *write* is mentioned in 62 chapters of the Bible. The phrase *unto you* occurs 162 times in the Synoptic Gospels. The phrase *unto you* is mentioned in 62 chapters of the Pauline, General, and Apocalyptic Epistles.

A central part of John's Letter comes as a warning to believers that they might be on guard against false teachers whose false teachings deny Christ's supremacy, even denying that He died and rose again at Jerusalem as God in the flesh. The first-century Jerusalem Church which was overseen by all the apostles regularly exposed heretics and made them repent or else depart. "They went out from us, but they were not of us; for if they had been of us, they would no doubt have continued with us: but they went out, that they might be made manifest that they were not all of us" (2:19). The Bible combination *they went out* (28 vs) and *he went out* (34 vs) = 62 verses. Again the word *went* occurs 1062 times in the Old Testament. Again the word *from* occurs 462 times in the NT Narrative. The word *us* is mentioned in 62 chapters of the Law.

Walking in Jerusalem's LOVE—Chapters 3 & 4

The heart of this 62nd book of the Bible is its middle chapter—chapter three—the 1162nd chapter of the Bible. Notice how John commences it: "Behold, what manner of love the Father hath bestowed upon us, that we should be called the sons of God" (3:1a). Born-again citizens belonging to New Jerusalem should walk in love even as Christ now does. Again the word *love* is mentioned in 162 chapters of the Bible.

"Whosoever is born of God doth not commit sin; for his seed remaineth in him: and he cannot sin, because he is born of God" (3:9). To better understand this 1162nd chapter and its mysterious connection to New Jerusalem, consider that John's only use of the word "seed" here refers to born-again children of God who now possess legal citizenship in the New Jerusalem! God can only produce a godly seed, and the King of Heaven can only produce royal children. The Major and Minor Prophets combination *seed* (60x), *seed's* (1x), *godly* (1x) = 62. The Major and Minor Prophets combination *seed* (60x) and *king's* (2x) = 62. The New Testament combination *born* (45 vs), *in Jerusalem* (16 vs), *doth not commit sin* (1 v) = 62 verses.

"Hereby perceive we the love of God, because he laid down his life for us: and we ought to lay down our lives for the brethren" (3:16). The Son of God laid His life down for us outside the walls of Jerusalem. First, He had to walk through Jerusalem's scornful streets carrying the cross. As believers now go without the holy camp they are to walk in love one toward another, even with that same love they hold for Jesus and for Jerusalem. The term *his brethren* (157x) and *his * brethren* (5x) occurs 162 combined times in the Bible.

The 62nd verse of First John describes how God's Jerusalemite children are born of His Jerusalem-descending Spirit: "And he that keepeth his commandments dwelleth in him, and he in him. And hereby we know that he abideth in us, by the Spirit which he hath given us" (3:24). John will never forget that notable day of Pentecost in Jerusalem. The title *the S/spirit* is mentioned in 162 chapters of the Bible.

Walking in Jerusalem's LIFE—Chapter 5

"And this is the record, that God hath given to us eternal life, and this life is in his Son. . . . These things have I written unto you that believe on the name of the Son of God; that ye may know that ye have eternal life, and that ye may believe on the name of the Son of God" (5:11, 13). As Jesus was raised in newness of life at Jerusalem, so has every born-again believer been spiritually and metaphorically raised along with Him. We are therefore to walk in His life and go in and out of the earthly Jerusalem with His glorious gospel upon our lips. The word *life* occurs 62 times in the Law. Again the phrase *his son* is mentioned in 162 verses of the Old Testament.

As John ends his Letter to the rightful citizens of New Jerusalem, he reminds them of the reason for Jesus' condescension to earthly Jerusalem. "And we know that the Son of God is <u>come</u>, and hath given us an understanding, that we may know him that is true, and we are in him that is true, even in his Son Jesus Christ. This is the true God, and eternal life" (5:20). Again the phrase *come to* is mentioned in 62 chapters of the OT Narrative. The Gospels combination *come to* (59x), *the holy city* (2x), *the city of Jerusalem* (1x) = 62.

Elect Lady—The Jerusalem Church

Through a metaphor the aged apostle addressed the New Testament mother church, the Jerusalem Church: "The elder unto the <u>elect</u> <u>lady</u> and <u>her children</u>, whom <u>I love</u> in <u>the truth</u>; and not I only, but also all they that have known <u>the truth</u>" (2 John 1:1). The Church at Jerusalem saw many conversions whereby children of God became born again by faith. The Bible combination *elect* (17x), *lady* (4x), *her children* (19x), *I love* (22x) = 62. The New Testament phrases *the truth* (61 vs) and *the truth's* (1 v) = 62 verses.

Jerusalem Church's Elect Sister—Church of Ephesus

"<u>The children</u> <u>of thy</u> <u>elect</u> <u>sister</u> <u>greet thee</u>. <u>Amen</u>" (2 John 1:13). John preferred to write with metaphors. Churches share in equality like sisters. They do not share a mother-and-daughter relationship but are rather like sisters to each other who share the same spiritual parentage of that Heavenly Jerusalem. Again the phrase *the children of* is mentioned in 62 verses of Nehemiah. Again the phrase *the children* occurs 62 times in the New Testament. The New Testament combination *of thy* (35x), *elect* (13x), *sister* (15x) – *greet thee* (1x) = 62. This verse presents the Bible's 62nd verse-mention of the word *Amen*.

New Jerusalem's Heavenly Dominion

"And hath made us kings and priests unto God and his Father; to him be glory and <u>dominion</u> for ever and ever. Amen" (Rev. 1:6). Again the word *dominion* occurs 62 times in the Bible, and this verse presents its 62nd occurrence.

The City of New Jerusalem

"Him that overcometh will I make a pillar in the temple of my God, and he shall go no more out: and I will write upon him the name of my God, and <u>the name of THE CITY OF MY GOD</u>, <u>which is new</u> JERUSALEM, which cometh down out of heaven from my God: and I will write upon him my new name" (Rev. 3:12). This verse presents the Bible's 762nd verse-mention of the name *Jerusalem*. The New Testament combination *which is* (261x) and *the name of the city of my God* (1x) = 262. The New Testament words *new* (61x) and *newborn* (1x) = 62. In this verse there are 62 words surrounding the keyword *Jerusalem*.

A Lamb Standing on Mount Sion

"And I looked, and, lo, a Lamb <u>stood</u> <u>on the mount SION</u>, and with him an hundred forty and four thousand, having his Father's name written in their foreheads" (Rev. 14:1). The Major and

Minor Prophets combination *stood* (60x), *upon mount Zion* (2x) = 62.

New Jerusalem's Bridal Adornment

"And I John saw THE HOLY CITY, NEW JERUSALEM, coming down from God out of heaven, <u>prepared as</u> <u>a bride adorned</u> <u>for her husband</u>" (Rev. 21:2). John envisioned the Holy City coming down to join proximity with the earthly Jerusalem. The Bible combination *prepared as* (2x), *a bride adorned for* (1x), *her husband* (59x) = 62.

New Jerusalem's Holy Fountain

"And he said unto me, It is done. I am Alpha and Omega, the beginning and the end. I will give unto him that is athirst of the fountain of the water of life freely" (Rev. 21:6). This is the 362nd verse of Revelation, and it refers to a holy fountain in the city of New Jerusalem.

New Jerusalem's Great Mountain

"And he carried me away in the spirit to a great and high <u>mountain</u>, and <u>shewed</u> me that <u>great</u> CITY, the holy JERUSALEM, descending out of heaven from God, Having the glory <u>of God</u>: and her light was like unto a stone most precious, even like a jasper stone, clear as crystal" (Rev. 21:10-11). Again the phrase *the mountain* occurs 62 times in the Bible. Again the word *shew* occurs 162 times in the Old Testament. The phrase *of God* occurs 162 times in the Gospels.

> The word *great* is mentioned in 62 chapters of the Law.
> The word *great* is mentioned in 162 verses of the Major Prophets.
> The word *great* occurs 962 times in the Bible.

New Jerusalem's Directional Gates

John saw the New Jerusalem and all of its glorious gates. "On the east three <u>gates</u>; on the north three <u>gates</u>; on the south three <u>gates</u>; and on <u>the west</u> three <u>gates</u>" (Rev. 21:13). Again the phrase *the west* occurs 62 times in Scripture. We repeat the following Jerusalem seals.

> The phrase *the gates* is mentioned in 62 verses of the OT.
> The phrase *the gate* occurs 162 times in the Bible.
> The phrase *the gate of* occurs 62 times in the Old Testament.
> The phrase *the gate of* is mentioned in 62 verses of the Bible.

New Jerusalem's Jasper Walls

"And he that talked with me had a golden reed to <u>measure</u> THE CITY, and <u>the gates</u> <u>thereof</u>, and <u>the wall</u> <u>thereof</u>" (Rev. 21:15). Again the word *measure* is mentioned in 62 verses of the Bible. The word *thereof* occurs naturally 62 times in the Minor Prophets. We repeat the following seals.

> The word *walls* is mentioned in 62 verses of the Old Testament.
> The phrase *wall(s) of* occurs 62 times in the Bible.

New Jerusalem's Four Sides

"And the city lieth foursquare, and the length is as large as the breadth: and he measured the city with the reed, twelve thousand furlongs. The length and the breadth and the height of it are equal" (Rev. 21:16). The Bible combination *the length* (60x), *and the breadth and* (1x), *the height of it are equal* (1x) = 62. Again the word *height* occurs 62 times in the Bible.

New Jerusalem's Golden Streets

"And the twelve gates were twelve pearls; every several gate was of one pearl: <u>and the street</u> of THE CITY <u>was pure gold</u>, as it were <u>transparent glass</u>" (Rev. 21:21). The Bible combination *and the street/s* (2 vs), *of the city* (158 vs), *was pure gold* (2 vs) = 162 verses. The Bible combination *gold* (361 vs) and *transparent glass* (1 v) = 362 verses.

New Jerusalem's Divine Glory

"And <u>THE CITY</u> had no need of the sun, neither of the <u>moon</u>, to shine in it: for <u>the glory of</u> God did lighten it, and the Lamb is the <u>light</u> thereof" (Rev. 21:23). The word *moon/s* occurs 62 combined times in the Bible. The Bible combination *the glory of the* (53x) and *the holy city* (9x) = 62. We repeat the following Jerusalem seals.

> The word *light* is mentioned naturally in 62 verses of the Wisdom Books.
> The word *light* occurs 62 times in the NT Narrative.
> The word *light* is mentioned in 162 chapters of the Bible.

New Jerusalem's Citizen Registry

"And there shall in no wise <u>enter</u> into <u>it</u> any thing that defileth, neither whatsoever worketh abomination, or maketh a lie: but they which are <u>written in the</u> Lamb's <u>book</u> of life" (Rev. 21:27). The Lamb's Book of Life is simply a registry of the New Jerusalem's legitimate residences. Yes, this eternal city will forever bear a public record of its eternal citizenry. Again the word *enter* is mentioned in 62 chapters of the Old Testament. The word *it* is mentioned in 62 verses of First Chronicles. The phrase *written in the book* occurs naturally 62 times in the Old Testament.

Go through the Gates of New Jerusalem!

"Blessed are they that do his commandments, that they may have right to the tree of life, and may enter in <u>through the gates</u> into THE CITY" (Rev. 22:14). Again the phrase *through the* occurs 62 times in the New Testament. Again the OT Narrative combination *through* (61x), *the gates of Jerusalem be opened* (1x) = 62. Again the NT Narrative combination *through* (61x), *the gates of* (1x) = 62.

63—God's Wrath

The dictionary gives us two definitions of the word WRATH: [1] strong, stern, or <u>fierce</u> <u>anger</u>, deeply resentful <u>indignation</u>; and [2] <u>vengeance</u> or <u>punishment</u> as the consequence of anger. The Bible uses the word WROTH as an adjective for wrath.

The Major/Minor Prophets combination: *vengeance* (27x), *wrath* (36x) = 63.
The Wisdom Books combination: *fierceness of his anger* (1x), *wrath* (62x) = 63.
All forms of the word *punish* are mentioned in 63 collective verses of the Bible.

God's wrath upon man is not arbitrary but rather based on His holy laws which have been made known unto man regarding His attitude toward our sin. Because wrath has such a permanent and devastating effect upon man, God often patiently holds it in reserve lest He seem to be a harsh God. However, all unrepentant sinners will one day become the object of God's eternal wrath.

The phrase *of God* is mentioned in 63 verses of Luke's Gospel.
The phrase *of God('s)* occurs 163 times in the Gospels.
The title *God* is found in 63 books of the Bible!
The title *God* is mentioned in 63 verses of Joshua.
The title *God* occurs 163 times in Romans.
The title *God* occurs naturally 63 times in First John.
The phrase *God/GOD of* is mentioned in 63 chapters of the Major Prophets.
The title *G/god* is mentioned in 663 verses of the Pauline Epistles.

~~~~

The title *LORD God/Lord GOD* occurs 163 times in the OT Narrative.
The title *Lord* occurs 63 times in the Wisdom Books.
The title *Lord* is mentioned in 63 verses of the Wisdom Books.
The title *Lord* occurs 463 times in the Old Testament.

Eve to Experience a Measure of God's Wrath

"<u>Unto the woman he said, I will greatly multiply thy sorrow and thy conception; in sorrow thou shalt bring forth children</u>" (Gen. 3:16a). The next time that Eve gave birth she would experience a very painful reminder of God's wrath toward her disobedience. The Bible combination *unto the woman he said* (1x), *I will greatly* (3x), *multiply thy* (4x), *sorrow and* (12x), *thy conception* (1x), *in sorrow* (4x), *thou shalt* (1250x), *bring forth* (85x), *children* (1803x) = 3163.

Adam to Experience a measure of God's Wrath

"<u>And unto Adam he said, Because thou hast hearkened unto the voice of thy wife, and hast eaten of the tree, of which I commanded thee, saying, Thou shalt not eat of it</u>: cursed is the ground for thy sake; in sorrow shalt thou eat of it all the days of thy life; Thorns also and thistles shall it bring forth to thee; and thou shalt eat the herb of the field; <u>In the sweat of thy face shalt thou eat bread, till thou return unto the ground</u>; for out of it wast thou taken: for <u>dust</u> thou art, and unto <u>dust</u> shalt thou return" (Gen. 3:17-19).

The Bible combination *and unto Adam he said* (1x), *because thou hast* (55x), *hearkened unto the* (4x), *voice of thy wife* (1x), *and hast eaten of* (1x), *the tree of knowledge of good and evil* (1x) = 63. The word *cursed* is mentioned in 63 verses of the Old Testament. The sentence *in the sweat of thy face shalt thou eat bread, till thou return unto the ground* consists of 63 letters!

The phrase *the dust* occurs 63 times in the Old Testament.
The phrase *the dust* is mentioned in 63 verses of the Bible.

Cain to Experience God's Wrath

"And now art thou <u>cursed</u> from the earth, which hath opened her mouth to receive thy brother's blood from thy hand; When thou tillest the ground, it shall not henceforth yield unto thee her strength; <u>a fugitive and a vagabond shalt thou be in the earth</u>. <u>And Cain said unto the LORD</u>, My PUNISHMENT is <u>greater than</u> <u>I can bear</u>" (Gen. 4:11-13). Again the word *cursed* is mentioned in 63 verses of the Old Testament. The Bible combination *a fugitive and a vagabond shalt thou be in the earth* (1x), *and Cain said unto the LORD* (1x), *punishment* (27x), *greater than* (33x), *I can bear* (1x) = 63.

God's Coming Wrath

"And GOD looked upon the earth, and, behold, it was corrupt; for all flesh had corrupted his way upon the earth. And GOD said unto Noah, The end of all flesh is come before me; for the earth is filled with violence through them; and, behold, <u>I will</u> <u>destroy them with the earth</u>" (Gen. 6:12-13). The Bible combination *I will* (562 chs), *destroy them with the earth* (1 ch) = 563 chapters. The Old Testament combination *I will* (1362 vs), *destroy them with the earth* (1 v) = 1363 verses.

God's Great Wrath

"And GOD saw that the <u>wickedness of man was</u> <u>great</u> in the earth, and that every imagination of the thoughts of his heart was only evil continually. And it repented the LORD that he had made man on the earth, and it grieved him at his heart. And <u>the LORD said, I will destroy man whom I have created from the face of the earth</u>; both man, and beast, and the creeping thing, and the fowls of the air; for it repenteth me that I have made them. But Noah found grace in the eyes of the LORD" (Gen. 6:5-8). Man's great wickedness deserves God's great wrath. The word *great* is mentioned in 163 verses of the Major Prophets. The Genesis combination *wickedness of man was* (1x), *great* (62x) = 63. The OT Narrative combination *the wickedness* (3x) and *great* (260x) = 263. The term *the wicked(ness)* occurs naturally 63 times in the Major and Minor Prophets. The words *the LORD said, I will destroy man whom I have created from the face of the earth* consist of 63 letters!

God's Destructive Wrath

"And, behold, I, even I, do <u>bring</u> a flood of waters upon the earth, to <u>destroy</u> <u>all flesh, wherein is the breath of life</u>, from under heaven; and <u>every thing that is in the earth</u> <u>shall die</u>" (Gen. 6:17). The word *bring* occurs 63 times in Leviticus. The word *destroy* is mentioned in 63 chapters of the Major and Minor Prophets. The Bible combination *destroy* (261x), *all flesh wherein is the breath of life* (2x) = 263. The Old Testament combination *every thing that is in the earth* (1 v), *shall die* (62 vs) = 63 verses.

God's Overflowing Wrath

"And, behold, I, even I, do bring a <u>flood</u> <u>of waters upon the earth</u>, to destroy all flesh, wherein is the breath of life, from under heaven; and every thing that is in the earth shall die" (Gen. 6:17). The Genesis combination *flood* (12x), *of waters* (3x), *upon the earth* (48x) = 63. The Bible combination *flood/s* (62x), *of waters upon the earth* (1x) = 63. The Bible combination *flood/s*

(62x), *overflowed with water* (1x) = 63.

God's Calculated Wrath

"In the six hundredth year of Noah's life, in the second month, the seventeenth day of the month, the same day were all the fountains of the great deep broken up, and the windows of heaven were opened. And the rain was upon the earth <u>forty</u> days and <u>forty</u> nights. . . . And all flesh died that moved upon the earth, both of fowl, and of cattle, and of beast, and of every creeping thing that creepeth upon the earth, and every man: All in whose nostrils was the breath of life, of all that was in the dry land, died" (Gen. 6:11-12, 21-22). The number *forty* occurs 63 times in the OT Narrative.

God's Scattering Wrath

"Therefore <u>is</u> the name of it called Babel; because the LORD did there confound the language of <u>all the earth</u>: and from thence did the LORD scatter them abroad upon the face of <u>all the earth</u>" (Gen. 11:9). When God brought this societal confusion upon mankind they became frightened. They felt His divine wrath in a very discomforting way. The phrase *all the earth* is mentioned in 63 verses Bible. The word *is* is the 63,663rd word of the Bible, and it pertains to God's wrath on Babel.

Sodom & Gomorrah Experienced God's Wrath

"Then the LORD rained <u>upon Sodom and upon Gomorrah</u> brimstone and <u>fire</u> <u>from the LORD</u> out of heaven; And he overthrew those cities, and all the plain, and all the inhabitants of the cities, and that which grew upon the ground" (Gen. 19:24-25). Altogether five cities in the region experienced fiery God's wrath that day. The Old Testament combination *upon Sodom and upon Gomorrah* (1x), *fire came* (2x), *from the LORD/Lord* (60x) = 63.

Egypt Will Experience God's Wrath

"And the Egyptians shall <u>know</u> that <u>I am the LORD</u>, when I <u>stretch forth</u> <u>mine hand</u> upon Egypt, and bring out the children of Israel from among them" (Exod. 7:5). The Bible oftentimes uses the word "know" to refer to experiential knowledge. Hence Egypt will experience God's wrath. The word *know* occurs 763 times in the Bible. The phrase *I am the LORD/Lord* occurs 163 times in the Old Testament. The Old Testament combination *stretch forth* (12 chs), *mine hand* (51 chs) = 63 chapters.

God's Hand of Wrath

"Then the LORD said unto Moses, Go in unto Pharaoh, and tell him, Thus saith the LORD GOD of the Hebrews, Let my people go, that they may serve me. For if thou refuse to let them go, and wilt hold them still, Behold, <u>the hand</u> of the LORD is upon thy cattle which is in the field, <u>upon the</u> horses, <u>upon the</u> asses, <u>upon the</u> camels, <u>upon the</u> oxen, and upon the sheep: there shall be a very grievous murrain" (Exod. 9:1-3). The phrase *upon the* is mentioned naturally in 63 verses of Genesis.

> The phrase *the hand* is mentioned in 363 verses of the Bible.
> The phrase *his hand* occurs naturally 63 times in the Law.
> The Bible: *my hand* (53 vs), *of wrath* (10 vs) = 63 verses.

"He that feared the word of the LORD among the servants of Pharaoh made his servants and his cattle flee into the houses" (Exod. 9:20). Some Egyptians did not want to experience God's wrath after hearing that a devastating hail storm was coming their way.

God's Wrath—One Fiery Hail Storm

"And Moses stretched forth his rod toward heaven: and the LORD sent thunder and hail, and the fire ran along upon the ground; and the LORD rained hail upon the land of Egypt. So there was hail, and fire mingled with the hail, very grievous, such as there was none like it in all the land of Egypt since it became a nation. And the hail smote throughout all the land of Egypt all that was in the field, both man and beast; and the hail smote every herb of the field, and brake every tree of the field" (Exod. 9:23-25).

The Exodus combination *and the LORD rained* (1x), *hail upon* (1x), *the land of Egypt* (60x), *and fire mingled with the hail* (1x) = 63.

Pharaoh Will Experience God's Wrath

"And the LORD said unto Moses, Pharaoh shall not hearken unto you; that my wonders may be multiplied in the land of Egypt" (Exod. 11:9). The combination *Almighty* (57x), *all might* (2x), *all power* (2x), *all my power* (1x), *all my wonders* (1x) = 63.

God's Wrath Demands Blood to Satiate It

"And the blood shall be to you for a token upon the houses where ye are: and when I see the blood, I will pass over you, and the plague shall not be upon you to destroy you, when I smite the land of Egypt" (Exod. 12:13). Even the firstborn among the Israelites would have suffered God's wrath had they not applied the blood of a lamb to their doorways. It was God's merciful design to allow an innocent substitute to become the recipient of the sinner's deserved wrath. The word *blood* occurs 163 times in the Law. The phrase *the plague* occurs 63 times in the Law. The phrase *upon you* is mentioned naturally in 63 verses of the Bible.

63rd Chapter of the Bible

Exodus chapter thirteen stands as a memorial of God's former wrath upon the firstborn of Egypt, whether they were men or beasts. This wrath-of-God chapter begins with Moses establishing a day of fearful remembrance.

"And the LORD spake unto Moses, saying, Sanctify unto me all the firstborn, whatsoever openeth the womb among the children of Israel, both of man and of beast: it is mine. And Moses said unto the people, Remember this day, in which ye came out from Egypt, out of the house of bondage; for by strength of hand the LORD brought you out from this place: there shall no leavened bread be eaten. This day came ye out in the month Abib" (Exod. 13:1-4). Egypt's strength was no match for God's strength. The word *strength* is mentioned in 163 chapters of the Bible.

The Israelites are reminded by the Lord that when they come into the Promised Land they are to observe this memorial week with great reverence and respect towards the Lord. "Unleavened bread shall be eaten seven days; and there shall no leavened bread be seen with thee, neither shall there be leaven seen with thee in all thy quarters" (v. 7). God had already warned that if any Hebrew was found with leaven in his house he would incur His divine wrath by being "cut off" from among the earth; so this injunction comes as a double warning (12:15, 19). The phrase *cut off* is mentioned in 189 verses of the Bible, a multiple of 63.

God also told the Hebrews "that thou shalt set apart unto the LORD all that openeth the matrix, and every firstling that cometh of a beast which thou hast; the males shall be the LORD'S. And every firstling of an ass thou shalt redeem with a lamb; and if thou wilt not redeem it, <u>then thou shalt break his neck</u>" (13:12-13). Future generations were to perform a ceremony which involves making a choice. If the wrong choice is made, God's wrath must be acted out in a tangible parabolic way. The Bible combination *then thou shalt break his* (1x), *neck* (62x) = 63.

"And it shall be when thy son asketh thee in time to come, saying, What is this? that thou shalt say unto him, By strength of hand the LORD brought us out from Egypt, from the house of bondage: And it came to pass, when Pharaoh would hardly let us go, that the LORD slew all the <u>firstborn</u> in the land of Egypt, both the <u>firstborn</u> of man, and the <u>firstborn</u> of beast: therefore I sacrifice to the LORD all that openeth the matrix, being males; but all the firstborn of my children I redeem" (vv. 14-15). The related Bible words *firstborn* (62 chs) and *firstbegotten* (1 ch) = 63 chapters.

Egyptian Army Experiences God's Wrath

"And Moses stretched forth his hand over the sea, and the sea returned to his strength when the morning appeared; and the Egyptians fled against it; and the LORD overthrew the Egyptians in the midst of the sea. And the waters returned, and covered the chariots, and the horsemen, and all the host of Pharaoh that came into the sea after them; there remained not so much as one of them. . . . and Israel saw the Egyptians <u>dead</u> upon the sea shore" (Exod. 14:27-28, 30b). All death is the resultant effect of God's judgments upon man's inherent sin nature. In this case Egypt's sin was exceeding, and therefore their death came prematurely. Egypt was never a great national power from this time forth. The word *dead* occurs naturally 363 times in the Bible.

God Sends Forth His Wrath

"And in the greatness of thine excellency thou hast overthrown <u>them that rose up against thee</u>: <u>thou sentest forth thy WRATH</u>, which <u>consumed them as stubble</u>" (Exod. 15:7). This verse presents the Bible's first mention of the word "wrath" as belonging to God. The Bible combination *them that rose* (4x), *up against thee* (8x), *thou sentest forth* (1x), *thy wrath* (16x), *consumed them* (14x), *as if they were* (2x), *stubble* (18x) = 63.

God's Voice of Wrath Expressed at Mount Sinai

"And it came to pass on the third day in the morning, that there were thunders and lightning, and a thick cloud upon the mount, and the <u>voice</u> of the trumpet exceeding loud; so that all the people that was in the camp trembled" (Exod. 19:16). The nature of God's awaiting wrath upon man's present sin was unmistakable at this time. When God uttered the words "Thou shalt not," Israel understood He meant exactly what He said! The word *voice* is mentioned in 63 chapters of the New Testament.

God's Wrath Will Wax Hot

"Ye shall not afflict any widow, or fatherless child. If thou afflict them in any wise, and they cry at all unto me, <u>I will surely hear their cry</u>; <u>And my WRATH shall wax hot, and I will kill you with the sword</u>" (Exod. 22:22-24a). The Bible combination *I will surely hear their cry* (1x), *and my wrath* (2x), *shall wax hot* (1x), *and I will kill you* (1x), *with the sword* (58x) = 63.

God Warns Israel of His Angel's Wrath

"Behold, I send <u>an Angel</u> before thee, to keep thee in the way, and to bring thee into the place which I have prepared. <u>Beware</u> of him, and obey his voice, <u>provoke him not</u>; for he will not pardon your transgressions: for my name is in him" (Exod. 23:20-21). Because God's name is in this Angel, this Angel's wrath is synonymous with God's wrath. The Bible combination *an angel* (34x), *beware* (28x), *provoke him not* (1x) = 63.

Breach of Sabbath Law Will Invoke God's Wrath

"Six days may work be done; but in the seventh is the sabbath of rest, holy to the LORD: whosoever doeth any work in the <u>sabbath day</u>, he shall surely be put to <u>death</u>" (Exod. 31:15). The title *sabbath day(s)* occurs 63 times in the Bible. The word *death* is mentioned in 63 verses of the Law.

Golden Calf Incident Invoked God's Wrath

When the nation fashioned a golden calf the people immediately invoked God's wrath. "And the LORD said unto Moses, I have seen <u>this people</u>, and, behold, it is a stiffnecked people: Now therefore let me alone, that my WRATH may wax hot against them, and that I may consume them: and I will make of thee a great nation" (Exod. 32:9-10). The title *this people* is mentioned in 63 chapters of the Old Testament.

Moses Seeks to Turn Away God's Wrath

"Wherefore should the Egyptians speak, and say, For mischief did he bring them out, to slay <u>them</u> in the mountains, and to consume <u>them</u> from the face of the earth? Turn from thy FIERCE WRATH, and repent of this evil against thy people" (Exod. 32:12).

The word *them* occurs 63 times in Ezra.
The word *them* occurs 63 times in Job.

The Sword of the Lord

"Thus saith <u>the LORD GOD</u> of Israel, Put every man his <u>sword</u> by his side, and go in and out from gate to gate throughout the camp, and slay every man his brother, and every man his companion, and every man his neighbour. And the children of Levi did according to the word of Moses: and there fell of the people that day about three thousand men" (Exod. 32:27-28). Had it not been for Moses' prior prayerful intervention the people would have incurred God's full wrath. Only a small portion of the nation died that day when Levites went out with swords in proxy for the Lord. Again the title *LORD God/Lord GOD* occurs 163 times in the OT Narrative.

The phrase *the sword* occurs 63 times in Ezekiel.
The phrase *the sword* is mentioned in 163 chapters of the Bible.

63rd Verse of Leviticus

"And if the whole <u>congregation</u> of Israel sin through ignorance, and the thing be hid from the eyes of the assembly, and they have done somewhat against any of the <u>commandments</u> of the LORD concerning things which should not be done, and are guilty" (Lev. 4:13). The Lord goes on to instruct Moses that the priesthood should lay their hands on a bullock's head to transfer the people's sin thereon and then to kill the bullock. After this, the priest would take of the bullock's blood and dip his finger in it and sprinkle it <u>seven</u> times before the Lord. This punishable act on their part would satisfy God's wrath in the matter. The word *congregation* occurs 363 times in the Old Testament. The word *seven* occurs 463 times in the Bible. The word *commandments* occurs 63 times in the Law.

God's Wrath against the Sin

"When the sin, which they have sinned against it, is known, then the congregation shall offer a young bullock for the sin, and bring him before the tabernacle of the congregation" (Lev. 4:14). The phrase *the sin* is mentioned naturally in 63 verses of the Bible.

A Sin Offering Satisfies God's Wrath

"And he shall do with the bullock as he did with the bullock for a sin offering, so shall he do with this: and the priest shall make an atonement for them, and it shall be forgiven them" (Lev. 4:20). Only an offering for sin can put away a sinner's sin and an angry God's wrath. The phrase *a sin offering* is mentioned in 63 verses of the Bible.

Fiery Trespassing Offering Subdues God's Wrath

"And the priest shall burn them upon the altar for an offering made by fire unto the LORD: it is a trespass offering" (Lev. 7:5). The word "trespass" refers to any guilty offense against God. To trespass against God is to breach any one of His commandments. Under this old dispensation such guilty offenses brought about God's wrath, and only an animal offering made by - could allay His wrath. All forms of the word *trespass* are mentioned in 63 chapters of the Bible. The word *offerings* occurs naturally 263 times in the Bible.

> The phrase *made by fire* occurs 63 times in the Bible.
> The phrase *by fire* occurs 63 times in the Law.

Nadab & Abihu Experienced God's Devouring Wrath

"And Nadab and Abihu, the sons of Aaron, took either of them his censer, and put fire therein, and put incense thereon, and offered strange fire before the LORD, which he commanded them not. And there went out fire from the LORD, and devoured them, and they died before the LORD" (Lev. 10:1-2). Willful disobedience can easily invoke God's wrath. The word *devour* occurs 63 times in the Old Testament.

Lest God's Wrath Return

"And Moses said unto Aaron, and unto Eleazar and unto Ithamar, his sons, Uncover not your heads, neither rend your clothes; lest ye die, and lest WRATH come upon all the people: but let your brethren, the whole house of Israel, bewail the burning which the LORD hath kindled" (Lev. 10:6). These close family members were not permitted to customarily mourn for Nadab and Abihu's deaths lest they show sorrow or regret over the punitive matter. They were rather to visibly vindicate the righteousness of God regarding this unfortunate event. Here the underlined word *lest* is the 163rd word of this chapter, and it supports the word keyword wrath. The word *lest* is mentioned naturally in 63 verses of the Law.

Making Idols Will Invoke God's Wrath

"Turn ye not unto idols, nor make to yourselves molten gods: I am the LORD your GOD" (Lev. 19:4). The word *idols* occurs 63 times in the Major and Minor Prophets.

Seven Increasing Degrees of God's Wrath

"But if ye will not hearken unto me, and will not do all these <u>commandments</u>; And if ye shall despise my statutes, or if your soul abhor my <u>judgments</u>, so that ye will not do all my <u>commandments</u>, but that ye break my covenant: I also will do this unto you; I will even appoint over you terror, consumption, and the burning ague, that shall consume the eyes, and cause sorrow of heart: and ye shall sow your seed in vain, for your enemies shall eat it. And I will set my face against you . . . And if ye will not be reformed by me by these things, but will walk contrary unto me; Then will I also walk contrary unto you, and will PUNISH you yet <u>seven</u> times for your sins. . . . And ye shall perish among the heathen, and the land of your enemies shall eat you up. And they that are left of you shall pine away in their iniquity in your enemies' lands; and also in the iniquities of their fathers shall they pine away with them" (Lev. 26:14-17a, 23-24, 38-39).

Again the word *commandments* occurs 63 times in the Law. The word *judgment(s)* occurs naturally 63 times in the Law. Again all forms of the word *punish* are mentioned in 63 collective verses of the Bible. Again the word *seven* occurs 463 times in the Bible.

Idol Worshipers Will Experience God's Wrath

"And I will destroy your high places, and cut down your images, <u>and cast</u> your carcases upon the carcases of your idols, and my soul shall abhor you" (Lev. 26:30). The phrase *and cast* occurs 63 times in the Old Testament and is mentioned in 63 verses thereof.

Punishment for Israel's Iniquities

"And that I also have walked contrary unto them, and have brought them into the land of their enemies; if then their uncircumcised hearts be humbled, and they then accept of <u>the</u> PUNISHMENT of their iniquity" (Lev. 26:41). Here the underlined word *the* is the 1063rd word of this chapter, and it is the definite article of *punishment*, a form of God's wrath.

Taberah

"And when the people complained, it displeased the LORD: and the LORD heard it; and his ANGER was <u>kindled</u>; and <u>the fire</u> of the LORD burnt among them, and consumed them that were in the uttermost parts of the camp. And the people cried unto Moses; and when Moses prayed unto the LORD, <u>the fire</u> was quenched. And he called the name of the place Taberah: because <u>the fire of the LORD</u> <u>burnt</u> among them" (Num. 11:1-3). The word *kindled* occurs 63 times in the Old Testament. The Bible's 63rd occurrence of the phrase *the fire* is found in Psalm twenty-one and lies beside the word "wrath." The Numbers combination *the fire of the LORD* (2x), *burnt* (61x) = 63.

Kadesh-Barnea

 "And while the flesh was yet between their teeth, ere it was chewed, the WRATH of the LORD was <u>kindled</u> against <u>the people</u>, and the LORD smote <u>the people</u> with a very great plague" (Num. 11:33). Again the word *kindled* occurs 63 times in the Old Testament. The phrase *the people* is mentioned in 63 verses of the Wisdom Books.

Miriam Experienced God's Kindled Wrath

God said to Miriam, "wherefore then were ye not afraid to speak against my servant Moses? And the ANGER of the LORD was <u>kindled</u> against them; and he departed. And the cloud departed from off the tabernacle; and, behold, Miriam became leprous, white as snow: and Aaron looked upon Miriam, and, behold, she was leprous" (Num. 12:8c-10). Again the word *kindled* occurs 63 times in the Old Testament.

Wilderness Generation Experienced God's Wrath for Forty Years

"And the LORD said unto Moses, How long will this people provoke me? and how long will it be ere they believe me, for all the signs which I have shewed among them? I will smite them with the pestilence, and disinherit them, and will make of thee a greater nation and mightier than they. . . . But as for you, your carcases, they shall fall in this wilderness. And your children shall wander in the wilderness forty years, and bear your whoredoms, until your carcases be wasted in the wilderness. After the number of the days in which ye searched the land, even forty days, each day for a year, shall ye bear your iniquities, even forty years, and ye shall know my breach of promise. I the LORD have said, I will surely do it unto all this evil congregation, that are gathered together against me: in this wilderness they shall be consumed, and there they shall die. And the men, which Moses sent to search the land, who returned, and made all the congregation to murmur against him, by bringing up a slander upon the land, Even those men that did bring up the evil report upon the land, died by the plague before the LORD (Num. 14:11-12, 32-37).

The ten men who arrogantly led this rebellion were suddenly visited with God's wrath. All the people who had thought to rebel against the Lord by returning to Egypt were randomly visited by God's wrath during the forty-year period. Again the number *forty* occurs 63 times in the OT Narrative. Again the title *this people* is mentioned in 63 chapters of the Old Testament. Again the word *congregation* occurs 363 times in the Old Testament. Again the phrase *the plague* occurs 63 times in the Law.

God's Consuming Wrath

"And the LORD spake unto Moses and unto Aaron, saying, Separate yourselves from among this congregation, that I may consume them in a moment. And they fell upon their faces, and said, O GOD, the GOD of the spirits of all flesh, shall one man sin, and wilt thou be WROTH with?" (Num. 16:20-22). The lead word of this wrath-of-God verse *And* is the 563rd word of this chapter.

Korah & His Band Experienced God's Wrath

"And the earth opened her mouth, and swallowed them up, and their houses, and all the men that appertained unto Korah, and all their goods. They, and all that appertained to them, went down alive into the pit, and the earth closed upon them: and they perished from among the congregation. . . . And there came out a fire from the LORD, and consumed the two hundred and fifty men that offered incense" (Num. 16:32-33, 35). The Old Testament combination *went down* (61x), *alive into the pit* (1x), *and the earth closed upon them* (1x) = 63.

God's Wrath

Because the people came to Moses the next day accusing him of being responsible for the deaths of Korah and his associates God's wrath became instantly stirred up. "And Moses said unto Aaron, Take a censer, and put fire therein from off the altar, and put on incense, and go quickly unto the congregation, and make an atonement for them: for there is WRATH gone out from the LORD; the plague is begun" (Num. 16:46). Again the word *congregation* occurs 363 times in the Old Testament. Again the phrase *the plague* occurs 63 times in the Law. The Old Testament combination *there/therefore is wrath* (3x) and *from the LORD/Lord* (60x) = 63.

4263rd Verse of the Bible

"And ye shall keep the charge of the sanctuary, and the charge of the altar: that there be no WRATH any more upon the children of Israel" (Num. 18:5). The keyword *wrath* actually occurs in this 63rd verse.

Israel Experienced God's Sent Wrath

"And the people spake against GOD, and against Moses, Wherefore have ye brought us up out of Egypt to die in the wilderness? for there is no bread, neither is there any water; and our soul loatheth this light bread. And the LORD sent fiery serpents among the people, and they bit the people; and much people of Israel died" (Num. 21:5-6). The Lord's wrath rose up against Israel from underneath the hot desert sands! Again the phrase *the people* is mentioned in 63 verses of the Wisdom Books. The word *sent* is mentioned in 63 verses of the Bible.

> The name *Israel* is mentioned in 63 verses of the Wisdom Books.
> The title *the children of Israel* is mentioned in 63 verses of Joshua.
> The phrase *of the children of Israel* occurs 163 times in the Bible.

God's Wrath Allayed by a Transfixed Brass Serpent

"And Moses made a serpent of brass, and put it upon a pole, and it came to pass, that if a serpent had bitten any man, when he beheld the serpent of brass, he lived" (Num. 21:9). In the Bible brass is representative of judgment, and thus here, by association of God's wrath. Here God's wrath upon the sinner is immediately allayed by a simple look of faith upon a crucified brazen serpent. This event wonderfully typifies the transfixed Messiah who takes upon Himself the sinner's guilt and shame whenever the sinner looks to Him in faith believing and calls upon His saving name. The Old Testament combination *like a serpent* (4 vs) and *of brass* (59 vs) = 63 verses. The Bible combination *of brass* (60 vs), *serpent upon* (1 v), *a pole* (2 vs) = 63 verses.

Balaam to Experienced God's Wrath

"And GOD'S ANGER was kindled because he went: and the angel of the LORD stood in the way for an adversary against him. Now he was riding upon his ass, and his two servants were with him" (Num. 22:2). In the very end, Balaam died by the sword. Here the word *stood* is the Bible's 116,463rd word of the Bible, and it pertains to God's awaiting wrath. Again the word *kindled* occurs 63 times in the Old Testament.

Baal-Peor

"And Israel abode in Shittim, and the people began to commit whoredom with the daughters of Moab. . . . And Israel joined himself unto Baal-peor: and the ANGER of the LORD was kindled against Israel. And the LORD said unto Moses, Take all the heads of the people, and hang them up before the LORD against the sun, that the FIERCE ANGER of the LORD may be turned away from Israel. And Moses said unto the judges of Israel, Slay ye every one his men that were joined unto Baal-peor. . . . And those that died in the plague were twenty and four thousand" (Num. 25:1, 3-5, 9).

Again the name *Israel* is mentioned in 63 verses of the Wisdom Books. Again the word *kindled* occurs 63 times in the Old Testament. Again the phrase *the plague* occurs 63 times in the Law.

Moses Worried About God's Recurring Wrath

Because the two and a half tribes did not want to enter the Promised Land but rather settle east of the Jordan, Moses feared that God would count them as rebels. Thus he exclaimed to them, "And, behold, ye are risen up in your fathers' stead, an increase of <u>sinful</u> <u>men</u>, to augment yet the FIERCE ANGER of the LORD toward Israel" (Num. 32:14). The Old Testament phrases *the sin* (62 vs) and *the sinful* (1 v) = 63 verses. The word *men* is found in 63 books of the Bible.

Moses Recounts God's Wrath on the Wilderness Generation

"For indeed the hand of the LORD was against them, to destroy them from among the host, until they were consumed. So it came to pass, when all the <u>men</u> of war were consumed and dead from among the people" (Deut. 2:15-16). Now that the new generation prepares to cross over Jordan they need to be reminded of the dangers of disobedience. Again the word *men* is found in 63 books of the Bible.

How to Provoke God to Wrath

"Take heed unto yourselves, lest ye forget the covenant of the LORD your God . . . When thou shalt beget children, and children's children, and ye shall have remained long in the land, and shall corrupt yourselves, and <u>make</u> a graven <u>image</u>, or the likeness of any thing, and shall <u>do evil in the sight of the LORD thy GOD, to</u> <u>provoke him</u> <u>to ANGER</u>" (Deut. 4:23a, 25). In this book, as Moses warns the new generation not to follow in their fathers' disobedient footsteps, he uses the word "anger" nearly one and a half dozen times. The Law combination *make an* (61x) and *image of God* (2x) = 63. The Bible combination *do evil in the sight of the LORD thy God to* (1x), *provoke him* (9x), *to anger* (53x) = 63.

5063rd Verse of the Bible

"Thou shalt not bow down thyself to them, nor serve them: for I the LORD thy God am a jealous GOD, visiting the iniquity of the fathers upon the children unto the third and fourth generation of them that hate me" (Deut. 5:9). This 63rd verse speaks of the wrath of God.

Other Gods

God instructs the next generation of Israelites not to give their sons in marriage to the heathen daughters of Canaan; "For they will turn away thy son from following me, that they may serve <u>other gods</u>: so will the ANGER of the LORD be kindled against you, and destroy thee suddenly" (Deut. 7:4).

The phrase *other gods* occurs 63 times in the Bible.
The phrase *other gods* is mentioned in 63 verses of the Bible.

5163rd Verse of the Bible

"Not for thy righteousness, or for the uprightness of thine heart, dost thou go to possess their land: but for <u>the wickedness</u> of these nations the LORD thy GOD doth drive them out from before thee, and that he may perform the word which the LORD sware unto thy fathers, Abraham, Isaac, and Jacob" (Deut. 9:5). This 63rd verse speaks of the wrath of God. Again the term *the wicked(ness)* occurs naturally 63 times in the Major and Minor Prophets.

Horeb

God reminded the new generation of Israelites, "Remember, and forget not, how thou provokedst the LORD thy GOD <u>to</u> WRATH in the wilderness: from the day that thou didst depart out of the land of Egypt, until ye came unto this place, ye have been rebellious against the LORD. Also in Horeb ye provoked the LORD <u>to</u> WRATH, so that the LORD was ANGRY with you to have destroyed you" (Deut. 9:7-8). Horeb is a name synonymous with Sinai; this is due to it being indistinguishable with Sinai in its geographic proximity. There the fathers provoked God to wrath.

The word *to* occurs 630 times in First Samuel.
The word *to* occurs 163 times in Nehemiah.
The word *to* occurs 13,563 times in the Bible.

The Mount of God

"So I turned and came down from the mount, and the mount burned with fire: and the two tables of <u>the covenant</u> were in my two hands. And I looked, and, behold, ye had sinned against the LORD your God, and had made you a molten calf: ye had turned aside quickly out of the way which the LORD had commanded you. And I took the two tables, and cast them out of my two hands, and brake them before your eyes" (Deut. 9:15-17). Through Moses, God's wrath was demonstrated to the wilderness generation in an alarming fashion. Business contracts can be broken, but covenants are not made so. According to the Near East custom, breach of a sacred blood-covenant pact was punishable by death. The phrase *the covenant* is mentioned in 63 chapters of the Bible.

God's Wrath Regarding the Golden Calf

<u>"For I was afraid of the ANGER and hot displeasure, wherewith the LORD was WROTH against you to destroy you</u>. But the LORD hearkened unto me at that time also" (Deut. 9:19). The Old Testament combination *for I was afraid* (1x), *afraid* (158x), *of the anger* (1x), *and hot displeasure* (1x), *wherewith the LORD was wroth* (1x), *against you to destroy you* (1x) = 163.

Lest God's Wrath Be Kindled & Ye Perish

"Take heed to yourselves, that your heart be not deceived, and ye turn aside, and serve other gods, and worship them; And then the LORD'S WRATH be <u>kindled</u> against you, and he shut up the heaven, that there be no rain, and that the land yield not her fruit; and <u>lest</u> ye perish quickly from off the good land which the LORD giveth you" (Deut. 11:16-17). Again the word *kindled* occurs 63 times in the Old Testament. Again the word *lest* is mentioned naturally in 63 verses of the Law.

163rd Chapter of the Bible

"Ye shall utterly <u>destroy</u> all the places, wherein the nations which ye shall possess served their gods, upon the high mountains, and upon the hills, and under every green tree: And ye shall overthrow their altars, and break their pillars, and burn their groves with fire; and ye shall hew down the graven images of their gods, and <u>destroy</u> the names of them out of that place. . . . Take heed to thyself that thou be not snared by following them, after that they be destroyed from before thee; and that thou enquire not after their gods, saying, How did these nations serve their gods? even so will I do likewise" (Deut. 12:2-3, 30).

Moses begins this chapter with instructions on how Israel is to display the wrath of God upon the Canaanite nations, and he ends this chapter with a warning to Israel how to avoid God's wrath. Again the word *destroy* is mentioned in 63 chapters of the Major and Minor Prophets.

Idolaters to Experience God's Wrath

"If there be found among you, within any of thy gates which the LORD thy God giveth thee, man or woman, that hath wrought wickedness in the sight of the LORD thy GOD, in transgressing his covenant, And hath gone and served <u>other gods</u>, and worshipped them, either the sun, or moon, or any of the host of heaven, which I have not commanded. . . . Then shalt thou bring forth that man or that woman, which have committed that wicked thing, unto thy gates, even that man or that woman, and shalt stone them with stones, till they die" (Deut. 17:2-3, 5). Again the phrase *other gods* occurs 63 times in the Bible.

5563rd Verse of the Bible

"But thou shalt have a perfect and just weight, a perfect and just measure shalt thou have: that thy days may be lengthened in the land which the LORD thy God giveth thee" (Deut. 25:15). The succeeding verse calls such activity an abomination unto God. This 63rd verse warns of God's wrath by way of cutting the abominable one's life short.

Cursed of God

"<u>Cursed</u> be he that confirmeth not all the words of this law to do them. And all the people shall say, Amen" (Deut. 27:26). Again the word *cursed* is mentioned in 63 verses of the Old Testament.

5663rd Verse of the Bible

"And he shall eat the fruit of thy cattle, and the fruit of thy land, until thou be destroyed: which also shall not leave thee either corn, wine, or oil, or the increase of thy kine, or flocks of thy sheep, until he have <u>destroyed</u> thee" (Deut. 28:50). The previous verse tells us who will eat Israel's agricultural blessings; "a nation of fierce countenance." The last five words of this 63rd verse foretell God's completed wrath upon disobedient Israel. Again the word *destroy* is mentioned in 63 chapters of the Major and Minor Prophets.

God's Exceeding Wrath

Israel's future disobedience will be rewarded in a dreadful way. "Also every sickness, and every plague, which is not <u>written in the book</u> of this <u>law</u>, them will the LORD bring upon thee, until thou be destroyed" (Deut. 28:61). The phrase *written in the book* occurs 63 times in the Old Testament. The word *law* occurs 63 times in the NT Narrative.

Deuteronomy 28:63

"And it shall come to pass, that as the LORD rejoiced over you to do you good, and to multiply you; so the LORD will rejoice over you to <u>destroy</u> you, and to bring you to nought; and ye shall be plucked from off the land whither thou goest to possess it" (Deut. 28:63). Such divine wrath will come as a fitting reward against Israel's unrepentant rebellion and sin. Again the word *destroy* is mentioned in 63 chapters of the Major and Minor Prophets.

When Israel Shall Have Experienced God's Wrath

"For they went and served <u>other gods</u>, and worshipped them, gods whom they knew not, and whom he had not given unto them: And the ANGER of the LORD was kindled against this land, to bring upon it all the <u>curses</u> that are written in this book: And the LORD rooted them out of their land in ANGER, and in WRATH, and in great INDIGNATION, and cast them into another land, as it is this day" (Deut. 29:26-28). Again the phrase *other gods* occurs 63 times in the Bible. The Old Testament combination *curse* (58 chs) and *curses* (5 chs) = 63 chapters.

The Day of God's Wrath

"To me belongeth VENGEANCE, and recompence; their foot shall slide in due time: for <u>the day of</u> their calamity is at hand, and the things that shall come upon them make haste" (Deut. 32:35). Man's wrath is often displayed out of hatred, but God's wrath is meted out because of His holy desire for divine justice. The phrase *the day of* occurs 163 times in the Bible!

Achan Experienced God's Wrath

"And ye, in any wise keep yourselves from the <u>accursed</u> thing, lest ye make yourselves <u>accursed</u>, when ye take of the <u>accursed</u> thing, and make the camp of Israel a curse, and trouble it. . . . But the children of Israel committed a trespass in the <u>accursed</u> thing: for Achan, the son of Carmi, the son of Zabdi, the son of Zerah, of the tribe of Judah, took of the <u>accursed</u> thing: and the ANGER of the LORD was <u>kindled</u> against <u>the children of Israel</u>. . . . And Joshua said, Why hast thou troubled us? the LORD shall trouble thee this day. And <u>all Israel stoned him with</u> <u>stones</u>, and burned them with fire, after they had stoned them with stones" (Josh. 6:18; 7:1, 25).

Again the word *cursed* is mentioned in 63 verses of the Old Testament. Again the word *kindled* occurs 63 times in the Old Testament. Again the title *the children of Israel* is mentioned in 63 verses of Joshua. The Old Testament combination *all Israel stoned him with* (2x), *stones* (161x) = 163.

The Valley of Achor

"And they raised over him <u>a great heap of</u> stones unto this day. So the LORD <u>turned</u> from the FIERCENESS of his ANGER. Wherefore the name of that place was called, The valley of Achor, unto this day" (Josh. 7:26). The Old Testament combination *a great heap of* (2x), *stones* (161x) = 163. The word *turned* is mentioned naturally in 63 chapters of the OT Narrative.

Breaking God's Law Invites God's Just Wrath

The narrative says of Joshua, "And afterward he read all the words of <u>the law</u>, the blessings and cursings, according to all that <u>is written</u> in the book of <u>the law</u>" (Josh. 8:24). Any breach of God's holy laws is viewed as a great offense to Him. He can respond accordingly if He chooses to do so. The phrase *the law(s)* occurs 63 times in the OT Narrative. Again the word *law* occurs 63 times in the NT Narrative.

> The phrase *it is written* occurs 63 times in the New Testament.
> The phrase *it is written* is mentioned in 63 verses of the New Testament.

Balaam Incurred God's Wrath

"<u>Balaam</u> also the son of Beor, the soothsayer, did the children of Israel slay with <u>the sword</u> among them that were slain by them" (Josh. 13:22). Balaam's intention was to go curse Israel for the benefit of money, yet the Lord turned his words into a fountain of blessings. In the end, the Lord judged the soothsayer according to his evil heart. The name *Balaam('s)* occurs 63 times in the Bible. Again the phrase *the sword* occurs 63 times in Ezekiel.

Joshua 15:63

"As for the Jebusites the inhabitants of Jerusalem, the children of Judah could not drive them out: but the Jebusites dwell with the children of Judah at Jerusalem unto this day" (Josh. 15:63). Israel's conquests fell short of their desired goal because of this one city's greatly fortified position. God's wrath upon this pagan city was reserved for a later date.

Joshua Warns Israel about God's Wrath

"But that ye must turn away this day from following the LORD? and it will be, seeing ye rebel to day against the LORD, that to morrow he will be WROTH with the whole congregation of Israel" (Josh. 22:18). Here the keyword *wroth* is the 663rd word of this chapter.

Congregation of Israel's Former Experience of God's Wrath

"Did not Achan the son of Zerah commit a trespass in the accursed thing, and WRATH fell on all the congregation of Israel? and that man perished not alone in his iniquity" (Josh. 22:20). Again the word *congregation* occurs 363 times in the Old Testament. Again the name *Israel* is mentioned in 63 verses of the Wisdom Books.

Aged Joshua Warns of God's Wrath

"When ye have transgressed the covenant of the LORD your God, which he commanded you, and have gone and served other gods, and bowed yourselves to them; then shall the ANGER of the LORD be kindled against you, and ye shall perish quickly from off the good land which he hath given unto you" (Josh. 23:16). Again the phrase *the covenant* is mentioned in 63 chapters of the Bible. Again the phrase *other gods* occurs 63 times in the Bible.

When God's Anger Gets Hot

"And the ANGER of the LORD was hot against Israel, and he delivered them into the hands of spoilers that spoiled them, and he sold them into the hands of their enemies round about, so that they could not any longer stand before their enemies" (Judg. 2:14). Here the key title *LORD* is the 636rd word of this chapter, and it is related to His wrath.

God's Anger Came against Israel

"And the ANGER of the LORD was hot against Israel; and he said, Because that this people hath transgressed my covenant which I commanded their fathers, and have not hearkened unto my voice" (Judg. 2:20). The Lord was angry with Israel for their partial obedience. They only subdued part of the Land. Again the name *Israel* is mentioned in 63 verses of the Wisdom Books. Again the title *this people* is mentioned in 63 chapters of the Old Testament. Again the phrase *the covenant* is mentioned in 63 chapters of the Bible.

6563rd Verse of the Bible

"And yet they would not hearken unto their judges, but they went a whoring after other gods, and bowed themselves unto them: they turned quickly out of the way which their fathers walked in, obeying the commandments of the LORD; but they did not so" (Judg. 2:17). This 63rd verse reveals the reason for God's anger and wrath toward the nation. Again the phrase *other gods* occurs 63 times in the Bible.

Other Nations Used for God's Wrath against Israel

"And the children of Israel did evil again in the sight of the LORD, and served Baalim, and Ashtaroth, and the gods of Syria, and the gods of Zidon, and the gods of Moab, and the gods of the children of Ammon, and the gods of the Philistines, and forsook the LORD, and served not him. And the ANGER of the LORD was hot against Israel, and he sold them into the hands of the Philistines, and into the hands of the children of Ammon" (Judg. 10:6-7). Again the title *the children of Israel* is mentioned in 63 verses of Joshua. Here the word *hot* is the 184,663rd word of the Bible, and it pertains to the wrath of the Lord.

"The Lord Hath Taken Vengeance"

"And she said unto him, My father, if thou hast opened thy mouth unto the LORD, do to me according to that which hath proceeded out of thy mouth; forasmuch as the LORD hath taken VENGEANCE for thee of thine enemies, even of the children of Ammon" (Judg. 11:36). The Bible combination *vengeance for thee of* (1x), *thine enemies* (62x) = 63.

63rd Verse of Ruth

"Then said she, Sit still, my daughter, until thou know how the matter will fall: for the man will not be in rest, until he have finished the thing this day" (Ruth 3:18). As the matter came to a conclusion later that day the unnamed near kinsman refused to perform the Mosaic custom commanded in the Mosaic Law. Long before the days of national Israel this was a custom among the patriarchs of Israel. When Judah's son Onan refused to fully perform this custom God became so angry with him that in His wrath He slew him. The same fearful thing could have befallen Ruth's uncooperative near kinsman, particularly so since it pertained to the matter of filling in a genealogical gap regarding the continuance of the Messianic Judean lineage. As it turned out, because Ruth's near kinsman did not marry her she visibly displayed her own wrath, according to the mandated law, by spitting in his face and removing one of his sandals that he might walk home shamefaced. The word *shame* is mentioned in 63 chapters of the Old Testament.

Hophni & Phinehas Experienced God's Wrath

"Now the sons of Eli were sons of Belial; they knew not the LORD. . . . Wherefore the sin of the young men was very great before the LORD: for men abhorred the offering of the LORD. . . . And this shall be a sign unto thee, that shall come upon thy two sons, on Hophni and Phinehas; in one day they shall die both of them. . . . And the ark of God was taken; and the two sons of Eli, Hophni and Phinehas, were slain" (1 Sam. 2:12, 17, 34; 4:11). The OT Narrative combination *Hophni and Phinehas* (5x) and *slain* (58x) = 63.

Philistine Cities Experienced God's Wrath

"And it was so, that, after they had carried it about, the hand of the LORD was against the city with a very great destruction: and he smote the men of the city, both small and great, and they had emerods in their secret parts. Therefore they sent the ark of God to Ekron. And it came to pass, as the ark of God came to Ekron, that the Ekronites cried out, saying, They have brought about the ark of the God of Israel to us, to slay us and our people" (1 Sam. 5:9-10). The Philistines suffered God's wrath in an excruciating way. The word *smitten* occurs 63 times in the Bible.

Looking into God's Ark Brought God's Wrath

"And he smote the men of Beth-shemesh, because they had looked into the ark of the LORD, even he smote of the people fifty thousand and threescore and ten men: and the people lamented, because the LORD had <u>smitten</u> many of the people with a great slaughter" (1 Sam. 6:19). Again the word *smitten* occurs 63 times in the Bible.

God Sent Thunder & Rain upon Israel

"Now therefore stand and see this great thing, which the LORD will do before your eyes. Is it not wheat harvest to day? I will call unto the LORD, and he shall send thunder and rain; that ye may perceive and see that your wickedness is great, which ye have done in the sight of the LORD, in asking you a king. So Samuel called unto the LORD; and the LORD <u>sent</u> thunder and rain that day: and all the people greatly feared the LORD and Samuel. And all the people said unto Samuel, Pray for thy servants unto the LORD thy GOD, that we die not: for we have added unto all our sins this evil, to ask us a king" (1 Sam. 12:17-19).

Again the word *sent* is mentioned in 63 verses of the Bible.

Nabal Experienced God's Wrath

"And there was a man in Maon, whose possessions were in Carmel; and the man was very great, and he had three thousand sheep, and a thousand goats: and he was shearing his sheep in Carmel. Now the name of the man was Nabal . . . the man was churlish and evil in his doings . . . such a son of Belial, that a man cannot speak to him . . . And it came to pass about ten days after, that the LORD <u>smote</u> Nabal, that he died" (1 Sam. 25:2-3a, 3d, 17c, 38). Again the word *smitten* occurs 63 times in the Bible.

Saul Spared Amalek from God's Wrath

"Then said Samuel. . . Because thou obeyedst not the voice of the LORD, nor executedst his FIERCE WRATH upon <u>Amalek</u>" (1 Sam. 28:16a, 18a). The Bible combination *spare* (40 vs) and *Amalek* (23 vs) = 63 verses. Here the keyword *wrath* is the 23,063rd word of First Samuel.

7963rd Verse of the Bible

"Moreover the LORD will also deliver Israel with thee into the hand of the Philistines: and to morrow shalt thou and thy sons be with me: the LORD also shall deliver the host of Israel into the hand of the Philistines. <u>Then Saul fell straightway all along on the earth, and was sore afraid, because of the words of Samuel: and there was no strength in him; for he had eaten no bread all the day, nor all the night</u>" (1 Sam. 28:19-20). The underlined words indicate the 7963rd verse of the Bible, and they reflect the results of receiving terrifying news of God's impending wrath. This came as a result of Saul seeking counsel from a witch.

Saul Experienced God's Wrath

"And the Philistines followed hard upon <u>Saul</u> and upon his sons; and the Philistines slew Jonathan, and Abinadab, and Malchi-shua, Saul's sons. And the battle went sore against <u>Saul</u>, and the archers hit him; and he was sore wounded of the archers. . . . So <u>Saul</u> died, and his three sons, and his armourbearer, and all his men, that same day together" (1 Sam. 31:2-3, 6). The name *Saul* occurs 363 times in the Old Testament.

Uzza Experienced God's Wrath

"And when they came to Nachon's threshingfloor, Uzzah put forth his hand to the ark of God,

349

and took hold of it; for the oxen shook it. And the ANGER of the LORD was kindled against Uzzah; and GOD <u>smote</u> him there for his error; and there he died by the ark of God" (2 Sam. 6:6-7). Uzza's action was instinctive rather than intuitive, for only the priesthood was permitted to handle the Ark. Again the word *kindled* occurs 63 times in the Old Testament. Again the word *smitten* occurs 63 times in Scripture.

David's House to Experience God's Wrath

"Now therefore <u>the sword</u> shall never depart from thine house . . . Behold, I will raise up evil against thee out of thine own house, and I will take thy wives before thine eyes, and give them unto thy neighbour, and he shall lie with thy wives in the sight of this sun. . . . the child also that is born unto thee shall surely die" (2 Sam. 12:10a, 11, 14b). Because David committed adultery and then had the husband killed in battle that he might take his wife to be his very own, God's wrath became greatly kindled against David. Again the phrase *the sword* is mentioned in 163 chapters of the Bible.

God's Wrath Falls upon the Innocent

"<u>And the LORD struck the child that Uriah's wife bare unto David, and it was very sick</u>. . . . And it came to pass on the seventh day, that the child died" (2 Sam. 12:15b, 18a). The OT Narrative combination *and the LORD* (155x), *struck* (4x), *the child* (2x), *that Uriah's wife bare unto David* (1x), *and it was very sick* (1x) = 163.

David Experiences God's Judgmental Wrath

"And the conspiracy was strong; for the people increased continually with Absalom. And there came a messenger to David, saying, The hearts of the men of Israel are after Absalom. And David said unto all his servants that were with him at Jerusalem, <u>Arise, and let us flee</u>; <u>for we shall not else</u> <u>escape</u> <u>from Absalom</u>: <u>make speed to depart</u>, lest he overtake us suddenly, and bring evil upon us, and smite the city with the edge of <u>the sword</u>" (2 Sam. 15:12b-14). The Bible combination *rise and let us flee* (1x), *for we shall not else* (1x), *escape* (59x), *from Absalom* (1x), *make speed to depart* (1x) = 63. Again the phrase *the sword* is mentioned in 163 chapters of the Bible.

David Continues to Experience God's Judgmental Wrath

"And as David and his men went by the way, Shimei went along on the hill's side over against him, and <u>cursed</u> as he went, and threw stones at him, and cast <u>dust</u>" (2 Sam. 16:13). Again the word *cursed* is mentioned in 63 verses of the Old Testament. Again the phrase *the dust* occurs 63 times in the Old Testament.

David Continues to Experience God's Judgmental Wrath

"Then said Joab, I may not tarry thus with thee. <u>And he took</u> <u>three darts in his hand</u>, <u>and thrust them through the heart of Absalom, while he was yet alive in the midst of the oak</u>. . . . And the king was much moved, and went up to the chamber over the gate, and wept: and as he went, thus he said, O my son Absalom, my son, my son Absalom! would God I had died for thee, O Absalom, my son, my son!" (2 Sam. 18:14, 33) David had given Joab instructions not to kill his son Absalom, but the Lord had determined to slay him. The Old Testament combination *and he took* (58x), *three darts in his hand* (1x), *and thrust them through* (1x), *the heart of Absalom* (1x), *while he was yet alive* (1x), *in the midst of the oak* (1x) = 63.

David Continues to Experience God's Judgmental Wrath

"And there happened to be there a man of Belial, whose name was Sheba, the son of Bichri, a Benjamite: and he blew a trumpet, and said, We have no part in David, neither have we inheritance in the son of Jesse: every man to his tents, O Israel. So every man of Israel went up from after David, and followed Sheba the son of Bichri . . . Sheba the son of Bichri by name, hath lifted up his hand against the king, even against David" (2 Sam. 20:1-2a, 21b). At this moment in time David's united kingdom became severed, but Joab quickly put down Sheba's revolt. The phrase *in his hand* occurs 63 times in the Old Testament.

Israel Experienced God's Wrath Because of Saul

"Then there was a famine in the days of David three years, year after year; and David enquired of the LORD. And the LORD answered, It is for Saul, and for his bloody house, because he slew the Gibeonites" (2 Sam. 21:1). Again the name *Saul* occurs 363 times in the Old Testament.

God's Wrath Stirred over David's Enemies

"The GOD of my rock; in him will I trust: he is my shield, and the horn of my salvation, my high tower, and my refuge, my saviour; thou savest me from violence. I will call on the LORD, who is worthy to be praised: so shall I be saved from mine enemies. . . . In my distress I called upon the LORD, and cried to my GOD: and he did hear my voice out of his temple, and my cry did enter into his ears. . . . Then the earth shook and trembled; the foundations of heaven moved and shook, because he was WROTH. There went up a smoke out of his nostrils, and fire out of his mouth devoured: coals were kindled by it" (2 Sam. 22:3-4, 7-9).

Again the word *devour* occurs 63 times in the Old Testament.

Israel Took Pride in Their Arm of Flesh

"And again the ANGER of the LORD was kindled against Israel, and he moved David against them to say, Go, number Israel and Judah, For the king said to Joab the captain of the host, which was with him, Go now through all the tribes of Israel, from Dan even to Beer-sheba, and number ye the people, that I may know the number of the people. . . . So the LORD sent a pestilence upon Israel from the morning even to the time appointed: and there died of the people from Dan even to Beer-sheba seventy thousand men" (2 Sam. 24:1, 15).

At this time Israel was at their zenith of military power. As a result, their pride had grown correspondingly. Therefore God sought to make a necessary correction. Again the name *Israel* is mentioned in 63 verses of the Wisdom Books. Again the phrase *the people* is mentioned in 63 verses of the Wisdom Books.

First Kings 8:63

"And Solomon offered a sacrifice of peace offerings, which he offered unto the LORD, two and twenty thousand oxen, and an hundred and twenty thousand sheep. So the king and all the children of Israel dedicated the house of the LORD" (1 Kings 8:63). Only a blood sacrifice offered in the ordained place could ever satisfy God's wrath against sin. The word *offered* occurs 63 times in the OT Narrative.

Solomon Invoked God's Wrath

"And Solomon did evil in the sight of the LORD . . . Then did Solomon build an high place for Chemosh, the abomination of Moab, in the hill that is before Jerusalem, and for Molech, the abomination of the children of Ammon. And likewise did he for all his strange wives, which burnt incense and sacrificed unto their <u>gods</u>. And the LORD was ANGRY with Solomon" (1 Kings 11:6a-9a). The Bible combination *build* (162x), *an high place for Chemosh* (1x) = 163. Again the phrase *other gods* occurs 63 times in the Bible.

Solomon Experienced God's Wrath

"Wherefore the LORD said unto Solomon, Forasmuch as this is done of thee, and thou hast not kept my covenant and my statutes, which I have commanded thee, I will surely <u>rend</u> the kingdom from thee, and will give it to thy servant. . . . And the LORD stirred up an adversary unto Solomon, Hadad the Edomite: he was of the king's seed in Edom" (1 Kings. 11:11, 14). Whenever a person became angry or stricken with grief, the Near East custom was to rend their garments. The Lord was both angry and grieved. The word *rent* is mentioned in 63 verses of the Bible.

463rd Verse of First Kings

"Whereupon the king took counsel, and made two calves of gold, and said unto them, It is too much for you to go up to Jerusalem: behold thy gods, O Israel, which brought thee up out of the land of Egypt. <u>And he set the one in Beth-el, and the other put he in Dan</u>" (1 Kings 12:28-29). The underlined words indicate the 63rd verse of First Kings, and they reveal Jeroboam's provoking of God's wrath. Again the word *idols* occurs 63 times in the Major and Minor Prophets.

Jeroboam Experienced God's Wrath

"And, behold, there came a man of God out of Judah by the word of the LORD unto Beth-el: and Jeroboam stood by the altar to burn incense. And he cried against the altar in the word of the LORD, and said, O altar, altar, thus saith the LORD; Behold, a child shall be born unto the house of David, Josiah by name; and upon thee shall he offer the priests of the high places that burn incense upon thee, and men's bones shall be burnt upon thee. And he gave a sign the same day, saying, This is the sign which the LORD hath spoken; Behold, the altar shall be <u>rent</u>, and the ashes that are upon it shall be poured out. And it came to pass, when king <u>Jeroboam</u> heard the saying of the man of God, which had cried against the altar in Beth-el, that he put forth his hand from the altar, saying, Lay hold on him. <u>And his hand</u>, <u>which he put forth</u> <u>against him</u>, <u>dried up</u>, so that he could not pull it in again to him. The altar also was rent, and the ashes poured out from the altar, according to the sign which the man of God had given by the word of the LORD" (1 Kings 13:1-5).

Second Chronicles tells us how this evil Israelite king died; the Lord struck him. Again the word *rent* is mentioned in 63 verses of the Bible. The First Kings combination *Jeroboam* (53x), *and his hand* (1x), *which he put forth* (1x), *against him* (6x), *dried up* (2x) = 63.

Disobedient Man of God Experiences God's Wrath

"And he cried unto the man of God that came from Judah, saying, Thus saith the LORD, Forasmuch as thou hast disobeyed the mouth of the LORD, and hast not kept the <u>commandment</u> which the LORD thy GOD commanded thee, But camest back, and hast eaten bread and drunk water in the place, of the which the LORD did say to thee, Eat no bread, and drink no water; thy carcase shall not come unto the sepulchre of thy fathers. And it came to pass, after he had eaten bread, and after he had drunk, that he saddled for him the ass, to wit, for the prophet whom he had brought back. And when he was gone, a lion met him by the way, and slew him" (1 Kings 13:21-24a).

Again the word *commandments* occurs 63 times in the Law.

Note: Throughout the remainder of First Kings and into Second Kings, we will only study the lives of the kings of Israel. They were all evil and each more or less deserved the wrath of God. For this reason, God's wrath came upon them so that their reigns were significantly shorter than those among the kings of Judah. We will observe the lives of the evil kings of Judah in Second Chronicles.

Nadab Experienced God's Wrath

"And <u>Nadab the son of Jeroboam</u> began to reign over Israel . . . and reigned over Israel two years. And he did evil in the sight of the LORD, and walked in the way of his father, and in <u>his sin</u> <u>wherewith he</u> <u>made Israel to sin</u>. And Baasha . . . conspired against him, and Baasha smote him at Gibbethon . . . and reigned in his stead" (1 Kings 15:25-27a, 28b). The Old Testament combination *Nadab the son of Jeroboam* (1x), *his sin* (29x), *wherewith* (16x), *made Israel to sin* (17x) = 63.

Baasha to Experience God's Wrath

"Then the word of the LORD came to Jehu the son of Hanani against Baasha, saying, Forasmuch as I exalted thee out of the dust, and made thee prince over my people Israel; and thou hast walked in the way of Jeroboam, <u>and hast made</u> <u>my people Israel to sin, to provoke me</u> <u>to ANGER</u> <u>with their sins</u>; Behold, I will take away the posterity of Baasha, and the posterity of his house; and will make thy house like the house of Jeroboam the son of Nebat. Him that dieth of Baasha in the city shall the dogs eat; and him that dieth of his in the fields shall the fowls of the air eat" (1 Kings 16:1-4).

The Old Testament combination *and hast made* (8x), *my people Israel to sin to provoke me* (1x), *to anger* (52x), *with their sins* (2x) = 63.

Elah Experienced God's Wrath

"Elah the son of Baasha to reign over Israel in Tirzah, two years. And his servant Zimri, captain of half his chariots, conspired against him, as he was in Tirzah, drinking himself <u>drunk</u> in the house of Arza steward of his house in Tirzah. And Zimri went in and smote him, and killed him . . . and <u>reigned in his stead</u>" (1 Kings 16:8b-10). Drunkenness is a sin which often provokes God to perform just judgment. The word *drunk(en)* occurs 63 times in the Bible. The phrase *reigned in his stead* occurs 63 times in the Bible and is mentioned in 63 verses thereof.

Zimri Executed God's Wrath upon Baasha's house

"And it came to pass, when he began to reign, as soon as he sat on his throne, that he slew all the house of Baasha: he left him not one that pisseth against a wall, neither of his kinsfolks, nor of his friends. Thus did Zimri <u>destroy</u> all the house of Baasha, according to the word of the LORD, which he spake against Baasha by Jehu the prophet, For all the sins of Baasha, and the sins of Elah his son, by which they sinned, and by which they made Israel to sin, in provoking the LORD GOD of Israel to ANGER with their vanities" (1 Kings 16:11-13).

Again the word *destroy* is mentioned in 63 chapters of the Major and Minor Prophets.

Zimri Experienced God's Wrath

"And the people that were encamped heard say, Zimri hath conspired, and hath also slain the king: wherefore all Israel made Omri, the captain of the host, king over Israel that day in the camp. And Omri went up from Gibbethon, and all Israel with him, and <u>they besieged Tirzah.</u> <u>And it came to pass, when Zimri saw that the city was taken, that he went into the palace of the king's house, and burnt the king's house over him with fire, and died, For his sins which he sinned in doing evil in the sight of the LORD, in walking in the way of Jeroboam, and in his sin</u>

which he did, to make Israel to sin" (1 Kings 16:16-19a).

King for only seven days, Zimri experienced a wrathful death as he committed suicide by burning. The Old Testament combination *they besieged Tirzah and it came to pass* (1x), *when Zimri* (1x), *saw that the city was taken* (1x), *that he went into* (1x), *the palace of the king's house* (2x), *and burnt the* (2x), *king's house over him* (1x), *with fire and died* (1x), *for his sins* (1x), *which he sinned* (2x), *in doing* (3x), *evil in the sight of the LORD* (44x), *in walking in the way of Jeroboam* (1x), *and in his sin which* (1x), *he did to make Israel to sin* (1x) = 63.

Omri Experienced God's Wrath

"But Omri wrought evil in the eyes of the LORD, and did worse than all that were before him. For he walked in all the way of Jeroboam the son of Nebat, and in his sin wherewith he made Israel to sin, to provoke the LORD GOD of Israel to ANGER with their vanities. . . . So Omri slept with his fathers, and was buried in Samaria: and Ahab his son reigned in his stead" (1 Kings 16:25-26, 28). Omri's life was cut short by God. Again the phrase *reigned in his stead* occurs 63 times in the Bible.

Ahab Greatly Provoked God's Wrath

"Ahab the son of Omri reigned over Israel in Samaria twenty and two years. And Ahab the son of Omri did evil in the sight of the LORD above all that were before him. And it came to pass, as if it had been a light thing for him to walk in the sins of Jeroboam the son of Nebat, that he took to wife Jezebel the daughter of Ethbaal king of the Zidonians, and went and served Baal, and worshipped him. And he reared up an altar for Baal in the house of Baal, which he had built in Samaria. And Ahab made a grove; and Ahab did more to provoke the LORD GOD of Israel to ANGER than all the kings of Israel that were before him" (1 Kings 16:29b-33).

This provoking-the-wrath-of-God passage presents the Bible's 63rd verse-mention of the word *anger*. The OT Narrative combination *Ahab the son of Omri reigned* (1x), *over Israel* (62x) = 63.

Drought Comes upon the Northern Kingdom

"And Elijah the Tishbite, who was of the inhabitants of Gilead, said unto Ahab, As the LORD GOD of Israel liveth, before whom I stand, there shall not be dew nor rain these years, but according to my word" (1 Kings 17:1). This judgment of God was a show of His wrath concerning Ahab's continued wickedness. The Old Testament combination *dry* (62 vs) and *great drought* (1 v) = 63 verses.

The Prophets of Baal & of the Groves
Experience God's Wrath

"Now therefore send, and gather to me all Israel unto mount Carmel, and the prophets of Baal four hundred and fifty, and the prophets of the groves four hundred, which eat at Jezebel's table. . . . And Elijah said unto them, Take the prophets of Baal; let not one of them escape. And they took them: and Elijah brought them down to the brook Kishon, and slew them there" (1 Kings 18:19, 40). The name *Baal* occurs 63 times in the Bible! The OT Narrative combination *and slew* (62x), *the prophets of the groves* (1x) = 63.

The Prophet of God Announced God's Wrath

"So the prophet departed, and waited for the king by the way, and disguised himself with ashes upon his face" (1 Kings 20:38). God generally foretold and forewarned of His wrath to come by way of a true prophet. The title *the prophet* occurs 163 times in the Bible.

Ahab Experienced God's Wrath

Elijah prophesied,

> "Thus saith the LORD, Hast thou killed, and also taken possession? And thou shalt speak unto him, saying, Thus saith the LORD, In the place where dogs licked the blood of Naboth shall dogs lick thy blood, even thine. . . . Behold, I will bring evil upon thee, and will take away thy posterity, and will cut off from Ahab him that pisseth against the wall, and him that is shut up and left in Israel, And will make thine house like the house of Jeroboam the son of Nebat, and like the house of Baasha the son of Ahijah, for the provocation wherewith thou hast provoked me to ANGER, and made Israel to sin" (1 Kings 21:19, 21-22).

Three years later God's wrath came upon Ahab.

> "And a certain man drew a bow at a venture, and smote the king of Israel between the joints of the harness . . . and the king was stayed up in his chariot against the Syrians, and died at even: and the blood ran out of the wound into the midst of the chariot . . . So the king died, and was brought to Samaria; and they buried the king in Samaria. And one washed the chariot in the pool of Samaria; and the dogs licked up his blood; and they washed his armour; according unto the word of the LORD which he spake" (22:34a, 37-38).

The title *the word of the LORD* occurs 63 times in the Kings and Chronicles.

Ahaziah Provoked God's Wrath

"Ahaziah the son of Ahab began to reign over Israel in Samaria . . . and reigned two years over Israel. And he did evil in the sight of the LORD, and walked in the way of his father, and in the way of his mother, and in the way of Jeroboam the son of Nebat, who made Israel to sin: For he served Baal, and worshipped him, and provoked to ANGER the LORD GOD of Israel, according to all that his father had done" (1 Kings 22:51-53). This wicked son of Ahab and Jezebel had his reign cut very short by an angry God. Again the name *Baal* occurs 63 times in the Bible!

Elijah the Prophet Calls for God's Fiery Wrath

"And Elijah answered and said to the captain of fifty, If I be a man of GOD, then let fire come down from heaven, and consume thee and thy fifty. And there came down fire from heaven, and consumed him and his fifty" (2 Kings 1:10). Elijah was God's instrument of wrath and indignation upon the continually apostatizing northern kingdom. The name *Elijah* is mentioned in 63 verses of the Bible. The phrase *from heaven* occurs 63 times in the New Testament.

Elisha's Mockers Experienced God's Wrath

"And he went up from thence unto Beth-el: and as he was going up by the way, there came forth little children out of the city, and mocked him, and said unto him, Go up, thou bald head; go up, thou bald head. And he turned back, and looked on them, and cursed them in the name of the LORD. And there came forth two she bears out of the wood, and tare forty and two children of them" (2 Kings 2:23-24). Again the word *cursed* is mentioned in 63 verses of the Old Testament.

Jehoram Provoked God's Wrath

"Now Jehoram the son of Ahab began to reign over Israel in Samaria . . . And he wrought evil in the sight of the LORD; but not like his father, and like his mother: for he put away the image of Baal that his father had made. Nevertheless he cleaved unto the sins of Jeroboam the son of Nebat, which made Israel to sin; he departed not therefrom" (2 Kings 3:1a, 2-3). The Old

Testament combination *he wrought* (6x), *evil in the sight of the* LORD (44x), *the sins of Jeroboam the son of Nebat* (10x), *which made Israel to sin* (3x) = 63.

Gehazi Experienced God's Wrath

"Is it a time to receive money, and to receive garments, and oliveyards, and vineyards, and sheep, and oxen, and menservants, and maidservants? The leprosy therefore of Naaman shall cleave unto thee, and unto thy seed for ever. And he went out from his presence a leper as white as snow" (2 Kings 5:26c-27). Gehazi's sin was covetousness. Again the phrase *the plague* occurs 63 times in the Law.

This Scoffer Experienced God's Wrath

"Then Elisha said, Hear ye the word of the LORD; Thus saith the LORD, To morrow about this time shall a measure of fine flour be sold for a shekel, and two measures of barley for a shekel, in the gate of Samaria. Then a lord on whose hand the king leaned answered the man of God, and said, Behold, if the LORD would make windows in heaven, might this thing be? And he said, Behold, thou shalt see it with thine eyes, but shalt not eat thereof. . . . And so it fell out unto him: for the people trode upon him in the gate, and he died" (2 Kings 7:1-2, 20).

Because this man scoffed at the prophet's prediction he incurred the wrath of God on the next day. The Bible combination *for the people* (10x), *trode upon him* (2x), *in the gate* (29x), *and he died* (22x) = 63.

Wrath of God Came upon the Syrians

The Syrians had laid siege upon Samaria. Having cut off the city's food supply for some time, starvation had set in. The Israelites were desperate for relief. To rescue Israel God's wrath came upon the Syrians' camp: "For the Lord had made the host of the Syrians to hear a noise of chariots, and a noise of horses, even the noise of a great host: and they said one to another, Lo, the king of Israel hath hired against us the kings of the Hittites, and the kings of the Egyptians, to come upon us. Wherefore they arose and fled in the twilight, and left their tents, and their horses, and their asses, even the camp as it was, and fled for their life" (2 Kings 7:6-7). The title *the Syrian(s)* occurs 63 combined times in the Bible.

God's Wrath Is Coming for Ahab's Sons

A young prophet anointed Jehu to be king over Israel and at the same time delivered a message of divine wrath regarding Ahab's remaining sons. "For the whole house of Ahab shall perish: and I will cut off from Ahab him that pisseth against the wall, and him that is shut up and left in Israel" (2 Kings 9:8). This verse presents the Bible's 63rd occurrence of the name *Ahab*, and we see its relation to the wrath of God upon his surviving household.

Jehoram Experienced God's Wrath

"And it came to pass, when Joram saw Jehu, that he said, Is it peace, Jehu? And he answered, What peace, so long as the whoredoms of thy mother Jezebel and her witchcrafts are so many? And Joram turned his hands, and fled . . . And Jehu drew a bow with his full strength, and smote Jehoram between his arms, and the arrow went out at his heart, and he sunk down in his chariot" (2 Kings 9:22-24). The OT Narrative combination *and Jehu* (17x), *drew a bow* (3x), *with his full* (1x), *strength* (32x), *and smote Jehoram* (1x), *between his* (3x), *arms* (4x), *and the arrow went out at his heart* (1x), *and he sunk down in his chariot* (1x) = 63.

"Then said Jehu to Bidkar his captain, Take up, and cast him in the portion of the field of Naboth the Jezreelite: for remember how that, when I and thou rode together after Ahab his father, the LORD laid this burden upon him; Surely I have seen yesterday the blood of Naboth, and the blood of his sons, saith the LORD; and I will requite thee in this plat, saith the LORD. Now therefore take and cast him into the plat of ground, according to the word of the LORD" (vv. 25-26).

Jehoram's body was not given a royal burial but was buried in a common manner in the ground which his father Ahab stole from Naboth. Thus was God's wrath satisfied. The Bible combination *take up* (40x), *and cast him* (16x), *in the portion* (5x), *of the field of Naboth the Jezreelite* (1x), *and I will requite thee in this plat saith the LORD* (1x) = 63.

Jehu Executed God's Wrath upon Baal Worshipers

Jehu gave the order for the prophets of Baal to be slain, "And they smote them with the edge of the sword; and the guard and the captains cast them out, and went to the city of the house of Baal. And they brought forth the images out of the house of Baal, and burned them. And they brake down the image of Baal, and brake down the house of Baal, and made it a draught house unto this day. Thus Jehu destroyed Baal out of Israel" (2 Kings 10:25b-28). Again the phrase *the sword* is mentioned in 163 chapters of the Bible. Again the name *Baal* occurs 63 times in the Bible.

Jehu Spared from God's Wrath

"Howbeit from the sins of Jeroboam the son of Nebat, who made Israel to sin, Jehu departed not from after them, to wit, the golden calves that were in Beth-el, and that were in Dan. And the LORD said unto Jehu, Because thou hast done well in executing that which is right in mine eyes, and hast done unto the house of Ahab according to all that was in mine heart, thy children of the fourth generation shall sit on the throne of Israel" (2 Kings 10:29-30). Jehu was not a good king, but he was better than most, and only one king of Israel reigned longer than him. Jehu was thus safeguarded from God's wrath. The Bible combination *Jehu departed not* (1 v), *from after them to wit* (1 v), *the golden calves that were in* (1 v), *Beth-el* (59 vs), *and that were in Dan* (1 v) = 63 verses.

Jehoahaz Experienced God's Wrath

"Jehoahaz the son of Jehu began to reign over Israel in Samaria, and reigned seventeen years. And he did that which was evil in the sight of the LORD, and followed the sins of Jeroboam the son of Nebat, which made Israel to sin; he departed not therefrom. And the ANGER of the LORD was kindled against Israel, and he delivered them into the hand of Hazael king of Syria, and into the hand of Ben-hadad the son of Hazael, all their days" (2 Kings 13:1b-3). Again the word *kindled* occurs 63 times in the Old Testament.

Jehoash Provokes God's Wrath

"Jehoash the son of Jehoahaz to reign over Israel in Samaria, and reigned sixteen years. And he did that which was evil in the sight of the LORD; he departed not from all the sins of Jeroboam the son of Nebat, who made Israel sin: but he walked therein" (2 Kings 13:10b-11).

The Old Testament combination *Jehoash the son of Jehoahaz* (3x), *reigned sixteen years and he did that which was* (1x), *evil in the sight of the LORD* (44x), *he departed not from all* (2x), *the sins of Jeroboam the son of Nebat* (10x), *who made Israel to sin* (2x), *but he walked therein* (1x)

= 63.

Jeroboam II Deserved God's Wrath

"Jeroboam the son of Joash king of Israel began to reign in Samaria, and reigned forty and one years. <u>And he did that which</u> <u>was evil in the sight of the LORD</u>: <u>he departed not from all</u> <u>the sins of Jeroboam the son of Nebat, who made Israel to sin</u>" (2 Kings 14:23b-24). The Old Testament combination *and he did that which* (28x), *was evil in the sight of the LORD* (21x), *he departed not from all* (2x), *the sins of Jeroboam the son of Nebat* (10x), *who made Israel to sin* (2x) = 63.

Zachariah Experiences God's Wrath

"<u>Zachariah the son of Jeroboam reign</u> <u>over Israel</u> in Samaria six months. And he did that which was evil in the sight of the LORD, as his fathers had done: he departed not from the sins of Jeroboam the son of Nebat, who made Israel to sin. And Shallum the son of Jabesh conspired against him, and smote him before the people, and slew him, and <u>reigned in his stead</u>" (2 Kings 15:8b-9). The OT Narrative combination *Zachariah the son of Jeroboam reign* (1x), *over Israel* (62x) = 63. Again the phrase *reigned in his stead* occurs 63 times in the Bible.

Shallum Experienced God's Wrath

"Shallum the son of Jabesh began to reign . . . and he reigned a full month in Samaria. For Menahem the son of Gadi went up from Tirzah, and came to Samaria, and <u>smote</u> Shallum the son of Jabesh in Samaria, and slew him, and <u>reigned in his stead</u>" (2 Kings 15:13-14). Shallum had killed his own brother to take the throne. For this he received his swift reward. His reign lasted only thirty days. Again the word *smitten* occurs 63 times in Scripture. Again the phrase *reigned in his stead* occurs 63 times in the Bible.

Menahem Deserved God's Wrath

"Then Menahem smote Tiphsah, and all that were therein, and the coasts thereof from Tirzah: because they opened not to him, therefore he smote it; and all the women therein that were with child he ripped up. . . . Menahem the son of Gadi . . . reigned ten years in Samaria. <u>And he did</u> <u>that which</u> <u>was evil in the sight of the LORD</u>: <u>he departed not all his days from</u> <u>the sins of Jeroboam the son of Nebat, who made Israel to sin</u>" (2 Kings 15:16-18). We are not told how Menahem died, but his life and reign was cut short lasting only ten years. This time is very short compared to the standard reign of Israel's first three kings who each ruled for forty years. The Old Testament combination *and he did that which* (28x), *was evil in the sight of the LORD* (21x), *he departed not all* (1x), *his days from* (1x), *the sins of Jeroboam the son of Nebat* (10x), *who made Israel to sin* (2x) = 63.

Pekahiah Experienced God's Wrath

"Pekahiah the son of Menahem began to reign over Israel in Samaria, and reigned two years. And he did that which was evil in the sight of the LORD: he departed not <u>from</u> the sins of Jeroboam <u>the</u> son of Nebat, who made Israel to sin. But Pekah the son of Remaliah, a captain of his, conspired against him, and smote him in Samaria, in the palace of the king's house, with Argob and Arieh, and with him fifty men of the Gileadites: and he killed him, and reigned in his room" (2 Kings 15:23b-25).

Here the the word *from* is the 663rd word of the chapter. Here the underlined definite article *the* is the 13,663rd word of Second Kings.

Pekah Experienced God's Wrath

"Pekah the son of Remaliah began to reign over Israel in Samaria, and reigned twenty years. And he did that which was evil in the sight of the LORD: he departed not from the sins of Jeroboam the son of Nebat, who made Israel to sin. In the days of Pekah king of Israel came Tiglath-pileser king of Assyria, and took Ijon, and Abel-beth-maachah, and Janoah, and Kedesh, and Hazor, and Gilead, and Galilee, all the land of Naphtali, and carried them captive to Assyria. And Hoshea the son of Elah made a conspiracy against Pekah the son of Remaliah, and <u>smote</u> him, and slew him, and <u>reigned in his stead</u>" (2 Kings 15:27b-30c). Again the word *smitten* occurs 63 times in Scripture. Again the phrase *reigned in his stead* occurs 63 times in the Bible.

Hoshea Experienced God's Wrath

"Hoshea the son of Elah to reign in Samaria over Israel nine years. And he did that which was evil in the sight of the LORD, but not as the kings of Israel that were before him. Against him came up Shalmaneser king of Assyria; and Hoshea became his servant, and gave him presents. And the king of Assyria found conspiracy in Hoshea: for he had sent messengers to So king of Egypt, and brought no present to the king of Assyria, as he had done year by year: therefore the king of Assyria shut him up, and <u>bound</u> him in prison" (2 Kings 17:1b-4). The word *bound* is mentioned in 63 verses of the Old Testament.

Nation of Israel Carried Away in God's Wrath

"And they left all the <u>commandments</u> of the LORD their God, and made them <u>molten images,</u> even two calves, and made a grove, and worshipped all the host of heaven, and served Baal. And they caused their sons and their daughters to pass through the fire, and used divination and enchantments, and sold themselves to do evil in the sight of the LORD, to provoke him to ANGER. Therefore the LORD was very angry with <u>Israel,</u> and removed them out of his sight: there was none left but the tribe of Judah only. . . . And the LORD rejected all the seed of <u>Israel,</u> and afflicted them, and delivered them into the hand of spoilers . . . Until the LORD removed <u>Israel</u> out of his sight, as he had said by all his servants the prophets. So was <u>Israel carried away</u> out of their own land to Assyria unto this day" (2 Kings 17:16-18, 20a, 32).

Again the word *commandments* occurs 63 times in the Law. Again the word *idols* occurs 63 times in the Major and Minor Prophets. Again the name *Israel* is mentioned in 63 verses of the Wisdom Books.

> The phrase *carried away* occurs 63 times in the Bible.
> The word *captivity* occurs 63 times in the Major Prophets.

Wrath of God Sent among Samarian Immigrants

"And the king of Assyria brought men from Babylon, and from Cuthah, and from Ava, and from Hamath, and from Sepharvaim, and placed them in the cities of Samaria instead of the children of Israel: and they possessed Samaria, and dwelt in the cities thereof. And so it was at the beginning of their dwelling there, that they feared not the LORD: therefore <u>the LORD sent</u> <u>lions among them, which slew some of them</u>" (2 Kings 17:24-25). Again the word *sent* is mentioned in 63 verses of the Bible. The combination *the LORD sent* (22 vs), *lions* (39 vs), *among them which slew* (1v), *slew some of them* (1v) = 63 verses.

Wrath of God Comes upon Assyrian Army

"And it came to pass that night, that the angel of the LORD went out, and smote in the camp of the Assyrians an hundred fourscore and five thousand: and when they arose early in the morning, behold, they were all <u>dead</u> corpses" (2 Kings 19:35). Again the word *dead* occurs naturally 363 times in the Bible.

Wrath of God Came upon Sennacherib

"So Sennacherib king of Assyria departed, and went and returned, and dwelt at Nineveh. And it came to pass, as he was worshipping in the house of Nisroch his god, that Adrammelech and Sharezer his sons smote him with <u>the sword</u>" (2 Kings 19:36-37b). Again the phrase *the sword* is mentioned in 163 chapters of the Bible.

10,163rd Verse of the Bible

"Because they have forsaken me, and have burned incense unto other gods, that they might provoke me to ANGER with all the works of their hands; therefore my WRATH shall be kindled against this place, and shall not be quenched" (2 Kings 22:17). The keyword *wrath* actually occurs in this 63rd verse.

God Turned Not From His Great Wrath against Judah

"Thus saith the LORD, Behold, I will bring evil upon this place, and upon the inhabitants thereof, even all the words of the book which the king of Judah hath read: Because they have forsaken me, and have burned incense unto other gods, that they might provoke me to ANGER with all the works of their hands; therefore my WRATH shall be kindled against this place, and shall not be quenched. . . . Notwithstanding the LORD turned not from the <u>FIERCENESS of his</u> <u>great</u> <u>WRATH</u>, wherewith his <u>ANGER</u> was <u>kindled</u> against Judah, because of all the provocations that Manasseh had provoked him withal" (2 Kings 23:16-17, 26).

God postponed His wrath until after Josiah's godly reign. Again the word *great* is mentioned in 163 verses of the Major Prophets. Again the Wisdom Books combination *fierceness of his anger* (1x) *wrath* (62x) = 63. Again the word *kindled* occurs 63 times in the Old Testament.

Wrath of God Came upon Jerusalem & Judah

"For through the ANGER of the LORD it came to pass <u>in Jerusalem</u> and <u>Judah,</u> until he had cast them out from his presence" (2 Kings 24:20ab).

> The name *Jerusalem* occurs 63 times in Second Kings.
> The phrase *in Jerusalem* is mentioned in 63 chapters of OTN.
> The phrase *in Jerusalem* occurs 163 times in the Bible.
> The name *Judah* occurs 63 times in the Minor Prophets.
> The name *Judah* is mentioned in 263 chapters of the OT.

Saul Reaped the Wrath of God

"So <u>Saul</u> died for his transgression which he committed against the LORD, even against the word of the LORD, which he kept not, and also for asking counsel of one that had a familiar spirit, to enquire of it; And enquired not of the LORD: therefore he slew him" (1 Chron. 10:13-14a). Again the name *Saul* occurs 363 times in the Old Testament.

Uzza Experienced the Wrath of God

"And when they came unto the threshingfloor of Chidon, Uzza put forth his hand to hold the ark;

for the oxen stumbled. <u>And</u> the ANGER of the LORD was kindled against Uzza, and he smote him, because he put his hand to the ark: and there he died before GOD" (1 Chron. 13:9-10). Here the lead word of this wrath-of-the-Lord verse *And* is the 263rd word of this chapter.

Wrath of God Came upon Jerusalem

"So the LORD <u>sent</u> <u>pestilence</u> upon Israel: and there fell of Israel seventy thousand men. And GOD <u>sent</u> an angel unto <u>Jerusalem</u> to destroy it: and as he was destroying, the LORD beheld, and he repented him of the evil, and said to the angel that destroyed, It is enough, stay now thine hand. And the angel of the LORD stood by the threshingfloor of Ornan the Jebusite. And David lifted up his eyes, and saw the angel of the LORD stand between the earth and the heaven, having a drawn <u>sword</u> <u>in his hand</u> stretched out over <u>Jerusalem</u>. Then David and the elders of Israel, who were clothed in sackcloth, fell upon their faces" (1 Chron. 21:14-16).

Again the word *sent* is mentioned in 63 verses of the Bible. Again the phrase *the plague* occurs 63 times in the Law. Again the phrase *the sword* is mentioned in 163 chapters of the Bible. Again the phrase *in his hand* occurs 63 times in the Old Testament. Again the name *Jerusalem* occurs 63 times in Second Kings.

Wrath of God Came upon Israel

"But David took not the number of them from twenty years old and under: because the LORD had said he would increase Israel like to the stars of the heavens. Joab the son of Zeruiah began to number, but he finished not, because there fell WRATH for it against <u>Israel</u>: neither was the number put in the account of the chronicles of king David" (1 Chron. 27:23- 24). Again the name *Israel* is mentioned in 63 verses of the Wisdom Books. In this verse of wrath there are 63 words surrounding the keyword *wrath*.

NOTE: We now examine the lives of the bad and evil kings of Judah. Out of the 21 kings who reigned in Jerusalem 11 of them provoked God's wrath.

Rehoboam Experienced the Wrath of God

"And it came to pass, when Rehoboam had established the kingdom, and had strengthened himself, he forsook the law of the LORD, and all Israel with him. And it came to pass, that in the fifth year of king Rehoboam Shishak king of Egypt came up against Jerusalem, because they had transgressed against the LORD. With twelve hundred chariots, and threescore thousand horsemen: and the people were without number that came with him out of Egypt; the Lubims, the Sukkiims, and the Ethiopians. . . . And when he humbled himself, the WRATH of the LORD <u>turned</u> from him, that he would not destroy him altogether: and also in Judah things went well" (2 Chron. 12:1-3; 12:12).

Again the word *turned* is mentioned naturally in 63 chapters of the OT Narrative.

Abijah Was Spared the Wrath of God

"And Rehoboam slept with his fathers, and was buried in the city of David: and <u>Abijah</u> his son reigned in his stead. . . . He reigned three years in Jerusalem" (2 Chron. 12:16; 13:2a). Abijah is called Abijam in First Kings, and Abia in Chronicles. We are informed in First Kings 15:3-4 that Abijam, "<u>walked in</u> <u>all the sins</u> <u>of his father, which he</u> <u>had done before him</u>: and his heart was not perfect with the LORD his God, as the heart of David his father. Nevertheless for David's sake did the LORD his God give him a lamp in Jerusalem, to set up his son after him, and to establish Jerusalem." The Bible combination *Abijam* (5x), *walked in* (51x), *all the sins* (5x), *of his father which he* (1x), *had done before him* (1x) = 63.

Jehoram Reaped the Wrath of God

Jehoram was married to Athaliah, the wicked daughter of Ahab and Jezebel.

"Now when Jehoram was risen up to the kingdom of his father, he strengthened himself, and slew all his brethren with the sword, and divers also of the princes of Israel. . . . Moreover the LORD stirred up against Jehoram the spirit of the Philistines, and of the Arabians, that were near the Ethiopians: And they came up into Judah, and brake into it, and carried away all the substance that was found in the king's house, and his sons also, and his wives; so that there was never a son left him, save . . . the youngest of his sons. And after all this the LORD smote him in his bowels with an incurable disease. And it came to pass, that in process of time, after the end of two years, his bowels fell out by reason of his sickness: so he died of sore diseases" (2 Chron. 21:4, 16-19a).

Again the word *smitten* occurs 63 times in Scripture. The sentence *and after all this the LORD smote him in his bowels with an incurable disease* consists of 63 letters!

Ahaziah Experienced God's Wrath

"Forty and two years old was Ahaziah when he began to reign, and he reigned one year in Jerusalem. His mother's name also was Athaliah . . . He also walked in the ways of the house of Ahab: for his mother was his counsellor to do wickedly. Wherefore he did evil in the sight of the LORD like the house of Ahab: for they were his counsellors after the death of his father to his destruction. . . . when Jehu was executing judgment upon the house of Ahab . . . And he sought Ahaziah: and they caught him, for he was hid in Samaria, and brought him to Jehu: and when they had slain him, they buried him" (2 Chron. 22:2-4, 8b, 9).

Ahaziah's reign was cut very short. The Old Testament combination *he also walked in the ways* (1x), *of the house of Ahab* (7x), *for his mother was* (1x), *his counsellor to* (1x), *do wickedly* (6x), *wherefore he did* (1x), *evil in the sight of the LORD* (44x), *like the house of Ahab* (1x), *for they were his counsellors* (1x) = 63. Again the word *judgment(s)* occurs naturally 63 times in the Law.

Queen Athaliah Greatly Deserved the Wrath of God

"But when Athaliah the mother of Ahaziah saw that her son was dead, she arose and destroyed all the seed royal of the house of Judah. . . . and Athaliah reigned over the land . . . So they laid hands on her; and when she was come to the entering of the horse gate by the king's house, they slew her there. . . . And all the people of the land rejoiced: and the city was quiet, after that they had slain Athaliah with the sword" (2 Chron. 23:10, 12b, 15, 21). Again the phrase *the sword* is mentioned in 163 chapters of the Bible.

Uzziah Incurred the Wrath of God

"But when he was strong, his heart was lifted up to his destruction: for he transgressed against the LORD his GOD, and went into the temple of the LORD to burn incense upon the altar of incense. . . . And Azariah the priest went in after him, and with him fourscore priests of the LORD, that were valiant men: And they withstood Uzziah the king . . . Then Uzziah was WROTH, and had a censer in his hand to burn incense: and while he was WROTH with the priests, the leprosy even rose up in his forehead . . . And Uzziah the king was a leper unto the day of his death, and dwelt in a several house, being a leper; for he was cut off from the house of the LORD" (2 Chron. 26:16, 17-18a, 19ab, 21a, b).

Uzziah was a good king over Judah but his pride caused him to fall. God smote him in His wrath. Again the word *smitten* occurs 63 times in Scripture. The Bible phrases *be cut off* (61x) and *am cut off* (2x) = 63.

Ahaz Experienced God's Wrath

"Ahaz was twenty years old when he began to reign, and he reigned sixteen years in Jerusalem: but he did [not] that which was right in the sight of the LORD, like David his father: For he walked in the ways of the kings of Israel, and made also molten <u>images</u> for Baalim. Moreover he burnt incense in the valley of the son of Hinnom, and burnt his children in the fire, after the abominations of the heathen whom the LORD had cast out before the children of Israel. He sacrificed also and burnt incense in the high places, and on the hills, and under every green tree. Wherefore the LORD his GOD delivered him into the hand of the king of Syria; and they smote him, and <u>carried away</u> a great multitude of them <u>captives</u>, and brought them to Damascus. And he was also delivered into the hand of the king of Israel, who smote him with a great slaughter" (2 Chron. 28:1-5).

The word *images* is mentioned in 63 verses of the Old Testament. Again the phrase *carried away* occurs 63 times in the Bible. Again the word *captivity* occurs 63 times in the Major Prophets.

Manasseh Experienced God's Wrath

"Manasseh was twelve years old when he began to reign, and he reigned fifty and five years in Jerusalem: But did that which was evil in the sight of the LORD, like unto the abominations of the heathen, whom the LORD had cast out before the children of Israel. . . . And he caused his children to pass through the fire in the valley of the son of Hinnom: also he observed times, and used enchantments, and used witchcraft, and dealt with a familiar spirit, and with wizards: he wrought much evil in the sight of the LORD, to provoke him to ANGER. And he set a carved image, the <u>idol</u> which he had made, in the house of GOD . . . Wherefore the LORD brought upon them the captains of the host of the king of Assyria, which took Manasseh among the thorns, and <u>bound</u> him with fetters, and carried him to Babylon" (2 Chron. 33:1-3, 6-7a, 11).

Again the word *idols* occurs 63 times in the Major and Minor Prophets. Again the word *bound* is mentioned in 63 verses of the Old Testament.

Amon Experienced God's Wrath

"Amon was two and twenty years old when he began to reign, and reigned two years in Jerusalem. But he did that which was evil in the sight of the LORD, as did Manasseh his father: for Amon sacrificed unto all the carved <u>images</u> which Manasseh his father had made, and served them; And humbled not himself before the LORD . . . but Amon trespassed more and more. And his servants conspired against him, and slew him in his own house" (2 Chron. 33:21-24). Again the word *images* is mentioned in 63 verses of the Old Testament.

Jehoahaz Experienced God's Wrath

"And the people of the land took Jehoahaz the son of Josiah, and anointed him, and made him king in his father's stead. Jehoahaz was twenty and three years old when he began to reign; and he reigned three months in Jerusalem . . . And the king of Egypt put him down at Jerusalem, and condemned the land in an hundred talents of silver and a talent of gold. And the king of Egypt made Eliakim his brother king over Judah and Jerusalem, and turned his name to Jehoiakim. And Necho took Jehoahaz his brother, and <u>carried</u> him to Egypt" (2 Chron. 36:30c-31b, 3-4).

Second Kings 23:32 informs us that Jehoahaz "did that which was evil in the sight of the LORD, according to all that his fathers had done." Again the phrase *carried away* occurs 63 times in the Bible.

Jehoiakim Experienced God's Wrath

"Jehoiakim was twenty and five years old when he began to reign, and he reigned eleven years in

Jerusalem: and he did that which was evil in the sight of the LORD his GOD. Against him came up Nebuchadnezzar king of Babylon, and <u>bound</u> him in fetters, to carry him to Babylon" (2 Chron. 36:5-6). Again the word *bound* is mentioned in 63 verses of the Old Testament.

Jehoiachin Experienced God's Wrath

"Jehoiachin was eight years old when he began to reign, and he reigned three months and ten days in Jerusalem: and he did that which was evil in the sight of the LORD. And when the year was expired, king Nebuchadnezzar sent, and <u>brought him to</u> Babylon" (2 Chron. 36:9-10a). Again the phrase *carried away* occurs 63 times in the Bible.

Zedekiah Experienced God's Wrath

"Zedekiah was one and twenty years old when he began to reign, and reigned eleven years in Jerusalem. And he did that which was evil in the sight of the LORD his GOD, and humbled not himself before Jeremiah the prophet speaking from the mouth of the LORD. And he also rebelled against king Nebuchadnezzar, who had made him swear by God: but he stiffened his neck, and hardened his heart from turning unto the LORD GOD of Israel. . . Therefore he brought upon them the king of the Chaldees, who slew their young men with <u>the sword</u> in the house of their sanctuary" (2 Chron. 36:11-13, 17).

Again the phrase *the sword* is mentioned in 163 chapters of the Bible.

Previous Generation Provoked God's Wrath

"But after that our fathers had provoked the GOD of heaven unto WRATH, he gave them into the hand of Nebuchadnezzar the king of Babylon, the Chaldean, who <u>destroyed</u> this house, and <u>carried</u> the people <u>away</u> into Babylon" (Ezra 5:12). Again the word *destroy* is mentioned in 63 chapters of the Major and Minor Prophets. Again the phrase *carried away* occurs 63 times in the Bible.

Ezra Feared the Wrath of God

Ezra was fearful because the nation had lost their separated position before the Lord through their intermarriage with strange wives. He was greatly worried about God's potential wrath. Thus he prayed, "And after all that is come upon us for our evil deeds, and for our great trespass, seeing that thou our GOD hast PUNISHED us less than our iniquities deserve, and hast given us such deliverance as this; Should we again break thy <u>commandments,</u> and join in affinity with the people of these abominations? wouldest not thou be ANGRY with us till thou hadst consumed us, so that there should be no remnant nor escaping?" (Ezra 9:13-14) Again all forms of the word *punish* are mentioned in 63 collective verses of the Bible. Again the word *commandments* occurs 63 times in the Law.

Ezra Works to Turn Away God's Wrath from the Remnant

"Let now our rulers of all the congregation stand, and let all them which have taken strange wives in our cities come at appointed times, and with them the elders of every city, and the judges thereof, until the FIERCE WRATH of our GOD for this matter be <u>turned</u> from us" (Ezra. 10:14). Again the word *turned* is mentioned naturally in 63 chapters of the OT Narrative.

The Jews of Jerusalem Experienced God's Wrath

"I asked them concerning the <u>Jews</u> that had escaped, which were left of the captivity, and concerning Jerusalem. And they said unto me, The remnant that are left of the captivity there in the province are in great affliction and reproach: the wall of Jerusalem also is broken down, and the gates thereof are burned with fire" (Neh. 1:2b-3).

The title *Jews* occurs 63 times in the OT Narrative.
The title *the Jews* occurs 63 times in John's Gospel.

God Is Slow to Anger & Wrath

Nehemiah confessed to God in prayer, "But they and our fathers dealt proudly, and hardened their necks, and hearkened not to thy commandments, And refused to obey, neither were mindful of thy wonders that thou didst among them; but hardened their necks, and in their rebellion appointed a captain to return to their bondage: but thou art a GOD ready to pardon, gracious and merciful, slow to ANGER, and of great kindness, and forsookest them not" (Neh. 9:16-17). The Old Testament combination *slow* (11x), *to anger* (52x) = 63.

Profaning the Sabbath Brings More of God's Wrath

"Did not your fathers thus, and did not our GOD bring all this evil upon us, and upon this city? yet ye bring more WRATH upon Israel by profaning the sabbath" (Neh. 13:18). Again the word *bring* occurs 63 times in Leviticus. The Isaiah combination *bring* (55x), *wrath* (8x) = 63. The word *more* is mentioned in 630 verses of the Bible, a visual multiple of 63.

Haman Reaps the Wrath of God

"So they hanged Haman on the gallows that he had prepared for Mordecai. Then was the king's WRATH pacified. . . . and they hanged Haman's ten sons" so that Esther's wrath would be pacified (Est. 7:10, 14c). Moreover, all this was done to pacify God's wrath upon Haman. The Esther combination *hanged* (7x), *Haman* (50x), *on the gallows* (3x), *then was the king's wrath* (1x), *pacified* (2x) = 63.

Job's Three Friends Kindled God's Wrath

"And it was so, that after the LORD had spoken these words unto Job, the LORD said to Eliphaz the Temanite, My WRATH is kindled against thee, and against thy two friends: for ye have not spoken of me the thing that is right, as my servant Job hath. Therefore take unto you now seven bullocks and seven rams, and go to my servant Job, and offer up for yourselves a burnt offering; and my servant Job shall pray for you: for him will I accept: lest I deal with you after your folly" (Job 42:7-8d). Again the word *kindled* occurs 63 times in the Old Testament.

Heathen Nations to Experience God's Wrath

"Why do the heathen rage, and the people imagine a vain thing? The kings of the earth set themselves, and the rulers take counsel together, against the LORD, and against his anointed. . . . He that sitteth in the heavens shall laugh: the Lord shall have them in derision. Then shall he speak unto them in his WRATH, and vex them in his sore displeasure" (Ps. 2:1-2, 4). The Wisdom Books combination *why do the heathen rage* (1x), *and the people imagine a vain thing* (1x), *the kings of the earth set themselves* (1x), *and the rulers take counsel together* (1x), *against the LORD and against his anointed* (1x), *he that sitteth in* (1x), *the heavens* (41x), *shall laugh* (3x), *the Lord shall have them* (1x), *in derision* (4x), *then shall he* (1x), *speak unto them* (1), *in his wrath* (4x), *and vex them* (1x), *in his sore displeasure* (1x) = 63.

What if the Son of God's Wrath Becomes Kindled?

"Kiss <u>the Son</u>, <u>lest</u> <u>he be</u> ANGRY, and ye perish from the way, when his WRATH is <u>kindled</u> but a little. Blessed are all they that put their trust in him" (Ps. 2:12).

> The case-sensitive title *the Son* occurs 163 times in the Bible.
> The title *T/the S/son* is mentioned in 63 chapters of the Gospels.
> The title *Son* is mentioned in 163 verses of the NT Narrative.
> The title *Son* occurs 63 times from Acts to the Apocalypse.
>
> ~~~~~
>
> The word *lest* is mentioned naturally in 63 verses of the Law.
> The phrase *he be* is mentioned in 63 verses Old Testament.
> The word *kindled* occurs 63 times in the Old Testament.

God's Latter-Time Wrath

"Thine hand shall find out all thine enemies: thy right hand shall find out those that hate thee. Thou shalt make them as a fiery oven in <u>the time of</u> thine ANGER: the LORD shall swallow them up in his WRATH, and <u>the fire</u> shall <u>devour</u> them" (Ps. 21:8-9). The Old Testament phrases *the time of* (62x) and *the latter time of* (1x) = 63. This verse presents the Bible's 63rd occurrence of the phrase *the fire* and describes a form of God's wrath. Again the word *devour* occurs 63 times in the Old Testament.

God's Temporary Chastening Wrath

"Sing unto the LORD, O ye saints of his, and give thanks at the remembrance of his holiness. <u>For his ANGER</u> <u>endureth</u> <u>but a moment</u>; in his favour is life: <u>weeping may</u> <u>endure for a night</u>, but joy cometh in the morning" (Ps. 30:4-5). Because believers sometimes fall into mischief the Lord must remind us of His wrath toward sin. In this way, we will quickly shape up. The Bible combination *for his anger* (1x), *endureth* (59x), *but a moment* (1x), *weeping may* (1x), *endure for a night* (1x) = 63.

God's Devouring Wrath

"<u>Our GOD</u> <u>shall come</u>, <u>and shall not keep silence</u>: <u>a fire</u> <u>shall devour before him</u>, <u>and it shall be very tempestuous round about him</u>" (Ps. 50:3). Again the word *devour* occurs 63 times in the Old Testament. Again the word *devour* occurs 63 times in the Old Testament. The Wisdom Books combination *our God* (31x), *shall come* (23x), *and shall not keep silence* (1x), *a fire* (6x), *shall devour before him* (1x), *and it shall be very tempestuous round about him* (1x) = 63.

The Wicked Will Go Down to Hell

"Let death seize upon them, and let them <u>go down</u> quick into hell: for wickedness is in their dwellings, and among them" (Ps. 55:15). The phrase *go down* is mentioned in 63 chapters of the Bible.

Psalm 63

David has many wonderful things to say of God's loving kindness; yet as he closes this psalm he says this of his enemies: "But those that seek my soul, to destroy it, shall go into <u>the lower parts</u> of the earth. They shall fall by <u>the sword</u>: they shall be a portion for foxes. But the king shall rejoice in GOD; every one that sweareth by him shall glory: but the mouth of them that speak lies shall be stopped" (Ps. 63:9-11). David is referring to hell, a place where the enemies of God experience His eternal wrath. The Bible combination *lowest part* (1x), *hell* (54x), *tormented* (8x) = 63. Again the phrase *the sword* is mentioned in 163 chapters of the Bible.

God's Wrath & the Sinner's Death

"He that is our God is the God of <u>salvation</u>; and unto GOD the Lord belong the issues from <u>death</u>" (Ps. 68:20). From an eternal perspective, the opposite of salvation is death. Similarly salvation is the escape from God's everlasting wrath. The word *salvation* occurs 63 times in the Psalms. Again the word *death* is mentioned in 63 verses of the Law.

Wilderness Israelites Experienced God's Wrath

"They were not estranged from their lust. But while their meat was yet in their mouths, <u>The WRATH OF GOD</u> came <u>upon them</u>, and slew the fattest of them, and smote down the chosen men of <u>Israel</u>" (Ps. 78:30-31). The word *came* occurs 63 times in John's Gospel. The naturally occurring Old Testament combination *the wrath of God* (1x), *upon them* (162x) = 163. Again the name *Israel* is mentioned in 63 verses of the Wisdom Books.

15,163rd Verse of the Bible

"He cast upon them the <u>FIERCENESS of his ANGER</u>, <u>WRATH</u>, and <u>INDIGNATION</u>, and trouble, by sending evil angels among them" (Ps. 78:49). This 63rd verse summarizes Egypt's harsh experience under God's wrath. Many keywords related to God's wrath actually occur in this 63rd verse. Again the Wisdom Books combination *fierceness of his anger* (1x) *wrath* (62x) = 63. Employing our two definitions of "wrath" we gather the following seal from Psalms: *fierce* (1x), *anger* (25x), *wrath* (28x), *indignation* (3x), *vengeance* (5x), *punishments* (1x) = 63.

God Was Wroth with Idolatrous Israel

"For they provoked him to ANGER with their high places, and moved him to jealousy with their graven images. <u>When God heard this, he was WROTH, and greatly abhorred Israel</u>. . . . He gave his people over also unto the sword; <u>and was WROTH</u> with his inheritance" (Ps. 78:58-59, 62). The Bible combination *when God heard this* (1x), *he was* (461x), *wroth and greatly abhorred Israel* (1x) = 463. The OT Narrative combination *and was* (46x), *wroth* (17x) = 63.

Psalm 78:63

"<u>The fire consumed their young men</u>; and their maidens were not given to marriage" (Ps. 78:63). This verse speaks of Israel's encounter with God's wrath after they entered Canaan and later became idolatrous. The Bible combination *the fire consumed their* (1 ch), *young men* (62 chs) = 63 chapters.

That Day When Israel Was Spared God's Wrath

"Therefore he said that he would destroy them, had not Moses his chosen stood before him in the breach, to <u>turn</u> away his WRATH, <u>lest</u> he should destroy them" (Ps. 106:23). Again the word *turned* is mentioned naturally in 63 chapters of the OT Narrative. Again the word *lest* is mentioned naturally in 63 verses of the Law.

God's Wrath against the Heathen

"To <u>execute VENGEANCE</u> upon <u>the heathen</u>, and <u>PUNISHMENTS</u> upon the people" (Ps.

149:7). The Major Prophets combination *he shall execute* (1x), *vengeance* (4x), *the heathen* (58x) = 63. Again all forms of the word *punish* are mentioned in 63 collective verses of the Bible.

"The Expectation of the Wicked"

"The desire of the righeous is only good: but the expectation <u>of the wicked</u> is WRATH" (Prov. 11:23). The phrase *of the wicked* is mentioned in 63 chapters of the Old Testament. Here the keyword *wrath* is the 427,463rd word of the Bible.

63rd Verse of Ecclesiastes

"I said in mine heart concerning the estate of the sons of <u>men</u>, that GOD might manifest them, and that they might see that they themselves are beasts" (Eccles. 3:18). Throughout the Bible we see the wrath of God falling indiscriminately at times upon both sinful men and wild beasts. Again the word *men* is found in 63 books of the Bible.

God's Wrath against His Sinful Children

"Ah sinful nation, a people laden with iniquity, a seed of evildoers, children that are corrupters: <u>they have forsaken the LORD, they have</u> <u>provoked</u> <u>the Holy One of Israel</u> unto ANGER, they are gone away backward" (Isa. 1:4). The Old Testament combination *they have forsaken the LORD they have* (1x), *provoked* (31x), *the Holy One of Israel* (30x), *unto anger* (1x) = 63.

Fear of God's Awakened Wrath

"And they shall go into the holes of the rocks, and into the caves of the earth, for <u>fear of</u> the LORD, and for the glory of his majesty, when he ariseth to shake terribly the earth" (Isa. 2:19). Here the word *fear* is the 463rd word of this chapter, and it pertains to fear of the Lord's awakened wrath. The phrase *fear of* is mentioned in 63 verses of the Old Testament.

17,863rd Verse of the Bible

"Wherefore it shall come to pass, that when the Lord hath performed his whole work upon mount Zion and on Jerusalem, I will <u>PUNISH</u> the fruit of <u>the stout heart of</u> <u>the king of Assyria</u>, and the glory of his high looks" (Isa. 10:12). Again all forms of the word *punish* are mentioned in 63 collective verses of the Bible. The related keyword *punish* actually occurs in this 63rd verse. The Old Testament equation *the king of Assyria* (64x) – *the stout heart of* (1x) = 63.

God's Day of Wrath against Sinners

"<u>Behold, the day of the LORD</u> <u>cometh,</u> <u>cruel both with</u> <u>WRATH and FIERCE ANGER</u>, to lay the land desolate: and he shall destroy the sinners thereof out of it" (Isa. 13:9). The Old Testament combination *behold the day of the LORD* (2x), *cometh* (159x), *cruel both with* (1x), *wrath and fierce anger* (1x) = 163.

263rd Verse of Isaiah

"And <u>I will PUNISH</u> <u>the world</u> <u>for their evil</u>, and the wicked for their iniquity; and I will cause the arrogancy of the proud to cease, and will lay low the haughtiness of the terrible" (Isa. 13:11). Again all forms of the word *punish* are mentioned in 63 collective verses of the Bible. The related key word *punish* actually occurs in this 63rd verse. The Old Testament combination *I will punish* (18x), *the world* (44x), *for their evil* (1x) = 63.

The Day of God's Fierce Anger & Wrath

"Therefore I will shake the heavens, and the earth shall remove out of her place, in the WRATH of the LORD of hosts, and in the day of his FIERCE ANGER" (Isa. 13:13). Again the phrase *the day of* occurs 163 times in the Bible.

God's Everlasting Burnings

"The sinners in Zion are afraid; fearfulness hath surprised the hypocrites. Who among us shall dwell with the devouring fire? who among us shall dwell with everlasting burnings?" (Isa. 33:14) The word *burning(s)* occurs 63 times in the Bible.

God's End-Time Indignation upon All Nations

"For the INDIGNATION of the LORD is upon all nations, and his FURY upon all their armies: he hath utterly destroyed them, he hath delivered them to the slaughter" (Isa. 34:2). The Bible combination *the indignation* (8x) and *all nations* (55x) = 63.

Messiah Smitten under the Wrath of God

"Surely he hath borne our griefs, and carried our sorrows: yet we did esteem him stricken, smitten of GOD, and afflicted" (Isa. 53:4). Again the word *smitten* occurs 63 times in the Bible.

1063rd Verse of Isaiah

"All we like sheep have gone astray; we have turned every one to his own way; and the LORD hath laid on him the iniquity of us all" (Isa. 53:6). The Lord's wrath came upon the Messiah to pacify His wrath toward mankind's endless sins.

The Wrathful Waters of Noah

"For a small moment have I forsaken thee; but with great mercies will I gather thee. In a little WRATH I hid my face from thee for a moment; but with everlasting kindness will I have mercy on thee, saith the LORD thy Redeemer. For this is as the waters of Noah unto me: for as I have sworn that the waters of Noah should no more go over the earth; so have I sworn that I would not be WROTH with thee, nor rebuke thee" (Isa. 54:7-9). The Law combination *is as the* (1 v), *waters* (55 vs), *of Noah* (7 vs) = 63 verses.

63rd Chapter of Isaiah

The theme of this chapter is, The Day of God's Vengeance. This favorable event for the house of Jacob will unfold in the lattermost days of Jacob's Trouble. Messiah will appear in His second advent to save Them. They will be ecstatic as they watch their enemies being scattered and destroyed by His strong arm and mighty Word.

> "Who is this that cometh from Edom, with dyed garments from Bozrah? this that is glorious in his apparel, travelling in the greatness of his strength? I that speak in righteousness, mighty to save. Wherefore art thou red in thine apparel, and thy garments like him that treadeth in the winefat? I have trodden the winepress alone; and of the people there was none with me: for I will tread them in mine ANGER, and trample them in my FURY; and their blood shall be sprinkled upon my garments, and I will stain all my raiment. For the day of VENGEANCE is in mine heart, and the year of my redeemed is come. And I looked, and there was none to help; and I wondered that there was none to uphold: therefore mine own

arm brought salvation unto me; and my <u>FURY</u>, it upheld me. And I will tread down the people in mine ANGER, and make them <u>drunk</u> in my <u>FURY</u>, and I will bring down their strength to the earth" (Isa. 63:1-6).

Again the word *great* is mentioned in 163 verses of the Major Prophets. Again the word *strength* is mentioned in 163 chapters of the Bible. The word *fury* is mentioned in 63 verses of the Major and Minor Prophets. Again the word *drunk(en)* occurs 63 times in the Bible. Again the phrase *the day of* occurs 163 times in the Bible!

The remainder of this chapter examines the remnant's hope in God as well as their proper fear of His vengeance even though they are the people of God. They still retain memories of the wilderness journey where they repeatedly became the objects of God's wrath. "But they rebelled, and vexed his holy Spirit: therefore he was <u>turned</u> to be their enemy, and he fought against them" (v. 10). Again the word *turned* is mentioned naturally in 63 chapters of the OT Narrative.

As the chapter closes Israel confesses her sin: "O LORD, why hast thou made us to err from thy ways, and hardened our heart from thy fear? Return for thy servants' sake, the <u>tribes</u> of thine inheritance" (v. 17). Back in the wilderness, not fearing God landed Israel in hot water. Here they pray to God asking Him to reverse the process lest they suffer His wrath yet again. Again the phrase *tribes of* occurs 63 times in the Law.

The Sinner's 100-Year Deadline

"There shall be no more thence an infant of days, nor an old man that hath not filled his days: for the child shall die an hundred years old; but the sinner being an hundred years old shall be <u>accursed</u>" (Isa. 65:20). During the Millennium, disobedient ones will not be permitted to live out the full one thousand years. Rather they will be judged unworthy at age one hundred and punished accordingly, even with sudden death. Again the word *cursed* is mentioned in 63 verses of the Old Testament.

18,963rd Verse of the Bible

"And I will utter my <u>judgments</u> against them touching all their wickedness, who have forsaken me, and have burned incense unto other gods, and worshipped the works of their own hands" (Jer. 1:16). Judah's judgment for their idolatry is wrath from heaven. Again the word *judgment(s)* occurs naturally 63 times in the Law.

63rd Verse of Jeremiah

"And I said after she had done all these things, Turn thou unto me. But she returned not. And her treacherous sister <u>Judah</u> saw it" (Jer. 3:7). The sequential verse reveals God's wrath upon the northern kingdom of Israel. He gave Israel a bill of divorcement after she continually rejected Him. God favored the sister tribe Judah, but in time He also had to display His wrath upon her. Again the name *Judah* occurs 63 times in the Major Prophets.

Judah & Jerusalem to Experience God's Wrath

Because a Gentile nation is on the way bringing death and destruction, the men of Judah and Jerusalem are to put on a spirit of humility and repentance. "For this gird you with sackcloth, lament and howl: for the FIERCE ANGER of the LORD is not <u>turned</u> back from us" (Jer. 4:8). Again the word *turned* is mentioned naturally in 63 chapters of the OT Narrative.

The Generation of God's Wrath

"Cut off thine hair, O Jerusalem, and cast it away, and take up a lamentation on high places; for the LORD hath rejected and forsaken the generation of his WRATH" (Jer. 7:29). God postponed His wrath during Josiah's generation but let it fall upon the generation after. The Jeremiah combination *take up a lamentation on high places* (1x), *for the Lord hath rejected and forsaken* (1x), *the generation* (1x), *of his* (52x), *wrath* (8x) = 63. The word *generation* occurs naturally 63 times in the Old Testament.

The Nations to Incur God's End-time Wrath

"But the LORD is the true GOD, he is the living GOD, and an everlasting king: at his WRATH the earth shall tremble, and the nations shall not be able to abide his INDIGNATION" (Jer. 10:10). The phrase *the nations* is mentioned in 63 chapters of the Major and Minor Prophets. In this verse there are 63 letters preceding the word *wrath*.

The Weapons of God's Wrath

"The LORD hath opened his armoury, and hath brought forth the weapons of his INDIGNATION: for this is the work of the Lord GOD of hosts in the land of the Chaldeans" (Jer. 15:25). The Bible combination *his armoury* (1x), *weapons* (21x), *indignation* (41x) = 63. The phrase *the Chaldeans* occurs 63 times in the Bible.

Jeremiah Seeks to Turn Away God's Wrath

Jeremiah tried to warn Jerusalem of wrath to come, but she rejected both him and his message. Thus he cries to God, "Shall evil be recompensed for good? for they have digged a pit for my soul. Remember that I stood before thee to speak good for them, and to turn away thy WRATH from them" (Jer. 18:20). Again the word *turned* is mentioned naturally in 63 chapters of the OT Narrative. The Bible combination *speak good for them and to* (1x), *turn away* (46x), *thy wrath* (16x) = 63.

463rd Verse of Jeremiah

"And go forth unto the valley of the son of Hinnom, which is by the entry of the east gate, and proclaim there the words that I shall tell thee" (Jer. 19:2). The next verse tells what words of wrath Jeremiah was to speak to the people: "Thus saith the LORD of hosts, the God of Israel; Behold, I will bring evil upon this place." The phrase *words of* is mentioned in 163 verses of the Old Testament.

God's Strong Arm of Wrath

"And I myself will fight against you with an outstretched hand and with a strong arm, even in ANGER, and in FURY, and in great WRATH" (Jer. 21:5). From Genesis to Jeremiah we find the following seal: *myself* (61x), *will fight against you* (1x), *with an outstretched hand* (1x) = 63. The word *arm* occurs 63 times in the Old Testament. Again the word *fury* is mentioned in 63 verses of the Major and Minor Prophets. Again the word *great* is mentioned in 163 verses of the Major Prophets.

God's Wrath Is Coming for Zedekiah

"But I will PUNISH you according to the fruit of your doings, saith the LORD: and I will kindle a fire in the forest thereof, and it shall devour all things round about it" (Jer. 21:14). Again the word *devour* occurs 63 times in the Old Testament.

Judah Carried Away under God's Wrath

"Thus saith the LORD, the GOD of Israel; Like these good <u>figs</u>, so will I acknowledge them that are <u>carried away</u> <u>captive</u> of <u>Judah</u>, whom I have sent out of this place into the land of <u>the Chaldeans</u> for their good" (Jer. 24:5). Again the phrase *carried away* occurs 63 times in the Bible. Again the word *captivity* occurs 63 times in the Major Prophets. Again the phrase *the Chaldeans* occurs 63 times in the Bible. Again the name *Judah* occurs 63 times in the Major Prophets. The Bible combination *captive* (59x), *naughty figs* (1x), *evil figs* (1x), *vile figs* (1x), *untimely figs* (1x) = 63.

Worshiping Idols Invokes God's Wrath

"Therefore now thus saith the LORD, the GOD of hosts, the God of Israel; Wherefore commit ye this great evil against your souls, to cut off from you man and woman, child and suckling, out of Judah, to leave you none to remain; In that ye provoke me unto WRATH with the works of your hands, burning incense unto <u>other gods</u> in the land of Egypt" (Jer. 44:7-8a). Again the phrase *other gods* occurs 63 times in the Bible.

A Day of Vengeance on God's Adversaries

"For this is the day of the Lord GOD of hosts, a day of VENGEANCE, that he may <u>avenge</u> <u>him of his</u> <u>adversaries</u>: and the sword shall devour, and it shall be satiate and made drunk with their blood: for the Lord GOD of hosts hath a sacrifice in the north country by the river Euphrates" (Jer. 46:10). The Bible combination *avenge* (17x), *him of his* (10x), *adversaries* (36x) = 63.

Elam to Experience God's Wrath

"For I will cause Elam to be dismayed before their enemies, and before them that seek their life: and I will <u>bring</u> evil upon them, even my FIERCE ANGER, saith the LORD; and I will send <u>the sword</u> after them, <u>till</u> I have consumed them" (Jer. 49:37). Elam was situated east of the Tigris River. Again the word *bring* occurs 63 times in Leviticus. Again the phrase *the sword* is mentioned in 163 chapters of the Bible. The word *till* occurs naturally 163 times in the Bible.

Babylon to Experience God's Wrath

"Behold, I am against thee, O destroying mountain, saith the LORD, which destroyest all the earth: <u>and I will stretch out mine hand upon thee, and roll thee down from the rocks,</u> and will make thee a burnt mountain" (Jer. 51:25). The phrases *and I will stretch out mine hand upon thee, and roll thee down from the rocks,* consist of 63 characters!

The Day of God's Anger

"<u>How hath the [Lord] covered the daughter of Zion with a cloud in his ANGER, and</u> cast down from heaven unto the earth the beauty of Israel, and remembered not his footstool in the day of his ANGER! The [Lord] hath swallowed up all the habitations of Jacob, and hath not pitied: he hath thrown down <u>in his WRATH</u> <u>the strong holds of the daughter of Judah;</u> <u>he hath brought them down to the ground</u>: he hath polluted the kingdom and the princes thereof" (Lam. 2:1-2). The Major and Minor Prophets combination *his wrath* (7x), *upon them* (56x) = 63. The Bible combination *how hath the Lord* (1x), *covered the daughter of* (1x), *Zion* (152x), *with a cloud* (6x), *in his anger and in his wrath* (1x), *the strong holds of the daughter of Judah* (1x), *he hath brought them down to the ground* (1x) = 163.

God's Wrath & Fury Accomplished in Jerusalem

"The LORD hath accomplished his FURY; he hath poured out his FIERCE ANGER, and hath kindled a fire in Zion, and it hath devoured the foundations thereof" (Lam. 4:11). Again the word *fury* is mentioned in 63 verses of the Major and Minor Prophets. Again the word *kindled* occurs 63 times in the Old Testament. The Major and Minor Prophets combination *kindled* (11x), *a fire* (31x), *in Zion* (20x), *and it hath devoured* (1x) = 63.

God's Wrath Entered the Gates of Jerusalem

"The kings of the earth, and all the inhabitants of the world, would not have believed that the adversary and the enemy should have entered into the gates of Jerusalem" (Lam. 4:12). This verse presents the Major Prophets' 163rd occurrence of the name *Jerusalem*, and it speaks of the city having fully suffered God's wrath.

The phrase *in Jerusalem* occurs 163 times in the Bible.
The name *Jerusalem* occurs 63 times in Second Kings.

20,463rd Verse of the Bible

"Wherefore dost thou forget us for ever, and forsake us so long time? Turn thou us unto thee, O LORD, and we shall be turned; renew our days as of old. But thou hast utterly rejected us; thou art very WROTH against us" (Lam. 5:21-22). The underlined 63rd verse corresponds with God's wrath.

63rd Verse of Ezekiel

"But thou, O son of man, behold, they shall put bands upon thee, and shall bind thee with them, and thou shalt not go out among them" (Ezek. 3:25). Before Judah's eyes, God makes Ezekiel a visible token of His continued wrath upon them. Jerusalem has already suffered one deportation. Two more waves of captivity are to come. All forms of the word bind reveal the seal of God's wrath: *bind* (49x), *bindeth* (9x), *binding* (5x) = 63. Again the word *bound* is mentioned in 63 verses of the Old Testament.

20,563rd Verse of the Bible

"When I shall send upon them the evil arrows of famine, which shall be for their destruction, and which I will send to destroy you: and I will increase the famine upon you, and will break your staff of bread" (Ezek. 5:16). This verse describes one form of God's coming wrath upon Jerusalem.

Idolatrous Jerusalem to Experience More of God's Wrath

"Behold, I, even I, will bring a sword upon you, and I will destroy your high places. And your altars shall be desolate, and your images shall be broken: and I will cast down your slain men before your idols" (Ezek. 6:3c-4). The sentence *Behold, I, even I, will bring a sword upon you, and I will destroy your high places* consists of 63 letters! Again the word *bring* occurs 63 times in Leviticus. Again the phrase *the sword* is mentioned in 163 chapters of the Bible. Again the phrase *upon you* is mentioned naturally in 63 verses of the Bible. Again the word *idols* occurs 63 times in the Major and Minor Prophets. Again the word *images* is mentioned in 63 verses of the

Old Testament.

False Prophets to Experience God's Wrath

"And they shall bear the PUNISHMENT of their iniquity: the PUNISHMENT of the prophet shall be even as the PUNISHMENT of him that seeketh unto him" (Ezek. 14:10). Again all forms of the word *punish* are mentioned in 63 collective verses of the Bible.

Judah's Idolatry Has Provoked God's Wrath

"Thou hast also committed fornication with the Egyptians thy neighbours, great of flesh; and hast increased thy whoredoms, to provoke me to ANGER" (Ezek. 16:26). This chapter is comprised of 63 verses.

Ezekiel 16:63

At the beginning of this chapter God tells Ezekiel to make Jerusalem to know her abominations. He wants to remind them now why His wrath has come. "That thou mayest remember, and be confounded, and never open thy mouth any more because of thy shame, when I am pacified toward thee for all that thou hast done, saith the Lord GOD" (Ezek. 16:63). This chapter on God's pacified wrath ends here in the 63rd verse. The word *shame* is mentioned in 63 chapters of the Old Testament.

God's Poured-Out Wrath

God speaks of the second or third wave of captivity. "And I will pour out mine INDIGNATION upon thee, I will blow against thee in the fire of my WRATH, and deliver thee into the hand of brutish men, and skilful to destroy" (Ezek. 21:31). The word *pour* occurs 63 times in the Bible. The Old Testament combination *pour out* (31x) and *indignation* (32x) = 63. The Major and Minor Prophets combination *and deliver thee* (1x), *into the hand of* (59x), *brutish men* (1x), *and skilful to destroy* (1x) = 63.

My Wrath

God speaks of the first captivity. "Therefore have I poured out mine INDIGNATION upon them; I have consumed them with the fire of my WRATH: their own way have I recompensed upon their heads, saith the Lord GOD" (Ezek. 22:31).

> The word *mine* occurs 63 times in Ezekiel.
> The word *my* occurs 63 times in Second Kings.
> The word *my* is mentioned in 163 chapters of the New Testament.
> The phrase *of my* occurs 463 times in the Bible.

Edom to Experience God's Wrath

"Therefore thus saith the Lord GOD; I will also stretch out mine hand upon Edom, and will cut off man and beast from it; and I will make it desolate from Teman; and they of Dedan shall fall by the sword. And I will lay my VENGEANCE upon Edom by the hand of my people Israel: and they shall do in Edom according to mine ANGER and according to my fury; and they shall know my VENGEANCE, saith the Lord GOD" (Ezek. 25:13-14). Again the phrase *the sword* is mentioned in 163 chapters of the Bible. Again the word *my* occurs 63 times in Second Kings. Again the word *mine* occurs 63 times in Ezekiel.

Philistines to Experience God's Wrath

"Therefore thus saith the Lord GOD; Behold, I will stretch out mine hand upon the Philistines, and I will cut off the Cherethims, and destroy the remnant of the sea coast. And I will execute great VENGEANCE upon them with furious rebukes; and they shall know that I am the LORD, when I shall lay my VENGEANCE upon them" (Ezek. 25:16-17). The word *when* is found in 63 books of the Bible. The naturally occurring Old Testament combination *I shall lay my vengeance* (1x), *upon them* (162x) = 163.

Gog & Magog to Experience God's Great Wrath

"And it shall come to pass at the same time when Gog shall come against the land of Israel, saith the Lord GOD, that my FURY shall come up in my face. For in my jealousy and in the fire of my WRATH have I spoken, Surely in that day there shall be a great shaking in the land of Israel" (Ezek. 38:18-19). Again the word *fury* is mentioned in 63 verses of the Major and Minor Prophets. Again the word *great* is mentioned in 163 verses of the Major Prophets.

63rd Verse of Daniel

"And as the toes of the feet were part of iron, and part of clay, so the kingdom shall be partly strong, and partly broken" (Dan. 2:42). A number of verses earlier, Daniel recounts Nebuchadnezzar's dream and speaks of God's coming wrath which will smash the image's two feet and thereby topple it to the ground: "Thou sawest till that a stone was cut out without hands, which smote the image upon his feet that were of iron and clay, and brake them to pieces . . . and the wind carried them away" (v. 34, 35c). Again the phrase *carried away* occurs 63 times in the Bible.

The word *them* occurs 63 times in Ezra.
The word *them* occurs 63 times in Job.

Belshazzar Feared God's Awakened Wrath

"In the same hour came forth fingers of a man's hand, and wrote over against the candlestick upon the plaister of the wall of the king's palace: and the king saw the part of the hand that wrote. Then the king's countenance was changed, and his thoughts troubled him, so that the joints of his loins were loosed, and his knees smote one against another. . . . And this is the writing that was written, MENE, MENE, TEKEL, UPHARSIN. This is the interpretation of the thing: MENE; GOD hath numbered thy kingdom, and finished it. TEKEL; Thou art weighed in the balances, and art found wanting. PERES; Thy kingdom is divided, and given to the Medes and Persians" (Dan. 5:5-6, 25-28).

The underlined verse indicates the 163rd verse of Daniel; it actually contains the keyword *God*, and it speaks of God's forthcoming wrath upon Babylon.

Praying for God's Wrath to Turn away from Jerusalem

"O [Lord], according to all thy righteousness, I beseech thee, let thine ANGER and thy FURY be turned away from thy city Jerusalem, thy holy mountain: because for our sins, and for the iniquities of our fathers, Jerusalem and thy people are become a reproach to all that are about us" (Dan. 9:16). Again the word *fury* is mentioned in 63 verses of the Major and Minor Prophets. Again the word *turned* is mentioned naturally in 63 chapters of the OT Narrative.

63rd Verse of Hosea

"And the pride of Israel doth testify to his face: therefore shall <u>Israel</u> and Ephraim fall in their iniquity; <u>Judah</u> also shall fall with them" (Hos. 5:5). God's wrath will cause both Israel and Judah to fall. Again the name *Israel* is mentioned in 63 verses of the Wisdom Books. Again the name *Judah* occurs 63 times in the Major Prophets.

22,163rd Verse of the Bible

"The princes of Judah were like them that remove the bound: therefore I will <u>pour</u> out my WRATH upon them like water" (Hos. 5:10). Again the word *pour* occurs 63 times in the Bible. The keyword *wrath* actually occurs in this 63rd verse.

God's Wrath Will Eventually Turn away from Israel

"I will heal their backsliding, I will love them freely: for mine ANGER is <u>turned</u> away from him" (Hos. 14:4). Again the word *turned* is mentioned naturally in 63 chapters of the OT Narrative.

The Day of the Lord Is at Hand!

"<u>Alas for the day</u>! <u>for the day of the LORD is at hand</u>, and as a <u>destruction from the</u> <u>Almighty</u> shall it come" (Joel 1:15). Again the phrase *the day of* occurs 163 times in the Bible! The Bible combination *alas for the day* (1x), *for the day of the LORD is at hand and as a* (1x), *destruction from the* (4x), *Almighty* (57x) = 63.

God's Anger Rises Slowly

"And rend your heart, and not your garments, and turn unto the LORD your GOD: for he is gracious and merciful, <u>slow</u> to ANGER, and of great kindness, and repenteth him of the evil" (Joel 2:13). Again the Old Testament combination *slow* (11x), *to anger* (52x) = 63.

God's Coming Wrath upon Judah

"But I will send a fire upon Judah, and it shall devour the palaces of JERUSALEM" (Amos 2:5). This wrath-of-God verse consists 63 letters!

King of Nineveh Seeks to Avoid God's Anger

"Who can tell if God will <u>turn</u> and repent, and <u>turn</u> away from his FIERCE ANGER, that we perish not" (Jonah 3:9). Again the word *turned* is mentioned naturally in 63 chapters of the OT Narrative.

God Will Execute Vengeance

"And I will execute VENGEANCE in ANGER and FURY upon the heathen, such as they have not heard" (Mic. 5:9, 15). The wrathful God will cut off anti-Israel nations during the Kingdom Age. Again the word *fury* is mentioned in 63 verses of the Major and Minor Prophets.

God Reserves His Wrath

"<u>God is jealous, and the LORD revengeth; the LORD revengeth, and is furious; the LORD will</u> <u>take VENGEANCE on his adversaries, and he reserveth WRATH for his enemies</u>" (Nhm. 1:2). The Major and Minor Prophets combination *God is jealous* (1x), *and the LORD revengeth* (1x), *the LORD revengeth* (2x), *and is furious* (1x), *the LORD will take* (2x), vengeance on his (1x), *adversaries* (15x), *and he reserveth* (1x), *wrath for his* (1x), *enemies* (38x) = 63.

Who Can Abide God's Wrath?

"The LORD is <u>slow</u> to ANGER, and great in power, and will not at all acquit the wicked: the LORD hath his way in the whirlwind and in the storm, and the clouds are the dust of his feet. . . . <u>Who can</u> stand before his INDIGNATION? and who can <u>abide</u> in the FIERCENESS of his ANGER? his FURY is poured out like fire, and the rocks are thrown down by him" (Nhm. 1:1, 6). Again the Old Testament combination *slow* (11x), *to anger* (52x) = 63. The Old Testament combination *Who can* (13x), *abide* (50x) = 63.

"In Wrath Remember Mercy"

"O LORD, I have heard thy speech, and was afraid: O LORD, revive thy work in the midst of the years, in the midst of the years make known; <u>in</u> WRATH remember mercy" (Hab. 3:2).

> The word *in* is mentioned in 263 verses of First Samuel.
> The word *in* occurs 63 times in Galatians.

God's Wrath Marched against Israel's Enemies

"The sun and moon stood still in their habitation: at the light of thine arrows they went, and at the shining of thy glittering spear. <u>Thou didst</u> <u>march</u> <u>through the land in</u> INDIGNATION, <u>thou didst thresh the heathen</u> <u>in ANGER</u>. <u>Thou wentest forth</u> for the salvation of thy people" (Hab. 3:11-13a). The Major and Minor Prophets combination *thou didst* (25x), *march* (4x), *through the land in* (1x), *indignation* (24), *thou didst thresh the heathen* (1x), *in anger* (7x), *thou wentest forth* (1x) = 63.

God's Wrath to Be Executed upon Judah for Baal Worship

"I will also stretch out mine hand upon Judah, and upon all the inhabitants of Jerusalem; and I will cut off the remnant of Baal from this place, and the name of the Chemarims with the priests;" I will also stretch out mine hand upon Judah, and upon all the inhabitants of <u>Jerusalem</u>; and I will cut off the remnant of <u>Baal</u> from this place, and the name of the Chemarims with the priests" (Zeph. 1:4). Again the name *Jerusalem* occurs 63 times in Second Kings. Again the name *Baal* occurs 63 times in the Bible!

God's Wrath Coming for Judah

"Neither their silver nor their gold shall be able to deliver them in the day of the LORD'S WRATH; but the whole land shall be <u>devoured</u> by the fire of his jealousy: for he shall make even a speedy riddance of all them that dwell in the land" (Zeph. 1:18). Again the word *devour* occurs 63 times in the Old Testament.

Seek the Lord Before His Anger Arrives

"Before the decree bring forth, before the day pass as the chaff, before the FIERCE ANGER of the LORD come upon you, before the day of the LORD'S ANGER come upon you. Seek ye the LORD, all ye meek of the earth, which have wrought his judgment; seek righteousness, seek meekness: it may be ye shall be hid in the day of the LORD'S ANGER" (Zeph. 2:2-3). In this verse there are 63 words surrounding the thrice occurring word *anger*.

God's Wrath upon the Kingdoms of this World

"And I will overthrow the throne of kingdoms, and I will destroy the strength of the kingdoms of the heathen; and I will overthrow the chariots, and those that ride in them; and the horses and their riders shall come down, every one by the sword of his brother" (Hag. 2:22). Again the phrase *the sword* is mentioned in 163 chapters of the Bible.

There Came Great Wrath from the Lord

"Yea, they made their hearts as an adamant stone, lest they should hear the law, and the words which the LORD of hosts hath sent in his spirit by the former prophets: therefore came a great WRATH from the LORD of hosts" (Zech. 7:12). Again the word *great* is mentioned in 163 verses of the Major Prophets.

The Lord's Perpetual Wrath against Edom

"Whereas Edom saith, We are impoverished, but we will return and build the desolate places; thus saith the LORD of hosts, They shall build, but I will throw down; and they shall call them, The border of wickedness, and, The people against whom the LORD hath INDIGNATION for ever" (Mal. 1:4). The Major and Minor Prophets combination *the people against whom* (1 v), *the LORD hath indignation* (1 v), *for ever* (61 vs) = 63 verses.

God's Wrath Will Come

"And I will come near to you to judgment; and I will be a swift witness against the sorcerers, and against the adulterers, and against false swearers, and against those that oppress the hireling in his wages, the widow, and the fatherless, and that turn aside the stranger from his right, and fear not me, saith the LORD of hosts" (Mal. 3:5). The phrase *will come* is mentioned in 63 verses of the Bible. Again the word *judgment(s)* occurs naturally 63 times in the Law.

The Great and Dreadful Day of the Lord

"Ye are cursed with a curse: for ye have robbed me, even this whole nation. . . . Behold, I will send you Elijah the prophet before the coming of the great and dreadful day of the LORD: And he shall turn the heart of the fathers to the children, and the heart of the children to their fathers, lest I come and smite the earth with a curse" (Mal. 3:9; 4:5). Again the word *cursed* is mentioned in 63 verses of the Old Testament. Again the word *great* is mentioned in 163 verses of the Major Prophets.

The New Testament

"The book of the generation of Jesus <u>Christ</u>, the <u>son</u> of David, the <u>son</u> of Abraham" (Matt. 1:1). Jesus Christ was both Son of Man and Son of God. He was both human and divine. He was of the earth and from heaven at the same time. He was both lowly and lofty. He died as the Lamb but rose again as the Lion. His first coming was to be given over unto judgment and condemnation for the sins of mankind, but His second coming will be for the purpose of judging the world and condemning all that are wicked and unbelieving. In other words, Christ came to earth the first time that He might take upon Himself the wrath of God for those who would be saved, but the next time He comes to earth it will be to pour out God's wrath upon the lost.

The title *Christ* is mentioned in 163 chapters of the New Testament.

The title *our Lord* occurs 63 times in the Pauline Epistles.

~~~~~

The title *son* is mentioned in 163 verses of First Chronicles.

The title *s/Son* occurs 63 times in John's Gospel.

The title *Son* is mentioned in 163 verses of the NT Narrative.

The title *Son of man/God* occurs 63 times in the Major Prophets.

A Warning to Flee from the Wrath to Come

"But when he saw many of <u>the Pharisees</u> <u>and Sadducees</u> come to his baptism, he said unto them, O generation of vipers, who hath warned you to flee <u>from the WRATH to come</u>?" (Matt. 3:7) The Son of God's fiery messenger never twisted his words. They were always straight and sharp like a sword. The NT Narrative combination *the Pharisees* (61x), *and the Sadducees* (2x) = 63. The phrase *from the* is found in 63 books of the Bible. The Wisdom Books combination *wrath* (62x) and *that is to come* (1x) = 63. The word *come* is mentioned in 63 verses of Exodus and occurs 63 times in Numbers.

Assigned to a Fiery Baptism

"And now also the axe is laid unto the root of the trees: therefore every tree which bringeth not forth good fruit is hewn down, <u>and cast</u> into the fire. I indeed baptize you with water unto repentance: but he that cometh after me is mightier than I, whose shoes I am not worthy to bear: he shall baptize you with the Holy Ghost, and <u>with fire</u>: Whose fan is in his hand, and he will throughly purge his floor, and gather his wheat into the garner; but he will burn up the chaff <u>with</u> unquenchable <u>fire</u>" (Matt. 3:10-12).

The Baptizer refers to two entirely different immersions, a holy one for the repentant and a horrible one for the unrepentant. Again the phrase *and cast* occurs 63 times in the Old Testament. Again the phrase *by fire* occurs 63 times in the Law.

In Danger of Hell Fire

"Ye have heard that it was said by them of old time, Thou shalt not kill; and whosoever shall kill shall be in danger of the judgment: But I say unto you, That whosoever is angry with his brother without a cause shall be in danger of the judgment: <u>and whosoever shall say to his brother, Raca, shall be in danger of the council</u>: but whosoever shall say, <u>Thou fool, shall be in danger of hell fire</u>" (Matt. 5:21-22). The sentence *and whosoever shall say to his brother, raca, shall be in danger of the council* consists of 63 letters! The Gospels combination *thou fool* (2x), *shall be in*

(9x), *danger of* (5x), *hell* (15x), *fire* (32x) = 63.

Judged Accordingly to God's Measured Wrath

"Judge not, that ye be not <u>judged</u>. For with what <u>judgment</u> ye judge, ye shall be <u>judged</u>: and with what measure ye mete, it shall be measured to you again" (Matt. 7:1-2). The angrier we are with another person the greater we judge that person. If God was angry with us would we not want Him to cool down first before judging us? The word *judged* occurs 63 times in the Bible. Again the word *judgment(s)* occurs naturally 63 times in the Law.

Devils Fear Son of God's Untimely Wrath

The devils at Gadara greatly feared Jesus when they saw Him coming straight at them. "And, behold, they cried out, saying, What have we to do with thee, Jesus, thou <u>Son</u> of God? art thou come hither to torment us before the <u>time</u>?" (Matt. 8:29) Again the title *Son* is mentioned in 163 verses of the NT Narrative. The Old Testament combination *the time of* (62x) and *wrath against the realm* (1x) = 63. The word *time* is mentioned in 163 verses of the New Testament!

A Day of Wrath & Judgment for Gospel-Resistant Cities

"And whosoever shall not receive you, nor hear your words, when ye depart out of that house or city, shake off <u>the dust</u> of your feet. Verily I say unto you, It shall be more tolerable for the land of Sodom and Gomorrha in <u>the day of</u> <u>judgment</u>, than for that <u>city</u>" (Matt. 10:14-15). Such cities will be laid in the dust and brought to desolation. God has done this before, and He will do it again. Again the phrase *the dust* occurs 63 times in the Old Testament and is mentioned in 63 verses of the Bible. Again the phrase *the day of* occurs 163 times in the Bible. Again the word *judgment(s)* occurs naturally 63 times in the Law. The word *city* is mentioned in 163 verses of the Major Prophets.

God's Fearful Wrath upon Lost Souls

"And <u>fear not</u> them which kill the body, but are not able to kill the soul: but rather fear him which is able to <u>destroy</u> both <u>soul</u> and body in hell" (Matt. 10:28). Before sending out His twelve apostles Christ reminded them not to fear the Pharisees' wrath, but rather to fear God's wrath which is appointed to all unbelievers. This would help them focus on things eternal. The phrase *fear not* occurs 63 times in the Bible and is mentioned in 63 verses thereof. Again the word *destroy* is mentioned in 63 chapters of the Major and Minor Prophets. The word *soul* is mentioned in 63 chapters of the Psalms.

Capernaum's Judgment Will be Worse than Sodom's

"Then began he to upbraid the cities wherein most of his mighty works were done, because they repented not: Woe unto thee, Chorazin! woe unto thee, Bethsaida! for if the mighty works, which were done in you, had been done in Tyre and Sidon, they would have repented long ago in sackcloth and ashes. But I say unto you, It shall be more tolerable for Tyre and Sidon at <u>the day of</u> <u>judgment</u>, than for you. And thou, Capernaum, which art exalted unto heaven, shalt be brought down to hell: for if the mighty works, which have been done in thee, had been done in Sodom, it would have remained until this day. But I say unto you, That it shall be more tolerable for the land of Sodom in <u>the day of</u> <u>judgment</u>, than for thee" (Matt. 11:20-24).

Again the phrase *the day of* occurs 163 times in the Bible! Again the word *judgment(s)* occurs naturally 63 times in the Law.

This Generation to Experience God's Wrath

"The men of Nineveh shall rise in <u>judgment</u> with this <u>generation</u>, and shall condemn it: because they repented at the preaching of Jonas; and, behold, a greater than Jonas is here" (Matt. 12:41). About forty years after Jesus spoke this prophecy God's wrath came upon the unbelieving nation. The Romans destroyed the Temple, killed hundreds of thousands in Israel, and the remaining Israelites were sold off as slaves. Believing Jews had taken Christ's warning to heart and fled for safety outside the country. Again the word *judgment(s)* occurs naturally 63 times in the Law. Again the word *generation* occurs naturally 63 times in the Old Testament.

Son of God's Wrath upon Kingdom Offenders

"As therefore the tares are gathered and <u>burned</u> in the fire; so shall it be in the end of this world. <u>The Son of man shall send forth his angels, and they shall gather out of his kingdom all things that offend, and them which do iniquity; And shall cast them into a furnace of fire: there shall be wailing and gnashing of teeth</u>" (Matt. 13:40-42). Again the word *burned* is mentioned in 63 chapters from Genesis to the Synoptic Gospels. The Bible combination *and them which do* (1 v), *iniquity* (262 vs) = 263 verses. The Bible combination *the Son of man shall send forth his angels* (1x), *and they shall gather out of his kingdom all things that offend and* (1x), *shall cast them into* (4x), *a furnace* (1x), *of fire* (54x), *there shall be wailing and gnashing of teeth* (2x) = 63.

Wicked Ones Will Go into the Furnace of Fire

"So shall it be at the end of the world: the angels shall come forth, and <u>sever the wicked</u> from among the just, And shall cast them into the <u>furnace of fire</u>: there shall be wailing and gnashing of teeth" (Matt. 13:49-50). On judgment day, angels will help the Son of God to execute wrath upon the wicked. The Bible combination *sever* (4x), *the wicked* (259x) = 263. The Old Testament combination *furnace* (26x), *of fire* (37x) = 63.

Child Offenders Will Suffer God's Severest Wrath

"But whoso shall offend one of these little ones which believe in me, it were better for him that <u>a millstone were hanged about his neck</u>, and that he were drowned in the depth of the sea" (Matt. 18:6). The Bible combination *a millstone were hanged about his* (3 vs), *neck* (60 vs) = 63 verses.

Crushed & Ground to Powder by Son of God's Wrath

"But last of all he sent unto them his son, saying, They will reverence my son. But when the husbandmen saw the son, they said among themselves, This is the heir; come, let us kill him, and let us seize on his inheritance. . . . When the lord therefore of the vineyard cometh, what will he do unto those husbandmen? They say unto him, He will miserably <u>destroy</u> those wicked men, and will let out his vineyard unto other husbandmen, which shall render him the fruits in their seasons. Jesus saith unto them . . . Therefore say I unto you, The kingdom of GOD shall be taken from you, and given to a nation bringing forth the fruits thereof. And whosoever shall fall <u>on this stone shall be broken: but on whomsoever it shall fall, it will grind him to powder</u>" (Matt. 21:37-38, 40-42a, 43-44).

Again the word *destroy* is mentioned in 63 chapters of the Major and Minor Prophets. The Gospels combination *on this stone* (1x), *shall be broken but* (2x), *on whomsoever* (2x), *it shall* (35x), *fall* (19x), *it will grind* (2x), *him to powder* (2x) = 63.

Armies of God Sent with God's Wrath to Jerusalem

"But when the king heard thereof, he was WROTH: and he <u>sent</u> forth his armies, and <u>destroyed</u>

those murderers, and <u>burned</u> up their city" (Matt. 22:7). One generation later the King of Heaven allowed Roman armies to destroy the Jewish resistance and to burn many buildings in Jerusalem including its prized Temple. Again the word *sent* is mentioned in 63 verses of the Bible. Again the word *destroy* is mentioned in 63 chapters of the Major and Minor Prophets. Again from Genesis to the Synoptic Gospels the word *burned* is mentioned in 63 chapters; this verse presents its 63rd chapter-mention.

Prophet-Killing Generation to Experience God's Wrath

"That <u>upon you</u> may come all the righteous blood shed upon the earth, from the blood of righteous Abel unto the blood of Zacharias son of Barachias, whom ye slew between the temple and the altar. Verily I say unto you, All these things shall come upon this <u>generation</u>" (Matt. 23:35-36). Again the phrase *upon you* is mentioned naturally in 63 verses of the Bible. Again the word *generation* occurs naturally 63 times in the Old Testament.

God's Temple-Destroying Wrath

"And Jesus went out, and departed from the temple: and his disciples came to him for to shew him <u>the buildings of</u> the temple. And Jesus said unto them, See ye not all these things? verily I say unto you, There shall not be left here one stone upon another, that shall not be thrown down" (Matt. 24:1-2). In AD 70 God's wrath came upon both the Temple and Jerusalem's citizens for their national rejection of Jesus as their rightful King. In AD 135 after putting down the Bar Kochba rebellion the Romans destroyed every remaining building at the Temple precinct and then pushed the rubble over the side of the foundation platform where it plummeted below thus fulfilling Jesus' prophetic words. The Gospels combination *the buildings of* (1x), *the temple* (62x) = 63.

God's End-Time Wrath upon Earth's Godless Tribes

"And then shall appear the sign of the <u>Son of man</u> in heaven: and then shall all the <u>tribes of</u> the earth mourn, and they shall see the <u>Son of man</u> coming in the clouds of heaven with power and great glory" (Matt. 24:30). Again the phrase *tribes of* occurs 63 times in the Law. Again the title *Son of man/God* occurs 63 times in Major Prophets.

Evil Servants to Experience God's Wrath

"But and if that evil servant shall say in his heart, My lord delayeth his coming; And shall begin to smite his fellowservants, and to eat and drink with the drunken; <u>The lord of that servant</u> shall come in a day when he looketh not for him, and in an hour that he is not aware of, And <u>shall cut him asunder, and appoint him his portion with the hypocrites</u>: there shall be <u>weeping</u> and <u>gnashing of teeth</u>" (Matt. 24:48-51). The Bible combination *the lord of that servant* (1x), *shall cut him asunder* (1x), *and appoint him* (1x), *his portion with the hypocrites* (1x), *weeping* (44x), *gnashing* (7x), *of teeth* (8x) = 63.

Unprofitable Servants to Experience God's Wrath

"And <u>cast ye the unprofitable servant into outer</u> <u>darkness</u>: there shall be weeping and gnashing of teeth" (Matt. 25:30). Jesus' preaching ministry functioned under the dispensation of the Law, a religious system which was based mostly upon works. The Bible combination *cast ye the unprofitable servant into outer* (1x), *darkness* (162x) = 163.

Anti-Christians to Experience God's Wrath

"When the Son of man shall come in his glory, and all the holy angels with him, then shall he sit upon the throne of his glory: And before him shall be gathered all nations: and he shall separate them one from another, as a shepherd divideth his sheep from the goats. And he shall set . . . the goats on the left . . . And these shall go away into everlasting PUNISHMENTS" (Matt. 25:31-33, 46a). Again all forms of the word *punish* are mentioned in 63 collective verses of the Bible.

Matthew 26:63

"But Jesus held his peace. And the high priest answered and said unto him, I adjure thee by the living GOD, that thou tell us whether thou be the Christ, the Son of GOD" (Matt. 26:63). The opposite of peace is wrath. Hence we see Christ withholding His wrath in this 63rd verse, yet in the very next verse the Son of God promises wrath to come. Again the title *Christ* is mentioned in 163 chapters of the Bible. Again the title *Son of God/Son of man* occurs 63 combined times in Major Prophets.

24,163rd Verse of the Bible

"And when they were come unto a place called Golgotha, that is to say, a place of a skull, They gave him vinegar to drink mingled with gall: and when he had tasted thereof, he would not drink. And they crucified him" (Matt. 27:33-35a). The underlined 63rd verse refers to the precise place where God's wrath against sin was to be poured upon Christ.

The Earth Rends Its Outer Garment

At the very moment of Jesus' death God's wrath was visibly released upon Jerusalem. "And, behold, the veil of the temple was rent in twain from the top to the bottom; and the earth did quake, and the rocks rent" (Matt. 27:51). As we mentioned earlier, rending garments was a Near Eastern custom to display one's emotions of grief or anger. God tore the Temple's hand-breadth-thick veil and the earth's hard outer crust. Again the word *rent* is mentioned in 63 verses of the Bible.

Matthew 27:63

"Saying, Sir, we remember that that deceiver said, while he was yet alive, After three days I will rise again" (Matt. 27:63). Perhaps the Pharisees secretly feared Christ's wrath if He did somehow rise again. The word *after* is mentioned in 63 verses of the Wisdom Books.

In Danger of Eternal Damnation

"Verily I say unto you, All sins shall be forgiven unto the sons of men, and blasphemies wherewith soever they shall blaspheme: But he that shall blaspheme against the Holy Ghost hath never forgiveness, but is in danger of eternal damnation" (Mark 3:28-29). The Bible combination *in danger of* (5x), *eternal* (47x), *damnation* (11x) = 63.

Legion of Demons Fear the Son of God's Wrath

"And when he was come out of the ship, immediately there met him out of the tombs a man with an unclean spirit . . . . But when he saw Jesus afar off, he ran and worshipped him, And cried with a loud voice, and said, What have I to do with thee, Jesus, thou Son of the most high GOD? I adjure thee by GOD, that thou torment me not. . . . My name is Legion: for we are many" (Mark 5:2, 6-7, 9c). Again the title *Son* is mentioned in 163 verses of the NT Narrative.

Cast into Hell Fire

"And if thine eye offend thee, pluck it out: it is better for thee to enter into the kingdom of GOD with one eye, than having two eyes to be cast into hell fire: Where their worm dieth not, and the fire is not quenched" (Mark 9:47-48). The Bible combination *rather than having two eyes to be cast into hell fire* (1x), *where their worm dieth not and* (3x), *the fire* (156x), *is not quenched* (3x) = 63.

1463rd Verse of the New Testament

"Thou knowest the commandments, Do not commit adultery, Do not kill, Do not steal, Do not bear false witness, Defraud not, Honour thy father and mother" (Mark 10:19). Jesus lists commandment-breaking sins which makes the sinner legally worthy of receiving God's wrath. Again the word *commandments* occurs 63 times in the Law.

463rd Verse of Mark

"And again he sent another; and him they killed, and many others; beating some, and killing some" (Mark 12:5). This evil action will certainly bring the wrath of God upon them.

Killing God's Son Will Bring God's Wrath

"What shall therefore the lord of the vineyard do? he will come and destroy the husbandmen, and will give the vineyard unto others" (Mark 12:9). Again the phrase *will come* is mentioned in 63 verses of the Bible. Again the word *come* occurs 63 times in Numbers. Again the word *destroy* is mentioned in 63 chapters of the Major and Minor Prophets.

The Days of God's Tribulation Wrath

"For in those days shall be affliction, such as was not from the beginning of the creation which GOD created unto this time, neither shall be. And except that the Lord had shortened those days, no flesh should be saved: but for the elect's sake, whom he hath chosen, he hath shortened the days" (Mark 13:19-20). The word *those* is mentioned in 263 chapters from Genesis to the NT Narrative. The phrase *the days* is mentioned in 263 verses in the Bible. The Bible combination *in those days* (61x), *shall be affliction* (1x), *such as was not from the beginning of the creation* (1x) = 63.

Judas the Betrayer to Incur God's Wrath

"And as they sat and did eat, Jesus said, Verily I say unto you, One of you which eateth with me shall betray me. . . . It is one of the twelve, that dippeth with me in the dish. The Son of man indeed goeth, as it is written of him: but woe to that man by whom the Son of man is betrayed! good were it for that man if he had never been born" (Mark 14:18, 20b-21). Again the phrase *it is written* occurs 63 times in the New Testament. The Gospels combination *one of you which eateth with me shall betray me* (1x), *the Son of man indeed goeth* (1x), *as it is written of him* (3x), *but woe* (10x), *to that man* (2x), *by whom* (7x), *the Son of man is* (15x), *betrayed* (18x), *good were it* (1x), *for that man* (2x), *if he had never* (1x), *been born* (2x) = 63.

563rd Verse of Mark

"And he said unto them, This is my blood of the new testament, which is shed for many" (Mark 14:24). Jesus' blood was to be sacrificially shed so that all those who believe in Him might escape God's wrath toward their sin.

384

The Wrath of God Begins to Overshadow Christ

"And saith unto them, My soul is exceeding sorrowful unto death: tarry ye here, and watch" (Mark 14:34). This verse presents the Bible's 163rd occurrence of the phrase *my soul*, and it pertains to the soon-coming wrath of God upon Jesus' sinless, sacrificial soul.

The Cup of Plagues

"And he went forward a little, and fell on the ground, and prayed that, if it were possible, the hour might pass from him. And he said, Abba, Father, all things are possible unto thee; take away this cup from me: nevertheless not what I will, but what thou wilt" (Mark 14:35-36). A Hebrew betrothal ceremony involved four symbolic cups. One of these was the cup of plagues. Both the groom-to-be and the bride-to-be drank from it. If either one of them ever became unfaithful to each other from that day forward they understood that they were inviting the other's wrath. Since Jesus had been completely faithful in the matter of His relationship to Israel He felt that He did not deserve to drink from this cup of wrath. Indeed He did not. But because Israel had been unfaithful to Him He must then drink it for her lest God force her to drink it and she die. God did not force Jesus to drink from the cup of plagues but rather gave Him no viable option. If Jesus were to forever be with His bride He must then cover for her faults, ever so painfully. Again the phrase *the plague* occurs 63 times in the Law.

1663rd Verse of the New Testament

"And they led Jesus away to the high priest: and with him were assembled all the chief priests and the elders and the scribes" (Mark 14:53). The lowly Son has submitted to undergo the God's wrath. He will soon feel the painful effects of it.

Mark 14:63

"Then the high priest rent his clothes, and saith, What need we any further witnesses?" (Mark 14:63) There was a Levitical command that the high priest never rend his garments. Any breach of this biblical injunction invoked a curse upon the whole nation. Caiaphas and his aged father Annas were the high priests at that time. The national curse that was brought on by the high priest's error came just hours later when the sun suddenly became darkened at noon day. The phrases *the high priest/s/'s* occurs 63 times from Genesis to the NT Narrative. The word *rent* is mentioned in 63 verses from Genesis to the end of the NT Narrative.

The Place of God's Outpoured Wrath

"And they bring him unto the place Golgotha, which is, being interpreted, The place of a skull" (Mark 15:22). This verse presents the Bible's 163rd occurrence of the phrase *the place*, and it refers to the place where God's wrath toward the world's sin was to be poured out.

Curse of Darkness over the World

"And when the sixth hour was come, there was darkness over the whole land until the ninth hour" (Mark 15:33). The Bible combination *darkness* (162x), *over the whole land* (1x) = 163.

This Man Absorbs God's Wrath

"And when the centurion, which stood over against him, saw that he so cried out, and gave up the ghost, he said, Truly this man was the Son of GOD" (Mark 15:39). This sinless Man endured the wrath of God which was otherwise intended for all humanity. The centurion recognized

God's wrath had been poured out on Jesus because of the various supernatural signs that he saw which were associated with Christ's death. The phrase *this man* is mentioned in 63 verses of the New Testament!

God Scatters the Wicked in His Wrath

"He hath shewed strength with his arm; he hath scattered the proud in the imagination of their hearts" (Luke 1:51). Again the word *strength* is mentioned in 163 chapters of the Bible. Again the word *arm* occurs 63 times in the Old Testament. The word *scattered* is mentioned in 63 verses from Genesis to the Gospels; this is its 63rd verse-mention, and it pertains to God's wrath.

God's Has an Axe to Grind

"And now also the axe is laid unto the root of the trees: every tree therefore which bringeth not forth good fruit is hewn down, and cast into the fire" (Luke 3:9). The Old Testament prophet had his stern gaze fixed upon the self-righteous leaders of Jerusalem when he pronounced this biblical mandate. He let them know that God was sharpening His axe for the new work ahead, and that they did not have long to amend their ways before His wrath arrived. Again the phrase *and cast* occurs 63 times in the Old Testament.

The Holy Destroyer from Nazareth

In the synagogue at Nazareth there was a man possessed with a devil, and he cried out with a loud voice, "Saying, Let us alone; what have we to do with thee, thou Jesus of Nazareth? art thou come to destroy us? I know thee who thou art; the Holy One of God" (Luke 4:34). This evil cabal feared the Son of God's immediate wrath. The Bible combination *the destroyer shall come* (1x), *the Holy One* (40x), *of Nazareth* (22x) = 63. Again the word *destroy* is mentioned in 63 chapters of the Major and Minor Prophets.

"Art Thou He That Should Come?"

"And John calling unto him two of his disciples sent them to Jesus, saying, Art thou he that should come? or look we for another?" (Luke 7:19) John had been urgently preaching about the Son of God's coming fiery wrath, but from his prison cell all John was presently seeing from Jesus was peace. The zealous prophet was perplexed as to why Jesus had not yet commenced His kingdom rule over the godless Gentiles with a rod of iron and sword of steel. Again the word *come* occurs 63 times in Numbers.

Results of Rejecting God's Counsel

"But the Pharisees and lawyers rejected the counsel of GOD against themselves, being not baptized of him" (Luke 7:30). Those who reject God's holy counsel to the very end are then left only with an inheritance of God's holy wrath. The NT Narrative combination *the Pharisees* (61x), *and lawyers* (1x), *rejected the counsel of God* (1x) = 63.

Son of God Drowns a Legion of Devils in His Wrath

"And Jesus asked him, saying, What is thy name? And he said, Legion: because many devils were entered into him. And they besought him that he would not command them to go out into the deep. And there was there an herd of many swine feeding on the mountain: and they besought him that he would suffer them to enter into them. And he suffered them. Then went the devils out of the man, and entered into the swine: and the herd ran violently down a steep place into the lake, and were choked" (Luke 8:30-33).

This legion suffered a lesser wrath than they deserved. The Bible combination *devils* (55x), *cometh out of the man and* (1x), *entered into the swine* (2x), *and the herd ran violently down a steep place* (1x), *and were choked* (2x) = 63.

Shall We Call Down Fire From Heaven?

A Samaritan village refused to offer Jesus and His evangelistic company the customary hospitality. "And when his disciples James and John saw this, they said, Lord, wilt thou that we command fire to <u>come down from heaven</u>, and <u>consume</u> them, even as Elias did?" (Luke 9:54) They thought the village was worthy of God's consummate wrath. The sons of thunder lost sight of grace and mercy and instead longed for fire and brimstone. Jesus gave them a stern reprimand. Again the phrase *from heaven* occurs 63 times in the New Testament. The Bible combination *come down from heaven* (7x) and *consume* (56x) = 63.

Condemnation & Wrath

"This is an evil generation: they seek a sign; and there shall no sign be given it, but the sign of Jonas the prophet. For as Jonas was a sign unto the Ninevites, so shall also the Son of man be to this generation. . . . The men of Nineve shall rise up in the <u>judgment</u> with this generation, and shall <u>condemn</u> it: for they repented at the preaching of Jonas; and, behold, a greater than Jonas is here" (Luke 11:29b-30, 32). Again the word *judgment(s)* occurs naturally 63 times in the Law. All forms of the word condemn show the seal of God's wrath in the following visual way: *condemnation* (12 vs), *condemn* (24 vs), *condemned* (20 vs), *condemnest* (1 v), *condemneth* (4 vs), *condemning* (2 vs) = 63 verses.

563rd Verse of Luke

"From the blood of Abel unto the blood of Zacharias, which perished between the altar and the temple: verily I say unto you, It shall be required of this <u>generation</u>" (Luke 11:51). About forty years following Jesus' ascension into heaven the Temple was destroyed along with its polluted altar and unbelieving religious leaders. This 563rd verse presents the Bible's 63rd chapter-mention of the word *generation*, and we see its relation to God's wrath. Again the word *generation* occurs naturally 63 times in the Old Testament.

Fear Him Who Has the Power to Cast into Hell

"Beware ye of the leaven of the Pharisees, which is hypocrisy. . . . And I say unto you my friends, Be not afraid of them that kill the body, and after that have no more that they can do. But I will forewarn you whom ye shall fear: Fear him, which after he hath killed hath <u>power to cast into hell</u>; yea, I say unto you, Fear him" (Luke 12:1, 4-5). The Bible combination *the power* (62x), *to cast into hell* (1x) = 63.

"The Son of Man Cometh"

"Be ye therefore ready also: for <u>the Son of man cometh</u> at an hour when ye think not" (Luke 12:40). Just as we see it here, the case-sensitive title *the Son of man* occurs 63 times in the Synoptic Gospels. Again the word *come* occurs 63 times in Numbers.

The Son of God's Wrath Will Come

"But and if that servant say in his heart, My lord delayeth his coming; and shall begin to beat the menservants and maidens, and to eat and drink, and to be drunken; The lord of that servant <u>will</u>

come in a day when he looketh not for him, and at an hour when he is not aware, and will cut him in sunder, and will appoint him his portion with the unbelievers" (Luke 12:45-46). The Son of God's wrath will come when sinners least expect it. Again the phrase *will come* is mentioned in 63 verses of the Bible!

God's Carefully Measured Wrath

"And that servant, which knew his lord's will, and prepared not himself, neither did according to his will, shall be beaten with many stripes" (Luke 12:47). Once again Jesus preached an Old Testament message. After His sacrificial death on the Cross was accomplished, there could be no more punishment for the believer's sins. In any case, this verse speaks of a lost person who has heard the gospel but will not obey it. The New Testament combination *that servant* (9x), *which knew his* (1x), *lord's will* (1x), *and prepared* (4x), *not himself* (5x), *neither did according to his will* (1x), *he shall be* (17x), *beaten* (6x), *with many* (10), *stripes* (9x) = 63.

2363rd Verse of the New Testament

"But he that knew not, and did commit things worthy of stripes, shall be beaten with few stripes" (Luke 12:48). All people have sin natures. This 63rd verse gives details concerning God's wrath upon a lost person who has never heard the gospel.

Repent or Perish

"I tell you, Nay: but, except ye repent, ye shall all likewise perish" (Luke 13:5). The Bible combination *I tell you nay but except* (2x), *except ye* (10x), *repent* (46x), *ye shall all* (3x), *likewise perish* (2x) = 63.

This Rich Man Went to Hell

"And it came to pass, that the beggar died, and was carried by the angels into Abraham's bosom: the rich man also died, and was buried; And in hell he lift up his eyes, being in torments, and seeth Abraham afar off, and Lazarus in his bosom. And he cried and said, Father Abraham, have mercy on me, and send Lazarus, that he may dip the tip of his finger in water, and cool my tongue; for I am tormented in this flame" (Luke 16:22-24). This rich man's sin was not love of money as much as it was lack of love for the poor and needy. The Bible combination *the rich man* (1x), *also died and was buried* (1x), *and being in* (3x), *hell* (54x), *he lift up his eyes* (2x), *being in torments* (1x), *for I am tormented in this flame* (1x) = 63.

Where the Eagles Gather

"I tell you, in that night there shall be two men in one bed; the one shall be taken, and the other shall be left. Two women shall be grinding together; the one shall be taken, and the other left. Two men shall be in the field; the one shall be taken, and the other left. And they answered and said unto him, Where, Lord? And he said unto them, Wheresoever the body is, thither will the eagles be gathered together" (Luke 16:34-37). An essential part of establishing Christ's earthly kingdom will be the rooting out of all offenders. After these offenders are executed by the wrath of God they will remain unburied. The Bible combination *the one shall* (6x), *be taken* (57x) = 63.

Noah & Lot's Generation Experienced God's Wrath

"And as it was in the days of Noe, so shall it be also in the days of the Son of man. They did eat, they drank, they married wives, they were given in marriage, until the day that Noe entered into the ark, and the flood came, and <u>destroyed</u> them all. Likewise also as it was in the days of Lot; they did eat, they drank, they bought, they sold, they planted, they builded; But the same day that Lot went out of Sodom it rained fire and brimstone from heaven, and <u>destroyed</u> them all. Even thus shall it be in the day when the <u>Son of man</u> is revealed" (Luke 17:26-30). Again the title *Son of man/God* occurs 63 times in Major Prophets. Again the word *destroy* is mentioned in 63 chapters of the Major and Minor Prophets.

63rd Chapter of the New Testament

At the very end of the parable of the ten pounds we read these words which speak of Christ's latter day judgment and wrath: "But those <u>mine enemies</u>, which would not that I should reign over them, <u>bring hither</u>, and slay them before me" (Luke 19:27). The Bible combination *mine enemies* (57x) and *bring hither* (6x) = 63.

Jerusalem's Latter-Day wrathful Destruction Foretold

"And when ye shall see <u>Jerusalem</u> compassed with armies, then know that the desolation thereof is nigh. Then let them which are <u>in Judæa</u> flee to the mountains; and let them which are in the midst of it depart out; and let not them that are in the countries enter thereinto. For these be <u>the days</u> of VENGEANCE, that all things which are written may be fulfilled. But woe unto them that are with child, and to them that give suck, in those days! for there shall be great distress in the land, and WRATH upon this people. And they shall fall by the edge of <u>the sword</u>, and shall be <u>led away captive</u> into all nations: and <u>Jerusalem</u> shall be trodden down of the Gentiles, until the times of the Gentiles be fulfilled" (Luke 21:20-24).

God's wrath upon Jerusalem came about in AD 70 as a result of Jerusalem's AD 30 rejection of Christ as King. Again the phrase *the days* is mentioned in 263 verses in the Bible. Again the phrase *the sword* is mentioned in 163 chapters of the Bible. Again the phrase *carried away* occurs 63 times in the Bible. We repeat the following two seals.

> The name *Jerusalem* occurs 63 times in Second Kings.
> The phrase *in Jerusalem* occurs 163 times in the Bible.

Unaware of God's Coming Wrath

"And take heed to yourselves, lest at any time your hearts be overcharged with surfeiting, and drunkenness, and cares of this life, and so that <u>day</u> <u>come</u> <u>upon you</u> unawares" (Luke 21:34). Again the phrase *the day of* occurs 163 times in the Bible. Again the word *come* occurs 63 times in Numbers. Again the phrase *upon you* is mentioned naturally in 63 verses of the Bible.

Luke 22:63

"And <u>the men</u> that held Jesus mocked him, and <u>smote</u> him" (Luke 22:63). Gentile soldiers become the instruments of God's wrath upon the sinless Son of Man. The lowercase phrase *the men* occurs 363 times in the Bible. Again the word *smitten* occurs 63 times in the Bible.

1063rd Verse of Luke

"Pilate therefore, willing to release Jesus, spake again to them. <u>But they cried, saying, Crucify him, crucify him.</u> And he said unto them the third time, Why, what evil hath he done? I have found no cause of death in him: I will therefore chastise him, and let him go. And they were instant with loud voices, requiring that he might be crucified. And the voices of them and of the chief priests prevailed. And Pilate gave sentence that it should be as they required" (Luke

23:20-24). The underlined verse indicates the 1063rd verse of the Bible, and it pertains to the predetermined verdict of God's wrath.

Christ Crucified Because of God's Wrath & Our Sins

"And when they were come to the place, which is called Calvary, there they <u>crucified</u> him" (Luke 23:33a). Christ Jesus took God's wrath upon Himself to spare humanity from it! The 63rd letter in this wrath-of-God verse—*i*—falls in the very middle of the word *crucified*.

The Messiah's Appointed Sufferings unto Wrath

"Then he said unto them, O fools, and slow of heart to believe all that the prophets have spoken: Ought not Christ to have <u>suffered</u> these things, and to enter into his glory? And beginning at Moses and all the prophets, he expounded unto them in all the scriptures the things concerning himself" (Luke 24:25-27). Jesus reflects upon the Scriptures which pertain to the wrath of God that the Messiah was to undergo. The word *suffer* occurs naturally 63 times in the New Testament.

The Sacrificial Lamb That Takes Away God's Wrath

"The next day John seeth Jesus coming unto him, and saith, Behold the Lamb of GOD, which taketh away <u>the sin</u> of the world" (John 1:29). From Genesis to the NT Narrative the phrase *the sin* is mentioned in 63 verses; this is its 63rd verse-mention, and by use of the accompanying word Lamb we see its relation to satisfying God's wrath against sin.

Son of God's Wrath upon the Money Changers

"And when he had made a scourge of small cords, he drove them all out of the temple, and the sheep, and the oxen; and poured out the changers' <u>money</u>, and overthrew the tables; And said unto them that sold doves, <u>Take these things hence</u>; <u>make not my Father's house</u> <u>an house of merchandise</u>. <u>And his disciples remembered</u> <u>that it was written</u>, <u>The zeal of</u> <u>thine house</u> <u>hath eaten</u> <u>me up</u>" (John 2:15-17). The Son of God's fierce anger was stirred over the great misuse of His Father's House of Prayer. The word *money* is mentioned naturally in 63 chapters of the Bible. The Bible combination *take these things hence* (1x), *make not my Father's house* (1x), *an house of merchandise* (1x), *and his disciples remembered* (1x), *that it was written* (1x), *the zeal of* (5x), *thine house* (51x), *hath eaten eaten me up* (2x) = 63.

Believers Shall Not Experience God's Wrath

"For God so loved the world, that he gave his only begotten Son, that whosoever believeth in him should <u>not</u> perish, but have everlasting life. For GOD sent <u>not</u> his Son into the world to condemn the world; but that the world through him might be saved. He that believeth on him is <u>not</u> condemned" (John 3:16-18a). The word *not* occurs 2063 times in the New Testament.

Wrath & Condemnation

"He that believeth on him is not <u>condemned</u>: but he that believeth not is <u>condemned</u> already, because he hath not believed in the name of the only begotten Son of GOD. And this is the <u>condemnation</u>, that light is come into the world, and men loved darkness rather than light, because their deeds were evil" (John 3:18-19). Again all forms of the word condemn show the seal of God's wrath in a delineated way: *condemnation* (12 vs), *condemn* (24 vs), *condemned* (20 vs), *condemnest* (1 v), *condemneth* (4 vs), *condemning* (2 vs) = 63 verses.

God's Abiding Wrath

"He that believeth on the Son hath everlasting life: and he that believeth not the Son shall not see life; but the WRATH OF GOD <u>abideth</u> on him" (John 3:36). The word *abide* is mentioned in 63 chapters of the Bible.

God's Judgment & Wrath Given unto the Son

"For the Father judgeth no man, but hath committed all <u>judgment</u> unto the <u>Son</u>. . . . He that heareth my word, and believeth on him that sent me, hath everlasting life, and shall not come into condemnation" (John 5:22, 24b). Again the word *judgment(s)* occurs naturally 63 times in the Law. Again the title *Son* is mentioned in 163 verses of the NT Narrative.

The Resurrection unto Damnation

"Marvel not at this: for the hour is coming, in the which all that are in the graves shall hear his voice, And shall come forth; they that have done good, unto the resurrection of life; and they that have <u>done evil</u>, unto the <u>resurrection</u> of <u>damnation</u>" (John 5:28-29). The Bible combination *done evil* (11x), *resurrection* (41x), *damnation* (11x) = 63.

John 6:63

"It is the spirit that quickeneth; <u>the flesh</u> profiteth nothing: the words that I speak unto you, they are spirit, and they are life" (John 6:63). Unless man becomes born of God's Spirit, God's wrath remains against man and his sinful flesh. The phrase *the flesh* occurs 63 times in the Pauline Epistles.

The Wrath of God Deferred

"When Jesus had lifted up himself, and saw none but the woman, he said unto her, Woman, where are those thine accusers? hath no man <u>condemned</u> thee? She said, No man, LORD. And Jesus said unto her, Neither do I condemn thee: go, and sin no more" (John 8:10-11). By Mosaic Law this adulteress had earned the wrath of God. Again all forms of the word *condemn* show the seal of God's wrath in their delineated 63 verse mentions.

563rd Verse of John

"Now is my soul troubled; and what shall I say? Father, save me from this hour: but for this cause came I unto this hour" (John 12:27). This 563rd verse of John is also concurrently the 3463rd verse of the New Testament, and it pertains to the hour of God's wrath upon His Son.

The Cup of Trembling

"Then said Jesus unto Peter, Put up thy sword into the sheath: <u>the cup</u> <u>which my Father</u> <u>hath given me, shall I not drink it</u>?" (John 18:11) We discussed the cup of plagues earlier. This cup was also known as the cup of trembling, for the one who was made to drink of it would fear exceedingly regarding the coming fury. The Bible combination *the cup* (37x), *of plague* (1x), *of trembling* (4x), *which my Father* (2x), *hath given me* (18x), *shall I not drink it* (1x) = 63.

763rd Verse of John

"And when he had thus spoken, one of the officers which stood by <u>struck</u> Jesus with the palm of his hand, saying, Answerest thou the high priest so?" (John 18:22) This 763rd verse of John is also concurrently the 3663rd verse of the New Testament, and it pertains to elements of God's wrath being administered unto the Son of God. Again the word *smitten* occurs 63 times in the Bible.

Burning Whips & Piercing Thorns

"Then Pilate therefore took Jesus, and scourged him. And the soldiers platted a crown of thorns, and put it on his head" (John 19:1-2a). This was only the beginning of God's wrath directed at the lowly Son of God. A cross still awaited Him. The Old Testament combination *crown of* (28x), *thorns* (34x), *set upon his head* (1x) = 63.

Jesus Died under God's Wrath

"When Jesus therefore had received the vinegar, he said, It is finished: and he bowed his head, and gave up the ghost" (John 19:30). Jesus could not have further suffered the fires of hell as some erring ones suggest, because He stated that God's wrath for sin was now finished. This verse presents the Bible's 63rd chapter-mention of the phrase *his head*, and we see its relation to the finished wrath of God upon the Son of God.

Wrath of God upon Christ's Soul Removed

"He seeing this before spake of the resurrection of Christ, that his soul was not left in hell, neither his flesh did see corruption" (Acts 2:31). Although Jesus' fleshly body never went to hell fire it did go into the place called hell which refers to the grave. God's wrath for sin put His sin-bearing flesh in the grave. Again from Genesis to the NT Narrative the word *flesh* is mentioned in 163 chapters; this verse presents its 163rd chapter-mention. Again the word *soul* is mentioned in 63 chapters of the Psalms.

Judas' Wrath-Filled Reward from God

"Now this man purchased a field with the reward of iniquity; and falling headlong, he burst asunder in the midst, and all his bowels gushed out. And it was known unto all the dwellers at Jerusalem; insomuch as that field is called in their proper tongue, Aceldama, that is to say, The field of blood. For it is written in the book of Psalms, Let his habitation be desolate, and let no man dwell therein: and his bishoprick let another take" (Acts 1:18-20). This betrayer took his own life by hanging himself. Then when his weight apparently broke the tree limb that he had hung himself on, he fell down to the cliff's rocky bottom where his blood was spattered. Then his iniquitous soul was taken to the lowest hell thereby pacifying God's wrath. The word *blood* occurs 163 times in the Law. Again the phrase *it is written* occurs 63 times in the New Testament.

Rejecting the Prophet Like Moses Will Reap God's Wrath

During Peter's second sermon he warned of God's particular wrath which awaited those who rejected Jesus' salvation message: "For Moses truly said unto the fathers, A prophet shall the Lord your GOD raise up unto you of your brethren, like unto me; him shall ye hear in all things whatsoever he shall say unto you. And it shall come to pass, that every soul, which will not hear that prophet, shall be destroyed from among the people" (Acts 3:22-23). Again the word *soul* is mentioned in 63 chapters of the Psalms. Again the word *destroy* is mentioned in 63 chapters of the Major and Minor Prophets.

Ananias & Sapphira Slain by God's Wrath

"But a certain man named Ananias, with Sapphira his wife, sold a possession, And kept back part of the price . . . But Peter said, Ananias, why hath Satan filled thine heart to lie to the Holy Ghost, and to keep back part of the price of the land? . . . Then Peter said unto her, How is it that ye have agreed together to tempt the Spirit of the LORD? behold, the feet of them which have buried thy husband are at the door, and shall carry thee out. Then fell she down straightway at his feet, and yielded up the ghost: and the young men came in, and found her dead, and, carrying her forth, buried her by her husband. And great fear came upon all the church, and upon as many as heard these things" (Acts 5:1-2a, 3, 9-11).

Underlined verse number three is the 26,063rd verse of the Bible. Again the word *dead* occurs naturally 363 times in the Bible.

Breaking the Law Brings God's Wrath

As Stephen closes out his fiery sermon he compares those who are about to kill him to those who beforetime killed other prophets, and "Who have received the law by the disposition of angels, and have not kept it" (Acts 7:53). God has promised great wrath for those who break His high and holy laws and refuse to repent. Again the word *law* occurs 63 times in the NT Narrative.

Herod Agrippa Eaten of Worms

"And upon a set day Herod, arrayed in royal apparel, sat upon his throne, and made an oration unto them. And the people gave a shout, saying, It is the voice of a god, and not of a man. And immediately the angel of the LORD smote him, because he gave not God the glory: and he was eaten of worms, and gave up the ghost" (Acts 12:21-23). Marcus Julius Agrippa never saw God's wrath coming, but he sure knew it when it arrived. Again the word *smitten* occurs 63 times in the Bible. The Bible combination *Herod* (40x), *the Lord smote him* (2x), *eaten of* (8x), *worms* (8x), *and gave up the ghost* (5x) = 63.

Beware Ye Despisers of God's Holy Work

Paul warns the Jews of Antioch Pisidia about the danger of God's wrath for rejecting His anointed messenger. "Beware therefore, lest that come upon you, which is spoken of in the prophets; Behold, ye despisers, and wonder, and perish: for I work a work in your days, a work which ye shall in no wise believe, though a man declare it unto you" (Acts 13:40-41). Again the word *come* occurs 63 times in Numbers. Again the phrase *upon you* is mentioned naturally in 63 verses of the Bible.

Son of Man Appointed a Day to Judge the World

"And the times of this ignorance GOD winked at; but now commandeth all men every where to repent: Because he hath appointed a day, in the which he will judge the world in righteousness by that man whom he hath ordained; whereof he hath given assurance unto all men, in that he hath raised him from the dead" (Acts 17:30-31). The New Testament combination *all men* (62x), *every where to repent* (1x) = 63. The Bible combination *and the times of this ignorance God winked at* (1x), *but now commandeth all men* (1x), *every where to repent* (1x), *hath appointed* (7x), *a day* (50x), *in the which he will judge the world* (1x), *by that man* (1x), *whom he hath ordained* (1x) = 63. The Bible combination *his Son whom he hath appointed* (1x), *a day* (50x), *to judge* (10x), *the world in righteousness* (2x) = 63.

Wrath of God Revealed from Heaven

"For the WRATH OF GOD is revealed <u>from heaven</u> against all ungodliness and unrighteousness of men, who hold the truth in unrighteousness" (Rom. 1:18). Again the phrase *from heaven* occurs 63 times in the New Testament.

Wrath of God Avoided through Repentance

"Or despisest thou the riches of his goodness and forbearance and longsuffering; not knowing that the goodness of God leadeth thee to repentance? But after thy hardness and impenitent heart treasurest up unto thyself WRATH against <u>the day of</u> WRATH and revelation of the righteous <u>judgment</u> of GOD; Who will render to every man according to his deeds. . . . But unto them that are contentious, and do not obey the truth, but obey unrighteousness, INDIGNATION and WRATH" (Rom. 2:4-6, 8).

Again the phrase *the day of* occurs 163 times in the Bible. Again the word *judgment(s)* occurs naturally 63 times in the Law. Here the wrath-related keyword *indignation* is the 163rd word of this chapter.

Saved from God's Wrath through God's Son

"Much more then, being now justified by his blood, we shall <u>be saved</u> <u>from WRATH</u> <u>through him</u>" (Rom. 5:9). This verse presents the Bible's 163rd occurrence of the word *wrath*. The 63rd letter of this wrath-verse commences immediately following the word *wrath*. The Bible combination *be saved* (55x), *from wrath* (1x), *through him* (7x) = 63.

Being in Christ Means No More Wrath

"There is therefore now no <u>condemnation</u> to them which are in Christ Jesus, who walk not after <u>the flesh</u>, but after the Spirit" (Rom. 8:1). Again all forms of the word *condemn* show the seal of God's wrath in their 63 delineated verse-mentions. Again the phrase *the flesh* occurs 63 times in the Pauline Epistles.

God Is Righteous When He Takes Vengeance

"But if our unrighteousness commend the righteousness of God, what shall we say? Is GOD unrighteous who taketh VENGEANCE? I speak as a man" (Rom. 3:5). Again the title *God* occurs 163 times in Romans.

Vengeance Is Mine Saith the Lord

"Dearly beloved, avenge not yourselves, but rather give place unto WRATH: for it is written, <u>VENGEANCE</u> is mine; I will repay, saith the LORD" (Rom. 12:19). The Old Testament combination *vengeance* (32 vs), *is mine* (31 vs) = 63 verses!

God's Ministers of His Governmental Wrath

"Let every soul be subject unto the higher powers. For there is no power but of GOD: the powers that be are ordained of GOD. Whosoever therefore resisteth the power, resisteth the ordinance of GOD: and they that resist shall receive to themselves damnation. For rulers are not a terror to good works, but to the evil. Wilt thou then not be afraid of the power? do that which is good, and thou shalt have praise of the same: For he is the minister of GOD to thee for good. But if thou do that which is evil, be afraid; for he beareth not <u>the sword</u> in vain: for he is the minister of GOD, a revenger to execute WRATH upon him that doeth evil" (Rom. 13:1-4).

God has established law and order in this fallen world. It is known as human government and is designed to combat anarchy. Again the phrase *the sword* is mentioned in 163 chapters of the Bible.

1063rd Chapter of the Bible

This key chapter emphasizes God's coming wrath in two regards; as it pertains to the Christ-adoring saints and as it pertains to the Christ-rejecting world. First Paul reminds the Corinthian believers that God will keep them safe in that dreadful day when His Son will judge the world. "Even as the testimony of Christ was confirmed in you: So that ye come behind in no gift; waiting for the coming of our Lord Jesus Christ: Who shall also confirm you unto the end, that ye may be blameless in the day of our LORD Jesus Christ" (1 Cor. 1:6-8). Again the phrase *the day of* occurs 163 times in the Bible. Again the title *our Lord* occurs 63 times in the Pauline Epistles. Again the title *Christ* is mentioned in 163 chapters of the New Testament.

Second Paul reminds them that unbelievers will eventually incur God's wrath for rejecting the gospel of Christ. "For the preaching of the cross is to them that perish foolishness . . . For it is written, I will destroy the wisdom of the wise, and will bring to nothing the understanding of the prudent. Where is the wise? where is the scribe? where is the disputer of this world? hath not GOD made foolish the wisdom of this world?" (vv. 18-20) Again the word *destroy* is mentioned in 63 chapters of the Major and Minor Prophets.

The Wrath of Christ the Destroyer

"Neither let us tempt Christ, as some of them also tempted, and were destroyed of serpents. Neither murmur ye, as some of them also murmured, and were destroyed of the destroyer. Now all these things happened unto them for ensamples: and they are written for our admonition, upon whom the ends of the world are come" (1 Cor. 10:9-11). Again the name *Christ* is mentioned in 163 chapters of the New Testament. Again the word *destroy* is mentioned in 63 chapters of the Major and Minor Prophets.

When the Cup of the Lord Becomes the Cup of Wrath

"Wherefore whosoever shall eat this bread, and drink this cup of the LORD, unworthily, shall be guilty of the body and blood of *the Lord*" (1 Cor. 11:27). This verse presents the Bible's 63rd mention of the word *cup*, and we see its relation to God's wrath. The Bible combination *guilty* (26x), *of the body* (20x), *and blood* (17x) = 63.

Judaizers & Legalizers Accursed of God

The chief apostle was stomping mad when he wrote saying, "But though we, or an angel from heaven, preach any other gospel unto you than that which we have preached unto you, let him be accursed" (Gal. 1:8). Those who preach the gospel of salvation with any admixture of works are an anathema to God. Faith in Christ's finished work on the cross is all that is necessary for salvation in this Dispensation of Grace. Works performed after one's day of salvation are simply a part of the believer's grateful service to God. The Greek word here for accursed is "anathema" and means assigned to damnation or destruction, even excommunication. Again the word *cursed* is mentioned in 63 verses of the Old Testament.

The Children of Disobedience

"Let no man deceive you with vain words: for because of these things cometh the WRATH OF

GOD upon the children of disobedience" (Eph. 5:6). Again the phrase *upon the* is mentioned naturally in 63 verses of Genesis. The New Testament combination *let no man deceive you with* (1x), *vain words* (1x), *for because of* (1x), *these things cometh* (1x), *the wrath of God upon* (2x), *the children of* (51x), *disobedience* (6x) = 63.

Their Destructive End Is Coming

"For many walk, of whom I have told you often, and now tell you even weeping, that they are the enemies of the cross of Christ: Whose end is destruction" (Phil. 3:18-19a). The word *is* is mentioned in 863 verses of the NT Narrative.

The Children of Disobedience

"For which things' sake the WRATH OF GOD cometh on the children of disobedience" (Col. 3:6). The phrase *on the* is mentioned in 63 chapters of the NT Narrative.

Believers Saved from the Wrath to Come

"And to wait for his Son from heaven, whom he raised from the dead, even Jesus, which delivered us from the WRATH to come" (1 Thess. 1:10). Again the phrase *from the* is found in 63 books of the Bible. Again the word *come* is mentioned in 63 verses of Exodus. Here the keyword *wrath* is the 753,963rd word of the Bible.

63rd Verse of First Thessalonians

"For yourselves know perfectly that the day of the LORD so cometh as a thief in the night" (1 Thess. 5:2). Again the phrase *the day of* occurs 163 times in the Bible.

Believers Not Appointed to God's Wrath

"For GOD hath not appointed us to WRATH, but to obtain salvation by our Lord Jesus Christ" (1 Thess. 5:9). Again the word *not* occurs 2063 times in the New Testament.

Taking Vengeance on Them That Obey Not the Gospel

"Seeing it is a righteous thing with GOD to recompense tribulation to them that trouble you; And to you who are troubled rest with us, when the Lord Jesus shall be revealed from heaven with his mighty angels, In flaming fire taking VENGEANCE on them that know not GOD, and that obey not the gospel of our LORD Jesus Christ: Who shall be PUNISHED with everlasting destruction from the presence of the LORD, and from the glory of his power" (2 Thess. 1:6-9). Again the phrase *from heaven* occurs 63 times in the New Testament. Again all forms of the word *punish* are mentioned in 63 collective verses of the Bible. Again the title *our Lord* occurs 63 times in the Pauline Epistles.

Son of God's Past, Present & Future Wrath

"And then shall that Wicked be revealed, whom the Lord shall consume with the spirit of his mouth, and shall destroy with the brightness of his coming" (2 Thess. 2:8). Again the word *destroy* is mentioned in 63 chapters of the Major and Minor Prophets. We present the following three wrath seals all at once: past, present, and future.

The word *came* occurs 63 times in John's Gospel.
The word *come* occurs 63 times in Numbers.

The term *will come* is mentioned in 63 verses of the Bible.

Sinners in the Hands of an Angry God

"Some men's sins are open beforehand, going before to <u>judgment</u>; and some men they follow after" (1 Tim. 5:24). Again the word *judgment(s)* occurs naturally 63 times in the Law.

The Judgment Day

"I charge thee therefore before God, and the <u>LORD Jesus Christ</u>, who shall <u>judge</u> the quick and the dead at his appearing and his kingdom" (2 Tim. 4:1). This verse presents the New Testament's 63rd occurrence of the title *Lord Jesus Christ*, and it. Again the word *judged* occurs 63 times in the Bible.

Reprobates to Experience God's Wrath

"Unto the pure all things are pure: but unto <u>them</u> that are defiled and unbelieving is nothing pure; but even their mind and conscience is defiled. <u>They</u> profess that they know GOD; but in works <u>they</u> deny him, being abominable, and disobedient, and unto every good work reprobate" (Titus 1:16). As a general rule, the Bible often refers to the disbelieving as "they" and "them" while referring to the believing as "we" and "us." Again the word *them* occurs 63 times in Ezra. The word *they* is mentioned in 263 verses of First and Second Samuel.

6863rd Verse of the New Testament

"Wherefore I was grieved with that generation, and said, They do alway err in their heart; and they have not known my ways. So I sware in my WRATH, They shall not enter into my rest. <u>Take heed, brethren, lest there be in any of you an evil heart of unbelief, in departing from the living GOD</u>" (Heb. 3:10-12). The underlined words indicate the 6863rd verse of the Bible, and this verse implies how to incur God's wrath.

"I Have Sworn in My Wrath"

"For we which have believed do enter into rest, as he said, As I have sworn in <u>my</u> WRATH, if they shall enter into my rest: although the works were finished from the foundation of the world" (Heb. 4:3). Here the word *my* is the 152,863rd word of the New Testament, and it supports the keyword wrath. Again the word *my* is mentioned in 163 chapters of the New Testament.

Thorns & Briers to Be Burned

"But that which beareth <u>thorns</u> and <u>briers</u> is rejected, and is nigh unto cursing; <u>whose end is to be burned</u>" (Heb. 6:8). The Bible combination *thorns* (50x), *briers* (12x), *whose end is to be burned* (1x) = 63. Again from Genesis to the Synoptic Gospels the word *burned* is mentioned in 63 chapters.

God Will Devour Presumptuous Sinners

"For if we sin wilfully after that we have received the knowledge of the truth, there remaineth no more sacrifice for sins, <u>But a certain fearful looking for of judgment and fiery</u> INDIGNATION, which shall devour the adversaries" (Heb. 10:26-27). Paul the learned rabbi was drawing from a mosaic passage in Numbers which refers to presumptuous sins. He was trying to put the fear of God in the hearts of these backsliding Hebrews as Moses had once tried to do with the Hebrews of his day. Yet these Hebrews were only guilty of trying to alleviate their suffering. The Bible combination *but a certain fearful* (1x), *looking for of judgment and* (1x), *fiery* (20x), *indignation* (41x) = 63.

30,163rd Verse of the Bible

"He that despised Moses' law died without mercy under two or three witnesses: <u>Of how much sorer PUNISHMENT, suppose ye, shall he be thought worthy, who hath trodden under foot the Son of GOD, and hath counted the blood of the covenant, wherewith he was sanctified, an unholy thing, and hath done despite unto the Spirit of grace?</u> For we know him that hath said, VENGEANCE belongeth unto me, I will recompense, saith the LORD. And again, The LORD shall <u>judge</u> his people. It is a fearful thing to fall into the hands of the living GOD" (Heb. 10:28-31).

Paul uses an Old Testament example to make a New Testament point. He looks for the strongest possible argument to make his case for turning the compromising Christians back to straight walking with God. * The book of Hebrews is not a thesis on salvation but rather on faith-living. The 30,163rd verse is underlined, and it pertains to God's wrath. Again the word *judged* occurs 63 times in the Bible.

The Sinner & the Wrath of God

"Brethren, if any of you do err from the truth, and one convert him; Let him know, that he which converteth the sinner from the error of his way shall save a soul from <u>death,</u> and shall hide a multitude of sins" (James 5:19-20). As a general rule, the Bible often refers to an unbeliever as "the sinner" while referring to a believer as "the saint." Nevertheless this passage refers to a believer who has fallen from grace. God's wrath can nonetheless be exacted upon a grossly wayward saint by cutting his or her life short. Again the word *death* is mentioned in 63 verses of the Law.

Sent Ones to Carry out God's Wrath against Evil Sinners

"Submit yourselves to every ordinance of man for the LORD'S sake: whether it be to the king, as supreme; Or unto governors, as unto them that are <u>sent</u> by him for the PUNISHMENTS of evildoers, and for the praise of them that do well" (1 Pet. 2:13-14). Again the word *sent* is mentioned in 63 verses of the Bible.

God's Judgment of the Ungodly

"For the time is come that <u>judgment</u> must begin at the house of GOD: and if it first begin at us, what shall the end be of them that obey not the gospel of GOD? And if the righteous scarcely be saved, where shall the ungodly and the sinner appear?" (1 Pet. 4:17-18) Again the word *judgment(s)* occurs naturally 63 times in the Law.

"The LORD knoweth how to deliver the godly out of temptations, and to reserve the unjust unto the day of judgment to be PUNISHED" (2 Pet. 2:9). Again all forms of the word *punish* are mentioned in 63 collective verses of the Bible.

The Day of God's Earthly Wrath

"But the day of the LORD <u>will come</u> as a thief in the night; in the which the heavens shall pass away with a great noise, and the elements shall melt with fervent heat, <u>the earth</u> also and the works that are therein shall be burned up" (2 Pet. 3:10). This wrath-filled event will come at the end of Christ's millennial reign, just after Satan is loosed to deceive the nations one last time.

God will purge the earth from all vestiges of evil. Again the phrase *will come* is mentioned in 63 verses of the Bible. The phrase *the earth* is mentioned in 63 chapters of the New Testament.

The Day of God's Heavenly Wrath

"Looking for and hasting unto the coming of the day of GOD, wherein the heavens being on fire shall be dissolved, and the elements shall melt with fervent heat?" (2 Pet. 3:12) After Satan and all his host are judged and banished to the lake of fire God will purge the lower heavens from all vestiges of evil. Again the phrase *the day of* occurs 163 times in the Bible. The word *wherein* is mentioned in 163 verses of the Bible.

> The word *day* is mentioned in 63 verses of Exodus.
> The word *day* is mentioned in 363 verses of the Law.
> The word *day* occurs 63 times in the Gospel of Luke.

63ʳᵈ Book of the Bible

SECOND JOHN is the 63ʳᵈ BOOK of the Bible. Its theme is Avoiding the Way of Antichrist. The antichrist is certainly appointed unto God's eternal wrath, and he wants to take with him to God's fiery judgment as many lost souls as possible. His method of capturing saved men's souls is deception. Even though he cannot take believers with him to hell he nevertheless attempts to do so just the same.

Second John contains two halves, the path of the believer and the peril of the believer. In the first half, John commends a certain church about their present proper Christian walk, that of truth and love.

In the second half of his Letter the aged apostle warns the church not to fall away from the truth of God's Word. This can happen through carelessness. Falling away can also happen when believers allow deceivers to steer them away from the truth. For such evil deceivers and antichrists, the wrath of God surely awaits them.

> "For many deceivers are entered into the world, who confess not that Jesus Christ is come in the flesh. This is a DECEIVER and an ANTICHRIST. Look to yourselves, that we lose not those things which we have wrought, but that we receive a full reward. Whosoever transgresseth, and abideth not in the doctrine of Christ, hath not GOD. He that abideth in the doctrine of Christ, he hath both the Father and the Son. If there come any unto you, and bring not this doctrine, receive him not into your house, neither bid him GOD speed: For he that biddeth him GOD speed is partaker of his evil deeds" (2 John 7-11).

These deceivers were either denying or undermining the doctrine of the Incarnation of the Son of God. Unless they repent, all deceivers will receive their full reward even the wrath of God. This passage contains the 63ʳᵈ occurrence of the word *not* in John's three Epistles. The word *neither* is mentioned in 63 verses of Ezekiel. The Bible's combined phrases *against the LORD/Lord* (52 chs) and *against God* (11 chs) = 63 chapters. The Bible combination *his evil* (11x), *deed/s* (52x) = 63.

Ordained to This Condemnation

"For there are certain men crept in unawares, who were before of old ordained to this condemnation, ungodly men, turning the grace of our God into lasciviousness, and denying the only LORD GOD, and our LORD Jesus Christ" (Jude 4). False teachers mix their little lies with a whole lot of truth so that they are not so easily detected and quickly removed from leadership.

Again all forms of the word *condemn* show the seal of God's wrath in their verse 63 mentions.

Recalling God's Wrath upon the Wilderness Generation

"I will therefore put you in remembrance, though ye once knew this, how that the LORD, having saved the people out of the land of Egypt, afterward <u>destroyed</u> them that believed not" (Jude 5). This verse presents the Bible's 163rd verse-mention of the word *destroyed*. Again the word *destroy* is mentioned in 63 chapters of the Major and Minor Prophets.

"The Vengeance of Eternal Fire"

"Even as Sodom and Gomorrha, and the cities about them in like manner, giving themselves over to fornication, and going after strange flesh, are set forth for an example, <u>suffering</u> the VENGEANCE of eternal fire" (Jude 7). The word *suffer* occurs naturally 63 times in the New Testament.

Eternal Wrath & Darkness Reserved for the Ungodly

"Raging waves of the sea, foaming out their own shame; wandering stars, to whom is reserved the blackness of darkness for ever. And Enoch also, the seventh from Adam, prophesied of these, saying, Behold, the LORD cometh with ten thousands of his saints, To execute <u>judgment</u> upon all, and to convince all that are ungodly among them of all their ungodly deeds which they have ungodly committed, and of all their hard speeches which ungodly sinners have spoken against him" (Jude 13-15).

The Lord Jesus is coming with the wrath of the Lord. Again the word *judgment(s)* occurs naturally 63 times in the Law.

Wrath of the Lamb

"And the kings of the earth, and the great men, and the rich men, and the chief captains, and the mighty men, and every bondman, and every free man, hid themselves in the dens and in the rocks of the mountains; And said to the mountains and rocks, Fall on us, and hide us <u>from</u> the face of <u>him</u> that sitteth on the throne, and from the WRATH of the Lamb: For <u>the</u> <u>great</u> <u>day of</u> his WRATH is <u>come</u>; and who shall be able to stand?" (Rev. 6:15-16) The phrase *from him* is naturally mentioned in 63 chapters in the Old Testament. Again the phrase *the day of* occurs 163 times in the Bible. Again the word *great* is mentioned in 163 verses of the Major Prophets. Again the word *come* occurs 63 times in Numbers.

Second Trumpet Bowl Judgment

"And the third part of the creatures which were in the sea, and had life, died; and the third part of the ships were <u>destroyed</u>" (Rev. 8:9). Outside this Apocalyptic Letter the word *destroyed* is mentioned in 163 verses.

"The Wine of the Wrath of God"

"The same shall <u>drink of</u> <u>the wine of</u> <u>the WRATH OF GOD</u>, <u>which is poured out</u> <u>without mixture</u> <u>into the cup of his INDIGNATION</u>; <u>and he shall be</u> <u>tormented</u> <u>with fire and brimstone</u> <u>in the</u> <u>presence of the holy angels</u>, <u>and in the presence of the Lamb</u>" (Rev. 14:10). The Bible phrases *to drink* (61x) and *to * drink* (2x) = 63. The Bible combination *drink of* (34x), *the wine of* (11x), *the wrath of God* (10x), *which is poured out* (1x), *without mixture* (1x), *into the cup of his indignation* (1x), *and he shall be tormented* (1x), *with fire and brimstone* (2x), *in the presence of* *the holy angels* (1x), *and in the presence of the Lamb* (1x) = 63.

"The Vials of the Wrath of God"

"And I heard a great voice out of the temple saying to the <u>seven</u> angels, Go your ways, and <u>pour</u> out the vials of the WRATH OF GOD upon the earth" (Rev. 16:1). Again the word *seven* occurs 463 times in the Bible. Again the word *pour* occurs 63 times in the Bible.

The Great Battle Day of God Almighty

"For they are the spirits of devils, working miracles, which go forth unto the kings of the earth and of the whole world, to gather them to the <u>battle</u> of that <u>great</u> <u>day</u> of GOD Almighty. (Rev. 16:14). Again the word *great* is mentioned in 163 verses of the Major Prophets. Again the word *day* is mentioned in 63 verses of Exodus. The word *battle* is mentioned in 163 verses of the Bible.

Christ's Rod of Iron

"And out of his mouth goeth a sharp <u>sword</u>, that with it he should smite the nations: and he shall rule them with <u>a rod</u> <u>of iron</u>: and he treadeth the winepress of the FIERCENESS and WRATH of Almighty GOD" (Rev. 19:15). Again the phrase *the sword* is mentioned in 163 chapters of the Bible. The Bible combination *a rod* (22x), *of iron* (41x) = 63!

The Wrath of God on Satan

"And I saw an angel come down <u>from heaven</u>, having the key of the bottomless pit and a great chain in his hand" (Rev. 20:1). Victors of battles often sported their top trophies by bringing them back robed in chains. The greater their trophy was, the greater or bigger the chains were which they bound them with. Again the phrase *from heaven* occurs 63 times in the New Testament.

Satan Bound in the Bottomless Pit for 1000 Years

"And he laid hold on the dragon, that old serpent, which is the Devil, and Satan, and <u>bound</u> him a thousand years, And cast him into the bottomless pit, and shut him up, and set a seal upon him" (Rev. 20:2-3b). Again the word *bound* is mentioned in 63 verses of the Old Testament.

Whose Names Were Not Written in the Book of Life

"And <u>whosoever</u> was <u>not found written</u> in the <u>book of life</u> was <u>cast into</u> the <u>lake of fire</u>" (Rev. 20:15). The word *whosoever* is mentioned in 163 verses of the Bible. The Bible combination *whose names* (6x), *not found written* (1x), *book of life* (8x), *cast into* (44x), *lake of fire* (4x) = 63.

God's Everlasting Wrath upon the Unholy Trinity

"And the <u>devil</u> <u>that deceived them</u> was <u>cast into the lake of fire and brimstone</u>, where <u>the beast</u> and <u>the false prophet</u> are, and shall be <u>tormented</u> <u>day and night for ever</u> and ever" (Rev. 20:10). The Bible combination *devil* (61x), *that deceived them* (1x), *cast into the lake of fire and brimstone* (1x) = 63. The Bible combination *the beast* (54x), *tormented* (8x), *day and night for ever* (1x) = 63.

God's Wrath—Man's Second Death

"But the fearful, and unbelieving, and the abominable, and murderers, and whoremongers, and sorcerers, and idolaters, and all liars, shall have their part in the lake which burneth with fire and brimstone: which is the second <u>death</u>" (Rev. 21:8). Again the word *death* is mentioned in 63 verses of the Law.

31,063rd Verse of the Bible

"And there came unto me one of the seven angels which had the seven vials full of the seven last <u>plagues,</u> and talked with me, saying, Come hither, I will shew thee the bride, the Lamb's wife" (Rev. 21:9). Again the phrase *the plague* occurs 63 times in the Law.

64—Broken Fellowship

The Creator made mankind in His holy image and character so He could enjoy daily fellowship with them. After the first man and woman sinned, their holy fellowship and relationship with God became severed and broken. Ever since that day, God has been trying to repair this breech. He longs for the common bond of Creator and creation to be restored.

When a believer commits a sin, even a great sin, he does not lose his salvation. He only loses his fellowship with God. Such lost fellowship can be quickly restored upon the sinner's heartfelt conviction of wrong, humble confession, and a prayer of repentance asking God for forgiveness and restoration.

> The Bible: *fellowship* (17x), *God and man* (4x), *be broken* (43x) = 64.
> The Bible's present-tense phrase *is broken* (21x) and *be broken* (43x) = 64.
> The word *broken* occurs 64 times from Genesis to the Psalms.
> All available tenses of *break* are mentioned in 64 verses of the Major Prophets.
> All Old Testament tenses of the word "break" show the seal of broken fellowship:
> *break* (130x), *breakest* (1x), *breaketh* (17x), *breaker* (1x), *breaking* (14x), *breakings* (1x) = 164.

Fellowship with another person comes by entering into some form of a covenant with that person whether formally or informally. Such covenants can be related to family, friendship, or marriage. Broken fellowship between two people is therefore a result of some broken covenant bond. Covenant and relationship are the basis of true fellowship.

Webster's Dictionary gives us several definitions of the word FELLOWSHIP:

> [1] companionship, company;
> [2] community of interest, activity, feeling, or experience, the state of being a fellow or associate;
> [3] a company of equals or friends, association; and
> [4] the quality or state of being comradely.

In this study we will see a wide variety of circumstances which brought about broken fellowships between people. Some broken fellowships were the result of different types of sin such as jealousy, strife, or hatred. Others were the result of unfortunate events, the giving away in marriage, or the result of a death. Some broken fellowships were needful and fruitful while others were unwelcome and unpleasant.

Man's Conditional Fellowship with God

"And the LORD God took the <u>man</u>, and put him into the garden of Eden to dress it and to keep it. And the LORD God commanded the <u>man</u>, saying, Of every tree of the garden thou mayest freely eat: But of the tree of the knowledge of good and evil, thou shalt not eat of it: for in the day that thou eatest thereof thou shalt surely die" (Gen. 2:15-16). Adam's relationship with God as Father and son would always remain constant, but their daily fellowship could only continue uninterrupted if Adam obeyed God's command.

The word *man* is mentioned in 64 chapters of the Synoptic Gospels.

The word *man* is mentioned in 64 verses of First Corinthians.

Adam & Eve Break Fellowship with God

"And the eyes of them both were opened, and <u>they</u> knew that <u>they</u> were naked; and <u>they</u> sewed fig leaves together, and made themselves aprons" (Gen. 3:7). Because the first couple knew they were now naked and that their fellowship with God was no longer holy, they quickly made some necessary adjustments which they thought were helpful. Their adjustments were insufficient to maintain proper fellowship with the Lord. Indeed a person can know when he is not in perfect fellowship with the Lord.

The word *they* occurs 364 times in Isaiah.

The word *they* is mentioned in 64 chapters of the Minor Prophets.

64th Verse of the Bible

"And they heard the voice of the LORD <u>God</u> walking in the <u>garden</u> in the cool of the day: and Adam and his wife hid themselves from the presence of the LORD <u>God</u> amongst the trees of the <u>garden</u>" (Gen. 3:8). Adam and Eve's face-to-face fellowship with God had become evidently broken. This was due to their garden-life disobedience. The word *garden(s)* occurs 64 combined times in the Bible. The title *LORD* is mentioned in 64 chapters of Isaiah. The title *God* occurs 64 times in First John.

Adam & Eve's Broken Fellowship with God Temporarily Restored

"Unto Adam also and to his wife did the LORD God make coats of skins, and clothed <u>them</u>" (Gen. 3:21). Adam and Eve's broken fellowship with God had become distinctly characterized by their undesirable nakedness and the works of their own hands. Their attempt to adjust their discomfort fell far short of true sanctification. God sought to remedy this problem with a solution of His own design; He clothed them with animal skins. In the process He shed animals' blood and made proper atonements for their sin. Herein acceptable fellowship between man and God was temporarily restored.

The word *them* occurs 264 times in Exodus.

The word *them* occurs 64 times in Romans.

The word *them* is found in 64 books of the Bible.

Adam's Right Hand of Fellowship with God Broken

"And the LORD God said, Behold, the man is become as one of us, to know good and evil: and now, lest he put forth <u>his hand</u>, and take also of the tree of life, and eat, and live for ever" (Gen. 3:22). Adam broke the right hand of fellowship with God when he put that hand to the forbidden fruit and ate from it. At this point in time the Lord was still worried about Adam's wayward hands and feet.

The phrase *his hand* occurs 64 times in the Law of Moses.

The phrase *his hand* is mentioned in 64 verses of Major/Minor Prophets.

Cain Breaks Fellowship with Abel

"And Abel was a keeper of sheep, but Cain was a tiller of the ground. And in process of time it came to pass, that Cain brought of the fruit of the ground an offering unto the LORD. And

Abel, he also brought of the firstlings of his flock and of the fat thereof. And the LORD had respect unto Abel and to his offering: But unto Cain and to his offering he had not respect. . . . And Cain talked with Abel his brother: and it came to pass, when they were in the field, that Cain rose up <u>against</u> Abel his brother, and <u>slew</u> him" (Gen. 4:2b-5a, 8).

Apparently Cain broke fellowship with his brother after a division of right and wrong was established between their religious approaches to God. Cain became jealous and it remained unresolved day by day. Thus it grew into hatred and eventually into homicide. The word *against* occurs 164 times in the Wisdom Books. The word *killed* is mentioned in 64 verses of the Bible.

Cain Confesses to His Broken Fellowship with His Brother

"<u>And the LORD said unto Cain, Where is Abel thy brother</u>? <u>And he said, I know not</u>: <u>Am I my brother's keeper</u>? <u>And he said, What hast thou done</u>? <u>the voice of thy brother's blood crieth unto me from the ground</u>" (Gen. 4:9-10). The Bible combination *and the LORD said unto Cain* (2x), *where is Abel thy brother* (1x), *and he said I know not* (1x), *am I my* (2x), *brother's* (35x), *keeper* (21x), *and he said what hast thou done* (1x), *the voice of thy brother's blood crieth unto me from the ground* (1x) = 64.

Broken Fellowship between Men & God

"And GOD saw that the wickedness of <u>man</u> was great in the earth, and that every imagination of the thoughts of his heart was only evil continually. And it repented the LORD that he had made <u>man</u> on the earth, and it grieved him at his <u>heart</u>. And the LORD said, I will destroy <u>man</u> whom I have created from the face of the earth" (Gen. 6:5-7a). Mankind had broken fellowship with God in such a way that it could not be repaired. God therefore sought to remedy the situation the only way He knew how—to start all over with the one godly family that had not broken fellowship with Him. The word *men* is mentioned in 640 chapters of the Bible, a vivid multiple of 64. The word *heart* is mentioned in 664 verses of the Old Testament.

Fellowship of Hearts Regained with Mankind

God had rightly broken off fellowship with humanity because of their continual wickedness. But after humanity's global judgment was complete and the Floodwaters abated, God sought to renew fellowship with humanity by directing Noah to make a sacrifice of peace.

> "And Noah builded an altar unto the LORD . . . and offered burnt offerings on the altar. And the LORD smelled a sweet savour; and the LORD said in his <u>heart</u>, I will not again curse the ground any more for man's sake; for the imagination of man's <u>heart</u> is evil from his youth; neither will I again smite any more every thing living, as I have done. While the earth remaineth, seedtime and harvest, and cold and heat, and summer and winter, and day and night shall not cease" (Gen. 8:20-22).

Again the word *heart* is mentioned in 664 verses of the Old Testament.

Noah & Ham

"And Noah began to be an husbandman, and he planted a vineyard: And he drank of the wine, and was drunken; and he was uncovered within his tent. And Ham, the father of Canaan, saw the nakedness of his father. . . . And <u>Noah awoke from his wine, and knew what his younger son had done unto him</u>. And he said, Cursed be Canaan; a servant of servants shall he be unto his brethren" (Gen. 9:20-22a, 24-25). In the following numeric seal we find the reason Noah broke fellowship with his son. The Genesis combination *Noah* (39x), *awoke* (4x), *from his* (7x), *wine*

(12x), *and knew what his younger son* (1x), *had done unto him* (1x) = 64.

Broken Fellowship between the Herdsmen

"And there was a strife between the herdmen of Abram's cattle and the herdmen of Lot's cattle" (Gen. 13:7a). Strife may lead to broken fellowship or it may at times be the result of broken fellowship. The Genesis combination *and there was a* (3x), *strife* (2x), *between the herdmen* (1x), *of Abram's cattle and* (1x), *the herdmen of* (3x), *Lot's* (1x), *cattle* (53x) = 64. The phrase *between the* is mentioned naturally in 64 verses of the Bible.

Abraham Prevents Possibility of Broken Fellowship with Lot

"And Abram said unto Lot, Let there be no strife, I pray thee, between me and thee, and between my herdmen and thy herdmen; for we be brethren. Is not the whole land before thee? separate thyself, I pray thee, from me: if thou wilt take the left hand, then I will go to the right; or if thou depart to the right hand, then I will go to the left" (Gen. 13:8-9). The Old Testament combination *be no* (63 chs) and *broken heart/s* (1 ch) = 64 chapters. The word *we* occurs 64 times in Numbers.

Abraham & Lot

"Then Lot chose him all the plain of Jordan; and Lot journeyed east: and they SEPARATED THEMSELVES from one another" (Gen. 13:11). Lot left his uncle on good terms, nevertheless they could no longer enjoy daily fellowship; this was all part of God's design. Lot was a man of little faith and low moral character. Thus it was determined that his seed should not mix with Abraham's faithful line. Again the word *they* is mentioned in 64 chapters of the Minor Prophets. The Bible combination *separated themselves from* (3x), *separated from* (7x), *one another* (54x) = 64.

Sarah & Hagar

"And Sarai . . . took Hagar her maid the Egyptian . . . and gave her to her husband Abram to be his wife. And he went in unto Hagar, and she conceived: and when she saw that she had conceived, her mistress was despised in her eyes. And Sarai said unto Abram, My wrong be upon thee: I have given my maid into thy bosom; and when she saw that she had conceived, I was despised in her eyes: the LORD judge between me and thee. But Abram said unto Sarai, Behold, thy maid is in thy hand; do to her as it pleaseth thee. And when Sarai dealt hardly with her, she fled from her face" (Gen. 16:3-6).

This broken fellowship began when Hagar suddenly changed her attitude toward her mistress. The phrase *from him* is mentioned naturally in 64 verses of the Old Testament.

Broken Covenant = Broken Fellowship

"And the uncircumcised man child whose flesh of his foreskin is not circumcised, that soul shall be cut off from his people; he hath BROKEN my covenant" (Gen. 17:14). Here the keyword *broken* is the 9600th word of the Bible, a multiple of 64.

Abraham & Ishmael

"And Sarah saw the son of Hagar the Egyptian, which she had born unto Abraham, mocking. Wherefore she said unto Abraham, Cast out this bondwoman and her son: for the son of this bondwoman shall not be heir with my son, even with Isaac. And the thing was very grievous in Abraham's sight because of his son. . . . And God said unto Abraham, Let it not be grievous in thy sight because of the lad, and because of thy bondwoman; in all that Sarah hath said unto thee, hearken unto her voice; for in Isaac shall thy seed be called. . . . And Abraham rose up early in the morning, and took bread, and a bottle of water, and gave it unto Hagar, putting it on her shoulder, and <u>the child</u>, and sent her <u>away</u>: and she departed, and wandered in the wilderness of Beer-sheba" (Gen. 21:9-10, 12, 14).

The phrase *the child* is mentioned in 64 verses of the Bible. The word *away* is mentioned in 64 chapters of the Law. The word *away* occurs 64 times in First and Second Kings.

Rebekah & Her Family

Eliezar said to Rebekah's family, "Send me <u>away</u> unto my master. And her brother and her mother said, Let the damsel abide with us a few days, at the least ten; after that she shall <u>go</u> And he said unto them, Hinder me not. . . . And they called Rebekah, and said unto her, Wilt thou <u>go</u> with this man? And she said, I will <u>go</u>. And they sent <u>away</u> Rebekah their sister" (Gen. 24:54c-56a, 58-59a). Rebekah's family was attempting to forestall an inevitable broken fellowship that was to come geographically by giving away a damsel in marriage. Again the word *away* is mentioned in 64 chapters of the Law. The word *go* occurs 64 times in Ezekiel.

Esau & Jacob

"<u>And Jacob</u> said, Sell me this day <u>thy birthright</u>. . . . and he sold his birthright unto Jacob. Then Jacob gave <u>Esau</u> bread and pottage of lentiles; and he did eat and drink, and rose up, and went his way: thus Esau despised his birthright" (Gen. 25:31, 33b-34). Esau quickly agreed to sell his birthright for Jacob's fresh-baked pita and hot lentil soup. In time Esau would despise his brother as much as he did his birthright. From this time forward the two brothers had a completely different kind of fellowship. The name *Esau* occurs 64 times in Genesis. The phrase *and Jacob* is mentioned in 64 verses of the Law.

Rachel & Leah

"And when Rachel saw that she bare Jacob no children, Rachel envied her sister. . . . And Rachel said, With great wrestlings have I wrestled with my sister. . . . Then <u>Rachel</u> said to <u>Leah</u>, Give me, I pray thee, of thy son's mandrakes. And she said unto her, Is it a small matter that thou hast taken my husband? and wouldest thou take away my son's mandrakes also" (Gen. 30:1a, 8a, 14d-15c). After Leah gave birth to her fourth son, childless Rachel turned her heart more and more against her sister. The wonderful fellowship they once shared as unmarried siblings would never be the same again. The Genesis combination *Rachel* (37 vs) and *Leah* (27 vs) = 64 verses.

Jacob & Laban—Rachel & Laban

"Then Jacob rose up, and set his sons and his wives upon camels; And he carried <u>away</u> all his cattle, and all his goods which he had gotten, the cattle of his getting, which he had gotten in Padan-aram, for to go to Isaac his father in the land of Canaan. And Laban went to shear his sheep: and Rachel had stolen the images that were her father's. And Jacob stole <u>away</u> unawares to Laban the Syrian, in that he told him not that he fled" (Gen. 31:17-20).

Jacob had grown weary with the long-running broken fellowship he was made to endure with his father-in-law. That Rachel stole her father's idols indicates her own weary, broken fellowship she had endured with her father. Here the Jacobeans broke fellowship permanently with the Labaneans. Again the word *away* is mentioned in 64 chapters of the Law.

Jacob seeks to Restore Fellowship with Esau by Grace

"And I have oxen, and asses, flocks, and menservants, and womenservants: and I have sent to tell my lord, that I may find <u>grace</u> in thy sight. . . . . And he said, What meanest thou by all this drove which I met? And he said, These are to find <u>grace</u> in the sight of my lord. And Esau said, I have enough, my brother; keep that thou hast unto thyself. And Jacob said, Nay, I pray thee, if now I have found <u>grace</u> in thy sight, then receive my present at my hand: for therefore I have seen thy face, as though I had seen the face of God, and thou wast pleased with me" (Gen. 32:5, 8-10). The word *grace* is mentioned in 64 chapters of the Pauline and General Epistles.

Joseph & His Half-Brothers

"Now Israel loved Joseph more than all his children, because he was the son of his old age: and he made him a coat of many colours. And when <u>his brethren</u> saw that their father loved him more than all <u>his brethren</u>, they hated him, and could not speak peaceably unto him. . . . And they said one to another, Behold, this dreamer cometh. Come now therefore, and let us slay him, and cast him into some pit, and we will say, Some evil beast hath devoured him: and we shall see what will become of his dreams" (Gen. 37:3-4, 19-20).

This visual token of Jacob's favoritism for his youngest son immediately severed any existing fellowship left between Joseph and his older half-brothers. From that time forward their fellowship became more and more distant. From Genesis to the Synoptic Gospels the phrase *his brethren* is mentioned in 64 chapters.

Jacob & His Favorite Son

"And he knew it, and said, It is my son's coat; an evil beast hath devoured him; Joseph is without doubt rent in pieces. And Jacob rent his clothes, and put sackcloth upon his loins, and mourned for his son many days. <u>And all his sons and all his daughters</u> <u>rose up to</u> <u>comfort him</u>; <u>but he refused to be</u> <u>comforted; and he said,</u> <u>For I will go down into</u> <u>the grave</u> <u>unto my son mourning</u>. Thus his father wept for him" (Gen. 37:33-35). The Bible combination *and all his sons and all his daughters* (1x), *rose up to* (11x), *comfort him* (7x), *but he refused to be comforted and he said* (1x), *I will go down into* (1x), *the grave* (42x), *unto my son mourning* (1x) = 64.

Joseph & the Chief Butler—A Forgotten Fellowship

Joseph had given the chief butler clear instructions to remember him after he returned to Pharaoh's court, "Yet did not the chief butler remember Joseph, but <u>forgat</u> him" (Gen. 40:23). The chief butler forgot Joseph not by chance but by choice. The Word *forget/forgat/forgot* is mentioned in 64 verses of the Bible.

Joseph Attempts to Restore Fellowship with His Half-Brothers

"And Joseph said unto his brethren, I am Joseph; doth my father yet live? And <u>his brethren could not answer him</u>; <u>for they were</u> <u>troubled</u> at <u>his presence</u>. And Joseph said unto his brethren, Come near to me, I pray you. And they came near. And he said, I am Joseph your brother, whom ye sold into Egypt. Now therefore be not grieved, nor angry with yourselves, that ye sold me hither: for God did send me before you to preserve life" (Gen. 45:3-5). Joseph had to plead with his half-brothers to draw closer to him. The Old Testament combination *his brethren could* (1x), *not answer him* (1x), *for they were troubled* (1x), *troubled* (45x), *his presence* (16x) = 64.

Half-Brothers Still Influenced by Their Sin of Broken Fellowship

"And when Joseph's brethren saw that their father was dead, they said, Joseph will peradventure hate us, and will certainly requite us all the evil which we did unto him. And they sent a messenger unto Joseph, saying, Thy father did command before he died, saying, So shall ye say unto Joseph, Forgive, I pray thee now, the trespass of thy brethren, and their sin; for they did unto thee evil: and now, we pray thee, forgive the trespass of the servants of the God of thy father. . . . And his brethren also went and fell down before his face; and they said, Behold, we be thy servants" (Gen. 50:15-18).

> The word *sin* is mentioned in 64 verses of the OT Narrative.
> The phrase *the sin* is mentioned in 64 verses of the Bible.
> The word *sins* is mentioned naturally in 164 verses of the Bible.

Egypt Breaks Longstanding Fellowship with Israel

"Now there arose up a new king over Egypt, which knew not Joseph. And he said unto his people, Behold, the people of the children of Israel are more and mightier than we: Come on, let us deal wisely with them; lest they multiply, and it come to pass, that, when there falleth out any war, they join also unto our enemies, and fight against us, and so get them up out of the land. Therefore they did set over them taskmasters to afflict them with their burdens" (Exod. 1:8-11a). The phrase *the people* is mentioned in 164 verses of the New Testament. From Genesis to the NT Narrative the word *fight* is mentioned in 64 chapters.

> The name *Israel* occurs 364 times in First/Second Kings.
> The phrase *of Israel* 64 times in Isaiah.

1564th Verse of the Bible

"And Pharaoh's daughter said unto her, Take this child away, and nurse it for me, and I will give thee thy wages. And the woman took the child, and nursed it" (Exod. 2:9). In this 64th verse, a mother who had just tearfully undergone a broken fellowship with her baby boy found it suddenly rekindled, albeit temporarily. Again the phrase *the child* is mentioned in 64 verses of the Bible.

Jochebed's Permanently Broken Fellowship with Her Little Boy

"And the child grew, and she brought him unto Pharaoh's daughter, and he became her son. And she called his name Moses: and she said, Because I drew him out of the water" (Exod. 2:10). Again the phrase *the child* is mentioned in 64 verses of the Bible.

Moses Breaks Fellowship with the Egyptians

"And it came to pass in those days, when Moses was grown, that he went out unto his brethren, and looked on their burdens: and he spied an Egyptian smiting an Hebrew, one of his brethren. And he looked this way and that way, and when he saw that there was no man, he slew the Egyptian, and hid him in the sand" (Exod. 2:11-12). It was on this particular day that Moses went out with a new favorable view of the Hebrews and a subsequent unfavorable view of the Egyptians. The Bible combination *in those days* (61x), *when Moses was grown* (1x), *that he went out unto his brethren* (1x), *and looked on their burdens* (1x) = 64.

Broken Fellowship between Two Hebrews

"And when he went out the second day, behold, two men of the Hebrews strove together: and he said to him that did the wrong, Wherefore smitest thou thy FELLOW?" (Exod. 2:13) The Bible combination *two men* (21x), *of the family of the* (5x), *Hebrews* (20x), *strove* (13x), *wherefore dost thou* (2x), *smitest thou* (2x), *thy fellow* (1x) = 64. The word *thy* is the 364th word in this chapter, and it concerns a fellow whom he was no longer in fellowship with.

64th Chapter of the Bible

This chapter closes out a long saga between two nations who had originally entered into a peaceful coexistence and somewhat marginalized fellowship with each other. Here in this chapter, some four hundred years later, Egypt is very protagonistic as she chases after her former Hebrew neighbors. Whereas these two nations were once neighbors, they are now notorious enemies. Their broken fellowship will become irreconcilable after God drowns the Egyptian army in the sea.

"And it was told the king of Egypt that <u>the people</u> <u>fled</u>: and the <u>heart</u> of Pharaoh and of his servants was <u>TURNED</u> <u>AGAINST</u> <u>the people</u>, and they said, Why have we done this, that we have let Israel go from serving us?" (Exod. 14:5) Here the narrative reveals a great change of heart in the house of Egypt. Just a day or two before the Egyptians had come to favor the Hebrews enough to lend them such things as they desired. Again the phrase *the people* is mentioned in 164 verses of the New Testament. Again the word *heart* is mentioned in 664 verses of the Old Testament. The word *turned* is mentioned in 64 chapters of the OT Narrative. Again the word *against* occurs 164 times in the Wisdom Books.

"And he made ready his chariot, and took his people with him: And he took six hundred chosen chariots, and all the chariots of Egypt, and captains over every one of them. And the LORD hardened the heart of Pharaoh king of Egypt, and he pursued after the children of Israel" (vv. 6-7). God intended for this fellowship of nations to remain broken apart for ages to come.

When the Hebrews saw the Egyptian army drawing close they were filled with fright and cried out to the Lord. They also cried out to Moses, "Is not this the word that we did tell thee in Egypt, saying, Let us alone, that we may serve the Egyptians? For it had been better for us to serve the Egyptians, than that we should die in the wilderness" (v. 12). Here the Hebrews break fellowship with Moses for the first time since he delivered them from their house of bondage.

After crossing the Red Sea on dry land and seeing it crash down upon the Egyptians, the Hebrews know that God has completely broken the strange fellowship between their two co-existing nations. "Thus the LORD saved Israel that day out of the hand of the Egyptians; and Israel saw the Egyptians dead upon the sea shore. And <u>Israel</u> saw that great work which the LORD did upon the Egyptians: and the people feared the LORD, and believed the LORD, and his servant Moses" (vv. 30-31). Again the name *Israel* occurs 364 times in First and Second Kings.

Fearful Existence of Broken Fellowship with God

"And all <u>the people</u> saw the thunderings, and the lightnings, and the noise of the trumpet, and the mountain smoking: and when the people saw it, they removed, and stood <u>afar off</u>. And they said unto Moses, Speak thou with us, and we will hear: but let not God speak with us, lest we die. And Moses said unto <u>the people</u>, Fear not: for God is come to prove you, and that his fear may be before your faces, that ye sin not. And <u>the people</u> stood <u>afar off</u>, and Moses drew near unto the thick darkness where God was" (Exod. 20:18-21). Again the phrase *the people* is mentioned in 164 verses of the New Testament. The phrase *far from* is mentioned in 64 verses of the Bible.

Broken Fellowship between Parents & Son

"And <u>he that curseth</u> <u>his father</u>, or <u>his mother</u>, shall surely be put to death" (Exod. 21:17). The Genesis combination *curse* (4x), *his father* (60x) = 64. The Old Testament combination *he that curseth* (2x), *his mother* (62x) = 64.

Broken Fellowship between Master & Servant

"And <u>if</u> a man smite the eye of his servant, or the eye of his maid, that it perish; he shall let him go free for his eye's sake" (Exod. 21:26). A master and servant are not equals or fellows, but they can exist in a state of fellowship and coexistence by living under the Lord's safekeeping guidelines. Here the word *if* is the 54,164th word of the Bible, and it refers to the broken-down fellowship between a master and his servant.

The Cherubim-Adorned Vail:
A Symbol of Humanity's Broken Fellowship with God

"And thou shalt make a vail of blue, and purple, and scarlet, and fine twined linen of cunning work: with <u>cherubims</u> shall it be made" (Exod. 26:31). In giving Moses the details on constructing the Tabernacle, God told him to create a massive curtain so there may be a safe separation between God and man. Moses was instructed to adorn the vail with cherubs. This was not purely for ornamental reasons; it was to remind Israel of man's great fall from holiness back in the Garden of God, a time when He was forced to put Adam and Eve outside the green sanctuary and block their way back in with cherubs and a flaming sword. From these two accounts we may surmise that cherubs signify God's guarded presence. The title *cherubims* occurs 64 times in Scripture.

The People Break Religious Fellowship with God

"And all <u>the people</u> brake off the golden earrings which were in their ears, and brought them unto Aaron. And he received them at their hand, and fashioned it with a graving tool, after he had made it a molten calf: and they said, These be thy gods, O <u>Israel</u>, which brought thee up out of the land of Egypt. And when Aaron saw it, he built an altar before it; and Aaron made proclamation, and said, To morrow is a feast to the LORD" (Exod. 32:3-5). Again the phrase *the people* is mentioned in 164 verses of the New Testament. Again the name *Israel* occurs 364 times in First and Second Kings.

Broken Fellowship Results in the Tabernacle's Removal

"And Moses took the tabernacle, and pitched it <u>without</u> <u>the camp</u>, <u>afar</u> off <u>from</u> the camp, and called it <u>the Tabernacle of the congregation</u>. And it came to pass, that every one which sought the LORD went out unto <u>the tabernacle of the congregation</u>, which was without the camp" (Exod. 33:7). The word *without* is mentioned in 64 verses of the Major Prophets. The Wisdom Books combination *without* (63x), *the camp* (1x) = 64. Again the phrase *far from* is mentioned in 64 verses of the Bible. The title *the tabernacle of the congregation* occurs 64 times in the paired law-giving books Exodus and Leviticus.

> The word *from* is mentioned in 64 verses of First Kings.
> The word *from* is mentioned in 64 verses of Ezra/Nehemiah.

An Offering to God Restores Broken Fellowship

"And the LORD called unto Moses, and spake unto him out of the tabernacle of the congregation, saying, Speak unto the children of Israel, and say unto them, <u>If any man of you</u> <u>bring</u> <u>an offering</u> unto the LORD, ye shall bring your <u>offering</u> of the cattle, even of the herd, and of the flock" (Lev. 1:1-2). Leviticus is about man's approach to God for man must come to God in a proper way. God welcomes fellowship with man, but man must first present God with a blood offering to atone for his sin and thereby alleviate any past or ongoing offenses toward God. The Leviticus combination *if any man of you* (1x), *bring* (63x) = 64.

> The term *an offering* occurs 64 times in the Old Testament.
> The word *offering* is mentioned in 64 verses of the OTN.

Salt a Covenant Symbol of Unbroken Fellowship

"And every oblation of thy meat offering shalt thou season with salt; neither shalt thou suffer the salt <u>of the covenant</u> of thy God to be lacking from thy meat offering: with all thine offerings thou shalt offer salt" (Lev. 2:13). This command was given to prevent a broken fellowship from occurring. The Near East custom of eating salt together was the bond of friendship. Neither could ever do the other harm from that time forward. The phrase *of the covenant* is mentioned in 64 verses of the Bible.

64th Verse of Leviticus

"When <u>the sin</u>, which they have <u>sinned against</u> it, is known, then the congregation shall offer a young bullock for <u>the sin</u>, and bring him before the tabernacle of the congregation" (Lev. 4:14). This was one of the sanctioned sin offerings for a priest who may have committed sin. The leading cause of broken fellowship with God is sin. Broken fellowship with God could only be restored through proper blood sacrifice, thus God gave all the necessary details. Again the phrase *the sin* is mentioned in 64 verses of the Bible. All tenses of *sin against* are mentioned in 64 verses of the Bible.

Priestly Atonement for Sin Restores Broken Fellowship

"And he shall burn all his fat upon the altar, as the fat of the sacrifice of peace offerings: and <u>the priest</u> shall make <u>an atonement</u> <u>for him as concerning his sin</u>, and it shall be forgiven him" (Lev. 4:26). The sinner could never directly approach God. The sanctified priest had to do this on his behalf to restore the sinner's broken fellowship with God. The title *the priest* occurs naturally 364 times in the Old Testament. The Law combination *an atonement* (62x), *for him as concerning/touching his sin* (2x) = 64.

Neighbor Breaks Fellowship with His Neighbor

"If a soul sin, and commit a trespass against the LORD, and lie unto <u>his neighbour</u> in that which was delivered him to keep, or in FELLOWSHIP, or in a thing taken away by violence, or hath deceived <u>his neighbour</u>" (Lev. 6:2). The phrase *his neighbor* occurs 64 times in the Old Testament!

Leper Endures Broken Fellowship with the Community

"When a man shall have in the skin of his flesh a rising, a scab, or bright spot, and it be in the skin of his flesh like <u>the plague</u> of <u>leprosy</u>; then he shall be brought unto Aaron the priest, or unto one of his sons the priests. . . . And if . . . He is a <u>leprous</u> man, he is unclean: the priest shall pronounce him utterly unclean; his plague is in his head. . . . All the days wherein the plague shall be in him he shall be defiled; he is unclean: <u>he shall dwell alone</u>; <u>without the</u>

camp shall his habitation be" (Lev. 13:2, 42a, 44, 46).

Until a leper was fully cleansed his fellowship with the community was entirely severed. All forms of the word leper show the seal of broken fellowship in the following delineated way: *leper* (16 vs), *lepers* (6 vs), *leprosy* (37 vs), *leprous* (5 vs) = 64 verses. The Law combination *the plague* (63x) and *he shall dwell alone* (1x) = 64. Again the word *without* is mentioned in 64 verses of the Major Prophets. Again the Wisdom Books combination *without* (63x), *the camp* (1x) = 64.

Strangers Endure Broken Fellowship with a Host Nation

"And if a stranger sojourn with thee in your land, ye shall not vex him. But the stranger that dwelleth with you shall be unto you as one born among you, and thou shalt love him as thyself; for ye were strangers in the land of Egypt: I am the LORD your God" (Lev. 19:33-34). The word *strangers* occurs 64 times in the Old Testament.

Slaves & Servants Reunite with Their Families

"And ye shall hallow the fiftieth year, and proclaim liberty throughout all the land unto all the inhabitants thereof: it shall be a jubile unto you; and ye shall return every man unto his possession, and ye shall return every man unto his family" (Lev. 25:10). Poor and indebted families routinely suffered broken fellowship when one or more family members were made to serve a creditor until their debt was paid off. The Law combination *every man* (63x), *unto his family* (1x) = 64.

Breaking Covenant with God

"And if ye shall despise my statutes, or if your soul abhor my judgments, so that ye will not do all my commandments, but that ye BREAK my covenant" (Lev. 26:15). Again all available tenses of the keyword *break* are mentioned in 64 verses of the Major Prophets.

3564th Verse of the Bible

"And they that are left of you shall pine away in their iniquity in your enemies' lands; and also in the iniquities of their fathers shall they pine away with them. If they shall confess their iniquity, and the iniquity of their fathers, with their trespass which they trespassed against me . . . Then will I remember my covenant with Jacob, and also my covenant with Isaac, and also my covenant with Abraham will I remember; and I will remember the land" (Lev. 26:39-40a, 42). The underlined verse indicates the 3564th verse of the Bible, and it describes the tragic results of breaking fellowship with God.

3764th Verse of the Bible

"Cut ye not off the tribe of the families of the Kohathites from among the Levites: But thus do unto them, that they may live, and not die, when they approach unto the most holy things: Aaron and his sons shall go in, and appoint them every one to his service and to his burden: But they shall not go in to see when the holy things are covered, lest they die" (Num. 4:18-20). The underlined verse indicates the 3764th verse of the Bible, and it is an injunction to prevent these particular workers from accidentally breaking fellowship with God.

Trespassing against the Lord

"Speak unto the children of Israel, When a man or woman shall commit any sin that men commit, to do a <u>trespass</u> <u>against the LORD</u>, and that person be guilty" (Num. 5:6). The Law combination *trespass* (45x), *against the LORD* (19x) = 64.

Numbers 7:64

"One kid of the goats for <u>a sin offering</u>" (Num. 7:64). The smallest of sins sever man's fellowship with God, but a sin offering allows the repentant sinner to come back into a harmonious relationship with God. The phrase *a sin offering* occurs 64 times in the Bible. The Bible combination *atonement* (33 chs) and *sin offering* (31 chs) = 64 chapters.

Levites Undergo Needful Broken Fellowship with the Other Tribes

"Take the Levites from among the children of Israel, and cleanse them" (Num. 8:6). The Levites routinely experienced broken fellowship with the other tribes as they had to keep themselves separate and ceremonially pure at all times.

> The name *Levi* occurs 64 times in the Old Testament.
> The title *Levites* occurs 264 times in the Old Testament.
> The title *Levites* is mentioned in 164 verses of OT Narrative.

4064th Verse of the Bible

"And the LORD spake suddenly unto Moses, and unto Aaron, and unto Miriam, Come out ye three unto the tabernacle of the congregation. And they three came out" (Num. 12:4). Moses' brother and sister had broken fellowship with him over the issue his sole leadership. They had entered into strife with him.

Broken Commandments = Broken Fellowship

"<u>Because he hath despised the word of the LORD</u>, and <u>hath BROKEN his commandment</u>, that soul shall utterly be cut off; his iniquity shall be upon him" (Num. 15:31). The joined phrases *because he hath despised the word of the LORD, and hath broken his commandment* consist of 64 letters! The Law combination *hath broken his* (1x), *commandments* (63x) = 64. The word *commandment* occurs 64 times in the OT Narrative.

Edomites' Broken Fellowship with the Jacobites

"And he said, Thou shalt not go through. And Edom came out against him with much people, and with a strong hand. Thus Edom refused to give Israel passage through his border: wherefore Israel <u>turned</u> <u>away</u> <u>from him</u>" (Num. 20:20-21). Edom's broken fellowship with the Jacobites goes all the way back to their founding father Esau. Again the word *turned* is mentioned in 64 chapters of the OT Narrative. Again the word *away* is mentioned in 64 chapters of the Law. Again the word *from* is mentioned in 64 verses of First Kings. The phrase *from him* is mentioned naturally in 64 chapters of the Old Testament.

Numbers 26:64

"But among these there was not a man of them whom Moses and Aaron the priest numbered, <u>when they numbered</u> <u>the children of Israel</u> in <u>the wilderness</u> of Sinai. For the LORD had said of them, They shall surely die in the wilderness. And there was not left a man of them, save Caleb the son of Jephunneh, and Joshua the son of Nun" (Num. 26:64-65). Israel's fellowship with God became broken when they refused to enter Canaan, the gracious inheritance He had granted them. The phrase *that were numbered* is mentioned in 64 verses of Numbers. The Bible combination *when they numbered* (1x), *of the children of Israel* (163x) = 164. The phrase *the wilderness* is mentioned in 264 verses of the Bible.

Wilderness Generation Breaks Fellowship in the Sight of the Lord

"And the LORD'S anger was kindled against Israel, and he made them wander in the wilderness forty years, until all the generation, that had done evil <u>in the sight of the LORD</u>, was consumed" (Num. 32:13). The Lord never loses sight of us, but broken fellowship on our part is exemplified by us losing sight of Him. The phrase *in the sight of the LORD* occurs 64 times in the Bible.

Lest the New Generation Forgets God & Breaks Fellowship

"Only take heed to thyself, and keep thy soul diligently, <u>lest</u> thou <u>forget</u> the things which thine eyes have seen, and <u>lest</u> they depart <u>from</u> thy heart all the days of thy life: but teach them thy sons, and thy sons' sons" (Deut. 4:9). The word *lest* is mentioned in 64 verses of the Law. All forms of the present-tense word *forget* are mentioned in 64 verses of the Bible. Again the word *from* is mentioned in 64 verses of Ezra and Nehemiah.

5064ᵗʰ Verse of the Bible

"Thou shalt not take the name of the LORD thy God in vain: for the LORD will not hold him guiltless that taketh his name in vain" (Deut. 5:11). A person who has broken fellowship with the Lord finds it not difficult to routinely misuse the Lord's name.

"Get You into Your Tents Again!"

Moses recalls God's lamentation regarding the broken fellowship He suffered with Israel at Mount Sinai when they urgently requested that He not speak directly to them but instead through Moses. "O that there were such an heart in them, that they would fear me, and keep all my commandments always, that it might be well with them, and with their children for ever! Go say to them, Get you into your <u>tents</u> again" (Deut. 5:29-30). The word *tents* is mentioned in 64 verses of the Bible.

264ᵗʰ Verse of Deuteronomy

"And it shall be, if thou do at all <u>forget</u> the LORD thy God, and walk after other gods, and serve them, and worship them, I testify against you this day that ye shall surely perish" (Deut. 8:19). Moses warns the new generation what will happen if they break fellowship with the Lord in the land of their inheritance. Again all forms of the present-tense word *forget* are mentioned in 64 verses of the Bible.

5164ᵗʰ Verse of the Bible

"Understand therefore, that the LORD thy God giveth thee not this good land to possess it for thy righteousness; for thou art a stiffnecked <u>people</u>" (Deut. 9:6). Moses reminds Israel that they are prone to breaking fellowship with the Lord. Again the phrase *the people* is mentioned in 164 verses of the New Testament.

564ᵗʰ Verse of Deuteronomy

"So shalt thou put away the guilt of innocent blood from among you, when thou shalt do that which is right <u>in the sight of the LORD</u>" (Deut. 21:9). The elders of a city were to perform a special ritual which would absolve that city from guilt of an anonymously slain person. Otherwise, by their omission, they will be breaking fellowship with the Holy One. Again the phrase *in the sight of the LORD* occurs 64 times in the Bible.

5464th Verse of the Bible

"Then it shall be, when he maketh his sons to inherit that which he hath, that he may not make the son of the beloved firstborn before the son of the hated, which is indeed the <u>firstborn</u>" (Deut. 21:16). A father must not break fellowship with his true firstborn son by giving his inheritance to the other firstborn son.

> The word *firstborn* occurs 64 times in the Law.
> The phrase *the firstborn* appears in 64 verses of Old Testament.

Thy Brother's Ox

"Thou shalt not see thy brother's <u>ox</u> or his sheep go astray, and hide thyself from them: thou shalt in any case bring them again unto thy brother. . . . Thou shalt not see thy brother's ass or his <u>ox</u> fall down by the way, and hide thyself from them: thou shalt surely help him to lift them up again" (Deut. 22:1, 4). Not to care for a fellow countryman's needy animal was to exemplify an existing broken fellowship with him. The word *ox* occurs 64 times in the Bible.

Broken Fellowship Evidenced by Loss of Favor

"When a man hath taken a wife, and married her, and it come to pass that she find no <u>favour</u> in his eyes, because he hath found some uncleanness in her: then let him write her a bill of divorcement, and give it in her hand, and send her out of his house" (Deut. 24:1). The word *favour* occurs 64 times in the Old Testament.

664th Verse of Deuteronomy

"<u>Then shall his brother's</u> <u>wife</u> come unto him in the presence of the elders, and loose his shoe from off his foot, and spit in his face, and shall answer and say, So shall it be done unto that man that will not build up his brother's house" (Deut. 25:9). A brother who will not help his deceased brother is one who has broken fellowship with him already, likely long ago. The Bible combination *then shall his brother's* (1 ch), *wife* (163 chs) = 164 chapters.

Deuteronomy 28:64

"And the LORD shall scatter thee among all people, from the one end of the earth even unto the other; and there thou shalt serve other gods, which neither thou nor thy fathers have known, even wood and stone" (Deut. 28:64). As continued punishment for Israel's broken fellowship and failure to repent, another sobering reward would come the nation's way—worldwide scattering.

Forsaking God & Breaking His Covenant

"And the LORD said unto Moses, Behold, thou shalt sleep with thy fathers; and this people will rise up, and go a whoring after the gods of the strangers of the land, whither they go to be among them, and will <u>forsake</u> me, and <u>BREAK my covenant</u> which I have made with them" (Deut. 31:16). The Bible combination *forsake* (57 vs) and *break my covenant* (7 vs) = 64 verses.

Two and a Half Tribes on the Other Side of Jordan

"For Moses had given the inheritance of two tribes and an half tribe on <u>the other side</u> Jordan"

(Josh. 14:3). Two and a half tribes had requested land on the other side of Jordan. Such a geographical divide could over time engender broken fellowship with the other tribes; on one occasion it almost did. The term "the other side" can be applied to mean on the opposing side. The phrase *the other side* occurs 64 times in Scripture.

The Schismatic Altar

"Then the children of Reuben and the children of Gad and the half tribe of Manasseh answered, and said unto the heads of the thousands of Israel . . . For the LORD hath made Jordan a border between us and you, ye children of Reuben and children of Gad; ye have NO PART in the LORD: so shall your children make our children cease from fearing the LORD. Therefore we said, Let us now prepare to build us an altar, not for burnt offering, nor for sacrifice: But that it may be a witness between us, and you, and our generations after us, that we might do the service of the LORD before him with our burnt offerings, and with our sacrifices, and with our peace offerings; that your children may not say to our children in time to come, Ye have NO PART in the LORD" (Josh. 22:21, 25-27).

This incident temporarily created a broken fellowship between the two and a half tribes and the nine and a half tribes. The very reason why the two and a half tribes had built this memorial altar was to prevent any possible future broken fellowship with the Lord. Borders have a tendency to break up unity. The phrase *the border of* occurs 64 times in the Bible.

The Angel of the Lord's Oath of Unbroken Fellowship

"And an angel of the LORD came up from Gilgal to Bochim, and said, I made you to go up out of Egypt, and have brought you unto the land which I sware unto your fathers; and I said, I will never BREAK my covenant with you" (Judg. 2:1). A broken covenant results in broken fellowship between the two covenant partners. The title *angel of the LORD/Lord* is mentioned in 64 verses of the Bible.

The Promised Land Generation's
Broken Fellowship in the Sight of the Lord

"And the children of Israel did evil in the sight of the LORD, and served Baalim" (Judg. 2:11). Again the phrase *in the sight of the LORD* occurs 64 times in the Bible. The joined phrases *and the children of Israel did evil in the sight of the LORD, and served Baalim* consist of 64 characters!

Baal Worship

"And they forsook the LORD, and served Baal and Ashtaroth" (Judg. 2:13). From the beginning Israel's descent into Baal worship caused a breach of fellowship with the Lord. The present-tense words *forsake* (58x) and *forsaketh* (6x) = 64. The name *Baal('s)* occurs 64 times in the Bible.

64th Verse of Judges

"And the children of Israel dwelt among the Canaanites, Hittites, and Amorites, and Perizzites, and Hivites, and Jebusites: And they took their daughters to be their wives, and gave their daughters to their sons, and served their gods" (Judg. 3:5-6). Israel broke close fellowship with God as they chose instead to begin new fellowships with their heathen neighbors. The Bible names *Canaanites* (11 bks), *Hittites* (11 bks), *Amorites* (14 bks), *Perizzites* (9 bks), *Hivites* (7 bks), *Jebusites* (12 bks) = 64 books.

Every Man against His Fellow

"And the three hundred blew the trumpets, and the LORD set <u>every man's</u> <u>sword against his</u> <u>FELLOW</u>, even throughout all the host: and the host fled to Beth-shittah in Zererath, and to the border of Abel-meholah, unto Tabbath" (Judg. 7:22). The Midianites were smitten with a supernatural broken fellowship whereby every man suddenly turned against fellow soldier. The Law combination *every man* (63x) and *smitest thou thy fellow* (1x) = 64.

Levite Man's Marital Partner Breaks Fellowship with Him

"And his concubine played the whore against him, and went away from him <u>unto her father's</u> <u>house</u> to Beth-lehem-judah, and was there four whole months. And her husband arose, and went after her, to speak friendly unto her, and to bring her again" (Judg. 19:2-3b). A concubine held the rights of legal marriage to a man, but her status remained that of a second-class wife. The Judges combination *and his* (34x), *concubine* (12x), *played* (1x), *the whore* (1x), *against him* (8x), *and went away* (3x), *from him* (4x), *unto her father's house* (1x) = 64.

Men of Israel against the Benjamites

"And the <u>men of Israel</u> turned again upon the children of Benjamin, and smote them with the edge of the sword, as well the men of every city, as the beast, and all that came to hand: also they set on fire all the cities that they came to" (Judg. 20:48). Because of Benjamin's great evil, fellowship became greatly broken between the northern tribes. The title *men of Israel* occurs 64 times in the Bible.

64th Verse of Ruth

"Then went Boaz up to the gate, and sat him down there: and, behold, the kinsman of whom Boaz spake came by; unto whom he said, Ho, such a one! turn aside, sit down here. And he turned aside, and sat down" (Ruth 4:1). On this day the unnamed kinsman of Naomi broke family fellowship with her and her daughter-in-law Ruth when he refused to perform the family custom concerning a dead brother. This man's name could never again be audibly spoken anywhere or at any time. From that day forward he would only be referred to as "the house of him that hath his shoe loosed" (Deut. 25:10).

Hannah's Broken Fellowship with Little Samuel

"And when she had weaned him, she took him up with her . . . and brought him unto the house of the LORD in Shiloh: and <u>the child</u> was young . . . and brought <u>the child</u> to Eli. And she said, Oh my lord, as thy soul liveth, my lord, I am the woman that stood by thee here, praying unto the LORD. For this child I prayed; and the LORD hath given me my petition which I asked of him: Therefore also I have lent him to the LORD; as long as he liveth he shall be lent to the LORD" (1 Sam. 1:24-28a).

After three wonderful, intimate years this mother and child underwent a broken fellowship. Again the phrase *the child* is mentioned in 64 verses of the Bible.

Hannah's Broken Fellowship Softened by a Yearly Visit

"Moreover <u>his mother</u> <u>made him a little coat,</u> <u>and brought it to him from year to year,</u> when she came up with her husband to offer the yearly sacrifice" (1 Sam. 2:19). The Old Testament combination *his mother* (62x), *made him a little coat* (1x), *and brought it to him from year to year* (1x) = 64.

Broken Fellowship Between Eli's House & God

"And the LORD said to Samuel, Behold, I will do a thing in Israel, at which both the ears of every one that heareth it shall tingle. In that day I will perform against <u>Eli</u> all things which I have spoken concerning his house: when I begin, I will also make an end. For I have told him that I will judge his house for ever for the iniquity which he knoweth; because his sons made themselves vile, and he restrained them not. And therefore I have sworn unto the house of <u>Eli</u>, that the iniquity of <u>Eli's</u> house shall not be purged with sacrifice nor offering for ever" (1 Sam. 3:11-12).

Eli's priestly dynasty fits our third definition of fellowship: an association. Again the title *the priest* occurs naturally 364 times in the Old Testament.

The Glory of God Departs from Israel

"And the Philistines fought, and Israel was smitten, and they fled every man into his tent: and there was a very great slaughter; for there fell of Israel thirty thousand footmen. And the ark of God was taken. . . . And she said, The glory is departed <u>from</u> Israel: for the ark of God is taken" (1 Sam. 4:10-11a, 22). The Ark symbolized God's presence. Because it was no longer in the Israelites' camp they were made to feel the broken fellowship between them and God. Again the word *from* is mentioned in 64 verses of First Kings.

164th Verse of First Samuel

"And the LORD said unto Samuel, Hearken unto the voice of <u>the people</u> in all that they say unto thee: for they have not rejected thee, but they have rejected me, that I should not reign over them" (1 Sam. 8:7). Israel was officially breaking fellowship with the Lord by their request for a different king. Again the phrase *the people* is mentioned in 164 verses of the New Testament.

Broken Fellowship between Daughters & Parents

"And he will take your <u>daughters</u> to be confectionaries, and to be cooks, and to be bakers" (1 Sam. 8:13). Broken fellowship between parents and their daughter typically occurs when they give her away in marriage. Here daughters would be summoned to work in the king's court, thus creating a long-term broken fellowship them and their parents. The word *daughters* occurs 64 times in the OT Narrative.

264th Verse of First Samuel

"<u>Now therefore stand and see this great thing, which the LORD will do before your eyes.</u> Is it not wheat harvest to day? I will call unto the LORD, and he shall send thunder and rain; that ye may perceive and see that your wickedness is great, which ye have done in the sight of the LORD, in asking you a king" (1 Sam. 12:16-17). The underlined verse indicates the 264th verse of the Bible, and it refers to a heavenly sign of Israel's broken fellowship with the Lord.

Philistine Fellows Violently Break Fellowship with One Another

For Israel's benefit God did a miracle that day. "And Saul and all the people that were with him assembled themselves, <u>and they came to the battle: and, behold, every man's sword was against his FELLOW</u>, and there was a very great discomfiture" (1 Sam. 14:20). The joined phrases *and they came to the battle: and, behold, every man's sword was against his fellow* consists of 64 letters!

Saul Break Fellowship with David in an Inward Way

"And Saul was very wroth, and the saying displeased <u>him</u>; and he said, They have ascribed unto David ten thousands, and to me they have ascribed but thousands: and what can he have more but the kingdom? And Saul eyed David from that day and forward" (1 Sam. 18:8-9). The word *him* is the 211,564th word of the Bible, and it refers to a king who decided to break fellowship with his champion fighter, chief army officer, and chief musician.

Saul Breaks Fellowship with David in a Recognizable Way

"And Saul was afraid of David, because the LORD was with him, and was departed from Saul. <u>Therefore Saul removed him from him, and made him his captain over a thousand</u>" (1 Sam. 18:13b). The joined phrases Therefore *Saul removed him from him, and made him his captain over a thousand* consist of 64 characters!

Saul's Broken Fellowship with David Becomes Permanent

"And Saul saw and knew that the LORD was with David. . . . And Saul was yet the more afraid of David; and Saul became <u>David's enemy</u> <u>continually</u>" (1 Sam. 18:28-29). How dreadful it is when one's friend breaks fellowship with him and then becomes his foe. The Bible combination *David's enemy* (1 ch), *continually* (63 chs) = 64 chapters. The name *David('s)* occurs a combined 264 times in First and Second Chronicles.

Saul's Broken Fellowship with His Son Jonathan

"Then Saul's <u>anger was kindled against</u> <u>Jonathan</u>, and he said unto him, <u>Thou son of the perverse rebellious woman</u>, do not I know that thou hast chosen the son of Jesse to thine own confusion" (1 Sam. 20:30a-c). After Jonathan suffered this public shame his relationship with his father was severely broken. The First Samuel combination *then Saul's* (1 v), *anger was kindled against* (2x), *Jonathan* (60 vs), *thou son of the perverse rebellious woman* (1 v) = 64 verses.

7764th Verse of the Bible

"And Saul cast a javelin at him to smite him: whereby Jonathan knew that it was determined of his father to slay David" (1 Sam. 20:33). This 64th verse reveals a severely broken family fellowship between father and son.

Saul Confesses to His Broken Fellowship with David

"Then said Saul, I have sinned: return, my son David: for I will no more do thee harm, because my soul was precious in thine eyes this day: behold, <u>I have</u> played the fool, and have erred exceedingly" (1 Sam. 26:21). The phrase *I have* occurs 864 times in the Old Testament.

264th Chapter of the Bible

This chapter is full of broken fellowships. Because David was put out of kingdom fellowship by Saul he went and joined affinity with the king of Gath. "And David said to Achish, Surely thou shalt know what thy servant can do. And Achish said to David, Therefore will I make thee keeper of mine head for ever" (1 Sam. 28:2).

Next we are reminded that the Israelite kingdom had suffered from broken fellowship with its most revered prophet. "Now Samuel was <u>dead</u>, and all Israel had lamented him, and buried him in Ramah, even in his own city" (v. 3a). Again the word *dead* occurs 364 times in the Bible.

Next the narrative reveals the negative results of Saul's broken fellowship with the Lord. The rift between them was so great that the Lord would not even give Saul military advice on Israel's behalf. "And when Saul saw the host of the Philistines, he was afraid, and his heart greatly trembled. And when Saul enquired of the LORD, the LORD answered him not, <u>neither</u> by dreams, nor by Urim, nor by prophets" (vv. 5-6). The word *neither* occurs naturally 164 times in the Law.

The bulk of this 264th chapter lays out a detailed story in which Saul tried to circumnavigate his broken relationship with the Lord by seeking divine counsel elsewhere. In the process he did something forbidden in the Law. He attempted to revive a broken fellowship with the nation's revered yet dead prophet by asking a witch to bring up his spirit from the dead. The witch succeeded in bringing up Samuel's spirit. When she did, Samuel lamented to Saul concerning his sudden broken fellowship with those righteous souls whom he was just resting with in paradise: "Why hast thou disquieted me, to bring me up?" (v. 15a) The last words the deceased prophet shared with Saul told of the king's forthcoming broken fellowship with all those in the land of the living: "to morrow shalt thou and thy sons be with me" (v. 19b). The 7964th verse of the Bible also occurs in this broken-fellowship chapter.

David Suffers Broken Fellowship with Jonathan

"Saul and Jonathan his son are <u>dead</u> also . . . And David lamented with this lamentation over Saul and over Jonathan. . . . O Jonathan, thou wast slain in thine high places. I am distressed for thee, my brother Jonathan: very pleasant hast thou been unto me: thy love to me was wonderful, passing the love of women. How are the mighty fallen, and the weapons of war perished!" (2 Sam. 1:4d, 17, 25b-27) Again the word *dead* occurs 364 times in the Bible.

Judah's Broken Fellowship with Israel

"Ish-bosheth Saul's son was forty years old when he began to reign over Israel, and reigned two years. But the house of <u>Judah</u> followed David" (2 Sam. 2:10).

The name *Judah* is mentioned in 264 chapters of the Bible.
The name *Judah* is mentioned in 164 verses of Jeremiah.

8064th Verse of the Bible

"And Abner said to Joab, Let the young men now arise, and play before us. And Joab said, Let them arise" (2 Sam. 2:14). This verse presents two warring factions who suffer broken fellowship on a national level—Israel and Judah.

Broken Fellowship Turns to Civil War

"Then there arose and went over by number twelve of Benjamin, which pertained to Ish-bosheth the son of Saul, and twelve of the servants of David. And they caught every one his FELLOW by the head, and thrust his sword in his FELLOW'S side; so they fell down together: wherefore that place was called Helkath-hazzurim, which is in Gibeon. And there was a very sore battle that day; and Abner was beaten, and the men of Israel, before the servants of David. . . . Then Abner called to Joab, and said, Shall the sword devour for ever? knowest thou not that it will be bitterness in the latter end? <u>how long</u> shall it be then, <u>ere thou bid the people return</u> <u>from following their brethren</u>?" (2 Sam. 2:15-17, 26)

Civil war between the northern and southern kingdoms erupted again after Saul's death. The Bible combination *how long* (61x), *shall it be then* (1x), *ere thou bid the people return* (1x), *from following their brethren* (1x) = 64.

Broken Fellowship Leads to Protracted Civil War

"Now there was long war <u>between the</u> house of Saul and the house of David: but David waxed stronger and stronger, and the house of Saul waxed weaker and weaker" (2 Sam. 3:1). Again the phrase *between the* is mentioned naturally in 64 verses of the Bible.

David & Michal Break Fellowship Permanently

"And as the ark of the LORD came into the city of David, Michal Saul's daughter looked through a window, and saw king David leaping and dancing before the LORD; and she despised him in her <u>heart</u>. . . . And Michal the daughter of Saul came out to meet David, and said, How glorious was the king of Israel to day, who uncovered himself to day in the eyes of the handmaids of his servants, as one of the vain fellows shamelessly uncovereth himself! And David said unto Michal . . . And I will yet be more vile than thus, and will be base in mine own sight: and of the maidservants which thou hast spoken of, of them shall I be had in honour. Therefore Michal the daughter of Saul had no child unto the day of her death" (2 Sam. 6:16, 20b-21a, 22-23).

Again the word *heart* is mentioned in 664 verses of the Old Testament. From Genesis to the NT Narrative the phrase *his wife* is mentioned in 64 chapters.

8264ᵗʰ Verse of the Bible

"<u>And David sent messengers, and took her; and she came in unto him, and he lay with her; for she was purified from her uncleanness: and she returned unto her house</u>" (2 Sam. 11:4). When David committed adultery he made the wife break the marital bonds of fellowship with her husband. The woman could have declined David's advance, but she refrained.

Absalom Pretends Not to Break Fellowship with Amnon

"And Absalom spake unto his brother Amnon neither good nor bad: <u>for Absalom</u> <u>hated</u> Amnon, because he had forced his sister Tamar. And it came to pass after two full years, that Absalom had sheepshearers in Baal-hazor, which is beside Ephraim: and Absalom invited all the king's sons. . . . Now Absalom had commanded his servants, saying, Mark ye now when Amnon's heart is merry with wine, and when I say unto you, Smite Amnon; then kill him, fear not: have not I commanded you? be courageous, and be valiant" (2 Sam. 13:22-23, 28).

Here the word *hated* is the 664ᵗʰ word in this chapter, and it refers to the broken fellowship which Absalom felt inwardly toward Amnon. The Bible combination *for Absalom* (4x), *hated* (60x) = 64.

8364ᵗʰ Verse of the Bible

"And, behold, the whole family is risen against thine handmaid, and they said, Deliver him that smote his brother, that we may <u>kill</u> him, for the life of his brother whom he slew; and we will destroy the heir also: and so they shall quench my coal which is left, and shall not leave to my husband neither name nor remainder upon the earth" (2 Sam. 14:7). Joab made a woman tell a story to King David of broken fellowship within her family. Again the word *killed* is mentioned in 64 verses of the Bible. This 8364ᵗʰ verse of the Bible pertains to a broken fellowship, and it consists of 64 words!

David Breaks Fellowship with Absalom

"And the king said unto Joab, Behold now, I have done this thing: go therefore, bring the young man Absalom again. . . . So Joab arose and went to Geshur, and brought Absalom to Jerusalem. And the king said, Let him turn to his own house, and let him not see <u>my face</u>. So Absalom returned to his own house, and saw not the king's face" (2 Sam. 14:21, 23-24). The phrase *my face* occurs 64 times in the Bible.

Absalom Breaks Fellowship with the House of Judah

"And it was so, that when any man came nigh to him to do him obeisance, he put forth his hand, and took him, and kissed him. And on this manner did Absalom to all Israel that came to the king for judgment: so Absalom stole the hearts of the men of Israel" (2 Sam. 15:5-6). Because Absalom was a prince of the house of Judah, this undermining action was a breach of fellowship with both his Judean tribe and royal house. Absalom's intentions were not to unite the two houses but rather to displace the house of Judah with an Israelite rule. Again the title *men of Israel* occurs 64 times in the Bible.

David Suffers Permanent Broken Fellowship with Absalom

"And the king was much moved, and went up to the chamber over the gate, and wept: and as he went, thus he said, O my son Absalom, my son, my son Absalom! would God I had died for thee, O Absalom, my son, my son!" (2 Sam. 18:33) The OT Narrative combination *O my son Absalom* (2x), *my son my son Absalom* (1x), *would God* (2x), *I had died for thee* (1x), *O Absalom* (2x), *my son* (56x) = 64.

Men of Israel Seek to Break Fellowship with Men of Judah

"And, behold, all the men of Israel came to the king, and said unto the king, Why have our brethren the men of Judah stolen thee away, and have brought the king, and his household, and all David's men with him, over Jordan? And all the men of Judah answered the men of Israel, Because the king is near of kin to us: wherefore then be ye angry for this matter? have we eaten at all of the king's cost? or hath he given us any gift? And the men of Israel answered the men of Judah, and said, We have ten parts in the king, and we have also more right in David than ye: why then did ye despise us, that our advice should not be first had in bringing back our king? And the words of the men of Judah were fiercer than the words of the men of Israel" (2 Sam. 19:41-43).

Just when things seems to be getting better between these two kingdoms the old strife began all over. The word *parts* occurs 64 times in the Bible. Again the title *men of Israel* occurs 64 times in the Bible.

Israel Temporarily Breaks Fellowship with Judah

"And there happened to be there a man of Belial, whose name was Sheba, the son of Bichri, a Benjamite: and he blew a trumpet, and said, We have NO PART in David, neither have we inheritance in the son of Jesse: every man to his tents, O Israel. So every man of Israel went up from after David, and followed Sheba the son of Bichri. . . . And David said to Abishai, Now shall Sheba the son of Bichri do us more harm than did Absalom: take thou thy lord's servants, and pursue after him, lest he get him fenced cities, and escape us. And there went out after him Joab's men, and the Cherethites, and the Pelethites, and all the mighty men: and they went out of Jerusalem, to pursue after Sheba the son of Bichri" (2 Sam. 20:1-2a, 6-7).

Again the word *from* is mentioned in 64 verses of First Kings.

First Kings 8:64

"The same day did the king hallow the middle of the court that was before the house of the LORD: for there he offered burnt offerings, and meat offerings, and the fat of the peace offerings: because the brasen altar that was before the LORD was too little to receive the burnt offerings, and meat <u>offerings</u>, and the fat of the peace <u>offerings</u>" (1 Kings 8:64). Solomon offered sacrifices on the nation's behalf and more than enough offerings to atone for any possible broken fellowship between the whole house of Israel and the Lord God. Again the word *offering* is mentioned in 64 verses of the OT Narrative.

464th Verse of First Kings

"And this thing became a sin: for <u>the people</u> went to worship before the one, even unto Dan" (1 Kings 12:30). The northern tribes broke fellowship with Jehovah when they worshiped the golden calves in honor of Baal. Again the phrase *the people* is mentioned in 164 verses of the New Testament.

Solomon Breaks Fellowship with the Lord

"For it came to pass, when Solomon was old, that his wives <u>turned</u> <u>away</u> his <u>heart</u> after other gods: and his <u>heart</u> was not perfect with the LORD his God, as was the heart of David his father. For Solomon went after Ashtoreth the goddess of the Zidonians, and after Milcom the abomination of the Ammonites. And Solomon did evil <u>in the sight of the LORD</u>, and went not fully after the LORD, as did David his father" (1 Kings 11:4-6). Again the word *turned* is mentioned in 64 chapters of the OT Narrative. Again the word *away* is mentioned in 64 chapters of the Law. Again the word *heart* is mentioned in 664 verses of the Old Testament. Again the phrase *in the sight of the LORD* occurs 64 times in the Bible.

Asa Seeks to Convince Ben-hadad to Break Fellowship with Baasha

"There is a league between me and thee, and between my father and thy father: behold, I have sent unto thee a present of silver and gold; <u>come and BREAK thy league with Baasha king of Israel, that he may depart from me</u>" (1 Kings 15:19). The First Kings combination *come and break thy* (1x), *league* (3x), *Baasha* (22x), *king of Israel* (38x) = 64. The sentence *come and break thy league with Baasha king of Israel, that he may depart from me* consists of 64 letters!

9564th Verse of the Bible

"And Elisha saw it, and he cried, My father, <u>my father,</u> <u>the chariot</u> of Israel, and <u>the horsemen</u> thereof. And he <u>saw him</u> <u>no more</u>: and he took hold of his own clothes, and <u>rent</u> <u>them in two pieces</u>" (2 Kings 2:12). Elisha tore his clothing into two pieces according to the Near East custom of grief and mourning, but this also stood as a token of the broken fellowship between him and his departed master. The lowercase phrase *my father* is mentioned in 64 verses of the OT Narrative. The New Testament combination *the chariot* (1x), *the horsemen* (2x), *saw him* (4x), *no more* (57x) = 64. The Bible combination *rent* (63 vs), *them in two pieces* (1 v) = 64 verses. The phrase *in pieces* is mentioned in 64 verses of the Old Testament.

Prophet's Wife Suffers Devastating Broken Fellowship

"Now there cried a certain woman of the wives of the sons of the prophets unto Elisha, saying, Thy servant my husband is <u>dead</u>; and thou knowest that thy servant did fear the LORD: and the creditor is come <u>to take</u> <u>unto him my two sons</u> to be bondmen" (2 Kings 4:1). Again the word *dead* occurs 364 times in the Bible. The Bible combination *to take* (63 chs), *unto him my two sons* (1 ch) = 64 chapters.

Hebrew Girl's Broken Fellowship with Her Parents

"And the Syrians had gone out by companies, and had <u>brought away</u> <u>captive</u> <u>out of the land of Israel</u> a little maid; and she waited on Naaman's wife" (2 Kings 5:2). The Bible combination *brought away* (3x), *captive* (59x), *out of the land of Israel* (2x) = 64.

Broken Fellowship between the Lord & His People Restored

"And Jehoiada made a covenant <u>between the</u> LORD and the king and <u>the people</u>, that they should be the LORD'S people" (2 Kings 11:17ab). Under Athaliah's wicked reign the people had not been able to properly worship the Lord. Thus the fellowship between God and His people had suffered a separation. Again the phrase *between the* is mentioned naturally in 64 verses of the Bible.

King Suffers Broken Fellowship with Dying Prophet

"Now Elisha was fallen sick of his sickness whereof he died. And Joash the king of Israel came down unto him, and wept over his face, and said, O <u>my father</u>, <u>my father</u>, the chariot of Israel, and the horsemen thereof" (2 Kings 13:14). Again the lowercase phrase *my father* is mentioned in 64 verses of the OT Narrative.

Israel Breaks Fellowship with Jehovah upon the Hills & High Places

God explained why Israel was carried away into captivity: "And they set them up images and groves in every high <u>hill</u>, and under every green tree: And there they burnt incense in all <u>the high places</u>, as did the heathen whom the LORD carried away before them; and wrought wicked things to provoke the LORD to anger" (2 Kings 17:10-11). The northern kingdom broke fellowship with God and chose for itself gods who could neither hear nor speak.

> The word *hill* is mentioned in 64 verses of the OT.
> The word *hills* occurs 64 times in the Old Testament.
> The term *the high places* occurs 64 times in the Bible.

Josiah Realizes Judah Has Broken Fellowship with the Lord

"And Hilkiah the high priest said unto Shaphan the scribe, I have found the book of the law in the house of the LORD. And Hilkiah gave the book to Shaphan. . . . And Shaphan read it before the king. And it came to pass, when the king had heard the words of the book of the law, that he rent his clothes. . . . Go ye, enquire of the LORD for me, and for the people, and for all <u>Judah</u>, concerning the words of this book that is found: for great is the wrath of the LORD that is kindled against us, because our fathers have not hearkened unto the words of this book, to do according unto all that which is written concerning us" (2 Kings 22:8, 10b-11, 13).

The Minor Prophets combination *Judah* (63x) and *break my covenant* (1x) = 64.

Josiah Reverses Judah's Broken Fellowship with the Lord

"And the king sent, and they gathered unto him all the elders of Judah and of Jerusalem. And the king . . . read in their ears all the words of the book <u>of the covenant</u> which was found in the house of the LORD. And the king stood by a pillar, and made a <u>covenant</u> before the LORD, to walk after the LORD, and <u>to keep</u> his commandments and his testimonies and his statutes with all their heart and all their soul, to perform the words of this <u>covenant</u> that were written in this book. And all the people stood to the covenant" (2 Kings 23:1-3).

> The phrase *to keep* occurs 64 times in the Old Testament.

The phrase *covenant of* is mentioned in 64 verses of the Bible.

The phrase *of the covenant* is mentioned in 64 verses of the Bible.

A Father & Firstborn Son Break Fellowship

"Now the sons of Reuben the firstborn of Israel, for he was the firstborn; but, forasmuch as he defiled his father's bed, his birthright was given unto the sons of Joseph the son of Israel" (1 Chron. 5:1).

The word *firstborn* occurs 64 times in the Law.

The phrase *the firstborn* is seen in 64 verses of Old Testament.

364th verse of First Chronicles

"So all Israel were reckoned by genealogies; and, behold, they were written in the book of the kings of Israel and Judah, who were carried away to Babylon for their transgression" (1 Chron. 9:1). Judah broke fellowship with the Lord through their persistent idolatry.

Israel Breaks Fellowship with Judah

"Rehoboam forsook the counsel of the old men, And answered them after the advice of the young men, saying, My father made your yoke heavy, but I will add thereto: my father chastised you with whips, but I will chastise you with scorpions. . . . And when all Israel saw that the king would not hearken unto them, the people answered the king, saying, What portion have we in David? and we have none inheritance in the son of Jesse: every man to your tents, O Israel: and now, David, see to thine own house. So all Israel went to their tents" (2 Chron. 10:13b-14, 16).

Again the phrase *the people* is mentioned in 164 verses of the New Testament. Again the name *Israel* occurs 364 times in First and Second Kings. Again the word *tents* is mentioned in 64 verses of the Bible.

Broken Fellowship with God Restored by Way of Repentance

Solomon prayed to God, saying, "When the heaven is shut up, and there is no rain, because they have sinned against thee; yet if they pray toward this place, and confess thy name, and turn from their sin, when thou dost afflict them; Then hear thou from heaven, and forgive the sin of thy servants, and of thy people Israel" (2 Chron. 6:26-27c). Again all tenses of *sin against* are mentioned in 64 verses of the Bible.

Later God proclaimed to Solomon, saying, "If my people, which are called by my name, shall humble themselves, and pray, and seek my face, and turn from their wicked ways; then will I hear from heaven, and will forgive their sin, and will heal their land" (7:14). Again the word *sin* is mentioned in 64 verses of the OT Narrative.

Asa Repairs Judah's Broken Fellowship with the Lord

Judah had fallen away from the Lord under Rehoboam's and Abijah's reigns. "And Asa did that which was good and right in the eyes of the LORD his God: For he took away the altars of the strange gods, and the high places, and brake down the images, and cut down the groves: And commanded Judah to seek the LORD God of their fathers, and to do the law and the commandment" (2 Chron. 14:2-4). The OT Narrative combination *and commanded Judah to seek* (1x), *seek* (49x), *the LORD God of their fathers* (14x) = 64.

564th Verse of Second Chronicles

"So Uzziah slept with his fathers, and they buried him with his fathers in the field of the burial which belonged to the kings; for they said, He is a leper: and Jotham his son reigned in his stead" (2 Chron. 26:23). Mosaic Law demanded that such a contagious person be removed from the community. Thus

Hezekiah Repairs Judah's Broken Fellowship with the Lord

Evil Ahaz had closed up the doors to God's House to prevent the people's daily fellowship with Him. Godly Hezekiah came along and reversed this Temple closure. "He in the first year of his reign, in the first month, opened the doors of the house of the LORD, and repaired them" (2 Chron. 29:3). The Bible combination *closed* (11x) and *the doors* (53x) = 64.

Hezekiah Reports on the Nation's Broken Fellowship with the Lord

Hezekiah informs all the Levites, saying, "Also they have shut up the doors of the porch, and put out the lamps, and have not burned incense nor offered burnt offerings in the holy place unto the God of Israel" (2 Chron. 29:7). The word *shut* is mentioned in 64 chapters of the Old Testament. Again the Bible combination *closed* (11x) and *the doors* (53x) = 64.

Hezekiah Fully Regains the Nation's Broken Fellowship with the Lord

"And they brought forth the he goats for the sin offering before the king and the congregation; and they laid their hands upon them: And the priests killed them, and they made reconciliation with their blood upon the altar, to make an atonement for all Israel: for the king commanded that the burnt offering and the sin offering should be made for all Israel" (2 Chron. 29:23-24). This atonement was to fully reinstate Israel's fellowship with the Lord which they had lost under Ahaz's ungodly reign. This passage presents the Bible's 64th occurrence of the phrase *an atonement*, and we see its relation to regaining broken fellowship. The phrase *a burnt offering* occurs 64 times in the Bible.

Josiah's Revival Brings the Nation Back into Fellowship with the Lord

Josiah's reforms greatly helped reinstate the nation's fellowship with the Lord which had been lost under Manasseh's and Amon's wicked reigns. "And Josiah took away all the abominations out of all the countries that pertained to the children of Israel, and made all that were present in Israel to serve, even to serve the LORD their God. And all his days they departed not from following the LORD, the God of their fathers" (2 Chron. 34:33). Again the name *Israel* occurs 364 times in First and Second Kings.

Judah Suffers Broken Fellowship with Godly Josiah

The king was killed in battle. "And all Judah and Jerusalem mourned for Josiah. And Jeremiah lamented for Josiah: and all the singing men and the singing women spake of Josiah in their lamentations to this day, and made them an ordinance in Israel: and, behold, they are written in the lamentations" (2 Chron. 35:24e-25). Again the word *killed* is mentioned in 64 verses of the Bible. The Bible combination *and all Judah and Jerusalem* (1x), *mourned for* (9x), *Josiah* (53x), *and Jeremiah lamented for Josiah* (1x) = 64.

Ezra 2:64

"The whole congregation together was forty and two thousand three hundred and threescore"

(Ezra 2:64). It had been seventy years since Israel was last able to offer up sacrifice to the Lord. Now that the remnant had returned to Jerusalem—the appointed place for sacrifice—they were anxious to begin religious fellowship with the Lord. The word *congregation* occurs 364 times in Scripture.

Should We Break Thy Commandments Again

"Should we again BREAK thy commandments, and join in affinity with the people of these abominations? wouldest not thou be angry with us till thou hadst consumed us, so that there should be no remnant nor escaping?" (Ezra 9:14) Here the related keyword *break* is the 6448th word of Ezra, a number from the 6400 range.

64th Verse of Nehemiah

"But it came to pass, that when Sanballat heard that we builded the wall, he was wroth, and took great indignation, and mocked the Jews" (Neh. 4:1). The phrase "the wall" is seen often in Nehemiah and stands as one of the keys to the whole book. The wall's broken-down state is a visible token of Judah's former breach of fellowship with the Lord. Hence, Nehemiah's theme of repairing the wall symbolizes restoring lost fellowship between the people of Israel and the God of Israel. The phrase *the wall* is mentioned in 64 chapters of the Bible.

Nehemiah 7:64

Certain of the remnant priests could not prove their pedigree. "These sought their register among those that were reckoned by genealogy, but it was not found: therefore were they, as polluted, put from the priesthood" (Neh. 7:64). On a working basis, these rejected priests soon began suffering from their broken fellowship with the approved priests. This verse fits our third definition of fellowship: an association. The word *from* is mentioned in 64 verses of Ezra and Nehemiah. Again the title *the priest* occurs naturally 364 times in the Old Testament.

64th Verse of Esther

"So Esther's maids and her chamberlains came and told it her. Then was the queen exceedingly grieved; and she sent raiment to clothe Mordecai, and to take away his sackcloth from him: but he received it not" (Est. 4:4). Mordecai's wearing ashes and a garment of sackcloth stood as greatly visible tokens of his sudden broken fellowship with his formerly amiable Persian citizenry.

Job Suffers Broken Fellowship with All Known Associates

"He hath put my brethren far from me, and mine acquaintance are verily ESTRANGED from me" (Job 19:13). Again the phrase *far from* is mentioned in 64 verses of the Bible.

Job's Relatives & Friends Broke Fellowship with Him

Job gave his sad testimony: "My kinsfolk have failed, and my familiar friends have forgotten me" (Job 19:14). Again the word *fail* occurs 64 times in Scripture.

Messiah Suffered Broken Fellowship with His Father

"My God, my God, why hast thou forsaken me? why art thou so far from helping me, and from the words of my roaring? . . . Be not far from me; for trouble is near; for there is none to help. . . . But be not thou far from me, O LORD: O my strength, haste thee to help me" (Ps. 22:1, 11, 19).

This psalm prophesied Messiah's suffering on the cross. Because the lowly Messiah was temporarily laden with the world's sins, there came a necessary yet temporary breaking of fellowship with the heavenly Father. Again the phrase *far from* is mentioned in 64 verses of the Bible.

David Feared Broken Fellowship with the Lord

"Hide not thy face <u>far from</u> me; put not thy servant away in anger: thou hast been my help; leave me not, neither forsake me, O God of my salvation. When my father and my mother forsake me, then the LORD will take me up" (Ps. 27:9-10). Again the phrase *far from* is mentioned in 64 verses of the Bible.

Messiah's Right-Hand Man to Break Fellowship with Him

"Yea, mine own familiar friend, in whom I trusted, which did eat of my bread, hath lifted up his heel <u>against</u> me" (Ps. 41:9). This is a prophecy concerning the Messiah and His apostate apostle. Again the word *against* occurs 164 times in the Wisdom Books.

David Laments His Broken Fellowship with the Lord

"Wash me throughly from mine iniquity, and cleanse me from my <u>sin</u>. For I acknowledge my transgressions: and my <u>sin</u> is ever before me. . . . Purge me with hyssop, and I shall be clean: wash me, and I shall be whiter than snow. Make me to hear joy and gladness; that the bones which thou hast BROKEN may rejoice. Hide thy face from my <u>sins</u>, and blot out all mine iniquities. Create in me a clean heart, O God; and renew a right spirit within me. Cast me not away from thy presence; and take not thy holy spirit from me. Restore unto me the joy of thy salvation" (Ps. 51:2-3, 7-12a).

Again the word *sin* is mentioned in 64 verses of the OT Narrative. Again the word *sins* is mentioned naturally in 164 verses of the Bible.

David's Enemies Broke Fellowship with Peaceful Coexisting Ones

"He hath put forth his hands against such as be at peace with him: he hath BROKEN his <u>covenant</u>" (Ps. 55:20). Again the phrase *covenant of* is mentioned in 64 verses of the Bible. Again the phrase *of the covenant* is mentioned in 64 verses of the Bible.

Psalm 64

This Psalm is about David's many enemies. Some of them used to be his friends, but they had broken fellowship with him, revolted against him, and now sought his life. As a consequence David prayed to God, "Hide me from the secret counsel of the wicked; from the insurrection of the workers of iniquity" (Ps. 64:2). After describing how his enemies shot bitter words at him like arrows, he brought a great contrast: "But God shall shoot at them with an arrow; suddenly shall they be wounded. So they shall make their own tongue to fall upon themselves: all that see them shall flee away. And all men shall fear, and shall declare the work of God; for they shall wisely consider of his doing" (vv. 7-9). Because these men had broken fellowship with God's anointed king, they showed how they had manifestly broken fellowship with God Himself. David longed for God to show them the error of their ways. Psalm 64 consists of 192 words, a multiple of 64.

Messiah's Many Broken Fellowships

"I am become a <u>stranger</u> unto my brethren, and an alien unto my mother's children" (Ps. 69:8).

This is a prophecy concerning the broken fellowship which the lowly Messiah was to endure with His half-brothers. Throughout His young adult life, the lowly Nazarene was likely held in admiration by all of His family and peers; yet when He entered into the ministry and proclaimed His Lordship over the nation all these familiar people began to quickly lose heart with Him. Again the word *strangers* occurs 64 times in the Old Testament.

The Lord Broke Fellowship with Wayward Israel

"So that he forsook the tabernacle of Shiloh, the <u>tent</u> which he placed among men" (Ps. 78:60). In the days of evil Saul the nation drifted so far away from God that He chose to abandon fellowship with them. Again the word *tents* is mentioned in 64 verses of the Bible.

Psalm 78:64

"Their <u>priests</u> fell by the sword; and their widows made no lamentation" (Ps. 78:64). This verse describes the broken Levite fellowships that the priests' wives had to suddenly cope with. Again the title *the priest* occurs naturally 364 times in the Old Testament.

Messiah's Suffers Broken Fellowships in His Hour of Darkness

"Lover and friend hast thou put <u>far from</u> me, and mine acquaintance into darkness" (Ps. 88:18). Again the phrase *far from* is mentioned in 64 verses of the Bible.

"If They Break My Statutes"

"If they BREAK my <u>statutes, and</u> keep not my commandments; Then will I visit their transgression with the rod, and their iniquity with stripes. Nevertheless my lovingkindness will I not utterly take from him, nor suffer my faithfulness to fail. My covenant will I not BREAK, nor alter the thing that is gone out of my lips. Once have I sworn by my holiness that I will not lie unto David" (Ps. 89:31-35).

> The phrase *statutes and* occurs 64 times in the Bible.
> The phrase *statutes and* is mentioned in 64 verses of the Bible.

Newly Found Favor Will Restore Broken Fellowship

"Thou shalt arise, and have mercy upon Zion: for the time to <u>favour</u> her, yea, the set time, is come" (Ps. 102:13). For more than nineteen centuries Israel was a wasteland. Having broken fellowship with Messiah, God broke off fellowship with them. Yet here we have a promise that He will show favor to them once again. Again the word *favour* occurs 64 times in the Old Testament.

The Brokenhearted

"He healeth the BROKEN in <u>heart</u>, and bindeth up their wounds" (Ps. 147:3). This verse presents the Bible's 64th occurrence of the word *broken*, and it refers to a remedy for Israel's broken fellowship with the Lord. Again the word *heart* is mentioned in 664 verses of the Old Testament.

Gossip Leads to Broken Fellowships

"<u>A whisperer</u> <u>separateth chief</u> FRIENDS. . . <u>he that repeateth a matter separateth very</u> FRIENDS" (Prov. 16:28b; 179b). This verse corresponds with our third definition of fellowship: a company of equals or friends. The Bible combination *a whisperer* (1x), *separateth chief* (1x), *friends* (49x), *he that repeateth* (1x), *a matter* (11x) *separateth very friends* (1x) = 64.

Forsake Not Thy Friends

"Thine own FRIEND, and thy father's FRIEND, forsake not; neither go into thy brother's house in the day of thy calamity: for better is a neighbour that is near than a brother far off" (Prov. 27:10a). The word *friend(s)* is mentioned in 64 verses of the Old Testament.

64th Verse of Solomon's Song

"I have put off my coat; how shall I put it on? I have washed my feet; how shall I defile them?" (Song 5:3) This speech reveals a separation of interest, even broken fellowship between a betrothed couple. The failure to engage in fellowship was the bride's. This greatly figures Israel's careless attitude and indifference toward her Messianic King at His first coming.

God Wants to Restore the Broken Fellowship

"Wash you, make you clean; put away the evil of your doings from before mine eyes; cease to do evil. . . . Come now, and let us reason together, saith the LORD: though your sins be as scarlet, they shall be as white as snow; though they be red like crimson, they shall be as wool" (Isa. 1:16, 18). The Bible combination *put away* (53x), *the evil of* (11x) = 64. Again the word *sins* is mentioned naturally in 164 verses of the Bible.

The Lord Hides His Face from Israel

"And I will wait upon the LORD, that hideth his face from the house of Jacob, and I will look for him" (Isa. 8:17). Because Israel remains unrepentant of their sins, the Lord continues His broken-off fellowship. Again the phrase *my face* occurs 64 times in the Bible. The phrase *the house* occurs 64 times in Jeremiah.

Strangers Reunited with Israel in the Golden Age

"For the LORD will have mercy on Jacob, and will yet choose Israel, and set them in their own land: and the strangers shall be joined with them, and they shall cleave to the house of Jacob" (Isa. 14:1). During the millennium Israel will finally enjoy close fellowship with the Gentiles. The opposite—broken fellowship—has been the norm over the past millennia. Again the word *strangers* occurs 64 times in the Old Testament.

The Nations Have Broken Fellowship with the Lord

"The earth also is defiled under the inhabitants thereof; because they have transgressed the laws, changed the ordinance, BROKEN the everlasting covenant" (Isa. 24:5). After the Fall of Man, God instilled His moral laws within the conscience of sinful mankind. This performance of law giving was for the purpose of preserving mankind from utter corruption. Nevertheless, the nations quickly rebelled against these holy laws and thus broke fellowship with the Lord. The Old Testament combination *broken* (161x), *his laws* (3x) = 164. The Old Testament combination *changed the ordinance* (1x), *broken* (161x), *the everlasting covenant* (2x) = 164.

Israel Has Refrained from Heartfelt Fellowship with the Lord

"Wherefore the Lord said, Forasmuch as this people draw near me with their mouth, and with their lips do honour me, but have removed their heart far from me, and their fear toward me is taught by the precept of men" (Isa. 29:13). Again the phrase *far from* is mentioned in 64 verses of the Bible.

Binding up Israel's Breach of Fellowship with the Lord

"Moreover the light of the moon shall be as the light of the sun, and the light of the sun shall be sevenfold, as the light of seven days, in <u>the day that the LORD</u> <u>bindeth up the</u> <u>breach</u> <u>of his</u> <u>people,</u> <u>and healeth the</u> <u>stroke</u> <u>of their wound</u>" (Isa. 30:26). The Bible combination *the day that the LORD* (8x), *bindeth up the* (2x), *breach* (22x), *of his people* (19x), *and healeth the* (1x), *stroke* (11x), *of their wound* (1x) = 64.

The Lord Can Not Have Fellowship with a Sinful Nation

"But your iniquities have separated between you and your God, and your <u>sins</u> have hid his face from you, that he will not hear" (Isa. 59:2). Again the word *sins* is mentioned naturally in 164 verses of the Bible.

64th Chapter of Isaiah

About twenty years has transpired since the northern kingdom began living in exile. They were warned repeatedly to turn from their Baal worship. After so long a battle with Israel's horribly broken fellowship, God finally gave them up to their vile affections. Then He raised an Assyrian army to come conquer them and carry them away with no possibility of return. These captives who are now suffering the retribution of their broken fellowship with God greatly long for restored fellowship. In their wishful thinking they say, "For since the beginning of the world men have not heard, nor perceived by the ear, neither hath the eye seen, O God, beside thee, what he hath prepared for him that waiteth for him. Thou meetest him that rejoiceth and worketh righteousness, those that remember thee in thy ways" (Isa. 64:4-5a). Whereas God had once waited for Israel to change their minds now Israel must wait for God to do the same.

Quickly moving away from such wishful thinking, these banished ones now confess the reality of their dismal, broken-fellowship situation to God: "behold, thou art wroth; for we have <u>sinned</u>. . . . we are all as an unclean thing, and all our righteousnesses are as filthy rags; and we all do fade as a leaf; and our iniquities, like the wind, have <u>taken us away</u>. And there is none that calleth upon thy name, that stirreth up himself to take hold of thee: for thou hast hid thy <u>face</u> from us, and hast consumed us, because of our iniquities" (vv. 5b-7). Again the word *sin* is mentioned in 64 verses of the OT Narrative. From Genesis to the NT Narrative the phrase *taken away* is mentioned in 64 verses. Again the phrase *my face* occurs 64 times in the Bible.

After confessing their waywardness the banished ones return again to their wishful thinking. "But now, O LORD, thou art our father; we are the clay, and thou our potter; and we all are the work of thy hand. Be not wroth very sore, O LORD, neither remember iniquity for ever: behold, see, we <u>beseech</u> thee, we are all thy people" (vv. 8-9). The word *beseech* is mentioned in 64 verses of the Bible. This 64th chapter ends with a great question to God regarding their broken fellowship with Him. "Wilt thou refrain thyself for these things, O LORD? wilt thou hold thy peace, and afflict us very sore?" (v. 12)

Jeremiah to Suffer Broken Fellowship with the Priests

"For, behold, I have made thee this day a defenced city, and an iron pillar, and brasen walls against the whole land, against the kings of Judah, against the princes thereof, against <u>the priests</u> thereof, and against the people of the land" (Jer. 1:18). Again the title *the priest* occurs naturally

364 times in the Old Testament.

They Have Broken Fellowship with Me

God testified this of backsliding Judah: "for <u>they</u> have turned their back unto me, and not their face: but in the time of their trouble <u>they</u> will say, Arise, and save us" (Jer. 2:27b). Again the word *they* is mentioned in 64 chapters of the Minor Prophets.

Jerusalem Has Forgotten the Lord

"Can a maid <u>forget</u> her ornaments, or a bride her attire? yet my people have <u>forgotten</u> me days without number" (Jer. 2:32). Again all forms of the present-tense word *forget* are mentioned in 64 verses of the Bible.

64th Verse of Jeremiah

"And I saw, when for all the causes whereby backsliding Israel committed <u>adultery</u> I had put her away, and given her a bill of divorce; yet her treacherous sister <u>Judah</u> feared not, but went and played the harlot also" (Jer. 3:8). The northern kingdom broke fellowship with God through their constant Baal worship. Judah, the southern kingdom, soon went down the same idolatrous path. Breaking fellowship with God is a dangerous path because it leads to apostasy. The Minor Prophets combination *Judah* (63x) and *played the harlot* (1x) = 64.

Man Is Prone to Break Fellowship with God

"O LORD, I know that the way of <u>man</u> is not in himself: it is not in <u>man</u> that walketh to direct his steps" (Jer. 10:23). Man is prone to break fellowship with God. He desperately needs God's constant intervention and help. Again the word *man* is mentioned in 64 verses of First Corinthians.

Judah Has Broken from the Covenant Fellowship

"They are turned back to the iniquities of their forefathers, which refused to hear my words; and <u>they</u> went after other gods to serve them: the house of Israel and the house of <u>Judah</u> have <u>BROKEN</u> <u>my covenant which I made with</u> their fathers" (Jer. 11:10). Jeremiah is comprised of 1364 verses. Again the word *they* is mentioned in 64 chapters of the Minor Prophets. Again the name *Judah* is mentioned in 164 verses of Jeremiah. The Old Testament combination *broken* (161x), *my covenant which I [had/have] made with* (3x) = 164.

Jeremiah's Plea for God Not to Break Covenant Fellowship with Judah

"We acknowledge, O LORD, our wickedness, and the iniquity of our fathers: <u>for we have sinned</u> <u>against thee</u>. Do not abhor us, for thy name's sake, do not disgrace the throne of thy glory: remember, BREAK not thy covenant with us" (Jer. 14:20-21). Judah is guilty of having first broken covenant fellowship with the Lord. The Major and Minor Prophets combination *for we have sinned* (3x), *against thee* (61x) = 64.

Judah Broke the Sacred Pact of Blood-Covenant Fellowship

"And I will give the men that have transgressed my covenant, which have not performed the words of the covenant which they had made before me, when they cut the calf in twain, and passed <u>between the</u> parts thereof" (Jer. 34:18). One step in performing the ancient blood-covenant ceremony was for two men to walk a figure-eight in the midst of two piles of slain animal parts. They would begin back to back and then finish their walk face to face at which time, while pointing down at the animal parts, they would say to each other, "God do so to me and more also if I ever break this covenant." Again the phrase *between the* is mentioned naturally in 64 verses of the Bible.

God Has Broken Fellowship with Judah & Jerusalem

"Let us search and try our ways, and <u>turn</u> again to the LORD. Let us lift up our <u>heart</u> with our hands unto God in the heavens" (Lam. 3:40-41). Judah had turned away her heart from God and now it was past time for her to turn back toward Him. Again the word *turned* is mentioned in 64 chapters of the OT Narrative. Again the word *heart* is mentioned in 664 verses of the Old Testament.

64th Verse of Ezekiel

God told Ezekiel, "And I will make thy tongue cleave to the roof of thy mouth, that thou shalt be dumb, and shalt not be to them a reprover: for they are a rebellious house" (Ezek. 3:26). Ezekiel's fellowship with his countrymen would become broken through the loss of his speech. Equally so God gave Israel this visual token of broken fellowship to the nation. Their leading prophet Ezekiel could not speak with them at will. He could only speak when God had something important to say to Israel through him.

Judah's Abominable Ways Lead to Broken Fellowship

"And mine eye shall not spare, neither will I have pity: I will recompense <u>thee according to thy ways</u> and thine abominations that are in the midst of thee; and ye shall <u>know that I am the LORD</u> that smiteth" (Ezek. 7:9). The Lord spoke of Judah's attitude of broken spiritual fellowship through her idol worship. There have been two deportations into Babylon thus far, yet one more remains. The Major Prophet combination *thee according to thy* (3x), *ways* (61x) = 64. The phrase *know that I am the LORD/Lord* occurs 64 times in the Major Prophets.

Judah's Breaking of Covenant Met with God's Broken Fellowship

"For thus saith the Lord GOD; I will even deal with thee as thou hast done, which <u>hast despised</u> the <u>oath</u> in <u>BREAKING the covenant</u>. . . . Therefore thus saith the Lord GOD; As I live, surely mine oath that he hath despised, and my covenant that he hath BROKEN, even it will I recompense upon his own head" (Ezek. 16:59; 17:19). The sacred blood-covenant ceremony was not valid unless the two men or parties made oaths before each other. They each promised to keep the covenant and did so by invoking a divine curse for any breach of the covenant. The Bible combination *hast despised* (3x), *oath* (59x), *breaking the covenant* (2x) = 64.

Broken Fellowship Caused by Israel's Stony Heart

"A new heart also will I give you, and a new spirit will I put within you: and I will take away the stony <u>heart</u> out of your flesh, and I will give you an heart of flesh. And I will put my spirit within you, and cause you to walk in my statutes, and ye shall keep my judgments, and do them" (Ezek. 36:26-27). Again the word *heart* is mentioned in 664 verses of the Old Testament.

Separated Fellows Israel & Judah to Be Restored

"Say unto them, Thus saith the Lord GOD; Behold, I will take the stick of Joseph, which is in the hand of Ephraim, and the tribes of <u>Israel</u> his FELLOWS, and will put them with him, even with the stick of <u>Judah</u>, and make them one stick, and they shall be one in mine hand" (Ezek. 37:19). We repeat the following seals.

The name *Israel* occurs 364 times in First/Second Kings.
The name *Judah* is mentioned in 164 verses of Jeremiah.

God's Broken Fellowship & Hidden Face to be Restored

"Neither will I hide <u>my face</u> any more from them: for I have poured out my spirit upon the house of Israel, saith the Lord GOD" (Ezek. 39:29). Again the phrase *my face* occurs 64 times in the Bible.

Rebellious House of Israel Has Broken the Covenant

"In that ye have brought into my sanctuary strangers, uncircumcised in heart, and uncircumcised in flesh, to be in my sanctuary, to pollute it, even my house, when ye offer my bread, the fat and the blood, and they have BROKEN my covenant because of all your abominations" (Ezek. 44:7). Here the keyword *broken* is the 564,037th word of the Bible, a number from the 564,000 range.

Three Hebrews Refuse to Break Covenant Fellowship with God

"If it be so, our God whom we serve is able to deliver us from the burning fiery furnace, and he will deliver us out of thine hand, O king. But if not, be it known unto thee, O king, that we will not <u>serve</u> thy <u>gods</u>, nor worship the golden image which thou hast set up" (Dan. 3:17-18). The Bible combination *to go and serve* (1x) and *other gods* (63x) = 64.

64th Verse of Hosea

Hosea prophesied to both the northern and southern kingdoms, "<u>They</u> shall go with their flocks and with their herds to seek the LORD; but <u>they</u> shall not find him; he hath withdrawn himself from them" (Hos. 5:6). The nation's broken fellowship with God is made apparent here. It was bad when they withdrew from God, but it would be far worse in the near future when He completely broke fellowship with them. Again the word *they* is mentioned in 64 chapters of the Minor Prophets.

Broken Fellowship with God Restored by Turning the Heart

"Therefore also now, saith the LORD, <u>turn</u> ye even to me with all your <u>heart</u>, and with fasting, and with weeping, and with mourning: And rend your <u>heart</u>, and not your garments, and <u>turn</u> unto the LORD your God: for he is gracious and merciful, slow to anger, and of great kindness, and repenteth him of the evil" (Joel 2:12-13). The heart once turned away from God; it must now turn back to God. Again the word *turned* is mentioned in 64 chapters of the OT Narrative. Again the word *heart* is mentioned in 664 verses of the Old Testament.

Disagreeableness Causes Broken Fellowship

"Hear this word that the LORD hath spoken <u>against</u> you, O children of <u>Israel</u>, against the whole family which I brought up from the land of Egypt, saying, You only have I known of all the families of the earth. . . . Can two walk together, except they be agreed?" (Amos 3:1-2a, 3) Again the word *against* occurs 164 times in the Wisdom Books. Again the name *Israel* occurs 364 times in First and Second Kings.

Run Away Prophet Breaks Fellowship Presence with the Lord

"But Jonah rose up to flee unto Tarshish <u>from</u> the presence of the LORD, and went down to Joppa; and he found a ship going to Tarshish: so he paid the fare thereof, and went down into it, to go with them unto Tarshish <u>from</u> the presence of the LORD" (Jonah 1:3). Again the word *from* is mentioned in 64 verses of First Kings.

Broken Fellowship between Israel & Her Messiah

The narrative says of Israel and the Messiah, "they shall smite the judge of Israel with a rod upon the cheek. . . . Therefore will he give them up, until the time that she which travaileth hath brought forth: then <u>the remnant of his brethren shall</u> <u>return</u> unto the children of <u>Israel</u>" (Mic. 5:3). Again the name *Israel* occurs 364 times in First and Second Kings. The following seal is right on cue. Again from Genesis to the Synoptic Gospels the phrase *his brethren* is mentioned in 64 chapters. The Bible combination *the remnant of his brethren shall* (1x), return (263x) = 264.

Jerusalem Has Broken Fellowship with the Lord

"I will also stretch out mine hand upon Judah, and upon all the inhabitants of <u>Jerusalem</u> . . . And them that are <u>turned</u> back <u>from</u> the LORD; and those that have not sought the LORD, nor enquired for him" (Zeph. 1:4a, 6). Again the word *turned* is mentioned in 64 chapters of the OT Narrative. Again the word *from* is mentioned in 64 verses of Ezra and Nehemiah.

> The name *Jerusalem* is mentioned in 764 verses of the Bible.
> The name *Jerusalem* occurs 264 times in the Major/Minor Prophets.
> The phrase *of Jerusalem* is mentioned in 164 verses of the Bible.

Remnant Refuses to Build the Lord's Fellowship House

"Thus speaketh the LORD of hosts, saying, This people say, The time is not come, the time that the LORD'S house should be built. Then came the word of the LORD by Haggai the prophet, saying, <u>Is it time for you</u>, <u>O ye</u>, <u>to dwell in your cieled houses</u>, <u>and this house</u> <u>lie waste</u>? Now therefore thus saith the LORD of hosts; Consider your ways" (Hag. 1:2-5). The remnant is challenged to consider their ways of broken fellowship for God feels slighted by their self-centeredness. The Old Testament combination *is it time for you* (1x), *O ye* (54x), *to dwell in your cieled houses* (1x), *and this house* (5x), *lie waste* (3x) = 64.

God Breaks Covenant Fellowship with Israel for Betraying the Messiah

"And I took my staff, even Beauty, and cut it asunder, that I might BREAK my covenant which I had made with all <u>the people</u>. And it was BROKEN in that day . . . And I said unto them, If ye think good, give me my price; and if not, forbear. So <u>they</u> weighed for my price thirty pieces of silver" (Zech. 11:10-12). This is a prophecy citing God's broken fellowship with Israel in retribution for their wicked rejection and betrayal of His heaven-sent Messiah. Again the phrase *the people* is mentioned in 164 verses of the New Testament. Again the word *they* is mentioned in 64 chapters of the Minor Prophets.

Judah and Israel's Long-Running Broken Fellowship

"Then I cut asunder mine other staff, even Bands, that I might BREAK THE BROTHERHOOD between <u>Judah</u> and <u>Israel</u>" (Zech. 11:14). One of the Bible's most pronounced broken fellowships was between the southern and northern tribes. This verse fits our third definition of fellowship: an association. Again the name *Judah* is mentioned in 164 verses of Jeremiah. Again the name *Israel* occurs 364 times in First and Second Kings.

"Wounded in the House of My Friends"

"And one shall say unto him, What are these wounds in thine hands? Then he shall answer, Those with which I was wounded in the house of my FRIENDS" (Zech. 13:6). This is a prophecy which tells of Messiah's Second Coming to Earth, a time when He will remind Israel of their former broken fellowship with Him at His first coming. The term "friends" refers to two covenant partners who had made a sacred blood-covenant pact together. Again the Old Testament combination *friend* (34 vs) and *friends* (30 vs) = 64 verses.

Broken Fellowship between God & His Fellow

"Awake, O sword, against my shepherd, and against the man that is my FELLOW, saith the LORD of hosts: smite the shepherd, and the sheep shall be scattered: and I will turn mine hand upon the little ones" (Zech. 13:7). Our introductory definition makes it clear that a fellow is an equal. The Lord God has but one equal—His eternal Son. Here the Son is incarnate and becomes the Smitten One for all Israel's sins.

The New Testament

"The book of the generation of <u>Jesus Christ</u>, the son of David, the son of Abraham" (Matt. 1:1). Jesus of Nazareth began to experience various levels of broken fellowships from the day of His very first sermon delivery which took place in His home town of Nazareth. From that time forward many individuals and groups would break fellowship with Him. Among others, this included His family and friends as well as His acquaintances and associates.

> The title *Lord Jesus Christ* is seen in 64 verses of Pauline Epistles.
> The phrase *Jesus answered* occurs 64 times in the Gospels.
> The title *God* occurs 64 times in the Epistle of First John.

Jesus Leaves the People to Go into the Wilderness

"Then was Jesus led up of the Spirit into <u>the wilderness</u> to be tempted of the devil" (Matt. 4:1). Jesus had just been baptized and was ready to minister and fellowship with the people, but His sudden calling to go into the wilderness brought an unexpected broken fellowship with the people. Again the phrase *the wilderness* is mentioned in 264 verses of the Bible.

James & John Left Their Father

"And going on from thence, he saw other two brethren, James the son of Zebedee, and John his brother, in a ship with Zebedee their father, mending their nets; and he called them. And they immediately <u>left</u> the ship and their father, and followed him" (Matt. 4:21-22). When these brothers left their father and his family fishing enterprise, it created a vacuum in their daily family life and made for broken fellowships. The word *left* is mentioned in 264 verses of the Old Testament.

Breaking the Least Little Commandment Leads to Broken Fellowship

"Whosoever therefore shall BREAK one of these least commandments, and shall teach men so, he shall be called the least in the kingdom of heaven" (Matt. 5:19a). Again the word *commandment* occurs 64 times in the OT Narrative. The Law combination *of the least* (1x), *commandments* (63x) = 64.

Be Reconciled to Thy Estranged Brother

"Therefore if thou bring thy gift to the altar, and there rememberest that thy brother hath ought against thee; Leave there thy gift before the altar, and go thy way; first be reconciled to thy brother, and then come and offer thy gift" (Matt. 5:23-24). Here the word "brother" is used to indicate a fellow countryman or fellow believer with whom fellowship has been previously broken. The New Testament combination *brother* (63 chs), *hath ought against thee* (1 ch) = 64 chapters. Again the word *against* occurs 164 times in the Wisdom Books. The Bible combination *leave there thy* (1x), *gift* (59x), *before the altar and go thy way* (1x), *first be reconciled to thy brother* (1x), *then come* (1x), *and offer thy gift* (1x) = 64.

Husband Breaks Fellowship with Wife

"It hath been said, Whosoever shall PUT AWAY his wife, let him give her a writing of divorcement: But I say unto you, That whosoever shall PUT AWAY his wife, saving for the cause of fornication, causeth her to commit adultery" (Matt. 5:31-32a). The Bible combination *shall put away his* (4 vs), *wife* (360 vs) = 364 verses.

Messianic Groom Will Be Taken Away from His Bride

"Then came to him the disciples of John, saying, Why do we and the Pharisees fast oft, but thy disciples fast not? And Jesus said unto them, Can the children of the bridechamber mourn, as long as the bridegroom is with them? but the days will come, when the bridegroom shall be taken from them, and then shall they fast" (Matt. 9:14-15). Jesus prophesied of His tragic death and the ensuing broken fellowship with His disciples. Again from Genesis to the NT Narrative the phrase *taken away* is mentioned in 64 verses. Again the word *from* is mentioned in 64 verses of First Kings.

> The word *children* occurs 64 times in the Synoptic Gospels.
> The word *children* appears naturally in 64 verses of Pauline/General Epistles.
> The phrase *children of* is mentioned in 64 chapters of the Bible.

Broken Fellowship between Loving Lord & Lost Israel

"These twelve Jesus sent forth, and commanded them, saying, Go not into the way of the Gentiles, and into any city of the Samaritans enter ye not: But go rather to the lost sheep of the house of Israel" (Matt. 10:5-6). Fellowship between the Shepherd and the sheep had been lost because the sheep had gone astray. Christ had come to gather them back to Himself. Again the name *Israel* occurs 364 times in First and Second Kings.

Broken Fellowships within a Partially Christian Household

"Think not that I am come to send peace on earth: I came not to send peace, but a sword. For I am come to set a man at variance <u>against</u> his father, and the daughter <u>against</u> her mother, and the daughter in law <u>against</u> her mother in law. And <u>a man's</u> <u>foes shall be they</u> <u>of his own</u> <u>household</u>" (Matt. 10:34-36). Again the word *against* occurs 164 times in the Wisdom Books. The Bible combination *a woman's* (1x), *foes shall be they* (1x), *of her own* (1x), *household* (61x) = 64.

This People's Heart Is Waxed Gross

"For <u>this people's</u> <u>heart is</u> <u>waxed gross, and their ears are dull of hearing, and their eyes they</u> <u>have closed; lest at any time they should see with their eyes, and hear with their ears, and should</u> <u>understand with their heart, and should be converted, and I should heal them</u>" (Matt. 13:15). Again the word *heart* is mentioned in 664 verses of the Old Testament. The Bible combination *this people's* (1x), *heart is* (53x), *waxed gross* (2x), *and their ears are dull of hearing and their eyes they have closed* (1x), *lest at any time they should see with their eyes and hear with their ears* (1x), *and should understand with their heart* (1x), *and should be converted* (2x), *and I should heal them* (3x) = 64.

This People's Heart Is Far from Me

"<u>This people</u> draweth nigh unto me with their mouth, and honoureth me with their lips; but their <u>heart</u> is <u>far from</u> me" (Matt. 15:8). This verse presents the Bible's 64th chapter-mention of the phrase *this people*, and we see its relation to the people's broken fellowship with the heaven-sent Son of God. Again the phrase *the people* is mentioned in 164 verses of the New Testament. Again the word *heart* is mentioned in 664 verses of the Old Testament. Again the phrase *far from* is mentioned in 64 verses of the Bible.

Master to Suffer Gravely Broken Fellowship with Disciples

"And while they abode in Galilee, Jesus said unto them, The Son of man shall be betrayed into the hands of men: And they shall <u>kill</u> him, and the third day he shall be raised again. And they were exceeding sorry" (Matt. 17:22-23). Again the word *killed* is mentioned in 64 verses of the Bible. The phrase *of death* is mentioned in 64 chapters of the Bible.

Lord Seeks to Restore Broken Fellowships within the Flock

"For the Son of man is come to <u>save</u> that which was lost. How think ye? if a man have an hundred sheep, and one of them be gone astray, doth he not leave the ninety and nine, and goeth into the mountains, and seeketh that which is gone astray? And if so be that he find it, verily I say unto you, he rejoiceth more of that sheep, than of the ninety and nine which went not astray" (Matt. 18:11-13). The word *save* is mentioned in 164 verses of the Old Testament. The word *flock* is mentioned in 64 chapters of the Bible.

How to Gain Back Thy Brother's Lost Fellowship

"Moreover if <u>thy brother</u> shall trespass against thee, go and tell him his <u>fault</u> between thee and him alone: <u>if he shall hear thee, thou hast gained</u> <u>thy brother</u>" (Matt. 18:15). As Jesus spoke on issues of the church's future daily life, He instructed them how to mend a broken fellowship between two believers. Again from Genesis to the Gospels the phrases *thy brother* (59 vs) and *thy * brother* (5 vs) = 64 verses. The lowercase word *brother* is mentioned in 364 verses of the Bible. Here the word *fault* is the 13,464th word of the New Testament, and it is the cause of broken fellowship with a brother. The Bible combination *if he shall hear thee* (1v), *thou hast gained* (1 v), *thy brother* (62 Vs) = 64 verses.

Broken Fellowship between Two Fellow Servants

"But the same servant went out, and found one of his FELLOWSERVANTS, which owed him an hundred pence: <u>and he laid hands on him, and took him by the throat, saying, Pay me that thou owest</u>. And his FELLOWSERVANT fell down at his feet, and besought him, saying, Have patience with me, and I will pay thee all. And he would not: but went and cast him into prison, till he should pay the debt. So when his FELLOWSERVANTS saw what was done, they were very sorry, and came and told unto their lord all that was done" (Matt. 18:28-31). The joined phrases *and he laid hands on him, and took him by the throat, saying, pay me that thou owest* consist of 64 letters!

Brotherly Forgiveness Restores Broken Fellowship

"So likewise shall my heavenly Father do also unto you, if ye from your hearts forgive not every one his <u>brother</u> their <u>trespasses</u>" (Matt. 18:35). The New Testament combination *brother* (63 chs) and *if he trespass against thee* (1 ch) = 64 chapters.

What God Hath Joined Together Do Not Put out of Fellowship

"The Pharisees also came unto him. . . . Is it lawful for a man to PUT AWAY <u>his wife</u> for every cause? And he answered and said unto them, Have ye not read, that he which made them at the beginning made them male and female, And said, For this cause shall a man LEAVE father and mother, and shall cleave to <u>his wife</u>: and they twain shall be one flesh? Wherefore they are no more twain, but one flesh. What therefore God hath joined together, let not man PUT ASUNDER" (Matt. 19:3-6).

Again from Genesis to the NT Narrative the phrase *his wife* is mentioned in 64 chapters.

Broken Fellowship between Religious Leaders & Lord Messiah

"<u>Behold, your house</u> <u>is left unto you desolate</u>. For I say unto you, <u>Ye shall not</u> <u>see me</u> <u>henceforth, till ye shall say</u>, <u>Blessed is he that</u> <u>cometh in the name of the Lord</u>" (Matt. 23:38-39). The New Testament combination *behold your house* (2x), *is left unto you desolate* (2x), *ye shall not* (13x), *see me* (12x), *henceforth* (19x), *till ye shall say* (1x), *blessed is he that* (8x), *cometh in the name of the Lord* (7x) = 64.

864th Verse of Matthew

"And shall cut him asunder, and appoint him his portion with the hypocrites: there shall be weeping and gnashing of teeth" (Matt. 24:51). This punishment will come to the evil person who broke fellowship with his fellow servants after becoming drunken and turning to beat them.

Judas Breaks Covenant & Fellowship with Messiah for Thirty Pieces of Silver

"Then one of the twelve, called Judas Iscariot, went unto the chief priests, And said unto them, What will ye give me, and I will deliver him unto you? And they <u>covenanted</u> with him <u>for thirty pieces of silver</u>. And from that time he sought opportunity to betray him" (Matt. 26:14-16). The number *thirty* is mentioned in 164 verses of the Bible! The Major and Minor Prophets combination *for my price thirty* (1x), *for thirty* (1x), *pieces of* (4x), *silver* (58x) = 64. We repeat the following two seals.

The phrase *of the covenant* is mentioned in 64 verses of the Bible.
The phrase *covenant of* is mentioned in 64 verses of the Bible.

Christ's Fellowship with His Father Suddenly Broken

"He went away again the second time, and prayed, saying, O <u>my Father</u>, if this cup may not pass away from me, except I drink it, thy will be done" (Matt. 26:42). Scholars debate whether Jesus was attempting to avoid the coming pain or the awaiting load of sin; both of which He was completely unfamiliar with. Yet a numeric seal places a spotlight on Jesus' desire to avoid broken fellowship with His Father which He would experience once He drank from this cup. The cup here symbolized the Cup of Plagues used in a Near East betrothal ceremony. Both the bride and groom drank of it as a pledge of faithfulness and an acknowledgment that should either one ever break their marriage vows, they would submit to drink the other's vengeful wrath. In this case Messiah was submitting to drink the Cup of Plagues in Israel's stead for her unfaithfulness. Again the lowercase phrase *my father* is mentioned in 64 verses of the OT Narrative.

Matthew 26:64

"Jesus saith unto him, Thou hast said: nevertheless I say unto you, Hereafter shall ye see the Son of man sitting on the right hand of power, and coming in the clouds of heaven" (Matt. 26:64). These words would cause the high priest to break fellowship with Messiah in an irreversible, violent manner.

Peter's Fellowship with Jesus Broken in a Proclaimed Way

"Now <u>Peter</u> <u>sat without</u> <u>in the palace</u>: <u>and a damsel came unto him, saying,</u> <u>Thou also wast with</u> <u>Jesus of Galilee. But he denied before them all</u>, saying, I know not what thou sayest. And when he was gone out into the porch, another maid saw him, and said unto them that were there, This FELLOW was also with Jesus of Nazareth. And again he denied with an oath, I do not know the man" (Matt. 26:69-72). The New Testament combination *Peter* (158x), *sat without* (1x), *in the palace* (2x), *and a damsel came unto him saying* (1x), *thou also wast with Jesus of Galilee* (1x), *but he denied before them all* (1x) = 164.

The Bitterness of Broken Fellowship

"And about the ninth hour Jesus cried with a loud voice, saying, Eli, Eli, lama sabachthani? that is to say, My God, my God, <u>why</u> hast thou <u>FORSAKEN</u> me?" (Matt. 27:46) Jesus acknowledged that God had broken fellowship with His Him in this dark hour. The Old Testament combination *why* (163 vs), *hast thou forsaken me* (1 v) = 164 verses.

Matthew 27:64

"Command therefore that the sepulchre be made sure until the third day, lest his disciples come by night, and steal him away, and say unto the people, He is risen from the <u>dead</u>: so the last error shall be worse than the first" (Matt. 27:64). A sepulcher stands as a sad token of a broken fellowship between the living and the dead. Again the word *dead* occurs 364 times in the Bible.

Christ Breaks Fellowship with Everyone to Pray Alone

"And straightway he constrained his disciples to get into the ship, and to <u>go</u> to the other side before unto Bethsaida, while he sent <u>away</u> the people. And when he had sent them <u>away</u>, he departed into a mountain to pray" (Mark 6:45-46). Again the word *go* occurs 64 times in Ezekiel.

Again the word *away* is mentioned in 64 chapters of the Law.

Hardness of Heart Causes Man & Wife
To Break Covenant Fellowship

"And the Pharisees came to him, and asked him, Is it lawful for a man to PUT <u>AWAY</u> his wife? tempting him. And he answered and said unto them, What did Moses command you? And they said, Moses suffered to write a bill of divorcement, and to PUT her <u>AWAY</u>. And Jesus answered and said unto them, For the hardness of your <u>heart</u> he wrote you this precept. But from the beginning of the creation God made them male and female. For this cause shall a man leave his father and mother, and cleave to his wife; And they twain shall be one flesh: so then they are no more twain, but one flesh. What therefore God hath joined together, let not man PUT ASUNDER" (Mark 10:2-10).

Again the word *away* is mentioned in 64 chapters of the Law. Again the word *heart* is mentioned in 664 verses of the Old Testament.

Little Children Kept Back from Fellowship with Jesus

"And they brought young <u>children</u> to him, that he should touch them: and his disciples rebuked those that brought them. But when Jesus saw it, he was much displeased, and said unto them, Suffer the little children to come unto me, and forbid them not: for of such is the kingdom of God" (Mark 10:13-14). Again the word *children* occurs 64 times in the Synoptic Gospels.

Leaving Family behind for the Great Commission

"Then Peter began to say unto him, Lo, we have <u>LEFT</u> all, and have followed thee. And Jesus answered and said, Verily I say unto you, There is no man that hath <u>LEFT</u> house, or brethren, or sisters, or father, or mother, or wife, or children, or lands, for my sake, and the gospel's, But he shall receive an hundredfold now in this time, houses, and brethren, and sisters, and mothers, and children, and lands, with persecutions; and in the world to come eternal life" (Mark 10:28-30). The gospel call separates loved ones from each other in a geographical way. Indeed it brings about measurable broken fellowship. Again the word *left* is mentioned in 264 verses of the Old Testament.

464th Verse of Mark

"Having yet therefore one son, his wellbeloved, he sent him also last unto them, saying, They will reverence my son" (Mark 12:6). This 64th verse sets the scene of broken fellowship between the heavenly Father and His heavenly Son after the Son was sent to Earth to gather in a harvest of souls.

Broken Fellowship with the Master by Way of His Death & Burial

"And being in Bethany in the house of Simon the leper, as he sat at meat, there came a woman having an alabaster box of ointment of spikenard very precious; and she brake the box, and poured it on his <u>head</u>" (Mark 14:3). Jesus went on to say that Mary had performed this deed in regard to His soon-awaiting burial. Here the word *head* is the 646,264th word of the Bible, and when the Master's precious head is at last laid to rest, fellowship with His disciples will become broken.

Judas' Broken Covenant & Fellowship Receives a Woeful Warning

"The Son of man indeed goeth, as it is written of him: but woe to that <u>man</u> by whom the Son of man is BETRAYED! good were it for that <u>man</u> if he had never been born" (Mark 14:21). Again the word *man* is mentioned in 64 chapters of the Synoptic Gospels.

564th Verse of Mark

"Verily I say unto you, I will drink no more of the fruit of the vine, until that day that I drink it new in the kingdom of God" (Mark 14:25). Jesus speaks of the broken fellowship which will geographically exist between them for an indefinite period of time.

Broken Fellowship between Messiah & Disciples
Commences in the Garden of Gethsemane

"And they came to a place which was named <u>Gethsemane</u>: and he saith to his <u>disciples</u>, Sit ye here, while I shall pray" (Mark 14:32). Jesus had been with the disciples side by side all evening, but their entrance into Gethsemane became a sudden turning point. He first separated Himself by prayer; then a short time later He separated Himself by being led off to prison and death. Again the word *garden(s)* occurs 64 times in the Bible. The word *disciples* occurs 64 times in John's Gospel.

Disciples Break Fellowship with Their Master Because of Fright

When the <u>disciples</u> saw that Jesus was actually being arrested they became afraid. "And <u>they</u> all FORSOOK him, and fled" (Mark 14:50). Again the word *disciples* occurs 64 times in John's Gospel. Again the word *they* is mentioned in 64 chapters of the Minor Prophets.

1664th Verse of the New Testament

"And Peter followed him <u>afar</u> off, even into the palace of the high priest: and he sat with the servants, and warmed himself at the fire" (Mark 14:54). Peter's current fellowship with his Master had been broken geographically. Again the phrase *far from* is mentioned in 64 verses of the Bible.

Mark 14:64

In a fit of rage the high priest declared, "Ye have heard the blasphemy: what think ye? And <u>they</u> all condemned him to be guilty of death" (Mark 14:64). Jesus' religious affiliation and association were more in line with the Pharisees than with the Sadducees or any of the other religious sects of that day, nearly a dozen in total. Here Messiah's fellowship became irreversibly and judiciously broken with Israel's religious hierarchy. Again the word *they* occurs 364 times in Isaiah.

Chief Priests' Broken Fellowship with the Melchizedek Priest

The narrative says of Pilate, "For he knew that the <u>chief priests</u> had delivered him for envy" (Mark 15:10). The chief priests envied Jesus because of His manifest power and authority. Although their envy had turned to hatred long before this dark day, their fellowship with Him was severely broken on this day of their final rejection of Him as Christ their King. Again the title *the priest* occurs naturally 364 times in the Old Testament. The phrase *chief priests* occurs 64 times in the New Testament.

Son of God Breaks Fellowship with Sons of Men
Through His Untimely Death

"And Jesus cried with a loud voice, and gave up the ghost" (Mark 15:37). Jesus' breathless state of existence naturally broke off fellowship with those in the land of the living. Again the word *dead* occurs 364 times in the Bible!

Christian Women Stand Afar off from Christ & His Cross

"There were also women looking on <u>afar off</u>: among whom was Mary Magdalene, and Mary the mother of James the less and of Joses, and Salome" (Mark 15:40). This verse presents both the Bible's 64th occurrence and 64th verse-mention of the phrase *far/afar off*, and it pertains to the mournful broken fellowship between Christ and His devoted lady disciples.

Come to Anoint Christ's Dead Body

"And when the sabbath was past, Mary Magdalene, and Mary the mother of James, and Salome, had bought sweet spices, that <u>they</u> might come and anoint him" (Mark 16:1). These lady disciples wanted to participate in a ceremony that pertained to broken fellowship with a dead loved one. They could visit their Master's body which was at rest, but they could not talk to Him. Again the word *they* occurs 364 times in Isaiah. The word *grave* is mentioned in 64 verses of the Bible. Again the word *dead* occurs 364 times in the Bible.

64th Verse of Luke

Zacharias had not audibly spoken to his friends or family for almost a year. After Zacharias wrote down John's name for all to see the narrative says, "And his mouth was opened immediately, and his tongue loosed, and he spake, and praised God" (Luke 1:64). Here we see the broken fellowship between a priest and his peers wonderfully restored.

The Christ Child Will Create both Blessed & Broken Fellowships

"And Simeon blessed them, and said unto Mary his mother, Behold, this <u>child</u> is set for the fall and rising again of many in Israel; and for a sign which shall be spoken against" (Luke 2:34). Again the phrase *the child* is mentioned in 64 verses of the Bible.

John the Baptist's Broken Fellowship with His Disciples

"But Herod the tetrarch, being reproved by him for Herodias his brother Philip's wife, and for all the evils which Herod had done, Added yet this above all, that he <u>shut</u> up John in prison" (Luke 3:19-20). John's fellowship was broken off with his associates while he was in prison. Again the word *shut* is mentioned in 64 chapters of the Old Testament.

Christ's Broken Fellowship in His Own Country

"And he said, Verily I say unto you, No prophet is accepted in <u>his own</u> country" (Luke 4:24). Jesus enjoyed wonderful years of fellowship with His hometown community of Nazareth up until the time He proclaimed His spiritual headship over them. At that time His fellowship with them immediately became broken. They even tried to push Him off a nearby cliff to prove their point. The phrase *his own* occurs naturally 164 times in the Old Testament.

Peter Suddenly Views His Sin as a Hindrance to Godly Fellowship

"When Simon Peter saw it, he fell down at Jesus' knees, saying, Depart <u>from</u> me; for I am a sinful man, O Lord" (Luke 5:8). Peter suddenly recognized his sinful nature in view of Messiah's manifested holy nature. Indeed sin separates man from God. Again the word *from* is mentioned in 64 verses of First Kings. We repeat the following seals. Again the phrase *the sin* is mentioned in 64 verses of the Bible.

Levi Breaks Fellowship with His Tax-Collecting Association

"And after these things he went forth, and saw a publican, named <u>Levi</u>, sitting at the receipt of custom: and he said unto him, Follow me. And he <u>LEFT</u> all, rose up, and followed him" (Luke 5:27-28). Levi suddenly started life anew. When he did he broke fellowship with his worldly friends. His name is drawn from the patriarch who founded the priestly tribe. Levi's tax-farming profession fits our third definition of fellowship: an association. Again the name *Levi* occurs 64 times in the Old Testament. Again the title *Levites* occurs 264 times in the Old Testament.

A Man's Withered Right Hand of Fellowship

"And it came to pass also on another sabbath, that he entered into the synagogue and taught: and there was a <u>man</u> whose right <u>hand</u> was withered" (Luke 6:6). The narrative offers an important detail concerning the man's misfortune; his right hand was withered—the one with which Near Eastern people traditionally greet and bless each other. This poor man experienced the repeated shame of not being able to offer his right hand of fellowship to friends and loved ones. Neither could he offer his left hand to others as that would invoke an offense. Jesus soon took care of this man's sad plight. Again the word *man* is mentioned in 64 verses of First Corinthians. Again the phrase *his hand* occurs 64 times in the Law and is mentioned in 64 verses of the Major and Minor Prophets.

Christians Will Experience Humiliating Broken Fellowships

"Blessed are ye, when men shall hate you, and when <u>they</u> shall SEPARATE you from their company, and shall reproach you, and cast out your name as evil, <u>for the Son of man's sake</u>" (Luke 6:22). The Gospels combination *they shall* (46x), *separate* (2x), *you from their* (1x), *company* (11x), *and shall reproach you* (1x), *and cast out your name* (1x), *as evil* (1x), *for the Son of man's sake* (1x) = 64.

Simon the Pharisee's Withdrawn Fellowship

"And he turned to the woman, and said unto Simon, Seest thou this woman? I entered into thine house, thou gavest me no water for my feet: but she hath washed my feet with tears, and wiped them with the hairs of her head. Thou gavest me no kiss: but this woman since the time I came in hath not ceased to kiss my feet. My head with oil thou didst not anoint: but this woman hath anointed my feet with ointment. Wherefore I say unto thee, Her sins, which are many, are forgiven; for she loved much: but to whom little is forgiven, the same <u>loveth little</u>" (Luke 7:44-47).

Pharisaic fellowship had been extended to Jesus through this Pharisee's personal invitation into his home. But true fellowship was denied Jesus upon His entrance into the house. Instead of being treated as an honored guest, the Great Rabbi was treated as less than ordinary. Not even the slightest show of hospitality was extended to Him at the feast. The title *the Pharisee(s)* occurs 64 times in the NT Narrative.

Maniac of Gadara's Lost Fellowship Regained

"Now the man out of whom the devils were departed besought him that he might be with him:

but Jesus sent him <u>away</u>, saying, Return to thine own house, and shew how great things God hath done unto thee. And he went his way, and published throughout the whole city how great things Jesus had done unto him" (Luke 8:38-39). This Gadarene man wanted to continue his newly found fellowship with Christ, but it was suddenly broken off upon receiving Christ's command to go back home. However, when he returned to his hometown his broken fellowship with the citizenry was suddenly restored. Again the word *away* is mentioned in 64 chapters of the Law.

Samaritans Break Fellowship with the Jerusalem-Bound Messiah

"And it came to pass, when the time was come that he should be received up, he stedfastly set his face to go to Jerusalem, And sent messengers before his face: and they went, and entered into a village of the <u>Samaritans,</u> to make ready for him. And they <u>did not</u> receive him, because his face was as though he would go to Jerusalem" (Luke 9:51-53). The Old Testament combination *Samaritans* (1x) and *did not* (63x) = 64.

Gospel Workers Must Be Willing
To Break Fellowship with Their Families

"And another also said, Lord, I will follow thee; but let me first go bid them farewell, which are at home at my house. And Jesus said unto him, No <u>man</u>, having put his hand to the plough, and looking back, is fit for the kingdom of God" (Luke 9:61-62). Jesus addressed this man's issue of having to go and gently break fellowship with his family. Jesus' haste to make it to Jerusalem did not afford the man any time for indecision. Messiah was marching forward. The disciples were therefore not to go backward. This proverb makes it clear that the gospel worker should hold no regrets or reservations, neither should he ever think of breaking fellowship with his Lord to retreat homeward until his gospel work is done. Again the word *man* is mentioned in 64 chapters of the Synoptic Gospels. The word *families* is mentioned in 164 verses of the Bible.

Becoming a Christian Will Cause Broken Fellowship within Household

"Suppose ye that I am come to give peace on earth? I tell you, Nay; <u>but rather division: For from henceforth there shall be five in one house divided, three against two, and two against three. The father shall be divided against the son, and the son against the father; the mother against the daughter, and the daughter against the mother; the mother in law against her daughter in law, and the daughter in law against her mother in law</u>" (Luke 12:51-53). Here we have underlined 64 particular words.

Many Refuse God's Fellowship Banquet

"Then said he unto him, A certain man made a great supper, and bade many: And sent his servant at supper time to say to them that were bidden, <u>Come</u>; for all things are now ready. And <u>they</u> all with one consent began to <u>make excuse</u>" (Luke 14:16-18a). Jesus' parable was quite descriptive of Israel's day. So many Jews were breaking fellowship with the Lord and His burgeoning kingdom plan. Again the word *they* is mentioned in 64 chapters of the Minor Prophets. The Bible combination *not come* (63x) and *make excuse* (1x) = 64.

Prodigal Son Returns Home & Is Received Back into Fellowship

"But the father said to his servants, Bring forth the best robe, and put it on him; and put a ring on his hand, and shoes on his feet: And bring hither the fatted calf, and kill it; and let us eat, and be merry: For this <u>my son</u> was <u>dead</u>, and is alive again; he was lost, and is found. And they began to be merry" (Luke 15:22-24). From Genesis to the NT Narrative the phrase *my son* is mentioned in 64 chapters. Again the word *dead* occurs 364 times in the Bible.

The Elder Brother Does Not Feel Like Fellowshipping

"Now his elder son was in the field: and as he came and drew nigh to the house, he heard musick and dancing. And he called one of the servants, and asked what these things meant. And he said unto him, Thy brother is come; and thy father hath killed the fatted calf, because he hath received him safe and sound. And he was angry, and would <u>not go</u> in" (Luke 15:25-28a). The elder brother's refusal to attend the welcome-home party shows he had inwardly broken-off fellowship with his younger brother. The phrase *not go* is mentioned in 64 verses of the Old Testament.

One Shall Be Taken Away & the Other Left

"I tell you, in that night there shall be two men in one bed; the one shall be <u>taken</u>, and the other shall be left. Two women shall be grinding together; the one shall be <u>taken</u>, and the other left. Two men shall be in the field; the one shall be <u>taken</u>, and the other left" (Luke 17:34-36). Many broken fellowships will suddenly come to pass at the end of days. As Jesus prepares to install His kingdom rule He will send forth angels to gather out the faithless ones. Again from Genesis to the NT Narrative the phrase *taken away* is mentioned in 64 verses.

2564th Verse of the New Testament

"Thou knowest the commandments, Do not commit adultery, Do not <u>kill</u>, Do not steal, Do not bear false witness, Honour thy father and thy mother" (Luke 18:20). To break any one of the Ten Commandments is to break fellowship with God. Again the word *killed* is mentioned in 64 verses of the Bible.

Judas Iscariot

"Then entered <u>Satan</u> into <u>Judas</u> surnamed <u>Iscariot</u>, being of the number of the twelve. And he went his way, and communed with the chief priests and captains, how he might betray him unto them. And they were glad, and covenanted to give him money. And he promised, and sought opportunity to BETRAY him unto them in the absence of the multitude" (Luke 22:3-6). Judas' fellowship with Jesus was already on shaky ground, but the moment Satan entered into Judas his fellowship with Christ was irreversibly broken. The Bible combination *Satan* (55x) and *Judas Iscariot* (9x) = 64.

The Last Supper

"And he said unto them, With desire I have desired to eat this <u>passover</u> with you before I suffer" (Luke 22:15). This Passover would mark the beginning of Christ's broken fellowship with His disciples. From Genesis to the Synoptic Gospels the word *passover* occurs 64 times; this is its 64th occurrence.

Luke 22:64

"And when they had blindfolded him, they struck him on the face, and asked him, saying, Prophesy, who is it that smote thee?" (Luke 22:64) After the high priest and the council condemned Jesus to death, the evidence of their broken fellowship began to manifest itself more and more.

King of the Jews Has Broken Fellowship with Jewish Leaders

"And the whole multitude of them arose, and led him unto Pilate. And they began to accuse him, saying, We found this FELLOW perverting the nation, and forbidding to give tribute to Cæsar, saying that he himself is <u>Christ</u> a King" (Luke 23:1-2). Again the title *Lord Jesus Christ* is seen in 64 verses of Pauline Epistles.

Sun Breaks Fellowship with Earth through Grief

"And it was about the sixth hour, and <u>there was a darkness over all</u> <u>the earth</u> until the ninth hour. And the sun was darkened, and the veil of the temple was rent in the midst" (Luke 23:44-45a). The Father's broken fellowship with His dying Son was revealed in a manifest way, by the celestial sun's broken fellowship with Earth. The New Testament combination *there was a darkness over all* (1 ch), *the earth* (63 chs) = 64 chapters.

Christ's Ascension Necessitated Broken Fellowship with His Disciples

"And it came to pass, while he blessed them, <u>he was PARTED FROM them,</u> and carried up into heaven" (Luke 24:51). From Genesis to the Gospels the combination *he was parted* (1x), *from them* (63x) = 64.

64th Verse of John

"And <u>the Jews'</u> passover was at hand, and Jesus went up to Jerusalem" (John 2:13). John's used the term "the Jews" signifies Judea's religious leaders. Jesus was not expecting to enjoy any real fellowship with them. From Genesis to the NT Narrative the phrase *the Jews* is mentioned in 64 chapters.

Man's Broken Fellowship with God at God's house

"And found in the temple those that sold oxen and sheep and doves, and the changers of money sitting: And when he had made a scourge of small cords, he drove them all out of the temple, and the sheep, and the oxen; and poured out the changers' money, and overthrew the tables; And said unto them that sold doves, Take these things hence; make not my <u>Father's house</u> an house of merchandise" (John 2:14-16). Here we see that true fellowship with God had been broken and replaced with commercialism. The OT Narrative combination *the house of the LORD* (162 vs) and *the house of God* (2 vs) = 164 verses.

Same Woman Divorced Five Times

"The woman answered and said, I have no <u>husband</u>. Jesus said unto her, Thou hast well said, I have no <u>husband</u>: For thou hast had five <u>husbands</u>; and he whom thou now hast is not thy <u>husband</u>: in that saidst thou truly" (John 4:17-18). This woman had suffered broken fellowship with five husbands. We are not told why, but the reasons can vary widely. We can conjecture that this woman's striking beauty easily secured her such successive husbands. The Bible combination *her husband* (59x), *bill of divorcement* (3x), *writing of divorcement* (2x) = 64.

John 6:64

"But there are some of you that believe not. For Jesus knew from the beginning who <u>they</u> were that believed not, and who should BETRAY him" (John 6:64). Jesus alerted some listeners concerning their poor standing with Him. He hoped they would not remain content in their state of broken fellowship with their advent King. Again the word *they* is mentioned in 64 chapters of the Minor Prophets.

"I Go unto Him That Sent Me"

The Pharisees and chief priests sent officers to take Jesus. "Then said Jesus unto them, Yet a little while am I with you, and then I go unto him that sent me. Ye shall seek me, and shall not find me: and where I am, thither ye cannot come" (John 7:33-34). Christ spoke of the soon coming broken fellowship between Him and them. The Bible combination *I go* (63x), *unto him that sent me* (1x) = 64.

The Pharisees Display Their Broken Fellowship with Christ

As the Pharisees were enquiring of the healed blind man, he gave them a strong admonition regarding their unbelief in the Great Physician. "Then they reviled him, and said, Thou art his disciple; but we are Moses' disciples. We know that God spake unto Moses: as for this FELLOW, we know not from whence he is" (John 9:28-29). Again the title *the Pharisee(s)* occurs 64 combined times in the NT Narrative.

Healed Blind Man Put out of Fellowship by the Council

The now-seeing man said, "If this man were not of God, he could do nothing. They answered and said unto him, Thou wast altogether born in sins, and dost thou teach us? And they CAST HIM OUT" (John 9:33-34). The healed blind man was ready to enjoy new fellowship with his countrymen, yet the leaders made him suffer broken fellowship and humiliation. The Old Testament combination *they cast* (15x), *him out* (43x), *of the temple of the LORD* (6x) = 64.

464th Verse of John

"My sheep hear my voice, and I know them, and they follow me: And I give unto them eternal life; and they shall never perish, neither shall any man pluck them out of my hand" (John 10:27-28). Jesus testifies to the nature of the Shepherd and sheep's unbreakable fellowship. This unbroken-fellowship verse is concurrently the 3364th verse of the New Testament.

Lazarus' Death & Burial

"The Jews then which were with her in the house, and comforted her, when they saw Mary, that she rose up hastily and went out, followed her, saying, She goeth unto the grave to weep there" (John 11:31). The grave stands between the living and the dead as an emblem of the departed and the living's broken fellowship. Again the word *grave* is mentioned in 64 verses of the Bible.

564th Verse of John

"And Jesus answered them, saying, The hour is come, that the Son of man should be glorified. . . . Now is my soul troubled; and what shall I say? Father, save me from this hour: but for this cause came I unto this hour. Father, glorify thy name. Then came there a voice from heaven, saying, I have both glorified it, and will glorify it again" (John 12:23, 27-28). The Incarnate Son had enjoyed unbroken fellowship with the Father all His life, yet in this hour of His suffering their fellowship would become severely broken. The word *hour* occurs 64 times in the Gospels. The underlined broken-fellowship verse is the 564th verse of John and concurrently the 3464th verse of the New Testament.

Master & Disciples' Broken Fellowship Only Transitory

"Simon Peter said unto him, Lord, whither goest thou? Jesus answered him, Whither <u>I go</u>, <u>thou canst not follow me now</u>; but thou shalt follow me afterwards. Peter said unto him, Lord, why cannot I follow thee now?" (John 13:36-37a) After Peter died he could regain face-to-face fellowship with Christ up in heaven. The Bible combination *I go* (63x), *thou canst not follow me now* (1x) = 64.

Bride & Groom's Broken Fellowship during Betrothal Period

"I <u>go</u> to prepare a place for you. And if I <u>go</u> and prepare a place for you, I will come again, and receive you unto myself; that where I am, there ye may be also" (John 14:2c-3). Jesus speaks in Near East terms of a betrothal. At her father's house, after the bride agreed to marry the groom he went away to build an addition onto his father's house. When it was finished he would return unannounced to the bride's house to take her away so she could be with him forevermore. Jesus was foretelling events surrounding the catching away of the saints, otherwise known as the Rapture. Again the word *go* occurs 64 times in Ezekiel.

Broken Fellowship with Christ Remedied by His Indwelling Spirit

"And I will pray the Father, and he shall give you another Comforter, that he may abide with you for ever. . . . I will not <u>LEAVE</u> <u>you</u> comfortless: I will come to you" (John 14:16, 18). The Greek word here for comfortless literally means orphaned. An orphan is a destitute child who in his misery is left without the everyday fellowship and comfort of a father and mother. The naturally occurring John combination *leave* (5x), *you* (159x) = 164.

Broken Fellowship for a Little While
During Christ's Death, Resurrection & Ascension

"A little while, and ye shall not see me: and again, a little while, and ye shall see me, because <u>I go</u> to the <u>Father</u>. . . . They said therefore, What is this that he saith, A little while? we cannot tell what he saith. Now Jesus knew that they were desirous to ask him, and said unto them . . . Verily, verily, I say unto you, That ye shall weep and lament, but the world shall rejoice: and ye shall be sorrowful, but your sorrow shall be turned into joy. . . . I will see you again, and your heart shall rejoice, and your joy no man taketh from you" (John 16:16, 18-19a, 20, 22b).

Again the word *go* occurs 64 times in Ezekiel. The Bible combination *I go* (63x) and *to my father's house in peace* (1x) = 64.

They Have Taken Away My Lord

Two angels talked with Mary Magdalene. "And they say unto her, Woman, why weepest thou? She saith unto them, Because they have <u>taken away</u> my Lord, and I know not where they have laid him" (John 20:13). Mary lamented her broken fellowship with the Master who had once so graciously saved her from indwelling devils. Again from Genesis to the NT Narrative the phrase *taken away* is mentioned in 64 verses.

Thomas Loathed His Broken Fellowship with Christ & As a Result
Broke Fellowship with the Apostles

"But Thomas, one of the twelve, called Didymus, was not with them when Jesus came. The other disciples therefore said unto him, We have seen the Lord. But he said unto them, Except I shall see in his hands the print of the nails, and put my finger into the print of the nails, and thrust my hand into his side, I will not believe" (John 20:24-25). In this broken-fellowship passage there are 64 words surrounding the name *Thomas*.

Galilean Apostles' Broken Fellowship with the Others

"After these things Jesus shewed himself again to the <u>disciples</u> at the sea of Tiberias; and on this wise shewed he himself. There were together Simon Peter, and Thomas called Didymus, and Nathanael of Cana in Galilee, and the sons of Zebedee, and two other of his disciples" (John 21:1-2). The twelve had been inseparable for three and a half years. But because there were only seven disciples banded together here, there was evident broken fellowship between the remainder of disciples—geographically. Not all of Christ's disciples were from Galilee. Again the word *disciples* occurs 64 times in John's Gospel.

864th Verse of John

"Jesus saith unto them, Bring of the fish which ye have now caught" (John 21:10). The disciples had all become disoriented with Jesus' resurrection appearances and disappearances. It was a broken fellowship that greatly disheartened them. Some of them even took up fishing again, thus forsaking their ministerial calling. They should have been telling the Galileans about Jesus' mighty resurrection. This broken-fellowship verse is concurrently the 3764th verse of the New Testament.

The Middle East Reconciliation Meal

"<u>Jesus saith unto them, Bring of the fish which ye have now caught.</u> . . . Jesus saith unto them, Come and dine. And none of the disciples durst ask him, Who art thou? knowing that it was the Lord. Jesus then cometh, and taketh bread, and giveth them, and fish likewise" (John 21:10, 12-13). The meal which Christ had prepared for the disciples is known in the Middle East as the Sulha, meaning table. It is a reconciliation meal whereby two disgruntled parties may work out their broken fellowship and differences peaceably over a table of food. There is little doubt that there was salt present at this meal, the customary token of friendship and peace. All the disciples had broken fellowship with the Lord on the night of His passion, and they needed to be reconciled to Him. The underlined words mark the 3764th verse of the New Testament, and they are part of Christ's plan to restore their broken fellowship with Him.

Christ Restores the Broken Fellowship between Him & Peter

"So when they had dined, Jesus saith to Simon <u>Peter</u>, <u>Simon, son of Jonas</u>, lovest thou me more than these? He saith unto him, Yea, Lord; thou knowest that I love thee. He saith unto him, Feed my lambs. He saith to him again the second time, Simon, son of Jonas, <u>lovest thou me?</u> He saith unto him, Yea, Lord; thou knowest that I love thee. He saith unto him, Feed my sheep. He saith unto him the third time, Simon, son of Jonas, <u>lovest thou me?</u> Peter was grieved because he said unto him the third time, <u>Lovest thou me?</u> And he said unto him, Lord, thou knowest all things; thou knowest that I love thee. Jesus saith unto him, Feed my sheep" (John 21:15-17).

The Bible combination *Peter* (158x), *Simon son of Jonas* (3x), *lovest thou me* (3x) = 164.

64th Verse of Acts

"Then Peter said unto them, Repent, and be baptized every one of you in the name of Jesus Christ for the <u>remission of sins</u>, and ye shall receive the gift of the Holy Ghost" (Acts 2:38). Mans' sin causes broken fellowship with God. This offense demands repentance toward the offended Person. Until true repentance is made before God, broken fellowship will persist with God. The New Testament combination *remission of* (9 chs), *sins* (55 chs) = 64 chapters.

4064th Verse of the New Testament

"The place of the scripture which he read was this, He was led as a sheep to the slaughter; and like a lamb dumb before his shearer, so opened he not his mouth" (Acts 8:32). The Messiah's broken fellowship with His generation is severely shown here.

Paul & Barnabas Break Fellowship

"And Barnabas determined to take with them John, whose surname was Mark. But Paul thought not good to take him with <u>them</u>, who <u>departed from</u> <u>them</u> from Pamphylia, and went not with <u>them</u> to the work. And the contention was so sharp between <u>them</u>, that they departed asunder one from the other: and so Barnabas took Mark, and sailed unto Cyprus; And Paul chose Silas, and departed" (Acts 15:37-40a). This broken fellowship was later restored. Again the word *them* occurs 64 times in Romans. The Gospels combination *departed* (51x) *from them* (13x) = 64.

Hebrew Crowd Violently Breaks Fellowship with Their Hebrew Preacher

"And they gave him audience unto this word, and then <u>lifted up their voices, and</u> said, <u>Away with such a FELLOW</u> <u>from the earth</u>: <u>for it is not fit that he</u> <u>should live</u>" (Acts 22:22). Since Paul spoke to the Hebrews in the Hebrew tongue they were all equals or fellows in that regard. The Bible combination *then lifted up their voices and* (4x), *away with* (22x), *such a fellow* (1x), *from the earth* (29x), *for it is not fit that he* (1x), *should live* (7x) = 64.

Paul Breaks the Fragile Fellowship Existing
Between Pharisees & Sadducees

"But when Paul perceived that the one part were Sadducees, and the other <u>Pharisees</u>, he cried out in the council, Men and brethren, I am a Pharisee, the son of a Pharisee: of the hope and resurrection of the dead I am called in question. And when he had so said, there arose a dissension <u>between the</u> <u>Pharisees</u> and the Sadducees: and the multitude was divided. For the Sadducees say that there is no resurrection, neither angel, nor spirit: but the <u>Pharisees</u> confess both. And there arose a great cry: and the scribes that were of the <u>Pharisees'</u> part arose, and strove, saying, We find no evil in this man: but if a spirit or an angel hath spoken to him, let us not fight against God. And when there arose a great dissension" (Acts 23:6-10a).

Again the title *the Pharisee(s)* occurs 64 combined times in the NT Narrative. Again the phrase *between the* is mentioned naturally in 64 verses of the Bible.

Pharisees of Pharisees' Broken Fellowship with the Pharisees

Paul's nephew spoke to the chief captain of the Roman guard. "The Jews have agreed to desire thee that thou wouldest bring down Paul to morrow into the council, as though <u>they</u> would enquire somewhat of him more perfectly. But do not thou yield unto <u>them</u>: for there lie in wait for him of <u>them</u> more than forty men, which have bound themselves with an oath, that <u>they</u> will neither eat nor drink till <u>they</u> have killed him: and now are <u>they</u> ready, looking for a promise from thee" (Acts 23:20-21). Again the title *the Pharisee(s)* occurs 64 combined times in the NT Narrative. Again the word *them* occurs 64 times in Romans. Again the word *they* is mentioned in 64 chapters of the Minor Prophets.

Paul's Imprisonment

"But after two years Porcius Festus came into Felix' room: and Felix, willing to shew the Jews a pleasure, left <u>Paul</u> bound" (Acts 24:27). Paul's normal day-to-day fellowship with believers was severely broken during his extended imprisonment at Caesarea Maritime. The New Testament combination *Paul* (153 vs) and *into prison* (11 vs) = 164 verses.

Broken Fellowship between Believing & Non-Believing Roman Jews

"And <u>some</u> <u>believed the things which were spoken, and</u> <u>some</u> <u>believed not</u>. And when <u>they</u> agreed not among themselves, they departed" (Acts. 28:24-25a). The New Testament combination *some believed the things which were spoken and* (1x), *some* (148x), *believed not* (14x), *and when they agreed not among themselves* (1x) = 164.

Breaking Fellowship with God's Covenant Law

Paul is making reference to unbelieving Jews when he writes, "Thou that makest thy boast of the law, through BREAKING the law dishonourest thou <u>God</u>?" (Rom. 2:23) Again the title *God* occurs 64 times in the Epistle of First John.

Old Testament Vine Suffers Broken Fellowship among Its Branches

"Thou wilt say then, The branches were BROKEN off, that I might be graffed in. Well; because of unbelief <u>they</u> were BROKEN off, and thou standest by faith. Be not highminded, but fear" (Rom. 11:19-20). Here the word *they* is the 114,664th word of the New Testament. Again the word *they* is mentioned in 64 chapters of the Minor Prophets.

Broken Fellowship between Two Believers

"But why dost thou judge thy brother? or why dost thou set at nought <u>thy brother</u>? for we shall all stand before the judgment seat of Christ" (Rom. 14:10). This verse presents the Bible's 64th occurrence of the phrase *thy brother*, and we see how it pertains to broken fellowship between two believers.

1064th Chapter of the Bible

This chapter analyzes the broken fellowship between the wisdom of men and the wisdom of God and between the foolish and the wise. "For I determined not to know any thing among you, save Jesus Christ, and him crucified. And . . . That your faith should not stand in the wisdom of <u>men</u>, but in the power of God. . . . But the natural <u>man</u> receiveth not the things of the Spirit of God: for they are foolishness unto him: neither can he know them, because they are spiritually discerned" (1 Cor. 2:2-3a, 5). The word *men* is mentioned in 640 chapters of the Bible, a vivid multiple of 64. Again the word *man* is mentioned in 64 verses of First Corinthians.

64th Verse of First Corinthians

"If any man <u>defile</u> the temple of God, him shall God destroy; for the temple of God is holy, which temple ye are" (1 Cor. 3:17). Here Paul warns the believer to be very careful with the use of his personal temple because it belongs to God for the purpose of unbroken fellowship. Paul drew from the Mosaic principle where defilement of any kind would put the defiled Israelite at a distance from the whole camp. That person would then suffer broken fellowship with his countrymen until the matter was resolved. From Genesis to the NT Narrative the word *defiled* is mentioned in 64 verses.

When Brother Breaks Fellowship with Brother

"But brother goeth to law with brother, and that before the unbelievers. Now therefore there is utterly a fault among you, because ye go to law one with another. Why do ye not rather take wrong? why do ye not rather suffer yourselves to be defrauded? Nay, <u>ye do wrong</u>, <u>and defraud</u>, <u>and that</u> <u>your brethren</u>" (1 Cor. 6:6-8). The Pauline Epistles combination *ye do* (8x), *wrong* (7x), *do wrong* (1x), *and defraud* (2x), *and that* (45x), *your brethren* (1x) = 64.

Broken Fellowship between Christian & Non-Christian Spouses

"<u>And unto the married I command</u>, yet not I, but the Lord, <u>Let not the wife DEPART FROM her husband</u>: <u>But and if she DEPART</u>, <u>let her remain unmarried, or be reconciled to her husband</u>: and let not the husband PUT AWAY his wife. But to the rest speak I, not the Lord: If any brother hath a wife that believeth not, and she be pleased to dwell with him, let him not PUT her AWAY. And the woman which hath an husband that believeth not, and if he be pleased to dwell with her, let her not LEAVE him" (1 Cor. 7:10-13).

The Bible combination *and unto the married I command* (1x), *let not the wife depart from* (1x), *her husband* (59x), *but and if she depart* (1x), *let her remain unmarried* (1x), *or be reconciled to her husband* (1x) = 64.

Corinthians Not to Be Careless & Break Fellowship with God

"But I say, that the things which the Gentiles sacrifice, <u>they sacrifice to devils</u>, and not to God: and <u>I would not that</u> <u>ye should have</u> <u>FELLOWSHIP with</u> <u>devils</u>" (1 Cor. 10:20). One cannot at the same time have fellowship with devils and with God. The New Testament combination *they sacrifice to devils* (1x), *I would not that* (3x), *ye should have* (5x), *fellowship with* (4x), *devils* (51x) = 64.

Broken Bread Representative of Christ's Geographically Broken Fellowship

"<u>And when he had given thanks, he BRAKE</u> <u>it, and said, Take, eat: this is</u> <u>my body</u>, <u>which is BROKEN</u> <u>for you</u>: <u>this do in remembrance of me</u>" (1 Cor. 11:24). The New Testament combination *and when he had given thanks he brake* (1x), *it and said* (2x), *take eat this is* (3x), *my body* (10x), *which is broken* (1x), *for you* (45x), *this do in remembrance of me* (2x) = 64.

Broken Fellowship between Righteousness & Unrighteousness

"Be ye not unequally yoked together with unbelievers: for what FELLOWSHIP hath <u>righteousness</u> with unrighteousness? and what communion hath light with darkness?" (2 Cor. 6:14) Here the word *righteousness* is the 129,564[th] word of the New Testament, and it pertains to a needful broken fellowship.

Under Duress, Peter Suddenly Breaks Fellowship with Gentile Believers

"For before that certain came from James, <u>he did eat with the Gentiles</u>: <u>but when they were come</u>, <u>he withdrew and</u> <u>separated himself</u>, <u>fearing them</u> <u>which were of the circumcision</u>" (Gal. 2:12). The New Testament combination *Peter* (158x), *did eat with the Gentiles* (1x), *but when they were come* (1x), *he withdrew and* (1x), *separated himself* (1x), *fearing them* (1x), *which were of the circumcision* (1x) = 164.

64th Verse of Galatians

"Wherefore then serveth the law? It was added because of transgressions, till the seed should come to whom the promise was made; and it was ordained by angels in the hand of a mediator" (Gal. 3:19). Because no man could keep the law, mankind stood in constant breach of fellowship with God. Only ordained blood sacrifices could restore such a breach.

Gentiles & Jews

"Wherefore remember, that ye being in time past <u>Gentiles</u> in the flesh, who are called <u>Uncircumcision</u> by that which is called the Circumcision in the flesh made by hands; That at that time ye were without Christ, being aliens from the commonwealth of <u>Israel</u>. . . . But now in Christ Jesus ye who sometimes were far off are made nigh by the blood of Christ. For he is our peace, who hath made both one, and hath broken down the middle wall of partition between us; Having abolished in his flesh the enmity, even the law of commandments contained in ordinances; for to make in himself of twain one new man, so making peace" (Eph. 2:11-12b, 13-15).

The Pauline Epistles combination *Gentiles* (48x) and *Uncircumcision* (16x) = 64. Again the name *Israel* occurs 364 times in First and Second Kings.

Holy Spirit & Believer

"And <u>grieve not</u> <u>the</u> holy <u>Spirit</u> of God, whereby ye are sealed unto the day of redemption. Let all bitterness, and wrath, and anger, and clamour, and evil speaking, be PUT AWAY from you, with all malice" (Eph. 4:30-31). Paul lists some sins among believers which will grieve the Holy Spirit. The Holy Spirit will never take flight from the offending believer, but He will break fellowship until the offending one acknowledges his or her error and asks for forgiveness. The New Testament combination *grieve not* (1x) and *the S/spirit* (163x) = 164.

Euodias & Syntyche

"I <u>beseech Euodias, and beseech Syntyche, that they be of the same mind in the Lord</u>" (Phil. 4:2). These two believers' broken fellowship was affecting the whole church, and Paul wanted them to quickly reconcile. The command *beseech Euodias, and beseech Syntyche, that they be of the same mind in the Lord* consist of 64 letters! The word *beseech* is mentioned in 64 verses of the Bible.

64th Verse of Colossians

"Put on therefore, as the elect of God, holy and beloved, bowels of mercies, kindness, humbleness of mind, meekness, <u>longsuffering</u>" (Col. 3:12). Performing the commands of this verse will help eliminate broken fellowship with another believer. The word *longsuffering* is mentioned in 64 chapters of the Bible.

Brother & Brother

"That no man go beyond and <u>defraud his brother</u> in any matter: because that the Lord is the avenger of all such, as we also have forewarned you and testified" (1 Thess. 4:6). The New Testament combination *defraud his* (1 ch), *brother* (63 chs) = 64 chapters.

64th Verse of First Thessalonians

"For when <u>they</u> shall say, Peace and safety; then sudden destruction cometh <u>upon them</u>, as travail upon a woman with child; and they shall not escape" (1 Thess. 5:3). If broken fellowship between unbelievers and a holy God remains unresolved without repentance on the sinners' part, then tribulation wrath will surely come upon them. Again the word *they* is mentioned in 64 chapters of the Minor Prophets. The phrase *upon them* occurs 164 times in the Old Testament.

Orderly & Disorderly

"Now we command you, brethren, in the name of our Lord Jesus Christ, that ye WITHDRAW yourselves <u>FROM</u> every brother that walketh disorderly, and not after the tradition which he received of us" (2 Thess. 3:6). Orderly believers are to withdraw their fellowship from disorderly believers. Again the word *from* is mentioned in 64 verses of First Kings.

Hymenaeus & Alexander

"Holding faith, and a good conscience; which some having PUT AWAY concerning faith have made shipwreck: Of whom is Hymenaeus and Alexander; whom I have delivered unto Satan, that <u>they</u> may learn not to blaspheme" (1 Tim. 1:19-20). These two Greek-minded believers were put out of church fellowship because of unrepentance concerning their false teaching on the resurrection of the saints. Again the word *they* is mentioned in 64 chapters of the Minor Prophets.

Demas & Paul

"For Demas hath FORSAKEN me, having loved this present world, and is DEPARTED unto Thessalonica" (2 Tim. 4:10a). Demas broke fellowship both with Paul and with the gospel because of his greater love for the world. The 64th letter in this broken-fellowship verse is the *r* in departed.

Heretic & House of God

"But avoid foolish questions, and genealogies, and contentions, and strivings about the law; for they are unprofitable and vain. <u>A man</u> <u>that is an heretick</u> <u>after the first and</u> <u>second</u> <u>admonition</u> <u>reject</u>; Knowing that he that is such is subverted, and sinneth, being condemned of himself" (Titus 3:9-11). Believers are to break fellowship with an unrepentant heretic. The Pauline and General Epistles combination *a man* (48x), *that is an heretick* (1x), *after the first and* (1x), *second* (10x), *admonition* (3x), *reject* (1x) = 64.

Philemon & Onesimus

Paul wroteto his frien,d saying, "Philemon our dearly beloved, and fellowlabourer . . . I beseech thee for my son Onesimus, whom I have begotten in my bonds: Which in time past was to thee unprofitable, but now profitable to thee and to me: Whom I have sent again: thou therefore receive him. . . . <u>For perhaps</u> he therefore <u>DEPARTED for a</u> <u>season</u>, that thou shouldest receive him for ever" (Philem. 1c, 10-12a, 15). This master and slave suffered broken fellowship when the slave ran away. Paul sought to right the wrong that had transpired. The Bible combination *for perhaps* (1x), *he therefore* (6x), *departed for a* (1x), *season* (56x) = 64.

Israel & Messiah

"For this is the covenant that I will make with the house of <u>Israel</u> after those days, saith the Lord; I will put my laws into their mind, and write them in their <u>hearts</u>: and I will be to them a God, and they shall be to me a people. . . . for all shall know me, from the least to the greatest. For I will be merciful to their unrighteousness, and their sins and their iniquities will I remember no more" (Heb. 8:10, 11b-12). When the King of the Jews returns to Israel, every Israelite will become an instant believer and be healed of his or her broken fellowship with the Lord. Again the name *Israel* occurs 364 times in First and Second Kings. Again the word *heart* is mentioned in 664 verses of the Old Testament.

Moses & Egypt

"By faith Moses, when he was come to years, refused to be called the son of Pharaoh's daughter; Choosing rather to suffer affliction with the people of God, than to enjoy the pleasures of sin for a season; Esteeming the reproach of Christ greater riches than the treasures in Egypt: for he had respect unto the recompence of the reward. By faith he FORSOOK Egypt, not fearing the wrath of the king: for he endured, as seeing him who is invisible" (Heb. 11:24-27). The phrase *out of Egypt* occurs 64 times from Genesis to the OT Narrative.

Rich Man & Poor Man

"For if there come unto your assembly a man with a gold ring, in goodly apparel, and there come in also a poor man in vile raiment; And ye have respect to him that weareth the gay clothing, and say unto him, Sit thou here in a good place; and say to the poor, Stand thou there, or sit here under my footstool: Are ye not then partial in yourselves" (James 2:2-4a). The Bible combination *there come in* (3x), *also a poor man* (1x), *in vile raiment* (1x), *and say to* (8x), *the poor* (145x), *stand thou there or sit* (1x), *here under* (2x), *my footstool* (3x) = 164.

Saint & Sinner

"Wherein they think it strange that ye run not with them to the same excess of riot, speaking evil of you" (1 Pet. 4:4). Again the word *them* is found in 64 books of the Bible.

Fellowship with God Broken by Walk of Darkness

"If we say that we have FELLOWSHIP with him, and walk in darkness, we lie, and do not the truth" (1 John 1:6). Again the word *we* occurs 64 times in Numbers.

Maintaining Unbroken Fellowship with God

The aged apostle said, "My little children, these things write I unto you, that ye sin not. And if any man sin, we have an advocate with the Father, Jesus Christ the righteous" (1 John 2:1). Just two verses earlier John stated, "If we confess our sins, he is faithful and just to forgive us our sins, and to cleanse us from all unrighteousness." In this New Testament dispensation Christ stands at the right hand of God, the Judge of all the Earth, and serves as the believer's only Advocate. The believer needs to be saved just once; however, he may need to be forgiven innumerable times. Christ stands ready to handle these matters whenever they arise. The believer's relationship with the Father never changes; only his fellowship with Him changes. Broken fellowship is corrected with the believer's simple confession and request for forgiveness. This should be done without delay. Again the word *sin* is mentioned in 64 verses of the OT Narrative. Again the word *sins* is mentioned naturally in 164 verses of the Bible.

64th Book of the Bible

THIRD JOHN is the 64th BOOK of the Bible by no coincidence. The heart of this brief letter pertains to one local pastor who refused to receive visiting evangelists including John himself, sparking broken fellowships between himself other Spirit-gifted leaders in Christ's church.

The beloved apostle condemned this evil pastor for breaking fellowship with such upstanding members of the church:

"We therefore ought to receive such, that we might be fellowhelpers to the truth. I wrote unto the church: but DIOTREPHES, who loveth to have the preeminence <u>among</u> them, receiveth us not. Wherefore, if I come, I will remember his deeds which he doeth, prating against us with malicious words: and not content therewith, <u>neither</u> doth he himself receive the brethren, and FORBIDDETH them that would, and casteth <u>them</u> out of the church" (3 John 1:8-10).

Diotrephese went so far as to put out of fellowship, to excommunicate, church members who gave lodging to visiting preachers of the gospel. How dreadful! Because of this evil pastor's attitude the whole church must have collectively sensed a spirit of broken fellowship with Lord. The word *among* is mentioned in 64 verses of Numbers. The word *neither* occurs naturally 164 times in the Law. Again the word *them* occurs 64 times in Romans.

With the following words John exhorted the church to continue on the right path regardless of Diotrephes' wrong path: "Beloved, follow not that which is <u>evil</u>, but that which is good" (v. 11). The word *evil* is mentioned in 64 verses of the Pauline and General Epistles.

The Fallen Angels

"And the <u>angels</u> which kept not their first estate, but LEFT their own habitation, he hath reserved in everlasting chains under darkness unto the judgment of the great day" (Jude 6). A sizable portion of the angels in heaven broke fellowship with God a short time after Lucifer did. This breach became irreversible. The title *angels* is mentioned in 64 chapters of the Bible.

64th Verse of Revelation

"I know thy <u>works</u>, that thou art neither cold nor hot: I would thou wert cold or hot" (Rev. 3:15). More than a generation had passed since the Laodicean church began with its fiery zeal. Now zeal had gone from this once-vibrant local church body. They had broken fellowship with the Savior through their half-heartedness and indifference. The word *works(')* is mentioned in 64 chapters of the New Testament.

Laodicea's Broken Fellowship with the Lord

"I counsel thee to buy of me gold tried in the fire, that thou mayest be rich; and white raiment, that thou mayest be clothed, and that the shame of thy nakedness do not appear; and anoint thine eyes with eyesalve, that thou mayest see. As many as I love, I rebuke and chasten: be zealous therefore, and repent" (Rev. 3:18-19). This verse presents the Bible's 64th occurrence of the word *clothed*, and in it the Lord advises wayward believers to cover their spiritual shame and thus restore the broken fellowship between them and Him.

65—Apostasy

Webster's Dictionary gives us the following two definitions of the word APOSTASY: [1] an act of <u>refusing</u> to continue <u>to follow</u>, <u>obey</u>, or recognize a religious faith; and [2] the abandonment of a previous loyalty, defection.

> The OT combination [all forms of the word] *refuse* (61x), *to follow* (4x) = 65.
> The OT combination [all forms of the word] *refuse* (61x), *to obey* (4x) = 65.

The word "apostasy" or variations of it do not appear in the Bible. However, we do see it in the New Testament's original Greek text. The Greek word *apostasia* means a defection from the truth. In Second Thessalonians 2:3 the KJV Bible renders this Greek noun as "<u>falling away</u>" and in Acts 21:21 as "<u>forsake</u>." The adjective *apostasion* means something separative and is rendered three times in the New Testament as "divorcement." The equivalent Hebrew root word *azab* occurs very frequently in the Old Testament and is rendered by the KJV translators as "forsake" or "<u>leave</u>."

> The Old Testament combination *falling* (8 vs), *away* (657 vs) = 665 verses.
> The Pauline and General Epistles combination *fall* (15x), *away* (50x) = 65.
> Various forms of the phrase *fall away* occur together five times in Scripture; one of these occurs is in the 365th verse of Luke.
> All forms of the word *fall* are mentioned in 65 verses of the New Testament.
> The word *fallen* is mentioned in 65 chapters of the Bible.
>
> ~~~~~
>
> The word *from* occurs 265 times in the Psalms.
> The word *from* is mentioned in 65 chapters of the Synoptic Gospels.
> The word *from* is found in 65 books of the Bible.
> The phrase *from the* is mentioned naturally in 165 verses of the Law.
> The phrase *from thy* occurs 65 times in the Bible.
> The phrase *from him* is mentioned in 65 chapters of the Old Testament.
> The phrase *far from* occurs 65 times in the Bible.
>
> ~~~~~
>
> All forms of the word forsake: *forsake* (57 vs), *forsaken* (74 vs), *forsaketh* (6 vs), *forsaking* (2 vs), *forsook* (24 vs), *forsookest* (2 vs) = 165 verses of the Bible.

An interesting numeric seal will be shown early in Genesis being associated with the number SIXTY AND FIVE.

Aftermath of Adam & Eve's Apostasy

"And they heard the voice of the LORD God walking in the garden in the cool of the day: and Adam and his wife hid themselves <u>FROM the</u> presence of the LORD God amongst the trees of the garden" (Gen. 3:8). The first couple was now ashamed of their apostasy. Again the phrase *from the* is mentioned naturally in 165 verses of the Law. Again the phrase *from him* is mentioned in 65 chapters of the Old Testament.

65th Verse of the Bible

"And the LORD God called unto Adam, and said unto him, Where art thou?" (Gen. 3:9) The metaphysical place where Adam currently existed was a state of apostasy. They had abandoned their previous loyalty to God and defected from the faith. Their guilt was now causing them great embarrassment.

The Man Makes Excuse for His Apostasy

"Hast thou eaten of the tree, whereof I commanded thee that thou shouldest not eat? And the man said, The woman whom thou gavest to be with me, she gave me of the tree, and I did eat" (Gen. 3:11b-12). The word *man* is mentioned in 65 verses of Numbers.

Cain's Apostasy

"And the LORD said unto Cain, Why art thou wroth? and why is thy countenance FALLEN? If thou doest well, shalt thou not be accepted? and if thou doest not well, sin lieth at the door. And unto thee shall be his desire, and thou shalt rule over him. And Cain talked with Abel his brother: and it came to pass, when they were in the field, that Cain rose up against Abel his brother, and slew him" (Gen. 4:6-8). The Lord sought to correct Cain's wrong approach to the altar by simply reminding him of the true religion He had established for mankind, yet Cain continued to depart from the known truth. Instead of moving closer to the truth he moved further away. Cain hated the truth so much that he chose to demonstrate his apostasy in a very violent way. Again the word *fallen* is mentioned in 65 chapters of the Bible. The word *sin* is mentioned in 195 chapters of the Bible, a multiple of 65.

Enoch's Apostasy from Earth at Age 365

"And Enoch lived SIXTY AND FIVE years, and begat Methuselah: And Enoch walked with God after he begat Methuselah three hundred years, and begat sons and daughters: And all the days of Enoch were THREE HUNDRED SIXTY AND FIVE years: And Enoch walked with God: and he was not; for God took him" (Gen. 5:21-24). The number *sixty and five* is seen only three times in Scripture, and two of these occurrences pertain to Enoch. According to our Greek definition of apostasy, Enoch became 'separated' from Earth geographically. The word *for* is the 365th word in this chapter, and it is part of an explanatory phrase which gives the reason Enoch became separated from the earth. The phrases *sixty and five years: and Enoch walked with God: and he was not; for God took him* consist of 65 characters!

The Worldwide Apostasy of Mankind

"And GOD saw that the wickedness of man was great in the earth, and that every imagination of the thoughts of his heart was only evil continually" (Gen. 6:5). The phrase *of man* is mentioned in 165 verses of the Old Testament.

> The word *evil* is mentioned in 65 chapters of the Major Prophets.
> The phrase *evil in* occurs 65 times in the Old Testament.

Waters of the Earth Apostatize Worldwide

"And it came to pass after seven days, that the waters of the flood were upon the earth. In the six hundredth year of Noah's life, in the second month, the seventeenth day of the month, the same day were all the fountains of the great deep broken up, and the windows of heaven were opened.

And the rain was upon the earth forty days and forty nights" (Gen. 7:10-12). According to our Greek definition of apostasy, the waters 'separated' themselves from their ordained abiding places. They dislodged from their fixed regions above and below the earth to move onward unto other geographic places. In the process they brought about great chaos to the inhabitants of the earth. The phrase *the waters* occurs 165 times in the Old Testament. The Old Testament combination *six hundred* (63x) and *six hundredth* (2x) = 65.

Canaan's Apostate Line

"And Noah awoke from his wine, and knew what his younger son had done unto him. And he said, Cursed be <u>Canaan</u>; a servant of servants shall he be unto his brethren" (Gen. 9:24-25). Ham abandoned his previous loyalty to family in a horrible way. He turned from sacredness to sacrilege. His apostasy from family values was rewarded with a perpetual family curse. The name *Canaan* occurs 65 times in the Law.

465th Verse of the Bible

"And said, I pray you, brethren, do not so <u>wickedly</u>" (Gen. 19:7). Lot expressed his abhorrence for the Sodomites' apostate ways. The word *wicked* is mentioned in 325 verses of the Bible, a multiple of 65.

Apostate Cities of the Plain Destroyed by Fire & Brimstone

"Then the LORD rained upon Sodom and upon Gomorrah brimstone and fire from the LORD out of heaven; And he overthrew those <u>cities</u>, and all the plain, and all the inhabitants of the <u>cities</u>, and that which grew upon the ground. . . . and lo, the smoke of the country went up as the smoke of a furnace" (Gen. 19:24-25, 28c). Cities are a breeding ground for eroding faith and apostasy. The word *cities* is mentioned in 65 chapters of the Major and Minor Prophets. The Bible combination *then the LORD rained upon* (1x), *Sodom* (48x), *and Gomorrah/ha* (15x), *brimstone and fire from the LORD* (1x) = 65.

Lot's Apostate Daughters

"And <u>Lot</u> went up out of Zoar, and dwelt in the mountain, and his two <u>daughters</u> with him; for he feared to dwell in Zoar: and he dwelt in a cave, he and his two daughters. And the firstborn said unto the younger, Our father is old, and there is not a man in the earth to come in unto us after the manner of all the earth: Come, let us make our father drink wine, and we <u>will lie with him</u>, that we may preserve seed of our father" (Gen. 19:30-32). These daughters abandoned their previous loyalty to family in a horrible way. Each of them turned from their understanding of what was sacred to willfully commit sacrilege. Their defection from the truth of family faith and values was rewarded with a perpetual family curse. Their two sons would become fathers of the Moabites and the Ammonites, fierce enemies of the Israelites—the people of God. The Genesis combination *Lot's* (1x), *daughters* (63x), *will lie with him* (1x) = 65.

665th Verse of the Bible

"But unto the sons of the concubines, which Abraham had, Abraham gave gifts, and sent them AWAY FROM Isaac his son, while he yet lived, eastward, unto the east country" (Gen. 25:6). Keturah was Abraham's wife, yet only held the status of a second-class wife. Her sons were made to apostatize from the camp, that is, to forsake camp.

Esau's Apostasy

"And Jacob said, Swear to me this day; and he sware unto him: and he <u>sold his birthright</u> unto Jacob. Then Jacob gave Esau bread and pottage of lentiles; and he did eat and drink, and rose up, and went his way: thus <u>Esau</u> <u>despised his birthright</u>" (Gen. 25:33-34). Esau's act was a token sign of his refusal to continue following his father's religious Hebrew faith. Being the firstborn son, he defected from a particular family truth of great value. The Genesis combination *Esau* (64x) and *sold his birthright* (1x) = 65. The Bible combination *despised* (60x), *his birthright* (5x) = 65.

Esau's Continued Apostasy

"And <u>Esau</u> was forty years old when he <u>took to wife Judith the daughter of Beeri the Hittite</u>, and Bashemath the daughter of Elon the Hittite: Which were a grief of mind unto Isaac and to Rebekah" (Gen. 26:34-35). The apostate son departed from an established family custom of only marrying within the Hebrew tribe. According to our second definition of apostasy, Esau 'defected' from his Hebrew people by marrying non-Hebrew wives. He would become the father of the Edomites, the Jacobites' enemies. The Genesis combination *Esau* (64x) and *took to wife Judith the daughter of Beeri the Hittite* (1x) = 65.

Jacob Apostatized from Laban's Land

Laban urgently enquired of Jacob, saying, "<u>Wherefore didst thou flee AWAY secretly, and steal AWAY FROM me; and didst not tell me</u>, that I might have sent thee away with mirth, and with songs, with tabret, and with harp?" (Gen. 31:27). The Law combination *wherefore* (57x), *didst thou* (4x), *flee away secretly* (1x), *and steal* (1x), *away from me* (1x), *and didst not tell me* (1x) = 65.

The Apostasy of Joseph's Half-Brothers

"And it came to pass, when Joseph was come unto his brethren, that they . . . took him and cast him into a pit. . . . And they sat down to eat bread. . . . and behold a company of Ishmeelites came from Gilead with their camels bearing spicery and balm and myrrh, going to carry it down to Egypt. And Judah said unto his brethren . . . Come, and let us sell him to the Ishmeelites, and let not our hand be upon him; for he is our brother and our flesh. And his brethren were content. Then there passed by Midianites merchantmen; and <u>they drew and lifted up Joseph out of the pit, and</u> <u>sold</u> <u>Joseph to</u> <u>the Ishmeelites</u> <u>for twenty pieces of silver</u>" (Gen. 37:23-28c).

These ten brothers abandoned their previous loyalty to family in a deplorable way. The Old Testament combination *they drew and lifted up Joseph out of the pit and* (1x), *sold* (56x), *Joseph to* (4x), *the Ishmeelites* (3x), *for twenty pieces of silver* (1x) = 65.

Judah's Apostasy

"And it came to pass at that time, that Judah went down from his brethren, and turned in to a certain Adullamite. . . . And <u>Judah</u> saw there <u>a daughter of a certain Canaanite</u>. . . . and he took her, and went in unto her. And <u>she conceived, and</u> <u>bare a son</u>; and he called his name Er. And she conceived again, and bare a son; and she called his name Onan. And she yet again conceived, and bare a son; and called his name Shelah" (Gen. 38:1-5a). In taking this Canaanitish woman to be his common-law wife, Judah abandoned his previous loyalty to the Hebrew family custom that Abraham established. The Minor Prophets combination *Judah* (63x) and *Canaanite/s* (2x) = 65. The Minor Prophets combination *Judah* (63x), *she conceived and* (1x), *bare a son* (1x) = 65.

The Old Testament combination *Judah* (263 chs), *a Canaanitish woman* (2 chs) = 265 chapters. The Bible combination *Judah* (264 chs) and *a daughter of a certain Canaanite* (1 ch) = 265 chapters.

1165th Verse of the Bible

"And it came to pass, when he heard that I lifted up my voice and cried, that he left his garment with me, and fled, and got him out" (Gen. 39:15). Potiphar's wife abandoned her previous loyalty to her husband when she attempted to commit adultery. Here she told a convincing truth to shelter her cold lie.

Sons Warned Not to Apostatize from Their Mission Objective

"So he sent his brethren away, and they departed: and he said unto them, See that ye FALL not OUT by the way" (Gen. 45:24). The Law combination *see that ye* (1 v), *fall not out by* (1 v), *the way* (63 vs) = 65 verses.

Reuben's Apostasy

"Reuben, thou art my firstborn, my might, and the beginning of my strength, the excellency of dignity, and the excellency of power: Unstable as water, thou shalt not excel; because thou wentest up to thy father's bed; then defiledst thou it: he went up to my couch" (Gen. 49:3-4). This son abandoned his previous loyalty to family when he committed an indecency. The Law combination *Reuben* (40x), *thou wentest up to thy father's bed* (1x), *then defiledst thou it* (1x), *he went up* (2x), *to my* (20x), *couch* (1x) = 65.

1565th Verse of the Bible

"And the child grew, and she brought him unto Pharaoh's daughter, and he became her son. And she called his name Moses: and she said, Because I drew him out of the water" (Exod. 2:10). A Hebrew mother was forced into abandoning her previous loyalty to her baby boy.

Moses' Apostasy from the House of Egypt

"And it came to pass in those days, when Moses was grown, that he went out unto his brethren, and looked on their burdens: and he spied an Egyptian smiting an Hebrew, one of his brethren. And he looked this way and that way, and when he saw that there was no man, he slew the Egyptian, and hid him in the sand. . . . Now when Pharaoh heard this thing, he sought to slay Moses. But Moses FLED FROM the face of Pharaoh, and dwelt in the land of Midian: and he sat down by a well" (Exod. 2:11-12, 15).

This adopted prince of Egypt radically abandoned his previous loyalty to the house of Egypt when he killed an Egyptian officer. This act visualized his mental decision to defect to the Hebrews. This immediately apostasy passage proceeds the 1565th verse of the Bible.

65th Chapter of the Bible

This chapter is a memorial of Egypt's final apostasy. After ten great judgments came upon Pharaoh he certainly knew the truth that Jehovah was the God over all other gods. God's aim was to make a believer out of Pharaoh, and indeed He did. This is why Pharaoh finally let the Hebrews go free. Yet afterward Pharaoh changed his mind about the God of the Hebrews, thinking he was somehow now strong enough to go wrest the Hebrews from their God's very hands. In accordance with our first definition of apostasy, Pharaoh's final act of war was a visible token of his refusal to continue recognizing the Hebrews' religious faith.

The Song of the Redeemed celebrates Jehovah's triumph over the apostate king of Egypt. "The LORD is a man of war: the LORD is his name. Pharaoh's chariots and his host hath he cast into the sea: his chosen captains also are drowned in the Red sea. The depths have covered them: they sank into the bottom as a stone. . . . And in the greatness of thine excellency thou hast overthrown them that rose up against thee: thou sentest forth thy wrath, which consumed them as stubble" (Exod. 15:3-5, 7). The title *Pharaoh* is mentioned in 65 verses of Genesis.

This chapter does not close until revealing Israel's own apostate heart and mindset of defection back to Egypt. They abandoned loyalty in both Moses and the Lord.

> "And when they came to Marah, they could not drink of the waters of Marah, for they were bitter. . . . And the people murmured against Moses, saying, What shall we drink? And he cried unto the LORD; and the LORD shewed him a tree, which when he had cast into the waters, the waters were made sweet: there he made for them a statute and an ordinance, and there he proved them, And said, If thou wilt diligently hearken to the voice of the LORD thy God, and wilt do that which is right in his sight, and wilt give ear to his commandments, and keep all his statutes, I will put none of these diseases upon thee, which I have brought upon the Egyptians: for I am the LORD that healeth thee" (vv. 23-26).

After performing a gracious miracle Moses challenged the people not to apostatize so easily but rather do what is right in God's eyes. The Law combination *and when they came* (3x), *to Marah* (1x), *they could not drink of the waters* (1x), *of Marah* (1x), *for they were bitter* (1x), *and the people* (28x), *murmured* (7x), *against Moses* (12x), *what shall* (9x), *we drink* (2x) = 65.

Israelites Apostatize from Law of Sabbath Rest

"And it came to pass, that there went out some of the people on the seventh day for to gather, and they found none. And the LORD said unto Moses, How long REFUSE ye TO keep my commandments and my laws?" (Exod. 16:27-28) The Old Testament combination *how long refuse ye* (1x), *to keep* (64x) = 65. The Old Testament combination *to keep* (64x), *my commandments and my laws* (1x) = 65.

Covenant Vows Lightly Made

At Mount Sinai God took Israel to Himself. There the marriage vows were stated. "And all the people answered together, and said, All that the LORD hath spoken we will do. And Moses returned the words of the people unto the LORD" (Exod. 19:8). Tragically it was only a short time until the people stopped doing as they said they would do; rather they began to do the opposite. From Genesis to the Gospels the phrase *did not* is mentioned in 65 chapters.

2065th Verse of the Bible

"Thou shalt not kill" (Exod. 20:13). To kill another human is to apostatize from the known truth God has divinely set forth. The Bible combination *thou shalt not* (240x), *kill* (125x) = 365.

A Son's Apostasy

"And he that curseth his father, or his mother, shall surely be put to death" (Exod. 21:17). Such abhorrent lack of loyalty to parents was to be rewarded most severely. The phrase *shall surely* occurs 65 times in the Bible. The word *death* is mentioned in 65 verses of the Wisdom Books. The Genesis combination *and he that* (2x), *curseth* (2x), *his father* (60x), *or his mother shall surely be put to death* (1x) = 65.

464

An Idolater's Apostasy

"He that sacrificeth unto any god, save unto the LORD only, he shall be utterly destroyed" (Exod. 22:20). The Bible combination *he that sacrificeth* (2x), *unto any* (6x), *god* (57x) = 65.

2465th Verse of the Bible:
Israel's Great Apostasy at Mount Sinai

"And when the people saw that Moses delayed to come down out of the mount, the people gathered themselves together unto Aaron, and said unto him, Up, make us gods, which shall go before us; for as for this Moses, the man that brought us up out of the land of Egypt, we wot not what is become of him" (Exod. 32:1). When Moses came down from the mountain the next day he saw the people's deplorable apostasy; they were celebrating around their newly fashioned golden calf. "Then Moses stood in the gate of the camp, and said, Who is on the LORD'S side? let him come unto me. And all the sons of Levi gathered themselves together unto him" (v. 26). Because they had fallen away from the truth they urgently needed to come back to the faith. They were to make their decision quickly and visibly come back to Moses and stand under his authoritative leadership. The underlined words indicate the 2465th verse of the Bible. The following seal uses the New Testament spelling for Sinai. The Bible combination *mount* (263x) and *Sina* (2x) = 265.

If Apostasy Be Done in the Congregation

"And if the whole congregation of Israel sin through ignorance, and the thing be hid from the eyes of the assembly, and they have done somewhat against any of the commandments of the LORD concerning things which should not be done, and are guilty; When the sin, which they have sinned against it, is known, then the congregation shall offer a young bullock for the sin, and bring him before the tabernacle of the congregation" (Lev. 4:13-14). The phrase *be done* is mentioned naturally in 65 verses of in the Bible. The phrase *have sinned* occurs 65 times from Genesis to the NT Narrative, and its 65th occurrence falls in the 2465th verse of the New Testament. The title *the congregation* is mentioned in 65 verses of the OT Narrative.

Nadab & Abihu's Apostasy

"And Nadab and Abihu, the sons of Aaron, took either of them his censer, and put fire therein, and put incense thereon, and offered strange fire before the LORD, which he commanded them not. And there went out fire from the LORD, and devoured them, and they died before the LORD" (Lev. 10:1-2). These two underling high priests knew the truth of their priestly religion yet totally departed from it. The word *strange* occurs 65 times in the Old Testament.

265th Verse of Leviticus

"And these are they which ye shall have in abomination among the fowls; they shall not be eaten, they are an abomination: the eagle, and the ossifrage, and the ospray" (Lev. 11:13). Any breach of this dietary religious law would be considered apostasy.

> The word *abomination* is mentioned in 65 verses of the Old Testament.
> The word *abomination(s)* occurs 65 times in the Major/Minor Prophets.

The Apostasy of Sacrificing to Devils

"And they shall no more offer their sacrifices unto devils, after whom they have gone a whoring.

This shall be a statute for ever unto them throughout their generations" (Lev. 17:7).

The word *they* is found in 65 books of the Bible.
The word *they* occurs 1965 times in the New Testament.

The Apostasy of Eating Blood
"And whatsoever man there be of <u>the house of Israel</u>, or of the strangers that sojourn among you, that <u>eateth any manner of</u> <u>blood</u>; I will even set my face against that soul that eateth blood, and will cut him off from among his people" (Lev. 17:10). The Law combination *eateth any manner of* (2x), *blood* (163x) = 165.

The title *the house of Israel* is mentioned in 65 verses of Ezekiel.
The title *the house of Israel* is mentioned in 65 chapters of the OT.

The Apostasy of Abominable Customs
"Therefore shall ye keep mine ordinance, that ye commit not any one of these abominable customs, which were <u>committed</u> before you, and that ye defile not yourselves therein: I am the LORD your God" (Lev. 18:30). The word *committed* occurs 65 times in the Old Testament.

The Apostasy of Profaning God's Name
"And ye shall not <u>swear</u> <u>by my name falsely</u>, <u>neither shalt thou profane</u> <u>the name of thy God</u>: I am the LORD" (Lev. 19:12). The phrase *the name of the LORD* is mentioned in 65 chapters of the Old Testament. The Bible combination *swear* (60x), *by my name falsely* (1x), *neither shalt thou profane* (2x), *the name of thy God* (2x) = 65.

565th Verse of Leviticus
"Do not prostitute thy daughter, to cause her to be a <u>whore</u>; lest the land FALL TO <u>whoredom</u>, and the land become full of wickedness" (Lev. 19:29). Whoredom is a base form of apostasy. All forms of the word *whore* is mentioned in 65 verses of the Bible.

You Shall Not Walk in Apostasy
"And ye <u>shall not</u> <u>walk</u> in the manners of the nation, which I cast out before you: for they <u>committed</u> all these things, and therefore I abhorred them" (Lev. 20:23). The word *walk* occurs 65 times in the New Testament. Again the word *committed* occurs 65 times in the Old Testament.

The phrase *shall not* occurs 65 times in Leviticus.
The phrase *shall not* occurs naturally 65 times in Jeremiah.
The phrase *shall not* occurs 65 times in the Synoptic Gospels.

If You Break My Covenant
"But if ye will not hearken unto me, and will not do all these commandments; <u>And if ye shall despise my statutes, or if your soul abhor my judgments, so that ye will not do all my commandments, but that ye break my covenant</u>" (Lev. 26:14). This scenario fits our first definition of apostasy: an act of refusing to continue to obey a religious faith. The Bible combination *and if ye shall despise my statutes* (1x), *or if your soul* (1x), *abhor my judgments* (1x), *so that ye* (6x), *will not do all my commandments* (1x), *but that ye break* (1x), *my covenant* (54x) = 65.

Punishment for Sins of Apostasy

"I also will do this <u>unto you</u>; I will even appoint over you terror, consumption, and the burning ague, that shall consume the eyes, and cause sorrow of heart: and ye shall sow your seed in vain, for your enemies shall eat it. And I will set my face against you, and ye shall be slain before your enemies: they that hate you shall reign over you; and ye shall flee when none pursueth you. And if ye will NOT yet for all this HEARKEN unto me, then I will punish you seven times more for your <u>sins</u>. And I will break the pride of your power; and I will make your heaven as iron, and your earth as brass: And your strength shall be spent in vain: for your land shall not yield her increase, neither shall the trees of the land yield their fruits" (Lev. 26:16-20).

The phrase *unto you* is mentioned in 65 verses of the Major and Minor Prophets. The word *sins* is mentioned naturally in 165 verses of the Bible.

3565th Verse of the Bible

"If they shall confess their iniquity, and the iniquity of their fathers, with their trespass which they trespassed against me, and that also they have contrary unto me" (Lev. 26:40). Repentance and confession of apostasy would be rewarded with national restoration and the return of God's favor. Again the word *walk* occurs 65 times in the New Testament.

Going Aside from One's Marriage Vows

"Speak unto the children of Israel, and say unto them, <u>If any man's wife go</u> <u>aside</u>, and <u>commit a trespass</u> against him" (Num. 5:12). Going aside is a deviation from the straight and narrow path of loyalty to one's marriage partner. The Old Testament combination *if any man's wife go* (1x), *aside* (60x), *commit a trespass* (4x) = 65.

> The word *go* occurs 65 times in Numbers.
> The word *go* occurs 65 times in Judges.
> The word *go* occurs 65 times in Isaiah.

The Law of Jealousies

"This is <u>the law of</u> jealousies, <u>when a wife</u> <u>goeth aside</u> <u>to another instead of</u> her husband, <u>and is defiled</u>" (Num. 5:29). The phrase *the law of* is mentioned in 65 chapters of the Bible. The Bible combination *when a wife* (1x), *goeth aside* (1x), *to another instead of* (2x), *her husband* (59x), *and is defiled* (2x) = 65.

465th Verse of Numbers

"And the cloud departed from off the tabernacle; and, behold, Miriam became leprous, white as snow: and Aaron looked upon Miriam, and, behold, she was leprous. And Aaron said unto Moses, Alas, my lord, I beseech thee, lay not <u>the sin</u> upon us, <u>wherein we have done foolishly</u>, and <u>wherein we have sinned</u>" (Num. 12:10-11). Verse ten is the 465th verse of Numbers, and it refers to the reward of Miriam's apostasy wherein she breached the expectation of loyalty to the nation's sole leader.

> The Bible: *the sin* (64 vs), *wherein we have done foolishly* (1 v) = 65 verses.
> The Bible: *the sin* (64 vs), *wherein we have sinned* (1 v) = 65 verses.

Apostate Spies Speak 65 Words of Descent

"And they brought up an evil report of the land which they had searched unto the children of

Israel, saying, <u>The land, through which we have gone to search it, is a land that eateth up the inhabitants thereof; and all the people that we saw in it are men of a great stature. And there we saw the giants, the sons of Anak, which come of the giants: and we were in our own sight as grasshoppers, and so we were in their sight</u>" (Num. 13:32-33).

Israel's Great Apostasy at Kadesh-Barnea

Joshua and Caleb had brought back from the Promised Land their good reports and fruitful tokens, but the other ten scouts gave an evil report. The people turned apostate as they began refusing to enter in the Promised Land as God had commanded them.

> "And all the children of Israel murmured against Moses and against Aaron: and the whole congregation said unto them, <u>Would God that we had died in the land of Egypt! or would God we had died in this wilderness! And wherefore hath the LORD brought us unto this land, to fall by the sword, that our wives and our children should be a prey? were it not better for us to return into Egypt?</u> And they said one to another, <u>Let us make a captain, and let us return into Egypt</u>" (Num. 14:2-4).

The people's apostate speech consists of 65 words plus one (1), hence—exceeding apostasy!

> The name *Israel* occurs 65 times in Leviticus.
> The name *Israel* is mentioned in 65 verses of Deuteronomy.
> The name *Israel* occurs 65 times in the Wisdom Books.
> The name *Israel* occurs 2565 times in the Bible.

Israel's Apostasy Punished with 40 Years x 365 Days of Dying in the Wilderness

God quickly passed down His great judgment upon the people for their great apostasy. "After the number of the days in which ye searched the land, even forty days, each day for a <u>year</u>, shall ye bear your iniquities, even forty <u>years</u> . . . I the LORD have said, I will surely do it unto all this <u>evil</u> congregation, that are gathered together against me: in this wilderness they shall be consumed, and there they shall die" (Num. 14:34-35). Again the word *evil* is mentioned in 65 chapters of the Major Prophets. The word *year* occurs naturally 365 times in the Bible!

Israel Guilty of Turning Away from the Lord

After Israel received their judicial sentencing for apostatizing, they endeavored to go up and fight. Moses warned the people not to go: "For the Amalekites and the Canaanites are there before you, and ye shall fall by the sword: because ye are TURNED AWAY <u>FROM the</u> LORD, therefore the LORD will not be with you" (Num. 14:43). Again the phrase *from the* is mentioned naturally in 165 verses of the Law.

A Personal Preventative against Apostasy

"Speak unto the children of Israel, and bid them that they make them fringes in the borders of their garments throughout their generations, and that they put upon the fringe of the borders a ribband of blue: And it shall be unto you for a fringe, <u>that ye may look upon it</u>, <u>and remember all the</u> commandments of the LORD, and do them; and that ye seek not after your own heart and your own eyes, after which ye use to go a whoring" (Num. 15:38-39). The blue fringe reminded the wearer of heaven and the One who watches over the wearer's daily walk, whether for good or for bad. The Law combination *that ye may look upon it* (1x), *and remember all the* (1x), *commandments* (63x) = 65.

Korah & His Band of Apostates

"Now Korah the son of Izhar, the son of Kohath, the son of Levi, and Dathan and Abiram, the sons of Eliab, and On, the son of Peleth, sons of Reuben, took men: And they rose up before Moses, with certain of the children of Israel, two hundred and fifty princes of the assembly, famous in the congregation, men of renown: And <u>they</u> gathered together against Moses and against Aaron, and said unto them, Ye take too much upon you, seeing all the congregation are holy, every one of them, and the LORD is among them: wherefore then lift ye up yourselves above the congregation of the LORD?" (Num. 16:1-3)

Again the word *they* is found in 65 books of the Bible.

Israel's Great Apostasy at Shittim

"And Israel abode in Shittim, and the people began to <u>commit</u> whoredom with the daughters of Moab. And they called <u>the people</u> unto the sacrifices of their gods: and <u>the people</u> did eat, and bowed down to their gods. And Israel joined himself unto Baal-peor: and the anger of the LORD was kindled against Israel" (Num. 25:1-3). The Bible's 65th occurrence of the word *commit* in First Corinthians 10:8 refers to this very incident of apostasy! The phrase *the people* occurs 165 times in the Major Prophets.

Numbers 26:65

The generation that departed from God's command to enter Canaan made a serious mistake: "For the LORD had said of them, They <u>shall</u> surely <u>die</u> in the wilderness. And there was not left a man of them, save Caleb the son of Jephunneh, and Joshua the son of Nun" (Num. 26:65).

> The phrase *shall die* occurs 65 times in the Old Testament.
> The phrase *shall die* also is mentioned in 65 verses of the Bible.

Israel's Apostasy Kindled God's Anger

Moses reminded the new generation of Reuben and Gad about the nation's former apostasy: "Thus did your fathers, when I sent them from Kadesh-barnea to see the land. For when they went up unto the valley of Eshcol, and saw the land, they discouraged the heart of the children of Israel, that they should not go into the land which the LORD had given them. And the LORD'S anger was <u>kindled</u> the same time" (Num. 32:8-10a). The word *kindled* is mentioned in 65 verses of the Bible.

Warning against Apostasy

"Only <u>take heed</u> to thyself, and <u>keep thy soul diligently,</u> <u>lest thou forget the things which thine eyes have seen,</u> <u>and lest they DEPART FROM thy heart all the days of thy life</u>: but teach them thy sons, and thy sons' sons" (Deut. 4:9). The word *forget/forgot/forgat* occurs 65 times in the Old Testament. The Bible combination *take heed* (55x), *to thyself and* (4x), *keep thy soul diligently* (1x), *lest thou forget* (2x), *the things which thine eyes have seen* (1x), *and lest they depart* (1x), *from thy heart all the days of thy life* (1x) = 65.

Take Heed

"<u>Take heed</u> unto yourselves, lest ye forget the covenant of the LORD your God, which he made with you, and make you a graven image, or the likeness of any thing, which the LORD thy God hath forbidden thee" (Deut. 4:23). In their natural occurrences all available forms of the phrase "take heed" show the seal of apostasy: *take heed* (54x), *take * heed* (7x), *takest heed* (1x), *taking* *heed* (1x), *took no heed* (2x) = 65. The word *heed* is mentioned naturally in 65 chapters of the Bible.

5065th Verse of the Bible

"Thou shalt not take <u>the name of the L</u>ORD thy God in vain: for the LORD will not hold him guiltless that taketh <u>his name</u> in vain" (Deut. 5:11). Great reverence and loyalty must be shown toward God's holy name lest a person commit apostasy. Again the phrase *the name of the LORD* is mentioned in 65 chapters of the Old Testament. The phrase *his name* occurs 165 times in the Bible.

265th Verse of Deuteronomy

"As <u>the nations</u> which the LORD destroyeth before your face, so shall ye perish; because ye WOULD NOT BE OBEDIENT unto the voice of the LORD your God" (Deut. 8:20). Moses warned the new generation what would happen if they apostatized like the Canaanite nations had already. The phrase *the nations* occurs 165 times in the Old Testament.

5165th Verse of the Bible

"Remember, and forget not, how thou provokedst the LORD thy God to wrath in the wilderness: from the day that thou didst depart out of the land of Egypt, until ye came unto this place, ye have been rebellious against the LORD" (Deut. 9:7). The apostate generation angered God time after time.

The People's Golden-Calf Apostasy

Moses reminded the young generation about their parents' former apostasy. "And I looked, and, behold, ye had sinned <u>against the L</u>ORD your God, and had made you a molten calf: ye had TURNED ASIDE quickly out of the way which the LORD had commanded you" (Deut. 9:16). The phrase *against the LORD* [where not immediately followed by the accompanying title "God"] occurs 65 times in Scripture.

The False Prophet's Apostasy

"And that prophet, or that dreamer of dreams, shall be put to death; because he hath spoken to TURN you <u>AWAY</u> <u>FROM the L</u>ORD your God . . . to thrust thee out of the way which the LORD thy God commanded thee to walk in. So shalt thou put the <u>evil</u> away from the midst of thee" (Deut. 13:5). Again the word *evil* is mentioned in 65 chapters of the Major Prophets.

The Law combination *away* (64 chs), *from the Lord your God* (1 ch) = 65 chapters.
The Law combination *away* (64 chs), *from the Lord our God* (1 ch) = 65 chapters.

The Children of Belial's Apostasy

"If thou shalt hear say in one of thy cities, which the LORD thy God hath given thee to dwell there, saying, Certain men, <u>the children of</u> Belial, are GONE OUT FROM among you, and have withdrawn the inhabitants of their city, saying, Let us go and serve other gods, which ye have not known; Then shalt thou enquire, and make search, and ask diligently; and, behold, if it be truth, and the thing certain, that such abomination is wrought among you; Thou shalt surely smite the inhabitants of that city with the edge of the sword, destroying it utterly, and all that is therein . . . with the edge of the sword. And thou shalt gather all the spoil of it into the midst of the street thereof, and shalt burn with fire the city, and all the spoil thereof every whit, for the LORD thy God: and it shall be an heap for ever; it shall not be built again"

(Deut. 13:12-16).

The phrase *the children of* is mentioned in 65 verses of Ezra.

The King's Preventative against Apostatizing

"<u>And</u> it shall be, when he sitteth upon the throne of his kingdom, that he shall write him a copy of this law in a book . . . And it shall be with him, and he shall read therein all the days of his life: that he may learn to fear the LORD his God, to keep all the words of this law and these statutes, to do them: That his heart be not lifted up above his brethren, and that he TURN not ASIDE FROM the commandment, to the right hand, or to the left: to the end that he may prolong his days in his kingdom, he, and his children, in the midst of Israel" (Deut. 17:18-20).

The lead word of this apostasy-preventative passage *And* is the 142,865th word of the Bible.

Witchcraft & Wizardry

"There shall not be found among you any one that maketh his son or his daughter to pass through the fire, or that useth divination, or an observer of times, or an enchanter, or a witch, Or a charmer, or a consulter with familiar spirits, or a wizard, or a necromancer. For all that do these things are an <u>abomination</u> unto the LORD" (Deut. 18:10-12a). Again the word *abomination* is mentioned in 65 verses of the Old Testament.

A Bill of Divorcement

"<u>When</u> a man hath taken a wife, and married her, and it come to pass that she find no favour in his eyes, because he hath found some uncleanness in her: then let him write her a bill of DIVORCEMENT, and give it in her hand, and send her out of his house" (Deut. 24:1). This scenario fits one definition of "apostasy" which properly means something separative. The lead word of this apostasy verse *when* is the 147,165th word of the Bible.

When a Brother Apostatizes from His Lawful Duty

"<u>And if the man like not</u> to take his brother's wife, then let his brother's wife go up to the gate unto the elders, and say, My husband's brother REFUSETH TO raise up unto his brother a name in Israel, he will not perform the duty of my husband's brother" (Deut. 25:7). The Bible combination *and if the man like not* (1x), *to take his brother's wife* (1x), *then let his brother's wife* (1x), *go up to the gate unto the elders and say* (1x), *my husband's brother* (2x), *refuseth to* (5x), *raise up* (35x), *unto his brother* (7x), *a name in Israel* (1x), *he will not perform the* (1x), *duty* (8x), *of my husband's brother* (2x) = 65.

665th Verse of Deuteronomy

"And <u>his name</u> shall be called in Israel, The house of him that hath his shoe loosed" (Deut. 25:10). A brother who will not help his deceased brother build his household is an apostate; he has broken his previous loyalty with his brother. Again the phrase *his name* occurs 165 times in the Bible.

Going after Other Gods

"And thou shalt not GO ASIDE FROM any of the words which I command thee this day, to the right hand, or to the left, <u>to GO after</u> <u>other gods</u> to serve them" (Deut. 28:14). The Bible combination *to go after* (2x), *other gods* (63x) = 65.

471

Deuteronomy 28:65

"And <u>among these nations</u> shalt thou find no ease, neither shall the sole of thy foot have rest: but the LORD shall give thee there a trembling heart, and failing of eyes, and sorrow of mind" (Deut. 28:65). Just one verse earlier the Lord mentioned the consequences of Israel's unrepentant apostasy: "and there thou shalt serve <u>other gods</u>." The combination *among these nations* (2x) and *other gods* (63x) = 65. This 65th verse refers to the tragic consequences of Israel's apostasy.

Israel's Canaan-Side Apostasy Foretold

"And the LORD said unto Moses, Behold, thou shalt sleep with thy fathers; and this people will rise up, and go a whoring after the gods of the <u>strangers</u> of the land, whither they go to be among them, and will FORSAKE me, and break my covenant which I have made with them" (Deut. 31:16). Again the word *strange* occurs 65 times in the Old Testament. The plural word *strangers(')* occurs 65 times in the Old Testament.

Write This Song of Apostasy

After informing Moses of the nation's forthcoming apostasy God gave Moses a special project to work on.

> "And I will surely hide my face in that day for all the evils which they shall have wrought, <u>in that they</u> <u>are turned unto</u> <u>other gods</u>. Now therefore write ye this song for you, and teach it the children of Israel: put it in <u>their</u> mouths, that this song may be a witness for me against the children of Israel. For when I shall have brought them into the land which I sware unto their fathers, that floweth with milk and honey; and they shall have eaten and filled themselves, and waxen fat; then <u>will they turn unto</u> <u>other gods</u>, and serve them, and provoke me, and break my covenant" (Deut. 31:18-20).

The word *their* is mentioned in 2365 verses of the Bible. The Bible combination *in that they are* (1x), *are turned unto* (1x), *other gods* (63x) = 65. The Bible combination *will turn unto* (2x), *other gods* (63x) = 65.

865th Verse of Deuteronomy

"For I know that after my death ye will utterly corrupt yourselves, and TURN ASIDE FROM the way which I have commanded you; and evil will befall you in the latter days; because ye will do evil in the sight of the LORD, to provoke him to anger through the work of your hands" (Deut. 31:29). Moses tells the Israelites of their forthcoming apostasy.

The Song of Apostasy

> "They have corrupted themselves, their spot is not the spot of his children: they are a perverse and crooked generation. . . . But Jeshurun waxed fat, and kicked: thou art waxen fat, thou art grown thick, thou art covered with fatness; then he FORSOOK God which made him, and lightly esteemed the Rock of his salvation. They provoked him to jealousy with strange gods, with abominations provoked they him to anger. They sacrificed unto devils, not to God; to gods whom they knew not, to new gods that came newly up, whom your fathers feared not. Of the Rock that begat thee thou art unmindful, and hast forgotten God that formed thee. And when the LORD saw it, he abhorred them, because of the provoking of his sons, and of his daughters. . . . I will see what their end shall be: for they are a very froward generation, children in whom is no faith. They have moved me to jealousy with that which is not God; they have provoked me to anger with their vanities: and I will move them to jealousy with those which are not a people; I will provoke them to anger with a foolish nation. For a fire is kindled in mine anger, and shall burn unto the lowest hell, and shall consume the earth with her increase, and set on fire the foundations of the mountains. I will

heap mischiefs upon them; I will spend mine arrows upon them. They shall be burnt with hunger, and devoured with burning heat, and with bitter destruction: I will also send the teeth of beasts upon them, with the poison of serpents of the dust. The sword without, and terror within, shall destroy both the young man and the virgin, the suckling also with the man of gray hairs. I said, I would scatter them into corners, I would make the remembrance of them to cease from among men. . . . For they are a nation void of counsel, neither is there any understanding in them. O that they were wise, that they understood this, that they would consider their latter end! . . . For their vine is of the vine of Sodom, and of the fields of Gomorrah: their grapes are grapes of gall, their clusters are bitter: Their wine is the poison of dragons, and the cruel venom of asps. . . . To me belongeth vengeance, and recompence; their foot shall slide in due time: for the day of their calamity is at hand, and the things that shall come upon them make haste. . . . I will render vengeance to mine enemies, and will reward them that hate me" (Deut. 32:5, 15-19, 20b-26, 28-29, 32-33, 35, 41c).

The entirety of this Song of Apostasy consists of 1065 words!

God Defines Apostasy

God instructed Joshua, "observe to do according to all the law, which Moses my servant commanded thee: turn not FROM it to the right hand or to the left" (Josh. 1:7b). God defines apostasy as any slight deviation from the law's perfectly prescribed way. The word *turn* is mentioned in 65 verses of the Major Prophets. The Bible combination *turn not to* (1 v), *the right hand* (58 vs), *nor to the left* (6 vs) = 65 verses.

65th Verse of Joshua

"That this may be a sign among you, that when your children ask their fathers in time to come, saying, What mean ye by these stones" (Josh. 4:6). In the event that future generations ever consider apostatizing from the Hebrews' religious faith, God establishes a visible monument so they will have something to bolster their faith and thereby continue following the God of Israel without hesitation. The Bible's 65th occurrence of the title *the fathers* falls in the 29,965th verse of the Bible.

Achan's Apostasy

"But the children of Israel committed a trespass in the accursed thing: for Achan, the son of Carmi, the son of Zabdi, the son of Zerah, of the tribe of Judah, took of the accursed thing: and the anger of the LORD was kindled against the children of Israel" (Josh. 7:1). Again the word *committed* occurs 65 times in the Old Testament. Again the word *kindled* is mentioned in 65 verses of the Bible. The Joshua combination *the children of Israel* (63 vs), *commit/ted a trespass in the accursed thing* (2 vs) = 65 verses.

Achan's Apostasy Transferred onto the Congregation

"Did not Achan the son of Zerah commit a trespass in the accursed thing, and wrath fell on all the congregation of Israel? and that man perished not alone in his iniquity" (Josh. 22:20). Again the title *the congregation* is mentioned in 65 verses of the OT Narrative.

Joshua Warns Israel against Future Apostasy

On his deathbed Joshua warned Israel not to make marriages with the heathen. He said of such apostasy, "When ye have transgressed the covenant of the LORD your God, which he commanded you, and have gone and served other gods, and bowed yourselves to them; then shall the anger of the LORD be kindled against you, and ye shall perish quickly from off the good land which he hath given unto you" (Josh. 23:16). The Bible combination *have/hath gone and served* (2x), *other gods* (63x) = 65.

Israelites Promise Not to Apostatize

"And the people answered and said, God forbid that we should FORSAKE the LORD, to serve other gods. . . . And Joshua said unto the people . . . If ye FORSAKE the LORD, and serve strange gods, then he will turn and do you hurt, and consume you, after that he hath done you good. And the people said unto Joshua, Nay; but we will serve the LORD" (Josh. 24:16, 19a, 20-21). Again the phrase *the people* occurs 165 times in the Major Prophets. Again all forms of the word *forsake* are mentioned in 165 combined verses of the Bible. Here the underlined word *serve* is the 665th word of this chapter, and it is related to the act of apostatizing.

Israel's Cycle of Apostasy & Deliverance

"And also all that generation were gathered unto their fathers: and there arose another generation after them, which knew not the LORD, nor yet the works which he had done for Israel. . . . Nevertheless the LORD raised up judges, which delivered them out of the hand of those that spoiled them. And yet they would NOT HEARKEN unto their judges, but they went a whoring after other gods. . . . And when the LORD raised them up judges, then the LORD was with the judge, and delivered them out of the hand of their enemies all the days of the judge: for it repented the LORD because of their groanings by reason of them that oppressed them and vexed them" (Judg. 2:10, 16-17a, 18).

The Old Testament combination *nevertheless the LORD* (2x), *raised up* (15x), *judges* (48x) = 65. The word *delivered* is mentioned in 65 chapters of the OT Narrative. The Old Testament combination *and went a whoring after* (2x), *other gods* (63x) = 65. The phrase *all the days* occurs 65 times in the Old Testament.

Israelites Forsook the Lord

"And they forsook the LORD God of their fathers, which brought them out of the land of Egypt, and followed other gods, of the gods of the people that were round about them, and bowed themselves unto them, and provoked the LORD to anger. And they FORSOOK the LORD, and served Baal and Ashtaroth" (Judg. 2:12-13). These two verses are situated as the 6558th and 6559th verses of the Bible, numbers from the 6500 range. The phrase *and they* occurs naturally 65 times in First Kings. Again the word *they* is found in 65 books of the Bible.

6565th Verse of the Bible

"And it came to pass, when the judge was dead, that they returned, and corrupted themselves more than their fathers, in following other gods to serve them, and to bow down unto them; they ceased not from their own doings, nor from their stubborn way" (Judg. 2:19). With divine precision this 6565th verse of the Bible completes the summary on Israel's full cycle of apostasy. The Major Prophets combination *corrupted* (2x), *themselves* (62x), *worse than their fathers* (1x) = 65. The Old Testament combination *in following* (2x), *other gods* (63x) = 65. The Bible combination *from their stubborn* (1x), *way* (664x) = 665.

Israel's First Apostasy

"And took their daughters to be their wives, and gave their daughters to their sons, and served their gods" (Judg. 3:6). This verse records Israel's first apostasy after Joshua and the elders passed away. The Bible combination *and served* (31x), *their gods* (34x) = 65. This account of

Israel's first apostasy is the 65th verse of Judges.

Israel's Second Apostasy

"And the children of Israel <u>did</u> evil again in the sight of the LORD: and the LORD strengthened Eglon the king of Moab against Israel, because <u>they</u> had done evil in the sight of the LORD" (Judg. 3:12). The phrase *they did* is mentioned in 65 verses of the Old Testament.

Israel's Third Apostasy

"And <u>the children of Israel again did evil in the sight of the LORD</u>, when Ehud was dead" (Judg. 4:1). The OT Narrative combination *the children of Israel again did evil* (1x), *in the sight of the LORD* (64x) = 65.

Israel's Fourth Apostasy

"And the children of Israel <u>did</u> evil in the sight of the LORD: and the LORD <u>delivered</u> them into the hand of Midian seven years" (Judg. 6:1). The word *did* is mentioned in 365 chapters of the Old Testament. Again the word *delivered* is mentioned in 65 chapters of the OT Narrative.

6665th Verse of the Bible

"And I said unto you, <u>I am the LORD your God; fear not</u> <u>the gods</u> of the Amorites, <u>in whose land ye dwell</u>: <u>but ye have NOT OBEYED</u> <u>my voice</u>" (Judg. 6:10). This verse fits our first definition of apostasy: an act of refusing to continue to obey. The OT Narrative combination *I am the LORD your God fear not* (1x), *the gods* (31x), *of the Amorites* (22x), *in whose land ye dwell* (2x), *but ye have not obeyed* (2x), *my voice* (7x) = 65.

Israel's Fifth Apostasy

"And it came to pass, as soon as Gideon was dead, that the children of <u>Israel</u> turned again, and went a whoring after Baalim, and made Baal-berith their god. And the children of Israel remembered not the LORD their God" (Judg. 8:33-34a). Again the name *Israel* occurs 2565 times in Scripture.

Israel's Sixth Apostasy

"And the children of Israel did evil again in the sight of the LORD, <u>and served Baalim, and Ashtaroth, and the gods of Syria, and</u> <u>the gods of Zidon, and the gods of Moab</u>, and the gods of the children of Ammon, and the gods of the Philistines, and FORSOOK the LORD, and served not him. . . . And the children of Israel cried unto the LORD, saying, We have sinned against thee, both because <u>we have FORSAKEN our God, and also served Baalim</u>. . . . Yet <u>ye have FORSAKEN me, and served</u> <u>other gods</u>: wherefore I will deliver you no more" (Judg. 10:6, 10, 13).

The Bible combination *we have* (263x), *forsaken our God* (1x), *and also served Baalim* (1x) = 265. The Old Testament combination *and served Baalim and Ashtaroth* (1x), *and the gods of Syria and* (1x), *the gods of* (41x), *Zidon* (21x), *and the gods of Moab* (1x) = 65. Again all forms of the word *forsake* are mentioned in 165 combined verses of the Bible. The Old Testament combination *ye have forsaken me and served* (2x), *other gods* (63x) = 65.

Israel's Seventh Apostasy

"And the children of Israel <u>did</u> <u>evil</u> again in the sight of the LORD; and the LORD <u>delivered</u> them <u>into the hand of the</u> Philistines forty years" (Judg. 13:1). Again the word *did* is mentioned in 365 chapters of the Old Testament. Again the word *evil* is mentioned in 65 chapters of the Major Prophets. Again the word *delivered* is mentioned in 65 chapters of the OT Narrative. The phrase *into the hand(s) of the* occurs 65 times in the Bible.

"Every Man Did That Which Was Right in His Own Eyes"

The book of Judges could easily be entitled the Book of Israel's Apostasies. It ends with this tragic declaration: "In those days there was no king in <u>Israel</u>: <u>every man</u> <u>did that which was</u> <u>right in his own eyes</u>" (Judg. 21:25). Again the name *Israel* occurs 2565 times in the Bible. The Law combination *every man* (63x), *whatsoever is right in his own eyes* (1x), *in his eyes* (1x) = 65.

65th Verse of Ruth

"And he took ten men of the elders of the city, and said, Sit ye down here. And they sat down" (Ruth 4:2). The kinsman refused to redeem Naomi's inheritance and raise up the name of his dead brother according to the ancient Mosaic custom. This near kinsman defected from the Mosaic faith. He abandoned his previous loyalty to his brother, thus apostatizing.

Hophni & Phinehas' Apostasy

"Now the sons of Eli were sons of Belial; they knew not the LORD. . . . Wherefore the sin of the young men was very great before the LORD: for men abhorred the offering of the LORD. . . . Now Eli was very old, and heard all that his sons did unto all Israel; and how they lay with the women that assembled at the door of the tabernacle of the congregation. . . . And there came a man of God unto Eli, and said unto him, Thus saith the LORD . . . And this shall be a sign unto thee, that shall come upon thy two sons, on Hophni and Phinehas; in one day <u>they shall die</u> both of them" (1 Sam. 2:12, 17, 22, 27a, 34).

Eli's two sons had greatly apostatized from the faith. Again the word *they* occurs 1965 times in the New Testament. Again the phrase *shall die* occurs 65 times in the Old Testament and is mentioned in 65 verses of the Bible.

Eli's Apostasy

"And . . . when Eli was laid down in his place . . . ere the lamp of God went out in the temple of the LORD. . . . And there came a man of God unto Eli, and said unto him, Thus saith the LORD . . . Wherefore kick ye at my sacrifice and at mine offering, which I have commanded in my habitation; and honourest thy sons above me, to make yourselves fat with the chiefest of all the offerings of Israel my people? . . . And I will raise me up a faithful <u>priest</u>" (1 Sam. 2:2-3a, 27a, 29, 35a).

Eli abandoned his previous loyalty to his religious duties. The title *priest* occurs 65 combined times in Kings and Chronicles. The Scofield Reference Bible places this apostate incident at circa 1165 BC.

65th Verse of First Samuel

"And the child Samuel ministered unto the LORD before Eli. And the word of the LORD was precious in those days; there was no open vision" (1 Sam. 3:1). The reason there was no open vision at that time was because the Lord was displeased with the priesthood's current state of apostasy.

Samuel's Counsel for Israel to Cease Apostatizing

"And Samuel spake unto all the house of Israel, saying, If ye do <u>return</u> unto the LORD with all your hearts, then PUT AWAY the strange gods and Ashtaroth from among you, and prepare your hearts unto the LORD, and serve him only: and he will deliver you out of the hand of the Philistines" (1 Sam. 7:3). Samuel was sent by God to help revive the nation and bring about its return to true, undefiled religion. The word *return* occurs 65 times in the OT Narrative. Again the word *strange* occurs 65 times in the Old Testament. The Bible combination *put away* (53x), *strange gods* (11x), *gods of the strangers of the land* (1x) = 65.

Joel & Abiah's Apostasy

"And it came to pass, when Samuel was old, that he made his sons judges over Israel. Now the name of his firstborn was Joel; and the name of his second, Abiah: they were judges in Beer-sheba. And his sons walked not in his ways, but TURNED ASIDE after lucre, and took bribes, and perverted judgment" (1 Sam. 8:1-3). The OT Narrative combination *turned* (64 chs), *aside after lucre* (1 ch) = 65 chapters. The joined phrases *and his sons walked not in his ways, but turned aside after lucre, and took bribes* consist of 65 letters!

Israel Divorces God to Seek another Ruling Head

"Then all the elders of Israel gathered themselves together, and came to Samuel unto Ramah, And said unto him, Behold, thou art old, and thy sons walk not in thy ways: now make us a king to judge us like all the nations. . . . And Samuel prayed unto the LORD. And the LORD said unto Samuel, Hearken unto the voice of the people in all that they say unto thee: for they have not rejected thee, but they have rejected me, that I should not reign over them" (1 Sam. 8:4-5, 6c-7).

This scenario fits one of our definitions of apostasy: something separative—divorcement. This passage serves as an introduction to the 165th verse of First Samuel.

165th Verse of First Samuel

"According to all the works which they have done since the day that I brought them up out of Egypt even unto this day, wherewith they have FORSAKEN me, and served other gods, so do they also unto thee" (1 Sam. 8:8). The apostasy-related keyword *forsaken* actually occurs in this 65th verse. The Wisdom Books combination *they have* (59x), *forsaken* (6x) = 65. The joined phrases *wherewith they have forsaken me, and served other gods, so do they also unto thee* consists of 65 letters!

The People Apostatize by Rejecting Their Heavenly King

Samuel warned the people about the difficulties they would face having an earthly king. "Nevertheless the people REFUSED TO OBEY the voice of Samuel; and they said, Nay; but we will have a king over us" (1 Sam. 8:19). The early part of this verse precisely matches our first definition of apostasy: an act of refusing to continue to obey. Again the phrase *the people* occurs 165 times in the Major Prophets. The Old Testament combination *nevertheless the people* (3x), *refused* (19x), *to obey* (43x) = 65.

The Apostasy of Worshipping Baalim & Ashtaroth

"And they cried unto the LORD, and said, We have sinned, because we have FORSAKEN the LORD, and have served Baalim and Ashtaroth: but now deliver us out of the hand of our enemies, and we will serve thee" (1 Sam. 12:10). The Bible combination *we have* (263x), *forsaken the Lord and* (1x), *have served Baalim and Ashtaroth* (1x) = 265.

265th Verse of First Samuel

"Is it not wheat harvest to day? I will call unto the LORD, and he shall send thunder and <u>rain</u>; that ye may perceive and see that your wickedness is great, which ye have done in the sight of the LORD, in asking you a king" (1 Sam. 12:17). Samuel wanted the people to understand God's anger toward their national apostasy. He used the example of rain "falling away from" its heavenly abiding place. The word *rain* is mentioned in 65 chapters of the Bible.

Saul's First Great Apostasy

"And Saul said, Bring hither a burnt offering to me, and peace offerings. And he offered the burnt offering. . . . And it came to pass, that as soon as he had made an end of offering the burnt offering, behold, Samuel came. . . . And Samuel said to Saul, Thou hast done foolishly: <u>thou hast not</u> <u>kept the</u> <u>commandment of the LORD</u> <u>thy God, which</u> <u>he commanded thee</u>" (1 Sam. 13:9, 10a, 13a). Saul defected or apostatized from his office of king when he intruded into the priest's office. This scenario also fits our first definition of apostasy. The OT Narrative combination *thou hast not* (10x), *kept the* (26x), *commandment of the LORD* (13x), *thy God which* (6x), *he commanded thee* (10x) = 65.

Saul's Second Great Apostasy

"<u>And Samuel said, When thou wast little in thine own sight, wast thou not made the head of the</u> <u>tribes of Israel, and the LORD anointed thee king over Israel</u>? And the LORD sent thee on a journey, and said, Go and utterly destroy the sinners the Amalekites, and fight against them until they be consumed. Wherefore then didst thou NOT OBEY the voice of the LORD, but didst fly upon the spoil, and didst <u>evil</u> in the sight of the LORD?" (1 Sam. 15:17-19) The underlined verse is the 365th verse of First Samuel, and it pertains to Saul's apostasy—his abandonment of previous loyalties to God. Again the word *evil* is mentioned in 65 chapters of the Major Prophets.

Saul, the Prototype Apostate Israelite King

"And the LORD said unto Samuel, How long wilt thou mourn for Saul, seeing I have REJECTED him from <u>reigning over</u> Israel?" (1 Sam. 16:1a) Saul's identity was with the northern tribes. He was the prototype Israelite king. Because he was constantly led by his self-will and accompanying anger, he became Israel's very first apostate king. All northern Israelite kings after him were apostates from the beginning of their reigns. The Old Testament combination *reigning* (1x), *over Israel* (64x) = 65.

The Lord Apostatizes from Saul

"But the Spirit of the LORD DEPARTED <u>FROM Saul</u>, and an <u>evil</u> <u>spirit</u> from the LORD troubled him. And Saul's servants said unto him, Behold now, an <u>evil</u> <u>spirit</u> from God troubleth thee" (1 Sam. 16:14-15). After the Lord pronounced His rejection of Saul, the Lord abandoned His previous loyalty to the king by withdrawing His Holy Spirit from him. Again the phrase *from him* is mentioned in 65 chapters of the Old Testament. Again the word *evil* is mentioned in 65 chapters of the Major Prophets.

> The lowercase title *spirit* occurs 65 times in the Wisdom Books.
> The lowercase title *spirit* occurs 65 times in the Major Prophets.
> The lowercase title *spirit* occurs 65 times in Pauline/General/Apocalyptic Epistles.
> The lowercase title *spirit of* is mentioned in 65 verses of the Bible.

Saul's Third Great Apostasy

"And the king said unto the footmen that stood about him, <u>Turn, and slay</u> the <u>priests of the LORD</u>; because their hand also is with David, and because they knew when he fled, and did not shew it to me. But the servants of the king would not put forth their hand to fall upon the priests of the LORD. And the king said to Doeg, <u>Turn</u> thou, and fall upon the priests. And Doeg the Edomite <u>turned</u>, and he fell upon the priests, and slew on that day fourscore and five persons that did wear a linen ephod. And Nob, the city of the priests, smote he with the edge of the sword, both men and women, children and sucklings, and oxen, and asses, and sheep, with the edge of the sword" (1 Sam. 22:17-19).

Again the word *turn* is mentioned in 65 verses of the Major Prophets. The Old Testament combination *turn* (258x), *and slay the* (2x), *the priests of the LORD* (5x) = 265.

7865th Verse of the Bible

"Now the name of the man was Nabal; and the name of his wife Abigail: and she was a woman of good understanding, and of a beautiful countenance: but the man was churlish and <u>evil</u> in his doings" (1 Sam. 25:2-3). This verse presents an apostate man whose name means fool. Again the word *evil* is mentioned in 65 chapters of the Major Prophets.

Saul's Fourth Great Apostasy

"Then said Saul unto his servants, Seek me a woman that hath a familiar <u>spirit</u>, that I may go to her, and enquire of her. And his servants said to him, Behold, there is a woman that hath a familiar <u>spirit</u> at Endor. And Saul disguised himself, and put on other raiment, and he went, and two men with him, and they came to the woman by night: and he said, I pray thee, divine unto me by the familiar <u>spirit</u>, and bring me him up, whom I shall name unto thee" (1 Sam. 28:7-8). By this action taken, Saul greatly apostatized from the Mosaic faith because it forbade necromancy—communication with the dead. The entirety of this apostasy narrative, found in verses 7-25, consists of 665 words! Again the lowercase word *spirit* occurs 65 times in the Major Prophets.

265th Chapter of the Bible

This entire chapter questions the possibility of David abandoning his loyalties to Saul the King of Israel and his potential loyalties to Achish the King of Gath. Great concern was expressed over an upcoming battle between these two nations. David had already defected from Israel when he fell away from Saul, but would he now apostatize from the Philistines and defect back to Israel? Would he continue to fall in line or would he again fall away?

"And the lords of the Philistines passed on by hundreds, and by thousands: but David and his men passed on in the rereward with Achish. Then said the princes of the Philistines, What do these Hebrews here? And Achish said unto the princes of the Philistines, Is not this David, the servant of Saul the king of Israel, which hath been with me these days, or these years, and I have found no fault in him since he FELL unto me unto this day? And the princes of the Philistines were wroth with him; and . . . said unto him, Make this fellow return, that he may go again to his place which thou hast appointed him, and let him not go down with us to <u>battle</u>, lest in the <u>battle</u> he be an adversary to us: for wherewith should he reconcile himself unto his master?" (1 Sam. 29: 2-4f)

Again all forms of the word *fall* show the seal of apostasy, mentioned collectively in 65 verses of the New Testament. The word *battle* occurs 165 times in the Old Testament.

David's Apostasy

"And it came to pass in an eveningtide, that David arose from off his bed, and walked upon the roof of the king's house: and from the roof he saw a woman washing herself; and the woman was very beautiful to look upon. And David sent and enquired after the woman. And one said, Is not this Bath-sheba, the daughter of Eliam, the wife of Uriah the Hittite? And David sent messengers, and took her; and she came in unto him, and he lay with her; for she was purified from her uncleanness: and she returned unto her house. <u>And the woman conceived, and sent and told David, and said, I am with child</u>" (2 Sam. 11:2-5).

David apostatized from the Ten Commandments when he committed adultery. The final verse of this apostasy passage is the 8265th verse of the Bible.

Abner's Apostasy

"So do God to Abner, and more also, except, as the LORD hath sworn to David, even so I do to him; To translate the kingdom <u>FROM the</u> house of Saul, and to set up the throne of David over Israel and over Judah, from Dan even to Beer-sheba. . . . And Abner sent messengers to David on his behalf, saying, Whose is the land? saying also, Make thy league with me, and, behold, my hand shall be with thee, to bring about all Israel unto thee" (2 Sam. 3:9-10, 12). Abner defected very suddenly from his previous loyalty to Ish-bosheth and the house of Saul. Again the phrase *from the* is mentioned naturally in 165 verses of the Law.

Amnon's Apostasy

"<u>And</u> it came to pass after this, that Absalom the son of David had a fair sister, whose name was Tamar; and Amnon the son of David loved her. And Amnon was so vexed, that he fell sick for his sister Tamar; for she was a virgin; and Amnon thought it hard for him to do any thing to her. But Amnon had a friend, whose name was Jonadab" (2 Sam. 13:1-3a). Amnon went on to defect from his previous royal-family loyalties and commit an evil deed. The lead word of this lengthy apostasy passage *And* is the 8665th word of Second Samuel.

Absalom's Apostasy

"And on this manner did <u>Absalom</u> to all Israel that came to the king for judgment: so Absalom stole the hearts of the men of Israel. . . . But Absalom sent spies throughout all the tribes of Israel, saying, As soon as ye hear the sound of the trumpet, then ye shall say, Absalom reigneth in Hebron" (2 Sam. 15:6, 10). Absalom abandoned his previous Judean loyalty to the house of David and covertly defected to the northern Israelites. The underlined apostate name *Absalom* is the 165th word in this apostasy chapter.

Sheba's Apostasy

"And there happened to be there a man of Belial, whose name was Sheba, the son of Bichri, a Benjamite: and he blew a trumpet, and said, We have no part in David, neither have we inheritance in the son of Jesse: every man to his tents, O <u>Israel</u>. So every man of <u>Israel</u> went up FROM after David, and followed Sheba the son of Bichri: but the men of Judah clave unto their king, from Jordan even to Jerusalem" (2 Sam. 20:1-2). Again the name *Israel* occurs 65 times in the Wisdom Books. Again the word *from* is found in 65 books of the Bible.

Adonijah's Apostasy

"<u>Then Adonijah the son of Haggith exalted himself</u>, saying, I will be king: and he prepared him chariots and horsemen, and fifty men to run before him. . . . And he conferred with Joab the son of Zeruiah, and with Abiathar the priest: and they following Adonijah helped him. . . . And Adonijah slew sheep and oxen and fat cattle by the stone of Zoheleth, which is by En-rogel, and called all his brethren the king's sons, and all the men of Judah the king's servants" (1 Kings 1:5, 7, 9). Adonijah abandoned his loyalty to his aged father when he stole his throne. His usurpation of power was quickly dealt with. The Kings and Chronicles combination *then Adonijah* (1x), *the son of Haggith exalted* (1x), *himself* (63x) = 65.

Abiathar's Apostasy

"And unto Abiathar the priest said the king, Get thee to Anathoth, unto thine own fields; for thou art worthy of <u>death</u>: but I will not at this time put thee to <u>death</u>, because thou barest the ark of the Lord GOD before David my father, and because thou hast been afflicted in all wherein my father was afflicted. So Solomon thrust out Abiathar FROM being priest unto the LORD; that he might fulfil the word of the LORD, which he spake concerning the house of Eli in Shiloh" (1 Kings 2:26-27).

Abiathar had loyally backed King David when Absalom tried to steal the throne, yet he turned and defected from David at the time of Adonijah's conspiracy. For this treasonous reason Solomon removed him from his high office. Again the word *death* is mentioned in 65 verses of the Wisdom Books.

Punishment Promised for Israel's Future Apostatizing

"And they shall answer, Because they FORSOOK the LORD their God, who brought forth their fathers out of the land of Egypt, and have taken hold upon <u>other gods, and have worshipped them</u>, and served them: therefore hath the LORD brought upon them all this evil" (1 Kings 9:9). The Old Testament combination *other gods* (63x), *and have worshipped them* (2x) = 65.

Solomon's Apostasy

"For it came to pass, when Solomon was old, that his wives <u>TURNED AWAY his heart</u> after <u>other gods</u>. . . . For Solomon went after Ashtoreth the goddess of the Zidonians, and after Milcom the <u>abomination</u> of the Ammonites. And Solomon did evil in the sight of the LORD. . . . Then did Solomon build an <u>high place</u> for Chemosh, the <u>abomination</u> of Moab, in the hill that is before Jerusalem, and for Molech, the <u>abomination</u> of the children of Ammon. And likewise did he for all his strange wives, which burnt incense and sacrificed unto their gods. And the LORD was angry with Solomon, because his heart was <u>TURNED</u> FROM the LORD God of Israel" (1 Kings 11:4-6a, 7-9b).

The Old Testament combination *turned away his heart* (2x), *other gods* (63x) = 65. Again the word *abomination* is mentioned in 65 verses of the Old Testament. The term *high places* is mentioned in 65 chapters of the Old Testament. Again the word *turn* is mentioned in 65 verses of the Major Prophets.

465th Verse of First Kings
Jeroboam's & Israel's Apostasy

"Then Jeroboam built Shechem in mount Ephraim, and dwelt therein . . . and made two calves of gold. . . . And he set the one in Beth-el, and the other put he in Dan. And this thing became a sin: for the people went to worship before the one, even unto Dan. <u>And he made an house of high places, and made priests of the lowest of the people, which were not of the sons of Levi</u>" (1 Kings 12:25a, 28b, 29-31). The underlined apostasy verse indicates the 465th verse of First Kings.

Rehoboam & Judah's Apostasy

"And Rehoboam the son of Solomon <u>reigned</u> in Judah. . . . And Judah <u>did</u> <u>evil</u> in the sight of the LORD, and they provoked him to jealousy with their <u>sins</u> which they had committed, above all that their fathers had done. For they also built them <u>high places</u>, and images, and groves, on every high hill, and under every green tree. And there were also sodomites in the land: and <u>they did</u> according to all the <u>abominations</u> of <u>the nations</u> which the LORD cast out before the children of Israel" (1 Kings 14:21a, 22-24).

The word *reigned* is mentioned in 65 chapters of the Old Testament. Again the phrase *they did* is mentioned in 65 verses of the Old Testament. Again the word *did* is mentioned in 365 chapters of the Old Testament. Again the word *evil* is mentioned in 65 chapters of the Major Prophets. Again the word *sins* is mentioned naturally in 165 verses of the Bible. Again the term *high places* is mentioned in 65 chapters of the Old Testament. Again the word *abomination* is mentioned in 65 verses of the Old Testament. Again the phrase *the nations* occurs 165 times in the Old Testament.

Abijam's Apostasy

"Now . . . <u>reigned</u> Abijam over Judah. Three years <u>reigned</u> he in Jerusalem. . . . And he <u>walked</u> in all the <u>sins</u> of his father, which he had done before him: and his heart was not perfect with the LORD his God, as the heart of David his father" (1 Kings 15:1-3). Half of the Judean kings were apostates. They departed from the godly Mosaic standards of faith and practice that the house of David had previously followed. Again the word *reigned* is mentioned in 65 chapters of the Old Testament. Again the word *walk* occurs 65 times in the New Testament. Again the word *sins* is mentioned naturally in 165 verses of the Bible.

NOTE: We do not discuss much about any of the twenty-one Israelite kings because from the beginning of their reigns they only followed the apostate patterns exhibited by their father-kings who reigned before them. Except for Saul and Jeroboam, the Israelite kings never abandoned previous loyalty to God as they were ever disobedient from the start of their reigns. Thus we will only examine the lives of the apostate Judean kings hereafter.

Elijah Laments the Israelites' Apostate Condition

"And he said, I have been very jealous for the LORD God of hosts: because the children of Israel have FORSAKEN thy covenant, thrown down thine altars, and slain thy prophets with the sword; and I, even I only, am left; and they seek my life, to take it away" (1 Kings 19:14). Here the keyword *forsaken* is the 465th word of this chapter.

Ahaziah's Apostasy

"Two and twenty years old was Ahaziah when he began to reign; and he <u>reigned</u> <u>one year</u> in Jerusalem. And his mother's name was Athaliah, the daughter of Omri king of Israel. And he walked in the way of the house of Ahab, and did evil in the sight of the LORD, as did the house of Ahab: for he was the son in law of the house of Ahab" (2 Kings 8:26-27). Like his wicked mother Athaliah, Ahaziah was also an apostate Judean king. Again the word *reigned* is mentioned in 65 chapters of the Old Testament. Ahaziah's one-year-long apostate reign would thus be equivalent to 365 solar days.

9765th Verse of the Bible

"For <u>the whole house of Ahab</u> shall perish: and I will <u>cut off from</u> <u>Ahab</u> him that pisseth against the wall, and him that is shut up and left in Israel" (2 Kings 9:8). The Bible combination *cut off from* (47x), *the whole house of Ahab* (1x), *the house of Ahab* (17x) = 65. The apostate name *Ahab* is mentioned naturally 65 in verses of First and Second Kings.

The Priests' Apostasy

"But it was so, that in the three and twentieth year of king Jehoash the priests had not repaired the breaches of the house. Then king Jehoash called for Jehoiada the priest, and the other priests, and said unto them, Why repair ye not the breaches of the house? now therefore receive no more money of your acquaintance, but deliver it for the breaches of the house" (2 Kings 12:6-7). For some unspecified reason these priests had refused to follow the prescribed religious faith concerning the Lord's House. They abandoned the care of it. Thus they had apostatized in measure. From Genesis to the Gospels the title *the priests* occurs 265 times. The title *priests* occurs 65 times in the Major and Minor Prophets. The Old Testament combination *have not* (164 vs), *repaired the breaches of the house* (1 v) = 165 verses.

9965th Verse of the Bible

"In the seventeenth year of Pekah the son of Remaliah Ahaz the son of Jotham king of Judah began to reign. Twenty years old was Ahaz when he began to reign, and reigned sixteen years in Jerusalem, and did not that which was right in the sight of the LORD his God, like David his father. But he walked in the way of the kings of Israel, yea, and made his son to pass through the fire, according to the abominations of the heathen, whom the LORD cast out from before the children of Israel. And he sacrificed and burnt incense in the high places, and on the hills, and under every green tree" (2 Kings 16:1-4).

Verse number one is the Bible's 9965th verse, and it names an apostate Judean king—Ahaz. The Old Testament combination *Ahaz the son of Jotham king of Judah* (1x), *did not* (63x), *that which was right in the sight of the LORD his God* (1x) = 65.

Apostate Northern Tribes Carried Away to Assyria

"In the ninth year of Hoshea the king of Assyria took Samaria, and carried Israel away into Assyria. . . . And the LORD rejected all the seed of Israel, and afflicted them, and delivered them into the hand of spoilers, until he had cast them out of his sight . . . as he had said by all his servants the prophets. So was Israel carried away out of their own land to Assyria unto this day" (2 Kings 17:6a, 20, 23bc). Again the word *delivered* is mentioned in 65 chapters of the OT Narrative. The Bible combination *carried away* (63x), *out of their own land* (2x) = 65.

465th Verse of Second Kings

"And they rejected his statutes, and his covenant that he made with their fathers, and his testimonies which he testified against them; and they followed vanity, and became vain, and went after the heathen that were round about them, concerning whom the LORD had charged them, that they should not do like them" (2 Kings 17:15). This verse describes in summary form the apostate condition of Israel's northern tribes.

10,065th Verse of the Bible

Hezekiah sent the elders of the priests to Isaiah concerning Rab-shakeh's terrifying words. "And they said unto him, Thus saith Hezekiah, This day is a day of trouble, and of rebuke, and blasphemy: for the children are come to the birth, and there is not strength to bring forth" (2 Kings 19:3). Rab-shakeh's terrifying words were an attempt to make the Judean citizens fearfully defect from the walled city of Jerusalem for a greater safety, coming to him in the spirit of surrender. These three terms—day of trouble, day of rebuke, day of blasphemy—all describe how apostasy is generally viewed.

Manasseh's Apostasy

"Manasseh . . . reigned fifty and five years in Jerusalem. . . . And he did that which was evil in the sight of the LORD, after the abominations of the heathen. . . . For he built up again the high places which Hezekiah his father had destroyed; and he reared up altars for Baal, and made a grove . . . and worshipped all the host of heaven, and served them. And he <u>built</u> <u>altars in the house of the LORD</u>. . . . And he <u>built</u> <u>altars for all the host of heaven</u> in the two courts of the house of the LORD. . . . And he made his son pass through the fire, and observed times, and used enchantments, and dealt with familiar spirits and wizards: he wrought much wickedness in the sight of the LORD, to provoke him to anger" (2 Kings 21:1-6).

Manasseh was considered the worst of the Judean kings. He abandoned his previous loyalty to his father Hezekiah's godly ways. The Bible combination *built* (163 vs), *altars in the house of the LORD* (2 vs) = 165 verses. The Bible combination *built* (163 vs), *altars for all the host of heaven* (2 vs) = 165 verses.

Amon's Apostasy

"<u>Amon was twenty and two years old when he began to reign, and he reigned two years in Jerusalem</u>. . . . And he did that which was evil in the sight of the LORD, as his father Manasseh did. And he walked in all the way that his father walked in, and served the idols that his father served, and worshipped them: And he FORSOOK the LORD God of his fathers, and walked not in the way of the LORD" (2 Kings 21:19-22). The Bible combination *Amon was twenty and two years old when he began to reign* (1x), *and he reigned two years* (1x), *in Jerusalem* (163x) = 165.

Because They of Jerusalem Have Forsaken Me

"Thus saith the LORD, Behold, I will bring evil upon this place, and upon the inhabitants thereof, even all the words of the book which the king of Judah hath read: <u>Because they have FORSAKEN me</u>, and have burned incense unto other gods, that they might provoke me to anger with all the works of their hands; therefore my wrath shall be kindled against this place, and shall not be quenched" (2 Kings 22:16-17). Huldah gave forth this prophecy concerning Jerusalem's apostate condition after the people had found a single copy of the Law. Knowledge of the Lord's ways had been lost under Manaesseh's and Amon's recent evil reigns. Again the word *they* is found in 65 books of the Bible. The Bible combination *because they have* (45x), *forsaken me* (20x) = 65.

The name *Jerusalem* occurs 65 times in the Minor Prophets.

Jehoahaz's Apostasy

"Jehoahaz was twenty and three years old when he began to reign; and he reigned three months in Jerusalem. . . . And he did that which was evil in the sight of the LORD, according to all that his fathers had done. <u>And Pharaoh-nechoh put him in bands at Riblah in the land of Hamath, that he might not reign in Jerusalem; Jerusalem; and put the land to a tribute of an hundred talents of silver, and a talent of gold</u>" (2 Kings 23:31-33). Jehoahaz was godly Josiah's son, yet he abandoned his loyalty to his father's faith and religion. The underlined verse indicates the 665th verse of Second Kings, and it describes the reward of Jehoahaz's apostasy.

Jehoiakim's Apostasy

"And Pharaoh-nechoh made Eliakim the son of Josiah king in the room of Josiah his father, and turned his name to Jehoiakim. . . . Jehoiakim was twenty and five years old when he began to reign; and he reigned eleven years in <u>Jerusalem</u>. . . . And he did that which was <u>evil in</u> the sight of the LORD, according to all that his fathers had done" (2 Kings 23:34ab, 36-37). This son also apostatized from the godly ways of his father Josiah. Again the phrase *evil in* occurs 65 times in the Old Testament. Again the name *Jerusalem* occurs 65 times in the Minor Prophets.

Jehoiachin's Apostasy

"Jehoiachin was eighteen years old when he began to reign, and he <u>reigned</u> in Jerusalem three months. . . . And he did that which was <u>evil in</u> the sight of the LORD, according to all that his father had done" (2 Kings 24:8-9). This apostate king was known by the alternate names Jeconiah, Jeconias, and Coniah. The Lord was so displeased with this apostate king that He placed a generational curse upon him. Again the word *reigned* is mentioned in 65 chapters of the Old Testament. Again the phrase *evil in* occurs 65 times in the Old Testament.

Zedekiah's Apostasy

"And the king of Babylon made Mattaniah . . . king in his stead, and changed his name to Zedekiah. Zedekiah was twenty and one years old when he began to reign, and he reigned eleven years in Jerusalem. . . . And he did that which was <u>evil in</u> the sight of the LORD, according to all that Jehoiakim had done. For through the anger of the LORD it came to pass in <u>Jerusalem</u> and Judah, until he had cast them out from his presence, that Zedekiah rebelled against the king of Babylon" (2 Kings 24:17-20).

Josiah's youngest son also apostatized from the godly ways of his Davidic father. Again the phrase *evil in* occurs 65 times in the Old Testament. Again the name *Jerusalem* occurs 65 times in the Minor Prophets.

Apostate Jerusalemites Carried Away to Babylon

"Nebuchadnezzar king of Babylon came, he, and all his host, against <u>Jerusalem</u>, and pitched eleventh year of king Zedekiah. . . . And he burnt the house of the LORD, and the king's house, and all the houses of Jerusalem, and every great man's house burnt he with fire. And all the army of the Chaldees, that were with the captain of the guard, brake down the walls of Jerusalem round about" (2 Kings 25:1b-2, 9-10). Jerusalem's apostate citizenry was carried away into captivity in a final third deportation. As they went they beheld their capital city going up in flames and smoke. The phrase *the city* is mentioned in 65 verses of First and Second Kings.

Apostasy of Reubenites, Gadites & Manasseh's Half Tribe

"<u>And they transgressed against the God of their fathers, and went a whoring after the gods of the people of the land, whom God destroyed before them</u>" (1 Chron. 5:25). The Old Testament combination *and they transgressed* (1x), *against the God of* (5x), *their fathers* (142x), *and went a whoring* (3x), *after the gods* (4x), *of the people of the land* (9x), *whom God destroyed before them* (1x) = 165.

Philistine Lords Feared David Would Fall Away

"And there fell some of Manasseh to David, when he came with the Philistines against Saul to battle: but they helped them not: for the lords of the Philistines upon advisement sent him away, saying, He will FALL to his master Saul to the jeopardy of our heads" (1 Chron. 12:19). Again the Pauline and General Epistles combination *fall* (15x), *away* (50x) = 65.

Uzza's Apostasy

"And when they came unto the threshingfloor of Chidon, Uzza put forth his hand to hold the ark; for the oxen stumbled. <u>And the anger of the LORD was kindled against</u> <u>Uzza, and he smote him, because</u> <u>he put</u> <u>his hand to</u> <u>the ark</u>: and there he died before God" (1 Chron. 13:8-9). Although Uzza meant well, either knowingly or unknowingly he abandoned the Levitical law which prescribed that only the priests handle the Holy Ark. The First and Second Chronicles combination *and the anger of the LORD was kindled against* (1x), *Uzza* (6x), *and he smote him because* (1x), *he put* (6x), *his hand to* (3x), *the ark* (48x) = 65.

Michal's Apostasy

"And it came to pass, as the ark of the covenant of the LORD came to the city of David, that Michal the daughter of Saul looking out at a window saw king David dancing and playing: and she despised him in her heart" (1 Chron. 15:29). David's wife abandoned her previous loyalties to her husband. First Chronicles contains 20,365 words.

David Warns Solomon about Apostatizing

"And thou, Solomon my son, know thou the God of thy father, and serve him with a perfect heart and with a willing mind: <u>for the LORD searcheth all hearts,</u> <u>and understandeth all</u> <u>the imaginations of the thoughts: if thou seek him,</u> <u>he will be found of thee: but</u> <u>if thou FORSAKE him,</u> <u>he will cast thee off for ever</u>" (1 Chron. 28:9). The Old Testament combination *for the LORD searcheth all hearts* (1x), *and understandeth all* (1x), *the imaginations of the thoughts* (1x), *if thou seek him* (2x), *he will be found of thee but* (1x), *if thou* (154x), *forever him* (4x), *he will cast thee off for ever* (1x) = 165.

The Lord Warns Solomon about Apostatizing

"And the LORD appeared to <u>Solomon</u> by night, and said unto him . . . according as I have covenanted with David thy father, saying, There shall not fail thee a man to be ruler in Israel. But if ye <u>TURN AWAY</u>, and FORSAKE my statutes and my commandments, which I have set before you, and <u>shall go and serve other gods, and</u> <u>worship</u> them; Then will I pluck them up by the roots out of my land which I have given them; and this house, which I have sanctified for my name, will I cast out of my sight, and will make it to be a proverb and a byword among all nations" (2 Chron. 7:12a, 18b-20).

The OT Narrative combination *Solomon* (261x), *turned away* (4x) = 265. The Old Testament combination *shall go and serve other gods and* (1x), *worship* (64x) = 65.

Rehoboam's Apostasy

"And it came to pass, when Rehoboam had established the kingdom, and <u>had strengthened himself, he FORSOOK the law of the LORD, and all Israel with him</u>" (2 Chron. 12:1). The joined phrase *had strengthened himself, he forsook the law of the LORD, and all Israel with him* consist of 65 letters!

The Princes of Judah Apostatized

Then came Shemaiah the prophet to Rehoboam, and to <u>the princes</u> of Judah, that were gathered together to Jerusalem because of Shishak, and said unto them, Thus saith the LORD, Ye have

FORSAKEN me, and therefore have I also left you in the hand of Shishak" (2 Chron. 12:5). The title *the princes* occurs 65 times in the OT Narrative. Here the keyword *forsaken* is the 318,665th word of the Bible.

11,465th Verse of the Bible

"And they burn unto the LORD every morning and every evening burnt sacrifices and sweet incense: the shewbread also set they in order upon the pure table; and the candlestick of gold with the lamps thereof, to burn every evening: for we keep the charge of the LORD our God; but ye have FORSAKEN him" (2 Chron. 13:11). King Abijah delivered this piercing word of exhortation to King Jeroboam concerning his apostasy.

Prophet Warns Asa about Judah & Benjamin's Continued Apostasy

"And he went out to meet Asa, and said unto him, Hear ye me, Asa, and all Judah and Benjamin; The LORD is with you, while ye be with him; and if ye seek him, he will be found of you; but if ye FORSAKE him, he will FORSAKE you. Now for a long season Israel hath been without the true God, and without a teaching priest, and without law. . . . Be ye strong therefore, and let not your hands be weak: for your work shall be rewarded. And when Asa heard these words, and the prophecy of Oded the prophet, he took courage, and PUT AWAY the abominable idols out of all the land of Judah and Benjamin" (2 Chron. 15:2-3, 7-8d).

Because the previous two kings had abandoned previous loyalty to the law, there was a great need for revival in the land. The Old Testament combination *and if ye seek him* (1x), *he will be found of you* (1x), *but if ye forsake him* (1x), *he will forsake you* (1x), *now for* (11x), *a long season* (2x), *Israel hath* (16x), *been without* (1x), *the true God* (1x), *and without* (28x), *a teaching priest* (1x), *and without law* (1x) = 65.

Asa's Apostasy

"And at that time Hanani the seer came to Asa king of Judah, and said unto him, Because thou hast relied on the king of Syria, and not relied on the LORD thy God, therefore is the host of the king of Syria escaped out of thine hand. . . . Herein thou hast done foolishly: therefore from henceforth thou shalt have wars. Then Asa was wroth with the seer, and put him in a prison house; for he was in a rage with him because of this thing. And Asa oppressed some of the people the same time" (2 Chron. 16:7, 9c-10).

Asa was a good king, but this event caused him to abandon his previous loyalty to God's true prophets. The Old Testament combination *Asa* (57x), *was wroth with the seer* (1x), *and put him in* (5x), *a prison house* (1x), *for he was in a rage with him because of this thing* (1x) = 65.

Apostate Prophets of Baal

"I saw the LORD sitting upon his throne, and all the host of heaven standing on his right hand and on his left. And the LORD said, Who shall entice Ahab king of Israel, that he may go up and fall at Ramoth-gilead? And one spake saying after this manner, and another saying after that manner. Then there came out a spirit, and stood before the LORD, and said, I will entice him. And the LORD said unto him, Wherewith? And he said, I will go out, and be a lying spirit in the mouth of all his prophets. And the LORD said, Thou shalt entice him, and thou shalt also prevail: go out, and do even so" (2 Chron. 18:18b-21).

Micaiah spoke these visionary words to Ahab. All but a handful of Israel's prophets were apostate. The word *prophets* is mentioned in 65 chapters of the Old Testament.

Jehoram's Apostasy

"And Jehoram his son reigned in his stead . . . he was the firstborn. Now when Jehoram was risen up to the kingdom of his father, he strengthened himself, and slew all his brethren with the sword, and divers also of the princes of Israel. Jehoram was thirty and two years old when he began to reign, and he reigned eight years in Jerusalem. And he walked in the way of the kings of Israel, like as did the house of Ahab: for he had the daughter of Ahab to wife: and he wrought that which was evil in the eyes of the LORD" (2 Chron. 21:1c, 3d-6).

This was a very bad Judean king; he abandoned loyalty to his own blood brothers by killing them. The OT Narrative combination *and he walked* (7x), *in the way of* (15x), *the kings of Israel* (39x), *like as did the house of Ahab* (1x), *for he had the* (1x), *daughter of Ahab to wife* (1x), *and he wrought that which was evil in the eyes of the LORD* (1x) = 65.

Jehoram's Apostasy Receives a Just Reward

"But hast walked in the way of the kings of Israel, and hast made Judah and the inhabitants of Jerusalem to go a whoring, like to the whoredoms of the house of Ahab, and also hast slain thy brethren of thy father's house, which were better than thyself. . . . And thou shalt have great sickness by disease of thy bowels, until thy bowels fall out by reason of the sickness day by day" (2 Chron. 21:13, 15). Elijah wrote this prophecy against King Jehoram and his Judean reign of apostasy. Jehoram had caused his people to continue to fall away from their true religion. Again the name *Jerusalem* occurs 65 times in the Minor Prophets. The phrase *to go* occurs 165 times in the Bible. Again the name *Ahab* is mentioned naturally in 65 verses of First and Second Kings. The Old Testament combination *hast walked in the way of the kings of Israel* (1x), *and hast made* (8x), *the inhabitants of Jerusalem* (39x), *the inhabitants of Judah* (1x), *to go a* (3x), *whoring like to* (1x), *the whoredoms* (3x), *of the house of Ahab* (7x), *and also hast slain thy* (1x), *brethren of thy father's house* (1x) = 65.

Apostate Princes of Judah Executed

"And it came to pass, that, when Jehu was executing judgment upon the house of Ahab, and found the princes of Judah, and the sons of the brethren of Ahaziah, that ministered to Ahaziah, he slew them" (2 Chron. 22:8). More detail on this event is given in Second Kings. These royal members of the house of Judah had divided loyalties. They were either blood relatives of Ahab's house or they had intermarried with it. Nevertheless they were on their way to Samaria to pay homage to the children of Ahab and Jezebel. Thus they were considered apostates in the true sense of the word. Again the title *the princes* occurs 65 times in the OT Narrative. All forms of the word *execute* occur 65 times in the Bible.

Apostate Athaliah Slain with the Sword

"Then Jehoiada the priest brought out the captains of hundreds that were set over the host, and said unto them, Have her forth of the ranges: and whoso followeth her, let him be slain with the sword. For the priest said, Slay her not in the house of the LORD. So they laid hands on her; and when she was come to the entering of the horse gate by the king's house, they slew her there" (2 Chron. 23:14-15).

The word *slain* occurs 165 times in the Old Testament.
The phrase *the sword* is mentioned in 65 chapters of the Major Prophets.

The Judean Princes Apostatize

"Now after the death of Jehoiada came the princes of Judah, and made obeisance to the king. Then the king hearkened unto them. And they LEFT the house of the LORD God of their fathers, and served groves and idols: and wrath came upon Judah and Jerusalem for this their trespass" (2 Chron. 24:17-18). These leaders abandoned or forsook loyalty to the Lord's House. Again the title *the princes* occurs 65 times in the OT Narrative. The OT Narrative combination *and they left* (3x), *the house of the LORD God of their fathers and* (1x), *served* (44x), *groves* (17x) = 65.

The Judean Princes' Apostasy Condemned

"And the Spirit of God came upon Zechariah the son of Jehoiada the priest, which stood above the people, and said unto them, Thus saith God, Why transgress ye the commandments of the LORD, that ye cannot prosper? because ye have FORSAKEN the LORD, he hath also FORSAKEN you" (2 Chron. 24:20). Because these princes abandoned their previous loyalty to God, God abandoned His previous loyalty to them. Again the title *the princes* occurs 65 times in the OT Narrative. The Bible combination *because ye* (64x), *have forsaken the LORD he hath also forsaken you* (1x) = 65.

Joash's Apostasy

"And they conspired against him, and stoned him with stones at the commandment of the king in the court of the house of the LORD. Thus Joash the king remembered not the kindness which Jehoiada his father had done to him, but slew his son. And when he died, he said, The LORD look upon it, and require it" (2 Chron. 24:21-22). Joash was a godly king, but he abandoned his loyalty to the high priest when he killed Zechariah. The First Chronicles combination *the LORD look* (1 v), *upon it and* (1 v), *require* (1 v), *it* (62 vs) = 65 verses.

Joash's Apostasy Rewarded

By years' end the Lord repaid Joash for his evil deed. "For the army of the Syrians came with a small company of men, and the LORD delivered a very great host into their hand, because they had FORSAKEN the LORD God of their fathers. So they executed judgment against Joash. And when they were departed from him, for they left him in great diseases, his own servants conspired against him for the blood of the sons of Jehoiada the priest, and slew him on his bed, and he died" (2 Chron. 24:24-25d). Here the word *the* is the 326,765th word of the Bible, and it supports the keyword forsaken.

Uzziah's Apostasy

"Sixteen years old was Uzziah when he began to reign. . . . And he did that which was right in the sight of the LORD, according to all that his father Amaziah did. And he sought God in the days of Zechariah, who had understanding in the visions of God: and as long as he sought the LORD, God made him to prosper. . . . But when he was strong, his heart was lifted up to his destruction: for he transgressed against the LORD his God, and went into the temple of the LORD to burn incense upon the altar of incense" (2 Chron. 26:3a, 4-5, 16).

The Old Testament combination *Uzziah* (27x), *for he transgressed against* (1x), *the LORD his God* (29x), *and went into the temple of the LORD* (1x), *to burn incense upon* (2x), *the altar of incense* (5x) = 65.

Judah's Recovery from Apostasy

"And Ahaz gathered together the vessels of the house of God, and cut in pieces the vessels of the house of God, and shut up the doors of the house of the LORD, and he made him altars in every corner of Jerusalem. And in every several city of Judah he made high places to burn incense unto other gods, and provoked to anger the LORD God of his fathers. . . . And Ahaz slept with his fathers, and they buried him. . . . Hezekiah began to reign. . . . He in the first year of his reign, in the first month, opened the doors of the house of the LORD, and repaired them. And he brought in the priests and the Levites, and gathered them together into the east street, And said unto them, Hear me, ye Levites, sanctify now yourselves, and sanctify the house of the LORD God of your fathers, and carry forth the filthiness out of the holy place. For our fathers have trespassed, and done that which was evil in the eyes of the LORD our God, and have FORSAKEN him, and have TURNED AWAY their faces FROM the habitation of the LORD, and TURNED their backs. . . . Now when all this was finished, all Israel that were present went out to the cities of Judah, and brake the images in pieces, and cut down the groves, and threw down the high places and the altars out of all Judah and Benjamin, in Ephraim also and Manasseh, until they had utterly destroyed them all" (2 Chron. 28:24-25, 27a; 29:1a, 3-6; 31:1).

Hezekiah brought about great reform in Judah; it had been in a degraded state of apostasy due to Ahaz's wicked reign. Again the term *high places* is mentioned in 65 chapters of the Old Testament. Again the word *turn* is mentioned in 65 verses of the Major Prophets. Again the phrase *from the* is mentioned naturally in 165 verses of the Law.

From Recovery Back to Apostasy
"Manasseh was twelve years old when he began to reign, and he reigned fifty and five years in Jerusalem: But did that which was evil in the sight of the LORD. . . . For he built again the high places which Hezekiah his father had broken down, and he reared up altars for Baalim, and made groves, and worshipped all the host of heaven, and served them" (2 Chron. 33:1-2a, 3). Over the centuries this type of apostate religious transition was a recurring cycle in the land of Judah. Again the word *reigned* is mentioned in 65 chapters of the Old Testament. Again the term *high places* is mentioned in 65 chapters of the Old Testament.

The Returned Remnant's Apostasy
"The people of Israel, and the priests, and the Levites, have not separated themselves from the people of the lands, doing according to their abominations, even of the Canaanites . . . and the Amorites. For they have taken of their daughters for themselves, and for their sons: so that the holy seed have mingled themselves with the people of those lands: yea, the hand of the princes and rulers hath been chief in this trespass" (Ezra 9:1b-2). Again the phrase *the people* occurs 165 times in the Major Prophets. The title *Levites* occurs 265 times in the Bible. Again the title *the princes* occurs 65 times in the OT Narrative.

Ezra's National Confession of Apostasy
"And now, O our God, what shall we say after this? for we have FORSAKEN thy commandments" (Ezra 9:10). The words *now, O our God, what shall we say after this? for we have forsaken thy commandments* consists of 65 letters!

Nehemiah 7:65
"And the Tirshatha said unto them, that they should not eat of the most holy things, till there stood up a priest with Urim and Thummim" (Neh. 7:65). The returning remnant sought to do things in the ordained way lest they apostatize from their prescribed religious faith. This contrasts with the apostate way their forefathers had conducted themselves seventy years earlier. The Old Testament combination *should not* (58x), *eat of the most holy things* (2x), *till there stood up* (2x), *a priest with* (2x), *Urim and Thummim* (1x) = 65.

Nehemiah Recalls the Wilderness Generation's Apostasy

"But they and our fathers dealt proudly, and hardened their necks, and hearkened not to thy commandments, And <u>REFUSED TO OBEY</u>, neither were mindful of thy wonders that thou didst among them; but hardened their necks, and in their rebellion appointed a captain to <u>return</u> to their bondage" (Neh. 9:16-17d). Again the word *return* occurs 65 times in the OT Narrative. Again the OT combination [all forms of the word] *refuse* (61x), *to obey* (4x) = 65.

Remnant's Oath to Cease from Their Apostasy

The people entered into an oath and invoked a curse upon themselves if they failed to remain holy. They ended their oath with these words: "and we will not FORSAKE the house of our God" (Neh. 10:39e). Again all forms of the word *forsake* are mentioned in 165 combined verses of the Bible.

The Remnant Forsook the Priest's Daily Needs

"And I perceived that the portions of the Levites had not been given them: for the Levites and the singers, that did the work, were fled every one to his field. Then contended I with the rulers, and said, Why is <u>the house of God</u> FORSAKEN? And I gathered them together, and set them in their place. Then brought all Judah the tithe of the corn and the new wine and the oil unto the treasuries" (Neh. 13:10-12). The mosaic commandment had been given not to ever forsake the Levite, the priest" (Deut. 12:19; 14:27). The people's forsaking of this commandment on tithing was thus counted as a form of apostasy. The title *the house of God* is mentioned in 65 verses of the OT Narrative.

Vashti's Apostasy

"But <u>the queen Vashti REFUSED TO come at the king's commandment by his chamberlains</u>: therefore was the king very wroth, and his anger burned in him" (Est. 1:12). The words *the queen Vashti refused to come at the king's commandment by his chamberlains* consist of 65 letters!

65th Verse of Job

"Thy words have upholden him that was <u>FALLING</u>, and thou hast strengthened the feeble knees" (Job 4:4). The spiritual words of wisdom Job often shared with others was very beneficial to those who were not as familiar with God's ways as Job was. Job must have kept many of his peers from falling away into apostasy and worshiping some god other than Jehovah. Here in this 65th verse an apostasy-related word occurs—*falling*, as in falling away from the faith.

Forsaking Fear of the Almighty

"To him that is afflicted pity should be shewed from his friend; but he FORSAKETH the fear of the Almighty" (Job 6:14). The Wisdom Books combination *to him that is afflicted pity should be shewed from his friend* (1x), *but he* (63x), *forsaketh the fear of the Almighty* (1x) = 65.

Apostates Are Not on the Right Road

"Serve the LORD with fear, and rejoice with trembling. Kiss the Son, lest he be angry, and ye perish <u>FROM the</u> way, when his wrath is kindled but a little. Blessed are all they that put their trust in him" (Ps. 2:11-12). In Hebrew the word way means the road. The term "from the way" refers to those who are walking the wrong way—the road of apostasy—having departed from the right way. Again the phrase *from the* is mentioned naturally in 165 verses of the Law.

Apostate Street

"Wickedness is in the midst thereof: deceit and guile depart not from her <u>streets</u>" (Ps. 55:11). The word *streets* occurs 65 times in the Bible.

65th Psalm

"Iniquities prevail against me: as for our transgressions, thou shalt purge them away. <u>Blessed is the man whom thou choosest, and causest to approach unto thee, that he may dwell in thy courts: we shall be satisfied with the goodness of thy house, even of thy holy temple</u>" (Ps. 65:3-4). The underlined verse marks the 14,865th verse of the Bible, and it stands as a beacon of hope when God shall have recovered Israel from her apostate ways!

Ephraim's Apostasy in the Day of Battle

"The children of <u>Ephraim</u>, being armed, and carrying bows, TURNED back in the day of <u>battle</u>. They kept not the covenant of God, and REFUSED TO walk in his law" (Ps. 78:9-10). All three forms of the name *Ephraim* are mentioned in 165 verses of the Bible. Again the word *battle* occurs 165 times in the Old Testament.

God Laments Israel's History of Apostatizing

"Oh that my people had hearkened unto me, and <u>Israel</u> had walked in my ways!" (Ps. 81:13) Again the name *Israel* occurs 2565 times in Scripture. Again the name *Israel* occurs 65 times in the Wisdom Books.

Forsaking God's Law

"If his children FORSAKE my law, and walk not in my judgments; <u>If they</u> break my statutes, and keep not my commandments; Then will I visit their transgression with the rod, and their iniquity with stripes. Nevertheless my lovingkindness will I not utterly take from him, nor suffer my faithfulness to fail" (Ps. 89:30-33). The phrase *if they* is mentioned naturally in 65 verses of the Bible.

Israel Refused to Follow Their Messiah

"<u>The stone</u> <u>which the builders</u> REFUSED is become the head stone of the corner" (Ps. 118:22). This verse fits our first definition of apostasy: an act of refusing to continue to follow or obey a religious faith. The Nazarene-born Messiah was that Prophet which Moses had foretold. The Bible combination *the stone* (32x) and *refused* (33x) = 65. The Old Testament combination *which the* (261x), *the builders* (4x) = 265.

Warning a Child against Apostatizing

"My son, hear the instruction of thy father, and FORSAKE not <u>the law of</u> thy mother" (Prov. 1:8). A child should never abandon his previous loyalty to parents. Again the phrase *the law of* is mentioned in 65 chapters of the Bible.

Apostates Refused to Turn & Walk Uprightly

"<u>TURN</u> you at my reproof: behold, I will pour out my spirit unto you, I will make known my words unto you. Because I have called, and ye REFUSED; I have stretched out my hand, and no man regarded; But ye have set at nought all my counsel, and would none of my reproof: I also will laugh at your calamity; I will mock when your fear cometh" (Prov. 1:23-26). Again the word

492

turn is mentioned in 65 verses of the Major Prophets.

The Apostate Ways of Man

"For the <u>ways</u> <u>of man</u> are before the eyes of the LORD, and he pondereth all his goings" (Prov. 5:21). Tragically the ways of man are prone to apostasy. He needs regular exhortation to walk in the way of the Lord. The word *ways* is mentioned in 65 verses of the Wisdom Books. Again the phrase *of man* is mentioned in 165 verses of the Old Testament.

Don't Apostatize from God's Clear & Instruction Word

"He <u>shall die</u> without <u>instruction</u>; and in the greatness of his folly he shall go ASTRAY" (Prov. 5:23). The Bible makes for a very good Instructor. If you learn to love God's Word you will not die a fool's death. Again the phrase *shall die* occurs 65 times in the Old Testament and is mentioned in 65 verses of the Bible. All forms of instruct show the seal of apostasy: *instruct* (9x), *instructed* (19x), *instructer* (1x), *instructers* (1x), *instructing* (1x), *instruction* (33x), *instructor* (1x) = 65.

Discord Causes Apostasy

"These six things doth the LORD hate: yea, seven are an <u>abomination</u> unto him. . . . and he that soweth discord among brethren" (Prov. 6:16, 19b). Discord causes people to needlessly separate themselves from one another. Again the word *abomination* is mentioned in 65 verses of the Old Testament.

The Way of Apostates Is Hard

"Good understanding giveth favour: but the <u>way</u> of transgressors is hard" (Prov. 13:15). The transgressor's hard way is established by his ever-hardening heart. Again the word *ways* is mentioned in 65 verses of the Wisdom Books.

65th Verse of Ecclesiastes

"All go unto one place; all are of <u>the dust,</u> and all turn to dust again" (Eccles. 3:20). Because all have sinned, all have apostatized from the faith at one time or another—some more than others or some less than others. Because we have all apostatized to some degree we must all die and go into the dust. From Genesis to the Gospels the phrase *the dust* occurs 65 times.

Marital Bonds & Apostasy

"Set me as a seal upon thine heart, as a seal upon thine arm: for love is strong as <u>death</u>; jealousy is cruel as the grave: the coals thereof are coals of fire, which hath a most vehement flame" (Song 8:6). The subject of jealousy arises here in the matter of love and marriage. The bridegroom wants his betrothed one to remain faithful in his absence. He mentions her wearing the covenant terms of their holy marriage covenant in a small ornamental compartment which will hang upon her chest or around her arm as an armband; this was according to a common custom in that time. This visible action is to her advantage as it reminds him of his obligations to her. Yet here the groom reversed the meaning. He does not want her to apostatize from him having already displayed a refusal to open the door of her house to let him in after he had knocked and patiently waited. Again the word *death* is mentioned in 65 verses of the Wisdom Books.

Sinful Nation Gone Away Backward

"Ah sinful nation, a people laden with iniquity, a seed of evildoers, children that are corrupters: they have FORSAKEN the LORD, they have provoked the Holy One of Israel unto anger, they are GONE AWAY BACKWARD" (Isa. 1:4). Again the word *they* is found in 65 books of the Bible.

17,665th Verse of the Bible

"Hear the word of the LORD, ye rulers of Sodom; give ear unto the law of our God, ye people of Gomorrah" (Isa. 1:10). The Lord calls Jerusalem by an apostate name. Again the name *Jerusalem* occurs 65 times in the Minor Prophets.

Apostates Will Be Punished with the Sword

"If ye be willing and OBEDIENT, ye shall eat the good of the land: But if ye REFUSE and rebel, ye shall be devoured with the sword: for the mouth of the LORD hath spoken it" (Isa. 1:19-20). Again the phrase *the sword* is mentioned in 65 chapters of the Major Prophets.

65th Verse of Isaiah

"As for my people, children are their oppressors, and women rule over them. O my people, they which lead thee cause thee to ERR, and destroy the way of thy paths" (Isa. 3:12). Since people are easily led astray, an apostate person will craftily work to this end.

Their Hearts Have Moved Far from God

"Wherefore the Lord said, Forasmuch as this people draw near me with their mouth, and with their lips do honour me, but have REMOVED their heart FAR FROM me, and their fear toward me is taught by the precept of men" (Isa. 29:13). Because Israel's heart has been drawn far away from God she needs to change her heart and humbly draw near to God once again. Again the phrase *far from* occurs 65 times in the Bible.

The Apostate Chaldeans

"Sit thou silent, and get thee into darkness, O daughter of the Chaldeans: for thou shalt no more be called, The lady of kingdoms" (Isa. 47:5). Babylon was the capital of Chaldea and the spiritual fountain for every false religion and apostate way. Isaiah prophesied its certain doom. The name *Chaldeans* occurs 65 times in the Bible.

Israel's Bill of Divorcement

"Thus saith the LORD, Where is the bill of your mother's DIVORCEMENT, whom I have PUT AWAY? or which of my creditors is it to whom I have sold you? Behold, for your iniquities have ye sold yourselves, and for your transgressions is your mother PUT AWAY" (Isa. 50:1). Because Israel refused to be a faithful and obedient wife God had to write her a bill of divorcement. The next verse following this apostate verse is the 18,665th verse of the Bible.

Departing Away from God

The prophet laid accusations of apostasy upon Israel: "In transgressing and lying against the LORD, and DEPARTING AWAY FROM our God, speaking oppression and revolt, conceiving and uttering from the heart words of falsehood" (Isa. 59:13). Again from Genesis to the Major

Prophets the phrase *away from* is mentioned in 65 chapters. The phrases *in transgressing and lying against the LORD, and departing away from our God,* consist of 65 characters!

Turning Away Backward from God

"And judgment is TURNED AWAY BACKWARD, and justice standeth afar off: for truth is <u>fallen</u> in the street, and equity cannot enter" (Isa. 59:14). Israel's judges were at this time apostates. Again the word *fallen* is also mentioned in 65 chapters of the Bible.

65th Chapter of Isaiah

Most of this chapter pertains to God's mercy at the time of Israel's final redemption; however, it begins with Israel's current abandoning of their previous loyalty to God.

"I have spread out my hands all the day unto a rebellious <u>people</u>, which <u>walketh</u> in a way that was not good, after their own thoughts" (Isa. 65:2). Here the Lord contrasts the Gentiles' coming to Him with the Israelites' apostatizing from Him. Again the phrase *the people* occurs 165 times in the Major Prophets. Again the word *walk* occurs 65 times in the New Testament.

God continues to describe Israel's horrible defection from the faith:

> "A people that provoketh me to anger continually to my face; that sacrificeth in gardens, and burneth incense upon altars of brick; Which remain among the graves, and lodge in the monuments, which eat swine's flesh, and broth of abominable things is in their vessels; Which say, Stand by thyself, come not near to me; for I am holier than thou. These are a smoke in my nose, a fire that burneth all the day. Behold, it is written before me: I will not keep silence, but will recompense, even recompense into their bosom, Your iniquities, and the iniquities of your fathers together, saith the LORD, which have burned incense upon the mountains, and blasphemed me upon the <u>hills</u>: therefore will I measure their former work into their bosom" (vv. 3-7).

The word *hills* occurs 65 times in Scripture.

"But ye are <u>they that FORSAKE the LORD, that forget my holy mountain</u>, that prepare a table for that troop, and that furnish the drink offering unto that number" (v. 11). The Old Testament combination *they that* (164 vs), *forsake the LORD that forget my holy mountain* (1 v) = 165 verses. The keyword *forsake* actually occurs in this 65th chapter.

Judah's Apostasy

"And I will utter my judgments against them touching all their wickedness, who <u>have FORSAKEN me, and have burned incense unto</u> <u>other gods</u>, and worshipped the works of their own hands" (Jer. 1:16). The Old Testament combination *they have forsaken me and have burned incense unto* (2x), *other gods* (63x) = 65.

Judah's Twofold Apostasy

"For my people have committed two evils; <u>they</u> have FORSAKEN me the fountain of living waters, and hewed them out cisterns, broken cisterns, that can hold no water" (Jer. 2:13). Again the word *they* occurs 1965 times in the New Testament.

65th Verse of Jeremiah

"And it came to pass through the lightness of her <u>whoredom</u>, that she <u>defiled</u> the land, and <u>committed</u> adultery with stones and with stocks" (Jer. 3:9). This 65th verse clearly speaks of apostasy. From Genesis to the NT Narrative the word *defiled* occurs 65 times. Again the word *committed* occurs 65 times in the Old Testament.

Judah's Apostate Ways of Worship

"Only acknowledge thine iniquity, that thou hast transgressed against the LORD thy God, and hast scattered thy <u>ways</u> to the strangers under every green tree, and ye <u>have</u> NOT OBEYED my voice, saith the LORD" (Jer. 3:13). Here the word *have* is the 484,465th word of the Bible. Again the word *ways* is mentioned in 65 verses of the Wisdom Books.

The Apostate Tribe Refuses to Return

"O LORD, are not thine eyes upon the truth? thou hast stricken them, but they have not grieved; thou hast consumed them, but they have REFUSED TO receive correction: they have made their faces harder than a rock; they have REFUSED TO <u>return</u>" (Jer. 5:3). Again the word *return* occurs 65 times in the OT Narrative.

19,065th Verse of the Bible

"Wherefore a lion out of the forest shall slay them, and a wolf of the evenings shall spoil them, a leopard shall watch over their <u>cities</u>: every one that goeth out thence shall be torn in pieces: because their transgressions are many, and their <u>BACKSLIDINGS</u> are <u>increased</u>" (Isa. 5:6). Again the word *cities* is mentioned in 65 chapters of the Major and Minor Prophets. The Bible combination *backsliding/s* (16x), *increased* (49x) = 65.

Apostates Love to Worship Strange Gods

"And it shall come to pass, when ye shall say, Wherefore doeth the LORD our God all these things unto us? then shalt thou answer them, Like as ye have FORSAKEN <u>me</u>, and served <u>strange</u> gods in your land, so shall ye serve strangers in a land that is not yours" (Jer. 5:19). In Hebrew the words serve and worship share the same root word. Here the word *me* is the 3765th word of Jeremiah, and it supports the keyword forsaken. Again the word *strange* occurs 65 times in the Old Testament.

Jerusalem Slides Backward Perpetually

"Why then is this people of <u>Jerusalem</u> SLIDDEN BACK by a perpetual BACKSLIDING? they hold fast <u>deceit</u>, they REFUSED TO return" (Jer. 8:5). Again the name *Jerusalem* occurs 65 times in the Minor Prophets. Here in this apostate verse the word *deceit* is the 6065th word of Jeremiah.

19,165th Verse of the Bible

"For they have healed the hurt of the daughter of my people slightly, saying, Peace, peace; when there is no peace" (Jer. 8:11). The apostate prophets in Judah readily prophesy lies.

Forsaking God's Law

"And the LORD saith, Because they have FORSAKEN <u>my</u> law which I set before them, and have NOT OBEYED my voice, neither walked therein" (Jer. 9:13). Refusing to obey is an act of apostasy. Here the word *my* is the 6965th word of Jeremiah, and it supports the keyword forsaken.

"They Went after Other Gods"

"They are TURNED BACK to the iniquities of their forefathers, which REFUSED TO hear my words; and they went after other gods to serve them: the house of Israel and the house of Judah have broken my covenant which I made with their fathers" (Jer. 11:10). The Old Testament combination *and they went after* (2x), *other gods* (63x) = 65.

They Served Other Gods

"This evil people, which refuse to hear my words, which walk in the imagination of their heart, and walk after other gods, to serve them, and to worship them, shall even be as this girdle, which is good for nothing" (Jer. 13:10). The Old Testament combination *other gods* (63x), *to serve them and to worship them* (2x) = 65.

Cursed Be the Man Who Departs from the Lord

"Thus saith the LORD; Cursed be the man that trusteth in man, and maketh flesh his arm, and whose heart DEPARTETH from the LORD" (Jer. 17:5). Again the word *man* is mentioned in 65 verses of Numbers. Again the phrase *from the* is mentioned naturally in 165 verses of the Law.

Judah Is Estranged from True Worship at the Lord's House

"Because they have FORSAKEN me, and have ESTRANGED this place, and have burned incense in it unto other gods, whom neither they nor their fathers have known, nor the kings of Judah, and have filled this place with the blood of innocents" (Jer. 19:4). Here the keyword *forsaken* is the 496,665th word of the Bible. The Old Testament combination *other gods* (63x), *whom neither they nor their fathers have known* (2x) = 65. The naturally occurring Old Testament combination *and have estranged* (1x), *this place* (64x) = 65.

Jerusalem to Be Destroyed because of Their Apostasy

"Then they shall answer, Because they have FORSAKEN the covenant of the LORD their God, and worshipped other gods, and served them" (Jer. 22:9). This apostasy verse immediately precedes the 19,465th verse of the Bible. The Old Testament combination *other gods* (63x), *worshipped them and served them* (2x) = 65.

19,465th Verse of the Bible

"Weep ye not for the dead, neither bemoan him: but weep sore for him that GOETH AWAY: for he shall return no more, nor see his native country" (Jer. 22:10). Many apostate Judeans will be killed and others will go away into captivity.

19,765th Verse of the Bible

"And they have TURNED unto me the back, and not the face: though I taught them, rising up early and teaching them, yet they have not hearkened to receive instruction" (Jer. 32:33). Failing to obey the Lord, hence apostatizing, is the theme of this verse.

19,865th Verse of the Bible

"Now the king sat in the winterhouse in the ninth month: and there was a fire on the hearth burning before him. (Jer. 36:22). After Jehudi had read a few leaves of it, he cut it with a penknife and cast it into the fire. The king's refusal to obey the Lord at Jeremiah's command, hence apostatizing, is the theme of this verse.

Jeremiah Accused of Apostatizing to the Chaldeans

"And when he was in the gate of Benjamin, a captain of the ward was there, whose name was Irijah, the son of Shelemiah, the son of Hananiah; and he took Jeremiah the prophet, saying, Thou FALLEST AWAY to the <u>Chaldeans</u>" (Jer. 37:13). Jeremiah was falsely accused of working with Babylon to deceive Judah. Again the Old Testament combination *falling* (8 vs) and *away* (657 vs) = 665 verses! Again the name *Chaldeans* occurs 65 times in the Bible.

Some Jews Obediently Apostatized to the Chaldeans

"And Zedekiah the king said unto Jeremiah, I am afraid of the <u>Jews</u> that are FALLEN <u>to</u> the Chaldeans, lest they deliver me into their hand, and they mock me" (Jer. 38:19). Here the word *to* is the 665th word of this chapter, and it supports the apostasy-related word fallen. The title *Jews(')* is mentioned in 65 verses of John's Gospel.

65th Verse of Lamentations

"This I recall to my mind, therefore have I hope" (Lam. 3:21). Speaking on behalf of the spiritually apostate citizenry of Jerusalem, the weeping prophet begins to recall the Lord's mercies. He hopes the Lord will not remember the city's apostasy for very long and therefore return to extending His mercies to them.

Judeans Refused to Obey the Lord's Judgments

"And she hath changed my judgments into wickedness more than the nations, and my statutes more than the countries that are round about her: for they have REFUSED <u>my</u> judgments and my statutes, they have not <u>walked</u> in them" (Ezek. 5:6). Here the word *my* is the 2665th word of Ezekiel, and it supports the apostasy-related word refused. Again the word *walk* occurs 65 times in the New Testament.

"Go No More Astray"

"<u>That the house of Israel may</u> GO no more ASTRAY FROM me, <u>neither be polluted any more</u> <u>with all their transgressions; but that they may be my people, and I may be their God</u>, saith the Lord GOD" (Ezek. 14:11). God longed for Judah's apostasy to come to an end. Again the title *the house of Israel* is mentioned in 65 verses of Ezekiel. The Bible combination *that the house of Israel may* (1x), *go no more* (4x), *astray* (22x), *from me* (129x), *neither be polluted* (1x), *any more with* (3x), *all their transgressions* (3x), *but that they may be my people* (1x), *and I may be their God* (1x) = 165.

Lucifer's Apostasy

"Thou art the anointed cherub that covereth; and I have set thee so: thou wast upon the holy mountain of God; thou hast walked up and down in the midst of the stones of fire. <u>Thou wast</u> <u>perfect in thy ways</u> <u>from the day</u> <u>that thou wast</u> <u>created</u>, <u>till iniquity was found in thee</u>" (Ezek. 28:14-15). The Ezekiel combination *thou wast perfect in thy ways* (1x), *from the day* (1x), *that thou wast* (3x), *created* (3x), *till* (9x), *iniquity* (47x), *was found in thee* (1x) = 65.

Be Ashamed for Your Apostasy

"Not for your sakes do I this, saith the Lord GOD, be it known unto you: <u>be ashamed</u> and confounded for your own ways, O house of Israel" (Ezek. 36:32). The phrase *be ashamed* is mentioned in 65 verses of the Bible.

Israel Shall Know Not to Apostatize Anymore

"So will I make my holy name known in the midst of my people Israel; and I will not let them pollute my holy name any more: and the heathen shall <u>know that I am the LORD</u>, the Holy One in Israel" (Ezek. 39:7). God sought to make an example of Israel for all other nations's benefit. Proper blessing and chastisement were needful if the nations were to turn to God from their heathen ways. The phrase *know that I am the LORD/Lord* occurs 65 times in the Major and Minor Prophets.

The Levites Went Astray Far from God

"And the <u>Levites</u> that are GONE AWAY <u>FAR FROM</u> me, when Israel WENT ASTRAY, which WENT ASTRAY AWAY FROM me after their idols; they shall even bear their iniquity" (Ezek. 44:10). Again the title *Levites* occurs 265 times in the Bible. Again the phrase *far from* occurs 65 times in the Bible.

Judeans Had Departed from God's Precepts

Daniel prayed on behalf of his apostate Hebrew countrymen. "We have sinned, and have <u>committed</u> iniquity, and have done wickedly, and have rebelled, even by DEPARTING <u>FROM thy</u> precepts and <u>from thy</u> judgments" (Dan. 9:5). In this verse the word *committed* is the 576,565th word of the Bible, and it refers to having committed apostasy. Again the word *committed* occurs 65 times in the Old Testament. Again the phrase *from thy* occurs 65 times in Scripture.

Departing from the Lord

"The beginning of the word of the LORD by Hosea. And the LORD said to Hosea, Go, take unto thee a wife of whoredoms and children of whoredoms: for <u>the land</u> hath <u>committed great whoredom</u>, departing <u>FROM the</u> LORD" (Hos. 1:2). The prophet was to visually demonstrate to Israel how the nation had apostatized from the Lord. A living parable was needed. Again the phrase *from the* is mentioned naturally in 165 verses of the Law. The Minor Prophets combination *the land* (63x), *committed great whoredom* (1x), *committed whoredom* (1x) = 65.

The Spirit of Apostasy

"My people ask counsel at their stocks, and their staff declareth unto them: for the <u>spirit of</u> whoredoms hath caused them to ERR, and they have GONE a whoring from under their God" (Hos. 4:12). Again the lowercase title *spirit of* is mentioned in 65 verses of the Bible.

65th Verse of Hosea

"They have dealt treacherously against the LORD: for they have begotten <u>strange</u> children: now shall a month devour them with their portions" (Hos. 5:7). As Israel apostatized and married strangers around them, their offspring were then born into apostasy. Again the word *strange* occurs 65 times in the Old Testament.

65th Verse of Joel

"Put ye in the sickle, for the harvest is ripe: come, get you down; for the press is full, the fats overflow; for their wickedness is great" (Joel 3:13). Full apostasy is the theme of this verse.

65th Verse of Amos

"Seek the LORD, and ye shall live; lest he break out like fire in the house of Joseph, and devour it, and there be none to quench it in Beth-el" (Amos 5:6). Joseph's tribe later split into two tribes. Occasionally the northern kingdom is referred to as Joseph but more often as the younger son Ephraim, the largest northern tribe. Bethel was one of the two cities where Jeroboam's apostate golden calves were set up. Great apostasy took place there on a daily basis as Israelites came there to kiss the golden calf representing Baal. Since the northern tribes had departed from Jehovah He told them to do the opposite—begin seeking Him. Again all three forms of the name *Ephraim* are mentioned in 165 verses of the Bible. The word *none* is mentioned in 65 verses of the New Testament.

Jonah's Apostasy

"But Jonah rose up to flee unto Tarshish FROM the presence of the LORD, and went down to Joppa; and he found a ship going to Tarshish" (Jonah 1:3a). Again the phrase *from the* is mentioned naturally in 165 verses of the Law.

Jerusalem's Apostasy

"For the transgression of Jacob is all this, and for the sins of the house of Israel. What is the transgression of Jacob? is it not Samaria? and what are the high places of Judah? are they not Jerusalem?" (Mic. 1:5) Again the word *sins* is mentioned naturally in 165 verses of the Bible. Again the name *Jerusalem* occurs 65 times in the Minor Prophets.

65th Verse of Micah

"And I will cut off the cities of thy land, and throw down all thy strong holds" (Mic. 5:11). Israel's religious defection from God caused His anger to boil. Again the word *cities* is mentioned in 65 chapters of the Major and Minor Prophets.

Nineveh's Apostasy

"The burden of Nineveh. The book of the vision of Nahum the Elkoshite. God is jealous, and the LORD revengeth; the LORD revengeth, and is furious; the LORD will take vengeance on his adversaries, and he reserveth wrath for his enemies. The LORD is slow to anger, and great in power, and will not at all acquit the wicked" (Nah. 1:1-3a). Some time ago the Assyrian capital had repented under Jonah's preaching. They had humbled themselves before God, but more than a century later they were living in apostasy. The sentence *the LORD is slow to anger, and great in power, and will not at all acquit the wicked* consists of 65 letters!

Woe unto Jerusalem for Her Apostasy

"Woe to her that is filthy and polluted, to the oppressing city! She OBEYED NOT the voice; she RECEIVED NOT correction; she trusted not in the LORD; she DREW NOT NEAR to her God" (Zeph. 3:1-2). Again the word *woe* is mentioned in 65 verses of the Old Testament. The word *she* occurs naturally 65 times in First and Second Samuel.

The Weary Remnant's Apostate Ways

"Then came the word of the LORD by Haggai the prophet, saying, Is it time for you, O ye, to dwell in your cieled houses, and this house lie waste? Now therefore thus saith the LORD of hosts; Consider your ways" (Hag. 1:3-5). Again the word *ways* is mentioned in 65 verses of the

Wisdom Books.

"They Went Their Way"

"For the idols have spoken vanity, and the diviners have seen a lie, and have told false dreams; they comfort in vain: therefore <u>they</u> WENT THEIR WAY as a flock, they were troubled, because there was no shepherd" (Zech. 10:2). The reality is they were apostate and estranged from Jehovah. Again the word *they* is found in 65 books of the Bible.

Woe to the Apostate Shepherds

"<u>Woe</u> to the idol shepherd that LEAVETH the flock! the sword shall be upon his arm, and upon his right eye: his arm shall be clean dried up, and his right eye shall be utterly darkened" (Zech. 11:17). Israel's apostasy was because of a lack of consistent strong teaching of gospel truth. The vacuum of truth by true shepherds would be quickly replaced with false shepherds' apostate teachings. Again the word *woe* is mentioned in 65 verses of the Old Testament; this is its 65th verse-mention.

Judah Has Married a Strange God

"Judah hath dealt treacherously, and an abomination is committed in Israel and in Jerusalem; for Judah hath profaned the holiness of the LORD which he loved, and hath married the daughter of a <u>strange</u> god" (Mal. 2:11). Again the word *strange* occurs 65 times in the Old Testament; this is its 65th occurrence.

Gone Away from God's Ordinances

"Even from the days of your fathers ye are GONE AWAY FROM mine ordinances, and have NOT KEPT them. Return unto me, <u>and</u> I will return unto you, saith the LORD of hosts. But ye said, Wherein shall we return?" (Mal. 3:7) This apostate chapter of Malachi contains 565 words.

The New Testament

"The book of the generation of <u>Jesus</u> <u>Christ</u>, the son of David, the son of Abraham" (Matt. 1:1). The nation of Israel had a perpetual problem with following and obeying God. The same was true when the Son of God came unto them. Jesus' message was both consistent and persistent: Follow Me! This presented the people with not only a great opportunity but also a great obstacle. Time after time crowds would listen to Messiah's message but then defect to what was more familiar to them—the Law of Moses.

> The title *Lord* is mentioned in 265 verses of the Pauline Epistles.
> The name *Jesus* is mentioned in 665 verses of the NT Narrative.
> The phrase *Jesus said* occurs 65 times in the New Testament.
> The title *Christ* occurs 65 times in First Corinthians.

Repent of Your Apostasy

"From that time Jesus began to preach, and to say, <u>Repent</u>: for the kingdom of heaven is at hand" (Matt. 4:17). Because the nation was not in the proper spiritual condition it should have been in, the people were therefore apostate in varying degrees. The Hebrew word for "repent" means to turn or to turn back. Again the word *turn* is mentioned in 65 verses of the Major Prophets.

When Your Salt Loses Its Saltiness

"<u>Ye are the salt of the earth</u>: <u>but if the salt</u> <u>have lost his</u> <u>savour</u>, <u>wherewith shall it be</u> <u>salted</u>? it is thenceforth good for nothing, but to be <u>cast out</u>, and to be trodden under foot of men" (Matt. 5:13). The Jews had not maintained a close walk with God. Rather than following the mosaic commandments they were merely following the twisted teachings of men. Thus, like salt, they had become ineffective through their apostatized condition. They had lost their savor as soul winners. The Bible combination *ye are the salt of the earth* (1x), *but if the salt* (3x), *have lost his saltness* (1x), *savour* (54x), *wherewith shall it be* (2x), *salted* (4x) = 65. From Genesis to the Gospels the phrase *cast out* is mentioned in 65 verses.

When Your Messianic Light Loses Its Luminescence

"Ye are the light of <u>the world</u>. A city that is set on an hill cannot be hid. Neither do men light a candle, and put it under a bushel, but on a candlestick; and it giveth light unto all that are in the house. Let your light so shine before men, that they may see your good works, and glorify your Father which is in heaven" (Matt. 5:14-16). The people had laid eyes on their long-awaited Messiah. But rather than go spread the good news like welcomed light in a fretful darkness, the people quickly fell away choosing to go back to their mundane lives. They apostatized. From Genesis to the Synoptic Gospels the title *the world* occurs 65 times.

When Your Marriage Loses Its Marriage Bonds

"It hath been said, Whosoever shall PUT AWAY his wife, let him give her a writing of DIVORCEMENT: But I say unto you, <u>That whosoever shall PUT AWAY his wife, saving for the cause of fornication, causeth her to commit adultery: and whosoever shall marry her that is divorced committeth adultery</u>" (Matt. 5:31-32). Mentioned earlier in the introduction, the Greek word apostasion properly means something separative—divorcement. Jesus makes provision for divorce but only in the case where the bride-to-be was unfaithful or apostate before the wedding day. The Bible combination *that whosoever shall put away his wife* (1x), *saving for the cause of fornication* (1x), *causeth her to commit adultery* (1x), *and whosoever shall marry* (1x), *her that is divorced* (2x), *committeth* (19x), *adultery* (40x) = 65.

When Your Pearls Are Cast before Apostate People

"Give not that which is holy unto the dogs, neither cast ye your pearls before swine, lest <u>they</u> trample them under <u>their</u> feet, and turn again and rend you" (Matt. 7:6). If apostates will not receive the simple teachings of God's Word, they will definitely not receive the deeper truths of the glorious gospel. Again the word *they* occurs 1965 times in the New Testament. Again the word *their* is mentioned in 2365 verses of the Bible.

When Your Father Gives You Unfit Things to Eat

"Or what man is there of you, whom if his son ask bread, <u>will he</u> give him a stone? Or if he ask a fish, <u>will he</u> give him a serpent? If ye then, being evil" (Matt. 7:9-11a). A hypothetical case is given here whereby an apostate father has deserted his previous duties of parental loyalty.

The Bible combination *will he* (63x), *give him a stone* (2x) = 65.
The Bible combination *will he* (63x), *give him a serpent* (2x) = 65.

When Apostate Prophets Speak Appealing Words

"Beware of <u>false</u> prophets, which come to you in sheep's clothing, but inwardly they are ravening wolves. Ye shall know them by their fruits. Do men gather grapes of thorns, or figs of thistles? Even so every good tree bringeth forth good fruit; but a corrupt tree bringeth forth evil fruit" (Matt. 7:15-17). Apostate prophets are easily identifiable by their apostate doings.

The Bible combination *false* (64x) and *feigned words* (1x) = 65.
The Bible combination *false* (64x) and *feigned lips* (1x) = 65.

Sheep Gone Astray

"How think ye? <u>if a man have</u> <u>an hundred</u> <u>sheep,</u> <u>and one of them</u> <u>be</u> <u>GONE</u> <u>ASTRAY</u>, doth he not leave the ninety and nine, and goeth into the mountains, and seeketh that which is GONE ASTRAY?" (Matt. 8:12) The New Testament combination *if a man have* (2x), *an hundred* (14x), *sheep* (42x), *and one of them be* (1x), *be gone* (1x), *astray* (5x) = 65.

When a Believer Falls Away from Giving Public Witness of Christ

"Whosoever therefore shall confess me before men, him will I confess also before my Father which is in heaven. But <u>whosoever shall</u> <u>DENY me</u> <u>before men,</u> <u>him will I</u> <u>also</u> <u>DENY</u> <u>before my Father which is in heaven</u>" (Matt. 10:32-33). The New Testament combination *whosoever shall* (46x), *deny me* (8x), *before men* (7x), *him will I also* (1x), *also deny* (1x), *before my Father which is in heaven* (2x) = 65.

Disciples Accused of Apostatizing from a Mosaic Law

"At that time Jesus went on the sabbath day through the corn; and his disciples were an hungred, and began to pluck the ears of corn, and to eat. But when the Pharisees saw it, they said unto him, Behold, <u>thy disciples</u> <u>do that which is not</u> <u>lawful to do</u> upon <u>the sabbath day</u>" (Matt. 12:1-2). Because Jesus was Lord of the Sabbath He made provision for His disciples to do this small bit of harvesting. The word *not* is mentioned in 1065 chapters of the Bible. The Bible combination *thy disciples* (10x), *do that which is not* (1x), *lawful to do* (4x), *the sabbath day* (50x) = 65.

Apostate Pharisees

After Jesus' performance of this miracle the people thought with great certainty that He was the Davidic Savior. "But when <u>the Pharisees</u> heard it, they said, <u>This fellow doth not cast out devils, but by Beelzebub the prince of the devils</u>" (Matt. 12:24). Only one Pharisee made this statement, yet all the other Pharisees immediately confirmed it. Their blasphemy toward Christ was an act of apostasy. The New Testament combination *the Pharisee* (3x), *the Pharisees* (61x), *the other Pharisees* (1x) = 65. The words *this fellow doth not cast out devils, but by Beelzebub the prince of the devils* consist of 65 characters!

Apostate Hearts

"For this people's heart is waxed gross, and <u>their</u> ears are dull of hearing, and <u>their</u> eyes they have closed; lest at any time they should see with their eyes, and hear with their ears, and should understand with their heart, and should be converted, and I should heal them" (Matt. 13:15). Jesus condemned the people regarding their apostate condition. Again the word *their* is mentioned in 2365 verses of the Bible.

Apostate Souls

"Again, the kingdom of heaven is like unto a net, that was cast into the sea, and gathered of every kind: Which, when it was full, they drew to shore, and sat down, and gathered the good into vessels, but cast the bad away. So shall it be at the end of the world: the angels shall come forth, and SEVER the wicked from among the just" (Matt. 13:47-49). The word *sever* corresponds with our definition of apostasy: something separative. The Bible combination *the angels shall come forth and* (1x), *sever* (4x), *the wicked* (259x), *from among the just* (1x) = 265.

Apostate Traditions

"Then came to Jesus scribes and Pharisees, which were of Jerusalem, saying, Why do thy disciples transgress the tradition of the elders? for they wash not their hands when they eat bread. But he answered and said unto them, Why do ye also transgress the commandment of God by your tradition?" (Matt. 15:1-3) Over time Israel's elders added many rules, regulations, commandments, keepings, ordinances, and observances to God's previously completed Law. These then became a hindrance to true faith and obedience to Moses' Law. After the religious leaders accused the disciples of apostatizing, Jesus pointed out that keeping their invalid traditions was actually a form of apostasy. The OT Narrative combination *why do thy disciples transgress* (1x), *the tradition of the* (3x), *elders* (59x), *for they wash not their hands* (1x), *when they eat bread* (1x) = 65.

Apostate Leaders

"Then came his disciples, and said unto him, Knowest thou that the Pharisees were offended, after they heard this saying? But he answered and said, Every plant, which my heavenly Father hath not planted, shall be rooted up. Let them alone: they be blind leaders of the blind. And if the blind lead the blind, both shall fall into the ditch" (Matt. 15:12-14). The blind are those who have refused the light of God's Word. The blind leaders are those who have also themselves refused it. Both together will fully fall away from the true religious faith. Again the word *fallen* is mentioned in 65 chapters of the Bible. The Bible combination *both* (263 chs) and *fall into the ditch* (2 chs) = 265 chapters.

Apostate Generation

"O ye hypocrites, ye can discern the face of the sky; but can ye not discern the signs of the times? A wicked and adulterous generation seeketh after a sign; and there shall no sign be given unto it, but the sign of the prophet Jonas" (Matt. 16:3b-4). Israel's religious apostasy was likened to marital unfaithfulness. God sent prophets to correct such apostate generations. The New Testament combination *wicked* (24x), *and adulterous* (2x), *generation* (37x), *seeketh after a sign* (2x) = 65.

Apostate Chief Priests

"Behold, we go up to Jerusalem; and the Son of man shall be BETRAYED unto the chief priests and unto the scribes, and they shall condemn him to death" (Matt. 20:18). Jesus foretold precisely how far the apostate priests would go in their apostasy. Again from Genesis to the Gospels the title *the priests* occurs 265 times. Again the title *priests* occurs 65 times in the Major and Minor Prophets. The title *chief priests* occurs 65 times in the Bible.

Apostate Hypocrites

"<u>Woe</u> unto you, scribes and Pharisees, hypocrites! for ye are like unto whited sepulchres, which indeed appear beautiful outward, but are within full of dead men's bones, and of all uncleanness. Even so ye also outwardly appear righteous unto men, but within ye are full of hypocrisy and iniquity" (Matt. 23:27-28). Again the word *woe* is mentioned in 65 verses of the Old Testament.

Apostate Stars

"Immediately after the tribulation of those days shall the sun be darkened, and the moon shall not give her light, and the <u>stars</u> shall FALL AWAY FROM heaven, and the powers of the heavens shall be shaken" (Matt. 24:29). The word *star(s)* is mentioned in 65 verses of the Bible.

Apostate Nations

"When the Son of man shall come in his glory, and all the holy angels with him, then shall he sit upon the throne of his glory: And before him shall be gathered all <u>nations</u>: and he shall separate them one from another, as a shepherd divideth his sheep from the goats: And he shall set the sheep on <u>his</u> right hand, <u>but the goats on</u> <u>the left</u>" (Matt. 25:33). These apostate nations will be judged by how they treated Jewish evangelists during the Tribulation. Again the phrase *the nations* occurs 165 times in the Old Testament. The Bible combination *but the goats on* (1x), *the left* (48x), *his left* (16x) = 65.

Apostatize Apostle

"Then one of <u>the twelve</u>, called <u>Judas</u> Iscariot, went unto the chief priests, And said unto them, What will ye give me, and I will deliver him unto you? And they <u>covenanted</u> <u>with him</u> <u>for thirty</u> <u>pieces of</u> <u>silver</u>. And from that time he sought opportunity to BETRAY him" (Matt. 26:14-16). The name Judas is the Greek rendering for the name Judah. The New Testament combination *the twelve* (32x) and *Judas* (33x) = 65. The Major and Minor Prophets combination *covenanted* (1x), *with Judah* (1x), *for thirty* (1x), *pieces of* (4x), *silver* (58x) = 65.

Apostate Apostle Betrays Christ with a Kiss

"And forthwith <u>he</u> came to Jesus, and said, Hail, <u>master</u>; and kissed him" (Matt. 26:49). Judas fully defected to the other side—the dark side. The Bible combination *Judas* (33x) and *his master* (32x) = 65.

All the Disciples Suddenly Apostatized from Christ

"But all this was done, that the scriptures of the prophets might be fulfilled. Then all <u>the disciples</u> FORSOOK him, and fled" (Matt. 26:56). The title *the disciples* occurs 65 times in the New Testament.

Matthew 26:65

"Then the high priest rent his clothes, saying, He hath spoken blasphemy; what further need have we of witnesses? behold, now ye have heard his blasphemy" (Mat. 26:65). The high priest was accusing Christ of apostatizing from the Mosaic faith.

Apostate Jury

"Pilate saith unto them, What shall I do then with Jesus which is called Christ? They all say unto him, Let him be crucified" (Matt. 27:22). Pilate was the Judge. Christ was the Accused. Judeans were the jury. The capitalized word *They* occurs 65 times in the NT Narrative.

Matthew 27:65

"Pilate said unto them, Ye have a watch: go your way, make it as sure as ye can" (Matt. 27:65). These chief priests were further apostatizing by attempting to fight against a biblical Old Testament truth of the resurrection. Their apostasy from the faith was growing by the hour. Again the title *chief priests* occurs 65 times in the Bible.

65th Verse of Mark

"But the days will come, when the bridegroom shall be TAKEN AWAY FROM them, and then shall they fast in those days" (Mark 2:20). Christ points to the dark day in the Pharisees' near future when they will greatly apostatize by taking Him away from the land of the living. They will create a separative event between the Master and His pupils. From Genesis to the NT Narrative the phrase *taken away* occurs 65 times. Again the word *from* is mentioned in 65 chapters of the Synoptic Gospels.

Citizens of Nazareth Apostatize Again from Jesus

"And he . . . came into his own country; and his disciples follow him. And when the sabbath day was come, he began to teach in the synagogue: and many hearing him were astonished, saying, From whence hath this man these things? . . . And they were offended at him. But Jesus said unto them, A prophet is not without honour, but in his own country, and among his own kin, and in his own house" (Mark 6:1-2d, 3e-4). Even though Nazareth had heard of Jesus' miracles over the past year or so, they still defected from Him after hearing His mighty words. Again the word *they* occurs 1965 times in the New Testament.

Cities of Israel Will Apostatize from the Gospel Message

"And he said unto them, In what place soever ye enter into an house, there abide till ye depart from that place. And whosoever shall not receive you, nor hear you, when ye depart thence, shake off the dust under your feet for a testimony against them. Verily I say unto you, It shall be more tolerable for Sodom and Gomorrha in the day of judgment, than for that city" (Mark 6:10-11). In this passage there are 65 words in Christ's speech, and they pertain to the apostles' needful reactions to any of the people's forthcoming apostasy.

Scribes & Pharisees Apostatize the Commandment of God

"For laying ASIDE the commandment of God, ye hold the tradition of men, as the washing of pots and cups: and many other such like things ye do. And he said unto them, Full well ye reject the commandment of God, that ye may keep your own tradition" (Mark 7:8-9). The words *full well ye reject the commandment of God, that ye may keep your own tradition* consist of 65 characters!

From Genesis to the Gospels the phrase *aside* occurs 65 times.
From Genesis to the NTN the phrase *aside* is mentioned in 65 verses.

465th Verse of Mark

"But those husbandmen said among themselves, This is the heir; come, let us kill him, and the inheritance shall be <u>ours</u>" (Mark 12:7). This verse tells of the husbandmen utterly abandoning previous loyalties to the land owner. The word *our* occurs 1165 times in the Bible.

Apostate Family Members

"Now <u>the brother</u> <u>shall BETRAY</u> <u>the brother</u> <u>to death,</u> <u>and the father the son;</u> <u>and children shall RISE UP AGAINST their parents,</u> <u>and shall cause them to be</u> <u>put to death</u>" (Mark 13:12). The New Testament combination *the brother* (12x), *shall betray* (6x), *the brother* (12x), *to death* (24x), *and the father the son* (1x), *and children shall rise up against their parents* (2x), *and shall cause them to be* (1x), *put to death* (7x) = 65.

Apostate Antichrist

"But when ye shall see the <u>abomination</u> of desolation, spoken of by Daniel the prophet, standing where it ought not, let him that readeth understand, then let them that be in Judæa flee to the mountains" (Mark 13:14). Suddenly the false messiah will abandon his previous loyalty to the Jewish people by erecting a blasphemous image in their Jewish temple. At that time the Jews will suddenly abandon their previous loyalties to him. Again the word *abomination* is mentioned in 65 verses of the Old Testament.

Judas Iscariot's Wicked Apostasy

"And <u>Judas</u> <u>Iscariot,</u> <u>one of the twelve,</u> <u>went unto the chief priests,</u> <u>to BETRAY him unto them.</u> <u>And when they heard it,</u> <u>they were glad,</u> <u>and promised to give him money</u>. And he sought how he might conveniently BETRAY him" (Mark 14:10-11). From this time forward Judas was a wicked and treacherous apostate. The Bible combination *Judas* (33x), *Iscariot* (11x), *one of the twelve* (8x), *went unto the chief priests* (2x), *to betray him unto them* (2x), *and when they heard it* (3x), *they were glad* (5x), *and promised to give him money* (1x) = 65.

The Apostles' Frightful Apostasy Predicted

"And Jesus saith unto them, All ye shall be offended because of me this night: for it is written, I will smite the shepherd, and the sheep shall be <u>scattered</u>" (Mark 14:27). Zechariah's prophecy foretold how Messiah's covenant men would suddenly depart from Him. Because of their fear of persecution all eleven disciples would abandon their previous loyalties to Christ. From Genesis to the Gospels the word *scattered* occurs 65 times.

The Apostles' Frightful Apostasy Performed

"And <u>they all</u> <u>FORSOOK him,</u> <u>and fled</u>" (Mark 14:50). Out of great fear the disciples apostatized from Christ. The Bible combination *they all* (33x), *forsook him* (2x), *the chief shepherd* (1x), *and fled* (29x) = 65.

The Father's Apostasy from Christ Prophesied

"And at the ninth hour Jesus cried with a loud voice, saying, Eloi, Eloi, lama sabachthani? which is, being interpreted, <u>My God, my God, why hast thou FORSAKEN me</u>?" (Mark 15:34) God had to forsake Christ for a little season because He had been ladened with the world's wretched sins. The verse which immediately precedes this direct quote in Psalm 22:1 is the 265th verse of the Psalms.

Mark 14:65

"And some began to spit on him, and to cover his face, and to buffet him, and to say unto him, Prophesy: and the servants did strike him with the palms of their hands" (Mark 14:65). The greatest apostasy in Israel's history was irreversibly underway here as the apostate priests cruelly mocked God's Son.

Peter's Apostasy

"And a little after, they that stood by said again to Peter, Surely thou art one of them: for thou art a Galilaean, and thy speech agreeth thereto. But he began to curse and to swear, saying, I know not this man of whom ye speak. And the second time the cock crew. And Peter called to mind the word that Jesus said unto him, Before the cock crow twice, thou shalt DENY me thrice. And when he thought thereon, he wept" (Mark 14:70b-72). The Bible combination *Peter* (158x), *called to mind the word that Jesus said* (1x), *unto him before the cock crow twice* (1x), *thou shalt deny* me *thrice* (5x) = 165.

Sun's Apostasy

"And when the sixth hour was come, there was darkness over the whole land until the ninth hour. And at the ninth hour Jesus cried with a loud voice, saying, Eloi, Eloi, lama sabachthani? which is, being interpreted, My God, my God, why hast thou FORSAKEN me?" (Mark 15:33-34) At this time, not only the very God of Heaven but also the light of heaven forsook Jesus. The sun refused to obey Christ's Genesis command to shine forth upon the earth. Angels were forbidden to come to His rescue. It was the hour of heaven's apostatizing from the earthly Son of God! The Gospels combination *hour* (64x), *was come to pass* (1x) = 65. The Bible combination *darkness* (162x), *over the whole land* (1x), *until the ninth hour* (2x) = 165. The Bible combination *sun* (160x), *refused to obey* (2x), *the creator* (3x) = 165. The Bible combination *which is being interpreted My God my God* (1 v), *why* (261 vs), *hast thou forsaken me* (3 vs) = 265 verses.

25,065th Verse of the Bible

"And Jesus being full of the Holy Ghost returned from Jordan, and was led by the Spirit into the wilderness, Being forty days tempted of the devil. And in those days he did eat nothing: and when they were ended, he afterward hungered. And the devil said unto him, If thou be the Son of God, command this stone that it be made bread" (Luke 4:1-3). Satan's goal was to cause the lowly Christ to abandon His previous loyalty to the Father. The Devil's goal was to get the weakened Christ to fall away from God and then fall down and worship him. The underlined 65th verse pertains to the Devil's wilderness attempt to make Jesus apostatize.

Satan's Second Attempt to Make Jesus Apostatize

"And the devil, taking him up into an high mountain, shewed unto him all the kingdoms of the world in a moment of time. And the devil said unto him, All this power will I give thee, and the glory of them: for that is delivered unto me; and to whomsoever I will I give it. If thou therefore wilt worship me, all shall be thine" (Luke 4:5-7). The underlined word *I* is the 42,665th word of the New Testament.

Nazarenes' Apostasy

"And he came to Nazareth, where he had been brought up: and, as his custom was, he went into the synagogue on the sabbath day, and stood up for to read. . . . And all they in the synagogue, when they heard these things, were filled with wrath, And rose up, and THRUST HIM OUT of the city, and led him unto the brow of the hill whereon their city was built, that they might cast him down headlong" (Luke 4:16, 28-29). The city in which Jesus had lived for nearly three decades suddenly abandoned its previous loyalty to Him in a most outrageous fashion. The Luke combination *cast him* (4x), *down* (60x), *headlong* (1x) = 65.

Scribes Accuse Christ of Apostasy

"And when he saw their faith, he said unto him, Man, thy sins are forgiven thee. And the scribes and the Pharisees began to reason, saying, Who is this which speaketh blasphemies? Who can forgive sins, but God alone?" (Luke 5:20-21) The religious leaders accused Christ of committing an act of clear apostasy, but He proved them wrong by performing a godly miracle. The New Testament combination *scribes* (62x), *began to reason* (1x), *who is this which speaketh blasphemies* (1x), *who can forgive sins but God alone* (1x) = 65.

Scribes Ready to Accuse Christ of Apostasy

"And the scribes and Pharisees watched him, whether he would heal on the sabbath day; that they might find an accusation against him" (Luke 6:7). The underlined word *the* is the 165th word in this chapter, and it pertains to those men who stood ready to accuse Christ of falling away from a Sabbath law.

365th Verse of Luke

"They on the rock are they, which, when they hear, receive the word with joy; and these have no root, which for a while believe, and in time of temptation FALL AWAY" (Luke 8:13). Just as Jesus predicted, history has shown that times of testing cause many believers to abandon the faith. The New Testament combination *time* (163 vs), *of temptations* (1 v), *shall fall away* (1 v) = 165 verses.

Being Ashamed of Christ

"For whosoever shall be ashamed of me and of my words, of him shall the Son of man be ashamed, when he shall come in his own glory, and in his Father's, and of the holy angels" (Luke 9:26). Christ called upon His people everywhere to publicly identify with Him even if He was not currently popular. Accordingly, to be ashamed of Christ at such times is to stand away from Christ and thus to apostatize from Him. Again the phrase *be ashamed* is mentioned in 65 verses of the Bible. The Bible combination *shall be ashamed of me and* (2x), *my words* (60x), *of him shall the Son of man be ashamed* (1x), *when he shall come in his own glory* (1x), *and in his Father's and of the holy angels* (1x) = 65.

Looking Back from Your Gospel Work

"And another also said, Lord, I will follow thee; but let me first go bid them farewell, which are at home at my house. And Jesus said unto him, No man, having put his hand to the plough, and looking back, is fit for the kingdom of God" (Luke 9:61-62). The kingdom of God includes holy service. Thus the gospel worker is to never think of defecting from his assigned gospel work but rather to embrace it until the gospel harvest is fully brought in. The Bible combination *plowing* (4x), *and looking* (7x), *back* (154x) = 165.

Lucifer's Apostatizing Fall from Heaven

"And he said unto them, <u>I beheld Satan</u> <u>as lightning FALL</u> <u>FROM heaven</u>" (Luke 10:18). Shortly after falling away from the holy faith, Satan was fittingly made to fall away from heaven by being cast out of it. The New Testament combination *I beheld Satan* (1x), *as lightning fall* (1x), *from heaven* (63x) = 65.

Refusing to Help Your Neighbor

"And Jesus answering said, A certain man went down from Jerusalem to Jericho, and fell among thieves, which stripped him of his raiment, and wounded him, and DEPARTED, LEAVING him half dead. And by chance there came down a certain priest that way: and when he saw him, <u>he passed by on</u> <u>the other side</u>. And likewise a Levite, when <u>he</u> was at the place, came and looked on him, and <u>passed by on</u> <u>the other side</u>" (Luke 10:30-32). The priest and the Levite of this parable both apostatized the Mosaic faith when they refused to help their neighbor in his great adversity. The Bible combination *he passed by on* (1x), *the other side* (64x) = 65.

Having Divided Loyalties

"If any man come to me, and hate not his father, and mother, and wife, and children, and brethren, and sisters, yea, and his <u>own life</u> also, he cannot be my disciple" (Luke 14:26). On several occasions the Bible uses the word "hate" to indicate a lesser love or preference. Our King seeks subjects for His kingdom work who will not be divided in their loyalties. The phrase *his own* occurs naturally 165 times in the Old Testament.

Living Riotously

"And he said, A certain man had two sons: And the younger of them said to his father, Father, give me the portion of goods that falleth to me. And he divided unto them his living. And not many days after the younger son gathered all together, and took his journey into a <u>far</u> country, and there <u>wasted</u> <u>his substance with riotous living</u>" (Luke 15:11-13). The prodigal son sought to abandon his previous loyalty to his father to take up another way of life. Again the phrase *far from* occurs 65 times in the Bible. The Bible combination *wasted* (64x), *his substance with riotous living* (1x) = 65.

2465th Verse of the New Testament

"And the son said unto him, Father, I <u>have sinned</u> against heaven, and in thy sight, and am no more worthy to be called thy son" (Luke 15:21). The son confessed his apostate behavior. The phrase *have sinned* occurs 65 times from Genesis to the NT Narrative; this 2465th verse of the New Testament presents its 65th occurrence.

Serving the Good Master No Longer

"No servant can serve two <u>masters</u>: for either he will hate the one, and love <u>the other</u>; or else he will hold to the one, and despise <u>the other</u>. Ye cannot serve God and mammon" (Luke 16:13). As sin can become a person's master so can money. Such infatuation with money causes the believer's heart to apostatize from God. Thus Jesus warns against apostatizing for the other side. Christ must be a believer's Master above all earthly others. The title *master* is mentioned in 65 verses of the NT Narrative. The phrase *the other* is mentioned in 65 verses of the New Testament.

Recalling the Apostasy of Lot's Wife

Jesus warns His listeners about the heart's tendency to apostatize God for one's greater love for the world. He sternly said, "Remember <u>Lot's</u> <u>wife</u>" (Luke 17:32). The Old Testament combination *wife of* (35 vs), *Lot* (29 vs), *became a pillar of salt* (1 v) = 65 verses. The Old Testament combination *wife of* (35 vs), *Lot/'s* (30 vs) = 65 verses.

Casting Out the Money Changers

Jesus beheld the ongoing apostasy concerning the nation's loss of true worship. "And he went into the temple, and began to <u>cast out</u> them that sold therein, and them that bought" (Luke 19:45). Again from Genesis to the Gospels the phrase *cast out* is mentioned in 65 verses; this is its 65th verse-mention.

Being Unaware of Your Apostasy

Jesus warned believers about the end-time apostasy: "And <u>take heed</u> to yourselves, <u>lest at any</u> <u>time</u> <u>your hearts be overcharged with surfeiting, and drunkenness, and cares of this life, and so</u> <u>that day come upon you unawares</u>" (Luke 21:34). The Bible combination *take heed* (55x), *lest at any time* (7x), *your hearts be overcharged with surfeiting* (1x), *and drunkenness and cares of this life* (1x), *so that day come upon you unawares* (1x) = 65.

Judas' Defecting-the-Faith Kiss

"<u>And while he yet spake</u>, <u>behold a multitude, and he that was called</u> <u>Judas</u>, <u>one of the twelve</u>, <u>went before them</u>, and <u>drew near</u> <u>unto Jesus</u> <u>to kiss him</u>" (Luke 22:47). Judas was an apostate from the beginning, yet here he sealed it with a departing kiss. The NT Narrative combination *and while he yet spake* (3x), *behold a multitude and he that was called* (1x), *Judas* (33x), *one of the twelve* (8x), *went before them* (3x), *drew near* (6x), *unto Jesus* (10x), *to kiss him* (1x) = 65.

Luke 22:65

"And many other things blasphemously <u>spake</u> they <u>against him</u>" (Luke 22:65). All three Synoptic Gospels overlay the chief priests' apostate behavior of mocking Jesus in a verse 65—Matt. 26:65, Mark 14:65, and Luke 22:65.

Refusing to Come to Christ

"<u>And ye will</u> <u>not come</u> to me, that ye might have life" (John 5:40). Jesus spoke of the leadership's refusal to show loyalty to Him. The Bible combination *and ye will* (2x), *not come* (63x) = 65.

Many Disciples Defected from Jesus

"From that time <u>many</u> of his disciples WENT BACK, and walked no more with him" (John 6:66) After Jesus delivered this strange teaching many disciples abandoned their previous loyalty to Him. The word *many* is mentioned naturally in 265 verses of the New Testament.

One Apostle Will Go Away

"Then said Jesus unto the twelve, Will ye also GO AWAY? Then Simon Peter answered him, Lord, to whom shall we go? thou hast the words of eternal life. And we believe and are sure that thou art that Christ, the Son of the living God. Jesus answered them, Have not I chosen you twelve, and <u>one of you</u> is a devil? He spake of Judas Iscariot the son of Simon: for he it was that <u>should BETRAY</u> him, being <u>one of the</u> twelve" (John 6:67-71).

One apostle would treacherously defect from Christ. Again the word *go* occurs 65 times in Numbers, 65 times in Judges, and 65 times in Isaiah. The Bible combination *one of them* (59x) and *shall betray* (6x) = 65. The phrase *one of the* is mentioned in 65 chapters of the Old Testament.

Because He Was an Apostate

"Then saith one of his disciples, Judas Iscariot, Simon's son, which should BETRAY him, Why was not this ointment <u>sold</u> for three hundred pence, and given to the poor? This he said, not that he cared for the poor; but because he was a thief, and had the bag, and bare what was put therein" (John 12:4-6). From Genesis to the Gospels the word *sold* is mentioned in 65 verses; this is its 65th verse-mention, and it refers to an apostate who held more loyalty for money than for his Master.

Apostate Thinking

"They shall put you out of the synagogues: yea, the time cometh, that whosoever killeth you will <u>think</u> that he doeth God service" (John 16:2). The word *think* occurs 65 times in the Bible.

3665th Verse of the New Testament

"Now Annas had sent him bound unto Caiaphas <u>the high priest</u>" (John 18:24). This verse describes the priesthood's high-handed apostasy against the Son of God. The title *the high priest('s)* occurs 65 times in the Bible.

Questioning Where Peter's Loyalty Rests

"So when they had dined, <u>Jesus saith to Simon Peter</u>, <u>Simon, son of Jonas</u>, <u>lovest</u> <u>thou me</u> <u>more than these</u>? He saith unto him, Yea, Lord; thou knowest that I love thee. He saith unto him, Feed my lambs" (John 21:15). Peter had abandoned his previous loyalty to his Master when he denied knowing Him and thereafter went back to his old fishing career. Peter had counted his great catch of fish one by one. Thus it was easy to see where his new loyalties rested. For this reason, after the meal Jesus felt compelled to ask Peter to declare where his loyalties were going to settle. The Bible combination *Jesus saith to* (2x), *Simon Peter* (18x), *Simon son of Jonas* (3x), *lovest* (12x), *thou me* (28x), *more than these* (2x) = 65.

Judas' Apostasy Infamously Memorialized

"Judas, which was guide to them that took Jesus. For he was numbered with us, and had obtained part of this ministry. Now this man purchased a field with the reward of iniquity; and FALLING headlong, he burst asunder in the midst, and all his bowels gushed out. And it was known unto all the dwellers at Jerusalem; insomuch as that field is called in their proper tongue, <u>Aceldama</u>, that is to say, <u>The field</u> <u>of</u> <u>blood</u>. <u>For it is written in</u> <u>the book of Psalms</u>, <u>Let his habitation be desolate</u>, <u>and let no man dwell therein</u>: <u>and his bishoprick let another take</u>" (Acts 1:16d-20).

Judas had evilly abandoned his ministry loyalty to Christ. The Bible combination *Aceldama* (1x), *the field of* (25x), *of blood* (32x), *for it is written in* (2x), *the book of Psalms* (2x), *let his habitation be desolate* (1x), *and let no man dwell therein* (1x), *and his bishoprick let another take* (1x) = 65.

27,065th Verse of the Bible

"And Ananias hearing these words FELL down, and gave up the ghost: and great fear came on all them that heard these things" (Acts 5:5). Unfortunately Ananias abandoned his previous loyalty to the Christian community when he lied about his financial donation to the church.

4065th Verse of the New Testament

"In his humiliation his judgment was taken away: and who shall declare his generation? for his life is taken from the earth" (Acts 8:33). This 65th verse refers to an Old Testament prophecy concerning Israel's future national apostasy—killing their heaven-sent Messiah.

Leading Others into Apostasy

"But Elymas the sorcerer for so is his name by interpretation withstood them, seeking to TURN AWAY the deputy FROM THE FAITH" (Acts 13:8). This man attempted to make a burgeoning believer apostatize from faith in Christ. Again the phrase *from the* is mentioned naturally in 165 verses of the Law.

Israel's Full Period of Apostasy under the Judges

"And after that he gave unto them judges about the space of four hundred and fifty years, until Samuel the prophet" (Acts 13:20). The period of the judges was a time in Israel's history marked by continual relapses into apostasy. The Bible combination *and after that he* (6x), *gave unto them* (7x), *judges* (52x) = 65.

Paul Accused of Teaching Jews Abroad to Apostatize from Moses

"And they are informed of thee, that thou teachest all the Jews which are among the Gentiles to FORSAKE Moses, saying that they ought not to circumcise their children, neither to walk after the customs" (Acts 21:21). This accusation was inaccurate. Again the word *walk* occurs 65 times in the New Testament.

Pharisees Fall Away from the Sadducees

"And when he had so said, there arose a DISSENSION between the Pharisees and the Sadducees: and the multitude was divided" (Acts 23:7). This divisive scene corresponds with our definition of apostasy: something separative. The word *between* is the 165th word in this chapter. The word *divided* is mentioned naturally in 65 and a half verses of the Bible.

The Gentiles' Digressive Apostasy

"Because that, when they knew God, they glorified him not as God, neither were thankful; but became vain in their imaginations, and their foolish heart was darkened. Professing themselves to be wise, they became fools, And changed the glory of the uncorruptible God into an image made like to corruptible man, and to birds, and fourfooted beasts, and creeping things" (Rom. 1:21-23). The combination *fools* (52x), *fool's heart* (1x), *foolishly* (12x) = 65.

The Result of the Gentile World's Apostasy

The following 65 segments reveal how the Lord left those religious apostates without remedy that they might only fall away further into sin.

> "[1] Wherefore God also [2] gave them up to uncleanness [3] through the lusts of their own hearts, [4] to dishonour their own bodies [5] between themselves: [6] Who changed the truth of God [7] into a lie, [8] and worshipped and served [9] the creature more than the Creator, [1] who is blessed for ever. Amen. [11] For this cause [12] God gave them up [13] unto vile affections:

[14] for even their women [15] did change the natural use [16] into that which is [17] against nature: [18)] And likewise also the men, [19] leaving the natural use [20] of the woman, [21] burned in their lust [22] one toward another; [23] men with men [24] working that which is unseemly, [25] and receiving in themselves [26] that recompence of their error [27] which was meet. [28] And even as [29] they did not like [30] to retain God in their knowledge, [31] God gave them over [32] to a reprobate mind, [33] to do those things [34] which are not convenient; [35] Being filled with [36] all unrighteousness, [37] fornication, [38] wickedness, [39] covetousness,[40] maliciousness; [41] full of [42] envy, [43] murder, [44] debate, [45] deceit, [46] malignity; [47] whisperers, [48] Backbiters, [49] haters of God, [50] despiteful, [51] proud, [52] boasters, [53] inventors of evil things, [54] disobedient to parents, [55] Without understanding, [56] covenantbreakers, [57] without natural affection, [58] implacable, [59] unmerciful: [60] Who knowing the judgment of God, [61] that they which commit such things [62] are worthy of death, [63] not only do the same, [64] but have pleasure in them [65] that do them" (Rom. 1:24-32).

65th Verse of Romans

"God forbid: yea, let God be true, but every man a liar; as it is written, That thou mightest be justified in thy sayings, and mightest overcome when thou art judged" (Rom. 3:4). Every person has told lies in their lifetime. Because God has given every soul a conscience of right and wrong, mankind inherently knows that telling a lie is wrong. Therefore, to lie is to apostatize or move away from the truth. The phrase *every man* occurs 65 times in the New Testament. The Law combination *every man* (63x), *lie unto his neighbour* (1x), *lie to one another* (1x) = 65. The New Testament combination *all men* (61 vs) and *liars* (4 vs) = 65 verses. The New Testament combination *all men* (61 vs), *speaketh a lie* (1 v), *maketh a lie* (2 vs), *changed the truth of God into a lie* (1 v) = 65 verses.

All Mankind Gone Out of the Way

"They are all GONE OUT OF THE WAY, they are together become unprofitable; there is none that doeth good, no, not one" (Rom. 3:12). Paul presented the doctrinal truth that all humanity remains in a state of apostasy until the Lord brings them back into the way of faith through His Spirit's guidance. Again the word *they* is found in 65 books of the Bible. The word *none* is mentioned in 65 verses of the New Testament.

5065th Verse of the New Testament

"But to Israel he saith, All day long I have stretched forth my hands unto a disobedient and gainsaying people" (Rom. 10:21). This verse speaks of Israel's Old Testament apostasy. It is a loose quotation of what God said about them in the opening verse of Isaiah's apostasy chapter—chapter 65. Again the name *Israel* occurs 2565 times in Scripture.

Gentile's Consolation for the Jews' Falling Away from Christ

"I say then, Have they stumbled that they should FALL? God forbid: but rather through their FALL salvation is come unto the Gentiles, for to provoke them to jealousy" (Rom. 11:11). Again the word *they* occurs 1965 times in the New Testament. Again the word *their* is mentioned in 2365 verses of the Bible.

1065th Chapter of the Bible

"And I, brethren, could not speak unto you as unto spiritual, but as unto carnal, even as unto babes in Christ. I have fed you with milk, and not with meat: for hitherto ye were not able to bear it, neither yet now are ye able. For ye are yet carnal: for whereas there is among you envying, and strife, and DIVISIONS, are ye not carnal, and <u>walk</u> as men? For while one saith, I am of Paul; and another, I am of Apollos; are ye not carnal?" (1 Cor. 3:1-4)

The chief apostle addressed a severe problem in the church at Corinth. The believers were apostatizing from one another by dividing into different sects. This scenario fits our definition of apostasy: something separative. Again from Genesis to the Synoptic Gospels the phrase *among you* is mentioned in 65 chapters. Again the word *divided* is mentioned naturally in 65 and a half verses of the Bible. Again the word *walk* occurs 65 times in the New Testament.

Take Heed Lest You Also Apostatize

"Wherefore let him that thinketh he standeth <u>take heed</u> lest he <u>FALL</u>" (1 Cor. 10:12). The naturally occurring New Testament combination *take heed* (25x), *fall* (40x) = 65.

A Schism in the Church Body

"That there should be no SCHISM in <u>the body</u>; but that the members should have the same care one for another (1 Cor. 12:25). Paul addressed another form of apostasy in the church. The Corinthians were apostatizing one from another according to their social status. This verse fits our definition of apostasy, meaning something separative. Webster's Dictionary defines the word "schism" as a formal division in or separation from a church or religious body. The word "schism" is therefore a synonym of apostasy. The term *the body* occurs 65 times in the New Testament.

165th Chapter of the New Testament

"O <u>foolish</u> <u>Galatians</u>, who hath bewitched you, that ye should <u>NOT OBEY</u> the truth, before whose eyes Jesus Christ hath been evidently set forth, crucified among you?" (Gal. 3:1, 3) The Galatians were quickly apostatizing from the sound doctrine Paul had previously given them. They were defecting from the New Covenant faith by turning back to Moses, from grace to works, from liberty to law. The Bible combination *foolish* (52x), *Galatians* (1x), *not obey* (12x) = 65.

Galatians Who Were Fallen from Grace

"Christ is become of no effect unto you, whosoever of you are justified by the law; ye are FALLEN FROM grace" (Gal. 5:4). Legalists were teaching Galatian believers that they should keep the law to keep their salvation. Those believers who turned back to the law were considered by Paul to be apostatizing. Again the word *fallen* is mentioned in 65 chapters of the Bible.

The Gentiles' Walk of Apostasy

"This I say therefore, and testify in the Lord, that ye henceforth <u>walk</u> not as other Gentiles <u>walk</u>, in the vanity of their mind, Having the understanding darkened, being ALIENATED FROM the life of God through the ignorance that is in them, because of the blindness of their heart: Who being past feeling have given themselves over unto lasciviousness, to work all uncleanness with greediness" (Eph. 4:17-19). Paul wanted this metropolitan Gentile church to maintain its current loyalty to the things of God and not its previous loyalty to the things of the world. Again the word *walk* occurs 65 times in the New Testament. This passage consists of 65 words.

6165th Verse of the New Testament

"For this ye know, that no whoremonger, nor unclean person, nor covetous man, who is an

515

idolater, hath any inheritance in the kingdom of Christ and of God" (Eph. 5:5). Just two verses earlier Paul gave his first warning to believers about committing apostasy: "But fornication, and all uncleanness, or covetousness, let it not be once named among you, as becometh saints."

Beware of Apostate Teachers

"Beware of dogs, beware of evil workers, beware of the concision. For we are the circumcision, which worship God in the spirit, and rejoice in Christ Jesus, and have no confidence in the flesh" (Phil. 3:2-3). Paul warned the Philippians to be on guard for false teachers—Judaizers and legalists—who would attempt to make them abandon their previous loyalty to the doctrine of grace and defect to the law. The Bible combination *beware of* (13x), *dogs* (24x), *beware of* (13x), *evil workers* (1x), *beware of* (13x), *the concision* (1x) = 65.

Don't Move Away from Gospel Truth

"If ye continue in the faith grounded and settled, and be not MOVED AWAY FROM the hope of the gospel, which ye have heard" (Col. 1:23a). The phrase *moved away from* perfectly describes apostasy. Again the phrase *from the* is mentioned naturally in 165 verses of the Law.

65th Verse of First Thessalonians

The apostle needfully informed believers about the day of sudden destruction which will come upon the apostate unbelieving world. He encouraged us, "But ye, brethren, are not in darkness, that that day should overtake you as a thief" (1 Thess. 5:4). Again the phrase *that day* occurs 65 times in the Major Prophets.

God's End-Time Vengeance on Apostates

"In flaming fire taking vengeance on them that know not God, and that OBEY NOT the gospel of our Lord Jesus Christ" (2 Thess. 1:8). This scenario fits our first definition of apostasy: an act of refusing to continue to obey a religious faith. The Bible combination *in flaming fire* (1x), *taking vengeance* (2x), *on them* (54x), *that know not God and that* (1x), *obey not* (6x), *the gospel of our Lord Jesus Christ* (1x) = 65.

The Church's Great End-Time Apostasy

"Let no man deceive you by any means: for that day shall not come, except there come a FALLING AWAY first, and that man of sin be revealed, the son of perdition" (2 Thess. 2:3). Here the phrase "falling away" is translated from the Greek word *apostasia*. The Tribulation will be marked by the professing church's widespread abandonment of loyalty to previously known Scriptural truth. They will rapidly fall away from the faith. The phrase *that day* is also mentioned in 65 verses of the Major Prophets. The Bible's only other occurrence of the phrase *fall away* is in the 365th verse of Luke.

Apostatizing from the Apostles' Doctrine

"And if any man OBEY NOT our word by this epistle, note that man, and have no company with him, that he may be ashamed" (2 Thess. 3:14). Again the phrase *be ashamed* is mentioned in 65 verses of the Bible.

Some Have Swerved from the Faith

"Now the end of the commandment is charity out of a pure heart, and of a good conscience, and of FAITH unfeigned: From which <u>some</u> having swerved have TURNED ASIDE unto vain jangling; Desiring to be teachers of the law; understanding neither what they say, nor whereof they affirm" (1 Tim. 1:5-7). The word *some* occurs 65 times in the Gospels.

Some Have Put Away the Faith
"Holding FAITH, and a good conscience; which <u>some</u> having put away concerning FAITH have made shipwreck" (1 Tim. 1:19). Again the word *some* occurs 65 times in the Gospels.

Some Shall Depart from the Faith
"Now the Spirit speaketh expressly, that in the latter times <u>some shall</u> <u>DEPART FROM</u> the <u>FAITH</u>, giving heed to seducing spirits, and doctrines of devils" (1 Tim. 4:1). Paul speaks of the professing church's latter-days apostasy. The Pauline Epistles combination *some shall* (1 v), *depart from* (4 vs), *faith* (160 vs) = 165 verses.

A Householder Worse Than an Infidel
"But if any provide not for his own, and specially for those of his own house, he hath <u>DENIED THE FAITH</u>, and <u>is worse than</u> an <u>INFIDEL</u>" (1 Tim. 5:8). A father who does not provide for his family's well-being is one who has abandoned his previous loyalty to his family. He has apostatized. An infidel is one who does not believe in or practice a religious faith. The New Testament combination *denied* (16x), *the faith* (43x), *is/be worse than* (4x), *an infidel* (2x) = 65.

Temptation Causes Believers to Fall Away from the Faith
"But they that will be rich FALL into temptation and a snare, and into many foolish and hurtful lusts, which drown men in destruction and perdition" (1 Tim. 6:9). Here the apostasy-related word *fall* is the 148,265th word of the New Testament.

Some Have Erred from the Faith
"For the love of <u>money</u> is the root of all evil: which while <u>some coveted after</u>, they have ERRED FROM THE FAITH, and pierced themselves through with many sorrows" (1 Tim. 6:10). Again the Bible combination *money* (64 chs) and *some coveted after* (1 ch) = 65.

Apostate Teachers Running Rampant
"O Timothy, keep that which is committed to thy trust, avoiding profane and vain babblings, and oppositions of <u>science falsely</u> so called" (1 Tim. 6:20). The believer must be careful not to adopt false doctrines into previously established New Testament beliefs. The Bible combination *science falsely* (1x) and *false* (64x) = 65.

6665th Verse of the New Testament
"<u>Which some</u> <u>professing have ERRED</u> <u>concerning</u> THE FAITH. Grace be with thee. Amen" (1 Tim. 6:21). This 65th verse actually contains a proper definition of apostasy. The Pauline Epistles combination *which some* (3x), *professing have erred* (3x), *concerning* (27x), *the faith* (32x) = 65. This verse of apostasy consists of 65 letters!

Opposing the Truth They Once Believed
"In meekness instructing those that oppose themselves; if God peradventure will give them repentance to the acknowledging of <u>the truth</u>" (2 Tim. 2:25). This verse presents the Bible's 65th

occurrence of the phrase *the truth*, and it refers to those believers who have defected from it.

Apostates Will Wax Worse & Worse

"But evil men and seducers shall <u>wax</u> worse and worse, deceiving, and being deceived" (2 Tim. 3:13). All delineated forms of wax show the seal of apostasy: *wax* (21 chs), *waxed* (33 chs), *waxen* (8 chs), *waxeth* (2 chs), *waxing* (1 ch) = 65 chapters.

65th Verse of Second Timothy

"<u>And they shall</u> TURN AWAY <u>their ears</u> FROM THE TRUTH, and shall be TURNED <u>unto fables</u>" (2 Tim. 4:4). Those who defect from the truth will have their minds disaffected by it. Having a lack of godly wisdom and discernment, such apostates will then easily believe in the world's most bazaar teachings. Again the word *they* occurs 1965 times in the New Testament. The Jeremiah combination *and they shall* (60x), *turn away* (5x) = 65. The Bible phrases *turn away* (46x), *their ears* (18x), *turned unto fables* (1x) = 65.

Demas' Apostasy

"For Demas <u>hath</u> FORSAKEN me, having loved this present <u>world</u>, and is DEPARTED unto Thessalonica; Crescens to Galatia, Titus unto Dalmatia" (2 Tim. 4:10). The word *hath* is mentioned in 165 verses of the Pauline Epistles. Again all forms of the word *forsake* are mentioned in 165 verses of the Bible. Again from Genesis to the Synoptic Gospels the title *the world* occurs 65 times.

Apostate Mouths

"For there are many unruly and vain talkers and deceivers, specially they of the circumcision: Whose <u>mouths</u> must be stopped, who subvert whole houses, teaching things which they ought not, for filthy lucre's sake" (Titus 1:10-11). Paul warned Titus about apostatizers who must be removed from their teaching positions in the church. Some would even need to be excommunicated. The word *mouth(s)* occurs 165 times in the Wisdom Books.

Apostate Slave

"<u>For perhaps</u> <u>he therefore</u> DEPARTED <u>for a</u> <u>season, that thou shouldest</u> <u>receive</u> <u>him for ever</u>" (Philem. 15). Philemon's slave Onesimus was guilty of abandoning his previous loyalty to his master. Paul wanted to send this saved slave back to his owner and set things right. The Bible combination *for perhaps* (1x), *he therefore* (6x), *departed for a* (1x), *season* (56x), *that thou shouldest receive* (1x), *receive him for ever* (1x) = 65.

29,965th Verse of the Bible

"God, who at sundry times and in divers manners spake in time past unto <u>the fathers</u> by the prophets" (Heb. 1:1). In times past Israel's leaders apostatized from the prophet's revealed truths rather than drew near to them. This 65th verse presents the Bible's 65th occurrence of the title *the fathers*.

Don't Depart from the Living God

Paul worried for the Jewish believers in Israel; he wanted them to remain victorious in their walk with Christ. Thus he said to them, "<u>Take heed, brethren, lest</u> there be in any of you an evil heart of unbelief, in DEPARTING FROM the living God" (Heb. 3:12). The Bible combination *take heed* (55x), *brethren lest* (3x), *there be in any of you an evil heart* (1x), *of unbelief* (5x), *in departing from the living God* (1x) = 65.

Moses Forsook Egypt

"By faith he FORSOOK Egypt, not fearing the wrath of the king: for he endured, as seeing him who is invisible" (Heb. 11:27). Paul recalls how Moses suddenly abandoned his previous loyalty to his royal family and the house of Egypt. Again all forms of the word *forsake* are mentioned in 165 combined verses of the Bible.

"If They Shall Fall Away"

"For it is impossible for those who were once enlightened, and have tasted of the heavenly gift, and were made partakers of the Holy Ghost, And have tasted the good word of God, and the powers of the world to come, If they shall FALL AWAY, to renew them again unto repentance; seeing they crucify to themselves the Son of God afresh, and put him to an open shame" (Heb. 6:4-6). Those who abandon their previous loyalty to Christ find it greatly difficult to return to Him. Again the phrase *if they* is mentioned naturally in 65 verses of the Bible.

Don't Turn Out of the Right Way

"And make straight paths for your feet, lest that which is lame be TURNED OUT OF THE WAY; but let it rather be healed" (Heb. 12:13). Paul encouraged the wavering Jewish believers to get spiritually healed and get back on the straight and narrow path the King of the Jews had established for them. The phrase *the way* is mentioned in 65 verses of the New Testament.

Don't Refuse to Hear the Heavenly Speaker

"See that ye REFUSE not him that speaketh. For if they escaped not who REFUSED him that spake on earth, much more shall not we escape, if we TURN AWAY FROM him that speaketh from heaven" (Heb. 12:25). The Bible combination *for if they escaped not* (1x), who *refused him that spake on earth* (1x), *much more shall not* (1x), *we escape if we* (2x), *turn away* (46x), *from him that* (13x), *speaketh from heaven* (1x) = 65.

Christ Promised to Never Apostatize from the Believer

"Let your conversation be without covetousness; and be content with such things as ye have: for he hath said, I will never leave thee, nor FORSAKE thee" (Heb. 13:5). The Hebrews combination *let your conversation* (1x), *be without covetousness* (1x), an*d be content with such things as ye have* (1x), *for he hath* (2x), *said* (16x), *I will* (16x), *never* (3x), *leave* (1x), *thee* (9x), *nor* (5x), *forsake* (1x), *thee* (9x) = 65.

Don't Be a Forgetful Hearer

"But whoso looketh into the perfect law of liberty, and continueth therein, he being not a forgetful hearer, but a doer of the work, this man shall be blessed in his deed" (James 1:25). A forgetful hearer tends to apostatize much sooner than one who remembers the Word. Accordingly the word *hearer* is 'not' found in 65 books of the Bible.

Past Apostasies

"That he no longer should live the rest of his time in the flesh to the lusts of men, but to the will of God. For the time past of our life may suffice us to have wrought the will of the Gentiles, when we walked in lasciviousness, lusts, excess of wine, revellings, banquetings, and abominable idolatries" (1 Pet. 4:2-3). The New Testament combination *that he no longer should live the rest of his time in the flesh* (1x), *to the lusts of men* (1x), *but to the will of God* (1x), *for the time past of our life* (1x), *may suffice us to have wrought* (1x), *the will of the Gentiles* (1x), *walked* (21x), *lasciviousness* (6x), *lusts* (24x), *excess of wine* (1x), *revellings* (2x), *banquetings* (1x), *abominable* (3x), *idolatries* (1x) = 65.

The Apostate's Bitter End

"For the time is come that judgment must begin at the house of God: and if it first begin at us, what shall the end be of them that OBEY NOT the gospel of God?" (1 Pet. 4:7) The General Epistles combination *them that obey not the gospel* (1 v), *of God* (64 vs) = 65 verses.

30,465th Verse of the Bible

"And if the righteous scarcely be saved, where shall the ungodly and the sinner appear?" (1 Pet. 4:18). This verse makes reference to ungodly people who could in their sinful lifestyles be considered apostates.

Make Sure That You Will Never Fall Away

"Wherefore the rather, brethren, give diligence to make your calling and election sure: for if ye do these things, ye shall never FALL" (2 Pet. 1:10). Again all forms of the word *fall* are mentioned in 65 verses of the New Testament.

Balaam, the Apostate Gainsayer

Peter spoke of money-coveting apostate teachers "which have FORSAKEN THE RIGHT WAY, and are GONE ASTRAY, following the way of Balaam the son of Bosor, who loved the wages of unrighteousness" (2 Pet. 2:15). The Bible combination *forsaken* (61 chs), *the right way* (4 chs) = 65 chapters. The Bible combination *Balaam* (60x) and *gone astray* (5x) = 65. The Bible combination *money* (64 chs) and *wages of unrighteousness* (1 ch) = 65 chapters.

Apostatizing after Knowing the Way

Peter spoke again of the money-coveting apostate teachers. "For it had been better for them not to have known the way of reighteousness than, after they have known it, to TURN FROM the holy commandment delivered unto them" (2 Pet. 2:21). Again the phrase *the way* is mentioned in 65 verses of the New Testament. Again the word *turn* is mentioned in 65 verses of the Major Prophets.

Don't Be Led Away from the Faith

"Ye therefore, beloved, seeing ye know these things before, beware lest ye also, being LED AWAY WITH THE ERROR of the wicked, FALL FROM your own stedfastness" (2 Pet. 3:17). The Pauline and General Epistles combination *beware* (5x), *lest* (50x), ye also being (1x), *led away with* (2x), *the error* (3x), *of the wicked* (3x), *fall from your own stedfastness* (1x) = 65.

65th Verse of First John

"They are of the world: therefore speak they of the world, and the world heareth them" (1 John 4:5). This verse speaks about the apostate teachers who possess the apostate spirit of the antichrist and gain an audience among other apostates. Again the word *they* is found in 65 books of the Bible.

Apostate Teachers Seek to Deceive

"For many deceivers are entered into the world, who confess not that Jesus Christ is come in the flesh. This is a deceiver and an antichrist" (2 John 1:7). The apostle of truth warned his children about the many apostate teachers roaming about. The Bible combination *of the world* (62 chs) and *antichrist* (3 chs) = 65 chapters.

65th Book of the Bible

JUDE is the 65th BOOK of the Bible because of its overriding theme regarding the eradication of apostasy within the church. Only in its second generation, the church of Christ was facing the challenge of dealing with roaming apostate teachers who were wreaking havoc in the church. Because Jude was so alarmed at Christianity's deteriorating situation, he wrote his letter to sanctified Christians encouraging them to unmask these apostate teachers within the church and then properly deal with them. Some of them may have repented and some may have continued to refuse to obey the faith. Nevertheless, if their heresies were not exposed and rooted out the church would suffer doctrinal destruction in the long run.

The Realization of Apostasy (3-4)

Jude begins with an eye-opening realization that apostasy does exists among the saints. "Beloved, when I gave all diligence to write unto you of the common salvation, it was needful for me to write unto you, and exhort you that ye should earnestly contend for the faith which was once delivered unto the saints" (Jude 3). The Bible combination *and exhort you that* (1 ch), *ye should earnestly* (1 ch), *contend for* (1 ch), *the faith* (36 chs), *which was once* (1 ch), *delivered unto* (16 chs), *to the saints* (9 chs) = 65 chapters.

Jude continues his church-apostasy realization: "For there are certain men crept in unawares, who were before of old ordained to this condemnation, ungodly men, turning the grace of our God into lasciviousness, and DENYING the only Lord God, and our Lord Jesus Christ" (4). The Bible combination *for there are certain men crept in unawares* (1x), *who were before* (1x), *of old* (59x), *ordained to this condemnation* (1x), *ungodly men turning the grace of our God* (1x), *into lasciviousness and denying* (1x), *the only Lord God and our Lord Jesus Christ* (1x) = 65.

The Reminder of Apostasy (5-16)

Jude now cites some historical instances of apostasy. First he mentions the exodus generation's departure from the faith. "I will therefore put you in remembrance, though ye once knew this, how that the Lord, having saved the people out of the land of Egypt, afterward destroyed THEM THAT BELIEVED NOT" (5). Again the phrase *the people* occurs 165 times in the Major Prophets.

Next Jude mentions a radical apostasy that once took place in heaven and subsequently affected earth: "the angels which kept not their first estate, but left their own habitation, he hath reserved in everlasting chains under darkness unto the judgment of the great day" (6). The plural words *angels* (64 chs) and *angels'* (1 ch) = 65 chapters of the Bible. Within the triad writings of Isaiah, Jeremiah, and Ezekiel, the word *judgment* occurs 65 times.

Jude cites a third instance of historical apostasy. "Sodom and Gomorrha, and the cities about them in like manner, giving themselves over to fornication, and going after strange flesh, are set forth for an example, suffering the vengeance of eternal fire" (7). Again the word *strange* occurs

65 times in the Old Testament.

The writer now shifts from describing groups of apostates to describing individual apostates. He first mentions the chief apostate Satan. "Yet Michael the archangel, when contending with the devil he disputed about the body of Moses, durst not bring against him a railing accusation, but said, The Lord rebuke thee" (9). The Devil is obviously in a class by himself.

Jude goes on to remind the church of three previous mortal apostates who, unlike Satan, believers could and should rebuke because of the corruption and destruction they breed.

> "But these speak evil of those things which <u>they</u> know not: but what <u>they</u> know naturally, as brute beasts, in those things <u>they</u> corrupt themselves. Woe unto them! for <u>they</u> have GONE IN THE WAY of [Cain], and ran greedily after the ERROR of [Balaam] for reward, and perished in the gainsaying of [Core]. These are spots in your feasts of charity, when <u>they</u> feast with you, feeding themselves without fear: clouds <u>they</u> are without water, carried about of winds; trees whose fruit withereth, without fruit, twice dead, plucked up by the roots; Raging waves of the sea, foaming out their own shame; wandering stars, to whom is reserved the blackness of darkness for ever. And Enoch also, the seventh from Adam, prophesied of these, saying, Behold, the Lord cometh with ten thousands of his saints, To execute judgment upon all, and to convince all that are ungodly among them of all their ungodly deeds which <u>they</u> have ungodly <u>committed</u>, and of all their hard speeches which ungodly <u>sinners</u> have spoken against him. These are murmurers, complainers, walking after their own lusts; and their mouth speaketh great swelling words, having men's persons in admiration because of advantage" (10-16).

Again the word *they* occurs 1965 times in the New Testament. Again the phrase *they did* is mentioned in 65 verses of the Old Testament. Again the word *committed* occurs 65 times in the Old Testament. The OT Narrative combination *sin* (64 vs) and *sinners* (1 v) = 65 verses.

The Remedy for Apostasy (17-25)

After instructing the church about why they should contend for the faith Jude proceeds to tell them how to contend for the faith. First they should contend with apostasy as a biblical duty. "But, beloved, remember ye the words which were spoken before of the apostles of our Lord Jesus Christ; How they told you there should be mockers in the last time, who should <u>walk</u> after their own ungodly lusts. These be they who SEPARATE themselves, sensual, having not the Spirit" (17-19). Again the word *walk* occurs 65 times in the New Testament.

Jude reminds the saints next how they should contend with apostasy from a sense of their own personal duty. Such personal Christian duty may save some unsuspecting apostates. "But ye, beloved, building up yourselves on your most holy faith, praying in the Holy Ghost, Keep yourselves in the love of God, looking for the mercy of our Lord Jesus Christ unto eternal life. And of <u>some</u> have compassion, making a difference: And others save with fear, pulling them out of the fire; hating even the garment spotted by the flesh" (20-23). Again the word *some* occurs 65 times in the Gospels.

As a final encouragement Jude reminds the saints Who it is that will keep them from ever falling into apostasy: "<u>Now unto him that is able to</u> <u>keep</u> <u>you from FALLING</u>, and to present you faultless before the presence of his glory with exceeding joy, To the only wise God our Saviour, be glory and majesty, dominion and power, both now and ever. Amen" (24-25). The New Testament *now unto him that is able to* (2x), *keep* (62x), *you from falling* (1x) = 65.

Fallen from Grace

"Remember therefore from whence thou art FALLEN, and repent, and do the first works; or else

I will come unto thee quickly, and will remove thy candlestick out of his place, except thou repent" (Rev. 2:5). Again the word *fallen* is mentioned in 65 chapters of the Bible.

The Dragon's, False Prophet's & Beast's Apostatizing Mouths

"And I saw three unclean spirits like frogs come out of the <u>mouth</u> of the dragon, and out of the <u>mouth</u> of the beast, and out of the <u>mouth</u> of the false prophet" (Rev. 16:13). The dragon, the beast, and the false prophet are three prevailing end-time apostates who will control the world. There will also be many thousands of other apostates in the last days whose mouths must be stopped. Again the word *mouth(s)* occurs 165 combined times in the Wisdom Books.

That Great Apostate Bound & Imprisoned for 1000 Years

"And he laid hold on the dragon, that old serpent, which is the Devil, and Satan, and <u>bound</u> him a thousand years" (Rev. 20:2). The word *bound* occurs 65 times in the Old Testament.

Triad Apostates Meet Their Eternal Doom

"And <u>the devil that deceived them was cast into the</u> <u>lake</u> <u>of fire</u> and brimstone, where the beast and the false prophet are, and shall be tormented day and night for ever and ever" (Rev. 20:10). The Bible combination *the devil that deceived them was cast into the* (1x), *lake* (10x), *of fire* (54x) = 65.

66—Idol Worship

Idolatry is nearly as old as mankind itself. The Bible uses the term "idolatry" to indicate the worship of gods other than Jehovah, the One True God. Such gods were represented by tangible objects made of clay, wood, stone, or metal. Men sometimes worshiped an object as if it were the actually deity, or they may have viewed it as a helpful representation of a deity. Oftentimes the distinction between these two ideas was blurred. The making and worshiping of an idol is man's failed attempt to communicate with God. God created the nation of Israel to teach all other nations how to approach and worship the one and only living God.

The Davis Dictionary of the Bible gives us the following definition of IDOLATRY:

> [1] an image, sculpture, or other representation of any person or being, intended as an object of worship, or as the embodiment and efficient presence of a deity.

The Merriam Webster Dictionary gives us the following definitions of IDOLATRY:

> [2] the worship of a physical object as a god; and
> [3] an immoderate attachment or devotion to something.

All forms of the word *worship* occur 198 times in the Bible, a multiple of 66.
All delineated forms of the word worship appear like this: *worship* (27 bks), *worshipped* (25 bks), *worshipper* (2 bks), *worshippers* (3 bks), *worshippeth* (4 bks), *worshipping* (5 bks) = 66 books.

~~~~

The word *gods* occurs naturally 66 times in the Law.
The term *the god(s)* occurs 66 times in the Old Testament.
The term *the idols/s* (27x) and *the image/s* (39x) occurs 66 times in the Bible.

~~~~

The OT combination *worship* (64x), *an idol in a grove* (2x) = 66.
The OT combination *worship* (64x), *carved image* (2x) = 66.
The OT combination *worship* (64x), *graven images of their gods* (2x) = 66.
The OT combination *worship* (64x), *gods of silver* (2x) = 66.
The OT combination *worship* (64x), *his idols of silver* (2x) = 66.
The OT combination *worship* (64x), *his idols of gold* (2x) = 66.
The OT combination *worship* (64x), *maketh a god* (2x) = 66.
The OT combination *worship* (64x), *molten gods* (2x) = 66.
The OT combination *worship* (64x), *molten images of* (2x) = 66.
The OT combination *worship* (64x), *their molten images* (2x) = 66.
The OT combination *worship* (64x), *the teraphim and the molten image* (2x) = 66.
The OT combination *worship* (64x), *the gods of the earth* (1x), *idolatry* (1x) = 66.
The OT combination *worship* (64x), *the carved images and the molten images* (2x) = 66.

The number SIXTY AND SIX only occurs once in the Bible, yet a numeric seal is found therein.
The word *six* occurs 66 times in the Law.

Cain's Idolatrous Approach to God

"Cain was a tiller of the ground. And in process of time it came to pass, that Cain brought of the fruit of the ground an offering unto the LORD. And the LORD had respect unto Abel and to his offering: But unto Cain and to his offering he had not respect. And Cain was very wroth, and his countenance fell" (Gen. 4:2c-5).

The word *brought* is mentioned in 66 chapters of the NT Narrative. The phrase *the fruit of* is mentioned in 66 verses of the Bible. The phrase *an offering* occurs 66 times in Scripture.

This is the Bible's first mention of the phrase "an offering," and it speaks of an idolatrous offering; according to our third definition of idolatry, Cain had an immoderate attachment or devotion to something—the works of his hands. Here in man's early history we see that idolatry began in its simplicity as false worship. Later it would develop more manifestly with the fashioning and adoration of idols. Cain worshiped the right God, but he did it in the wrong way. He took the wrong approach. He brought no blood. Thus he offended God in his attempt to worship Him. This is hardly different from offering the right sacrifice to the wrong god. Cain was familiar with the rule of worship—bring God a sanctioned animal and shed its blood. Instead Cain brought to God the product of his own self-praising labors, something that he was immoderately devoted to and that God had not ordained. Cain's attitude before God was typical of an idolater: proud, lacking true religious character, self-willed, and defiant toward God.

Babel's Idolatrous Approach to God

"And the whole earth was of one language, and of one speech. And it came to pass, as they journeyed from the east, that they found a plain in the land of Shinar; and they dwelt there. . . And they said, Go to, let us build us a city and a tower, whose top may reach unto heaven; and let us make us a name, lest we be scattered abroad upon the face of the whole earth. . . . Therefore is the name of it called Babel; because the LORD did there confound the language of all the earth" (Gen. 11:1-2, 4, 9a).

The underlined word *earth* is the 6166th word of the Bible. The word *they* is mentioned in 166 chapters of the Law. The Bible combination *scattered abroad upon* (2x) and *all the earth* (64x) = 66.

Babel was a city which undertook an idolatrous approach to worshiping God. As a result God chose to cease its operation and disperse its citizenry. The people had undertaken construction of a mountaintop worship center which God had not ordained. In antiquity men understood that the gods preferred to dwell in the mountains. For this reason men were inclined to build ziggurats and pyramids as welcoming high places for the gods to descend upon and inhabit. Although the multitude was scattered from Babel, not everyone left the city. One language group apparently continued dwelling there or later returned to it. This city would therefore continue to become the country of Babylonia and over time develop into a world center for false religion. As this city was cursed with confusion, all their future attempts to worship God would be met with confusion. Whether idols and images existed before this time is difficult to know, yet it is certain that in time religious objects were indeed fashioned in Babel.

Abram's Idolatrous Ancestry

"And Terah lived seventy years, and begat Abram, Nahor, and Haran. . . . And Terah took Abram his son, and Lot the son of Haran his son's son, and Sarai his daughter in law, his son Abram's wife; and they went forth with them from Ur of the Chaldees, to go into the land of Canaan; and they came unto Haran, and dwelt there. . . . and Terah died in Haran" (Gen. 11:26, 31, 32b). Idolatry is a vain or empty religious practice. It offends God and does not fill the human soul's true need. Under God's express instruction Abram left this idolatrous city and set out for a new life of faith and obedience. It would seem that his father Terah was so impressed by the Lord's visitation that he decided to take his whole family and journey along with his youngest son Abram. This whole chapter which documents Babel's idolatrous fall and Abram's departure from Mesopotamian's cradle of idolatry consists of 606 words, a 66 with an empty place in its midst. The Bible combination *Abram* (54x), *Abram's* (7x), *Ur* (5x) = 66. The plural name *Chaldeans(')* occur 66 times in the Bible.

Abram's Departure from the Mesopotamian Cradle of Idolatry Resumes

"Now the LORD had said unto Abram, Get thee out of thy country, and from thy kindred, and from thy father's house, unto a land that I will shew thee: And I will make of thee a great nation. . . . So Abram departed, as the LORD had spoken unto him; and Lot went with him: and Abram was seventy and five years old when he departed out of Haran. And Abram took Sarai his wife, and Lot his brother's son, and all their substance that they had gathered, and the souls that they had gotten in Haran; and they went forth to go into the land of Canaan; and into the land of Canaan they came" (Gen. 12:1-2a, 4-5).

Terah and his family had traveled northward from Ur until reaching the upper regions of Mesopotamia where there was a city called Haran. Terah decided to settle there. Abram's allegiance to father caused him to tarry with him until his father died many years later. If Terah had initially undertaken this journey on faith, one thing is sure: he lacked persistence because he stopped halfway in their long route to Canaan. The Genesis combination *now the LORD had said* (1x), *unto Abram get thee* (1x), *out of* (62x), *thy country* (2x) = 66. The OT Narrative combination *Abram* (2x) and *country* (64x) = 66.

Ur of the Chaldees

"After these things the word of the LORD came unto Abram in a vision, saying, Fear not, Abram: I am thy shield, and thy exceeding great reward. . . . And he believed in the LORD; and he counted it to him for righteousness. And he said unto him, I am the LORD that brought thee out of Ur of the Chaldees, to give thee this land to inherit it" (Gen. 15:1, 6-7). The Lord reminded Abram of his divine deliverance from idol worship. Ur was a metropolitan city located on the Euphrates River, one of great importance in religion and industry. It was conquered and plundered many times by various nations and empires over the centuries. At one time the Chaldeans held control of the city. During their occupation of Ur it became a religious center for moon worship. They also worshiped Bel-marduk. The Bible combination *worshipped the* (15x) and *moon* (51x) = 66. The Genesis combination *out of* (62x), *Ur of the Chaldees* (3x), *to give thee this land* (1x) = 66.

A Standing Image of Lot's Wife

Lot reluctantly walked away from Sodom. "But his wife looked back from behind him, and she became a pillar of salt" (Gen. 19:26). Sodom had become an idol in the heart of Lot's wife. Her longing after Sodom fits our third definition of idolatry: an immoderate attachment or devotion to something. In great irony she was turned into an idol—a standing image. The phrase *and she* occurs 266 times in the Old Testament. The Bible combination *Lot's* (2 chs), *wife* (163 chs), *became a pillar of salt* (1 ch) = 166 chapters.

Laban Wanted His Stolen Idols Back

Laban spoke with Jacob: "Wherefore hast thou stolen my <u>GODS</u>? And Jacob answered and said to Laban . . . With whomsoever thou findest thy <u>GODS</u>, let him not live: before our brethren discern thou what is thine with me, and take it to thee. For Jacob knew not that Rachel had stolen <u>them</u>. And Laban went into Jacob's tent, and into Leah's tent, and into the two maidservants' tents; but he found <u>them</u> not. Then went he out of Leah's tent, and entered into Rachel's tent" (Gen. 31:30c-31a, 32-33). Family idols could be small yet still greatly valued. These religious objects were small figurines known as teraphim meaning healers and were inexpensive and easy to transport. For Rachel they were easy to hide being so small. People became personally attached to their idols. These belonged to the father not the children. Again the word *gods* occurs naturally 66 times in the Law. The word *them* occurs 466 times in Jeremiah.

The phrase *his own* occurs 166 times in the Old Testament.
The phrase *his own* is mentioned in 66 chapters of the NT.

Laban's Idols Hidden in Rachel's Tent

"Now Rachel had taken <u>the IMAGES</u>, and put <u>them</u> in the camel's furniture, and sat upon <u>them</u>. And Laban searched all the <u>tent</u>, but found <u>them</u> not. And she said to <u>her</u> father, Let it not displease my lord that I cannot rise up before thee; for the custom of women is upon me. And he searched, but found not <u>the IMAGES</u>" (Gen. 31:34-35). An image was an idol which bore the likeness of some supposed deity. Gentiles who dwelled in tents must have constantly felt the pressure of their vulnerability both to the elements of the earth and to the possibility of invaders. For this reason such tent-dwellers felt especially compelled to keep idols for their protection. Rachel should not have felt the need to follow the Gentiles' custom because she knew of her husband's personal encounters with the One True God Jehovah. Nevertheless, she continued in her idolatry. The portable idols were Laban's but Rachel felt they should now be hers. Again the word *them* occurs 466 times in Jeremiah. The word *tents* occurs 66 times in Scripture. The word *her* occurs 66 times in Isaiah. Again the Bible combination *the idols/s* (27x) and *the image/s* (39x) = 66.

Jacob's Clan Buries Their Idols

"Then Jacob said unto his household, and to all that were with him, Put away the <u>strange GODS that are among you</u>, and be clean. . . . And let us arise, and go up to Beth-el; and I will make there an altar unto God. . . . And they gave unto Jacob all the <u>strange GODS which were in their hand</u>, and all their earrings which were in their ears; and Jacob hid <u>them</u> under the oak which was by Shechem" (Gen. 35:2ab, 3a, 4). Earrings were not always worn for mere ornamental purposes. Some were designed with idolatrous symbols or shapes and rested on the idol's own ears while the worshipper slept at night. Other styles were worn as amulets to guard against superstition. Jacob understood that they must all be put away if the people were to attain unto sanctification. Again the word *them* occurs 466 times in Jeremiah.

The Old Testament: *strange* (65x), *gods that are among you* (1x) = 66.
The Old Testament: *strange* (65x), *gods which were in their hand* (1x) = 66.

66 Hebrews Enter the Land of Colossal Idols

"All the souls that came with Jacob into Egypt, which came out of his loins, besides Jacob's sons' wives, all the souls were THREESCORE AND SIX" (Gen. 46:26). It was in Egypt that the

Hebrew clan underwent a cultural submergence in idolatry for four centuries. At the end of four centuries the Living God taught the Hebrew nation a lesson in trusting idols: it is a vain and worthless thing to do. However, the Hebrews did not learn this godly lesson.

Deliverance out of the Hand of Idol Worshipers

The Lord told Moses, "I am come down to deliver them <u>out of the hand of</u> the Egyptians, and to bring them up <u>out of</u> that land unto a good land and a large, unto a land flowing with milk and honey" (Exod. 3:8a). At this ordained time the Lord wanted to deliver the Hebrews from their extended sojourn in the land of colossal idols. The phrase *out of the hand of* occurs 66 times in the Bible.

The Lord's Plan to Judge Egypt for Her Idolatry

"And I will harden Pharaoh's heart, and multiply my signs and my wonders in the land of Egypt. But Pharaoh shall not hearken unto you, that I may lay my hand upon Egypt, and bring forth mine armies, and my people the children of Israel, out of the land of Egypt by great judgments. And the Egyptians shall know that I am the LORD, when I stretch forth mine hand upon Egypt, and bring out the children of Israel from among them. . . . and against all <u>the GODS</u> of Egypt I will execute judgment: I am the LORD" (Exod. 7:3-5; 12:12c).

Again the term *the god(s)* occurs 66 times in the Bible. The Lord's plan was to lay a devastating judgment upon all of Egypt's gods. This would have a temporary and negative effect on the idolatrous people, but it would also have a positive and lasting effect on Egypt by causing her to turn from her idolatry if she were so willing. The land was full of idols and images depicting a host of false deities, ten in particular. The end result of God's judgment would be both Egypt and Israel knowing for certain that Jehovah alone was God, the only God the nations should fear and serve. Let's look at these judgments upon idolatrous Egypt's false gods.

Hapi—Egyptian God of the Nile

This god was responsible for the Nile's annual rise of water levels which replenished the delta with rich silt and supplied water to its annually planted crops. In His anger Jehovah turned the Nile waters to blood, cursing it. "And Moses and Aaron did so, as the LORD commanded; <u>and he lifted up the rod, and smote</u> <u>the waters</u> <u>that were in the river</u>, <u>in the sight of Pharaoh</u>, <u>and in the sight of his servants</u>; <u>and all the waters that were in the river were turned to blood</u>. And the fish that was in the river died; and the river stank, and the Egyptians could not drink of the water of the river" (Exod. 7:20-21b). The Law combination *and he lifted up the rod and smote* (1x), *the waters* (59x), *that were in the river* (2x), *in the sight of Pharaoh* (2x), *and in the sight of his servants* (1x), *and all the waters that were in the river were turned to blood* (1x) = 66.

Heket—Egyptian Goddess of Fertility

Heket was responsible for renewal and fertility. She was depicted with the head of a frog. In His anger Jehovah inundated the land with a curse of frogs. "<u>And Aaron stretched out his hand over</u> <u>the waters of Egypt</u>; and the <u>frogs</u> <u>came up, and covered</u> <u>the land of Egypt</u>. . . . <u>and the frogs died</u> out of the houses, out of the villages, and out of the fields. <u>And they gathered them together upon heaps</u>: <u>and the land stank</u>" (Exod. 8:6, 13b-14). The Law combination *and Aaron stretched out his hand over* (1x), *the waters of Egypt* (2x), *frogs* (11x), *came up* (13x), *and covered* (8x), *all the land of Egypt* (28x), *and the frogs died* (1x), *and they gathered them together upon heaps* (1x), *and the land stank* (1x) = 66.

Geb—Egyptian God of the Earth

Geb ruled over the dusty earth and with his added blessing allowed the crops to grow. He was also considered to be the father of snakes. In His anger Jehovah cursed Egypt's dusty soil and covered it with lice. "And the LORD said unto Moses, Say unto Aaron, Stretch out thy rod, and smite <u>the dust</u> of the land, that it may become lice throughout all the land of Egypt. And they did so" (Exod. 8:16-17a). The phrase *the dust* occurs 66 times in the Bible.

Khepri—Egyptian God of Creation

Khepri was responsible for the rising of the morning sun and by association brought rebirth and renewal. He was depicted as an insect-faced god. In His anger Jehovah cursed Egypt with swarms of one species of insect. "And the LORD said unto Moses, Rise up early in the morning, and stand before Pharaoh . . . and say unto him . . . if thou wilt not let my people go, behold, <u>I will send</u> <u>swarms</u> <u>of flies upon thee</u>, and upon thy servants, and upon thy people, and into thy houses: <u>and the houses of the Egyptians</u> <u>shall be full of swarms</u> <u>of flies</u>, and also the ground whereon they are" (Exod. 8:20-21). The Old Testament combination *I will send* (49x), *swarms* (5x), *of flies upon thee* (1x), *and the houses of the Egyptians* (1x), *shall be full of swarms* (1x), *of flies* (9x) = 66.

Hathor—Egyptian Goddess of Love & Protection

This goddess was normally depicted with a crown of cow horns upon her head. On occasion she was personified as an entire cow. In His anger Jehovah plagued Egypt's livestock to bring about their deaths. "Behold, the hand of the LORD is upon thy cattle which is <u>in the field</u>, upon the horses, upon the asses, upon the camels, upon the oxen, and upon the sheep: there shall be a very grievous murrain" (Exod. 9:3). The phrase *in the field* is mentioned in 66 verses of the Old Testament.

Isis—Egyptian Goddess of Life & Magic

Isis protected women and children and healed the sick. In His anger Jehovah plagued the Egyptians with boils and sores, taking away their health and healing. "And they took ashes of the furnace, and stood before Pharaoh; <u>and Moses sprinkled it up toward heaven</u>; <u>and it became a boil</u> <u>breaking forth with blains upon man, and upon beast</u>. And <u>the magicians could not stand before Moses because of the boils</u>; <u>for the boil</u> <u>was upon the</u> <u>magicians</u>, <u>and upon all the Egyptians</u>" (Exod. 9:10-11). The Bible combination *and Moses sprinkled it up toward heaven* (1x), *and it became a boil* (1x), *breaking forth with blains upon man and upon beast* (2x), *the magicians* (15x), *could not stand* (4x), *before Moses* (6x), *because of the boils* (1x), *for the boil* (1x), *was upon the* (19x), *magicians* (15x), *and upon all the Egyptians* (1x) = 66.

Nut—Egyptian Goddess of the Sky & Cosmos

This goddess was often depicted as a nude woman arching over the sky. She was also depicted with a water pot upon her head. In His anger Jehovah cursed the sky by raining down a hailstorm laced with fire. "And Moses stretched forth his rod toward heaven: and the LORD sent thunder and hail, and the fire ran along upon the ground; and the LORD rained hail upon the land of Egypt. So there was hail, and fire mingled with the hail, very grievous, such as there was none like it in all the land of Egypt since it became a nation" (Exod. 9:23-24). The Old Testament combination *a woman* (65x) and *waterpot* (1x) = 66.

Set—Egyptian God of Chaos & Storms

This god was responsible for <u>war</u>. He was depicted with a distinctive animal head resembling that of a jackal. In His anger Jehovah sent forth an innumerable army of locusts to destroy everything that was green. "And the LORD said unto Moses, Stretch out thine hand over the land of Egypt for the <u>locusts, that they may come up upon the land of Egypt</u>, and eat every herb of the land, even all that the hail hath left. . . . very grievous were they; before them there were no such <u>locusts</u> as they, neither after them shall be such. For they covered the face of the whole earth, so that the land was darkened" (Exod. 10:12, 14b-15a). The Bible combination *make war with* (5x), *armies* (43x), *locusts* (17x), *that they may come up upon the land of Egypt* (1x) = 66.

Ra—Egyptian God of the Sun

Ra was the most important god ruling over the sky, universe, and even the underworld. He was portrayed with a falcon's head and a sun suspended over him. In His anger Jehovah brought three days of utter darkness upon Egypt. "<u>And the LORD said unto Moses, Stretch out thine hand toward heaven, that there may be darkness over the land of Egypt, even darkness which may be felt</u>. And Moses stretched forth his hand toward heaven; and there was a thick darkness in all the land of Egypt three days" (Exod. 10:21-11). The underlined words indicate the 266th verse of Exodus.

Pharaoh—The Incarnate God of Egypt

The king of Egypt was worshiped by the Egyptians because he was considered to be the greatest Egyptian god of all. It was believed that he was actually the son of Ra himself, manifest in the flesh. In His anger Jehovah brought about the deaths of all Egypt's firstborn sons, particularly Pharaoh's firstborn son. "And Moses said, Thus saith the LORD, About midnight will I go out into the midst of Egypt: And all the firstborn in the land of Egypt shall die, from <u>the firstborn of Pharaoh that sitteth upon his throne</u>, even unto the firstborn of the maidservant that is behind the mill; and all the firstborn of beasts. And there shall be a great cry throughout all the land of Egypt, such as there was none like it, nor shall be like it any more" (Exod. 12:4-5). The Old Testament combination *the firstborn* (64 vs), *of Pharaoh that sitteth upon his throne* (1 v), *of Pharaoh that sat on his throne* (1 v) = 66 verses.

66th Chapter of the Bible

Exodus chapter sixteen is the 66th chapter of the Bible because of its offer of true spiritual food and spiritual rest as a remedy against idol worship's emptiness. As Scripture will show in a moment, while in Egypt Israel did not know the Lord. Israel was therefore guilty of idol worship by default. Idol worship is difficult work and always leaves the idol worshiper spiritually drained and dissatisfied. Here Israel's ongoing spiritual journey brings them from a test of thirst to a test of hunger. Are they hungry to know the One True Living God or will they remain indifferent? In this chapter holy manna becomes the perfect cure for Israel's idol-worshiping tendencies. This new spiritual food was also warmly accompanied with their new religious rest—the Sabbath.

> "And they took their journey from Elim, and all the congregation of the children of <u>Israel</u> came unto the wilderness of Sin . . . after their departing out of the land of Egypt. And the whole congregation of the children of Israel murmured against Moses and Aaron in the wilderness: And the children of Israel said unto them, Would to God we had died by the hand of the LORD <u>in the land of Egypt</u>, when we sat by the flesh pots, and when we did eat bread to the full; for ye have brought us forth into this wilderness, to kill this whole assembly with <u>hunger</u>" (Exod. 16:1-3).

This scenario fits our third definition of idolatry: an immoderate attachment or devotion to something. Here Israel revealed her sudden longing to go back to a land filled with colossal idols. They were not presently controlled by their heart but rather their bellies. They preferred gorging themselves under the shadow of idols rather than eating modestly under the shadow of the Almighty. The underlined name Israel is the 50,066th word of the Bible, and it falls in the 66th chapter of the Bible. The related Bible phrases *in the land of Egypt* (58x), *into the land of Egypt* (6x), *unto the land of Egypt* (2x) = 66. All forms of the word hunger show the seal of idol worship: *hunger* (24x), *hungered* (2x), *hungred* (9x), *hungry* (30x), *hungerbitten* (1x) = 66.

Israel's new spiritual rest from idolatry's hardship came to the nation through God's gift of the Sabbath Day. Moses said, "To morrow is the rest of the holy sabbath unto the LORD. . . . See, for that the LORD hath given you the sabbath, therefore he giveth you on the sixth day the bread of two days; abide ye every man in his place, let no man go out of his place on the <u>seventh</u> day. So the people <u>rested</u> on the <u>seventh</u> day" (vv. 23, 29-30). The great Sabbath miracle was that they ate manna on this day without having to gather it; the double portion given on the sixth day made this possible. The word *seventh* is mentioned in 66 chapters of the Old Testament. The word *rest* is mentioned naturally in 166 chapters of the Old Testament.

Jethro Turned from His Idolatry

"And Jethro rejoiced for all the goodness which the LORD had done to Israel, whom he had delivered out of the hand of the Egyptians. And Jethro said, Blessed be the LORD. . . . Now I know that the LORD is greater than all <u>GODS</u>. . . . And Jethro, Moses' father in law, took a burnt offering and sacrifices for God: and Aaron came, and all the elders of Israel, to eat bread with Moses' father in law before God" (Exod. 18:9-10a, 11a, 12). Again the word *gods* occurs naturally 66 times in the Law.

No Other Gods

"Thou shalt have no <u>other GODS</u> before me" (Exod. 20:3). At the forefront of the Ten Commandments is the issue of idolatry. The word *other* is mentioned in 66 chapters of the Law. Again the phrase *other god(s)* occurs 66 times in the Bible.

Not Any Likeness of God

"Thou shalt not <u>make</u> unto thee any GRAVEN IMAGE, or <u>any</u> likeness of <u>any</u> thing that is in heaven above, or that is <u>in the earth</u> beneath, or that is in the water under the earth" (Exod. 20:4). The Second Commandment also deals with the issue of idolatry. The word *make* is mentioned in 66 verses of Ezekiel. The word *any* occurs 66 times in the Wisdom Books. The phrase *in the earth* occurs 66 times in the Bible.

No Bowing to or Serving Other Gods

"<u>Thou shalt not</u> BOW DOWN <u>thyself to them</u>, nor SERVE <u>them</u>" (Exod. 20:5a). In the Hebrew text the word "serve" shares the same root word with worship, thus we place this word in all capitals. Service is something a person devotes his full attention to. Bowing down before a deity is an act of worship, thus we place this phrase in all capitals. The word *serve* occurs 66 times in the Law. The Law combination *thou shalt not* (153x), *bow down* (9x), *thyself to them* (1x), *nor serve them* (3x) = 166. The Job combination *serve* (3x), *them* (63x) = 66.

Make No Mention of Other Gods' Names

"And in all things that I have said unto you be circumspect: and <u>make no mention of the name of</u> <u>other GODS,</u> <u>neither</u> let it be heard out of thy mouth" (Exod. 23:13). Again the word *other* is mentioned in 66 chapters of the Law. The Bible combination *make no mention of the name of* (1x), *neither make mention of the name of* (1x), *not make mention of the name of* (1x), *other gods* (63x) = 66.

Hebrews Turned Golden Earrings into Golden Calf

Apis was Egypt's highly regarded bull deity and was worshiped in Memphis. When the Israelites pondered Moses' long absence they suddenly found opportunity to craft this idol they were somewhat familiar with. "Up, <u>make</u> us GODS, which shall go before us; for as for this Moses, the man that brought us up out of the land of Egypt, we wot not what is become of him. And Aaron said unto them, Break off the <u>golden</u> earrings, which are in the ears of your wives, of your sons, and of your daughters, and bring them unto me. And all <u>the people</u> . . . brought them unto Aaron. And he received them at their hand, and fashioned it with a graving tool, after he had made it a MOLTEN CALF: and they said, These be thy GODS, O Israel, which brought thee up out of the land of Egypt" (Exod. 32:2c-4). Again the word *make* is mentioned in 66 verses of Ezekiel. Again the phrase *the people* occurs 66 times in Joshua.

> The word *golden* occurs 66 times in the Bible.
> The word *gold* occurs naturally 166 times in the OT Narrative.

Moses turned Golden Calf into Golden Dust

God told Moses to get down to the people. "And it came to pass, as soon as he came nigh unto the camp, that he saw the CALF, and the dancing: and Moses' anger waxed hot, and he cast the tables out of his hands, and brake them beneath the mount. And he took the CALF_which they had made, and <u>burnt</u> it in the fire, and ground it to powder, and strawed it upon the water, and made the children of Israel <u>drink</u> of it" (Exod. 32:19-20). The word *burnt* occurs 366 times in the Bible. The word *drink* is mentioned in 266 verses of the Old Testament!

When dissolved in water, gold dust nanoparticles create a solution known as colloidal gold. A variety of colors can be produced depending on the size and amount of the particles. If the particles are smaller than one hundred nanometers the liquid solution is an intense red color. Over the centuries this product has been assumed to hold a measure of curative powers, including improvements in mental health. Perhaps Moses made Israel drink the solution not only as a punitive measure but also as a preventative measure against a future mindset of idolatry.

2466th Verse of the Bible

"And he said unto them, Thus saith the LORD God of Israel, Put every man his sword by his side, and go in and out from gate to gate throughout the camp, and slay every man his brother, and every man his companion, and every man his neighbour" (Exod. 32:27). Judgment was to be given out for the people's sinful worship of the golden calf. Three thousand idolaters were put to death.

Moses Prayed for Israel's Great Sin of Idolatry

"And it came to pass on the morrow, that Moses said unto the people, Ye have <u>sinned</u> a great <u>sin</u>: and now I will go up unto the LORD; peradventure I shall make an atonement for your <u>sin</u>. And

Moses returned unto the LORD, and said, Oh, this people have <u>sinned</u> a great <u>sin</u>, and have made them GODS OF <u>gold</u>. Yet now, if thou wilt forgive their <u>sin</u>—; and if not, blot me, I pray thee, out of thy book which thou hast written" (Exod. 32:30-32). The word *sins* is mentioned in 166 verses of the Bible. Again the word *gold* occurs naturally 166 times in the OT Narrative.

God Plagued Israel for Making the Golden Calf

"And the LORD plagued the people, because <u>they made</u> <u>the CALF, which Aaron made</u>" (Exod. 32:35). The word *made* is mentioned in 266 verses of the New Testament. The Bible combination *they made* (65x), *the calf which Aaron made* (1x) = 66.

Take Heed to Worship No Other God

As the Lord wrote the Decalogue on tables of stone for the second time He reminded the nation, "Take <u>heed</u> to thyself, lest thou make a covenant with the inhabitants of the land whither thou goest, lest it be for a snare in the midst of thee: But ye shall destroy their altars, break their IMAGES, and cut down their GROVES: For thou shalt WORSHIP no <u>other GOD</u>: for the LORD, whose name is Jealous, is a jealous God" (Exod. 34:12-14). The word *heed* is mentioned in 66 chapters of the Bible. Again the word *other* is mentioned in 66 chapters of the Law. The Bible phrases *other g/God* (3x) and *other gods* (63x) = 66.

Whoring after Other Gods

"Lest thou make a covenant with the inhabitants of the land, and they go a WHORING after their gods, and do sacrifice unto their gods, and one call thee, and thou eat of his sacrifice; And thou take of their daughters unto thy sons, and their daughters <u>go a WHORING after their</u> <u>GODS</u>, and make thy sons <u>go a WHORING after their</u> <u>GODS</u>. Thou shalt make thee no molten GODS" (Exod. 34:15-16). The Old Testament combination *go a whoring after their* (3x), *other gods* (63x) = 66.

Sacrificing unto Devils

"And they shall <u>no more</u> <u>offer</u> <u>their sacrifices unto devils</u>, after whom they have gone a WHORING" (Lev. 17:7ab). Any sacrifice offered to a god other than Jehovah God is an act of idolatry. Behind such false gods are unseen devilish spirits. The phrase *no more* is mentioned in 66 verses of the Major and Minor Prophets. The Leviticus combination *offer* (65 vs), *their sacrifices unto devils* (1 v) = 66 verses.

Sacrificing outside the Appointed Place

"This shall be a statute for ever unto them throughout their generations. And thou shalt say unto them, <u>Whatsoever man</u> <u>there be of the house of Israel</u>, <u>or of the strangers which sojourn among</u> <u>you, that offereth a</u> <u>burnt offering or sacrifice</u>, <u>And bringeth it not unto the door of the tabernacle</u> <u>of the congregation</u>, <u>to offer it unto the LORD</u>; <u>even that man</u> <u>shall be cut off</u> <u>from among his</u> <u>people</u>" (Lev. 17:7c-9). After this commandment was given, any sacrifice offered other than at Jehovah's holy altar would be considered an idolatrous practice. The Bible combination *whatsoever man* (4x), *there be of the house of Israel* (3x), *or of the strangers which sojourn among you that offereth a* (1x), *burnt offering or sacrifice* (2x), *and bringeth it not unto the door of the tabernacle of the congregation* (2x), *to offer it unto the LORD* (1x), *even that man* (3x), *shall be cut off* (39x), *from among his people* (11x) = 66.

Sacrificing an Animal & Drinking Its Blood

"And <u>whatsoever man there be of the house of Israel</u>, <u>or of the strangers that sojourn among you,</u> <u>that</u> <u>eateth</u> <u>any manner</u> <u>of blood;</u> I will even set my face against that soul that eateth blood, and will cut him off from among his people" (Lev. 17:10). Drinking a sacrifice's blood was common practice among the idolatrous nations. Israel was not to do this. The Old Testament combination *and whatsoever man there be of the house of Israel* (1x), *or of the strangers that sojourn among you which/that* (2x), *eateth* (32x), *any manner* (10x), *of blood* (21x) = 66.

Canaan's Idolatrous Doings

"After the <u>doings</u> of the land of Egypt, wherein ye dwelt, shall ye not do: and after the <u>doings</u> of the <u>land of Canaan</u>, whither I bring you, shall ye not do: neither shall ye walk in their ordinance" (Lev. 18:3). Both Egypt and Canaan were filled with standing images carved from wood and stone. The word *doing(s)* is mentioned naturally in 66 verses of the Old Testament. The title *land of Canaan* occurs 66 times in Scripture.

Committing Idolatry

"Therefore shall ye keep mine ordinance, that ye <u>commit</u> not any one of these abominable customs, which were <u>committed</u> before you, and that ye defile not yourselves therein: I am the LORD your God" (Lev. 18:30).

> The word *commit* is mentioned naturally in 66 verses of the Bible.
> The word *committed* is mentioned in 66 chapters of the Bible.

Turning unto Idols

"<u>Turn</u> ye not <u>unto</u> IDOLS, nor <u>make</u> to yourselves molten GODS: I am the LORD your God" (Lev. 19:4). This verse gives us the Bible's first mention of the plural word idols. The word *turn* is mentioned in 66 chapters of the Major and Minor Prophets. The word *unto* is found in 66 books of the Bible. Again the word *make* is mentioned in 66 verses of Ezekiel.

Worshiping Molech

"<u>Whosoever he be</u> of the children of Israel, or of the strangers that sojourn in Israel, <u>that giveth</u> <u>any of his seed unto Molech;</u> <u>he shall surely be</u> <u>put to death</u>: <u>the people of the land</u> <u>shall stone</u> <u>him with stones</u>. . . . Then I will set my face against that man, and against his family, and will cut him off, and all that go a WHORING after him, to commit WHOREDOM with Molech, from among their people" (Lev. 20:2, 5). Child sacrifice was a horrible idolatrous practice in Canaan. The Law combination *whosoever he be* (4x), *that giveth any of his seed unto Molech* (1x), *he shall surely be* (6x), *put to death* (44x), *the people of the land* (8x), *shall stone him with stones* (3x) = 66.

Making a Graven Image

"Ye shall <u>make</u> you no IDOLS nor <u>GRAVEN IMAGE</u>, neither rear you up a STANDING IMAGE, neither shall ye set up any IMAGE OF STONE in your land, to BOW DOWN unto it: for I am the LORD your God" (Lev. 21:6). Again the word *make* is mentioned in 66 verses of Ezekiel. The Leviticus combination *make* (65x) and *graven image* (1x) = 66.

Idolatry in High Places

"I will destroy your <u>HIGH PLACES</u>, and cut down your IMAGES, and cast your carcases upon the carcases of your IDOLS, and my soul shall abhor you" (Lev. 26:30). Ancient people often built shrines for their idols on the hilltops. The Bible treats hills and mountains the same; they are both elevated places. Such territory was understood by the heathen to be suitably situated territory for gods to come and dwell in. Knowing that Israel would fall into such idolatry after they settled among the Canaanites, the Lord strongly warned Israel against doing so. The word *image(s)* is mentioned in 66 chapters from Genesis to the Major Prophets. The idol-worshiping term *high places* is mentioned in 66 chapters of the Bible.

Yet Again Israel Commits Idolatry in the Wilderness

"And Israel abode in Shittim, and the people began to commit whoredom with the daughters of Moab. And they called the people unto the sacrifices of their GODS: and the people did eat, and BOWED DOWN to their GODS. And Israel joined himself unto <u>BAAL-PEOR</u>: and the anger of the LORD was kindled against Israel. And the LORD said unto Moses, Take all the heads of the people, and hang <u>them</u> up before the LORD against the sun, that the fierce anger of the LORD may be turned away from Israel" (Num. 25:1-4).

The Old Testament combination *Baal* (62x) and *Peor* (4x) = 66. Again the word *them* occurs 466 times in Jeremiah.

The Idolatrous Inhabitants of Canaan

"Then ye shall drive out all <u>the inhabitants</u> of the land from before you, and destroy all their PICTURES, and destroy all their MOLTEN IMAGES, and quite pluck down all their HIGH PLACES" (Num. 33:52).

The phrase *the inhabitants* is mentioned in 166 verses of the Old Testament.
The phrase *inhabitants of* is mentioned in 66 verses of the OT Narrative.

66th Verse of Deuteronomy

"That also was accounted a land of giants: giants dwelt therein in old time; and the Ammonites call them Zamzummims" (Deut. 2:20). The chief deity of the Ammonites was Moloch also spelled Molech, Milcom, or Malcam. Moloch was the fire god. His name means king, and he demanded human sacrifice.

An Image in the Likeness of Anything

Moses reminded the new generation, "<u>Take ye</u> therefore <u>good heed unto yourselves</u> . . . <u>Lest ye corrupt yourselves, and</u> <u>make you a GRAVEN IMAGE</u>, <u>the similitude of any figure</u>, <u>the likeness of male or female</u>, <u>The likeness of any beast that is on the earth</u>, <u>the likeness of any winged fowl that flieth</u> <u>in the air</u>, <u>The likeness of any thing that creepeth on the ground</u>, <u>the likeness of any fish that is in the waters</u> <u>beneath the earth</u>" (Deut. 4:15a, 16-18). Idols generally took on one of two forms; some were made in the image of a man called anthropomorphic, and others were made in the image of animal or as a fusion of animal and human called zoomorphic. The Bible combination *take ye* (20x), *good heed unto yourselves* (2x), *lest ye corrupt yourselves and* (1x), *make you a graven image* (2x), *the similitude of any figure* (1x), *the likeness of* (24x), *male or female* (4x), *the likeness of any beast that is on the earth* (1x), *the likeness of any winged fowl* (1x), *that flieth* (3x), *in the air* (3x), *the likeness of any thing that creepeth on the ground* (1x), *the likeness of any fish that is in the waters* (1x), *beneath the earth* (2x) = 66.

Lest Ye Forget

Again Moses gave a similar warning: "Take heed unto yourselves, <u>lest ye forget the covenant of the LORD your God</u>, <u>which he made with you</u>, and <u>make you a GRAVEN IMAGE</u>, or <u>the likeness of any thing</u>, <u>which the LORD thy God hath forbidden thee</u>" (Deut. 4:23). Again the word *make* is mentioned in 66 verses of Ezekiel. Here the word *graven* is the 766th word of the chapter. The Bible combination *lest ye forget the covenant of the LORD your God* (1x), *which he made with you* (1x), *make* (1055x), *you a graven image* (2x), *likeness of any thing* (5x), *which the LORD thy God hath forbidden thee* (1x) = 1066.

Gods That Neither See Nor Hear Nor Eat Nor Drink

"And there ye shall SERVE GODS, the work of men's hands, wood and stone, which <u>neither see</u>, <u>nor hear</u>, <u>nor eat</u>, <u>nor smell</u>" (Deut. 4:28). The Law combination *neither* (165x), *see nor hear* (1x) = 166. The Isaiah combination *neither* (65x), *smell* (1x) = 66. The NT Narrative combination *neither* (64 chs), *eat nor* (2 chs) = 66 chapters. The NT Narrative combination *neither* (64 chs), *eat nor drink* (2 chs) = 66 chapters.

Serving Other Gods

"<u>For they will turn away thy son from following me, that they may SERVE other GODS</u>: so will the anger of the LORD be kindled against you, and destroy thee suddenly" (Deut. 7:4). Again the word *serve* occurs 66 times in the Law. Again the word *other* is mentioned in 66 chapters of the Law. The sentence *for they will turn away thy son from following me, that they may serve other gods* consists of 66 characters.

Israel's Mandated Idol-Destruction Policy

"But thus shall ye deal with them; ye shall <u>destroy</u> their altars, and break down their IMAGES, and cut down their GROVES, and <u>burn their GRAVEN IMAGES with fire</u>" (Deut. 7:5). The word *destroyed* occurs 66 times in the OT Narrative. The Law combination *destroy* (56x), *their altars* (3x), *burn with fire* (6x), *their graven images* (1x) = 66. The underlined word *images* is the 166th word of this chapter.

5166th Verse of the Bible

"Also in Horeb ye <u>provoked</u> the LORD to <u>wrath</u>, so that the LORD was angry with you to have destroyed you" (Deut. 9:8). This verse refers to God's former wrath concerning Israel's idolatrous golden calf. The Wisdom Books combination *provoked him* (4x), *wrath* (62x) = 66.

Turning Aside to Serve Other Gods

"Take heed to yourselves, that your heart be not deceived, <u>and ye turn aside</u>, <u>and SERVE other GODS</u>, and WORSHIP them" (Deut. 11:16). The Old Testament combination *and ye turn* (1x), *aside* (60x), *and serve other gods* (5x) = 66.

Idolatry upon the Hills

"Ye shall utterly destroy all the places, wherein the nations which ye shall possess SERVED <u>their GODS</u>, upon the high mountains, <u>and upon the hills</u>, and under every green tree: And ye shall overthrow their altars, and break their pillars, and burn their GROVES with fire; and ye shall hew down the GRAVEN IMAGES of their GODS, and destroy the names of them out of that place" (Deut. 12:2-3). The phrase *and upon the* occurs 66 times in the Bible. The Bible

537

combination *hills* (65x) and *hill top* (1x) = 66.

166ᵗʰ Chapter of the Bible

"If thy brother . . . or thy friend, which is as thine own soul, entice thee secretly, saying, Let us go and SERVE other GODS, which thou hast not known, thou, nor thy fathers; Namely, of the GODS of the people which are round about you, nigh unto thee, or far off from thee, from the one end of the earth even unto the other end of the earth; Thou shalt not consent unto him, nor hearken unto him; neither shall thine eye pity him, neither shalt thou spare, neither shalt thou conceal him: But thou shalt surely kill him" (Deut. 13:6-9a). The phrase *thy brother* occurs 66 times in the whole Bible.

Idolaters Who Worship the Host of Heaven to Be Stoned with Stones

"If there be found among you, within any of thy gates which the LORD thy God giveth thee, man or woman, that hath . . . gone and SERVED other GODS, and WORSHIPPED them, either the sun, or moon, or any of the host of heaven, which I have not commanded; And it be told thee, and thou hast heard of it, and enquired diligently, and, behold, it be true, and the thing certain, that such abomination is wrought in Israel: Then shalt thou bring forth that man or that woman, which have committed that wicked thing, unto thy gates . . . and shalt stone them with stones, till they die" (Deut. 17:2-5).

These verses immediately follow the 5366ᵗʰ verse of the Bible. The phrase *the host of* is mentioned in 66 verses of the Old Testament. The Law combination *bring forth that man or that woman* (1x), *which have committed that wicked thing* (1x), *unto thy gates even* (1x), *stone* (57x), *them with stones* (5x), *till they die* (1x) = 66. The Bible combination *bring forth that man or that woman* (1 v), *unto thy gates* (1v), *stone them with* (5 vs), *stones* (158 vs), *till they die* (1 v) = 166 verses. The Old Testament combination *stone them with* (5x), *stones* (161x) = 166.

Idolatrous Practices Warned Against

"There shall not be found among you any one that maketh his son or his daughter to pass through the fire, or that useth divination, or an observer of times, or an enchanter, or a witch, Or a charmer, or a consulter with familiar spirits, or a wizard, or a necromancer. For all that do these things are an abomination unto the LORD: and because of these abominations the LORD thy God doth drive them out from before thee" (Deut. 18:10-12). The Bible combination *there shall not be found among you any* (1x), *divination* (12x), *observer of times* (1x), *enchanter* (1x), *witch* (2x), *charmer* (1x), *consulter* (1x), *familiar spirits* (9x), *wizard* (2x), *necromancer* (1x), *for all that do these things are* (1x), *an abomination* (34x) = 66.

Idolatrous Work of the Craftsman's Hands

"Cursed be the man that maketh any GRAVEN or MOLTEN IMAGE, an abomination unto the LORD, the work of the hands of the craftsman, and putteth it in a secret place. And all the people shall answer and say, Amen" (Deut. 27:15). The Old Testament combination *the work of the* (42x), *hands of the* (23x), *craftsman* (1x) = 66. Here the word *work* is the 366ᵗʰ word of the chapter, and it is the work of an idolater. The word *it* occurs 6066 times outside the apocalyptic 66ᵗʰ book of the Bible.

Gods Made of Wood & Stone

"The LORD shall bring thee, and thy king which thou shalt set over thee, unto a nation which neither thou nor thy fathers have known; and there shalt thou SERVE other GODS, wood and stone" (Deut. 28:36). The Law combination *wood* (61x), *and stone* (5x) = 66. The Bible combination *and there shalt thou* (2x), *serve other gods* (12x), *wood* (140x), *and stone* (12x) = 166.

Deuteronomy 28:66
"And thy life shall hang in doubt before thee; and thou shalt fear day and night, and shalt have none assurance of thy life" (Deut. 28:66). This verse describes how idols bring the worshiper no assurance of salvation but rather the opposite. Just two verses earlier the Lord mentioned idolatry.

Idols Made of Silver & Gold
"For ye know how we have dwelt in the land of Egypt; and how we came through the nations which ye passed by; And ye have seen their abominations, and their IDOLS, wood and stone, silver and gold, which were among them" (Deut. 29:16-17). The Bible combination *and how we came through the nations* (1x), *which ye passed by* (1x), *and ye have seen their abominations and* (3x), *their idols* (23x), *wood and stone* (8x), *silver and gold* (29x), *which were among them* (1x) = 66. The word *silver* is mentioned in 66 verses of the Law.

Old Gods & New Gods All the Same
"They provoked him to jealousy with STRANGE GODS, with abominations provoked they him to anger. They sacrificed unto devils, not to God; to GODS whom they knew not, to new GODS that came newly up, whom your fathers feared not" (Deut. 32:16-17). Again the word *gods* occurs naturally 66 times in the Law.

Idolatrous City of Jericho Accursed
"And the city shall be accursed, even it, and all that are therein. . . . And ye, in any wise keep yourselves from the accursed thing, lest ye make yourselves accursed, when ye take of the accursed thing, and make the camp of Israel a curse, and trouble it. But all the silver, and gold, and vessels of brass and iron, are consecrated unto the LORD: they shall come into the treasury of the LORD" (Josh. 6:17a). The Bible combination *Jericho* (64x) and *shall be accursed* (2x) = 66. The Bible combination *keep yourselves from idols* (1 ch), *the thing* (65 chs) = 66 chapters. The phrase *of brass* occurs 66 times in the Bible.

Achan Had an Idolatrous Heart
"And Achan answered Joshua, and said, Indeed I have sinned against the LORD God of Israel, and thus and thus have I done: When I saw among the spoils a goodly Babylonish garment, and two hundred shekels of silver, and a wedge of gold of fifty shekels weight, then I coveted them, and took them; and, behold, they are hid in the earth in the midst of my tent, and the silver under it" (Josh. 7:20-21). Achan's longing after the silver and gold he saw and taking it for himself fits our third definition of idolatry: an immoderate attachment or devotion to something. Using all available forms, the phrase *sin/ned/ners/neth/ning against* occurs 66 times in the Bible. Again the word *silver* is mentioned in 66 verses of the Law. Again the word *gold* occurs naturally 166 times in the OT Narrative. Again the word *tents* occurs 66 times in Scripture.

6466th Verse of the Bible
"And the LORD your God, he shall expel them from before you, and drive them from out of your

sight; and ye shall possess their land, as the LORD your God hath promised unto you" (Josh. 23:5). The chief reason for the heathens' expulsion from the land was their idolatrous ways. Again the word *them* occurs 466 times in Jeremiah. The phrase *them out of* occurs 66 times in the Bible and is mentioned in 66 verses thereof.

Joshua Warns the People about Falling into Idolatry

On the day of his passing Joshua counseled the people not to fall into idolatry after his death. He warned them, "When ye have transgressed the covenant of the LORD your God, which he commanded you, and have gone and <u>SERVED</u> other GODS, and BOWED yourselves to <u>them</u>; then shall the anger of the LORD be kindled against you, and ye shall perish quickly from off the good land which he hath given unto you" (Josh. 23:16). Again the word *serve* occurs 66 times in the Law. Again the word *them* occurs 466 times in Jeremiah.

Abraham's Idol-Worshiping Fathers

"And Joshua said unto all the people, Thus saith the LORD God of Israel, Your fathers dwelt on the other side of the flood in old time, even Terah, the father of Abraham, and the father of Nachor: and they SERVED other GODS. And I took <u>your father Abraham</u> from <u>the other side</u> of the flood, and led him throughout all the land of Canaan" (Josh. 24:2-3ab). God brought the nation's forefather Abram out of the cradle of idolatry, Mesopotamia, meaning the land between two rivers. This regional plain flooded from time to time. Ur was situated right on the Euphrates River. The Bible combination *your father Abraham* (2x) and *the other side* (64x) = 66.

Some People Need to Put Away their Strange Gods

"And Joshua said unto <u>the people</u>, Ye are witnesses against yourselves that ye have chosen you the LORD, to SERVE him. And they said, We are witnesses. Now therefore put away, said he, the <u>STRANGE</u> <u>GODS which are among you</u>, and incline your heart unto the LORD God of Israel" (Josh. 24:22-23). Joshua knew the people needed repentance and revival. Because some of them were harboring idols he did what Jacob once did with his clan—he told them to put away their strange gods and be clean. Again the phrase *the people* occurs 66 times in Joshua. The Old Testament combination *strange* (65x), *gods which are among you* (1x) = 66.

Idolatrous Children of Israel

"And <u>the children of</u> Israel did evil in the sight of the LORD, and SERVED Baalim: And they forsook the LORD God of their fathers, which brought them out of the land of Egypt, and followed other GODS, of the GODS of the people that were round about them, and BOWED themselves unto them, and provoked the LORD to anger. And they forsook the LORD, and SERVED BAAL and Ashtaroth. And the anger of the LORD was hot against Israel, and he delivered them into the hands of spoilers that spoiled them. . . . Nevertheless the LORD raised up judges, which delivered them out of the hand of those that spoiled them. And yet they would not hearken unto their judges, but <u>they went a WHORING after</u> <u>other GODS</u>, and BOWED themselves unto them: they turned quickly out of the way which their fathers walked in, obeying the commandments of the LORD; but they did not so" (Judg. 2:11-14a, 16-17).

The phrase *the children* is mentioned in 366 chapters of the Bible. The phrase *of the children of* occurs 366 times in the Old Testament. The OT Narrative combination *they went* (61 vs), *a whoring* (5 vs) = 66 verses. The Old Testament combination *went a whoring after their* (3x), *other gods* (63x) = 66.

6566th Verse of the Bible

"And the anger of the LORD was hot against Israel; and he said, Because that this people hath transgressed my covenant which I commanded their fathers, and have not hearkened unto my voice" (Judg. 2:20). The Bible combination *the anger of the LORD* (24x) and *against Israel* (42x) = 66. The Major and Minor Prophets combination *this people* (48x), *transgressed* (16x), *my covenant which I* (2x) = 66.

Idolatrous Followers

"And it came to pass, when the judge was dead, that they returned, and corrupted themselves more than their fathers, in following other GODS to SERVE them, and to BOW DOWN unto them; they ceased not from their own doings, nor from their stubborn way" (Judg. 2:19). The Old Testament combination *in following* (2x), *other gods* (63x) *to serve them and to bow down unto them* (1x) = 66.

66th Verse of Judges

"And the children of Israel did evil in the sight of the LORD, and forgat the LORD their God, and SERVED Baalim and the GROVES" (Judg. 3:7). The phrase *in the sight of the* occurs 66 times in the OT Narrative.

Idolatrous Altars

The Lord gave Gideon an initiation test. "And it came to pass the same night, that the LORD said unto him, Take thy father's young bullock, even the second bullock of seven years old, and throw down the altar of BAAL that thy father hath, and cut down the GROVE that is by it" (Judg. 6:25).

> The phrase *the altar* is mentioned in 66 verses of the OTN.
> The phrase *altar of* occurs 66 times in the Old Testament.

Idolatrous Rulers

The Israelites recognized God's hand upon Gideon. This is why they wanted to create a dynastic line through him. "And Gideon said unto them, I will not rule over you, neither shall my son rule over you: the LORD shall rule over you" (Judg. 8:23). The reason God wanted to maintain His theocracy over Israel was that earthly kings were prone to lead their people into idolatry. The word *rule* occurs 66 times in the Bible.

Idolatrous Object

Gideon's initial reservation to become a king may have come from his own understanding that he, like his father, was prone to worship idols. Gideon stood firm in his refusal to become king, but it seems he set himself up to be a spiritual high priest over them. This was an unsanctioned thing to do. From his portion of the Midianite spoils, even of the "ornaments, and collars, and purple raiment that was on the kings of Midian, and beside the chains that were about their camels' necks . . . Gideon made an EPHOD thereof, and put it in his city, even in Ophrah: and all Israel went thither a whoring after it: which thing became a snare unto Gideon, and to his house" (Judg. 8:26b-27). Rather than have the people come directly to him for spiritual discernment he set up the ephod as an idol and had the people seek it out and pray before it. Again the OT Narrative combination *they went* (61 vs) and *a whoring* (5 vs) = 66 verses. Again the word *it* occurs 6066 times outside the apocalyptic 66th book of the Bible.

Idolatrous Nations

"And the children of Israel did evil again in the sight of the LORD, and SERVED Baalim, and Ashtaroth, and the GODS of Syria, and the GODS of Zidon, and the GODS of Moab, and the GODS of the children of Ammon, and the GODS of the Philistines, and forsook the LORD, and SERVED not him" (Judg. 10:6). The Judges combination *the children of Israel* (60x), *did evil again in the sight of the LORD* (3x), *and served Baalim* (3x) = 66. The word *again* is mentioned in 266 chapters of the Old Testament.

Philistine Lords Worship Dagon for His Victory

"Then the lords of the Philistines gathered them together for to offer a great sacrifice unto DAGON their GOD, and to rejoice: for they said, Our GOD hath delivered Samson our enemy into our hand. And when the people saw him, they PRAISED their GOD: for they said, Our GOD hath delivered into our hands our enemy, and the destroyer of our country, which slew many of us" (Judg. 16:23-24). Again the phrase *the people* occurs 66 times in Joshua. Again the worship-related word *praise* is mentioned in 66 chapters of the Wisdom Books.

Micah's House of Images

"And when he had restored the eleven hundred shekels of silver to his mother, his mother said, I had wholly dedicated the silver unto the LORD from my hand for my son, to make a GRAVEN IMAGE and a MOLTEN IMAGE: now therefore I will restore it unto thee. Yet he restored the money unto his mother; and his mother took two hundred shekels of silver, and gave them to the founder, who made thereof a GRAVEN IMAGE and a MOLTEN IMAGE: and they were in the house of Micah" (Judg. 17:3-4). The phrase *in the house* occurs 166 times in the Bible. Again the word *silver* is mentioned in 66 verses of the Law.

Idolatrous Houses

"Then answered the five men that went to spy out the country of Laish, and said unto their brethren, Do ye know that there is in these houses an EPHOD, and TERAPHIM, and a GRAVEN IMAGE, and a MOLTEN IMAGE? now therefore consider what ye have to do" (Judg. 18:14). The phrase *do ye* is mentioned in 66 verses of the Bible.

Idolatrous Priests

The Danites were passing through. "And these went into Micah's house, and fetched the CARVED IMAGE, the EPHOD, and the TERAPHIM, and the MOLTEN IMAGE. Then said the priest unto them, What do ye?" (Judg. 18:18) Teraphim were figurines depicting human forms. These were commonly made of clay and served as a person's household gods. Teraphim is derived from the word *rapha* meaning healer. The word *priest* is mentioned in 66 verses of the paired books Numbers and Deuteronomy. Again the phrase *do ye* is mentioned in 66 verses of the Bible.

Idolatrous Danites

"And they built a city, and dwelt therein. And they called the name of the city Dan. . . . And the children of Dan set up the GRAVEN IMAGE: and Jonathan, the son of Gershom, the son of Manasseh, he and his sons were priests to the tribe of Dan until the day of the captivity of the land. And they set them up Micah's GRAVEN IMAGE, which he made, all the time that the house of God was in Shiloh" (Judg. 18:28d-29c, 30-31).

Modern archaeology has uncovered evidence of this unique Israelite cult worship: a large four-horned altar, an olive-oil press for carrying out libations, and several small incense shovels. The Danites wanted to worship Jehovah in their own way, but this was strictly forbidden and idolatrous in nature. The Bible combination *Dan* (64 vs), *Dannah* (1 v), *tribe of the Danites* (1 v) = 66 verses. Again the word *priest* is mentioned in 66 verses of the paired books Numbers and Deuteronomy.

Idolatrous Eyes

"In those days there was no king in Israel: every man did that which was right in his own eyes" (Judg. 21:25). The people's self-rule philosophy easily led them to delve into idolatry. The book of Judges consists of 18,966 words. Here, *eyes* is the 18,966th word of Judges.

> The phrase *his eyes* occurs 66 times in the Old Testament.
> The phrase *his own* occurs 166 times in the Old Testament.
> The phrase *his own* is mentioned in 66 chapters of the NT.

66th Verse of Ruth

"And he said unto the kinsman, Naomi, that is come again out of the country of Moab, selleth a parcel of land, which was our brother Elimelech's" (Ruth 4:3). This verse mentions the Israelite woman's sojourn in the land of idols as Moab worshiped Chemosh. The Old Testament combination *is come again out of* (1x), *the country* (65x) = 66.

The Lord's Holy Ark in Dagon's Idolatrous House

"When the Philistines took the ark of God, they brought it into the house of Dagon, and set it by Dagon. And when they of Ashdod arose early on the morrow, behold, Dagon was fallen upon his face to the earth before the ark of the LORD. And they took Dagon, and set him in his place again. And when they arose early on the morrow morning, behold, Dagon was fallen upon his face to the ground before the ark of the LORD; and the head of Dagon and both the palms of his hands were cut off upon the threshold; only the stump of Dagon was left to him" (1 Sam. 5:2-4).

The Lord desired to teach the Philistines a life lesson on the folly of idol worship. Just after the Lord smote Dagon's image He smote the Philistines with a plague. The joined phrases *when the Philistines took the ark of God, they brought it into the house of Dagon* consist of 66 characters!

Philistines Fashion Golden Images of Mice

"Then said they, What shall be the trespass offering which we shall return to him? They answered, Five golden emerods, and five golden mice, according to the number of the lords of the Philistines: for one plague was on you all, and on your lords. Wherefore ye shall make IMAGES of your emerods, and IMAGES of your mice that mar the land" (1 Sam. 6:4-5b). Again the word *golden* occurs 66 times in the Bible. Again the word *make* is mentioned in 66 verses of Ezekiel. The Old Testament combination *shall make* (64 chs), *images of your emrods* (1 ch), *images of your mice* (1 ch) = 66 chapters.

Israelites Put Away Images of Baalim & Ashtaroth

"And Samuel spake unto all the house of Israel, saying, If ye do return unto the LORD with all your hearts, then put away the strange GODS and Ashtaroth from among you, and prepare your hearts unto the LORD, and SERVE him only: and he will deliver you out of the hand of the

Philistines. Then the children of Israel did put away Baalim and Ashtaroth, and SERVED the LORD only" (1 Sam. 7:3-4). The Old Testament combination *then put away the* (1x), *strange* (65x) = 66. The Old Testament combination *put away* (37x), *Baalim* (18x), *Ashtaroth* (11x) = 66.

Idols Are Vain Things

Samuel warned the people about choosing an earthly king to rule over them. "And turn ye not aside: for then should ye go after vain things, which cannot profit nor deliver; for they are vain" (1 Sam. 12:21). From Genesis to the Gospels the word *vain* is mentioned in 66 chapters.

Stubbornness Is Akin to Idolatry

Samuel said to Saul, "For rebellion is as the sin of witchcraft, and stubbornness is as iniquity and IDOLATRY. Because thou hast rejected the word of the LORD, he hath also rejected thee from being king" (1 Sam. 15:23). This verse presents the Old Testament's only occurrence of the singular word idolatry. The *d* in idolatry is the 66th letter in this idol-worshiping verse. The Old Testament combination *iniquity* (160 chs), *stubbornness* (2 chs), *stubborn* (4 chs) = 166 chapters.

A Large Heavy Image

"And Michal took an IMAGE, and laid it in the bed, and put a pillow of goats' hair for his bolster, and covered it with a cloth" (1 Sam. 19:13). Here the idol-related keyword *image* is the 212,566th word of the Bible.

King Saul Rids the Land of Witches & Wizards

"Now Samuel was dead, and all Israel had lamented him, and buried him in Ramah, even in his own city. And Saul had put away those that had familiar spirits, and the wizards, out of the land" (1 Sam. 28:3). It seems that Saul took Samuel's advice to the next level by eliminating idolatrous practices such as wizardry and witchcraft in Israel. From Genesis to First Samuel the combination *those that had familiar spirits* (1x), *and the wizards* (2x), *out of the land* (63x) = 66.

David Burned the Philistines' Idols

When the Philistines heard that David now wore the crown they sought to come against Israel but were sorely defeated. "And there they left their IMAGES, and David and his men burned them" (2 Sam. 5:21). The Old Testament combination *burned* (61 chs) and *their images* (5 chs) = 66 chapters.

The Giant's Digital Identification of 66

"And there was yet a battle in Gath, where was a man of great stature, that had on every hand SIX fingers, and on every foot SIX toes, four and twenty in number; and he also was born to the giant" (2 Sam. 21:20). This giant was undoubtedly idolized by the Philistines because they felt the gods were in favor of him. When this giant held up both hands he made a visual display of the number 66 with all of his digits. Again the word *six* occurs 66 times in the Law.

God Warns Solomon against Turning Idolatrous

"But if ye shall at all turn from following me, ye or your children, and will not keep my commandments and my statutes which I have set before you, but go and SERVE other GODS, and WORSHIP them: Then will I cut off Israel out of the land which I have given them; and this house, which I have hallowed for my name, will I cast out of my sight; and Israel shall be a proverb and a byword among all people" (1 Kings 9:6-7). Again the word *them* occurs 466 times in Jeremiah.

9066ᵗʰ Verse of the Bible

"And Hiram <u>sent to the king</u> SIXSCORE talents <u>of gold</u>" (1 Kings 9:14). Hiram was an idol-worshiping king, but he loved David and Solomon. The name Hiram means exaltation of life. The Bible combination *to king Solomon* (7x) and *of gold* (159x) = 166. Again the word *gold* occurs naturally 166 times in the OT Narrative.

Solomon's 666 Talents of Gold

"Now the weight of <u>gold</u> that came to Solomon in one year was SIX HUNDRED THREESCORE AND SIX talents of <u>gold</u>" (1 Kings 10:14). This verse fits our third definition of idolatry: an immoderate attachment or devotion to something.

Solomon loved gold. In some respects Solomon stands as a type of the antichrist because he was the first king in Jerusalem to set up an abominable idol. The world brought to Jerusalem their annual estimation of Solomon's worth. A small part of the world idolizing this man can be seen in the Queen of Sheba's awe and wonder of him. Solomon's annual levy of the nations was in reality an idolatrous offering to himself as the most powerful king in the earth. Solomon could not help but think of himself more highly than he ought; thus he idolized himself. This fact can be observed by his owning 700 wives and 300 second-class wives. The number 666 is not a multiple of 66, but it is a personification of 66 and idolatry. The combination *threescore and six* (5x), *sixty and six* (1x) = 6, a factor of 66. Again the word *six* occurs 66 times in the Law. Again the word *gold* occurs naturally 166 times in the OT Narrative.

Solomon's Idolatry

"For it came to pass, when <u>Solomon</u> was old, that his wives turned away his heart after <u>other</u> GODS: and <u>his heart</u> <u>was not</u> perfect with the LORD his God, as was the heart of David his father" (1 Kings 11:4). The name *Solomon('s)* is mentioned in 266 verses of the Old Testament. Again the word *other* is mentioned in 66 chapters of the Law. The New Testament combination *his heart* (13x), *was not* (53x) = 66.

Solomon's Introduction of Idolatry to Jerusalem

"For <u>Solomon</u> went after Ashtoreth the GODDESS of the Zidonians, and after Milcom the abomination of the Ammonites. And Solomon did evil in the sight of the LORD, and went not fully after the LORD, as did David his father. Then did Solomon build an HIGH PLACE for Chemosh, the abomination of Moab, in the <u>hill</u> that is before <u>Jerusalem</u>, and for Molech, the abomination of the children of Ammon" (1 Kings 11:5-7). Solomon did not bring idolatrous practices into Jerusalem but rather just outside its eastern border. Again the name *Solomon('s)* is mentioned in 266 verses of the Old Testament. The Old Testament singular combination *hill* (64 vs), *hill's* (1 v), *hill top* (1 v) = 66 verses.

> The name *Jerusalem* is in 266 verses from Genesis to Second Chronicles.
> The name *Jerusalem* occurs naturally 666 times in the Old Testament.
> The phrase *to Jerusalem* occurs 66 times in the OT Narrative.
> The phrase *of Jerusalem* occurs 166 times in the Bible.

Because They Worshiped Ashtoreth

The prophet told Jeroboam about Solomon's coming judgment. "Behold, I will rend the kingdom out of the hand of Solomon . . . Because that they have forsaken me, and have <u>WORSHIPPED</u> Ashtoreth the GODDESS of the Zidonians, Chemosh the GOD of the Moabites, and Milcom the GOD <u>of the children of</u> Ammon, and have not walked in my ways, to do that which is right in mine eyes, and to keep my statutes and my judgments, as did David his father" (1 Kings 11:33). Again all forms of the word *worship* occur 198 times in the Bible, a multiple of 66. Again the phrase *of the children of* occurs 366 times in the Old Testament.

King Jeroboam's Two Golden Calves

"Whereupon <u>the king</u> took counsel, and made two <u>CALVES</u> of gold, and said unto them, It is too much for you to go up to Jerusalem: behold thy GODS, O Israel, which brought thee up out of the land of Egypt. And he set <u>the</u> one in <u>Beth-el</u>, and <u>the</u> other put he in <u>Dan</u>" (1 Kings 12:28-29). King Jeroboam greatly increased idolatry in the land by sanctioning the worship of a golden calf. The title *the king* occurs 166 times in Second Kings. The Bible combination *the calves* (7x), *of gold* (159x) = 166. The name *Beth-el* occurs 66 times in the Bible. The Bible combination *Dan* (64 vs) and *golden calves* (2 vs) = 66 verses. Again the word *gold* occurs naturally 166 times in the OT Narrative.

466th Verse of First Kings

"And Jeroboam ordained a feast in the eighth month, on the fifteenth day of the month, like unto the feast that is in Judah, and he offered upon the altar. So did he in Beth-el, sacrificing unto the CALVES that he had made: and he placed in Beth-el <u>the priests</u> of the <u>HIGH PLACES</u> which he had made" (1 Kings 12:32). The title *the priests* occurs naturally 266 times in the Bible. Again the term *high places* is mentioned in 66 chapters of the Bible.

Jeroboam's Idolatrous Altar

"And, behold, there came a man of God out of Judah by the word of the LORD unto <u>Beth-el</u>: and Jeroboam stood by <u>the altar</u> to burn incense. And he cried against the altar . . . and said, O <u>altar, altar</u>, thus saith the LORD; Behold, a child shall be born unto the house of David, Josiah by name; and upon thee shall he offer <u>the priests</u> of the HIGH PLACES that burn incense upon thee, and men's <u>bones</u> shall be burnt upon thee. And he gave a sign the same day, saying, This is the sign which the LORD hath spoken; Behold, <u>the altar</u> shall be rent, and the ashes that are upon it shall be poured out" (1 Kings 13:1-3).

Again the name *Beth-el* occurs 66 times in the Bible. Again the phrase *the altar* is mentioned in 66 verses of the OT Narrative. Again the title *the priests* occurs naturally 266 times in the Bible. The word *bones* is mentioned in 66 chapters of the Bible.

The Lord's Zeal to Destroy Jeroboam's Idolatry

"After this thing Jeroboam returned not from his evil way, but made again of the lowest of the people priests of the HIGH PLACES: whosoever would, he consecrated him, and he became one of the priests of the HIGH PLACES. . . . And this thing became sin unto the house of Jeroboam, even to cut it off, and <u>to destroy</u> it from off the face of the earth" (1 Kings 13:33-34). The phrase *to destroy* is mentioned in 66 verses of the Old Testament.

Jeroboam's Idolatry Receives Divine Judgment

The prophet told Jeraboam's wife to give him the following message: "<u>But hast done evil above</u>

all that were before thee: for thou hast gone and made thee other GODS, and MOLTEN IMAGES, to provoke me to anger, and hast cast me behind thy back: Therefore, behold, I will bring evil upon the house of Jeroboam, and will cut off. . . . Him that dieth of Jeroboam in the city shall the dogs eat; and him that dieth in the field shall the fowls of the air eat: for the LORD hath spoken it" (1 Kings 14:9-10a, 11). The Bible combination *but hast done* (1x), *done evil* (11x), *above all* (53x), *that were before thee* (1x) = 66. The present-tense Bible phrases *be cut off* (59 vs) and *is cut off* (7 vs) = 66 verses.

The Idolatrous Kings of Israel & Judah

"For the LORD shall smite Israel . . . and shall scatter them beyond the river, because they have made their GROVES, provoking the LORD to anger. And he shall give Israel up because of the sins of Jeroboam, who did sin, and who made Israel to sin. . . . And the rest of the acts of Jeroboam, how he warred, and how he reigned, behold, they are written in the book of the chronicles of the kings of Israel" (1 Kings 14:15-16, 19). Jeroboam was the first northern king to introduce idol worship in the land, but all his successors would work to reinforce the observance of idolatry. All the northern kings of Israel were guilty of idolatry. Even Saul committed an idolatrous act when he enquired of the Lord by a familiar spirit. Half of Judah's kings were also guilty of being idolaters.

The word *kingdom* is mentioned in 166 verses of the Old Testament.
The title *king* is mentioned in 366 chapters of the Old Testament.
The title *king of* occurs 266 times in First and Second Kings.
The title *king of the* is mentioned in 66 verses of the Bible.
The title *king of Judah* is mentioned in 66 chapters of Old Testament.
The title *the king* occurs 166 times in Second Kings.
The title *the king* occurs 966 times in the OT Narrative.
The title *the king of* occurs 66 times in Joshua and Judges.
The title *the kings* occurs 66 times in First and Second Kings.
The title *of the king* occurs 66 times in the OT Narrative.
The title *of the kings* occurs 66 times in the OT Narrative.
The title *of the kings of* occurs 66 times in the Bible.
The title *all the kings of Israel* (2x), *over Israel* (64x) = 66x in the Bible.

Rehoboam's Idolatry

"And Rehoboam the son of Solomon reigned in Judah. . . . And Judah did evil in the sight of the LORD, and they provoked him to jealousy with their sins which they had committed, above all that their fathers had done. For they also built them HIGH PLACES, and IMAGES, and GROVES, on every high hill, and under every green tree" (1 Kings 14:21a, 22-23). The OT Narrative combination *and Judah did* (1x), *evil in the sight of the LORD* (64x), *and they provoked him to jealousy* (1x) = 66. The word *sins* is mentioned in 166 verses of the Bible. Here the underlined word *and* is the 258,366th word of the Bible; it sits between the idolatrous words images and groves.

Abijam's Idolatry

"Abijam over Judah. Three years reigned he in Jerusalem. . . . And he walked in all the sins of his father, which he had done before him: and his heart was not perfect with the LORD his God" (1

Kings 15:1b-3c). Again the word *sins* is mentioned in 166 verses of the Bible. The phrase *his father/'s/s/s'* is mentioned in 166 collective verses of the OT Narrative.

King Asa Cleanses the Land of Idolatry

"And he took away the sodomites out of the land, and removed all the IDOLS that his fathers had <u>made</u>. And also Maachah his mother, even her he removed from being queen, because she had <u>made</u> an IDOL in a grove; and Asa destroyed her IDOL, and burnt it by the brook Kidron" (1 Kings 15:12-13). Again the word *made* is mentioned in 266 verses of the New Testament.

Nadab's Idolatry

"And Nadab the son of Jeroboam began to reign over Israel . . . and reigned <u>over Israel</u> two years. <u>And he did evil in the sight of the LORD</u>, <u>and walked in the</u> <u>way of his father</u>, <u>and in his sin</u> <u>wherewith he</u> <u>made Israel</u> <u>to sin</u>" (1 Kings 15:25-26). The OT Narrative combination *and he did evil in the sight of the LORD and* (3x), *and walked in the* (6x), *way of his father* (2x), *and in his sin* (4x), *wherewith he* (9x), *made Israel* (20x), *to sin* (22x) = 66.

Baasha's Idolatry

"And Baasha . . . of the house of Issachar . . . smote . . . Nadab . . . and reigned in his stead. . . . <u>And he did evil in the sight of the LORD, and walked in the way of Jeroboam, and in his sin</u> <u>wherewith he made Israel to sin</u>" (1 Kings 15:27-28, 34). Baasha's idolatry is summarized in the underlined verse, the 566th verse of First Kings.

Elah's Idolatry

"<u>Began Elah the son of</u> <u>Baasha to reign</u> <u>over Israel</u> in Tirzah, two years. And his servant Zimri, captain of half his chariots, conspired against him, as he was in Tirzah, drinking himself drunk in the house of Arza steward of his house in Tirzah. And Zimri went in and smote him, and killed him . . . For all the sins of Baasha, and the sins of Elah his son, by which they sinned, and by which they made Israel to sin, in provoking the LORD God of Israel to anger with their vanities" (1 Kings 16:8-10a, 13). The Bible combination *began Elah the son of* (1x), *Baasha to reign* (1x), *over Israel* (64x) = 66.

The phrase *to reign* occurs 66 times in the OT Narrative.
The phrase *to reign* is mentioned in 66 verses of the OTN.

Zimri's Idolatry

"Zimri reign seven days in Tirzah. . . . And it came to pass, when Zimri saw that the city was taken, that he went into the palace of the king's house, and burnt the king's house over him with fire, and died, For his sins which he sinned in doing evil in the sight of the LORD, in walking <u>in the way of Jeroboam</u>, <u>and in his sin which</u> <u>he did</u>, to make Israel to sin" (1 Kings 16:5b, 18-19). The First and Second Kings combination *in the way of Jeroboam* (4x), *and in his sin which* (1x), *he did* (61x) = 66.

Tibni's Idolatry

"Then were the people <u>of Israel</u> divided into two parts: half of the people followed Tibni the son of Ginath, to make him <u>king</u>; and half followed Omri. But the people that followed Omri prevailed against the people that followed Tibni the son of Ginath: so Tibni died" (1 Kings

16:21-22b). The narrative does not give us specific information of Tibni's idolatrous way while he reigned for more than four years, but we know that all Israel's kings were idol worshipers. Again the Bible combination *all the kings of Israel* (2x) and *over Israel* (64x) = 66.

Omri's Idolatry

"But Omri wrought evil in the eyes of the LORD, and did worse than all that were before him. For he walked in all the way of Jeroboam the son of Nebat, and in his sin wherewith he made Israel to sin, to provoke the LORD God of Israel to <u>anger</u> with their vanities" (1 Kings 16:25-26). The word *anger* occurs 66 times from Genesis to First Kings.

Ahab's Idolatry

"And <u>Ahab</u> <u>the son of Omri did evil</u> <u>in the sight of the LORD</u> <u>above all that were before him</u>. And it came to pass, as if it had been a light thing for him to walk in the sins of Jeroboam the son of Nebat, that he took to wife Jezebel the daughter of Ethbaal king of the Zidonians, and went and SERVED BAAL, and WORSHIPPED him. And he reared up <u>an altar for BAAL in the house of BAAL</u>, which he had built in Samaria. And Ahab made a GROVE; and Ahab did more to provoke the LORD God of Israel to anger than <u>all the kings of Israel</u> that were before him" (1 Kings 16:30-33).

The name *Ahab* is mentioned in 66 verses of First and Second Kings. The OT Narrative combination *the son of Omri did evil* (1x), *in the sight of the LORD* (64x), *above all that were before him* (1x) = 66. The Bible combination *an altar for* (2x), *Baal* (63x), *in the house of Baal* (1x) = 66. Again the Bible combination *all the kings of Israel* (2x) and *over Israel* (64x) = 66. Again the phrase *in the house* occurs 166 times in the Bible.

Elijah Seeks to Stamp out Baal Worship

"And Elijah came unto all the people, and said, <u>How long halt ye between two opinions? if the LORD be God, follow him: but if BAAL, then follow him</u>. And the people answered him not a word. Then said Elijah unto the people, I, even I only, remain a prophet of the LORD; but <u>BAAL'S</u> <u>prophets</u> are four hundred and fifty men" (1 Kings 18:21-22). The northern tribes believed in Jehovah, but they exalted Baal over Him. They were guilty of syncretism, the attempted union of different or opposing religions. When the fire from heaven fell on Jehovah's altar the northern tribes quickly acknowledged that Jehovah was Chief among the gods. The Bible combination *how long halt ye between two opinions* (1x), *if the LORD be God follow him but if* (1x), *Baal* (63x), *then follow him* (1x) = 66. The Old Testament combination *Baal's* (1 ch), *prophets* (65 chs) = 66 chapters.

Elijah Slays the Idolatrous Prophets of Baal

"<u>And Elijah said unto them, Take the prophets of BAAL; let not one of them escape.</u> And they took <u>them</u>: and Elijah brought <u>them</u> down to the brook Kishon, and slew <u>them</u> there" (1 Kings 18:40). The sentence *and Elijah said unto them, take the prophets of BAAL; let not one of them escape.* consists of 66 characters! Here the word *prophets* is the 19,666th word of First Kings. Again the word *them* occurs 466 times in Jeremiah.

Jezebel Hears of the Idolatrous Prophet's Mass Execution

"And Ahab told Jezebel all that Elijah had done, and withal <u>how</u> he had slain all the prophets with the sword" (1 Kings 19:1). Here the word *how* is the 262,666th word of the Bible.

Jezebel's Idolatry

"Then Jezebel sent a messenger unto Elijah, saying, So let <u>the GODS</u> do to me, and more also, if I make not thy life as the life of one of them by to morrow about this time" (1 Kings 19:2). Jezebel was a wicked and idolatrous queen, a Zidonian by birth. She lived her royal life by her gods' decree. Again the term *the god/s* occurs 66 combined times in the Bible.

Ahab & Jezebel's Idolatry

"But there was none like unto Ahab, which did sell himself to work wickedness in the sight of the LORD, whom <u>Jezebel</u> his wife stirred up. And he did very abominably in following IDOLS, according to all things as did the Amorites, whom the LORD cast out before the children of Israel" (1 Kings 21:25-26). Here *Jezebel* is the 265,666th word of the Bible.

Ahaziah's Idolatry

"Ahaziah the son of Ahab began <u>to reign</u> over Israel in Samaria . . . and reigned two years over Israel. And he did evil in the sight of the LORD, and walked in the way of his father, and in the way of his mother, and in the way of Jeroboam the son of Nebat, who made Israel to sin: For he SERVED BAAL, and WORSHIPPED him, and provoked to <u>anger</u> the LORD God of Israel, according to all that his father had done" (1 Kings 22:51-53). Again the phrase *to reign* occurs 66 times in the OT Narrative. Again the word *serve* occurs 66 times in the Law. This verse presents the Bible's 66th occurrence of the word *anger*, and it relates to God's anger over a king's idolatry.

Ahaziah's Idolatrous Enquiry of Baal-Zebub

"And Ahaziah fell down through a lattice in his upper chamber that was in Samaria, and was sick: and he sent messengers, and said unto them, <u>Go, ENQUIRE OF BAAL-ZEBUB, the GOD of Ekron whether I shall recover of this disease</u>" (2 Kings 1:2-4c). Ahaziah's idolatrous request consists of 66 letters!

Jehoram's Idolatry

"Now <u>Jehoram the son of Ahab began to reign over Israel in Samaria</u> the eighteenth year of Jehoshaphat king of Judah, and reigned twelve years. <u>And he wrought evil in the sight of the LORD</u>; but not like his father, and like his mother: for he put away the IMAGE of BAAL that his father had made. Nevertheless he cleaved unto the sins of Jeroboam the son of Nebat, which made Israel to sin; he departed not therefrom" (2 Kings 3:1-3). The Old Testament combination *Jehoram* (23x), *Joram* (27x), *the son of Ahab* (10x), *began to reign over Israel in Samaria* (5x), *and he wrought evil in the sight of the LORD* (1x) = 66.

9666th Verse of the Bible

"In this thing the LORD pardon thy servant, that when my master goeth into the house of RIMMON to WORSHIP there, and he leaneth on my hand, and I BOW myself in the house of RIMMON: when I BOW DOWN myself <u>in the house</u> of Rimmon, the LORD pardon thy servant in this thing" (2 Kings 5:18). Naaman's healing led to his instant conversion to Jehovah worship. Here he reveals his repentant heart by apologizing for his continued service to the idolatrous king of Syria. Rimmon was Damascus' local representation of BAAL-HADAD, her chief Aramean deity, the god of storm, rain, thunder, and sun. Again the phrase *in the house* occurs 166 times in the Bible.

Baal Worship Destroyed in Israel

"And it came to pass, as soon as he had made an end of offering the burnt offering, that Jehu said to the guard and to the captains, Go in, and slay them; let none come forth. And they smote them with the edge of the sword; and the guard and the captains cast them out, and went to the city of the house of BAAL. And they brought forth the IMAGES out of the house of BAAL, and burned them. And they brake down the IMAGE of BAAL, and brake down the house of BAAL, and made it a draught house unto this day. Thus Jehu destroyed BAAL out of Israel" (2 Kings 10:25-28).

The underlined idol-worshiping verse number twenty-five consists of 66 words! Again the word *destroyed* occurs 66 times in the OT Narrative.

Jehu's Idolatry

"Howbeit from the sins of Jeroboam the son of Nebat, who made Israel to sin, Jehu departed not from after them, to wit, the GOLDEN CALVES that were in Beth-el, and that were in Dan" (2 Kings 10:29). The two golden calves had originally been fashioned as objects honoring Jehovah. This was done to prevent the northern tribes from traveling to the religious center in Judea. Again the word *sins* is mentioned in 166 verses of the Bible. Again the Bible combination *Dan* (64 vs) and *golden calves* (2 vs) = 66 verses. Again the name *Beth-el* occurs 66 times in the Bible.

Athaliah's Idolatry:
Jehoiada Destroys Baal Worship in Jerusalem

Athaliah's six-year reign of terror and cult worship in Jerusalem had just come to an end with her execution. The evil queen and daughter of Jezebel had been slain through the high priest's conspiracy. "And Jehoiada made a covenant between the LORD and the king and the people, that they should be the LORD'S people; between the king also and the people. And all the people of the land went into the house of BAAL, and brake it down; his altars and his IMAGES brake they in pieces thoroughly, and slew Mattan the priest of BAAL before the altars. And the priest appointed officers over the house of the LORD" (2 Kings 11:17-18). The Old Testament combination *in the house of Baal* (1x) and *the priest* (365x) = 366. Again the phrase *the altar* is mentioned in 66 verses of the OT Narrative. The phrase *in pieces* is mentioned in 66 verses of the Bible.

High Places Not Taken away in Judah

Joash did that which was good in God's eyes. "But the HIGH PLACES were not taken away: the people still sacrificed and burnt incense in the HIGH PLACES" (2 Kings 12:3). The high places were unsanctioned places used to worship Jehovah. These places remained a temptation wherein idolatrous practices could be reintroduced. Most Judean kings did not bother to take them away because they were usually very quickly put back into use. Again the term *high places* is mentioned in 66 chapters of the Bible. Again the phrase *the people* occurs 66 times in Joshua. The phrase *taken away* is mentioned in 66 verses of the Bible.

Jehoahaz's Idolatry

"Jehoahaz the son of Jehu began to reign over Israel in Samaria, and reigned seventeen years. And he did that which was evil in the sight of the LORD, and followed the sins of Jeroboam the son of Nebat, which made Israel to sin; he departed not therefrom" (2 Kings 13:1b-2). Again the Bible combination *all the kings of Israel* (2x) and *over Israel* (64x) = 66. Again the word *sins* is mentioned in 166 verses of the Bible.

Jehoash's Idolatry

And then "began <u>Jehoash</u> the son of Jehoahaz to reign over Israel in Samaria, and reigned sixteen years. And he did that which was evil in the sight of the LORD; he departed not from all the sins of Jeroboam the son of Nebat, who made Israel sin: but he walked therein. . . . And Joash slept with his fathers. . . . and <u>Joash</u> was buried in Samaria with the kings of Israel" (2 Kings 13:10b-11, 13). The alternate Bible names *Jehoash* (49x) and *Joash* (17x) = 66.

Jeroboam II's Idolatry

"Jeroboam the son of Joash king of Israel began <u>to reign</u> in Samaria, and reigned forty and one years. And he did that which was evil in the sight of the LORD: he departed not from all the <u>sins</u> of Jeroboam the son of Nebat, who made Israel to sin" (2 Kings 14:23b-24). Again the phrase *to reign* occurs 66 times in the OT Narrative. Again the word *sins* is mentioned in 166 verses of the Bible.

Zachariah's Idolatry

And then "did <u>Zachariah the son of</u> <u>Jeroboam reign</u> <u>over Israel</u> in Samaria six months. And he did that which was evil in the sight of the LORD, as his fathers had done: he departed not from the <u>sins</u> of Jeroboam the son of Nebat, who made Israel to sin" (2 Kings 15:8b-9). The Bible combination *Zachariah the son of* (1x), *Jeroboam reign* (1x), *over Israel* (64x) = 66.

Shallum's Idolatry

"Shallum the son of Jabesh began <u>to reign</u>. . . . and he reigned a full month in Samaria. For Menahem the son of Gadi went up from Tirzah, and came to Samaria, and smote Shallum . . . in Samaria, and slew him, and reigned in his stead" (2 Kings 15:13-14). This northern king was an idolater like all those before him, yet the narrative gives us no details because his reign was so short-lived. Speaking of short-lived, the full account of Shallum's reign is covered in verses ten through fifteen and consists of 165 words—one word short-lived of 166. Again the phrase *to reign* occurs 66 times in the OT Narrative.

Menahem's Idolatry

And then "began <u>Menahem the son of Gadi</u> to reign over Israel, and reigned ten years in Samaria. And he did that which was evil <u>in the sight of the LORD</u>: he departed not all his days from the <u>sins</u> of Jeroboam the son of Nebat, who made Israel to sin" (2 Kings 15:17b-18). Again the word *sins* is mentioned in 166 verses of the Bible. The OT Narrative combination *Menahem the son of Gadi* (2x), *in the sight of the LORD* (64x) = 66.

Pekahiah's Idolatry

"<u>Pekahiah his son reigned in his stead</u> . . . <u>over Israel</u> <u>in Samaria, and reigned two years</u>. And he did that which was evil in the sight of the LORD: he departed not from the sins of Jeroboam the son of Nebat, who made Israel to sin" (2 Kings 15:22b-24). The Bible combination *Pekahiah his son reigned in his stead* (1x), *over Israel* (64x), *in Samaria and reigned two years* (1x) = 66.

Israel's Idolatrous Kings Routinely Assassinated

"But <u>Pekah</u> the son of Remaliah, <u>a captain of his</u>, <u>conspired against him</u>, <u>and smote him in</u>

Samaria, in the palace of the king's house, with Argob and Arieh, and with him fifty men of the Gileadites: and he killed him, <u>and reigned in his room</u>" (2 Kings 15:25). Pekah assassinated Pekiah and was afterward himself assassinated by Hoshea. The OT Narrative combination *Pekah* (10x), *a captain of his* (1x), *conspired against him* (9x), *and smote him* (7x), *in Samaria* (33x), *and reigned in his room/stead* (6x) = 66.

Pekah's Idolatry

"<u>Pekah the son of Remaliah began to reign</u> over Israel <u>in Samaria, and reigned twenty years</u>. And he did that which was evil in the sight of the LORD: he departed not from the sins of Jeroboam the son of Nebat, who made Israel to sin" (2 Kings 15:27b-28). The Bible combination *Pekah the son of Remaliah began to reign* (1x), *over Israel* (64x), *in Samaria and reigned twenty years* (1x) = 66.

9966th Verse of the Bible

"Twenty years old was Ahaz when he began <u>to reign,</u> and reigned sixteen years in Jerusalem, and did not that which was right in the sight of the LORD his God, like David his father" (2 Kings 16:2). Again the phrase *to reign* occurs 66 times in the OT Narrative.

Hoshea's Idolatry

And then "began Hoshea the son of Elah <u>to reign in Samaria</u> over Israel nine years. And he did that which was evil in the sight of the LORD, but not as the kings of Israel that were before him" (2 Kings 17:1b-2). Hoshea was the last northern king. The Bible combination *to reign in Samaria* (2x) and *over Israel* (64x) = 66.

Assyria's Idolatrous Worship of Asshur

"And the covert for the sabbath that they had built in the house, and the king's entry without, turned he from the house of the LORD for the king of <u>Assyria</u>" (2 Kings 16:18). Because the evil Judean king Ahaz wanted the Assyrians to protect him against Israel and Syria, he set aside a special place for the Assyrian king to worship his god inside Jerusalem's Temple precinct. The Assyrian's chief god was Ashur, god of the mountains and sky. They also worshiped Marduk. The name *Assyria* occurs 66 times in the OT Narrative.

Israel Carried Away into Permanent Captivity for Her Idolatry

"For they SERVED IDOLS, <u>whereof</u> the LORD had said unto them, Ye shall not do this thing . . . . And they rejected his statutes, and his covenant that he made with their fathers, and his testimonies which he testified against them; and they followed vanity, and became <u>vain</u>, and went after the heathen that were round about them. . . . <u>And they left all the commandments of the LORD their God, and made them MOLTEN IMAGES, even TWO CALVES, and made a GROVE, and WORSHIPPED all the host of heaven, and SERVED BAAL</u>. And they caused their sons and their daughters to pass through the fire, and used divination and enchantments, and sold themselves to do evil in the sight of the LORD, to provoke him to anger" (2 Kings 17:12, 15ab, 16-17).

Here the word *whereof* is the 282,366th word of the Bible, and it refers to the northern tribes' idolatry. Again from Genesis to the Gospels the word *vain* is mentioned in 66 chapters. The underlined words indicate the 466th verse of Second Kings, and the verse expressly pertains to idol worship. Again the phrase *the host of* is mentioned in 66 verses of the Old Testament.

Hezekiah Breaks the Brazen Serpent in Pieces

"He removed the HIGH PLACES, and brake the IMAGES, and cut down the GROVES, and brake in pieces the BRASEN SERPENT that Moses had made: for unto those days the children of Israel did burn incense to it: and he called it Nehushtan" (2 Kings 18:4). Here we discover that a thing of holy reverence was turned into a thing of unholy religion. The word "Nehushtan" means a thing made of brass or copper. Again the phrase *of brass* occurs 66 times in Scripture. Again the word *it* occurs 6066 times outside the apocalyptic 66th book of the Bible. Again the phrase *in pieces* is mentioned in 66 verses of the Bible.

Idols—The Works of Men's Hands

"And have cast their GODS into the fire: for they were no GODS, but the work of men's hands, wood and stone: therefore they have destroyed them" (2 Kings 19:18). Hezekiah speaks of Assyria destroying other nations' idols. The following seal includes words such as "work," "works," "workers," "workmen," "workmanship," and "working": The phrase *the work* of* is mentioned in 166 verses of the Bible. The word *men* is mentioned in 166 chapters of the New Testament. Again the Law combination *wood* (61x), *and stone* (5x) = 66.

The word *hands* is mentioned in 66 verses of the Law.
The word *hands* is mentioned in 66 chapters of Major/Minor Prophets.

Judah's Idolatrous Kings

"And the LORD spake by his servants the prophets, saying, Because Manasseh king of Judah hath done these abominations, and hath done wickedly above all that the Amorites did, which were before him, and hath made Judah also to sin with his IDOLS: Therefore thus saith the LORD God of Israel, Behold, I am bringing such evil upon Jerusalem and Judah, that whosoever heareth of it, both his ears shall tingle" (2 Kings 21:10-12). Again the title *king of Judah* is mentioned in 66 chapters of the Old Testament.

Manasseh's Idolatry Described in 566 Words

"Manasseh was twelve years old when he began to reign, and reigned fifty and five years in Jerusalem. . . . And he did that which was evil in the sight of the LORD, after the abominations of the heathen. . . . And Manasseh slept with his fathers, and was buried in the garden of his own house, in the garden of Uzza: and Amon his son reigned in his stead" (2 Kings 21:1a, 2a, 18). The entirety of this historical passage on Manasseh's idolatry, verses one through eighteen, consists of 566 words.

Manasseh Turns the Temple into an Idolatrous Worship Center

"And he built altars in the house of the LORD, of which the LORD said, In Jerusalem will I put my name. And he built altars for all the host of heaven in the two courts of the house of the LORD" (2 Kings 21:4). Again the phrase *in the house* occurs 166 times in the Bible. Again the phrase *altar of* occurs 66 times in the Old Testament. Again the phrase *the host of* is mentioned in 66 verses of the Old Testament.

Idolatry Kindles God's Wrath

Huldah prophesied the Word of the Lord: "Because they have forsaken me, and have burned incense unto other GODS, that they might provoke me to anger with all the works of their hands;

therefore my wrath <u>shall be</u> <u>kindled</u> against this place, and shall not be quenched" (2 Kings 22:17). The Bible combination *and have burned incense unto* (3x), *other gods* (63x) = 66. The phrase *shall be* is mentioned in 666 chapters of the Bible. The word *kindled* occurs 66 times in Scripture.

Idols & Idolaters Removed from the Lord's Temple
"And the king commanded Hilkiah the high priest, and the priests of the second order, and the keepers of the door, to bring forth out of <u>the temple</u> of the LORD all the vessels that were <u>made</u> for <u>BAAL</u>, and for the <u>GROVE</u>, and for all the host of heaven: and he burned them without Jerusalem in the fields of Kidron, and carried the ashes of them unto Beth-el" (2 Kings 23:4). The phrase *the temple* occurs 66 times in the Old Testament! Again the word *made* is mentioned in 266 verses of the New Testament. The combination *Baal* (63x) and *made a grove* (3x) = 66.

Josiah Deposed the Idolatrous Priests
"And he put down <u>the</u> IDOLATROUS <u>priests</u>, whom the kings of Judah had ordained to burn incense in the high places in the cities of Judah, and in the places round about Jerusalem" (2 Kings 23:5a). Again the title *the priests* occurs naturally 266 times in the Bible.

Idolatrous Altars Turned to Dust
King Josiah wanted to rid Jerusalem and all Judea of idol worship. "And the altars that were on the top of the upper chamber of Ahaz, which the kings of Judah had made, and the altars which Manasseh had made in the two courts of the house of the LORD, did the king beat down, and brake them down from thence, and cast <u>the dust</u> of them into the brook Kidron" (2 Kings 23:12). Again the phrase *the dust* occurs 66 times in Scripture.

Josiah Deposed the Idolatrous Workers
"Moreover the workers with familiar spirits, and the wizards, and the images, and the IDOLS, <u>and all the abominations that were spied in the land of Judah and in Jerusalem,</u> did Josiah put away, that he might perform the words of the law which were written in the book that Hilkiah the priest found in the house of the LORD" (2 Kings 23:24). The clause *and all the abominations that were spied in the land of Judah and in Jerusalem,* consists of 66 characters!

666th Verse of Second Kings
"And Pharaoh-nechoh made Eliakim the son of Josiah king in the room of Josiah his father, and turned his name to Jehoiakim, and took Jehoahaz away: and he came to Egypt, and died there" (2 Kings 23:34). Jehoiakim was not godly like his father but was rather an idolater.

Northern Tribes Carried Away Because of Their Idolatry
"And <u>they</u> transgressed against the God of their fathers, and <u>went</u> <u>a whoring</u> after the GODS of <u>the people</u> of the land, whom God destroyed before them. And the God of Israel stirred up the spirit of Pul king of Assyria, and the spirit of Tilgath-pilneser king of Assyria, and he carried them away" (1 Chron. 5:25-26ab). Again the OT Narrative combination *they went* (61 vs), *a whoring* (5 vs) = 66 verses. Again the phrase *the people* occurs 66 times in Joshua.

The Idolatrous Temple of Dagon
"And they put his armour <u>in the house</u> of their GODS, and fastened his head in <u>the temple</u> of

DAGON" (1 Chron. 10:10). Again the phrase *in the house* occurs 166 times in the Bible. Again the phrase *the temple* occurs 66 times in the Old Testament. The *m* in temple is the 66th letter of this verse.

King Saul's Lone Episode of Idolatry

"So Saul died for his transgression which he <u>committed</u> against the LORD, even against the word of the LORD, which he kept not, and also for asking counsel of one that had a familiar spirit, to enquire of it; And enquired not of the LORD: therefore he slew him" (1 Chron. 10:13-14a). Again the word *committed* is mentioned in 66 chapters of the Bible.

King David Denounces Idolatry

David's psalm of thanksgiving denounced idolatry outright. "For great is the LORD, and greatly to be praised: he also is to be feared above all <u>GODS</u>. For all the <u>GODS</u> of <u>the people</u> are IDOLS: but the LORD made the heavens" (1 Chron. 16:25-26). Again the word *gods* occurs naturally 66 times in the Law. Again the phrase *the people* occurs 66 times in Joshua.

Idolatry to Be Repented of & Forgiven

"<u>If my people, which are called by my name, shall humble themselves, and pray, and seek my face, and turn from their wicked ways; then will I hear from heaven, and will forgive their sin</u>, and will heal their land" (2 Chron. 7:14). The OT Narrative combination *If my people which are called by my name* (1x), *shall humble themselves and* (1x), *pray and seek my face and* (1x), *turn from* (5x), *from their* (16x), *wicked* (13x), *ways* (28x), *then will I hear from heaven and will forgive their sin* (1x) = 66.

The Lord's Warning to Solomon

"But if ye turn away, and forsake my statutes and my commandments, which I have set before you, and shall go and SERVE other GODS, and WORSHIP <u>them</u>; Then will I pluck <u>them</u> up by the roots out of my land which I have given <u>them</u>; and this house, which I have sanctified for my name, will I cast out of my sight, and will make it to be a proverb and a byword among all nations" (2 Chron. 7:19-20). Again the word *them* occurs 466 times in Jeremiah.

Rehoboam's Idolatry

Rehoboam was a bad Judean king. "And it came to pass, when Rehoboam had established the <u>kingdom</u>, and had strengthened himself, he forsook the law of the LORD, and all Israel with him" (2 Chron. 12:1). Rehoboam had been raised by his Ammonite mother Naamah. Since she was an idolater she most likely taught him to worship Milcom and Molech. Turning from Jehovah, Rehoboam probably took up worshiping his mother's gods. Again the word *kingdom* is mentioned in 166 verses of the Old Testament.

Asa Banished Abominable Idols from Judah

Asa was a good Judean king. "And when Asa heard these words, and the prophecy of Oded the prophet, he took courage, and put away the abominable IDOLS out of all the land of Judah and Benjamin, and out of <u>the cities</u> which he had taken from mount Ephraim, and renewed the altar of the LORD, that was before the porch of the LORD" (2 Chron. 15:8). The Major and Minor Prophets combination *the cities* (55 vs) and *the * cities* (11 vs) = 66 verses.

"And also concerning Maachah the mother of Asa the king, he removed her from being queen, because she had <u>made</u> an IDOL in a grove: and Asa cut down her IDOL, and stamped it, and burnt it at the brook Kidron" (v. 16). Here the word *made* is the 9366th word of Second Chronicles, and it refers to the making of an idol. Again the word *made* is mentioned in 266 verses of the New Testament.

Jehoshaphat Banished Idolatry in the High Places

Jehoshaphat was a good Judean king. "And the LORD was with Jehoshaphat, because he walked in the first ways of his father David, and sought not unto BAALIM; But sought to the LORD God of his father, and walked in his commandments, and not after the doings of Israel. . . . And his heart was lifted up in the ways of the LORD: moreover he took away the <u>HIGH PLACES</u> and GROVES out of Judah" (2 Chron. 17:3-4, 6). Again the term *high places* is mentioned in 66 chapters of the Bible.

Jehoram's Idolatry

Jehoram was a bad Judean king. "Now Jehoshaphat slept with his fathers, and was buried with his fathers in the city of David. And Jehoram his son reigned in his stead. . . . And he <u>walked</u> <u>in the way of</u> the kings of Israel, like as did the house of <u>Ahab</u>: for he had the daughter of <u>Ahab</u> to wife: and he wrought that which was evil in the eyes of the LORD" (2 Chron. 21:1, 6). The OT Narrative combination *walked* (51x), *in the way of* (15x) = 66. Again the name *Ahab* is mentioned in 66 verses of First and Second Kings.

Ahaziah's Idolatry

"So Ahaziah the son of Jehoram <u>king of Judah</u> reigned. . . . and he reigned one year in Jerusalem. His mother's name also was Athaliah the daughter of Omri. He also walked in the ways of the house of <u>Ahab</u>: for his mother was his counsellor to do wickedly. Wherefore he did evil in the sight of the LORD like the house of <u>Ahab</u>: for they were his counsellors after the death of his father to his destruction" (2 Chron. 22:1c-4). Ahaziah feared his wicked mother and her idolatrous cabal more than he feared the Lord. Again the title *king of Judah* is mentioned in 66 chapters of the Old Testament. Again the name *Ahab* is mentioned in 66 verses of First and Second Kings.

Amaziah's Idolatry

Amaziah was a mostly good Judean king, but he eventually turned to worship idols. "Now it came to pass, <u>after that Amaziah was come from</u> <u>the slaughter of the Edomites, that he brought</u> <u>the GODS</u> of <u>the children of Seir, and set them up to be his GODS, and BOWED DOWN</u> <u>himself before them, and burned incense unto them</u>" (2 Chron. 25:14). This evil Judean king suddenly took confidence in powerless gods who were unable to deliver Edom. The Bible combination *after that Amaziah was come from* (1x), *the slaughter of the Edomites that he brought* (1x), *the gods* (58x), *the children of Seir* (3x), *and set them up to be his gods* (1x), *and bowed down himself before them* (1x), *and burned incense unto them* (1x) = 66.

Ahaz's Idolatry

Ahaz was a wicked Judean king. A detailed account of his idolatrous ways begins with the 11,766th verse of the Bible, underlined.

"Ahaz was twenty years old when he began to reign, and he reigned sixteen years in Jerusalem: but he did not that which was right in the sight of the LORD, like David his father: For he walked in the ways of the kings of Israel, and made also molten IMAGES for Baalim. Moreover he burnt incense in the valley of the son of Hinnom, and burnt his children in the fire, after the abominations of the heathen whom the LORD had cast out before the children of Israel. He sacrificed also and burnt incense in the high places, and on the hills, and under every green tree. . . . And in the time of his distress did he trespass yet more against the LORD: this is that king Ahaz. For he sacrificed unto the GODS of Damascus, which smote him: and he said, Because the GODS of the kings of Syria help them, therefore will I sacrifice to them, that they may help me. But they were the ruin of him, and of all Israel. And Ahaz gathered together the vessels of the house of God, and cut in pieces the vessels of the house of God, and shut up the doors of the house of the LORD, and he made him altars in every corner of Jerusalem. And in every several city of Judah he made HIGH PLACES to burn incense unto other GODS, and provoked to anger the LORD God of his fathers" (2 Chron. 28:2-4, 22-25).

Again the word *other* is mentioned in 66 chapters of the Law. Again the word *gods* occurs naturally 66 times in the Law. Again the phrase *in pieces* is mentioned in 66 verses of the Bible.

Hezekiah Cleansed Temple of Idols for Passover
"And the priests went into the inner part of the house of the LORD, to cleanse it, and brought out all the uncleanness that they found in the temple of the LORD into the court of the house of the LORD. And the Levites took it, to carry it out abroad into the brook Kidron" (2 Chron. 29:16). The Bible combination *and the priests went* (1x), *into the inner part* (1x), *of the house of the LORD* (64x) = 66.

Hezekiah Cleansed the Cities of Judah
"Now when all this was finished, all Israel that were present went out to the cities of Judah, and brake the IMAGES in pieces, and cut down the GROVES, and threw down the HIGH PLACES and the altars out of all Judah and Benjamin, in Ephraim also and Manasseh, until they had utterly destroyed them all. Then all the children of Israel returned, every man to his possession, into their own cities" (2 Chron. 31:1). Again the phrase *in pieces* is mentioned in 66 verses of the Bible. The word *destroyed* occurs 66 times in the OT Narrative.

Manasseh's Idolatry
Manasseh was the worst of Judah's kings. "And he caused his children to pass through the fire in the valley of the son of Hinnom: also he observed times, and used enchantments, and used witchcraft, and dealt with a familiar spirit, and with wizards: he wrought much evil in the sight of the LORD, to provoke him to anger. And he set a CARVED IMAGE, the IDOL which he had made, in the house of God" (2 Chron. 33:6-7a). The Law combination *and he set up* (1 v), *standing image* (1 v), *he made* (64 vs) = 66 verses.

Amon's Idolatry
Amon was also among the worst of Judah's kings. "Amon was two and twenty years old when he began to reign, and reigned two years in Jerusalem. But he did that which was evil in the sight of the LORD, as did Manasseh his father: for Amon sacrificed unto all the CARVED IMAGES which Manasseh his father had made, and SERVED them" (2 Chron. 33:21-22). Again the word *serve* occurs 66 times in the Law.

Josiah Burned the Idolatrous Priests' Bones

Josiah was a very good Judean king. He fulfilled the prophecy that was spoken of him nearly 200 years earlier.

> "And they brake down the altars of BAALIM in his presence; and the IMAGES, that were on high above them, he cut down; and the GROVES, and the CARVED IMAGES, and the MOLTEN IMAGES, he brake in pieces, and made dust of them, and strowed it upon the graves of them that had sacrificed unto them. And he burnt the bones of the priests upon their altars, and cleansed Judah and Jerusalem. And so did he in the cities of Manasseh, and Ephraim, and Simeon, even unto Naphtali, with their mattocks round about" (2 Chron. 34:4-6).

Again the phrase *in pieces* is mentioned in 66 verses of the Bible. Again the phrase *the dust* occurs 66 times in Scripture. Again the word *bones* is mentioned in 66 chapters of the Bible. Again the title *the priests* occurs naturally 266 times in the Bible.

Adonikam

"The children of Adonikam, SIX HUNDRED SIXTY AND SIX" (Ezra 2:13). In Hebrew Adonikam's name means lord of rising or our lord arose. This combination of name meaning and triple-six number assignment presents a prophetic picture of Israel's future false messiah who after receiving a deadly sword wound to the head will rise from the dead to become lord over all the end-time earth. After this deceiver arises from his deadly wound an idol will be fashioned and placed inside the Third Temple. Many around the world will ignorantly worship both him and it. These same idolaters will receive his image which is known as the mark of the beast. Those who receive his identifying mark will thereby become his adopted children. The false messiah's resurrection and worshipful image are described in Revelation 13:14 wherein occurs the 6666th word of Revelation, the 66th book of the Bible. Again the word *six* occurs 66 times in the Law.

The Remnant

"And they said unto me, The remnant that are left of the captivity there in the province are in great affliction and reproach: the wall of Jerusalem also is broken down, and the gates thereof are burned with fire" (Neh. 1:3). The wall was broken down more than seventy years earlier as judgment from God for Jerusalem's unrepentant idol worship. The term "remnant" refers either to Jews who were left behind in Jerusalem or, as here, to Jews who return to Jerusalem. After their Babylonian captivity the Jews solidly learned not to worship idols. The phrase *the remnant* is mentioned in 66 verses of the Old Testament. Again the phrase *of Jerusalem* occurs 166 times in the Bible.

Many Remnant Jews Marry Idolatrous Wives

"In those days also saw I Jews that had married wives of Ashdod, of Ammon, and of Moab: And their children spake half in the speech of Ashdod, and could not speak in the Jews' language, but according to the language of each people. And I contended with them, and cursed them, and smote certain of them, and plucked off their hair, and made them swear by God, saying, Ye shall not give your daughters unto their sons, nor take their daughters unto your sons, or for yourselves. Did not Solomon king of Israel sin by these things? . . . even him did outlandish women cause to sin" (Neh. 13:23-26a, 26d).

Nehemiah recalls the manner in which Solomon's pagan wives turned his heart to worship idols. The Jew at this time were repeating Solomon's great mistake. The phrase *the Jews* occurs 66 times in the Old Testament.

The Ways of Man Are Prone to Idol Worship

Elihu said of the Almighty, "For <u>his eyes</u> are upon <u>the ways</u> of <u>man</u>, and he <u>seeth all his goings</u>" (Job 34:21). The ways of man are generally prone to idol worship. This is evidenced throughout the earth. The phrase *his eyes* occurs 66 times in the Old Testament. The Major Prophets combination *seeth all his* (1x), *ways* (61x), *goings* (4x) = 66. The word *ways* occurs 66 times in the Psalms. The phrase *of man* occurs 166 times in the Old Testament.

The Fool & His Idols

"The <u>fool</u> hath said in his heart, There is no God. Corrupt are they, and have <u>done abominable iniquity</u>: there is none that doeth good" (Ps. 53:1). Only a foolish person will worship a statue or image—an inanimate object. The word *fool* occurs 66 times in Scripture. The Bible combination *done* (565x), *abominable iniquity* (1x) = 566.

Psalm 78:66

"And he smote his <u>enemies</u> in the hinder parts: he put them to a perpetual reproach" (Ps. 78:66). This verse speaks of that time when God smote the idolatrous Philistines with emerods for stealing His Ark and placing it inside Dagon's idol-standing temple.

The word *enemies* occurs 266 times in the Bible.
The word *enemies* is mentioned in 166 chapters of the Bible.

The Nations' Gods

"For all the <u>GODS</u> of the <u>nations</u> are IDOLS: but the LORD made the heavens" (Ps. 96:5). Again the word *gods* occurs naturally 66 times in the Law. The Law combination *nations* (65x) and *molten images* (1x) = 66. The word *nations* is mentioned naturally in 166 chapters of the Old Testament.

Historical Summary of Israel's Idolatry in the Wilderness

"<u>They made</u> a CALF in Horeb, and WORSHIPPED the MOLTEN IMAGE" (Ps. 106:19). Again the word *they* is mentioned in 166 chapters of the Law. The Bible combination *they made* (65x), *a calf in Horeb* (1x) = 66.

Historical Summary of Israel's Idolatry in Canaan

"They did not destroy the <u>nations,</u> concerning whom the LORD commanded them: But were mingled among the heathen, and learned their works. And they <u>SERVED</u> their IDOLS: which were a snare unto them. Yea, they sacrificed their sons and their daughters unto devils" (Ps. 106:34-37). Again the word *nations* is mentioned naturally in 166 chapters of the Old Testament. Again the word *serve* occurs 66 times in the Law.

Idols—They Speak Not, See Not, Hear Not, Handle Not, Walk Not

"But our God is in the heavens: he hath done whatsoever he hath pleased. Their IDOLS are silver and gold, the work of men's hands. <u>They</u> have <u>mouths,</u> but <u>they</u> speak <u>not</u>: eyes have <u>they,</u> but <u>they</u> see <u>not</u>: <u>They</u> have ears, but <u>they</u> hear <u>not</u>: noses have <u>they,</u> but <u>they</u> smell <u>not</u>: <u>They</u> have <u>hands,</u> but <u>they</u> handle <u>not</u>: feet have <u>they,</u> but <u>they</u> walk <u>not</u>: neither speak <u>they</u> through their throat. <u>They</u> that <u>make</u> them are like unto them; so is every one that trusteth <u>in</u>

them" (Ps. 115:3-8).

Again the word *they* is mentioned in 166 chapters of the Law. The word *mouth* is mentioned in 66 verses of the New Testament. Again the phrase *his eyes* occurs 66 times in the Old Testament. Again the word *hands* is mentioned in 66 verses of the Law. The word *not* is found in 66 books of the Bible. Again the word *make* is mentioned in 66 verses of Ezekiel. The phrase *in them* is mentioned naturally in 66 verses of the Old Testament.

The Idols of the Heathen

"The IDOLS of the heathen are <u>silver</u> and <u>gold</u>, the work of men's hands" (Ps. 135:15). Again the word *silver* is mentioned in 66 verses of the Law. Again the word *gold* occurs naturally 166 times in the OT Narrative.

Only a Fool Puts Idols in His Own House

"He that troubleth <u>his own</u> house shall inherit the wind: and the <u>fool</u> shall be servant to the wise of heart" (Prov. 11:29). Again the phrase *his own* occurs 166 times in the Old Testament and is mentioned in 66 chapters of the New Testament. Again the word *fool* occurs 66 times in the Bible.

Solomon's Idolatrous Works Vexed Him

"Then I looked on all the works that my hands had wrought, and on the <u>labour</u> <u>that I had</u> <u>laboured to do</u>: and, behold, all was vanity and vexation of spirit, and there was no profit under the sun" (Eccles. 2:11). Solomon's worldly endeavors correspond with our third definition of idolatry: an immoderate attachment or devotion to something. Part of Solomon's labors literally included the building of idolatrous altars to other gods. The Old Testament combination *labour* (65x), *that I had laboured to do* (1x) = 66.

End-Time Idols Shall Be Cast Away in the Caves

"And they shall go into the holes of the rocks, and into the caves of the earth, for fear of the LORD, and for the glory of his majesty, when he ariseth to shake terribly the earth. In that day <u>a</u> <u>man shall cast</u> <u>his</u> IDOLS of silver, and his IDOLS of gold, which they made each one for himself to WORSHIP, to the moles and to the bats" (Isa. 2:19-20). In their frustration and fury these end-time idolaters will cast their useless idols to the unclean creatures dwelling alongside them in the caves. Here we find the keywords *idols* and *worship* in the same verse. The Bible combination *a man shall cast* (1 bk), *his* (65 bks) = 66 books. The word *his* occurs 66 times in Esther.

Idols Will Fall & Bow before the Lord's Earthly Presence

"The burden of Egypt. Behold, the LORD rideth upon a swift cloud, and shall come into Egypt: and the <u>IDOLS</u> <u>of Egypt shall be moved</u> <u>at his presence,</u> and the heart of Egypt shall melt in the midst of it" (Isa. 19:1). The Lord's end-time coming will shake the earth terribly, causing idols to fall prostrate before Him. The dark-spirit forces behind these idols will be fearful as their doom readily awaits them. The Major and Minor Prophets combination *idols* (63x), *of Egypt shall be moved* (1x), *at his presence* (2x) = 66.

The Workman's Idol Work

"The workman melteth a GRAVEN IMAGE, and the goldsmith spreadeth it over with gold, and casteth silver chains" (Isa. 40:19). The Bible combination *the workman* (5x), *melteth* (7x), *a graven image* (12x), *and the goldsmith spreadeth it over* (1x), *with gold* (36x), *and casteth* (4x), *silver chains* (1x) = 66.

No Praise to Be Given to Graven Images

"I am the LORD: that is my name: and my glory will I not give to another, neither my PRAISE to GRAVEN IMAGES" (Isa. 42:8). Again the worship-related word *praise* is mentioned in 66 chapters of the Wisdom Books.

Men's Idols Are Unprofitable

"Who hath formed a GOD, or MOLTEN a GRAVEN IMAGE that is profitable for nothing?" (Isa. 44:10) The Old Testament combination *formed* (33x), *a god* (33x) = 66.

Idolater Falls Down & Prays to His Idol

"And the residue thereof he maketh a GOD, even his GRAVEN IMAGE: he falleth down unto it, and WORSHIPPETH it, and prayeth unto it, and saith, Deliver me; for thou art my GOD" (Isa. 44:17). To fashion a wooden idol, all an idolater needed was a small piece of wood—the residue of a hewn tree. Again the word *it* occurs 6066 times outside the apocalyptic 66th book of the Bible.

> The word *pray* is mentioned in 66 verses of the Law.
> The word *pray* is mentioned in 66 verses of the NT.

Idolaters & Idol Makers to Be Ashamed

"They shall be ashamed, and also confounded, all of them: they shall go to confusion together that are makers of IDOLS" (Isa. 45:16). The phrase *they shall be* is mentioned naturally in 66 verses of the Major Prophets. Again the word *make* is mentioned in 66 verses of Ezekiel.

The Burden-Bearers of Idols

"BEL BOWETH DOWN, NEBO STOOPETH, their IDOLS were upon the beasts, and upon the cattle: your carriages were heavy loaden; they are a burden to the weary beast. They stoop, they BOW DOWN together; they could not deliver the burden, but themselves are gone into captivity" (Isa. 46:1-2). Bel was another name for Marduk, god of the sun. Nebo was the son of Marduk, and he represented the god of literature and science. Large images of these gods were paraded about on Babylon's New Year's Day festival. Idolatry may at times impose a physical burden upon animals, but it always imposes a spiritual burden upon man. From Genesis to the NT Narrative the word *burden* occurs 66 times; this is its 66th occurrence.

Walking in Darkness

"Therefore is judgment far from us, neither doth justice overtake us: we wait for light, but behold obscurity; for brightness, but we walk in darkness" (Isa. 59:9). Idolatry can be described as walking in spiritual darkness. The New Testament combination *walk in* (21 vs), *darkness* (45 vs) = 66 verses.

66th Chapter of Isaiah

This chapter has a lot to say about Israel's future blessings in the millennial kingdom age, yet it begins and ends with matters pertaining to their present and prevalent sin of idolatry.

God condemned Israel's idolatrous heart by describing their mere external ritualism in relation to their daily sacrifices. "He that killeth an ox is as if he slew a man; he that sacrificeth a lamb, as if he cut off a dog's neck; he that offereth an oblation, as if he offered swine's blood; he that burneth incense, as if he blessed an IDOL. Yea, they have chosen their own ways, and their soul delighteth in their abominations" (Isa. 66:3-4). The keyword *idol* actually occurs in this 66th chapter.

The Lord then made it clear that He sees what idolaters do in their secrets places, and He lets them know the penalty for doing so is most severe. "A voice of noise from the city, a voice from the temple, a voice of the LORD that rendereth recompence to his enemies. . . . For, behold, the LORD will come with fire, and with his chariots like a whirlwind, to render his anger with fury, and his rebuke with flames of fire. . . . They that sanctify themselves, and purify themselves in the gardens behind one tree in the midst, eating swine's flesh, and the abomination, and the mouse, shall be consumed together, saith the LORD" (vv. 6, 15, 17). Again the word *enemies* occurs 266 times in the Bible. The word *fury* is mentioned in 66 verses of the Bible. The Bible combination *garden* (52x), *gardens* (12x), *swine's flesh* (2x) = 66.

During the millennium, nations from around the world will make pilgrimage to Jerusalem not just annually but monthly. In contrast to the way they used to worship idols they will worship the One True God. "And it shall come to pass, that from one new moon to another, and from one sabbath to another, shall all flesh come to WORSHIP before me, saith the LORD" (Isa. 66:23). God said these same groups of Gentile visitors will receive a lesson on idolatry while in the Holy Land as they "shall go forth, and look upon the carcases of the men that have transgressed against me: for their worm shall not die, neither shall their fire be quenched; and they shall be an abhorring unto all flesh" (v. 24). Indeed Isaiah's closing words were a warning against idolatry both to Israel and also to the world. The keyword *worship* actually occurs in this 66th chapter.

The Works of Their Own Hands

"And I will utter my judgments against them touching all their wickedness, who have forsaken me, and have burned incense unto other GODS, and WORSHIPPED the works of their own hands" (Jer. 1:16). The Bible combination *burned incense unto other gods and worshipped* (1x), *the works of* (61x), *their own hands* (4x) = 66. Again the word *hands* is mentioned in 66 chapters of the Major and Minor Prophets.

Idolatry under Every Green Tree

The prophet recalls the Lord's words to him in the days of Josiah's reign. "Hast thou seen that which backsliding Israel hath done? she is gone up upon every high mountain and under every green tree, and there hath played the harlot" (Jer. 3:6bc). Green trees with their low hanging branches served their useful purpose of outdoor temples. The word *under* is mentioned naturally in 66 verses of the Major and Minor Prophets. The Major Prophets combination *she is gone up* (1 v), *upon every high mountain and* (2 vs), *under* (56 vs), *green tree* (7 vs) = 66 verses.

66th Verse of Jeremiah

The prophet recalled the Lord's recent words concerning Judah's sin of idolatry. "And yet for all this her treacherous sister <u>Judah</u> hath not turned unto me with her whole heart, but feignedly, saith the LORD" (Jer. 3:10). The title *Judah('s)* is mentioned in 166 verses of Jeremiah.

Idolatrous Jerusalem

God said to the idolatrous city, "Cut off thine hair, O <u>Jerusalem</u>, and cast it away, and take up a lamentation on HIGH PLACES; for the LORD hath rejected and forsaken the generation of his wrath" (Jer. 7:29). Jehovah directed Jerusalem's citizens to go to their former high places of idol worship and lament their current judgment from Him. Again the name *Jerusalem* occurs naturally 666 times in the Old Testament.

Idolatrous Nations Shall Tremble

"But the LORD is the true God, he is the living God, and an everlasting king: at his wrath <u>the earth</u> <u>shall tremble</u>, and the nations shall not be able to abide his indignation" (Jer. 10:10). The Bible combination *the earth shall* (37x), *tremble* (29x) = 66.

Idols Have No Breath in Them

"Every man is brutish in his knowledge: every founder is confounded by the GRAVEN IMAGE: for his <u>MOLTEN IMAGE is</u> <u>falsehood,</u> and <u>there</u> is no breath <u>in them</u>" (Jer. 10:14). The Bible combination *molten image is* (2x), *false* (64x) = 66. Here the word *there* is the 490,666th word of the Bible. Again the phrase *in them* is mentioned naturally in 66 verses of the Old Testament.

Woe to the Adulterated Idolaters

The Lord said to His idolatrous people, "I have seen thine adulteries, and thy neighings, the lewdness of thy WHOREDOM, and thine abominations on the hills in the fields. <u>Woe</u> unto thee, O Jerusalem! wilt thou not be made clean? when shall it once be?" (Jer. 13:27) Throughout the Old and New Testaments, the words idolatry and adultery are used interchangeably because they both exemplify unfaithfulness to God. The word *woe* occurs 66 times in the Old Testament.

Your Father Have Been Idolatrous

"Then shalt thou say unto them, Because <u>your fathers</u> <u>have forsaken me, saith the LORD</u>, and <u>have walked after</u> <u>other GODS,</u> <u>and have SERVED</u> them, and <u>have WORSHIPPED</u> them, and have forsaken me, <u>and have not kept my law</u>" (Jer. 16:11). The Major and Minor Prophets combination *your fathers* (39x), *have forsaken me saith the LORD* (1x), *have walked after* (3x), *have worshipped* (2x), *and have served* (1x), *other gods* (19x), *and have not kept my law* (1x) = 66.

Israel's Idolatrous Land Made Desolate of People

"Because my people hath forgotten me, they have burned incense to vanity, and they have caused them to stumble in their ways from the ancient paths, to walk in paths, in a way not cast up; To make their land <u>desolate,</u> and a perpetual hissing; every one that passeth thereby shall be astonished, and wag his head" (Jer. 18:15-16). The word *desolate* is mentioned in 66 chapters of the Major and Minor Prophets.

Judean King Taken to the Chaldeans' Idol-Worshiping Land

"But the <u>Chaldeans'</u> army pursued after them, and overtook Zedekiah in the plains of Jericho: and when they had taken him, they brought him up to Nebuchadnezzar king of Babylon to

Riblah in the land of Hamath, where he gave judgment upon him" (Jer. 39:5). Again the plural name *Chaldeans(')* occurs 66 combined times in the Bible.

Judah Would Not Turn from Her Idol Worship

"But they hearkened not, nor inclined their ear to <u>turn</u> from their wickedness, to burn no incense unto <u>other</u> GODS" (Jer. 44:5). Again the word *turn* is mentioned in 66 chapters of the Major and Minor Prophets. Again the word *other* is mentioned in 66 chapters of the Law.

Judah's Reproach for Practicing Idolatry in Egypt

"Therefore now . . . Wherefore commit ye this great evil against your souls . . . In that ye provoke me unto wrath with the works of your hands, burning incense unto other GODS in the land of Egypt, whither ye be gone to dwell . . . that ye might be a curse and a <u>reproach</u> among all the nations of the earth? . . . He shall break also the IMAGES of Beth-shemesh, that is in the land of Egypt; and the houses of the GODS of the Egyptians shall he burn with fire" (Jer. 44:7-8, 13)

Many Jews fled to assumed safety in Egypt to avoid the Babylonian incursion, yet they did not turn from idolatry. The word *reproach* is mentioned in 66 chapters of the Old Testament.

The Queen of Heaven

"And when we burned incense to the queen of heaven, and poured out drink offerings unto her, did we make her cakes to WORSHIP her, and pour out drink offerings <u>unto</u> her, without our men?" (Jer. 44:19). Here in this idolatry verse the underlined word *unto* is the 517,166th word of the Bible.

20,166th Verse of the Bible

"And I will set my throne in Elam, and will destroy from thence the king and the princes, saith the LORD" (Jer. 49:38). The Lord threatened to destroy the idolatrous Elamites and displace them.

Babylon's Images of Bel to Be Broken in Pieces

"Declare ye among the nations, and publish, and set up a standard; publish, and conceal not: say, Babylon is taken, BEL is confounded, MERODACH is broken in pieces; her IDOLS are confounded, her IMAGES are broken <u>in pieces</u>" (Jer. 50:2). Again the phrase *in pieces* is mentioned in 66 verses of the Bible.

Lamentation 3:66

"Persecute and <u>destroy them</u> in anger from under the heavens of the LORD" (Lam. 3:66). Jeremiah referred to his adversaries who opposed his godly counsel and instead persecuted him for it. Many of these princes and rulers were idolaters. This 66th verse presents the Bible's 66th verse-mention of the phrase *destroy them*, and it pertains to idolatrous rulers.

Judah's High Places Shall Be Made Desolate

"In all your dwellingplaces the cities shall be laid waste, and the HIGH PLACES shall be <u>desolate</u>; that your altars may be laid waste and made <u>desolate</u>, and your IDOLS may be broken and cease, and your IMAGES may be cut down, and your <u>WORKS</u> may be abolished" (Ezek. 6:6). Again the word *desolate* is mentioned in 66 chapters of the Major and Minor Prophets. Here the word *works* is the 3266th word of Ezekiel.

They Did Worship Idols upon Every High Hill

God pledged to Israel that after He brought His mighty destruction upon the land, "then shall ye know that I am the LORD, when their slain men shall be among their IDOLS round about their altars, upon every HIGH HILL, in all the tops of the mountains, and under every green tree, and under every thick oak, the place where they did offer sweet savour to all their IDOLS" (Ezek. 6:13). The Major Prophets combination *green* (12x), *tree* (54x) = 66. The phrase *they did* occurs naturally 66 times in the Old Testament.

Ezekiel Sees Profane Idolatry in the Temple

"And he brought me to the door of the court; and when I looked, behold a hole in the wall. Then said he unto me, Son of man, dig now in the wall: and when I had digged in the wall, behold a door. And he said unto me, Go in, and behold the wicked abominations that they do here. So I went in and saw; and behold every form of creeping things, and abominable beasts, and all the IDOLS of the house of Israel, portrayed upon the wall round about. And there stood before them seventy men of the ancients of the house of Israel, and in the midst of them stood Jaazaniah the son of Shaphan, with every man his censer in his hand; and a thick cloud of incense went up" (Ezek. 8:7-11).

Again the phrase *the temple* occurs 66 times in the Old Testament.

Idolatrous Love for Tammuz

"Then he brought me to the door of the gate of the LORD'S house which was toward the north; and, behold, there sat women weeping for TAMMUZ" (Ezek. 8:14). Child worship began to circulate soon after Nimrod's death but perhaps earlier. According to one myth, after Nimrod died his wife Semiramis became pregnant in his absence. She named her son Tammuz, and they considered him a demigod. Mythology also portrayed Tammuz as Ishtar's husband. It was supposed that Tammuz died annually upon the winter solstice and was reborn three days later. This rebirth of the sun god on December 25th became known as the Venerable Day of the Sun. Ezekiel reveals that Israelite women still idolized this child who was worshiped as the sun god. Today ancient Tammuz altars can be found around Jerusalem having the letter T inscribed on them. The word *child* is mentioned in 66 chapters of the Old Testament. The Bible combination *worshipping* (5x), *Tammuz* (1x), *sun* (160x) = 166.

Sun Worship

"Then said he unto me, Hast thou seen this, O son of man? turn thee yet again, and thou shalt see greater abominations than these. And he brought me into the inner court of the LORD'S house, and, behold, at the door of the temple of the LORD, between the porch and the altar, were about five and twenty men, with their backs toward the temple of the LORD, and their faces toward the east; and they WORSHIPPED the sun toward the east" (Ezek. 8:15-16). Again the word *they* is mentioned in 166 chapters of the Law. The Major Prophets combination *worshipped the sun toward* (1x), *the east* (65x) = 66.

Repent of All Your Idolatries

"Therefore say unto the house of Israel, Thus saith the Lord GOD; Repent, and turn yourselves from your IDOLS; and turn away your faces from all your abominations" (Ezek. 14:6). All forms of the word *repent* occur a combined 66 times in the New Testament. Again the word *turn* is mentioned in 66 chapters of the Major and Minor Prophets. The phrase *all your* occurs 66 times in the Bible!

The Two Idolatrous Women

"Then said I unto her that was old in adulteries, Will they now commit WHOREDOMS with her, and she with them? Yet they went in unto her, as they go in unto a woman that playeth the harlot: so went they in unto Aholah and unto Aholibah, the lewd women" (Ezek. 23:43-44). These two guilty parties were Israel and Judah. The underlined word *they* is the 546,666th word of the Bible. Again the word *her* occurs 66 times in Isaiah.

Idols of Egypt to Be Divinely Destroyed

"Thus saith the Lord GOD; I will also destroy the IDOLS, and I will cause their IMAGES to cease out of Noph; and there shall be no more a prince of the land of Egypt: and I will put a fear in the land of Egypt" (Ezek. 30:13). Again the word *destroyed* occurs 66 times in the OT Narrative.

Among the Heathen

"And I scattered them among the heathen, and they were dispersed through the countries: according to their way and according to their doings I judged them" (Ezek. 36:19). Because Israel loved idols the Lord sent them into captivity among the heathen, a people who regularly worshiped idols. There Judah learned their lesson the hard way. The combination *among the heathen* (46x) and *among the Gentiles* (20x) = 66.

"All Your Idols"

"Then will I sprinkle clean water upon you, and ye shall be clean: from all your filthiness, and from all your IDOLS, will I cleanse you" (Ezek. 36:25). The phrase *all your* occurs 66 times in the Bible.

Idolatrous Kingdoms Broken in Pieces

Daniel recounted the king of Babylon's dream about his colossal idol made of amalgamated metals. "Thou sawest till that a stone was cut out without hands, which smote the IMAGE upon his feet that were of iron and clay, and brake them to pieces" (Dan. 2:34). The dream ended with Messiah smashing the idol, an object that symbolized the world's idolatrous and empirical kingdoms. Again the word *kingdom* is mentioned in 166 verses of the Old Testament.

66th Verse of Daniel

"Forasmuch as thou sawest that the stone was cut out of the mountain without hands, and that it brake in pieces the iron, the brass, the clay, the silver, and the gold; the great God hath made known to the king what shall come to pass hereafter: and the dream is certain, and the interpretation thereof sure" (Dan. 2:45). Daniel concluded his analysis of the king's idolatrous dream. Again the phrase *in pieces* is mentioned in 66 verses of the Bible.

Nebuchadnezzar's Colossal, 66-Cubits Idol

"Nebuchadnezzar the king made an IMAGE of gold, whose height was THREESCORE cubits, AND the breadth thereof SIX cubits: he set it up in the plain of Dura, in the province of Babylon" (Dan. 3:1). The title *the king* occurs 166 times in Second Kings. Again the word *made* is mentioned in 266 verses of the New Testament. The combined frontal dimensions of Nebuchadnezzar's massive idol were 66 cubits. The naturally occurring Major and Minor Prophets combination *height* (25x) and *breadth* (41x) = 66. Again the word *it* occurs 6066 times outside the apocalyptic 66th book of the Bible.

Worship of the King's Colossal Idol Is Mandatory
Certain Chaldeans came to inform Nebuchadnezzar that three Jews would not bow before his great image. They said, "Thou, O king, hast made a decree, that every man that shall hear the sound of the cornet, flute, harp, sackbut, psaltery, and dulcimer, and all kinds of musick, shall FALL DOWN and WORSHIP the golden IMAGE: And whoso FALLETH not DOWN and WORSHIPPETH, that he should be cast into the midst of a burning fiery furnace" (Dan. 3:10-11). The phrase *shall fall* is mentioned in 66 chapters of the Bible. Again the word *golden* occurs 66 times in the Bible.

Three Jews Refused to Worship the King's Colossal Idol
The Chaldeans' report continues: "There are certain Jews whom thou hast set over the affairs of the province of Babylon, Shadrach, Meshach, and Abed-nego; these men, O king, have not regarded thee: they SERVE not thy GODS, nor WORSHIP the golden IMAGE which thou hast set up" (Dan. 3:12). Again the word *serve* occurs 66 times in the Law.

Jews Given a Second Chance to Worship the King's Colossal Idol
"Then Nebuchadnezzar in his rage and fury commanded to bring Shadrach, Meshach, and Abed-nego. Then they brought these men before the king. Nebuchadnezzar spake and said unto them, Is it true, O Shadrach, Meshach, and Abed-nego, do not ye SERVE my GODS, nor WORSHIP the golden IMAGE which I have set up? Now if ye be ready that at what time ye hear the sound of the cornet, flute, harp, sackbut, psaltery, and dulcimer, and all kinds of musick, ye FALL DOWN and WORSHIP the IMAGE which I have made; well: but if ye WORSHIP not, ye shall be cast the same hour into the midst of a burning fiery furnace; and who is that God that shall deliver you out of my hands?" (Dan. 3:13-15)

Again the word *image(s)* is mentioned in 66 chapters from Genesis to the Major Prophets.

Three Steadfastly Refuse to Worship the Golden Image
"Shadrach, Meshach, and Abed-nego, answered and said to the king, O Nebuchadnezzar, we are not careful to answer thee in this matter. If it be so, our God whom we serve is able to deliver us from the burning fiery furnace, and he will deliver us out of thine hand, O king. But if not, be it known unto thee, O king, that we will not SERVE thy GODS, nor WORSHIP the golden IMAGE which thou hast set up" (Dan. 3:16-18). The Bible combination *but if not be it known* (1x), *unto thee O king that* (1x), *we will not* (28x), *serve thy gods nor* (1x), *worship the* (27x), *golden image* (6x), *which thou hast set up* (2x) = 66.

Gods of Silver, Brass, Iron, Wood & Stone
"Belshazzar the king made a great feast to a thousand of his lords. . . . They drank wine, and PRAISED the GODS of gold, and of silver, of brass, of iron, of wood, and of stone" (Dan. 5:1, 4). Idols can be made from any variety of materials. The word *of* is found in 66 books of the Bible. Again the word *silver* is mentioned in 66 verses of the Law. Again the phrase *of brass* occurs 66 times in the Bible. The Law combination *the gods of* (5x) and *wood* (61x) = 66. Again the worship-related word *praise* is mentioned in 66 chapters of the Wisdom Books.

Abominable Idol Causes the Temple's End-Time Desolation

"And he shall confirm the covenant with many for one week: and in the midst of the week he shall cause the sacrifice and the oblation to cease, and for the overspreading of abominations he shall make it <u>desolate</u>, even until the consummation" (Dan. 9:27abc). The last-days false messiah will set up an idol of himself inside the Temple at Jerusalem. This abominable act will cause the priests and Jewish people to flee as they know their lives are in grave danger. They will only be safe once the true Messiah comes to take over Jerusalem and the world, a waiting period of three and a half years. The word *desolate* is mentioned in 66 chapters of the Major and Minor Prophets.

866th Chapter of the Bible

"For they shall eat, and not have enough: they shall <u>commit</u> WHOREDOM, and shall not increase: because they have left off to take <u>heed</u> to the LORD" (Hos. 4:10). Again the word *commit* is mentioned naturally in 66 verses of the Bible. Again the word *heed* is mentioned in 66 chapters of the Bible.

Ephraim Is Joined to Idols

The Lord said of the unrepentant northern tribes, "<u>Ephraim</u> is joined to IDOLS: let him alone" (Hos. 4:17). The name *Ephraim* occurs 66 times in the Major and Minor Prophets.

The Sin of Idolatry

"<u>And now they sin more and more, and have made them molten IMAGES of their silver,</u> and IDOLS according to their own understanding, all of it the work of the craftsmen: they say of them, Let the men that sacrifice kiss the calves" (Hos. 13:2). Again the word *sins* is mentioned in 166 verses of the Bible. The joined phrases *and now they sin more and more, and have made them molten images of their silver,* consist of 66 characters!

Outwardly Religious; Inwardly Idolatrous

"<u>Have ye offered unto me sacrifices and offerings in the wilderness forty years</u>, O house of Israel? But ye have borne the tabernacle of your MOLOCH and CHIUN your IMAGES, the star of your GOD, which ye made to yourselves" (Amos 5:25-26). Jehovah emphasized Israel's religious hypocrisy dating back to their exodus beginnings. The people worshiped God outwardly but worshiped other gods inwardly. The Old Testament combination *offered unto me* (1x), *sacrifices* (65x) = 66. The question *have ye offered unto me sacrifices and offerings in the wilderness forty years* consists of 66 letters!

66th Verse of Micah

"And I will cut off witchcrafts out of thine hand; and thou shalt have <u>no more</u> soothsayers" (Mic. 5:12). At the end of days the Lord promises to rid Israel of every idolatrous temptation. Again the phrase *no more* is mentioned in 66 verses of the Major and Minor Prophets.

No More Worshiping of Your Idolatrous Works

"Thy GRAVEN IMAGES also will I cut off, and thy STANDING IMAGES out of the midst of thee; and thou shalt the work of thine hands" (Mic. 5:13). Again the phrase *no more* is mentioned in 66 verses of the Major and Minor Prophets.

Idolatrous Nineveh to Be Destroyed

"And the LORD hath given a commandment concerning thee, that no more of thy name be sown: out of the house of thy GODS will I cut off the GRAVEN IMAGE and the molten IMAGE: I will make thy grave; for thou art vile" (Nah. 1:14). The Old Testament combination *out of the house of* (21x), *thy gods* (10x), *will I cut off* (5x), *graven image* (26x), *and the molten image* (3x), *for thou art vile* (1x) = 66.

Burning Incense to Their Dragnet

"Therefore they sacrifice unto their net, and burn incense unto their drag; because by them their portion is fat, and their meat plenteous" (Hab. 1:16). This verse presents the Bible's 66th chapter-mention of the word *incense*, and we see its association with an idolatrous practice.

The Maker of Dumb Idols

"What profiteth the GRAVEN IMAGE that the maker thereof hath graven it; the molten IMAGE, and a teacher of lies, that the maker of his work trusteth therein, to make dumb IDOLS? Woe unto him that saith to the wood, Awake; to the dumb stone, Arise, it shall teach! Behold, it is laid over with gold and silver, and there is no breath at all in the midst of it" (Hab. 2:18-19). Again the word *make* is mentioned in 66 verses of Ezekiel. Again the Leviticus combination *make* (65x) and *graven image* (1x) = 66. Again the word *it* occurs 6066 times outside the apocalyptic 66th book of the Bible.

"I will also stretch out mine hand upon Judah, and upon all the inhabitants of Jerusalem; and I will cut off the remnant of BAAL from this place, and the name of the CHEMARIMS with the priests; And them that WORSHIP the host of heaven upon the housetops; and them that WORSHIP and that swear by the LORD, and that swear by MALCHAM" (Zeph. 1:4-5). The priests of the Lord wore white, but the prophets of Baal, the Chemarims, wore black. Again the phrase *the inhabitants* is mentioned in 166 verses of the Old Testament. Again the phrase *of Jerusalem* occurs 166 times in the Bible. Again the title *the priests* occurs naturally 266 times in the Bible. Again the phrase *the host of* is mentioned in 66 verses of the Old Testament.

Idolatrous Kingdoms to Be Overthrown

The Lord declared, "And I will overthrow the throne of kingdoms, and I will destroy the strength of the kingdoms of the heathen" (Hag. 2:22a). Again the word *destroyed* occurs 66 times in the OT Narrative. Again the word *kingdom* is mentioned in 166 verses of the Old Testament.

66th Verse of Zechariah

Zechariah asked the angel what the object was. "And he said, This is wickedness. And he cast it into the midst of the ephah; and he cast the weight of lead upon the mouth thereof" (Zech. 5:8). The vision goes on to speak of an idolatrous woman who turned into two women with wings which then took up the ephah and flew to Shinar where they built a shrine to place it in. Again the word *it* occurs 6066 times outside the apocalyptic 66th book of the Bible.

The Lord Will Cut off the Idols' Names

"And it shall come to pass in that day, saith the LORD of hosts, that I will cut off the names of the IDOLS out of the land, and they shall no more be remembered: and also I will cause the prophets and the unclean spirit to pass out of the land" (Zech. 13:2). The Bible combination *and it shall come to pass in that day saith the* LORD *of hosts* (1x), *that I will cut off* (4) *the names of* (40) *the idols* (21) = 66.

The New Testament

"The book of the generation of <u>Jesus Christ,</u> the son of David, the son of Abraham" (Matt. 1:1). No form of the word idolatry occurs in the Gospels, but the related word *image* does. After their Babylonian captivity was over Israel learned to put away her idolatry. However, the Gentiles who were to be engrafted into the spiritual commonwealth still needed to learn their lesson on the folly and foolishness of idol worship. Jesus would die for this common sin among the Gentiles so they might be saved from it. The Romans who occupied Israel were steeped in idolatry. The idolatrous Roman eagle insignia was seen throughout the land, particularly so in Jerusalem where the provincial governor ruled. Regarding Christ, the religious leaders viewed Jesus as an apostate Who was attempting to deceive the unsuspecting Israelite masses into idolatrously worshiping Him.

> The name *Jesus Christ* is mentioned in 166 verses of the Pauline/General/Apocalyptic Epistles.
> The title *Lord* is mentioned in 66 chapters of the Gospels.

"Fall Down and Worship Me"
"Again, the <u>DEVIL</u> taketh him up into an exceeding high mountain, and sheweth him all the kingdoms of the world, and the glory of them; And saith unto him, All these things will I give thee, if thou wilt FALL DOWN and WORSHIP me" (Matt. 4:8-9). Ever since Lucifer apostatized through pride he has desired that both angels and mankind worship him. Here he foolishly thought he could get the Incarnate Son of God to worship him. Devil worship is an overt form of idolatry. The title *Devil* is the 166th word in this chapter, and he was attempting to seduce someone to idolize him.

Galilee of the Gentiles
"The land of Zabulon, and the land of Nephthalim, by the way of the sea, beyond Jordan, <u>Galilee</u> of <u>the Gentiles;</u> <u>The people</u> which sat in darkness saw great light; and to <u>them which</u> sat in the region and shadow of death light is sprung up" (Matt. 4:15-16). After Assyria carried away the northern tribes it repopulated Galilee with Gentiles of varying nationalities. Seven centuries later Christ came and set up His ministry headquarters in this idolatrous region. When He did the Gentiles seemed to be more responsive to His ministry than the Jews were. Once he healed them of their diseases they went home and abandoned trust in their useless idols. Again the phrase *the people* occurs 66 times in Joshua. The name *Galilee* occurs 66 times in the New Testament. The term *the Gentiles* is mentioned in 66 chapters outside the 66th apocalyptic book of the Bible. The phrase *them which* is mentioned in 66 chapters of the New Testament.

Vain Repetitions

"But when ye pray, use not vain repititions, as the heathen do: for they think that they shall be heard for their much speaking" (Matt. 6:7). The heathen have a tendency to pray to idols and to pray repetitiously, like walking in circles and getting nowhere. Again the word *pray* is mentioned naturally in 66 chapters of the OT Narrative. Again the word *they* is mentioned in 166 chapters of the Law. The phrase *speak unto* occurs 66 times in the Law.

The word *pray* is mentioned in 66 verses of the Law.
The word *pray* is mentioned in 66 verses of the NT.

Jesus Accused of an Evil & Idolatrous Practice

"As they went out, behold, they brought to him a dumb man possessed with a devil. And when the devil was cast out, the dumb spake: and the multitudes marvelled, saying, It was never so seen in Israel. But the Pharisees said, He casteth out devils through the prince of the devils" (Matt. 9:34). The religious leaders accused Jesus of the idolatrous practice of sorcery. The New Testament combination *it was never so seen in Israel* (1x), *but the Pharisees said* (1x), *he casteth out* (2x), *devils through* (2x), *the prince of the* (5x), *devils* (51x), *Baal-zebub* (4x) = 66.

366th Verse of New Testament

"And in his name shall the Gentiles trust" (Matt. 12:21). This 66th verse draws from an Old Testament prophecy which prophesied of the idol-worshiping Gentiles turning from their idolatry to trust in the Lord's chosen Servant, the Incarnate Son of God. Again the term *the Gentiles* is mentioned in 66 chapters outside the 66th apocalyptic book of the Bible.

Again Jesus Accused of an Evil, Idolatrous Practice

"Then was brought unto him one possessed with a devil, blind, and dumb: and he healed him, insomuch that the blind and dumb both spake and saw. And all the people were amazed, and said, Is not this the son of David? But when the Pharisees heard it, they said, This fellow doth not cast out devils, but by *BEELZEBUB* the prince of the devils" (Matt. 12:22-24). The Pharisees' accusation against Christ concerned idolatry. Their thinking was that He somehow implored the name of a certain false god to summon His curative powers. Baal-Zebub was a special deity worshiped by the Philistines at Ekron. The name means lord of the fly and is a parody on the dung god. The New Testament combination *Beelzebub* (7x), *the prince of the* (5x), *devils* (51x), *fly* (3x) = 66. The sentence *This fellow doth not cast out devils, but by Beelzebub the prince of the devils.* consists of 66 characters.

When Rich Men Idolize Their Treasure

"Jesus said unto him, If thou wilt be perfect, go and sell that thou hast, and give to the poor, and thou shalt have treasure in heaven: and come and follow me. But when the young man heard that saying, he went away sorrowful: for he had great possessions. Then said Jesus unto his disciples, Verily I say unto you, That a rich man shall hardly enter into the kingdom of heaven" (Matt. 19:21-22). This ruler's love of money fits our third definition of idolatry: immoderate attachment or devotion to something. All forms of the word *treasure* are mentioned naturally in 66 chapters of the Old Testament.

Caesar Worship
(Part 1)

"Tell us therefore, What thinkest thou? Is it lawful to give tribute unto Caesar, or not? But Jesus perceived their wickedness, and said, Why tempt ye me, ye hypocrites? Shew me the tribute money. And they brought unto him a penny. And he saith unto them, Whose is this IMAGE and superscription?" (Matt. 22:17-20) In keeping with the mosaic prohibition, the Jews did not strike coins with man's image upon them. The Romans however did, seeking to venerate and worship their rulers. Such idolization of man was principally founded at the death of Augustus Caesar whereupon the Roman senate declared him to be a god. It is presumed by many scholars that the coin Jesus held in His hand was the Roman denarius. At that time it had on its obverse side a profile of Tiberius' head, crowned with laurel leaves. Around his head it bore the superscription, "Caesar Tiberius, son of the divine Augustus." Caesar was emperor of the Roman world, thus king of the world. Again the title *king of the* is mentioned in 66 verses of the Bible.

False Christs Will Deceive Many into Idolizing Them

"And Jesus answered and said unto them, Take <u>heed</u> that no man deceive you. For many shall come in my name, saying, I am <u>Christ</u>; and shall deceive many" (Matt. 24:4-5). Such last-days deceivers will draw unsuspecting souls into a blasphemous form of idolatry. Deceived ones will ignorantly bow and worship these false christs. Again the word *heed* is mentioned in 66 chapters of the Bible. Again the name *Jesus Christ* is mentioned in 166 verses of the Pauline, General, and Apocalyptic Epistles.

Antichrist's Abominable Idol to Cause Temple's Desolation

"When ye therefore shall see the <u>abomination</u> of <u>desolation</u>, spoken of by Daniel the prophet, stand in the holy place, whoso readeth, let him understand: Then let them which be in Judaea flee into the mountains" (Matt. 24:15). The antichrist will place a standing idol of his likeness inside the Temple. This verse presents the Bible's 66th verse-mention of the word *abomination*. Again the word *desolate* is mentioned in 66 chapters of the Major and Minor Prophets.

Idolatrous Image of the Antichrist

"So likewise ye, when ye <u>shall see</u> all these things, know that it is near, even at the doors" (Matt. 24:33). This verse presents the Bible's 66th occurrence of the phrase *shall see*, and it partly refers to the idolatrous image of the antichrist mentioned earlier in the chapter.

Judas' Idolatry of Money

"Then one of the twelve, called Judas Iscariot, went unto the chief priests, And said unto them, What will ye give me, and I will deliver him unto you? And they covenanted with him for thirty pieces of <u>silver</u>. And from that time he sought opportunity to betray him" (Matt. 26:14-16). This passage fits our third definition of idolatry: immoderate attachment or devotion to something. Judas' money bag was never full enough. Again the word *silver* is mentioned in 66 verses of the Law.

Matthew 26:66

"What think ye? They answered and said, <u>He is guilty of death</u>" (Matt. 26:66). Their guilty charge was one of idolatrous blasphemy, a crime punishable by death. This false charge was based upon Jesus' claim to God's throne where He specifically described Himself in terms of

Deity and made Himself the object of peoples' true adoration and worship. The Law combination *he is* (59x), *guilty of* (2x), *of death* (5x) = 66.

Teach All Nations to Abandon Their Idolatrous Practices

"Go ye therefore, and teach all <u>nations</u>, baptizing them in the name of the Father, and of the Son, and of the Holy Ghost: Teaching them to observe all things whatsoever I have commanded you" (Matt. 28:19-20a). The Lord Jesus wants all nations to turn from idolatry and find true religion and spiritual life through Him. Again the word *nations* is mentioned naturally in 166 chapters of the Old Testament.

Idolatrous Decapolis

The maniac of Gadara wanted to follow Jesus now that he was healed, but Jesus told him, "Go home to thy friends, and tell them how great things the Lord hath done for thee, and hath had compassion on thee. And he departed, and began to publish in <u>Decapolis</u> how great things Jesus had done for him: and all men did marvel" (Mark 5:19-20). Decapolis was an association of ten Gentile cities extending from Galilee as far as Damascus. Standing idols would have been commonplace in all these cities. The Major and Minor Prophets combination *the cities* (55 vs) and *the * cities* (11 vs) = 66 verses.

Worshiping the Commandments of Men

Jesus spoke to the Pharisees and scribes: "Well hath Esaias prophesied of you hypocrites, as it is written, This people <u>honoureth me with their lips, but</u> <u>their heart</u> <u>is far from me</u>. Howbeit in <u>vain</u> do they WORSHIP me, teaching for doctrines the commandments of men" (Mark 7:6-7). This passage fits our third definition of idolatry: immoderate attachment or devotion to something. The religious leaders elevated men's commandments over God's commandments. The word *vain* is mentioned in 66 chapters from Genesis to the Gospels; this is its 66th chapter-mention. The Bible combination *honoureth me with their lips but* (2x), *their heart* (59x), *is far from me* (5x) = 66.

966th Chapter of the Bible

"And there appeared unto them Elias with Moses: and they were talking with Jesus. And Peter answered and said to Jesus, Master, it is good for us to be here: and <u>let us</u> <u>make</u> three tabernacles; one for thee, and one for Moses, and one for Elias. For he wist not what to say; for they were sore afraid" (Mark 9:4-6). Peter had a disposition to speak without knowledge. Here he unintentionally lapsed into idolatry by ignorantly suggesting that Moses and Elijah be given glory by erecting shrines on their behalf. This was misplaced worship, perhaps even idolatrous worship. At that time a cloud passed over their heads. God spoke aloud from it in judgment against Peter's hasty plan of action. The expression *let us* occurs 66 times in the New Testament. Again the word *make* is mentioned in 66 verses of Ezekiel.

Idolatrous Commercial Practices in the Temple

"And they come to Jerusalem: and Jesus went into <u>the temple</u>, and began to cast out them that sold and bought in <u>the temple</u>, and overthrew the tables of the moneychangers, and the seats of them that sold doves; And would not suffer that any man should carry any vessel through <u>the temple</u>. And he taught, saying unto them, <u>Is it not written</u>, <u>My house shall be called of all nations the house of prayer</u>? <u>but ye have</u> <u>made it a</u> <u>den of</u> <u>thieves</u>" (Mark 11:15-17). This passage fits our third definition of idolatry: immoderate attachment or devotion to something. Through their greed the priesthood hierarchy had allowed the temple precinct to become too commercialized. Again the phrase *the temple* occurs 66 times in the Old Testament. The Bible combination *is it not written* (2x), *my house shall be called of all nations* (1x), *the house of prayer* (3x), *but ye have* (24x), *made it a* (9x), *den of* (11x), *thieves* (16x) = 66.

Caesar Worship
(Part 2)

"And they brought it. And he saith unto them, Whose is this IMAGE and superscription? And they said <u>unto</u> him, Cæsar's. And Jesus answering said unto them, Render to Cæsar the things that are Cæsar's, and to God the things that are God's. And they marvelled at him" (Mark. 12:16-17). Here in this idolization-of-man passage the underlined word *unto* is the 644,666th word of the Bible.

Latter-Day False Christs Will Seek Men to Idolize Them

"And Jesus answering them began to say, Take heed lest any man deceive you: For many shall come in my name, saying, I am <u>Christ</u>; and shall deceive many" (Mark 13:5-6). Here the name *Christ* is the 645,466th word of the Bible. Again the name *Jesus Christ* is mentioned in 166 verses of the Pauline, General, and Apocalyptic Epistles.

Power of the Gospel Saves Idolaters from Vain Worship

"So then after the Lord had spoken unto them, he was received up into heaven, and sat on the right hand of God. . . . And they went forth, and preached every where, the Lord working with them, and confirming the word with signs following. Amen" (Mark 16:15, 19-20). The apostles' testimony of Christ's recent miracles, message of saving grace, and bodily ascension helped turn tens of thousands of Gentiles from worshiping idols to worshiping the Living God. These are the last words in Mark's Gospel, a gospel consisting of 15,166 words.

25,066th Verse of the Bible

"Being forty days <u>tempted</u> of <u>the devil</u>. And in those days he did eat nothing: and when they were ended, he afterward hungered" (Luke 4:2). Satan's goal was to attack Jesus at His weakest moment and draw Him into idolatrous worship of himself by making Him bow before him. Details of this attempt are described in verses five through seven. The Bible combination *tempted* (22 vs) and *the devil* (44 vs) = 66 verses.

Satan's Idolatrous Ways

"<u>And he said unto them, I</u> beheld Satan as <u>lightning fall</u> <u>from heaven</u>" (Luke 10:18). Satan's pride led to a burning desire that the angels idolize or worship him. The New Testament combination *and he said unto them I* (2x), *beheld Satan as lightning fall* (1x), *from heaven* (63x) = 66.

Covetousness Is Idolatry

"And he said unto them, Take heed, and beware of COVETOUSNESS: for a man's life consisteth not in the <u>abundance</u> of the things which he possesseth" (Luke 12:15). Webster defines covetous as being marked by inordinate desire for wealth or possessions or for another's possessions. This passage therefore fits our third definition of idolatry: immoderate attachment or devotion to something. Here *abundance* is the 13,666th word in Luke's Gospel.

Serving Mammon Is Idolatry

"No servant can <u>serve</u> two masters: for <u>either</u> he will hate <u>the one</u>, and love <u>the other</u>; or else he will hold to <u>the one</u>, and despise <u>the other</u>. Ye cannot <u>serve</u> God and mammon. And the Pharisees also, who were covetous, heard all these things: and they derided him" (Luke 16:13-14). Jesus emphasized the idolatrous nature of immoderately desiring an abundance of money. You will recall what was earlier stated: in the Hebrew text the word serve shares the same root word with worship. There is a distinct difference between working for money and worshiping money. The former is unnecessary but the latter is not. The underlined word *either* is the 666,566th word of the Bible. Again the word *serve* occurs 66 times in the Law.

The phrase *the one* is mentioned in 66 chapters of the OT.
The phrase *the other* occurs 66 times in the New Testament.

Rich Young Ruler's Idolatrous Heart

"Now when Jesus heard these things, he said unto him, Yet lackest thou one thing: sell all that thou hast, and distribute unto the poor, and thou shalt have <u>treasure</u> in heaven: and come, follow me. And when he heard this, he was very sorrowful: for he was very rich" (Luke 18:22-23). The rich young ruler had an immoderate attachment to money and material things he possessed. This was behavior was idolatrous. Again all forms of the word *treasure* are mentioned naturally in 66 chapters of the Old Testament.

Caesar Worship
(Part 3)

"Shew me a penny. Whose IMAGE and superscription hath it? They answered and <u>said</u>, Cæsar's" (Luke 20:24). Here the word *said* is the 670,266th word of the Bible, and it supports the idolatrous name Caesar's.

66th Chapter of the New Testament

"Then entered Satan into Judas surnamed Iscariot, being of the number of the twelve. And he went his way, and communed with the chief priests and captains, how he might betray him unto them. And they were glad, and covenanted to give him money" (Luke 22:3-4). In this 66th chapter we see the religious leaders appealing to Judas' idolatrous heart. They could tell by his comportment that he was a 'mover and shaker'—a man about town.

Jesus Treated by the Council as a Blasphemous Idolater

"Pilate therefore, willing to release Jesus, spake again to them. But they cried, saying, Crucify him, crucify him. And he said unto them the third time, Why, what evil hath he done? I have found no cause of death in him: I will therefore chastise him, and let him go. And they were instant with loud voices, requiring that he might be crucified. And the voices of them and of the chief priests prevailed. <u>And Pilate gave sentence that it should be as they required</u>" (Luke 23:20-24).

The religious leaders viewed Jesus not as a Great Healer but rather as an apostate blasphemer Who was attempting to deceive the ignorant people into worshiping or idolizing Him. They felt He was worthy of the most severe punishment. The underlined words indicate the 1066th verse of Luke's Gospel.

Preaching That Men Repent of Idolatry

"And said unto them, Thus it is written, and thus it behoved Christ to suffer, and to rise from the dead the third day: And that repentance and remission of <u>sins</u> should be preached in his name among all nations, beginning at <u>Jerusalem</u>" (Luke 24:46-47). The disciples would soon begin preaching the gospel to the heathen and encouraging them to repent from their sin of idolatry. Again the word *sins* is mentioned in 166 verses of the Bible. Again the name *Jerusalem* occurs naturally 666 times in the Old Testament.

66th Verse of John

"And when he had made a scourge of small cords, he drove them all out of the temple, and the sheep, and the oxen; and poured out the <u>changers' money,</u> and overthrew the tables" (John 2:15). The Temple precinct merchantmen were guilty of greatly misplaced worship because they adored money more than they adored God. Their hearts were therefore idolatrous. The Bible combination *moneychangers* (2 chs) and *money* (64 chs) = 66 chapters.

Idolatrous Men Prefer Doing Evil Deeds

"And this is the condemnation, that light is come into the world, and men loved darkness rather than light, because their deeds were evil. For every one that <u>doeth evil</u> <u>hateth the light,</u> neither cometh to the light, lest his deeds should be reproved" (John 3:19-20). The following seal employs all forms of the phrase "do evil." The Bible combination *do evil* (25x), *doest evil* (1x), *doeth evil* (6x), *doing evil* (1x), *done evil* (11x), *did evil* (20x), *didst evil* (1x), *hateth the light* (1x) = 66.

Samaritans' Idolatrous Worship

"<u>Ye WORSHIP ye know not what: we know what we WORSHIP: for salvation is of the Jews</u>. But the hour cometh, and now is, when the true WORSHIPPERS shall WORSHIP the Father in spirit and in truth: for the Father seeketh such to WORSHIP him. God is a Spirit: and they that WORSHIP him must WORSHIP him in spirit and in truth" (John 4:22-24). Jesus addressed the Samaritans' corruption of true worship. They adhered only to the five books of Moses and rejected all the prophet's guiding words. Only a few centuries earlier they had built an unsanctioned temple in Samaria and for centuries had carried out unauthorized sacrifices there. Hence their worship was idolatrous. Their temple now lay desolate, but they worshiped the memory of it. Idolatrous worship is sincere worship, but it is sacrilegious in the Lord's eyes. The joined phrases *ye worship ye know not what: we know what we worship: for salvation is of the Jews* consists of 66 characters!

Some in Israel Think Christ to Be an Idolater

"<u>And</u> there was much murmuring among the people concerning him: for some said, He is a good man: others said, Nay; but he deceiveth the people" (John 7:12). The lead word of this verse *And* is the 70,866th word of the New Testament, and in this verse some of the people felt Jesus was an apostate idolater trying to lead Israelites into a new form of false worship.

The Idol's Servant

"Jesus answered them, Verily, verily, I say unto you, Whosoever <u>committeth</u> sin is <u>the servant</u> of sin" (John 8:34). When a person bows himself before an idol he displays his servanthood spirit to that idol and the god it represents. Such a servant performs other duties to the idol such as offering it foods, burning incense before it, and maintaining its shrine. As stated earlier, in the Hebrew text the word *serve* shares the same Hebrew root with worship. Again the word *commit* is mentioned naturally in 66 verses of the Bible.

> The title *the servant('s)* is mentioned in 66 verses of the Bible.
> The word *servant* is mentioned in 66 verses of the Law.
> The phrase *his servant* is mentioned in 66 verses of the Old Testament.
> The phrase *my servant* occurs 66 times in the Old Testament.

The Idol's House

"And the servant abideth not <u>in the house</u> for ever" (John 8:35a). Men have always loved to build houses for their false gods. Such an idolatrous structure is called a shrine and has a servant to attend to its needs. Again the phrase *in the house* occurs 166 times in the Bible.

Judas Immoderately Worshiped Money

"This he said, not that he cared for the poor; but because he was a thief, and <u>had the bag</u>, and bare what was put therein" (John 12:6). Judas put gain before God and mammon before Messiah. He had an immoderate attachment or devotion to money and was thus an idolater. The Bible combination *money* (64 chs) and *had the bag* (2 chs) = 66 chapters.

The Idolater's Walk

"Then Jesus said unto them, Yet a little while is the light with you. Walk while ye have the light, lest darkness come upon you: for he that <u>walketh</u> <u>in darkness</u> knoweth not whither he goeth" (John 12:35). Jesus contrasted the in-Christ walk with the idolatrous walk. The New Testament combination *walk* (65x) and *with idolaters* (1x) = 66.

The Chief Priests Idolize a Roman God

"But they cried out, Away with him, away with him, crucify him. Pilate saith unto them, Shall I crucify your King? <u>The</u> chief <u>priests</u> answered, We have no <u>king</u> but Cæsar" (John 19:15). As these priests pledged allegiance to Rome they committed idolatry by paying great homage to a man who was routinely worshiped as god. Their offense to the Lord did not go unpunished; about six hours later their Temple suffered significant damage in an earthquake. Again the title *the priests* occurs naturally 266 times in the Bible. Again the title *king* is mentioned in 366 chapters of the Old Testament.

66th Verse of Acts

"And with many other words did he testify and exhort, saying, Save yourselves from this untoward <u>generation</u>" (Acts 2:40). The apostle boldly compared the current leadership of Israel to that of the former idolatrous wilderness generation. The Greek word for "untoward" is *skolios* meaning warped. This word also figuratively means perverse. Peter's admonition reflected on some of the opening words of Moses' song of apostasy about the golden-calf-worshiping generation: "They have corrupted themselves. . . . they are a perverse and crooked generation" (Deut. 32:5). From Genesis to the Synoptic Gospels the word *generation* is mentioned in 66 chapters.

Worshiping the Host of Heaven

"To whom our fathers would not obey, but thrust him from them, and in their hearts turned back <u>again</u> into Egypt, Saying unto Aaron, <u>Make</u> us GODS to go before us: for as for this Moses, which brought us out of the land of Egypt, we wot not what is become of him. And they made a CALF in those days, and <u>offered sacrifice unto the IDOL, and rejoiced in the work of</u> <u>their own hands</u>. Then God turned, and gave them up to WORSHIP <u>the host of</u> heaven; as it is written in the book of the prophets, O ye house of Israel, have ye offered to me slain beasts and sacrifices by the space of forty years in the wilderness? Yea, ye took up the tabernacle of MOLOCH, and the <u>star</u> of your GOD REMPHAM, FIGURES which ye <u>made</u> to WORSHIP them: and I will carry you away beyond Babylon" (Acts 7:39-43).

Stephen testified concerning Israel's diso0bedient leadership in that idol-worshiping wilderness generation. The word *again* is the 699,666th word of the Bible, and it refers to going back to a land full of idolatry. Again the word *make* is mentioned in 66 verses of Ezekiel. The Bible combination *offered sacrifice unto the idol* (1x), *and rejoiced in the works of* (61x), *their own hands* (4x) = 66. Again the phrase *the host of* is mentioned in 66 verses of the Old Testament. The word *star(s)* occurs 66 times in the Bible. Again the word *made* is mentioned in 266 verses of the New Testament.

Immoderate Worship of a King

"And Herod was highly displeased with them of Tyre and Sidon: but they came with one accord to him, and . . . desired peace; because their country was nourished by the king's country. And upon a set day Herod, arrayed in royal apparel, sat upon his throne, and made an oration unto them. <u>And</u> the people gave a shout, saying, It is the voice of a GOD, and not of a man" (Acts 12:20-22). The leading word of the idolatrous-people verse *And* is the 94,166th word of the New Testament.

Salvation Sent to the Idol-Worshiping Gentiles

"For so hath the Lord commanded us, saying, I have set thee to be a light of the Gentiles, that thou shouldest be for <u>salvation</u> <u>unto the ends of</u> the earth" (Acts 13:47). Idol worship can be found from one end of the earth to the other. The Bible combination *salvation* (58 vs), *unto the ends of* (8 vs) = 66 verses.

Jupiter & Mercury

"And when <u>the people</u> saw what Paul had done, they lifted up their voices, saying in the speech of Lycaonia, <u>The GODS</u> <u>are come down</u> <u>to us in the</u> <u>likeness of men</u>. And they called Barnabas, JUPITER; and Paul, MERCURIUS, because he was the chief speaker. Then the priest of JUPITER, which was before their city, brought oxen and garlands unto the gates, and would have done sacrifice with the people" (Acts 14:11-13). These two evangelists corrected the people's idolatrous error. Again the phrase *the people* occurs 66 times in Joshua. The Bible combination *the gods* (58x), *are come down* (3x), *to us in the* (3x), *likeness of men* (2x) = 66. Here the word *come* is the 11,866th word of Acts.

Gentile Christians & Prohibitions against Idolatrous Practices

When the Jerusalem Church discovered from Paul and Barnabas' missionary report that the Gentiles had turned to the new Jewish faith they issued an edict. The Jerusalem council wanted to ensure that Christians living in heathen communities took measurable precautions to keep themselves from idolatrous practices. James declared, "Wherefore my sentence is, that we trouble not them, which from among the Gentiles are turned to God. But that we write unto them, that they abstain from pollutions of IDOLS, and from fornication, and from things strangled, and from blood" (Acts 15:19-20). This verse presents the Bible's 66th occurrence of the term *the Gentiles*, and we see its relationship to idol worship. Again the term *the Gentiles* is mentioned in 66 chapters outside the 66th apocalyptic book of the Bible.

Athens—The City of Idols

"Now while Paul waited for them at Athens, his spirit was stirred in him, when he saw the city wholly given to IDOLATRY" (Acts 17:16). Images of gods and heroes adorned Athens and were particularly visible on the Acropolis, the highest part of the city. The phrase *the city of* is mentioned naturally in 66 chapters of the Old Testament. The Old Testament *wholly* (26x), *given to* (36x), *idolatry* (1x) = 66!

The Greeks' Ignorant Worship

"Then Paul stood in the midst of MARS' hill, and said, Ye men of Athens, I perceive that in all things ye are too superstitious. For as I passed by, and beheld your devotions, I found an altar with this inscription, TO THE UNKNOWN GOD. Whom therefore ye ignorantly WORSHIP, him declare I unto you. . . . Forasmuch then as we are the offspring of God, we ought not to think that the Godhead is like unto gold, or silver, or stone, GRAVEN by art and man's device. And the times of this ignorance God winked at; but now commandeth all men every where to repent" (Acts 17:22-23, 29-30).

Because the Greeks perceived themselves as the most advanced and cultured of all civilizations, their idols and images were anthropomorphic—in man's likeness. The phrase *like unto* is mentioned in 66 chapters of the Bible. Again the word *gold* occurs naturally 166 times in the OT Narrative. Again the word *silver* is mentioned in 66 verses of the Law.

Idol Making Is a Profitable Craft

"For a certain man named Demetrius, a silversmith, which made silver SHRINES for DIANA, brought no small gain unto the CRAFTSMEN; Whom he called together with the workmen of like occupation, and said, Sirs, ye know that by this CRAFT we have our wealth" (Acts 19:24-25). The Bible combination *Demetrius* (3x), *silversmith* (1x), *Diana* (5x), *gain* (30x), *wealth* (27x) = 66. The word *craft* occurs 6 times in Scripture, a visual factor of 66. Again the word *made* is mentioned in 266 verses of the New Testament.

Temple of the Great Goddess Diana

"So that not only this our CRAFT is in danger to be set at nought; but also that the temple of the great GODDESS DIANA should be despised, and her magnificence should be destroyed, whom all Asia and the world WORSHIPPETH" (Acts 19:27). Here the word *great* is the 16,266th word of Acts. Again the phrase *the temple* occurs 66 times in the Old Testament.

Image of the Great Goddess Diana

Because the pagan assembly was confused, "all with one voice about the space of two hours cried out, Great is DIANA of the Ephesians. . . . And when the townclerk had appeased the people, he said, Ye men of Ephesus, what man is there that knoweth not how that the city of the Ephesians is a WORSHIPPER of the great GODDESS DIANA, and of the IMAGE which fell down from JUPITER?" (Acts 19:34b-35) The entirety of this idol-worshiping passage runs from verses twenty-three to forty-one and consists of 466 words surrounding the keyword *image*.

Turning the Gentiles from Their Idolatry

Christ had spoken to Paul with these instructions: "Delivering . . . from <u>the Gentiles</u>, unto whom now I send thee, To open their eyes, and to <u>turn them from darkness</u> to light, and <u>from the power of</u> Satan unto God, that they may receive forgiveness of sins, and inheritance among them which are sanctified by faith that is in me" (Acts 26:17b-18). The following three seals show that idol worship is the general sin implied in the text. Again the word *turn* is mentioned in 66 chapters of the Major and Minor Prophets. The Bible combination *turn from the* (4x) and *darkness* (162x) = 166. The Bible combination *from the darkness* (2x), *from the power of* (9x), *Satan* (55x) = 66. Again the term *the Gentiles* is mentioned in 66 chapters outside the 66th apocalyptic book of the Bible.

The Barbarians of Melita

"And he shook off the beast into the fire, and felt no harm. Howbeit they looked when he should have swollen, or fallen down dead suddenly: but after they had looked a great while, and saw no harm come to him, they changed their minds, and said that <u>he</u> was a GOD" (28:5-6). Here the underlined word *he* is the 107,466th word of the New Testament, and it refers to the man whom the barbarians suddenly began to idolize.

Creepy Idols Made by Foolish Men

"Because that, when they knew God, they glorified him not as God, neither were thankful; but became vain in their <u>imaginations</u>, and their foolish heart was darkened. Professing themselves to be wise, they became <u>fools</u>, And changed the glory of the uncorruptible God into an IMAGE made like to <u>corruptible</u> man, and to <u>birds</u>, and <u>fourfooted beasts</u>, and <u>creeping things</u>. Wherefore God also gave them up to uncleanness through the lusts of their own hearts . . . Who . . . WORSHIPPED and <u>SERVED</u> the <u>creature</u> more than the Creator, who is blessed for ever. Amen" (Rom. 1:21-25).

This passage mentions both anthropomorphic and zoomorphic idols. Again the word *fool* occurs 66 times in the Bible. Again the word *serve* occurs 66 times in the Law. The Bible combination *imaginations* (6x), *corruptible* (7x), *birds* (24x), *fourfooted beasts* (3x), *creeping things* (14x), *creatures* (12x) = 66.

The Abhorrence of Idols

"Thou that sayest a man should not commit adultery, dost thou commit adultery? thou that abhorrest IDOLS, dost <u>thou</u> <u>commit</u> sacrilege?" (Rom. 2:22). Here the word *thou* is the 1166th word of Romans, and refers to a person having idolatrous behavior. Again the word *commit* is mentioned naturally in 66 verses of the Bible.

Most Israelites Once Bowed to Baal's Image

"But what saith the answer of God unto him? I have reserved to myself <u>seven thousand men</u>, <u>who have not BOWED</u> <u>the knee</u> to <u>the IMAGE of</u> <u>BAAL</u>" (Rom. 11:4). The Old Testament combination *seven thousand men* (1x), *who have not bowed* (1x), *the knee* (1x), *Baal* (62x), *his image* (1x) = 66.

1066th Chapter of the Bible

"Moreover it is required in stewards, that a man be found faithful. . . . but he that judgeth me is the Lord. Therefore judge nothing before the time, until the Lord come, who both will bring to light the <u>hidden things</u> of <u>darkness</u>, and will make manifest the counsels of the hearts: and then shall every man have praise of God" (1 Cor. 4:2, 4c-5). Believers can have idols in their hearts, but the Lord will one day bring such hidden idolatry into the open. The Bible combination *hidden things* (4x) and *darkness* (162x) = 166.

Once more in this 1066th chapter of the Bible, Paul addresses the problem of idolizing men. "And these things, brethren, I have in a figure transferred to myself and to Apollos for your sakes; that ye might learn in us not to think of <u>men</u> above that which is written, that no one of you be puffed up for one against another" (v. 6). Again the word *men* is mentioned in 166 chapters of the New Testament.

28,466th Verse of the Bible

"But now I have written unto you not to keep company, if any man that is called a brother be a fornicator, or covetous, or an IDOLATER, or a railer, or a drunkard, or an extortioner; with such an one no not to eat" (1 Cor. 5:11). Corinth was ancient Greek metropolis port city. Worldly amusements were readily available for merchantmen and navies who came there on business or leisure. It was a city full of idolatrous temples and fulfillments for every sinner's vice. This 66th verse presents the keyword *idolater*.

No Entry into the Kingdom for Idolaters

"Know ye not that the unrighteous shall not inherit the kingdom of God? Be not deceived: <u>neither</u> fornicators, nor IDOLATERS . . . shall inherit the kingdom of God" (1 Cor. 6:9-10). Here the word *neither* is the 120,066th word of the New Testament, and it pertains to idolaters.

Idolatry Akin to Lustful Behavior

"Now these things were our examples, to the intent we should not <u>lust after evil things</u>, as they also lusted. Neither be ye IDOLATERS, as were some of <u>them</u>; as it is written, <u>The people</u> sat down to eat and drink, and <u>rose up</u> to play. Neither let us commit <u>fornication</u>, as some of <u>them committed</u>, and fell in one day three and twenty thousand" (1 Cor. 10:6-8). Paul brought across the Old Testament analogy that idolatry's spiritual perversions are akin to one's physical immorality. Corinth had pagan temples in which temple prostitution played an integral part. The Corinthian church had to be fully reformed from such behavior. Again the phrase *the people* occurs 66 times in Joshua. The phrase *rose up* is mentioned in 66 chapters of the Old Testament. The Bible combination *lust after evil things* (1 v), *fornication* (32 vs), *adultery* (33 vs) = 66 verses. Again the word *them* occurs 466 times in Jeremiah. Again the word *committed* is mentioned in 66 chapters of the Bible.

Flee from Idolatry

"Wherefore, my dearly beloved, <u>flee</u> from IDOLATRY" (1 Cor. 10:14). The word *flee* is mentioned naturally in 66 chapters of the Old Testament.

Be Careful of Eating Meat Sacrificed to Idols

"What say I then? that the IDOL is any thing, or that which is offered in sacrifice to IDOLS is any thing? But I say, that the things which the Gentiles sacrifice, they sacrifice to DEVILS, and not to God: and I would not that ye should have fellowship with DEVILS, Ye cannot drink the cup of the Lord, and the cup of DEVILS: ye cannot be partakers of the Lord's table, and of <u>the table of DEVILS</u>. . . . Whatsoever is sold in the shambles, that eat, asking no question for conscience sake: For the earth is the Lord's, and the fulness thereof. If any of them that believe not bid you to a <u>feast</u>, and ye be disposed to go; whatsoever is set before you, eat, asking no question for conscience sake. But if any man say unto you, This is offered in sacrifice unto IDOLS, eat not for his sake that shewed it, and for conscience sake" (1 Cor. 10:19-20, 25-28c).

The Bible combination *the table of devils* (1 v), *the feast* (59 vs), *the feasts* (6 vs) = 66 verses. The entirety of chapter ten is a warning against idolatrous behavior and consists of 667 words, a number from the 66-hundred range.

The Temple of Idols

"Be ye not unequally yoked together with unbelievers: for what fellowship hath righteousness with unrighteousness? and what communion hath light with darkness? And what concord hath Christ with Belial? or what part hath he that believeth with an infidel? And what agreement hath the temple of God with IDOLS?" (2 Cor. 6:14-16a) As Paul draws analogies about impure Christian relationships he again equates it with idolatrous behavior. Again the phrase *the temple* occurs 66 times in the Old Testament.

166th Chapter of the New Testament

"Now I say, That the heir, as long as he is a child, differeth nothing from a servant, though he be lord of all; But is under tutors and governors until the time appointed of the father. Even so we, when we were children, were in bondage under the elements of the world" (Gal. 4:1-3). The spiritual elements of this world are steeped in idolatry. Thus the world is in spiritual bondage to idolatry. The New Testament combination *were in bondage under* (1x), *the elements* (3x), *of the world* (62x) = 66.

Paul recalls the Galatians' former custom of idolatry. "Howbeit then, when ye knew not God, ye did service unto them which by nature are no GODS" (v. 8). Again the word *them* occurs 466 times in Jeremiah.

In accordance with our third definition of idolatry, the apostle now speaks of the Galatian's current immoderate attachment to Jewish observances that have been errantly forced upon them by the Judaizers. "But now, after that ye have known God, or rather are known of God, how turn ye again to the weak and beggarly elements, whereunto ye desire again to be in bondage? Ye observe days, and months, and times, and years. I am afraid of you" (vv. 9-11a). The Bible combination *ye observe days* (1x), *and months* (1x), *and times and years* (1x), *I am afraid* (7x), *of you* (156x) = 166.

No Idolatrous Works of the Flesh

"Now the works of the flesh are manifest, which are these; Adultery, fornication, uncleanness, lasciviousness, IDOLATRY" (Gal. 5:19-20a). Because Galatia was a Gentile church Paul had to warn the people about idolatrous practices. The Bible combination *the works of* (61x) and *idolatry* (5x) = 66.

No Idolatrous Souls in God's Kingdom

"But fornication, and all uncleanness, or COVETOUSNESS, let it not be once named among you, as becometh saints; Neither filthiness, nor foolish talking, nor jesting, which are not convenient: but rather giving of thanks. For this ye know, that no WHOREMONGER, nor unclean person, nor COVETOUS man, who is an IDOLATER, hath any inheritance in the kingdom of Christ and of God" (Eph. 5:3-5). Once more the apostle reminds believers about the

583

Old Testament parallel between immorality and idolatry. Because Ephesus was a Gentile church Paul had to warn the people also about engaging in idolatrous practices. This idolatrous verse number five precedes the 6166th verse of the New Testament.

6166th Verse of the New Testament

"Let no man deceive you with <u>vain</u> words: for because of these things cometh the wrath of God upon the children of disobedience" (Eph. 5:6). The words of an idolatrous man are the subject of this 66th verse. Again from Genesis to the Gospels the word *vain* is mentioned in 66 chapters.

No Idolatrous Talking

"Do all things without murmurings and disputings: That ye may be blameless and harmless, the sons of God, without rebuke, in the <u>midst of a crooked and perverse</u> nation, among whom ye shine as lights in the world" (Phil. 2:14-15). Because Philippi was a Roman colony it had plenty of images of gods and heroes on display to worship. Once again the words crooked and perverse signify idolatrous behavior, something that the Gentile Christians at Philippi were to stay clear of at all times. The Bible combination *midst* (364x), *of a crooked and perverse* (1x), *perverse and crooked* (1x) = 366.

The Immoderate Devotion of Angel Worship

"Let no man beguile you of your reward in a voluntary humility and WORSHIPPING of <u>angels,</u> intruding into those things which he hath not seen, vainly puffed up by his fleshly mind" (Col. 2:18). The phrase "voluntary humility" refers to one's willingness to bow before. Here the word *angels* is the 752,766th word of the Bible.

A Laundry List of Immoderate Behaviors

"<u>Mortify</u> therefore your members which are upon the earth; fornication, uncleanness, INORDINATE AFFECTION, evil concupiscence, and COVETOUSNESS, which is IDOLATRY" (Col. 3:5). Because Colossae was a Gentile church the people also needed warnings against idolatry. The word *mortify* is the 142,666th word of the New Testament. Here the keyword *idolatry* is the 752,966th word of the Bible.

No More Serving Idols

"<u>For they themselves shew of us what manner of entering in we had unto you, and how ye turned to God from IDOLS to SERVE the living and true God</u>" (1 Thess. 1:9). The Pauline Epistles combination *turned to God* (1 v), *from* (156 vs), *idols* (9 vs) = 166 verses. The New Testament combination *for they themselves shew of us* (1x), *what manner of entering in we had* (1x), *unto you and how* (1x), *ye turned* (1x), *to God* (56x), *from idols* (2x), *to serve* (3x), *the living and true God* (1x) = 66.

No Participation in Fornication

"For this is the <u>will of God, even your sanctification, that ye should abstain from fornication</u>" (1 Thess. 4:3). Because Thessalonica was a Gentile church the people also needed exhortation to remain free from idolatrous, spiritual strongholds. The Bible combination *will of God* (23x), *even your sanctification that ye should* (1x), *abstain from* (6x), *fornication* (36x) = 66.

66th Verse of First Thessalonians

"Ye are all the children of light, and the children of the day: we are not of the night, nor of darkness" (1 Thess. 5:5). The apostle compares the children of light with children of darkness. Instead of worshiping the invisible God as the children of the day do, the children of darkness worship the various visible things of this world. Again the phrase *the children* is mentioned in 366 chapters of the Bible. The phrase *the night* is mentioned naturally in 66 verses of the Old Testament.

The Idolatrous End-Time Man of Sin

"Let no man deceive you by any means: for that day shall not come, except there come a falling away first, and that MAN OF SIN be revealed, the SON OF PERDITION" (2 Thess. 2:3). The antichrist will seek to lead the world into the darkest depths of damnable idolatry the world has ever known—the worship of his personal name and image. The phrase *the man of* occurs 66 times in the Old Testament.

29,666th Verse of the Bible

"Who opposeth and exalteth himself above all that is called God, or that is WORSHIPPED; so that he as God sitteth in the temple of God, shewing himself that he is God" (2 Thess. 2:4) This evil man will sit in a rebuilt temple of God and expect to be worshiped and adored as God, to be idolized by the world. The antichrist or false Messiah will carry in his soul a damnable degree of pride. Underlined word *that* is the 145,666th word of the New Testament. The keyword *worshipped* actually occurs in this 666th verse. The *i* in "worshipped" is the 66th letter in this idolatrous verse. Again the phrase *the temple* occurs 66 times in the Old Testament. The word *himself* occurs 66 times in the Major and Minor Prophets.

The Image of Him Who Is the Antichrist

"Even him, whose coming is after the working of Satan with all power and signs and lying wonders" (2 Thess. 2:9). Here the word "him" refers to the idolatrous man of sin, the antichrist, the world's most infamous idolater. He will attempt to kill all people who refuse to show idolatrous allegiance to him. The word *him* occurs 6661 times in the Bible.

End-Time False Teachers & Idolatry

"Now the Spirit speaketh expressly, that in the latter times some shall depart from the faith, giving heed to seducing spirits, and doctrines of DEVILS; Speaking lies in hypocrisy; having their conscience seared with a hot iron" (1 Tim. 4:1-2). Such willful apostasy leads men to become false teachers of idolatry and perverseness. These false teachers and false prophets will help propagate the global mandate of souls to receive the idolatrous mark of the beast. The Bible combination *now the Spirit* (1x), *speaketh expressly* (1x), *that in the latter times* (1x), *some shall depart from the faith* (1x), *giving heed to* (2x), *seducing* (1x), [lowercase only] *spirits* (42x), *doctrines* (5x), *of devils* (5x), *speaking lies* (2x), *in hypocrisy having* (1x), *their conscience* (3x), *seared with a hot iron* (1x) = 66.

No Vain Babblings

"But shun profane and vain babblings: for they will increase unto more ungodliness" (2 Tim. 2:16). Men first began to babble at Babel when God confused mankind's common language. Again the word *they* is mentioned in 166 chapters of the Law. The lead word of this idolatry verse *but* is the 759,566th word of the Bible. The Old Testament combination *profane and* (1 ch), *vain* (63 chs), *Babel* (2 chs) = 66 chapters.

All Men Hold Tendency toward Idolatry

"For the grace of God that bringeth salvation hath appeared to <u>all men</u>" (Titus 2:11). All humanity inherit Adam's original sin through his sin-tainted blood line. All men are therefore born with pride, having a me-first syndrome. It can be said that anything which comes before God is considered idolatry. Tragically idolatrous man loves himself very much and without even giving it much thought. He must therefore be taught to love God. The phrase *all men* is mentioned in 66 chapters of the Bible.

Jesus Was Once Tempted to Idolize Lucifer

"<u>For we have not an high priest</u> which cannot be touched with <u>the feeling of our infirmities; but was in all</u> <u>points</u> <u>tempted</u> <u>like as we are,</u> <u>yet without sin</u>" (Heb. 4:15). Two gospel accounts bear record of the devil attempting to tempt Christ to fall down and worship him. That test was genuine and real, but Jesus could have never failed this trial because He was God incarnate. The Bible combination *for we have not an high priest* (1x), *which cannot be touched with* (1x), *the feeling of our infirmities* (1x), *but was in all* (1x), *points* (2x), *tempted* (25x), *like as* (28x), *as we are* (6x), *yet without sin* (1x) = 66.

66th Verse of James

"Who is a wise man and endued with knowledge among you? let him shew out of a good conversation his works with meekness of wisdom" (James 3:13). The opposite of meekness and wisdom is pride and foolishness. James' letter is an exhortation on exhibiting true religion and thereby true worship. This would stand in contrast to idolatrous worship. The Bible words *pride* (46 vs) and *foolishness* (20 vs) = 66 verses.

No Immoderate Fleshly Lusts in Your Soul

"Dearly beloved, I beseech you as strangers and pilgrims, <u>abstain</u> <u>from</u> <u>fleshly</u> <u>lusts,</u> <u>which war against the soul</u>" (1 Pet. 2:11). When a man lusts after a woman he is idolizing that woman. This is so because he has become immoderately attached or devoted to her body. The General Epistles combination *abstain* (1x), *from* (52x), *fleshly* (1x), *lusts* (10x), *which war against* (1x), *the soul* (1x) = 66.

A Past Life of Idolatrous Behavior

"<u>For the time</u> <u>past</u> <u>of our life may suffice us to have wrought the will of the Gentiles,</u> when we walked in lasciviousness, lusts, excess of wine, revellings, banquetings, and abominable IDOLATRIES" (1 Pet. 4:3). The Bible combination *for the time* (14x), *past* (51x), *of our life may suffice us to have wrought the will of the Gentiles* (1x) = 66.

No Idols in the Church, on the Church, or Outside the Church

"<u>The church</u> that is at Babylon, elected together with you, saluteth you; and so doth Marcus my son" (1 Pet. 5:13). Whether Peter used Babylon as a covert name for Rome, Jerusalem, or for the actual city of Babylon, these cities were nevertheless rife with idol worship. Wherever the church was found in the first century, idols were certainly visible in every city. Early in the fourth century Rome adopted Christianity as its chief religion. At that time Rome turned its idolatrous temples into church buildings. The tragedy was that the people let their idols remain inside the churches and merely changed the names of the gods and goddesses to represent Christian figures mentioned in the gospels. Thus was the Roman-style church taken hostage by unsaved Gentiles and immersed into idolatry. This fact is attested by the following seal. The title *the church* occurs naturally 66 times in the New Testament.

Entangled in Idolatry's Dark Web

"For if after they have escaped the pollutions of the world through the knowledge of the Lord and Saviour Jesus Christ, they are <u>again</u> entangled therein, and overcome, the latter end is worse with them than the beginning" (2 Pet. 2:20). The term "the pollutions of the world" refers to all forms of idolatry. This idolatrous verse presents the Bible's 666th occurrence of the word *again*, and it refers to falling back again into idolatry.

Don't Let the Wicked Lead You away into Idolatry

"Ye therefore, beloved, seeing ye know these things before, beware lest ye also, being led away with the error <u>of the wicked,</u> fall from your own stedfastness" (2 Pet. 3:17). The phrase *of the wicked* is mentioned naturally in 66 chapters of the Bible.

The Spirit of Antichrist

"And every spirit that confesseth not that Jesus Christ is come in the flesh is not of God: and this is that <u>spirit of</u> <u>antichrist</u>, whereof ye have heard that it should come; and even now already is it in the world" (1 John 4:3). In the past two verses John warned about the idolatrous false prophets in the world, and now he draws attention to the spirit of idolatry which is borne out of the spirit of doctrinal error. The Bible combination *spirit of* (65 vs), *antichrists* (1 v) = 66 verses.

"Keep Yourselves from Idols"

"Little children, <u>keep</u> <u>yourselves from</u> <u>IDOLS.</u> Amen" (1 John 5:21). The New Testament combination *keep* (62x), *yourselves from* (3x), *idols of gold and silver and brass and stone and of wood* (1x) = 66.

1166th Chapter of the Bible

"I wrote unto the church: but Diotrephes, who loveth to have the preeminence among them, receiveth us not" (3 John 1:9). Diotrephes was an arrogant church bishop. He idolized himself. Accordingly his name means 'nourished by Zeus.'

Ungodliness & Lewdness

"How that they told you there should be <u>mockers</u> <u>in the last time,</u> <u>who should</u> <u>walk after their own</u> <u>ungodly</u> <u>lusts.</u> These be they who separate themselves, sensual, having not the Spirit" (Jude 18-19). Idolatrous or immoderate behavior is in view here. A sensual person is one who lacks moral restraints and is lewd and unchaste. Ungodly idolaters will always mock what is true and of the Spirit of truth. The Bible combination *mockers* (5x), *in the last time* (2x), *who should* (7x), *walk after their own* (1x), *ungodly* (27x), *lusts* (24x) = 66.

66th Book of the Bible

REVELATION is the 66th BOOK of the Bible for two reasons: its major theme is end-time idolatry which reaches beyond all previous historical or spiritual boundaries, and its major theme is Christ's all-powerful return to put away idolatry from the face of the earth.

Idolatrous Things to Be Revealed—"The Revelation of Jesus Christ, which God gave unto him, <u>to shew unto his servants</u> <u>things</u> <u>which must</u> <u>shortly come to pass</u>; and he sent and signified it by his angel unto his servant John" (Rev. 1:1). The word *shew* is the 778,866th word of the Bible. The Bible combination *to shew unto his servants things* (1x), *things* (1161x), *which must* (3x), *shortly come to pass* (1x) = 1166.

Idolatrous Souls in the Church's Midst—"But I have a few things against thee, because thou hast there them that hold the doctrine of BALAAM, who taught Balac to cast a stumblingblock before the children of Israel, to eat things sacrificed unto IDOLS, and to <u>commit</u> fornication" (2:14). This local first-century church found itself caught up in a wicked form of idolatrous behavior. The Lord warned the church at Pergamos about its ongoing evil. The keyword *idols* actually occurs in this 66th book of the Bible. Again the word *commit* is mentioned naturally in 66 verses of the Bible.

Idolatrous False Prophetess in the Church—"Notwithstanding I have a few things against thee, because thou sufferest that woman Jezebel, which calleth herself a prophetess, to teach and to seduce my servants to commit fornication, and to eat things sacrificed unto IDOLS. And I gave her space to repent of her <u>fornication</u>; and she repented not. Behold, I will cast her into a bed, and <u>them that commit</u> <u>adultery</u> with her into great tribulation, except they repent of their deeds" (2:20-22). The church at Thyatira was also caught up in idolatrous behavior. The keyword *idols* occurs again in this 66th book of the Bible. The Bible combination *them that commit* (1 v), *adultery* (33 vs), *fornication* (32 vs) = 66 verses.

Idolatrous World Leader's Victory Day & Worship as a King—"And I saw, and behold a white horse: and he that sat on him had a bow; and a <u>crown</u> was given unto him: and he went forth conquering, and to conquer" (6:2). The word *crown* occurs 66 times in the Bible.

7666th Verse of the New Testament—"For the great day of his wrath is come; and who shall be able to stand?" (6:17) In that day those who have not repented of their idolatrous ways will suffer greatly at the Lord's hand. Idolaters will not be able to withstand the judgment.

Idolatrous Souls Still Refuse to Repent—"And the rest of the <u>men</u> which were not killed by these plagues yet repented not of the works of their hands, that they should not WORSHIP DEVILS, and <u>IDOLS</u> of gold, and silver, and brass, and stone, and of wood: which neither can see, nor hear, nor walk" (9:20). A list of idolatrous behavior which defiant ones refuse to repent of is given here. As mentioned several times heretofore, idol worship is associated with vanity, a word which means empty or useless. Again the word *men* is mentioned in 166 chapters of the New Testament. The keywords *idols* and *worship* are mentioned together in this verse of the 66th book of the Bible.

Idolatrous Worldwide Party Lasts Three Days—"And <u>they</u> that dwell upon the earth shall rejoice over them, and make merry, and shall send gifts one to another; because these two prophets tormented them that dwelt on the earth" (11:10). This idolatrous celebration will take place immediately following the deaths of the two witnesses. Again the word *they* is mentioned in 166 chapters of the Law.

Idolatrous Kingdoms of This World Lose Their Power—"And the seventh angel sounded; and there were great voices in heaven, saying, The <u>kingdoms</u> of this world are become the kingdoms of our Lord, and of his Christ; and he shall reign for ever and ever" (11:15). All kingdoms of this fallen world system possess some measure of idolatry. Again the word *kingdom* is mentioned in 166 verses of the Old Testament.

Idolatrous Angels That Follow Satan—"And his tail drew the third part of the <u>stars</u> of heaven, and did cast them to the earth: and the dragon stood before the woman which was ready to be delivered, for to devour her child as soon as it was born" (12:4). Here the word *stars* is the 5866th word of Revelation. Again the word *star(s)* occurs 66 times in the Bible.

7766th Verse of the New Testament—"And the beast which I saw was like unto a leopard, and his feet were as the feet of a bear, and his mouth as the mouth of a lion: and the dragon gave him his power, and his seat, and great authority" (13:2). By his great power and control, the beast system will forcibly spread antichrist's idolatry all over the world.

Antichrist Becomes Idolized after He Rises from the Dead—"And I saw one of his heads as <u>it</u> were wounded to death; and his deadly wound was healed: and all the world wondered after the beast" (13:3). As we saw back in the book of Ezra, Adonikam's name means lord of rising or our lord arose, and the number associated with his name was precisely 666. This combination of name meaning and number assignment presents a prophetic pattern of the antichrist, a man who will in the last days rise from the dead after receiving a deadly sword wound and as a result will be worshiped as 'lord of all the earth.' Again the word *it* occurs 6066 times outside the apocalyptic 66th book of the Bible.

Idolatry of Satan & Antichrist Intensifies—"And they WORSHIPPED the dragon which gave power unto the beast: and they <u>WORSHIPPED</u> the beast, saying, Who is like unto the beast? who is able to make war with him? . . . And all that dwell upon the earth shall WORSHIP him, whose names are not written in the book of life of the Lamb slain from the foundation of the world" (13:4, 8). When referring to a person the word "beast" means a cruel, coarse, and filthy person. Such a definition describes an idolatrous person. The one mentioned here is the historically feared antichrist. Again the keywords *worship* and *worshipped* actually occur in this 66th book of the Bible. The underlined word *worshipped* presents the Bible's 66th occurrence of the word, and it falls here in the 66th book of the Bible.

Empowered False Prophet Facilitates Antichrist Worship—"And I beheld another beast <u>coming</u> up out of the earth; and he had two horns like a lamb, and he spake as a dragon. And he exerciseth all the power of the first beast before him, and causeth the earth and them which dwell therein to WORSHIP the first beast, whose deadly wound was healed" (13:11-12). This passage presents the New Testament's 66th occurrence of the word *coming*, and it refers to a coming end-time idolater. Again the keyword *worship* actually occurs in this 66th book of the Bible.

Empowered False Prophet Furthers Antichrist Worship—"And deceiveth them that dwell on the earth by the means of those miracles which he had <u>power</u> to do in the sight of the beast; saying to them that dwell on the earth, that they should <u>make an IMAGE to the beast</u>, which had the wound by a sword, and did live" (13:14). The underlined word *power* is the 6666th word of this 66th book of the Bible, and it refers to an idolater's satanic empowerment. Again the word *make* is mentioned in 66 verses of Ezekiel. The Bible combination *made an* (65x), *image to the beast* (1x) = 66.

Empowered False Prophet Forces Antichrist Worship—"And he had power to give life unto the IMAGE of the beast, that the IMAGE of the beast should both speak, and cause that as <u>many</u>

as would not WORSHIP the IMAGE of the beast should be killed" (13:15). Again the keywords *worship* and *image* actually occur within a single verse of this 66th book of the Bible. The word *many* is mentioned in 266 verses of the New Testament.

Empowered False Prophet Forces Antichrist's Idolatrous Mark—"And he causeth all, both small and great, rich and poor, free and bond, to <u>receive</u> a mark in their <u>right hand</u>, or in their foreheads" (13:16). The word *receive* is mentioned naturally in 166 verses of the Bible.

> The term *right hand* occurs naturally 166 times in the Bible.
> The word *right* is mentioned in 266 verses of the Old Testament.
> The word *right* occurs 66 times in the New Testament.

Idolatrous Number of the Antichrist—"And that no man might buy or sell, save he that had the mark, or the name of the beast, or the <u>number</u> of his name. Here is wisdom. Let him that hath understanding count the <u>number</u> of the beast: for <u>it is the</u> <u>number of</u> <u>a man</u>; and his number is SIX HUNDRED THREESCORE <u>AND SIX</u>" (13:17-18). Implantable microchips were perfected at the very beginning of the 21st century. These information-based and sometimes economic-based objects are routinely implanted under the skin of a person's hand. They are being used for business-related purposes, military purposes, and more. During the idolatrous reign of US President Barak Hussein Obama, three-dimensional nano-carbon images were produced with his likeness. His three-dimensional graven image was the same size as the period at the end of this sentence and could easily, if so desired, be inserted into a microchip which itself is about the size of a grain of rice. Here in this 66th book of the Bible the number *66* is actually found.

> The word *number* is mentioned in 166 verses of the Bible.
> The Synoptic Gospels: *it is the* (3x), *number of* (2x), *a man* (61x) = 66.
> Again the word *six* occurs 66 times in the Law.
> The phrase *and six* occurs 66 times in the Bible; seen for the 66th time.

Idolatrous Babylon's Doom Announced—"<u>And there followed another angel, saying, Babylon is fallen, is fallen, that great city, because she made all nations drink of the wine of the wrath of her fornication</u>" (14:8). Here idolatry is likened unto fornication. The Bible combination *and there followed another angel saying* (1x), *Babylon is fallen is fallen* (2x), *that great city because* (1x), *she made* (6x), *all nations drink* (1x), *of the wine* (9x), *of the wrath of* (9x), *of hers* (1x), *fornication* (36x) = 66.

Eternal Doom for Worshiping Antichrist—"And the third angel followed them, saying with a loud voice, If any man WORSHIP the beast and his IMAGE, and receive his mark in his forehead, or in his hand, The same shall drink of the wine of the wrath of God, which is poured out without mixture into the cup of his indignation; and he <u>shall be</u> tormented with fire and brimstone" (14:9-10c). Unlike idol worship in the past, anyone who participates in this end-time false-worship system will in no way be forgiven. Again the keywords *worship* and *image* occur in this 66th book of the Bible. Again the phrase *shall be* is mentioned in 666 chapters of the Bible.

Eternal Reward for Not Worshiping Antichrist—"And I saw as it were a sea of glass mingled with fire: and them that had gotten the victory over the beast, and over his IMAGE, and over <u>his</u> mark, and over the number of <u>his name</u>, stand on the sea of glass, having the harps of God" (15:2). Those faithful ones who trust God and refuse to submit to the antichrist's system of false worship will be beheaded for their faith. The Bible combination *his name* (165x) and *that* *antichrist* (1x) = 166.

266th Verse of Revelation—"And men were scorched with great heat, and blasphemed the name of God, which hath power over these plagues: and <u>they</u> repented not to give him glory" (16:9). They repented not from their idolatrous ways. Again the word *they* is mentioned in 166 chapters of the Law.

Mystery Babylon's Destruction for Propagating Idolatry—"And <u>the woman </u>was arrayed in <u>purple</u> and <u>scarlet</u> colour, and decked with gold and precious stones and pearls, having a golden cup in her hand full of abominations and filthiness of her fornication. . . . the fear of her torment, saying, Alas, alas, that great city Babylon, that mighty city! for in one hour is thy judgment come" (17:4; 18:10).   The New Testament combination *the woman* (51x), *purple* (9x), *scarlet* (6x) = 66.

Eternal Doom of the Beast & the False Prophet—"And the beast was taken, and with him the false prophet that wrought miracles before him, with which he deceived them that had received the mark of the beast, and them that WORSHIPPED his IMAGE. These both were cast alive into a lake of <u>fire</u> <u>burning</u> with <u>brimstone</u>" (19:20). Again the keywords *worshipped* and *image* actually occur in this 66th book of the Bible. The Bible combination *fire and brimstone* (6x) and *burning* (60x) = 66.

Eternal Doom of All Idolaters— "But the fearful, and unbelieving, and the abominable, and murderers, and whoremongers, and sorcerers, and IDOLATERS, and <u>all</u> liars, shall have their part in the lake which burneth with fire and brimstone: which is the second death. . . . For without are dogs, and sorcerers, and WHOREMONGERS, and murderers, and, IDOLATERS and whosoever loveth and maketh a lie" (21:8, 15). The word *all* occurs 166 times in the Minor Prophets, and is found in 66 books of the Bible.

APPENDIX

100: Heaven
1000: Glory
1611: King James Version
The Jesus Litmus Test

100—Heaven

The Bible uses the term HEAVEN and HEAVENS to indicate three different realms. The first realm is the lower heaven which envelops Earth with its fresh air, blue sky, and rain clouds. The second realm is the outer heaven which stretches across the universe's expanse of space being filled with bright stars, flaming suns, and planetary bodies. The third realm is that holy heaven wherein the Creator God dwells with all His holy angels, seraphim, cherubim, and saints.

All delineated forms of heaven point to the seal of heaven: *heaven* (550 vs), *heaven's* (1 v), *heavens* (127 vs), *heavenly* (22 vs) = 700 verses, a multiple of 100. The phrases *in heaven* (99 vs) and *in the heavenly places* (1 v) = 100 Bible verses. The phrase *from heaven* is found in 100 verses of the Bible.

The number ONE HUNDRED occurs only three times in Scripture, yet two amazing numeric seals are found in the last host verse. This find is revealed in Ezra.

The capitalized word *One* is mentioned in 100 verses of the Old Testament. The word *hundred* is mentioned in 101 chapters of the OT Narrative. The phrase *an hundred(fold)* is mentioned in 101 chapters of the Bible.

God Created the First Heaven

"In the beginning <u>God</u> <u>created</u> <u>the</u> <u>HEAVEN</u> and the <u>earth</u>" (Gen. 1:1). The word *the* occurs 100 times in Jonah and is mentioned in 100 chapters of the Pauline Epistles. The Revelation combination *God* (99x), *created heaven* (1x) = 100.

The word *earth* occurs 100 times in the OT Narrative.
The word *earth* occurs 200 times in the Law, a multiple of 100.

God Created the Second Heaven

"And God said, Let there be lights in the FIRMAMENT <u>of the</u> HEAVEN to divide the day from the night; and let them be for signs, and for seasons, and for days, and years: And let them be for lights in the FIRMAMENT <u>of the</u> HEAVEN to give light upon the earth: and it was so. And God made two great lights; the greater light to rule the day, and the lesser light to rule the night: he made the stars also" (Gen. 1:14-16). The phrase *of the* is mentioned naturally in 100 verses of Mark's Gospel.

100th Word of the Bible

"And God said, Let there be a FIRMAMENT in <u>the MIDST of</u> the waters, and let it divide the waters from the waters. And God made the firmament, and divided the waters which were under the FIRMAMENT from the waters which were above the FIRMAMENT: and it was so. And God called the FIRMAMENT HEAVEN" (Gen. 1:6-8). Here the word *midst* is the 100th word of the Bible, and it pertains to the creative placement of the first heaven. The phrase *the midst of* is mentioned in 200 chapters of the Bible, a multiple of 100.

Man Was Made in God's Heavenly Image

"So God created man in his own <u>image</u>, in the <u>image</u> of God created he him; male and female created he them" (Gen. 1:27). The word *image* occurs 100 times in the Bible.

Enoch Walked with God All the Way to Heaven

"And Enoch <u>walked</u> with God after he begat Methuselah three HUNDRED years, and begat sons and daughters. . . . And Enoch <u>walked</u> with God: and he was not; for God took him" (Gen. 5:22, 24). Enoch walked with God for exactly 300 years until the day God took him up to heaven, even without dying. The number 300 is a multiple of 100. The word *walked* is mentioned in 100 verses of the Old Testament.

The Windows of Heaven

"The fountains also of the deep and the windows <u>of</u> HEAVEN were stopped, and the rain from HEAVEN was restrained" (Gen. 8:2).

> The word *of* is mentioned in 100 chapters of the Pauline Epistles.
> The word *of* is mentioned naturally in 100 verses of First/Second Timothy.
> The word *of* occurs 6100 times in the New Testament.

God Spoke to Noah from Heaven

"And God <u>spake unto</u> Noah, saying, Go forth of the ark, thou, and thy wife, and thy sons, and thy sons' wives with thee" (Gen. 8:15-16). The phrase *spake unto* is mentioned in 100 chapters of the Law.

God's Rainbow in the Heaven

"<u>I do set my</u> bow in the CLOUD, and it shall be for a token of a covenant between me and the earth" (Gen. 9:13). The Bible combination *I do set my* (1x), *bow* (99x) = 100.

Building a Tower unto Heaven

"And they said, Go to, let us build us a city and a tower, whose top may reach <u>unto</u> HEAVEN; and let us make us a name, lest we be scattered abroad upon the face of the whole earth" (Gen. 11:4).

> The word *unto* is mentioned in 100 verses of Nehemiah.
> The word *unto* occurs 100 times in Job.

Possessor of Heaven

"And he blessed him, and said, <u>Blessed be</u> Abram of the most high God, possessor <u>of</u> HEAVEN and earth" (Gen. 14:19). The phrases *blessed is* (37x) and *blessed be* (63x) = 100. Again the word *of* is mentioned in 100 chapters of the Pauline Epistles.

Will of God in Heaven

"And Abram said, Lord <u>GOD</u>, what <u>wilt thou</u> give me, seeing I go childless, and the steward of my house is this Eliezer of Damascus?" (Gen. 15:2) The will of God originates in heaven. The phrase *wilt thou* occurs 100 times in the Old Testament. The phrase *wilt thou* is mentioned in 100 chapters of the Bible.

> The all-capitalized title *GOD* is mentioned in 300 verses of the Bible, multiple of 100.
> The all-capitalized title *GOD* is mentioned in 100 chapters of the Old Testament.

As for Me, God in Heaven
"<u>As for</u> me, behold, my covenant is with thee, and thou shalt be a father of many nations" (Gen. 17:4). The phrase *as for* is mentioned in 100 chapters of the Old Testament.

Based on a Heavenly Promise,
Isaac Was Born unto an Aged 100-Year-Old Father
"And when Abram was ninety years old and nine, the LORD appeared to Abram, and said unto him . . . As for Sarai thy wife, thou shalt not call her name Sarai, but Sarah shall her name be. And I will bless her, and give thee a son also of her: yea, I will bless her, and she shall be a mother of nations; kings of people shall be of her. <u>Then Abraham fell upon his face, and laughed, and said in his heart, Shall a child be born unto him that is an HUNDRED years old</u>? and shall Sarah, that is ninety years old, bear? . . . And Abraham called the name of his son that was born unto him, whom Sarah bare to him, Isaac. And Abraham circumcised his son Isaac being eight days old, as God had commanded him. <u>And Abraham</u> was <u>an HUNDRED years old, when his son Isaac was born</u> unto him" (Gen. 17:1a, 15b-17; 21:3-5).

By scholars of old, Isaac has been referred to as the Son of Promise. Indeed it was the God of Heaven who made this gracious promise to the aged earthly pilgrim called Abraham. The sentence *then Abraham fell upon his face, and laughed, and said in his heart, shall a child be born unto him that is an hundred years old* consists of 100 letters! The Law combination *and Abraham* (44x), *an hundred* (55x), *years old when his son Isaac was born* (1x) = 100.

Went up to Heaven
"And he left off talking with him, and God <u>went up</u> from Abraham" (Gen. 17:22). The phrase *went up* is mentioned in 100 verses of the OT Narrative.

Out of Heaven
"Then the LORD rained upon Sodom and upon Gomorrah brimstone and fire from the LORD <u>out of</u> HEAVEN" (Gen. 19:24). The phrase *out of* occurs 100 times in the Synoptic Gospels.

The God of Heaven
"And I will make thee swear by the <u>LORD</u>, the <u>God of</u> HEAVEN, and the God of the earth, that thou shalt not take a wife unto my son of the daughters of the Canaanites, among whom I dwell" (Gen. 24:3). The title *LORD God* is mentioned in 100 verses of the Kings and Chronicles. Again the word *of* is mentioned in 100 chapters of the Pauline Epistles.

Vision of a Ladder to Heaven
"And he dreamed, <u>and behold a ladder set up on the earth, and the top of it reached to heaven: and behold the angels of God ascending and descending on it</u>" (Gen. 28:12). The words *and behold a ladder set up on the earth, and the top of it reached to heaven: and behold the angels of God ascending and descending on it* consist of 100 letters!

The Blessings of Heaven
"Even by <u>the God of thy father, who shall help thee; and by the Almighty, who shall bless thee with blessings of HEAVEN above</u>" (Gen. 49:25a). The Law combination *the God of thy father* (5x), *who shall help thee* (1x), *and by the Almighty* (1x), *who shall bless thee with* (1x), *blessings* (6x), *of heaven* (30x), *above* (56x) = 100.

God's Eternal Existence in Heaven

"And God said unto Moses, I AM THAT I AM: and he said, Thus shalt thou say unto the children of Israel, I AM hath sent me unto you" (Exod. 4:14). The phrase *I am* is mentioned in 200 verses of the New Testament, a multiple of 100.

100th Verse of Exodus

"And the people believed: and when they heard that the LORD had visited the children of Israel, and that he had looked upon their affliction, then they bowed their heads and worshipped" (Exod. 4:31). The Old Testament combination *and that he had* (3 chs), *looked* (96 chs), *upon their affliction* (1 ch) = 100 chapters.

Moses Sprinkles Ashes toward Egypt's Heaven

"And they took ashes of the furnace, and stood before Pharaoh; and Moses sprinkled it up toward HEAVEN; and it became a boil breaking forth with blains upon man, and upon beast" (Exod. 9:10). The word *toward* in the phrase "toward the" occurs naturally 100 times in the Major and Minor Prophets.

Egypt's Heaven Suddenly Turns Violent

"And Moses stretched forth his rod toward HEAVEN: and the LORD sent thunder and hail, and the fire ran along upon the ground; and the LORD rained hail upon the land of Egypt" (Exod. 9:23). The Old Testament combination *burning fiery* (8x), *rain* (92x) = 100. The Old Testament combination *rain* (92x), *great hailstones* (3x), *upon the land of Egypt* (5x) = 100.

Egypt's Heaven Suddenly Turns Dark

"And Moses stretched forth his hand toward HEAVEN; and there was a thick darkness in all the land of Egypt three days" (Exod. 10:22). The Old Testament combination *and Moses stretched forth his hand toward heaven* (1 v), *and there was a thick* (1 v), *darkness* (97 vs), *in all the land of Egypt three days* (1 v) = 100 verses.

The Cloud Rider
(Part 1)

"And they took their journey from Succoth, and encamped in Etham, in the edge of the wilderness. And the LORD went before them by day in a pillar of a CLOUD, to lead them the way; and by night in a pillar of fire, to give them light; to go by day and night: He took not away the pillar of the CLOUD by day, nor the pillar of fire by night, from before the people" (Exod. 13:20-22). This passage presents the Bible's first mention of the word *cloud* as it relates to the glorious concept of God traveling accompanied by a cloud or clouds. In this mode of transport commentators have given Him an appropriate title—the Cloud Rider. Moses will emphasize this theme upon his departure song. In this opening scene of the Cloud Rider the underlined word *to* is the 10,100th word of Exodus, and it rests next to the heaven-related word cloud.

The Cloud Rider
(Part 2)

"And the angel of God, which went before the camp of Israel, removed and went behind them; and the pillar of the CLOUD went from before their face, and stood behind them: And it came between the camp of the Egyptians and the camp of Israel; and it was a CLOUD and darkness to them, but it gave light by night to these: so that the one came not near the other all the night" (Exod. 14:19-20). The Bible combination *the pillar of the* (5 vs), *cloud* (94 vs), *went from before their face* (1 v) = 100 verses.

Strong Heavenly Wind Parts the Red Sea

"And Moses stretched out his hand over the sea; <u>and the LORD caused the sea to go back by a strong east WIND</u> all that night, and made the sea dry land, and the waters were divided. . . . and the waters were a wall unto them on their right hand, and on their left" (Exod. 14:21-22). The Old Testament combination *the LORD caused the sea to go back by a* (1x), *strong wind* (2x), *strong east* (1x), *wind* (96x) = 100. The Old Testament combination *wind/s* (99x), *windy* (1x) = 100.

The Cloud Rider
(Part 3)

"And Moses went up unto God, and the LORD called unto him out of the mountain . . . And the LORD said unto Moses, <u>Lo, I come</u> <u>unto thee in a thick CLOUD,</u> <u>that the people may hear when I speak with thee,</u> and believe thee for ever. And Moses told the words of the people unto the LORD" (Exod. 19:3a, 9). The thick cloud shielded the people from looking upon God in their sinful, unsanctified flesh. The Bible combination *Lo* (42x), *I come* (56x), *unto thee in a thick cloud* (1x), *that the people may hear when I speak with thee* (1x) = 100.

Manna—Bread from Heaven

"And it came to pass, that at even the quails came up, and covered the camp: and in the morning the dew lay round about the host. And when the dew that lay was gone up, behold, upon the face of the wilderness there lay a small round thing, as small as the hoar frost on the ground. And when the children of Israel saw it, they said one to another, It is MANNA: for they wist not what it was. And Moses said unto them, This is the <u>bread</u> which the LORD hath given you to eat" (Exod. 16:13-15).

We will see later where one of the psalmists describes this food as "the corn of heaven." This passage consists of just two words short of 100.

The naturally occurring OTN combination *bread* (81x), *from heaven* (19x) = 100.
The Gospels combination *rain/ed* (4x), *bread* (62x), *from heaven* (34x) = 100.

Heavenly Refreshment Out of the Rock

"Behold, I will stand before thee there upon the <u>rock</u> in Horeb; and thou shalt smite the rock, and there shall come water out of it, that the people may drink. And Moses did so in the sight of the elders of Israel" (Exod. 17:6). This miraculous life-giving water is a picture of that eternal spring which ever flows in heaven. The Rock is a pre-figure of Christ, out of Whose riven side flowed life-saving water.

The lowercase word *rock* occurs 100 times in the Old Testament.
The lowercase word *rock* is mentioned in 100 verses of the Bible.

Canaan Land—Type of Heaven
(Part 1: A Prepared Place)

"Behold, I send an Angel before thee, to keep thee <u>in the way,</u> <u>and to bring thee into the place which I have</u> <u>prepared</u>" (Exod. 23:20). The goal was to bring Israel into Canaan Land, a type of heaven. The phrase *way of* is mentioned in 100 chapters of the Bible. The Bible combination *in the way* (99x), *and to bring thee into the place* (1x) = 100.

The past-tense word *prepared(st)* is mentioned in 100 verses of the Bible.
The Bible: *the place which I have* (1 v), *prepared* (99 vs) = 100 verses.

God Came down from Heaven Above

"And they saw the God of Israel: and there was under his feet as it were a paved work of a sapphire stone, and as it were the body of HEAVEN in his clearness" (Exod. 24:10). The color of sapphire is a rich blue like the heavens above! The Bible combination *down from* (91 vs), *heaven above* (9 vs) = 100 verses. The Old Testament combination *and they saw the* (1 v), *God of Israel* (199 vs) = 200 verses, a multiple of 100. The Bible combination *sapphire* (9x), *stone* (191x) = 200, a multiple of 100.

The Cloud Rider
(Part 4)

"And Moses went up into the mount, and a CLOUD covered the mount. And the glory of the LORD abode upon mount Sinai, and the CLOUD covered it six days: and the seventh day he called unto Moses out of the midst of the CLOUD. And the sight of the glory of the LORD was like devouring fire on the top of the mount in the eyes of the children of Israel. And Moses went into the midst of the CLOUD, and gat him up into the mount: and Moses was in the mount forty days and forty nights" (Exod. 24:15-18).

This passage consists of 99 heavenly words, a number that breathlessly waits to become 100.

The Cloud Rider
(Part 5)

Moses had ascended the mount of God to receive from Him a replacement copy of the Ten Laws which he had earlier cast out of his hands. "And the LORD descended in the CLOUD, and stood with him there, and proclaimed the name of the LORD. And the LORD passed by before him, and proclaimed, The LORD, The LORD God, merciful and gracious, longsuffering, and abundant in goodness and truth" (Exod. 34:5-6). The Old Testament combination *descended* (12x) and *cloud* (88x) = 100.

Symbolic Cherubim to Guard God's Heaven-on-Earth Throne

"And make one CHERUB on the one end, and the other CHERUB on the other end: [even] of the mercy seat shall ye make the CHERUBIMS on the two ends thereof. And the CHERUBIMS shall stretch forth [their] wings on high, covering the mercy seat with their wings, and their faces [shall look] one to another; toward the mercy seat shall the faces of the CHERUBIMS be. And thou shalt put the mercy seat above upon the ark; and in the ark thou shalt put the testimony that I shall give thee. And there I will meet with thee, and I will commune with thee from above the mercy seat, from between the two CHERUBIMS which are upon the ark of the testimony" (Exod. 25:19-22c).

God's throne in heaven is guarded by cherubim so others know it is directly unapproachable. This theme was to be exemplified inside the wilderness Tabernacle. In this passage there are 100 naturally occurring words from *cherub* to *cherubims*; bracketed words were supplied by the translators.

100 Loops of the Curtain

"Fifty loops shalt thou make in the one curtain, and fifty loops shalt thou make in the edge of the curtain that is in the coupling of the second; that the loops may take hold one of another. And thou shalt make fifty taches of gold, and couple the curtains together with the taches: and it shall be one tabernacle" (Exod. 26:5-6). The theme of *heaven* is seen here in the curtain's fashioning: 50 + 50 = 100.

The Most Heavenly Place

"And thou shalt hang up the vail under the taches, that thou mayest bring in thither within the vail the ark of the testimony: and the vail shall divide unto you between the holy place and THE MOST HOLY. And thou shalt put the mercy seat upon the ark of the testimony in the most holy place" (Exod. 26:33-34). Like heaven, the veiled Most Holy Place was unapproachable by mortal men. The term *most holy place* only occurs twice in the Law, yet its host verse here reveals the underlined and associated 20,100th word of Exodus.

Tabernacle's Tent Door to Be Heavenly Adorned

"And thou shalt make an hanging for the door of the tent, of blue, and purple, and scarlet, and fine twined linen, wrought with needlework" (Exod. 26:36). The Bible combination *purple* (48x) and *scarlet* (52x) = 100. The word *door* is mentioned in 100 verses of the Law. The Bible combination *tent* (98x), *of blue and purple and scarlet and fine twined linen wrought with needlework* (2x) = 100.

Tabernacle's Length to Be 100 Cubits

"The length of the court shall be AN HUNDRED cubits, and the breadth fifty every where, and the height five cubits of fine twined linen, and their sockets of brass" (Exod. 27:18). The Old Testament combination *length* (69 vs), *of the court* (30 vs), *shall be an hundred cubits* (1 v) = 100 verses.

Smoke of Sweet-Smelling Incense Ascends Heavenward

"And Aaron shall burn thereon sweet incense every morning: when he dresseth the lamps, he shall burn incense upon it. And when Aaron lighteth the lamps at even, he shall burn incense upon it, a perpetual incense before the LORD throughout your generations" (Exod. 30:7-8). The Major and Minor Prophets combination *the priest shall* (1x), *burn* (46x), *sweet* (16x), *incense* (37x) = 100. The Law combination *sweet* (54 vs), *incense* (42 vs), *every morning* (4 vs) = 100 verses.

Heavenly Blessing Bestowed upon You This Day

"For Moses had said, Consecrate yourselves to day to the LORD, even every man upon his son, and upon his brother; that he may bestow upon you a blessing this day" (Exod. 32:29). The Lord's daily blessings are bestowed upon His children from His holy dwelling place in heaven. The Bible combination *that he may* (98x), *bestow upon you* (1x), *a blessing this day* (1x) = 100. The phrase *this day* is mentioned in 100 verses of the Law.

Tabernacle's Hangings Were 100 Cubits

"And he made the court: on the south side southward the hangings of the court were of fine twined linen, AN HUNDRED cubits: Their pillars were twenty, and their brasen sockets twenty;

the hooks of the pillars and their fillets were of silver. And for the north side the hangings were AN HUNDRED cubits" (Exod. 38:9-11a). The Old Testament combination *the hangings of the court were of* (1 v), *fine* (99 vs) = 100 verses.

Tabernacle's Heavenly Sum of Silver—100 Talents

"This is the sum of the tabernacle, even of the tabernacle of testimony, as it was counted, according to the commandment of Moses. . . . And the silver of them that were numbered of the congregation was AN HUNDRED talents, and a thousand seven hundred and threescore and fifteen shekels, after the shekel of the sanctuary" (Exod. 38:21ab, 25).

A Doorway to Heaven in the Wilderness

"And he shall kill the bullock before the LORD: and the priests, Aaron's sons, shall bring the blood, and sprinkle the blood round about upon the altar that is by the door of the tabernacle of the congregation" (Lev. 1:5). This outer doorway could not be approached without first presenting the God of Heaven a sacrifice upon His holy altar. The word *altar* is mentioned in 300 verses of the Old Testament, a multiple of 100. The Leviticus-Numbers combination *altar that is by the door of* (1x), *the tabernacle of the congregation* (99x) = 100.

When Disobedient Israel's Heaven Turns to Iron

"And if ye will not yet for all this hearken unto me, then I will punish you seven times more for your sins. And I will break the pride of your power; and I will make your HEAVEN as iron, and your earth as brass: And your strength shall be spent in vain: for your land shall not yield her increase, neither shall the trees of the land yield their fruits" (Lev. 26:18-20). This promise simply means God will cause their rain to cease, causing their soil to turn hard like brass. The metallic word *iron* occurs 100 times in the Bible!

100th Verse of Numbers

"And I, behold, I have taken the Levites from among the children of Israel instead of all the firstborn that openeth the matrix among the children of Israel: therefore the Levites shall be mine" (Num. 3:12). The Kings and Chronicles combination *Levites* (98x), *be mine* (1x), *they are holy* (1x) = 100.

Heavenly Cloud Covered the Holy Tabernacle & Children

"And on the day that the tabernacle was reared up the CLOUD covered the tabernacle, namely, the tent of the testimony: and at even there was upon the tabernacle as it were the appearance of fire, until the morning. So it was alway: the CLOUD covered it by day, and the appearance of fire by night. And when the CLOUD was taken up from the tabernacle, then after that the children of Israel journeyed: and in the place where the CLOUD abode, there the children of Israel pitched their tents" (Num. 9:15-17).

The word *covered* is mentioned in 100 verses of the Bible.

Canaan Land—Type of Heaven
(Part 2: A Fruitful Land)

"And they came unto the brook of Eshcol, and cut down from thence a branch with one cluster of grapes, and they bare it between two upon a staff; and they brought of the pomegranates, and of the figs" (Num. 13:23). Canaan is a type of heaven, having wonderful provisions of so many goodly things. The Bible combination *and they came unto* (9x), *the brook of Eshcol* (1x), *and cut down from thence* (1x), *a branch* (6x), *with one cluster of* (1x), *grapes* (37x), *and they bare it between* (1x), *two upon a* (1x), *staff* (43x) = 100. The Bible combination *fig tree* (33x), *fig/s* (66x), *fruit of the land of Canaan* (1x) = 100.

4100ᵗʰ Verse of the Bible

"The place was called the brook Eshcol, because of the cluster of grapes which the children of Israel cut down from thence" (Num. 13:24). Here we see the fruit of the vines in Canaan being especially blessed of heaven: excluding the period at the end of this verse, it consists of 100 characters!

Canaan Land—Type of Heaven
(Part 3: A Land Flowing with Milk & Honey)

"<u>If the LORD delight</u> <u>in us, then he</u> <u>will bring us into this land</u>, <u>and give it us</u>; <u>a land which floweth with</u> <u>milk</u> and <u>honey</u>" (Num. 14:8). The Old Testament combination *if the LORD delight* (1x), *in us then* (1x), *he will bring us into this land* (1x), *and give it us* (1x), *a land which floweth with* (1x), *milk* (43x), *honey* (52x) = 100.

Purification from Sin

"And a man that is clean shall gather up the ashes of the heifer, and lay them up without the camp in a clean place, and it shall be kept for the congregation of the children of Israel for a water of separation: it is <u>a purification for</u> <u>sin</u>" (Num. 19:9). This purification by holy water was needed to enter the whole Israelite encampment. It is also typical of the needed water purification to enter heaven. The believer is presently washed from sin by the water of God's Word and the washing of regeneration by the Holy Ghost, an action made possible only by Messiah's blood atonement once for the sinner. The Old Testament combination *a purification for* (1 v), *sin* (299 vs) = 300 verses, a multiple of 100.

Canaan Land—Type of Heaven
(Part 4: A Desirable Land)

"And I besought the LORD at that time, saying, O Lord GOD . . . <u>I pray thee</u>, <u>let me</u> <u>go over</u>, <u>and see the good</u> <u>land that is</u> <u>beyond Jordan</u>, that goodly <u>mountain</u>, and Lebanon" (Deut. 3:23-25). The beautiful mountain Moses yearned to see was Mount Hermon which lies on Israel's northernmost border and rises 10,000 feet above sea level. Indeed it towers up through the first heaven. The word *mountain* is mentioned in 100 chapters of the Bible. The Law combination *I pray thee* (51x), *let me* (25x), *go over* (17x), *and see the good* (1x), *land that is* (2x), *beyond Jordan* (4x) = 100.

From One Side of Heaven to the Other

"For ask now of the days that are past, which were before thee, since the day that God created man upon the earth, and ask from the one <u>side of</u> HEAVEN unto the other, whether there hath been any such thing as this great thing is, or hath been heard like it?" (Deut. 4:32) The word *side* in the phrase "side of" occurs naturally 100 times in the Old Testament. The word *side* occurs 400 times in the Old Testament, a multiple of 100.

The Heaven of Heavens

"Behold, <u>the HEAVEN and the</u> <u>HEAVEN of HEAVENS</u> <u>is the LORD'S thy God</u>, the earth also, with all that <u>therein</u> is" (Deut. 10:14). Moses' figure of speech "heaven of heavens" is a summary description of heaven's grandeur and surpassing nature. The Old Testament combination *the heaven and the* (1x), *heaven of* (5x), *heavens* (93x), *is the LORD'S thy God* (1x) = 100. The word *therein* occurs 200 times in the Old Testament, a multiple of 100.

Canaan Land—Type of Heaven
(Part 5: A Land of Hills & Valleys)

"But <u>the land, whither ye go to possess</u> it, <u>is a land of hills</u> and <u>valleys, and drinketh water of the rain of heaven</u>: A land which the LORD thy God careth for: the eyes of the LORD thy God are always upon it, from the beginning of the year even unto the end of the year" (Deut. 11:11-12). The phrase *the land* occurs 300 times in the OT Narrative, a multiple of 100. The Bible combination *the land whither ye go to possess* (4x), *is a land of* (1x,) *hills* (65x), *valleys* (28x), *and drinketh water of* (1x), *the rain of heaven* (1x) = 100.

Promised Days of Heaven on Earth

"<u>That your days may be multiplied</u>, and the days of your children, in <u>the land which the LORD sware unto your fathers</u> to <u>give them, as the days of heaven</u> <u>upon the earth</u>" (Deut. 11:21). The Wisdom Books combination *that your days may be multiplied* (1 v), *days* (87 vs), *of heaven* (12 vs) = 100 verses. The New Testament combination *the LORD sware* (1x), *to give them* (2x), *the days* (39x), *of heaven* (58x) = 100. The Bible combination *the land which the LORD sware unto your fathers* (4x), *to give them as the days of heaven* (1x), *upon the earth* (95x) = 100. The phrase *the day(s) of* is mentioned in 300 verses of the Old Testament, a multiple of 100.

The Lord's Heavenly Habitation

"<u>Look down from</u> <u>thy holy habitation, from</u> <u>HEAVEN, and bless thy people Israel, and the land which thou hast given us</u>, as thou swarest unto our fathers, a land that floweth with milk and honey" (Deut. 26:15). Again the phrase *from heaven* is found in 100 verses of the Bible. The Law combination *look down* (1x), *down from* (13x), *thy holy habitation from* (1x), *heaven* (83x), *and bless thy people Israel* (1x), *and the land which thou hast given us* (1x) = 100.

"Give Ear, O Ye Heavens"

"Give <u>ear</u>, O ye HEAVENS, and I will speak; and hear, O earth, the words of my mouth" Deut. 32:1). These are the opening words of Moses' swan song. The word *ear* occurs 100 times in the Old Testament.

Precious Things of Heaven

"And of Joseph he said, Blessed of the LORD be his land, for the precious <u>things</u> of HEAVEN, for the dew, and for the deep that coucheth beneath" (Deut. 33:13). The Old Testament *blessed of the LORD be* (1x), *his land for the* (2x), *precious* (59x), *things of heaven for the* (1x), *dew* (37x) = 100. The word *things* is mentioned in 100 verses of the OT Narrative.

The Cloud Rider
(Part 6)

"There is none like unto <u>the God of Jeshurun, who RIDETH upon</u> <u>the HEAVEN in thy help,</u> and in his <u>excellency on</u> the SKY" (Deut. 33:26). Moses' song emphasizes the Lord's heavenly mode of transport. The Old Testament combination *the God of Jeshurun who rideth upon* (1x), *the heaven* (66x), *in thy help* (1x), *and in his* (29x), *excellency on* (1x), *the sky* (2x) = 100.

The Heavenly Land of Gilead

"And Moses went up from the plains of Moab unto the mountain of Nebo, to the top of Pisgah, that is over against Jericho. And the LORD shewed him all the land of <u>Gilead</u>, unto Dan" (Deut. 34:1). Gilead is a mountainous region full of thick forests, rolling hills, and fresh running rivers. Its highest peak reaches into the lowers heavens, 3900 feet above sea level. This land further qualifies as heavenly for it yields sufficient rainfall to sustain daily life. Although it is situated east of Jordan outside of the land Canaan, it properly belongs to Israel's fuller heavenly inheritance from the Lord. The name *Gilead* occurs 100 times in the Bible, all in the Old Testament.

Canaan Land—Type of Heaven
(Part 6: Passing over Jordan, a Type of Entering into Heaven)

"Pass through the host, and command the people, saying, Prepare you victuals; for within three days ye shall <u>pass over this</u> <u>Jordan, to go in</u> <u>to possess the land</u>, which the LORD your God giveth you to possess it" (Josh. 1:11). The name *Jordan* is mentioned in 103 verses of the OT Narrative, a number from the one-hundred range. The word *pass* is mentioned in 100 verses of the NT Narrative. Employing all tenses of the verb, the phrase *pass* over* occurs 100 times in the Bible. The Bible combination *pass over this* (3x), *Jordan to go in* (2x), *go in* (88x), *to possess the land* (7x) = 100. The Ecclesiastes combination *in* (99x), *an inheritance* (1x) = 100. The Esther combination *to go* (3x), *in* (97x) = 100. The Hebrews combination *go* (94x), *in* (3x), *inheritance* (3x) = 100.

> The word *in* occurs 600 times in Genesis, a multiple of 100.
> The word *in* is mentioned in 100 chapters of the Pauline Epistles.
> The word *in* occurs 2900 times in the New Testament, a multiple of 100.

The Midst of Heaven

"And the sun stood still, and the moon stayed, until the people had avenged themselves upon their enemies. Is not this written in the book of Jasher? So the sun stood still in <u>the midst of</u> HEAVEN, and hasted not to go down about a whole day" (Josh. 10:13). The phrase *the midst of* is mentioned in 200 chapters of the Bible, a multiple of 100.

Israel Began to Possess Her Heavenly Inheritance

"So Joshua took the whole land, according to all that the LORD said unto Moses; and Joshua gave it for an <u>inheritance</u> unto Israel according to their divisions by their tribes. And the land rested from war" (Josh. 11:23). The word *inheritance* is mentioned in 101 chapters of the Old Testament, a number resting so comfortably near 100 and being in the one-hundred range.

Canaan Land—Type of Heaven
(Part 7: A Land of Eternal Possession)

"And the children of Reuben and the children of Gad and the half tribe of Manasseh returned, and departed from the children of Israel out of Shiloh, which is <u>in the land of</u> <u>Canaan</u>, to go unto the country of Gilead, to <u>the land of their</u> <u>possession</u>, whereof they were possessed, according to the word of the LORD by the hand of Moses" (Josh. 22:9). The phrase *in the land of* occurs 200 times in the Old Testament, a multiple of 100. The Bible combination *that land* (17x), *of Canaan* (83x) = 100. The Old Testament combination *the land of their* (13 vs), *possession* (87 vs) = 100 verses. The word *possession* occurs 100 times in the Old Testament.

Spiritual Warfare in the Heavens

"They fought from HEAVEN; the stars in their courses fought against Sisera" (Judg. 5:20). The OT Narrative combination *they fought from heaven* (1x), *the stars* (4x), *in their* (77x), *courses* (17x), *fought against Sisera* (1x) = 100.

Sacrificial Flames Ascend toward Heaven

"For it came to pass, when the flame went up toward HEAVEN from off the altar, that the angel of the LORD ascended in the flame of the altar" (Judg. 13:20a). Again the word *toward* in the phrase "toward the" occurs naturally 100 times in the Major and Minor Prophets. Again the word *altar* is mentioned in 300 verses of the Old Testament, a multiple of 100.

The Lord's Protective Heavenly Wings

"The LORD recompense thy work, and a full reward be given thee of the LORD God of Israel, under whose wings thou art come to trust" (Judg. 2:12). Wings are made for soaring across the heavens. Here they are spoken of metaphorically. The OT Narrative combination *the LORD God of Israel* (81x), *under whose* (1x), *wings* (11x), *thou art come* (6x), *to trust* (1x) = 100.

Out of Heaven Shall God Thunder

"The adversaries of the LORD shall be broken to pieces; out of HEAVEN shall he thunder upon them: the LORD shall judge the ends of the earth; and he shall give strength unto his king, and exalt the horn of his anointed" (1 Sam. 2:10). Again the phrase *out of* occurs 100 times in the Synoptic Gospels.

Their Cry Went Up to Heaven

"And the men that died not were smitten with the emerods: and the cry of the city went up to HEAVEN" (1 Sam. 5:12).

The word *went* occurs 1400 times in the Bible, a multiple of 100.
The phrase *up to* is mentioned naturally in 200 verses of Bible, a multiple of 100.

Israel Seeks to Replace Her Heavenly King

"But the thing displeased Samuel, when they said, Give us a king to judge us. And Samuel prayed unto the LORD. And the LORD said unto Samuel, Hearken unto the voice of the people in all that they say unto thee: for they have not rejected thee, but they have rejected me, that I should not reign over them" (1 Sam. 8:6-7). The lowercase title *the king of* occurs 100 times in Second Kings. The word *me* occurs naturally 100 times in Judges.

From Heaven the Lord Said

"Will the men of Keilah deliver me up into his hand? will Saul come down, as thy servant hath heard? O LORD God of Israel, I beseech thee, tell thy servant. And the LORD said, He will come down. Then said David, Will the men of Keilah deliver me and my men into the hand of Saul? And the LORD said, They will deliver thee up" (1 Sam. 23:11-12). On this occasion the Lord spoke from heaven to answer David by the high priest who possessed the Urim and Thumim. At other times the Lord may have spoken aloud directly to the enquiring individual. The phrase *and the LORD/Lord said* is mentioned in 100 chapters of the Bible.

The Cloud Rider
(Part 7)

"Then the earth shook and trembled; the foundations of HEAVEN moved and shook, because he was wroth. There went up a smoke out of his nostrils, and fire out of his mouth devoured: coals were kindled by it. He bowed the HEAVENS also, and came down; and darkness [was] under his feet. And he RODE upon a cherub, and did fly: and he was seen upon the wings of the WIND. And he made darkness pavilions round about him, dark waters, [and] thick CLOUDS of the skies. Through the brightness before him were coals of fire kindled. The LORD thundered from HEAVEN, and the most High uttered his voice" (2 Sam. 22:8-14).

In this selected passage there are 100 naturally occurring words from the beginning unto its last mention of *heaven*; the bracketed words were supplied by the translators.

Into the Lord's Heavenly Hand

"And David said unto Gad, I am in a great strait: let us fall now into the hand of the LORD; for his mercies are great: and let me not fall into the hand of man" (2 Sam. 24:14). The phrase *into the hand of* is mentioned in 100 verses of the Bible, all in the Old Testament.

Heavenly Cloud Filled the Temple

"And it came to pass, when the priests were come out of the holy place, that the CLOUD filled the house of the LORD, So that the priests could not stand to minister because of the CLOUD: for the glory of the LORD had filled the house of the LORD" (1 Kings 8:10-11). The word *filled* occurs 100 times in Old Testament. The Old Testament combination *and it came to pass when the priests* (3x), *were come out of the holy place that the* (1x), *cloud* (88x), *filled the house of the LORD* (3x), *so that the priests* (2x), *could not stand to minister* (2x), *because of the cloud* (1x) = 100.

Solomon Spread Forth His Hands toward Heaven

"And Solomon stood before the altar of the LORD in the presence of all the congregation of Israel, and spread forth his hands toward HEAVEN" (1 Kings 8:22). The Bible combination *Solomon stood before the altar of the LORD* (1x), *and spread forth* (4x), *his hands* (83x), *toward heaven* (12x) = 100.

An Earthly House for the King of Heaven

"But will God indeed dwell on the earth? behold, the HEAVEN and HEAVEN of HEAVENS cannot contain thee; how much less this house that I have builded?" (1 Kings 8:27) Here the word *of* is the 8400th word of First Kings, a multiple of 100; it even rests comfortably between the keywords "heaven" and "heavens." The Ezra combination *God* (97x), *dwell* (2x), *the earth* (1x) = 100. The Bible combination *this house* (53 vs) and *builded* (47 vs) = 100 verses.

Praying toward God's Lower Heavenly House

"And hearken thou to the supplication of thy servant, and of thy people Israel, when they shall pray toward this place: and hear thou in HEAVEN thy dwelling place: and when thou hearest, forgive" (1 Kings 8:30). Again the word *ear* occurs 100 times in the Old Testament. The OT

Narrative combination *when they* (9x), *shall pray toward this place* (1x) = 100.

When Heaven Is Shut Up
"When HEAVEN is shut up, and there is no rain, because they have sinned against thee" (1 Kings 8:35a). The word *shut* occurs 100 times from Genesis to the NT Narrative.

> The word *when* is mentioned in 100 verses of Deuteronomy.
> The word *when* occurs 100 times in John's Gospel.

Praying with Hands Spread toward Heaven
"And it was so, that when Solomon had made an end of praying all this prayer and supplication unto the LORD, he arose from before the altar of the LORD, from kneeling on his knees with his hands spread up to HEAVEN" (1 Kings 8:54). The word *spread* is mentioned in 100 verses of the Old Testament. Again the phrase *up to* is mentioned naturally in 200 verses of the Bible, a multiple of 100.

All the Host of Heaven
Micaiah was speaking to Ahab's false prophets. "And he said, Hear thou therefore the word of the LORD: I saw the LORD sitting on his throne, and all the host of HEAVEN standing by him on his right hand and on his left" (1 Kings 22:19). The term *the host* occurs 100 times in the OT Narrative! The OT Narrative combination *I saw the LORD sitting on his throne* (1x), *and all the host of* (5x), *heaven* (93x), *standing by him on his right hand and on his left* (1x) = 100.

Elijah's Master Will Be Taken to heaven Today
"And the sons of the prophets that were at Beth-el came forth to Elisha, and said unto him, Knowest thou that the LORD will take away thy master from thy head to day? And he said, Yea, I know it; hold ye your peace" (2 Kings 2:3). As we see it here, the lowercase title *master* occurs 100 times in the Bible.

Elijah's Translation to Heaven
"And it came to pass, as they still went on, and talked, that, behold, there appeared a chariot of fire, and horses of fire, and parted them both asunder; and Elijah went up by a WHIRLWIND into HEAVEN. And Elisha saw it, and he cried, My father, my father, the chariot of Israel, and the horsemen thereof" (2 Kings 2:11-12a). The word *chariots* occurs naturally in 100 verses of the Old Testament. Again the phrase *went up* is mentioned in 100 verses of the OT Narrative. The word *into* is mentioned in 100 verses of Acts.

> Second Kings: *gone* (9x), *up* (90x), *by a whirlwind into heaven* (1x) = 100.
> The Chronicles combination *gone* (2x), *up* (96x), *unto heaven* (2x) = 100.
> The OT Narrative combination *go* up* (96x), *into/unto heaven* (4x) = 100.
> The Major/Minor Prophets: *gone up* (10 vs), *heaven* (90 vs) = 100 verses.
> The Acts combination *up* (94x), *into heaven* (6x) = 100.

100th Verse of Second Kings
"And the mother of the child said, As the LORD liveth, and as thy soul liveth, I will not leave thee. And he arose, and followed her" (2 Kings 4:30). The word *as* is mentioned in 100 verses of Genesis. This 100th verse which talks of the Heavenly Lord consists of 100 letters!

The Lord Made the Heavens
"For all the gods of the people are idols: but the LORD <u>made</u> <u>the HEAVENS</u>" (1 Chron. 16:26). The Gospels combination *made* (94x), *the heaven/s* (6x) = 100. Again the word *the* occurs 100 times in Jonah and is mentioned in 100 chapters of the Pauline Epistles.

Let the Heavens Be Glad & Earth Rejoice
"Let <u>the HEAVENS</u> <u>be glad, and</u> let the earth <u>rejoice</u>: <u>and let men say among the nations, The LORD reigneth</u>" (1 Chron. 16:31). The Old Testament combination *the heavens* (93x), *be glad and rejoice* (6x), *and let men say among the nations the LORD reigneth* (1x) = 100.

David Received an Answer from Heaven
"And David built there an altar unto the LORD, and offered burnt offerings and peace offerings, and called upon the LORD; and he <u>answered</u> him <u>from HEAVEN</u> by fire upon the altar of burnt offering" (1 Chron. 21:26). The word *answer* is mentioned naturally in 100 verses of the Old Testament. Again the phrase *from heaven* is found in 100 verses of the Bible.

Heaven's Exalted Head
"Thine, O LORD, is the greatness, and the power, and the glory, and the victory, and the majesty: for all that is in the HEAVEN and in the earth is thine; thine is the kingdom, O LORD, <u>and thou art</u> <u>exalted as</u> <u>head</u> <u>above all</u>" (1 Chron. 29:11). All forms of the word *exalt* occur 100 times in the Bible. The OT Narrative combination *and thou art* (2x), *exalted as* (1x), *head* (84x), *above all* (13x) = 100.

100ᵗʰ Verse of Second Chronicles
"And he stood before the altar of the LORD in the presence of all the congregation of Israel, and spread forth his hands" (2 Chron. 6:12). The next sequential verse tells us that Solomon spread forth his hands toward *heaven*.

Fire from Heaven
"Now when Solomon had made an end of praying, the <u>fire</u> <u>came down</u> <u>from HEAVEN, and consumed the burnt offering and the sacrifices</u>; and the glory of the LORD filled the house" (2 Chron. 7:1). The OT Narrative combination *fire* (75x), *came down* (24x), *from heaven and consumed the burnt offering and the sacrifices* (1x) = 100.

God in Heaven
"And Jehoshaphat stood in the congregation of Judah and Jerusalem, in the house of the LORD, before the new court, And said, O LORD God of our fathers, art not thou <u>God in</u> HEAVEN? and rulest not thou over all the kingdoms of the heathen? and in thine hand is there not power and might, so that none is able to withstand thee?" (2 Chron. 20:5-6) The phrase *God in* is mentioned naturally in 100 verses of the Bible.

Jehoiada Served the God of Heaven for 100 Years
"But Jehoiada waxed old, and was full of days when he died; an hundred and thirty years old was he when he died" (2 Chron. 24:15). As all Levites did, Jehoiada began his priesthood service at age 30. He later became high priest and lived to be 130 years old before dying, thus completing 100 years of service to the Lord.

Even unto Heaven

"Then the priests the Levites arose and blessed the people: and their voice was heard, and their prayer came up to his holy dwelling place, <u>even unto</u> HEAVEN" (2 Chron. 30:27). The phrase *even unto* is mentioned in 100 chapters of the Old Testament. Again the word *unto* occurs 100 times in Job.

Hezekiah Cried unto Heaven

"And for this cause Hezekiah the king, and the prophet Isaiah the son of Amoz, prayed and <u>cried</u> to HEAVEN" (2 Chron. 32:20). The Bible words *cried* (199x) and *cries* (1x) = 200, a multiple of 100.

100 Priests' Garments

"<u>They gave after their ability</u> unto the treasure of the work threescore and one thousand drams of gold, and five thousand pound of silver, and <u>ONE HUNDRED</u> priests' <u>garments</u>" (Ezra 2:69). The word *garments* occurs 100 times from Genesis to the NT Narrative where the Aaronic Priesthood came to an end with the advent of the Melchizedek Priest. The Old Testament combination *they gave after their ability* (1x), *one hundred* (3x), *priests'* (9x), *garments* (87x) = 100.

Burnt Offerings unto the God of Heaven

"And that which they have need of, both young bullocks, and rams, and lambs, <u>for the burnt offerings</u> of <u>the God of heaven</u>, wheat, salt, wine, and oil, according to the appointment of the priests which are at Jerusalem, let it be given them day by day without fail" (Ezra 6:9). The Old Testament combination *for the burnt* (9x), *offering/s unto* (73x), *the God of heaven* (18x) = 100.

Laws Decreed by the God of Heaven

"And I, even I Artaxerxes the king, do make a decree to all the treasurers which are beyond the river, that whatsoever Ezra the priest, the scribe of <u>the law of</u> the God of HEAVEN, shall require of you, it be done speedily" (Ezra 7:21).

> The phrase *the law* is mentioned in 100 verses of the Pauline Epistles.
> The phrase *the law of* occurs 100 times in the Bible.
> The phrase *law of* is mentioned in 100 verses of the Bible.

Beseeching the God of Heaven

"And said, I beseech thee, O L<small>ORD</small> God of HEAVEN, the great and terrible God, that keepeth covenant and mercy for them that love him and observe his commandments" (Neh. 1:5). Again the title *L<small>ORD</small> God* is mentioned in 100 verses of the Kings and Chronicles.

The Uttermost Part of Heaven

"But if ye turn unto me, and keep my commandments, and do them; <u>though there were of you cast out</u> <u>unto the uttermost</u> <u>part of</u> the HEAVEN, <u>yet</u> <u>will I gather</u> <u>them from thence</u>, and will bring them unto the place that I have chosen to set my name there" (Neh. 1:9). The Old Testament combination *though there were* (1x), *of you cast out* (1x), *unto the uttermost* (3x), *part of* (89x), *the heaven yet* (1x), *yet will I gather* (2x), *them from thence* (3x) = 100.

The Cloud Rider
(Part 8)

"Moreover thou leddest them in the day by a CLOUDY pillar; and in the night by a pillar of fire, to give them light in the way wherein they should go" (Neh. 9:12).The OT Narrative combination *moreover thou* (3x), *leddest them* (1x), *in the day* (10x), *by a* (14x), *cloudy* (1x), *pillar* (15x), *and in the night by a* (1x), *pillar* (15x), *of fire* (6x), *to give them* (4x), *light* (28x), *the way wherein they should go* (2x) = 100.

The Height of Heaven

"Is not God in the height of HEAVEN? and behold the height of the stars, how high they are! And thou sayest, How doth God know? can he judge through the dark CLOUD? Thick CLOUDS are a covering to him, that he seeth not; and he walketh in the circuit of HEAVEN" (Job 22:12-14). The OT Narrative combination *the height of the* (6x), *heaven* (93x), *the most High* (1x) = 100. The Bible combination *can he judge through the dark cloud* (1x), *thick* (39x), *clouds* (49x), *are a covering* (1x), *to him that he* (4x), *seeth not* (3x), *and he walketh* (2x), *in the circuit of heaven* (1x) = 100.

Look unto the Heavens

"Look unto the heavens, and see; and behold the CLOUDS which are higher than thou" (Job 35:5). The Old Testament combination *look unto* (8 vs), *the heavens* (91 vs), *and see and behold the clouds* (1 v) = 100 verses.

Sky Lights in the Lower Heavens

"Hearken unto this, O Job: stand still, and consider the wondrous works of God. Dost thou know when God disposed them, and caused the light of his CLOUD to shine? . . . Hast thou with him spread out the SKY?" (Job 37:14-15, 18a) Oftentimes clouds reflect the sun's light in such a heavenly fashion that a majestic sky is created, bringing God much glory. Again the word *spread* is mentioned in 100 verses of the Old Testament. The Bible combination *the light* (96x), *of a cloud* (4x) = 100.

Heavenly Sleep upon Heavenly Beds

"I will both lay me down in peace, and sleep: for thou, LORD, only makest me dwell in safety" (Ps. 4:8). The word *bed(s)* occurs 100 times in the Bible. All forms of the word "sleep" occur like this: *sleep* (82x), *sleeper* (1x), *sleepest* (4x), *sleepeth* (7x), *sleeping* (6x) = 100.

Consider the Heavens

"When I consider thy HEAVENS, the work of thy fingers, the moon and the stars, which thou hast ordained" (Ps. 8:3). The Old Testament combination *consider the* (6x), *the heavens* (93x), *the work of thy fingers* (1x) = 100.

The Throne of Heaven

"The LORD is in his holy temple, the LORD'S throne is in HEAVEN: his eyes behold, his eyelids try, the children of men" (Ps. 11:4). The phrase *is in* occurs 101 times in the New Testament.

The word *is* is mentioned in 100 chapters of the Pauline Epistles.

The word *is* occurs 100 times in the Apocalyptic Epistle.

Waking up with Heavenly Satisfaction

"As for me, I will behold thy <u>face</u> in righteousness: I shall be <u>satisfied, when I awake</u>, with thy likeness" (Ps. 17:15). The phrase *face of* is mentioned in 100 verses of the Bible. The Bible phrases *thine eyes* (94 vs) and *his beauty* (6 vs) = 100 verses. The Bible combination *satisfied when I awake* (1 v), *in heaven* (99 vs) = 100 verses.

The Cloud Rider
(Part 9)

"<u>He bowed the HEAVENS also, and came down: and darkness was under his feet. And he RODE upon a cherub, and did fly: yea, he did fly upon the wings of the WIND</u>" (Ps. 18:9-10). The darkness under the Lord's feet was His dark thunder clouds. The Old Testament combination *darkness* (97 vs), *was under his feet* (3 vs) = 100 verses. The Old Testament combination *he bowed the heavens also* (2x), *and came down* (6x), *and darkness was under his feet* (2x), *and he rode upon a* (2x), *cherub* (30x), *and did fly* (2x), *yea he did fly upon* (1x), *the wings of* (12x), *the wind* (43x) = 100.

Pathway to Heaven Ventures through the Valley of Death

"Yea, though I walk <u>through the</u> valley of the shadow of death, I will fear no evil: for thou art with me; thy rod and thy staff they comfort me" (Ps. 23:4). The phrase *through the* is mentioned in 100 chapters of the Old Testament.

The Lord's Heavenly Touch

"Thou preparest a table before me in the presence of mine enemies: thou <u>anointest</u> <u>my head with oil</u>; my cup runneth over" (Ps. 23:5). The Bible combination *anoint* (98x), *my head with oil* (2x) = 100.

The Lord's Heavenly House

"Surely goodness and mercy shall follow me all the days of my life: and I will dwell in <u>the house of the LORD</u> for ever" (Ps. 23:6). The phrase *the house of the LORD* is mentioned in 100 chapters of the Bible.

The Lord's Heavenly Heart

"The counsel of the LORD standeth for ever, the thoughts of <u>his heart</u> to all generations" (Ps. 33:11). Whose heart could be more heavenly than the Lord's?

> The lowercase phrase *his heart* is mentioned in 100 chapters of the Bible.
> The word *heart* occurs 100 times in the Law.

The Heavens Shall Declare God's Righteousness

"<u>And the heavens shall declare his righteousness: for God is judge himself</u>. Selah" (Ps. 50:6). The Bible combination *and the heavens shall* (4x), *declare* (95x), *his righteousness for God is judge himself* (1x) = 100. The Wisdom Books combination *and the heavens shall declare his righteousness* (1x), *for God is* (9x), *judge* (33x), *himself* (57x) = 100.

God Is Exalted above the Heavens

"Be thou <u>exalted</u>, <u>O God</u>, above the HEAVENS; let thy glory be above all the earth" (Ps. 57:5).

Again all forms of the word *exalt* occur 100 times in the Bible. The expression *O God/GOD* is mentioned naturally in 100 verses of the Old Testament. The expression *O God* is mentioned naturally in 100 verses of the Bible.

The Cloud Rider
(Part 10)

"Sing unto God, sing praises to his name: extol <u>him that RIDETH</u> <u>upon the</u> <u>HEAVENS by</u> <u>his name JAH</u>, and rejoice before him" (Ps. 68:4). The Wisdom Books combination *him that rideth* (2 vs), *upon the* (95 vs), *heavens by* (2 vs), *his name JAH* (1 v) = 100 verses.

The Cloud Rider
(Part 11)

"Sing unto God, ye kingdoms of the earth; O sing praises unto the Lord; Selah: To <u>him that RIDETH</u> <u>upon the</u> <u>HEAVENS of HEAVENS,</u> <u>which were of old</u>; lo, he doth send out his voice, and that a mighty voice. Ascribe ye strength unto God: his excellency is over Israel, and his strength is in the CLOUDS" (Ps. 68:32-34). The Psalms combination *upon the* (61x), *heavens* (39x) = 100. The Wisdom Books combination *him that rideth* (2 vs), *upon the* (95 vs), *heavens of heavens* (2 vs), *which were of old* (1 v) = 100 verses.

The Cloud Rider
(Part 12)

"The <u>chariots</u> of God are twenty thousand, even thousands of angels: the Lord is among them, as in Sinai, in the holy place. Thou hast ascended on high, thou hast led captivity captive" (Ps. 68:17-18b). As at Sinai, here God was shrouded by dark clouds. Again the word *chariots* is mentioned naturally in 100 verses of the Old Testament.

Wilderness Generation Fed with Heavenly Food

"Though he had commanded the CLOUDS from above, and <u>opened</u> <u>the doors of</u> <u>HEAVEN, And had rained down manna</u> upon them to eat, and had given them of the corn of HEAVEN. Man did eat angels' food" (Ps. 78:23-25a). The Old Testament combination *opened* (71 vs), *the doors of* (29 vs), *heaven and had rained down manna* (1 v) = 100 verses.

Wilderness Generation Visited with Heavenly Winds

The passage continues, "he sent them meat to the full. He caused an east <u>WIND</u> to blow in the HEAVEN: and by his power he brought in the south <u>WIND</u>" (Ps. 78:25b-26). The Old Testament combination *wind* (87x), *winds* (12x), *windy* (1x) = 100.

The Congregation of Saints in Heaven

"And the HEAVENS shall praise thy wonders, O LORD: thy faithfulness also in <u>the congregation of the saints</u>. . . . God is greatly to be feared in the assembly of the <u>saints</u>, and to be had in reverence of all them that are about him" (Ps. 89:5, 7). The phrase *the congregation(s)* is mentioned in 300 verses of the Bible, a multiple of 100. The word *saint(s)* occurs 100 times in the Bible.

A Faithful Witness in Heaven

The psalmist says of the David's household, "It shall be established for ever as the moon, and <u>as</u>

a faithful witness <u>in</u> HEAVEN. Selah" (Ps. 89:37). The phrase *as a* occurs 100 times in the Wisdom Books. Again the word *in* is mentioned in 100 chapters of the Pauline Epistles.

The 100ᵗʰ Psalm

A Psalm of praise.

"Make a joyful noise unto the LORD, all ye lands. Serve the LORD with gladness: come before his presence with singing. Know ye that the LORD he is God: it is he that hath made us, and not we ourselves; we are his people, and the <u>sheep</u> of his pasture. <u>Enter into</u> his gates with thanksgiving, and into his <u>courts</u> with praise: be thankful unto him, and bless his name" (Ps. 100:1-4). Among the complete five volumes of Psalms, this 100ᵗʰ Psalm is the only Psalm bearing the word "praise," an action that never ceases in heaven. All forms of the sword *sheep* occur 200 times in the Bible. The Bible combination *flock* (99 vs) and *sheepmaster* (1 v) = 100 verses. Courteous behavior is appropriate in heaven's holy court. The Bible words *court* (99 vs) and *courteous* (1 v) = 100 verses. The phrase *enter* into* is mentioned in 100 verses of the New Testament. The Bible combination *enter* (99 chs) and *entrances* (1 ch) = 100 chapters.

The Cloud Rider
(Part 13)

"Bless the LORD, O my soul. O LORD my God, thou art very great; thou art clothed with honour and majesty. Who coverest thyself with light as with a garment: who stretchest out the HEAVENS like a curtain: Who layeth the beams of his chambers in the waters: who maketh the CLOUDS his <u>chariot</u>: <u>who walketh</u> <u>upon the wings of the WIND</u>" (Ps. 104:1-3). Again the word *chariots* is mentioned naturally in 100 verses of the Old Testament. The Old Testament combination *who walketh* (1x), *upon the wings of the* (3x), *wind* (96x) = 100.

God's Word Is Forever Settled in Heaven

"For ever, O LORD, <u>thy word is settled</u> <u>in HEAVEN</u>" (Ps. 119:89). The Bible combination *thy word is settled* (1 v), *in heaven* (99 vs) = 100 verses.

Lift Up Your Eyes unto the Heavenly Hills

"I will <u>lift</u> up mine eyes unto the hills, from whence cometh my help. My help cometh from the LORD, which made HEAVEN and earth" (Ps. 121:1-2). The word *lift* is mentioned in 100 verses of the Bible.

The God of Heaven Is Merciful

"O give thanks unto the God of HEAVEN: for his <u>mercy</u> endureth for ever" (Ps. 136:26). The word *mercy* occurs 100 times in the Psalms.

Heaven—God Is There

"If I ascend up <u>into</u> HEAVEN, thou art <u>there</u>: if I make my bed in hell, behold, thou art there" (Ps. 139:8). Again the word *into* is mentioned in 100 verses of Acts.

The word *there* is mentioned in 100 verses of the Chronicles.
The word *there* is occurs 100 times in Jeremiah.

Heaven & All That Is Therein

"Which made HEAVEN, and earth, the sea, and all that <u>therein</u> is: which keepeth truth for ever" (Ps. 146:6). The word *therein* occurs 200 times in the Old Testament, a multiple of 100.

The Lord Established the Heavens

"<u>The LORD by wisdom hath founded the earth; by understanding hath he established the HEAVENS</u>" (Prov. 3:19). The Old Testament combination *the LORD by wisdom* (1x), *hath founded the earth by* (1x), *understanding hath* (2x), *he established* (3x), *the heavens* (93x) = 100.

100th Verse of Proverbs

"Hear, O my son, and receive my <u>sayings</u>; and the years of thy life shall be many" (Prov. 4:10). By divine Authorship these proverbial sayings belong to the God of Heaven. The word *saying(s)* occurs 1000 times in the Old Testament, a very visual multiple of 100.

Heaven's Pureness

"He that loveth <u>pureness</u> of heart, for the grace of his lips the king shall be his friend" (Prov. 22:11). The King of Heaven seeks friends that are pure in heart. The word *pure(ness)* occurs 100 times in the Bible.

God's Son Hath Ascended Up into Heaven

"Who hath ascended up <u>into</u> HEAVEN, or descended? who hath gathered the WIND in his fists? who hath bound the waters in a garment? who hath established all the ends of the earth? what is his name, and what is his son's name, if thou canst tell?" (Prov. 30:4) Again the word *into* is mentioned in 100 verses of Acts.

Trust in the Lord's Heavenly Salvation

"Behold, God is my salvation; I will <u>trust</u>, and not be afraid: for the LORD JEHOVAH is my strength and my song; he also is become my salvation" (Isa. 12:22). The word *trust* is mentioned in 100 chapters of the Bible.

The Cloud Rider
(Part 14)

"The burden of Egypt. <u>Behold, the LORD RIDETH upon a swift CLOUD</u>, and shall come into Egypt: and the idols of Egypt shall be moved at his presence, and the heart of Egypt shall melt in the midst of it" (Isa. 19:1). The Isaiah combination *behold* (93 vs), *the LORD rideth upon a swift* (1 v), *cloud* (6 vs) = 100 verses.

God Stretches Out the Heavens like a Curtain

"It is he that sitteth upon the circle <u>of the earth</u>, and the inhabitants thereof are as grasshoppers; that stretcheth out the HEAVENS <u>as a</u> curtain, and spreadeth them out as a tent to dwell in" (Isa. 40:22). The phrase *of the earth* occurs 300 times in the Bible, a multiple of 100. Again the phrase *as a* occurs 100 times in the Wisdom Books.

The First Person to Exist in Heaven

"Thus saith the LORD the King of Israel, and his redeemer the LORD of hosts; I am <u>the first</u>, and I am the last; and beside me there is no God" (Isa. 44:6). The phrase *the first* occurs 300 times in the Bible, a multiple of 100.

The Sent One from Heaven

"Come ye near unto me, hear ye this; I have not spoken in secret from the beginning; from the time that it was, there am I: and now the Lord GOD, and his Spirit, hath sent me" (Isa. 48:16). The Son of God speaks of His previous existence in heaven. The pronoun *me* is mentioned in 100 chapters of the NT Narrative.

The Eternal Nature of Heaven

"For thus saith the high and lofty One that inhabiteth eternity, whose name is Holy; I dwell in the high and holy place, with him also that is of a contrite and humble spirit, to revive the spirit of the humble, and to revive the heart of the contrite ones" (Isa. 57:15). The Bible combination *eternity* (1x), *everlasting* (97x), *without end* (2x) = 100. The New Testament combination *my name is called* (1x), *Holy* (99x) = 100.

God Stretched Out the Heavens by His Discretion

"He hath made the earth by his power, he hath established the world by his wisdom, and hath stretched out the HEAVENS by his discretion. When he uttereth his voice, there is a multitude of waters in the HEAVENS, and he causeth the vapours to ascend from the ends of the earth; he maketh lightnings with rain, and bringeth forth the WIND out of his treasures" (Jer. 10:12-13). The Old Testament combination *he hath established* (4x), *the world by his wisdom and hath stretched out* (2x), *the heavens* (93x), *by his discretion* (1x) = 100. The Major Prophets combination *a multitude of* (4x), *waters* (92x), *in the heavens* (4x) = 100. The Old Testament combination *and bringeth forth the* (2x), *wind* (96x), *out of his treasures* (2x) = 100.

Israel Protected by the Immeasurable Heaven

"Thus saith the LORD; If HEAVEN above can be measured, and the foundations of the earth searched out beneath, I will also cast off all the seed of Israel for all that they have done, saith the LORD" (Jer. 31:37). The Jeremiah combination *if* (55x), *heaven* (24x), *above* (6x), *can be* (1x), *measured* (2x), *and the foundations of the earth* (1x), *searched* (2x), *out beneath* (1x), *I will also* (3x), *cast off all* (1x), *the seed of Israel for all* (1x), *that they have done* (3x) = 100.

The Heavenly Father Will Answer Your Call

"Call unto me, and I will answer thee, and shew thee great and mighty things, which thou knowest not" (Jer. 33:3). The Bible combination *call* (190 vs) and *answer thee* (10 vs) = 200 verses, a multiple of 100.

Till the Lord Beholds Jerusalem from Heaven with Pity

"Mine eye trickleth down, and ceaseth not, without any intermission, Till the LORD look down, and behold from HEAVEN" (Lam. 3:50). Again the phrase *from heaven* is mentioned in 100 verses of the Bible. The Major and Minor Prophets combination *mine eye trickleth down and ceaseth not* (1x), *without any* (2x), *intermission* (1x), *till the LORD* (1x), *look down* (2x), *and behold from* (2x), *heaven* (91x) = 100.

Ezekiel Had Visions of an Opened Heaven

"Now it came to pass in the thirtieth year, in the fourth month, in the fifth day of the month, as I was among the captives by the river of Chebar, that the HEAVENS were opened, and I saw visions of God" (Ezek. 1:1). In his opening remarks the prophet testifies that while he was in exile from Israel, the heavens became opened to him. The Old Testament combination *the heavens were* (2x), *open* (97x), *and I saw visions of God* (1x) = 100.

The Cloud Rider
(Part 15)

"And I looked, and, behold, a WHIRLWIND came out of the north, a great CLOUD, and a fire infolding itself, and a brightness was about it, and out of the midst thereof as the colour of amber, out of the midst of the fire. Also out of the midst thereof came the likeness of four living creatures" (Ezek. 1:4-5a). The Priestly prophet beheld visions of God's Son descending in heavenly glory. Here the heavens-related word *whirlwind* is the 100th Word of Ezekiel.

The Cloud Rider
(Part 16)

"And above the FIRMAMENT that was over their heads was the likeness of a throne, as the appearance of a sapphire stone: and upon the likeness of the throne was the likeness as the appearance of a man above upon it. And I saw as the colour of amber, as the appearance of fire round about within it, from the appearance of his loins even upward, and from the appearance of his loins even downward, I saw as it were the appearance of fire, and it had brightness round about. As the appearance of the bow that is in the CLOUD in the day of rain, so was the appearance of the brightness round about. This was the appearance of the likeness of the glory of the LORD. And when I saw it, I fell upon my face, and I heard a voice of one that spake" (Ezek. 1:26-28).

Sapphire is the color of heaven—brilliant blue. The cloud rider in this vision is none other than the Son of God. The phrase *a man* occurs 100 times in the NT Narrative! In this Cloud Rider passage which at last introduces the Person of interest, there are precisely 100 words preceding the heaven-related word *cloud*.

God's Heavenly Mountain

"By the multitude of thy merchandise they have filled the midst of thee with violence, and thou hast sinned: therefore I will cast thee as profane out of the mountain of God: and I will destroy thee, O covering cherub, from the midst of the stones of fire" (Ezek. 28:16). Again the word *mountain* is mentioned in 100 chapters of the Bible.

Vision of a Tree That Reached unto Heaven

"The tree grew, and was strong, and the height thereof reached unto HEAVEN, and the sight thereof to the end of all the earth. The leaves thereof were fair" (Dan. 4:11-12a). Again the word *unto* occurs 100 times in Job. The Bible combination *the tree* (38x), *grew* (28x), *and was strong* (2x), *and the height* (15x), *thereof reached* (1x), *unto heaven* (12x), *and the sight thereof* (2x), *to the end of all the earth* (1x), *the leaves thereof were fair* (1x) = 100.

The King of Heaven

"Now I Nebuchadnezzar praise and extol and honour the King of HEAVEN, all whose works are truth, and his ways judgment: and those that walk in pride he is able to abase" (Dan. 4:37). The title *king* is mentioned in 400 verses of the Major and Minor Prophets, a multiple of 100.

The Lord of Heaven

"But hast lifted up thyself against the <u>Lord of</u> HEAVEN" (Dan. 5:23a). The title *LORD/Lord of* occurs 100 times in the Minor Prophets.

The Cloud Rider
(Part 17)

"I saw in the night visions, and, behold, one like the Son of man came with <u>the</u> CLOUDS of HEAVEN, and came to the Ancient of days, and they brought him near before him" (Dan. 7:13). Like Ezekiel's vision, this vision reveals the glory of God's Son. Here the underlined word *the* is the 575,100th word of the Bible, and it serves as the definition article for the heaven-related word "clouds." The Bible words *cloud* (94 vs) and *cloudy* (6 vs) = 100 verses.

The Heavens Shall Hear the Earth

"And it shall come to pass in that day, I will hear, saith the LORD, I will <u>hear</u> the HEAVENS, and they shall <u>hear</u> the earth" (Hos. 2:21). When Israel is at last reconciled to her Creator, heaven and earth shall also be reconciled. They will begin afresh enjoying the unity they once gladly held. Again the word *ear* occurs 100 times in the Old Testament.

End-Time Wonders in the Heavens

"And <u>I will shew</u> wonders <u>in the HEAVENS</u> <u>and in the earth,</u> <u>blood, and fire, and</u> <u>pillars of</u> <u>smoke</u>" (Joel 2:30). The Bible combination *I will shew* (24x), *wonders* (55x), *in the heaven* (15x), *and in the earth* (3x), *beneath blood and fire and* (1x), *pillars of smoke* (2x) = 100.

The Lord's Heavenly Recipe for Rain

"<u>It is he that</u> <u>buildeth his</u> <u>stories in the</u> HEAVEN, and hath founded his troop in the earth; he <u>that</u> <u>calleth for the waters of the sea,</u> <u>and poureth them out upon the face of the earth</u>: The LORD is his name" (Amos 9:6). The Major and Minor Prophets combination *it is he that* (2x), *buildeth his* (2x), *stories in the* (1x), *heaven* (91x), *that calleth for the waters of the sea* (2x), *and poureth them out upon the face of the earth* (2x) = 100.

Jerusalem Destined to Become a Heavenly Mountain

"But in the last days it shall come to pass, that <u>the mountain of the house of the LORD</u> shall be established in the top of the mountains, and it shall be exalted above the hills; and people shall flow unto it" (Mic. 4:1). Again the word *mountain* is mentioned in 100 chapters of the Bible. The phrases *the mount* (99x) and *the mountain of the house of the LORD* (1x) = 100.

The Cloud Rider
(Part 18)

"The LORD is slow to anger, and great in power, and will not at all acquit the wicked: the LORD hath his way in the WHIRLWIND and in the storm, and the CLOUDS are the <u>dust</u> of his feet" (Nah. 1:3). Climatologists have discovered that every drop of mist in the air has a speck of dust for its nucleus. The word *dust* occurs naturally 100 times in the Old Testament.

The Cloud Rider
(Part 19)

"God came from Teman, and the Holy One from mount Paran. Selah. His glory covered the

HEAVENS, and the earth was full of his praise. . . . Was the LORD displeased against the rivers? was thine anger against the rivers? was thy wrath against the sea, that thou didst RIDE upon thine horses and thy <u>chariots</u> <u>of</u> salvation? Thy bow was made quite naked, according to the oaths of the tribes, even thy word. Selah" (Hab. 3:3, 8-9b). Again the word *chariots* is mentioned naturally in 100 verses of the Old Testament. Here the underlined word *of* is the 599,000th word of the Old Testament, a multiple of 100.

God Will Shake the Heavens in the Last Days

"For thus saith the LORD of hosts; Yet once, it is a little while, and <u>I will shake</u> the HEAVENS, and the earth, and the sea, and the dry land" (Hab. 2:6). The Minor Prophets combination *I will shake* (2x), *the heavens* (98x) = 100.

The Heavenly King Will Come to Live in Jerusalem

"Yea, many people and strong nations shall come to seek the LORD of hosts <u>in Jerusalem</u>, and to pray before the LORD" (Zech. 8:22). The phrase *in Jerusalem* is mentioned in 100 chapters of the Bible.

The New Testament

The book of the generation of <u>Jesus</u> <u>Christ</u>, <u>the son</u> of David, the son of Abraham" (Matt. 1:1). By genealogy Jesus was not only the son of David and the son of Abraham but also the eternal Son of God. He came from heaven to usher in the kingdom of heaven. Because of His countrymen refusing His kingship, He went back to heaven until they should be ready to fully receive Him.

> The name *Jesus(')* occurs 100 times in Luke's Gospel.
> The title *Christ* is mentioned in 100 verses of First/Second Corinthians.
> The uppercase title *Son* is mentioned in 100 chapters of the New Testament.

Mary's Heavenly Baby Was Born

"And Jacob begat Joseph the husband of Mary, of whom <u>was</u> born Jesus, who is called Christ" (Matt. 1:16). The word *was* occurs 1000 times in the NT Narrative, a multiple of 100.

The Heavenly Voice of One Nazarene

"And he came and dwelt in a city called Nazareth: that it might be fulfilled which was spoken by the prophets, He shall be called <u>a Nazarene</u>" (Matt. 2:23). The Bible combination *voice of* (199x) and *a Nazarene* (1x) = 200. This title only occurs once in Scripture.

Christ's Heavenly Baptism

"And Jesus, when he was <u>baptized</u>, went up straightway out of the water: and, lo, the HEAVENS were opened unto him, and he saw the Spirit of God descending like a dove, and lighting upon him" (Matt. 3:16). John had baptized thousands of Jews, but this One was different. He had a heavenly glow about Him. All forms of the word baptize show the seal of heaven: *baptize* (9x), *baptized* (61x), *baptizeth* (2x), *baptizest* (1x), *baptizing* (4x), *baptism* (22x), *baptisms* (1x) = 100.

The Kingdom of Heaven

"From that time Jesus began to preach, and to say, Repent: for the kingdom of HEAVEN is at hand" (Matt. 4:17). The phrase *the kingdom* occurs 100 times in the Gospels!

The 100th verse of the New Testament

"Blessed are they which are persecuted for righteousness' sake: for theirs is the kingdom of HEAVEN" (Mat. 5:10). The keyword *heaven* actually occurs in this 100th verse.

Everyone Is Perfect in Heaven

"Be ye therefore perfect, even as your Father which is in HEAVEN is perfect" (Matt. 5:48). The Bible words *perfect* (99x) and *perfectness* (1x) = 100.

Doing the Will of the Father in Heaven

"Thy kingdom come. Thy will be done in earth, as it is in HEAVEN" (Matt. 6:10). Again the phrase *the kingdom* occurs 100 times in the Gospels. The word *will* is mentioned in 100 chapters of the Psalms.

Not Every Professor of Christ Shall Enter Heaven

"Not every one that saith unto me, Lord, Lord, shall enter into the kingdom of HEAVEN; but he that doeth the will of my Father which is in HEAVEN" (Matt. 7:21). Jesus preached under the dispensation of the Law not Grace. Thus He demanded works as clear evidence of one's faith. The Bible combination *not every one that saith unto me Lord Lord shall* (1 ch) *enter* (99 chs) = 100 chapters.

The Father Which Is in Heaven

"For whosoever shall do the will of my Father which is in HEAVEN, the same is my brother, and sister, and mother" (Matt. 12:50). The phrase *which is/be in* occurs 100 times the Bible. Again the word *is* occurs 100 times in Revelation. Again the phrase *is in* occurs 101 times in the New Testament. Again the word *in* is mentioned in 100 chapters of the Pauline Epistles.

Looking Up to Heaven

"And he commanded the multitude to sit down on the grass, and took the five loaves, and the two fishes, and looking up to HEAVEN, he blessed, and brake, and gave the loaves to his disciples, and the disciples to the multitude" (Matt. 14:19).

Heaven's New Covenant Church Gates

"And I say also unto thee, That thou art Peter, and upon this rock I will build my church; and the gates of hell shall not prevail against it" (Matt. 16:18). This verse presents the Bible's 100th occurrence of the phrase *the gate(s) of*; here it makes its first appearance in the New Testament.

The Cloud Rider
(Part 20)

"While he yet spake, behold, a bright CLOUD overshadowed them: and behold a voice <u>out of</u> the CLOUD, which said, This is my beloved Son, in whom I am well pleased; hear ye him. And when the disciples heard it, they fell on their face, and were sore afraid" (Matt. 17:5-6). Again the phrase *out of* occurs 100 times in the Synoptic Gospels.

Children's Guardian Angels in Heaven

"Take heed that ye despise not one of these little ones; for I say unto you, <u>That in HEAVEN their angels do always behold the face of my Father</u> which is in HEAVEN" (Matt. 18:10). The Bible combination *that in heaven their* (1x), *angels* (93x), *do always* (3x), *behold the face of* (3x) = 100. The Bible combination *angels* (93x), *do always* (3x), *behold the face* (3x), *face of my Father* (1x) = 100.

Jesus Speaks about Heavenly Treasure

"<u>JESUS</u> said unto him, If thou wilt be perfect, go and sell that thou hast, and give to the poor, and thou shalt have treasure in HEAVEN: and come and follow me" (Matt. 19:21). This verse presents the Bible's 100th occurrence of the name *Jesus*, and its host verse reveals the accompanying word "heaven."

The Prophet from Heaven

"And the multitude said, This is Jesus <u>the prophet</u> of Nazareth of Galilee" (Matt. 21:11). The phrase *the prophet* is mentioned in 100 chapters of the Bible.

The Cloud Rider
(Part 21)

"Immediately after the tribulation of those days shall the sun be darkened, and the moon shall not give her light, and the stars <u>shall fall from HEAVEN, and the powers of the HEAVENS shall be shaken</u>: And then shall appear the sign of the Son of man in HEAVEN: and then shall all the tribes of the earth mourn, and they shall see the Son of man <u>coming</u> in the CLOUDS of HEAVEN with power and great glory. And he shall send his angels with a great sound of a trumpet, and they shall gather together his elect from the four WINDS, from one end of HEAVEN to the other" (Matt. 24:29-31).

Jesus' use of the Old Testament Cloud-Rider theme was His clear claim to divinity. For this the Priesthood condemned Him to death. The Bible combination *shall fall* (99x), *from heaven and the powers of the heavens shall be shaken* (1x) = 100. The word *coming* occurs 100 times in the Bible.

Be Ready for the Son of Man's Heavenly Coming

"Therefore be ye also <u>ready</u>: for in such an hour as ye think not the Son of man <u>cometh</u>" (Matt. 24:44). The word *ready* occurs 100 times. The word *cometh* occurs 100 times in the Gospels.

The Cloud Rider
(Part 22)

"But Jesus held his peace. And the high priest answered and said unto him, I adjure thee by the living God, that thou tell us whether thou be the Christ, the <u>Son</u> of God. Jesus saith unto him, Thou hast said: nevertheless I say unto you, Hereafter shall ye see the <u>Son</u> of man sitting on the right hand of power, and <u>coming</u> in the CLOUDS of HEAVEN" (Matt. 26:63-64). Again the uppercase title *Son* is mentioned in 100 chapters of the New Testament. Again the word *coming* occurs 100 times in the Bible.

A Voice from Heaven

"And straightway coming up out of the water, <u>he saw the heavens opened,</u> <u>and the Spirit like a</u> <u>dove descending upon him</u>: <u>And there came</u> <u>a voice</u> <u>from HEAVEN, saying, Thou art my</u> <u>beloved Son</u>, in whom I am well pleased" (Mark 1:10-11). Here *heaven* is the 23,900th word of the New Testament, a multiple of 100. The New Testament combination *he saw the heavens opened* (1x), *and the Spirit like a dove descending upon him* (1x), *and there came* (13x), *a voice* (21x), *from heaven* (63x), *saying thou art my beloved Son* (1x) = 100.

Jesus Looked Up to Heaven to Pray

"And when he had taken the five loaves and the two fishes, he looked <u>up to</u> HEAVEN, and blessed, and brake the loaves, and gave them to his disciples to set before them; and the two fishes divided he among them all" (Mark 6:41). Again the phrase *up to* is mentioned naturally in 200 verses of the Bible, a multiple of 100.

Pharisees Were Seeking a Sign from Heaven

"And the Pharisees came forth, and began to question with him, seeking of him <u>a sign</u> from HEAVEN, tempting him" (Mark 8:11). The First Corinthian combination *a* (99x), *sign not to them that believe but to them that believe not* (1x) = 100. The First Corinthian combination *the Jews require a sign* (1x), *a* (99x) = 100.

A Poor Widow Lays Up Treasure in Heaven

"And Jesus sat over against the treasury, and beheld how the people cast money into the treasury: and many that were rich cast in much. And there came a certain poor widow, and she threw in two mites, which make a farthing. And he called unto him his disciples, and saith unto them, Verily I say unto you, That this poor widow hath cast more in, than all they which have cast into the treasury: For all they did cast in of their abundance; but she of her want did cast in all that she had, even all her living" (Mark 12:41-44).

This story of the poor widow and her last two mites consists of 100 words.

The Cloud Rider
(Part 23)

"Again the high priest asked him, and said unto him, Art thou the <u>Christ</u>, the <u>Son</u> of the Blessed? And Jesus said, I am: and ye shall see the Son of man sitting on the right hand of power, and coming in the CLOUDS of HEAVEN" (Mark 14:61b-62). Again the title *Christ* is mentioned in 100 verses of First and Second Corinthians. Again the uppercase title *Son* is mentioned in 100 chapters of the New Testament.

Jesus Welcomed Back into Heaven

"<u>So then after the Lord had spoken</u> <u>unto them,</u> he was <u>received</u> <u>up into</u> HEAVEN, <u>and sat on</u> <u>the</u> <u>right hand of God</u>" (Mark 16:19). The NT Narrative combination *so then after the Lord had spoken* (1x), *unto them he was* (1x), *received* (72x), *up into* (21x), *heaven and sat on* (1x), *the right hand of God* (4x) = 100.

The Son of the Highest in Heaven

"He shall be great, and shall be called the <u>Son of the Highest</u>: and the Lord God shall give unto him the throne of his father David" (Luke 1:32). The Bible words *prince* (99 vs) and *Son of the Highest* (1 v) = 100 verses.

The Way of Heavenly Peace

"To give light to them that sit in darkness and in the shadow of death, to guide our feet into the way of <u>peace</u>" (Luke 1:79). The word *peace* is mentioned in 400 verses, a multiple of 100.

The Heavenly Host Praising God

"And suddenly there was with the angel a multitude of <u>the</u> HEAVENLY <u>host</u> praising God, and saying, Glory to God in the highest, and on earth peace, good will toward men" (Luke 2:13-14). Again the term *the host* occurs 100 times in the OT Narrative.

The Holy Ghost from Heaven

"Now when all the people were baptized, it came to pass, that Jesus also being baptized, and praying, the HEAVEN was opened, And <u>the Holy Ghost</u> <u>descended</u> in a bodily shape <u>like a dove</u> upon him, and a voice came from HEAVEN, which said, Thou art my beloved Son; in thee I am well pleased" (Luke 3:21-22). The New Testament combination *the Holy Ghost* (89x), *descended* (7x), *like a dove* (4x) = 100.

The Heavenly Words That Jesus Said

"And all bare him witness, and wondered at the gracious <u>words which proceeded out of his mouth</u>. And they <u>said</u>, Is not this Joseph's son?" (Luke 4:27) The Bible combination *said* (3999x) and *words which proceeded out of his mouth* (1x) = 4000, a multiple of 100. The words *say* (1001x) and *said* (3999x) = 5000, a multiple of 100. Again the phrase *and the LORD/Lord said* is mentioned in 100 chapters of the Bible.

The Way of the Cross Leads Heavenward

"And he said to them all, If any man will come after me, let him deny himself, and <u>take up</u> his <u>cross</u> daily, and follow me" (Luke 9:23). The Bible combination *carry* (90x), *his cross* (10x) = 100.

Is Your Name Written in Heaven?

"Notwithstanding in this rejoice not, that the spirits are subject unto you; but rather rejoice, because <u>your names</u> are <u>written</u> in HEAVEN" (Luke 10:20). The word *name* occurs 100 times in the Psalms. The combination *your names* (1 v) and *in heaven* (99 vs) = 100 verses. The NT Narrative combination *written* (58x), *in heaven* (42x) = 100.

A Heavenly Portion for Every Faithful Servant

"And the Lord said, Who then is that faithful and wise steward, whom his lord shall make ruler over his household, to give them their <u>portion</u> of meat in due season?" (Luke 12:42) The word *portion* occurs 100 times in the Bible.

The Cloud Rider
(Part 24)

"Men's hearts failing them for fear, and for looking after those things which are coming on the earth: for the powers of HEAVEN shall be shaken. <u>And then shall they see</u> *the Son of man coming in a CLOUD with power and great glory*" (Luke 21:26-27). The Bible combination *and then shall they see* (2x), *the s/Son of man* (97x), *coming in a cloud with power and great glory* (1x) = 100.

Jesus Was Carried Up into Heaven

"And it came to pass, while he blessed them, he was parted from them, and carried up <u>into</u> HEAVEN" (Luke 24:51). Again the word *into* is mentioned in 100 verses of Acts.

Windows of Heaven Will Open for Jesus

"And he saith unto him, Verily, verily, I say unto you, Hereafter ye shall see HEAVEN open, and the angels of God ascending and <u>descending</u> <u>upon</u> the Son of man" (John 1:51). The Bible combination *descending* (8x) and *on him* (92x) = 100 times. The phrase *upon me* occurs 100 times.

Need for a Heavenly Birth

"Jesus answered and said unto him, Verily, verily, I say unto thee, Except a man be <u>born</u> <u>again</u>, he cannot see the kingdom of God" (John 3:3). The Bible words *born* (149x) and *again* (651x) = 800, a new-beginnings multiple of 100. The naturally occurring Major Prophets combination *born* (9x), *again* (91x) = 100.

"I Tell You of Heavenly Things"

"If I have told you earthly things, and ye believe not, how shall ye believe, if I <u>tell</u> you <u>of</u> HEAVENLY <u>things</u>?" (John 3:12) The word *tell* is mentioned in 100 chapters of the Old Testament. Again the word *of* is mentioned in 100 chapters of the Pauline Epistles. Again the word *things* is mentioned in 100 verses of the OT Narrative.

Christ Came to Finish the Father's Heavenly Work

"Jesus saith unto them, My meat is to do the will of him that sent <u>me, and to finish</u> his <u>work</u>" (John 4:34). Again the pronoun *me* is mentioned in 100 chapters of the NT Narrative. The Bible combination *and to finish* (1 v), *the work of* (99 vs) = 100 verses.

Everlasting Life in Heaven

"Verily, verily, I say unto you, He that heareth my word, and <u>believeth on him that sent me, hath everlasting life, and shall not come into condemnation; but is passed from death unto life</u>" (John 5:24). The Bible combination *believeth on him that sent me hath* (1x), *everlasting* (97x), *life and shall not come into condemnation* (1x), *but is passed from death unto life* (1x) = 100.

The Heavenly Bread of Life

"And Jesus said unto them, I am <u>the bread of</u> <u>life</u>: he that cometh to me shall never hunger; and he that believeth on me shall never thirst" (John 6:35). The naturally occurring Wisdom Books combination *the bread of* (6x), *life* (94x) = 100.

I Came Down from Heaven Above

"And they said, Is not this Jesus, the son of Joseph, whose father and mother we know? how is it then that <u>he saith</u>, I came <u>down from</u> <u>HEAVEN</u>?" (John 6:42) The phrase *he saith* occurs 100 times in the Bible. Again the Bible combination *down from* (91 vs), *heaven above* (9 vs) = 100 verses.

I Am the Door of Heaven

"Then said Jesus unto them again, Verily, verily, I say unto you, <u>I am the</u> door of the sheep. . . . <u>I am the</u> door: by me if any man enter in, he shall be saved, and shall go in and out, and find pasture" (John 10:7, 9). The phrase *I am the* is mentioned in 200 verses of the Bible, a multiple of 100. All forms of the word "feed" show the seal of heaven: *feed* (81x), *feedest* (2x), *feedeth* (8x), *feeding* (8x), *feedingplace* (1x) = 100.

Forever Young in Heaven

"And whosoever liveth and believeth in me shall never die. Believest thou this?" (John 11:26) The word *young* occurs 300 times in the Bible, a multiple of 100.

A Prepared Place Reserved for You in Heaven

"In my Father's house are many mansions: if it were not so, I would have told you. I go to <u>prepare</u> a <u>place</u> for you. And if I go and <u>prepare</u> a <u>place</u> for you, I will come again, and receive you <u>unto myself</u>; that where I am, there ye may be also" (John 14:2-3). The past-tense word *prepared(st)* is mentioned in 100 verses of the Bible. Again the phrases *in heaven* (99 vs) and *in the heavenly places* (1 v) = 100 Bible verses. The word *place* is mentioned in 100 verses of the New Testament.

> The phrase *unto me* is mentioned in 100 chapters of the Major Prophets.
> The phrase *unto me* occurs 100 times in New Testament.

Your Covenant Friend in Heaven

"Greater love hath no man than this, that a man lay down his life for his <u>friends</u>. Ye are my <u>friends</u>, if ye do whatsoever I command you" (John 15:13-14). The Bible words *friend* (49 vs), *friends* (48 vs), and *friendly* (3 vs) = 100 verses.

The Giver of Heavenly Life

"As thou hast given him power over all flesh, that he should <u>give</u> eternal life to as many as thou hast given him. And this is life eternal, that they might know thee the only true God, and Jesus Christ, whom thou hast sent" (John 17:2-3). The New Testament words *give* (199x) and *giver* (1x) = 200, a multiple of 100.

> The word *give* is mentioned in 100 chapters of the Law.
> The word *give* is mentioned in 100 verses of the Wisdom Books.

I Come to Thee in Heaven

"And now I am no more in the world, but these are in the world, and I come <u>to thee</u>" (John 17:11a). The phrase *to thee* is mentioned in 100 chapters of the Bible.

The Cloud Rider
(Part 25)

"And when he had spoken these things, while they beheld, he was taken up; and a CLOUD received him out of their sight. . . . Which also said, Ye men of Galilee, why stand ye gazing <u>up into HEAVEN</u>? this same Jesus, which is taken up from you into HEAVEN, shall so come in like manner as ye have seen <u>him go into HEAVEN</u>" (Acts 1:11). The NT combination *seen* (99x), *him go into heaven* (1x) = 100. The uppercase word *Go* occurs 100 times in the OT Narrative. Again the word *into* is mentioned in 100 verses of Acts. Again the Acts combination *up* (94x), *into heaven* (6x) = 100.

The Third Heaven Must Receive Jesus

"Repent ye therefore, and be converted, that your sins may be blotted out, when the times of refreshing shall come from the presence of the Lord; And he shall send Jesus Christ, which before was preached unto you: Whom <u>the HEAVEN</u> <u>must</u> <u>receive</u> <u>until the times</u> of restitution of all things" (Acts 3:19-21a). The phrase *things which* is mentioned in 100 verses of the NT. The Gospels combination *the heaven* (3x), *must* (36x), *receive* (58x), *until the time/s* (3x) = 100.

Jesus Christ Exalted in Heaven

"Him hath God <u>exalted</u> with his right hand to be a Prince and a Saviour, for to give repentance to Israel, and forgiveness of sins" (Acts 5:31). All forms of "exalt" show the seal of heaven: *exalt* (26x), *exalted* (64x), *exaltest* (1x), *exalteth* (9x) = 100.

Christ's Heavenly Light & Voice Comes to Saul of Tarsus

"And as he journeyed, he came near Damascus: and suddenly there shined round about him a light from HEAVEN: And he fell to the earth, and heard a voice saying unto him, Saul, Saul, why persecutest thou me? And he said, Who art thou, Lord? <u>And the Lord said</u>, I am Jesus whom thou persecutest: it is hard for thee to kick against the pricks" (Acts 9:3-5). Again the phrase *and the LORD/Lord said* is mentioned in 100 chapters of the Bible.

100th Chapter of the New Testament

Peter recalls his heavenly vision whereby a great sheet was "let down <u>from HEAVEN</u>" being full of all manner of unkosher creatures (Acts 11:5c). "And I heard a voice saying unto me, Arise, Peter; slay and eat. But I said, Not so, Lord: for nothing common or unclean hath at any time entered into my mouth. But the voice answered me again <u>from HEAVEN</u>, What God hath cleansed, that call not thou common" (vv. 7-9). This was God's way of signifying to the Jews that it was His heavenly ordained plan and time to graft in the Gentiles. Again the phrase *from heaven* is mentioned in 100 verses of the Bible.

Rain from Heaven

"Nevertheless he left not himself without witness, in that he did good, and gave us <u>rain</u> <u>from HEAVEN</u>, and fruitful seasons, filling our hearts with food and gladness" (Acts 14:17). All available tenses of the word *rain* occur 100 times in the Old Testament. The word *from* is mentioned naturally in 100 verses of Exodus.

Jews & Gentiles Invited to Heaven

"Even us, whom he hath called, not of <u>the Jews</u> only, but also <u>of the Gentiles</u>?" (Rom. 9:24) The case-sensitive phrases *the Jews* (199x) and *precious jewel* (1x) = 200, a multiple of 100. The Bible phrases *of the people* (199 vs) and *of the Gentile* (1 v) = 200 verses, a multiple of 100.

You Get to Heaven by Believing the Gospel

"Moreover, brethren, I declare unto you the gospel which I preached unto you, which also ye have received, and wherein ye stand; By which also ye are saved . . . For I delivered unto you first of all that which I also received, how that Christ died for our sins according to the scriptures; And that he was buried, and that he <u>rose again</u> <u>the third day</u> according to the scriptures" (1 Cor. 15:1-2a, 3-4). The New Testament combination *from the dead* (52 vs), *the third day* (48 vs) = 100 verses.

A Heavenly Body Is Needful to Be Fit for Heaven

"And as we have borne the image of the earthy, we shall also bear the <u>image</u> of the HEAVENLY. Now this I say, brethren, that flesh and blood cannot inherit the kingdom of God" (1 Cor. 15:49-50a). Again the word *image* occurs 100 times in the Bible.

The Judgment Seat of Christ in Heaven

"<u>For we must all</u> <u>appear</u> <u>before the</u> <u>judgment seat of Christ;</u> <u>that every one may receive the things</u> <u>done in his body</u>, according to that he hath done, whether it be good or bad" (2 Cor. 5:10). Our bad works will eventually bring shame when we stand before the Judge. We will not lose our salvation, only some of our rewards. The word *shame* occurs 100 times in the Bible. The New Testament combination *for we must all* (1x), *appear* (25x), *before the* (70x), *judgment seat of Christ* (2x), *that every one may receive the things* (1x), *done in his body* (1x) = 100.

The Third Heaven

"I knew a man in Christ above fourteen years ago, (whether in the body, I cannot tell; or whether out of the body, I cannot tell: God knoweth;) such an one caught up to <u>the third</u> HEAVEN" (2 Cor. 12:2). The phrase *the third* is mentioned in 100 chapters from Genesis to the Gospels. The phrase *the third* is mentioned in 100 verses of the Old Testament!

That Heavenly Mother Called Jerusalem

"But <u>Jerusalem</u> which is above is free, which is <u>the mother of</u> us all" (Gal. 4:26). Again the phrase *in Jerusalem* is mentioned in 100 chapters of the Bible. The Jeremiah combination *Jerusalem* (99 vs) and *the mother of* (1 v) = 100 verses. The word *mother* is mentioned in 100 chapters of the Old Testament.

The Israel of God

"And as many as walk according to this rule, peace be on them, and mercy, and upon the <u>Israel</u> of God" (Gal. 6:16). The name Israel belongs to those elected ones which are destined to experience all the blessings of heaven.

> The name *Israel* is mentioned in 100 verses of Second Samuel.
> The phrase *all Israel* is mentioned in 100 chapters of the Bible.
> The phrase *of Israel* is mentioned in 100 verses of Joshua.

Believers Given a Heavenly Inheritance

"Which is the earnest of our inheritance until the redemption of the purchased <u>possession</u>, unto the praise of his glory" (Eph. 1:14). Christ purchased the church with His own blood, and so it is His possession. Thus no believer can lose his or her salvation. Christ will see to it that each believer at last receives a new heavenly body to complete the whole transaction. Then and only then will the believer be able to live a sinless life to Christ's pleasing. Again the word *possession* occurs 100 times in the Old Testament.

Christ Is Set to Reign in the Heavenly Places

"Which he <u>wrought</u> in Christ, when he raised him from the dead, and <u>set</u> him at his own right hand <u>in the HEAVENLY places</u>" (Eph. 1:20). The word *wrought* occurs 100 times. Again the phrases *in heaven* (99 vs) and *in the heavenly places* (1 v) = 100 Bible verses. The Kings and Chronicles combination *set* (98x) and *in the heaven* (2x) = 100.

1100th Chapter of the Bible

"For this cause I bow my knees unto the Father of our Lord Jesus Christ, Of whom the whole <u>family</u> in HEAVEN and earth is named" (Eph. 3:14-15). The words *family* (123x), *families* (174x), and *kinsfolks* (3x) = 300, a multiple of 100. Just within the book of Numbers, the combination *the families of the* (75x) and *the family of the* (25x) = 100. 1100th chapter of the Bible.

Heavenly Bodies of Flesh & Bones

"For no man ever yet hated his own flesh; but nourisheth and cherisheth it, even as the Lord the church: For we are members of his body, of his flesh, and of his <u>bones</u>" (Eph. 5:30). Christ's resurrected body was fashioned with flesh and bones according to His own words. Our heavenly bodies will be equipped just the same. The word *bone(s)* is mentioned in 100 verses of the Bible.

High Places in Heaven

"For we wrestle not against flesh and blood, but against principalities, against powers, against the rulers of the darkness of this world, against spiritual wickedness in <u>high places</u>" (Eph. 6:12). The Bible phrases *high places* (98x), *highest part* (1x), and *highest room* (1x) = 100.

The Day of Christ & Our Upward Call to Heaven

"That ye may approve things that are excellent; that ye may be sincere and without offence till <u>the day of</u> Christ" (Phil. 1:10). The Day of Christ refers to that day when He will appear in the air and catch us up in the air to go be with Him. This event is commonly called the Rapture of the Church. The phrase *the day of* is mentioned in 100 chapters of the Old Testament.

Our Desire to Be with Christ in Heaven

"For I am in a strait betwixt two, having a <u>desire</u> to depart, and <u>to be</u> with Christ; which is far better" (Phil. 1:23). All tenses and forms of the word "desire" look like this: *desire* (111x), *desired* (50x), *desiredst* (2x), *desires* (3x), *desirest* (2x), *desireth* (17x), *desirable* (3x), *desiring* (12x) = 200, a multiple of 100. The phrase *to be* occurs 100 times in the Pauline Epistles.

Every Creature in Heaven Bows the Knee to Christ

"That at the name of Jesus every knee should bow, of <u>things</u> in HEAVEN, and things in earth, and things under the earth; And that every tongue should confess that Jesus Christ is Lord, to the glory of God the Father" (Phil. 2:10-11). Again the word *things* is mentioned in 100 verses of the OT Narrative.

Christ Created All Things in Heaven

"For by him were all things created, that are in heaven, and that are in earth, visible and invisible, whether they be thrones, or dominions, or principalities, or powers: all things were created by him, and for him" (Col. 1:16). The Pauline Epistles combination *for by him were* (1x), *all things* (98x), *created that are in heaven* (1x) = 100.

The Godhead in Heaven

"For in him dwelleth all the fulness of the Godhead bodily" (Col. 2:9). The phrases *of God* (399 chs) and *of the Godhead* (1 ch) = 400 chapters, a multiple of 100.

We Have a Master in Heaven

"Masters, give unto your servants that which is just and equal; knowing that ye also have a Master in HEAVEN" (Col. 4:1). The Gospels combination *also have* (2x), *ye have a* (2x), *Master* (55x), *in heaven* (41x) = 100.

Wait for God's Son from Heaven

"And to wait for his Son from HEAVEN, whom he raised from the dead, even Jesus, which delivered us from the wrath to come" (1 Thess. 1:10). The naturally occurring Bible combination *wait* (99 vs), *for his Son from heaven* (1 v) = 100 verses. Again the word *from* is mentioned naturally in 100 verses of Exodus. Again the phrase *from heaven* is mentioned in 100 verses of the Bible.

The Cloud Rider
(Part 26)

"For the Lord himself shall descend from HEAVEN with a shout, with the voice of the archangel, and with the trump of God: and the dead in Christ shall rise first: Then we which are alive and remain shall be caught up together with them in the CLOUDS, to meet the Lord in the air: and so shall we ever be with the Lord" (1 Thess. 4:16). The New Testament combination *for the Lord himself* (1x), *shall descend* (2x), *from heaven* (63x), *with a shout* (1x), *with the voice of* (1x), *the archangel* (2x), *and with the* (8x), *trump of God* (1x), *and the dead in Christ* (1x), *shall rise first* (1x), *then we* (3x), *which are alive* (2x), *and remain* (2x), *shall be caught up* (1x), *together with them* (2x), *in the clouds* (5x), *to meet the Lord* (1x), *in the air* (1x), *and so shall we ever* (1x), *be with the Lord* (1x) = 100.

"The Lord Jesus Shall Be Revealed from Heaven"

"And to you who are troubled rest with us, when the Lord Jesus shall be revealed from HEAVEN with his mighty angels" (2 Thess. 1:7). The Pauline and General Epistles combination *and to you who are troubled* (1x), *rest with us when the* (1x), *Lord Jesus* (96x), *shall be revealed from heaven* (1x), *with his mighty angels* (1x) = 100.

Christ's Heavenly Kingdom Is Forever & Ever

"And the Lord shall deliver me from every evil work, and will preserve me unto his HEAVENLY kingdom: to whom be glory <u>for ever and</u> ever. Amen" (2 Tim. 4:18). Again the phrase *the kingdom* occurs 100 times in the Gospels. The phrase *for ever and* is mentioned in 100 chapters of the Bible.

Justified by God's Heavenly Grace

"That being <u>justified by his grace</u>, we should be made heirs according to the hope of eternal life" (Titus 3:7). The Pauline Epistles combination *justified by his* (1x), *grace* (99x) = 100.

This Heavenly Day

"For unto which of the angels said he at any time, Thou art my Son, <u>this day</u> have I begotten thee? And again, I will be to him a Father, and he shall be to me a Son?" (Heb. 1:5) The phrase *this day* is mentioned in 100 verses of the Law.

Heavenly Ministers

"Are they not all <u>ministering spirits</u>, sent forth to minister for them who shall be heirs of salvation?" (Heb. 1:14) The phrases *the mighty* (99 vs) and *ministering spirits* (1 v) = 100 verses.

We Labor with a Heavenly Love

"For God is not unrighteous to forget your work and <u>labour of love</u>, which ye have shewed toward his name, in that ye have ministered to the saints, and do minister" (Heb. 6:10). The combination *labour* (87 vs), *of love* (13 vs) = 100 verses.

A Heavenly Rest

"For if Jesus had given them <u>rest</u>, then would he not afterward have spoken of another day. There remaineth therefore a rest to the people of God. For he that is entered into his <u>rest</u>, he also hath ceased from his own works, as God did from his. Let us labour therefore to enter into that <u>rest</u>, lest any man fall after the same example of unbelief" (Heb. 8:4-11). The word *rest* is mentioned in 200 chapters of the Bible, a multiple of 100.

Christ Now Appearing in Heaven for Us

"<u>For Christ is not entered into the holy places made with hands, which are the figures of the true; but into HEAVEN itself, now to appear in the presence of God for us</u>" (Heb. 9:24). Again the word *into* is mentioned in 100 verses of Acts. The New Testament combination *for Christ* (7x), *is not entered into* (1x), *the holy places* (1x), *made with hands* (7x), *which are the* (6x), *figures* (2x), *of the true* (2x), *but into heaven* (1x), *itself* (2x), *now to* (4x), *appear* (25x), *in the presence of God* (2x), *for us* (39x) = 99; this writer is unable to reach 100.

Looking for Christ to Come from Heaven

"So Christ was once offered to bear the sins of many; and unto them that look <u>for him</u> shall he appear the second time without sin unto salvation" (Heb. 9:28). The phrase *for him* is mentioned in 100 chapters.

Pilgrim Abraham Sought for a Heavenly City

"By faith he sojourned in the land of promise, as in a strange country, dwelling in tabernacles with Isaac and Jacob, the heirs with him of the same promise: For he <u>looked for</u> a city which hath foundations, whose builder and maker is God" (Heb. 11:9-10). The word *sought* is mentioned in

100 chapters of Bible.

The Church in Heaven

"To the general assembly and church of the <u>firstborn</u>, which are <u>written</u> in HEAVEN, and to God the Judge of all, and to the <u>spirits of just men made perfect</u>" (Heb. 12:23). The word *firstborn* is mentioned in 100 verses of the Bible. Again the NT Narrative combination *written* (58x), *in heaven* (42x) = 100. The Bible combination *spirit of* (99 chs) and *spirits of just men made perfect* (1 ch) = 100 chapters.

The Father Sends Us Perfect Gifts from Heaven

"Every good gift and every <u>perfect</u> gift is from above, and cometh down from the Father of lights, with whom is no variableness, neither shadow of turning" (James 1:17). Again the words *perfect* (99x) and *perfectness* (1x) = 100.

Act Heavenly toward Your Neighbor

"<u>If ye</u> fulfil the royal law according to the scripture, Thou shalt love thy <u>neighbour</u> as thyself, ye do well" (James 2:8). The phrase *if ye* is mentioned in 100 chapters. The word *neighbour* is mentioned in 100 verses.

Heaven Will Be Brought Nigh to You

"Draw nigh to God, and he will draw <u>nigh</u> <u>to you</u>. Cleanse your hands, ye sinners; and purify your hearts, ye double minded" (James 4:8).

The word *nigh* occurs 100 times in the Bible.
The phrase *to you* occurs 100 times in the Bible.

The Heaven Gave Earth Rain

"And he prayed again, and the HEAVEN gave <u>rain</u>, and the earth brought forth her fruit" (James 5:18). Again all available tenses of the word *rain* occur 100 times in the Old Testament.

Your Inheritance Is Reserved in Heaven

"To an <u>inheritance</u> incorruptible, and undefiled, and that fadeth not away, reserved <u>in</u> HEAVEN for you" (1 Pet. 1:4). The Hebrews combination *go* (94x), *in* (3x), *inheritance* (3x) = 100.

Speak Like a Heavenly Minister

"If any man speak, let him speak as the oracles of God; if any man <u>minister</u>, let him do it as of the ability which God giveth: that God in all things may be glorified through Jesus Christ, to whom be praise and dominion for ever and ever. Amen" (1 Pet. 4:11). The word *minister* occurs 100 times in the Bible.

Old Heavens Dissolved to Make Way for the New

"Looking for and hasting unto the <u>coming</u> of the day of God, wherein the HEAVENS being on fire shall be dissolved, and the elements shall melt with fervent heat? Nevertheless we, according to his promise, look for new HEAVENS and a new earth, wherein dwelleth righteousness" (2 Pet. 3:12-13). Again the word *coming* occurs 100 times in the Bible.

Jesus Christ's Former Heavenly Walk on Earth

"He that saith he abideth in him ought himself also so to walk, even as he <u>walked</u>" (1 John 2:6). Again the word *walked* is mentioned in 100 verses of the Old Testament.

When He Shall Appear from Heaven

"Beloved, now are we the <u>sons</u> of God, and it doth not yet appear what we shall be: but we know that, when he shall appear, we shall be like him; for we shall see him as he is" (1 John 3:2). The word *sons* is mentioned in 300 chapters of the Bible, a multiple of 100.

These THREE Bear Record in Heaven

"<u>For there are</u> <u>three</u> <u>that bear</u> <u>record in HEAVEN, the Father, the Word, and the Holy Ghost</u>: and <u>these three</u> <u>are one</u>" (1 John 5:7). Behold the following threefold numeric witness. The Bible combination *three that bear record* (1 v), *in heaven* (99 vs) = 100 verses. The New Testament combination *for there are* (4x), *three* (75x), *that bear* (3x), *record in heaven* (1x), *the Father the Word* (1x), *and the Holy Ghost* (3x), *these three* (6x), *are one* (7x) = 100. The phrase *and these* occurs naturally 100 times in the Bible.

Clothed in Heaven's Whitest

"He that overcometh, the same shall be <u>clothed</u> in white raiment" (Rev. 3:5a). The word *covered* is mentioned in 100 verses.

Listen for The Holy Spirit's Heavenly Voice

"He that hath an <u>ear</u>, let him hear what the Spirit <u>saith</u> unto the churches" (Rev. 3:6). Again the word *ear* occurs 100 times in the Old Testament. The phrase *he saith* occurs 100 times in the Bible.

That Heavenly City

"Him that overcometh will I make a pillar in the temple of my God, and he shall go no more out: and I will write upon him the name of my God, and the name of <u>the city of</u> my God, which is new Jerusalem, which cometh down out of HEAVEN from my God: and I will write upon him my new name" (Rev. 3:12). The phrase *the city of* is mentioned in 100 verses of the Bible.

The Elders in Heaven

"And round about the throne were four and twenty seats: and upon the seats I saw four and twenty <u>elders</u> sitting, clothed in white raiment; and they had on their heads crowns of gold" (Rev. 4:4). The Bible combination *elder/s* (199x) and *very aged men* (1x) = 200, a multiple of 100.

The Sea of Glass in Heaven

"And before the throne <u>there was a</u> <u>sea of glass</u> like unto crystal: and in the midst of the throne, and round about the throne, were four beasts full of eyes before and behind" (Rev. 4:6). The Bible combination *there was a* (97x), *sea of glass* (3x) = 100.

The Book of Judgments in Heaven

"And <u>I saw</u> <u>a strong angel</u> <u>proclaiming with a loud voice,</u> <u>Who is worthy to open the book,</u> <u>and to loose the seals thereof?</u>" (Rev. 5:2) The word *book* occurs 100 times in the OT Narrative. The Bible combination *I saw* (96x), *a strong angel* (1x), *proclaiming with a loud voice* (1x), *who is worthy to open the book* (1x), *and to loose the seals thereof* (1x) = 100.

Remnant of All Peoples to Be in Heaven

"And they sung a new song, saying, Thou art worthy to take the book, and to open the seals thereof: for thou wast slain, and hast redeemed us to God by thy <u>blood</u> out of every kindred, and <u>tongue</u>, and <u>people</u>, and <u>nation</u>" (Rev. 5:9). The word *blood* (199 chs) and the phrase *the Lamb's* (1 ch) = 200 chapters, a multiple of 100. The word *people* occurs 300 times in Scripture, a multiple of 100. The word *tongue* is mentioned in 100 chapters. The words *tongue* (129x), *tongues* (36x), *language* (27x), *languages* (7x), and *speakings* (1x) = 200, a multiple of 100. The word *nation* (99 chs) and phrase *kindreds of the nations* (1 ch) = 100.

The Altar in Heaven

"And when he had opened the fifth seal, I saw under the <u>altar</u> the souls of them that were slain for the word of God, and for the testimony which they held" (Rev. 6:9). Again the word *altar* is mentioned in 300 verses of the Old Testament, a multiple of 100.

The Glorious God of Heaven

"And the same hour was there a great earthquake, and the tenth part of the city fell, and in the earthquake were slain of men seven thousand: and the remnant were affrighted, <u>and gave glory to the</u> God of HEAVEN" (Rev. 11:13). Here the name *God* is the 5600th word of Revelation, a multiple of 100. The Revelation combination *gave glory to the* (1x), *God* (99x) = 100.

Time for the Heavenly King's Kingdom Reign on Earth

"And the seventh angel sounded; and there were great voices in HEAVEN, saying, The kingdoms of this world are become <u>the kingdoms of</u> our Lord, and of his <u>Christ</u>; and he shall reign <u>for ever and</u> ever" (Rev. 11:15). Again the phrase *the kingdom* occurs 100 times in the Gospels. The NT Narrative combination *the kingdom/s of* (99x), *of our Lord Jesus Christ* (1x) = 100. Again the phrase *for ever and* is mentioned in 100 chapters of the Bible.

The Temple & Ark in Heaven

"And <u>the temple</u> of God was opened in HEAVEN, and there was seen in his temple the <u>ark of his testament</u>: and there were lightnings, and voices, and thunderings, and an earthquake, and great hail" (Rev. 11:19). The phrase *the temple* is mentioned in 100 verses of the New Testament. The Bible combination *ark* (199 vs), *of his testament* (1 v) = 200 verses, a multiple of 100.

Angel Flying in the Midst of Heaven

"And I saw another angel fly in <u>the midst of</u> HEAVEN, having the everlasting gospel to preach unto them that dwell on the earth, and to every nation, and kindred, and tongue, and people," (Rev. 14:6). Again the phrase *the midst of* is mentioned in 200 chapters, a multiple of 100.

Heaven's Unequalled King

"These shall make war with the Lamb, and the Lamb shall overcome them: for he is Lord of lords, and King of <u>kings</u>: and they that are with him are called, and chosen, and faithful" (Rev. 17:14). The lowercase word *kings* is mentioned in 300 verses.

A Grand Wedding Celebration in Heaven

"And he saith unto me, Write, Blessed are they which are called unto the marriage supper of the Lamb" (Rev. 19:9ab). Before the disciples, Jesus ate food in His resurrected body—and so shall we even with Him. The phrase *did eat* occurs 100 times in the Bible. The word *drink* occurs 300 times in the Old Testament, a multiple of 100. The word *vessel(s)* occurs 200 times in the Bible, a multiple of 100.

The Cloud Rider
(Part 27)

"And I saw HEAVEN opened, and behold a white horse; and he that sat upon him was called Faithful and True, and in righteousness he doth judge and make war. His eyes were as a flame of fire, and on his head were many crowns; and he had a name written, that no man knew, but he himself. And he was clothed with a vesture dipped in blood: and his name is called The Word of God. And the armies which were in HEAVEN followed him upon white horses, clothed in fine linen, white and clean. And out of his mouth goeth a sharp sword, that with it he should smite the nations: and he shall rule them with a rod of iron: and he treadeth the winepress of the fierceness and wrath of Almighty God. And he hath on his vesture and on his thigh a name written, KING OF KINGS, AND LORD OF LORDS" (Rev. 19:11-16).

The naturally occurring Bible combination *followed him upon white* (1 v), *horses* (99 vs) = 100 verses.

1000-Year Kingdom of Heaven Commences on Earth

"Blessed and holy is he that hath part in the first resurrection: on such the second death hath no power, but they shall be priests of God and of Christ, and shall reign with him a thousand years" (Rev. 20:6). The millennial kingdom of Christ is a beautiful blending of heaven and earth. It will last 1000 years, a glorious multiple of 100. The number 100 is derived from the multiplication of 10 x 10, ten being the Bible's number for Ordinal Perfection. The number 1000 is derived from the multiplication of 10 x 100—that is to say, perfection x 100. The Bible combination *but they shall be priests of* (1x), *God and of Christ* (1x), *and shall reign* (1x), *reign with him* (2x), *a thousand* (95x) = 100.

That Heavenly City Called New Jerusalem

"And he carried me away in the spirit to a great and high mountain, and shewed me that great city, the holy Jerusalem, descending out of HEAVEN from God" (Rev. 21:10). This heavenly city will hover over the earthly Jerusalem. Again the word *earth* occurs 100 times in the OT Narrative. Again the phrase *out of* occurs 100 times in the Synoptic Gospels.

Heavenly City's Walls—Garnished with Precious Gemstones

"And the wall of the city had twelve foundations, and in them the names of the twelve apostles of the Lamb. . . . And the foundations of the wall of the city were garnished with all manner of precious stones. The first foundation was jasper; the second, sapphire; the third, a chalcedony; the fourth, an emerald; The fifth, sardonyx; the sixth, sardius; the seventh, chrysolite; the eighth, beryl; the ninth, a topaz; the tenth, a chrysoprasus; the eleventh, a jacinth; the twelfth, an amethyst" (Rev. 21:14, 19-20).

The Bible combination *foundations* (32x), *of the wall of the city* (1x), *were garnished* (1x), *with all manner of* (2x), *precious stones* (19x), *jasper* (7x), *sapphire* (9x), *chalcedony* (1x), *emerald* (5x), *sardonyx* (1x), *sardius* (4x), *chrysolite* (1x), *beryl* (6x), *topaz* (5x), *chrysoprasus* (1x), *jacinth* (2x), *amethyst* (3x) = 100.

Gates of the Heavenly City Ever Open

"And the gates of it shall not be shut at all by day: for there shall be no night there" (Rev. 21:25). The phrase *shall(t) not* occurs 1000 times in the Bible, a beautiful multiple of 100.

No Defilement to Enter the Heavenly City

"And there shall in no wise enter into it any thing that defileth, neither whatsoever worketh abomination, or maketh a lie: but they which are written in the Lamb's book of life" (Rev. 21:27). Again the word *book* occurs 100 times in the OT Narrative.

Main Street in Heaven & the Tree of Life

"And he shewed me a pure river of water of life, clear as crystal, proceeding out of the throne of God and of the Lamb. In the midst of the street of it, and on either side of the river, was there the tree of life, which bare twelve manner of fruits, and yielded her fruit every month: and the leaves of the tree were for the healing of the nations" (Rev. 22:1-2). The naturally occurring Major Prophets combination *in the midst of* (96x), *the street* (4x) = 100. The New Testament combination *and on either side* (1x), *of the river* (1x), *was there the* (1x), *tree* (50x), *of life* (37x), *which bare* (1x), *twelve manner of fruits* (1x), *and yielded her fruit every month* (1x), *and the leaves* (1x), *of the tree* (2x), *were for the healing* (1x), *of the nations* (3x) = 100.

The Servants of God in Heaven

"And there shall be no more curse: but the throne of God and of the Lamb shall be in it; and his servants shall serve him" (Rev. 22:3). The word *servants* occurs 100 times in First and Second Samuel.

1000—Glory

The Bible uses the number one THOUSAND, as well as its plural THOUSANDS, to indicate the glory of some thing or some person. Such glory in this large numeric value is sometimes attributed to exemplary men or reigning kings but more importantly to the Almighty God.

The number 1000 is a multiple of 100 by a factor of 10. One hundred represents heaven, and ten represents ordinal perfection, thus one thousand typifies the ordinal perfection of heaven—and when we see it we will call it glory!

Webster's Dictionary gives us a handful of definitions of the word GLORY:

> [1] a: praise, honor, or distinction extended by common consent; Renown
> b: worshipful praise, honor, and thanksgiving
> *Ex. giving glory to God*
> [2] a: something that secures praise or renown
> *Ex. the glory of a brilliant career*
> b: a distinguished quality or asset
> *Ex. The glory of the city is its Gothic cathedral.*
> [3] a: a state of great gratification or exaltation
> *Ex. When she's acting she's in her glory.*
> b: a height of prosperity or achievement
> *Ex. ancient Rome in its glory*
> [4] a: great beauty and splendor; Magnificence
> *Ex. the glory that was Greece and the grandeur that was Rome*
> b: the splendor and beatific happiness of heaven; *broadly*: eternity
> [5] a: a ring or spot of light such as an aureole
> b: a halo appearing around the shadow of an object

The Glory of Adam

"And the LORD God formed man of the dust of the ground, and breathed into his nostrils the breath of life; and man became a living soul. And the LORD God planted a garden eastward in Eden; and there he put the man whom he had formed" (Gen. 2:7-8). The Lord had formed a human creature that reflected His own spiritual image and heavenly glory. Adam was the son of God; all other humans are merely the sons of men. The final word of this passage *formed* is the 1000th word of the Bible. The Bible combination *and the LORD God formed man of the dust of the ground* (1 v), *and breathed into* (1 v), *his nostrils the breath of life* (1 v), *and man became a living soul* (1 v), *and the LORD God planted* (1 v), a *garden eastward* (1 v), *in Eden* (2 vs), *and there he put* (1 v), *the man* (293 vs), *whom* (697 vs), *he had formed* (1 v) = 1000 verses.

Adam Fell Short of His Glorious 1000th Birthday

"And all the days that Adam lived were nine hundred and thirty years: and he died" (Gen. 5:5). Adam would have lived to see his 1000th birthday and many more had he not disobeyed God's thou-shalt-not commandment in eating of the tree of knowledge of good and evil.

Men of Renown

"There were giants in the earth in those days; and also after that, when the sons of God came in unto the daughters of men, and they bare children to them, the same became mighty men which were of old, men of RENOWN" (Gen. 6:4). The Law combination *there were* (12x), *giants in the* (1x), *earth* (200x), *in those days* (5x), *and also* (22x), *after that* (30x), *when the* (77x), *sons of God* (2x), *came in unto the* (1x), *came in unto the daughters of* (1x), *men* (162x), *and they bare children* (2x), *to them* (15x), *the same* (52x), *became* (25x), *mighty* (33x), *men* (162x), *which were* (30x), *of old* (4x), *men* (162x), *of renown* (2x) = 1000.

The Glory of God's Heavenly Rainbow

"And God said, This is the token of the covenant which I make between me and you and every living creature that is with you, for perpetual generations: I do set my bow in the cloud, and it shall be for a token of a covenant between me and the earth. And it shall come to pass, when I bring a cloud over the earth, that the bow shall be seen in the cloud" (Gen. 9:12-14). The Genesis combination *I do set* (1x), *my bow* (2x), *in the cloud* (3x), *and it shall be* (3x), *for a token of a covenant* (1x), *between me and the earth* (1x), *and it shall* (9x), *come to pass* (9x), *when I* (3x), *bring a cloud* (1x), *over the* (18x), *earth* (121x), *that the bow* (1x), *shall* (259x), *be* (257x), *seen* (11x), *in the* (296x), *cloud* (4x) = 1000.

The Glory of Abraham's High Appointment

"And I will make of thee a great nation, and I will bless thee, and make thy name great; and thou shalt be a blessing: And I will bless them that bless thee, and curse him that curseth thee: and in thee shall all families of the earth be blessed" (Gen. 12:2-3). The Old Testament combination *and I will make of thee* (4x), *a great* (160x), *nation* (114x), *and I will bless thee and* (1x), *make thy name* (3x), *great* (708x), *and thou shalt be a blessing* (1x), *and I will bless them that bless thee and curse him that curseth thee* (1x), *and in thee* (3x), *shall all families of* (1x), *the earth be blessed* (4x) = 1000.

The Glory of Abraham's Beautiful Wife

"And it came to pass, when he was come near to enter into Egypt, that he said unto Sarai his wife, Behold now, I know that thou art a fair woman to look upon: Therefore it shall come to pass, when the Egyptians shall see thee, that they shall say, This is his wife: and they will kill me, but they will save thee alive" (Gen. 12:11-12). The Bible combination *Sarah Abraham's wife* (1x), *she* (982x), *was fair* (3x), *was very fair* (3x), *was exceeding fair* (1x), *was fair and beautiful* (1x), *a fair woman* (2x), *to look on/upon* (7x) = 1000.

The Glory of Abraham's Redeemed Life

"And unto Sarah he said, Behold, I have given thy brother a THOUSAND pieces of silver: behold, he is to thee a covering of the eyes, unto all that are with thee, and with all other: thus she was reproved" (Genesis 20:16). The king was happy to take Sarah into his harem because she was so exceeding fair. In the king's presence Sarah had continued to guard the secret of her marital status with Abraham; thus she needed correction. The Bible combination *and unto Sarah* (2x), *Sarah* (37x), *he said behold* (18x), *I have given* (7x), *thy brother* (66x), *thousand* (520x), *pieces of* (26x), *silver* (320x), *behold he is to thee a covering of the eyes* (1x), *unto all that are with thee* (1x), *and with all other* (1x), *thus she was reproved* (1x) = 1000.

The Glory of a Mother in Israel

"And they blessed Rebekah, and said unto her, Thou art our sister, be thou the mother of THOUSANDS of millions, and let thy seed possess the gate of those which hate them" (Genesis 24:60). Sarah was the first of Israel's four matriarchs. Rebekah became the second. The manifold number of offspring they wish upon her is to ascribe glory to her matriarchal calling. The Law combination *and they* (443x), *blessed* (75x), *Rebekah and said unto* (1x), *her* (468x), *thou art our sister* (1x), *be thou* (6x), *the mother* (3x), *of thousands of* (1x), *millions* (1x) = 1000.

The Glory of Isaac's Divinely Chosen Bride

"And Rebekah arose, and her damsels, and they rode upon the camels, and followed the man: and the servant took Rebekah, and went his way. And Isaac came from the way of the well Lahai-roi; for he dwelt in the south country. And Isaac went out to meditate in the field at the eventide: and he lifted up his eyes, and saw, and, behold, the camels were coming" (Gen. 24:61-63). The Law combination *and Rebekah arose* (1x), *and her* (31x), *damsels* (1x), *and they* (443x), *rode upon* (1x), *the camels* (10x), *and followed the man* (1x), *and the servant* (8x), *took* (182x), *Rebekah* (28x), *and went* (38x), *his way* (8x), *and Isaac* (31x), *came from the* (3x), *way of the well Lahai-roi* (1x), *for he dwelt* (2x), *in the south country* (1x), *and Isaac went out to meditate* (1x), *in the field at* (1x), *the eventide* (1x), *and he lifted up his* (3x), *eyes* (95x), *and saw* (7x), *and behold* (97x), *the camels were* (1x), *coming* (4x) = 1000.

Jacob's Glorious Dream of a Ladder Reaching to Heaven

"And he dreamed, and behold a ladder set up on the earth, and the top of it reached to heaven: and behold the angels of God ascending and descending on it. And, behold, the LORD stood above it, and said, I am the LORD God of Abraham thy father, and the God of Isaac" (Gen. 28:12-13b). The Bible combination *and he dreamed and* (1x), *behold a ladder* (1x), *set up on the earth* (1x), *and the top of it* (1x), *reached to heaven* (1x), *and behold the angels* (1x), *of God* (984x), *ascending* (5x), *and descending on it* (1x), *and behold the LORD* (3x), *stood above it* (1x) = 1000.

Glory of All That Jacob Had Gotten in Padan-Aram

"And he heard the words of Laban's sons, saying, Jacob hath taken away all that was our father's; and of that which was our father's hath he gotten all this GLORY" (Gen. 31:1). The Genesis combination *and he heard the words of Laban's sons saying* (1x), *Jacob* (166x), *hath taken away* (1x), *all that* (43x), *was our* (2x), *father's* (32x), *and of* (31x), *that* (521x), *which* (199x), *was our father's* (1x), *hath he gotten all this* (1x), *glory* (2x) = 1000.

1000th Verse of the Bible

"And the young man deferred not to do the thing, because he had delight in Jacob's daughter: and he was more honourable than all the house of his father" (Gen. 34:19). This 1000th verse speaks of the son of Hamor, Shechem, who was more glorious than the others.

The Glorious Son of Jacob's Old Age

"Now Israel loved Joseph more than all his children, because he was the son of his old age: and he made him a coat of many colours" (Gen. 37:3). The Old Testament combination *now* (949x), *Israel loved* (1x), *Joseph more than all* (1x), *his children* (32x), *because he was* (12x), *the son of his old age* (1x), *and he made him a* (1x), *coat of many colours* (3x) = 1000.

Joseph's First Dream of Future Glory

"And Joseph dreamed a dream, and he told it his brethren: and they hated him yet the more. And he said unto them, Hear, I pray you, this dream which I have dreamed: <u>For</u>, <u>behold</u>, <u>we were</u> <u>binding</u> <u>sheaves</u> <u>in the field</u>, <u>and, lo, my</u> <u>sheaf arose, and also</u> <u>stood upright;</u> <u>and, behold, your</u> <u>sheaves</u> <u>stood round about, and made obeisance</u> <u>to my sheaf</u>. And his brethren said to him, Shalt thou indeed reign over us? or shalt thou indeed have dominion over us? And they hated him yet the more for his dreams, and for his words" (Gen. 37:5-8).

The Law combination *For* (135x), *behold* (239x), *we were* (5x), *binding* (4x), *sheaves* (2x), *in the field* (30x), *and lo* (12x), *my* (565x), *sheaf arose and also* (1x), *stood upright* (2x), *and behold your sheaves* (1x), *stood round about* (1x), *and made obeisance* (2x), *to my sheaf* (1x) = 1000.

Joseph's Second Dream of Future Glory

"<u>And he dreamed yet another dream, and told</u> <u>it his brethren, and said, Behold, I have dreamed a</u> <u>dream more; and, behold, the sun and the moon and the eleven stars made obeisance to me. And</u> <u>he told it to his father, and to his brethren: and his father rebuked him, and said unto him, What is</u> <u>this dream that thou hast dreamed? Shall I and thy mother and thy brethren indeed come to bow</u> <u>down ourselves to thee to the earth</u>?" (Gen. 37:9-10)

The Law combination *and he dreamed* (2x), *yet another dream* (1x), *and told* (15x), *it his brethren* (2x), *and said behold* (5x), *I have* (168x), *dreamed a* (6x), *dream* (30x), *more* (75x), *and behold* (97x), *the sun* (21x), *and the moon* (2x), *and the eleven* (2x), *stars* (10x), *made obeisance to* (2x), *me* (549x), *and he told it* (2x), *to his father* (3x), *and to his brethren* (1x), *and his father rebuked him and said unto him* (1x), *what is this dream* (1x), *that thou hast dreamed* (1x), *shall I and thy mother and thy brethren* (1x), *indeed come to* (1x), *bow down ourselves* (1x), *to thee to the earth* (1x) = 1000.

Joseph Attains Glorious Rule over Egypt

"And Pharaoh said unto Joseph, Forasmuch as God hath shewed thee all this, there is none so discreet and wise as thou art: Thou shalt be over my house, and according unto thy word shall all my people be ruled: only in the throne will I be greater than thou. And Pharaoh said unto Joseph, See, I have set thee over all the land of Egypt. <u>And Pharaoh</u> <u>took off his ring</u> <u>from his hand, and</u> <u>put it</u> <u>upon Joseph's</u> <u>hand, and arrayed him</u> <u>in vestures of</u> <u>fine linen</u>, <u>and put a gold chain about</u> <u>his neck; And he made him</u> <u>to ride</u> <u>in the second chariot</u> <u>which he had; and they cried</u> <u>before him,</u> <u>Bow the knee: and he made him</u> <u>ruler</u> <u>over all</u> <u>the land of</u> <u>Egypt</u>" (Gen. 41:39-43).

The Law combination *and Pharaoh* (32x), *took off his* (1x), *ring* (3x), *from his hand* (1x), *and put it* (17x), *upon Joseph's* (2x), *hand* (311x), *and arrayed him* (1x), *in vestures of* (1x), *fine linen* (14x), *and put a* (3x), *gold chain* (1x), *about his* (1x), *neck* (15x), *and he made him* (5x), *to ride* (1x), *in the second chariot* (1x), *which he had* (16x), *and they cried* (2x), *before him bow the knee* (1x), *and he made him* (5x), *ruler* (6x), *over all* (11x), *the land of* (260x), *Egypt* (289x) = 1000.

All the Glory Joseph Had Attained in Egypt

"<u>And ye shall tell my</u> <u>father</u> <u>of all</u> <u>my</u> <u>GLORY in Egypt,</u> <u>and of all that ye have</u> <u>seen; and ye shall</u> <u>haste and bring down</u> <u>my father</u> <u>hither</u>" (Gen. 45:13). The Law combination *and ye shall tell my* (1x), *father* (238x), *of all* (110x), *my* (565x), *glory in Egypt* (1x), *and of all that ye have* (1x), *seen* (46x), *and ye shall haste and bring down* (1x), *my father* (31x), *hither* (6x) = 1000.

The Glorious Mountain of God

"Now Moses kept the flock of Jethro his father in law, the priest of Midian: and he led the flock to the backside of the <u>desert</u>, and came <u>to the mountain of</u> God, even to <u>Horeb</u>" (Exod. 3:1). The Bible treats Sinai and Horeb as indistinguishable places. Even if they were in proximity to each other, they yet remained part of the Mountain of God. The Deuteronomy combination *unto the mountain* (3x), *of* (996x) *Sinai* (1x) = 1000. The Deuteronomy combination *desert* (1x), *unto the mountain* (3x), *of* (996x) = 1000.

Moses Finds Himself Standing on Glorious Ground

"And the angel of the LORD appeared unto him in a flame of fire out of the midst of a bush: and he looked, and, behold, the bush burned with fire, and the bush was not consumed. And Moses said, I will now turn aside, and see this great sight, why the bush is not burnt. And when the LORD saw that he turned aside to see, <u>God called unto him out of the midst of the bush, and said, Moses, Moses. And he said, Here am I. And he said, Draw not nigh hither: put off thy shoes from off thy feet, for the place whereon thou standest is holy ground</u>" (Exod. 3:2-5).

The Law combination *God* (799x), *called* (145x), *unto him out of* (5x), *the midst of the bush* (1x), *and said Moses Moses* (1x), *and he said here am I* (5x), *and he said draw not nigh hither* (1x), *put off thy shoes* (1x), *from off thy* (2x), *feet* (25x), *for the place* (1x), *whereon* (12x), *thou standest* (1x), *is holy ground* (1x) = 1000. The Bible combination *draw not nigh hither* (1x), *put off thy shoes from off thy feet* (2x), *the place* (184x), *whereon thou* (4x), *standest* (6x), *holy* (611x), *ground* (192x) = 1000.

Lord Provides a Glorious Red Sea Crossing for Israel

"<u>And Moses stretched out his hand over the sea; and the LORD caused the sea to go back by a strong east wind all that night, and made the sea dry land, and the waters were divided. And the children of Israel went into the midst of the sea upon the dry ground: and the waters were a wall unto them on their right hand, and on their left</u>" (Exod. 14:21-22). The Law combination *and Moses* (224x), *stretched out* (10x), *his hand* (64x), *over* (204x), *the sea* (45x), *and the LORD* (309x), *caused the sea* (1x), *to go back by* (1x), *a strong* (6x), *east wind* (1x), *all that night* (3x), *and made* (23x), *the sea dry land* (1x), *and the waters* (12x), *were divided* (1x), *and the children of Israel* (41x), *went into the* (9x), *midst of the sea* (7x), *upon the dry ground* (1x), *and the waters* (12x), *were a* (10x), *wall* (11x), *unto them on their right hand* (2x), *and on their left* (2x) = 1000.

Lord's Glorious Triumph over Egypt's Chariot Army

"<u>Then sang Moses and the children of Israel this song unto the LORD, and spake, saying, I will sing unto the LORD, for he hath triumphed GLORIOUSLY: the horse and his rider hath he thrown into the sea</u>" (Gen. 15:1). The Bible combination *then sang Moses and the children of Israel* (1x), *this song unto the LORD* (1x), *and spake* (58x), *saying I will* (14x), *sing* (119x), *unto the LORD for* (28x), *he hath* (531x), *triumphed* (2x), *gloriously* (3x), *the horse* (24x), *and his rider* (6x), *hath he* (67x), *thrown* (19x), *into the sea* (27x) = 1000.

Glory of the Lord Appears in the Cloud

"<u>And Moses spake unto Aaron, Say unto all the congregation of the children of Israel, Come near before the LORD: for he hath heard your murmurings. And it came to pass, as Aaron spake unto the whole congregation of the children of Israel, that they looked toward the wilderness, and, behold, the GLORY of the LORD appeared in the cloud</u>" (Exod. 16:10). The Bible combination *and Moses spake unto Aaron* (2x), *say unto all the congregation of the children of Israel* (1x), *come near before the* LORD (1x), *for he hath* (42x), *heard/heareth your murmurings* (3x), *and it came to pass* (396x), *as Aaron* (3x), *spake unto* (271x), *the whole congregation* (16x), *of the children of Israel* (163x), *that they looked* (2x), *toward the wilderness* (4x), *and behold the* (59x), *glory of the* LORD/Lord (36x), *appeared in the cloud* (1x) = 1000.

Moses Goes Nearer to the Lord's Mountaintop Glory

"And when the voice of the trumpet sounded long, and waxed louder and louder, Moses spake, and God answered him by a voice. And the LORD came down upon mount Sinai, on the top of the mount: and the LORD called Moses up to the top of the mount; and Moses went up" (Exod. 19:19-20). The Bible combination *and when the voice* (2x), *of the trumpet* (20x), *sounded long* (1x), *and waxed* (6x), *louder and louder* (1x), *Moses spake and* (1x), *God answered him* (1x), *by a voice* (1x), *and the* LORD *came* (5x), *down upon* (21x), *mount Sinai* (19x), *on the top* (13x), *of the mount* (13x), *and the* LORD *called* (5x), *Moses* (828x), *up to the* (52x), *top of the mount* (6x), *and Moses went up* (5x) = 1000.

Moses Privileged to Enter the Lord's Glory Cloud

"And Moses went up into the mount, and a cloud covered the mount. And the GLORY of the LORD abode upon mount Sinai, and the cloud covered it six days: and the seventh day he called unto Moses out of the midst of the cloud. And the sight of the GLORY of the LORD was like devouring fire on the top of the mount in the eyes of the children of Israel. And Moses went into the midst of the cloud, and gat him up into the mount: and Moses was in the mount forty days and forty nights" (Exod. 24:15-18).

The Bible combination *and Moses went up into the mount* (2x), *and a cloud* (2x), *covered the mount* (1x), *and the glory of the* LORD (15x), *abode upon mount Sinai* (1x), *and the cloud* (6x), *covered it* (5x), *six days* (19x), *and the seventh day* (2x), *he called unto* (5x), *Moses out of the midst of the cloud* (1x), *and the sight of* (1x), *the glory of the* LORD (34x), *was like* (26x), *devouring fire* (5x), *on the top of* (13x), *the mount* (99x), *in the eyes of the children of Israel* (2x), *and Moses went* (13x), *into the midst* (33x), *of the cloud* (14x), *and gat him* (4x), *up into* (71x), *the mount* (99x), *and Moses* (234x), *was in* (183x), *the mount* (99x), *forty days and forty nights* (11x) = 1000.

The High Priest's Glorious Golden Garments

"And thou shalt make holy garments for Aaron thy brother for GLORY and for beauty. . . . And these are the garments which they shall make; a breastplate, and an ephod, and a robe, and a broidered coat, a mitre, and a girdle. . . . And thou shalt make a plate of pure gold, and grave upon it, like the engravings of a signet, HOLINESS TO THE LORD. And thou shalt put it on a blue lace, that it may be upon the mitre; upon the forefront of the mitre it shall be" (Exod. 28:2-4a, 36-37).

The Old Testament combination *and thou shalt make* (48x), *make* (909x), *holy garments* (11x), *for Aaron* (14x), *thy brother for* (2x), *glory and* (3x), *for beauty* (3x), *and these are the garments* (1x), *which they shall make* (2x), *a breastplate* (2x), *and an ephod* (1x), *and a robe* (1x), *and a broidered coat* (1x), *a mitre and a girdle* (1x), *a plate of pure gold* (1x) = 1000.

God's Glory Revealed in a Grave Manner

"And the children of Levi did according to the word of Moses: and there fell of the people that day about three THOUSAND men" (Exod. 32:28). The following equation employs both plus and minus symbols. The Bible combination *three* (485x) + *thousand* (520x) = 1005 – *and there fell of* (3x) – *the people that day* (2x) = 1000.

Moses Pleads to See the Lord's Glory

"And he said, I beseech thee, shew me thy GLORY. . . . And he said, Thou canst not see my face: for there shall no man see me, and live. And the LORD said, Behold, there is a place by me, and thou shalt stand upon a rock: And it shall come to pass, while my GLORY passeth by, that I will put thee in a clift of the rock, and will cover thee with my hand while I pass by: And I will take away mine hand, and thou shalt see my back parts: but my face shall not be seen" (Exod. 33:18, 20-23).

The Bible combination *and he said* (510x), *I beseech thee* (34x), *shew me thy* (3x), *glory* (402x), *and he said thou canst not see my face* (1x), *for there shall no man* (1x), *see me and live* (1x), *and the LORD said behold* (2x), *there is a place by me* (1x), *and thou shalt stand upon a rock* (1x), *and it shall come to pass while* (1x), *my glory passeth by* (1x), *that I will put thee* (1x), *in a clift of the rock* (1x), *and will cover thee with my hand* (1x), *while I pass by* (1x), *and I will take away mine hand* (1x), *and thou shalt see* (6x), *my back parts* (1x), *but my face shall not be seen* (1x) = 1000.

1000th Verse of Exodus

"And Moses gathered all the congregation of the children of Israel together, and said unto them, These are the words which the LORD hath commanded, that ye should do them" (Exod. 35:1). This 1000th verse refers to the Lord's fearfully glorious words.

Glory of the Lord Fills the Tabernacle

"And he reared up the court round about the tabernacle and the altar, and set up the hanging of the court gate. So Moses finished the work. Then a cloud covered the tent of the congregation, and the GLORY of the LORD filled the tabernacle. And Moses was not able to enter into the tent of the congregation, because the cloud abode thereon" (Exod. 40:33-35b). The Old Testament combination *and he reared up* (5x), *the court round about the tabernacle and the altar* (1x), *and set up the hanging of the court gate* (1x), *so Moses finished the work* (1x), *then a cloud covered the tent of the congregation* (1x), *and the glory of the LORD filled the tabernacle* (2x), *and Moses was not* (1x), *able to enter into* (1x), *the tent of the congregation* (13x), *because* (908x), *the cloud* (47x), *abode thereon* (1x) = 1000.

Wilderness Generation's Journeys & Encampments under the Glory Cloud

"And when the cloud was taken up from over the tabernacle, the children of Israel went onward in all their journeys: But if the cloud were not taken up, then they journeyed not till the day that it was taken up. For the cloud of the LORD was upon the tabernacle by day, and fire was on it by night, in the sight of all the house of Israel, throughout all their journeys" (Exod. 40:36-38). The Law combination *but if the cloud* (1x), *were not taken up* (1x), *then they journeyed not* (1x), *till the day that it was* (1x), *taken up* (8x), *For* (135x), *the cloud* (36x), *of the LORD* (250x), *was upon* (17x), *the tabernacle* (245x), *by day* (13x), *and fire was* (1x), *on it* (5x), *by night* (16x), *in the sight* (38x), *of all* (110x), *the house of Israel* (7x), *throughout* (68x), *all their* (38x), *journeys* (9x) = 1000.

Aaron's Glorious Consecration for the Ministry

"And Moses took the anointing oil, and anointed the tabernacle and all that was therein, and sanctified them. And he sprinkled thereof upon the altar seven times, and anointed the altar and all his vessels, both the laver and his foot, to sanctify them. And he poured of the anointing oil upon Aaron's head, and anointed him, to sanctify him" (Lev. 8:10-12). The Law combination *and he poured* (3x), *of the anointing* (7x), *oil* (111x), *upon* (758x), *Aaron's* (29x), *head* (91x), *and anointed him to sanctify him* (1x) = 1000.

The Lord's Blessing & Glory

"And Moses and Aaron went into the tabernacle of the congregation, and came out, and blessed the people: and the GLORY of the LORD appeared unto all the people" (Lev. 9:23). The Leviticus combination *and Moses and Aaron went* (1x), *into the tabernacle of the congregation* (4x), *and came* (2x), *out and* (7x), *blessed the people* (1x), *and the* (311x), *glory of* (2x), *the LORD* (307x), *appeared* (1x), *unto* (359x), *all the people* (5x) = 1000.

"I Will Be Glorified"

"Then Moses said unto Aaron, This is it that the LORD spake, saying, I will be sanctified in them that come nigh me, and before all the people I will be GLORIFIED. And Aaron held his peace" (Lev. 10:3). The Leviticus combination *this is it that the LORD spake saying* (1x), *I will* (36x), *be* (528x), *sanctified* (6x), *in* (375x), *them that* (7x), *come nigh* (4x), *me* (17x), *and before all* (1x), *the people* (17x), *I will be glorified* (1x), *and Aaron held* (1x), *his peace* (6x) = 1000. The NT Narrative combination *this is that which was spoken* (1x), *before all the people* (1x), *I will* (110x), *be* (862x), *glorified* (26x) = 1000.

A Hundred Israelites Shall Put Ten Thousand Enemies to Flight,
Thus Bringing Glory to God

"And five of you shall chase an hundred, and an hundred of you shall put TEN THOUSAND to flight: and your enemies shall fall before you by the sword" (Lev. 26:8). Here we see the word *thousand* in relation to God's greater glory.

O Lord, Return in Glory to the Many Thousands in Israel

"And the cloud of the LORD was upon them by day, when they went out of the camp. And it came to pass, when the ark set forward, that Moses said, Rise up, LORD, and let thine enemies be scattered; and let them that hate thee flee before thee. And when it rested, he said, Return, O LORD, unto the many THOUSANDS of Israel" (Num. 10:34-36). The Numbers combination *and it came to pass* (10x), *when the* (21x), *ark* (6x), *set forward* (13x), *that Moses said* (1x), *rise up LORD* (1x), *and let thine* (1x), *enemies* (1x), *be scattered* (1x), *and let them that* (1x), *hate thee* (1x), *flee before thee* (1x), *and when* (28x), *it rested* (1x), *he said* (11x), *return* (7x), *O* (7x), *LORD* (387x), *unto* (499x), *the many* (1x), *thousands of Israel* (1x) = 1000.

All Earth Shall Be Filled with the Glory of the Lord

"But as truly as I live, all the earth shall be filled with the GLORY of the LORD. Because all those men which have seen my GLORY, and my miracles, which I did in Egypt and in the wilderness, and have tempted me now these ten times, and have not hearkened to my voice; Surely they shall not see the land which I sware unto their fathers, neither shall any of them that provoked me see it" (Num. 14:21-23). The Law combination *but as* (8x), *truly as I* (2x), *live* (45x), *all the* (523x), *earth* (200x), *shall be filled* (2x), *with the* (156x), *glory of the LORD* (13x), *because all those men which have seen* (1x), *my glory* (4x), *and my miracles* (1x), *which I did in*

644

Egypt (1x), *and in the wilderness* (2x), *and have tempted me* (1x), *now these* (8x), *ten times* (3x), *and have not hearkened* (1x), *to my voice* (13x), *surely they* (1x), *shall not see* (3x), *the land which I sware unto their fathers* (3x), *neither shall any* (4x), *of them that provoked me* (1x), *see it* (4x) = 1000.

Men of Renown

"Now Korah, the son of Izhar, the son of Kohath, the son of Levi, and Dathan and Abiram, the sons of Eliab, and On, the son of Peleth, sons of Reuben, took men: And they rose up before Moses, with certain of the children of Israel, two hundred and fifty princes of the assembly, famous in the congregation, men of RENOWN" (Num. 16:1-2). The Law combination *now* (167x), *Korah the son of Izhar* (1x), *the son of Kohath the son of Levi* (1x), *and Dathan and Abiram the sons of Eliab* (1x), *and On the son of Peleth sons of Reuben* (1x), *took men* (1x), *and they rose up* (6x), *before Moses* (6x), *with certain of* (1x), *the children of Israel* (369x), *two hundred and fifty* (6x), *princes* (29x), *of the assembly* (7x), *famous in* (2x), *the congregation* (238x), *men of* (162x), *renown* (2x) = 1000.

A Glorious Star to Arise Out of Jacob

"I shall see him, but not now: I shall behold him, but not nigh: there shall come a Star out of Jacob, and a Sceptre shall rise out of Israel, and shall smite the corners of Moab, and destroy all the children of Sheth. . . . Out of Jacob shall come he that shall have dominion" (Num. 24:17, 19a). The Law combination *I shall see him* (1x), *but not now* (1x), *I shall* (23x), *behold him* (2x), *but not nigh* (1x), *there shall* (50x), *come a* (1x), *star* (1x), *out of Jacob* (2x), *and a sceptre shall* (1x), *rise* (23x), *out of* (316x), *Israel* (576x), *and shall smite* (1x), *the corners of Moab* (1x), *and destroy all the children of Sheth* (1x) = 1000.

Moses' Blessing of a Glorious Thousandfold Multiplication of Israel

"The LORD your God hath multiplied you, and, behold, ye are this day as the stars of heaven for multitude. The LORD God of your fathers make you a THOUSAND times so many more as ye are, and bless you, as he hath promised you!" (Deut. 1:10-11) The Old Testament combination *the LORD God* (196x), *of your* (175x), *fathers* (480x), *make you a thousand* (1x), *times* (117x), *so many more as ye are and* (1x), *bless you* (3x), *as he hath* (25x), *promised you* (3x) = 1000.

The Glorious God Is Faithful to a Thousand Generations

"Know therefore that the LORD thy God, he is God, the faithful God, which keepeth covenant and mercy with them that love him and keep his commandments to a THOUSAND generations; And repayeth them that hate him to their face" (Deut. 7:9-10a). The Law combination *know therefore* (2x), *that the LORD thy God* (13x), *he is God* (3x), *the faithful* (1x), *God* (786x), *which keepeth* (1x), *covenant and mercy* (1x), *with them that* (2x), *love him* (3x), *and keep his commandments* (2x), *to a* (6x), *thousand* (106x), *generations* (72x), *and repayeth them that hate him* (1x), *to their face* (1x) = 1000.

"He Is Thy Praise"

"He is thy PRAISE, and he is thy God, that hath done for thee these great and terrible things, which thine eyes have seen" (Deut. 10:21). This declaration fits our first definition of the word glory: praise or distinction extended by common consent. The Bible combination *He* (754x), *praise* (246x) = 1000.

The Lord's Glorious & Fearful Name

"If thou wilt not <u>observe to do all the words of this law</u> <u>that are written</u> <u>in this book,</u> <u>that thou mayest fear this</u> <u>GLORIOUS</u> <u>and fearful</u> <u>name,</u> <u>THE LORD THY GOD</u>" (Deut. 28:58). The Bible combination *observe to do all the words of this law* (3x), *that are written* (8x), *in this book* (12x), *that thou mayest fear this* (1x), *glorious* (45x), *and fearful* (2x), *name* (928x), *THE LORD THY GOD* (1x) = 1000.

Heavenly Glory of the King of Jehurun

"And he said, The LORD came from Sinai, and rose up from Seir unto them; he shined forth from mount Paran, and he came with <u>TEN THOUSANDS</u> of <u>saints:</u> from his right hand went a fiery law for them. Yea, he loved the people; all his saints are in thy hand: and they sat down at thy feet; every one shall receive of thy words. . . . And he was king in Jeshurun" (Deut. 33:2). The Deuteronomy combination *ten thousands* (2x), *of* (996x), *saints* (2x) = 1000.

Joseph's Glory to Continue through Ephraim & Manasseh

Moses blesses two special tribes which came of Joseph: "<u>let the blessing</u> <u>come</u> <u>upon the</u> <u>head of</u> <u>Joseph,</u> <u>and upon</u> <u>the top</u> of <u>the head</u> <u>of him</u> <u>that was separated</u> <u>from his brethren.</u> <u>His GLORY</u> is <u>like</u> <u>the firstling</u> <u>of his</u> <u>bullock,</u> <u>and his</u> <u>horns</u> <u>are like</u> <u>the horns of</u> <u>unicorns:</u> <u>with them</u> <u>he shall</u> <u>push</u> <u>the people</u> <u>together</u> <u>to</u> <u>the ends of</u> <u>the earth:</u> <u>and they</u> <u>are the</u> <u>TEN</u> <u>THOUSANDS</u> of <u>Ephraim,</u> <u>and they</u> <u>are</u> <u>the THOUSANDS</u> <u>of Manasseh</u>" (Deut. 33:16c-17). The Deuteronomy combination *let the blessing* (1x), *come* (56x), *upon the* (34x), *head of* (2x), *Joseph* (3x), *and upon* (7x), *the top* (4x), *of the head* (2x), *of him* (7x), *that was separated* (1x), *from his brethren* (1x), *his glory* (1x), *is like* (2x), *the firstling* (4x), *of his* (37x), *bullock* (3x), *and his* (36x), *horns* (2x), *are like* (1x), *the horns of* (1x), *unicorns* (1x), *with them* (12x), *he shall* (46x), *push* (1x), *the people* (45x), *together* (8x), *to* (479x), *the ends of* (1x), *the earth* (32x), *and they* (33x), *are the* (10x), *ten* (6x), *thousands* (5x), *of Ephraim* (2x), *and they* (33x), *are* (76x), *the thousands* (1x), *of Manasseh* (4x) = 1000.

Ark of the Covenant's Two Thousandfold Glory

"And it came to pass after three days, that the officers went through the host; <u>And they</u> <u>commanded the people, saying, When ye see</u> <u>the ark of the covenant of the LORD</u> <u>your God, and</u> <u>the priests the Levites</u> <u>bearing it,</u> <u>then ye shall</u> <u>remove</u> <u>from your</u> <u>place, and go</u> <u>after it.</u> <u>Yet there</u> <u>shall be</u> <u>a space between</u> <u>you and it,</u> <u>about</u> <u>TWO THOUSAND</u> <u>cubits</u> <u>by measure:</u> <u>come not near</u> <u>unto it,</u> <u>that ye may know</u> <u>the way</u> <u>by which</u> <u>ye must go:</u> <u>for ye</u> <u>have not passed</u> <u>this way</u> <u>heretofore</u>" (Josh. 3:2-4).

The OT Narrative combination *and they commanded the people saying* (1x), *when ye see* (1x), *the ark of the covenant of the LORD* (24x), *your God and* (6x), *the priests the Levites* (6x), *bearing it* (1x), *then ye shall* (8x), *remove* (6x), *from your* (2x), *place and go* (10x), *after it* (3x), *yet there shall be* (1x), *a space between* (1x), *you and it* (4x), *about* (159x), *two* (308x), *thousand* (281x), *cubits* (74x), *by measure* (1x), *come not near* (1x), *unto it* (4x), *that ye may know* (1x), *the way* (82x), *by which* (8x), *ye must go* (1x), *for ye* (9x), *have not passed* (1x), *this way* (2x), *heretofore* (3x) = 1000.

Lord Provides a Glorious Jordan River Crossing for Israel

"<u>And as they that bare</u> <u>the ark</u> <u>were come unto</u> <u>Jordan,</u> <u>and the feet of</u> <u>the priests</u> <u>that bare</u> <u>the ark</u> <u>were dipped in</u> <u>the brim of</u> <u>the water,</u> (for Jordan overfloweth all his banks all the time of harvest,) <u>That the</u> <u>waters</u> <u>which came</u> <u>down from</u> <u>above</u> <u>stood and rose up upon an heap</u> <u>very far</u>

from the city Adam, that is beside Zaretan: and those that came down toward the sea of the plain, even the salt sea, failed, and were cut off: and the people passed over right against Jericho. And the priests that bare the ark of the covenant of the LORD stood firm on dry ground in the midst of Jordan, and all the Israelites passed over on dry ground, until all the people were passed clean over Jordan" (Josh. 3:15-17).

The OT Narrative combination *and as they that bare* (1x), *the ark* (152x), *were come unto* (1x), *Jordan* (120x), *and the feet of* (1x), *the priests* (185x), *that bare* (20x), *the ark* (152x), *were dipped in the brim of* (1x), *the water* (23x), *that the* (228x), *waters* (32x), *which came* (13x), *down from* (24x), *above* (45x), *stood and rose up upon an heap* (1x), *very far from the city Adam* (1x) = 1000.

Joshua Magnified in the Eyes of Israel

"On that day the LORD MAGNIFIED Joshua in the sight of all Israel; and they feared him, as they feared Moses, all the days of his life" (Josh. 4:14). This magnification fits our fourth definition of glory: great splendor; magnificence. The Bible combination *on that day* (20x), *the LORD magnified* (2x), *Joshua* (216x), *magnified Joshua* (1x), *in the sight of* (159x), *all Israel and they* (2x), *feared him* (3x), *as they* (130x), *feared Moses* (1x), *all the days of his* (16x), *life* (450x) = 1000.

Achan Broke Fellowship with the God of Israel
But Must Now Give Him the Glory

"And Joshua said unto Achan, My son, give, I pray thee, GLORY to the LORD God of Israel, and make confession unto him; and tell me now what thou hast done; hide it not from me" (Josh. 7:19). The Old Testament combination *give* (681x), *I pray thee* (156x), *glory* (225x), *to the LORD God of Israel* (2x) = 1064 – 64 [Bible number for 'broken fellowship'] = 1000.

The Glory of God in Israel's Battles

"One man of you shall chase a THOUSAND: for the LORD your God, he it is that fighteth for you, as he hath promised you. Take good heed therefore unto yourselves, that ye love the LORD your God" (Josh. 23:10-11). The Joshua combination *one* (46x), *man* (30x), *of you* (7x), *shall* (104x), *chase a* (1x), *thousand* (8x), *for* (169x), *the LORD/Lord* (222x), *your* (87x), *God* (73x), *he* (131x), *it is that* (2x), *fighteth* (1x), *for you* (7x), *as* (77x), *he hath* (7x), *promised you* (2x), *take good heed therefore unto* (1x), *yourselves* (10x), *that ye* (14x), *love the LORD your God* (2x) = 1000.

Barak Forfeits His Guaranteed Wartime Glory

"And Deborah, a prophetess, the wife of Lapidoth, she judged Israel at that time. . . . And she sent and called Barak the son of Abinoam out of Kedesh-naphtali, and said unto him, Hath not the LORD God of Israel commanded, saying, Go and draw toward mount Tabor, and take with thee TEN THOUSAND men of the children of Naphtali and of the children of Zebulun? And I will draw unto thee to the river Kishon Sisera, the captain of Jabin's army, with his chariots and his multitude; and I will deliver him into thine hand. And Barak said unto her, If thou wilt go with me, then I will go: but if thou wilt not go with me, then I will not go. And she said, I will surely go with thee: notwithstanding the journey that thou takest shall not be for thine honour; for the LORD shall sell Sisera into the hand of a woman. And Deborah arose, and went with Barak to Kedesh" (Judg. 4:4, 6-9).

The OT Narrative combination *hath not the* (3x), *LORD God of Israel commanded saying* (1x), *go and* (40x), *draw* (12x), *toward* (87x), *mount Tabor* (3x), *and take* (25x), *with thee* (81x), *ten*

(112x), *thousand* (281x), *men of* (255x), *the children of Naphtali* (4x), *and of the children of Zebulun* (1x), *and I will draw unto thee to the river Kishon* (1x), *Sisera* (20x), *the captain of Jabin's army with his* (1x), *chariots* (64x), *and his multitude* (1x), *and I will deliver* (3x), *him into thine hand* (1x), *and Barak said unto her* (1x), *if thou wilt go with me then I will go* (1x), *but if thou wilt not go with me* (1x), *then I will not go* (1x) = 1000.

Deborah Glories in the Lord

"Then sang Deborah and Barak the son of Abinoam on that day, saying, PRAISE ye the LORD for the avenging of Israel, when the people willingly offered themselves. Hear, O ye kings; give ear, O ye princes; I, even I, will sing unto the LORD; I will sing PRAISE to the LORD God of Israel" (Judg. 5:1-3). Deborah's words here fit our first definition of the word glory: worshipful praise, honor, and thanksgiving. The OT Narrative combination *then sang Deborah* (1x), *and Barak* (3x), *the son of Abinoam* (3x), *on that day* (17x), *saying* (393x), *praise ye the LORD* (1x), *for the* (460x), *avenging of Israel* (1x), *when the people* (6x), *willingly* (15x), *offered themselves* (3x), *hear O ye kings* (1x), *give ear* (3x), *O ye princes* (1x), *I even I* (5x), *will sing unto the LORD* (1x), *I will sing* (3x), *praise to* (1x), *the LORD God of Israel* (81x) = 1000.

Israelites Deprived of Obtaining Anytime Wartime Glory

"And the LORD said unto Gideon, The people that are with thee are too many for me to give the Midianites into their hands, lest Israel vaunt themselves against me, saying, Mine own hand hath saved me. . . . And the LORD said unto Gideon, By the three hundred men that lapped will I save you, and deliver the Midianites into thine hand: and let all the other people go every man unto his place" (Judg. 7:2, 7). The OT Narrative combination *and the LORD said* (47x), *unto Gideon* (6x), *the people that* (80x), *are with thee* (2x), *are* (359x), *too many for me* (1x), *to give* (32x), *the Midianites* (17x), *into their hands* (2x), *lest Israel* (1x), *vaunt themselves* (1x), *against me* (27x), *saying mine own* (1x), *hand hath* (2x), *saved me* (1x), *and the LORD said* (47x), *unto Gideon* (6x), *by the* (205x), *three hundred* (44x), *men that* (66x), *lapped* (2x), *will I* (50x), *save you* (1x) = 1000.

Manoah Glories over the Angel of the Lord's Sayings

"And Manoah said unto the angel of the LORD, What is thy name, that when thy sayings come to pass we may do thee HONOUR?" (Judg. 13:17) Manoah's words correspond with our first definition of glory: worshipful praise, honor, and thanksgiving. The word *saying(s)* occurs 1000 times in the Old Testament.

Samson Glories in His Supernatural Strength
Whereby He Killed 1000 Men in One Day!

"And when he came unto Lehi, the Philistines shouted against him: and the Spirit of the LORD came mightily upon him, and the cords that were upon his arms became as flax that was burnt with fire, and his bands loosed from off his hands. And he found a new jawbone of an ass, and put forth his hand, and took it, and slew a THOUSAND men therewith. And Samson said, With the jawbone of an ass, heaps upon heaps, with the jaw of an ass have I slain a THOUSAND men" (Judg. 15:14-16).

The Bible combination *with the jawbone* (1x), *of an ass* (8x), *heaps upon* (1x), *heaps* (20x), *with the* (960x), *jaw* (4x), *of an ass have I slain* (1x), *a thousand men* (5x) = 1000.

Hannah Glories in the Lord

"And Hannah prayed, and said, My heart rejoiceth in the LORD, mine horn is exalted in the LORD: my mouth is enlarged over mine enemies; because I rejoice in thy salvation. There is none holy as the LORD: for there is none beside thee: neither is there any rock like our God" (1 Sam. 2:1-2). The Old Testament combination *and Hannah* (2x), *prayed and said* (2x), *my heart* (81x), *rejoiceth* (13x), *in the LORD* (64x), *mine horn* (1x), *is exalted* (6x), *in the LORD* (64x), *my mouth* (65x), *is enlarged* (1x), *over mine enemies* (1x), *because I* (48x), *rejoice* (147x), *in thy salvation* (6x), *there is* (341x), *none holy* (1x), *as the LORD* (152x), *for there is none beside* (1x), *thee neither is there any* (3x), *rock like our God* (1x) = 1000.

When Poor & Humble Men Inherit the Throne of Glory

"He raiseth up the poor out of the dust, and lifteth up the beggar from the dunghill, to set them among princes, and to make them inherit the throne of GLORY: for the pillars of the earth are the LORD'S, and he hath set the world upon them" (1 Sam. 2:8). The Bible combination *he raiseth up the* (2x), *poor* (205x), *out of the dust* (6x), *and lifteth up* (2x), *the beggar* (2x), *from the dunghill* (1x), *to set* (36x), *them among* (11x), *princes* (273x), *and to make them inherit* (1x), *the throne* (96x), *of glory* (22x), *for the pillars* (3x), *of the earth* (300), *are the LORD'S* (3x), *and he hath* (36x), *set the world upon them* (1x) = 1000.

"The Glory Is Departed from Israel"

"And she named the child I-chabod, saying, The GLORY is departed from Israel: because the ark of God was taken, and because of her father in law and her husband. And she said, The glory is departed from Israel: for the ark of God is taken" (1 Sam. 4:21-22). The OT Narrative combination *and she* (26x), *named* (3x), *the child* (22x), *I-chabod* (1x), *saying* (98x), *the glory* (2x), *is* (284x), *departed* (20x), *from* (214x), *Israel* (261x), *because the* (15x), ark of God (25x), *was taken* (10x), *and because* (4x), *of her* (7x), *father in law* (2x), *and her husband* (3x), *and she said the glory is departed from Israel for* (1x), *the ark of God is taken* (2x) = 1000.

Philistine Lords Instructed to Give the God of Israel Glory

"Wherefore ye shall make images of your emerods, and images of your mice that mar the land; and ye shall give GLORY unto the God of Israel: peradventure he will lighten his hand from off you, and from off your gods, and from off your land. . . . And take the ark of the LORD, and lay it upon the cart; and put the jewels of gold, which ye return him for a trespass offering, in a coffer by the side thereof; and send it away, that it may go" (1 Sam. 6:5, 8).

Here the word *put* is 201,000th word of the Bible, and it speaks of where to put their sacred tokens of glory.

David Ascribed with More Glory Than Saul

"And it came to pass as they came, when David was returned from the slaughter of the Philistine, that the women came out of all cities of Israel, singing and dancing, to meet king Saul, with tabrets, with joy, and with instruments of musick. And the women answered one another as they played, and said, Saul hath slain his THOUSANDS, and David his TEN THOUSANDS. And Saul was very wroth, and the saying displeased him; and he said, They have ascribed unto David TEN THOUSANDS, and to me they have ascribed but THOUSANDS: and what can he have more but the kingdom? And Saul eyed David from that day and forward" (1 Sam. 18:6-9).

The Old Testament combination *and the women answered one another* (1x), *as they played and said* (1x), *Saul hath* (3x), *slain his* (3x), *thousands and* (27x), *David* (953x), *hath slain his* (2x), *ten thousands* (10x) = 1000.

Saul Attempts to Reduce David's Glory to 1000

"Therefore Saul <u>removed him</u> from him, and made him his captain over a THOUSAND; and he went out and came in before the people. . . . But all Israel and Judah loved <u>David</u>, because he went out and came in before them" (1 Sam. 18:13, 16). The name *David('s)* occurs naturally 1001 times in the Old Testament. The naturally occurring Old Testament combination *David* (949x) + *David's* (52x) – *removed him* (1x) = 1000.

David, the Glorious King of Israel

"Then David returned to bless his household. <u>And Michal the daughter of Saul came out</u> <u>to meet</u> <u>David, and said, How</u> <u>GLORIOUS was</u> <u>the king</u> <u>of Israel to day</u>, who uncovered himself to day in the eyes of the handmaids of his servants, as one of the vain fellows shamelessly uncovereth himself!" (2 Sam. 6:20) The OT Narrative combination *and Michal* (5x), *the daughter of Saul came out* (1x), *to meet David and said* (1x), *How* (25x), *glorious was* (1x), *the king* (966x), *of Israel to day* (1x) = 1000.

David Reckoned to Be More Glorious Than Any Judean
By a Factor of Ten Thousand

"<u>But the people answered, Thou shalt not go forth: for if we flee away, they will not care for us;</u> <u>neither if half of us die, will they care for us: but now thou art worth</u> TEN THOUSAND <u>of us:</u> <u>therefore now it is better that thou succour us out of the city</u>" (2 Sam. 18:3). The Old Testament combination *but the people answered* (1x), *for if we flee away* (1x), *they will not care for us* (1x), *neither if half of us die* (1x), *will they care for us* (1x), *but now* (24x), *thou art worth* (1x), *ten thousand of* (4x), *us* (961x), *therefore now it* (1x), *is better that* (2x), *thou succour* (1x), *us out of the city* (1x) = 1000.

The Glory of Having 1000 Silver Shekels

"<u>I would have given thee ten shekels of silver, and a girdle. And the man said unto Joab, Though</u> <u>I should receive</u> a THOUSAND <u>shekels of silver in mine hand, yet would I not put forth mine</u> <u>hand against the king's son</u>: for in our hearing the king charged thee and Abishai and Ittai, saying, Beware that none touch the young man Absalom" (2 Sam. 18:11c-12). This declaration fits our third definition of glory: a state of great gratification or exaltation. The Bible combination *I would have given thee ten shekels of silver and a girdle* (1x), *and the man* (54x), *said unto Joab* (3x), *though I should* (3x), *receive* (176x), *thousand* (520x), *shekels* (96x), *of silver* (133x), *in mine hand* (12x), *yet would I not put forth* (1x), *mine hand against the king's son* (1x) = 1000.

Solomon's Day of Crowning Glory

"And Zadok the priest took an horn of oil out of the tabernacle, and anointed Solomon. <u>And they</u> <u>blew the trumpet; and all the people said, God save king Solomon. And all the people came up</u> <u>after him, and the people piped with pipes, and rejoiced with great joy, so that the earth rent with</u> <u>the sound of them</u>" (1 Kings 1:39-40). The First and Second Kings combination *and they blew the* (1x), *trumpet* (3x), *and all the* (58x), *people said* (2x), *God* (170x), *save* (18x), *king* (567x), *Solomon* (151x), *and all the people* (15x), *came up after him* (1x), *and the people piped with pipes and* (1x), *rejoiced* (4x), *with great* (2x), *joy* (1x), *so that the* (4x), *earth rent* (1x), *with the sound of them* (1x) = 1000.

Solomon Offers 1000 Burnt Offerings to the Glory of God

"And the king went to Gibeon to sacrifice there; for that was the great high place: A THOUSAND burnt offerings did Solomon offer upon that altar" (1 Kings 3:4). The Bible combination *and the king went* (6x), *to Gibeon to sacrifice there* (1x), *for that was the great* (1x), *high place* (22x), *a thousand* (95x), *burnt* (366x), *offerings* (265x), *did Solomon* (7x), *offer* (236x), *upon that altar* (1x) = 1000.

God Made Solomon's Reign Exceeding Glorious

"And God gave Solomon wisdom and understanding exceeding much, and largeness of heart, even as the sand that is on the sea shore. And Solomon's wisdom excelled the wisdom of all the children of the east country, and all the wisdom of Egypt. For he was wiser than all men; than Ethan the Ezrahite, and Heman, and Chalcol, and Darda, the sons of Mahol: and his fame was in all nations round about. And he spake THREE THOUSAND proverbs: and his songs were A THOUSAND and five" (1 Kings 4:29-32).

The Bible combination *and God gave* (3x), *Solomon* (279x), *wisdom and* (72x), *understanding* (160x), *exceeding much* (5x), *and largeness* (1x), *of heart* (29x), *even as the sand* (2x), *that is on* (12x), *the sea shore* (8x), *and Solomon's* (4x), *wisdom excelled* (1x), *the wisdom of* (24x), *all the children of* (40x), *the east country* (4x), *and all the wisdom of Egypt* (1x), *for he was* (37x), *wiser than* (6x), *all men* (74x), *than Ethan the Ezrahite* (1x), *and Heman and Chalcol and Darda the sons of Mahol* (1x), *and his fame* (4x), *was in all* (3x), *nations round about* (2x), *and he spake three thousand* (1x), *proverbs* (9x), *and his songs were* (1x), *a thousand* (95x), *and five* (121x) = 1000.

The Glory of the Lord Filled the House

"And it came to pass, when the priests were come out of the holy place, that the cloud filled the house of the LORD, So that the priests could not stand to minister because of the cloud: for the GLORY of the LORD had filled the house of the LORD. Then spake Solomon, The LORD said that he would dwell in the thick darkness" (1 Kings 8:10-12). The Bible combination *and it came to pass when the priests were* (2x), *come out of* (43x), *the holy place* (44x), *that the cloud* (6x), *filled* (159x), *the house of the LORD* (234x), *so that the priests* (2x), *could not stand* (4x), *to minister* (40x), *because of the* (115x), *cloud* (107x), *for the glory of the LORD* (2x), *had filled* (4x), *the house of the LORD* (234x), *then spake Solomon* (1x), *the LORD said that* (1x), *he would dwell in the thick darkness* (2x) = 1000.

King Solomon Had 1000 Wives Altogether

"But king Solomon loved many strange women . . . Solomon clave unto these in love. . . And he had seven hundred wives, princesses, and three hundred concubines" (1 Kings 11:1a, 2e, 3a). Concubines were regarded as second-class wives as their role was more servant oriented; thus Solomon had 1000 wives altogether. The OT Narrative combination *but king Solomon* (1x), *loved many* (1x), *strange women* (1x), *Solomon clave unto these* (1x), *in love* (1x), *and he* (915x), *had seven hundred* (1x), *wives* (62x), *princesses* (1x), *and three hundred* (5x), *concubines* (11x) = 1000.

651

Seven Thousand Israelites Still Glorify the Lord

"Yet I have left me SEVEN THOUSAND in Israel, all the knees which have not bowed unto Baal, and every mouth which hath not kissed him" (1 Kings 19:18). The First Kings combination *yet* (15x), *I have* (37x), *left* (20), *me* (110x), *seven* (14x), *thousand* (21x), *in* (459x), *Israel* (203x), *all the* (100x), *knees* (3x), *which have not bowed* (1x), *unto Baal* (1x), *and every* (4x), *mouth* (11x), *which hath not kissed him* (1x) = 1000.

Glorious Ones Carried Away into Captivity

"And he carried away Jehoiachin to Babylon, and the king's mother, and the king's wives, and his officers, and the mighty of the land, those carried he into captivity from Jerusalem to Babylon. And all the men of might, even SEVEN THOUSAND, and craftsmen and smiths A THOUSAND, all that were strong and apt for war, even them the king of Babylon brought captive to Babylon" (2 Kings 24:15-16). The Old Testament combination *and he carried away Jehoiachin* (1x), *to Babylon* (34x), *and the king's* (16x), *mother* (159x), *and the king's* (16x), *wives* (199x), *and his officers and* (2x), *the mighty* (93x), *of the land* (310x), *those carried he* (1x), *into captivity* (35x), *from Jerusalem* (21x), *to Babylon* (34x), *and all the men* (25x), *of might* (6x), *even seven thousand* (1x), *and craftsmen* (1x), *and smiths a thousand* (1x), *all that were* (41x), *strong and apt for war* (1x), *even them the king of Babylon brought* (1x), *captive to Babylon* (2x) = 1000.

Lord, Let Thy Name Be Magnified

"Therefore now, LORD, let the thing that thou hast spoken concerning thy servant and concerning his house be established for ever, and do as thou hast said. Let it even be established, that thy name may be MAGNIFIED for ever, saying, The LORD of hosts is the God of Israel, even a God to Israel: and let the house of David thy servant be established before thee" (1 Chron. 17:23-24). This magnification fits our fourth definition of glory: great splendor; magnificence. The Bible combination *therefore now LORD* (2x), *let the thing* (1x), *that thou hast spoken concerning* (2x), *thy servant and concerning his house be established for ever* (1x), *and do as thou hast said* (3x), *let it even be established* (1x), *that thy* (49x), *name* (928x), *may be magnified for ever* (1x), *saying the LORD of hosts* (2x), *is the God of Israel* (1x), *even a God to Israel* (1x), *and let the house of David* (1x), *thy servant be* (4x), *established before thee* (3x) = 1000.

The Magnifical Fame & Glory of God's House

"And David said, Solomon my son is young and tender, and the house that is to be builded for the LORD must be exceeding MAGNIFICAL, of fame and of GLORY throughout all countries: I will therefore now make preparation for it. So David prepared abundantly before his death" (1 Chron. 22:5). The OT Narrative combination *and David said* (63x), *Solomon my son* (7x), *is young and tender and* (1x), *the house* (634x), *that is* (100x), *to be builded* (1x), *for the LORD* (70x), *must be* (5x), *exceeding* (11x), *magnifical of fame* (1x), *and of glory* (1x), *throughout* (59x), *all countries* (2x), *I will therefore* (1x), *now make* (3x), *preparation* (1x), *for it* (38x), *so David prepared abundantly* (1x), *before his death* (1x) = 1000.

11,000th Verse of the Bible

"Of the sons of Gershom, Shebuel was the chief" (1 Chron. 23:16). This ten thousandth plus one thousandth verse speaks of one man who held the position of glory among his people.

Solomon Magnified in the Eyes of Israel

"And the LORD MAGNIFIED Solomon exceedingly in the sight of all Israel, and bestowed upon him such royal majesty as had not been on any king before him in Israel" (1 Chron. 29:24-25). The Old Testament combination *and the LORD* (530x), *magnified* (18x), *Solomon* (270x), *exceedingly* (39x), *in the sight of all Israel* (7x), *and bestowed* (2x), *upon him such royal majesty* (1x), *as had* (4x), *not been* (31x), *on any* (3x), *king before him* (2x), *in Israel* (93x) = 1000.

The Temple's Glorious Brasen Sea

"Also he made a molten sea of ten cubits from brim to brim, round in compass, and five cubits the height thereof; and a line of thirty cubits did compass it round about. And under it was the similitude of oxen, which did compass it round about: ten in a cubit, compassing the sea round about. Two rows of oxen were cast, when it was cast. It stood upon twelve oxen, three looking toward the north, and three looking toward the west, and three looking toward the south, and three looking toward the east: and the sea was set above upon them, and all their hinder parts were inward. And the thickness of it was an handbreadth, and the brim of it like the work of the brim of a cup, with flowers of lilies; and it received and held THREE THOUSAND baths" (2 Chron. 4:2-5).

The OT Narrative combination *and the thickness of it was an handbreadth* (1x), *and the brim of it* (1x), *like* (93x), *the work* (57x), *of the brim* (1x), *of a cup* (2x), *with flowers* (2x), *of lilies* (2x), *and it* (312x), *received* (14x), *and held* (2x), *three* (225x), *thousand* (281x), *baths* (7x) = 1000.

The Levites Glorify the Lord

"It came even to pass, as the trumpeters and singers were as one, to make one sound to be heard in PRAISING and THANKING the LORD; and when they lifted up their voice with the trumpets and cymbals and instruments of musick, and PRAISED the LORD, saying, For he is good; for his mercy endureth for ever: that then the house was filled with a cloud, even the house of the LORD" (2 Chron. 5:13). The OT Narrative combination *it came even to pass* (2x), *as the* (127x), *trumpeters* (3x), *and singers* (1x), *were as one to make one sound* (1x), *to be* (113x), *heard in* (7x), *praising* (3x), *and thanking the LORD* (1x), *and when they* (50x), *lifted up their voice* (6x), *with the trumpets* (13x), *and cymbals* (3x), *and instruments* (2x), *of musick* (6x), *and praised the LORD* (4x), *saying for he is good* (2x), *for his mercy* (5x), *endureth for ever* (7x), *that then* (4x), *the house* (634x), *was filled* (4x), *with a cloud* (1x), *even the house of the LORD* (1x) = 1000.

Glory of the Lord Was upon the House

"And when all the children of Israel saw how the fire came down, and the GLORY of the LORD upon the house, they bowed themselves with their faces to the ground upon the pavement, and worshipped, and PRAISED the LORD, saying, For he is good; for his mercy endureth for ever" (2 Chron. 7:3). The Bible combination *and when all* (16x), *the children of Israel* (635x), *saw how* (1x), *the fire* (156x), *came down* (62x), *and the GLORY of the LORD/Lord* (16x), *upon the house* (11x), *they bowed themselves* (3x), *with their faces* (5x), *to the ground* (48x), *upon the pavement* (2x), *and worshipped* (44x), *and praised the LORD saying for he is good for his mercy endureth for ever* (1x) = 1000.

Egypt's Glorious Army of a Thousand Thousand

"And there came out against them Zerah the Ethiopian with an host of a THOUSAND THOUSAND, and three hundred chariots; and came unto Mareshah" (2 Chron. 14:9). This Egyptian king brought along with his great army many Libyan fighters. It was a million-man army. The Old Testament combination *and there came* (27x), *out against them* (5x), *Zerah the* (5x), *Ethiopian* (8x), *with an host of a* (1x), *thousand* (466x), *thousand* (466x), *and three hundred chariots* (1x), *and came unto* (14x), *Mareshah* (8x) = 1001.

Hezekiah Magnified in the Sight of All Nations

"And many brought gifts unto the LORD to Jerusalem, and presents to Hezekiah king of Judah: so that he was MAGNIFIED in the sight of all nations from thenceforth" (2 Chron. 32:23). The OT Narrative combination *many* (62x), *brought* (304x), *gifts unto the LORD to* (1x), *Jerusalem* (373x), *and presents to* (1x), *Hezekiah* (89x), *king of Judah* (86x), *to Hezekiah king of Judah* (2x), *so that he was magnified* (1x), *in the sight of* (80x), *all nations from thenceforth* (1x) = 1000.

1000 Silver Platters & 1000 Other Vessels

"And this is the number of them: thirty chargers of gold, A THOUSAND chargers of silver, nine and twenty knives, Thirty basons of gold, silver basons of a second sort four hundred and ten, and other vessels A THOUSAND" (Ezra 1:9-10). The Ezra combination *And* (85x), *this* (64x), *is* (49x), *the number of* (3x), *them* (63x), *a* (64x), *thousand* (19x), *chargers* (2x), *of* (642x), *silver* (18x) = 1009, a number rooted in the first-generation 1000s family.

Glorious Basons of Gold Weighing 1000 Drams

"Also twenty basons of gold, of A THOUSAND drams; and two vessels of fine copper, precious as gold" (Ezra 8:27). The Old Testament combination *also twenty* (1x), *basons* (18x), *of gold* (153x), *of a* (366x), *thousand* (466x), *drams* (6x) = 1010, a number rooted in the first-generation 1000s family.

1000 Drams of Gold

"And some of the chief of the fathers gave unto the work. The Tirshatha gave to the treasure A THOUSAND drams of gold, fifty basons, five hundred and thirty priests' garments" (Neh. 7:70). The Old Testament combination *the Tirshatha gave to* (1x), *the treasure* (8x), *of a* (366x), *thousand* (466x), *drams* (6x), *of gold* (153x) = 1000.

Blessed Is Thy Glorious Name

"Then the Levites, Jeshua, and Kadmiel, Bani, Hashabniah, Sherebiah, Hodijah, Shebaniah, and Pethahiah, said, Stand up and bless the LORD your God for ever and ever: and blessed be thy GLORIOUS name, which is exalted above all blessing and PRAISE" (Neh. 9:5). The Old Testament combination *then the Levites* (2x), *Jeshua and Kadmiel* (2x), *Bani Hashabniah Sherebiah* (1x), *Hodijah Shebaniah and* (1x), *Pethahiah said* (1x), *stand up and bless* (1x), *the LORD your God* (145x), *for ever and ever* (25x), *and blessed* (27x), *be thy glorious* (1x), *name* (755x), *which is exalted* (1x), *above all* (38x), *blessing and praise* (1x) = 1000.

Songs of Praise & Thanksgiving to God

"For in the days of David and Asaph of old there were chief of the singers, and songs of PRAISE and THANKSGIVING unto God" (Neh. 12:46). The Bible combination *for in* (74x), *the days of* (221x), *David and* (168x), *Asaph of* (2x), *old* (380x), *there were chief of the* (1x), *singers* (38x), *and songs of praise and* (1x), *thanksgiving* (28x), *unto God/GOD* (86x) = 1000.

Ahasuerus' Proud Display of His Glorious Kingdom

"In the third year of his reign, he made a feast unto all his princes and his servants; the power of Persia and Media, the nobles and princes of the provinces, being before him: When he shewed the riches of his GLORIOUS kingdom and the honour of his excellent MAJESTY many days, even an hundred and fourscore days" (Est. 1:3-4). The Old Testament combination *in the third year of his reign* (2x), *he made a feast unto all his* (2x), *princes and his servants* (2x), *the power of Persia and Media* (1x), *the nobles and princes of the provinces* (1x), *being before him* (1x), *when he shewed* (2x), *the riches* (7x), *of his* (927x), *glorious kingdom* (1x), *and the honour of his excellent* (1x), *majesty* (25x), *many days* (27x), *even an hundred and fourscore days* (1x) = 1000.

You Cannot Answer One of 1000 Questions
Coming from the Glorious God

"Then Job answered and said, I know it is so of a truth: but how should man be just with God? If he will contend with him, he cannot answer him one of a THOUSAND" (Job 9:1-3).

The Bible combination *if he will* (9x), *contend with him* (4x), *he cannot* (13x), *answer him one* (1x), *of a* (454x), *thousand* (520x) = 1001 – 1 = 1000.

Job Stripped of His Glory

"Then Job answered and said. . . . Know now that God hath overthrown me, and hath compassed me with his net. . . . He hath stripped me of my GLORY, and taken the crown from my head" (Job 19:1, 6, 9). The Job combination *then Job answered* (6x), *and said* (38x), *know now* (1x), *that God* (6x), *hath overthrown me* (1x), *and hath* (4x), *compassed me* (1x), *with his* (14x), *net* (2x), *he hath* (28x), *stripped* (2x), *me* (252x), *of* (538x), *my glory* (2x), *and taken the crown* (1x), *from* (101x), *my head* (3x) = 1000.

The Heavens Declare God's Glory

"The heavens declare the GLORY of God; and the firmament sheweth his handywork. Day unto day uttereth speech, and night unto night sheweth knowledge" (Ps. 19:1-2). The Bible combination *the glory of God* (16x), *of God* (984x) = 1000.

The King of Glory

"Lift up your heads, O ye gates; and be ye lift up, ye everlasting doors; and the King of GLORY shall come in. Who is this King of GLORY? The LORD strong and mighty, the LORD mighty in battle. Lift up your heads, O ye gates; even lift them up, ye everlasting doors; and the King of GLORY shall come in. Who is this King of GLORY? The LORD of hosts, he is the King of GLORY. Selah" (Ps. 24:7-10). The Bible combination *lift up* (88x), *your heads* (6x), *O ye* (62x), *gates* (144x), *and be ye* (9x), *lift up* (88x), *ye everlasting* (2x), *doors* (71x), *the king* (472x), *of glory* (22x), *shall come in* (17x), *who is this* (14x), *king of glory* (5x) = 1000.

God Owns the Cattle on a Thousand Hills

"I will take no bullock out of thy house, nor he goats out of thy folds. For every beast of the forest is mine, and the cattle upon a THOUSAND hills" (Ps. 50:9-10). The Wisdom Books combination *I will take no bullock out of thy house nor he goats out of thy folds for* (1x), *every* (96x), *beast of the forest is* (1x), *mine* (202x), *and the* (305x), *cattle* (7x), *upon* (354x), *a thousand* (14x), *hills* (20x) = 1000.

A Divine Place Called Glory

"Thou shalt <u>guide me</u> <u>with thy</u> <u>counsel</u>, <u>and afterward</u> <u>receive</u> <u>me</u> to GLORY. <u>Whom have I in</u> <u>heaven</u> <u>but thee</u>? <u>and there</u> <u>is none upon</u> <u>earth</u> <u>that I</u> <u>desire</u> <u>beside thee</u>" (Ps. 73:24-25). The Psalms combination *thou shalt* (35x), *guide me* (2x), *with thy* (22x), *counsel* (17x), *and afterward* (1x), *receive* (5x), *me* (662x), *to glory* (1x), *whom have I in* (1x), *heaven* (38x), *but thee* (1x), *and there* (10x), *is none upon* (1x), *earth* (141x), *that I* (46x), *desire* (18x), *beside thee* (1x) = 1002, a number resting in the glorious realm of 1000.

Enter His Gates with a Glorifying Heart

"<u>Enter into</u> <u>his</u> gates <u>with</u> THANKSGIVING, and into his courts with PRAISE: be THANKFUL <u>unto him</u>, <u>and bless</u> <u>his name</u>" (Ps. 100:4). The Psalms combination *enter into* (4x), *his* (610x), *gates* (11x), *with* (342x), *thanksgiving* (8x), *and into his courts with praise* (1x), *be thankful unto him* (1x), *and bless* (4x), *his name* (19x) = 1000.

God Has Glorified His Word above His Name

"<u>I will</u> WORSHIP <u>toward</u> <u>thy holy temple</u>, <u>and</u> PRAISE <u>thy name</u> <u>for thy lovingkindness</u> <u>and for</u> <u>thy truth</u>: <u>for thou hast</u> MAGNIFIED <u>thy word</u> <u>above all thy</u> <u>name</u>" (Ps. 138:2). The Bible combination *I will worship toward* (1x), *thy holy temple* (5x), *and praise thy name* (2x), *for thy lovingkindness* (3x), *and for thy truth* (1x), *for thou hast magnified* (1x), *thy word* (58x), *above all thy* (1x), *name* (928x) = 1000.

It Is the Glory of God to Conceal a Thing

"<u>It is the</u> GLORY <u>of God</u> <u>to conceal</u> <u>a thing</u>: <u>but</u> <u>the honour of kings</u> <u>is to search out</u> <u>a matter</u>" (Prov. 25:2). The Bible combination *it is the glory* (1x), *of God* (984x), *to conceal* (1x), *a thing but* (1x), *the honour of kings* (1x), *is to search out* (1x), *a matter* (11x) = 1000.

One Righteous Man Gloriously Found Among a Thousand

"Which yet my soul seeketh, but I find not: <u>one</u> <u>man</u> among <u>a THOUSAND</u> <u>have</u> <u>I found</u> . . . Lo, this only have I found, that God hath made man upright; but they have sought out many inventions" (Eccles. 7:28-29). The Wisdom Books combination *one* (129x), *man* (403x), *have* (474x), *I found* (8x) = 1014 – *a thousand* (14x) = 1000.

Tower of David's Glorious Armory of 1000 Bucklers

"<u>Thy neck is like the tower of</u> <u>David</u> <u>builded</u> <u>for an</u> <u>armoury</u>, <u>whereon</u> <u>there</u> <u>hang</u> <u>A THOUSAND</u> <u>bucklers</u>, <u>all</u> <u>shields of</u> <u>mighty</u> <u>men</u>" (Song 4:4). The groom dotes about his bride's beautifully formed neck. Hers was especially receptive for an array of attractive royal ornaments. The Wisdom Books combination *thy neck is like the tower of* (1x), *David* (15x), *builded* (6x), *for an* (7x), *armoury* (1x), *whereon* (2x), *there* (260x), *hang* (1x), *a thousand* (14x), *bucklers* (2x), *all* (482x), *shields of* (2x), *mighty* (49x), *men* (154x) = 1000.

Eliakim to Become Glorious in Jerusalem

"<u>And it shall come to pass in that day</u>, <u>that I will call</u> <u>my servant</u> Eliakim <u>the son of Hilkiah</u>: And I will clothe him with thy robe, and strengthen him with thy girdle, <u>and I will commit thy</u> <u>government into his hand</u>: and he shall be a father to the inhabitants of Jerusalem, and to the house of Judah. <u>And the key of the house of David</u> will I <u>lay upon his shoulder; so he shall open, and none</u> <u>shall shut; and he shall</u> <u>shut, and none shall open. And I will</u> <u>fasten</u> *him* <u>as a nail in a sure</u> <u>place; and he shall be</u> <u>for a</u> GLORIOUS <u>throne to his father's house. And they shall hang</u>

upon him all the GLORY of his father's house" (Isa. 22:20-24a).

The Isaiah combination *and it shall come to pass in that day* (11x), *that I will call* (1x), *my servant* (15x), *Eliakim* (5x), *the son of Hilkiah* (2x), *and I will commit* (1x), *thy government into his hand* (1x), *and the key* (1x), *of the house of* (6x), *David* (9x), *will I* (33x), *lay upon his* (1x), *shoulder* (5x), *so he* (3x), *shall open* (2x), *and none* (12x), *shall shut* (3x), *and he shall* (38x), *shut* (11x), *and none* (12x), *shall open* (2x), *and I will* (61x), *fasten* (1x), *him* (169x), *as a* (62x), *nail* (2x), *in a sure* (1x), *place* (37x), *and he shall be* (5x), *for a* (42x), *glorious* (12x), *throne* (7x), *to his* (347x), *father's* (3x), *house* (60x), *and they shall hang* (1x), *upon him* (12x), *all the glory* (3x), *of his father's house* (1x) = 1000.

1000th Verse of Isaiah

"Lift up thine eyes round about, and behold: all these gather themselves together, and come to thee. As I live, saith the LORD, thou shalt surely clothe thee with them all, as with an ornament, and bind them on thee, as a bride doeth" (Isa. 49:18). A promise is given that glory and honor will come again to Zion. The Major Prophets combination *lift up* (34x), *thine eyes* (21x), *round about* (96x), *and behold all these* (1x), *gather themselves together and* (1x), *come to thee* (4x), *as I live* (19x), *saith the LORD* (396x), *thou shalt* (213x), *surely* (78x), *clothe thee* (1x), *with them all* (3x), *as with an ornament* (1x), *and bind them* (2x), *on thee* (5x), *as a* (103x), *bride* (8x), *doeth* (13x) = 1000.

God's Crucified Servant-Son to Be Greatly Glorified

"Behold, my servant shall deal prudently, he shall be EXALTED and EXTOLLED, and be very high. As many were astonied at thee; his visage was so marred more than any man, and his form more than the sons of men: So shall he sprinkle many nations; the kings shall shut their mouths at him: for that which had not been told them shall they see; and that which they had not heard shall they consider" (Isa. 52:13-15). The Major Prophets combination *behold* (367x), *my servant* (30x), *shall deal* (6x), *prudently* (1x), *he shall* (240x), *be exalted* (9x), *and extolled* (1x), *and be* (44x), *very* (45x), *high* (96x), *as many* (1x), *were astonied* (2x), *at thee* (9x), *his visage* (2x), *was so* (2x), *marred* (3x), *more than* (14x), *any man* (3x), *and his form* (1x), *more than* (14x), *the sons of men* (4x), *so shall* (28x), *he sprinkle* (1x), *many nations* (7x), *the kings* (34x), *shall shut* (4x), *their mouths* (2x), *at him* (2x), *for that* (9x), *which had not been told them* (1x), *shall they see* (1x), *and that which* (12x), *they had not* (4x), *heard shall they consider* (1x) = 1000. The word *was* occurs 1000 times in the NT Narrative.

Glory of the Lord Has Risen upon Zion

"Arise, shine; for thy light is come, and the GLORY of the LORD is risen upon thee. For, behold, the darkness shall cover the earth, and gross darkness the people: but the LORD shall arise upon thee, and his GLORY shall be seen upon thee. And the Gentiles shall come to thy light, and kings to the BRIGHTNESS of thy rising" (Isa. 60:1-3). The Isaiah combination *arise* (8x), *shine* (2x), *for thy* (11x), *light* (31x), *is come* (6x), *and the glory* (5x), *of the LORD* (103x), *is* (391x), *risen* (1x), *upon* (166x), *thee* (241x), *and the Gentiles* (2x), *shall come to* (31x), *thy light* (5x), *and kings to the brightness* (1x), *of thy rising* (1x) = 1000.

"That I May Be Glorified"

"Thy people also shall be all righteous: they shall inherit the land for ever, the branch of my planting, the work of my hands, that I may be GLORIFIED" (Isa. 60:21). The Old Testament combination *thy people also shall be all* (1x), *righteous* (195x), *they shall inherit* (4x), *the land for ever the* (1x), *branch* (31x), *of my planting* (1x), *the work of my hands* (3x), *that I* (601x), *may be* (151x), *glorified* (13x) = 1001, a number rooted in the first-generation 1000s family.

"A Little One Shall Become a Thousand"

"A little one shall become A THOUSAND, and a small one a strong nation: I the LORD will hasten it in his time" (Isa. 60:22). The Major and Minor Prophets combination *a little* (17x), *one* (389x), *shall become a* (6x), *thousand* (58x), *and a small* (1x), *one* (389x), *a strong* (10x), *nation* (63x), *I the LORD* (40x), *will hasten* (2x), *it in* (34x), *his time* (1x) = 1008, a number rooted in the first-generation 1000s family.

Jerusalem to Become a Glory in the Earth

"I have set watchmen upon thy walls, O Jerusalem, which shall never hold their peace day nor night: ye that make mention of the LORD, keep not silence, And give him no rest, till he establish, and till he make Jerusalem a PRAISE in the earth" (Isa. 62:6-7). The following seal substitutes the synonymous phrase "a praise" with "a glory." The Bible combination *I have set watchmen* (1x), *upon thy walls* (3x), *O Jerusalem* (16x), *which shall never* (2x), *hold their peace* (5x), *day nor night* (5x), *ye that* (78x), *make mention of the LORD* (1x), *keep not silence* (2x), *and give him* (5x), *no rest* (1x), *till he establish* (1x), *and till he make* (1x), *Jerusalem* (811x), *a glory* (2x), *in the earth* (66x) = 1000.

No Man Should Glory in Himself

"Thus saith the LORD, Let not the wise man GLORY in his wisdom, neither let the mighty man GLORY in his might, let not the rich man GLORY in his riches: But let him that GLORIETH GLORY in this, that he understandeth and knoweth me, that I am the LORD which exercise lovingkindness, judgment, and righteousness, in the earth: for in these things I delight, saith the LORD" (Jer. 9:23-24). The Old Testament combination *thus saith the LORD let not* (1x), *the wise man* (4x), *glory* (225x), *in his wisdom* (1x), *neither let* (18x), *the mighty man* (7x), *glory* (225x), *in his might* (2x), *let not* (81x), *the rich man* (5x), *glory in his riches* (1x), *but let him that glorieth* (1x), *glory in this* (1x), that he *understandeth and knoweth me* (1x), *that I am the LORD* (76x), *which exercise* (1x), *lovingkindness* (26x), *judgment and* (58x), *righteousness* (205x), *in the earth* (61x) = 1000.

1000th Verse of Jeremiah

"Now while he was not yet gone back, he said, Go back also to Gedaliah the son of Ahikam the son of Shaphan, whom the king of Babylon hath made governor over the cities of Judah, and dwell with him among the people: or go wheresoever it seemeth convenient unto thee to go. So the captain of the guard gave him victuals and a reward, and let him go" (Jer. 40:5). Jeremiah had been despised and mistreated by the rulers of Jerusalem throughout his long ministry because they thought he was a false prophet. Now he begins to experience a little bit of the glory in being recognized as a true prophet serving in his ordained office.

Jerusalem in Ruins & No Longer the Perfection of Beauty

"All that pass by clap their hands at thee; they hiss and wag their head at the daughter of Jerusalem, saying, Is this the city that men call The perfection of beauty, The joy of the whole earth?" (Lam. 2:15) These names for Jerusalem correspond with our fourth definition of glory: great beauty and splendor. The Bible combination *all that pass by* (3x), *clap* (6x), *their hands* (80x), *at thee they hiss and wag their head* (1x), *at the daughter of* (1x), *Jerusalem* (811x), *saying is this the city that* (1x), *men call* (2x), *the perfection of* (2x), *beauty* (49x), *the joy of* (16x), *the whole earth* (28x) = 1000.

The Glorious Aureole Appearance of the Manifest Lord

"And above the firmament that was over their heads was the likeness of a throne, as the appearance of a sapphire stone: and upon the likeness of the throne was the likeness as the appearance of a man above upon it. And I saw as the colour of amber, as the appearance of FIRE ROUND ABOUT within it, from the appearance of his loins even upward, and from the appearance of his loins even downward, I saw as it were the appearance of fire, and it had BRIGHTNESS ROUND ABOUT. As the appearance of the bow that is in the cloud in the day of rain, so was the appearance of the BRIGHTNESS ROUND ABOUT. This was the appearance of the likeness of the GLORY of the LORD" (Ezek. 1:26-28c).

This passage corresponds with our fifth definition of glory: a halo appearing around the shadow of an object. The Bible combination *and above* (17x), *the firmament* (15x), *that was over* (8x), *their heads* (38x), *was the likeness* (2x), *of a throne as* (1x), *the appearance of* (29x), *a sapphire stone* (3x), *and upon the* (82x), *likeness of the throne* (1x), *was the likeness as* (1x), *the appearance of* (29x), *a man* (530x), *above upon it* (3x), *and I saw* (35x), *as the colour of* (6x), *amber* (3x), *as the appearance of* (12x), *fire round about within it from* (1x), *the appearance of* (29x), *his loins* (18x), *even upward* (2x), *and from the appearance of* (1x), *his loins* (18x), *even downward* (2x), *as the appearance of* (12x), *the bow* (19x), *that is in the cloud* (1x), *in the day of rain* (1x), *so was the appearance of* (1x), *the brightness round about* (1x), *this was the* (28x), *appearance of the* (10x), *likeness of the* (5x), *glory of the LORD/Lord* (36x) = 1000.

Glory of the Lord Departs from Solomon's Temple

"Then the GLORY of the LORD departed from off the threshold of the house, and stood over the cherubims. . . . But as for them whose heart walketh after the heart of their detestable things and their abominations, I will recompense their way upon their own heads, saith the Lord GOD. . . . And the GLORY of the LORD went up from the midst of the city, and stood upon the mountain which is on the east side of the city" (Ezek. 10:18, 21, 23). The Major Prophets combination *then* (355x), *the glory of the LORD* (13x), *departed* (12x), *from off* (14x), *the threshold of* (7x), *the house* (225x), *and stood* (7x), *over the cherubims and the glory of the LORD* (1x), *went* (112x), *up from* (19x), *the midst of* (135x), *the city* (85x), *and stood upon* (1x), *the mountain* (11x), *which is on* (2x), *the east side of the city* (1x) = 1000.

Glory of the Lord Enters into Messiah's Millennial Temple

"Afterward he brought me to the gate, even the gate that looketh toward the east: And, behold, the GLORY of the God of Israel came from the way of the east: and his voice was like a noise of many waters: and the earth shined with his GLORY. . . . And the GLORY of the LORD came into the house by the way of the gate whose prospect is toward the east. So the spirit took me up, and brought me into the inner court; and, behold, the GLORY of the LORD filled the house" (Ezek. 43:1-2, 4-5).

Here in this passage the glory-related word *filled* is the 563,000th word of the Bible, a multiple of 1000.

Glorious Living Waters Flow from Messiah's Millennial Temple

"Afterward he brought me again unto the door of the house; and, behold, waters issued out from under the threshold of the house eastward . . . And when the man that had the line in his hand went forth eastward, he measured A THOUSAND cubits, and he brought me through the waters; the waters were to the ankles. Again he measured A THOUSAND, and brought me through the waters; the waters were to the knees. Again he measured A THOUSAND, and brought me through; the waters were to the loins. Afterward he measured A THOUSAND; and it was a river that I could not pass over: for the waters were risen, waters to swim in, a river that could not be passed over" (Ezek. 47:3-5).

The Bible combination *afterward he brought me* (3x), *again unto the* (15x), *door of the house* (8x), *and behold waters issued* (1x), *out from under* (4x), *the threshold of the house* (4x), *eastward* (40x), *and when the man* (6x), *that had the line* (1x), *in his hand* (70x), *went forth* (76x), *eastward* (40x), *he measured a* (4x), *thousand* (520x), *cubits* (213x) = 1001.

The Glory of Messiah's All-Victorious Kingdom

"Thou sawest till that a stone was cut out without hands, which smote the image upon his feet that were of iron and clay, and brake them to pieces. Then was the iron, the clay, the brass, the silver, and the gold, broken to pieces together, and became like the chaff of the summer threshingfloors; and the wind carried them away, that no place was found for them: and the stone that smote the image became a great mountain, and filled the whole earth" (Dan. 2:34-35).

Here in this glorious Messianic kingdom passage the word *the* is the 570,000th word of the Bible, a multiple of 1000.

Belshazzar Puts on a Glorious Feast for 1000 of His Lords

"Belshazzar the king made a great feast to a THOUSAND of his lords, and drank wine before the THOUSAND. . . . They drank wine, and praised the gods of gold, and of silver, of brass, of iron, of wood, and of stone" (Dan. 5:1, 4). The Major and Minor Prophets combination *Belshazzar the* (2x), *king* (504x), *made* (221x), *a great feast to* (1x), *a thousand* (10x), *of his* (236x), *lords* (10x), *and drank wine before* (1x), *the thousand* (2x), *they drank wine and praised* (1x), *the gods of* (10x), *gold and of silver of brass of iron of wood* (1x), *and of stone* (1x) = 1000.

Messiah's Coronation Day & Installation of His Glorious World Kingdom

"I saw in the night visions, and, behold, one like the Son of man came with the clouds of heaven, and came to the Ancient of days, and they brought him near before him. And there was given him dominion, and GLORY, and a kingdom, that all people, nations, and languages, should serve him: his dominion is an everlasting dominion, which shall not pass away, and his kingdom that which shall not be destroyed" (Dan. 7:13-14). The Major and Minor Prophets combination *I saw in the* (4x), *night visions* (2x), *and behold one like the* (2x), *s/Son of man* (101x), *came with the clouds of* (1x), *heaven* (91x), *and came to* (2x), *the Ancient of days* (3x), *and they brought* (4x), *him near* (1x), *before him* (29x), *and there* (113x), *was given him* (2x), *dominion* (24), *and glory* (4x), *and a kingdom* (1x), *that all* (8x), *people* (548x), *nations and languages* (5x), *should serve him* (1x), *his dominion* (10x), *is an* (14x), *everlasting dominion* (2x), *which shall not* (7x), *pass away and* (1x), *his kingdom* (8x), *that which shall not* (2x), *be destroyed* (10x) = 1000.

Israel's God Is Renown in the Earth

"And now, O Lord our God, that hast brought thy people forth out of the land of Egypt with a mighty hand, and hast gotten thee RENOWN, as at this day; we have sinned, we have done wickedly" (Dan. 9:15). The Old Testament combination *and now* (84x), *O Lord* (49x), *our God that hast* (1x), *brought* (730x), *thy people* (127x), *forth out of the land of Egypt with a mighty hand* (1x), *and hast gotten thee* (1x), *renown* (7x) = 1000.

God Will Turn Israel's Glory into Shame

"As they were increased, so they sinned against me: therefore will I change their GLORY into shame" (Hos. 4:7). The following numeric seal falls short of 1000 similarly to Israel's glory falling short of God's righteousness. The Minor Prophets combination *as* (207x), *they* (354x), *were* (33x), *increased* (4x), *so* (52x), *they sinned against me* (1x), *therefore* (67x), *will I* (44x), *change* (4x), *their* (232x), *glory into shame* (1x) = 999.

Northern Tribes to Lose Their National Glory & Blessing

"For thus saith the Lord GOD; The city that went out by A THOUSAND shall leave an hundred, and that which went forth by an hundred shall leave ten, to the house of Israel" (Amos 5:3). The Major and Minor Prophets combination *for thus* (53x), *saith the Lord GOD* (228x), *the city* (103x), *that went out* (2x), *by* (554x), *a thousand* (10x), *shall leave* (6x), *an hundred* (17x), *and that which went forth* (1x), *by an hundred* (17x), *shall leave ten* (1x), *to the house of Israel* (8x) = 1000.

Sennacherib Will Come & Take Away Israel's Glory

"Yet will I bring an heir unto thee, O inhabitant of Mareshah: he shall come unto Adullam the GLORY of Israel" (Mic. 1:15). The Major and Minor Prophets combination *yet will I* (12x), *bring an* (3x), *heir* (3x), *unto thee* (126x), *O inhabitant of* (7x), *Mareshah* (1x), *Sennacherib king of Assyria* (3x), *he shall* (286x), *come unto Adullam* (1x), *the glory of* (42x), *Israel* (516x) = 1000.

Under Judgment, Nineveh to Lose All Her Glory

"Take ye the spoil of silver, take the spoil of gold: for there is none end of the store and GLORY out of all the pleasant furniture" (Nah. 2:9). The Minor Prophets combination *take* (47x), *ye* (209x), *the spoil of* (3x), *silver* (21x), *take* (47x), *the spoil of gold* (1x), *for* (402x), *there* (84x), *is none* (9x), *end* (11x), *of the store and* (1x), *glory* (20x), *out of* (72x), *all the* (63x), *pleasant* (9x), *furniture* (1x) = 1000.

Earth Shall Be Filled with Knowledge of the Lord's Glory

"For the earth shall be filled with the knowledge of the GLORY of the LORD, as the waters cover the sea" (Hab. 2:14). The Major and Minor Prophets combination *for the* (388x), *earth* (276x), *shall be filled* (5x), *with the* (230x), *knowledge of* (5x), *of the glory of the LORD* (2x), *as the waters cover* (2x), *the sea* (88x), *when he cometh* (3x), *thy king cometh* (1x) = 1000.

God's Glory Covered the Heavens

"God came from Teman, and the Holy One from mount Paran. Selah. His GLORY covered the heavens, and the earth was full of his PRAISE. And his brightness was as the light; he had horns coming out of his hand: and there was the hiding of his power" (Hab. 3:3-4). Again the word *was* occurs 1000 times in the NT Narrative.

Remnant Uninterested in Building a Glorious House for the Lord

"Thus speaketh the LORD of hosts, saying, This people say, The time is not come, the time that the LORD'S house should be <u>built</u>" (Hag. 1:2). Here the glory-related word *built* is the 601,000th word of the Old Testament.

Building the Lord's House Will Bring Him Glory

"Thus saith the LORD of hosts; Consider your ways. Go up to the mountain, and bring wood, and build the house; and I will take pleasure in it, and I will be GLORIFIED, saith the LORD" (Hag. 1:7-8). The Major and Minor Prophets combination *thus saith* (357x), *the LORD of hosts* (217x), *consider* (23x), *your ways* (11x), *go up* (22x), *to the mountain* (3x), *and bring* (15x), *wood* (25x), *and build* (4x), *the house* (301x), *and I will take* (6x), *pleasure in it* (1x), *and I will be* (17x), *glorified saith the LORD* (1x) = 1003.

The Greater Glory of This Latter House

"<u>And I will shake all nations, and the desire of all nations shall come: and I will fill this house with glory</u>, saith the LORD of hosts. The silver is mine, and the gold is mine, saith the LORD of hosts. <u>The glory of this latter house shall be greater than of the former, saith the LORD of hosts: and in this place will I give peace, saith the LORD of hosts</u>" (Hag. 2:7-9). The Major and Minor Prophets combination *and I will shake* (2x), *all nations* (18x), *and the desire of all nations* (1x), *shall come and* (11x), *I will fill* (5x), *this house* (12x), *with glory* (2x), *the glory* (48x), *of this latter* (1x), *house* (459x), *shall be greater than* (1x), *of the former* (1x), *saith the LORD of hosts* (120x), *and in* (166x), *this place* (32x), *will I give peace* (1x), *saith the LORD of hosts* (120x) = 1000.

Messiah Shall Bear the Glory of the Millennial Temple

"<u>Thus speaketh the LORD of hosts, saying, Behold the man whose name is The BRANCH; and he shall grow up out of his place, and he shall build the temple of the LORD: Even he shall build the temple of the LORD; and he shall bear the GLORY, and shall sit and rule upon his throne; and he shall be a priest upon his throne: and the counsel of peace shall be between them both</u>" (Zech. 6:12b-13). The Bible combination *thus speaketh the LORD of hosts saying* (3x), *behold the man* (6x), *whose name* (50x), *is the branch* (1x), *and he shall grow up out of his place* (1x), *and he shall build* (1x), *the temple of the LORD/Lord* (24x), *even he shall build* (1x), *the temple of the LORD/Lord* (24x), *and he shall bear* (215x), *the glory* (132x), *and shall sit and* (1x), *rule* (66x), *upon his* (159x), *throne* (176x), *and he shall be* (34x), *a priest* (17x), *upon his throne* (8x), *and the counsel* (3x), *of peace* (65x), *shall be between* (1x), *them both* (12x) = 1000.

The Lord Will Be Magnified

"And your eyes shall see, and ye shall say, The LORD will be MAGNIFIED from the border of Israel" (Mal. 5:1). The Major and Minor Prophets combination *and your* (52x), *eyes shall* (10x), *see and ye shall say* (1x), *the LORD will* (36x), *be magnified* (1x), *from the* (360x), *border of* (27x), *Israel* (516x) = 1003.

The New Testament

"The book of the <u>generation</u> of <u>Jesus</u> Christ, the son of David, the son of Abraham" (Matt. 1:1). Jesus Christ's generation saw more of God's manifest glory than any other generation in Israel's history. Through Christ's miraculous deeds they saw the lame walk again, the blind see again, and the paralyzed move again. They saw sick folk become strong and lepers become clean. They saw demon-possessed souls made whole again, the downcast rejoice again, and the dead live again! They also saw God's glory through His lowly incarnate Son's wise words.

The New Testament combination *Jesus* (973x) + *generation* (37x) = 1010 — *Jesus'* (10x) = 1000.

For Thine Is the Kingdom, the Power & the Glory

"<u>For thine is</u> <u>the kingdom, and the power, and the GLORY, for</u> <u>ever. Amen</u>" (Matt. 6:13b). The Gospels combination *for thine is* (1x), *thine is* (2x), *the kingdom* (100x), *and the power* (4x), *and the* (10x), *glory* (36x), *for* (846x), *ever amen* (1x) = 1000.

Lilies of the Field Gloriously Arrayed

"<u>And why take ye</u> <u>thought for raiment</u>? <u>Consider</u> <u>the lilies</u> <u>of the</u> <u>field</u>, <u>how they grow</u>; <u>they toil not</u>, <u>neither</u> <u>do they</u> <u>spin: And yet</u> <u>I say unto you</u>, <u>That even Solomon</u> <u>in all his GLORY</u> <u>was not arrayed like one</u> <u>of these</u>" (Matt. 6:28-29). The Gospels combination *and why take ye* (1x), *thought for raiment* (1x), *consider* (4x), *the lilies* (2x), *of the* (642x), *field* (22x), *how they grow* (2x), *they toil not* (2x), *neither* (101x), *do they* (5x), *spin and yet* (1x), *I say unto you* (121x), *that even* (7x), *Solomon* (8x), *in all his* (2x), *glory* (36x), *was not* (23x), *arrayed like one* (2x), *of these* (18x) = 1000.

People Astonished at Jesus' Glorious Sayings

"And it came to pass, when Jesus had ended these <u>sayings</u>, the people were astonished at his doctrine" (Matt. 7:28). Again the word *saying(s)* occurs 1000 times in the Old Testament.

They Glorified the God of Israel

"<u>And great multitudes came unto him, having with them those that were lame, blind, dumb, maimed, and many others, and cast them down at Jesus' feet; and he healed them: Insomuch that the multitude wondered, when they saw the dumb to speak, the maimed to be whole, the lame to walk, and the blind to see: and they GLORIFIED the God of Israel</u>" (Matt. 15:30-31). The Gospels combination *and great multitudes came unto him* (1x), *having with them* (1x), *those that were* (2x), *lame blind dumb maimed* (1x), *and many others* (3x), *and cast them* (3x), *down at* (6x), *Jesus' feet and he healed them* (1x), *insomuch* (13x), *that the* (69x), *multitude* (65x), *wondered* (8x), *when they* (111x), *saw* (140x), *the dumb* (4x), *to speak* (13x), *the maimed* (3x), *to be* (68x), *whole* (61x), *the lame* (4x), *to walk* (2x), *and the blind* (3x), *to see* (22x), *and they* (345x), *glorified* (21x), *the God* (13x), *of Israel* (17x) = 1000.

The Son of Man Will Return in the Glory of His Father

"<u>For the</u> <u>Son of man</u> <u>shall come</u> <u>in the GLORY</u> <u>of his</u> <u>Father</u> <u>with his</u> <u>angels; and then he shall reward</u> <u>every man</u> <u>according to</u> <u>his works</u>" (Matt. 16:27). The Gospels combination *for the*

(101x), *Son of man* (84x), *shall come* (26x), *in the* (374x), *glory* (36x), *of his* (79x), *Father* (180x), *with his* (20x), *angels* (29x), *and then he shall* (1x), *reward* (17x), *every man* (15x), *according to his* (3x), *works* (34x), *his works* (1x) = 1000.

The Son of Man Will Sit upon His Throne of Glory

"When the Son of man shall come in his GLORY, and all the holy angels with him, then shall he sit upon the throne of his GLORY" (Matt. 25:31). The Matthew combination *the Son of man shall come* (2x), *when the* (36x), *Son of man shall* (6x), *come* (89x), *in his glory* (1x), *and all the* (4x), *holy angels with* (1x), *him* (378x), *then shall* (17x), *he* (412x), *sit* (11x), *upon* (32x), *the throne of his* (2x) *glory* (9x) = 1000.

They Glorified God in Their Amazement

"I say unto thee, Arise, and take up thy bed, and go thy way into thine house. And immediately he arose, took up the bed, and went forth before them all; insomuch that they were all amazed, and GLORIFIED God, saying, We never saw it on this fashion" (Mark 2:11-12). The Gospels combination *I say unto thee arise and take up* (2x), *thy bed and go* (2x), *thy way into thine house* (1x), *and immediately* (25x), *he arose* (15x), *took up the bed* (1x), *and went* (46x), *forth* (129x), before (125x), *them all* (19x), *insomuch that they were* (2x), *all amazed and glorified* (1x), *God* (312x), *saying* (317x), *we never* (1x), *saw it on* (1x), *this fashion* (1x) = 1000.

The Son of Man to Return in Clouds of Glory

"But in those days, after that tribulation, the sun shall be darkened, and the moon shall not give her light, And the stars of heaven shall fall, and the powers that are in heaven shall be shaken. And then shall they see the Son of man coming in the clouds with great power and GLORY" (Mark 13:24-26). The Gospels combination *but in those days after that tribulation* (1x), *the sun shall be darkened* (1x), *and the moon* (2x), *shall not give* (2x), *her light* (2x), *and the stars* (2x), *of heaven* (42x), *shall fall and the powers* (1x), *that are in heaven* (1x), *shall be* (230x), *shaken* (6x), *and then* (21x), *shall they* (17x), *see* (127x), *the Son of man* (83x), *coming* (35x), *in the* (374x), *clouds* (4x), *with great* (3x), *power and* (10x), *glory* (36x) = 1000.

Glory of the Lord Shone Round about the Shepherds

"And there were in the same country shepherds abiding in the field, keeping watch over their flock by night. And, lo, the angel of the Lord came upon them, and the GLORY of the Lord shone round about them: and they were sore afraid" (Luke 2:8-9). The Gospels combination *and there were in* (1x), *the same country* (1x), *shepherds abiding in the field* (1x), *keeping watch* (1x), *over their flock by night* (1x), *and lo* (7x), *the angel of the Lord* (5x), *came upon* (2x), *them* (978x), *and the glory of the Lord* (1x), *shone round about them* (1x), *and they were sore afraid* (1x) = 1000.

In the Night Sky, a Multitude of Angels Glorify God

"And suddenly there was with the angel a multitude of the heavenly host praising God, and saying, GLORY to God in the highest, and on earth peace, good will toward men. And it came to pass, as the angels were gone away from them into heaven, the shepherds said one to another, Let us now go even unto Bethlehem, and see this thing which is come to pass, which the Lord hath made known unto us" (Luke 2:13-15). In the midst of this glorifying passage, the word *as* is the 651,000th word of the Bible.

Jesus' Transfiguration unto Divine Glory

"And it came to pass about an eight days after these sayings, he took Peter and John and James, and went up into a mountain to pray. And as he prayed, the fashion of his countenance was altered, and his raiment was white and glistering. . . . But Peter and they that were with him were heavy with sleep: and when they were awake, they saw his GLORY" (Luke 9:28-29, 32ab). The Gospels combination *and as he prayed the* (1x), *fashion* (2x), *of his countenance* (1x), *was altered* (1x), *and his raiment* (4x), *was white* (2x), *and glistering* (1x), *but Peter* (4x), *and they that were* (11x), *with him* (73x), *were heavy* (3x), *with sleep* (1x), *and when they were* (15x), *awake* (3x), *they saw* (24x), *his* (818x), *glory* (36x) = 1000.

Healed Blind Man Glorifies God

"What wilt thou that I shall do unto thee? And he said, Lord, that I may receive my sight. And Jesus said unto him, Receive thy sight: thy faith hath saved thee. And immediately he received his sight, and followed him, GLORIFYING God: and all the people, when they saw it, gave PRAISE unto God" (Luke 18:41-43). The Gospels combination *what wilt thou* (3x), *that I shall* (6x), *do unto thee and he said Lord* (1x), *that I may* (7x), *receive my* (2x), *sight* (20x), *and Jesus said unto him* (12x), *receive* (58x), *thy sight* (4x), *thy faith hath* (7x), *saved thee* (2x), *and immediately* (25x), *he received* (4x), *his sight* (5x), *and followed him* (10x), *glorifying* (3x), *God* (312x), *and all the people* (8x), *when they* (111x), *saw it* (17x), *gave* (70x), *praise unto* (1x), *God* (312x) = 1000.

Centurion Stationed at the Cross Glorified God

"Now when the centurion saw what was done, he GLORIFIED God, saying, Certainly this was a righteous man" (Luke 23:47). The Gospels combination *now* (164x), *when* (568x), *the centurion* (8x), *saw* (140x), *what was* (10x), *done* (88x), *he glorified God* (1x), *saying certainly this was a* (1x), *righteous* (19x), *was a righteous man* (1x) = 1000.

The Word Was Made Gloriously Incarnate

"And the Word was made flesh, and dwelt among us, and we beheld his GLORY, the GLORY as of the only begotten of the Father, full of grace and truth" (John 1:14). Again the word *was* occurs 1000 times in the NT Narrative.

Jesus' Glory Manifested through the First of Many Miracles

"This beginning of miracles did Jesus in Cana of Galilee, and manifested forth his GLORY; and his disciples believed on him" (John 2:11). The John's Gospel combination *this beginning* (1x), *of* (474x), *miracles* (9x), *did* (39x), *Jesus in* (5x), *Cana of Galilee and* (2x), *manifested forth* (1x), *his* (176x), *glory and* (2x), *his* (176x), *disciples* (64x), *believed* (27x), *on him* (25x) = 1001.

1000th Chapter of the Bible

In this glorious chapter, a Sanhedrin member gives glory to Jesus by acknowledging that God's presence is most certainly with Him. "There was a man of the Pharisees, named Nicodemus, a ruler of the Jews: The same came to Jesus by night, and said unto him, Rabbi, we know that thou art a teacher come from God: for no man can do these miracles that thou doest, except God be with him" (John 3:1-2). The Gospels combination *the same* (62x), *came to* (97x), *Jesus* (617x), *by night* (7x), *and said unto him* (55x), *Rabbi* (8x), *we know* (19x), *that thou* (52x), *art a teacher* (1x), *come from God* (2x), *for no man can* (1x), *do these miracles* (1x), *that thou doest* (4x), *except God be* (1x), *with him* (73x) = 1000.

Jesus expounds upon His salvation teaching with a revelation on the glorious nature of God's active Spirit. "Marvel not that I said unto thee, Ye must be born again. The wind bloweth where it listeth, and thou hearest the sound thereof, but canst not tell whence it cometh, and whither it goeth: so is every one that is born of the Spirit" (vv. 7-8). The Gospels combination *marvel not that* (1x), *I* (955x), *said unto thee* (3x), *ye must be born again* (1x), *the wind bloweth* (1x), *where it* (4x), *listeth* (1x), *and thou hearest the sound* (1x), *thereof* (17x), *but canst not tell* (1x), *whence it cometh* (1x), *and whither* (4x), *it goeth* (1x), *so is every one* (1x), *that is born* (2x), *of the Spirit* (6x) = 1000.

Jesus digresses from His salvation talk to tell this ruler of His unique heavenly glory. "If I have told you earthly things, and ye believe not, how shall ye believe, if I tell you of heavenly things? And no man hath ascended up to heaven, but he that came down from heaven, even the Son of man which is in heaven" (vv. 12-13). The Gospels combination *if I have* (3x), *told you* (11x), *earthly things and ye* (1x), *believe not* (11x), *how shall* (5x), *ye believe* (12x), *if I tell you of* (2x), *heavenly* (8x), *things* (273x), *and no man* (12x), *hath ascended* (1x), *up to* (21x), *heaven* (143x), *but he that came* (1x), *came down from* (9x), *heaven* (143x), *even* (96x), *the Son of man* (83x), *which is in* (22x), *heaven* (143x) = 1000.

Lazarus' Resurrection for God's Glory & the Son of God's Glory

"When Jesus heard that, he said, This sickness is not unto death, but for the GLORY of God, that the Son of God might be GLORIFIED thereby" (John 11:4). The Gospels combination *when Jesus* (55x), *heard that* (28x), *he said* (191x), *this* (392x), *sickness is* (1x), *not unto* (11x), *death* (44x), *but for the glory* (1x), *of God* (162x), *that the* (69x), *the Son of God* (24x), *might be* (28x), *glorified* (21x), *thereby* (1x) = 1000.

Dark Hour Has Come for the Son of Man to Be Glorified

"And Jesus answered them, saying, The hour is come, that the Son of man should be GLORIFIED. Verily, verily, I say unto you, Except a corn of wheat fall into the ground and die, it abideth alone: but if it die, it bringeth forth much fruit" (John 12:23-24). The Gospels combination *and Jesus* (131x), *answered them* (20x), *saying* (317x), *the hour is* (6x), *come* (332x), *that the* (69x), *Son of man* (84x), *should be glorified* (1x), *verily verily I say unto you* (20x), *except a corn of wheat fall into* (1x), *the ground* (15x), *and die* (1x), *it abideth alone* (1x), *but if it die* (1x), *it bringeth forth much fruit* (1x) = 1001.

Thousands Respond Positively to the Glorious Preached Word

"And with many other words did he testify and exhort, saying, Save yourselves from this untoward generation. Then they that gladly received his word were baptized: and the same day there were added unto them about THREE THOUSAND souls" (Acts 2:41). The Acts combination *and with many other words* (1x), *did he testify and exhort saying* (1x), *save yourselves from this untoward generation* (1x), *then* (95x), *they* (389x), *that gladly* (1x), *received* (26x), *his* (146x), *word* (40x), *were baptized* (5x), *and the* (126x), *same* (21x), *day* (59x), *there were added* (1x), *unto them* (49x), *about* (38x), *three thousand souls* (1x) = 1000.

Stephen Speaks of the God of Glory

"And he said, Men, brethren, and fathers, hearken; The God of GLORY appeared unto our father

666

Abraham, when he was in Mesopotamia, before he dwelt in Charran" (Acts 7:2). The title 'God of Glory' occurs only once in the Old Testament and once in the New Testament. The Acts combination *and he said men* (1x), *brethren* (53x), *and fathers* (2x), *hearken* (5x), *the God of* (12x), *glory* (4x), *appeared unto our* (1x), *father* (10x), *Abraham* (8x), *when* (224x), *he* (380x), *was* (247x), *in Mesopotamia* (1x), *before* (51x), *he dwelt in Charran* (1x) = 1000.

Stephen Saw the Glory of God & Jesus Christ

"But he, being full of the Holy Ghost, looked up stedfastly into heaven, and saw the GLORY of God, and Jesus standing on the right hand of God, And said, Behold, I see the heavens opened, and the Son of man standing on the right hand of God" (Acts 7:55-56). The Acts combination *but he* (8x), *martyr Stephen* (1x), *being* (31x), *full of* (10x), *the Holy Ghost* (41x), *looked* (6x), *up* (94x), *stedfastly* (5x), *into* (103x), *heaven* (24x), *and saw* (7x), *the glory of* (2x), *God* (170x), *and Jesus* (1x), *standing* (8x), *on* (94x), *the right* (5x), *hand* (29x), *of God* (53x), *and said* (47x), *behold* (24x), *I see* (1x), *the heavens* (2x), *opened* (15x), *and the* (126x), *Son of man* (1x), *standing* (8x), *on the right* (2x), *hand* (29x), *of God* (53x) = 1000.

Saul of Tarsus Beheld the Glorious Light of the Heavenly Christ

"And it came to pass, that, as I made my journey, and was come nigh unto Damascus about noon, suddenly there shone from heaven a great light round about me. And I fell unto the ground, and heard a voice saying unto me, Saul, Saul, why persecutest thou me? . . . And they that were with me saw indeed the light, and were afraid; but they heard not the voice of him that spake to me. . . And when I could not see for the GLORY of that light, being led by the hand of them that were with me, I came into Damascus" (Acts 22:6-7, 9, 11).

The Bible combination *and they that were with me* (1x), *saw indeed the light* (1x), *and were afraid but they heard not* (1x), *the voice of him that* (4x), *spake to me* (2x), *and when I could not* (1x), *see* (597x), *for the glory* (12x), *of that* (101x), *light* (272x), *being led* (2x), *by the hand of them* (1x), *that were with me* (4x), *I came into Damascus* (1x) = 1000.

1000th Verse of Acts

"And some believed the things which were spoken, and some believed not" (Acts 28:24). The things Paul had spoken pertained to the glorious kingdom of God and of Christ Jesus.

Suffering & the Glory That Follows

"The Spirit itself beareth witness with our spirit, that we are the children of God: And if children, then heirs; heirs of God, and joint-heirs with Christ; if so be that we suffer with him, that we may be also GLORIFIED together. For I reckon that the sufferings of this present time are not worthy to be compared with the GLORY which shall be revealed in us" (Rom. 8:16-18). The New Testament combination *the Spirit itself beareth witness with our spirit* (1x), *that we are the children of God* (1x), *and if children* (1x), *then heirs* (1x), *heirs of God* (1x), *and joint-heirs with* (1x), *Christ* (555x), *if so be* (7x), *that we* (116x), *suffer with him* (1x), *that we may* (16x), *be also* (10x), *glorified* (37x), *together* (137x), *for I reckon that the* (1x), *sufferings* (10x), *of this* (79x), *present time* (3x), *are not worthy* (1x), *to be compared* (1x), *with the glory* (2x), *which shall be revealed* (1x), *in us* (17x) = 1000.

They Crucified the Lord of Glory

"Which none of the princes of this world knew: for had they known it, they would not have crucified the Lord of GLORY" (1 Cor. 2:8). The New Testament combination *none/nor of the princes of this* (2x), *world* (241x), *knew* (74x), *for had they* (1x), *known it* (2x), *they would not have* (1x), *crucified the* (2x), *Lord* (667x), *of glory* (10x) = 1000.

The Former Glory of the Mosaic Law
"But if the ministration of death, written and engraven in stones, was GLORIOUS, so that the children of Israel could not steadfastly behold the face of Moses for the glory of his countenance; which GLORY was to be done away: How shall not the ministration of the spirit be rather GLORIOUS?" (2 Cor. 3:7-8) The Exodus combination the commandments (0x), of the (611x), LORD (389X) = 1000.

The Glorious Gospel of Christ
"But if our gospel be hid, it is hid to them that are lost: In whom the god of this world hath blinded the minds of them which believe not, lest the light of the GLORIOUS gospel of Christ, who is the image of God, should shine unto them" (2 Cor. 4:4). The New Testament combination *but if our* (2x), *gospel* (101x), *be hid it is hid* (1x), *to them that are lost* (1x), *in whom* (22x), *the god* (1x), *of this* (79x), *world* (241x), *hath blinded* (3x), *the minds* (1x), *of them* (170x), *which believe not* (1x), *lest* (90x), *the light* (35x), *of the glorious* (1x), *gospel* (101x), *of Christ* (90x), *who is* (59x), *the image of God should shine unto them* (1x) = 1000.

The Glory of the Cross
"But God forbid that I should GLORY, save in the cross of our Lord Jesus Christ, by whom the world is crucified unto me, and I unto the world" (Gal. 6:14). The Pauline Epistles combination *but God forbid* (1x), *that I should* (4x), *glory save in* (1x), *the cross* (9x), *of our* (54x), *Lord* (289x), *Jesus* (233x), *Christ* (404x), *by whom the* (1x), *world is* (2x), *crucified unto me* (1x), *and I unto the world* (1x) = 1000.

The Father of Glory
"That the God of our Lord Jesus Christ, the Father of GLORY, *may give unto you* the spirit of wisdom and revelation in the knowledge of him" (Eph. 1:17). The Pauline Epistles combination *that the God of our* (1x), *Lord* (289x), *Jesus* (233x), *Christ* (404x), *the Father* (23x), *of glory* (5x), *may give unto you* (1x), *the spirit of wisdom and* (1x), *revelation* (8x), *the knowledge* (12x), *of him* (23x) = 1000.

A Glorious Church
"That he might sanctify and cleanse it with the washing of water by the word, That he might present it to himself a GLORIOUS church, not having spot, or wrinkle, or any such thing; but that it should be holy and without blemish" (Eph. 5:26-27). The Pauline Epistles combination *that he might* (18x), *sanctify* (3x), *and cleanse* (1x), *it with* (4x), *the washing of* (2x), *water* (4x), *by the word* (7x), *that he* (86x), *might present it* (1x), *to himself a* (1x), *glorious* (12x), *church* (44x), *not* (784x), *having spot or wrinkle* (1x), *or any such thing* (1x), *but that* (15x), *it should* (3x), *be holy* (5x), *and without* (7x), *blemish* (1x) = 1000.

To the Glory of God
Every Tongue Shall Proclaim Jesus as Lord
"Wherefore God also hath highly exalted him, and given him a name which is above every

name: That at the name of Jesus every knee should bow, of things in heaven, and things in earth, and things under the earth; And that every tongue should confess that Jesus Christ is Lord, to the GLORY of God the Father" (Phil. 2:9-11). The Pauline Epistles combination *wherefore* (58x), *God also* (4x), *hath highly* (1x), *exalted* (4x), *him* (271x), *and given him a* (1x), *name* (25x), *which is* (125x), *above* (26x), *every name* (2x), *that at* (2x), *the name of* (14x), *Jesus* (233x), *every knee should bow* (1x), *of things* (12x), *in heaven* (12x), *and things* (6x), *in earth* (4x), *and things* (6x), *under the earth* (1x), *and that every tongue* (1x), *should confess that* (1x), *Jesus Christ* (134x), *is Lord* (1x), *to the glory* (5x), *of God the* (3x), *Father* (47)x = 1000.

Appearing with Christ in Glory

"When Christ, who is our life, shall appear, then shall ye also appear with him in GLORY" (Col. 3:4). The Pauline Epistles combination *when* (126x), *Christ* (404x), *who* (192x), *is our life shall appear* (1x), *then shall ye also appear with* (1x), *him* (271x), *in glory* (5x) = 1000.

We Are Called unto God's Kingdom & Glory

"As ye know how we exhorted and comforted and charged every one of you, as a father doth his children, That ye would walk worthy of God, who hath called you unto his kingdom and GLORY" (1 Thess. 2:11-12). The Pauline Epistles combination *as ye know* (5x), *how we exhorted* (1x), *and comforted and charged* (1x), *every one* (23x), *of you* (52x), *as a father* (2x), *doth* (16x), *his children* (64x), *that ye would walk worthy* (1x), *of God* (276x), *who* (192x), *hath called you unto* (1x), *his* (264x), *kingdom and* (1x), *glory* (101x) = 1000.

Christ's Name Glorified

"That the name of our Lord Jesus Christ may be GLORIFIED in you, and ye in him, according to the grace of our God and the Lord Jesus Christ" (2 Thess. 1:12). The Pauline Epistles combination *that the name of our* (1x), *Lord* (289x), *Jesus* (233x), *Christ* (404x), *may be glorified* (1x), *in you and ye in him* (1x), *according to the* (49x), *grace of our God and* (1x), *the Lord Jesus Christ* (21x) = 1000.

The Incarnate God Received up into Glory

"And without controversy great is the mystery of godliness: God was manifest in the flesh, justified in the Spirit, seen of angels, preached unto the Gentiles, believed on in the world, received up into GLORY" (1 Tim. 3:16). The Pauline Epistles combination *and without* (7x), *controversy* (1x), *great is the mystery of* (1x), *godliness* (11x), *God* (630x), *was manifest* (1x), *in the flesh* (21x), *justified* (21x), *in the Spirit* (8x), *seen of* (5x), *angels* (23x), *preached* (20x), *unto the* (77x), *Gentiles* (48x), *believed* (23x), *on in* (1x), *the world* (56x), *received* (45x), *up into glory* (1x) = 1000.

To Whom Be Glory for Ever & Ever

"And the Lord shall deliver me from every evil work, and will preserve me unto his heavenly kingdom: to whom be GLORY for ever and ever. Amen" (2 Tim. 4:18). The Pauline Epistles combination *and the Lord* (16x), *shall deliver me* (2x), *from every* (2x), *evil* (45x), *work* (39x), *and will* (10x), *preserve me* (1x), *unto his* (8x), *heavenly* (14x), *kingdom* (16x), *to whom* (24x), *be* (668x), *glory* (101x), *for ever* (19x), *and ever* (6x), *Amen* (29x) = 1000.

The Glorious Appearing of Jesus Christ

"Looking for that blessed hope, and the GLORIOUS appearing of the great God and our Saviour Jesus Christ" (Titus 2:13). The Pauline Epistles combination *looking* (4x), *for that* (18x), *blessed* (18x), *hope* (46x), *and the* (114x), *glorious* (12x), *appearing of the great* (1x), *God* (631x), *and our* (11x), *Saviour* (11x), *Jesus Christ* (134x) = 1000.

God & the Brightness of His Son's Glory

"God, who at sundry times and in divers manners spake in time past unto the fathers by the prophets, Hath in these last days spoken unto us by his Son, whom he hath appointed heir of all things, by whom also he made the worlds; Who being the brightness of his GLORY, and the express image of his person, and upholding all things by the word of his power, when he had by himself purged our sins, sat down on the right hand of the Majesty on high" (Heb. 1:1-3).

The Pauline Epistles combination *God* (631x), *who* (192x), *at sundry times* (1x), *and in divers* (1x), *manners* (2x), *spake in time* (1x), *past* (14x), *unto the fathers* (2x), *by the prophets* (1x), *hath in these last days* (1x), *spoken* (17x), *unto us* (16x), *by his* (14x), *Son* (28x), *whom he hath* (2x), *appointed* (9x), *heir* (6x), *of all things* (3x), *by whom* (10x), *also he* (5x), *made the worlds* (1x), *who being the* (1x), *brightness* (2x), *of his glory* (5x), *and the express image of his* (1x), *person* (6x), *and upholding all things* (1x), *by the word* (7x), *of his power* (4x), *when he had* (4x), *by himself* (2x), *purged our sins* (1x), *sat down* (3x), *on the right hand* (5x), *of the Majesty on high* (1x) = 1000.

Jesus Christ, the Lord of Glory

"My brethren, have not the faith of our Lord Jesus Christ, the Lord of GLORY, with respect of persons" (James 2:1). The General Epistles combination *my brethren* (9x), *have* (94x), *not the faith* (1x), *of our* (11x), *Lord* (44x), *Jesus* (41x), *Christ* (49x), *the* (632x), *Lord* (44x), *of glory* (4x), *with* (71x), *respect of persons* (2x) = 1002.

Suffering Patiently for the Glory of God

"Servants, be subject to your masters with all fear; not only to the good and gentle, but also to the froward. For this is thankworthy, if a man for conscience toward God endure grief, suffering wrongfully. For what GLORY is it, if, when ye be buffeted for your faults, ye shall take it patiently? but if, when ye do well, and suffer for it, ye take it patiently, this is acceptable with God" (1 Pet. 2:18-20). Here in this passage the word *toward* is the 1000th word of First Peter, and it refers to the believer having a mindset of glory toward God.

Christ's Sufferings & His Revealed Glory

"But rejoice, inasmuch as ye are partakers of Christ's sufferings; that, when his GLORY shall be revealed, ye may be glad also with exceeding joy" (1 Pet. 4:13). The General Epistles combination *but* (112x), *rejoice* (5x), *inasmuch* (1x), *as* (83x), *ye* (145x), *are* (79x), *partakers* (2x), *of* (404x), *Christ's* (1x), *sufferings* (3x), *that when* (3x), *his* (87x), *glory* (20x), *shall be* (17x), *revealed* (4x), *ye may* (11x), *may be* (10x), *glad* (1x), *also with* (1x), *exceeding* (3x), *joy* (8x) = 1000.

At His Baptism
Jesus Received Honor & Glory from the Father

"For we have not followed cunningly devised fables, when we made known unto you the power and coming of our Lord Jesus Christ, but were eyewitnesses of his MAJESTY. <u>For he received from God the Father honour and GLORY, when there came such a voice to him from the excellent GLORY, This is my beloved Son, in whom I am well pleased</u>" (2 Pet. 1:16-17). The General Epistles combination *for* (138x), *he* (136x), *received* (6x), *from* (52x), *God* (138x), *the Father* (24x), *honour* (5x), *and* (431x), *glory* (20x), *when there came such a voice* (1x), *to him* (9x), *from the excellent* (1x), *glory* (20x), *this is my beloved Son* (1x), *in whom* (2x), *I am* (4x), *well* (11x), *pleased* (1x) = 1000.

1000 Years Is Merely as One Day with the Timeless Lord

"<u>But, beloved, be not ignorant of this one thing, that one day is with the Lord as a THOUSAND years, and a THOUSAND years as one day</u>" (2 Pet. 3:8). The General Epistles combination *but beloved* (3x), *be not* (186x), *ignorant of* (7x), *one thing* (17x), *that one day* (1x), *is with* (67x), *the Lord as* (46x), *a thousand* (95x), *years* (537x), *and a thousand* (11x), *years as* (5x), *one day* (25x) = 1000.

The Lord Will Come with Tens of Thousands of His Saints

"<u>And Enoch also, the seventh from Adam, prophesied of these, saying, Behold, the Lord cometh with TEN THOUSANDS of his saints, To execute judgment upon all, and to convince all that are ungodly among them of all their ungodly deeds which they have ungodly committed, and of all their hard speeches which ungodly sinners have spoken against him</u>" (Jude 14). The General Epistles combination *and Enoch* (1x), *also* (43x), *the seventh* (1x), *from* (52x), *Adam* (1x), *prophesied of* (2x), *these* (25x), *saying* (2x), *behold* (12x), *the* (632x), *Lord* (44x), *cometh* (2x), *with* (71x), *ten thousands of* (1x), *his* (87x), *saints* (2x), *to execute* (1x), *judgment* (11x), *upon all* (1x), *and to convince all* (1x), *that are ungodly among them* (1x), *of all their ungodly deeds* (1x), *which they have* (1x), *ungodly committed* (1x), *and of all their* (1x), *hard speeches* (1x), *which ungodly sinners* (1x), *have spoken against him* (1x) = 1000.

Before the Presence of His Glory

"<u>Now unto him that is able to keep you from falling, and to present you faultless before the presence of his GLORY with exceeding joy</u>" (Jude 24). The General Epistles combination *now* (24x), *unto* (96x), *him* (107x), *that is* (19x), *able to* (3x), *keep you* (1x), *from* (52x), *falling* (1x), *and to* (13x), *present you faultless* (1x), *before* (13x), *the* (632x), *presence* (1x), *of his* (15x), *glory* (20x), *with exceeding joy* (2x) = 1000.

Glory Be to Our Only Savior

"<u>To the only wise God our Saviour, be GLORY and majesty, dominion and power, both now and ever. Amen</u>" (Jude 25). The General Epistles combination *to* (156x), *the* (632x), *only* (9x), *wise* (2x), *God* (138x), *our* (38x), *Saviour* (7x), *be glory* (3x), *and majesty* (1x), *dominion and power* (1x), *both* (5x), *now and ever* (1x), *amen* (7x) = 1000.

Ten Thousand Times Ten Thousand Angels Glorify the Lamb

"<u>And I beheld, and I heard the voice of many angels round about the throne and the beasts and the elders: and the number of them was TEN THOUSAND times TEN THOUSAND, and THOUSANDS of THOUSANDS; Saying with a loud voice, Worthy is the Lamb that was slain to receive power, and riches, and wisdom, and strength, and honour, and GLORY</u>, and blessing" (Rev. 5:11-12). The Bible combination *and I beheld* (6x), *and I heard the voice of* (2x), *many angels* (1x), *round about the throne* (5x), *and the beasts and the elders* (1x), *and the number of them was* (1x), *ten* (248x), *thousand* (520x), *times* (146x), *ten thousand* (48x), *and thousands of thousands* (1x), *saying with a loud voice* (4x), *worthy is the Lamb that was slain to* (1x), *receive power* (3x), *and riches* (5x), *and wisdom and strength and* (1x), *honour and glory* (5x), *and blessing* (2x) = 1000.

The Glorious 1000-Year Reign of Christ

"Blessed and holy is he that hath part in the first resurrection: on such the second death hath no power, but they shall be priests of God and of Christ, and shall reign with him A THOUSAND years" (Rev. 20:6). The Bible combination *blessed and holy is* (1x), *he that hath* (53x), *part in* (6x), *the first resurrection* (2x), *on such* (5x), *the second death hath no* (1x), *power* (272x), *but they shall* (26x), *be priests of God and of Christ* (1x), *and shall reign with him* (1x), *a thousand* (95x), *years* (537x) = 1000.

1611—King James Version

(The Holy Bible)

The term 'Holy Bible' is derived from the Latin words *biblia sacra*, meaning holy books. Usage of the term 'Holy Bible' began sometime in the Middle Ages, yet it became renown in 1611 when the Church of England revealed it with embossed gold letters upon their newly authorized version of the Bible. This new Protestant Bible did not take on the title King James Bible for many years thereafter. Throughout this study, here a little and there a little, we will present various details which pertain to the King James Bible's making. Such explanations will only lightly address the topic. We leave the reader to discover a much greater depth of information on the King James Bible's making from other helpful sources, those who have written diligently on the subject.

Since the word BIBLE does not occur in the King James Version, we will cite many verses which pertain to it such as employing the words BOOK, WORD, or SCRIPTURE. Identified as key words of our study, these will be placed in all-capital letters for easier recognition.

The King James Bible project spanned seven years. It was conceived in 1604. Early stages of its development required much planning and preparation. Thereafter, the greater work of translating could begin in earnest sometime around 1607. The body of its formal English text was fully developed by 1610 and ready to be birthed in 1611. With these dates in mind, a few numeric seals will be shown presenting these meaningful numbers.

The number 1611 bears upon it the Golden Ratio number 1.61. See the introduction of chapter 61 for a brief summary of the Golden Ratio and its connection with the God number 61. The Golden Ratio is a ratio of 1 to 1.61, a series of numbers which, when inverted visually, comprise the number 1611. Below are two random numeric seals which paint a picture of the 1611 Bible Translation.

~~~~

The Bible combination *the book of the LORD* (1x), *holy* (611x) = a visual 1611.

The Bible combination *of the LORD/Lord* (1610 vs), *the author and finisher* (1 v) = a visual 1611.

The OT Narrative combination *in the* (1299x), *year* (139x), *sixteen* (15x), *eleven* (8x), *the word of the LORD* (76x), *was written* (12x), *for the people* (22x), *by the hand* (37x), *of the living God* (2x), *and they stood up in their place and read in the book* (1x) = 1611.

The Word of the Lord

"After these things the WORD of the LORD came unto Abram in a vision, saying, Fear not, Abram: I am thy shield, and thy exceeding great reward" (Gen. 15:1). This verse presents the Bible's first occurrence of the phrase "word of the Lord." The Bible combination *after these things the word* (1 v), *of the Lord/LORD* (1610 vs) = a visual 1611 verses. The Bible combination *the word of the Lord/LORD* (161 chs) and *came unto Abram* (1 ch) = a visual 1611 chapters.

Genesis 16:11

"And the angel of the LORD said unto her, Behold, thou art with child, and shalt bear a son, and shalt call his name Ishmael; because the LORD hath heard thy affliction" (Gen. 16:11). The Bible combination *and the angel of the LORD* (24x), *said unto her* (89x), *behold* (1326x), *thou art with child* (1x), *with child* (26x), *and shalt* (77x), *bear a* (8x), *son and shalt call his name Ishmael* (1x), *Ishmael* (47x), *because the LORD hath* (11x), *heard thy affliction* (1x) = 1611.

1611th Verse of the Bible

"And it shall come to pass, if they will not believe also these two signs, neither hearken unto thy voice, that thou shalt take of the water of the river, and pour it upon the dry land: and the water which thou takest out of the river shall become blood upon the dry land" (Exod. 4:9). The Major and Minor Prophets combination *and it shall come to pass* (64x), *if they will* (2x), *not* (1384x), *believe* (4x), *also these two signs* (0x), *neither hearken* (1x), *unto thy* (7x), *voice* (141x), *that thou shalt take of the water of the river* (0x), *and pour* (4x), *it upon the dry land* (0x), *and the water which thou takest* (0x), *out of the river* (0x), *shall become blood upon* (0x), *the dry land* (4x) = 1611.

Exodus 16:11

"And the LORD spake unto Moses, saying" (Exod. 16:11). "I have heard the murmurings of the children of Israel: speak unto them, saying, At even ye shall eat flesh, and in the morning ye shall be filled with bread; and ye shall know that I am the LORD your God" (v. 12). The Exodus combination *and the* (407x), *LORD* (389x), *spake* (37x), *unto* (448x), *Moses* (278x), *saying* (47x), *at even ye shall eat flesh* (1x), *and in the morning ye shall* (1x), *be filled with bread* (1x), *and ye shall know that I am the LORD your God* (2x) = 1611.

1611 KJV Is a Book like No Other

"And the LORD said unto Moses, WRITE this for a memorial in a BOOK, and rehearse it in the ears of Joshua: for I will utterly put out the remembrance of Amalek from under heaven" (Exod. 17:14). The Law combination *and the LORD* (312x), *said unto* (386x), *Moses write* (2x), *this* (550x), *for a* (244x), *memorial* (22x), *in a* (68x), *book* (16x), *and rehearse it* (1x), *in the ears* (8x), *of Joshua* (1x), *for I will utterly put out the remembrance of Amalek from under heaven* (1x) = 1611.

1611 KJV Contains All the Words of the Lord

"And Moses WROTE all the WORDS of the LORD, and rose up early in the morning, and builded an altar under the hill, and twelve pillars, according to the twelve tribes of Israel" (Exod. 24:4). The New Testament combination *and Moses* (3x), *wrote* (22x), *all* (1130x), *the words of* (14x), *the Lord* (433x), *and rose up* (2x), *early in the morning and* (1x), *builded* (4x), *an altar* (2x), *under the hill* (0x), *and twelve pillars* (0x), *according to the twelve tribes of Israel* (0x) =1611.

1611 KJV Was Designed to Read in Churches

"And he took the BOOK of the covenant, and read in the audience of the people: and they said, All that the LORD hath said will we do, and be obedient" (Exod. 24:7). The Law combination *and he* (746x), *Moses the man of God* (1x), *took the book* (1x), *of the covenant* (18x), *the book of the law* (1x), *and read* (1x), *in the audience of* (4x), *the people* (236x), *and they said* (40x), *all*

674

that (179x), *the LORD hath said* (8x), *will we* (11x), *do* (308x), *and be* (53x), *obedient* (4x) = 1611.

The expression 'Appointed to be read in Churches' was placed on the title page of the 1611 Holy Bible. This declaration was to clearly show the king's approval for its widespread use throughout the Church of England. Moreover, it was King James' specific desire that this new translation sound good when read aloud. The company chiefs who had oversight of the translation work listened carefully as the finished verses were individually read aloud for their approval.

1611 Version of the Holy Bible Is Unchangeable

"And the tables were the work of God, and the WRITING was the WRITING of God, graven upon the tables" (Exod. 32:16). God did not write the Ten Commandments upon animal's skin, clay, or wood. He chose stone for its enduring and unchangeable quality. The only alterations made to the 1769 edition of the KJV were merely spelling and capitalization; no words were ever changed. The following 1611 numeric seals are only visually oriented.

The Old Testament: *engraven* (1x), *set* (611x) = 1611.
The Old Testament: *hewn in stone* (1x), *set* (611x) = 1611.
The Old Testament: *it was finished* (1x), *set* (611x) = 1611.
The Old Testament: *unchangeable* (1x), *set* (611x) = 1611.
The Old Testament: *written and concluded* (1x), *set* (611x) = 1611.
The Old Testament: *graven upon the tables* (1x), *set* (611x) = 1611.
The Old Testament: *work of an engraver in stone* (1x), *set* (611x) = 1611.
The Old Testament: *written and engraven in stones* (1x), *set* (611x) = 1611.
The Old Testament: *words in the book of the law of God* (1x), *set* (611x) = 1611.
The Old Testament: *wrote these words in the book of the law of God* (1x), *set* (611x) = 1611.

1611 KJV Was Written after the Tenor of the English Language's Poetic Past

"And the LORD said unto Moses, WRITE thou these WORDS: for after the tenor of these WORDS I have made a covenant with thee and with Israel" (Exod. 34:27). The Old Testament combination *And the LORD said unto Moses* (51x), [uppercase only] *Write thou* (1x), *these words* (833x), *for after* (1x), *the tenor* (2x), *of these words* (3x), *I have made a covenant* (2x), *with thee* (256x), *with Israel* (13x) = 1611.

By the turn of the 1600s, the English language was changing rapidly and already declining regarding its former poetic peak of Elizabethan beauty. At the present time, society's vernacular use of the singular words 'thee' and 'thou' as well as the plural 'ye' had mostly been replaced with the word 'you.' Despite its archaic tone, the translators were moved of God to skillfully employ the tenor of the Old Elizabethan English in making their new Bible. Much of that formal wording was drawn from William Tyndale's 1526 translation. Today English professors and journalists alike readily agree that the King James Bible is the most beautiful work of English prose ever written.

The Words of Moses

"And ye shall not go out from the door of the tabernacle of the congregation, lest ye die: for the anointing oil of the LORD is upon you. And they did according to the WORD of Moses" (Lev. 10:7). The Acts combination *and they did* (0x), *according to* (7x), *the* (1555x), *words of* (5x), *word* (40x), *of Moses* (4x) = 1611.

My Word

"And the L<small>ORD</small> said unto Moses, Is the L<small>ORD</small>'<small>S</small> hand waxed short? thou shalt see now whether my WORD shall come to pass unto thee or not" (Num. 11:23). The Major and Minor Prophets combination *and the L<small>ORD</small> said unto* (11x), *Moses* (7x), [uppercase only] *Is the* (1x), *L<small>ORD</small>'<small>S</small>* (45x), *L<small>ORD</small>'<small>S</small> hand* (4x), *waxed* (5x), *short* (0x), *thou shalt see now whether* (0x), *my* (1093x), *word* (241x), *shall come to pass* (78x), *unto thee* (126x), *or not* (0x) = 1611.

The Lord's written Word came to pass over the course of time. It was a work in progress. It began with Moses who wrote in the Hebrew tongue and continued with the apostles who wrote in Greek. Nearly 1500 years had elapsed, yet the Lord was not through with His holy Word. Some 1500 years after the New Testament words were penned, the Lord decided to make a triad creation combining the two languages into one new common language. Thus He gave the world the Holy Bible in a universal language—English.

He Who Heard the Words of God

"He hath said, which heard the WORDS of God, which saw the vision of the Almighty, falling into a trance, but having his eyes open" (Num. 24:4). The Bible combination *He hath said* [uppercase only] (4x), *which heard the* (4x), *words* (456x), *of God* (84x), *which saw* (6x), *the vision of the* (3x), *Almighty* (57x), *falling into a trance* (2x), *but having his* (2x), *eyes open* (3x) = 1611.

Ye Shall Not Add to Nor Diminish from the Word of God

"Now therefore hearken, O Israel, unto the statutes and unto the judgments, which I teach you, for to do them, that ye may live, and go in and possess the land which the LORD God of your fathers giveth you. Ye shall not add unto the word which I command you, neither shall ye diminish ought from it, that ye may keep the commandments of the LORD your God which I command you" (Deut. 4:1-2). Law combination *now therefore hearken O Israel* (1x), *unto the statutes and unto the judgments* (1x), *which I teach you* (1x), *for to do them* (1x), *that ye may live and go in* (1x), *and possess the land* (6x), *which the L<small>ORD</small> God of your fathers giveth you* (1x), *ye* (844x), *shall not* (186x), *add* (14x), *unto the word* (1x), *which I* (105x), *command you* (11x), *neither shall* (49x), *ye diminish* (1x), *ought* (24x), *from it* (6x), *that ye may* (23x), *keep* (123x), *the commandments of* (14x), *the L<small>ORD</small> your God* (82x), *which I* (105x), *command you* (11x) = 1611.

Deuteronomy 16:11

"And thou shalt rejoice before the [L<small>ORD</small>] thy God, thou, and thy son, and thy daughter, and thy manservant, and thy maidservant, and the Levite that is within thy gates, and the stranger, and the fatherless, and the widow, that are among you, in the place which the L<small>ORD</small> thy God hath chosen to place his name there" (Deut. 16:11). The New Testament combination *in the place where he* (1x), *hath chosen to place* (0x), *his* (1473x), *name* (173x) = 1611. The New Testament combination *his* (1473x), *name* (173x), *name there* (1x) = 1611.

*To the divine Author's glory and praise, this 16:11th verse of Deuteronomy presents the Bible's 1611th mention of the title *lord/Lord/LORD* and is seen here in the added brackets.

A New Israelite King's Newly Written Copy of the Bible

"And it shall be, when he sitteth upon the throne of his kingdom, that he shall WRITE him a copy of this law in a BOOK out of that which is before the priests the Levites" (Deut. 17:18). The Law combination *the king* (81x), *and it shall be* (71x), *when* (470x), *he sitteth* (2x), *upon the* (358x), *throne* (4x), *of his* (242x), *kingdom* (11x), *that he* (166x), *shall write him* (1x), *a copy* (1x), *of this* (36x), *law* (82x), *in a* (68x), *book* (16x), *out of that which is* (1x), *before the priests the Levites* (1x) = 1611.

A New Israelite King's Personal Copy of the Holy Bible

"And it shall be with him, and he shall READ therein all the days of his life: that he may learn to fear the LORD his God, to keep all the WORDS of this law and these statutes, to do them" (Deut. 17:19). The Law combination *a king* (2x), *a new king* (1x), *and it shall be* (71x), *with him* (96x), *and he* (746x), *shall read* (1x), *therein* (68x), *all the days* (25x), *of his* (242x), *life* (62x), *that he may* (32x), *learn* (7x), *to fear* (7x), *the LORD his God* (5x), *to keep* (23x), *all the words* (17x), *of this* (36x), *law* (82x), *and these* (36x), *statutes* (45x), *to do them* (7x) = 1611.

When the translators finished their 1611 edition, the recently installed English King James was presented with his personal copy wherein he could read, study, and meditate.

God Made a Final End of His Long-Running Bible Project
(Part 1)

"And it shall be, when the officers have made an end of speaking unto the people, that they shall make captains of the armies to lead the people" (Deut. 20:9). Here the word *end* is the 16,111th word of Deuteronomy.

Jesus Was Accursed of God upon the Tree

"His body shall not remain all night upon the tree, but thou shalt in any wise bury him that day; for he that is hanged is accursed of God; that thy land be not defiled, which the LORD thy God giveth thee for an inheritance" (Deut. 21:23). This critical verse presents the King James Bible's 1611th mention of the title *LORD*.

God Made a Final End of His Long-Running Bible Project
(Part 2)

"And it came to pass, when Moses had made an end of WRITING the WORDS of this law in a BOOK, until they were finished" (Deut. 31:24). The First Chronicles combination *an* (41x), *end* (1x), *of* (1532x), *writing* (1x), *the words of* (1x), *this* (31x), *law* (4x) = 1611. The Exodus combination *And* [uppercase only] (858x), *it* (415x), *came* (75x), *to pass* (35x), *when* (101x), *Moses* (278x), *had made* (4x), *an end* (1x), *of writing* (0x), *the words of this law* (3x), *in a book until they were* (0x), *finished* (2x) = 1769.

Dr. Benjamin Blayney presented his Oxford Standardized Revision of the 1611 King James Bible in 1769. He used Dr. Samuel Johnson's 1755 printing of the Johnson Dictionary to accomplish his new work. The spelling, punctuation, and grammar of the English language had become standardized at this time, and Blayney desired to bring the Holy Bible in line with this new standard. "Citie" was spelled "city," and "powred" became "poured." Blayney also updated the 1611 edition's Gothic type to now appear in Roman letters, giving it an updated look. From 1769 onward this revised edition became God's final and finished work.

All the Words of This Book

"If thou wilt not observe to do all the WORDS of this law that are WRITTEN in this BOOK, that thou mayest fear this glorious and fearful name, THE LORD THY GOD; Then the LORD will make thy plagues wonderful, and the plagues of thy seed, even great plagues, and of long continuance, and sore sicknesses, and of long continuance" (Deut. 28:58). The Law combination *if thou* (61x), *wilt* (36), *not observe* (1x), *to do all* (10x), *the words* (46x), *of this* (36x), *law* (82), *that are* (47x), *written* (14x), *in this* (25x), *book* (16x), *that thou* (138x), *mayest fear* (1x), *this* (550x), *glorious* (3x), *and fearful* (1x), *name* (193x), *the LORD thy God* (243x), *then the* (67x), *LORD will make thy* (1x), *plagues* (7x), *wonderful and the* (1x), *plagues* (7x), *of thy seed* (7x), *even great* (1x), *plagues* (7x), *and of long* (2x), *continuance* (2x), *and sore* (2x), *sicknesses* (2x), *and of long continuance* (2x) = 1611.

KJV Bible Project Commenced in 1604

"And the LORD thy God will . . . again rejoice over thee for good, as he rejoiced over thy fathers: If thou shalt hearken unto the voice of the LORD thy God, to keep his commandments and his statutes which are WRITTEN in this BOOK of the law, and if thou turn unto the LORD thy God with all thine heart, and with all thy soul" (Deut. 30:9-10). The Exodus combination [uppercase only] *This* (16x), *book* (4x), *of* (1579x), *the law* (0x), *of the LORD thy God* (5x) = 1604.

The idea to create a new translation of the Bible came about at Hampton Court Palace in January 1604 when two Puritan ministers presented their request to the King. He liked the idea. By June 1604 King James had approved a list 54 Bible scholars fit for the scholarly work at hand. Not all of these Oxford and Cambridge scholars desired to accept the challenging task; only 47 of them are known to have actually undertaken this translation work. Their individual names can be found on an extant list.

Divine Witness of the 1611 Holy Bible

"Take this book of the law, and put it in the side of the ark of the covenant of the LORD your God, that it may be there for a witness against thee" (Deut. 31:26). The Deuteronomy combination *take* (43x), *this* (169x), *book* (9x), *of* (996x), *the law* (5x), *and put* (2x), *it* (243x), *in the side of the ark of the covenant* (1x), *of the LORD* (82x), *your God* (47x), *that it* (12x), *may be there* (1x), *for a witness against thee* (1x) = 1611.

All That Is Written in the 1611 KJV Translation
(Part 1)

"This BOOK of the law shall not depart out of thy mouth; but thou shalt meditate therein day and night, that thou mayest observe to do according to all that is WRITTEN therein: for then thou shalt make thy way prosperous, and then thou shalt have good success" (Josh. 1:8). The Joshua combination *this* (89x), *book* (7x), *of the* (415x), *law* (9x), *shall* (104x), *not depart* (1x), *out of* (71x), *thy* (29x), *mouth* (6x), *but* (59x), *thou shalt* (11x), *meditate* (1x), *therein* (15x), *day and night* (1x), *that* (276x), *thou mayst* (3x), *observe* (2x), *to do* (6x), *according* (48x), *to* (365x), *all that* (32x), *is written* (4x), *therein* (15x), *for then* (1x), *thou shalt* (11x), *make* (14x), *thy way* (1x), *prosperous and then* (1x), *thou shalt* (13x), *have good success* (1x) = 1611.

All That Is Written in the 1611 KJV Translation
(Part 2)

"And he wrote there upon the stones a copy of the law of Moses, which he WROTE in the presence of the children of Israel. . . And afterward he read all the WORDS of the law, the blessings and cursings, according to all that is WRITTEN in the BOOK of the law" (Josh. 8:32-34). The Deuteronomy combination *and he wrote* (3x), *there upon* (0x), *the stones* (2x), *a copy* (1x), *of the law* (4x), *of Moses* (0x), *which he wrote* (0x), *in the presence of* (1x), *the children of Israel* (20x), *And* [uppercase only] (336x), *afterward* (2x), *he* (302x), *read* (2x), *all* (284x), *the words* (24x), *of the* (31x), *law* (24x), *the blessings* (0x), *and cursings* (0x), *according to* (29x), *all* (284x), *that is* (44x), *written* (8x), *in the* (177x), *book of* (4x), *the law* (5x) = 1611.

The Lord's Great 1611 Work—A Perfect English Translation

"And the people served the LORD all the days of Joshua, and all the days of the elders that outlived Joshua, who had seen all the great works of the LORD, that he did for Israel" (Judg. 2:7). The Judges combination *And the* [uppercase only] (124x), *people* (69x), *served* (13x), *the LORD* (168x), *all* (125x), *the days of* (7x), *Joshua* (7x), *and all* (31x), *the days of* (7x), *the elders that outlived* (1x), *Joshua* (7x), *who* (21x), *had seen* (1x), *all* (125x), *the great* (1x), *works* (2x), *of the LORD* (56x), *that* (303x), *he* (254x), *did* (51x), *for* (119x), *Israel* (184x) = 1611.

Ruth's Devoted Declaration to the Bible People

"And Ruth said, Intreat me not to leave thee, or to return from following after thee: for whither thou goest, I will go; and where thou lodgest, I will lodge: thy people shall be my people, and thy God my God" (Ruth 1:16). The OT Narrative combination *and Ruth said intreat me* (1x), *not to* (24x), *leave thee* (5x), *or to* (12x), *return from* (4x), *following after thee* (1x), *for whither thou goest I will go* (1x), *and where* (5x), *thou lodgest* (1x), *I will* (249x), *lodge* (12x), *thy people* (45x), *shall be* (179x), *my people* (46x), *and thy* (60x), *God* (924x), *my God* (42x) = 1611.

That I May Show Thee the Word of God

"And as they were going down to the end of the city, Samuel said to Saul, Bid the servant pass on before us, (and he passed on,) but stand thou still a while, that I may shew thee the WORD of God" (1 Sam. 9:27). The following numeric seal uses only the words of Samuel to complete the equation. The OT Narrative combination *bid the servant* (1x), *pass on before us* (1x), *but stand thou* (1x), *still* (32x), *a while* (3x), *that I* (139x), *may* (197x), *shew* (47x), *thee* (842x), *the word* (93x), *of God* (255x) = 1611.

Samuel Wrote It in a Book

"Then Samuel told the people the manner of the kingdom, and WROTE it in a BOOK, and laid it up before the LORD. And Samuel sent all the people away, every man to his house" (1 Sam. 10:25). The Isaiah combination *then Isaiah* (1x), *told the people* (0x), *the manner of* (2x), *the kingdom* (2x), *and wrote* (0x), *it* (369x), *in* (562x), *a* (518x), *book* (5x), *and laid it* (0x), *up* (150x), *before the LORD* (2x) = 1611.

Behold It Is Written in the Book

"Also he bade them teach the children of Judah the use of the bow: behold, it is WRITTEN in the BOOK of Jasher" (2 Sam. 1:18). The Old Testament combination *also he* (29x), *bade them teach* (1x), *the children of Judah* (43x), *the use of the* (1x), *of the bow* (1x), *behold* (1104x), *it is* [lowercase only] (367x), *written in the book* (63x), *of Jasher* (2x) = 1611.

Second Samuel 16:11

"And David said to Abishai, and to all his servants, Behold, my son, which came forth of my bowels, seeketh my life: how much more now may this Benjamite do it? let him alone, and let him curse; for the LORD hath <u>bidden</u> him" (2 Sam. 16:11). Like King David, King James' own countrymen also sought after his life on numerous occasions. For the purposes of our study, the keyword in this verse is "bidden." Indeed the Lord hath clearly bidden the 1611 translation to be written! He put it in King James' heart to authorize such an English enterprise.

Lord's Performance of the 1611 Translation

"<u>Concerning</u> <u>this house</u> <u>which thou art in</u> <u>building</u>, <u>if</u> <u>thou wilt</u> <u>walk</u> <u>in my</u> <u>statutes</u>, <u>and execute my</u> <u>judgments</u>, <u>and keep</u> <u>all my</u> <u>commandments</u> <u>to walk</u> <u>in them</u>; <u>then will I</u> PERFORM <u>my WORD</u> <u>with thee</u>, <u>which I spake</u> <u>unto David thy father</u>" (1 Kings 6:12). The OT Narrative combination *concerning* (68x), *this house* (41x), *which thou art* (4x), *in building* (7x), *if* (241x), *thou wilt* (29x), *walk* (31x), *in my* (40x), *statutes* (33x), *and execute my* (1x), *judgments* (17x), *and keep* (6x), *all my* (9x), *commandments* (38x), *to walk* (15x), *in them* (12x), *then will I* (6x), *perform* (10x), *my* (780x), *word* (135x), *with thee* (81x), *which I spake* (1x), *unto David thy father* (1x) = 1606.

The translation work of the Lord's epic English Bible was well underway during the year 1606. It was being performed without further hindrance since the Catholic conspirators' diabolical Gunpowder Plot of 1605 had been foiled. Thirty-six barrels of gunpowder had been stored in a rented space under the Parliament House as the conspirators anxiously awaited the reconvening day of all the English heads of state. Had their plot been successful, thousands of people would have died that day and there would be no King James Bible. We will see the number 1605 many times in this study.

The Lord's 1611 Translation Is Proven & True

"<u>And now</u>, <u>O</u> <u>God of Israel</u>, <u>let</u> <u>thy WORD</u>, <u>I pray thee</u>, <u>be VERIFIED</u>, <u>which</u> <u>thou</u> <u>spakest</u> <u>unto thy</u> <u>servant</u> <u>David my father</u>" (1 Kings 8:26). The First and Second Kings combination *and now* (8x), *O* (34x), *God of Israel* (28x), *let* (73x), *thy word* (3x), *I pray thee* (34x), *be verified* (1x), *which* (326x), *thou* (280x), *spakest* (3x), *unto* (469x), *thy* (266x), *servant* (71x), *David my father* (14x) = 1610.

King James felt that some English translations such as the Bishop's Bible and the Geneva Bible "were corrupt and not answerable to the truth of the original." He wanted a Bible that was true to both the original texts and the analogy of the faith. Six companies undertook the diligent work of translation, during which they cross-checked each other's work for grammatical and literary accuracy. Doctrinal conventions were also convened at times to ensure that appropriate theological and ecclesiastical standards were being met. These oversight committees, Bible scholars in their own right, carefully scrutinized the translators' work to achieve perfection. Alas, their work was verified and completed sometime near the end of the year 1610 and thus ready to send to the printers.

The Words of God Came to the KJV Translators

"<u>But</u> <u>the WORD of God</u> <u>came unto Shemaiah</u> <u>the man of God, saying, Speak unto Rehoboam,</u>

the son of Solomon, king of Judah, and unto all the house of Judah and Benjamin, and to the remnant of the people, saying" (1 Kings 12:22-23). The Bible combination *But* [uppercase only] (1558x), *the word of God* (46x), *came unto Shemaiah* (1x), *the man of God saying* (3x), speak *unto Rehoboam the son of Solomon king of Judah* (2x), *and unto all the house of Judah and Benjamin and to the remnant of the people* (1x) = 1611.

It is without question that the Lord was present to aid the King James translators in their holy work. This fact is borne out through tens of thousands of numeric seals found within this voluminous resource book.

First Kings 16:11

"And it came to pass, when he began to reign, as soon as he sat on his throne" (1 Kings 16:11a). The Old Testament combination *came* (1587x), *to pass when he began to reign* (1x), *as soon as he sat* (1x), *on his throne* (8x), *that the king of Israel* (1x), *made a decree* (8x), *to translate* (1x), *the word of God* (3x), *and that it should be published* (1x) = 1611.

As soon as he sat upon the throne of England in March 1603, King James was ready to work. Soon after he gave his reigning approval for a new Bible translation during a solemn meeting with Puritan leaders where he was to address their many grievances. The Anglican bishops present at this conference protested the thought of their beloved Bishop's Bible being replaced, but the king insisted. This meeting took place at Hampton Court Palace in January 1604 but was intended to be held months earlier, delayed because of the ongoing plague in London.

Enquiring at the Divine Words of This 1611 Book

"And the KING commanded Hilkiah the priest . . . saying, Go ye, enquire of the LORD for me, and for the people, and for all Judah, concerning the WORDS of this BOOK that is found: for great is the wrath of the LORD that is kindled against us, because our fathers have not hearkened unto the WORDS of this BOOK, to do according unto all that which is WRITTEN concerning us" (2 Kings 22:12-13). The Second Kings combination *and the king commanded* (3x), *go ye* (2x), *enquire* (10x), *of the LORD for me* (1x), *and for the people* (1x), *and for all Judah* (1x), *concerning* (6x), *the words* (15x), *of* (1421x), *this* (88x), *book* (34x), *that is* (10x), *found* (19x) = 1611.

First Chronicles 16:11

"Seek the LORD and his strength, seek his face continually" (1 Chron. 16:11). The OT Narrative combination *seek the* (vs), *LORD* (vs), *and his strength* (vs) = 1611 intersecting verses.

Note: The individual phrase totals are thus intentionally omitted here. The believer's strength in the Lord can be found within the pages of His 1611 Holy Bible.

Second Chronicles 16:11

"And, behold, the acts of Asa, first and last, lo, they are WRITTEN in the BOOK of the kings of Judah and Israel" (2 Chron. 16:11). The First and Second Kings combination *and behold* (22x), *behold* (105x), *the acts of* (35x), *Asa* (25x), *first* (5x), *and last* (0x), *lo* (5x), *they* (386x), *are* (77x), *written* (41x), *in the* (411x), *book of* (39x), *the kings* (66x), *of Judah and* (26x), *Israel* (364x) = 1607.

Search in the 1611 Book & Thou Shalt Find

"Now because we have maintenance from the king's palace, and it was not meet for us to see the king's dishonour, therefore have we sent and certified the king; That search may be made in the BOOK of the records of thy fathers: so shalt thou find in the BOOK of the records" (Ezra 4:14-15b). The Old Testament combination *that search* (2x), *may be made* (2x), *in the book of the records* (2x), *of thy fathers so* (1x), *shalt* (1510x), *thou find* (5x), *find in the book* (1x), *the book of* (87x), *the records* (2x) = 1611.

As It Is Written in the 1611 Book

"And they set the priests in their [divisions] and the Levites in their courses for the service of God which is at Jerusalem; as it is WRITTEN in the BOOK of Moses" (Ezra 6:18). The Kings and Chronicles combination *and they set* (6x), *the priests in their [charges]* (1x), *and the Levites in their courses* (1x), *for the service* (7x), *of God* (140x), *which is at* (0x), *Jerusalem* (241x), *as* (274x), *it is* (31x), *written* (70x), *in the* (747x), *book of* (62x), *Moses* (31x) = 1611.

Distinct Sound of the 1611 Bible When Read Aloud

"So they READ in the BOOK in the law of God distinctly, and gave the sense, and caused them to understand the reading" (Neh. 8:8). The OT Narrative combination **sixteen** (15x), **eleven** (8x), *so they* (51x), *read* (19x), *in the* (1299x), *book* (100x), *in the law of God* (1x), *distinctly* (1x), *and gave* (34x), *the sense and* (1x), *caused* (19x), *them to* (62x), *understand the reading* (1x) = 1611.

As stated earlier, in the very middle of the 1611 translation's title page, a grand declaration went forth: 'Appointed to be read in churches.' Bibles were expensive, and the common people were unable to afford one. This drought situation made it vitally important that the new Bible translation be read aloud for their hearing. As its distinct sound began to go forth in the churches, the people began to happily discuss it among themselves, even during the church-service readings. Not long afterward, a rule was made that there could be no talking during the reading times.

Divine Seal of the King's 1611 Translation

"WRITE ye also for the Jews, as it liketh you, in the king's name, and seal it with the king's ring: for the WRITING which is WRITTEN in the king's name, and sealed with the king's ring, may no man reverse" (Est. 8:8). The OT Narrative combination *write ye also* (1x), *for the Jews* (3x), *as it liketh* (1x), *you in the king's name* (1x), *and seal* (1x), *it with* (27x), *the king's ring* (4x), *for the* (460x), *writing* (17x), *which is* (119x), *written in* (82x), *the king's* (223x), *name* (277x), *and sealed with the king's* (2x), *ring* (6x), *may* (197x), *no* (195x), *man reverse* (1x) = 1611.

The King of Kings has placed His divine seal upon every perfect page of His 1611 translation. Such heavenly seals are revealed to us in their numeric form.

And It Was Written in the 1611 Book

"And the decree of Esther, confirmed these matters of Purim; and it was WRITTEN in the BOOK" (Est. 9:32). The OT Narrative combination *and the decree of* (1x), *Esther* (53x), *confirmed these* (1x), *matters of Purim* (1x), *and it was* (53x), *written* (103x), *in the* (1299x), *book* (100x) = 1611.

God's English Words Forever Printed in a 1611 Book

"Oh that my WORDS were now WRITTEN! Oh that they were PRINTED in a BOOK! That they were graven with an iron pen and lead in the rock for ever!" (Job 19:23-24) The Wisdom Books combination *oh* (21x), *that* (1356x), *my words* (18x), *were now* (1x), *written* (9x), *oh that* (18x), *they were* (24x), *printed in a book* (1x), *that they were graven* (1x), *with an* (8x), *iron* (13x), *pen and lead* (1x), *in the rock* (1x), *for ever* (139x) = 1611.

The 1611 Words of the Lord Are Pure Words

"The WORDS of the LORD are pure WORDS: as silver tried in a furnace of earth, purified seven times" (Ps. 12:6). The Psalms combination *The* [uppercase only] (219x), *words* (25x), *of the* (423x), *LORD* (715x), *are pure* (1x), *pure words* (1x), *as* (196x), *silver* (8x), *tried* (6x), *in a furnace* (1x), *of earth* (1x), *purified* (1x), *seven* (2x), *times* (12x) = 1611.

Like pure silver coming out of its repetitious, dross-removing process, the King James Bible rises to the surface as the last in a series of seven Protestant translations, each one gaining more and more purity under each passing trial of fire: Tyndale Bible 1526, Coverdale Bible 1536, Matthew Bible 1537, Great Bible 1539, Geneva Bible 1560, Bishop's Bible 1568, King James Bible 1611. The first trial of fire became a literal one for William Tyndale; the Catholic church burned him at the stake. It is Tyndale's translation which stands as the basis for most of the King James Bible's wording and phraseology.

Psalm 16:11

"Thou wilt shew me the path of life: in thy presence is fullness of joy; at thy right hand there are pleasures for evermore" (Ps. 16:11). The Psalms combination *Thou* [uppercase only] (113x), *wilt* (43x), *shew me* (3x), *the path* (2x), *of* (1380x), *life* (26x), *in thy presence* (2x), *is fullness of* (1x), *joy* (19x), *at thy right hand* (3x), *there are* (3x), *pleasures* (2x), *for evermore* (14x) = 1611.

The Lord's 1611 Bible translation highly effectively reveals the path of life to its reader. The sincere seeker of eternal life will never go away disappointed from this holy and inspired book.

Perfect Volume of the 1611 Bible

"Then said I, Lo, I come: in the volume of the BOOK it is WRITTEN of me" (Ps. 40:7). The Wisdom Books combination *Then said* [uppercase only] (4x), *I* (1347x), *Lo I* [uppercase only] (2x), *come* (130x), *in the volume* (1x), *of the book* (2x), *it is* (116x), *written of* (1x), *of me* (8x) = 1611.

Great Was the Company That Published the 1611 Translation

"The Lord gave the WORD: great was the company of those that PUBLISHED it" (Ps. 68:11). The Wisdom Books combination *the Lord* (27x), *gave* (33x), *the word* (12x), *great* (115x), *was the* (4x), *company of* (5x), *those* (55x), *that* (1356x), *published it* (1x) = 1608.

In the year 1608 the King James translators were in the midst of their scholarly research and writing. An extant list reveals the names of 47 men who are known to have labored in this holy work. They were divided up into six companies with chiefs presiding over each company and their specific work assignment.

FIRST WESTMINSTER COMPANY
Genesis - 2 Kings
FIRST CAMBRIDGE COMPANY
1 Chronicles - Song of Solomon
FIRST OXFORD COMPANY
Isaiah - Malachi
SECOND CAMBRIDGE COMPANY
Apocrypha
SECOND OXFORD COMPANY
Gospels, Acts & Book of Revelation
SECOND WESTMINSTER COMPANY
Epistles

In Thy 1611 Book

"Thine eyes did see my substance, yet being unperfect; and in thy BOOK all my members were WRITTEN, which in continuance were fashioned, when as yet there was none of them" (Ps. 139:16). The Wisdom Books combination *and in* [lowercase only] (50x), *thy* (1070x), *book* (6x), *all* (482x), *my members* (2x), *were written* (1x) = 1611. The following numeric seal employs only lowercase letters and words. The Psalms combination *in* (831x), *thy* (759x), *book* (4x), *all my* (15x), *members* (1x), *were written* (1x) = 1611.

Proverbs 16:11

"A just weight and balance are the LORD'S: all the weights of the bag are his work" (Prov. 16:11). The Second Samuel combination *a just* (0x), *weight* (4x), *and balance are* (0x), *the* [lowercase only] (1597x), *LORD'S* (4x), *all the weights* (0x), *of the bag* (0x), *are his* (0x), *work* (0x) = 1605.

The translators were just beginning to weigh the Lord's words, mostly Hebrew and Greek, against the English language in the year 1605. They sought to weigh the Lord's words carefully and deliberately.

Do Not Add to the Lord's Words

"Add thou not unto his WORDS, lest he reprove thee, and thou be found a liar" (Prov. 30:6). The Wisdom Books combination *add* (3x), *add thou* (1x), *not unto* (7x), *his* (1326x), *words* (117x), *lest* (37x), *he reprove* (2x), *thee and* (57x), *thou be* (16x), *found* (38x), *a liar* (4x) = 1608.

King James' Powerful Translation of the Word of God

"Where the WORD of a KING is, there is power: and who may say unto him, What doest thou?" (Eccles. 8:4) The Bible combination *Where* [uppercase only] (72x), *the word of* (351x), *a king is* (4x), *there is* (421x), *power* (272x), *and who may* (22x), *say unto him* (60x), *What* [uppercase only] (336x), *doest* (45x), *thou O king* (4x), *James* (4x), *his excellent majesty* (1x), *that sitteth upon the throne* (1x) = 1611.

What made King James' translation of the Bible so powerful is chiefly the divine power which presided behind him, even "the LORD of the king that sitteth upon the throne." Still James is considered the most educated and linguistic king to ever sit on England's throne. His literary accomplishments included the writing of many godly books.

Take a Great Roll & Write in It with a Man's Pen

"Moreover the LORD said unto me, Take thee a great ROLL, and WRITE in it with a man's pen concerning Maher-shalal-hash-baz" (Isa. 8:1). The Major Prophets combination *Moreover* [uppercase only] (41x), *the LORD* (1308x), *said unto me* (44x), *take thee* (11x), *a great* [lowercase only] (38x), *roll* (20x), *and write in it* (2x), *with a* (63x), *man's* (13x), *pen* (3x), *concerning* (66x), *Maher-shalal-hash-baz* (2x) = 1611.

Seek Ye Out of the Lord's 1611 Book & Read

"Seek ye out of the BOOK of the LORD, and READ: no one of these shall fail, none shall want her mate: for my mouth it hath commanded, and his spirit it hath gathered them" (Isa. 34:16). The Major Prophets combination *seek ye* (3x), *out of the* (128x), *book of* (2x), *the LORD* (1308x), *and read* (4x), *no one* (1x), *of these* (10x), *shall fail* (6x), *none* (109x), *shall want her mate* (1x), *for my* (32x), *mouth it* (2x), *hath commanded* (4x), *and his spirit hath gathered them* (1x) = 1611.

My 1611 Word Shall Not Return to Me Void

"So shall my WORD be that goeth forth out of my mouth: it shall not return unto me void, but it shall accomplish that which I please, and it shall prosper in the thing whereto I sent it" (Isa. 55:11). The Major Prophets combination *so shall* (28x), *my* (923x), *word* (201x), *be that* (7x), *goeth forth* (5x), *out of* (239x), *my mouth* (19x), *it shall not return unto me* (1x), *void* (3x), *but it shall accomplish* (1x), *that which* (63x), *I please* (1x), *and it shall* (97x), *prosper* (21x), *in the thing* (1x), *whereto I sent it* (1x) = 1611.

Jeremiah 16:11

"Then shalt thou say unto them, Because your fathers have forsaken me, saith the LORD, and have walked after other gods, and have served them, and have worshipped them, and have forsaken me, and have not kept my LAW" (Jer. 16:11). We do not reveal any further numeric seals here other than to use this 16:11 position to point out that the 1611 KJV translation is surely a perfect rendering of God's Law.

All That Is Written in This Book

"And I will bring upon that land all my WORDS which I have pronounced against it, even all that is WRITTEN in this BOOK, which Jeremiah hath prophesied against all the nations" (Jer. 25:13). The New Testament combination *and I will bring* (0x), *upon that* (5x), *that land* (2x), *all my words* (0x), *which I have pronounced* (0x), *against it* (4x), *even* (275x), *all* (1130x), *that is* (159x), *written in* (29x), *this book* (7x) = 1611.

Write All the Words That God Has Spoken

"Thus speaketh the LORD God of Israel, saying, WRITE thee all the WORDS that I have spoken unto thee in a BOOK" (Jer. 30:2). A covenant is usually expressed in words which are so ratified by the covenant maker. Covenant terms are also typically written down for safe keeping and future reference. The Law combination *a* (1768x), *book of the covenant* (1x) = 1769.

Jeremiah Wrote All of the Lord's Spoken Words

"Take thee a ROLL of a BOOK, and WRITE therein all the WORDS that I have spoken unto thee against Israel, and against Judah, and against all the nations, from the day I spake unto thee, from the days of Josiah, even unto this day . . . Then Jeremiah called Baruch the son of Neriah:

and Baruch WROTE from the mouth of Jeremiah all the WORDS of the LORD, which he had spoken unto him, upon a ROLL of a BOOK" (Jer. 36:2, 4). The Major Prophets combination *Take* [uppercase only] (21x), *thee a roll* (1x), *of a* (115x), *book* (22x), *and write* (7x), *therein* (50x), *all the words* (14x), *that I* (234x), *have spoken* (33x), *unto thee* (105x), *against Israel* (1x), *and against Judah* (1x), *and against all the nations* (1x), *from the day* (4x), *I spake unto thee* (2x), *from the days of Josiah* (1x), *even unto this day* (8x), *Then* [uppercase only] (262x), *Then Jeremiah* (6x), *called* (71x), *Baruch* (23x), *the son of Neriah* (10x), *and Baruch* (3x), *wrote from* (1x), *the mouth of* (18x), *Jeremiah* (131x), *all the words* (14x), *of the LORD* (340x), *which he* (24x), *had spoken* (5x), *unto him* (51x), *upon a* (7x), *roll* (20x), *of a book* (4x) = 1610.

The Published 1611 King James Bible—A Set Standard

"The WORD that the LORD spake against Babylon and against the land of the Chaldeans by Jeremiah the prophet. Declare ye among the nations, and PUBLISH, and set up a standard; PUBLISH, and conceal not: say, Babylon is taken" (Jer. 50:1-2a). The Jeremiah combination *the word* (76x), *that* (651x), *the LORD* (671x), *spake* (29x), *against Babylon* (9x), *and against* (19x), *the land of the Chaldeans* (8x), *by Jeremiah* (1x), *the prophet* (49x), *declare ye* (3x), *among* (41x), *the nations* (33x), *and publish* (5x), *and set* (4x), *up a standard* (2x), *publish* (8x), *and conceal not* (1x), *say Babylon is taken* (1x) = 1611.

Ezekiel 16:11

"I decked thee also with ornaments, and I put bracelets upon thy hands, and a chain on thy neck" (Ezek. 16:11). The Law combination *I* (1263x), *decked thee* (0x), *also with* (7x), *ornaments* 3(x), *and I* (213x), *put bracelets* (0x), *upon thy hands* (0x), *and a* [lowercase only] (108x), *chain* (1x), *on thy* (0x), *neck* (15x) = 1611. The Lord beautified His 1611 English Bible with the most beautiful English words and prose.

The Scripture of Truth

"But I will shew thee that which is noted in the SCRIPTURE of truth: and there is none that holdeth with me in these things, but Michael your prince" (Dan. 10:21). This verse presents the Old Testament's only occurrence of the word "scripture," either singular or plural. The Major and Minor Prophets combination *But* [uppercase only] (217x), *I will shew thee* (2x), *that which* (74x), *is noted* (1x), *in the* (1226x), *scripture of* (1x), *truth* (43x), *and there is* [lowercase only] (26x), *none that* (10x), *holdeth* (3x), *with me in* (2x), *these things but* (1x), *Michael* (3x), *your prince* (1x) = 1610.

Seal the Words of the 1611 Book

"But thou, O Daniel, shut up the words, and seal the BOOK, even to the time of the end: many shall run to and fro, and knowledge shall be increased" (Dan. 12:4). The Major Prophets combination *But* [uppercase only] (170x), *thou* (971x), *O* (290x), *Daniel* (78x), *shut up* (9x), *the words* (47x), *and seal* (2x), *the book* (12x), *even to the* (21x), *time of the end* (5x), *many shall run to and fro* (1x), *and knowledge* (4x), *shall be increased* (1x) = 1611.

1611 Translation of the Lord's Words

"The WORD of the LORD that came unto Hosea, the son of Beeri, in the days of Uzziah, Jotham, Ahaz, and Hezekiah, kings of Judah, and in the days of Jeroboam the son of Joash, king of Israel. The beginning of the WORD of the LORD by Hosea. And the LORD said to Hosea" (Hos. 1:1-2a).

The Old Testament combination *of the word* (6x), *of the LORD/Lord* (1605x) = 1611.

"As the Lord Hath Said"
"And it shall come to pass, that whosoever shall call on the name of the LORD shall be delivered: for in mount Zion and in Jerusalem shall be deliverance, as the LORD hath said, and in the remnant whom the LORD shall call" (Joel 2:32). The Minor Prophets combination *And it shall* [uppercase only] (24x), *come to pass* (28x), *that whosoever* (1x), *shall call* (6x), *on* (46x), *the name* (10x), *of the LORD* (112x), *shall be delivered* (1x), *for in* (2x), *mount Zion* (4x), *and in* (27x), *Jerusalem* (65x), *shall be deliverance* (2x), *as the* (64x), *LORD* (468x), *hath* (102x), *said* (96x), *and in* (27x), *the remnant* (18x), *whom* (16x), *the LORD* (485x), *shall call* (6x) = 1610.

End-Time Famine of the Lord's 1611 Words
"Behold, the days come, saith the Lord GOD, that I will send a famine in the land, not a famine of bread, nor a thirst for water, but of hearing the WORDS of the LORD" (Amos 8:11). The Old Testament combination *behold the days come saith the Lord* (15x), *that I will send* (3x), *a famine in the land* (4x), *not a famine of bread* (1x), *nor a thirst* (1x), *for water* (3x), *but of hearing the words* (1x), *of the LORD* (1583x) = 1611.

Preaching the 1611 Translation of God's Word
"And the word of the LORD came unto Jonah the second time, saying, Arise, go unto Nineveh, that great city, and preach unto it the preaching that I bid thee" (Jonah 3:1). The Old Testament combination *And the word* [uppercase only] (25x), *of the LORD* (1583x), *came unto Jonah the second time saying* (1x), *arise go unto Nineveh that great city* (1x), *and preach unto it the preaching that I bid thee* (1x) = 1611.

KJV Shall Be Exalted above All Other Versions
"But in the last days it shall come to pass, that the mountain of the house of the LORD shall be established in the top of the mountains, and it shall be exalted above the hills; and people shall flow unto it" (Mic. 4:1). The Old Testament combination *but in the last days* (1x), *it shall come to pass that the* (6x), *mountain of the house* (3x), *of the LORD* (1583x), *shall be established in* (4x), *the top of the mountains* (6x), *and it shall be exalted* (1x), *above the hills* (2x), *and people* (4x), *shall flow unto it* (2x) = 1612.

The Lord's exaltation process of the King James Bible began in the years following its 1611 release. By 1650 it had become so widely popular that all other Protestant English Bibles simply went out of print.

The 1611 Publishing of Peace & Good Tidings
"Behold upon the mountains the feet of him that bringeth good tidings, that PUBLISHETH peace!" (Nah. 1:15a) The Major and Minor Prophets combination *behold* (428x), *upon* (816x), *the mountains* (72x), *the feet of* (5x), *him that* (91x), *bringeth* (18x), *good* (86x), *tidings* (12x), *that publisheth* (3x), *peace* [lowercase only] (80x) = 1611.

Plain Reading of the Visionary 1611 Translation
"And the LORD answered me, and said, WRITE the vision, and make it plain upon tables, that he may run that READETH it" (Hab. 2:1). The Bible combination *and the LORD* (vs), *answered me*

(vs), *and said* (vs), *write the* (vs), *vision* (vs), *and make* (vs), *it plain* (vs), *upon tables* (vs), *that he may run* (vs), *that readeth it* (vs) = 1611 intersecting verses!

Indeed the 1611 translators were not only scholarly but also visionary. Their high aim was to create an English Bible that would never need replacing—one that could stand the test of time.

Time Came for the Lord's Word to be Reconstructed with Lasting English

"Then came the WORD of the LORD by Haggai the prophet, saying, Is it time for you, O ye, to dwell in your cieled houses, and this house lie waste?" (Hag. 1:3-4) The Old Testament combination *then* (1580x), *came the word of the LORD* (18x), *by Haggai* (3x), *the prophet saying* (6x), *is it time for you O ye* (1x), *to dwell in your* (1x), *cieled houses* (1x), *and this house lie waste* (1x) = 1611.

Then Came the 1611 Word of the Lord unto England

"In the eighth month, in the second year of Darius, came the word of the LORD unto Zechariah, the son of Berechiah, the son of Iddo the prophet, saying" (Zech. 1:1). The Old Testament combination *In the eighth month* [uppercase only] (1x), *in the second year of Darius* (5x), *came the word* (18x), *of the LORD* (1583x), *unto Zechariah the son of Berechiah* (2x), *the son of Iddo the prophet saying* (2x) = 1611.

KJV Translators Finished Their Burden in 1610

"The burden of the word of the LORD to Israel by Malachi" (Mal. 1:1). The Old Testament combination *the burden of the word* (3x), *of the LORD/Lord* (1605x), *to Israel by* (1x), *Malachi* (1x) = 1610.

The New Testament

"The BOOK of the generation of Jesus Christ, the son of David, the son of Abraham" (Matt. 1:1). The New Testament combination *Jesus* (973x), *Christ* (555x), *our Lord* (80x), *Saviour of the world* (2x), *and only Potentate* (1x) = 1611.

Every Jot & Tittle of the KJV Holy Bible

"For verily I say unto you, Till heaven and earth pass, one jot or one tittle shall in no wise pass from the law, till all be fulfilled" (Matt. 5:18). The Matthew combination *for verily I say unto you* (4x), *till heaven* (1x), *and* (1552x), *earth* (27x), *pass* (15x), *one jot or one tittle* (1x), *shall in no wise pass from* (1x), *the law* (9x), *till all be fulfilled* (1x) = 1611.

The Cornerstone 1611 Scriptures

"Jesus saith unto them, Did ye never READ in the SCRIPTURES, The stone which the builders rejected, the same is become the head of the corner: this is the Lord's doing, and it is marvellous in our eyes?" (Matt. 21:42) This verse presents the Bible's 1611th occurrence of the capitalized definite article *The*. By divine order, this same underlined word *The* is the 1611th word in this chapter of Matthew, and it rests next to the related keyword of our study *scriptures*.

The King James Bible has for so long been the chief cornerstone of the Lord's completed written creation, yet so many modern religious leaders or Bible scholars reject this divinely rendered piece of architecture, saying it needs to be greatly adjusted or replaced altogether. There are even those at this present day who admire the KJV but seek to modernize certain words so it will seem to fit better into today's society.

Gospel Translated & Published in Its 1611 KJV Form

"And the gospel must first be PUBLISHED among all nations" (Mark 13:10). The NT Narrative combination *and the gospel* (1x), *must first* (4x), *be* (862x), *published among* (1x), *among* (131x), *all* (595x), *nations* (13x) = 1607.

The modern Missions Era, which began in the late 18th century, awakened Bible societies to begin mass printing the KJV Bible for its worldwide distribution. It has been estimated that approximately 5 billion copies of the King James Bible have been printed to date. During the British colonial era, they used their beloved 1611 Version to teach nations the English language.

God's 1611 Book of English Words

"As it is WRITTEN in the BOOK of the WORDS of Esaias the prophet, saying, The voice of one crying in the wilderness, Prepare ye the way of the Lord, make his paths straight" (Luke 3:4). The New Testament combination *as* (1040x), *it is* (276x), *written* (132x), *in the book of* (10x), *the words* (22x), *of Esaias* (3x), *the prophet* (33x), *saying the* (19x), *voice of* (25x), *one crying* (4x), *in the wilderness* (23x), *prepare* (15x), *ye the* (15x), *way of the Lord* (5x), *make his* (4x), *paths* (4x), *straight* (10x) = 1607.

Luke 16:11

"If therefore ye have not been faithful in the unrighteous mammon, who will commit to your trust the true riches?" (Luke 16:11) The NT Narrative combination *If* [uppercase only] (97x), *therefore* (216x), *ye* (916x), *have not* (29x), *been faithful* (5x), *in the unrighteous* (1x), *mammon* (4x), *who* (135x), *will commit to* (1x), *your* (198x), *trust the true* (1x), *riches* (7x) = 1610.

In 1604 the Lord committed unto a company of scholarly English men the true riches of His Holy Word to take it from its Hebrew, Aramaic, and Greek settings and therewith reset it to English.

Open the Heart-Warming 1611 Scriptures

"And they said one to another, Did not our heart burn within us, while he talked with us by the way, and while he opened to us the SCRIPTURES?" (Luke 24:32) The Luke combination *and they* (123x), *said one to another* (2x), *did not our* (1x), *heart* (12x), *burn within us* (1x), *while* (19x), *he talked with us* (1x), *by the way and* (2x), *while he* (8x), *opened* (8x), *to us* (3x), *the* (1428x), *scriptures* (3x) = 1611.

Countless King James Bible readers and enthusiasts testify that there is something very special about this translation. They also say it is easier to commit verses and passages to memory. Further, they say it is also easier to sing the lines of this blessed translation. Many have testified of their minds turning from a confused state to a suddenly peaceful one from reading this particular Bible. In more ways than one, the KJV translation remains heartwarming and endearing.

Son of God Speaks the Words of God

"For he whom God hath sent speaketh the WORDS of God: for God giveth not the Spirit by measure unto him" (John 3:34). The New Testament combination *For he* [uppercase only] (54x), *whom God hath* (5x), *sent* (196x), *speaketh the words of* (1x), *God* (1349x), *for God giveth not the* (1x), *S/spirit by* (4x), *measure unto him* (1x) = 1611.

1611 Word of God Was Published throughout the World

"And when the Gentiles heard this, they were glad, and glorified the word of the Lord: and as many as were ordained to eternal life believed. And the WORD of the Lord was PUBLISHED throughout all the region" (Acts 13:49). The New Testament combination *and when the Gentiles heard this* (1x), *they were glad* (3x), *and glorified the word of the Lord* (1x), *and as many as were* (2x), *ordained to eternal* (1x), *life believed and* (1x), *the word of the Lord* (13x), *was* (1349x), *published* (5x), *throughout* (29x), *all the* (196x), *region* (10x) = 1611.

To date, the 1611 King James Version Bible is still the best-selling, most widely published, and most freely distributed book in the world.

The Sound & Hearing of the 1611 KJV Bible

"So then faith cometh by hearing, and hearing by the word of God. But I say, Have they not heard? Yes verily, their sound went into all the earth, and their WORDS unto the ends of the world" (Rom. 10:17-18). The New Testament combination *so then* (17x), *faith* (245x), *cometh* (123x), *by* (810x), *hearing* (25x), *and hearing* (6x), *by the* (267x), *word of God* (45x), *but I say* (18x), *have they* (5x), *not heard* (6x), *yes verily* (1x), *their sound* (1x), *went into* (35x), *all the earth* (4x), *and their words* (2x), *unto the ends of the world* (1x) = 1611.

Hope-Filled 1611 Translation Brings Patience & Comfort

"For whatsoever things were written aforetime were WRITTEN for our learning, that we through patience and comfort of the SCRIPTURES might have hope" (Rom. 15:4). The New Testament combination *For* [uppercase only] (771x), *whatsoever things* (7x), *were written* (5x), *aforetime* (2x), **the old testament** (1x), *were* (784x), *written for our* (2x), *learning* (3x), *that we through* (1x), *patience and* (10x), *comfort* (24x), *of the scriptures might have hope* (1x) = 1611.

According to the 1611 KJV Scriptures

"For I delivered unto you first of all that which I also received, how that Christ died for our sins according to the SCRIPTURES; And that he was buried, and that he rose again the third day according to the SCRIPTURES" (1 Cor. 15:3-4). The New Testament combination *for I* (123x), *delivered* (73x), *unto you* (381x), *first of all* (5x), *that which* (110x), *I also* (21x), *received* (128x), *how that* (25x), *Christ* (555x), *died* (35x), *for our sins* (4x), *according to the* (67x), *scriptures* (21x), *and that he* (19x), *was buried* (2x), *and that he* (19x), *that he rose again* (1x), *rose again* (3x), *the third day* (16x), *according to the scripture/s* (3x) = 1611.

Those Who Corrupt the King James Translation of God's Word

"For we are not as many, which corrupt the WORD of God: but as of sincerity, but as of God, in the sight of God speak we in Christ" (2 Cor. 2:17). The Pauline Epistles combination *for* (1002x), *we* (452x), *are not* (34x), *as many* (11x), *which corrupt* (1x), *the word of God* (15x), *but as* (20x), *of sincerity but* (1x), *as of God* (1x), *in the sight of God* (7x), *speak* (63x), *we in* (3x), *we in Christ* (1x) = 1611.

So thorough, perfect, and fully accepted was the King James translation that no one dared change it for over 250 years. However, in 1881 the Revised Standard Version was proudly published. This modern English version, like most all others which would follow after it, came from the corrupt Alexandrian line of texts. The received text, from which the King James Bible was graciously crafted, came from the Antioch line. Among the corrupt texts from which Westcott and Hort knowingly derived their Revised Standard Version were the Catholic works known as Vaticanus and Sianaticus.

What Saith the KJV Scriptures?

"Nevertheless what saith the SCRIPTURE? Cast out the bondwoman and her son: for the son of the bondwoman shall not be heir with the son of the freewoman" (Gal. 4:30). The New Testament combination *nevertheless* (33x), *what* (408x), *saith* (307x), *the scripture* (25x), *cast* (167x), *out* (508x), *the bondwoman* (4x), *Agar* (2x), *and her son* (1x), [no mention of his name] (0x), *for the son* (11x), *of the bondwoman* (3x), *shall not* (108x), *be heir with* (1x), *Isaac* (20x), *the son of the* (7x), *freewoman* (3x), *Sara* (3x) = 1611.

Whole Armor of God Includes the 1611 KJV Bible

"And take the helmet of salvation, and the sword of the Spirit, which is the WORD of God" (Eph. 6:17). The Ephesians combination *armour* (2x), *and take* (1x), *the* (241x), *helmet* (1x), *of* (159x), *salvation* (2x), *and* [lowercase only] (103x), *the* (241x), *sword* (1x), *of* (159x), *the* (241x), *Spirit* [uppercase only] (12x), *which is* (12x), *the* (241x), *word* (3x), *of* (159x), *God* (33x) = 1611.

Dispensation of the King James Bible

"Whereof I am made a minister, according to the dispensation of God which is given to me for you, to fulfil the WORD of God" (Col. 1:25). The Pauline Epistles combination *whereof* (16x), *I am* (58x), *made* (123x), *a minister* [lowercase only] (4x), *according* (83x), *to the* (157x), *dispensation* (4x), *of God* (276x), *which* (508x), *is given* (13x), *to me* (18x), *for you* (29x), *to fulfil* (2x), *the word* (44x), *of God* (276x) = 1611.

The dispensation of the King James Bible was accompanied by a keen interest across the British Isles to learn about God's Word. To fulfill their new desire to read and study God's Word, the people needed to enroll in literacy classes, and these were soon commonplace in England. Over time and as a direct result, England became the most literate nation on Earth. Moreover, the great revivals in England, Scotland, and America took place under the sound of the preaching of the King James Bible.

Power of the Lord's 1611 Word

"For our gospel came not unto you in WORD only, but also in power, and in the Holy Ghost, and in much assurance; as ye know what manner of men we were among you for your sake. And ye became followers of us, and of the Lord, having received the WORD in much affliction, with joy

691

of the Holy Ghost: So that ye were ensamples to all that believe in Macedonia and Achaia" (1 Thess. 1:5-6). The New Testament combination *for our* (19x), *gospel* (101x), *came not* (12x), *unto you in* (8x), *word* (206x), *only* (98x), *but also in* (4x), *power* (152x), *and in the* (53x), *Holy Ghost* (90x), *and in* (133x), *much* (130x), *assurance* (5x), *as ye know* (6x), *what manner of men* (1x), *we were* (31x), *among you* (59x), *for your sake* (1x), *and ye* (109x), *became* (24x), *followers* (8x), *of us* (23x), *and of the Lord* (2x), *having received the* (4x), *word* (206x), *in much* (7x), *affliction* (14x), *with joy of the* (1x), *Holy Ghost* (90x), *so that ye* (4x), *were ensamples* (1x), *to all that* (4x), *believe in Macedonia* (1x), *and Achaia* (4x) = 1611.

That the 1611 Word May Have Free Course

"Finally, brethren, pray for us, that the WORD of the Lord may have free course, and be glorified, even as it is with you: And that we may be delivered from unreasonable and wicked men: for all men have not faith" (2 Thess. 3:1). The Pauline Epistles combination *finally* (5x), *brethren* (109x), *pray* (18x), *for us* (23x), *that the* (69x), *word* (62x), *of the* (523x), *Lord* (289x), *may* (145x), *have free* (1x), *course* (4x), *and be* (15x), *glorified* (8x), *even* (121x), *as it is* (29x), *with you* (39x), *and that we* (1x), *may be* (52x), *delivered from unreasonable* (1x), *and wicked men* (1x), *for all men* (2x), *have not* (33x), *faith* (171x) = 1611.

At first the Authorized Version held copyright protections, but in due time these restrictions were canceled. Such wide printing freedom made it possible to give out the Word of God without hindrance! Most all of the modern versions retain their copyright privileges and thus restrict their otherwise free use.

For the King James Scripture Saith So

"Let the elders that rule well be counted worthy of double honour, especially they who labour in the word and doctrine. For the SCRIPTURE saith, Thou shalt not muzzle the ox that treadeth out the corn. And, The labourer is worthy of his reward" (1 Tim. 5:7-18). The Old Testament combination *Let the* [uppercase only] (51x), *elders* (119x), *that rule well be* (0x), *counted* (25x), *worthy of* (6x), *double* (20x), *honour especially* (0x), *they who* (2x), *labour in* (4x), *the word and* (2x), *doctrine* (6x), *For the* [uppercase only] (192x), *scripture* (1x), *saith* (955x), *thou shalt not* (218x), *muzzle* (1x), *the ox when he* (1x), *treadeth* (7x), *out the corn* (1x), *and the labourer* (0x), *is worthy of* (4x), *his reward* (3x) = 1611.

Bring the KJV Books

"The cloke that I left at Troas with Carpus, when thou comest, bring with thee, and the BOOKS, but especially the PARCHMENTS" (2 Tim. 4:13). The Pauline Epistles combination *cloke* (2x), *that I* (73x), *left* (9x), *at* (78x), *Troas* (2x), *with* (412x), *Carpus* (1x), *when thou comest* (1x), *bring* (20x), *with* (412x), *thee* (74x), *and the* (114x), *books* (1x), *but* [lowercase only] (408x), *especially* (3x), *the parchments* (1x) = 1611.

God's Forever-Preserved 1611 Word

"And the Lord shall deliver me from every evil work, and will PRESERVE me unto his heavenly kingdom: to whom be glory for ever and ever. Amen" (2 Tim. 4:18). Here the word *ever* is the 1611th word of Second Timothy and rests within a verse that mentions the word "preserve," by itself relating to God's eternally preserved Word.

Prophecy in the KJV Scripture

"<u>Knowing</u> <u>this</u> <u>first</u>, <u>that</u> <u>no prophecy</u> <u>of the</u> <u>SCRIPTURE</u> <u>is</u> <u>of any private interpretation</u>. <u>For the</u> <u>prophecy</u> <u>came</u> <u>not</u> <u>in</u> <u>old time</u> <u>by the</u> <u>will of man</u>: <u>but</u> <u>holy men</u> <u>of God</u> <u>spake</u> <u>as</u> <u>they were</u> <u>moved</u> <u>by the Holy Ghost</u>" (2 Pet. 1:20-21). The General Epistles combination *knowing* (7x), *this* (51x), *first* (6x), *that* (294x), *no* (23x), *prophecy* (3x), *of the* (95x), *scripture* (5x), *is* (210x), *of any private interpretation* (1x), *for* (138x), *the prophecy* (1x), *came* (5x), *not* (160x), *in* (210x), *old time* (1x), *by the* (19x), *will of* (7x), *man* (45x), *but* (112x), *holy men* (1x), *of God* (73x), *spake* (1x), *as* (83x), *they were* (5x), *moved* (1x), *by* (50x), *the Holy Ghost* (4x) = 1611.

The Holy Bible Commandments

"<u>For it</u> <u>had been</u> <u>better</u> <u>for them</u> <u>not to</u> <u>have</u> <u>known</u> <u>the way of righteousness</u>, <u>than</u>, <u>after they</u> <u>have known it</u>, <u>to turn</u> <u>from the HOLY COMMANDMENT</u> <u>delivered unto them</u>" (2 Pet. 2:21). The New Testament combination *for it* (26x), *had been* (41x), *better* (35x), *for them* (27x), *not to* (70x), *have* (1084x), *known* (90x), *the way of righteousness* (2x), *than* (139x), *after they have known it* (1x), *to turn* (5x), *from the holy* (2x), *commandment/s* (88x), *commandment delivered unto them* (1x) = 1611.

1611 Version Stirs the Mind to Better Remembrance

"<u>This</u> <u>second epistle, beloved,</u> <u>I now</u> <u>WRITE</u> <u>unto you;</u> <u>in both</u> <u>which I</u> <u>stir</u> <u>up</u> <u>your</u> <u>pure</u> <u>minds</u> <u>by way of remembrance</u>" (2 Pet. 3:1). The Pauline and General Epistles combination *This* [uppercase only] (26x), *second epistle beloved* (1x), *I now* (4x), *write* (30x), *unto* (545x), *you* (619x), *in both* (1x), *which I* (23x), *stir* (3x), *up* (79x), *your* (254x), *pure* (16x), *minds* (9x), *by way of remembrance* (1x) = 1611.

Begotten of the Father's True & Holy Bible

"<u>Of his</u> <u>own will</u> <u>begat he us with the WORD of</u> <u>truth,</u> <u>that we should be</u> <u>a kind of firstfruits of his creatures</u>" (James 1:18). The New Testament combination *Of* [uppercase only] (42x), *his* (1479x), *own will* (6x), *begat he us with the word of* (1x), *truth* (118x), *that we should be* (6x), *a kind of firstfruits of his creatures* (1x) = 1611.

Keep the King James Version's Perfect Wording

"<u>But</u> whoso keepeth his WORD, in him verily is the love of God perfected: hereby know we that we are in him" (1 John 2:5). This verse presents the Bible's 1611th occurrence of the word *but*, and it is associated with God's Word—the Holy Bible. Many seek to replace it in one way or another.

The King James Bible Written with Paper & Ink

"<u>Having</u> <u>many</u> <u>things</u> <u>to WRITE</u> <u>unto you,</u> <u>I would not</u> <u>WRITE</u> <u>with</u> <u>paper</u> <u>and ink</u>: <u>but I trust</u> <u>to come unto you,</u> <u>and speak</u> <u>face to face,</u> <u>that our</u> <u>joy may</u> <u>be full</u>" (2 John 1:12). The New Testament combination *having* (155x), *many* (286x), *things* (728x), *to write* (11x), *unto you* (381x), *I would not* (12x), *write with* (1x), *paper* (1x), *and ink* (1x), *but I trust* [lowercase only] (2x), *to come unto you* (6x), *and speak* (3x), *face to face* (4x), *that our* (8x), *joy may* (3x), *be full* (9x) = 1611.

Written 1611 Translation Is a True Record

"<u>Demetrius</u> <u>hath</u> <u>good</u> <u>report</u> <u>of all men</u>, <u>and of the</u> <u>truth</u> <u>itself</u>: <u>yea</u>, <u>and</u> <u>we</u> <u>also</u> <u>BEAR</u>

RECORD; and ye know that our RECORD is true. I had many things to WRITE, but I will not with ink and pen write unto thee" (3 John 12-13a). The Bible combination *Demetrius* (3x), *hath good report* (1x), *of all men* (14x), *and of the* (232x), *truth itself* (1x), *yea and* (30x), *we also* (18x), *bear record* (4x), *and ye know that* (4x), *our* (1165x), *record* (30x), *is true* (22x), *I had* (72x), *many things to write* (2x), *but I will not* (6x), *with ink* (3x), *and pen* (1x), *write unto thee* (2x), *I John who also am your brother and companion* (1x) = 1611.

The Diligent King James Translation Writers

"Beloved, when I gave all diligence to WRITE unto you of the common salvation, it was needful for me to WRITE unto you, and exhort you that ye should earnestly contend for the faith which was once delivered unto the saints" (Jude 3). The Bible combination *beloved when I* (1x), *gave all* (3x), *diligence to* (5x), *write* (91x), *unto you* (580x), *of the common* (4x), *common salvation* (1x), *it was needful* (2x), *for me to write* (2x), *unto you* (580x), *and exhort you* (2x), *that ye should earnestly* (1x), *contend for* (3x), *the faith* (43x), *which was once* (1x), *delivered* (290x), *unto the saints* (2x) = 1611.

Curse for Adding Words unto the Lord's 1611-Translation Book

"For I testify unto every man that heareth the WORDS of the prophecy of this BOOK, If any man shall add unto these things, God shall add unto him the plagues that are written in this BOOK" (Rev. 22:18). The Bible combination *and I John saw these things and heard them* (1x), *for I testify unto* (1x), *every man* (274x), *that heareth* (18x), *the words* (221x), *of the prophecy* (3x), *of this* (198x), *book* (188x), *if any man shall add unto* (1x), *these things* (293x), *God shall add* (1x), *unto him the* (49x), *plagues* (24x), *that are written* (8x), *in this* [lowercase only] (142x), *book* (188x), *the Revelation of Jesus Christ which God gave unto him* (1x) = 1611.

In her book *New Age Bible Versions*, Gail Riplinger testifies to this urgent warning, saying that some editors of modern Bible versions have actually wound up in insane asylums.

The JESUS Litmus Test
Jesus' Name & the Bible Numbers Chart

The Lord has revealed a truly exciting discovery for us regarding His signature upon the King James Version of the Bible. The first 66 consecutive occurrences of the name JESUS in the Gospel of Matthew are found to correspond with the Bible Numbers Chart in a very precise manner! Within each host verse of JESUS' name, the full subject matter of the verse or parts therein will correspond in meaning with the established numeric pattern. This divine blueprint is breathtaking and further confirms that our Bible Numbers Chart can be thoroughly trusted as a perfect standard. If there ever was a name that should fit the Bible Numeric pattern, it is the name JESUS! In each chronological verse the name *Jesus* will be shown in all capital letters for visual emphasis.

This presentation does not duplicate the various numeric seals of Jesus' name; the reader can reference those multiple findings at the introduction page of each New Testament study. Neither do we repeat numeric seals of the 66 keywords; those can be cited at the introduction page of each Old Testament study.

The Gospel of Matthew

Jesus #1—UNITY
"The book of the generation of JESUS Christ, the son of David, the son of Abraham" (Matt. 1:1).

Jesus shared a genealogical UNITY with both the house of David and the family of Abraham. The phrase *the generation of Jesus Christ* occurs 1 time in the Bible.

Jesus #2—UNION (Witness)
"And Jacob begat Joseph the husband of Mary, of whom was born JESUS, who is called Christ" (Matt. 1:16).

The infant Christ-child enjoyed a very warm UNION with His adoptive father Joseph. Like all babies, the infant Christ-child enjoyed a very loving UNION with His birth mother Mary. His miracle birth itself was a WITNESS to all that the angel Gabriel had recently foretold of Him. Further Jesus would grow up to become the greatest WITNESS the heavenly Father ever sent to Israel. The phrase *born Jesus* occurs 2 times in the Bible.

Jesus #3—DIVINE PERFECTION (New Life)
"Now the birth of JESUS Christ was on this wise: When as his mother Mary was espoused to Joseph, before they came together, she was found with child of the Holy Ghost" (Matt. 1:18).

This verse describes Jesus' conception as being PERFECTLY DIVINE. Even though He had an earthly mother, His blood type—like all children—was determined by His biological father. Jesus had only the Holy Ghost as His paternal Father. Thus He had no sin in His blood and was therefore DIVINELY PERFECT as a man. The concept of NEW LIFE is seen here through Jesus' conception into the world. The phrase *the birth* is found in 3 books of the Old Testament. The title *of the Holy Ghost* occurs 3 times in Matthew's Gospel.

Jesus #4—EARTH (The World)

"And she <u>shall bring forth</u> a son, and thou shalt <u>call his name</u> JESUS: for he <u>shall save</u> <u>his people</u> from their sins" (Matt. 1:21).

A prophecy is given to Joseph that his virgin bride will bring forth a Son into the WORLD. As an adult Jesus will save His EARTHLY kinsmen from their peril. The phrase *shall bring forth* is mentioned in 4 chapters of the Major Prophets. The phrase *call his name* occurs 4 times in the New Testament. The phrase *shall save* is mentioned in 4 chapters of the New Testament. The earthly phrase *his people* is mentioned in 104 chapters of the Old Testament and occurs 4 times in the Gospels.

Jesus #5—Grace (God's Goodness)

"And knew her not till she had brought forth her <u>firstborn son</u>: and he called his name JESUS" (Matt. 1:25).

God demonstrated GRACE to Joseph by giving him understanding of the situation. GOD'S GOODNESS was demonstrated to Mary by her husband's patience and kindness. Firstborn sons always come as a grace gift to married couples. Like the word grace, the name *Jesus* is comprised of 5 letters. This verse presents the Bible's 5th occurrence of the phrase *firstborn son*. The word *firstborn* is found in 5 books of the New Testament.

Jesus #6—MAN (Weakness, Manifestation of Sin, Evils of Satan)

"Now when JESUS <u>was born</u> in Bethlehem of Judaea in the days of Herod the king, behold, there came wise men from the east to Jerusalem" (Matt. 2:1).

Jesus' human WEAKNESS is seen here in His infant state of existence. Herod the Great was a king who himself was ruled over by the WEAKNESS of his own fear and paranoia. The MANIFESTATION OF his SIN and the EVILS OF SATAN were seen through his sanctioned murders of his various family members. The phrase *was born* occurs 6 times in the Gospels.

Jesus #7—Spiritual Perfection (Completeness)

"Then cometh JESUS from Galilee <u>to Jordan</u> unto John, to <u>be baptized</u> of him" (Matt. 3:13).

This day was the beginning of Jesus' public ministry. He was not undergoing this baptism to achieve spiritual perfection but rather to demonstrate His SPIRITUAL PERFECTION as a learned Prophet. Before any such leaders could begin public ministry, he had to undergo a ritual baptism. Thus for Jesus this event was not a baptism of repentance but rather one of commencement into His holy office. Jesus' inaugural baptism wonderfully demonstrated His COMPLETENESS of education, maturity, and readiness for public ministry. The phrase *to Jordon* occurs 7 times in the Old Testament. The phrase *be baptized* occurs 7 times in Acts.

Jesus #8—New Beginnings

"And JESUS answering said unto him, Suffer it to be <u>so now</u>: for thus it <u>becometh</u> us <u>to fulfil</u> all righteousness. Then he suffered him" (Matt. 3:15).

Because John resisted Jesus' initial request, Jesus gave him specific instructions to baptize Him so He might have His ceremonial NEW BEGINNING as the nation's Holy Prophet and Son of Righteousness as Malachi foretold. The term *the ministry* occurs 8 times in the Pauline Epistles.

The phrase *so now* occurs 8 times in the Bible. The word *becometh* is mentioned in 8 chapters of the New Testament. The phrase *to fulfil* occurs 8 times in the Bible.

Jesus #9—Spirit (Fruit-Bearing)

"And JESUS, when he was baptized, went up straightway out of the water: and, lo, <u>the heavens</u> were opened unto him, <u>and he saw</u> <u>the Spirit of God</u> <u>descending</u> like <u>a dove</u>, and lighting upon him" (Matt. 3:16).

Jesus possessed an absolute sinless nature; thus He was fit to be embodied with all the fullness of THE SPIRIT. Having now been baptized with water and THE SPIRIT, Jesus was ready to begin a FRUIT-BEARING ministry. The title *the heavens* occurs 109 times in the Bible. The phrase *and he saw* is found in 9 books of the Bible. The title *the Spirit of God* is mentioned in 9 chapters of the New Testament. The phrase *a dove* occurs 9 times in the Bible. The Bible combination *and he saw the Spirit of God* (1x), *descending* (8x) = 9.

Jesus #10—Ordinal Perfection (Order)

"Then was JESUS led up of the Spirit <u>into the wilderness</u> to be <u>tempted</u> of the devil" (Matt. 4:1).

The word ordinal means 'of or relating to order, rank, or position in a series.' The devil—Satan—once held the highest rank of any angel in heaven; here he is seen to hold ORDINAL PERFECTION over earthly mortals. In the wilderness Jesus was severely tested to manifestly prove Jesus' ORDINAL PERFECTION over all mortals. The phrase *into the wilderness* is mentioned in 10 chapters of the New Testament. The word *tempted* is mentioned in 10 verses of the Pauline and General Epistles.

Jesus #11—Judgment (Disorder)

"JESUS said unto him, <u>It is written</u> again, Thou shalt not tempt the Lord thy God" (Matt. 4:7).

Satan was doing what he does best—acting DISORDERLY and causing DISORDER. Tempting any person to commit sin is itself a sin and worthy of God's JUDGMENT. Indeed Jesus laid judgment against Satan with this biblical proclamation from God's Word. Whenever a person breaks one of God's "thou shalt not" commandments, he becomes worthy of God's righteous JUDGMENT. When that dreadful time comes he or she will be JUDGED on the basis of what is written in God's Word. The phrase *it is written* is found in 11 books of the New Testament.

Jesus #12—Governmental Perfection

"Then saith JESUS unto him, Get thee hence, Satan: for it is written, Thou shalt <u>worship</u> <u>the Lord thy God</u>, and him only shalt thou <u>serve</u>" (Matt. 4:10).

Because of His GOVERNMENTAL PERFECTION, the Lord God is worthy of man's worship and man's service. The word *worship* occurs 12 times in the OT Narrative. The title *the LORD thy God* is mentioned in 12 chapters of the Major Prophets. The word *serve* is mentioned in 12 chapters of Exodus, in 12 verses of Joshua, in 12 verses of First and Second Samuel, and occurs 12 times in the Synoptic Gospels.

Jesus #13—Rebellion (Anger)

"Now when JESUS had heard that John was <u>cast into prison</u>, he departed into Galilee" (Matt. 4:12).

After making Herod Antipas angry by giving him a bold reminder that he was acting as a profane sinner, John was cast into prison. Herod had REBELLED against the Mosaic command by marrying his living brother's wife. Prisons cells are typically reserved for those who rebel against known law. John did not deserve to be cast into prison, but Herod did. The phrase *cast into* is found in 13 books of the Bible. The phrase *in prison* occurs 13 times in the New Testament.

Jesus #14—Deliverance (Salvation)

"From that time JESUS began <u>to preach</u>, and to say, <u>Repent</u>: for <u>the kingdom of heaven is</u> <u>at hand</u>" (Matt. 4:17).

Jesus had come to bring mankind DELIVERANCE from sin. His SALVATION was and still is sure to come to all those who faithfully heed His message and repent of their sins. The phrase *to preach* is mentioned naturally in 14 verses of the New Testament. The word *preach* is mentioned in 14 chapters of the NT Narrative. The word *repent* occurs 14 times in the NT Narrative. The phrase *the kingdom of heaven is* occurs 14 times in the Bible. The phrase *at hand* occurs 14 times in the NT Narrative.

Jesus #15—Rest (Peace)

"And JESUS, walking by <u>the sea</u> of Galilee, saw two brethren, Simon called Peter, and Andrew his brother, casting a net into the <u>sea</u>: for they were fishers" (Matt. 4:18).

The sea provides a place of REST and PEACE for people to enjoy a bit of leisure time. In fact, time itself seems to rest whenever you get near a sea shore. The title *Galilee* occurs 15 times in Luke's Gospel. The title *the sea* occurs 15 times in Ezekiel. The word *sea* is mentioned in 215 chapters of the Bible.

Jesus #16—Love (Obedience)

"And JESUS went about all Galilee, teaching in their synagogues, and preaching the gospel of the kingdom, and <u>healing</u> <u>all manner of sickness</u> and <u>all manner of disease</u> among the people" (Matt. 4:23).

Jesus showed His genuine LOVE for the people through unconditionally healing them. In gratitude for the great LOVE and benevolence they had been shown, the people were to respond with their OBEDIENCE to His preaching and teaching. The Bible combination *healing* (14x), *all manner of sickness* (2x) = 16. The Bible combination *healing* (14x), *all manner of disease* (2x) = 16.

Jesus #17—Victory (Joy)

"And it came to pass, when JESUS had ended these sayings, <u>the people were</u> astonished at his doctrine" (Matt. 7:28).

Jesus had just finished delivering His beautiful Sermon on the Mount. His wise philosophy of life informed the people how they could gain the VICTORY and JOY mankind so desperately seeks like by knocking on heaven's door until your request is answered. The phrase *the people were* is mentioned in 17 chapters of the Old Testament.

Jesus #18—Bondage (Oppression)

"And JESUS put forth his hand, and touched him, saying, I will; be thou clean. And immediately his leprosy was cleansed" (Matt. 8:3).

Leprosy is a horrible, disfiguring disease that eats away at one's body, thus placing such a one in mental BONDAGE. The leprous one's isolation from society only adds to his existing level of DEPRESSION. These benighted souls desperately sought to find the Great Physician to obtain an instant cure for their condition. Jesus loosed this leper from both his bondage and his depression. The word *loosed* is mentioned in 18 verses of the New Testament.

Jesus #19—Faith (Trust)
"And JESUS saith unto him, See thou tell no man; but go thy way, shew thyself to the priest, and offer the gift that Moses commanded, for a testimony unto them" (Matt. 8:4).

When Jesus delivered this charge to the cleansed leper, He TRUSTED him to keep the charge. Other such healed subjects usually went and did the exact opposite by blazing the matter abroad, yet this cleansed leper acted in good FAITH by doing as he was commanded. Sacrificial gifts were to be offered unto the Lord in FAITH, believing He would graciously accept both the gift and giver. The phrase *go thy way* occurs 19 times in the Bible. The word *gift* is mentioned in 19 verses of the Old Testament.

Jesus #20—Redemption (Wisdom)
"And when JESUS was entered into Capernaum, there came unto him a centurion, beseeching him" (Matt. 8:5).

This centurion's servant was grievously tormented with a neurological ailment which caused paralysis. What the centurion desperately longed for was his servant's REDEMPTION from a life of pain. Whenever Jesus entered into any town or village, it was certain that REDEMPTION had come! The title *centurion* occurs 20 times in the Bible. The combination *was entered* (4x) and *Capernaum* (16x) = 20. The phrase *came unto him* occurs 20 times in the New Testament, all occurring in the NT Narrative.

Jesus #21—Sin (Lawlessness)
"And JESUS saith unto him, I will come and heal him" (Matt. 8:7).

The poor servant's body was in a state of anatomical LAWLESSNESS as it was under the strong, paralyzing influence of palsy. Since all men are SINNERS, the greatest need they have is to be healed from their life-threatening disease of SIN. Jesus greatly desires to help us with this spiritual malady. Whenever Jesus healed someone He gave them adamant instruction to go and sin no more. The phrase *I will come* is mentioned in 21 verses of the Bible. The word *heal* occurs 21 times in the Old Testament. The word *healed* is found in 21 books of the Bible.

Jesus #22—Understanding (Light)
"When JESUS heard it, he marvelled, and said to them that followed, Verily I say unto you, I have not found so great faith, no, not in Israel" (Matt. 8:10).

This centurion had perfect UNDERSTANDING that Jesus need not come under his roof but instead simply send forth His authoritative, healing word. This believing centurion's spiritual LIGHT had come to him as reward for his activated daily faith. The word *marvellous* is mentioned in 22 verses of the Bible. The phrase *by faith* occurs 22 times in the Bible. This verse presents the Bible's 22nd book-mention of the phrase *in Israel*.

Jesus #23—Death

"And JESUS said unto the centurion, Go thy way; and as thou hast believed, so be it done unto thee. And his <u>servant</u> was healed in the selfsame hour" (Matt. 8:13).

Servants were not generally cared for as well as the family members were. They often lacked the proper diet, rest, and medical care to live long, prosperous lives. Whereas the centurion's servant had been lying at DEATH'S door, here the servant was marvelously pulled away from DEATH'S door. The near-death title *servant* is the 23rd word in this verse.

Jesus #24—Priesthood

"And when <u>JESUS</u> was come <u>into</u> Peter's <u>house,</u> he saw his wife's mother laid, and sick of a fever" (Matt. 8:14).

Wherever Jesus resided He became the high PRIEST of that house; no one knew God better than He did. One of the Old Testament PRIESTHOOD'S duties was to pray for the people's healing. Fulfilling the priestly type, any time Jesus was in a house, that place constituted a healing temple. As we read on in the sequential verse we see that Jesus "touched her hand, and the fever left her." The word *touched* occurs 24 times in the New Testament; most all of these pertain to Jesus' healing power. The Gospels combination *Jesus went* (20x), *went into the house* (4x) = 24.

Jesus #25—Forgiveness

"Now when <u>JESUS saw great</u> <u>multitudes</u> about him, he gave commandment to depart unto the other side" (Matt. 8:18).

The leading word of this verse "now" is a connecting word; it reflects on the prior verse where the narrative speaks of Jesus' power to heal mankind's infirmities and sicknesses. To qualify man's healing from his fatal sin-sickness, Jesus' FORGIVENESS must also be directly applied. Other scriptures confirm that whenever Jesus saw the multitudes He was moved with compassion. Such divine compassion is what makes His forgiveness possible. The Bible combination *Jesus saw great* (1x) and *multitudes* (24x) = 25.

Jesus #26—Gospel (Good News)

"And JESUS saith unto him, The <u>foxes</u> have <u>holes,</u> and the <u>birds</u> of the air have <u>nests;</u> but the Son of man <u>hath not</u> where to lay <u>his head</u>" (Matt. 8:20).

Jesus had stationary GOSPEL headquarters in Capernaum, yet it was only a shared accommodation. He sometimes used this for brief periods of rest, but Jesus' GOSPEL ministry consisted of itinerates preaching. His circuit travels lasted for months at a time. From one location to the next Jesus made His home under the stars. All that was important to Jesus at this time was sharing the GOOD NEWS. Nothing else mattered. The Bible words *foxes* (7 chs) and *birds* (19 chs) = 26 chapters. The Bible words *holes* (11x) and *nest* (15x) = 26. The phrase *hath not* is mentioned in 126 verses. The phrase *his head* occurs 26 times in the Law.

Jesus #27—Preaching (Holy Truth)

"But JESUS said unto him, <u>Follow me;</u> and <u>let the dead bury their dead</u>" (Matt. 8:22).

Jesus wanted this man to follow Him and assist in PREACHING the gospel of the kingdom. Jesus needed many helpers to reach the hundreds of villages scattered about Israel. Josephus estimated there were 240 villages just in the Galilee area. When Jesus gave this hard-hitting maxim He was simply speaking a HOLY TRUTH. What He meant was this: do not let family obligations hinder you from doing the greater work of God. The Bible combination *follow me* (25x) and *let the dead bury their dead* (2x) = 27.

Jesus #28—Eternal Life

"And, behold, they cried out, saying, What have we to do with thee, JESUS, thou Son of God? art thou come hither to torment us before the time?" (Matt. 8:29)

The legion called the lowly incarnate Son of Man by His grander, past ETERNAL title—Son of God. They also refer to that golden future time when ETERNITY will begin without evil influence dwelling upon the earth. Indeed the Son of God is the only One Who can grant mortals ETERNAL LIFE. This eternal-Son-of-God verse consists of 28 words! The title *thou son/Son* is mentioned in 28 chapters of the Bible. The title *son/Son of God* occurs 28 times in the Gospels. The phrase *the time of* is found in 28 books of the Bible.

Jesus #29—Departure

"And, behold, the whole city came out to meet JESUS: and when they saw him, they besought him that he would DEPART out of their coasts" (Matt. 8:34).

This city's entire Gentile population obligates Jesus to quickly DEPART from them. The keyword *depart* actually occurs in this 29th location. The word *coasts* is mentioned in 29 chapters of the Old Testament.

Jesus #30—Dedication (Blood)

"And, behold, they brought to him a man sick of the palsy, lying on a bed: and JESUS seeing their faith said unto the sick of the palsy; Son, be of good cheer; thy sins be forgiven thee" (Matt. 9:2).

Several men performed a great service for their friend. Their great show of DEDICATION caused Jesus to reward them by healing their friend. Jesus was DEDICATED to bringing the people good cheer, particularly the cheerful news of sin's forgiveness. Jesus' forgiveness was based upon His own forthcoming outpoured BLOOD. The word *forgive* is mentioned in 30 chapters of the Bible.

Jesus #31—Family (Children)

"And JESUS knowing their thoughts said, Wherefore think ye evil in your hearts?" (Matt. 9:4)

Jesus was talking to some scribes who were standing nearby. These men, like Jesus, were Hebrew and thus members of the FAMILY of Israel. The sad truth is not everyone in your natural or extended FAMILY always likes you; some will even hate you. Like a parent who attempts to correct his erring CHILDREN, Jesus began to reason with them. The New Testament combination *wherefore think ye* (1x), *evil in* (2x), *your hearts* (28x) = 31.

Jesus #32—Covenant (Fellowship)

"And as JESUS passed forth from thence, he saw a man, named Matthew, sitting at the receipt of custom: and he saith unto him, Follow me. And he arose, and followed him" (Matt. 9:9) .

Jesus invited this business man to enter into COVENANT with Him, a COVENANT which would now require his full-time commitment to conducting the King's business. After this man partners with the King of the Jews they will eat together, talk together, walk together, pray together, preach together, reason together, and rest together. Such activities are considered true FELLOWSHIP. Together they will share joys and sorrows, laughter and tears, life and death. Covenants are not made while sitting; one must rise and stand for the occasion. The phrase *he arose* is mentioned in 32 chapters of the Bible. The phrase *followed him* occurs 32 times in the Gospels. There are 32 words in this covenant-fellowship verse.

Jesus #33—Promise

"And it came to pass, as JESUS sat at meat in the house, behold, many publicans and sinners came and sat down with him and his disciples" (Matt. 9:10).

One of the Old Testament titles of God is the Hope of Israel. This title also appropriately pertains to Israel's great Messianic hope of which Jesus was its promised fulfillment. Jesus held out great hope and PROMISE for the sick, the outcasts, and society's underprivileged. These were all attracted to Him because He so readily and gladly received them. The word *sinners* is mentioned in 33 chapters of the Bible.

Jesus #34—Man's Religion

"But when JESUS heard that, he said unto them, They that be whole need not a physician, but they that are sick" (Matt. 9:12).

Having watched Jesus eating with publicans and sinners, the Pharisees complained about it to His disciples. Because they loved their elders' manmade RELIGION, these RELIGIOUS bigots rejected Christ's simple RELIGION which is based on godly love of neighbor and peace with fellow man. The title *the Pharisees* is mentioned in 34 chapters of the Bible.

Jesus #35—Hope (Suffering)

"And JESUS said unto them, Can the children of the bridechamber mourn, as long as the bridegroom is with them? but the days will come, when the bridegroom shall be taken from them, and then shall they fast" (Matt. 9:15).

These castaways were currently being drawn to the wonderful saving HOPE that Jesus alone freely offered. Jesus' metaphor implied that His devoted followers were currently full of HOPE because of His kingly and joyful presence but would one day SUFFER great emotional lows because of His violent death. The Old Testament combination *the children of the* (34 vs), *bridegroom coming out of his chamber* (1 v) = 35 verses.

Jesus #36—Enemy (Exaltation of Man)

"And JESUS arose, and followed him, and so did his disciples" (Matt. 9:19).

A certain ruler whose daughter had just died came to Jesus, anxiously desiring that He would return to his house to touch her and make her instantly live again. Having such certainty and confidence, this man had likely seen Jesus do this before. Man's greatest ENEMY is death. Jesus arose and, as the ENEMY of Death, headed toward the ENEMY'S territory. The word *arose* occurs 36 times in the Gospels.

Jesus #37—Word of God

"But JESUS turned him about, and when he saw her, he said, Daughter, be of good comfort; thy

702

<u>faith</u> hath made thee <u>whole</u>. And the woman was made <u>whole</u> from that hour" (Matt. 9:22).

This hemorrhagic woman was desperate to touch the hem of Jesus' garment. The four tassels on the edge of the Jews' outer garments represented the mosaic commandments and symbolized the WORD OF GOD. As it turned out, this woman had a pleasant encounter with the spoken WORD OF GOD. The phrase *Jesus said* is mentioned in 37 chapters of the Bible. The word *turned* is mentioned in 37 verses of the New Testament and mostly pertain to Jesus turning Himself about. The phrase *by faith* occurs 37 times in the Bible, all in the New Testament. The word *whole* is mentioned in 37 chapters of the Gospels.

Jesus #38—Unbelief
"And when JESUS came into the ruler's house, and saw the minstrels and the people making a noise" (Matt. 9:23).

This verse reveals the people's earliest UNBELIEF in the Great Physician's power to raise the dead back to life. The ruler of the house believed, but the noisy mourners did NOT BELIEVE despite Jesus' arrival. Then after Jesus told them that the girl was only sleeping, they began to make a different kind of noise, turning their mournful cries into humiliating laughter. All forms of the word *laugh* are mentioned in 38 verses of the Bible.

Jesus #39—Disease (Adultery)
"And when JESUS departed thence, two <u>blind</u> men followed him, crying, and saying, Thou Son of David, <u>have mercy</u> on us" (Matt. 9:27).

Among the various causes for blindness is DISEASE. These two men were desperate for the Great Physician's cure. The phrase *the blind* occurs 39 times in the Bible. The phrase *have mercy* is mentioned in 39 chapters from Genesis to the NT Narrative.

Jesus #40—Temptation (Testing)
"And when he was come into the house, <u>the blind</u> men came to him: and JESUS saith unto them, Believe ye that <u>I am able</u> to do this? <u>They said unto him, Yea, Lord</u>" (Matt. 9:28).

Jesus now completes the TEST of faith He had earlier placed these two frail men under. Rather than immediately answering their cries for mercy, He had made them follow Him all the way to His house in Capernaum, likely a considerable distance for blind men and all the while ignoring their continual pleas for help. It seems He was stretching their faith. In very deed, they did not lose heart. At the last they passed His profound TEST-question with their profound two-word answer. The Bible combination *is able* (31x), *am able* (2x), *was able* (7x) = 40. The Bible combination *the blind* (39x) and *they said unto him yea Lord* (1x) = 40.

Jesus #41—Rule of Man
"And their eyes were opened; and JESUS straitly <u>charged</u> them, saying, See that no MAN know it" (Matt. 9:30).

The Son of Man demonstrated His loving RULE over these MEN in two ways: by healing them and by giving them a strict charge. The phrase *the charge* occurs 41 times in Scripture. The phrase *commanded(st) them* occurs 41 times in the Bible. The keyword *man* actually occurs in this 41st verse.

Jesus #42—Israel's Oppression

"And JESUS went about <u>all the cities</u> and villages, teaching in their synagogues, and preaching the gospel of the kingdom, and healing every sickness and every disease among the people" (Matt. 9:35).

Jesus' teaching and preaching on the kingdom's arrival brought fresh spiritual hope to the nation that was living under an OPPRESSIVE occupation. His miraculous healings also greatly helped alleviate the nation's physical OPPRESSION. The phrase *all the cities* is mentioned in 42 verses of the Old Testament.

Jesus #43—Contention

"These twelve JESUS sent forth, and commanded them, saying, Go not <u>into the way</u> <u>of the</u> <u>Gentiles,</u> and into any city of the Samaritans enter ye not" (Matt. 10:5).

Jesus sought to eliminate needless CONTENTIONS during their mission. If they went to the Gentiles, those people might become CONTENTIOUS over whose god was greater. And if they went to the half-Jew Samaritans, those people might become CONTENTIOUS over the issue of the true place of worship. Sharp contention had existed between the Jews and Samaritans for more than century. The people of Israel were Jesus' present concern. The Bible combination *into the way* (5x), *of the Gentiles* (38x) = 43.

Jesus #44—Chosen Ones

"And it came to pass, when Jesus had made an end of commanding <u>his</u> twelve <u>disciples,</u> he departed thence to teach and to preach in their cities" (Matt. 11:1).

These twelve men were especially CHOSEN to be key leaders and authoritative figures in Jesus' kingdom. At this moment they were assigned with some important kingdom work. The phrase *his disciples* occurs 144 times in the Bible, all in the Gospels.

Jesus #45—Preserved Life

"JESUS answered and said unto them, <u>Go</u> and <u>shew John again those things which ye do hear</u> <u>and see</u>" (Matt. 11:4).

While John was sitting deep down in Herod Antipas's prison, he greatly feared for the PRESERVATION of his LIFE. Because kingdom events were not unfolding as he had supposed, John had sent two of his disciples to go ask Jesus for some clarification. John needed some reassurance. Jesus's answer concerned LIFE PRESERVATION of many but strangely enough, not particularly of John's life: "The blind receive their sight, and the lame walk, the lepers are cleansed, and the deaf hear, the dead are raised up, and the poor have the gospel preached to them" (v. 5). The words *go shew John again those things which ye do hear and see* consist of 45 letters!

Jesus #46—Reconstructed Life (Temple)

"And as they departed, JESUS began to say unto the multitudes concerning John, What went ye out into the wilderness to see? A reed shaken with <u>the wind</u>?" (Matt. 11:7)

Jesus begins to speak of John the Baptist, and as He continues His speech he references the violence which John has recently incurred. The prophet's LIFE was undergoing RECONSTRUCTION in a negative way. He and his thundering voice were being removed from the public to go sit silently and obscurely in prison. The wind is oftentimes used as a metaphor to describe the Holy Spirit's stirring nature. Jesus also went on to describe John in terms of the RECONSTRUCTED LIFE of Elijah. The phrase *the wind* is mentioned in 46 chapters from Genesis to the NT Narrative.

Jesus #47—Humility

"At that time JESUS answered and said, I thank thee, O Father, Lord of heaven and earth, because thou hast hid these things from the wise and prudent, and hast <u>revealed</u> them unto <u>babes</u>" (Matt. 11:25).

As you know, the word "babes" refers to very little children. Jesus gladly chose this group to signify them as tokens of true HUMILITY. Pride is a predominate attitude that is missing in small children. The Bible combination *revealed* (38x) and *babes* (9x) = 47.

Jesus #48—Father's Blessing

"At that time JESUS went on the <u>sabbath day</u> through the corn; and his disciples were an hungred, and began to pluck the ears of corn, and to eat" (Matt. 12:1).

The hungry disciples readily enjoyed their heavenly FATHER'S convenient BLESSING of fresh-from-the-farm food. But onlooking Pharisees questioned the disciples' supposed Sabbath-breaking dietary activity. Religious leaders like these had turned the FATHER'S Sabbath BLESSING into a Sabbath curse through their many added prohibitions. The Sabbath meaning to be a blessing to Israel can be seen in the following numeric seal. The title *sabbath day* is mentioned in 48 verses of the Bible.

Jesus #49—Father's Love

"But when JESUS knew it, he withdrew himself from thence: and <u>great multitudes followed him</u>, and he <u>healed</u> them all" (Matt. 12:15).

Jesus was the incarnate expression of the FATHER'S exponential LOVE. Even though the Pharisees had just gathered and plotted against Jesus, He continued all the same to demonstrate the FATHER'S heavenly LOVE by healing more sick folk. The New Testament combination *great multitudes followed him* (3x) and *healed* (46x) = 49.

Jesus #50—Purification (Persecution)

"And JESUS knew their thoughts, and said unto them, Every kingdom <u>divided</u> against itself is brought to desolation; and every city or house <u>divided</u> against itself shall not stand" (Matt. 12:25).

Jesus wanted to PURIFY the Pharisees' highly impure thoughts concerning the origin of His power to heal because they thought He was using a powerful, devilish spirit. They were PERSECUTING Him with their humiliating insults—a crafty approach they had hoped would also divide Him from His followers. The word *divided* is mentioned in 50 verses of the Old Testament.

Jesus #51—Praise

"The same day went JESUS out of the house, and <u>sat</u> by the sea side" (Matt. 13:1).

The Sea of Galilee is a beautiful body of water surrounded by mountains. A peaceful place to worship God, Jesus likely went there to enjoy some PRAISE time with His heavenly Father. The word *sat* occurs 51 times in the Synoptic Gospels—Matthew, Mark, and Luke.

Jesus #52—Gospel Work

"All these things spake JESUS unto the multitude in parables; and without a parable spake he not unto them" (Matt. 13:34).

Because the Pharisees had recently accused Jesus of conspiring with Beelzebub to accomplish His healing work, Jesus' GOSPEL WORK needed some adjustment. He would no longer continue casting His pearls before swine. Thus He began to teach in a different way by using parables. The word *spake* is mentioned in 52 chapters of the Gospels!

Jesus #53—Faithful Witness

"Then JESUS sent the multitude away, and went into the house: and his disciples came unto him, saying, Declare unto us the parable of the tares of the field" (Matt. 13:36).

Parables were easy-to-remember stories, yet they were not always so easily understood. They were designed to be accompanied with further explanation from the FAITHFUL WITNESS who witnessed it. Jesus was always glad to privately explain His parables to genuinely interested listeners so His FAITHFUL WITNESS might be better received. The Bible combination *and his disciples came unto him saying* (1x), *declare unto us the* (2x), *parable* (49x), *of the tares of the field* (1x) = 53.

Jesus #54—False Witness

"JESUS saith unto them, Have ye understood all these things? They say unto him, Yea, Lord" (Matt. 13:51).

Jesus had just explained the parable of the Wheat and the Tares as being about the gospel's enemies who as FALSE WITNESSES come afterward, sowing their confusing FALSE teachings where the true gospel had been recently sown. The word *teach* is mentioned in 54 chapters of the Old Testament.

Jesus #55—Resist the Truth

"And it came to pass, that when JESUS had finished these parables, he departed thence" (Matt. 13:53).

He departed for Nazareth. Thus this verse introduces a narrative section concerning Jesus' Synagogue visit at Nazareth where the people were amazed with His wisdom and TRUTH yet stubbornly RESISTED it. Their RESISTANCE to Jesus' divine TRUTH is emphasized a few verses later where we read that "he did not many mighty works there because of their unbelief."

Jesus #56—Hard Heart

"And they were offended in him. But JESUS said unto them, A prophet is not without honour, save in his own country, and in his own house" (Matt. 13:57).

The offense the Nazarenes took from Jesus' authoritative teaching was born within their own HARDENED HEARTS. They were simply too familiar with this hometown Citizen. Many times in soul-winning people will not receive a gospel witness directly from fellow family members, but they will respond positively to a complete stranger. The Bible combination *a prophet* (52x), *in his own country* (4x) = 56.

Jesus #57—Depart the Faith

"At that time Herod the tetrarch heard of the fame of JESUS" (Matt. 14:1).

When Herod first heard news of Jesus, he thought He might be John the Baptist having come back from the dead. The next many verses recall how Herod had recently DEPARTED THE FAITH by killing Israel's mighty wilderness prophet John the Baptist.

Jesus #58—Worldly Life

"And his disciples came, and took up the body, and buried it, and went and told JESUS" (Matt. 14:12).

The verse prior to this one tells precisely who was at the root of this WORLDLY evil which befell John the Baptist. It was Herod the Tetrarch's wife *Herodias*, Herod the Great's granddaughter. She lived a very WORLDLY LIFE in many respects. The historian Josephus records that she had three husbands of which Antipas was the last. She was so WORLDLY that she allowed her daughter Salome, from her first marriage, to perform an immoderate dance before Antipas. It seems that the daughter was cut from the same worldly cloth as her mother.

Jesus #59—Oppressor

"When JESUS heard of it, he departed thence by ship into a desert place apart: and when the people had heard thereof, they followed him on foot out of the cities" (Matt. 14:13).

Jesus became OPPRESSED after hearing news about John's horrific death. These two had been familiar cousins. Being mentally afflicted and pained in His heart, Jesus wanted to be alone for a while. Thus He sought a place of solitude. Behind John the Baptist's tragic beheading was Satan, the invisible OPPRESSOR. The Gospels combination *when Jesus* (55x), *heard of it* (3x), *he departed thence by ship into a desert place* (1x) = 59.

Jesus #60—Earthly King

"And JESUS went forth, and saw a great multitude, and was moved with compassion toward them, and he healed their sick" (Matt. 14:14).

This EARTHLY KING was particularly interested in His kingdom subjects' earthly needs. The word compassion has a synonym—mercy. The New Testament combination *mercy* (59x) and *he healed their sick* (1x) = 60. The John combination *Jesus* (253x), *went forth* (7x) = 260.

Jesus #61—God (King of the Jews)

"But JESUS said unto them, They need not depart; give ye them to eat" (Matt. 14:16).

This KING OF THE JEWS would never let His devoted citizenry go hungry. Since a king is ultimately responsible for feeding his people, Jesus initiates a process whereby He will soon miraculously feed a large crowd. The phrase *to eat* is mentioned in 61 chapters from Genesis to the NT Narrative. The Bible combination *they need not depart* (1x), *loaves* (32x), *fishes* (27x), *bring them hither to me* (1x) = 61. The word *eaten* is mentioned in 61 chapters of the Old Testament.

Jesus #62—Jerusalem

"And straightway JESUS constrained his disciples to get into a ship, and to go <u>before him</u> unto the other side, <u>while he sent</u> <u>the multitudes</u> <u>away</u>" (Matt. 14:22).

Not everyone in this crowd was from the Galilee region. Some of the people would have begun to make their way southward back to JERUSALEM. The NT Narrative combination *while he sent* (2x), *the multitudes* (10x), *away* (150x) = 162.

Jesus #63—God's Wrath

"And in the fourth watch of the night JESUS went unto them, walking on the sea" (Matt. 14:25).

At this point the storm-drenched disciples were beyond all hope they would reach the other side for we are told that "the <u>ship</u> was now in the midst of the sea, tossed with waves." Hence the setting here is one of great fear and trepidation. Nature's powerful wrath is often likened to the WRATH OF GOD. Ships regularly experiencing the wrath of God upon tempestuous seas can be seen in the following numeric seal. The word *ship* is mentioned in 63 verses of the New Testament.

Jesus #64—Broken Fellowship

"But straightway JESUS spake unto them, saying, Be of good cheer; it is I; be not afraid" (Matt. 14:27).

The disciples' FELLOWSHIP with Jesus had been temporarily BROKEN as a result of their geographical separation, yet it begins to come to an end here in this verse as Jesus draws near them both in proximity and in the spirit of peace. The phrase *other side* occurs 64 times in the Bible. The word *ship* occurs 64 times in the New Testament.

Jesus #65—Apostasy

"And he said, Come. And when Peter was come down <u>out of</u> the ship, he walked on the water, to go to JESUS" (Matt. 14:29).

The Greek word *apostasia* means 'a defection from the truth; to forsake.' It also implies 'a departure out or away from.' At this point the sea was still raging and boisterous, and the boat was taking on water and sinking. Peter suddenly got an idea that he would DEFECT from the sinking ship and FORSAKE his fellow shipmen to go to Jesus for certain refuge. The phrase *out of* occurs 65 times in Judges, 65 times in Second Chronicles, and is mentioned in 65 verses of Ezekiel.

Jesus #66—Idol Worship

"And immediately Jesus stretched forth his hand, and caught him, and said unto him, O thou of little faith, wherefore didst thou doubt?" (Matt. 14:31)

Webster's Dictionary gives us one definition of idolatry: an immoderate attachment or devotion to something. Peter had a blind spot—he was too devoted to himself. Thus he IDOLIZED himself. We do know that he regularly exalted himself above his peers. Here Peter walks on the water with great pride, and soon after this "me-first" type of apostle begins to quickly sink. Peter's trust and confidence in himself became his downfall. You will remember that it was Peter's idea to walk on water; Jesus simply allowed him to set himself up for a fall.

www.ingramcontent.com/pod-product-compliance
Lightning Source LLC
Chambersburg PA
CBHW061833260326
41914CB00005B/975